Microsoft Certification Books from Sybex

Azure Certifications

MC Microsoft Certified Azure Data Fundamentals Study Guide: Exam DP-900—ISBN 978-1-119-85583-5, April 2022

Edition with accompanying online labs—ISBN 978-1-394-15845-4, August 2022

Microsoft Azure Architect Technologies and Design Complete Study Guide: Exams AZ-303 and AZ-304—ISBN 978-1-119-55953-5, December 2020

MCA Microsoft Certified Associate Azure Administrator Study Guide: Exam AZ-104—ISBN 978-1-119-70515-4, April 2022

Edition with accompanying online labs—ISBN 978-1-394-15847-8, August 2022

Microsoft Certified Azure Fundamentals Study Guide: Exam AZ-900—ISBN 978-1-119-77092-3, April 2021

MCA Microsoft Certified Associate Azure Network Engineer Study Guide: Exam AZ-700—ISBN 978-1-119-87292-4, September 2022

MCA Microsoft Certified Associate Azure Security Engineer Study Guide: Exam AZ-500—ISBN 978-1-119-87037-1, November 2022

Microsoft 365 Certifications

MCA Microsoft 365 Teams Administrator Study Guide: Exam MS-700—ISBN 978-1-119-77334-4, September 2021

MCA Modern Desktop Administrator Complete Study Guide with 900 Practice Test Questions: Exam MD-100 and Exam MD-101, 2nd Edition—ISBN 978-1-119-98464-1, January 2023

MCE Microsoft Certified Expert Cybersecurity Architect Study Guide: Exam SC-100—ISBN 978-1-394-18021-9, April 2023

Microsoft Office 365 Certifications

MCA Microsoft Office Specialist (Office 365 and Office 2019) Complete Study Guide: Word Exam MO-100, Excel Exam MO-200, and PowerPoint Exam MO-300—ISBN 978-1-119-71849-9, June 2021

MCA Microsoft Office Specialist (Office 365 and Office 2019) Study Guide: Word Associate Exam MO-100—ISBN 978-1-119-71826-0, December 2020

MCA Microsoft Office Specialist (Office 365 and Office 2019) Study Guide: Excel Associate Exam MO-200—ISBN 978-1-119-71824-6, March 2021

MCA Microsoft Office Specialist (Office 365 and Office 2019) Study Guide: PowerPoint Associate Exam MO-300—ISBN 978-1-119-71846-8, May 2021

Microsoft® Certified Associate
Windows Server® Hybrid
Administrator Complete

Study Guide

MCA
Microsoft® Certified Associate
Windows Server® Hybrid
Administrator Complete

Study Guide
Exam AZ-800 and Exam AZ-801

William Panek

This book is dedicated to the three ladies of my life: Crystal, Alexandria, and Paige.

Acknowledgments

I would like to thank my wife and best friend, Crystal. She is always the light at the end of my tunnel. I want to thank my two daughters, Alexandria and Paige, for all of their love and support during the writing of all my books. The three of them are my support system and I couldn't do any of this without them.

I want to thank my family, and especially my brothers, Rick, Gary, and Rob. They have always been there for me. I want to thank my father, Richard, who helped me become the man I am today, and my mother, Maggie, for all of her love and support.

I would like to thank all of my friends and co-workers at StormWind Studios (www .stormwindstudios.com). Thanks to all of you for everything that you do. I would not have been able to complete this book without all of your help and support.

I want to thank everyone on my Sybex team, especially my development editor, Kim Wimpsett, who helped me make this the best book possible, and Rodney Fournier, who was the technical editor and an outstanding resource on this book. It's always good to have the very best technical person backing you up. I want to thank Magesh Elangovan, who was my production editor, and Elizabeth Welch, the copyeditor.

Special thanks to my acquisitions editor, Kenyon Brown, who was the lead for the entire book. Finally, I want to thank everyone else behind the scenes who helped make this book possible. It's truly an amazing thing to have so many people work on my books to help make them the very best. I can't thank you all enough for your hard work.

About the Author

William Panek holds the following certifications: MCP, MCP+I, MCSA, MCSA+ Security and Messaging, MCSE-NT (3.51 and 4.0), MCSE (2000, 2003, 2012/2012 R2), MCSE+Security and Messaging, MCDBA, MCT, MCTS, MCITP, CCNA, CCDA, and CHFI. Will is also a five-time and current Microsoft MVP winner.

After many successful years in the computer industry, Will decided that he could better use his talents and his personality as an instructor. He began teaching for schools such as Boston University and the University of Maryland, just to name a few. He has done consulting and training for some of the biggest government and corporate companies in the world, including the United States Secret Service, Cisco, United States Air Force, and United States Army.

In 2015, Will became a Sr. Microsoft Instructor for StormWind Studios (www .stormwindstudios.com). He currently lives in New Hampshire with his wife and two daughters. Will was also a Representative in the New Hampshire House of Representatives from 2010 to 2012. In his spare time, he likes to do blacksmithing, shooting (trap and skeet), snowmobiling, playing racquetball, and riding his Harley. Will is also a commercially rated helicopter pilot.

About the Technical Editor

Rodney Fournier has worked with Microsoft technologies as a consultant for decades. He is a huge Detroit Red Wings fan and a father.

Contents at a Glance

Contents

Chapter 9   Introduction to Microsoft Azure   465

Chapter 10   Understanding Azure Active Directory   499

Table of Exercises

Introduction

This book was written from over 25 years of IT experience. I have taken that experience and translated it into a Windows Server book that will help you not only prepare for the Microsoft Certified Associate Windows Server Hybrid Administrator exams but also develop a clear understanding of how to install and configure Windows Server 2022 while avoiding all the possible configuration pitfalls.

Many Microsoft books just explain the Windows Server operating system, but with *MCA® Microsoft Certified Associate Windows Server® Hybrid Administrator Complete Study Guide: Exam AZ-800 and Exam AZ-801*, I will go a step further, providing many in-depth, step-by-step procedures to support my explanations of how the operating system performs at its best.

The exams AZ-800, Administering Windows Server Hybrid Core Infrastructure, and AZ-801, Configuring Windows Server Hybrid Advanced Services, cover Windows Server 2022. This is Microsoft's Windows Server operating system software. Windows Server 2022 is the newest version released by Microsoft.

This book takes you through all the ins and outs of Windows Server 2022, including integrating Windows Server environments with Azure services, managing Windows Server in on-premises networks, and so much more.

When all is said and done, this is a technical book for IT professionals who want to take Windows Server 2022 to the next step and get certified. With this book, you will not only learn Windows Server 2022 and hopefully pass the exams, you will also become a Windows Server expert.

The Microsoft Certification Program

Since the inception of its certification program, Microsoft has certified more than 2 million people. As the computer network industry continues to increase in both size and complexity, this number is sure to grow—and the need for proven ability will also increase. Certifications can help companies verify the skills of prospective employees and contractors.

The Microsoft certification track for Windows Server includes this certification:

Microsoft Certified: Windows Server Hybrid Administrator Associate   The Microsoft Certified: Windows Server Hybrid Administrator Associate is now the highest-level certification you can achieve with Microsoft in relation to Windows Server. It requires passing exams AZ-800 and AZ-801. This book assists in your preparation for both exams.

How Do You Become Certified on Windows Server?

Attaining Microsoft certification has always been a challenge. In the past, students have been able to acquire detailed exam information—even most of the exam questions—from online "brain dumps" and third-party "cram" books or software products. For the new generation of exams, this is simply not the case.

Microsoft has taken strong steps to protect the security and integrity of its certifications. Now prospective candidates must complete a course of study that develops detailed knowledge about a wide range of topics. It supplies them with the true skills needed, derived from working with the technology being tested.

The new generations of Microsoft certification programs are heavily weighted toward hands-on skills and experience. It is recommended that candidates have troubleshooting skills acquired through hands-on experience and working knowledge.

Fortunately, if you are willing to dedicate the time and effort to learn Windows Server 2022, you can prepare yourself well for the exam by using the proper tools. By working through this book, you can successfully meet the requirements to pass the Windows Server exams.

Microsoft Certified: Windows Server Hybrid Administrator Associate Exam Requirements

Candidates for MCA certification for Windows Server must pass two exam:

- AZ-800: Administering Windows Server Hybrid Core Infrastructure
- AZ-801: Configuring Windows Server Hybrid Advanced Services

Microsoft provides exam objectives to give you a general overview of possible areas of coverage on the Microsoft exams. Keep in mind, however, that exam objectives are subject to change at any time without prior notice and at Microsoft's sole discretion. Please visit the Microsoft Learning website (https://learn.microsoft.com/en-us/certifications/windows-server-hybrid-administrator) for the most current listing of exam objectives.

> For a more detailed description of the Microsoft certification programs, including a list of all the exams, visit the Microsoft Learning website at https://learn.microsoft.com/en-us/certifications/browse.

Types of Exam Questions

In an effort to both refine the testing process and protect the quality of its certifications, Microsoft has focused its latest certification exams on real experience and hands-on proficiency. There is a greater emphasis on your past working environments and responsibilities and less emphasis on how well you can memorize. In fact, Microsoft says that certification candidates should have hands-on experience before attempting to pass any certification exams.

Microsoft will accomplish its goal of protecting the exams' integrity by regularly adding and removing exam questions, limiting the number of questions that any individual sees in a beta exam, limiting the number of questions delivered to an individual by using adaptive testing, and adding new exam elements.

Exam questions may be in a variety of formats. Depending on which exam you take you may see multiple-choice questions as well as select-and-place and prioritize-a-list questions. Simulations and case study–based formats are included as well. Let's take a look at the types of exam questions so that you'll be prepared for all the possibilities.

Multiple-Choice Questions

Multiple-choice questions come in two main forms. One is a straightforward question followed by several possible answers of which one or more is correct. The other type of multiple-choice question is more complex and based on a specific scenario. The scenario may focus on several areas or objectives.

Select-and-Place Questions

Select-and-place exam questions involve graphical elements that you must manipulate to successfully answer the question. For example, you might see a diagram of a computer network. A typical diagram will show computers and other components next to boxes that contain the text "Place here." The labels for the boxes represent various computer roles on a network, such as a print server and a file server. Based on information given for each computer, you are asked to select each label and place it in the correct box. You need to place *all* of the labels correctly. No credit is given for the question if you correctly label only some of the boxes.

In another select-and-place problem, you might be asked to put a series of steps in order by dragging items from boxes on the left to boxes on the right and placing them in the correct order. One other type requires that you drag an item from the left and place it under an item in a column on the right.

For more information on the various exam question types, go to https://docs.microsoft.com/en-us/certifications/exam-duration-question-types.

Simulations

Simulations are the kinds of questions that most closely represent actual situations and test the skills you use while working with Microsoft software interfaces. These exam questions include a mock interface on which you are asked to perform certain actions according to a given scenario. The simulated interfaces look nearly identical to what you see in the actual product.

Because of the number of possible errors that can be made on simulations, be sure to consider the following recommendations from Microsoft:

- Do not change any simulation settings that don't pertain to the solution directly.
- When related information has not been provided, assume that the default settings are used.
- Make sure that your entries are spelled correctly.
- Close all the simulation application windows after completing the set of tasks in the simulation.

The best way to prepare for simulation questions is to spend time working with the graphical interface of the product on which you will be tested.

Case Study–Based Questions

These questions present a scenario with a range of requirements. Based on the information provided, you answer a series of multiple-choice and select-and-place questions. The interface for case study–based questions have a number of tabs, each of which contains information about the scenario. At present, this type of question appears only in most of the Design exams.

Tips for Taking the Windows Server Exams

Here are some general tips for achieving success on your certification exam:

- Arrive early at the exam center so that you can relax and review your study materials. During this final review, you can look over tables and lists of exam-related information.
- Read the questions carefully. Do not be tempted to jump to an early conclusion. Make sure that you know *exactly* what the question is asking.
- Answer all questions. If you are unsure about a question, mark it for review and come back to it at a later time.
- On simulations, do not change settings that are not directly related to the question. Also, assume default settings if the question does not specify or imply which settings are used.
- For questions that you're not sure about, use a process of elimination to get rid of the obviously incorrect answers first. This improves your odds of selecting the correct answer when you need to make an educated guess.

Exam Registration

At the time this book was released, Microsoft exams are given using more than 1,000 Authorized VUE Testing Centers around the world. For the location of a testing center near you, go to VUE's website at https://home.pearsonvue.com. If you are outside the United States and Canada, contact your local VUE registration center.

Find out the number of the exam you want to take, and then register with the VUE registration center nearest to you. At this point, you will be asked for advance payment for the exam. The exams are $165 each and you must take them within one year of payment. You can schedule exams up to six weeks in advance or as late as one working day prior to the date of the exam. You can cancel or reschedule your exam if you contact the center at least two working days prior to the exam. Same-day registration is available in some locations, subject to space availability. Where same-day registration is available, you must register a minimum of two hours before test time.

When you schedule the exam, you will be provided with instructions regarding appointment and cancellation procedures, ID requirements, and information about the testing center location. In addition, you will receive a registration and payment confirmation letter from VUE.

Microsoft requires certification candidates to accept the terms of a nondisclosure agreement before taking certification exams.

 Exam policies can change from time to time. We highly recommend that you check both the Microsoft and Pearson VUE sites for the most up-to-date information when you begin your preparing, when you register, and again a few days before your scheduled exam date.

Who Should Read This Book?

This book is intended for individuals who want to earn their Microsoft Certified: Windows Server Hybrid Administrator Associate certification.

Not only will this book help anyone who is looking to pass the Microsoft exams, it will also help anyone who wants to learn the real ins and outs of the Windows client operating system.

What's Inside?

Here is a glance at what's in each chapter.

Chapter 1: Introduction to Windows Server 2022   You've decided to start down the track of Windows Server 2022. In the first chapter, I explain what's new about the Windows Server 2022 features and benefits that are available and how these features can help improve your organization's network.

Chapter 2: Understanding Hyper-V   This chapter talks about virtualization and how it works. We will focus most of our attention on Microsoft's version of virtualization called Hyper-V. I'll explain how to install, configure, and build virtual machines.

Chapter 3: Installing Windows Server 2022   In this chapter, I will show you how to install Windows Server 2022. I will show you how to install the Desktop (GUI) version of Server 2022 as well as the Server Core version of Server 2022.

Chapter 4: Understanding IP   In this chapter, I will discuss the most important protocol used in a Microsoft Windows Server 2022 network: *Transmission Control Protocol/ Internet Protocol (TCP/IP)*. TCP/IP is actually multiple protocols bundled together: Transmission Control Protocol (TCP) and the Internet Protocol (IP).

Chapter 5: Implementing DNS   This chapter talks about the Domain Name System (DNS). DNS is one of the most important networking services that you can put on your network, and it's also one of the key topics that you'll need to understand if you plan to take any of the Microsoft Azure exams.

Chapter 6: Configuring DHCP and IPAM   In this chapter, I will show you the different methods of setting up an IP address network. If you want systems to be able to share network resources, the computers must all talk the same type of language. This is where DHCP comes into play.

Chapter 7: Understanding Active Directory   One of the most important tasks that you will complete on a network is setting up your domain. To set up your domain properly, you must know how to install and configure your domain controllers. Once you understand how to plan properly for your domain environment, you will learn how to install Active Directory, which you will accomplish by promoting a Windows Server 2022 computer to a domain controller. We will look at the difference between setting up Active Directory on a Server Core machine versus Windows Server 2022 with the Desktop Experience. I will also discuss a feature in Windows Server 2022 called a *read-only domain controller (RODC)*, and I will show you how to install Active Directory using Windows PowerShell.

Chapter 8: Understanding Group Policies   Two of the most important system administration features in Windows Server 2022 and Active Directory are *Group Policy* and *security policy*. By using *Group Policy Objects (GPOs)*, you can quickly and easily define restrictions on common actions and then apply them at the site, domain, or organizational unit (OU) level. In this chapter, you will see how group and security policies work.

Chapter 9: Introduction to Microsoft Azure   Before we actually connect the network to the cloud, it's important to understand how the cloud works and the different types of cloud setups that you can choose from. In this chapter, I will explain the different types of cloud setups and the terminology that you will need to understand so that you can build your cloud network.

Chapter 10: Understanding Azure Active Directory   In this chapter, it is time for us to start diving into the world of Azure Active Directory (AD). Azure AD is a cloud-based identity and access management service. The Azure environment is controlled by the Azure Resource Manager. It can be controlled by templates, PowerShell, the Azure portal, CLI, and APIs. Azure AD controls access to resources using RBAC and conditional access.

Chapter 11: Configuring Storage   This chapter explains how to set up your servers so that your network users have something to access. Before you can set up a server, you have to determine its purpose. Is it going to be a print server, a file storage server, a remote access server, or a domain controller?

Chapter 12: Building an Azure Infrastructure   In this chapter, I will talk about building an Azure infrastructure. We will start by talking about a smaller type of virtual environment called a container. I will then talk about using the different Azure components that will allow you to build and secure your Azure infrastructure.

Chapter 13: Managing Data in a Hybrid Network   In this chapter, I will introduce you to some of the techniques and components of high availability. I will explain how to set up high availability using network load balancing (NLB). I will talk about some of the reasons why you would choose to use NLB over using a failover cluster and which applications or servers work better with NLB. I will also show you how to use PowerShell for NLB.

Chapter 14: Hybrid Data and Servers   In this chapter, I will talk about the benefits of using Microsoft Endpoint and the tools and applications that will help IT administrators manage their software and applications. I will also talk about Autopilot and how you can use Autopilot to deploy operating systems to new or repurposed machines. It is truly a zero-touch installation.

Chapter 15: Implementing Security   In this chapter, you'll learn how to defend your Windows systems by using the built-in security features called Windows Security. I will show you the different ways that you can protect your system using Windows Security. I will show you how to protect your Windows client and server devices by using the Windows Defender Firewall.

Chapter 16: Understanding Monitoring   In this chapter, I'll cover the tools and methods used for measuring performance and troubleshooting failures in Windows Server 2022. Before you dive into the technical details, however, you should thoroughly understand what you're trying to accomplish and how you'll meet this goal.

Chapter 17: Understanding Disaster Recovery   In this chapter, I will talk about some of the ways to protect your data and your systems by using Azure. Azure has a number of tools available to help identify and remediate security issues. I will briefly discuss some of them and delve into how to identify and remediate Windows Server security issues by using Azure services such as Microsoft Sentinel and Microsoft Defender for Cloud.

What's Included with the Book

There are many helpful items intended to prepare you for the Microsoft Certified: Windows Server Hybrid Administrator Associate certification included in this book:

Assessment Test   There is an assessment test at the conclusion of the introduction that can be used to quickly evaluate what you know about Windows Server 2022. This test should be taken prior to beginning your work in this book and should help you identify areas in which you are either strong or weak. Note that these questions are purposely more simplistic than the types of questions you may see on the exams.

Opening List of Objectives   Most of the chapters include a list of the exam objectives that are covered in that chapter. However, a few chapters might only provide an introduction to a topic and not cover any objectives.

Helpful Exercises   Throughout the book, I have included step-by-step exercises of some of the more important tasks you should be able to perform. Some of these exercises have corresponding videos that can be downloaded from the book's website. Also, later in this introduction you'll find a recommended home lab setup that will be helpful in completing these tasks.

Exam Essentials   The end of each chapter also includes a listing of exam essentials. These are essentially repeats of the objectives, but remember that any objective on the exam blueprint could show up on the exam.

Chapter Review Questions   Each chapter includes review questions. These are used to assess your understanding of the chapter and are taken directly from the chapter. These questions are based on the exam objectives and are similar in difficulty to items you might encounter on the actual AZ-800 and AZ-801 exams.

The Sybex Interactive Online Test Bank, flashcards, videos, and glossary can be accessed at www.wiley.com/go/sybextestprep.

Interactive Online Learning Environment and Test Bank

The interactive online learning environment that accompanies *MCA Microsoft Certified Associate Windows Server Hybrid Administrator Complete Study Guide: Exam AZ-800 and Exam AZ-801* provides a test bank with study tools to help you prepare for the certification exams and increase your chances of passing the exam the very first time! The test bank includes the following elements:

Sample Tests   All of the questions in this book are provided, including the assessment test, which you'll find at the end of this introduction, and the chapter tests that include the review questions at the end of each chapter. In addition, there are two practice exams. Use these questions to test your knowledge of the study guide material. The online test bank runs on multiple devices.

Electronic Flashcards   The flashcards are included for quick reference and are great tools for learning quick facts. You can even consider them additional simple practice questions, which is essentially what they are.

PDF of Glossary of Terms   A glossary is included that covers the key terms used in this book.

Like all exams, the MCA certification from Microsoft is updated periodically and may eventually be retired or replaced. At some point after Microsoft is no longer offering this exam, the old editions of our books and online tools will be retired. If you have purchased this book after the exam was retired, or are attempting to register in the Sybex online learning environment after the exam was retired, please know that we make no guarantees that this exam's online Sybex tools will be available once the exam is no longer available.

Recommended Home Lab Setup

To get the most out of this book, you will want to make sure that you complete the exercises throughout the chapters. To complete the exercises, you will need one of two setups. First, you can set up a machine with Windows 10/11 and complete the exercises using a regular Windows client machine.

The second way to set up Windows 10/11 is by using virtualization. I set up Windows 10/11 as a virtual hard disk (VHD) and I did all the exercises this way. The advantages of using virtualization are that you can always just wipe out the system and start over without losing a real server. Plus, you can set up multiple virtual servers and create a full lab environment on one machine.

I created a video for this book showing you how to set up a virtual machine and how to install Windows 10 onto that virtual machine. This video can be seen at www.youtube .com/c/williampanek.

How to Contact Sybex or the Author

Sybex strives to keep you supplied with the latest tools and information you need for your work. Please check the website at www.wiley.com/go/sybextestprep, where I'll post additional content and updates that supplement this book should the need arise.

You can contact me by going to my website at www.willpanek.com. I also have videos and test prep information at www.youtube.com/c/williampanek. I also have a Twitter account, @AuthorWillPanek.

Objective Mapping

Tables I.1 and I.2 provide a handy objective map that shows you at a glance in what chapter each objective is covered.

TABLE I.1 Exam AZ-800 Objective Map: Administering Windows Server Hybrid Core Infrastructure.

Objective	Chapter
Deploy and manage Active Directory Domain Services (AD DS) in on-premises and cloud environments (30–35%)	
Deploy and manage AD DS domain controllers	**Chapter 7**
▪ Deploy and manage domain controllers on-premises	
▪ Deploy and manage domain controllers in Azure	
▪ Deploy Read-Only Domain Controllers (RODCs)	
▪ Troubleshoot flexible single master operations (FSMO) roles	
Configure and manage multi-site, multi-domain, and multi-forest environments	**Chapter 7**
▪ Configure and manage forest and domain trusts	Chapter 4
▪ Configure and manage AD DS sites	
▪ Configure and manage AD DS replication	
Create and manage AD DS security principals	**Chapter 7**
▪ Create and manage AD DS users and groups	Chapter 4
▪ Manage users and groups in multi-domain and multi-forest scenarios	
▪ Implement group managed service accounts (gMSAs)	
▪ Join Windows Servers to AD DS, Azure AD DS, and Azure AD	
Implement and manage hybrid identities	**Chapter 10**
▪ Implement Azure AD Connect	
▪ Manage Azure AD Connect Synchronization	
▪ Implement Azure AD Connect cloud sync	
▪ Integrate Azure AD, AD DS, and Azure AD DS	
▪ Manage Azure AD DS	
▪ Manage Azure AD Connect Health	
▪ Manage authentication in on-premises and hybrid environments	
▪ Configure and manage AD DS passwords	
Manage Windows Server by using domain-based Group Policies	**Chapter 8**
▪ Implement Group Policy in AD DS	
▪ Implement Group Policy Preferences in AD DS	
▪ Implement Group Policy in Azure AD DS	

Objective	Chapter

Manage Windows Servers and workloads in a hybrid environment (10–15%)

Manage Windows Servers in a hybrid environment — **Chapter 16**

- Deploy a Windows Admin Center gateway server — Chapter 2
- Configure a target machine for Windows Admin Center
- Configure PowerShell Remoting
- Configure CredSSP or Kerberos Delegation for second hop remoting
- Configure JEA for PowerShell Remoting

Manage Windows Servers and workloads by using Azure services — **Chapter 12**

- Manage Windows Servers by using Azure Arc
- Assign Azure Policy Guest configuration
- Deploy Azure services using Azure Virtual Machine extensions on non-Azure machines
- Manage updates for Windows machines
- Integrate Windows Servers with Log Analytics
- Integrate Windows Servers with Azure Security Center
- Manage IaaS virtual machines (VMs) in Azure that run Windows Server
- Implement Azure Automation for hybrid workloads
- Create runbooks to automate tasks on target VMs
- Implement DSC to prevent configuration drift in IaaS machines

Manage virtual machines and containers (15–20%)

Manage Windows Servers and workloads by using Azure services — **Chapter 12**

- Manage Windows Servers by using Azure Arc
- Assign Azure Policy guest configuration
- Deploy Azure services using Azure VM extensions on non-Azure machines
- Manage updates for Windows machines
- Integrate Windows Servers with Log Analytics
- Integrate Windows Servers with Microsoft Defender for Cloud
- Manage IaaS VMs in Azure that run Windows Server
- Implement Azure Automation for hybrid workloads
- Create runbooks to automate tasks on target VMs
- Implement Azure Automation State Configuration to prevent configuration drift in IaaS machines

TABLE I.1 Exam AZ-800 Objective Map: Administering Windows Server Hybrid Core Infrastructure *(continued)*

Objective	Chapter
Create and manage containers	**Chapter 12**
▪ Create Windows Server container images	Chapter 2
▪ Manage Windows Server container images	
▪ Configure container networking	
▪ Manage container instances	
Manage Azure Virtual Machines that run Windows Server	**Chapter 12**
▪ Manage data disks	Chapter 2
▪ Resize Azure VM	
▪ Configure continuous delivery for an Azure VM	
▪ Configure connections to VMs	
▪ Manage Azure VM network configuration	
Implement and manage an on-premises and hybrid networking infrastructure (15–20%)	
Implement on-premises and hybrid name resolution	**Chapter 5**
▪ Integrate DNS with AD DS	Chapter 7
▪ Create and manage DNS zones and records	
▪ Configure DNS forwarding/conditional forwarding	
▪ Integrate Windows Server DNS with Azure DNS private zones	
▪ Implement DNSSEC	
Manage IP addressing in on-premises and hybrid scenarios	**Chapter 4**
Implement and manage IPAM	Chapter 1
▪ Implement and configure the DHCP server role (on-premises only)	
▪ Resolve IP address issues in hybrid environments	
▪ Create and manage scopes	
▪ Create and manage IP reservations	
▪ Implement DHCP high availability	

- Implement and manage Azure Network Adapter
- Implement and manage Azure extended network
- Implement and manage Network Policy Server role
- Implement Web Application Proxy
- Implement Azure Relay
- Implement site-to-site VPN
- Implement Azure Virtual WAN
- Implement Azure AD Application Proxy

Manage storage and file services (15–20%)

- Create Azure File Sync Service
- Create sync groups
- Create cloud endpoints
- Register servers
- Create server endpoints
- Configure cloud tiering
- Monitor File Sync
- Migrate DFS to Azure File Sync

- Configure Windows Server file share access
- Configuring file screens
- Configure FSRM quotas
- Configure BranchCache
- Implement and configure Distributed File System (DFS)

TABLE I.1   Exam AZ-800 Objective Map: Administering Windows Server Hybrid Core Infrastructure   *(continued)*

Objective	Chapter
Configure Windows Server storage	**Chapter 3**

- Configure disks and volumes
- Configure and manage Storage Spaces
- Configure and manage Storage Replica
- Configure Data Deduplication
- Configure SMB direct
- Configure Storage QoS
- Configure file systems

TABLE I.2   AZ-801 Objective Map: Configuring Windows Server Hybrid Advanced Services

Objective	Chapter
Secure Windows Server on-premises and hybrid infrastructures (25-30%)	
Secure Windows Server operating system	**Chapter 15**

- Configure and manage Exploit Protection
- Configure and manage Windows Defender Application Control
- Configure and manage Microsoft Defender for Endpoint
- Configure and manage Windows Defender Credential Guard
- Configure SmartScreen
- Implement operating system security by using Group Policies

| **Secure a hybrid Active Directory infrastructure** | **Chapter 7** |

- Configure password policies
- Enable password block lists
- Manage protected users
- Manage account security on an RODC
- Harden domain controllers
- Configure authentication policies silos
- Restrict access to domain controllers
- Configure account security
- Manage AD built-in administrative groups
- Manage AD delegation
- Implement and manage Microsoft Defender for Identity

Objective	Chapter

Identify and remediate Windows Server security issues by using Azure Services   Chapter 17

- Monitor on-premises servers and Azure IaaS VMs by using Microsoft Sentinel
- Identify and remediate security issues on-premises servers and Azure IaaS VMs by using Microsoft Defender for Cloud

Secure Windows Server networking   Chapter 15

- Manage Windows Defender Firewall
- Implement domain isolation
- Implement connection security rules

Secure Windows Server storage   Chapter 11

- Manage Windows BitLocker Drive Encryption (BitLocker)
- Manage and recover encrypted volumes
- Enable storage encryption by using Azure Disk Encryption
- Manage disk encryption keys for IaaS virtual machines

Implement and manage Windows Server high availability (10–15%)

Implement a Windows Server failover cluster   Chapter 13

- Implement a failover cluster on-premises, hybrid, or cloud-only
- Create a Windows failover cluster
- Stretch cluster across datacenter or Azure regions
- Configure storage for failover clustering
- Modify quorum options
- Configure network adapters for failover clustering
- Configure cluster workload options
- Configure cluster sets
- Configure Scale-Out File servers
- Create an Azure witness
- Configure a floating IP address for the cluster
- Implement load balancing for the failover cluster

TABLE I.2 AZ-801 Objective Map: Configuring Windows Server *(continued)*

Objective	Chapter
Manage failover clustering	**Chapter 13**

- Implement cluster-aware updating
- Recover a failed cluster node
- Upgrade a node to Windows Server 2022
- Failover workloads between nodes
- Install Windows updates on cluster nodes
- Manage failover clusters using Windows Admin Center

Implement and manage Storage Spaces Direct	**Chapter 13**

- Create a failover cluster using Storage Spaces Direct
- Upgrade a Storage Spaces Direct node
- Implement networking for Storage Spaces Direct
- Configure Storage Spaces Direct

Implement disaster recovery (10–15%)

Manage backup and recovery for Windows Server	**Chapter 17**

Back up and restore files and folders to Azure Recovery Services Vault

- Install and manage Azure Backup Server
- Back up and recover using Azure Backup Server
- Manage backups in Azure Recovery Services Vault
- Create a backup policy
- Configure backup for Azure VM using the built-in backup agent
- Recover VM using temporary snapshots
- Recover VMs to new Azure VMs
- Restore a VM

Implement disaster recovery by using Azure Site Recovery	**Chapter 17**

- Configure Azure Site Recovery networking
- Configure Site Recovery for on-premises VMs
- Configure a recovery plan
- Configure Site Recovery for Azure VMs
- Implement VM replication to secondary datacenter or Azure region
- Configure Azure Site Recovery policies

Objective	Chapter

Protect virtual machines by using Hyper-V replicas   **Chapter 2**

- Configure Hyper-V hosts for replication
- Manage Hyper-V replica servers
- Configure VM replication
- Perform a failover

Migrate servers and workloads (20–25%)

Migrate on-premises storage to on-premises servers or Azure   **Chapter 14**

- Transfer data and share
- Cut over to a new server by using Storage Migration Service (SMS)
- Use Storage Migration Service to migrate to Azure VMs
- Migrate to Azure file shares

Migrate on-premises servers to Azure   **Chapter 14**

Deploy and configure Azure Migrate appliance

- Migrate VM workloads to Azure IaaS
- Migrate physical workloads to Azure IaaS
- Migrate by using Azure Migrate

Migrate workloads from previous versions to Windows Server 2022   **Chapter 14**

- Migrate IIS
- Migrate Hyper-V hosts
- Migrate RDS host servers
- Migrate DHCP
- Migrate print servers

Migrate IIS workloads to Azure   **Chapter 14**

- Migrate IIS workloads to Azure Web Apps
- Migrate IIS workloads to containers

TABLE I.2   AZ-801 Objective Map: Configuring Windows Server *(continued)*

Objective	Chapter
Migrate an AD DS infrastructure to Windows Server 2022 AD DS	**Chapter 7**

- Migrate AD DS objects, including users, groups and Group Policies using AD Migration Tool
- Migrate to a new Active Directory forest
- Upgrade an existing forest

Monitor and troubleshoot Windows Server environments (20–25%)

Monitor Windows Server by using Windows Server tools and Azure services	**Chapter 16**

- Monitor Windows Server by using Performance Monitor
- Create and configure Data Collector Sets
- Monitor servers and configure alerts by using Windows Admin Center
- Monitor by using System Insights
- Manage event logs
- Deploy Azure Monitor agents
- Collect performance counters to Azure
- Create alerts
- Monitor Azure VMs by using Azure diagnostics extension
- Monitor Azure VMs performance by using VM Insights

Troubleshoot Windows Server on-premises and hybrid networking	**Chapter 16**

- Troubleshoot hybrid network connectivity
- Troubleshoot on-premises connectivity

Troubleshoot Windows Server virtual machines in Azure	**Chapter 17**

- Troubleshoot deployment failures
- Troubleshoot booting failures
- Troubleshoot VM performance issues
- Troubleshoot VM extension issues
- Troubleshoot disk encryption issues
- Troubleshoot storage
- Troubleshoot VM connection issues

How to Contact the Publisher

If you believe you have found a mistake in this book, please bring it to our attention. At John Wiley & Sons, we understand how important it is to provide our customers with accurate content, but even with our best efforts an error may occur.

To submit your possible errata, please email it to our Customer Service Team at wileysupport@wiley.com with the subject line "Possible Book Errata Submission."

Assessment Test

1. You are speaking to a co-worker regarding using Classless Inter-Domain Routing (CIDR). Which of the following subnet masks are represented with the CIDR of /28?

    A. 255.255.255.224

    B. 255.255.255.240

    C. 255.255.255.248

    D. 255.255.255.254

2. You have a large number of Windows client computers. All of the computers in the network are joined to Microsoft Azure Active Directory (Azure AD). All of the computers are configured differently in terms of update settings. Some of them are configured for manual updates. You want to configure Windows Update for these machines. You must meet the following requirements:

    - The computers must be managed from a central location.

    - You must minimize traffic across the Internet.

    - You must keep costs to a minimum.

    What Windows Update technology should you use to meet your requirements?

    A. Microsoft Configuration Manager (MCM)

    B. Windows Server Update Service (WSUS)

    C. Windows Update for Business

    D. Windows Update Management Center

3. You and a colleague are discussing managing volumes. What type of volume are we discussing when we say that it is a simple volume that spreads data across multiple disks?

    A. Mirrored volume

    B. RAID-5 volume

    C. Spanned volume

    D. Striped volume

4. A user contacts you to let you know that they cannot connect to the Internet. You examine the `ipconfig` results as shown here:

    ```
    IPv4 Address. . . . . . . .: 10.254.254.1
    Subnet Mask . . . . . . .  : 255.255.255.0
    Default Gateway . . . . . .: 10.254.254.255
    ```

    What is most likely the cause of the issue given the `ipconfig` results?

    A. The subnet mask is incorrect.

    B. The IP address is incorrect.

    C. The default gateway is incorrect.

    D. The subnet mask and the IP address are incorrect.

5. You have a Windows client machine that needs to be able to communicate with all computers on the internal network. The company decides to add 15 new segments to its IPv6 network. How should you configure the IPv6 address so that the server can communicate with all of the segments?

   A. Configure the address as `fd00::2b0:e0ff:dee9:4143/8`.

   B. Configure the address as `fe80::2b0:e0ff:dee9:4143/32`.

   C. Configure the address as `ff80::2b0:e0ff:dee9:4143/64`.

   D. Configure the address as `fe80::2b0:e0ff:dee9:4143/64`.

6. You are worried that your network's security may have been compromised. You want to set up a policy that will not allow hackers to be able to continuously attempt user logons using different passwords. What Local Security policy should you set to accomplish this goal?

   A. An Account Lockout policy

   B. An Audit policy

   C. A Password policy

   D. Security Options

7. You are troubleshooting a network connectivity problem, and you are reviewing the following results:

```
1     15 ms     19 ms     19 ms   10.21.80.1
2     12 ms     22 ms     12 ms   208.59.252.1
3    152 ms    216 ms    149 ms   207.172.15.38
4     14 ms     24 ms     37 ms   207.172.19.222
5     21 ms     16 ms     25 ms   207.172.19.103
6     17 ms     23 ms     30 ms   207.172.9.126
7     15 ms     14 ms     15 ms   72.14.238.232
8     15 ms     35 ms     18 ms   209.85.241.148
9     30 ms     23 ms     44 ms   66.249.91.104
```

   What command was used to acquire these results?

   A. `ipconfig`

   B. `pathping`

   C. `netstat`

   D. `tracert`

8. You have a Windows client computer that is used to test new Windows features. You want to configure this computer to receive preview builds of Windows Server 2022 as soon as they are available. In the Settings app, what should you configure from Update & Security to set this up?

   A. Delivery Optimization

   B. For Developers

   C. Windows Insider Program

   D. Windows Update

9. You are a system administrator for a medium-sized Active Directory network. You have a few new applications that will be deployed throughout the organization using Registry-based settings. You want to control the Registry settings by using Group Policy and create a standard set of options for these applications and allow other system administrators to modify them using the standard Active Directory tools. Which of the following can you use to meet your needs? (Choose two.)

    A. Create administrative templates.

    B. Implement delegation of specific objects within Active Directory.

    C. Implement the inheritance functionality of GPOs.

    D. Implement the No Override functionality of GPOs.

    E. Provide administrative templates to the system administrators who are responsible for creating Group Policy for the applications.

10. You are a systems administrator for your corporate network. Because of the unusual growth of TCP/IP devices on your corporate network over the last year, you need to scale out your IPAM database capabilities. You are currently using a Windows Internal Database (WID) for your IPAM infrastructure, and you want to migrate your IPAM database to a Microsoft SQL Server. Which PowerShell cmdlet should you use?

    A. `Get-IpamMigrationSettings`

    B. `Move-IpamDatabase`

    C. `Show-IpamDatabaseConfig`

    D. `Show-IpamStatistics`

11. Your network contains two servers named Server1 and Server2 that run Windows Server 2022. Server1 is a DHCP server that is configured to have a scope named Scope1. Server2 is configured to obtain an IP address automatically. In the scope on Server1, you create a reservation named Server2_Reservation for Server2. You replace the network adapter on Server2 and you need to ensure that Server2 can obtain the same IP address as it did before the network card got replaced. What should you modify on Server1?

    A. The Advanced settings of Server2_Reservation

    B. The MAC address of Server2_Reservation

    C. The Name Protection settings of Scope1

    D. The Network Access Protection Settings of Scope1

12. You want to ensure that only the GPOs set at the OU level affect the Group Policy settings for objects within the OU. Which option can you use to do this (assuming that all other GPO settings are the defaults)?

    A. The Enforced option

    B. The Block Policy Inheritance option

    C. The Disable option

    D. The Deny permission

13. You are the administrator for your company network. The network has an Active Directory domain. The domain contains several thousand Windows client computers. You implement hybrid Microsoft Azure Active Directory (Azure AD) and Microsoft Intune. You have to register all of the existing computers automatically to Azure AD and enroll the computers in Intune. What should you do while using the least amount of administrative effort?

   A. Configure an Autodiscover address record.

   B. Configure an Autodiscover service connection point (SCP).

   C. Configure a Group Policy Object (GPO).

   D. Configure a Windows Autopilot deployment profile.

14. You want to view your Azure AD directory settings for an Azure AD subscription. What PowerShell command should you use?

   A. `Add-AzureADDirectorySetting`

   B. `Get-AzureADDirectorySetting`

   C. `Set-AzureADDirectorySetting`

   D. `View-AzureADDirectorySetting`

15. You and a colleague are discussing a tool that is virtualization-based security to help isolate critical files so that only system software that is privileged can access those critical files. What is this tool called?

   A. Windows Defender Application Control

   B. Windows Defender Credential Guard

   C. Windows Defender Exploit Guard

   D. Windows Defender Firewall with Advanced Security

16. You and a colleague are discussing the different Intune profile types that you can create. These profiles are used to allow or prevent some features on the devices. One of the profile types includes hundreds of settings that can be configured for Microsoft Edge, OneDrive, Remote Desktop, Word, Excel, and more. What profile type is being discussed?

   A. Administrative templates

   B. Certificates

   C. Custom profiles

   D. Device restrictions

17. You have a user who is a member of the Sales, R&D, and HR groups. There is a folder called `MyShare` on the server. The current permissions of the folder are as follows:

Group/user	NTFS permission
Sales	Read
Marketing	Modify
R&D	Modify

Group/user	NTFS permission
HR	Deny
Admin	Full Control

What is this user's effective NTFS permission?

A. Deny

B. Full Control

C. Modify

D. Read

18. You and a colleague are discussing the wide variety of Windows client recovery techniques that Microsoft provides. One of these techniques shows a log of application and system messages, including errors, informational messages, and warnings. What is this recovery technique called?

A. Backup and Restore

B. Driver Rollback

C. Event Viewer

D. Safe Mode

E. Startup Repair Tool

F. System Restore

19. You and a colleague are discussing the Microsoft Defender Application Guard. You know that there are a few hardware requirements that must be met to be able to utilize this feature. What is the minimum amount of RAM that Microsoft recommends to use Application Guard?

A. 2 GB

B. 4 GB

C. 8 GB

D. 12 GB

20. You company is planning to migrate a web application to Azure. The web application is accessed by external users. You need to recommend a cloud deployment solution to minimize the amount of administrative effort used to build and manage the web application. What should you include in the recommendation?

A. Database as a service (DaaS)

B. Infrastructure as a service (IaaS)

C. Platform as a service (PaaS)

D. Software as a service (SaaS)

21. You and a colleague are discussing the ability of Azure AD users to roam their profile data between multiple devices, allowing the user and app settings to sync between the devices regardless of where the user is located. What is this called?

   A. Azure Readiness Roaming

   B. Enterprise State Roaming

   C. Mandatory User Profile

   D. Roaming User Profile

22. You and a colleague are discussing a tool that allows an organization to automate the detection and remediation of identity-based risks. What is this tool called?

   A. Azure AD User Security

   B. Azure AD Identity Protection

   C. Azure AD Security add-on

   D. Azure Identity Protection

23. You and a colleague are discussing roles and permissions. You are using Azure AD, and you want to assign permissions to users for maintaining conditional access. What role should you assign to the users if you'd like them to be able to view, create, modify, and delete conditional access policies?

   A. Application Administrator role

   B. Compliance Administrator role

   C. Conditional Access Administrator role

   D. Conditional Admission Administrator role

Answers to Assessment Test

1. **B.** The CIDR /28 tells you that 28 1s are turned on in the subnet mask. Twenty-eight 1s equals 11111111.11111111.11111111.11110000. This would then equal 255.255.255.240.

2. **B.** Windows Update is a tool that connects to the Microsoft website or to a local update server called a Windows Server Update Services (WSUS) server. This will ensure that the Windows client operating system and other Microsoft products have the most up-to-date version. An advantage to using WSUS is that administrators can approve the updates prior to them being deployed onto the network. Another advantage is that the clients only need to download updates locally, without using Internet bandwidth. Microsoft offers WSUS for free.

3. **C.** A spanned volume is a simple volume that spans multiple disks. You can create a spanned volume from free space that exists on a minimum of 2 to a maximum of 32 physical drives. When the spanned volume is initially created in Windows Server 2022, it can be formatted with either FAT32 or NTFS. If you extend a volume that already contains data, then the partition must be formatted with NTFS.

4. **C.** The `ipconfig` results are showing that this is a Class A address that is being used as a Class C network. On a Class C network, you *cannot* use the first or last numbers in the IP range (0 and 255). The first number of any range represents the network ID. The last number of any range represents the broadcast ID (255). So, having the default gateway set as .255 is not correct. The highest number on a Class C network that can be issued to a device is 254.

5. **A.** When you look at an IPv6 address, the first sections tell you the IPv6 address space prefix. `fd00::` /8 is the unique local unicast prefix, and this allows the server to communicate with all local machines within your intranet.

6. **A.** You will want to configure an Account Lockout policy. This policy is used to specify options that will prevent a user from attempting multiple failed logon attempts. If the Account Lockout Threshold value is surpassed, the account will be locked. The account can be reset based on a specified amount of time or through administrator involvement. An Account Lockout policy is a useful method of slowing down online password-guessing attacks.

7. **D.** Tracert is a diagnostic utility that determines the route to a destination by sending Internet Control Message Protocol (ICMP) echo packets to the destination. In these packets, the `tracert` command uses varying IP time-to-live (TTL) values. You can use `tracert` to find out where a packet has stopped on a network.

8. **C.** The Windows Insider Program allows you to preview builds of Windows 10 (and above) and Windows Server 2019 (and above). It allows you to try new features and provide feedback directly to Microsoft. On the Windows client computer, go to Settings ↻ Update & Security ↻ Windows Insider Program. You will need to have administrator rights to the computer.

9. **A, E.** Administrative templates are used to specify the options available for setting Group Policy. By creating new administrative templates, you can specify which options are available

for the new applications. You can then distribute these templates to other system administrators in the environment.

10. B. The `Move-IpamDatabase` command allows you to move an IPAM database to a SQL server database.

11. B. Reservations are set up by using the machine's network adapter's MAC address. Every network adapter has its own MAC address. So, when the network card is replaced, the new MAC address needs to be put into the current reservation.

12. B. The Block Policy Inheritance option prevents group policies of higher-level Active Directory objects from applying to lower-level objects as long as the Enforced option is not set.

13. D. Using Microsoft Intune and Windows Autopilot, you can give devices to your end users without the need to build, maintain, and apply custom operating system images. When you use Intune to manage Autopilot devices, you can manage policies, profiles, applications, and more.

14. B. Azure Active Directory (Azure AD) simplifies the way that you manage your applications by providing a single identity system for your cloud and on-premises apps. You can use the `Get-AzureADDirectorySetting` command to get the directory setting from Azure AD.

15. B. Windows Defender Credential Guard is a virtualization-based security tool to help isolate critical files so that only system software that is privileged can access those critical files. Once it's enabled, a Windows client machine that is part of Active Directory or Azure AD will have the system's credentials protected by Windows Defender Credential Guard. Windows Defender Credential Guard can be enabled by using Group Policy, the Registry, or the Hypervisor-Protected Code Integrity (HVCI) and Windows Defender Credential Guard hardware readiness tool.

16. A. Microsoft Intune includes settings and features that allow you to enable or disable features for different devices. These settings and features are added to configuration profiles. Once you create a configuration profile, you will then use Intune to assign the profile to the devices. There is a wide variety of profile types. Administrative templates include hundreds of settings that can be configured for Microsoft Edge, OneDrive, Remote Desktop, Word, Excel, and more. These templates provide you with a simplified view of settings similar to Group Policy, and they are all cloud-based.

17. A. Permissions are additive among themselves. This means you get the highest level of permissions among the group membership. In this question, the user is a member of three different groups, which consist of Read, Modify, and Deny. Since the permissions are additive and the user will get the highest level of permission, the user's effective permission will be Deny. Because the user has been denied access through the HR membership, the deny permissions override the allowed permissions.

18. C. The Windows Event Viewer shows a log of application and system messages. It also includes errors, informational messages, and warnings. It is a handy tool for troubleshooting. Event Viewer is a useful tool for monitoring network information. You can use the logs to view any information, warnings, or alerts related to the functionality of the network. Event Viewer can display hundreds of events.

19. C. Microsoft Defender Application Guard uses a hardware isolation approach. This lets untrusted site navigation launch inside a container, thus safeguarding corporate networks and data. The administrator determines which sites are trusted sites, cloud resources, and internal networks. Anything that is not on the trusted sites list is considered untrusted. If a user goes to an untrusted site, Microsoft Edge opens the site in an isolated Hyper-V-enabled container, which is separate from the host operating system.

20. C. According to Microsoft, "platform as a service (PaaS) is a complete development and deployment environment in the cloud, with resources that enable you to deliver everything from simple cloud-based apps to sophisticated, cloud-enabled enterprise applications."

21. B. Azure AD users have the ability to securely synchronize their user settings and application settings data to the cloud using Enterprise State Roaming. Enterprise State Roaming provides users with a unified experience across their Windows devices and diminishes the time required for configuring a new device. To enable Enterprise State Roaming, perform the following steps:

   1. Sign into the Azure AD Admin Center.

   2. Select Azure Active Directory ➢ Devices ➢ Enterprise State Roaming.

   3. Select Users May Sync Settings And App Data Across Devices.

   When you enable Enterprise State Roaming, your organization is automatically granted a free, limited-use license for Azure Rights Management protection from Azure Information Protection.

22. B. Azure AD Identity Protection is a tool that allows a company to achieve these three key tasks:

   ■ Automate the detection and remediation of identity-based risks.

   ■ Investigate risks using data in the portal.

   ■ Export risk detection data to third-party utilities for further analysis.

   Azure AD Identity Protection identifies risks. The risk signals that can trigger remediation efforts may include requiring users to perform Azure Multifactor Authentication, requiring users to reset their password by using self-service password reset, or blocking until an administrator takes action.

23. C. Conditional access is a feature used by Azure AD to bring signals together, to make decisions, and to enforce policies. To manage conditional access abilities, you should assign the Conditional Access Administrator role. Users that have the Conditional Access Administrator role have permissions to view, create, modify, and delete conditional access policies. The Conditional Access Administrator can perform the following tasks in Azure AD:

   ■ Create: Create conditional access policies

   ■ Read: Read conditional access policies

   ■ Update: Update conditional access policies

   ■ Delete: Delete conditional access policies

Chapter

1

Introduction to Windows Server 2022

So, you have decided to start down the track of Windows Server 2022. The first question we must ask ourselves is, what's the first step? Well, the first step is to learn what's new about the Windows Server 2022 features and benefits that are available and how these features can help improve your organization's network.

So that's where I am going to start. I will talk about the different Windows Server 2022 versions and what version may be best for you. In this chapter, I will introduce you to Windows Server 2022, but you probably won't see too many questions on the exam for this chapter. But it's important you understand the features that have been added and removed so that you can do the job properly and not just pass the exams.

So, let's dive right into the server by talking about some of the features and advantages of Windows Server 2022.

Features and Advantages of Windows Server 2022

Before you decide to install and configure Windows Server 2022, it's first important to learn about some of the features and the advantages it offers. Windows Server 2022 is built off the solid foundation of Windows Server 2016 and Windows Server 2019, but Microsoft has stated that Windows Server 2022 is "the cloud-ready operating system." This means that many of the features of Windows Server 2022 are built and evolve around cloud-based software and networking.

I will talk about all of these features in greater detail throughout this book. What follows are merely brief descriptions of some of the features of Windows Server 2022:

Built-in Security Microsoft has always tried to make sure that their operating systems are as secure as possible, but with Windows Server 2022, Microsoft has included Windows Defender Advanced Threat Protection (ATP). This feature helps stop attackers on your system and allows your company to meet any compliance requirements.

Active Directory Certificate Services *Active Directory Certificate Services (AD CS)* provides a customizable set of services that allow you to issue and manage *public key infrastructure (PKI) certificates*. These certificates can be used in software security systems that employ public key technologies.

Active Directory Domain Services *Active Directory Domain Services (AD DS)* includes new features that make deploying domain controllers simpler and that let you implement them faster. AD DS also makes the domain controllers more flexible, both to audit and to authorize for access to files. Moreover, AD DS has been designed to make performing administrative tasks easier through consistent graphical and scripted management experiences.

Active Directory Federation Services *Active Directory Federation Services (AD FS)* provides Internet-based clients with a secure identity access solution that works on both Windows and non-Windows operating systems. AD FS gives users the ability to do a *single sign-on (SSO)* and access applications on other networks without needing a secondary password. Federation Services is one of the ways that you can connect your on-site domain with the cloud.

Active Directory Lightweight Directory Services *Active Directory Lightweight Directory Services (AD LDS)* is a *Lightweight Directory Access Protocol (LDAP)* directory service that provides flexible support for directory-enabled applications, without the dependencies and domain-related restrictions of AD DS.

Active Directory Rights Management Services *Active Directory Rights Management Services (AD RMS)* provides management and development tools that let you work with industry security technologies, including encryption, certificates, and authentication. Using these technologies allows you to create reliable information protection solutions.

Application Server *Application Server* provides an integrated environment for deploying and running custom, server-based business applications.

BitLocker *BitLocker* is a tool that allows you to encrypt the hard drives of your computer. By encrypting the hard drives, you can provide enhanced protection against data theft or unauthorized exposure of your computers or removable drives that are lost or stolen.

BranchCache *BranchCache* allows data from files and web servers on a wide area network (WAN) to be cached on computers at a local branch office. By using BranchCache, you can improve application response times while also reducing WAN traffic. Cached data can be either distributed across peer client computers (distributed cache mode) or centrally hosted on a server (hosted cache mode). BranchCache is included with Windows Server 2022 and Windows 10/11.

Containers Windows Server 2022 has continued focusing on an isolated operating system environment called *Dockers*. Dockers allow applications to run in isolated environments called *containers*. Containers are separate locations where applications can operate without affecting other applications or other operating system resources. To understand Dockers and containers, think of virtualization.

Virtual machines are operating systems that run in their own space on top of another operating system. Dockers and containers allow an application to run in its own space, and because of this, it doesn't affect other applications. There are two different types of containers you should focus on:

Windows Server Containers   Windows Server 2022 allows an isolated application to run by using a technology called process and namespace isolation. Windows Server 2022 containers allow applications to share the system's kernel with their container and all other containers running on the same host.

Hyper-V Containers   Windows Server 2022 Hyper-V containers add another virtual layer by isolating applications in their own optimized virtual machine. Hyper-V containers work differently than Windows Server containers in that the Hyper-V containers do not share the system's kernel with other Hyper-V containers.

Credential Guard   Credential Guard helps protect a system's credentials, and this helps avoid pass-the-hash attacks. Credential Guard offers better protection against advanced persistent threats by protecting credentials on the system from being stolen by a compromised administrator or malware.

Credential Guard can also be enabled on Remote Desktop Services servers and Virtual Desktop Infrastructure so that the credentials for users connecting to their sessions are protected.

DHCP   *Dynamic Host Configuration Protocol (DHCP)* is an Internet standard that allows organizations to reduce the administrative overhead of configuring hosts on a TCP/IP-based network. Some of the features are DHCP failover, policy-based assignment, and the ability to use Windows PowerShell for DHCP Server.

DNS   *Domain Name System (DNS)* services are used in TCP/IP networks. DNS will convert a computer name or fully qualified domain name (FQDN) to an IP address. DNS also has the ability to do a reverse lookup and convert an IP address to a computer name. DNS allows you to locate computers and services through user-friendly names.

Failover Clustering   *Failover Clustering* gives an organization the ability to provide high availability and scalability to networked servers. Failover clusters can include file share storage for server applications, such as Hyper-V and Microsoft SQL Server, and for applications that run on physical servers or virtual machines.

File Server Resource Manager   *File Server Resource Manager* is a set of tools that allows you to manage and control the amount and type of data stored on the organization's servers. By using File Server Resource Manager, you have the ability to set up file management tasks, use quota management, get detailed reports, set up a file classification infrastructure, and configure file-screening management.

File and Storage Services   *File and Storage Services* allows you to set up and manage one or more file servers. These servers can provide a central location on your network where you can store files and then share those files with network users. If users require access to the same files and applications or if centralized backup and file management are important issues for an organization, you should set up network servers as a file server.

Group Policy   *Group Policies* are a set of rules and management configuration options that you can control through the Group Policy settings. These policy settings can be placed on users' computers throughout the organization.

Hyper-V   *Hyper-V* is one of the most changed features in Windows Server 2022. Hyper-V allows you to consolidate servers by creating and managing a virtualized computing environment. It does this by using virtualization technology that is built into Windows Server 2022.

Hyper-V allows you to run multiple operating systems simultaneously on one physical computer. Each virtual operating system runs in its own virtual machine environment.

Windows Server 2022 Hyper-V now allows you to protect your corporate virtual machines using the feature called *Shielded Virtual Machine*. Shielded Virtual Machines are encrypted using BitLocker and the VMs can only run on approved Hyper-V host systems.

Hyper-V also now includes a feature called *containers*. Containers add a new unique additional layer of isolation for containerized applications.

IPAM   *IP Address Management (IPAM)* is one of the features first introduced with Windows Server 2012. IPAM allows you to customize and monitor the IP address infrastructure on a corporate network.

Kerberos Authentication   Windows Server 2022 uses the *Kerberos authentication* protocol and extensions for password-based and public key authentication. The Kerberos client is installed as a *security support provider (SSP)*, and it can be accessed through the *Security Support Provider Interface (SSPI)*.

Managed Service Accounts   Stand-alone *managed service accounts*, originally created for Windows Server 2008 R2 and Windows 7, are configured domain accounts that allow automatic password management and *service principal names* (SPNs) management, including the ability to delegate management to other administrators.

Nested Virtualization   Windows Server 2022 allows you to use a Hyper-V feature called *Nested Virtualization*. Nested Virtualization allows you to create virtual machines within virtual machines. As an instructor, I find this to be an awesome new feature. Now I can build a Windows Server 2022 Hyper-V Server with a training virtual machine. Then when I get to the part when I need to teach Hyper-V, I can just do that right on the classroom virtual machine. There are numerous possibilities, and we will talk more about them throughout this book.

Nano Server   Windows Server 2022 allows you to set up a unique type of server installation called Nano Server. Nano Server requires you to remotely administer the server operating system. It was primarily designed and optimized for private clouds and datacenters. Nano Server is very similar to Server Core, but the Nano Server operating system uses significantly smaller hard drive space, has no local logon capability, and only supports 64-bit applications and tools.

Networking   There are many networking technologies and features in Windows Server 2022, including BranchCache, Data Center Bridging (DCB), NIC Teaming, and many more.

Network Load Balancing   The *Network Load Balancing (NLB)* feature dispenses traffic across multiple servers by using the TCP/IP networking protocol. By combining two or more computers that are running applications in Windows Server 2022 into a single virtual cluster, NLB provides reliability and performance for mission-critical servers.

Network Policy and Access Services   Use the *Network Policy Server (NPS) and Access Services* server role to install and configure *Network Access Protection (NAP)*, secure wired and wireless access points, and use RADIUS servers and proxies.

Print and Document Services   *Print and Document Services* allows you to centralize print server and network printer tasks. This role also allows you to receive scanned documents from network scanners and route the documents to a shared network resource, Windows SharePoint Services site, or email addresses. Print and Document Services also provides fax servers with the ability to send and receive faxes while also giving you the ability to manage fax resources such as jobs, settings, reports, and fax devices on the fax server.

PowerShell Direct   Windows Server 2022 includes a simple way to manage Hyper-V virtual machines called PowerShell Direct. PowerShell Direct is a powerful set of parameters for the `PSSession` cmdlet called `VMName`. This will be discussed in greater detail in the Hyper-V chapters, and it is included with Windows Server 2022.

Remote Desktop Services   Before Windows Server 2008, we used to refer to this as Terminal Services. *Remote Desktop Services* allows users to connect to virtual desktops, RemoteApp programs, and session-based desktops. Using Remote Desktop Services allows users to access remote connections from within a corporate network or from the Internet.

Security Auditing   *Security auditing* gives you the ability to help maintain the security of your enterprise. By using security audits, you can verify authorized or unauthorized access to machines, resources, applications, and services. One of the best advantages of security audits is to verify regulatory compliance.

Smart Cards   Using *smart cards* (referred to as *two-factor authentication*) and their associated *personal identification numbers (PINs)* is a popular, reliable, and cost-effective way to provide authentication. When using smart cards, the user not only must have the physical card but must also know the PIN to be able to gain access to network resources. This is effective because even if the smart card is stolen, thieves can't access the network unless they know the PIN.

Software-Defined Networking   The Software-Defined Networking (SDN) solution allows you to centrally configure and manage your physical and virtual network devices. These devices include items such as routers, switches, and gateways in your datacenter.

Telemetry   The *Telemetry* service allows the Windows Feedback Forwarder to send feedback to Microsoft automatically by deploying a Group Policy setting to one or more organizational units. Windows Feedback Forwarder is available on all editions of Windows Server 2022, including Server Core.

TLS/SSL (Schannel SSP)   *Schannel* is a security support provider (SSP) that uses the *Secure Sockets Layer (SSL)* and *Transport Layer Security (TLS)* Internet standard authentication protocols together. The Security Support Provider Interface is an API used by Windows systems to allow security-related functionality, including authentication.

Volume Activation   Windows Server 2022 *Volume Activation* will help your organization benefit from using this service to deploy and manage volume licenses for a medium to large number of computers.

Web Server (IIS)   The *Web Server (IIS)* role in Windows Server 2022 allows you to set up a secure, easy-to-manage, modular, and extensible platform for reliably hosting websites, services, and applications.

Windows Deployment Services   *Windows Deployment Services* allows you to install Windows operating systems remotely. You can use Windows Deployment Services to set up new computers by using a network-based installation.

Windows PowerShell Desired State Configuration   Windows Server 2022 allows you to create a PowerShell management platform called Windows PowerShell Desired State Configuration (DSC). DSC enables the deployment and management of configuration data for software services and also helps you manage the environment in which these services run.

DSC allows you to use Windows PowerShell language extensions along with new Windows PowerShell cmdlets and resources. DSC lets you declaratively specify how your corporation wants their software environment to be configured and maintained.

DSC allows you to automate tasks like enabling or disabling server roles and features, manage Registry settings, manage files and directories, manage groups and users, deploy software, and run PowerShell scripts, to name just a few.

Windows Server Backup Feature   The *Windows Server Backup* feature gives your organization a way to back up and restore Windows servers. You can use Windows Server Backup to back up the entire server (all volumes), selected volumes, the system state, or specific files or folders.

Windows Server Update Services   *Windows Server Update Services (WSUS)* allows you to deploy application and operating system updates. By deploying WSUS, you have the ability to manage updates that are released through Microsoft Windows Update to computers in your network. This feature is integrated with the operating system as a server role on a Windows Server 2022 system.

Deciding Which Windows Server 2022 Version to Use

You may be wondering which version of Windows Server 2022 is best for your organization. After all, Microsoft offers the following four versions of Windows Server 2022:

Windows Server 2022 Datacenter   This version is designed for organizations that are looking to migrate to a highly virtualized, private cloud environment. Windows Server 2022 Datacenter has full Windows Server functionality with unlimited virtual instances.

Windows Server 2022 Standard   This version is designed for organizations with physical or minimally virtualized environments. Windows Server 2022 Standard has full Windows Server functionality with two virtual instances.

Windows Server 2022 Datacenter: Azure Edition   Windows Server Azure Edition is a Windows Server version designed specifically to operate either as an Azure IaaS VM or as a VM on an Azure Stack HCI cluster.

Windows Server 2022 Essentials   This version is ideal for small businesses that have as many as 25 users and 50 devices. Windows Server 2022 Essentials has a simpler interface and preconfigured connectivity to cloud-based services but no virtualization rights.

Table 1.1 shows the locks and limitations of Windows Server 2022 Standard and Windows Server 2022 Datacenter. The information in this chart was taken directly from Microsoft's website.

TABLE 1.1   Windows Server 2022 locks and limits

Locks and Limits	Windows Server 2022 Standard	Windows Server 2022 Datacenter
Maximum number of users	Based on CALs	Based on CALs
Maximum SMB connections	16,777,216	16,777,216
Maximum RRAS connections	Unlimited	Unlimited
Maximum IAS connections	2,147,483,647	2,147,483,647
Maximum RDS connections	65,535	65,535

Locks and Limits	Windows Server 2022 Standard	Windows Server 2022 Datacenter
Maximum number of 64-bit sockets	64	64
Maximum number of cores	Unlimited	Unlimited
Maximum RAM	24 TB	24 TB
Can be used as virtualization guest	Yes, two virtual machines, plus one Hyper-V host per license	Yes, unlimited virtual machines, plus one Hyper-V host per license
Server can join a domain	Yes	Yes
Edge network protection/firewall	No	No
DirectAccess	Yes	Yes
DLNA codecs and web media streaming	Yes, if installed as Server with Desktop Experience	Yes, if installed as Server with Desktop Experience

Table 1.2 shows the differences between Windows Server 2022 Standard and Windows Server 2022 Datacenter. The information in this chart was also taken directly from Microsoft's website.

TABLE 1.2   Windows Server 2022 Standard vs. Datacenter

Windows Server roles available	Windows Server 2022 Standard	Windows Server 2022 Datacenter
Active Directory Certificate Services	Yes	Yes
Active Directory Domain Services	Yes	Yes
Active Directory Federation Services	Yes	Yes
AD Lightweight Directory Services	Yes	Yes

TABLE 1.2 Windows Server 2022 Standard vs. Datacenter *(Continued)*

Windows Server roles available	Windows Server 2022 Standard	Windows Server 2022 Datacenter
AD Rights Management Services	Yes	Yes
Device Health Attestation	Yes	Yes
DHCP Server	Yes	Yes
DNS Server	Yes	Yes
Fax Server	Yes	Yes
File and Storage Services	Yes	Yes
Host Guardian Service	Yes	Yes
Hyper-V	Yes	Yes, including Shielded Virtual Machines
Network Controller	No	Yes
Network Policy and Access Services	Yes, when installed as Server with Desktop Experience	Yes, when installed as Server with Desktop Experience
Print and Document Services	Yes	Yes
Remote Access	Yes	Yes
Remote Desktop Services	Yes	Yes
Volume Activation Services	Yes	Yes
Web Services (IIS)	Yes	Yes
Windows Deployment Services	Yes*	Yes
Windows Server Essentials Experience	No	No
Windows Server Update Services	Yes	Yes

Table 1.3 shows the features of Windows Server 2022 Standard and Windows Server 2022 Datacenter. The information in this chart was also taken directly from Microsoft's website.

TABLE 1.3   Windows Server 2022 Standard vs. Datacenter

Windows Server features installable with Server Manager (or PowerShell)	Windows Server 2022 Standard	Windows Server 2022 Datacenter
.NET Framework 3.5	Yes	Yes
.NET Framework 4.7	Yes	Yes
Background Intelligent Transfer Service (BITS)	Yes	Yes
BitLocker Drive Encryption	Yes	Yes
BitLocker Network Unlock	Yes, when installed as Server with Desktop Experience	Yes, when installed as Server with Desktop Experience
BranchCache	Yes	Yes
Client for NFS	Yes	Yes
Containers	Yes (unlimited Windows containers; up to two Hyper-V containers)	Yes (unlimited Windows and Hyper-V containers)
Data Center Bridging	Yes	Yes
Direct Play	Yes, when installed as Server with Desktop Experience	Yes, when installed as Server with Desktop Experience
Enhanced Storage	Yes	Yes
Failover Clustering	Yes	Yes
Group Policy Management	Yes	Yes
Host Guardian Hyper-V Support	No	Yes
I/O Quality of Service	Yes	Yes
IIS Hostable Web Core	Yes	Yes

TABLE 1.3   Windows Server 2022 Standard vs. Datacenter *(Continued)*

Windows Server features installable with Server Manager (or PowerShell)	Windows Server 2022 Standard	Windows Server 2022 Datacenter
Internet Printing Client	Yes, when installed as Server with Desktop Experience	Yes, when installed as Server with Desktop Experience
IPAM Server	Yes	Yes
iSNS Server service	Yes	Yes
LPR Port Monitor	Yes, when installed as Server with Desktop Experience	Yes, when installed as Server with Desktop Experience
Management OData IIS Extension	Yes	Yes
Media Foundation	Yes	Yes
Message Queueing	Yes	Yes
Multipath I/O	Yes	Yes
MultiPoint Connector	Yes	Yes
Network Load Balancing	Yes	Yes
Peer Name Resolution Protocol	Yes	Yes
Quality Windows Audio Video Experience	Yes	Yes
RAS Connection Manager Administration Kit	Yes, when installed as Server with Desktop Experience	Yes, when installed as Server with Desktop Experience
Remote Assistance	Yes, when installed as Server with Desktop Experience	Yes, when installed as Server with Desktop Experience
Remote Differential Compression	Yes	Yes
RSAT	Yes	Yes
RPC over HTTP Proxy	Yes	Yes

Windows Server features installable with Server Manager (or PowerShell)	Windows Server 2022 Standard	Windows Server 2022 Datacenter
Setup and Boot Event Collection	Yes	Yes
Simple TCP/IP Services	Yes, when installed as Server with Desktop Experience	Yes, when installed as Server with Desktop Experience
SMB 1.0/CIFS File Sharing Support	Installed	Installed
SMB Bandwidth Limit	Yes	Yes
SMTP Server	Yes	Yes
SNMP Service	Yes	Yes
Software Load Balancer	Yes	Yes
Storage Replica	Yes	Yes
Telnet Client	Yes	Yes
TFTP Client	Yes, when installed as Server with Desktop Experience	Yes, when installed as Server with Desktop Experience
VM Shielding Tools for Fabric Management	Yes	Yes
WebDAV Redirector	Yes	Yes
Windows Biometric Framework	Yes, when installed as Server with Desktop Experience	Yes, when installed as Server with Desktop Experience
Windows Defender features	Installed	Installed
Windows Identity Foundation 3.5	Yes, when installed as Server with Desktop Experience	Yes, when installed as Server with Desktop Experience
Windows Internal Database	Yes	Yes
Windows PowerShell	Installed	Installed

TABLE 1.3 Windows Server 2022 Standard vs. Datacenter *(Continued)*

Windows Server features installable with Server Manager (or PowerShell)	Windows Server 2022 Standard	Windows Server 2022 Datacenter
Windows Process Activation Service	Yes	Yes
Windows Search Service	Yes, when installed as Server with Desktop Experience	Yes, when installed as Server with Desktop Experience
Windows Server Backup	Yes	Yes
Windows Server Migration Tools	Yes	Yes
Windows Standards-Based Storage Management	Yes	Yes
Windows TIFF IFilter	Yes, when installed as Server with Desktop Experience	Yes, when installed as Server with Desktop Experience
WinRM IIS Extension	Yes	Yes
WINS Server	Yes	Yes
Wireless LAN Service	Yes	Yes
WoW64 support	Installed	Installed
XPS Viewer	Yes, when installed as Server with Desktop Experience	Yes, when installed as Server with Desktop Experience

Features available generally	Windows Server 2022 Standard	Windows Server 2022 Datacenter
Best Practices Analyzer	Yes	Yes
Direct Access	Yes	Yes
Dynamic Memory (in virtualization)	Yes	Yes
Hot Add/Replace RAM	Yes	Yes

Features available generally	Windows Server 2022 Standard	Windows Server 2022 Datacenter
Microsoft Management Console	Yes	Yes
Minimal Server Interface	Yes	Yes
Network Load Balancing	Yes	Yes
Windows PowerShell	Yes	Yes
Server Core installation option	Yes	Yes
Server Manager	Yes	Yes
SMB Direct and SMB over RDMA	Yes	Yes
Software-Defined Networking	No	Yes
Storage Migration Service	Yes	Yes
Storage Replica	Yes, (1 partnership and 1 resource group with a single 2TB volume)	Yes, unlimited
Storage Spaces	Yes	Yes
Storage Spaces Direct	No	Yes
Volume Activation Services	Yes	Yes
VSS (Volume Shadow Copy Service) integration	Yes	Yes
Windows Server Update Services	Yes	Yes
Windows System Resource Manager	Yes	Yes
Server license logging	Yes	Yes
Inherited activation	As guest if hosted on Datacenter	Can be a host or a guest
Work Folders	Yes	Yes

Once you choose what roles are going on your server, you must then decide how you're going to install Windows Server 2022. There are two ways to install Windows Server 2022: you can upgrade a Windows Server 2012 R2 (or above) machine to Windows Server 2022, or you can do a clean install of Windows Server 2022. If you are running any version of Server before 2012 R2, you must first upgrade to Windows Server 2012 R2 or 2016 before upgrading to Windows Server 2022. If you decide that you are going to upgrade, you must follow specific upgrade paths.

> Microsoft best practice recommendation for installing servers is to always do a clean install and not an upgrade. Upgrading from Windows Server 2012 R2 and higher is possible. But Microsoft recommends that you always do a clean install of a server.

Your choice of Windows Server 2022 version is dictated by how your current network is designed. If you are building a network from scratch, then it's pretty straightforward. Just choose the Windows Server 2022 version based on your server's tasks. However, if you already have a version of Windows Server 2012 installed, you should follow the recommendations in Table 1.4, which briefly summarize the supported upgrade paths to Windows Server 2022.

TABLE 1.4   Supported Windows Server 2022 upgrade path recommendations

Current system	Upgraded system
Windows Server 2012 Standard	Windows Server 2016 Standard or Datacenter
Windows Server 2012 Datacenter	Windows Server 2016 Datacenter
Windows Server 2012 R2 Standard	Windows Server 2022 Standard or Datacenter
Windows Server 2012 R2 Datacenter	Windows Server 2022 Datacenter
Windows Server 2012 R2 Essentials	Windows Server 2022 Essentials
Windows Storage Server 2016 Standard	Windows Storage Server 2022 Standard
Windows Storage Server 2016 Datacenter	Windows Storage Server 2022 Datacenter

Deciding on the Type of Installation

One of the final choices you must make before installing Windows Server 2022 is what type of installation you want. There are three ways to install Windows Server 2022, which we'll look at next.

Windows Server 2022 (Desktop Experience)

This is the version with which most administrators are familiar. This is the version that uses *Microsoft Management Console (MMC)* windows, and it is the version that allows the use of a mouse to navigate through the installation.

Windows Server 2022 Server Core

This is a bare-bones installation of Windows Server 2022. You can think of it this way: if Windows Server 2022 (Desktop Experience) is a top-of-the-line luxury car, then Windows Server 2022 Server Core is the stripped-down model with manual windows, cloth seats, and no air-conditioning. It might not be pretty to look at, but it gets the job done.

🌐 Real World Scenario

Server Core

Here is an explanation of Server Core that I have used ever since it was introduced in Windows Server 2008.

I am a *huge* sports fan. I love watching sports on TV, and I enjoy going to games. If you have ever been to a hockey game, you know what a hockey goal looks like. Between hockey periods, the stadium workers often bring out a huge piece of Plexiglas onto the ice. There is a tiny square cut out of the bottom of the glass. The square is just a bit bigger than a hockey puck itself.

Now they pick some lucky fan out of the stands, give them a puck at center ice, and then ask them to shoot the puck into the net with the Plexiglas in front of it. If they get it through that tiny little square at the bottom of the Plexiglas, they win a car or some such great prize.

Well, Windows Server 2022 (Desktop Experience) is like regular hockey with an open net, and Windows Server 2022 Server Core is the Plexiglas version. Because Windows Server 2022 Server Core has the plexiglass, Microsoft refers to this as a smaller attack surface.

Server Core supports a limited number of roles:

- Active Directory Certificate Services (AD CS)
- Active Directory Domain Services (AD DS)
- Active Directory Federation Services (AD FS)
- Active Directory Lightweight Directory Services (AD LDS)
- Active Directory Rights Management Services (AD RMS)
- Application Server
- DHCP Server
- DNS Server

- Fax Server
- File and Storage Services
- BITS Server
- BranchCache
- Hyper-V
- Network Policy and Access Services
- Print and Document Services
- Remote Access
- Remote Desktop Services
- Volume Activation Services
- Web Server (IIS)
- Windows Deployment Services
- Windows Server Update Services
- .NET Framework 3.5 Features
- .NET Framework 4.5 Features
- Streaming Media Services
- Failover Clustering
- iSCSI
- Network Load Balancing
- MPIO
- qWave
- Telnet Server/Client
- Windows Server Migration Tools
- Windows PowerShell 5.0

Server Core does not have the normal Windows interface or GUI. Almost everything has to be configured via the command line or, in some cases, using the Remote Server Administration Tools from a full version of Windows Server 2022. Although this might scare off some administrators, it has the following benefits:

Reduced Management   Because Server Core has a minimum number of applications installed, it reduces management effort.

Minimal Maintenance   Only basic systems can be installed on Server Core, so it reduces the upkeep you would need to perform in a normal server installation.

Smaller Footprint   Server Core requires only 1 GB of disk space to install and 2 GB of free space for operations.

Tighter Security   With only a few applications running on a server, it is less vulnerable to attacks.

Server Core App Compatibility Features on Demand   Windows Server 2022 now includes the Server Core App Compatibility Features on Demand (FODs). This feature drastically improves the application compatibility of the Windows Server Core installation. It does this by containing a subset of components from Windows Server 2022 with the Desktop Experience but without adding the Windows Server Desktop Experience graphical environment. The advantage is that this helps increase the functionality and compatibility of Windows Server 2022 Server Core while keeping it as lean as possible.

The prerequisites for Server Core are basic. It requires the Windows Server 2022 installation media, a product key, and the hardware on which to install it.

After you install the base operating system, you use PowerShell or the remote administrative tools to configure the network settings, add the machine to the domain, create and format disks, and install roles and features. It takes only a few minutes to install Server Core, depending on the hardware.

🌐 Real World Scenario

Better Security

When I started in this industry more than 20 years ago, I was a programmer. I used to program computer hospital systems. When I switched to the networking world, I continued to work under contract with hospitals and with doctors' offices.

One problem I ran into is that many doctors are affiliated with hospitals, but they don't actually have offices within the hospital. Generally, they have offices either near the hospital or, in some cases, right across the street.

Here is the issue: do we put servers in the doctors' offices, or do we make the doctor log into the hospital network through a remote connection? Doctors' offices normally don't have computer rooms, and we don't want to place a domain controller or server on someone's desk. It's just unsafe!

This is where Windows Server 2022 Server Core can come into play. Since it is a slimmed-down version of Windows and there is no GUI, it makes it harder for anyone in the office to hack into the system. Also, Microsoft introduced a new domain controller in Windows Server 2008 called a *read-only domain controller (RODC)*. As its name suggests, it is a read-only version of a domain controller (explained in detail later in this book).

With Server Core and an RODC, you can feel safer placing a server on someone's desk or in any office. Server Core systems allow you to place servers in areas that you would never have placed them before. This can be a great advantage to businesses that have small, remote locations without full server rooms.

Windows Server 2022 Nano Server

Windows Server 2022 allows you to set up a type of server installation called Nano Server. Nano Server lets you remotely administer the server operating system. It was primarily designed and optimized for private clouds and datacenters. Nano Server is very similar to Server Core, but the Nano Server operating system uses significantly smaller hard drive space, has no local logon capability, and only supports 64-bit applications and tools. Nano Server has no local logon and must be administered remotely.

Removed Features

As with all new versions of Windows Servers, Microsoft decided to remove or retire features or services that are no longer needed. The following are features and services that were replaced starting with Windows Server 2022:

IIS 6 Management Compatibility   The following features were removed in the first release of Windows Server 2022: IIS 6 Metabase Compatibility (Web-Metabase), IIS 6 Management Console (Web-Lgcy-Mgmt-Console), IIS 6 Scripting Tools (Web-Lgcy-Scripting), and IIS 6 WMI Compatibility (Web-WMI).

IIS Digest Authentication   Microsoft plans to replace the IIS Digest Authentication method. You should use other authentication methods. These methods include Client Certificate Mapping and Windows Authentication.

Internet Storage Name Service (iSNS)   iSNS is being replaced by the Server Message Block (SMB) feature. This feature offers basically the same functionality with additional features.

RSA/AES Encryption for IIS   The RSA/AES Encryption for IIS method is being replaced by the improved Cryptography API: Next Generation (CNG) method.

Windows PowerShell 2.0   The Windows PowerShell 2.0 version has been surpassed by several more recent versions. You can get the superior features and performance if you use Windows PowerShell 5.0 or later.

The following are features and services that are being replaced starting with Windows Server 2022 version 1803:

File Replication Service   File Replication Services were first introduced in Windows Server 2003 R2. They have now been replaced by DFS Replication.

Hyper-V Network Virtualization (HNV)   Hyper-V Network Virtualization (HNV) has been replaced because Network Virtualization is now included in Windows Server 2022 as part of the Software-Defined Networking (SDN) solution. SDN also includes items such as the Network Controller, Software Load Balancing, User-Defined Routing, and Access Control Lists.

Table 1.5 shows all the features and roles that are no longer being developed. The information in the next two charts was taken directly from Microsoft's website.

TABLE 1.5 Features and roles no longer being developed

Feature or roles	You can use . . .
Business Scanning, also called Distributed Scan Management (DSM)	The Scan Management functionality was introduced in Windows Server 2008 R2 and enabled secure scanning and the management of scanners in an enterprise. Microsoft is no longer investing in this feature, and there are no devices available that support it.
IPv4/6 Transition Technologies (6to4, ISATAP, and Direct Tunnels)	6to4 has been disabled by default since Windows 10/11, version 1607 (the Anniversary Update), ISATAP has been disabled by default since Windows 10/11, version 1703 (the Creators Update), and Direct Tunnels has always been disabled by default. Please use native IPv6 support instead.
MultiPoint Services	Microsoft is no longer developing the MultiPoint Services role as part of Windows Server. MultiPoint Connector services are available through Features on Demand for both Windows Server and Windows 10/11. You can use Remote Desktop Services, in particular the Remote Desktop Services Session Host, to provide RDP connectivity.
Offline symbol packages (Debug symbol MSIs)	Microsoft is no longer making the symbol packages available as a downloadable MSI. Instead, the Microsoft Symbol Server is moving to be an Azure-based symbol store. If you need the Windows symbols, connect to the Microsoft Symbol Server to cache your symbols locally or use a manifest file with SymChk.exe on a computer with Internet access.
Remote Desktop Connection Broker and Remote Desktop Virtualization Host in a Server Core installation	Most Remote Desktop Services deployments have these roles co-located with the Remote Desktop Session Host (RDSH), which requires Server with Desktop Experience; to be consistent with RDSH Microsoft is changing these roles to also require Server with Desktop Experience. Microsoft is no longer developing these RDS roles for use in a Server Core installation. If you need to deploy these roles as part of your Remote Desktop infrastructure, you can install them on Windows Server 2016 with Desktop Experience.

These roles are also included in the Desktop Experience installation option of Windows Server 2022. You can test them in the Windows Insider build of Windows Server 2022 — just be sure to choose the LTSC image.

RemoteFX 3D Video Adapter (vGPU)	Microsoft is developing new graphics acceleration options for virtualized environments. You can also use Discrete Device Assignment (DDA) as an alternative.

TABLE 1.5 Features and roles no longer being developed *(Continued)*

Feature or roles	You can use . . .
Software Restriction Policies in Group Policy	Instead of using the Software Restriction Policies through Group Policy, you can use AppLocker or Windows Defender Application Control to control which apps users can access and what code can run in the kernel.
Storage Spaces in a Shared configuration using an SAS fabric	Deploy Storage Spaces Direct instead. Storage Spaces Direct supports the use of HLK-certified SAS enclosures, but in a nonshared configuration, as described in the Storage Spaces Direct hardware requirements.
Windows Server Essentials Experience	Microsoft is no longer developing the Essentials Experience role for the Windows Server Standard or Windows Server Datacenter SKUs. If you need an easy-to-use server solution for small-to-medium businesses, check out the new Microsoft 365 for Business solution, or use Windows Server 2016 Essentials.

Table 1.6 shows the features that are no longer being developed starting with Windows Server 2022.

TABLE 1.6 Features no longer being developed in Server 2022

Feature	Instead, you can use . . .
Hyper-V vSwitch on LBFO	In a future release, the Hyper-V vSwitch will no longer have the capability to be bound to an LBFO team. Instead, it must be bound via Switch Embedded Teaming (SET).
XDDM-based remote display driver (new)	Starting with this release the Remote Desktop Services uses a Windows Display Driver Model (WDDM)-based Indirect Display Driver (IDD) for a single session remote desktop. The support for Windows 2000 Display Driver Model (XDDM)-based remote display drivers will be removed in a future release. Independent software vendors (ISVs) that use the XDDM-based remote display driver should plan a migration to the WDDM driver model. For more information on implementing remote display indirect display drivers, ISVs can reach out to rdsdev@microsoft.com.
UCS log collection tool (new)	The UCS log collection tool, while not explicitly intended for use with Windows Server, is nonetheless being replaced by the Feedback hub on Windows 10/11.

Feature	Instead, you can use . . .
Key Storage Drive in Hyper-V	Microsoft is no longer working on the Key Storage Drive feature in Hyper-V. If you're using generation 1 VMs, check out Generation 1 VM Virtualization Security for information about options going forward. If you're creating new VMs, use Generation 2 virtual machines with TPM devices for a more secure solution.
Trusted Platform Module (TPM) management console	The information previously available in the TPM management console is now available on the Device security page in the Windows Defender Security Center.
Host Guardian Service Active Directory attestation mode	Microsoft is no longer developing Host Guardian Service Active Directory attestation mode—instead, they have added a new attestation mode, host key attestation, that's far simpler and equally as compatible as Active Directory–based attestation. This new mode provides equivalent functionality with a setup experience, simpler management, and fewer infrastructure dependencies than the Active Directory attestation. Host key attestation has no additional hardware requirements beyond what Active Directory attestation required, so all existing systems will remain compatible with the new mode.
OneSync service	The OneSync service synchronizes data for the Mail, Calendar, and People apps. Microsoft has added a sync engine to the Outlook app that provides the same synchronization.
Remote Differential Compression API support	Remote Differential Compression API support enabled synchronizing data with a remote source using compression technologies, which minimized the amount of data sent across the network.
WFP lightweight filter switch extension	The WFP lightweight filter switch extension enables developers to build simple network packet filtering extensions for the Hyper-V virtual switch. You can achieve the same functionality by creating a full filtering extension. As such, Microsoft will remove this extension in the future.

Summary

In this chapter, you studied the latest advantages of using Windows Server 2022. You also learned about the different roles and features you can install on a Windows Server 2022 machine. We explored how to migrate those roles and features from a Windows Server 2008, 2008 R2, 2012, 2012 R2, 2016, and Windows Server 2019 machine to a Windows Server 2022 machine.

I discussed the different upgrade paths that are available and which upgrades are best for your current network setup. You learned that another important issue to decide when installing Windows Server 2022 is whether to use Server Core, Nano, or the GUI installation.

I discussed a feature called Features on Demand, which allows you to remove roles and features from the operating system and remove the associated files completely from the hard drive, thus saving disk space.

Exam Essentials

Understand the upgrade paths.   It's important to make sure you understand the various upgrade paths from Windows Server 2012 R2 and higher to Windows Server 2022.

Understand Windows Server 2022 server roles.   Understand what the Windows Server 2022 server roles do for an organization and its users.

Understand Features On Demand.   Understand the purpose of Features on Demand. Microsoft loves to ask exam questions about its new features, and this will be no exception. Understand how features and roles stay on the system until you physically remove them from the hard drive.

Review Questions

1. You are the administrator for ABC Company. You are looking to install Windows Server 2022, and you need to decide which version to install. You need to install a version of Windows that is just for logon authentication and nothing else. You want the most secure option, and cost is not an issue. What should you install?

    A. Windows Server 2022 Datacenter (Desktop Experience)

    B. Windows Server 2022 Datacenter Server Core

    C. Windows Server 2022 Standard (Desktop Experience)

    D. Windows Server 2022 Web Server Core

2. You are the IT manager for a large organization. One of your co-workers installed a new Windows Server 2022 Datacenter Server Core machine, but now the IT team has decided that it should be a Windows Server 2022 Datacenter (Desktop Experience). What should you do?

    A. Reinstall Windows Server 2022 Datacenter Server Core on the same machine.

    B. Install a new machine with Windows Server 2022 Datacenter Server Core.

    C. Convert the current Windows Server 2022 Datacenter Server Core to the Windows Server 2022 Datacenter (Desktop Experience) version.

    D. Dual-boot the machine with both Windows Server 2022 Datacenter Server Core and Windows Server 2022 Datacenter (Desktop Experience).

3. You are the administrator for your company, and you are looking at upgrading your Windows Server 2012 R2 Standard with GUI to Windows Server 2022. Which version of Windows Server 2022 does Microsoft recommend you use to keep the GUI interface?

    A. Windows Server 2022 Datacenter (Desktop Experience)

    B. Windows Server 2022 Standard (Desktop Experience)

    C. Windows Server 2022 Datacenter

    D. Windows Server 2022 Standard

4. You are looking at upgrading your Windows Server 2012 R2 Datacenter with GUI machine to Windows Server 2022. Your organization is considering virtualizing its entire server room, which has 25 servers. To which version of Windows Server 2022 would you upgrade while keeping the GUI interface?

    A. Windows Server 2022 Datacenter (Desktop Experience)

    B. Windows Server 2022 Standard (Desktop Experience)

    C. Windows Server 2022 Datacenter

    D. Windows Server 2022 Standard

5. You have been hired to help a small company set up its first Windows network. It has had the same 13 users for the entire two years it has been open, and the company has no plans to expand. What version of Windows Server 2022 would you recommend?

   A. Windows Server 2022 Datacenter (Desktop Experience)

   B. Windows Server 2022 Standard (Desktop Experience)

   C. Windows Server 2022 Datacenter

   D. Windows Server 2022 Essentials

6. You have been hired to help a small company set up its Windows network. It has 20 users, and it has no plans to expand. What version of Windows Server 2022 would you recommend?

   A. Windows Server 2022 Datacenter

   B. Windows Server 2022 Standard

   C. Windows Server 2022 Essentials

   D. Windows Server 2022 Datacenter (Desktop Experience)

7. Which of the following are benefits of using Windows Server 2022 Server Core? (Choose all that apply.)

   A. Reduced management

   B. Minimal maintenance

   C. Smaller footprint

   D. Tighter security

8. You are a server administrator, and you are trying to save hard drive space on your Windows Server 2022 Datacenter machine. Which feature can help you save hard disk space?

   A. HDSaver.exe

   B. Features on Demand

   C. ADDS

   D. WinRM

9. You are the IT director for your company. Your company needs to install a version of Windows Server 2022 that uses the Current Branch for Business servicing model. What version would you install?

   A. Windows Server 2022 Datacenter

   B. Windows Server 2022 Standard

   C. Windows Server 2022 Essentials

   D. Windows Server 2022 Nano Server

10. What type of server would you install into an area where physical security is a concern?

   A. Windows Server 2022 Datacenter (Desktop Experience)

   B. Windows Server 2022 Standard (Desktop Experience)

   C. Windows Server 2022 Datacenter

   D. Do not install servers into a nonsecure location.

11. You are the network administrator for a large training company. You need to install a way to automate the installation of Windows operating systems by using an image or through the network. What can you install to complete this task using Windows Server 2022?

    A. WSUS

    B. WDS

    C. RIS

    D. WRIS

12. Which version of Windows Server 2022 would you install if you want reduced management, minimal installation files, and tighter security? (Choose all that apply.)

    A. Windows Server 2022 Datacenter (Desktop Experience)

    B. Windows Server 2022 Standard (Desktop Experience)

    C. Windows Server 2022 Datacenter

    D. Windows Server 2022 Standard

13. Which version of Windows Server 2022 has no local logon and must be administered remotely?

    A. Windows Server 2022 Datacenter

    B. Windows Server 2022 Standard

    C. Windows Server 2022 Nano Server

    D. Windows Server 2022 Essentials

14. You are the administrator for a large company. Your manager has approached you and asked you about the Current Branch for Business servicing model. He wants to know which version of Windows Server 2022 uses this model. What version would you tell him uses the CBB servicing model?

    A. Windows Server 2022 Datacenter

    B. Windows Server 2022 Standard

    C. Windows Server 2022 Essentials

    D. Windows Server 2022 Nano Server

15. You are the administrator for StormWind Studios. You are looking to install Windows Server 2022 and you need to decide which version to install. You have to install a version of Windows into a remote location that does not have a server room, so security is an issue. You want the most secure option, and cost is not an issue. What should you install?

    A. Windows Server 2022 Datacenter (Desktop Experience)

    B. Windows Server 2022 Datacenter (Server Core)

    C. Windows Server 2022 Standard (Desktop Experience)

    D. Windows Server 2022 Essentials

Chapter

2

Understanding Hyper-V

THE FOLLOWING AZ-800 EXAM OBJECTIVES ARE COVERED IN THIS CHAPTER:

✓ **Manage Hyper-V and guest virtual machines**

- Enable VM Enhanced Session Mode
- Manage VM using PowerShell Remoting, PowerShell Direct, and HVC.exe
- Configure nested virtualization
- Configure VM memory
- Configure Integration Services
- Configure Discrete Device Assignment
- Configure VM Resource Groups
- Configure VM CPU Groups
- Configure hypervisor scheduling types
- Manage VM Checkpoints
- Implementing high availability for virtual machines
- Manage VHD and VHDX files
- Configure Hyper-V network adapter
- Configure NIC teaming
- Configure Hyper-V switch

THE FOLLOWING AZ-801 EXAM OBJECTIVES ARE COVERED IN THIS CHAPTER:

✓ **Protect virtual machines by using Hyper-V replicas**

- Configure Hyper-V hosts for replication
- Manage Hyper-V replica servers
- Configure VM replication
- Perform a failover

One of the greatest advancements in servers over the last decade has been the ability to have one physical server but run multiple servers on top of that one physical box. This is known as *virtualization*.

In this chapter, I will talk about virtualization and how it works. We will focus most of our attention on Microsoft's version of virtualization called Hyper-V.

Hyper-V is a server role in Windows Server 2022 that allows you to virtualize your environment and therefore run multiple virtual operating system instances simultaneously on a physical server. This not only helps you improve server utilization but also helps you create a more cost-effective and dynamic system.

Hyper-V allows an organization of any size to act and compete with other organizations of any size. A small company can buy a single server and then virtualize that server into multiple servers. Hyper-V gives a small company the ability to run multiple servers on a single box and compete with a company of any size.

For the large organizations, an administrator can consolidate multiple servers onto Hyper-V servers, thus saving an organization time and money by using fewer physical boxes but still having all the servers needed to run the business.

In this chapter, you will also get a solid understanding of what is important in virtualization and in what areas of your work life you can use it.

Introduction to Virtualization

Virtualization is a method for abstracting physical resources from the way that they interact with other resources. For example, if you abstract the physical hardware from the operating system, you get the benefit of being able to move the operating system between different physical systems.

This is called *server virtualization*. But other forms of virtualization are available, such as presentation virtualization, desktop virtualization, and application virtualization. I will now briefly explain the differences between these forms of virtualization:

Server Virtualization This basically enables multiple servers to run on the same physical host server. Hyper-V is Microsoft's server virtualization tool that allows you to turn physical machines into virtual machines and manage them on fewer physical servers. Thus, you will be able to consolidate physical servers. So, you can have less physical hardware but just as many individual servers that are needed to run your entire network. The individual machines that run on the host server are called virtual machines. Virtual machines are just guest servers that run on top of the Hyper-V host server system.

Presentation Virtualization   When you use *presentation virtualization*, your applications run on a different computer, and only the screen information is transferred to your computer. An example of presentation virtualization is Microsoft Remote Desktop Services in Windows Server 2022.

Desktop Virtualization   *Desktop virtualization* provides you with a virtual machine on your desktop, comparable to server virtualization. You run your complete operating system and applications in a virtual machine so that your local physical machine just needs to run a very basic operating system. An example of this form of virtualization is Microsoft Virtual PC.

Application Virtualization   *Application virtualization* helps prevent conflicts between applications on the same PC. Thus, it helps you isolate the application running environment from the operating system installation requirements by creating application-specific copies of all shared resources. It also helps reduce application-to-application incompatibility and testing needs. An example of an application virtualization tool is Microsoft Application Virtualization (App-V).

When it comes to server virtualization, there are many different players in the game. The original king of virtualization is VMware. VMware was the first company to take server virtualization to the next level.

At the same time, Microsoft had smaller versions of virtualization such as Virtual Server. In 2008 Microsoft released its first version of Hyper-V. To say that Windows Server 2008 Hyper-V had flaws would be a kind way of putting it.

But as Microsoft continued to release versions of server, it kept improving Hyper-V. When Microsoft released Windows Server 2012 and 2012 R2, it made huge leaps and bounds. Then Windows Server 2016 and Server 2019 took Hyper-V to another level—a level where they could actually compete with VMware and other virtual vendors. The big advantage of Hyper-V is that it comes included with Windows Server.

So how do we get a Windows Server to allow multiple servers to all run on the same machine? Well, the great thing about virtualization is that it is all done for us using the Microsoft Windows Hypervisor.

The Windows *hypervisor* is a thin layer of software that sits between the hardware and the Windows Server 2022 operating system. This thin layer allows one physical machine to run multiple operating systems in different virtual machines at the same time. The hypervisor is the mechanism that is responsible for maintaining isolation between the different Hyper-V partitions.

The hypervisor allows the Hyper-V host server to have multiple virtual machines running on the same machine at one time. So now you may be wondering how many virtual machines you can run at the same time. This is all going to depend on your machine's hardware and the licensing that you own. For example, physical memory and processors are just two examples of hardware that would need to be increased depending on how many virtual machines you want to run. Also, other features loaded into the virtual environment may require even higher hardware demands like clustering. We will talk more about the hypervisor later in the chapter.

So since we are going to be focusing on Microsoft's version of virtualization, let's take a look at some of the Hyper-V features that you get.

Hyper-V Features

As a lead-in to the virtualization topic and Hyper-V, I will start with a list of key features, followed by a list of supported guest operating systems. This should provide you with a quick, high-level view of this feature before you dig deeper into the technology.

Key Features of Hyper-V

The following are the key features of Hyper-V:

Architecture   The hypervisor-based architecture, which has a 64-bit micro-kernel, provides a new array of device support as well as performance and security improvements.

Automatic Virtual Machine Activation (AVMA)   *Automatic Virtual Machine Activation (AVMA)* is a feature that allows you to install virtual machines on a properly activated Windows Server 2022 system without the need to manage individual product keys for each virtual machine. When using AVMA, virtual machines get bound to the licensed Hyper-V server as soon as the virtual machine starts. The virtual machines can move the AVMA-licensed VM to other hosts, but the VM can only run one instance and it can only be on a host set up for AVMA. It is bound to the host it is running on, but it can move from host to host as long as the hosts are AVMA.

Discrete Device Assignment   One feature of Windows Server 2022 is the ability to use Discrete Device Assignment (DDA). DDA allows you to take full advantage of performance and application compatibility improvements in the user experience by allowing the system's graphic cards to be directly assigned to a virtual machine. This allows the graphic card processor to be fully available to the virtual desktops that are utilizing the native driver of the graphics card processor as well as the network card's storage features.

Dynamic Memory   *Dynamic Memory* is a feature of Hyper-V that allows it to balance memory automatically among running virtual machines. Dynamic Memory allows Hyper-V to adjust the amount of memory available to the virtual machines in response to the needs of the virtual machines. It is currently available for Hyper-V in Windows Server 2022.

Enhanced Session Mode   *Enhanced Session Mode* enhances the interactive session of the Virtual Machine Connection for Hyper-V administrators who want to connect to their virtual machines. It gives administrators the same functionality as a remote desktop connection when the administrator is interacting with a virtual machine.

In previous versions of Hyper-V, the virtual machine connection gave you limited functionality while you connected to the virtual machine screen, keyboard, and mouse. You could use an RDP connection to get full redirection abilities, but doing so would require a network connection to the virtual machine host.

Enhanced Session Mode gives you the following benefits for local resource redirection:

- Display configuration
- Audio
- Printers
- Clipboard
- Smart cards
- Drives
- USB devices
- Supported Plug and Play devices

Fibre Channel   The virtual Fibre Channel feature allows you to connect to the Fibre Channel storage unit from within the virtual machine. *Virtual Fibre Channel* allows you to use your existing Fibre Channel to support virtualized workloads. Hyper-V users have the ability to use Fibre Channel storage area networks (SANs) to virtualize the workloads that require direct access to SAN logical unit numbers (LUNs).

Hardware Architecture   Hyper-V's architecture provides improved utilization of resources such as networking, memory, and disks.

Hyper-V Nesting   Windows Server 2022 has a feature of Hyper-V called *Hyper-V nesting*. Hyper-V nesting allows you to run a virtual machine in a virtual machine. So, let's say that you build a new 2016 Hyper-V server. You install Windows Server 2022 into a virtual machine. Then in that virtual machine, you can install Hyper-V and build other virtual machines within the first virtual machine. You can install a Windows Server 2022 virtual machine and still show others how to install and create virtual machines in the original virtual machine. To enable Hyper-V nesting, you would run the following PowerShell command on the Hyper-V Host. The virtual machines must be in the OFF State when this command is run (this means the virtual machines must be turned off).

```
Set-VMProcessor -VMName <VMName> -ExposeVirtualizationExtensions $true
```

Network Isolation   One nice feature of using Microsoft Hyper-V network virtualization is the ability of Hyper-V to keep virtual networks isolated from the physical network infrastructure of the hosted system. Because you can set up Hyper-V software–defined virtualization policies, you are no longer limited by the IP address assignment or VLAN isolation requirements of the physical network. Hyper-V allows for built-in network isolation to keep the virtual network separated from the virtual network.

Network Load Balancing Hyper-V provides support for *Windows Network Load Balancing (NLB)* to balance the network load across virtual machines on different servers.

Non-Uniform Memory Access Non-Uniform Memory Access (NUMA) is a multiprocessor memory architecture that allows a processor to access its local memory quicker than memory located on another processor. NUMA allows a system to access memory quickly by providing separate memory on each processor. Processors can access their local assigned memory, thus speeding the system performance. Normally a multiprocessor system runs into performance issues when multiple processors access the same memory at the same time. NUMA helps prevent this by allowing processors to access their own memory. Memory that is dedicated to a processor is referred to as a NUMA node.

Operating System Support Both 32-bit and 64-bit operating systems can run simultaneously in Hyper-V. Also, different platforms like Windows, Linux, and others are supported.

Quick Migration Hyper-V's *quick migration* feature provides you with the functionality to run virtual machines in a clustered environment with switchover capabilities when there is a failure. Thus, you can reduce downtime and achieve higher availability of your virtual machines.

Resource Metering Hyper-V *resource metering* allows your organization to track usage within the businesses departments. It allows you to create a usage-based billing solution that adjusts to your provider's business model and strategy.

RemoteFX Windows Server 2022 Hyper-V RemoteFX allows for an enhanced user experience for RemoteFX desktops by providing a 3D virtual adapter, intelligent codecs, and the ability to redirect USB devices in virtual machines.

Scripting Using the Windows Management Instrumentation (WMI) interfaces and APIs, you can easily build custom scripts to automate processes in your virtual machines.

Shared Virtual Hard Disk Windows Server 2022 Hyper-V has a feature called Shared Virtual Hard Disk. *Shared Virtual Hard Disk* allows you to cluster virtual machines by using shared virtual hard disk (VHDX) files.

Shared virtual hard disks allow you to build a high availability infrastructure, which is important if you are setting up either a private cloud deployment or a cloud-hosted environment for managing large workloads. Shared virtual hard disks allow two or more virtual machines to access the same VHDX file.

Shielded Virtual Machines Shielded Virtual Machines are a generation 2 virtual machine that uses a virtual Trusted Platform Module chip and is encrypted using Windows BitLocker. Shielded Virtual Machines allow enterprise administrators to provide a more secure environment for their tenant virtual machines.

Support for Symmetric Multiprocessors   Support for up to 64 processors in a virtual machine environment provides you with the ability to run applications as well as multiple virtual machines faster.

Virtual Machines   Virtual machines are the operating systems that run on the virtual server. They can be full operating systems or smaller versions of operating systems. The virtual machines are the actual virtual environment that these operating systems run in. They can communicate and operate on a network the same way a physical server can.

Virtual Machine Snapshot   You can take snapshots of running virtual machines, which provides you with the capability to recover to any previous virtual machine snapshot state quickly and easily.

Virtual Machine Queue   Windows Server 2022 Hyper-V includes a feature called *Virtual Machine Queue (VMQ)* as long as the hardware is VMQ-compatible network hardware. VMQ uses packet filtering to provide data from an external virtual machine network directly to virtual machines. This helps reduce the overhead of routing packets from the management operating system to the virtual machine.

Once VMQ is enabled on Hyper-V, a dedicated queue is created on the physical network adapter for each virtual network adapter to use. When data arrives for the virtual network adapter, the physical network adapter places that data in a queue and once the system is available, all the data in the queue is delivered to the virtual network adapter.

To enable the virtual machine queue on a specific virtual machine, enter the settings for the virtual machine and expand Network Adapter. Click Hardware Acceleration in the right window; then select Enable Virtual Machine Queue.

Supported Guest Operating Systems

Guest operating systems are the operating systems that run in the virtual environment. Depending on your version of Windows Server 2022, the number of guest operating systems depends on how many virtual machines can be loaded based on licensing. Windows Server 2022 Standard allows you to have the host system and two virtual machines. You can purchase additional licensing to allow more virtual machines, but the default is two virtual machines.

Windows Server 2022 Datacenter can have unlimited virtual machines along with the Hyper-V Host system. The maximum number of VMs that can run at once is 1,024.

Once you purchase the appropriate version of Windows Server and licensing, you can start creating virtual machines with guest operating systems.

The following guest operating systems have been successfully tested on Hyper-V and are hypervisor aware. Table 2.1 shows all of the guest server operating systems and the maximum number of virtual processors. Table 2.2 shows all of the guest client operating systems and the maximum number of virtual processors.

TABLE 2.1 Hyper-V guest server operating systems

Guest operating system (server)	Maximum number of virtual processors
Windows Server 2022	64 for Generation 1 VMs and 240 for Generation 2 VMs
Windows Server 2019	64 for Generation 1 VMs and 240 for Generation 2 VMs
Windows Server 2016	64 for Generation 1 VMs and 240 for Generation 2 VMs
Windows Server 2012 and Server 2012 R2	64
Windows Server 2008 R2 with Service Pack 1 (SP1)	64
Windows Server 2008 R2	64
Windows Server 2008 with Service Pack 2 (SP2)	8
Red Hat Enterprise Linux 5.7 and 5.8	64
Red Hat Enterprise Linux 6.0–6.3	64
SUSE Linux Enterprise Server 11 SP2	64
Open SUSE 12.1	64

TABLE 2.2 Hyper-V guest client operating systems

Guest operating system (client)	Maximum number of virtual processors
Windows 11	32
Windows 10	32
Windows 8.1	32
CentOS 5.7 and 5.8	64
CentOS 6.0–6.3	64
Red Hat Enterprise Linux 5.7 and 5.8	64

Guest operating system (client)	Maximum number of virtual processors
Red Hat Enterprise Linux 6.0–6.3	64
SUSE Linux Enterprise Server 11 SP2	64
Open SUSE 12.1	64

The list of supported guest operating systems may always be extended. Please check the official Microsoft Hyper-V site to obtain a current list of supported operating systems: `https://docs.microsoft.com/en-us/windows-server/virtualization/hyper-v/hyper-v-on-windows-server`.

Hyper-V Architecture

This section will provide you with an overview of the Hyper-V architecture (see Figure 2.1). I'll explain the differences between a hypervisor-aware and a non-hypervisor-aware child partition.

FIGURE 2.1 Hyper-V architecture

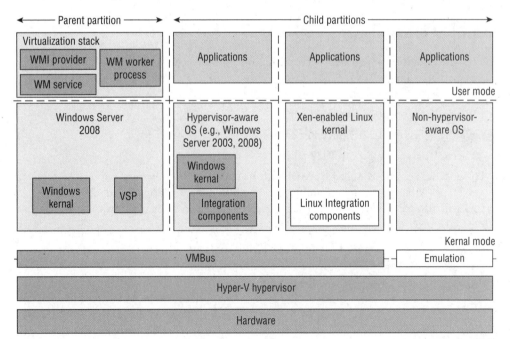

As you can see, Hyper-V is based on the microkernel architecture. As I stated earlier in the chapter, Hyper-V provides a virtualization layer called a hypervisor that runs directly on the system hardware. You can see that the hypervisor is similar to what the kernel is to Windows. It is a software layer responsible for the interaction with the core hardware and works in conjunction with an optimized instance of Windows Server 2022 that allows running multiple operating systems on a physical server simultaneously. The Hyper-V architecture consists of the hypervisor and parent and child partitions.

The Windows Server 2022 operating system runs in the parent partition, and it delivers the WMI provider for scripting as well as the VM service.

Virtual machines each run in their own child partitions. Child partitions do not have direct access to hardware resources; instead, they have a virtual view of the resources, which are called *virtual devices*.

If you're running a hypervisor-aware operating system like Windows Server 2008, Windows Server 2008 R2, Windows Server 2012, Windows Server 2016, Windows Server 2019, or Windows Server 2022 in your virtual machine, any request to the virtual devices is redirected via the high-speed bus to the devices in the parent partition, which will manage the requests.

By default, only Windows Server 2008 R2 and newer are hypervisor-aware operating systems. Once you install Hyper-V Integration Components on an operating system other than Windows Server 2008 R2 and newer, it will be hypervisor aware. Microsoft provides a hypervisor adapter to make Linux hypervisor aware.

Non-hypervisor-aware operating systems (for example, Windows NT 2003) use an emulator to communicate with the Windows hypervisor, which is slower than molasses in the winter.

Hyper-V Operating Systems

To use virtualization in Windows Server 2022, you need to consider the basic software requirements for Hyper-V. Hyper-V runs only on the following editions of the Windows Server 2022 operating system:

- Windows Server 2022 Standard edition
- Windows Server 2022 Datacenter edition
- Microsoft Hyper-V Server 2022 edition

Hyper-V was first introduced by Microsoft in 2008 and with every version of Windows Server, Hyper-V has gotten better and better. The following Windows Server 2016/2019 servers will also run Hyper-V. Many administrators may run both Windows Server 2016 and Server 2019 together.

- Windows Server 2016/2019 Standard edition
- Windows Server 2016/2019 Datacenter edition
- Microsoft Hyper-V Server 2016/2019 edition

Linux and FreeBSD Image Deployments

One of the features of Windows Server 2022 is the ability for Hyper-V to support Linux and FreeBSD virtual machines. Hyper-V now can support these new virtual machines because Hyper-V has the ability to emulate Linux and FreeBSD devices. Because Hyper-V now has the ability to emulate these two devices, no additional software needs to be installed on Hyper-V.

Unfortunately, because Hyper-V has to emulate these devices, you lose some of the Hyper-V functionality like high performance and full management of the virtual machines. So, it's a trade-off—you get to run Linux and FreeBSD type Hyper-V virtual machines, but you lose some of the benefits of Hyper-V.

But wait; there is a way to get your Hyper-V functionality back. This issue can be resolved as long as you install Hyper-V on machines that can support Linux and FreeBSD operating systems. The drivers that are needed on Hyper-V are called Linux Integration Services (LIS) and FreeBSD Integrated Services (FIS). By putting these drivers on a device that can handle Linux and FreeBSD, you can then have Hyper-V with all of the features Microsoft offers.

To get these drivers and make Hyper-V work will all of its functionality, you must make sure that you install a newer release of Linux that includes LIS. To get the most out of FreeBSD, you must get a version after 10.0. For FreeBSD versions that are older than 10.0, Microsoft offers ports that work with BIS drivers that need to be installed. Hyper-V will work with Linux and FreeBSD without the need of any additional drivers or equipment. By having drivers and equipment that supports Linux and FreeBSD, you just get all of the Hyper-V features that your organization may need.

Hyper-V Installation and Configuration

This section explains how to install the Hyper-V role using Server Manager in Windows Server 2022 Full installation mode or the command-line mode in Windows Server 2022 Server Core. We will then take a look at Hyper-V as part of Server Manager before discussing how to use the Hyper-V Manager. Finally, we will look at the Hyper-V server settings and then cover two important areas for Hyper-V: virtual networks and virtual hard disks.

Hyper-V Requirements

The following subsections will describe the hardware and software requirements for installing the Hyper-V server role. It is important to understand these requirements for obtaining your software license as well as for planning for server hardware. When you understand the requirements, you can design and configure a Hyper-V solution that will meet the needs of your applications.

Hardware Requirements

In addition to the basic hardware requirements for Windows Server 2022, there are requirements for running the Hyper-V server role on your Windows server. They are listed in Table 2.3.

TABLE 2.3   Hardware requirements for Hyper-V

Requirement area	Definition
CPU	x64-compatible processor with Intel VT or AMD-V technology enabled. Hardware Data Execution Prevention (DEP), specifically Intel XD bit (execute disable bit) or AMD NX bit (no execute bit), must be available and enabled. Minimum: 1.4 GHz. Recommended: 2 GHz or faster.
Memory	Minimum: 1 GB of RAM. Recommended: 4 GB of RAM or greater. (Additional RAM is required for each running guest operating system.) Maximum: 1 TB.
Hard disk	Minimum: 8 GB. Recommended: 20 GB or greater. (Additional disk space needed for each guest operating system.)

The Add Roles Wizard in Server Manager additionally verifies the hardware requirements. A good starting point is to check your hardware against the Microsoft hardware list to make sure that Windows Server 2022 supports your hardware. If you try to install the Hyper-V server role on a computer that does not meet the CPU requirements, you'll get a warning window that looks like Figure 2.2.

FIGURE 2.2   Warning window that Hyper-V cannot be installed

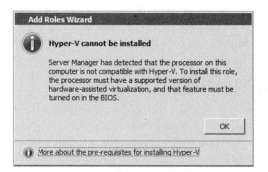

Install the Hyper-V Role

Now it's time to see how to install the Hyper-V server role on the two installation options of Windows Server 2022: a Full installation and a Server Core installation.

Installing Hyper-V in Full Installation Mode

You can install the Hyper-V server role on any Windows Server 2022 installation for which the Full option was chosen. In addition, the server must meet both the hardware and software requirements. The installation process is simple, as Exercise 2.1 demonstrates.

EXERCISE 2.1

Installing Hyper-V in Full Installation Mode

1. Open Server Manager.

2. In Server Manager, choose option 2, Add Roles And Features.

3. At the Select Installation Type page, choose the role-based or feature-based installation. Click Next.

4. On the Select Destination Server screen, choose Select A Server From The Server Pool and select the server to which you want to add this role. Click Next.

5. On the Select Server Roles screen, click the check box next to Hyper-V (see Figure 2.3). When the Add Features dialog box appears, click the Add Features button. Then click Next.

FIGURE 2.3   Server Manager Add Features

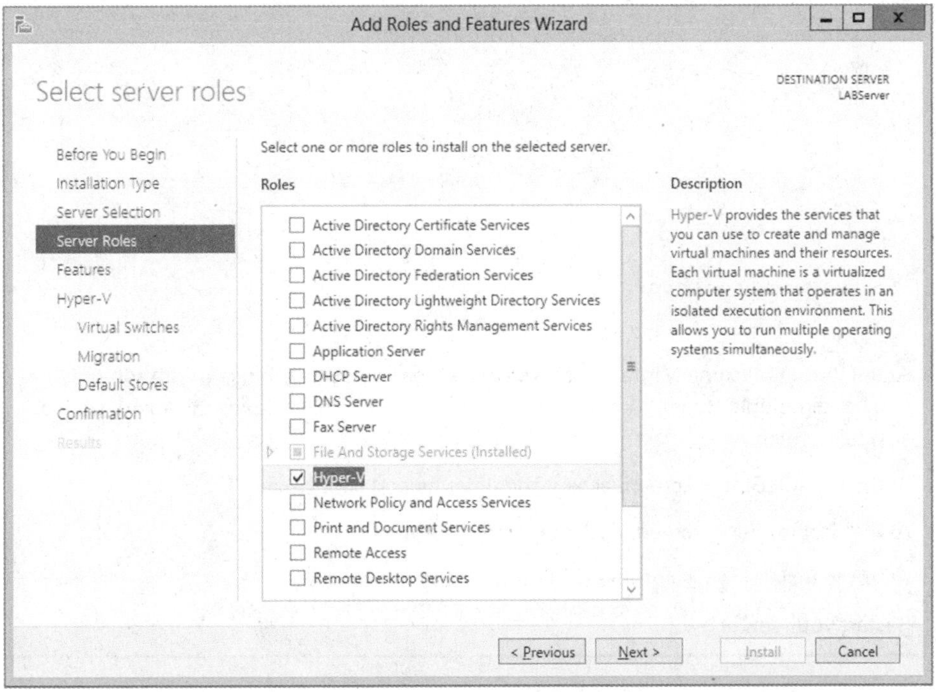

EXERCISE 2.1 *(continued)*

6. At the Select Features screen, click Next.
7. At the Hyper-V introduction screen, click Next.
8. At the Create Virtual Switches screen (see Figure 2.4), choose your adapter and click Next.

FIGURE 2.4 Create Virtual Switch screen

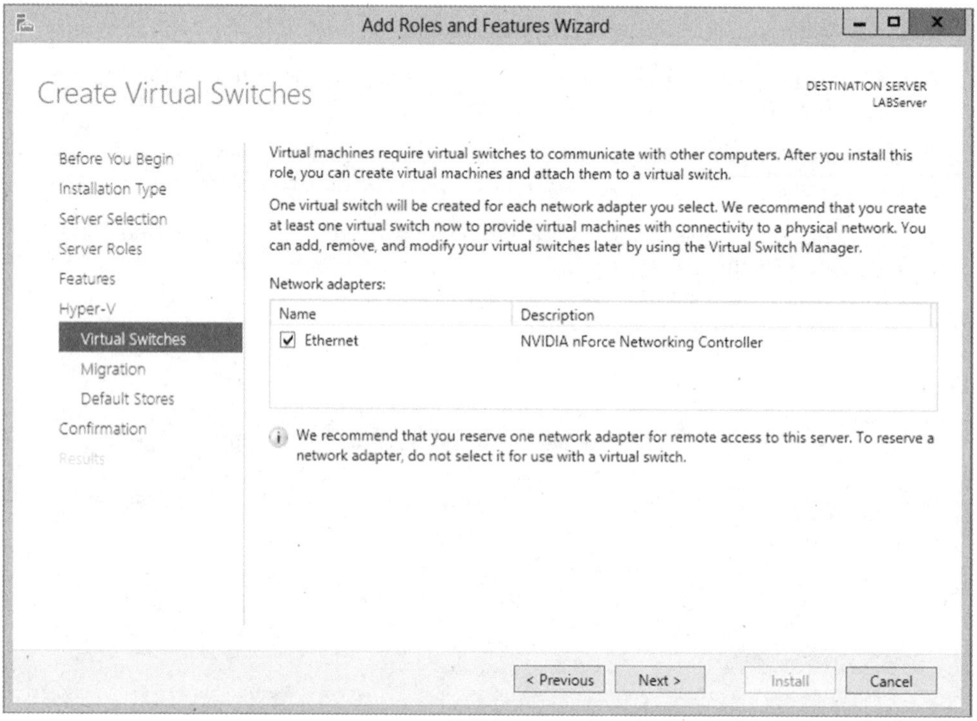

9. At the Virtual Machine Migration screen, click Next. You want to use migration only if you have multiple Hyper-V servers. Since we will have only one for this exercise, just skip this screen.
10. At the Default Stores screen, accept the defaults and click Next.
11. At the Confirmation screen, click the Install button.
12. After the installation is complete, click the Close button.
13. Restart your server.

Installing Hyper-V in Server Core

The Server Core installation option is included in Windows Server 2022. It creates an operating system installation without a GUI shell. You can either manage the server remotely from another system or use the Server Core's command-line interface.

This installation option provides the following benefits:

- Reduces attack surface (because fewer applications are running on the server)
- Reduces maintenance and management (because only the required options are installed)
- Requires less disk space and produces less processor utilization
- Provides a minimal parent partition
- Reduces system resources required by the operating system as well as the attack surface

By using Hyper-V on a Server Core installation, you can fundamentally improve availability because the attack surface is reduced and the downtime required for installing patches is optimized. It will thus be more secure and reliable with less management.

To install Hyper-V for a Windows Server 2022 installation, you must execute the following command in the command-line interface:

```
Dism /online /enable-feature /featurename:Microsoft-Hyper-V
```

Hyper-V in Server Manager

As with all of the other Windows Server 2022 roles, the Hyper-V role neatly integrates into Server Manager. Server Manager filters the information just for the specific role and thus displays only the required information. As you can see in Figure 2.5, the Hyper-V Summary page shows related event log entries, the state of the system services for Hyper-V, and useful resources and support.

FIGURE 2.5 Hyper-V in Server Manager

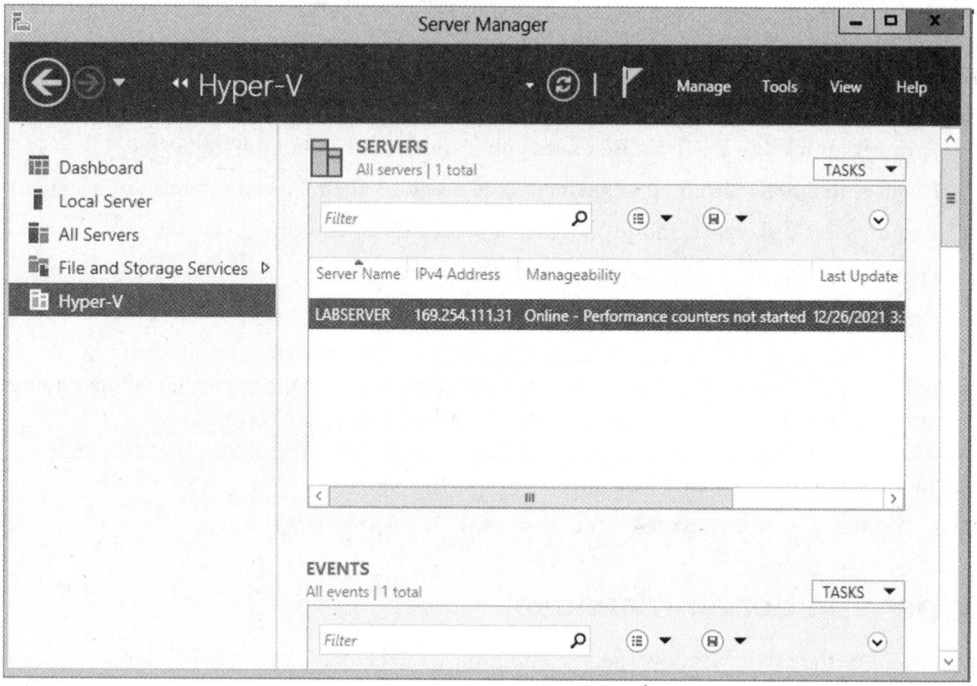

Using Hyper-V Manager

Hyper-V Manager is the central management console to configure your server and create and manage your virtual machines, virtual networks, and virtual hard disks. Unlike Virtual Server 2005, where you managed all virtual machines through a web interface, Hyper-V Manager is managed through a Microsoft Management Console (MMC) snap-in. You can access it either in Server Manager or by using Administrative Tools ➢ Hyper-V Manager. Figure 2.6 shows how Hyper-V Manager looks once you start it.

FIGURE 2.6   Hyper-V Manager

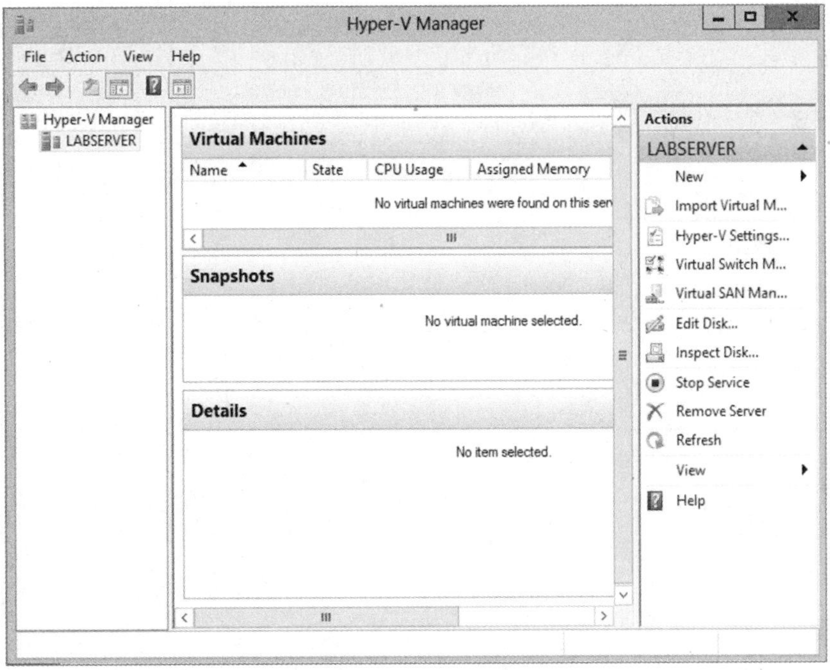

Hyper-V Manager is available for the following current operating systems:

- Windows Server 2022
- Windows Server 2019
- Windows Server 2016
- Windows Server 2012 R2
- Windows Server 2012
- Windows 10/Windows 11

You can use Hyper-V Manager to connect to any Full or Server Core installation remotely. Besides Hyper-V Manager, you can use the WMI interface for scripting Hyper-V.

Configure Hyper-V Settings

In this section, you will get an overview of the available Hyper-V settings for the server. You configure all server-side default configuration settings like default locations of your configuration files or the release key. You can open the Hyper-V Settings page (see Figure 2.7) in Hyper-V Manager by clicking Hyper-V Settings in the Actions pane.

FIGURE 2.7 Hyper-V Settings

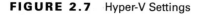

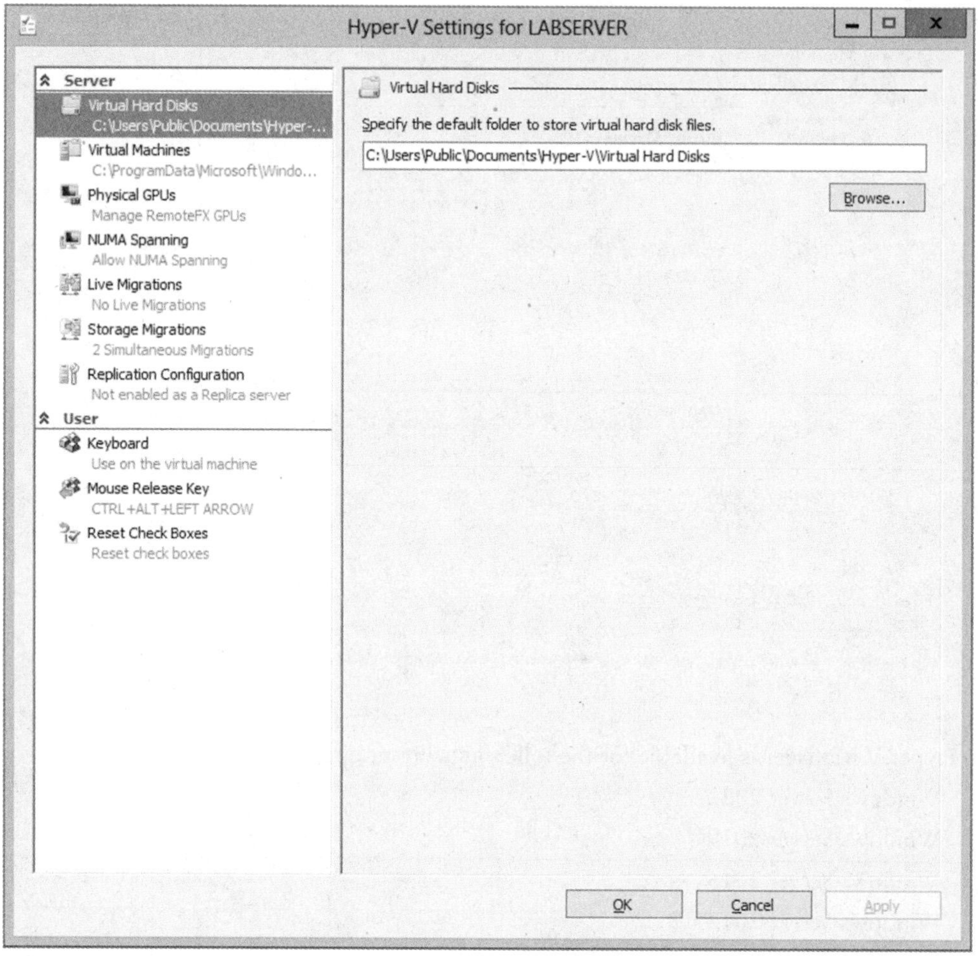

The Hyper-V Settings page includes the following settings:

Virtual Hard Disks   Specifies the default location of your virtual hard disk files (those with the extension .vhd or .vdhx).

Virtual Machines   Specifies the default location of your virtual machine configuration files. It includes the Virtual Machine XML configuration files (part of the Virtual Machines folder) as well as related snapshots (part of the Snapshot folder).

Physical GPUs   This feature allows for graphical processing unit (GPU) accelerated video within a virtual machine. The GPU will allow you to support 3D GPU accelerated graphics.

NUMA Spanning   You can configure Hyper-V to allow virtual machines to span non-uniform memory architecture (NUMA) nodes. When the physical computer has NUMA nodes, this setting provides virtual machines with additional computing resources. Spanning NUMA nodes can help you run more virtual machines at the same time. However, using NUMA can decrease overall performance.

Live Migrations   *Live migration* allows a Hyper-V administrator to relocate running virtual machines easily from one node of the failover cluster to another node in the same cluster. Live Migration is explained in more detail later in this chapter.

Storage Migrations   *Storage Migration* allows you to move your virtual machine storage from one location to another. This setting allows you to specify how many storage migrations can be performed at the same time on this system.

Replication Configuration   This setting allows you to configure this computer as a Replica Server to another Hyper-V server. Hyper-V Replica allows you to replicate your Hyper-V virtual machines from one Hyper-V host at a primary site to another Hyper-V host at the Replica site.

Each node of the failover cluster that is involved in Replica must have the Hyper-V server role installed. One of the servers in the Hyper-V replication needs to be set up as a Replica Broker to allow the replication to work properly.

Keyboard   Defines how to use Windows key combinations. Options are Physical Computer, Virtual Machine, and Virtual Machine Only When Running Full Screen.

Mouse Release Key   Specifies the key combination to release the mouse in your virtual machine. Options are Ctrl+Alt+Left Arrow, Ctrl+Alt+Right Arrow, Ctrl+Alt+Space, and Ctrl+Alt+Shift.

Reset Check Boxes   Resets any check boxes that hide pages and messages when checked. This will bring any window up again on which you checked the Do Not Show This Window Again check box.

Manage Virtual Switches

A *virtual network* provides the virtual links between nodes in either a virtual or physical network. Virtual networking in Hyper-V is provided in a secure and dynamic way because you can granularly define virtual network switches for their required usage. For example, you can define a private or internal virtual network if you don't want to allow your virtual machines to send packages to the physical network.

To allow your virtual machines to communicate with each other, you need virtual networks. Just like normal networks, virtual networks exist only on the host computer and allow you to configure how virtual machines communicate with each other, with the host, and with the network or the Internet. You manage virtual networks in Hyper-V using *Virtual Switch Manager*, as shown in Figure 2.8.

FIGURE 2.8   Virtual Network Manager

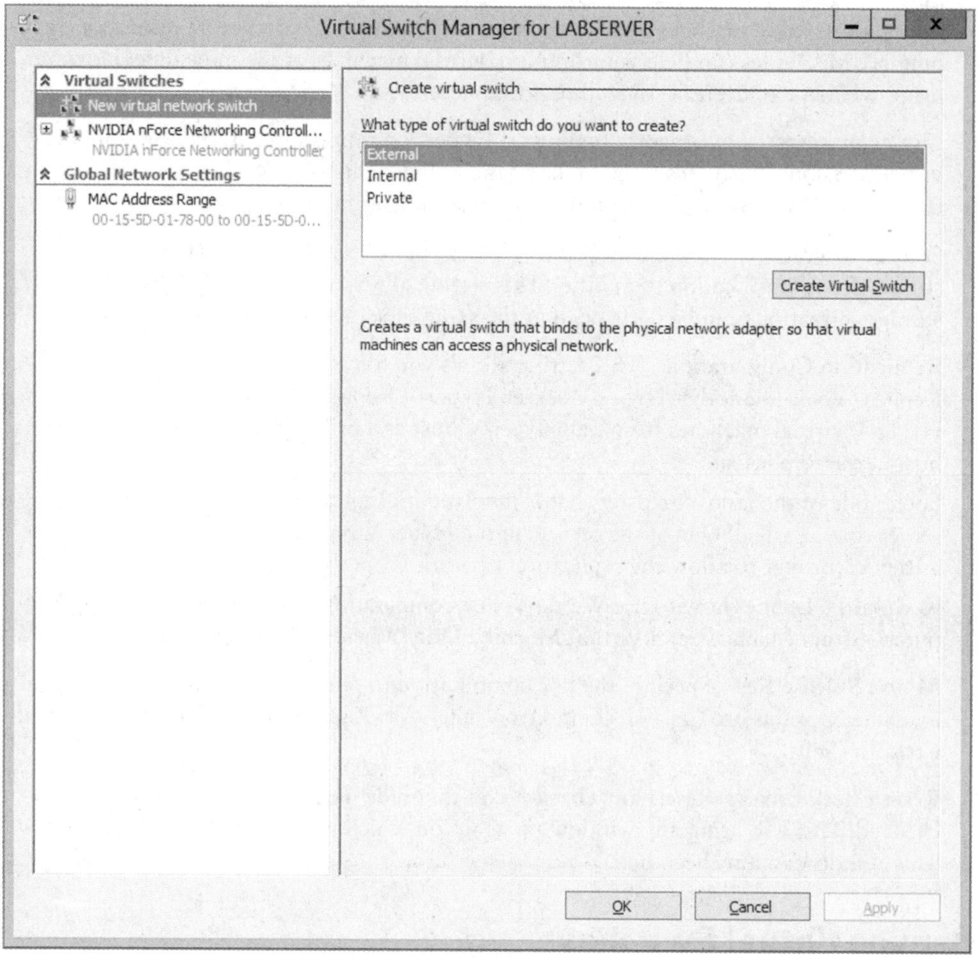

Using Virtual Switch Manager, you can create, manage, and delete virtual switches. You can define the network type as external, internal only, or private:

External   Any virtual machine connected to this virtual switch can access the physical network. You would use this option if you want to allow your virtual machines to access, for example, other servers on the network or the Internet. This option is used in production environments where your clients connect directly to the virtual machines.

Internal   This option allows virtual machines to communicate with each other as well as the host system but not with the physical network. When you create an internal network, it also creates a local area connection in Network Connections that allows the host machine to communicate with the virtual machines. You can use this option if you want to separate your host's network from your virtual networks.

Private   When you use this option, virtual machines can communicate with each other but not with the host system or the physical network; thus, no network packets are hitting the wire. You can use this option to define internal virtual networks for test environments or labs, for example.

On the external and internal-only virtual networks, you also can enable virtual LAN (VLAN) identification. You can use VLANs to partition your network into multiple subnets using a VLAN ID. When you enable virtual LAN identification, the NIC that is connected to the switch will never see packets tagged with VLAN IDs. Instead, all packets traveling from the NIC to the switch will be tagged with the access mode VLAN ID as they leave the switch port. All packets traveling from the switch port to the NIC will have their VLAN tags removed. You can use this if you are already logically segmenting your physical machines and also use it for your virtual ones.

Exercise 2.2 explains how to create an internal-only virtual switch.

EXERCISE 2.2

Creating an Internal Virtual Network

1.   Click Windows Key ➢ Administrative Tools ➢ Hyper-V Manager.

2.   In Hyper-V Manager, in the Actions pane, choose Virtual Switch Manager.

3.   On the Virtual Switch page, select Private and click the Create Virtual Switch button.

4.   On the New Virtual Switch page, enter **Private Virtual Network** in the Name field.

5.   Click OK.

When you create the internal virtual switch, a network device is created in Network Connections, as shown in Figure 2.9.

FIGURE 2.9 Virtual network card

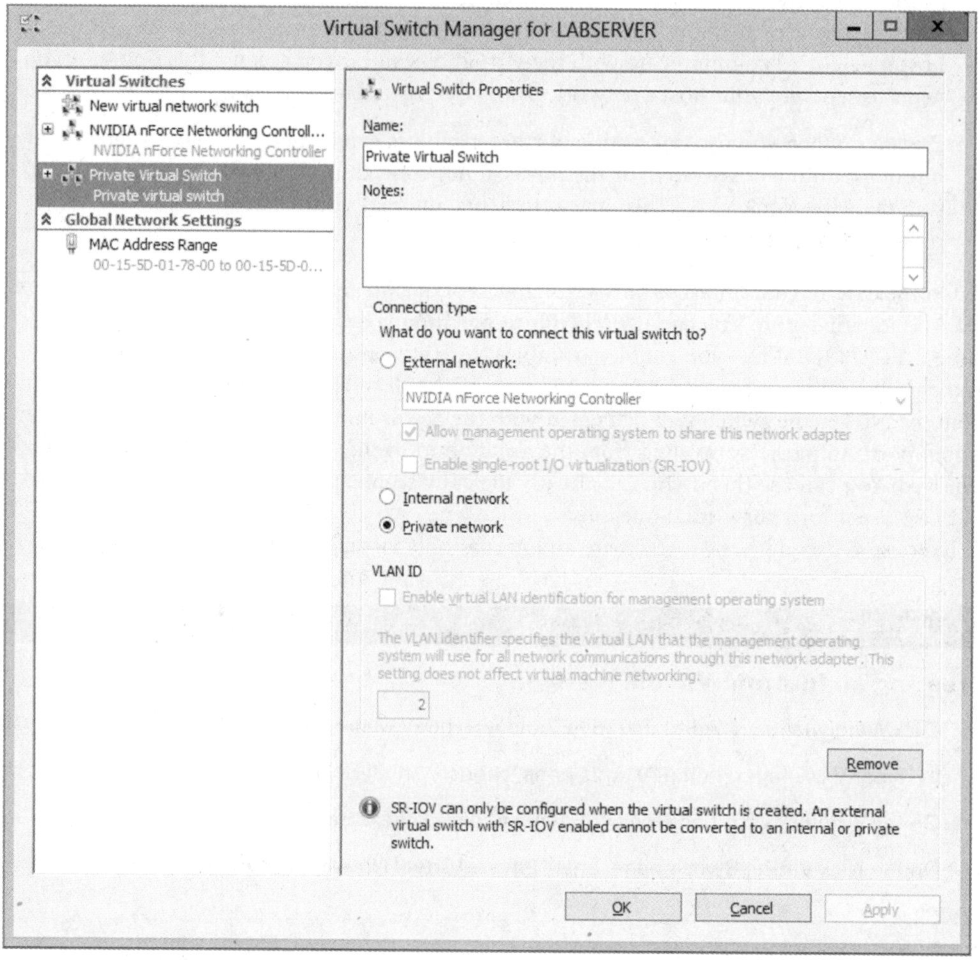

This is also the case when you create an external virtual network because it will replace the physical network card of the host machine to give the parent partition a virtual network card that is also used in the child partitions.

Unlike with Virtual Server 2005, Hyper-V binds the virtual network service to a physical network adapter only when an external virtual network is created. The benefit of this is that the performance is better if you do not use the external virtual network option. The downside, however, is that there will be a network disruption when you create or delete an external virtual network.

Communication between the virtual machine and the local host computer is not configured automatically. Once you install a virtual machine, you need to make sure that the TCP/IP settings are in agreement with the settings you define in the virtual network card. Start with a ping from your host machine to the virtual machines to verify that communication is working.

Managing Virtual Hard Disks

In addition to virtual networks, you need to manage virtual hard disks that you attach to your virtual machines. A virtual hard disk in Hyper-V, apart from a pass-through disk, is a VHD or VHDX file that basically simulates a hard drive on your virtual machine.

The following subsections will first show you what types of virtual hard disks are available and then show you how to create them. You will also learn what options are available to manage virtual hard disks.

Types of Hard Disks

Depending on how you want to use the disk, Hyper-V offers various types, as described in Table 2.4.

TABLE 2.4 Virtual hard disks in Hyper-V

Type of disk	Description	When to use it
Dynamically expanding	This disk starts with a small VHD file and expands it on demand once an installation takes place. It can grow to the maximum size you defined during creation. You can use this type of disk to clone a local hard drive during creation.	This option is effective when you don't know the exact space needed on the disk and when you want to preserve hard disk space on the host machine. Unfortunately, it is the slowest disk type.
Fixed size	The size of the VHD file is fixed to the size specified when the disk is created. This option is faster than a dynamically expanding disk. However, a fixed-size disk uses up the maximum defined space immediately. This type is ideal for cloning a local hard drive.	A fixed-size disk provides faster access than dynamically expanding or differencing disks, but it is slower than a physical disk.
Differencing	This type of disk is associated in a parent-child relationship with another disk. The differencing disk is the child, and the associated virtual disk is the parent. Differencing disks include only the differences to the parent disk. By using this type, you can save a lot of disk space in similar virtual machines. This option is suitable if you have multiple virtual machines with similar operating systems.	Differencing disks are most commonly found in test environments and should not be used in production environments.

TABLE 2.4   Virtual hard disks in Hyper-V *(continued)*

Type of disk	Description	When to use it
Physical (or pass-through disk)	The virtual machine receives direct pass-through access to the physical disk for exclusive use. This type provides the highest performance of all disk types and thus should be used for production servers where performance is the top priority. The drive is not available for other guest systems.	This type is used in high-end datacenters to provide optimum performance for VMs. It's also used in failover cluster environments.

Creating Virtual Hard Disks

To help you gain practice in creating virtual hard disks, the following three exercises will teach you how to create a differencing hard disk, how to clone an existing disk by creating a new disk, and how to configure a physical or pass-through disk to your virtual machine. First, in Exercise 2.3, you will learn how to create a differencing virtual hard disk.

EXERCISE 2.3

Creating a Differencing Hard Disk

1. Open Hyper-V Manager.

2. In Hyper-V Manager, in the Actions pane, choose New ➤ Hard Disk.

3. In the New Virtual Hard Disk Wizard, click Next on the Before You Begin page.

4. At the Choose Disk Format screen, choose VHDX and click Next. The size of your VHDs depends on which format you choose. If you're going to have a VHD larger than 2,040 GB, use VHDX. If your VHD is less than 2,040 GB, then you should use VHD.

5. On the Choose Disk Type page, select Fixed Size and click Next.

6. On the Specify Name And Location page, enter the new name of the child disk (for example, **newvirtualharddisk.vhd**). You can also modify the default location of the new VHD file if you want. Click Next to continue.

7. Next, on the Configure Disk page, you need to specify the size of the VHD file. Choose a size based on your hard disk and then click Next to continue. I used 60 GB as our test size.

8. On the Completing The New Virtual Hard Disk Wizard page, verify that all settings are correct and click Finish to create the hard disk.

The process to add a physical or pass-through disk to a virtual machine is quite different. For this, first you need to create the virtual machine, and then you open the virtual machine settings to configure the physical disk. If you want to add a physical disk to a virtual machine, the physical disk must be set as Offline in Disk Management, as shown in Figure 2.10.

FIGURE 2.10   In Disk Management, you can set disks as Offline.

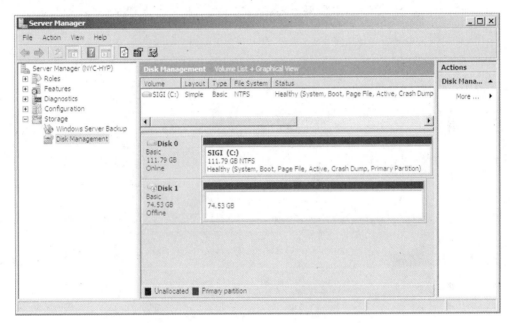

To access Disk Management, click the Windows Key, choose Administrative Tools ➤ Computer Management, expand Storage in the left pane, and click Disk Management.

 You cannot share a physical disk among multiple virtual machines or with the host system.

Physical or pass-through disks might not be that important if your use of virtualization is based on test environments, but they become crucial when you need to plan for highly available virtual datacenters. This is especially true if you consider using failover clusters to provide the Quick Migration feature, which is when you should consider matching one logical unit number (LUN) from your enterprise storage system or storage area network (SAN) as one physical disk. This provides you with the optimum performance you need in such an environment.

Managing Virtual Hard Disks

Hyper-V also provides two tools to manage virtual hard disks: Inspect Disk and Edit Disk. These tools are available in the Actions pane in Hyper-V Manager.

Inspect Disk   This provides you with information about the virtual hard disk. It shows you not only the type of the disk but also information such as the maximum size for dynamically expanding disks and the parent VHD for differencing disks.

Edit Disk   This provides you with the Edit Virtual Hard Disk Wizard, which you can use to compact, convert, expand, merge, or reconnect hard disks. Figure 2.11 shows you the wizard's options when you select a dynamically expanding disk.

FIGURE 2.11   The Edit Virtual Hard Disk Wizard

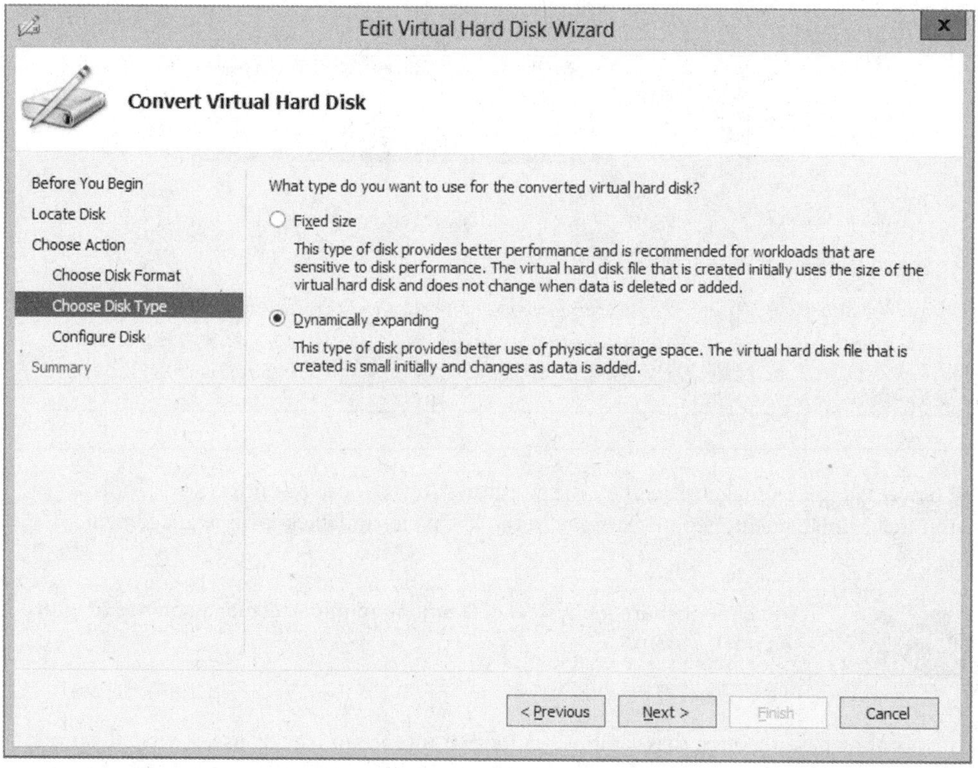

Table 2.5 provides you with an overview of what you can do with the wizard.

TABLE 2.5   Edit Virtual Hard Disk Wizard overview

Action	Description
Compact	Reduces the size of a dynamically expanding or differencing disk by removing blank space from deleted files.
Convert	Converts a dynamically expanding disk to a fixed disk or vice versa.
Expand	Increases the storage capacity of a dynamically expanding disk or a fixed virtual hard disk.
Merge	Merges the changes from a differencing disk into either the parent disk or another disk (applies to differencing disks only!).
Reconnect	If a differencing disk no longer finds its referring parent disk, this option can reconnect the parent to the disk.

Generation 1 vs. Generation 2 VHDs

Previous versions of Hyper-V had some pretty major drawbacks. One big drawback was that Hyper-V could not boot a virtual machine from a virtual hard drive that was SCSI. Believe it or not, SCSI controllers were not even recognized by Hyper-V unless you installed the Integration Services component.

Another issue that the previous versions of Hyper-V had was the inability to copy files from the Hyper-V host to the virtual machines without the use of a network connection in the virtual machine. The older versions of Hyper-V, prior to Windows Server 2016, are now considered Generation 1 versions. Why is it so important to know which generations of Hyper-V you should use or need to use?

Hyper-V generations help determine what functionality and what virtual hardware you can use in your virtual machine. Windows Server 2022 Hyper-V supports both virtual machine generations: Generation 1 and Generation 2.

As already explained, previous versions of Hyper-V are considered Generation 1, and this provides the same virtual hardware to the virtual machine as in previous versions of Hyper-V.

Generation 2 is included with Windows Server 2022, and it provides better functionality on the virtual machines including secure boot (which is enabled by default), the ability to boot from a SCSI virtual hard disk or boot from a SCSI virtual DVD, the ability to use a standard network adapter to PXE boot, and Unified Extensible Firmware Interface (UEFI) firmware support. Generation 2 now gives you the ability to support UEFI firmware instead of BIOS-based firmware. On a virtual machine that is Generation 2, you can configure Secure Boot, enable TPM, and set security policies by selecting the Security section of the virtual machine's properties.

So, when you create VHDs in Windows Server 2022, one of your choices will be the ability to create the VHDs as a Generation 1 or Generation 2 VHD. If you need the ability to have your VHDs run on older versions of Hyper-V, make them a Generation 1 VHD. If they are going to run only on Windows Server 2012 R2 and above, make your VHDs Generation 2 and take advantage of all the new features and functionality.

Configuring Virtual Machines

This section covers the topics of creating and managing virtual machines as well as how to back up and restore virtual machines using features such as Import and Export and Snapshot. We'll also briefly look at Hyper-V's Live Migration feature.

Creating and Managing Virtual Machines

It is important to learn how to create a virtual machine, how to change its configuration, and how to delete it. Let's take a look at the Virtual Machine Connection tool and install the Hyper-V Integration Components onto a virtual machine.

Virtual Machines

Virtual machines define the child partitions in which you run operating system instances. Each virtual machine is separate and can communicate with the others only by using a virtual network. You can assign hard drives, virtual networks, DVD drives, and other system components to it. A virtual machine is similar to an existing physical server, but it no longer runs on dedicated hardware—it shares the hardware of the host system with the other virtual machines that run on the host.

Exercise 2.4 shows you how to create a new virtual machine. Before completing this exercise, download an eval copy of Windows Server from Microsoft's website (www.microsoft.com/downloads). Make sure the file downloaded is an image file (with the extension .iso). You will use this image to install the operating system into the virtual machine.

EXERCISE 2.4

Creating a New Virtual Machine

1. Open Hyper-V Manager (see Figure 2.12).

FIGURE 2.12   Hyper-V Manager

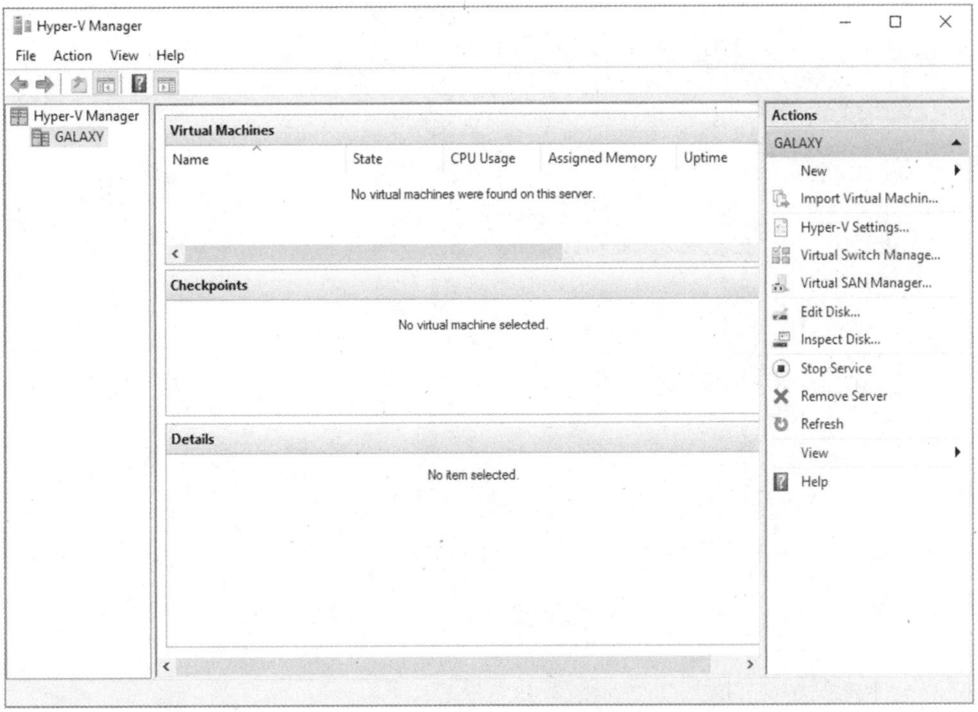

2. In Hyper-V Manager, in the Actions pane, choose New ➢ Virtual Machine.

3. In the New Virtual Machine Wizard, click Next on the Before You Begin page.

4. On the Specify Name And Location page, give your virtual machine a name and change the default location of the virtual machine configuration files. Click Next to continue.

5. The Specify Generation screen is next. Choose Generation 2 (see Figure 2.13) and click Next.

FIGURE 2.13 Specify Generation screen

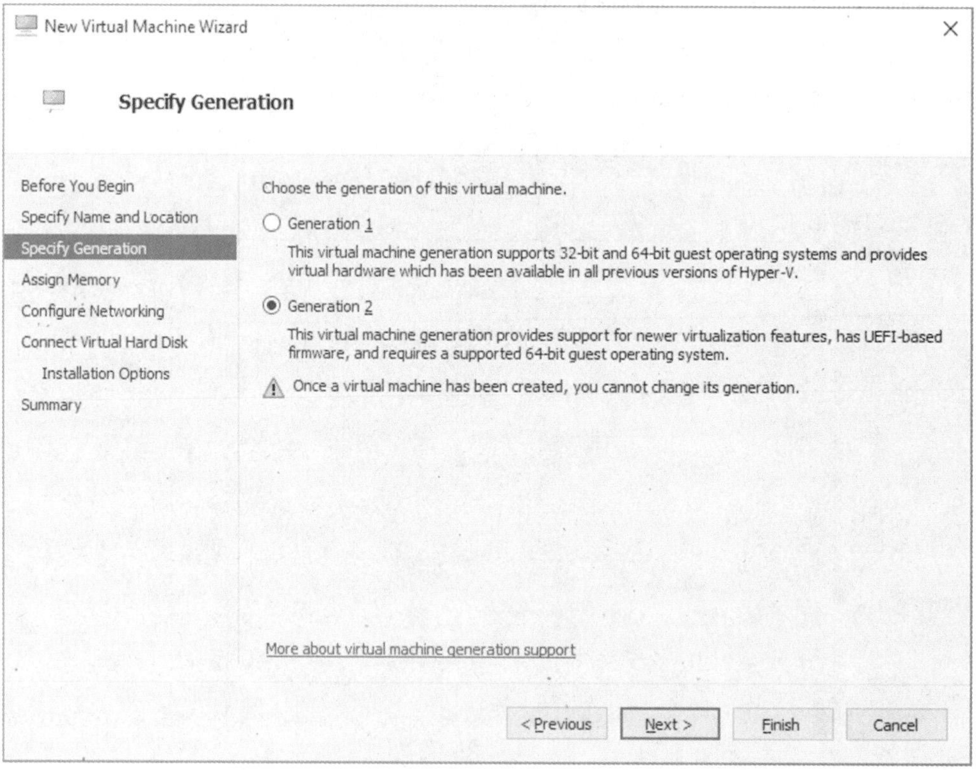

New Virtual Machine Wizard   ×

Specify Generation

Before You Begin
Specify Name and Location
Specify Generation
Assign Memory
Configure Networking
Connect Virtual Hard Disk
  Installation Options
Summary

Choose the generation of this virtual machine.

○ Generation 1

This virtual machine generation supports 32-bit and 64-bit guest operating systems and provides virtual hardware which has been available in all previous versions of Hyper-V.

⦿ Generation 2

This virtual machine generation provides support for newer virtualization features, has UEFI-based firmware, and requires a supported 64-bit guest operating system.

⚠ Once a virtual machine has been created, you cannot change its generation.

More about virtual machine generation support

      < Previous   Next >   Finish   Cancel

6. On the Assign Memory page (see Figure 2.14), define how much of your host computer's memory you want to assign to this virtual machine. Remember that once your virtual machine uses up all of your physical memory, it will start swapping to disk, thus reducing the performance of all virtual machines. Click Next to continue.

FIGURE 2.14   VM RAM

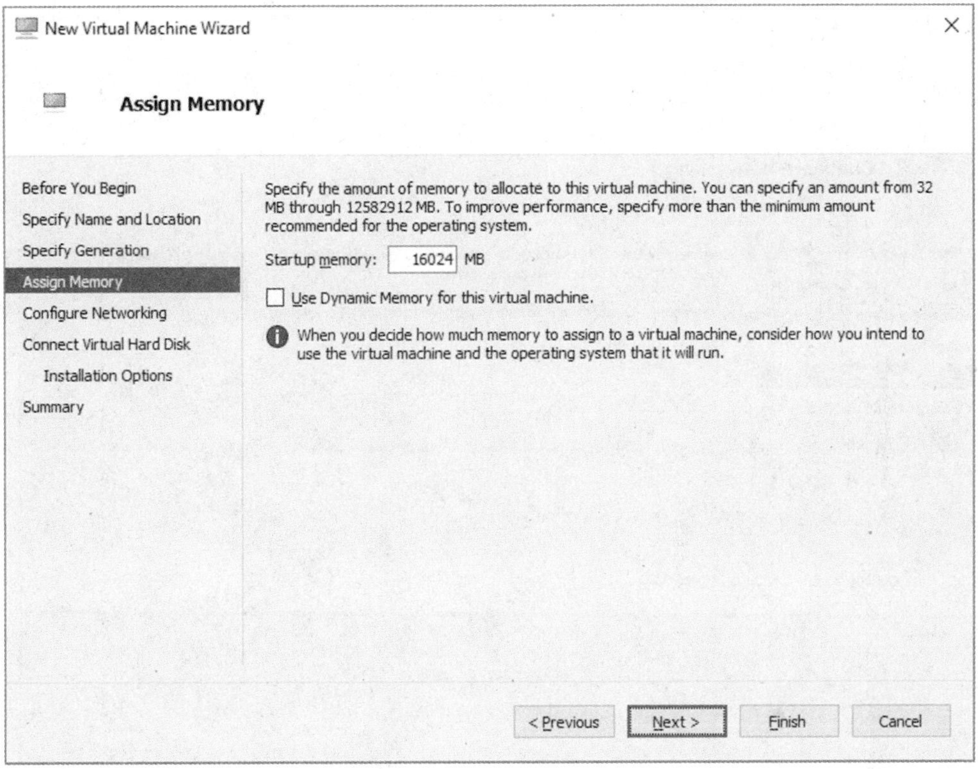

7. On the Configure Networking page (see Figure 2.15), select the virtual network that you previously configured using Virtual Network Manager. Click Next to continue.

EXERCISE 2.4 *(continued)*

FIGURE 2.15 Configure Networking page

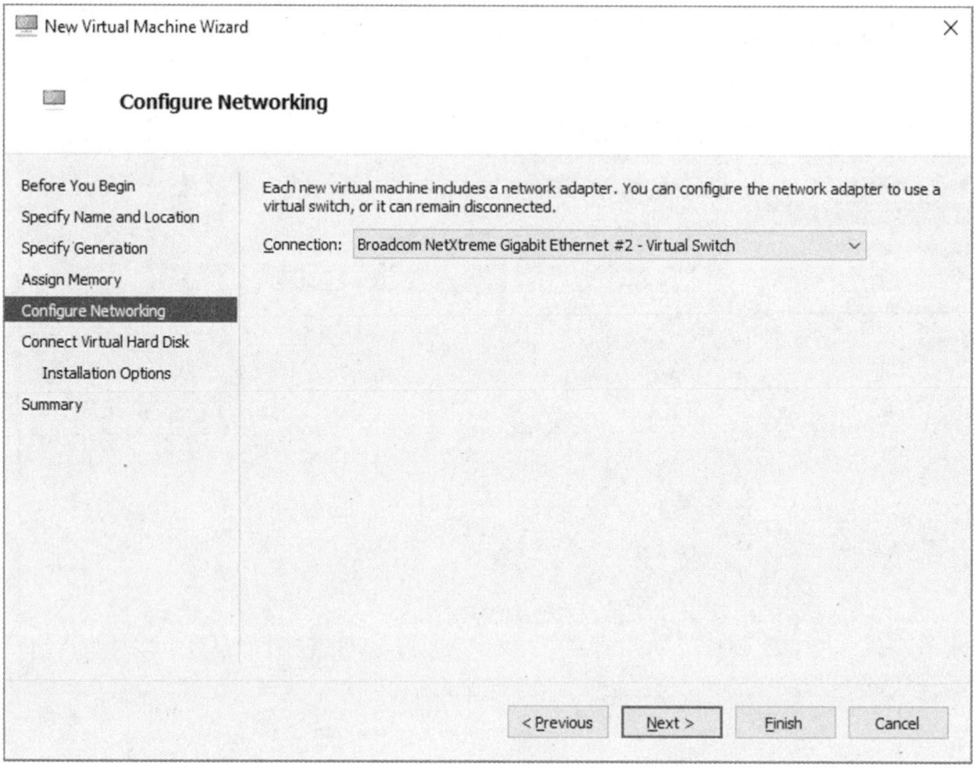

8. On the next page, you configure your virtual hard disk (see Figure 2.16). You can create a new virtual hard disk, select an existing disk, or choose to attach the hard disk later. Be aware that you can create only a dynamically expanding virtual disk on this page; you cannot create a differencing, physical, or fixed virtual hard disk there. However, if you created the virtual hard disk already, you can, of course, select it. Click Next to continue.

FIGURE 2.16   Connect Virtual Hard Disk page

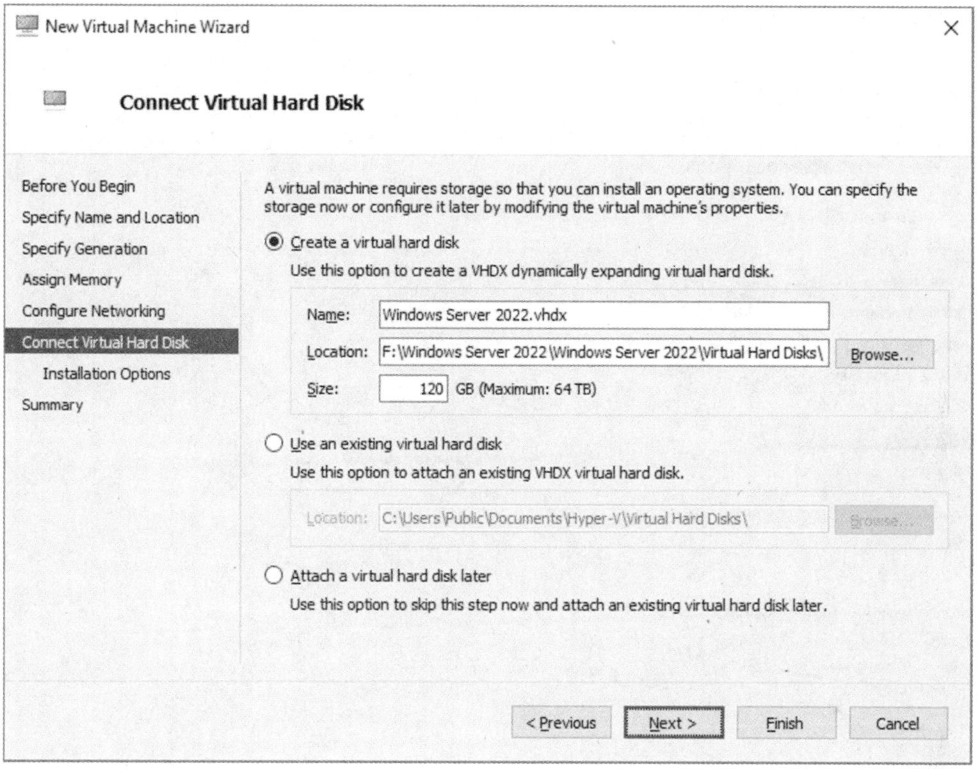

9. On the Installation Options page (see Figure 2.17), you can select how you want to install your operating system. You have the option to install an operating system later, install the operating system from a boot CD/DVD-ROM where you can select a physical device or an image file (ISO file), install an operating system from a floppy disk image (VFD file, or a virtual boot floppy disk), or install an operating system from a network-based installation server. The last option will install a legacy network adapter to your virtual machine so that you can boot from the network adapter. Select Install An Operating System from a bootable CD/DVD-ROM and choose Image File (.iso). Then click Next.

EXERCISE 2.4 *(continued)*

FIGURE 2.17 Installing OS screen

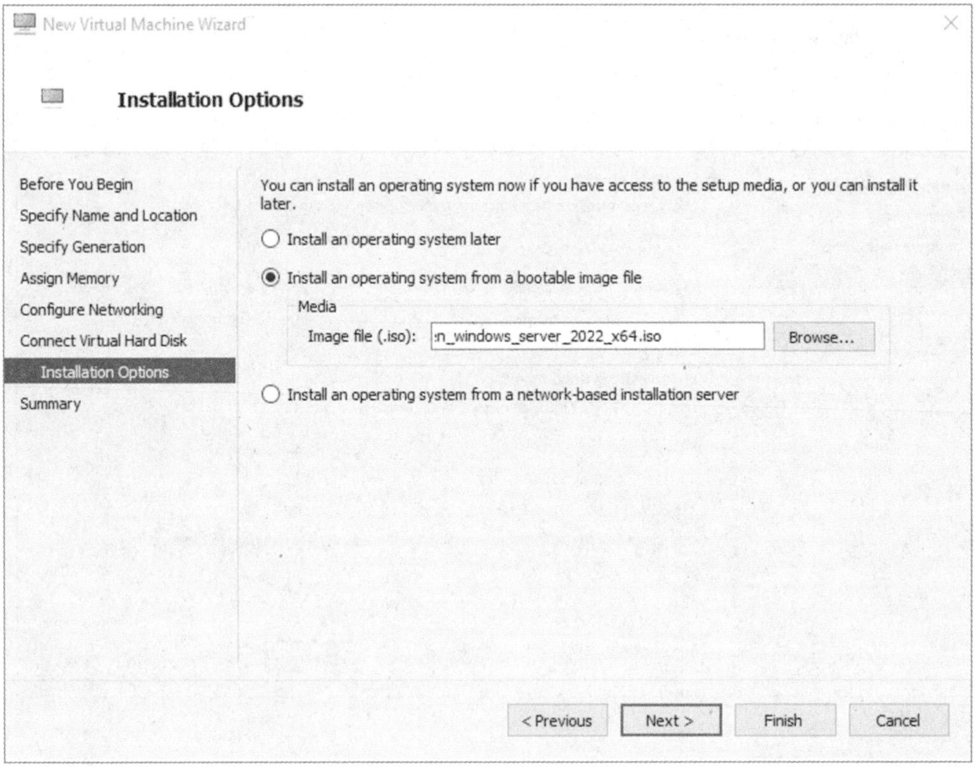

10. On the Completing The New Virtual Machine Wizard summary page (see Figure 2.18), verify that all settings are correct. You also have the option to start the virtual machine immediately after creation. Click Next to create the virtual machine.

FIGURE 2.18   Completing the New Virtual Machine Wizard screen

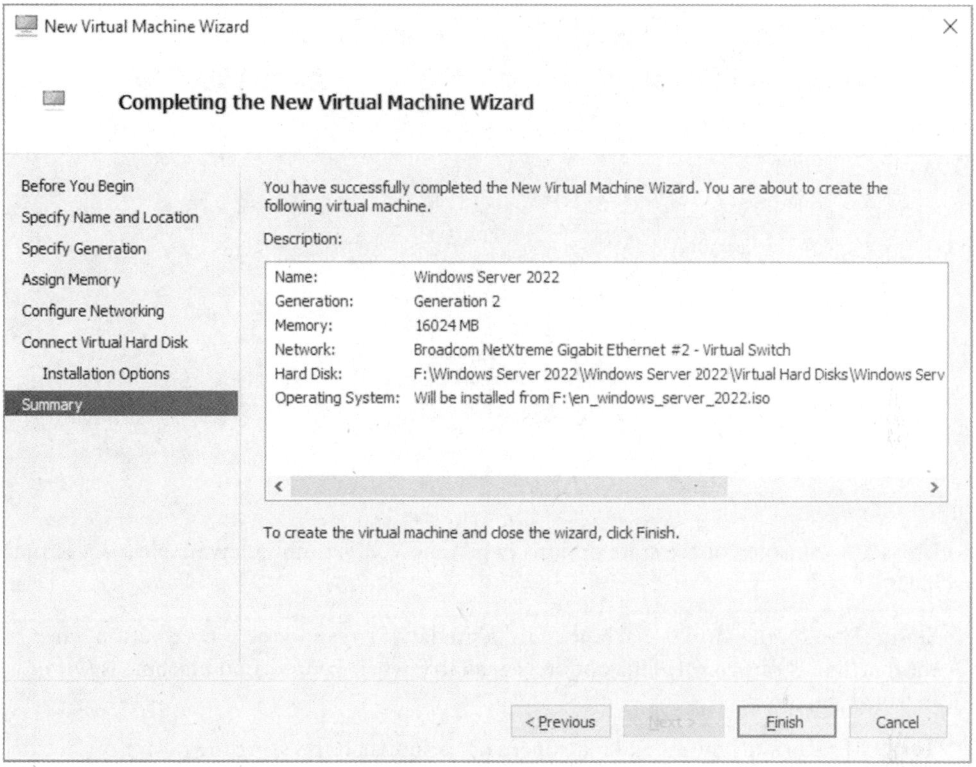

11.   Repeat this process and create a few more virtual machines.

After completing Exercise 2.4, you will have a virtual machine available in Hyper-V Manager. Initially, the state of the virtual machine will be Off. Virtual machines can have the following states: Off, Starting, Running, Paused, and Saved. You can change the state of a virtual machine in the Virtual Machines pane by right-clicking the virtual machine's name, as shown in Figure 2.19, or by using the Virtual Machine Connection window.

FIGURE 2.19   Options available when right-clicking a virtual machine

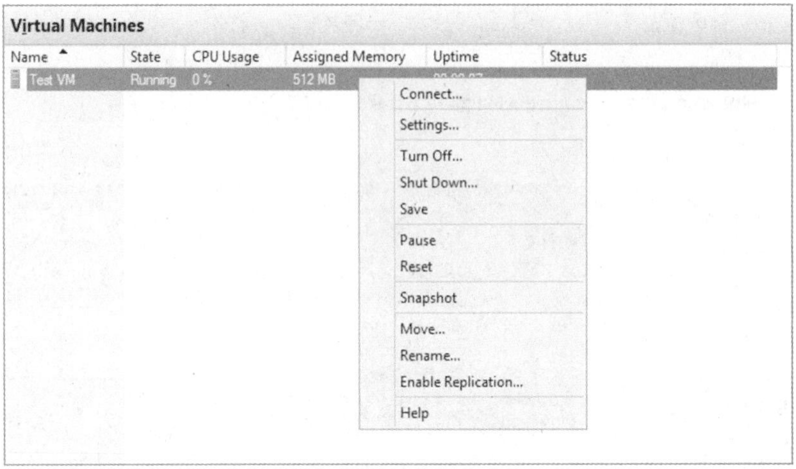

Here is a list of some of the state options (when the VM is running) available for a virtual machine:

Start   Turn on the virtual machine. This is similar to pressing the power button when the machine is turned off. This option is available when your virtual machine is Off or in Saved state.

Turn Off   Turn off the virtual machine. This is similar to pressing the power-off button on the computer. This option is available when your virtual machine is in Running, Saved, or Paused state.

Shut Down   This option shuts down your operating system. You need to have the Hyper-V Integration Components installed on the operating system; otherwise, Hyper-V will not be able to shut down the system.

Save   The virtual machine is saved to disk in its current state. This option is available when your virtual machine is in Running or Paused state.

Pause   Pause the current virtual machine, but do not save the state to disk. You can use this option to release processor utilization quickly from this virtual machine to the host system.

Reset   Reset the virtual machine. This is like pressing the reset button on your computer. You will lose the current state and any unsaved data in the virtual machine. This option is available when your virtual machine is in Running or Paused state.

Resume   When your virtual machine is paused, you can resume it and bring it online again.

Changing Configuration on an Existing Virtual Machine

To change the configuration settings on an existing virtual machine, you right-click your virtual machine's name in the Virtual Machines pane in Hyper-V Manager and choose Settings. You can change settings such as memory allocation and hard drive configuration. All items that you can configure are described in the following list:

Add Hardware   Add devices to your virtual machine, such as a SCSI controller, a network adapter, or a legacy network adapter. A legacy network adapter is required if you want to perform a network-based installation of an operating system.

BIOS   This is the replacement of the virtual machine's BIOS. Because you can no longer enter the BIOS during startup, you need to configure it with this setting. You can turn Num Lock on or off and change the basic startup order of the devices.

Memory   Change the amount of random access memory (RAM) allocated to the virtual machine.

Processor   Change the number of logical processors this virtual machine can use and define resource control to balance resources among virtual machines by using a relative weight.

IDE Controller   Add/change and remove devices from the IDE controller. You can have hard drives or DVD drives as devices. Every IDE controller can have up to two devices attached, and by default, you have two IDE controllers available.

Hard Drive   Select a controller to attach to this device as well as to specify the media to use with your virtual hard disk. The available options are Virtual Hard Disk File (with additional buttons labeled New, Edit, Inspect, and Browse that are explained in the virtual hard disk section) and Physical Hard Disk. You can also remove the device here.

DVD Drive   Select a controller to attach to this device and specify the media to use with your virtual CD/DVD drive. The available options are None, Image File (ISO Image), and Physical CD/DVD Drive Connected To The Host Computer. You also can remove the device here.

SCSI Controller   Configure all hard drives that are connected to the SCSI controller. You can add up to 63 hard drives to each SCSI controller, and you can have multiple SCSI controllers available.

Network Adapter   Specify the configuration of the network adapter or remove it. You can also configure the virtual network and MAC address for each adapter and enable virtual LAN identification. The network adapter section also allows you to control Bandwidth Management.

Bandwidth Management allows you to specify how the network adapter will utilize network bandwidth. You have the ability to set a minimum network bandwidth that a network adapter can use and a maximum bandwidth. This gives you greater control over how much bandwidth a virtual network adapter can use.

COM1 and COM2   Configure the virtual COM port to communicate with the physical computer through a named pipe. You have COM1 and COM2 available.

Diskette   Specify a virtual floppy disk file to use.

Name   Edit the name of the virtual machine and provide some notes about it.

Integration Services   Define what integration services are available to your virtual machine. Options are Operating System Shutdown, Time Synchronization, Data Exchange, Heartbeat, and Backup (Volume Snapshot).

Snapshot File Location   Define the default file location of your snapshot files.

Smart Paging File Location   This area allows you to set up a paging file for your virtual machine. Windows Server 2022 has a Hyper-V feature called *Smart Paging*. If you have a virtual machine that has a smaller amount of memory than what it needs for startup memory, when the virtual machine gets restarted, Hyper-V then needs additional memory to restart the virtual machine. Smart Paging is used to bridge the memory gap between minimum memory and startup memory. This allows your virtual machines to restart properly.

Automatic Start   Define what this virtual machine will do when the physical computer starts. Options are Nothing, Automatically Start If The Service Was Running, and Always Start This Virtual Machine. You also can define a start delay here.

Automatic Stop   Define what this virtual machine will do when the physical computer shuts down. Options are Save State, Turn Off, and Shut Down.

Please be aware that only some settings can be changed when the virtual machine's state is Running. It is best practice to shut down the virtual machine before you modify any setting.

Deleting Virtual Machines

You can also delete virtual machines using Hyper-V Manager. This deletes all of the configuration files, as shown in Figure 2.20.

FIGURE 2.20   Delete Virtual Machine warning window

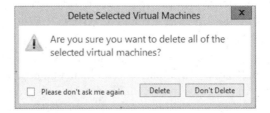

Make sure you manually delete any virtual disks that were part of the virtual machines to free up disk space. Virtual disks are *not* deleted when you delete a virtual machine.

Virtual Machine Connection

Similar to the Virtual Machine Remote Control (VMRC) client that was available with Virtual Server 2005 R2 and previous versions, Hyper-V comes with Virtual Machine Connection to connect to virtual machines that run on a local or remote server.

You can use it to log on to the virtual machine and use your computer's mouse and keyboard to interact with the virtual machine. You can open Virtual Machine Connection in Hyper-V Manager by double-clicking a virtual machine or by right-clicking a virtual machine and selecting Connect. If your virtual machine is turned off, you might see a window similar to the one in Figure 2.21.

FIGURE 2.21   Virtual Machine Connection window when the machine is turned off

Virtual Machine Connection not only provides you with functionality similar to that of Hyper-V Manager, such as being able to change the state of a virtual machine, but also provides you with additional features that are especially useful when you want to work with a virtual machine:

> **File Access Settings or Exit Virtual Machine Connection**   Change the state of a virtual machine and create or revert a snapshot. Additionally, you have the options to send Ctrl+Alt+Delete to your virtual machine and Insert Integration Services Setup Disk.

Context-Sensitive Buttons Provide Quick Access to Key Features   These buttons are available under the menu bar to provide you with fast access to the most important features. It shows the connection of a running VM, but the VM has not had an operating system installed yet, so the figure 2.21 shows the Windows Server 2022 Setup screen.

NIC Teaming

NIC Teaming, also known as load balancing and failover (LBFO), gives you the ability to allow multiple network adapters on a system to be placed into a team. Independent hardware vendors (IHVs) have required NIC Teaming, but until Windows Server 2012, NIC Teaming was *not* part of the Windows Server operating system.

To be able to use NIC Teaming, make sure the computer system has at least one Ethernet adapter. If you want to provide fault protection, you must have a minimum of two Ethernet adapters. One advantage of Windows Server 2022 is that you can set up 32 network adapters in a NIC team.

NIC Teaming is a common practice when setting up virtualization. This is one way that you can have load balancing with Hyper-V.

NIC Teaming gives you the ability to allow a virtual machine to use virtual network adapters in Hyper-V. The advantage of using NIC Teaming in Hyper-V is that you can use NIC Teaming to connect to more than one Hyper-V switch. This allows Hyper-V to still have connectivity even if the network adapter under the Hyper-V switch gets disconnected.

You can configure NIC Teaming in either Server Manager or PowerShell. NIC teaming can be configured in different configuration models, including Switch Independent or Switch Dependent.

Switch Independent means the switch is unaware of the NIC team and the NIC team is responsible for figuring out how to distribute the traffic without the switches help or knowledge. They can be on the same switch or different switches. They do have to be in the same VLAN/subnet/broadcast domain.

Switch Dependent means that the switch determines how to distribute traffic. They can be on the same switch or in a multichassis switch with a shared ID between the various chassis.

If you use Switch Independent NIC Teaming, your NICs can be on different switches but both switch ports must be on the same subnet.

Remote Direct Memory Access

When most of us think of Hyper-V, we think of a group of virtual machines sharing access to a systems resource. With Windows Server 2022, Hyper-V includes Remote Direct Memory Access (RDMA).

RDMA allows one computer to directly access memory from the memory of another computer without the need of interfacing with either one's operating system. This gives systems the ability to have high throughput and low-latency networking. This is useful when it comes to clustering systems (including Hyper-V).

Windows Server 2012 R2 RDMA services couldn't be bound to a Hyper-V Virtual Switch and because of this, Remote Direct Memory Access and Hyper-V had to be on the same computer as the network adapters. Because of this, there was a need for a higher number of physical network adapters that were required to be installed on the Hyper-V host.

Because of the improvements of RDMA on Windows Server 2022, you can use fewer network adapters while using RDMA.

Switch Embedded Teaming

Earlier we discussed NIC Teaming, but we also have the ability to do Switch Embedded Teaming (SET). SET can be an alternative to using NIC Teaming in environments that include Hyper-V and the Software-Defined Networking (SDN) stack in Windows Server 2022. SET is available in all versions of Windows Server 2022 that include Hyper-V and SDN stack.

SET does use some of the functionality of NIC Teaming into the Hyper-V Virtual Switch, but SET allows you to combine a group of physical adapters (minimum of 1 adapter and a maximum of 8 adapters) into software based virtual adapters.

By using virtual adapters, you get better performance and greater fault tolerance in the event of a network adapter going bad. For SET to be enabled, all of the physical network adapters must be installed on the same physical Hyper-V host.

One of the requirements of SET is that all network adapters that are members of the SET group be identical adapters. This means that they need to be the same adapter types from the same manufacturers.

One main difference between NIC Teaming and SET is that SET only supports Switch Independent mode setups. Again, this means that Switch Independent mode means the NICs control the teaming. They could be on the same or different switches.

You need to create a SET team at the same time you create the Hyper-V virtual switch. You can do this by using the Windows PowerShell command `New-VMSwitch`.

At the time you create a Hyper-V virtual switch, you must include the `EnableEmbeddedTeaming` parameter in your command syntax. The following example shows a Hyper-V switch named StormSwitch:

```
New-VMSwitch -Name StormSwitch -NetAdapterName "NIC 1","NIC 2"
-EnableEmbeddedTeaming $true
```

You also have the ability to remove a SET team by using the following PowerShell command. This example removes a virtual switch named StormSwitch:

```
Remove-VMSwitch "StormSwitch"
```

Storage Quality of Service

Windows Server 2022 Hyper-V includes a feature called *Storage Quality of Service (QoS)*. Storage QoS allows a Hyper-V administrator to manage how virtual machines access storage throughput for virtual hard disks.

Storage QoS gives you the ability to guarantee that the storage throughput of a single VHD cannot adversely affect the performance of another VHD on the same host. It does this by giving you the ability to specify the maximum and minimum I/O loads based on I/O operations per second (IOPS) for each virtual disk in your virtual machines.

To configure Storage QoS, you would set the maximum IOPS values (or limits) and set the minimum values (or reserves) on virtual hard disks for virtual machines.

If you are using shared virtual hard disks, Storage QoS will not be available.

Installing Hyper-V Integration Components

Hyper-V *Integration Components*, also called *Integration Services*, are required to make your guest operating system hypervisor-aware. Similar to the VM Additions that were part of Microsoft Virtual Server 2005, these components improve the performance of the guest operating system once they are installed. From an architectural perspective, virtual devices are redirected directly via the VMBus; thus, quicker access to resources and devices is provided.

If you do not install the Hyper-V Integration Components, the guest operating system uses emulation to communicate with the host's devices, which of course makes the guest operating system slower.

Exercise 2.5 shows you how to install Hyper-V Integration Components on one of your virtual machines running Windows Server 2022.

EXERCISE 2.5

Installing Hyper-V Integration Components

1. Open Hyper-V Manager.

2. In Hyper-V Manager, in the Virtual Machines pane, right-click the virtual machine on which you want to install Hyper-V Integration Components and click Start.

3. Right-click the virtual machine again and click Connect. Meanwhile, your virtual machine should already be booting.

4. If you need to log into the operating system of your virtual machine, you should do so.

5. Starting with Windows Server 2012 R2, Integration Services aren't installed via an emulated floppy like it was prior to Windows Server 2016. Instead, they are installed as a Windows update. So now that the virtual machine is set up, do your updates on the Hyper-V host along with the updates for the Hyper-V guest. After you reboot, Integration Components should be installed and ready to go.

Linux and FreeBSD Image Deployments

One of the features of Windows 2022 is the ability for Hyper-V to support Linux and FreeBSD virtual machines. Hyper-V now can support these new virtual machines because Hyper-V has the ability to emulate Linux and FreeBSD devices. Because Hyper-V now has the ability to emulate these two devices, no additional software needs to be installed on Hyper-V.

Unfortunately, because Hyper-V has to emulate these devices, you lose some of the Hyper-V functionality like high performance and full management of the virtual machines. So it's a trade-off. You get to run Linux and FreeBSD type Hyper-V virtual machines, but you lose some of the benefits of Hyper-V.

But wait; there is a way to get your Hyper-V functionality back. This issue can be resolved as long as you install Hyper-V on machines that can support Linux and FreeBSD operating systems. The drivers that are needed on Hyper-V are called Linux Integration Services (LIS) and FreeBSD Integrated Services (FIS). By putting these drivers on a device that can handle Linux and FreeBSD, you can then have Hyper-V with all of the features Microsoft offers.

To get these drivers and make Hyper-V work with all of its functionality, you must make sure that you install a newer release of Linux that includes LIS. To get the most out of FreeBSD you must get a version after 10.0. For FreeBSD versions that are older than 10.0, Microsoft offers ports that work with BIS drivers that need to be installed. Hyper-V will work with Linux and FreeBSD without the need of any additional drivers or equipment. By having drivers and equipment that supports Linux and FreeBSD, you just get all of the Hyper-V features that your organization may need.

I have personally installed Kali Linux and Parrot Linux on Windows Server 2022 Hyper-V. So, you have many different options when installing Linux. The installation screens will be different but the installation of these versions of Linux can be easily done. The only issue that I have encountered when installing Kali and Parrot is that I need to choose Generation 1 when installing these versions.

In Exercise 2.6, I will show you how to install Linux into a virtual machine. I will then walk you through a full installation of a Linux server. Before you complete this lab, you must download a copy of Linux. For this exercise, I downloaded a free copy of Linux Ubuntu as an image file (ISO). If you choose a different version of Linux, the installation screens during the exercise may be different.

EXERCISE 2.6

Creating a Linux Virtual Machine

1. Open Hyper-V Manager.

2. In the right-hand window under Actions, click New ➢ Virtual Machine.

3. At the Before You Begin screen, just choose Next.

4. At the Specify Name and Location screen, enter the name of the Linux virtual machine and the location you would like to store the virtual machine files. Then click Next.

5. At the Generation screen, choose Generation 2 and click Next.

EXERCISE 2.6 *(continued)*

6. At the Assign Memory screen, enter in the amount of memory you want to allocate to this virtual machine. I am using 12 GB (12,000 MB). Click Next.

7. Choose which network connection you want to use and click Next.

8. At the Connect Virtual Hard Disk screen, choose Create A Virtual Hard Disk. Set the location of where you want the files to reside and also how much space you want to use (I chose 127 GB). Click Next.

9. At the Installation Options screen, choose Install An Operating System From A Bootable Image File and point to your Linux ISO download. Click Next.

10. At the Completing the New Virtual Machine Wizard screen, make sure all of the settings are correct and click Finish.

11. After the virtual machine is created, click the virtual machine and on the right side under Linux, click Start.

12. When the Linux installation starts, click Your Language.

13. At the Ubuntu menu, choose Install Ubuntu Server.

14. Again, you will need to choose your language for the installation.

15. Choose your country.

16. At the Detect Keyboard Layout screen, click No. Choose your keyboard (ours is US Normal). The installation will continue.

17. Next, choose a hostname. I am keeping the default of Ubuntu. Click Continue.

18. Enter your user account (full name) and click Continue.

19. Enter your username. The first name is fine. Click Continue.

20. Type your password and click Continue. Do not choose to show your password in clear. You will then be asked to reenter your password and click Continue.

21. When you're asked whether to encrypt your home directory, choose No.

22. The installation will try to figure out your time zone. If it picks correct, choose Yes. If it doesn't, choose No and enter your time zone.

23. The next screen will ask you about setting up a partition disk. I am going to allow Linux to configure the disk (Guided) and I will allow it to use the entire drive with a Logical Volume Manager (LVM). So I am choosing Guided – Use Entire Disk And Set Up LVM.

24. The installation will then ask about partition type. I am choosing SCSI3.

25. The next screen will verify your choices for partitioning. Click Yes.

26. The installation will then verify your disk size and ask whether you want to continue. Choose the disk size and then choose Yes to continue.

27. The next screen will ask you if you use a proxy server for Internet access. If you use a proxy, enter it, and if you don't, just click Continue.

28. You will be asked about updates for Linux. Choose how you want to do your updates. Since this is a test virtual machine, I am choosing No Automatic Updates.

29. At the Software Selection screen, choose what software you want installed during this process. I chose DNS, Samba File Server, and Standard System Utilities. Click Continue.

30. At the GRUB Boot screen, click Yes to install the GRUB boot loader. This is fine since we have no other operating system on this virtual machine.

31. Once the installation is complete, click Continue. At this point, Linux will restart and ask you for your login and password. After you enter them, you will be at a Linux prompt.

32. Type **shutdown** at the prompt to shut down the virtual machine.

Now that you have installed Linux (or FreeBSD), the next step is to help improve the Hyper-V performance. As I stated earlier, this issue will be resolved as long as you install the drivers that are needed on Hyper-V called Linux Integration Services (LIS) and FreeBSD Integrated Services (FIS). By putting these drivers on a device that can handle Linux and FreeBSD, you can then have Hyper-V with all of the features Microsoft offers.

Depending on what version of Linux or FreeBSD that you installed, you will need to download some additional updates to get the best performance out of Hyper-V. The following Microsoft website has a list of links for the different versions of Linux and FreeBSD updates: https://docs.microsoft.com/en-us/windows-server/virtualization/hyper-v/Supported-Linux-and-FreeBSD-virtual-machines-for-Hyper-V-on-Windows.

In Exercise 2.7, I will show you how to install the additional updates needed for the Linux Ubuntu version (20.10) that you installed in Exercise 2.6.

EXERCISE 2.7

Updating Linux Ubuntu 20.10

1. Open Hyper-V Manager.

2. Start the Linux virtual machine by clicking the Linux virtual machine and choosing Start from the right-hand menu.

3. At the Ubuntu login, enter the login and password that you created in Exercise 2.6.

4. Since we are using Ubuntu 20.10, we need to install the latest virtual kernel to have up-to-date Hyper-V capabilities. To install the virtual HWE kernel, run the following commands as root (or sudo):

    ```
    sudo apt-get update
    ```

5. You will be asked for your password. Enter your password.

6. Next type the following command:

    ```
    sudo apt-get install linux-image-virtual
    ```

7. You will be asked to confirm your choice. Type **Y** and press Enter.

8. Type the following command:

    ```
    sudo apt-get install linux-tools-virtual linux-cloud-tools-virtual
    ```

9. You will be asked to confirm your choice. Again, type **Y** and press Enter .

10. After everything is installed, you are ready to go. You can clear the screen by typing **Clear** and pressing Enter. To shut down the system, type **shutdown**.

Finally, if you want to set up the Linux or FreeBSD virtual machines to use the advantages of secure boot, you would need to run the following PowerShell command on the Hyper-V server:

```
Set-VMFirmware -VMName "VMname" -EnableSecureBoot Off
```

PowerShell Commands

One of the things that Microsoft has stated is that the exams are going to be more Power-Shell intensive. So, I wanted to add a PowerShell section showing the different PowerShell commands that you can use for Hyper-V. The information in Table 2.6 has been taken directly from Microsoft's websites. The table explains just some of the PowerShell commands that you can use with Hyper-V.

Table 2.6 shows you just some of the PowerShell commands for Hyper-V. To see a more comprehensive list, please visit Microsoft's website at https://docs.microsoft.com/en-us/powershell/module/hyper-v/?view=win10-ps.

TABLE 2.6   Hyper-V PowerShell commands

Command	Explanation
Add-VMDvdDrive	Adds a DVD drive to a virtual machine
Add-VMHardDiskDrive	Adds a hard disk drive to a virtual machine
Add-VMMigrationNetwork	Adds a network for virtual machine migration on one or more virtual machine hosts
Add-VMNetworkAdapter	Adds a virtual network adapter to a virtual machine
Add-VMSwitch	Adds a virtual switch to an Ethernet resource pool
Checkpoint-VM	Creates a checkpoint of a virtual machine
Convert-VHD	Converts the format, version type, and block size of a virtual hard disk file
Copy-VMFile	Copies a file to a virtual machine
Debug-VM	Debugs a virtual machine
Disable-VMConsoleSupport	Disables keyboard, video, and mouse for virtual machines
Disable-VMMigration	Disables migration on one or more virtual machine hosts
Dismount-VHD	Dismounts a virtual hard disk
Enable-VMConsoleSupport	Enables keyboard, video, and mouse for virtual machines
Enable-VMMigration	Enables migration on one or more virtual machine hosts
Enable-VMReplication	Enables replication of a virtual machine
Enable-VMResourceMetering	Collects resource utilization data for a virtual machine or resource pool
Export-VM	Exports a virtual machine to disk
Export-VMSnapshot	Exports a virtual machine checkpoint to disk

TABLE 2.6   Hyper-V PowerShell commands *(Continued)*

Command	Explanation
Get-VHD	Gets the virtual hard disk object associated with a virtual hard disk
Get-VHDSet	Gets information about a VHD set
Get-VHDSnapshot	Gets information about a checkpoint in a VHD set
Get-VM	Gets the virtual machines from one or more Hyper-V hosts
Get-VMDvdDrive	Gets the DVD drives attached to a virtual machine or snapshot
Get-VMHardDiskDrive	Gets the virtual hard disk drives attached to one or more virtual machines
Get-VMMemory	Gets the memory of a virtual machine or snapshot.
Get-VMNetworkAdapter	Gets the virtual network adapters of a virtual machine, snapshot, management operating system, or of a virtual machine and management operating system
Get-VMProcessor	Gets the processor of a virtual machine or snapshot
Get-VMReplication	Gets the replication settings for a virtual machine
Get-VMSwitch	Gets virtual switches from one or more virtual Hyper-V hosts
Merge-VHD	Merges virtual hard disks
Mount-VHD	Mounts one or more virtual hard disks
Move-VM	Moves a virtual machine to a new Hyper-V host
New-VHD	Creates one or more new virtual hard disks
New-VM	Creates a new virtual machine
New-VMGroup	Creates a virtual machine group
New-VMSwitch	Creates a new virtual switch on one or more virtual machine hosts

Command	Explanation
Remove-VHDSnapshot	Removes a snapshot from a VHD set file
Remove-VM	Deletes a virtual machine
Remove-VMHardDiskDrive	Deletes one or more virtual hard disks (VHDs) from a virtual machine
Remove-VMNetworkAdapter	Removes one or more virtual network adapters from a virtual machine
Remove-VMReplication	Removes the replication relationship of a virtual machine
Remove-VMSan	Removes a virtual storage area network (SAN) from a Hyper-V host
Remove-VMSwitch	Deletes a virtual switch
Rename-VM	Renames a virtual machine
Rename-VMGroup	Renames virtual machine groups
Resize-VHD	Resizes a virtual hard disk
Restart-VM	Restarts a virtual machine
Save-VM	Saves a virtual machine
Set-VHD	Sets properties associated with a virtual hard disk
Set-VM	Configures a virtual machine
Set-VMBios	Configures the BIOS of a Generation 1 virtual machine
Set-VMMemory	Configures the memory of a virtual machine
Set-VMNetworkAdapter	Configures features of the virtual network adapter in a virtual machine or the management operating system
Set-VMProcessor	Configures one or more processors of a virtual machine
Set-VMReplicationServer	Configures a host as a Replica server
Set-VMSan	Configures a virtual storage area network (SAN) on one or more Hyper-V hosts

TABLE 2.6   Hyper-V PowerShell commands *(Continued)*

Command	Explanation
Set-VMSwitch	Configures a virtual switch
Stop-VM	Shuts down, turns off, or saves a virtual machine
Suspend-VM	Suspends, or pauses, a virtual machine

Summary

Virtualization is quickly becoming a hot topic in information technology. The potential for consolidation is tremendous, and thus it will become more and more important.

After reading this chapter, you should have a good understanding of the Hyper-V architecture and what is required to install Hyper-V.

The section about installation and configuration covered various basic aspects of configuring the virtualization environment. You learned about the types of virtual networks that are available, the options for installing the Hyper-V role, and the types of virtual hard disks that you can use to optimize virtualization for your specific scenario.

You also learned how to configure virtual machines using the Hyper-V environment and how to create your own virtual datacenter on top of your Hyper-V machines. I showed you how to create and manage virtual machines, how to use Virtual Machine Connection to control a virtual machine remotely, and how to install Hyper-V Integration Components. You also learned how to export and import virtual machines as well as how to do snapshots of your virtual machine.

If you have never worked with virtualization software before, the information in this chapter may have been completely new to you. You should now be well prepared to try Hyper-V in your own environment.

Exam Essentials

Understand Hyper-V's architecture.   When you have a good understanding of Hyper-V's architecture, especially when an operating system in a virtual machine is hypervisor aware versus non-hypervisor aware, you have a solid understanding of what is important from an architectural perspective.

You should know about the Hyper-V Integration Components and how they change the behavior of a virtual machine. Also know for which operating systems the integration components are available.

Know Hyper-V's requirements and how to install it.   Know the hardware and software requirements as well as how to install Hyper-V. Hyper-V requires an x64-based processor and Data Execution Protection (DEP). Hardware-assisted virtualization must be enabled—don't forget this! Also remember that you can install Hyper-V two ways: using Server Manager or using the command line in Server Core.

Understand virtual networks and virtual hard disks.   Virtual networks and hard disks are the two most tested topics. You definitely should know the types of virtual networks available (that is, external, internal only, and private virtual network) as well as all types of virtual hard disks (dynamically expanding, fixed size, differential, and physical or pass-through). You should be able to apply the correct one when needed. Don't forget the Edit Virtual Hard Disk Wizard, which is also a good source for questions in the exam.

Know how to create and manage virtual machines.   You should be able to explain how to create a virtual machine, what options are available to install an operating system in a virtual machine, and how to install the Hyper-V Integration Components on a virtual machine. Don't forget about the virtual machine states and the virtual machine settings!

Understand how to back up and restore virtual machines.   Have a good understanding of the concept of exporting and importing virtual machines, how snapshots work, and what lies behind a quick migration. Understand how you can export a virtual machine, what you should consider when moving it to a new host machine, and what happens after importing it to the import folder. The same applies to snapshots: you need to know what options you have available and what each option will do. Especially recognize the difference between applying and reverting a snapshot.

Review Questions

1. On which of the following x64 editions of Windows Server 2022 does Hyper-V run? (Choose all that apply.)

   A. Windows Server 2022 Web Edition

   B. Windows Server 2022 Standard Edition

   C. Windows Server 2022 Itanium Edition

   D. Windows Server 2022 Datacenter Edition

2. You want to build a test environment based on virtual machines on a single Windows Server 2022 machine, but you also want to make sure the virtual machines communicate with only each other. What type of virtual network do you need to configure?

   A. External

   B. Internal only

   C. Private virtual machine network

   D. Public virtual machine network

3. Andy wants to change the memory of a virtual machine that is currently powered up. What does he need to do?

   A. Shut down the virtual machine, use the virtual machine's settings to change the memory, and start it again.

   B. Use the virtual machine's settings to change the memory.

   C. Pause the virtual machine, use the virtual machine's settings to change the memory, and resume it.

   D. Save the virtual machine, use the virtual machine's settings to change the memory, and resume it.

4. You want to make sure the hard disk space for your virtual machines is occupied only when needed. What type of virtual hard disk would you recommend?

   A. Dynamically expanding disk

   B. Fixed-size disk

   C. Differencing disk

   D. Physical or pass-through disk

5. How do you add a physical disk to a virtual machine?

   A. Use the Virtual Hard Disk Wizard.

   B. Use the Edit Virtual Hard Disk Wizard.

   C. Use the virtual machine's settings.

   D. Use the New Virtual Machine Wizard.

6. Rich bought a new server with an Itanium IA-64 processor, 4 GB of RAM, and a SAN that provides 1 TB of hard disk space. After installing Windows Server 2022 for Itanium-based systems, he wants to install Hyper-V on this server. Can Hyper-V be installed on this system?

    A. Yes

    B. No

7. What are the minimum CPU requirements for running Hyper-V on a machine? (Choose all that apply.)

    A. An x64-based processor (Intel or AMD).

    B. Hardware Data Execution Protection (DEP) must be enabled.

    C. Hardware-assisted virtualization must be enabled.

    D. The processor must at least have a dual core.

8. What is the command to install Hyper-V on a Windows Server 2022 machine that was installed in Server Core?

    A. `start /w ocsetup Hyper-V`

    B. `start /w ocsetup microsoft-hyper-v`

    C. `start /w ocsetup Microsoft-Hyper-V`

    D. `start /w ocsetup hyper-v`

9. On what operating systems can you install the Hyper-V Manager MMC? (Choose all that apply.)

    A. Windows Server 2022

    B. Windows Server 2003

    C. Windows 10

    D. Windows 11

10. What statement is correct for an external virtual network?

    A. The virtual machines can communicate with each other and with the host machine.

    B. The virtual machines can communicate with each other only.

    C. The virtual machines can communicate with each other, with the host machine, and with an external network.

    D. The virtual machines cannot communicate with each other.

11. You have a Windows Server 2022 server. The server has the Hyper-V server role installed. You create a virtual machine on the server named VM01, which has a legacy network adapter. You need to assign a specific amount of available network bandwidth to the virtual machine. What should you do first?

   A. The legacy network adapter needs to be removed, and then the `Set-VMNetworkAdapter` cmdlet must be run.

   B. The legacy network adapter needs to be removed, and then another network adapter should be added.

   C. Add another legacy network adapter, and then the `Set-VMNetworkAdopter` cmdlet must be run.

   D. Add another legacy network adapter, and then configure network adapter teaming.

12. Your company has decided to use Microsoft Hyper-V for its entire virtualized environment. You are trying to learn about all the issues surrounding Hyper-V. You start reading about Integration Services. You need to find out all of the services that Integrated Services use. Which of the following does Integrated Services offer? (Choose all that apply.)

   A. Time Synchronization

   B. Data Exchange

   C. Heartbeat

   D. Backup (volume snapshot)

13. You want to create a virtual disk that clones a local drive available on your host machine. What types of disks can you use to copy a physical disk to a virtual disk using Hyper-V Manager? (Choose all that apply.)

   A. Dynamically expanding

   B. Fixed size

   C. Differencing

   D. Physical or pass-through

14. What is a legacy network adapter in Hyper-V?

   A. A virtual network adapter that can be configured when the Hyper-V Integration Components are installed

   B. A virtual network adapter that can connect to the virtual networks

   C. A virtual network adapter that you need in order to boot from the network

   D. A virtual network adapter that connects your virtual machine to the host machine

15. How do you move virtual machines between host machines?

   A. Use the Export And Import Virtual Machine command in Hyper-V.

   B. Move the virtual machine files to the target host, and add them to Hyper-V.

   C. Create a snapshot of the virtual machine, and apply it to a different machine.

   D. Use the Save command in Hyper-V.

16. You are the administrator of a large company that has decided to switch from Virtual Server to Microsoft Hyper-V. You have created a Hyper-V virtual machine with Windows Server 2022. You want to be able to do Time Synchronization in the virtual machine. What do you need to install to get the volume snapshots?

    A. Virtual Machine Additions

    B. Integration Services

    C. Virtual Integration

    D. Virtual Machine Services

17. You are the administrator of a mid-sized company that has decided to switch from Virtual Server to Microsoft Hyper-V. You have created a Hyper-V virtual machine with Windows Server 2022. You are having issues when the virtual machine's data gets exchanged. What do you need to install to solve your problem?

    A. Virtual Machine Additions

    B. Run a V2V conversion

    C. Virtual Integration

    D. Integration Services

18. You are the administrator for a large organization that has a Windows Server 2022 machine named Panek1. The Hyper-V role has been installed on the server named Panek1. You have created a fixed-size VHD named `DiskA.vhd`. As an administrator, you need to make the data in `DiskA.vhd` available to several virtual machines. You must also

    ▪ Ensure that if the contents are changed on any virtual machine the changes are not reflected on the other virtual machines.

    ▪ Minimize the amount of disk space used.

    What should you do?

    A. Create a fixed-size VHDX. Transfer the information from `DiskA.vhd` to the new VHDX file.

    B. Convert `DiskA.vhd` to a dynamically expanding VHD.

    C. Create a dynamically expanding VHDX. Transfer the information from `DiskA.vhd` to the new VHDX file.

    D. Create differencing VHDs that use `DiskA.vhd` as the parent disk.

19. You are the administrator on a mid-sized company network. You have a server named Stellacon1 that runs Windows Server 2022. Stellacon1 has the Hyper-V server role installed. On Stellacon1, you create a virtual machine named VM2022. VM2022 has a legacy network adapter. You need to assign a specific amount of available network bandwidth to VM2022. What should you do first?

    A. Remove the legacy network adapter, and then run the `Set-VMNetworkAdapter` cmdlet.

    B. Add a second legacy network adapter, and then run the `Set-VMNetworkAdapter` cmdlet.

    C. Add a second legacy network adapter, and then configure network adapter teaming.

    D. Remove the legacy network adapter, and then add a newer network adapter.

20. You are a network administrator for a small company that uses Hyper-V. You need to reboot your virtual machine. What PowerShell command can you use?

A. Restart-VM

B. Reboot-VM

C. Shutdown-VM

D. ShutStateOff

Chapter 3

Installing Windows Server 2022

THE FOLLOWING AZ-800 EXAM OBJECTIVES ARE COVERED IN THIS CHAPTER:

✓ **Configure Windows Server storage**

- Configure disks and volumes
- Configure and manage Storage Spaces

So, now it's time to install Windows Server 2022. In this chapter, you'll learn how to install Windows Server 2022. I will show you how to install the Desktop (GUI) version of Server 2022 as well as the Server Core version of Server 2022.

I will also show you how to get updates for the Windows Server and how to set up Windows Server Update Services (WSUS). Finally, I will talk about using Features on Demand.

In Chapter 2, "Understanding Hyper-V," I explained how to install, configure, and build virtual machines. If you have a Windows Hyper-V server, you can install Windows Server 2022 into a new virtual machine. If you don't have a Hyper-V server, you can install Windows Server 2022 onto a new machine and then install the Hyper-V role (following the steps in Chapter 2).

After installing Hyper-V, you can do an installation of Windows Server 2022 into a new virtual machine, and then you can use that virtual machine for labs throughout this book.

I will also show you how to choose and configure a filesystem (FAT32, NTFS, ReFS) that best fits your server needs.

The Windows Server 2022 installation can be done on a virtual server. You can use any virtualization software as long as it supports Windows Server 2022 and 64-bit processors. This is the reason I explained virtualization in the previous chapters. I will be installing Windows Server 2022 on Windows Hyper-V. The installation is exactly the same as installing Windows Server 2022 on a physical machine.

Installing the Windows Server 2022 OS

In this section, I'll walk you through two different types of installations: a full install of Windows Server 2022 Datacenter (Desktop Experience), and installing the Server Core version of the same software.

For these labs, I am using the full release of Windows Server 2022 Datacenter, but you can use Windows Server 2022 Standard.

Installing with the Desktop Experience

In Exercise 3.1, you'll install Windows Server 2022 Datacenter (Desktop Experience). This installation will have a graphical user interface (GUI), which means that an administrator will be able to control the applications on the desktop and the operating system functions with a mouse.

Windows Installation

As of this writing, I used a full release of Windows Server 2022 Datacenter that I downloaded from my MSDN account. Microsoft is constantly releasing new versions of Windows Server 2022. For this reason, there may be some screens that have changed somewhat since this book was published. But the installation should be very close to what I will do here.

EXERCISE 3.1

Installing Windows Server 2022 Datacenter (Desktop Experience)

1. Insert the Windows Server 2022 installation media and restart the machine. You may be asked to press any key to start the installation.

2. At the first screen, Windows Server 2022 (see Figure 3.1) will ask you to configure your language, time and currency, and keyboard. Make your selections and click Next.

FIGURE 3.1 Windows Server 2022 Setup

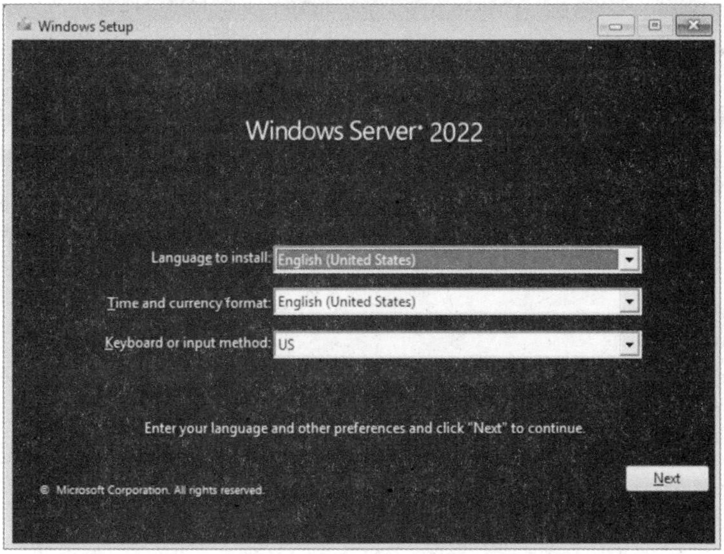

EXERCISE 3.1 *(continued)*

3. At the next screen (see Figure 3.2), click the Install Now button.

FIGURE 3.2 Install Now screen

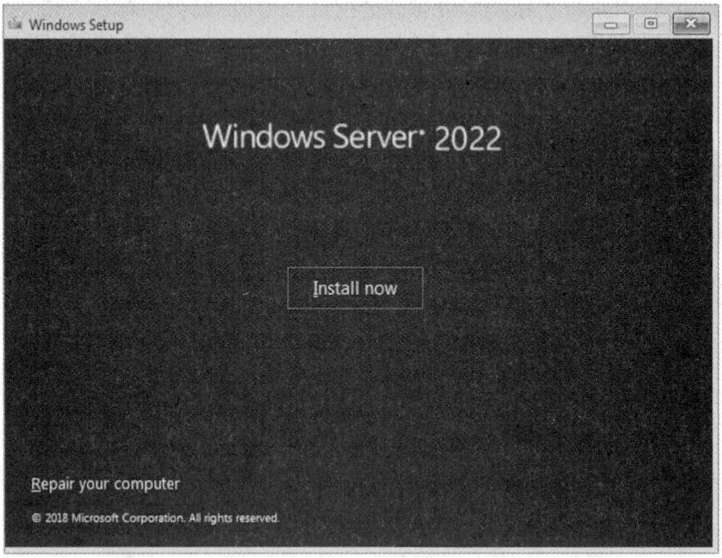

4. Depending on what version of Windows Server 2022 you have (MSDN, TechNet, and so on), you may be asked to enter a product key. If this screen appears, enter your product key and click Next. If this screen does not appear, just go to step 5.
5. The Select The Operating System That You Want To Install screen then appears. Choose Windows Server 2022 Datacenter (Desktop Experience) (see Figure 3.3) and click Next.

FIGURE 3.3   Windows Server Edition

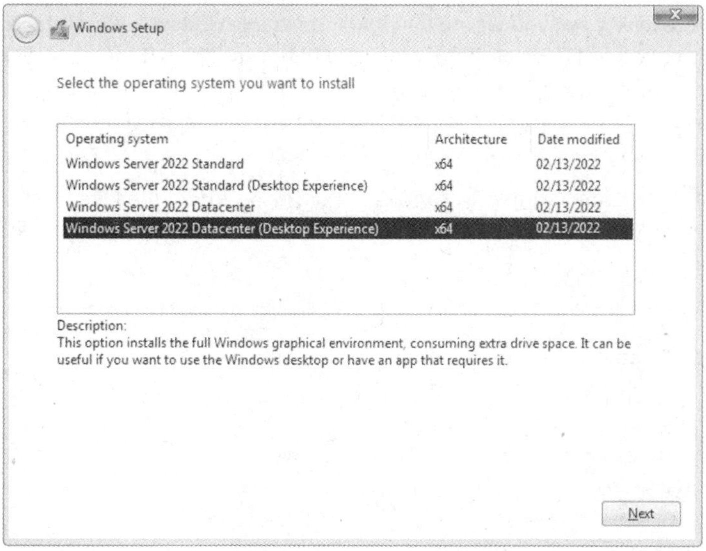

6. The license terms screen appears. After reading the Windows Server 2022 license agreement, check the I Accept The License Terms check box and click Next.

7. On the Which Type Of Installation Do You Want? screen (see Figure 3.4), choose Custom: Install Windows Only (Advanced).

FIGURE 3.4   Choosing Custom: Install Windows Only

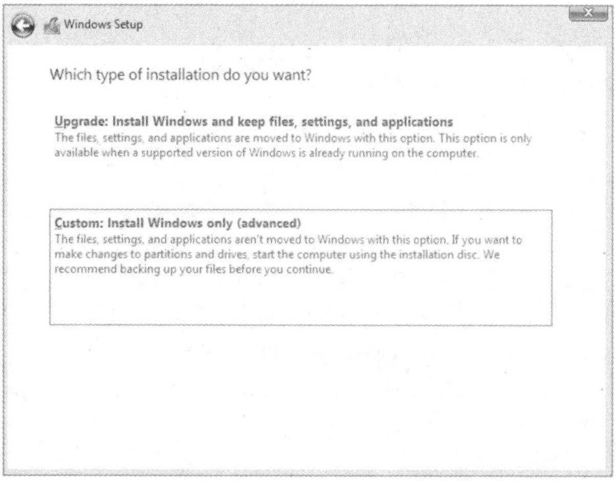

8. The next screen will ask you where you want to install Windows. If your hard disk is already formatted as NTFS, click the drive and then click Next. If the hard disk is not yet set up or formatted, click the New link and create a partition. After creating the partition, choose the Primary partition and click the Format link. Once the format is done, make sure you choose the new partition and click Next.

9. The Installing Windows screen will appear next. This is where the files from your media will be installed onto the system (see Figure 3.5). The machine will reboot during this installation.

FIGURE 3.5   Installing Windows screen

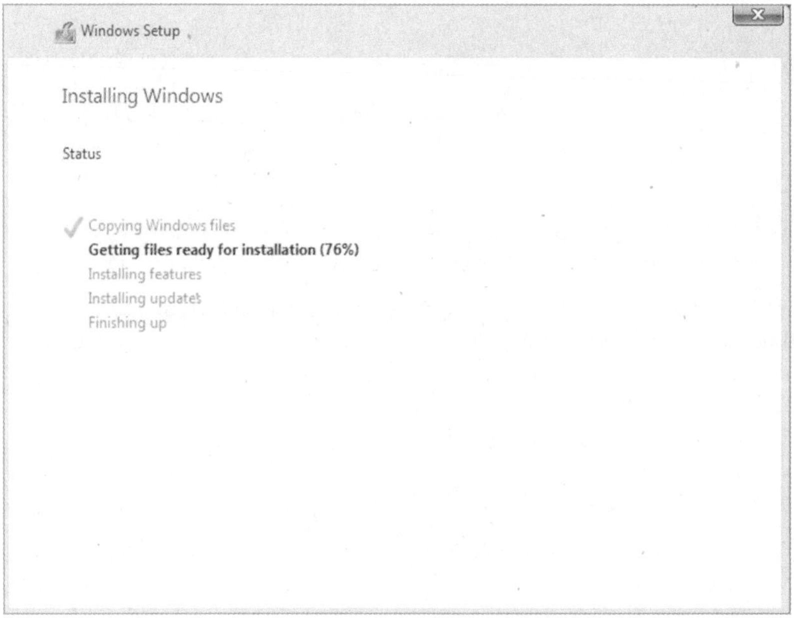

10. After the machine has finished rebooting, a screen requesting the administrator password will appear (see Figure 3.6). Type in your password. (P@ssword is used in this exercise. *Do not* use this password in a live environment.) Your password must meet the password complexity requirements (three of the following four are needed for complexity: one capitalized, one lowercase, one number, and/or one special character). Click Finish.

FIGURE 3.6   Customize Settings screen

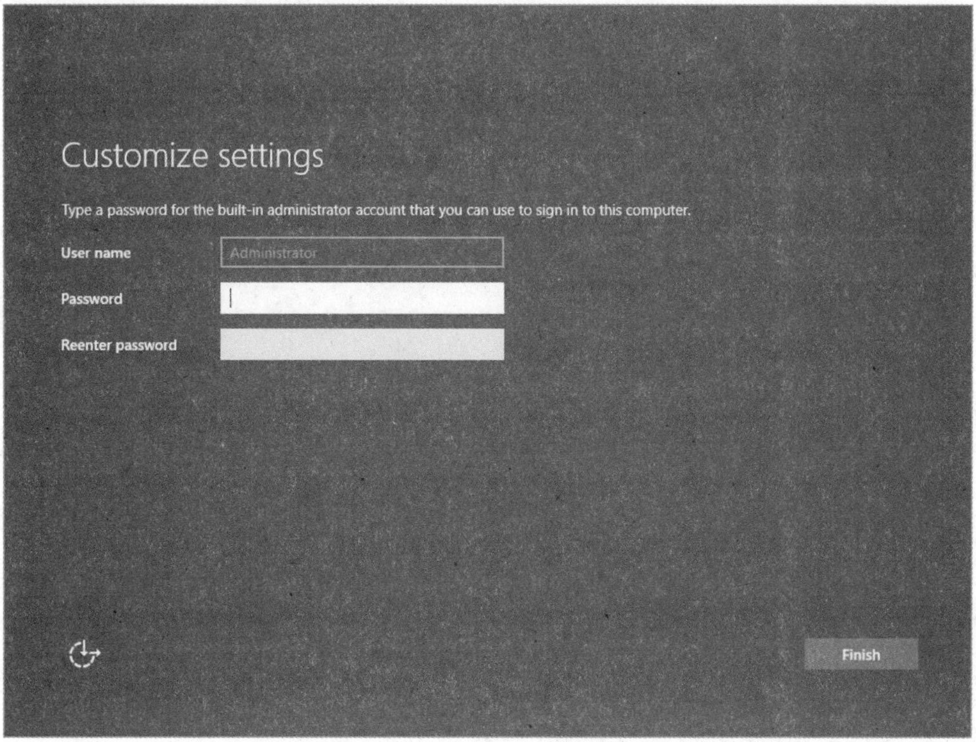

Customize settings

Type a password for the built-in administrator account that you can use to sign in to this computer.

User name	Administrator
Password	
Reenter password	

Finish

11. Next, log into the system. Press Ctrl+Alt+Del, and type the administrator password. The machine will set up the properties of the administrator account.

12. Notice that the Server Manager dashboard automatically appears (see Figure 3.7). You may receive a message about using the Windows Admin Center. Just close that message. We will use the Windows Admin Center later in this book. Your Windows Server 2022 installation is now complete.

EXERCISE 3.1 *(continued)*

FIGURE 3.7   Windows Server Manager Dashboard

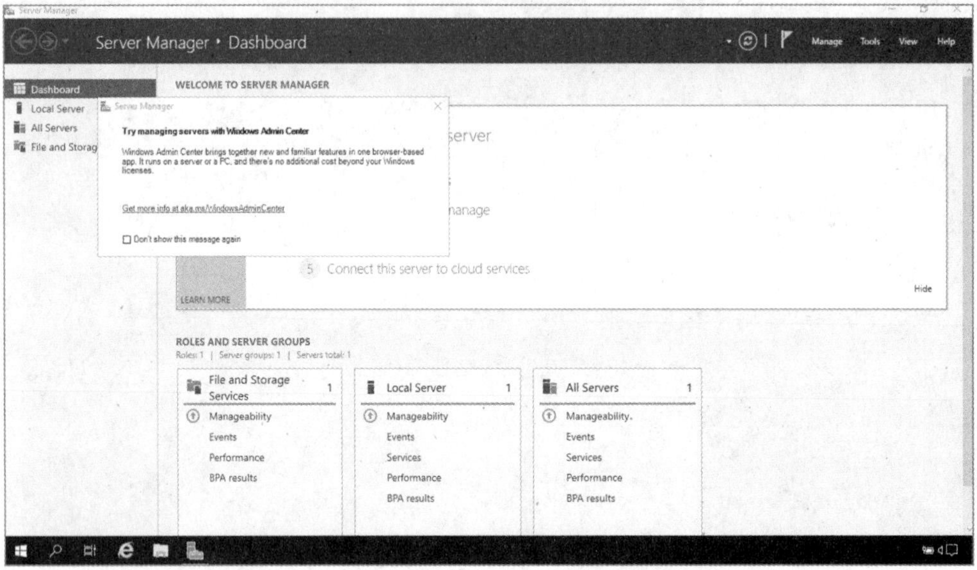

13. Close Server Manager.

After you have logged into the Windows Server 2022 Datacenter system, you will notice some features right away. The first is that there is a Start button in the lower-left corner of the screen. We will be using the Start Menu a lot throughout this book.

> **NOTE**   Administrators can also access the Start button by clicking the Windows Key on a standard keyboard.

So now that we have installed the Windows Server 2022 Datacenter (Desktop version), we are going to install Windows Server 2022 Datacenter Server Core.

Installing Windows Server 2022 Server Core

In Chapter 1, "Introduction to Windows Server 2022," I talked about the difference between the Desktop version and the Server Core version of Windows Server 2022. The Server Core version of Server does not have a GUI interface. This means that there are no wizards, Start Menus, or user desktops. Once the system boots up, you need to use the command prompt or PowerShell commands to configure the system.

In Exercise 3.2, you will learn how to install Windows Server 2022 Server Core. You'll notice that the steps are similar to the ones in Exercise 3.1, with a couple of exceptions. As mentioned earlier, Server Core is a command-line configuration of Windows Server 2022.

EXERCISE 3.2

Installing Windows Server 2022 Using Server Core

1. Insert the Windows Server 2022 installation media and restart the machine. You may be asked to press any key to start the installation.

2. At the first screen, Windows Server 2022 will prompt you to configure your language, time and currency, and keyboard. Make your selections and click Next.

3. At the next screen, click the Install Now button.

4. Depending on what version of Windows Server 2022 you have (MSDN, TechNet, and so on), you may be asked to enter a product key. If this screen appears, enter your product key and click Next. If this screen does not appear, just go to step 5.

5. The Select The Operating System That You Want To Install screen then appears. Choose Windows Server 2022 Datacenter (see Figure 3.8) and click Next.

FIGURE 3.8   Windows Server Edition

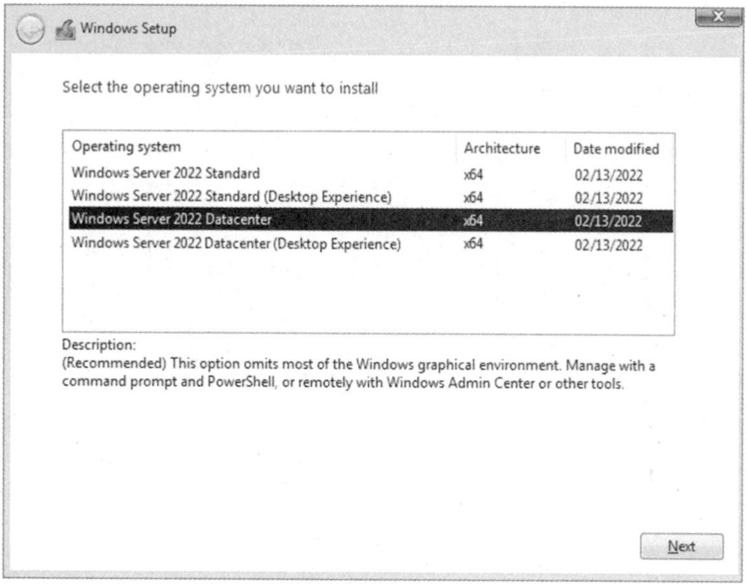

Windows Setup

Select the operating system you want to install

Operating system	Architecture	Date modified
Windows Server 2022 Standard	x64	02/13/2022
Windows Server 2022 Standard (Desktop Experience)	x64	02/13/2022
Windows Server 2022 Datacenter	x64	02/13/2022
Windows Server 2022 Datacenter (Desktop Experience)	x64	02/13/2022

Description:
(Recommended) This option omits most of the Windows graphical environment. Manage with a command prompt and PowerShell, or remotely with Windows Admin Center or other tools.

Next

6. The license terms screen appears. After reading the Windows Server 2022 license agreement, check the I Accept The License Terms check box and click Next.

7. At the Which Type Of Installation Do You Want? screen, choose Custom: Install Windows Only (Advanced).

8. The next screen will ask you where you want to install Windows. If your hard disk is already formatted as NTFS, click the drive and then click Next. If the hard disk is not set up or formatted, click the New link and create a partition. After creating the partition, choose the Primary partition and click the Format link. Once the partition is formatted, make sure you choose the new partition and click Next.

9. The Installing Windows screen will appear next. This is where the files from your media will be installed onto the system. The machine will reboot during this installation.

10. After the machine is finished rebooting, a screen requesting the administrator password will appear. Click OK (see Figure 3.9) and then type your password. (P@ssword is used in this exercise. *Do not* use this password in a live environment.) You will be asked to enter your password in a second time. Your password must meet the password complexity requirements (one capitalized letter, one number, and/or one special character).

FIGURE 3.9   Change Password screen

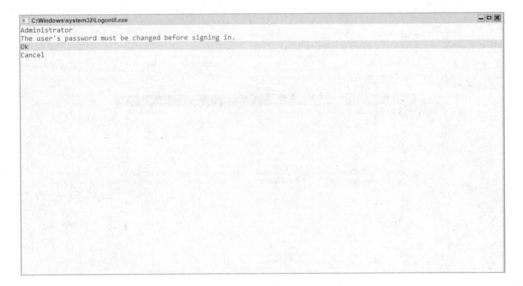

11. After the password is changed, a screen will appear telling you that the password has changed (see Figure 3.10). Press the Enter key.

FIGURE 3.10   Password Changed screen

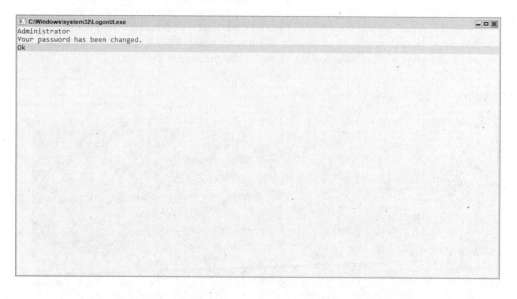

12. You will be automatically logged in. You will notice that the command prompt will appear (see Figure 3.11). Your Windows Server 2022 Server Core installation is now complete.

FIGURE 3.11   Server Core command prompt

EXERCISE 3.2 *(continued)*

13. If you want to do a quick configuration of Server Core, type **PowerShell** and press Enter. This will put you into a PowerShell prompt. Type **sconfig** and press Enter. You will now be able to do some basic configuration of the Server Core system (see Figure 3.12). You can run `sconfig` in the command prompt, but I recommend that you start using PowerShell for all of your configuration. PowerShell is a much more powerful tool and you should use it every time you can to get used to it.

FIGURE 3.12   Server Core `sconfig` command

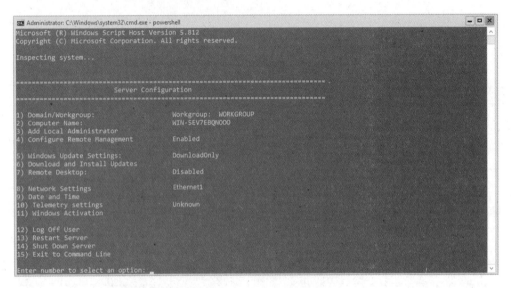

14. Choose option 15 and press Enter to exit this screen.

15. To turn off the machine, type **Shutdown /s /t 0**.

You'll use many PowerShell commands throughout this book. I will show you the PowerShell commands needed to configure and maintain Windows Server 2022 Server Core throughout this entire book.

Activating and Servicing Windows

After you complete the installation of Windows Server 2022, the next step is activating the operating system. Windows Server 2022 gives you a few different options when it comes to activation.

In the past, many administrators would use the Volume Activation Management Tool (VMAT) to activate both Microsoft operating systems and Microsoft products like Office. You can still use VMAT to activate Microsoft products like Office, but with the release of Windows Server 2022, there are some new ways to help you activate the operating systems.

So let's take a look at some of the different activation options that you have with Windows Server 2022 operating system.

Key Management Service

Windows Server 2022 Key Management Service (KMS) gives your Windows computers an easy and automated way for them to get activated. KMS allows your computers to get activated right on your local network without you having to contact Microsoft. For this to happen, you must set up a KMS client-server network. KMS clients are able to contact KMS servers as long as your network uses either a static TCP/IP configuration or you have a Domain Name System (DNS) server setup.

To configure KMS hosts systems, you must configure and retrieve Volume Activation information. Do so by using a Software License Manager (referred to as SL Manager) script (Slmgr.vbs). You can run this script on a local system or on a remote system, but it needs to be run from a user's account that uses an elevated command prompt. KMS host systems can be any Windows client operating system running Windows Vista or higher and any Server above Windows Server 2003.

To create or modify the Slmgr.vbs script, you can use either the Wscript.exe or the Cscript.exe application. Slmgr.vbs uses the Wscript.exe scripting engine by default. After you make any changes to the Slmgr.vbs script, you must restart the Software Licensing Service. You can do so by using the Services Microsoft Management Console (MMC) or by running the net stop and net start commands at an elevated command prompt (net stop sppsvc and net start sppsvc).

The Slmgr.vbs script has different command-line switches that you can use. Table 3.1 describes some of those switches.

TABLE 3.1   Slmgr.vbs switches

Parameter	Description
/ato	This switch is used for retail and volume system editions with a KMS host key or a Multiple Activation Key (MAK) installed. The /ato command prompts Windows to try to do an online activation. For any systems that are using a Generic Volume License Key (GVLK), this will make the system attempt to do a KMS activation.
/cdns	This switch allows you to disable KMS host automatic DNS publishing.
/cpri	You can use this switch to lower the priority of KMS host processes.

TABLE 3.1   Slmgr.vbs switches *(continued)*

Parameter	Description
/dli	You can use this switch on the KMS host to view the current KMS activation count.
/dlv	When you use this switch, the license information for the installed operating system is displayed.
/ipk	This command will try to install a 5x5 product key.
/sai activationInterval	This switch allows you to change how often a KMS client attempts to activate itself when it cannot find a KMS host. The default setting is 120 minutes, but you can change the interval by replacing ActivationInterval with the number of minutes you want to set.
/sdns	This switch allows you to enable KMS host automatic DNS publishing.
/spri	This switch allows you to set the CPU priority of the KMS host processes to Normal.
/sprt PortNumber	Using this switch allows you to change the default TCP communications port on a KMS host from 1688 to whichever port you want to use. To change the default port number, replace the PortNumber switch with the TCP port number you want to use.
/sri RenewalInterval	This switch allows you to change how often a KMS client attempts to renew its activation by contacting a KMS host. If you need to change the default of 10080 (7 days), just replace RenewalInterval with the number of minutes you want to use.

To run Slmgr.vbs remotely, you must supply additional parameters. You must include the computer name of the target computer as well as a username and password of a user account that has local administrator rights on the target computer. If run remotely without a specified username and password, the script uses the credentials of the user running the script:

```
slmgr.vbs TargetComputerName [username] [password] /parameter [options]
```

Automatic Virtual Machine Activation

Another Windows Server 2022 activation method is called Automatic Virtual Machine Activation (AVMA). The main advantage of AVMA is that it works the same way a proof-of-purchase works. Once there is proof that the Windows Server 2022 operating system is used in accordance with Microsoft Software License terms, AVMA allows you to install virtual machines on that Windows Server operating system without using or managing product keys for each virtual machine.

AVMA attaches the virtual machine activation to the properly activated Hyper-V machine during the startup process. One of the nice advantages to using AVMA is that AVMA will provide you with real-time reporting data. When your virtual servers are properly activated using volume or OEM licensing, AVMA gives your organization many benefits, like the ability to activate virtual machines in remote areas as well as activate virtual machines even if no Internet connection is present.

Another advantage of AVMA activations is that virtual machines are activated as long as the Hyper-V server is legally licensed. This helps consulting companies in the fact that they do not need to access client virtual machines to activate the machines as long as the Hyper-V server is properly licensed. Also, hosting companies can use the server logs to help keep the virtual machines running properly.

AVMA requires Windows Server 2022 with the Hyper-V role installed. AVMA can also run on Windows Server 2012, Windows Server 2012 R2, Windows Server 2016, and Windows Server 2019 if needed. Table 3.2 shows the Windows Server 2022 AVMA (5x5) Keys that are available from Microsoft's website along with the keys for Windows Server 2019 (https://docs.microsoft.com/en-us/windows-server/get-started-19/vm-activation-19).

TABLE 3.2   Windows Server AVMA keys

Windows Server 2022	AVMA Key
Datacenter	W3GNR-8DDXR-2TFRP-H8P33-DV9BG
Standard	YDFWN-MJ9JR-3DYRK-FXXRW-78VHK

Windows Server 2019	AVMA Key
Datacenter	H3RNG-8C32Q-Q8FRX-6TDXV-WMBMW
Standard	TNK62-RXVTB-4P47B-2D623-4GF74
Essentials	2CTP7-NHT64-BP62M-FV6GG-HFV28

Active Directory–Based Activation

One of the best advantages of using Windows Servers is the ability to install Active Directory onto your corporate network. Active Directory is just a centralized database of objects for a corporation; that centralized database is called a domain.

If your company is running Active Directory, you can use this to your advantage when it comes to activation. Active Directory–Based Activation (ADBA) allows you to activate computers right through the domain connection.

Many organizations have remote locations and at these locations there is company-owned software that needs to be registered. Normally administrators would use a retail key or a Multiple Activation Key (MAK) to get these products activated. The nice thing about ADBA is that as long as the computers are connected to the domain, the software and products can be activated through the domain.

When you join a Windows computer to the domain, the ADBA will automatically activate the computer's version of Windows either online with Microsoft or through the use of an activation proxy.

Servicing Windows Server 2022

Now that we've looked at some of the ways to activate you Windows Server 2022 systems, let's take a look at how you can service your Windows Server systems. Table 3.3 shows the various versions for Windows Server 2022 and which servicing model each version uses.

TABLE 3.3   Servicing models for Windows Server 2022

Installation option	LTSB servicing	Semi-annual servicing
Desktop Experience	Yes	No
Server Core	Yes	Yes
Nano Server	No	Yes

Long-Term Servicing Branch

Before the release of Windows Server 2022, Windows operating systems used the 5+5 servicing models. What this meant was there were five years of mainstream support and five years of extended support for the different versions of the Windows operating systems. This model will continue to be used in Windows Server 2022 (Desktop Support and Server Core), but it will be known as Long-Term Servicing Branch (LTSB).

Semi-annual Channel

The Semi-annual Channel is an excellent option for administrators who want to take advantage of the new operating system capabilities in Server Core or Nano Server containers. Windows Server 2022 products in the Semi-Annual Channel will have new releases of the server available twice a year. One will get released in the spring and one will get released in the fall. Each release will be supported for 18 months from the initial release date.

Many of the features included with the Semi-Annual Channel will be rolled into the following Long-Term Servicing Channel release of Windows Server. The editions, functionality, and supporting content may vary from each release depending on customer feedback.

The Semi-Annual Channel will be available to volume-licensed customers that have Software Assurance, as well as customers using the Azure Marketplace or other cloud-based service providers and loyalty programs like organizations having Visual Studio Subscriptions.

Configuring Windows Server Updates

When Microsoft releases a new operating system, users will encounter issues and security deficiencies. Both of these can cause your network to have many problems. So to help fix these issues, Microsoft will release updates and security fixes on a weekly basis. It is important for an IT department to keep their network systems up to date with these fixes.

Well, there are two main ways to do this. You can let your users all connect to Microsoft's website one at a time and grab updates, or you can set up a Windows Server Update Services (WSUS) server to get these updates. Then that WSUS server can release the updates to your users. This helps a company because when all your users connect to Microsoft to get the same updates, it's a waste of bandwidth and time. Also, as an IT person, you may not want all of the Microsoft updates to be deployed to your clients without viewing and testing them first.

I can tell you from firsthand experience that there have been times when I deployed an update from Microsoft and it caused more issues than it fixed. So having the ability to view and test updates on a test system ensures that the updates that we are deploying work the way that they are supposed to. So let's take a look at some of the tools you need to understand when dealing with updates:

Windows Update This utility attaches to the Microsoft website through a user-initiated process, and it allows Windows users to update their operating systems by downloading updated files (critical and noncritical software updates).

Windows Server Update Services (WSUS) This utility is used to deploy a limited version of Windows Update to a corporate server, which in turn provides the Windows updates to client computers within the corporate network. This allows clients who are limited to what they can access through a firewall to be able to keep their Windows operating systems up-to-date.

Windows Update

Windows Update is available for most Windows operating systems, and it allows the system to receive updates from Microsoft. Examples of updates include security fixes, critical updates, updated help files, and updated drivers.

If you (as an administrator) want to use Windows Update, click Start ➤ Settings ➤ Update And Security. You would then see the following options:

When The Last Updates Were Done   When you enter the Windows Update settings, the first thing you will see is when the last updates were done (if any).

Check For Updates Button   This feature allows you to manually check if any updates are available for the operating system. When you click this button (shown in Figure 3.13), the system will check for updates. If any updates are found, they will be downloaded and installed.

FIGURE 3.13   Windows Update control panel

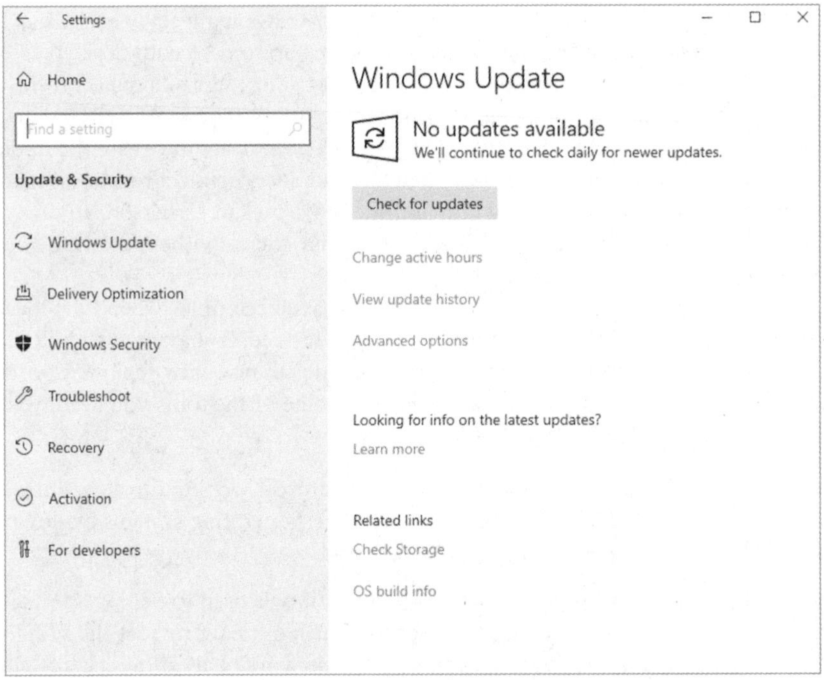

Update History   This allows you to track all the updates that you have applied to your server.

Change Active Hours   This setting allows you to set your active hours on the system. So, for example, if you worked on this system or the server was most active from 8:00 a.m. to 6:00 p.m., you can set those hours so that Windows Update knows when to download and install updates.

Restart Options   This setting allows you to customize when the system will restart after the machine receives its updates.

Advanced Options   You can use this option to customize what updates you receive when you use Windows Update.

> **NOTE** The information that is collected by Windows Update includes the operating system and version number, the Internet Explorer version, the version information for any software that can be updated through Windows Update, the Plug and Play ID numbers for installed hardware, and the region and language settings. Windows Update will also collect the product ID and product key to confirm that you are running a licensed copy of Windows, but this information is retained only during the Windows Update session and it is not stored. No personal information that can be used to identify users of the Windows Update service is collected.

Windows Server 2022 updates will recognize when you have a network connection and will automatically search for any updates for your computer from the Windows Update website (as long as an Internet connection is available) or from a WSUS server (explained in the next section).

If any updates are identified, they will be downloaded using *Background Intelligent Transfer Services (BITS)*. BITS is a bandwidth-throttling technology that allows downloads to occur using idle bandwidth only. This means that downloading automatic updates will not interfere with any other Internet traffic.

If Windows Update detects any updates for your computer, you will see an update icon in the notification area of the Taskbar.

As stated before, you can configure Windows Update by selecting Start ➢ Settings ➢ Update And Security. You can manually check for updates by clicking the Check For Updates button.

After the updates get downloaded to the server, you will see a status window showing you the update status of the updates being downloaded and installed (see Figure 3.14).

FIGURE 3.14   Viewing the update status

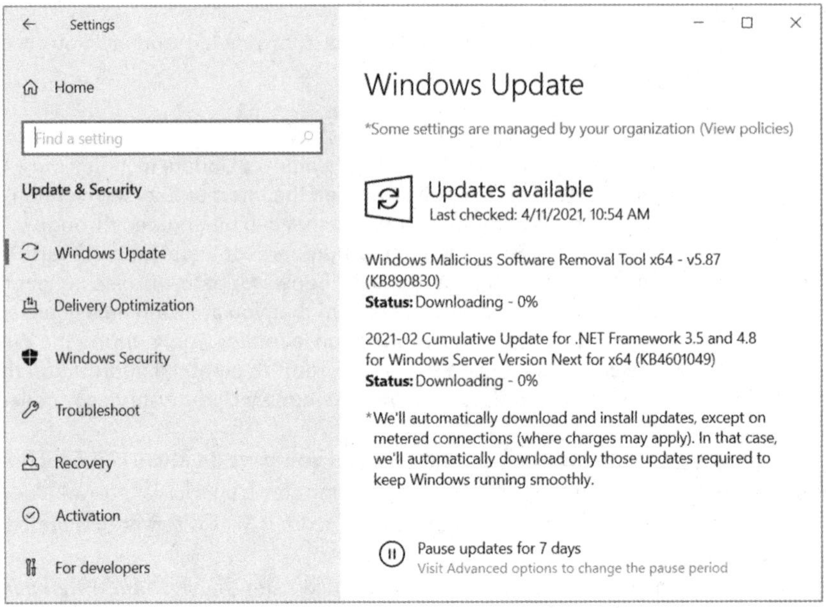

After some updates are downloaded and installed, you may be required to reboot the server. As seen in Figure 3.15, you can choose to reboot the server now or you can click the Schedule The Restart link and choose when you want the server to reboot. Scheduling the server to reboot after hours can be a good option for organizations that can't have the server taken down during the day. I recommend that an administrator be nearby in the event that an update prevents the server from restarting properly. This situation is rare, but it does happen.

FIGURE 3.15   The Restart Now button

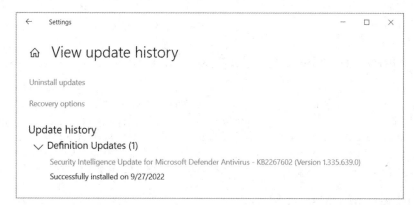

Once updates have been installed, you can click the Update History link to see all the previous updates. When you click this link, you will be shown the updates that have been installed and also have the ability to uninstall any updates (see Figure 3.16).

FIGURE 3.16   Viewing your update history

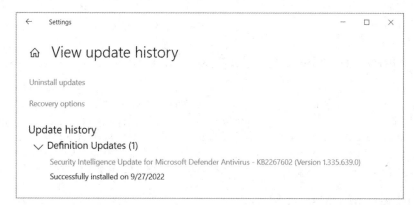

You also have the ability to set advanced options in the Updates section. One of the advanced options is to download other Microsoft updates for other Microsoft products (for example, you get Office updates at the same time you get operating system updates). You also have the ability to defer upgrades (see Figure 3.17).

When you decide to defer upgrades, new Windows features will not be downloaded or installed during the upgrade process. Deferring upgrades will not affect the Windows Server 2022 system from getting security updates. Deferring upgrades will only prevent you from getting the newest Windows features as soon as they are released.

FIGURE 3.17   Viewing Advanced Options

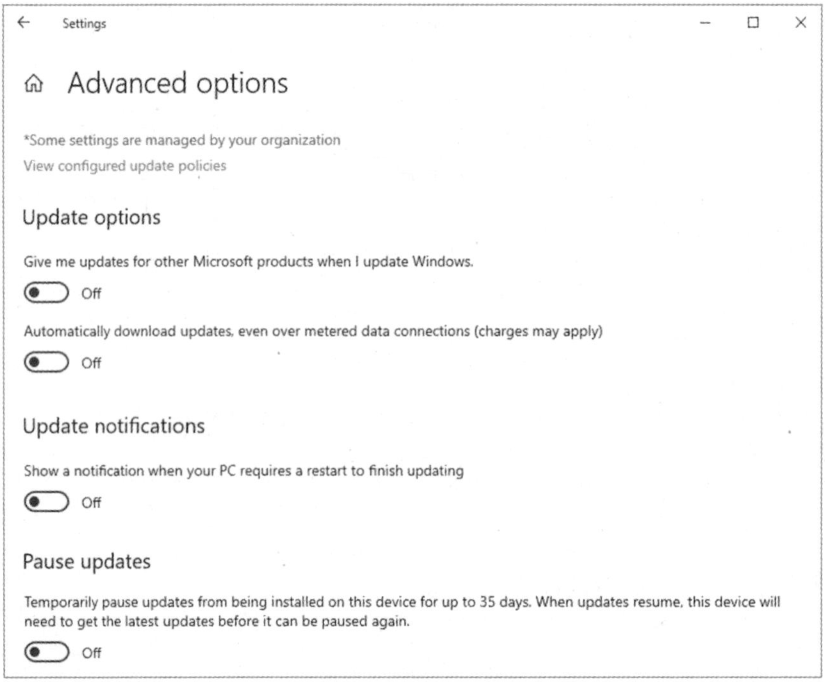

Using Windows Server Update Services

Windows Server Update Services (WSUS), formerly known as Software Update Services (SUS), is used to leverage the features of Windows Update within a corporate environment. WSUS downloads Windows updates to a corporate server, which in turn provides the updates to the internal corporate clients. This allows you to test and have full control over what updates are deployed within your corporate environment. WSUS is designed to work in medium-sized corporate networks that are not using System Center.

Advantages of Using WSUS

Using WSUS has many advantages:

- It allows an internal server within a private intranet to act as a virtual Windows Update server.

- You have selective control over what updates are posted and deployed from the public Windows Update site. No updates are deployed to client computers unless you first approve them.
- You can control the synchronization of updates from the public Windows Update site to the WSUS server either manually or automatically.
- You can configure Automatic Updates on client computers to access the local WSUS server as opposed to the public Windows Update site.
- WSUS checks each update to verify that Microsoft has digitally signed it. Any updates that are not digitally signed are discarded.
- You can selectively specify whether clients can access updated files from the intranet or from Microsoft's public Windows Update site, which is used to support remote clients.
- You can deploy updates to clients in multiple languages.
- You can configure client-side targeting to help client machines get updates. Client-side targeting allows your organization's computers to automatically add themselves to the computer groups that were created in the WSUS console.
- You can configure a WSUS statistics server to log update access, which allows you to track which clients have installed updates. The WSUS server and the WSUS statistics server can coexist on the same computer.
- You can manage WSUS servers remotely using HTTP or HTTPS.

WSUS Server Requirements

To act as a WSUS server, the server must meet the following requirements:

- It must be running Windows Server 2008, Windows Server 2008 R2, Windows Server 2012, Windows Server 2012 R2, Windows Server 2016, Windows Server 2019, or Windows Server 2022.
- It must have all of the most current security patches applied.
- It must be running Internet Information Services (IIS) 6.0 or newer.
- It must be connected to the network.
- It must have an NTFS partition with 100 MB of free disk space to install the WSUS server software, and it must have 6 GB of free space to store all the update files.
- It must use BITS version 2.0.
- It must use Microsoft Management Console 3.0.
- It must use Microsoft Report Viewer Redistributable 2008 or higher.
- Windows Defender should be enabled on the WSUS server.

   If your WSUS server meets the following system requirements, it can support up to 15,000 WSUS clients:

- Pentium III 700 MHz processor
- 512 MB of RAM

Installing the WSUS Server

WSUS should run on a dedicated server, meaning that the server will not run any other applications except IIS, which is required. Microsoft recommends that you install a clean or new version of Windows Server 2008, Windows Server 2008 R2, Windows Server 2012, Windows Server 2012 R2, Windows Server 2016, Windows Server 2019, or Windows Server 2022 and apply any service packs or security-related patches.

Exercise 3.3 walks you through the installation process for WSUS.

EXERCISE 3.3

Installing a WSUS Server

1. Choose Server Manager by clicking the Server Manager icon on the Taskbar.

2. Click option number 2, Add Roles And Features. If the Before You Begin screen appears, just click Next.

3. Choose role-based or featured-based installation and click Next.

4. Select your server and click Next.

5. Choose Windows Server Update Services (see Figure 3.18). Click the Add Features button when the dialog box appears. Then click Next.

FIGURE 3.18 Choosing to install WSUS

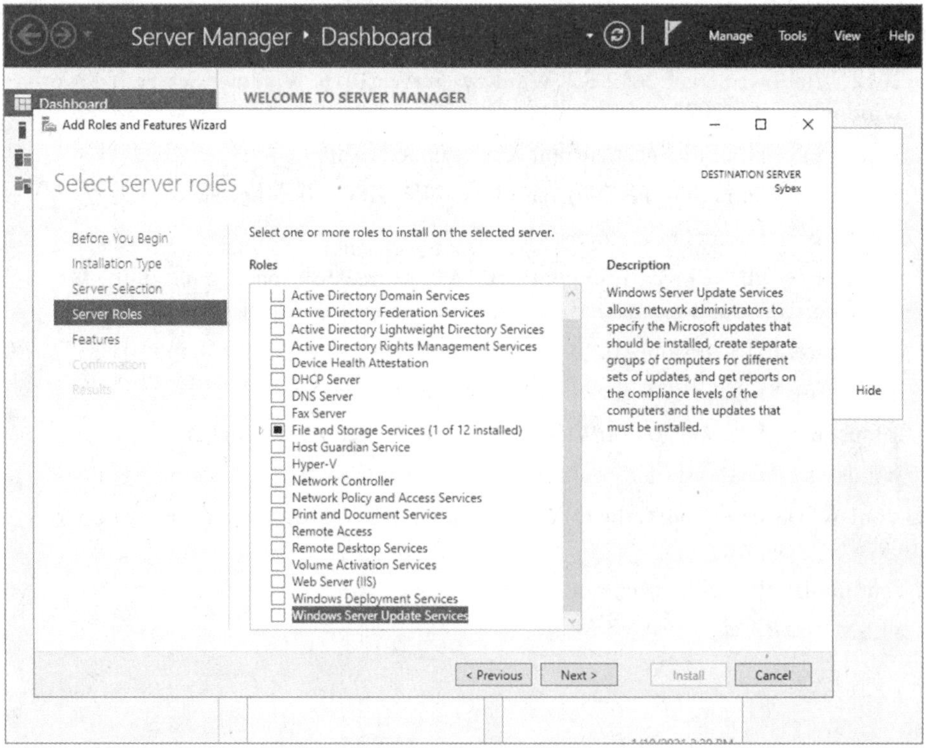

6. At the Select Features screen, just click Next.

7. At the Windows Server Update Services screen, click Next.

8. At the Select Role Services screen, make sure that WID Connectivity and WSUS Services are both checked (see Figure 3.19). Click Next.

FIGURE 3.19   Select Role screen

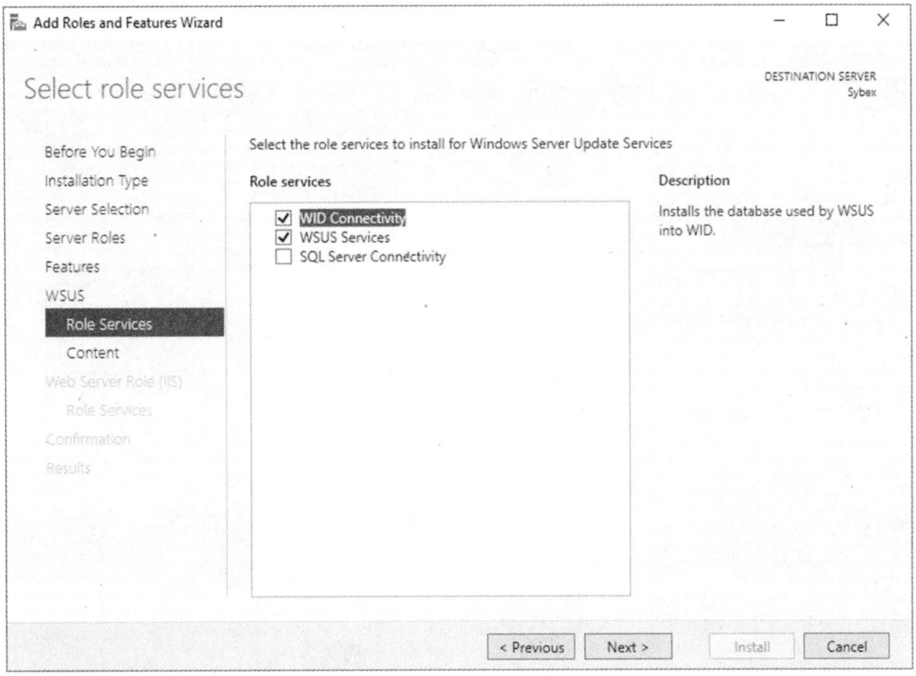

9. At the Content Location Selection screen, make sure the check box Store Updates In The Following Location is checked and enter the path of where you want your updates stored. After you do this, click Next (see Figure 3.20). If you deselect this box, updates are not stored locally. They are downloaded from Microsoft only once they are approved. This will help save hard drive space. But we are going to store our updates locally.

EXERCISE 3.3 ***(continued)***

FIGURE 3.20 Content Location Selection screen

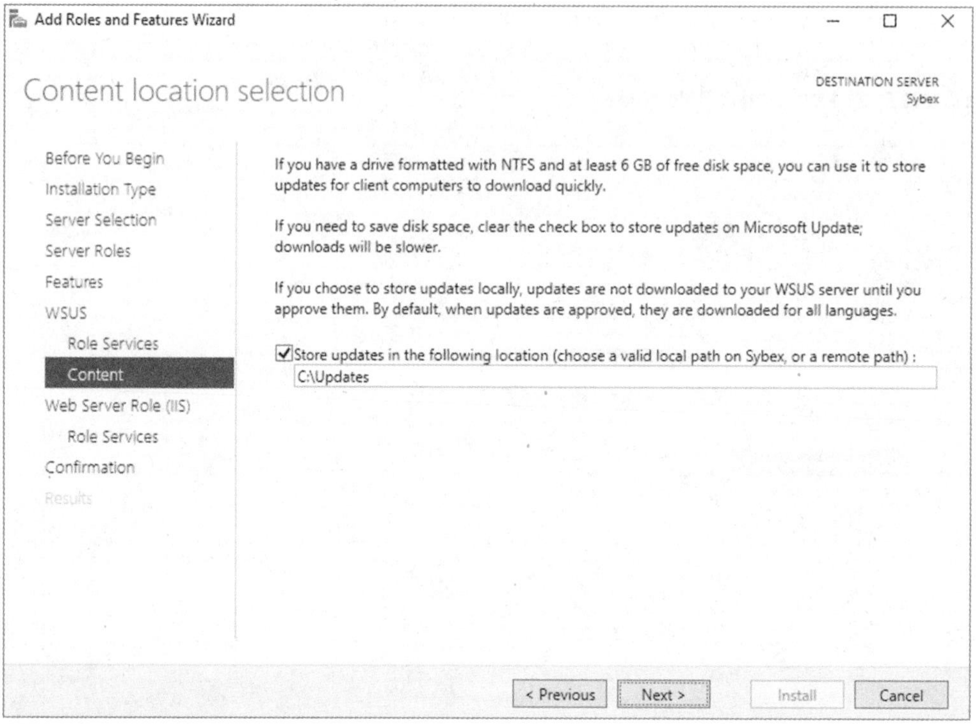

10. At the Web Server Role screen, click Next.
11. At the Role Services screen, accept the defaults and click Next.
12. At the Confirmation screen, shown in Figure 3.21, select Restart The Destination Server Automatically If Required. Then click the Install button.

FIGURE 3.21   Confirmation screen

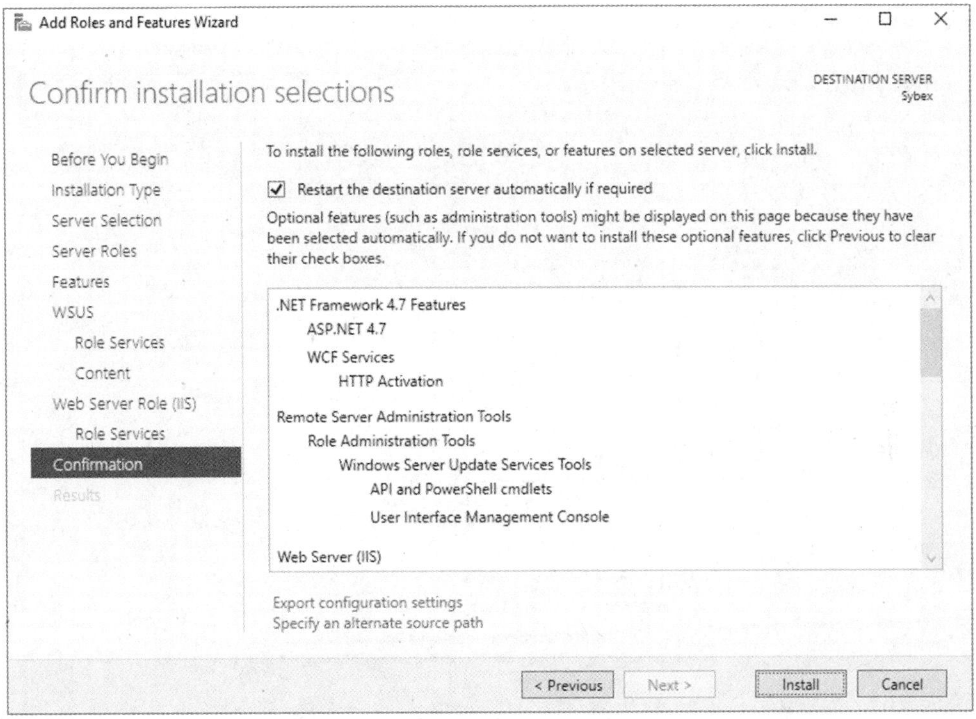

13. The installation will begin (shown in Figure 3.22), and you will see the progress. Once the installation is complete, click Close.

EXERCISE 3.3 *(continued)*

FIGURE 3.22 Status screen

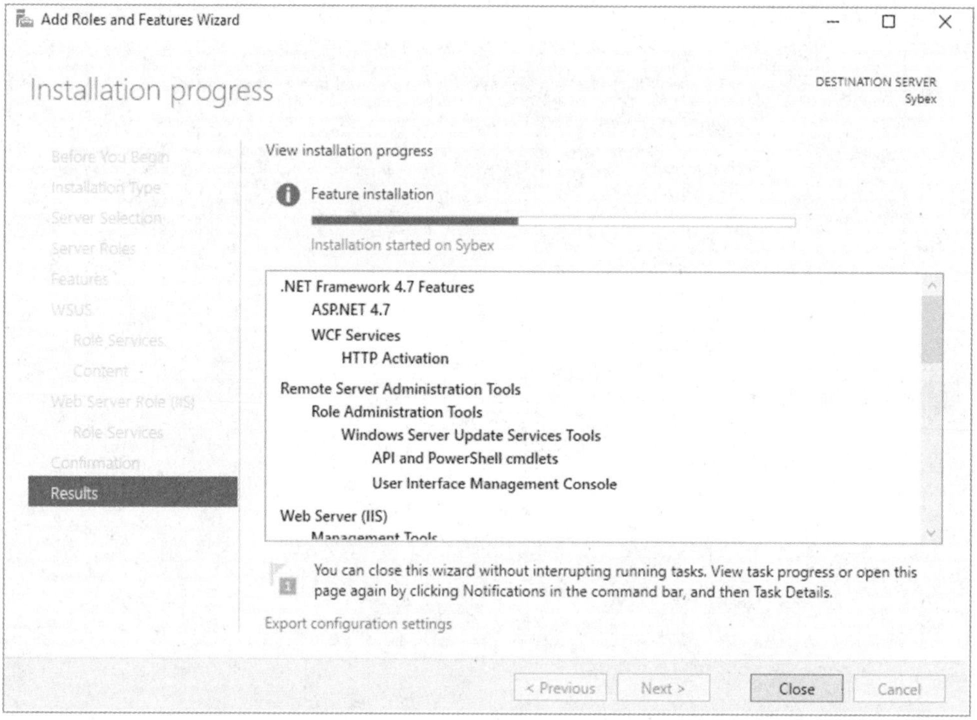

14. In Server Manager, click the WSUS link on the left side. Then click the More link (see Figure 3.23) next to Configuration Required For Windows Server Update Services.

FIGURE 3.23   Status screen more link

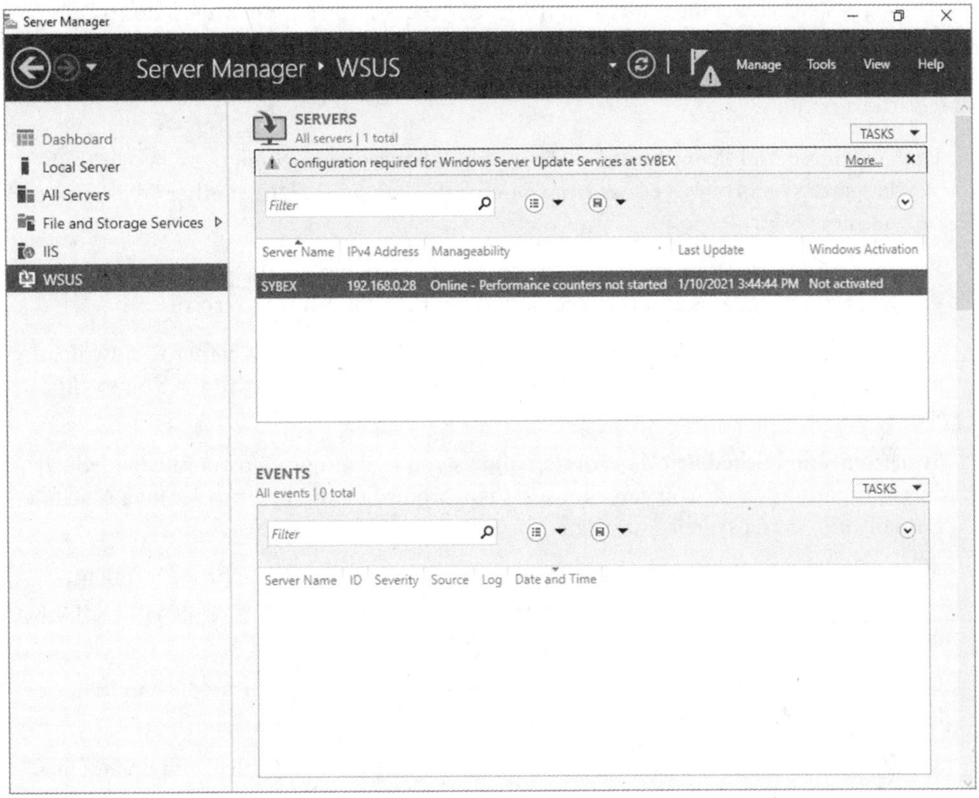

15. At the All Servers Task Details And Notifications screen, click the Launch Post-Installation Tasks link.

16. The installation process will automatically continue. Once it is finished, you will see Complete under Stage. Close the All Servers Task Details And Notifications screen.

17. Close Server Manager.

18. If a WSUS Configure Options box appears, just close it. You will set options in the next exercise.

Configuring a WSUS Server

Configuring a WSUS machine is a straightforward process. The easiest way to do so is to use the WSUS Server Configuration Wizard. This wizard walks you through the WSUS setup process, and it makes it easy to configure WSUS. When in the WSUS snap-in, you can configure various options:

Update Source And Proxy Server   This option allows you to configure whether this WSUS server synchronizes either from Microsoft Update or from another WSUS server on your network.

Products And Classifications   This option allows you to select the products for which you want to get updates and the type of updates that you want to receive.

Update Files And Languages   This option allows you to choose whether to download update files and where to store those update files. This option also allows you to choose which update languages you want downloaded.

Synchronization Schedule   This option allows you to configure how and when you synchronize your updates. You can choose to synchronize manually or to set up a schedule for daily automatic synchronization.

Automatic Approvals   This option allows you to specify how to approve installation of updates automatically for selected groups and how to approve revisions to existing updates.

Computers   This option allows you to set computers to groups or use Group Policy or Registry settings on the computer to receive updates.

Server Cleanup Wizard   This option allows you to clean out updates, and update files from your server.

Reporting Rollup   This option allows you to choose whether to have replica downstream servers roll up computer and update status to this WSUS server.

Email Notifications   This option allows you to set up email notifications for WSUS. You can be notified when new updates are synchronized, or you can get email status reports. This option also allows you to set up the email server's information on your WSUS server.

Microsoft Update Improvement Program   This option allows you to choose whether you want to participate in the Microsoft Update Improvement program. When you choose to participate in this program, your WSUS server will automatically send information to Microsoft about the quality of your updates. This following information is included:

- How many computers are in the organization
- How many computers successfully installed each update
- How many computers failed to install each update

Personalization   This option allows you to personalize the way information is displayed for this server. This option also allows you to set up a to-do list for WSUS.

WSUS Server Configuration Wizard   This option allows you to set up many of the preceding options by just using this one setup wizard.

In Exercise 3.4, you will learn how to set up some of the WSUS server options. To complete this exercise, you need to have an Internet connection that can communicate with Microsoft.

EXERCISE 3.4

Setting WSUS Server Options

1. Open the Windows Server Update Services snap-in from Administrative Tools by clicking Start and then choosing Administrative Tools (see Figure 3.24). The Windows Server Update Services snap-in will be at the bottom of the list alphabetically. Double-click the Windows Server Update Services snap-in.

FIGURE 3.24   Administrative Tools

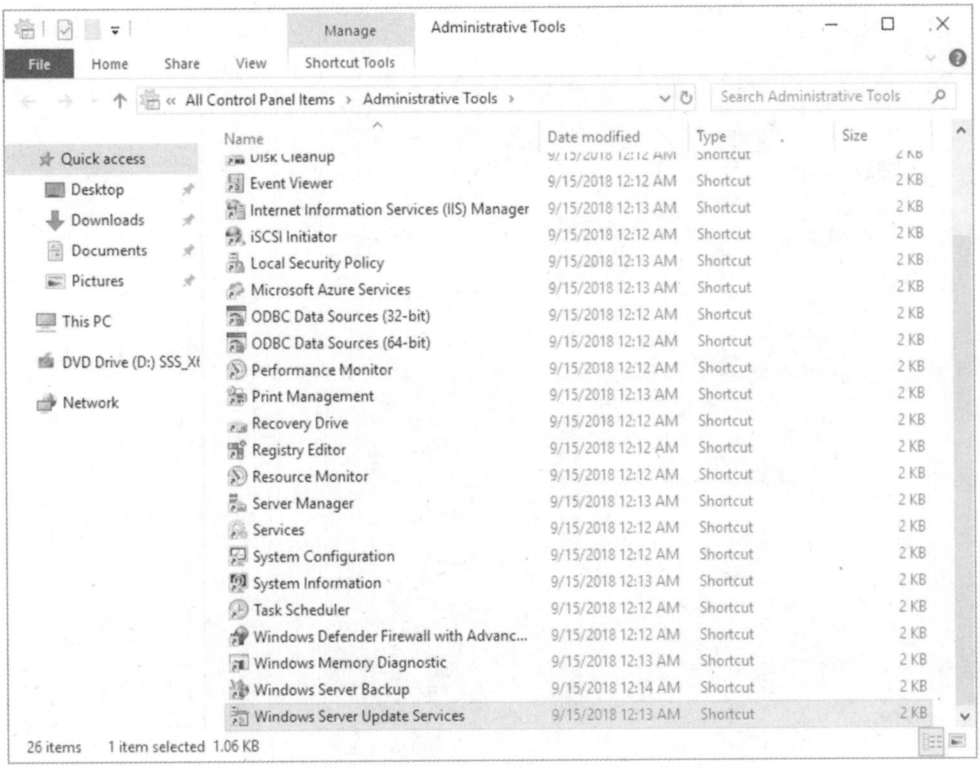

EXERCISE 3.4 *(continued)*

2. The WSUS Server Configuration Wizard appears. Click Next at the Before You Begin screen.

3. At the Join Microsoft Update Improvement Program screen, deselect the Yes box and click Next. If you want to participate in the program, keep the check box selected.

4. At the Choose Upstream Server screen, choose Synchronize From Microsoft Update and click Next.

5. Fill in the information at the Specify Proxy Server screen if you need to use a proxy server. If you do not need a proxy server, just click Next.

6. At the Connect To Upstream Server screen, click the Start Connecting button (see Figure 3.25). This step can take a while depending on your connection speed. Once it's finished connecting, click Next.

FIGURE 3.25   Connect To Upstream Server screen

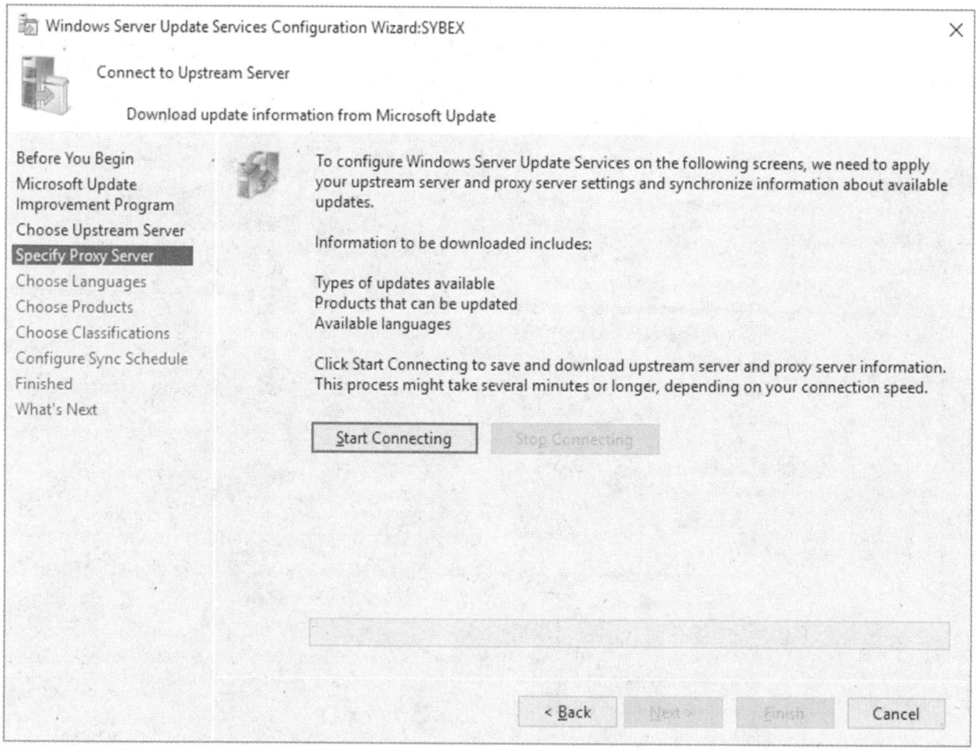

7. At the Language screen, choose which languages that you need updates for and click Next.

8. At the Choose Products screen (Figure 3.26), scroll down and choose the products for which you want to receive updates. Then click Next. You should only choose the products that you have in your organization. The more items you choose, the more space your network will need.

FIGURE 3.26　Choose Products screen

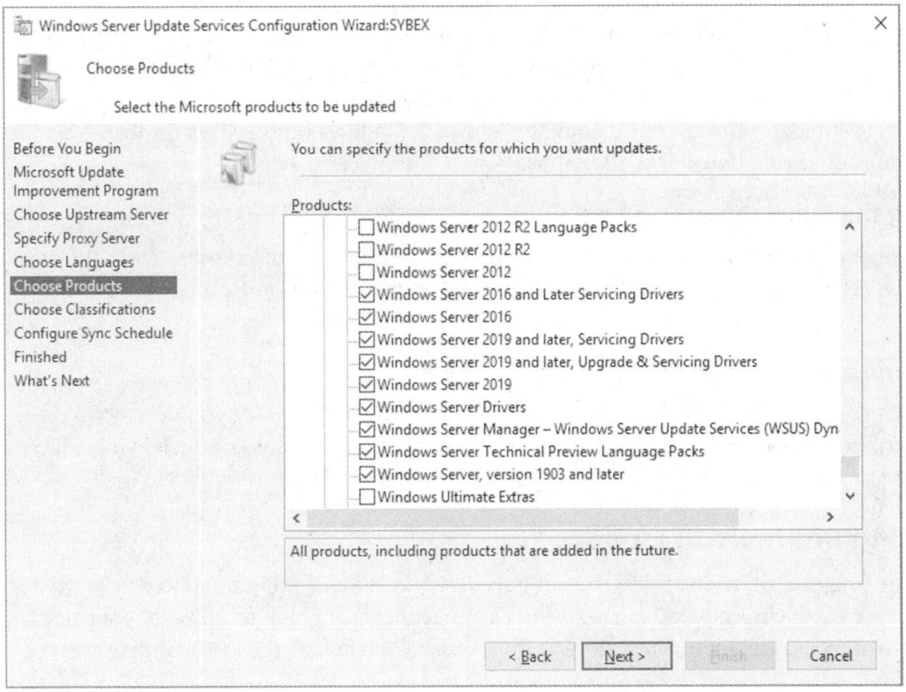

9. At the Choose Classifications screen, choose the classifications of updates you would like and click Next.

10. The Set Sync Schedule screen will appear next. At this screen, you can choose whether you want manual or automatic synchronizations. For this exercise, choose Synchronize Manually and click Next.

11. At the Finish screen, you can click Begin Initial Synchronization and click Finish. Be advised that this initial sync can take some time to finish. So if you don't have time to complete it now, you can always synchronize later.

12. Close WSUS.

Testing and Approving Updates

You should test and approve updates before they are deployed to WSUS clients. The testing should be done on a test machine that is not used for daily tasks.

You also want to make sure that the WSUS test client has Windows Defender or a third-party antivirus type software on it. This ensures that when the updates are loaded onto this test system, the updates will be checked against possible viruses, antimalware, spyware, or any other type of malicious software.

There are many reasons why you should pre-test the updates. There have been times in the past (and it doesn't happen a lot) when Microsoft has released an update that has caused issues on a network. Microsoft does its best to ensure that all updates are tested before deploying them, but depending on how your network is set up, the update may not perform the same way as it was intended. So by testing updates before deploying them, you ensure that the updates will not cause your network any unseen unforeseen problems.

To approve updates, from the welcome screen, click Updates on the site's toolbar. Make your settings on the Updates page that appears.

Viewing the Synchronization Log

To view the synchronization log, click the Reports button on the site's toolbar from the welcome screen. The Reports page will appear. Click Synchronization Results to view the results.

Configuring a Disconnected Network

You have the ability to use WSUS on a disconnected network. To do so, you download the updates to the Internet-connected WSUS server. After the download is complete, you can export the updates and then import the updates to the disconnected network.

Choosing Products to Update

One of the toughest decisions that you will have to make when setting up a network and a WSUS server is which products you (and the IT department) is going to allow in your network environment. The more Microsoft products that you choose, the more updates you will need.

But you have to make sure you choose the products that are needed and make sure those updates get done. Some of the products that we, as IT professionals, need to look at may not be things we think of right away. For example, we want to make sure that when we choose our products, we include Windows Defender.

As stated in the section "Testing and Approving Updates" earlier in this chapter, Windows Defender protects your systems against viruses, spyware, antimalware, and other malicious software. As new viruses get released, we need to make sure we protect our network systems against those viruses. Making sure we always have the up-to-date protection ensures that we can battle these attacks.

Also, as new operating systems come out (for example, Windows Server 2022), we as IT members want to make sure we have the latest security updates and improvements. This will not only ensure that our networks run at peak performance, but it will also ensure that we fix any security loopholes that hackers may have figured out in the operating system.

WSUS Client Requirements

WSUS clients run a special version of Automatic Updates that is designed to support WSUS. The following enhancements to Automatic Updates are included:

- Clients can receive updates from a WSUS server as opposed to the public Microsoft Windows Update site.
- You can schedule when the downloading of updated files will occur.
- Clients can be configured via Group Policy or through editing the Registry.
- Updates can occur when an administrative account or nonadministrative account is logged on.

The following current client platforms are the only ones that WSUS currently supports:

- Windows 7
- Windows 8
- Windows 10
- Windows 11
- Windows Server 2008 and 2008 R2
- Windows Server 2012 and 2012 R2
- Windows Server 2016
- Windows Server 2019
- Windows Server 2022

Configuring the WSUS Clients

You can configure WSUS clients in two ways. The method you use depends on whether you use Active Directory in your network.

In a non-enterprise network (not running Active Directory), you would configure Automatic Updates through the Control Panel. Each client's Registry would then be edited to reflect the location of the server providing the automatic updates.

Within an enterprise network, using Active Directory, you would typically see Automatic Updates configured through Group Policy. Group Policy is used to manage configuration and security settings via Active Directory. Group Policy is also used to specify what server a client will use for Automatic Updates. If Automatic Updates is configured through Group Policy, the user will not be able to change Automatic Updates settings by choosing Control Panel ➢ System (for XP) or Windows Update (for Windows 8, Windows 7, Windows Vista, Windows Server 2008, Windows Server 2008 R2, Windows Server 2012, Windows Server 2012 R2, Windows Server 2016, Windows Server 2019, and Windows Server 2022).

Configuring a Client in a Non–Active Directory Network

The easiest way to configure the client to use Automatic Updates is through the Control Panel. However, you can also configure Automatic Updates through the Registry. The Registry is a database of all your server settings. You can access it by choosing

Start ➤ Run and entering **regedit** in the Run dialog box. Automatic Updates settings are defined through HKEY_LOCAL_MACHINE\Software\Policies\Microsoft\Windows\WindowsUpdate\AU.

Table 3.4 lists some of the Registry options that you can configure for Automatic Updates.

TABLE 3.4   Selected Registry keys and values for Automatic Updates

Registry key	Options for values
NoAutoUpdate	0: Automatic Updates are enabled (default).
	1: Automatic Updates are disabled.
	2: Notify of download and installation.
	3: Autodownload and notify of installation.
	4: Autodownload and schedule installation.
	5: Automatic Updates is required, but end users can configure.
ScheduledInstallDay	1: Sunday.
	2: Monday.
	3: Tuesday.
	4: Wednesday.
	5: Thursday.
	6: Friday.
	7: Saturday.
UseWUServer	0: Use public Microsoft Windows Update site.
	1: Use server specified in WUServer entry.

To specify what server will be used as the Windows Update server, you edit two Registry keys, which are found here:

HKEY_LOCAL_MACHINE\Software\Policies\Microsoft\Windows\WindowsUpdate

- The WUServer key sets the Windows Update server using the server's HTTP name—for example, http://intranetSUS.

- The WUStatusServer key sets the Windows Update intranet WSUS statistics server by using the server's HTTP name—for example, http://intranetSUS.

Configuring a Client in an Active Directory Network

If the WSUS client is part of an enterprise network using Active Directory, you would configure the client via Group Policy. In Exercise 3.5, we will walk you through the steps needed to configure the Group Policy Object (GPO) for WSUS clients. The *Group Policy Management Console (GPMC)* must be installed for you to complete this exercise. If you don't have the GPMC installed, you can install it using the Server Manager utility.

EXERCISE 3.5

Configuring a GPO for WSUS

1. Open the GPMC by pressing the Windows Key and selecting Administrative Tools ➤ Group Policy Management.

2. Expand the forest, domains, and your domain name. Under your domain name, click Default Domain Policy. Right-click and choose Edit.

3. Under the Computer Configuration section, expand Policies ➤ Administrative Templates ➤ Windows Components ➤ Windows Update.

4. In the right pane, double-click the Configure Automatic Updates option. The Configure Automatic Updates Properties dialog box appears. Click the Enabled button. Then, in the drop-down list, choose Auto Download And Notify For Install. Click OK.

5. Double-click Specify Intranet Microsoft Update Service Location Properties. This setting allows you to specify the server from which the clients will get the updates. Click Enabled. In the two server name boxes, enter **//servername** (the name of the server on which you installed WSUS in Exercise 3.3). Click OK.

6. To configure the rescheduling of automatic updates, double-click Reschedule Automatic Updates Scheduled Installations. You can enable and schedule the amount of time that Automatic Updates waits after system startup before it attempts to proceed with a scheduled installation that was previously missed. Click Enabled. Enter **10** in the Startup (Minutes) box. Click OK.

7. To configure auto-restart for scheduled Automatic Updates installations, double-click No Auto-Restart For Scheduled Automatic Updates Installations. When you enable this option, the computer is not required to restart after an update. Enable this option and click OK.

8. Close the GPMC.

Configuring Client-Side Targeting

You can use a GPO to enable client-side targeting. Client machines can be automatically added into the proper computer group once the client computer connects to the WSUS server. Client-side targeting can be a useful tool when you have multiple client computers and you need to automate the process of assigning those computers to computer groups.

You can enable client-side targeting on the WSUS server by clicking the Use Group Policy Or Registry Settings On Client Computers option on the Computers Options page.

1. On the WSUS console toolbar, click Options and then click Computer Options.

2. In Computer Options, choose one of the following options:

   ▪ If you want to create groups and assign computers through the WSUS console (server-side targeting), click Use The Move Computers Task In Windows Server Update Services.

   ▪ If you want to create groups and assign computers by using Group Policy settings on the client computer (client-side targeting), click Use Group Policy Or Registry Settings On Computers.

3. Under Tasks, click the Save Settings button and then click OK.

Microsoft has announced that many of their configuration options will eventually be moving to PowerShell, so I will show you some of the available PowerShell commands for updates. Table 3.5 describes PowerShell commands that are available for WSUS administration.

 Table 3.5 is just a partial list of PowerShell commands for WSUS. To see a complete list, visit Microsoft's website at https://docs.microsoft.com/en-us/powershell/module/updateservices/?view=win10-ps.

TABLE 3.5   WSUS administration commands

PowerShell command	Description
Add-WsusComputer	This command allows you to add a client computer to a WSUS target group.
Approve-WsusUpdate	This allows you to approve an update that can then be applied to clients.
Deny-WsusUpdate	This allows you to deny an update.
Get-WsusClassification	You can use this command to get the list of all WSUS classifications available on the server.
Get-WsusComputer	This command allows you to view the WSUS computer object that represents the client computer.

PowerShell command	Description
Get-WsusProduct	You can use this command to get the list of all WSUS products available on the server.
Get-WsusUpdate	This command shows you the WSUS update object and the details about that update.
Get-WsusServer	This command allows you to view the WSUS update server object.
Invoke-WsusServerCleanup	This command allows you to initiate the cleanup process on the WSUS server.
Set-WsusClassification	This command sets whether the classifications of updates are enabled on the WSUS server.

Understanding Features On Demand

One of the problems in previous versions (prior to Windows Server 2012) of Windows Server was how roles and features were stored on the hard disk. Before the introduction of Windows Server 2012, even if a server role or feature was disabled on a server, the binary files for that role or feature were still present on the disk. The problem with this approach is that, even if you disable the role, it still consumes space on your hard drive.

Features on Demand in Windows Server 2012 solves this issue because not only can you disable a role or feature, you can also completely remove the role or feature's files. Windows Server 2022 has continued with Features on Demand and you can choose what roles and features you want to use, when you want to use them.

Once this is done, a state of Removed is shown in Server Manager, or the state of Disabled With Payload Removed is shown in the Deployment Image Servicing and Management (Dism.exe) utility. To reinstall a role or feature that has been completely removed, you must have access to the installation files.

 We talk about the Deployment Image Servicing and Management (Dism .exe) utility throughout this book. DISM will be discussed in great detail when we discuss Windows imaging.

If you want to remove a role or feature completely from the system, use -Remove with the Windows PowerShell Uninstall-WindowsFeature cmdlet.

If you want to reinstall a role or feature that has been removed completely, use the Windows PowerShell -Source option of the Install-WindowsFeature Server

Manager cmdlet. Using the -Source option states the path where the WIM image files and the index number of the image will be located. If you decide not to use the -Source option, Windows will use Windows Update by default.

When you're using the Features on Demand configuration, if feature files are not available on the server computer and the installation requires those feature files, Windows Server 2022 can be directed to get those files from a side-by-side feature store, which is a shared folder that contains feature files. It is available to the server on the network, from Windows Update, or from installation media. This shared folder can be overwritten using the -Source option in the Windows PowerShell utility.

Source Files for Roles or Features

Offline virtual hard disks (VHDs) cannot be used as a source for installing roles or features that have been completely removed. Only sources for the same version of Windows Server 2022 are supported.

To install a removed role or feature using a WIM image, follow these steps:

1. Run the following command:

   ```
   Get-windowsimage -imagepath \install.wim
   ```

   In step 1, *imagepath* is the path where the WIM files are located.

2. Run the following command:

   ```
   Install-WindowsFeature featurename -Source wim: path:index
   ```

   In step 2, *featurename* is the name of the role or feature from `Get-WindowsFeature`. *path* is the path to the WIM mount point, and *index* is the index of the server image from step 1.

To add or remove a role or feature, you must have administrative rights to the Windows Server 2022 machine.

Understanding Filesystems

When we start the discussion about understanding Windows filesystems, we have to first think about how the Windows Server 2022 machine will be used. There are four supported filesystems: FAT, FAT32, NTFS, and ReFS. FAT and FAT32 partitions may not always be an available option. As you can see in Figure 3.27, all four filesystems are available because the partition is under 4 GB.

FIGURE 3.27   Format options on Windows Server 2022

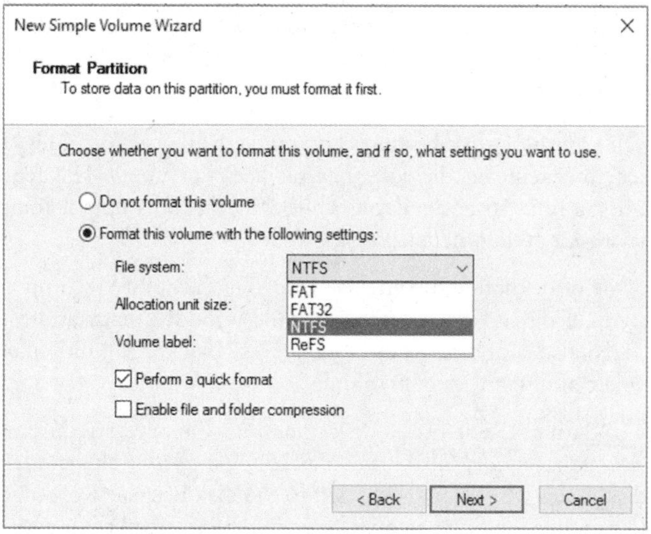

FAT has a maximum partition size of 4 GB and FAT32 has a maximum partition size of 32 GB. In Figure 3.27, since it's a 3 GB partition, all four options are available. But because most drives today are much larger than 32 GB, we will continue our focus on just NTFS and ReFS.

When you're planning your Active Directory deployment, the filesystem that the operating system uses is an important concern for two reasons. First, the filesystem can provide the ultimate level of security for all the information stored on the server itself. Second, it is responsible for managing and tracking all of this data. The Windows Server 2022 platform supports two main filesystems:

- Windows NT File System (NTFS)
- Resilient File System (ReFS)

Although ReFS was new to Windows Server 2012, NTFS has been around for many years, and NTFS in Windows Server 2022 has been improved for better performance.

Resilient File System (ReFS)

Windows Server 2022 includes a filesystem called *Resilient File System (ReFS)*. ReFS was created to help Windows Server 2022 maximize the availability of data and online operation. ReFS allows the Windows Server 2022 system to continue to function despite some errors that would normally cause data to be lost or the system to go down. ReFS uses data integrity to protect your data from errors and also to make sure that all of your important data is online when that data is needed.

One of the issues that IT members have had to face over the years is the problem of rapidly growing data sizes. As we continue to rely more and more on computers, our data continues to get larger and larger. This is where ReFS can help an IT department. ReFS was designed specifically with the issues of scalability and performance in mind, which resulted in some of the following ReFS features:

Availability   If your hard disk becomes corrupted, ReFS has the ability to implement a salvage strategy that removes the data that has been corrupted. This feature allows the healthy data to continue to be available while the unhealthy data is removed. All of this can be done without taking the hard disk offline.

Scalability   One of the main advantages of ReFS is the ability to support volume sizes up to 2^{78} bytes using 16 KB cluster sizes, while Windows stack addressing allows 2^{64} bytes. ReFS also supports file sizes of $2^{64}-1$ bytes, 2^{64} files in a directory, and the same number of directories in a volume.

Robust Disk Updating   ReFS uses a disk updating system referred to as an *allocate-on-write transactional model* (also known as *copy on write*). This model helps to avoid many hard disk issues while data is written to the disk because ReFS updates data using disk writes to multiple locations in an atomic manner instead of updating data in place.

Data Integrity   ReFS uses a check-summed system to verify that all data that is being written and stored is accurate and reliable. ReFS always uses allocate-on-write for updates to the data, and it uses checksums to detect disk corruption.

Application Compatibility   ReFS allows for most NTFS features and also supports the Win32 API. Because of this, ReFS is compatible with most Windows applications.

As of this writing, ReFS has some limitations on what the filesystem can handle. To check out ReFS features and limitations, visit Microsoft's website to see if any changes have been made for ReFS (https://learn.microsoft.com/en-us/windows-server/storage/refs/refs-overview).

The following are some of the features currently not available using ReFS:

- Filesystem compression
- Filesystem encryption
- Transactions
- Object IDs
- Offloaded data transfer (ODX)
- Short names
- Extended attributes
- Disk quotas
- Bootable
- Page file support
- Supported on removable media

NTFS

Let's start with some of the features of NTFS. There are many benefits to using NTFS, including support for the following:

Disk Quotas   To restrict the amount of disk space used by users on the network, system administrators can establish *disk quotas*. By default, Windows Server 2022 supports disk quota restrictions at the volume level. That is, you can restrict the amount of storage space that a specific user uses on a single disk volume. Third-party solutions that allow more granular quota settings are also available.

Filesystem Encryption   One of the fundamental problems with network operating systems (NOSs) is that system administrators are often given full permission to view all files and data stored on hard disks, which can be a security and privacy concern. In some cases, this is necessary. For example, to perform backup, recovery, and disk management functions, at least one user must have all permissions. Windows Server 2022 and NTFS address these issues by allowing for *filesystem encryption*. Encryption essentially scrambles all of the data stored within files before they are written to the disk. When an authorized user requests the files, they are transparently decrypted and provided. By using encryption, you can prevent the data from being used in case it is stolen or intercepted by an unauthorized user—even a system administrator.

Dynamic Volumes   Protecting against disk failures is an important concern for production servers. Although earlier versions of Windows NT supported various levels of Redundant Array of Independent Disks (RAID) technology, software-based solutions had some shortcomings. Perhaps the most significant was that you needed to perform server reboots to change RAID configurations. Also, you could not make some configuration changes without completely reinstalling the operating system. With Windows Server 2022 support for *dynamic volumes*, you can change RAID and other disk configuration settings without having to reboot or reinstall the server. The result is greater data protection, increased scalability, and increased uptime. Dynamic volumes are also included with ReFS.

Mounted Drives   By using *mounted drives*, you can map a local disk drive to an NTFS directory name. This helps you organize disk space on servers and increase manageability. By using mounted drives, you can mount the `C:\Users` directory to an actual physical disk. If that disk becomes full, you can copy all the files to another, larger drive without changing the directory path name or reconfiguring applications.

Remote Storage   System administrators often notice that as soon as they add more space, they must plan the next upgrade. One way to recover disk space is to move infrequently used files to external hard drives. However, backing up and restoring these files can be quite difficult and time-consuming. You can use the *remote storage* features supported by NTFS to offload seldom-used data automatically to a backup system or other devices. The files, however, remain available to users. If a user requests an archived file,

Windows Server 2022 can automatically restore the file from a remote storage device and make it available. Using remote storage like this frees up system administrators' time and allows them to focus on tasks other than micromanaging disk space.

Self-Healing NTFS   In previous versions of the Windows Server operating system, if you had to fix a corrupted NTFS volume, you used a tool called `Chkdsk.exe`. The disadvantage of this tool is that the Windows Server's availability was disrupted. If this server was your domain controller, that could stop domain logon authentication.

To help protect the Windows Server 2022 NTFS filesystem, Microsoft now uses a feature called self-healing NTFS. *Self-healing NTFS* attempts to fix corrupted NTFS filesystems without taking them offline. Self-healing NTFS allows an NTFS filesystem to be corrected without running the `Chkdsk.exe` utility. New features added to the NTFS kernel code allow disk inconsistencies to be corrected without system downtime.

Security   NTFS allows you to configure not only folder-level security but also file-level security. NTFS security is one of the biggest reasons most companies use NTFS. ReFS also allows folder- and file-level security.

Setting Up the NTFS Partition

Although the features mentioned in the previous section likely compel most system administrators to use NTFS, additional reasons make using it mandatory. The most important reason is that the Active Directory data store must reside on an NTFS partition. Therefore, before you begin installing Active Directory, make sure you have at least one NTFS partition available. Also, be sure you have a reasonable amount of disk space available (at least 4 GB). Because the size of the Active Directory data store will grow as you add objects to it, also be sure that you have adequate space for the future.

Exercise 3.6 shows you how to use the administrative tools to view and modify disk configuration.

 Before you make any disk configuration changes, be sure you completely understand their potential effects; then perform the test in a lab environment and make sure you have good, verifiable backups handy. Changing partition sizes and adding and removing partitions can result in a total loss of all information on one or more partitions.

If you want to convert an existing partition from FAT or FAT32 to NTFS, you need to use the CONVERT command-line utility. For example, the following command converts the `C:` partition from FAT to NTFS:

```
CONVERT c: /fs:ntfs
```

EXERCISE 3.6

Viewing Disk Configurations

1. Right-click the Start button and choose Disk Management (shown in Figure 3.28).

FIGURE 3.28   Disk Management

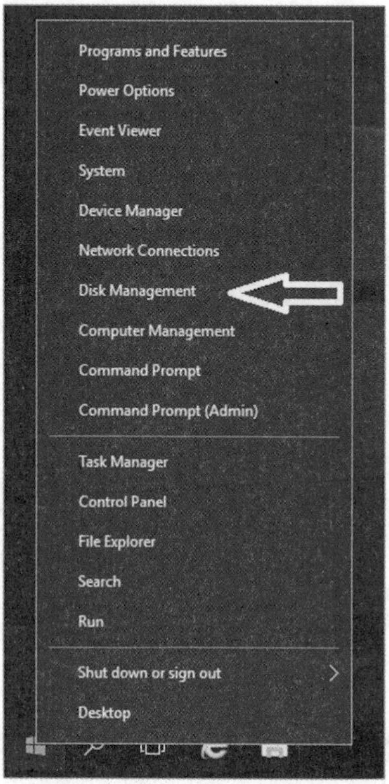

The Disk Management program shows you the logical and physical disks that are currently configured on your system. Note that information about the size of each partition is also displayed (in the Capacity column).

2. To see the available options for modifying partition settings, right-click any of the disks or partitions and choose Properties. This step is optional.

3. Close Computer Management.

Storage in Windows Server 2022

As an IT administrator, you'll need to ask many questions before you start setting up a server. What type of disks should be used? What type of RAID sets should be made? What type of hardware platform should be purchased? These are all questions you must ask when planning for storage in a Windows Server 2022 server. In this section, I will answer these questions so that you can make the best decisions for storage in your network's environment.

Initializing Disks

To begin, let's first discuss how to add disk drives to a server. Once a disk drive has been physically installed, it must be initialized by selecting the type of partition. Different types of partition styles are used to initialize disks: *Master Boot Record (MBR)* and *GUID Partition Table (GPT)*.

MBR has a partition table that indicates where the partitions are located on the disk drive, and with this particular partition style, only volumes up to 2 TB (2,048 GB) are supported. An MBR drive can have up to four primary partitions or it can have three primary partitions and one extended partition that can be divided into unlimited logical drives.

Windows Server 2022 can only boot off an MBR disk unless it is based on the Extensible Firmware Interface (EFI); then it can boot from GPT. An Itanium server is an example of an EFI-based system. GPT is not constrained by the same limitations as MBR. In fact, a GPT disk drive can support volumes of up to 18 EB (18,874,368 million terabytes) and 128 partitions. As a result, GPT is recommended for disks larger than 2 TB or disks used on Itanium-based computers. Exercise 3.7 demonstrates the process of initializing additional disk drives to an active computer running Windows Server 2022. If you're not adding a new drive, then stop after step 4. I am completing this exercise using Computer Management, but you also can do this exercise using Server Manager.

EXERCISE 3.7

Initializing Disk Drives

1. Open Computer Management under Administrative Tools.

2. Select Disk Management.

3. After disk drives have been installed, right-click Disk Management and select Rescan Re-scan Disks.

4. A pop-up box appears indicating that the server is scanning for new disks. If you did not add a new disk, go to step 9.

5. After the server has completed the scan, the new disk appears as Unknown.

6. Right-click the Unknown disk and select Initialize Disk.

7. A pop-up box appears asking for the partition style. For this exercise, choose MBR.

8. Click OK.

9. Close Computer Management.

The disk will now appear online as a basic disk with unallocated space.

Configuring Basic and Dynamic Disks

Windows Server 2022 supports two types of disk configurations: basic and dynamic. Basic disks are divided into partitions and can be used with previous versions of Windows. Dynamic disks are divided into volumes and can be used with Windows 2000 Server and newer releases.

When a disk is initialized, it is automatically created as a basic disk, but when a new fault-tolerant (RAID) volume set is created, the disks in the set are converted to dynamic disks. Fault-tolerance features and the ability to modify disks without having to reboot the server are what distinguish dynamic disks from basic disks.

 Fault tolerance (RAID) is discussed in detail later in this chapter in the "Redundant Array of Independent Disks" section.

A basic disk can simply be converted to a dynamic disk without loss of data. When a basic disk is converted, the partitions are automatically changed to the appropriate volumes. However, converting a dynamic disk back to a basic disk is not as simple. First, all the data on the dynamic disk must be backed up or moved. Then, all the volumes on the dynamic disk have to be deleted. The dynamic disk can then be converted to a basic disk. Partitions and logical drives can be created, and the data can be restored.

The following are actions that can be performed on basic disks:

- Formatting partitions
- Marking partitions as active
- Creating and deleting primary and extended partitions
- Creating and deleting logical drives
- Converting from a basic disk to a dynamic disk

The following are actions that can be performed on dynamic disks:

- Creating and deleting simple, striped, spanned, mirrored, or RAID-5 volumes
- Removing or breaking a mirrored volume
- Extending simple or spanned volumes
- Repairing mirrored or RAID-5 volumes
- Converting from a dynamic disk to a basic disk after deleting all volumes

In Exercise 3.8, you'll convert a basic disk to a dynamic disk.

EXERCISE 3.8

Converting a Basic Disk to a Dynamic Disk

1. Open Computer Management under Administrative Tools.

2. Select Disk Management.

3. Right-click a basic disk that you want to convert and select Convert To Dynamic Disk (see Figure 3.29).

FIGURE 3.29   Converting a disk

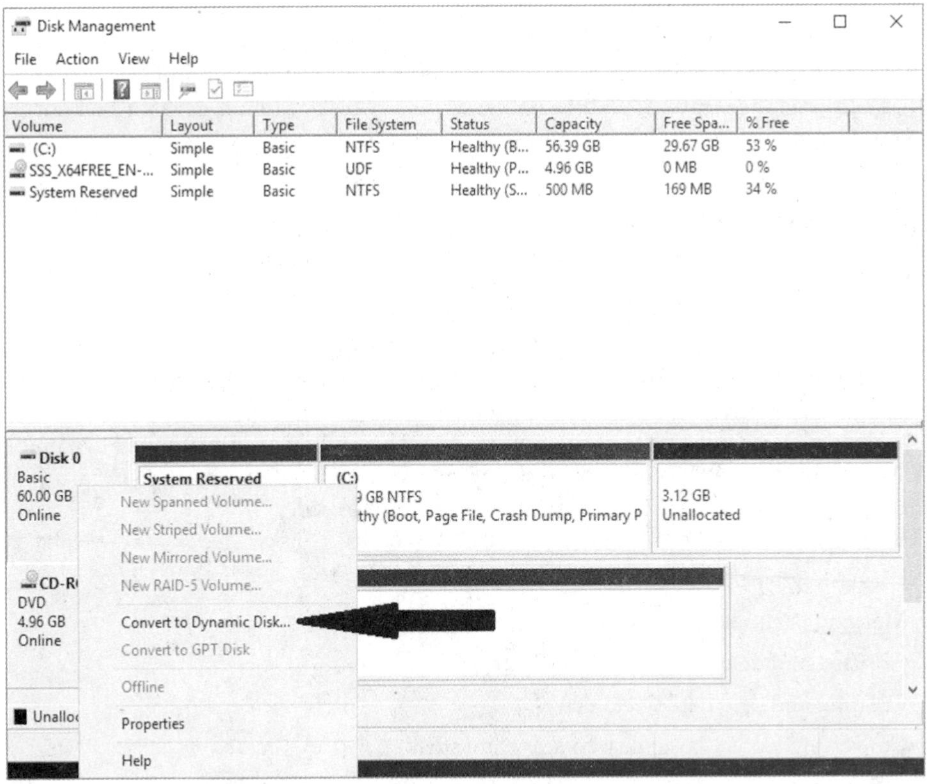

4. The Convert To Dynamic Disk dialog box appears. From here, select all the disks that you want to convert to dynamic disks. In this exercise, only one disk will be converted.

5. Click OK.

6. The Convert To Dynamic Disk dialog box changes to the Disks To Convert dialog box and shows the disk/disks that will be converted to dynamic disks.

7. Click Convert.

8. Disk Management will warn that if you convert the disk to dynamic, you will not be able to start the installed operating system from any volume on the disk (except the current boot volume). Click Yes.

9. Close Computer Management.

The converted disk will now show as Dynamic in Disk Management.

Managing Volumes

A *volume set* is created from volumes that span multiple drives by using the free space from those drives to construct what will appear to be a single drive. The following list includes the various types of volume sets and their definitions:

- *Simple volume* uses only one disk or a portion of a disk.

- *Spanned volume* is a simple volume that spans multiple disks, with a maximum of 32. Use a spanned volume if the volume needs are too great for a single disk.

- *Striped volume* stores data in stripes across two or more disks. A striped volume gives you fast access to data but is not fault tolerant, nor can it be extended or mirrored. If one disk in the striped set fails, the entire volume fails.

- *Mirrored volume* duplicates data across two disks. This type of volume is fault tolerant because if one drive fails, the data on the other disk is unaffected.

- *RAID-5 volume* stores data in stripes across three or more disks. This type of volume is fault tolerant because if a drive fails, the data can be re-created from the parity off the remaining disk drives. Operating system files and boot files cannot reside on the RAID-5 disks.

Exercise 3.9 illustrates the procedure for creating a volume set.

EXERCISE 3.9

Creating a Volume Set

1. Open Computer Management under Administrative Tools.

2. Select Disk Management.

3. Select and right-click a disk that has unallocated space. If there are no disk drives available for a particular volume set, that volume set will be grayed out as a selectable option. In this exercise, you'll choose a spanned volume set, but the process after the volume set selection is the same regardless of which kind you choose. The only thing that differs is the number of disk drives chosen.

4. The Welcome page of the New Spanned Volume Wizard appears and explains the type of volume set chosen. Click Next.

5. The Select Disks page appears. Select the disk that will be included with the volume set and click Add. Repeat this process until all of the desired disks have been added. Click Next.

6. The Assign Drive Letter Or Path page appears. From here you can select the desired drive letter for the volume, mount the volume in an empty NTFS folder, or choose not to assign a drive letter. The new volume is labeled as E. Click Next.

7. The Format Volume page appears. Choose to format the new volume. Click Next.

8. Click Finish.

9. If the disks have not been converted to dynamic, you will be asked to convert the disks. Click Yes.

The new volume will appear as a healthy spanned dynamic volume with the new available disk space of the new volume set.

Storage Spaces in Windows Server 2022

Windows Server 2022 includes a technology called *Storage Spaces*. Windows Server 2022 allows you to virtualize storage by grouping disks into storage pools. These storage pools can then be turned into virtual disks called *storage spaces*.

The Storage Spaces technology allows you to have a highly available, scalable, low-cost, and flexible solution for both physical and virtual installations. Storage Spaces allows you to set up this advantage on either a single server or in scalable multinode mode. So, before going any further, let's look at these two terms:

Storage Pools   *Storage pools* are a group of physical disks that allows you to delegate administration, expand disk sizes, and group disks together.

Storage Spaces   *Storage Spaces* allows you to take free space from storage pools and create virtual disks called storage spaces. Storage spaces give you the ability to have precise control, resiliency, and storage tiers.

Storage spaces and storage pools can be managed by an administrator through the use of the Windows Storage Management API, Server Manager, or Windows PowerShell.

One of the advantages of using the Storage Spaces technology is the ability to set up resiliency. There are three types of Storage Space resiliency: mirror, parity, and simple (no resiliency).

Fault tolerance (RAID) is discussed in detail in the "Redundant Array of Independent Disks" section.

Now that you understand what storage spaces and storage pools do, let's take a look at some of the other advantages of using these features in Windows Server 2022:

Availability   One advantage to the Storage Spaces technology is the ability to fully integrate the storage space with failover clustering. This advantage allows you to achieve service deployments that are continuously available. You have the ability to set up storage pools to be clustered across multiple nodes within a single cluster.

Tiered Storage   The Storage Spaces technology allows virtual disks to be created with a two-tier storage setup. For data that is used often, you have an SSD tier; for data that is not used often, you use an HDD tier. The Storage Spaces technology will automatically transfer data at a subfile level between the two different tiers based on how often the data is used. Because of tiered storage, performance is greatly increased for data that is used most often, and data that is not used often still gets the advantage of being stored on a low-cost storage option.

Delegation   One advantage of using storage pools is that you have the ability to control access by using access control lists (ACLs). What is nice about this advantage is that each storage pool can have its own unique access control lists. Storage pools are fully integrated with Active Directory Domain Services.

Redundant Array of Independent Disks

The ability to support drive sets and arrays using *Redundant Array of Independent Disks (RAID)* technology is built into Windows Server 2022. RAID can be used to enhance data performance, or it can be used to provide fault tolerance to maintain data integrity in case of a hard disk failure. Windows Server 2022 supports three types of RAID technologies:

RAID-0 (Disk Striping)   *Disk striping* is using two or more volumes on independent disks created as a single striped set. There can be a maximum of 32 disks. In a striped set, data is divided into blocks that are distributed sequentially across all the drives in the set. With RAID-0 disk striping, you get very fast read and write performance because multiple blocks of data can be accessed from multiple drives simultaneously. However, RAID-0 does not offer the ability to maintain data integrity during a single disk failure. In other words, RAID-0 is not fault tolerant; a single disk event will cause the entire striped set to be lost, and it will have to be re-created through some type of recovery process, such as a tape backup.

RAID-1 (Disk Mirroring)   *Disk mirroring* is two logical volumes on two separate identical disks created as a duplicate disk set. Data is written on two disks at the same time; that way, in the event of a disk failure, data integrity is maintained and available. Although this fault tolerance gives administrators data redundancy, it comes with a price because it diminishes the amount of available storage space by half. For example, if you want to create a 300 GB mirrored set, you would have to install two 300 GB hard drives into the server, thus doubling the cost for the same available space.

RAID-5 Volume (Disk Striping with Parity)   With a RAID-5 volume, you have the ability to use a minimum of three disks and a maximum of 32 disks. RAID-5 volumes allow data to be striped across all the disks with an additional block of error-correction called parity. *Parity* is used to reconstruct the data in the event of a disk failure. RAID-5 has slower write performance than the other RAID types because the OS must calculate the parity information for each stripe that is written, but the read performance is equivalent to a stripe set, RAID-0, because the parity information is not read. Like RAID-1, RAID-5 comes with additional cost considerations. For every RAID-5 set, roughly an entire hard disk is consumed for storing the parity information. For example, a minimum RAID-5 set requires three hard disks, and if those disks are 300 GB each, approximately 600 GB of disk space is available to the OS and 300 GB is consumed by parity information, which equates to 33.3 percent of the available space. Similarly, in a five-disk RAID-5 set of 300 GB disks, approximately 1,200 GB of disk space is available to the OS, which means that 20 percent of the total available space is consumed by the parity information. The words *roughly* and *approximately* are used when calculating disk space because a 300 GB disk will really be only about 279 GB of space. This is because vendors define a gigabyte as 1 billion bytes, but the OS defines it as 2^{30} (1,073,741,824) bytes. Also, remember that filesystems and volume managers have overhead as well.

Software RAID is a nice option for a small company, but hardware RAID is definitely a better option if the money is available.

Table 3.6 breaks down the various aspects of the supported RAID types in Window Server 2022.

TABLE 3.6   Supported RAID-level properties in Windows Server 2022

RAID level	RAID type	Fault tolerant	Advantages	Minimum number of disks	Maximum number of disks
0	Disk striping	No	Fast reads and writes	2	32
1	Disk mirroring	Yes	Data redundancy and faster writes than RAID-5	2	2
5	Disk striping with parity	Yes	Data redundancy with less overhead and faster reads than RAID-1	3	32

Creating RAID Sets

Now that you understand the concepts of RAID and how to use it, you can look at the creation of RAID sets in Windows Server 2022. The process of creating a RAID set is the same as the process for creating a simple or spanned volume set, except for the minimum disk requirements associated with each RAID type.

Creating a mirrored volume set is basically the same as creating a volume set except that you will select New Mirrored Volume. It is after the Select Disks page of the New Mirrored Volume Wizard appears that you'll begin to see the difference. Since a new mirrored volume is being created, the volume requires two disks.

During the disk selection process, if only one disk is selected, the Next button will be unavailable because the disk minimum has not been met. Refer to Figure 3.30 to view the Select Disks page of the New Mirrored Volume Wizard during the creation of a new mirrored volume and notice that the Next button is not available.

FIGURE 3.30   Select Disks page of the New Mirrored Volume Wizard

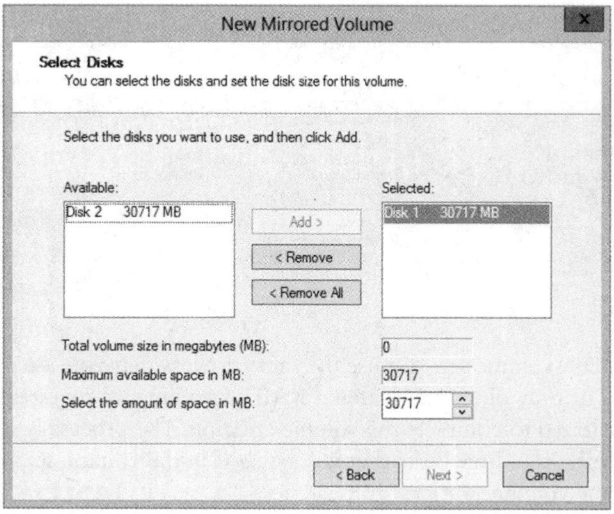

To complete the process, you must select a second disk by highlighting the appropriate disk and adding it to the volume set. Once the second disk has been added, the Next button is available to complete the mirrored volume set creation.

A drive letter will have to be assigned, and the volume will need to be formatted. The new mirrored volume set will appear in Disk Management. In Figure 3.31, notice that the capacity of the volume equals one disk even though two disks have been selected.

FIGURE 3.31 Newly created mirrored volume set

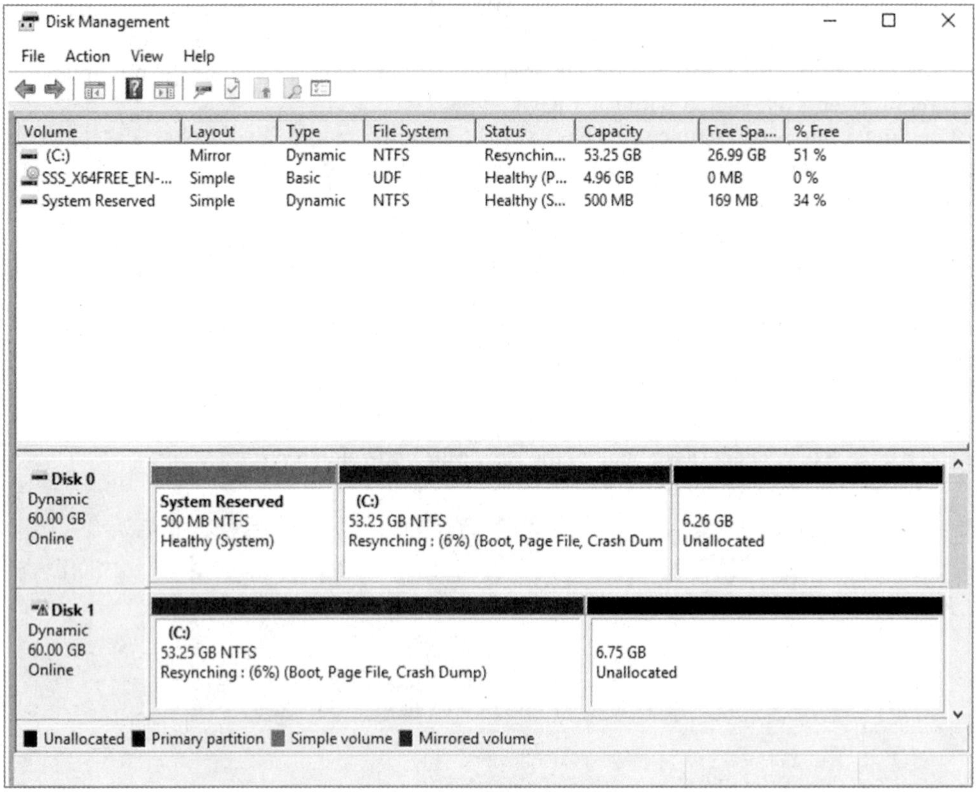

To create a RAID-5 volume set, you use the same process that you use to create a mirrored volume set. The only difference is that a RAID-5 volume set requires that a minimum of three disks be selected to complete the volume creation. The process is simple: select New RAID-5 Volume, select the three disks that will be used in the volume set, assign a drive letter, and format the volume.

Mount Points

With the ever-increasing demands of storage, mount points are used to surpass the limitation of 26 drive letters and to join two volumes into a folder on a separate physical disk drive. A *mount point* allows you to configure a volume to be accessed from a folder on another existing disk.

Through Disk Management, a mount point folder can be assigned to a drive instead of using a drive letter, and it can be used on basic or dynamic volumes that are formatted with NTFS. However, mount point folders can be created only on empty folders within a volume. Additionally, mount point folder paths cannot be modified; they can be removed only once they have been created. Exercise 3.10 shows the steps to create a mount point.

EXERCISE 3.10

Creating Mount Points

1. Right-click the Start button and select Disk Management.

2. Right-click the volume where the mount point folder will be assigned, and select Change Drive Letter And Paths.

3. Click Add.

4. Either type the path to an empty folder on an NTFS volume or click Browse to select or make a new folder for the mount point.

When you explore the drive, you'll see the new folder created. Notice that the icon indicates that it is a mount point.

Microsoft MPIO

Multipath I/O (MPIO) is associated with high availability because a computer will be able to use a solution with redundant physical paths connected to a storage device. Thus, if one path fails, an application will continue to run because it can access the data across the other path.

The MPIO software provides the functionality needed for the computer to take advantage of the redundant storage paths. MPIO solutions can also load-balance data traffic across both paths to the storage device, virtually eliminating bandwidth bottlenecks to the computer. What allows MPIO to provide this functionality is the new native *Microsoft Device Specific Module (Microsoft DSM)*. The Microsoft DSM is a driver that communicates with storage devices—iSCSI, Fibre Channel, or Serial-Attached SCSI (SAS)—and it provides the chosen load-balancing policies. Windows Server 2022 supports the following load-balancing policies:

Failover   In a failover configuration, there is no load balancing. There is a primary path that is established for all requests and subsequent standby paths. If the primary path fails, one of the standby paths will be used.

Failback   This is similar to failover in that it has primary and standby paths. However, with failback you designate a preferred path that will handle all process requests until it fails, after which the standby path will become active until the primary reestablishes a connection and automatically regains control.

Round-Robin   In a round-robin configuration, all available paths will be active and will be used to distribute I/O in a balanced round-robin fashion.

Round-Robin with a Subset of Paths   In this configuration, a specific set of paths will be designated as a primary set and another as standby paths. All I/O will use the primary set of paths in a round-robin fashion until all of the sets fail. Only at this time will the standby paths become active.

Dynamic Least Queue Depth   In a dynamic least queue depth configuration, I/O will route to the path with the least number of outstanding requests.

Weighted Path   In a weighted path configuration, paths are assigned a numbered weight. I/O requests will use the path with the least weight—the higher the number, the lower the priority.

Exercise 3.11 demonstrates the process of installing the Microsoft MPIO feature for Windows Server 2022.

EXERCISE 3.11

Installing Microsoft MPIO

1. Choose Server Manager by clicking the Server Manager icon on the Taskbar.

2. Click number 2, Add Roles And Features.

3. Choose role-based or feature-based installation and click Next.

4. Choose your server and click Next.

5. Click Next on the Roles screen.

6. On the Select Features screen, select the Multipath I/O check box (see Figure 3.32). Click Next.

FIGURE 3.32   Multipath I/O

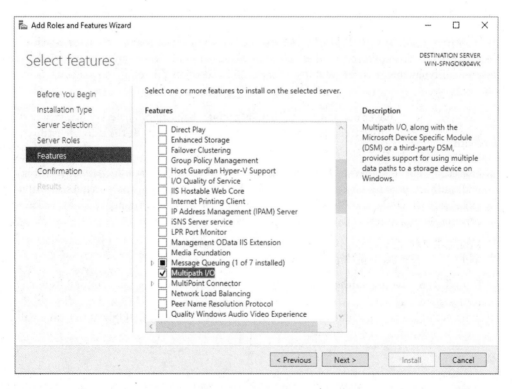

7.   On the Confirm Installation Selections page, verify that Multipath I/O is the feature that will be installed. Click Install.

8.   After the installation completes, the Installation Results page appears, stating that the server must be rebooted to finish the installation process.

9.   Click Close.

10. Restart the system.

Typically, most storage arrays work with the Microsoft DSM. However, some hardware vendors require DSM software that is specific to their products. Third-party DSM software is installed through the MPIO utility as follows:

1.   Open Administrative Tools ➢ MPIO.

2.   Select the DSM Install tab.

3.   Add the path of the INF file and click Install.

Configuring iSCSI Target

Internet Small Computer System Interface (iSCSI) is an interconnect protocol used to establish and manage a connection between a computer (initiator) and a storage device (target). It does this by using a connection through TCP port 3260, which allows it to be used over a LAN, a WAN, or the Internet. Each initiator is identified by its iSCSI Qualified Name (iQN), and it is used to establish its connection to an iSCSI target.

iSCSI was developed to allow block-level access to a storage device over a network. This is different from using a network attached storage (NAS) device that connects through the use of Common Internet Filesystem (CIFS) or Network Filesystem (NFS).

Block-level access is important to many applications that require direct access to storage. Microsoft Exchange and Microsoft SQL are examples of applications that require direct access to storage.

By being able to leverage the existing network infrastructure, iSCSI was also developed as an alternative to Fibre Channel storage by alleviating the additional hardware costs associated with a Fibre Channel storage solution.

iSCSI also has another advantage over Fibre Channel in that it can provide security for the storage devices. iSCSI can use Challenge Handshake Authentication Protocol (CHAP or MS-CHAP) for authentication and Internet Protocol Security (IPsec) for encryption. Windows Server 2022 is able to connect an iSCSI storage device out of the box with no additional software or hardware needing to be installed. This is because the Microsoft iSCSI initiator is built into the operating system.

Windows Server 2022 supports two different ways to initiate an iSCSI session:

-   Through the native Microsoft iSCSI software initiator that resides on Windows Server 2022

-   Using a hardware iSCSI host bus adapter (HBA) that is installed in the computer

Both the Microsoft iSCSI software initiator and iSCSI HBA present an iSCSI quali-fied name that identifies the host initiator. When the Microsoft iSCSI software initiator is used, the CPU utilization may be as much as 30 percent higher than on a computer with a hardware iSCSI HBA. This is because all of the iSCSI process requests are handled within the operating system. Using a hardware iSCSI HBA, process requests can be offloaded to the adapter, thus freeing the CPU overhead associated with the Microsoft iSCSI software initi-ator. However, iSCSI HBAs can be expensive, whereas the Microsoft iSCSI software initiator is free.

It is worthwhile to install the Microsoft iSCSI software initiator and perform load test-ing to see how much overhead the computer will have prior to purchasing an iSCSI HBA or HBAs, depending on the redundancy level. Exercise 3.12 explains how to install and con-figure an iSCSI connection.

EXERCISE 3.12

Configuring iSCSI Storage Connection

1. Right-click the Start button ➢ Control Panel ➢ Administrative Tools ➢ iSCSI Initiator.

2. If a dialog box appears, click Yes to start the service.

3. Click the Discovery tab.

4. In the Target Portals portion of the page, click Discover Portal.

5. Enter the IP address of the target portal and click OK.

6. The IP address of the target portal appears in the Target Portals box. Click OK.

Internet Storage Name Service

Internet Storage Name Service (iSNS) allows for central registration of an iSCSI environment because it automatically discovers available targets on the network. The purpose of iSNS is to help find available targets on a large iSCSI network.

The Microsoft iSCSI initiator includes an iSNS client that is used to register with the iSNS. The iSNS feature maintains a database of clients that it has registered either through DCHP discovery or through manual registration. iSNS DHCP is available after the instal-lation of the service, and it is used to allow iSNS clients to discover the location of the iSNS. However, if iSNS DHCP is not configured, iSNS clients must be registered manually with the iscsicli command.

To execute the command, launch a command prompt on a computer hosting the Microsoft iSCSI and type **iscsicli addisnsserver *server_name***, where ***server_name*** is the name of the computer hosting iSNS. Exercise 3.13 walks you through the steps required to install the iSNS feature on Windows Server 2022, and then it explains the differ-ent tabs in iSNS.

EXERCISE 3.13

Installing the iSNS Feature

1. Choose Server Manager by clicking the Server Manager icon on the Taskbar.

2. Click number 2 ➢ Add Roles And Features.

3. Choose role-based or featured-based installation and click Next.

4. Select your server and click Next.

5. Click Next on the Roles screen.

6. On the Select Features screen, choose the iSNS Server Service check box. Click Next.

7. On the Confirmation screen, click the Install button.

8. Click the Close button. Close Server Manager and reboot.

9. Log in and open the iSNS server under Administrative Tools.

10. Click the General tab. This tab displays the list of registered initiators and targets. In addition to their iSCSI qualified name, it lists storage node type (Target or Initiator), alias string, and entity identifier (the fully qualified domain name [FQDN] of the machine hosting the iSNS client).

11. Click the Discovery Domains tab (see Figure 3.33). The purpose of Discovery Domains is to provide a way to separate and group nodes. This is similar to zoning in Fibre Channel. The following options are available on the Discovery Domains tab:

    - *Create* is used to create a new discovery domain.

    - *Refresh* is used to repopulate the Discovery Domain drop-down list.

    - *Delete* is used to delete the currently selected discovery domain.

    - *Add* is used to add nodes that are already registered in iSNS to the currently selected discovery domain.

    - *Add New* is used to add nodes by entering the iSCSI Qualified Name (iQN) of the node. These nodes do not have to be currently registered.

    - *Remove Used* is used to remove selected nodes from the discovery domain.

EXERCISE 3.13 *(continued)*

FIGURE 3.33 Discovery Domains tab

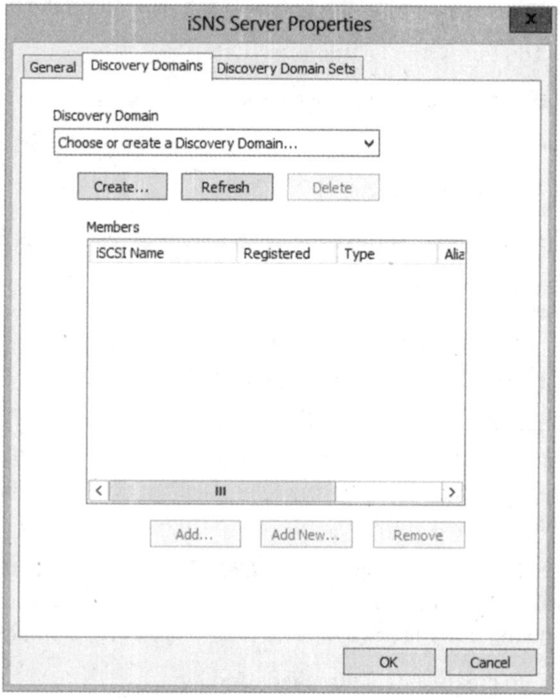

12. Click the Discovery Domain Sets tab. The purpose of discovery domain sets is to separate further discovery domains. Discovery domains can be enabled or disabled, giving you the ability to restrict further the visibility of all initiators and targets. The options on the Discovery Domains tab are as follows:
    - The *Enable* check box is used to indicate the status of the discovery domain sets and to turn them off and on.
    - *Create* is used to create new discovery domain sets.
    - *Refresh* is used to repopulate the Discovery Domain Sets drop-down list.
    - *Delete* is used to delete the currently selected discovery domain set.
    - *Add* is used to add discovery domains to the currently selected discovery domain set.
    - *Remove* is used to remove selected nodes from the discovery domain sets.
13. Close the iSNS server.

Implement Thin Provisioning and Trim

Thin provisioning and trim can be useful features that allow organizations to get the most out of their storage arrays. These solutions apply directly to a virtualized environment using virtual disks that are thin provisioned.

Thin provisioning is a way of providing what is known as just-in-time allocations. Blocks of data are written to disk only as they are used instead of zeroing out all the blocks of data that have been allocated to the virtual disk configuration. Thin provisioning is tricky to manage properly because you could easily find yourself in a position where you have an overprovisioned environment because of overallocation.

For example, say you have 100 VMs that are all provisioned with 40 GB thin-provisioned virtual disks. Each VM is currently utilizing only 20 GB of the total 40 GB that has been allocated. The problem is that you have only 2 TB worth of storage. Without realizing it, you've overprovisioned your environment by 200 percent because of thin provisioning.

This is where trim comes in to help us manage thin provisioning. *Trim* automatically reclaims free space that is not being used. In addition to trim, Windows Server 2022 provides standardized notifications that will alert administrators when certain storage thresholds are crossed.

Fibre Channel

Fibre Channel storage devices are similar to iSCSI storage devices in that they both allow block-level access to their data sets and can provide MPIO policies with the proper hardware configurations. However, Fibre Channel requires a Fibre Channel host bus adapter (HBA), fiber-optic cables, and Fibre Channel switches to connect to a storage device.

A *World Wide Name (WWN)* from the Fibre Channel HBA is used from the host and device so that they can communicate directly with each other, similar to using a NIC's MAC address. In other words, a logical unit number (LUN) is presented from a Fibre Channel storage device to the WWN of the host's HBA. Fibre Channel has been the preferred method of storage because of the available connection bandwidth between the storage and the host.

Fibre Channel devices support 1 Gb/s, 2 Gb/s, and 4 Gb/s connections, and they soon will support 8 Gb/s connections, but now that 10 Gb/s Ethernet networks are becoming more prevalent in many datacenters, iSCSI can be a suitable alternative. It is important to consider that 10 Gb/s network switches can be more expensive than comparable Fibre Channel switches.

N-Port Identification Virtualization (NPIV) is a Fibre Channel facility allowing multiple N-Port IDs to share a single physical N-Port. This allows multiple Fibre Channel initiators to occupy a single physical port. By using a single port, this eases hardware requirements in storage area network (SAN) design.

Network-Attached Storage

The concept of a *network-attached storage (NAS)* solution is that it is a low-cost device for storing data and serving files through the use of an Ethernet LAN connection. A NAS device accesses data at the file level via a communication protocol such as NFS, CIFS, or even HTTP, which is different from iSCSI or FC Fibre Channel storage devices that access the data at the block level. NAS devices are best used in file-storing applications, and they do not require a storage expert to install and maintain the device. In most cases, the only setup that is required is an IP address and an Ethernet connection.

Virtual Disk Service

Virtual Disk Service (VDS) was created to ease the administrative efforts involved in managing all of the various types of storage devices. Many storage hardware providers used their own applications for installation and management, and this made administering all of these various devices very cumbersome.

VDS is a set of application programming interfaces (APIs) that provides a centralized interface for managing all the various storage devices. The native VDS API enables the management of disks and volumes at an OS level, and hardware vendor-supplied APIs manage the storage devices at a RAID level. These are known as software and hardware providers.

A *software provider* is host based, and it interacts with Plug and Play Manager because each disk is discovered and operates on volumes, disks, and disk partitions. VDS includes two software providers: basic and dynamic. The basic software provider manages basic disks with no fault tolerance, whereas the dynamic software providers manage dynamic disks with fault management. A hardware provider translates the VDS APIs into instructions specific to the storage hardware. This is how storage management applications are able to communicate with the storage hardware to create LUNs or Fibre Channel HBAs to view the WWN. The following are Windows Server 2022 storage management applications that use VDS:

- The *Disk Management snap-in* is an application that allows you to configure and manage the disk drives on the host computer. You have already seen this application in use when you initialized disks and created volume sets.

- DiskPart is a command-line utility that configures and manages disks, volumes, and partitions on the host computer. It can also be used to script many of the storage management commands. DiskPart is a robust tool that you should study on your own because it is beyond the scope of this book. Figure 3.34 shows the various commands and their function in the DiskPart utility.

- DiskRAID is also a scriptable command-line utility that configures and manages hardware RAID storage systems. However, at least one VDS hardware provider must be installed for DiskRAID to be functional. DiskRAID is another useful utility that you should study on your own because it's beyond the scope of this book.

FIGURE 3.34 DiskPart commands

```
                    Administrator: Command Prompt - diskpart         _  □  X

DISKPART> help

Microsoft DiskPart

ACTIVE        - Mark the selected partition as active.
ADD           - Add a mirror to a simple volume.
ASSIGN        - Assign a drive letter or mount point to the selected volume.
ATTRIBUTES    - Manipulate volume or disk attributes.
ATTACH        - Attaches a virtual disk file.
AUTOMOUNT     - Enable and disable automatic mounting of basic volumes.
BREAK         - Break a mirror set.
CLEAN         - Clear the configuration information, or all information, off the
                disk.
COMPACT       - Attempts to reduce the physical size of the file.
CONVERT       - Convert between different disk formats.
CREATE        - Create a volume, partition or virtual disk.
DELETE        - Delete an object.
DETAIL        - Provide details about an object.
DETACH        - Detaches a virtual disk file.
EXIT          - Exit DiskPart.
EXTEND        - Extend a volume.
EXPAND        - Expands the maximum size available on a virtual disk.
FILESYSTEMS   - Display current and supported file systems on the volume.
FORMAT        - Format the volume or partition.
GPT           - Assign attributes to the selected GPT partition.
HELP          - Display a list of commands.
IMPORT        - Import a disk group.
INACTIVE      - Mark the selected partition as inactive.
LIST          - Display a list of objects.
MERGE         - Merges a child disk with its parents.
ONLINE        - Online an object that is currently marked as offline.
OFFLINE       - Offline an object that is currently marked as online.
RECOVER       - Refreshes the state of all disks in the selected pack.
                Attempts recovery on disks in the invalid pack, and
                resynchronizes mirrored volumes and RAID5 volumes
                that have stale plex or parity data.
REM           - Does nothing. This is used to comment scripts.
REMOVE        - Remove a drive letter or mount point assignment.
REPAIR        - Repair a RAID-5 volume with a failed member.
RESCAN        - Rescan the computer looking for disks and volumes.
RETAIN        - Place a retained partition under a simple volume.
SAN           - Display or set the SAN policy for the currently booted OS.
SELECT        - Shift the focus to an object.
SETID         - Change the partition type.
SHRINK        - Reduce the size of the selected volume.
UNIQUEID      - Displays or sets the GUID partition table (GPT) identifier or
                master boot record (MBR) signature of a disk.

DISKPART>
```

Understanding Data Center Bridging

I think the easiest way to understanding Data Center Bridging (DCB) is to understand NIC bridging. Many of us who have used laptops have used both wireless and wired networks at the same time. This involves bridging network adapter cards to work as one. Well, Data Center Bridging is the same thing but just done on a larger scale.

The Institute of Electrical and Electronic Engineers (IEEE) created a suite of standards called Data Center Bridging. DCB allows the same Ethernet infrastructure to work throughout the datacenter. This means that all the network servers, clusters, and datacenters will share the same Ethernet infrastructure. DCB works through the use of hardware-based bandwidth allocation. The hardware controls the flow of data through DCB.

DCB is nice because when you set up the hardware-based flow control, you can determine which type of traffic gets a higher priority to the allocated bandwidth. DCB can be very useful for data that bypasses the operating system and accesses the network adapters directly (as virtualization can). DCB can work with different types of network adapters, including Remote Direct Memory Access (RDMA) over Converged Ethernet, Internet Small Computer System Interface (iSCSI), or Fibre Channel over Ethernet (FCoE).

The reason that the IEEE has developed the DCB standard is because many third-party and hardware manufacturers do not work together well. By having an industry-standard hardware-based flow control protocol, many IT datacenters can use DCB to make different vendors work together. Also, Windows Server 2022 makes it very easy to deploy and manage DCB. There are a couple of requirements when deploying DCB through Windows Server 2022:

- The Ethernet adapters installed into the Windows Server 2022 systems must be DCB compatible.

- The hardware switches that are deployed to your infrastructure must also be DCB compatible.

DCB can be installed onto a Windows Server two ways; through Server Manager or through PowerShell. Here are the steps for both ways.

Installing DCB Using PowerShell

To install and use DCB through PowerShell, complete the following steps:

1. Click the Start button, then right-click Windows PowerShell, and select More ➤ Run As Administrator.

2. In the Windows PowerShell console, enter **Install-WindowsFeature data-center-bridging** and press Enter.

Installing DCB Using Server Manager

To install and use DCB through Server Manager, follow these steps:

1. On the Windows Server 2022 system, open Server Manager.

2. Click the Add Roles And Features link.

3. At the Before You Begin screen, click Next.

4. At the Select Installation Type screen, choose role-based or feature-based installation and then click Next.

5. On the Select Destination Server screen, make sure the server that you want to install DCB on is selected and then click Next.

6. On the Select Server Roles screen, click Next.

7. On the Select Features screen, select the Data Center Bridging option. If a dialog box appears asking to install additional features, click the Add Feature button. Then click Next.

8. At the Confirmation screen, verify that everything is okay and then click Install.

Using PowerShell

Table 3.7 defines a few of the cmdlets available in Windows PowerShell. Again, there are hundreds of cmdlets, and the ones listed in the table are just some of the more common ones. You can retrieve a list of all the cmdlets starting here:

http://technet.microsoft.com/en-us/scriptcenter/dd772285.aspx

TABLE 3.7   Windows PowerShell cmdlets

Cmdlet	Definition
Add-VMHardDiskDrive	Allows you to add a VHD file to a virtual machine.
Block-SmbShareAccess	This cmdlet allows you to add a deny access control entry (ACE) to the security descriptor for the Server Message Block (SMB) share.
Clear-History	Deletes entries from the command history.
Close-SmbOpenFile	This allows you to forcibly close an open file by one of the clients of the Server Message Block (SMB) server.
Close-SmbSession	This allows you to forcibly kill a Server Message Block (SMB) session.
Format-table	Shows the results in a table format.
Get-Date	Shows the date and time.
Get-event	Shows an event in the event queue.
Get-Help Install-WindowsFeature	Shows the syntax and accepted parameters for the Install-WindowsFeature cmdlet.
Get-NetIPAddress	Shows information about IP address configuration.
Get-NfsClientConfiguration	Shows configuration settings for an NFS client.
Get-NfsMappedIdentity	Shows an NFS mapped identity.
Get-NfsMappingStore	Shows the configuration settings for the identity mapping store.
Get-NfsNetgroup	Shows the netgroup.
Get-NfsSession	Shows the information about client systems that are currently connected to a share on an NFS server.
Get-NfsShare	Shows an NFS share on the NFS server.
Get-NfsSharePermission	Shows you the NFS shares permissions that are on an NFS server.
Get-SmbOpenFile	Allows you to see basic information about the files that are open on the Server Message Block (SMB) server.

TABLE 3.7 Windows PowerShell cmdlets *(continued)*

Cmdlet	Definition
Get-SmbShare	Allows you to see the Server Message Block (SMB) shares on the computer.
Get-WindowsFeature	Shows a list of available and installed roles and features on the local server.
Get-WindowsFeature –ServerName	Shows a list of available and installed roles and features on a remote server.
Import-Module	Adds modules to the current session.
Invoke-command	Runs commands on local or remote computers.
New-NfsShare	Allows you to create an NFS file share.
New-event	Creates a new event.
New-SmbShare	Allows you to create a new SMB share.
New-VHD	Allows you to create a new VHD file.
Out-file	Sends the job results to a file.
Receive-job	Gets the results of a Windows PowerShell background job.
Remove-job	Deletes a Windows PowerShell background job.
Remove-NfsShare	Allows you to delete an NFS file share.
Remove-SmbShare	Allows you to delete an SMB share.
Set-Date	Sets the system time and date on a computer.
Set-NetIPAddress	Modifies IP address configuration properties of an existing IP address.
Set-NetIPv4Protocol	Modifies information about the IPv4 protocol configuration.
Set-SmbShare	Allows you to modify the properties of the Server Message Block (SMB) share.
Set-VM	Allows you to configure some virtual machine settings like configuring the locations for snapshot storage and smart paging.

Cmdlet	Definition
Set-VMDvdDrive	Allows you to set a virtual machine to use a DVD or ISO file.
Set-VMMemory	Allows you to set the RAM for a virtual machine.
Start-job	Starts a Windows PowerShell background job.
Stop-job	Stops a Windows PowerShell background job.
Trace-command	Configures and starts a trace of a command on a machine.
Uninstall-WindowsFeature	Removes a role or feature.

Summary

In this chapter, you learned how to install Windows Server 2022 Datacenter (Desktop Experience), and you installed the Windows Server 2022 Server Core. Remember, Server Core is a slimmed-down version of Windows Server. With no GUI desktop available, it's a safer alternative to a normal Windows installation. As discussed, a nice advantage of Windows Server 2022 is that you can change from Server Core to the GUI version and back again.

I talked about installing updates and how to install and configure WSUS. I also discussed Features on Demand, which allows you to remove roles and features from the operating system and remove the associated files completely from the hard drive, thus saving disk space.

Finally, I discussed how configuring file and storage solutions can be highly effective in your organization. You now have a better understanding of how Windows Server 2022 can provide you with extended functionality for effectively controlling corporate data.

Exam Essentials

Understand Windows Server 2022 Desktop Experience vs. Server Core. Understand the difference between the Windows Server 2022 Desktop Experience version and the Windows Server 2022 Server Core version.

Understand Features on Demand. Understand the feature called Features on Demand. Microsoft loves to ask exam questions about its new features, and this will be no exception. Understand how features and roles stay on the system until you physically remove them from the hard drive.

Know how to configure NTFS security.   One of the major advantages of using NTFS over FAT32 is access to additional security features. NTFS allows you to put security at the file and folder layers. NTFS security is in effect whether the user is remote or local to the computer with the data.

Understand Windows PowerShell.   Understanding Windows PowerShell is not only important for the exam, but it will also allow you to configure Server Core more efficiently. Windows PowerShell is a command-line utility that allows you to run single cmdlets as well as run complex tasks to exploit the full power from PowerShell.

Review Questions

1. You are the administrator for the ABC Company. You are looking to install Windows Server 2022, and you need to decide which version to install. You want to install a version of Windows that is just for logon authentication and nothing else. You want the most secure option and cost is not an issue. What should you install?

   A. Windows Server 2022 Datacenter (Desktop Experience)

   B. Windows Server 2022 Datacenter Server Core

   C. Windows Server 2022 Standard (Desktop Experience)

   D. Windows Server 2022 Web Server Core

2. You are the IT manager for a large company. You have a file server named FileServer1. FileServer1 runs Windows Server 2022 and is configured with the following volumes shown:

   Volume C NTFS

   Volume D NTFS

   Volume E ReFS

   On which volumes can you use file encryption and disk quotas?

   A. Volume C Only

   B. Volume D Only

   C. Volume E Only

   D. Volume C and D

   E. Volume C, D, and E

3. You are the administrator for your company, and you are looking at upgrading your Windows Server 2012 R2 Standard with GUI to Windows Server 2022. Which version of Windows Server 2022 does Microsoft recommend you use to keep the GUI interface?

   A. Windows Server 2022 Datacenter (Desktop Experience)

   B. Windows Server 2022 Standard (Desktop Experience)

   C. Windows Server 2022 Datacenter

   D. Windows Server 2022 Standard

4. You are looking at upgrading your Windows Server 2012 R2 Datacenter with GUI machine to Windows Server 2022. Your organization is considering virtualizing its entire server room, which has 25 servers. To which version of Windows Server 2022 would you upgrade while keeping the GUI interface?

   A. Windows Server 2022 Datacenter (Desktop Experience)

   B. Windows Server 2022 Standard (Desktop Experience)

   C. Windows Server 2022 Datacenter

   D. Windows Server 2022 Standard

5. You have been hired to help a small company set up its first Windows network. It has had the same 13 users for the entire two years it has been open, and the company has no plans to expand. What version of Windows Server 2022 would you recommend?

   A. Windows Server 2022 Datacenter (Desktop Experience)

   B. Windows Server 2022 Standard (Desktop Experience)

   C. Windows Server 2022 Datacenter

   D. Windows Server 2022 Essentials

6. You have been hired to help a small company set up its Windows network. It has 20 users, and it has no plans to expand. What version of Windows Server 2022 would you recommend?

   A. Windows Server 2022 Datacenter

   B. Windows Server 2022 Standard

   C. Windows Server 2022 Essentials

   D. Windows Server 2022 Datacenter (Desktop Experience)

7. Which of the following are benefits of using Windows Server 2022 Server Core? (Choose all that apply.)

   A. Reduced management

   B. Minimal maintenance

   C. Smaller footprint

   D. Tighter security

8. You are a server administrator, and you are trying to save hard drive space on your Windows Server 2022 Datacenter machine. Which feature can help you save hard disk space?

   A. `HDSaver.exe`

   B. Features on Demand

   C. ADDS

   D. WinRM

9. Which version of Windows Server 2022 would you install if you want reduced management, minimal installation files, and tighter security? (Choose all that apply.)

   A. Windows Server 2022 Datacenter (Desktop Experience)

   B. Windows Server 2022 Standard (Desktop Experience)

   C. Windows Server 2022 Datacenter

   D. Windows Server 2022 Standard

10. You are working on a Windows Server 2022 Datacenter Server system. You need to view which roles and services are installed on the machine. Which PowerShell cmdlet can you use to see this?

    A. `Get-event`

    B. `New-event`

    C. `Trace-command`

    D. `Get-WindowsFeature`

11. You are the administrator for StormWind Studios. You are looking to install Windows Server 2022 and you need to decide which version to install. You need to install a version of Windows into a remote location that does not have a server room. So security is an issue. You want the most secure option and cost is not an issue. What should you install?

    A. Windows Server 2022 Datacenter (Desktop Experience)

    B. Windows Server 2022 Datacenter

    C. Windows Server 2022 Standard (Desktop Experience)

    D. Windows Server 2022 Essentials

12. What is the default TCP port for iSCSI?

    A. 3260

    B. 1433

    C. 21

    D. 3389

13. A system administrator is trying to determine which filesystem to use for a server that will become a Windows Server 2022 file server and domain controller. The company has the following requirements:

    ▪ The filesystem must allow for file-level security from within Windows 2022 Server.

    ▪ The filesystem must make efficient use of space on large partitions.

    ▪ The domain controller SYSVOL must be stored on the partition.

    Which of the following filesystems meets these requirements?

    A. FAT

    B. FAT32

    C. HPFS

    D. NTFS

14. For security reasons, you have decided that you must convert the system partition on your removable drive from the FAT32 filesystem to NTFS. Which of the following steps must you take in order to convert the filesystem? (Choose two.)

    A. Run the command CONVERT /FS:NTFS from the command prompt.

    B. Rerun Windows Server 2016 Setup, and choose to convert the partition to NTFS during the reinstallation.

    C. Boot Windows Server 2016 Setup from the installation CD-ROM, and choose Rebuild Filesystem.

    D. Reboot the computer.

15. Your company has decided to implement a Windows 2022 server. The company IT manager before you always used FAT32 as the system partition. Your company wants to know whether it should move to NTFS. Which of the following are some advantages of NTFS? (Choose all that apply.)

  A. Security

  B. Quotas

  C. Compression

  D. Encryption

16. You are the administrator of your network, which consists of two Windows Server 2022 systems. One of the servers is a domain controller, and the other server is a file server for data storage. The hard drive of the file server is starting to fill up. You do not have the ability to install another hard drive, so you decide to limit the amount of space everyone gets on the hard drive. What do you need to implement to solve your problem?

  A. Disk spacing

  B. Disk quotas

  C. Disk hardening

  D. Disk limitations

17. You are working on a Windows Server 2022 Datacenter Server system. You need to view the roles and services installed on the machine. Which PowerShell cmdlet can you use to see this?

  A. `Get-event`

  B. `New-event`

  C. `Trace-command`

  D. `Get-WindowsFeature`

18. What command would be used to register an iSCSI initiator manually to an iSNS server?

  A. `iscsicli refreshisnsserver server_name`

  B. `iscsicli listisnsservers server_name`

  C. `iscsicli removeisnsserver server_name`

  D. `iscsicli addisnsserver server_name`

19. You are an IT administrator who manages an environment that runs multiple Windows Server 2022 servers from multiple site locations across the United States. Your Windows Server 2022 machines use iSCSI storage. Other administrators report it is difficult to locate available iSCSI resources on the network. You need to make sure that other administrators can easily access iSCSI resources using a centralized repository. What feature should you deploy?

  A. The iSCSI Target Storage Provider feature

  B. The Windows Standards-Based Storage Management feature

  C. The iSCSI Target Server role feature

  D. The iSNS Server service feature

20. You are the IT manager for a large company. You have a file server named FileServer1. FileServer1 runs Windows Server 2022 and is configured with the following volumes shown:

Volume C NTFS

Volume D NTFS

Volume E ReFS

On which volumes can you use BitLocker?

- **A.** Volume C only
- **B.** Volume D only
- **C.** Volume E only
- **D.** Volumes C and D
- **E.** Volumes C, D, and E

Understanding IP

**THE FOLLOWING AZ-800 EXAM
OBJECTIVES ARE COVERED
IN THIS CHAPTER:**

✓ Manage IP addressing in on-premises and hybrid scenarios

✓ Resolve IP address issues in hybrid environments

In this chapter, I will discuss the most important protocol used in a Microsoft Windows Server 2022 network: *Transmission Control Protocol/Internet Protocol (TCP/IP)*.

TCP/IP is actually two protocols bundled together: Transmission Control Protocol (TCP) and the Internet Protocol (IP). TCP/IP is a suite of protocols developed by the U.S. Department of Defense's Advanced Research Projects Agency in 1969.

This chapter is divided into two main topics. First, I'll talk about TCP/IP version 4 (IPv4), and then I'll discuss TCP/IP version 6 (IPv6). IPv4 is still used in Windows Server 2022, and it was the primary version of TCP/IP in all previous versions of Windows. However, IPv6 is the most recent version of TCP/IP. IPv6 has been out for many years, and it has become more popular with every new release of Windows.

On the AZ-800 and AZ-801 exams, you will encounter many topics that require that you know and understand IP and how it works. Network services like DNS, DHCP, and Active Directory sites are just a few topics that require detailed knowledge of IP and how it works. You can't configure these services properly unless you understand IP.

Plus, as you continue to take Microsoft exams after AZ-800 and AZ-801, you will need to know how to properly understand and configure IP for those exams. IP is the protocol that allows us all to communicate over our on-site network and the Internet.

Understanding TCP/IP

The easiest way to understand how IP works is to think about telephone numbers. IP addresses are just telephone numbers assigned to a computer. When one computer wants to talk to another computer, you can connect to it by using its telephone number (IP address).

I mentioned that TCP/IP is actually two protocols bundled together: TCP and IP. These protocols sit on a four-layer TCP/IP model.

Details of the TCP/IP Model

The four layers of the TCP/IP model are as follows (see Figure 4.1):

Application Layer The *Application layer* is where the applications that use the protocol stack reside. These applications include File Transfer Protocol (FTP), Trivial File Transfer Protocol (TFTP), Simple Mail Transfer Protocol (SMTP), and Hypertext Transfer Protocol (HTTP).

Transport Layer   The *Transport layer* is where the two Transport layer protocols reside. These are TCP and the User Datagram Protocol (UDP). TCP is a connection-oriented protocol, and delivery is guaranteed. UDP is a connectionless protocol. This means that UDP does its best job to deliver the message, but there is no guarantee.

Internet Layer   The *Internet layer* is where IP resides. *IP* is a connectionless protocol that relies on the upper layer (Transport layer) for guaranteeing delivery. *Address Resolution Protocol (ARP)* also resides on this layer. ARP turns an IP address into a Media Access Control (MAC) address. All upper and lower layers travel through the IP protocol.

Link Layer   The data link protocols like Ethernet and Token Ring reside in the *Link layer*. This layer is also referred to as the *Network Access layer*.

FIGURE 4.1   TCP/IP model

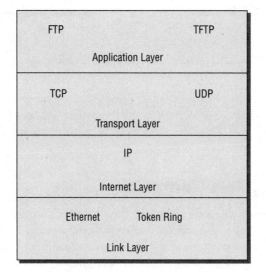

How TCP/IP Layers Communicate

When an application like FTP is called upon, the application moves down the layers and TCP is retrieved. TCP then connects itself to the IP protocol and gets released onto the network through the Link layer (see Figure 4.2). This is a connection-oriented protocol because TCP is the protocol that guarantees delivery.

FIGURE 4.2 TCP/IP process

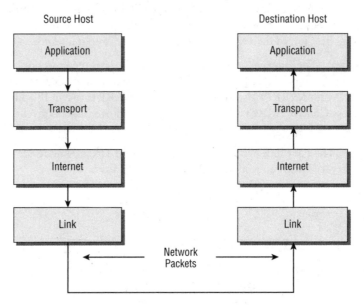

When an application like TFTP gets called, the application moves down the layers and UDP is retrieved. UDP then connects itself to the IP protocol and gets released onto the network through the Link layer. This is a connectionless protocol because UDP does not have guaranteed delivery.

Understanding Port Numbers

TCP and UDP rely on port numbers assigned by the *Internet Assigned Numbers Authority (IANA)* to forward packets to the appropriate application process. Port numbers are 16-bit integers that are part of a message header. They identify the application software process with which the packet should be associated. For example, let's say that a client has a copy of Internet Explorer and a copy of Mail open at the same time. Both applications are sending TCP requests across the Internet to retrieve web pages and email, respectively. How does the computer know which return packets to forward to Internet Explorer and which packets to forward to Mail?

When making a connection, the client chooses a source port for the communication that is usually in the range 1024–65535 (or sometimes in the range 1–65535). This source port then communicates with a destination port on the server side. Every packet destined for unsecure Internet traffic has a source port number of 80 in the header, and every packet destined for Mail has a source port number of 110 in the header.

Table 4.1 describes the most common port numbers (you might need to know these for the exam). You can visit www.iana.org to get the most current and complete list of port numbers. It's good to become familiar with specific port numbers because it's a benefit to be able to determine from memory the ports that, for example, allow or block specific protocols in a firewall. Allowing only port 80, for instance, does not ensure that all web traffic will be allowed. You must also allow port 443 for certain secure web traffic.

> **NOTE**   Simply because a port is "well known" doesn't mean that a given service must run on it. It's technically valid to run any service on any port, but doing so is usually a bad idea. For example, if you chose to run your web server on TCP port 25, clients would need to type www.example.com:25 to reach your website from most browsers.

TABLE 4.1   Common port numbers

Port number	Description
20	FTP data
21	FTP control
22	Secure Shell (SSH)
23	Telnet
25	Simple Mail Transfer Protocol (SMTP)
53	Domain Name System (DNS)
80	Hypertext Transfer Protocol (HTTP), Web
88	Kerberos Network Authentication
110	Post Office Protocol v3 (POP3)
443	Secure HTTP (HTTPS)
464	Kerberos Changes (for example, setting a password)
902	VMware ESXi

Understanding IP Addressing

Understanding IP addressing is critical to understanding how IP works. An IP address is a numeric identifier assigned to each device on an IP network. This type of address is a logical software address that designates the device's location on the network. It isn't the physical hardware address hard-coded in the device's network interface card.

In this section, you will see how IP addresses are used to identify uniquely every machine on the network (MAC address).

The Hierarchical IP Addressing Scheme

An IP address consists of 32 bits of information. These bits are divided into four sections (sometimes called *octets* or *quads*) containing 1 byte (8 bits) each. There are three common methods for specifying an IP address:

- Dotted decimal, as in 130.57.30.56
- Binary, as in 10000010.00111001.00011110.00111000
- Hexadecimal, as in 82 39 1E 38

All of these examples represent the same IP address.

The 32-bit IP address is a structured, or hierarchical, address as opposed to a flat, or nonhierarchical, address. Although IP could have used either *flat addressing* or *hierarchical addressing*, its designers elected to use the latter for a very good reason, as you will now see.

IP Address Structure

IP addressing works the same way. Instead of the entire 32 bits being treated as a unique identifier, one part of the IP address is designated as the network address (or network ID) and the other part as a node address (or host ID), giving it a layered, hierarchical structure. Together, the IP address, the network address, and the node address uniquely identify a device within an IP network.

The network address—the first two sets of numbers in an IP address—uniquely identifies each network. Every machine on the same network shares that network address as part of its IP address, just as the address of every house on a street shares the same street name. In the IP address 130.57.30.56, for example, 130.57 is the network address.

The node address—the second two sets of numbers—is assigned to, and uniquely identifies, each machine in a network, just as each house on the same street has a different house number. This part of the address must be unique because it identifies a particular machine—an individual, as opposed to a network. This number can also be referred to as a *host address*. In the sample IP address 130.57.30.56, the node address is .30.56.

Understanding Network Classes

The designers of the Internet decided to create classes of networks based on network size. For the small number of networks possessing a very large number of nodes, they created the Class A network. At the other extreme is the Class C network, reserved for the numerous networks with small numbers of nodes. The class of networks in between the very large and very small ones is predictably called the Class B network.

The default subdivision of an IP address into a network and node address is determined by the class designation of your network. Table 4.2 summarizes the three classes of networks, which will be described in more detail in the following sections.

TABLE 4.2 Network address classes

Class	Mask bits	Leading bit pattern	Decimal range of first octet of IP address	Assignable networks	Maximum nodes per network
A	8	0	1–126	126	16,777,214
B	16	10	128–191	16,384	65,534
C	24	110	192–223	2,097,152	254

Classless Inter-Domain Routing (CIDR), explained in detail later in this chapter, has effectively done away with these class designations. You will still hear and should still know the meaning behind the class designations of addresses because they are important to understanding IP addressing. However, when you're working with IP addressing in practice, CIDR is more important to know.

To ensure efficient routing, Internet designers defined a mandate for the leading bits section of the address for each different network class. For example, because a router knows that a Class A network address always starts with a 0, it can quickly apply the default mask, if necessary, after reading only the first bit of the address. Table 4.2 illustrates how the leading bits of a network address are defined. When considering the subnet masking between network and host addresses, the number of bits to mask is important. For example, in a Class A network, 8 bits are masked, making the default subnet mask 255.0.0.0; in a Class C, 24 bits are masked, making the default subnet mask 255.255.255.0.

Some IP addresses are reserved for special purposes and shouldn't be assigned to nodes. Table 4.3 describes some of the reserved IP addresses. See RFC 3330 for others.

TABLE 4.3   Special network addresses

Address	Function
Entire IP address set to all 0s	Depending on the mask, this network (that is, the network or subnet of which you are currently a part) or this host on this network.
A routing table entry of all 0s with a mask of all 0s	Used as the default gateway entry. Any destination address masked by all 0s produces a match for the all 0s reference address. Because the mask has no 1s, this is the least desirable entry, but it will be used when no other match exists.
Network address 127	Reserved for loopback tests. Designates the local node, and it allows that node to send a test packet to itself without generating network traffic.
Node address of all 0s	Used when referencing a network without referring to any specific nodes on that network. Usually used in routing tables.
Node address of all 1s	Broadcast address for all nodes on the specified network, also known as a *directed broadcast*. For example, 128.2.255.255 means all nodes on the Class B network 128.2. Routing this broadcast is configurable on certain routers.
169.254.0.0 with a mask of 255.255.0.0	The "link-local" block used for autoconfiguration and communication between devices on a single link. Communication cannot occur across routers. Microsoft uses this block for Automatic Private IP Addressing (APIPA).
Entire IP address set to all 1s (same as 255.255.255.255) 10.0.0.0/8172.16.0.0 to 172.31.255.255	Broadcast to all nodes on the current network; sometimes called a limited broadcast or an all-1s broadcast. *This broadcast is not routable.*
192.168.0.0/16	The private-use blocks for Classes A, B, and C. As noted in RFC 1918, the addresses in these blocks must never be allowed into the Internet, making them acceptable for simultaneous use behind NAT servers and non-Internet-connected IP networks.

In the following subsections, we will look at the three network types.

Class A Networks

In a Class A network, the first byte is the network address, and the remaining 3 bytes are used for the node addresses. The Class A format is Network.Node.Node.Node.

For example, in the IP address 49.22.102.70, 49 is the network address, and 22.102.70 is the node address. Every machine on this particular network would have the distinctive network address of 49. Within that network, however, you could have a large number of machines.

There are 126 possible Class A network addresses. Why? The length of a Class A network address is 1 byte, and the first bit of that byte is reserved, so 7 bits in the first byte remain available for manipulation. This means that the maximum number of Class A networks is 128. (Each of the 7 bit positions that can be manipulated can be either a 0 or a 1, and this gives you a total of 2^7 positions, or 128.) But to complicate things further, it was also decided that the network address of all 0s (0000 0000) would be reserved. This means that the actual number of usable Class A network addresses is 128 minus 1, or 127. Also, 127 is a reserved number (a network address of 0 followed by all 1s [0111 1111]), so you actually start with 128 addresses minus the 2 reserved, and you're left with 126 possible Class A network addresses.

Each Class A network has 3 bytes (24 bit positions) for the node address of a machine, which means that there are 2^{24}, or 16,777,216, unique combinations. Because addresses with the two patterns of all 0s and all 1s in the node bits are reserved, the actual maximum usable number of nodes for a Class A network is 2^{24} minus 2, which equals 16,777,214.

Class B Networks

In a Class B network, the first 2 bytes are assigned to the network address, and the remaining 2 bytes are used for node addresses. The format is Network.Network.Node.Node.

For example, in the IP address 130.57.30.56, the network address is 130.57, and the node address is 30.56.

The network address is 2 bytes, so there would be 2^{16} unique combinations. But the Internet designers decided that all Class B networks should start with the binary digits 10. This leaves 14 bit positions to manipulate; therefore, there are 16,384 (or 2^{14}) unique Class B networks.

This gives you an easy way to recognize Class B addresses. If the first 2 bits of the first byte can be only 10, that gives you a decimal range from 128 up to 191 in the first octet of the IP address. Remember that you can always easily recognize a Class B network by looking at its first byte, even though there are 16,384 different Class B networks. If the first octet in the address falls between 128 and 191, it is a Class B network, regardless of the value of the second octet.

A Class B network has 2 bytes to use for node addresses. This is 2^{16} minus the two patterns in the reserved-exclusive club (all 0s and all 1s in the node bits) for a total of 65,534 possible node addresses for each Class B network.

Class C Networks

The first 3 bytes of a Class C network are dedicated to the network portion of the address, with only 1 byte remaining for the node address. The format is Network.Network.Network.Node.

In the example IP address 198.21.74.102, the network address is 198.21.74, and the node address is 102.

In a Class C network, the first three bit positions are always binary 110. Three bytes, or 24 bits, minus 3 reserved positions leaves 21 positions. There are therefore 2^{21} (or 2,097,152) possible Class C networks.

The lead bit pattern of 110 equates to decimal 192 and runs through 223. Remembering our handy easy-recognition method, this means you can always spot a Class C address if the first byte is in the range 192–223, regardless of the values of the second and third bytes of the IP address.

Each unique Class C network has 1 byte to use for node addresses. This leads to 2^8, or 256, minus the two special patterns of all 0s and all 1s, for a total of 254 node addresses for each Class C network.

NOTE   Class D networks, used for multicasting only, use the address range 224.0.0.0 to 239.255.255.255 and are used, as in broadcasting, as destination addresses only. Class E networks (reserved for future use at this point) cover 240.0.0.0 to 255.255.255.255. Addresses in the Class E range are considered within the experimental range.

Subnetting a Network

If an organization is large and has lots of computers or if its computers are geographically dispersed, it makes good sense to divide its colossal network into smaller ones connected by routers. These smaller networks are called *subnets*. The benefits of using subnets are as follows:

Reduced Network Traffic   We all appreciate less traffic of any kind, and so do networks. Without routers, packet traffic could choke the entire network. Most traffic will stay on the local network—only packets destined for other networks will pass through the router and to another subnet. This traffic reduction also improves overall performance.

Simplified Management   It's easier to identify and isolate network problems in a group of smaller networks connected together than within one gigantic one.

Understanding the Benefits of Subnetting

To understand one benefit of subnetting, consider a hotel or office building. Say that a hotel has 1,000 rooms with 75 rooms to a floor. You could start at the first room on the first floor and number it 1; then when you get to the first room on the second floor, you could number it 76 and keep going until you reach room 1,000. But someone looking for room 521 would have to guess on which floor that room is located. If you were to "subnet" the hotel, you would identify the first room on the first floor with the number 101 (1 = Floor 1 and 01 = Room 1), the first room on the second floor with 201, and so on. The guest looking for room 521 would go to the fifth floor and look for room 21.

An organization with a single network address (comparable to the hotel building mentioned in the sidebar "Understanding the Benefits of Subnetting") can have a subnet address for each individual physical network (comparable to a floor in the hotel building). Each subnet is still part of the shared network address, but it also has an additional identifier denoting its individual subnetwork number. This identifier is called a *subnet address*.

Subnetting solves several addressing problems:

- If an organization has several physical networks but only one IP network address, it can handle the situation by creating subnets.

- Because subnetting allows many physical networks to be grouped together, fewer entries in a routing table are required, notably reducing network overhead.

- These things combine collectively to yield greatly enhanced network efficiency.

The original designers of the Internet Protocol envisioned a small Internet with only tens of networks and hundreds of hosts. Their addressing scheme used a network address for each physical network. As you can imagine, this scheme and the unforeseen growth of the Internet created a few problems. The following are two examples:

Not Enough Addresses   A single network address can be used to refer to multiple physical networks, but an organization can request individual network addresses for each one of its physical networks. If all of these requests were granted, there wouldn't be enough addresses to go around.

Gigantic Routing Tables   If each router on the Internet needed to know about every physical network, routing tables would be impossibly huge. There would be an overwhelming amount of administrative overhead to maintain those tables, and the resulting physical overhead on the routers would be massive (CPU cycles, memory, disk space, and so on). Because routers exchange routing information with each other, an additional, related consequence is that a terrific overabundance of network traffic would result.

Although there's more than one way to approach these problems, the principal solution is the one that I'll cover in this book—subnetting. As you might guess, *subnetting* is the process of carving a single IP network into smaller logical subnetworks. This trick is achieved by subdividing the host portion of an IP address to create a subnet address. The actual subdivision is accomplished through the use of a subnet mask (covered later in the chapter).

In the following sections, you will see exactly how to calculate and apply subnetting.

Implementing Subnetting

Before you can implement subnetting, you need to determine your current requirements and plan on how best to implement your subnet scheme.

How to Determine Your Subnetting Requirements

Follow these guidelines to calculate the requirements of your subnet:

1. Determine the number of required network IDs: one for each subnet and one for each wide area network (WAN) connection.

2. Determine the number of required host IDs per subnet: one for each TCP/IP device, including, for example, computers, network printers, and router interfaces.

3. Based on these two data points, create the following:

   - One subnet mask for your entire network

   - A unique subnet ID for each physical segment

   - A range of host IDs for each unique subnet

How to Implement Subnetting

Subnetting is implemented by assigning a subnet address to each machine on a given physical network. For example, in Figure 4.3, each machine on subnet 1 has a subnet address of 1.

FIGURE 4.3   A sample subnet

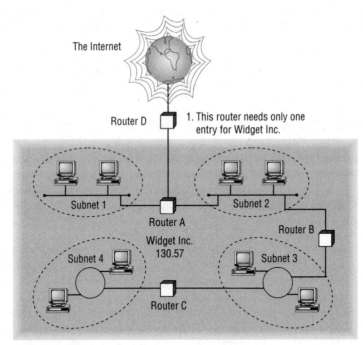

The default network portion of an IP address can't be altered without encroaching on another administrative domain's address space, unless you are assigned multiple consecutive classful addresses. To maximize the efficient use of the assigned address space, machines on a particular network share the same network address. In Figure 4.3, you can see that all of the Widget Inc. machines have a network address of 130.57. That principle is constant. In subnetting, it's the host address that's manipulated—the network address doesn't change. The subnet address scheme takes a part of the host address and recycles it as a subnet address. Bit positions are stolen from the host address to be used for the subnet identifier. Figure 4.4 shows how an IP address can be given a subnet address.

FIGURE 4.4   Network vs. host addresses

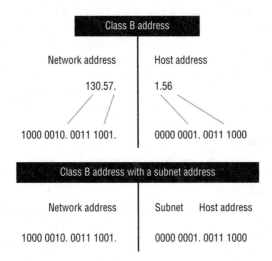

Class B address	
Network address	Host address
130.57.	1.56
1000 0010. 0011 1001.	0000 0001. 0011 1000

Class B address with a subnet address		
Network address	Subnet	Host address
1000 0010. 0011 1001.	0000 0001.	0011 1000

Because the Widget Inc. network is a Class B network, the first 2 bytes specify the network address and are shared by all machines on the network, regardless of their particular subnet. Here every machine's address on the subnet must have its third byte read 0000 0001. The fourth byte, the host address, is the unique number that identifies the actual host within that subnet. Figure 4.5 illustrates how a network address and a subnet address can be used together.

FIGURE 4.5   The network address and its subnet

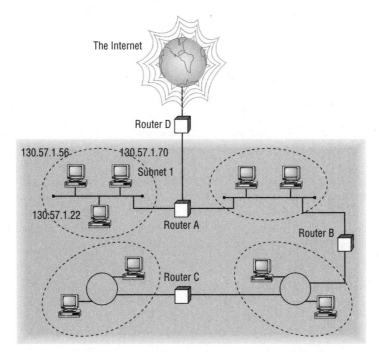

When implementing subnetting, you need some type of hardware installed onto the network. Most of us will just use a router. But if you do not want to purchase an expensive router, there is another way.

One way that you can implement subnetting is by using a Windows Server 2022 machine with multiple NIC adapters configured with routing enabled on the server. This type of router is called a *multihomed router*. This is an inexpensive way to set up a router using a Microsoft server, but it may not be the best way. Many companies specialize in routers, and these routers offer many more features and more flexibility than a multihomed router.

How to Use Subnet Masks

For the subnet address scheme to work, every machine on the network must know which part of the host address will be used as the network address. This is accomplished by assigning each machine a subnet mask.

The network administrator creates a 32-bit subnet mask consisting of 1s and 0s. The 1s in the subnet mask represent the positions in the IP address that refer to the network and subnet addresses. The 0s represent the positions that refer to the host part of the address. Figure 4.6 illustrates this combination.

FIGURE 4.6 The subnet mask revealed

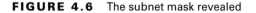

Subnet mask code

1s = Positions representing network or subnet addresses
0s = Positions representing the host address

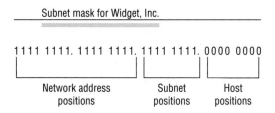

Subnet mask for Widget, Inc.

1111 1111. 1111 1111. 1111 1111. 0000 0000

Network address positions   Subnet positions   Host positions

In the Widget Inc. example, the first two bytes of the subnet mask are 1s because Widget's network address is a Class B address, formatted as Network.Network.Node.Node. The third byte, normally assigned as part of the host address, is now used to represent the subnet address. Hence, those bit positions are represented with 1s in the subnet mask. The fourth byte is the only part of the example that represents the host address.

The subnet mask can also be expressed using the decimal equivalents of the binary patterns. The binary pattern of 1111 1111 is the same as decimal 255. Consequently, the subnet mask in the example can be denoted in two ways, as shown in Figure 4.7.

FIGURE 4.7   Different ways to represent the same mask

Subnet mask in binary: 1111 1111. 1111 1111. 1111 1111. 0000 0000

Subnet mask in decimal: 255   .   255   .   255   .   0

(The spaces in the above example are only for illustrative purposes.
The subnet mask in decimal would actually appear as 255.255.255.0.)

Not all networks need to have subnets, and therefore they don't need to use custom subnet masks. In this case, they are said to have a *default* subnet mask. This is basically the same as saying that they don't have any subnets except for the one main subnet on which the network is running. Table 4.4 shows the default subnet masks for the different classes of networks.

TABLE 4.4   Default subnet masks

Class	Format	Default subnet mask
A	Network.Node.Node.Node	255.0.0.0
B	Network.Network.Node.Node	255.255.0.0
C	Network.Network.Network.Node	255.255.255.0

Once the network administrator has created the subnet mask and has assigned it to each machine, the IP software applies the subnet mask to the IP address to determine its subnet address. The word *mask* carries the implied meaning of "lens" in this case; that is, the IP software looks at its IP address through the lens of its subnet mask to see its subnet address. Figure 4.8 illustrates an IP address being viewed through a subnet mask.

FIGURE 4.8   Applying the subnet mask

Subnet mask code

1s = Positions representing network or subnet addresses
0s = Positions representing the host address

Positions relating to the subnet address

Subnet mask: 1111 1111. 1111 1111. 1111 1111. 0000 0000

IP address of a machine on subnet 1:   1000 0010. 0011 1001. 0000 0001. 0011 1000
(Decimal: 130.57.1.56)

Bits relating to the subnet address

In this example, the IP software learns through the subnet mask that, instead of being part of the host address, the third byte of its IP address is now going to be used as a subnet address. The IP software then looks in its IP address at the bit positions that correspond to the mask, which are 0000 0001.

The final step is for the subnet bit values to be matched up with the binary numbering convention and converted to decimal. In the Widget Inc. example, the binary-to-decimal conversion is simple, as illustrated in Figure 4.9.

FIGURE 4.9   Converting the subnet mask to decimal

Binary numbering convention

Position/value: ◄── (continued)	128 64 32 16 8 4 2 1
Widget third byte:	0 0 0 0 0 0 0 1
Decimal equivalent:	0 + 1 = 1
Subnet address:	1

By using the entire third byte of a Class B address as the subnet address, it is easy to set and determine the subnet address. For example, if Widget Inc. wants to have a subnet 6, the third byte of all machines on that subnet will be 0000 0110 (decimal 6 in binary).

Using the entire third byte of a Class B network address for the subnet allows for a fair number of available subnet addresses. One byte dedicated to the subnet provides eight bit positions. Each position can be either a 1 or a 0, so the calculation is 2^8, or 256. Thus, Widget Inc. can have up to 256 total subnetworks, each with up to 254 hosts.

Although RFC 950 prohibits the use of binary all 0s and all 1s as subnet addresses, today almost all products actually permit this usage. Microsoft's TCP/IP stack allows it, as does the software in most routers (provided you enable this feature, which sometimes is not the case by default). This gives you two additional subnets. However, you should not use a subnet of 0 (all 0s) unless all the software on your network recognizes this convention.

How to Calculate the Number of Subnets

The formulas for calculating the maximum number of subnets and the maximum number of hosts per subnet are as follows:

$2 \times$ number of masked bits in subnet mask = maximum number of subnets

$2 \times$ number of unmasked bits in subnet mask $- 2$ = maximum number of hosts per subnet

In the formulas, *masked* refers to bit positions of 1, and *unmasked* refers to bit positions of 0. The downside to using an entire byte of a node address as your subnet address is that you reduce the possible number of node addresses on each subnet. As explained earlier, without a subnet, a Class B address has 65,534 unique combinations of 1s and 0s that can be used for node addresses. The question then is why would you ever want 65,534 hosts on a single physical network?

The trade-off is acceptable to most who ask themselves this question. If you use an entire byte of the node address for a subnet, you then have only 1 byte for the host addresses, leaving only 254 possible host addresses. If any of your subnets are populated with more than 254 machines, you'll have a problem. To solve it, you would then need to shorten the subnet mask, thereby lengthening the number of host bits and increasing the number of host addresses. This gives you more available host addresses on each subnet. A side effect of this solution is that it shrinks the number of possible subnets.

Figure 4.10 shows an example of using a smaller subnet address. A company called Acme Inc. expects to need a maximum of 14 subnets. In this case, Acme does not need to take an entire byte from the host address for the subnet address. To get its 14 different subnet addresses, it needs to snatch only 4 bits from the host address ($2^4 = 16$). The host portion of the address has 12 usable bits remaining ($2^{12} - 2 = 4,094$). Each of Acme's 16 subnets could then potentially have a total of 4,094 host addresses, and 4,094 machines on each subnet should be plenty.

FIGURE 4.10   An example of a smaller subnet address

Acme, Inc.

Network address:	132.8 (Class B; net.net.host.host)
Example IP address:	1000 0100. 0000 1000. 0001 0010. 0011 1100
Decimal:	132 . 8 . 18 . 60

Subnet Mask Code

1s = Positions representing network or subnet addresses
0s = Positions representing the host address

Subnet mask:

Binary:	1111 1111. 1111 1111. 1111 0000. 0000 0000
Decimal:	255 . 255 . 240 . 0

(The decimal 240 is equal to the binary 1111 0000.)

Positions relating to the subnet address

Subnet mask: 1111 1111. 1111 1111. 1111 0000. 0000 0000

IP address of a Acme machine: 1000 0100. 0000 1000. 0001 0010. 0011 1100
(Decimal: 132.8.18.60)

Bits relating to the subnet address

Binary-to-Decimal Conversions for Subnet Address

Subnet mask positions:	1	1	1	1	0	0	0	0
Position/value: ←— (continue)	128	64	32	16	8	4	2	1
Third byte of IP address:	0	0	0	1	0	0	1	0
Decimal equivalent:					0 + 16 = 16			
Subnet address for this IP address:					16			

An Easier Way to Apply Subnetting

Now that you have the basics of how to subnet down, you'll learn an easier way. If you have learned a different way and it works for you, stick with it. It does not matter how you get to the finish line, just as long as you get there. But if you are new to subnetting, Figure 4.11 will make it easier for you.

FIGURE 4.11   Will Panek's IPv4 subnetting chart

Subnet Mask	128	64	32	16	8	4	2	1
255	1	1	1	1	1	1	1	1
254	1	1	1	1	1	1	1	0
252	1	1	1	1	1	1	0	0
248	1	1	1	1	1	0	0	0
240	1	1	1	1	0	0	0	0
224	1	1	1	0	0	0	0	0
192	1	1	0	0	0	0	0	0
128	1	0	0	0	0	0	0	0
0	0	0	0	0	0	0	0	0

0 = HOSTS   1 = SUBNETS   **Will Panek's Chart**

	Power		Subnets		Hosts
2 ×	2	=	4	−2	2
2 ×	3	=	8	−2	6
2 ×	4	=	16	−2	14
2 ×	5	=	32	−2	30
2 ×	6	=	64	−2	62
2 ×	7	=	128	−2	126
2 ×	8	=	256	−2	254
2 ×	9	=	512	−2	510
2 ×	10	=	1024	−2	1022
2 ×	11	=	2048	−2	2046
2 ×	12	=	4096	−2	4094
2 ×	13	=	8192	−2	8190
2 ×	14	=	16384	−2	16382
2 ×	15	=	32768	−2	32766

This chart may look intimidating, but it's really simple to use once you have done it a few times.

> **TIP**   Remember that, on this chart, 1s equal subnets and 0s equal hosts. If you get this confused, you will get wrong answers in the following exercises.

Watch the Hosts column on the lower end of the chart. This represents the number of addresses available to you after the two reserved addresses have been removed. The following exercises provide some examples.

SUBNET MASK EXERCISE 4.1

Class C, 10 Hosts per Subnet

You have a Class C address, and you require 10 hosts per subnet.

1. Write down the following:

    255.255.255.____

    The blank is the number you need to fill in.

2. Look under the Hosts column and choose the first number that is larger than 10 (the number of hosts per subnet you need). You should have come up with 14.

3. Move across the page and look at the number in the Power column. The power number is 4.

4. Go to the top of the chart and look for the row with exactly four 0s (hosts). Find the number at the beginning of the row.

The number at the beginning of the row is 240. That's your answer. The subnet mask should be 255.255.255.240.

SUBNET MASK EXERCISE 4.2

Class C, 20 Hosts per Subnet

You have a Class C address, and you need 20 hosts per subnet.

1. Write down the following:

    255.255.255.___

2. Look under the Hosts column and find the first number that covers 20. (This should be 30.)

3. Go across to the power number (5).

4. Go to the top part of the chart and find the row with exactly five 0s from right to left.

The number at the beginning of the row is 224. Your answer should be 255.255.255.224.

SUBNET MASK EXERCISE 4.3

Class C, Five Subnets

Now you have a Class C address, and you need five subnets. Remember that subnets are represented by 1s in the chart.

1. Write down the following:

    255.255.255.___

2. Look under the Subnets column and find the first number that covers 5. (This should be 8.)

3. Go across to the power number. (This should be 3.)

4. Go to the top part of the chart and find out which row has exactly three 1s (remember, 1s are for subnets) from left to right.

Your answer should be 255.255.255.224.

SUBNET MASK EXERCISE 4.4

Class B, 1,500 Hosts per Subnet

This one is a bit harder. You have a Class B address, and you need 1,500 hosts per subnet. Because you have a Class B address, you need to fill in the third octet of numbers. The fourth octet contains eight 0s.

1. Write down the following:

   255.255.___.0

2. Look at the Hosts column and find the first number that covers 1,500. (This should be 2,046.)

3. Go across and find the power number. (This should be 11.)

4. Remember, you already have eight 0s in the last octet. So, you need only three more. Find the row with three 0s.

You should come up with an answer of 255.255.248.0. This actually breaks down to 11111111.11111111.11111000.00000000, and that's how you got the 11 zeros.

SUBNET MASK EXERCISE 4.5

Class B, 3,500 Hosts per Subnet

You have a Class B address, and you need 3,500 hosts per subnet.

1. Write down the following:

   255.255.___.0

2. Look at the Hosts column and find the first number that covers 3,500. (This should be 4,094.)

3. Go across and find the power number. (This should be 12.)

4. Remember, you already have eight 0s in the last octet, so you need only four more. Count for four 0s from right to left.

You should come up with an answer of 255.255.240.0. Again, this actually breaks down to 11111111.11111111.11110000.00000000, and that's how you got the 12 zeros.

> If you get a question that gives you both the hosts and the subnets, always figure out the larger number first. Then, depending on the mask you have decided to use, make sure that the lower number is also correct with that mask.

Now try some more subnet mask exercises using the data that follows:

Class B address	**Class B address**
1,000 hosts per subnet	25 subnets
Class C address	**Class B address**
45 hosts per subnet	4,000 hosts per subnet
192.168.0.0	**Class B address**
10 subnets	2,000 hosts per subnet
	25 subnets

Here are the answers. If any of your answers are wrong, follow the previous examples and try to work through them again.

Class B address	**Class B address**
1,000 hosts per subnet 255.255.252.0	25 subnets 255.255.248.0
Class C address	**Class B address**
45 hosts per subnet 255.255.255.192	4,000 hosts per subnet 255.255.240.0
192.168.0.0	**Class B address**
10 subnets 255.255.255.240	2,000 hosts per subnet
	25 subnets 255.255.248.0

Applying Subnetting the Traditional Way

Sometimes subnetting can be confusing. After all, it can be quite difficult to remember all of those numbers. You can step back a minute and take a look at the primary classes of networks and how to subnet each one. Let's start with Class C because it uses only 8 bits for the node address, so it's the easiest to calculate. In the following sections, I will explain how to subnet the various types of networks.

Subnetting Class C

If you recall, a Class C network uses the first 3 bytes (24 bits) to define the network address. This leaves you 1 byte (8 bits) with which to address hosts. So, if you want to create subnets, your options are limited because of the small number of bits available.

If you break down your subnets into chunks smaller than the default Class C, then fig-uring out the subnet mask, network number, broadcast address, and router address can be confusing. To build a sturdy base for subnetting, study the following techniques for deter-mining these special values for each subnet, but also learn and use the more efficient tech-nique presented in the later section "Quickly Identifying Subnet Characteristics Using CIDR" and the earlier section "An Easier Way to Apply Subnetting." Table 4.5 summarizes how you can break down a Class C network into one, two, four, or eight smaller subnets, and it gives you the subnet masks, network numbers, broadcast addresses, and router addresses. The first 3 bytes have simply been designated x.y.z. (Note that the table assumes you can use the all-0s and all-1s subnets too.)

TABLE 4.5   Setting up Class C subnets

Number of desired subnets	Subnet mask	Network number	Router address	Broadcast address	Remaining number of IP addresses
1	255.255.255.0	x.y.z.0	x.y.z.1	x.y.z.255	253
2	255.255.255.128	x.y.z.0	x.y.z.1	x.y.z.127	125
	255.255.255.128	x.y.z.128	x.y.z.129	x.y.z.255	125
4	255.255.255.192	x.y.z.0	x.y.z.1	x.y.z.63	61
	255.255.255.192	x.y.z.64	x.y.z.65	x.y.z.127	61
	255.255.255.192	x.y.z.128	x.y.z.129	x.y.z.191	61
	255.255.255.192	x.y.z.192	x.y.z.193	x.y.z.255	61
8	255.255.255.224	x.y.z.0	x.y.z.1	x.y.z.31	29
	255.255.255.224	x.y.z.32	x.y.z.33	x.y.z.63	29
	255.255.255.224	x.y.z.64	x.y.z.65	x.y.z.95	29
	255.255.255.224	x.y.z.96	x.y.z.97	x.y.z.127	29
	255.255.255.224	x.y.z.128	x.y.z.129	x.y.z.159	29
	255.255.255.224	x.y.z.160	x.y.z.161	x.y.z.191	29
	255.255.255.224	x.y.z.192	x.y.z.193	x.y.z.223	29
	255.255.255.224	x.y.z.224	x.y.z.225	x.y.z.255	29

For example, suppose you want to chop up a Class C network, 200.211.192.*x*, into two subnets. As you can see in the table, you'd use a subnet mask of 255.255.255.128 for each subnet. The first subnet would have the network number 200.211.192.0, router address could be the first available host address of 200.211.192.1, and broadcast address 200.211.192.127. You could assign IP addresses 200.211.192.2 through 200.211.192.126—that's 125 additional different IP addresses.

Heavily subnetting a network results in the loss of a progressively greater percentage of addresses to the network number, broadcast address, and router address.

The second subnet would have the network number 200.211.192.128, router address 200.211.192.129, and broadcast address 200.211.192.255.

Determining the Subnet Numbers for a Class C Subnet

The first subnet always has a 0 in the interesting octet. In the example, it would be 200.211.192.0, the same as the original nonsubnetted network address. To determine the subnet numbers for the additional subnets, first you have to determine the incremental value:

1. Begin with the octet that has an interesting value (other than 0 or 255) in the subnet mask. Then subtract the interesting value from 256. The result is the incremental value.

   If again you use the network 200.211.192.*x* and a mask of 255.255.255.192, the example yields the following equation: 256 – 192 = 64. Thus, 64 is your incremental value in the interesting octet—the fourth octet in this case. Why the fourth octet? That's the octet with the interesting value, 192, in the mask.

2. To determine the second subnet number, add the incremental value to the 0 in the fourth octet of the first subnet.

   In the example, it would be 200.211.192.64.

3. To determine the third subnet number, add the incremental value to the interesting octet of the second subnet number.

   In the example, it would be 200.211.192.128.

4. Keep adding the incremental value in this fashion until you reach the actual subnet mask number.

   For example, 0 + 64 = 64, so your second subnet is 64. And 64 + 64 is 128, so your third subnet is 128. And 128 + 64 is 192, so your fourth subnet is 192. Because 192 is the subnet mask, this is your last subnet. If you tried to add 64 again, you'd come up with 256, an unusable octet value, which is always where you end up when you've gone too far. This means your valid subnets are 0, 64, 128, and 192 (total of 4 subnets on your network).

The numbers between the subnets are your valid host and broadcast addresses. For example, the following are valid hosts for two of the subnets in a Class C network with a subnet mask of 192:

- The valid hosts for subnet 64 are in the range 65–126, which gives you 62 hosts per subnet.

  (You can't use 127 as a host because that would mean your host bits would be all 1s. The all-1s format is reserved as the broadcast address for that subnet.)

- The valid hosts for subnet 128 are in the range 129–190, with a broadcast address of 191.

As you can see, this solution wastes a few addresses—six more than not subnetting at all, to be exact. In a Class C network, this should not be hard to justify. The 255.255.255.128 subnet mask is an even better solution if you need only two subnets and expect to need close to 126 host addresses per subnet.

Calculating Values for an Eight-Subnet Class C Network

What happens if you need eight subnets in your Class C network?

By using the calculation of $2x$, where x is the number of subnet bits, you would need 3 subnet bits to get eight subnets ($2^3 = 8$). What are the valid subnets, and what are the valid hosts of each subnet? Let's figure it out.

11100000 is 224 in binary, and it would be the interesting value in the fourth octet of the subnet mask. This must be the same on all workstations.

To figure out the valid subnets, subtract the interesting octet value from 256 (256 − 224 = 32), so 32 is your incremental value for the fourth octet. Of course, the 0 subnet is your first subnet, as always. The other subnets would be 32, 64, 96, 128, 160, 192, and 224. The valid hosts are the numbers between the subnet numbers, except the numbers that equal all 1s in the host bits. These numbers would be 31, 63, 95, 127, 159, 191, 223, and 255. Remember that using all 1s in the host bits is reserved for the broadcast address of each subnet.

The valid subnets, hosts, and broadcasts are as follows:

Subnet	Hosts	Broadcast
0	1–30	31
32	33–62	63
64	65–94	95
96	97–126	127
128	129–158	159
160	161–190	191
192	193–222	223
224	225–254	255

You can add one more bit to the subnet mask just for fun. You were using 3 bits, which gave you 224. By adding the next bit, the mask now becomes 240 (11110000).

By using 4 bits for the subnet mask, you get 16 subnets because $2^4 = 16$. This subnet mask also gives you only 4 bits for the host addresses, or $2^4 - 2 = 14$ hosts per subnet. As you can see, the number of hosts per subnet gets reduced rather quickly for each host bit that gets reallocated for subnet use.

The first valid subnet for subnet 240 is 0, as always. Because $256 - 240 = 16$, your remaining subnets are then 16, 32, 48, 64, 80, 96, 112, 128, 144, 160, 176, 192, 208, 224, and 240. Remember that the actual interesting octet value also represents the last valid subnet, so 240 is the last valid subnet number. The valid hosts are the numbers between the subnets, except for the numbers that are all 1s—the broadcast address for the subnet.

Table 4.6 shows the numbers in the interesting (fourth) octet for a Class C network with eight subnets.

TABLE 4.6   Fourth octet addresses for a Class C network with eight subnets

Subnet	Hosts	Broadcast
0	1–14	15
16	17–30	31
32	33–46	47
48	49–62	63
64	65–78	79
80	81–94	95
96	97–110	111
112	113–126	127
128	129–142	143
144	145–158	159
160	161–174	175
176	177–190	191
192	193–206	207
208	209–222	223
224	225–238	239
240	241–254	255

Subnetting Class B

Because a Class B network has 16 bits for host addresses, you have plenty of available bits to play with when figuring out a subnet mask. Remember that you have to start with the leftmost bit and work toward the right. For example, a Class B network would look like x.y.0.0, with the default mask of 255.255.0.0. Using the default mask would give you one network with 65,534 hosts.

The default mask in binary is 11111111.11111111.00000000.00000000. The 1s represent the corresponding network bits in the IP address, and the 0s represent the host bits. When you're creating a subnet mask, the leftmost bit(s) will be borrowed from the host bits (0s will be turned into 1s) to become the subnet mask. You then use the remaining bits that are still set to 0 for host addresses.

If you use only 1 bit to create a subnet mask, you have a mask of 255.255.128.0. If you use 2 bits, you have a mask of 255.255.192.0, or 11111111.11111111.11000000.00000000.

As with subnetting a Class C address, you now have three parts of the IP address: the network address, the subnet address, and the host address. You figure out the subnet mask numbers the same way as you did with a Class C network (see the previous section, "Calculating Values for an Eight-Subnet Class C Network"), but you'll end up with a lot more hosts per subnet.

There are four subnets, because $2^2 = 4$. The valid third-octet values for the subnets are 0, 64, 128, and 192 (256 − 192 = 64, so the incremental value of the third octet is 64). However, there are 14 bits (0s) left over for host addressing. This gives you 16,382 hosts per subnet ($2^{14} − 2 = 16,382$).

The valid subnets and hosts are as follows:

Subnet	Hosts	Broadcast
x.y.0.0	x.y.0.1 through x.y. 63.254	x.y.63.255
x.y.64.0	x.y.64.1 through x.y.127.254	x.y.127.255
x.y.128.0	x.y.128.1 through x.y.191.254	x.y.191.255
x.y.192.0	x.y.192.1 through x.y.255.254	x.y.255.255

You can add another bit to the subnet mask, making it 11111111.11111111.1110000 0.00000000, or 255.255.224.0. This gives you eight subnets ($2^3 = 8$) and 8,190 hosts. The valid subnets are 0, 32, 64, 96, 128, 160, 192, and 224 (256 − 224 = 32). The subnets, valid hosts, and broadcasts are listed here:

Subnet	Hosts	Broadcast
x.y.0.0	x.y.0.1 through x.y.31.254	x.y.31.255
x.y.32.0	x.y.32.1 through x.y.63.254	x.y.63.255
x.y.64.0	x.y.64.1 through x.y.95.254	x.y.95.255
x.y.96.0	x.y.96.1 through x.y.127.254	x.y.127.255
x.y.128.0	x.y.128.1 through x.y.159.254	x.y.159.255
x.y.160.0	x.y.160.1 through x.y.191.254	x.y.191.255
x.y.192.0	x.y.192.1 through x.y.223.254	x.y.223.255
x.y.224.0	x.y.224.1 through x.y.255.254	x.y.255.255

The following are the breakdowns for a 9-bit mask and a 14-bit mask:

- If you use 9 bits for the mask, it gives you 512 subnets (2^9). With only 7 bits for hosts, you still have 126 hosts per subnet ($2^7 - 2 = 126$). The mask looks like this:

    11111111.11111111.11111111.10000000, or 255.255.255.128

- If you use 14 bits for the subnet mask, you get 16,384 subnets (2^{14}) but only two hosts per subnet ($2^2 - 2 = 2$). The subnet mask would look like this:

    11111111.11111111.11111111.11111100, or 255.255.255.252

🌐 Real World Scenario

Subnet Mask Use in an ISP

You may be wondering why you would use a 14-bit subnet mask with a Class B address. This approach is actually very common. Let's say you have a Class B network and use a subnet mask of 255.255.255.0. You'd have 256 subnets and 254 hosts per subnet. Imagine also that you are an Internet service provider (ISP) and have a network with many WAN links, a different one between you and each customer. Typically, you'd have a direct connection between each site. Each of these links must be on its own subnet or network. There will be two hosts on these subnets—one address for each router port. If you used the mask described earlier (255.255.255.0), you would waste 252 host addresses per subnet. But by using the 255.255.255.252 subnet mask, you have more subnets available, which means more customers—each subnet with only two hosts, which is the maximum allowed on a point-to-point circuit.

You can use the 255.255.255.252 subnet mask only if you are running a routing algorithm such as Enhanced Interior Gateway Routing Protocol (EIGRP) or Open Shortest Path First (OSPF). These routing protocols allow what is called *Variable Length Subnet Masking (VLSM)*. VLSM allows you to run the 255.255.255.252 subnet mask on your interfaces to the WANs and run 255.255.255.0 on your router interfaces in your local area network (LAN) using the same classful network address for all subnets. It works because these routing protocols transmit the subnet mask information in the update packets that they send to the other routers. Classful routing protocols, such as RIP version 1, don't transmit the subnet mask and therefore cannot employ VLSM.

Subnetting Class A

Class A networks have even more bits available than Class B and Class C networks. A default Class A network subnet mask is only 8 bits, or 255.0.0.0, giving you a whopping 24 bits for hosts to play with. Knowing which hosts and subnets are valid is a lot more complicated than it was for either Class B or Class C networks.

If you use a mask of 11111111.1111111.00000000.00000000, or 255.255.0.0, you'll have 8 bits for subnets, or 256 subnets (2^8). This leaves 16 bits for hosts, or 65,534 hosts per subnet ($2^{16} - 2 = 65534$).

If you split the 24 bits evenly between subnets and hosts, you would give each one 12 bits. The mask would look like this: 11111111.11111111.11110000.00000000, or 255.255.240.0. How many valid subnets and hosts would you have? The answer is 4,096 subnets each with 4,094 hosts ($2^{12} - 2 = 4,094$).

The second octet will be somewhere between 0 and 255. However, you will need to figure out the third octet. Because the third octet has a 240 mask, you get 16 ($256 - 240 = 16$) as your incremental value in the third octet. The third octet must start with 0 for the first subnet, the second subnet will have 16 in the third octet, and so on. This means that some of your valid subnets are as follows (not in order):

Subnet	Hosts	Broadcast
x.0-255.0.0	x.0-255.0.1 through x.0-255.15.254	x.0-255.15.255
x.0-255.16.0	x.0-255.16.1 through x.0-255.31.254	x.0-255.31.255
x.0-255.32.0	x.0-255.32.1 through x.0-255.47.254	x.0-255.47.255
x.0-255.48.0	x.0-255.48.1 through x.0-255.63.254	x.0-255.63.255

They go on in this way for the remaining third-octet values through 224 in the subnet column.

Working with Classless Inter-Domain Routing

Microsoft uses an alternate way to write address ranges, called *Classless Inter-Domain Routing* (*CIDR*; pronounced "cider"). CIDR is a shorthand version of the subnet mask. For example, an address of 131.107.2.0 with a subnet mask of 255.255.255.0 is listed in CIDR as 131.107.2.0/24 because the subnet mask contains 24 1s. An address listed as 141.10.32.0/19 would have a subnet mask of 255.255.224.0, or 19 1s (the default subnet mask for Class B plus 3 bits). This is the nomenclature used in all Microsoft exams (see Figure 4.12).

FIGURE 4.12   Subnet mask represented by 1s

Subnet mask in binary: 1111 1111. 1111 1111. 1111 1111. 0000 0000

Subnet mask in decimal: 255   .   255   .   255   .   0

(The spaces in the above example are only for illustrative purposes.
The subnet mask in decimal would actually appear as 255.255.255.0.)

Let's say an Internet company has assigned you the following Class C address and CIDR number: 192.168.10.0/24. This represents the Class C address of 192.168.10.0 and a subnet mask of 255.255.255.0.

Again, CIDR represents the number of 1s turned on in a subnet mask. For example, a CIDR number of /16 stands for 255.255.0.0 (11111111.11111111.00000000.00000000).

The following is a list of all of the CIDR numbers (starting with a Class A default subnet mask) and their corresponding subnet masks:

CIDR	Mask	CIDR	Mask	CIDR	Mask
/8	255.0.0.0	/17	255.255.128.0	/25	255.255.255.128
/9	255.128.0.0	/18	255.255.192.0	/26	255.255.255.192
/10	255.192.0.0	/19	255.255.224.0	/27	255.255.255.224
/11	255.224.0.0	/20	255.255.240.0	/28	255.255.255.240
/12	255.240.0.0	/21	255.255.248.0	/29	255.255.255.248
/13	255.248.0.0	/22	255.255.252.0	/30	255.255.255.252
/14	255.252.0.0	/23	255.255.254.0	/31	255.255.255.254
/15	255.254.0.0	/24	255.255.255.0	/32	255.255.255.255
/16	255.255.0.0				

Quickly Identifying Subnet Characteristics Using CIDR

Given the limited time you have to dispatch questions in the structured environment of a Microsoft certification exam, every shortcut to coming up with the correct answer is a plus. The following method, using CIDR notation, can shave minutes off the time it takes you to complete a single question. Since you already understand the underlying binary technology at the heart of subnetting, you can use the following shortcuts, one for each address class, to come up with the correct answer without working in binary.

Identifying Class C Subnet Characteristics

Consider the host address 192.168.10.50/27. The following steps flesh out the details of the subnet of which this address is a member:

1. Obtain the CIDR-notation prefix length for the address by converting the dotted-decimal mask to CIDR notation.

   In this case, /27 corresponds to a mask of 255.255.255.224. Practice converting between these notations until it becomes second nature.

2. Using the closest multiple of 8 that is greater than or equal to the prefix length, compute the interesting octet (the octet that increases from one subnet to the next in increments other than 1 or 0). Divide this multiple by 8. The result is a number corresponding to the octet that is interesting.

   In this case, the next multiple of 8 greater than 27 is 32. Dividing 32 by 8 produces the number 4, pointing to the fourth octet as the interesting one.

3. To compute the incremental value in the interesting octet, subtract the prefix length from the next higher multiple of 8, which in this case is 32. The result (32 − 27) is 5. Raise 2 to the computed value ($2^5 = 32$). The result is the incremental value of the interesting octet.

4. Recall the value of the interesting octet from the original address (50 in this case). Starting with 0, increment by the incremental value until the value is exceeded. The values then are 0, 32, 64, and so on.

5. The subnet in question extends from the increment that is immediately less than or equal to the address's interesting octet value to the address immediately before the next increment. In this example, 192.168.10.50/27 belongs to the subnet 192.168.10.32, and this subnet extends to the address immediately preceding 192.168.10.64, which is its broadcast address, 192.168.10.63.

   Note that if the interesting octet is not the fourth octet, all octets after the interesting octet must be set to 0 for the subnet address.

6. The usable range of addresses for the subnet in question extends from one higher than the subnet address to one less than the broadcast address, making the range for the subnet in question 192.168.10.33 through 192.168.10.62. As you can see, 192.168.10.50/27 definitely falls within the subnet 192.168.10.32/27.

Identifying Class B Subnet Characteristics

Using the steps in the previous section, find the subnet in which the address 172.16.76.12 with a mask of 255.255.240.0 belongs.

1. The corresponding CIDR notation prefix length is /20.

2. The next multiple of 8 that is greater than 20 is 24. 24/8 = 3. Octet 3 is interesting.

3. 24 − 20 = 4, so the incremental value is $2^4 = 16$.

4. The increments in the third octet are 0, 16, 32, 48, 64, 80, and so on.

5. The increments of 64 and 80 bracket the address's third-octet value of 76, making the subnet in question 172.16.64.0, after setting all octets after the interesting octet to 0. This subnet's broadcast address is 172.16.79.255, which comes right before the next subnet address of 172.16.80.0.

6. The usable address range then extends from 172.16.64.1 through 172.16.79.254.

Identifying Class A Subnet Characteristics

Try it one more time with 10.6.127.255/14. Combine some of the related steps if possible:

1. The prefix length is 14. The next multiple of 8 that is greater than or equal to 14 is 16. 16/8 = 2, so the second octet is interesting.

2. 16 − 14 = 2, so the incremental value in the second octet is $2^2 = 4$.

3. The corresponding second-octet value of 6 in the address falls between the 4 and 8 increments. This means that the subnet in question is 10.4.0.0 (setting octets after the second one to 0) and its broadcast address is 10.7.255.255.

4. The usable address range is from 10.4.0.1 through 10.7.255.254.

Determining Quantities of Subnets and Hosts

The general technique described in the previous sections is also useful when trying to determine the total number of subnets and hosts produced by a given mask with respect to the default mask of the class of address in question.

For example, consider the Class B address 172.16.0.0 with a subnet mask of 255.255.254.0. This is a prefix length of 23 bits. When you subtract the default prefix length for a Class B address of 16 from 23, you get the value 7. Raising 2 to the 7th power results in the value 128, which is the number of subnets you get when you subnet a Class B address with the 255.255.254.0 mask.

Determining the number of hosts available in each of these 128 subnets is simple because you always subtract the prefix length that the subnet mask produces, 23 in this example, from the value 32, which represents the total number of bits in any IP address. The difference, 9, represents the remaining number of 0s, or host bits, in the subnet mask. Raising 2 to this value produces the total possible number of host IDs per subnet that this subnet mask allows. Remember to subtract 2 from this result to account for the subnet and broadcast addresses for each subnet. This gives you the actual number of usable host IDs per subnet. In this case, this value is $2^9 - 2 = 510$.

Repeated practice with this technique will reduce your time to obtain the desired answer to mere seconds, leaving time for the more challenging tasks in each question. You have a wealth of examples and scenarios in this chapter, as well as in the review questions, on which to try your technique and build your trust in this faster method.

Supernetting

Let's take a look at a different type of subnetting. Class B addresses give you 65,534 addresses, but let's say that you have 1,000 users. Would you really need a Class B address? Not if you use supernetting.

Supernetting allows you to have two or more blocks of contiguous subnetwork addresses. So, what does that actually mean? Class C addresses give you 254 usable addresses. So, if you needed 1,000 users, you could set up supernetting of four Class C addresses that are contiguous:

    Example:

    192.168.16.0

    192.168.17.0

    192.168.18.0

    192.168.19.0

When you set up supernetting for a Class C, you would use a Class B subnet mask. When you set up supernetting for a Class B, you would use a Class A subnet mask. This allows you to use multiple classes to get a larger number of hosts without taking up an entire class.

So, the subnet mask for the previous example would be 255.255.252.0, or /22. The reason we used this subnet mask is because a 252 subnet mask allows for four subnets. Each of those Class C numbers would equal one subnet on this network.

Understanding IPv6

Internet Protocol version 6 (IPv6) is the first major revamping of IP since RFC 791 was accepted in 1981. Yes, the operation of IP has improved, and there have been a few bells and whistles added (such as NAT, for example), but the basic structure is still being used as it was originally intended. IPv6 has actually been available to use in Microsoft operating systems since NT 4.0, but it always had to be manually enabled. Windows Vista was the first Microsoft operating system to have it enabled by default. It is also enabled by default in Windows 7, Windows 10, Windows 11, Windows Server 2008, Windows Server 2008 R2, Windows Server 2012/2012 R2, Windows Server 2016, Windows Server 2019, and Windows Server 2022, and it probably will be in all Microsoft operating systems from this point on.

TCP and UDP—as well as the IP applications, such as HTTP, FTP, SNMP, and the rest—are still being used in IPv4. So, you might ask, why change to the new version? What does IPv6 bring to your networking infrastructure? What is the structure of an IPv6 address? How is it implemented and used within Windows Server 2022? I'll answer all of those questions and more in this section.

IPv6 History and Need

In the late 1970s, as the IP specifications were being put together, the vision of the interconnected devices was limited compared to what we actually have today. To get an idea of the growth of the Internet, take a look at Hobbes's Internet Timeline in RFC 2235 (www.faqs.org/rfcs/rfc2235.html). As you can see, in 1984, the number of hosts finally surpassed 1,000—two years after TCP and IP were introduced. With 32 bits of addressing available in IPv4, it handled the 1,000+ hosts just fine. And even with the number of hosts breaking the 10,000 mark in 1987 and then 100,000 in 1989, there were still plenty of IP addresses to go around. But when the number of hosts exceeded 2 million in 1992 and 3 million in 1994, concern in the industry started to build. So in 1994, a working group was formed to come up with a solution to the quickly dwindling usable address availability in the IPv4 space. Internet Protocol next generation (IPng) was started.

Have you heard of IP address depletion being a problem today? Probably not as much. When the working group realized that it could not have IPv6 standardized before the available addresses might run out, they developed and standardized *Network Address Translation (NAT)* as an interim solution. NAT, or more specifically an implementation of NAT called *Port Address Translation (PAT)*, took care of a big portion of the problem.

NAT works very well, but it does have some limitations, including issues of peer-to-peer applications with their IPv4 addresses embedded in the data, issues of end-to-end traceability, and issues of overlapping addresses when two networks merge. Because all devices in an IPv6 network will have a unique address and no network address translation will take place, the global addressing concept of IPv4 will be brought back (the address put on by the source device will stay all the way to the destination). Thus, with the new-and-improved functionality of IPv6, the drawbacks of NAT and the limitations of IPv4 will be eliminated.

New and Improved IPv6 Concepts

Several elements of the IPv4 protocol could use some enhancements. Fortunately, IPv6 incorporates those enhancements as well as new features directly into the protocol specification to provide better and additional functionality.

The following list includes new concepts and new implementations of old concepts in IPv6:

- Larger address space (128-bit vs. 32-bit).

- Autoconfiguration of Internet-accessible addresses with or without DHCP. (Without DHCP, it's called *stateless autoconfiguration*.)

- More efficient IP header (fewer fields and no checksum).

- Fixed-length IP header (the IPv4 header is variable length) with extension headers beyond the standard fixed length to provide enhancements.

- Built-in IP mobility and security. (Although available in IPv4, the IPv6 implementation is a much better implementation.)

- Built-in transition schemes to allow integration of the IPv4 and IPv6 spaces.

- ARP broadcast messages replaced with multicast request.

Here are more details about these features:

128-Bit Address Space   The new 128-bit address space will provide unique addresses for the foreseeable future. Although I would like to say that we will never use up all of the addresses, history may prove me wrong. The number of unique addresses in the IPv6 space is 2^{128}, or 3.4×10^{38}, addresses. How big is that number? It's enough for toasters and refrigerators (and maybe even cars) to all have their own addresses.

As a point of reference, the nearest black hole to Earth is 1,600 light years away. If you were to stack 4mm BB pellets from here to the nearest black hole and back, you would need 1.51×10^{22} BBs. This means you could uniquely address each BB from Earth to the black hole and back and still have quite a few addresses left over.

Another way to look at it is that the IPv6 address space is big enough to provide more than 1 million addresses per square inch of the surface area of the earth (oceans included).

Autoconfiguration and Stateless Autoconfiguration   Autoconfiguration is another added/improved feature of IPv6. We've used DHCP for a while to assign IP addresses to client machines. You should even remember that APIPA can be used to assign addresses automatically to Microsoft DHCP client machines in the absence of a DHCP server. The problem with APIPA is that it confines communication between machines to a local LAN (no default gateway). What if a client machine could ask whether there was a router on the LAN and what network it was on? If the client machine knew that, it could not only assign itself an address, it could also choose the appropriate network and default gateway. The stateless autoconfiguration functionality of IPv6 allows the clients to do this.

Improved IPv6 Header   The IPv6 header is more efficient than the IPv4 header because it is fixed length (with extensions possible) and has only a few fields. The IPv6 header consists of a total of 40 bytes:

32 bytes   Source and destination IPv6 addresses

8 bytes   Version field, traffic class field, flow label field, payload length field, next header field, and hop limit field

You don't have to waste your time with a checksum validation anymore, and you don't have to include the length of the IP header (it's fixed in IPv6; the IP header is variable length in IPv4, so the length must be included as a field).

IPv6 Mobility   IPv6 is only a replacement of the OSI layer 3 component, so you'll continue to use the TCP (and UDP) components as they currently exist. IPv6 addresses a TCP issue, though. Specifically, TCP is connection oriented, meaning that you establish an end-to-end communication path with sequencing and acknowledgments before you ever send any data, and then you have to acknowledge all of the pieces of data sent. You do this through a combination of an IP address, port number, and port type (socket).

If the source IP address changes, the TCP connection may be disrupted. But then how often does this happen? Well, it happens more and more often because more people are walking around with a wireless laptop or a wireless voice over IP (VoIP) telephone. IPv6 mobility establishes a TCP connection with a home address and, when changing networks, it continues to communicate with the original endpoint from a care-of address as it changes LANs, which sends all traffic back through the home address. The handing off of network addresses does not disrupt the TCP connection state (the original TCP port number and address remain intact).

Improved Security   Unlike IPv4, IPv6 has security built in. *Internet Protocol Security (IPsec)* is a component used today to authenticate and encrypt secure tunnels from a source to a destination. This can be from the client to the server or between gateways. IPv4 lets you do this by enhancing IP header functionality (basically adding a second IP header while encrypting everything behind it). In IPv6, you add this as standard functionality by using extension headers. Extension headers are inserted into the packet only if they are needed. Each header has a "next header" field, which identifies the next piece of information. The extension headers currently identified for IPv6 are Hop-By-Hop Options, Routing, Fragment, Destination Options, Authentication, and Encapsulating Security Payload. The Authentication header and the Encapsulating Security Payload header are the IPsec-specific control headers.

IPv4 to IPv6 Interoperability   Several mechanisms in IPv6 make the IPv4-to-IPv6 transition easy:

> A simple dual-stack implementation where both IPv4 and IPv6 are installed and used is certainly an option. In most situations (so far), this doesn't work so well because most of us aren't connected to an IPv6 network and our Internet connection is not IPv6 even if we're using IPv6 internally. Therefore, Microsoft includes other mechanisms that can be used in several different circumstances.

> *Intra-Site Automatic Tunnel Addressing Protocol (ISATAP)* is an automatic tunneling mechanism used to connect an IPv6 network to an IPv4 address space (not using NAT). ISATAP treats the IPv4 space as one big logical link connection space.

> *6to4* is a mechanism used to transition to IPv4. This method, like ISATAP, treats the IPv4 address space as a logical link layer with each IPv6 space in transition using a 6to4 router to create endpoints using the IPv4 space as a point-to-point connection (kind of like a WAN, eh?). 6to4 implementations still do not work well through a NAT, although a 6to4 implementation using an Application layer gateway (ALG) is certainly doable.

> *Teredo* is a mechanism that allows users behind a NAT to access the IPv6 space by tunneling IPv6 packets in UDP.

Pseudo-interfaces are used in these mechanisms to create a usable interface for the operating system. Another interesting feature of IPv6 is that addresses are assigned to interfaces (or pseudo-interfaces), not simply to the end node. Your Windows Server 2022 will have several unique IPv6 addresses assigned.

New Broadcast Methods   IPv6 has moved away from using broadcasting. The three types of packets used in IPv6 are unicast, multicast, and anycast. IPv6 clients then must use one of these types to get the MAC address of the next Ethernet hop (default gateway). IPv6 makes use of multicasting for this along with the new functionality called *neighbor discovery*. Not only does ARP use new functionality, but ICMP (also a layer 3 protocol) has been redone and is now known as ICMP6. *ICMP6* is used for messaging (packet too large, time exceeded, and so on) as it was in IPv4, but now it's also used for the messaging of IPv6 mobility. ICMP6 echo request and ICMP6 echo reply are still used for ping.

IPv6 Addressing Concepts

You need to consider several concepts when using IPv6 addressing. For starters, the format of the address has changed. Three types of addresses are used in IPv6, with some predefined values within the address space. You need to get used to seeing these addresses and be able to identify their uses.

IPv6 Address Format

For the design of IPv4 addresses, you present addresses as octets or the decimal (base 10) representation of 8 bits. Four octets add up to the 32 bits required. IPv6 expands the address space to 128 bits, and the representation is for the most part shown in hexadecimal (a notation used to represent 8 bits using the values 0–9 and A–F). Figure 4.13 compares IPv4 to IPv6.

FIGURE 4.13   IPv4/IPv6 comparison

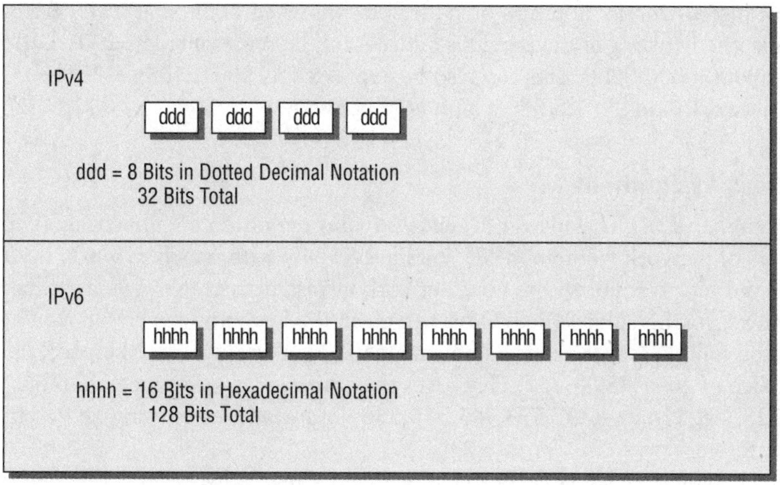

A full IPv6 address looks like this example:

2001:0DB8:0000:0000:1234:0000:A9FE:133E

You can tell the implementation of DNS will make life a lot easier even for those who like to ping the address in lieu of the name. Fortunately, DNS already has the ability to handle IPv6 addresses with the use of an AAAA record. (*A* is short for *alias*.) An A record in IPv4's addressing space is 32 bits, so an AAAA record, or four *A*s, is 128 bits. The Windows Server 2022 DNS server handles the AAAA and the reverse pointer (PTR) records for IPv6.

IPv6 Address Shortcuts

There are several shortcuts for writing an IPv6 address. These are described in the following list:

- :0: stands for :0000:.

- You can omit preceding 0s in any 16-bit word. For example, :DB8: and :0DB8: are equivalent.

- :: is a variable standing for enough zeros to round out the address to 128 bits. :: can be used only once in an address.

You can use these shortcuts to represent the example address 2001:0DB8:0000:0000 :1234:0000:A9FE:133E, as shown here:

- Compress :0000: into :0::

    2001:0DB8:0000:0000:1234:0:A9FE:133E

- Eliminate preceding zeros:

    2001:DB8:0000:0000:1234:0:A9FE:133E

- Use the special variable shortcut for multiple 0s:

    2001:DB8::1234:0:A9FE:133E

You now also use prefix notation or slash notation when discussing IPv6 networks. For example, the network of the previous address can be represented as 2001:DB8:0000: 0000:0000:0000:0000:0000. This can also be expressed as 2001:DB8:: /32. The /32 indicates 32 bits of network, and 2001:DB8: is 32 bits of network.

IPv6 Address Assignment

So, do you subnet IPv6? The answer depends on your definition of subnetting. If you are given 32 bits of network from your ISP, you have 96 bits with which to work. If you use some of the 96 bits to route within your network infrastructure, then you are subnetting. In this context, you do subnet IPv6. However, given the huge number of bits you have available, you will no longer need to implement VLSM. For example, Microsoft has a network space of 2001:4898:: /32. That gives the administrators a space of 96 bits (2^{96} = 79,228,162,514,264,337,593,543,950,336 unique addresses using all 96 bits) with which to work.

You can let Windows Server 2022 dynamically/automatically assign its IPv6 address, or you can still assign it manually (see Figure 4.14). With dynamic/automatic assignment, the IPv6 address is assigned either by a DHCPv6 server or by the Windows Server 2022 machine. If no DHCPv6 server is configured, the Windows Server 2022 machine can query the local LAN segment to find a router with a configured IPv6 interface. If so, the server will assign itself an address on the same IPv6 network as the router interface and set its default gateway to the router interface's IPv6 address. Figure 4.14 shows that you have the same dynamic and manual choices as you do in IPv4; however, the input values for IPv6 must conform to the new format.

FIGURE 4.14   TCP/IPv6 Properties window

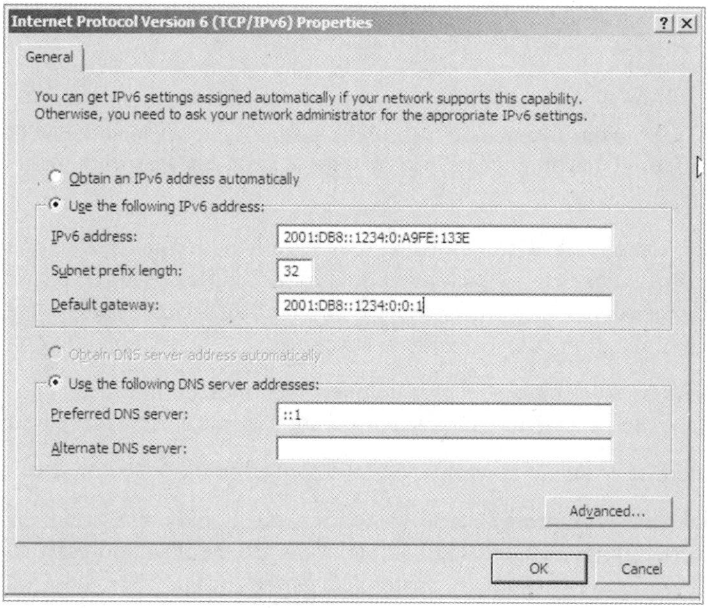

To see your configured IP addresses (IPv4 and IPv6), you can still use the `ipconfig` command. For example, I have configured a static IPv4 address and an IPv6 address on my server. The IPv6 address is the same as the one used in the earlier IPv6 example address. Figure 4.15 shows the result of this command on Windows Server 2022 for my server.

FIGURE 4.15   IPv6 configuration as seen from the command prompt

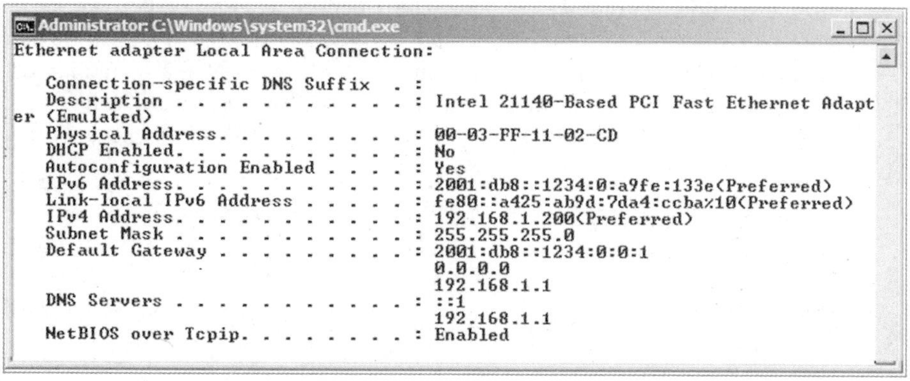

IPv6 Address Types

As stated earlier, there are three types of addresses in IPv6: anycast, unicast, and multicast. A description of each of these types of IPv6 addresses follows:

> **NOTE** Note the absence of the broadcast type, which is included in IPv4. You can't use broadcasts in IPv6; they've been replaced with multicasts.

Anycast Addresses   Anycast addresses are not really new. The concept of anycast existed in IPv4 but was not widely used. An *anycast address* is an IPv6 address assigned to multiple devices (usually different devices). When an anycast packet is sent, it is delivered to one of the devices, usually the closest one.

Unicast Addresses   A *unicast packet* uniquely identifies an interface of an IPv6 device. The interface can be a virtual interface or pseudo-interface or a real (physical) interface.

Unicast addresses come in several types, as described in the following list:

Global Unicast Address   As of this writing, the global unicast address space is defined as 2000:: /3. The 2001::/32 networks are the IPv6 addresses currently being issued to business entities. As mentioned, Microsoft has been allocated 2001:4898:: /32. A Microsoft DHCPv6 server would be set up with scopes (ranges of addresses to be assigned) within this address space. There are some special addresses and address formats that you will see in use as well. You'll find most example addresses listed as 2001:DB8:: /32; this space has been reserved for documentation. Do you remember the loopback address in IPv4, 127.0.0.1? In IPv6 the loopback address is ::1 (or 0:0:0:0:0:0:0:0001). You may also see an address with dotted-decimal used. A dual-stack Windows Server 2022 machine may also show you FE80::5EFE:192.168.1.200. This address form is used in an integration/migration model of IPv6 (or if you just can't leave the dotted-decimal era, I suppose).

Link-Local Address   Link-local addresses are defined as FE80:: /10. If you refer to Figure 4.15 showing the `ipconfig` command, you will see the link-local IPv6 address as fe80::a425:ab9d:7da4:ccba. The last 8 bytes (64 bits) are random to ensure a high probability of randomness for the link-local address. The link-local address is to be used on a single link (network segment) and should never be routed.

There is another form of the local-link IPv6 address called the *Extended User Interface 64-bit (EUI-64)* format. This is derived by using the MAC address of the physical interface and inserting an FFFE between the third and fourth bytes of the MAC. The first byte is also made 02 (this sets the universal/local, or U/L, bit to 1 as defined in IEEE 802 frame specification). Again looking at Figure 4.15, the EUI-64 address would take the physical (MAC) address 00-03-FF-11-02-CD and make the link-local IPv6 address FE80::0203:FFFF:FE11:02CD. (I've left the preceding zeros in the link-local IPv6 address to make it easier for you to pick out the MAC address with the FFFE inserted.)

AnonymousAddress Microsoft Server 2022 uses the random address by default instead of EUI-64. The random value is called the *AnonymousAddress* in Microsoft Server 2022. It can be modified to allow the use of EUI-64.

Unique Local Address The *unique local address* can be Fc00 or FD00, and it is used like the private address space of IPv4. RFC 4193 describes unique local addresses. They are not expected to be routable on the global Internet. They are used for private routing within an organization.

Multicast Address *Multicast addresses* are one-to-many communication packets. Multicast packets are identifiable by their first byte (most significant byte, leftmost byte, leftmost 2 nibbles, leftmost 8 bits, and so on). A multicast address is defined as FF00::/8.

In the second byte shown (the 00 of FF00), the second 0 is what's called the *scope*. Interface-local is 01, and link-local is 02. FF01:: is an interface-local multicast.

There are several well-known (already defined) multicast addresses. For example, if you want to send a packet to all nodes in the link-local scope, you send the packet to FF02::1 (also shown as FF02:0:0:0:0:0:0:1). The all-routers multicast address is FF02::2.

You can also use multicasting to get the logical link layer address (MAC address) of a device with which you are trying to communicate. Instead of using the ARP mechanism of IPv4, IPv6 uses the ICMPv6 neighbor solicitation (NS) and neighbor advertisement (NA) messages. The NS and NA ICMPv6 messages are all part of the new *Neighbor Discovery Protocol (NDP)*. This new ICMPv6 functionality also includes router solicitation and router advertisements as well as redirect messages (similar to the IPv4 redirect functionality).

Table 4.7 outlines the IPv6 address space known prefixes and some well-known addresses.

Unicast vs. Anycast

Unicast and anycast addresses look the same and may be indistinguishable from each other; it just depends on how many devices have the same address. If only one device has a globally unique IPv6 address, it's a unicast address. If more than one device has the same address, it's an anycast address. Both unicast and anycast are considered one-to-one communication, although you could say that anycast is one-to-"one of many."

TABLE 4.7 IPv6 address space known prefixes and addresses

Address prefix	Scope of use
2000:: /3	Global unicast space prefix
FE80:: /10	Link-local address prefix
FC00:: /7	Unique local unicast prefix
FD00:: /8	Unique local unicast prefix
FF00:: /8	Multicast prefix
2001:DB8:: /32	Global unicast prefix used for documentation
::1	Reserved local loopback address
2001:0000: /32	Teredo prefix (discussed later in this chapter)
2002:: /16	6to4 prefix

IPv6 Integration/Migration

It's time to get into the mindset of integrating IPv6 into your existing infrastructure with the longer goal of migrating to IPv6. In other words, this is not going to be an "OK, Friday the Internet is changing over" rollout. You have to bring about the change as a controlled implementation. It could easily take three to five years before a solid migration occurs and probably longer. I think the migration will take slightly less time than getting the world to migrate to the metric system on the overall timeline. The process of integration/migration consists of several mechanisms.

Dual Stack   Simply running both IPv4 and IPv6 on the same network, utilizing the IPv4 address space for devices using only IPv4 addresses and utilizing the IPv6 address space for devices using IPv6 addresses

Tunneling   Using an encapsulation scheme for transporting one address space inside another

Address Translation   Using a higher-level application to change one address type (IPv4 or IPv6) to the other transparently so that end devices are unaware one address space is talking to another

I elaborate on these three mechanisms in the following sections.

IPv6 Dual Stack

The default implementation in Windows Server 2022 is an enabled IPv6 configuration along with IPv4; this is dual stack. The implementation can be dual IP layer or dual TCP/IP stack. Windows Server 2022 uses the dual IP layer implementation (see Figure 4.16). When an application queries a DNS server to resolve a hostname to an IP address, the DNS server may respond with an IPv4 address or an IPv6 address. If the DNS server responds with both, Windows Server 2022 will prefer the IPv6 address. Windows Server 2022 can use both IPv4 and IPv6 addresses as necessary for network communication. When looking at the output of the `ipconfig` command, you will see both address spaces displayed.

FIGURE 4.16   IPv6 dual IP layer diagram

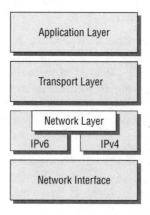

IPv6 Tunneling

Windows Server 2022 includes several tunneling mechanisms for tunneling IPv6 through the IPv4 address space. They include the following:

- Intra-Site Automatic Tunnel Addressing Protocol (ISATAP), which is used for unicast IPv6 communication across an IPv4 infrastructure. ISATAP is enabled by default in Windows Server 2022.

- 6to4, which is used for unicast IPv6 communication across an IPv4 infrastructure.

- Teredo, which is used for unicast IPv6 communication with an IPv4 NAT implementation across an IPv4 infrastructure.

With multiple tunneling protocols available and enabled by default, you might ask, what's the difference, and why is one used over the others? They all allow you to tunnel IPv6 packets through the IPv4 address space (a really cool thing if you're trying to integrate/migrate). Here are the details of these tunneling mechanisms:

ISATAP   *Intra-Site Automatic Tunnel Addressing Protocol (ISATAP)* is the automatic tunnel addressing protocol providing IPv6 addresses based on the IPv4 address of the end interface (node). The IPv6 address is automatically configured on the local device, and the dual stack machine can use either its IPv4 or IPv6 address to communicate on the local network (within the local network infrastructure). ISATAP can use the neighbor discovery mechanism to determine the router ID and network prefix where the device is located, thus making intrasite communication possible even in a routed infrastructure.

The format of an ISATAP address is as follows:

[64 bits of prefix] [32 bits indicating ISATAP] [32 bits IPv4 address]

The center 32 bits indicating ISATAP are actually 0000:5EFE (when using private IPv4 addresses). The ISATAP address of the example Windows Server 2022 machine using the link-local IPv6 address is FE80::5EFE:192.168.1.200. Each node participating in the ISATAP infrastructure must support ISATAP. If you're routing through an IPv4 cloud, a border router (a router transitioning from an IPv6 to IPv4 space) must support ISATAP. Windows Server 2022 can be configured as a border router, and it will forward ISATAP packets. ISATAP is experimental and is defined in RFC 4214.

6to4   *6to4* specifies a procedure for IPv6 networks to communicate with each other through an IPv4 space without the IPv6 nodes having to know what's happening. The IPv6 nodes do not need to be dual stacked to make this happen. The border router is the device responsible for knowing about the IPv6-to-IPv4 transition. The IPv6 packets are encapsulated at the border router (and decapsulated at the other end or on the way back). There is an assigned prefix for the 6to4 implementation: 2002:: /16. 6to4 is defined in RFC 3056.

Teredo   *Teredo* (named after a kind of shipworm that drills holes in the wood of ships) is a protocol designed to allow IPv6 addresses to be available to hosts through one or more layers of NAT. Teredo uses a process of tunneling packets through the IPv4 space using UDP. The Teredo service encapsulates the IPv6 data within a UDP segment (packet) and uses IPv4 addressing to get through the IPv4 cloud. Having layer 4 (Transport layer) available to use as translation functionality is what gives you the ability to be behind a NAT. Teredo provides host-to-host communication and dynamic addressing for IPv6 nodes (dual stack), allowing the nodes to have access to resources in an IPv6 network and the IPv6 devices to have access to the IPv6 devices that have only connectivity to the IPv4 space (like home users who have an IPv6-enabled operating system connecting to IPv6 resources while their home ISP has only IPv4 capabilities). Teredo is defined in RFC 4380.

In Windows Server 2022, an IPv4 Teredo server is identified and configured (using the `netsh` command interface). The Teredo server provides connectivity resources (address) to the Teredo client (the node that has access to the IPv4 Internet and needs access to an IPv6 network/Internet). A Teredo relay is a component used by the IPv6 router to receive traffic destined for Teredo clients and forward the traffic appropriately. The defined prefix for a Teredo address is 2001:0000:: /32. Teredo does add overhead like all the other implementations discussed. It is generally accepted that you should use the simplest model available. However, in the process of integration/migration for most of us behind a NAT, Teredo will be the process to choose.

From Windows Server 2022, use the `ipconfig /all` command to view the default configurations including IPv4 and IPv6. You may notice a notation that I didn't discuss, the percent sign at the end of the IPv6 address (see Figure 4.17). The number after the percent sign is the virtual interface identifier used by Windows Server 2022.

FIGURE 4.17   IPv6 interface identifier for `ipconfig` display

```
Link-local IPv6 Address . . . . . : fe80::a425:ab9d:7da4:ccba%10
```

Useful IPv6 Information Commands

You can use numerous commands to view, verify, and configure the network parameters of Windows Server 2022. Specifically, you can use the `netsh` command set and the `route` command set as well as the standard `ping` and `tracert` functions.

Use the `netsh` command interface (as well as the provided dialog boxes, if you want) to examine and configure IPv6 functionality. The `netsh` command issued from the command interpreter changes into a network shell (`netsh`) where you can configure and view both IPv4 and IPv6 components.

Don't forget to use the ever-popular `route print` command to see the Windows Server 2022 routing tables (IPv4 and IPv6). The other diagnostic commands are still available for IPv4 as well as IPv6. In previous versions of Microsoft operating systems, `ping` was the IPv4 command, and `ping6` was the IPv6 command. This has changed in Windows Server 2022; `ping` works for both IPv4 and IPv6 to test layer 3 connectivity to remote devices. The IPv4 `tracert` command was `tracert6` for IPv6. The command is now `tracert` for both IPv4 and IPv6, and it will show you every layer 3 (IP) hop from source to destination. (This assumes that all of the administrators from here to there want you to see the hops and are not blocking ICMP. It also assumes that there are no IP tunnels, which your packets are traversing; you won't see the router hops in the tunnel either.)

Overall, the consortium of people developing the Internet and the Internet Protocol have tried to make all of the changes to communication infrastructures easy to implement. (This is a daunting task with the many vendors and various infrastructures currently in place.) The goal is not to daze and confuse administrators; it's designed to provide maximum flexibility with the greatest functionality. IPv6 is going to provide the needed layer 3 (Network layer, global addressing layer, logical addressing layer . . . call it what you like) functionality for the foreseeable future.

IPv6 Address Breakdown

The final thing that you need to understand about IPv6 is how the address breaks down. As I have stated previously, there are different sections of an IPv6 address. For example, the first group of numbers can show you the site prefix and what type of message that you are dealing with. The ending part of the IPv6 address shows the computer's interface ID. So, let's take a look at an IPv6 address and how each section shows you about the network and computer system:

2001:0db8:6d4c:2116:0000:0000:1996:5acb

In this IPv6 address, there are actually multiple sections. As I have stated, an IPv6 address is 128 bits. The first 64 bits explain the Site Prefix and Subnet ID and the final 64 bits shows the Interface ID.

So, using the previous IPv6 address, let's break down the sections:

2001:0db8:6d4c:2116   :   0000:0000:1996:5acb

64 bits   64 bits

2001:0db8:6d4c   :   2116   :   0000:0000:1996:5acb

Site Prefix Subnet ID   Interface ID

Summary

In this chapter, I explained the importance of properly configuring both computer ports and using the IP protocol. Knowing the most common computer ports is very important when configuring both computers and firewalls.

The Internet Protocol (IP) is the primary protocol in use today. I showed how the 32-bit IPv4 address is a structured and hierarchical one that is used to identify uniquely every machine on a network. You learned how to determine available IP addresses and implement subnetting.

In addition, you learned how the new layer 3 IPv6 protocol is implemented, including the structure of the IPv6 address. Finally, I discussed the new functionality included in IPv6 addressing as well as several Windows Server 2022 integration/migration implementations.

Exam Essentials

Know the most commonly used port numbers.   When making a connection, the client chooses a source port for the communication that is usually in the range 1024–65535 (or sometimes in the range 1–65535). This source port then communicates with a destination port on the server side.

Understand what subnetting is and when to use it.   If an organization is large and has many computers or if its computers are geographically dispersed, it's sensible to divide its large network into smaller ones connected by routers. These smaller networks are called *subnets*. Subnetting is the process of carving a single IP network into smaller, logical subnetworks.

Understand subnet masks.   For the subnet address scheme to work, every machine on the network must know which part of the host address will be used as the subnet address. The network administrator creates a 32-bit subnet mask consisting of 1s and 0s. The 1s in the subnet mask represent the positions that refer to the network or subnet addresses. The 0s represent the positions that refer to the host portion of the address.

Understand IPv6.   Understand the structure of an IPv6 address and how it's displayed. Know the shortcuts and rules (such as for displaying 0s) for writing IPv6 addresses. Know the integration/migration components for IPv6 included in Windows Server 2022, including tunneling and dual stack.

Review Questions

1. Your company has a main office and a branch office. The two offices are connected by using a WAN link. Each office contains a firewall that filters WAN traffic. The network in the branch office contains 10 servers that run Windows Server 2022. You need to configure the firewall in the branch office to allow for secure inbound connections. Which inbound TCP port should you allow?

    A. 443

    B. 80

    C. 20

    D. 21

2. Your network contains an Active Directory Domain Services (AD DS) domain named WillPanek.com. You need to configure the server port to allow for Secure Shell (SSH).

    Solution: On the server's firewall, you configure ports 20 and 21 for both inbound and outbound communications. Does this meet the goal?

    A. Yes

    B. No

3. Your network contains multiple Exchange servers located in multiple locations. You need to configure the server port to allow for Simple Mail Transfer Protocol (SMTP).

    Solution: On the Exchange servers, you configure port 53 for both inbound and outbound communications. Does this meet the goal?

    A. Yes

    B. No

4. Your network contains multiple clients that use external mail servers. You need to configure the firewall port to allow for Post Office Protocol version 3 (POP3).

    Solution: On the firewall, you configure port 110 for both inbound and outbound communications. Does this meet the goal?

    A. Yes

    B. No

5. You are the network administrator for ABC Company. You have an IPv6 prefix of 2001:DB8:BBCC:0000::/53, and you need to set up your network so that your IPv6 addressing scheme can handle 1,000 more subnets. Which network mask would you use?

    A. /60

    B. /61

    C. /62

    D. /63

    E. /64

6. You are the network administrator for WillPanek.com Corporation. WillPanek.com has a Windows Server 2022 machine that needs to be able to communicate with all computers on the internal network. WillPanek.com has decided to add 15 new segments to its IPv6 network. How would you configure the IPv6 so that the server can communicate with all the segments?

A. Configure the IPv6 address as fd00::2b0:e0ff:dee9:4143/8.

B. Configure the IPv6 address as fe80::2b0:e0ff:dee9:4143/32.

C. Configure the IPv6 address as ff80::2b0:e0ff:dee9:4143/64.

D. Configure the IPv6 address as fe80::2b0:e0ff:dee9:4143/64.

7. You are the network administrator for a mid-sized organization that has installed Windows Server 2022 onto the network. You are thinking of moving all machines to Windows 10 and IPv6. You decide to set up a test environment with four subnets. What type of IPv6 addresses do you need to set up?

A. Global addresses

B. Link-local addresses

C. Unique local addresses

D. Site-local addresses

8. You have a large IP-routed network using the address 137.25.0.0; it is composed of 20 subnets, with a maximum of 300 hosts on each subnet. Your company continues on a merger-and-acquisitions spree, and your manager has told you to prepare for an increase to 50 subnets, with some containing more than 600 hosts. Using the existing network address, which of the following subnet masks would work for the requirement set by your manager?

A. 255.255.252.0

B. 255.255.254.0

C. 255.255.248.0

D. 255.255.240.0

9. Your company is growing dramatically via acquisitions of other companies. As the network administrator, you need to keep up with the changes because they affect the workstations and you need to support them. When you started, there were 15 locations connected via routers, and now there are 25. As new companies are acquired, they are migrated to Windows Server 2022 and brought into the same domain as another site. Management says that they are going to acquire at least 10 more companies in the next two years. The engineers have also told you that they are redesigning the company's Class B address into an IP addressing scheme that will support these requirements and that there will never be more than 1,000 network devices on any subnet. What is the appropriate subnet mask to support this network when the changes are completed?

A. 255.255.252.0

B. 255.255.248.0

C. 255.255.255.0

D. 255.255.255.128

10. You work for a small printing company that has 75 workstations. Most of them run stand-ard office applications such as word processing, spreadsheet, and accounting programs. Fif-teen of the workstations are constantly processing huge graphics files and then sending print jobs to industrial-sized laser printers. The performance of the network has always been an issue, but you have never addressed it. You have now migrated your network to Windows 10 and Windows Server 2022 and have decided to take advantage of the routing capability built into Windows Server 2022. You choose the appropriate server and place two NICs in the machine, but you realize that you have only one network address, 201.102.34.0, which you obtained years ago. How should you subnet this address to segment the bandwidth hogs from the rest of the network while giving everyone access to the entire network?

    A. 255.255.255.192

    B. 255.255.255.224

    C. 255.255.255.252

    D. 255.255.255.240

11. You work for Carpathian Worldwide Enterprises, which has more than 50 administrative and manufacturing locations around the world. The size of these organizations varies greatly, with the number of computers per location ranging from 15 to slightly fewer than 1,000. The sales operations use more than 1,000 facilities, each of which contains 2 to 5 computers. Carpathian is also in merger talks with another large organization. If the merger materializes as planned, you will have to accommodate another 100 manufacturing and administrative locations, each with a maximum of 600 computers, as well as 2,000 additional sales facilities. You don't have any numbers for the future growth of the company, but you are told to keep growth in mind. You decide to implement a private addressing plan for the entire organiza-tion. More than half of your routers don't support Variable Length Subnet Masking. Which subnet masks would work for this situation? (Choose all that apply.)

    A. 255.255.224.0

    B. 255.255.240.0

    C. 255.255.248.0

    D. 255.255.252.0

    E. 255.255.254.0

12. Which of the following subnet masks are represented with the CIDR of /27?

    A. 255.255.255.254

    B. 255.255.255.248

    C. 255.255.255.224

    D. 255.255.255.240

13. You have 3,500 client computers on a single subnet. You need to select a subnet mask that will support all the client computers. You need to minimize the number of unused addresses. Which subnet mask should you choose?

    A. 255.255.248.0

    B. 255.255.254.0

    C. 255.255.240.0

    D. 255.255.252.0

14. You ask one of your technicians to get the IPv6 address of a new Windows Server 2022 machine, and she hands you a note with FE80::0203:FFFF:FE11:2CD on it. What can you tell from this address? (Choose two.)

A. This is a globally unique IPv6 address.

B. This is a link-local IPv6 address.

C. This is a multicast IPv6 address.

D. In EUI-64 format, you can see the MAC address of the node.

E. In EUI-64 format, you can see the IPv4 address of the node.

15. Your network contains an Active Directory Domain Services (AD DS) domain named WillPanek.com. You need to configure the server port to allow for DNS communications.

Solution: On the server's firewall, you configure port 80 for both inbound and outbound communications. Does this meet the goal?

A. Yes

B. No

Chapter

5

Implementing DNS

THE FOLLOWING AZ-800 EXAM OBJECTIVES ARE COVERED IN THIS CHAPTER:

✓ **Implement on-premises and hybrid name resolution**

- ▪ Integrate DNS with AD DS

- ▪ Create and manage zones and records

- ▪ Configure DNS forwarding/conditional forwarding

- ▪ Integrate Windows Server DNS with Azure DNS private zones

- ▪ Implement DNSSEC

As we move closer to connecting your onsite network with Azure, we still have features and services required to make this happen. That brings us to DNS.

The Domain Name System (DNS) is one of the most important networking services that you can put on your network, and it's also one of the key topics that you'll need to understand if you plan to take any of the Microsoft Azure exams.

By the end of this chapter, you should have a deeper understanding of how DNS works, how to set it up properly, how to configure DNS, proper management of the DNS server, and how to troubleshoot DNS issues quickly and easily in Microsoft Windows Server 2022.

Introducing DNS

The *Domain Name System (DNS)* is a service that allows you to resolve a hostname to an Internet Protocol (IP) address. One of the inherent complexities of operating in networked environments is working with multiple protocols and network addresses. Owing largely to the tremendous rise in the popularity of the Internet, however, most environments have transitioned to use *Transmission Control Protocol/Internet Protocol (TCP/IP)* as their primary networking protocol. Microsoft is no exception when it comes to supporting TCP/IP in its workstation and server products. All current versions of Microsoft's operating systems support TCP/IP, as do most other modern operating systems.

An easy way to understand DNS is to think about making a telephone call. If you wanted to call Microsoft and did not know the phone number, you could call information, tell the operator the name (Microsoft), and get the telephone number. You would then make the call. Now think about trying to connect to Server1. You don't know the TCP/IP number (the computer's telephone number), so your computer asks DNS (information) for the number of Server1. DNS returns the number, and your system makes the connection (call). DNS is your network's 411, or information, and it returns the TCP/IP data for your network.

TCP/IP is actually a collection of different technologies (protocols and services) that allow computers to function together on a single, large, and heterogeneous network. Some of the major advantages of this protocol are widespread support for hardware, software, and network devices; reliance on a system of standards; and scalability. TCP handles tasks such as sequenced acknowledgments. IP involves many jobs, such as logical subnet assignment and routing.

Hosts File

Nowadays, most computer users are quite familiar with navigating to DNS-based resources, such as WillPanek.com. To resolve these "friendly" names to TCP/IP addresses that the network stack can use, you need a method for mapping them. Originally, ASCII flat files (often called *HOSTS files*, as shown in Figure 5.1) were used for this purpose. In some cases, they are still used today in small networks, and they can be valuable in helping to troubleshoot name resolution problems.

FIGURE 5.1　HOSTS file

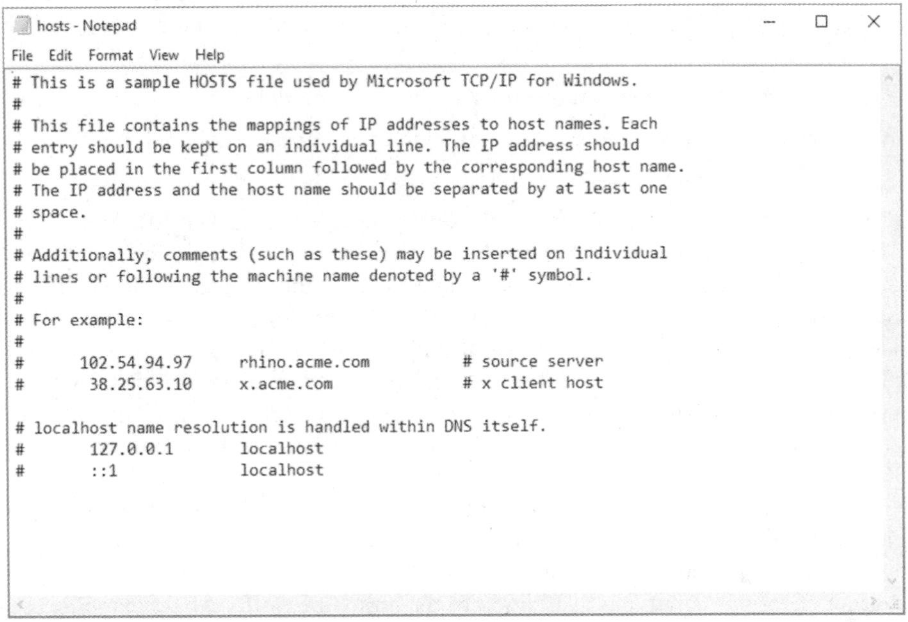

```
hosts - Notepad                                              —    □    ×
File  Edit  Format  View  Help
# This is a sample HOSTS file used by Microsoft TCP/IP for Windows.
#
# This file contains the mappings of IP addresses to host names. Each
# entry should be kept on an individual line. The IP address should
# be placed in the first column followed by the corresponding host name.
# The IP address and the host name should be separated by at least one
# space.
#
# Additionally, comments (such as these) may be inserted on individual
# lines or following the machine name denoted by a '#' symbol.
#
# For example:
#
#      102.54.94.97     rhino.acme.com          # source server
#      38.25.63.10      x.acme.com              # x client host

# localhost name resolution is handled within DNS itself.
#      127.0.0.1        localhost
#      ::1              localhost
```

As the number of machines and network devices grew, it became unwieldy for administrators to manage all of the manual updates required to enter new mappings to a master HOSTS file and distribute it. Clearly, a better system was needed.

As you can see from the sample HOSTS file in Figure 5.1, you can conduct a quick test of the email server's name resolution as follows:

1. Open the HOSTS file: `C:\Windows\Systems32\drivers\etc`.

2. Add the IP-address-to-hostname mapping.

3. Try to ping the server using the hostname to verify that you can reach it using an easy-to-remember name.

Following these steps should drive home the concept of DNS for you because you can see it working to make your life easier. Now you don't have to remember 10.0.0.10; you only need to remember `exchange03`. However, you can also see how this method can become unwieldy if you have many hosts that want to use easy-to-remember names instead of IP addresses to locate resources on your network.

When dealing with large networks, users and network administrators must be able to locate the resources they require with minimal searching. Users don't care about the actual physical or logical network address of the machine; they just want to be able to connect to it using a simple name that they can remember.

From a network administrator's standpoint, however, each machine must have its own logical address that makes it part of the network on which it resides. Therefore, some scalable and easy-to-manage method for resolving a machine's logical name to an IP address and then to a domain name is required. DNS was created just for this purpose.

DNS is a hierarchically distributed database. In other words, its layers are arranged in a definite order, and its data is distributed across a wide range of machines, each of which can exert control over a portion of the database. DNS is a standard set of protocols that defines the following:

- A mechanism for querying and updating address information in the database

- A mechanism for replicating the information in the database among servers

- A schema of the database

DNS was originally developed in the early days of the Internet (called ARPAnet at the time) when it was a small network created by the Department of Defense for research purposes. Before DNS, computer names, or hostnames, were manually entered into a HOSTS file located on a centrally administered server. Each site that needed to resolve hostnames outside of its organization had to download this file. As the number of computers on the Internet grew, so did the size of this HOSTS file—and along with it the problems of its management. The need for a new system that would offer features such as scalability, decentralized administration, and support for various data types became more and more obvious. DNS, introduced in 1984, became this new system.

With DNS, the hostnames reside in a database that can be distributed among multiple servers, decreasing the load on any one server and providing the ability to administer this naming system on a per-partition basis. DNS supports hierarchical names and allows for the registration of various data types in addition to the hostname-to-IP-address mapping used in HOSTS files. Database performance is ensured through its distributed nature as well as through caching.

The DNS distributed database establishes an inverted logical tree structure called the *domain namespace*. Each node, or domain, in that space has a unique name. At the top of the tree is the root. This may not sound quite right, which is why the DNS hierarchical model is described as being an inverted tree, with the root at the top. The root is represented by the null set: "". When written, the root node is represented by a single dot (.).

Each node in the DNS can branch out to any number of nodes below it. For example, below the root node are a number of other nodes, commonly referred to as *top-level domains (TLDs)*. These are the familiar .com, .net, .org, .gov, .edu, and other such names. Table 5.1 lists some of these TLDs.

TABLE 5.1   Common top-level DNS domains

Domain name	Type of organization
com	Commercial (for example, `stormwind.com` for StormWind Training Corporation).
edu	Educational (for example, `gatech.edu` for the Georgia Institute of Technology).
gov	Government (for example, `whitehouse.gov` for the White House in Washington, D.C.).
int	International organizations (for example, `nato.int` for NATO); this top-level domain is fairly rare.
mil	Military organizations (for example, `usmc.mil` for the Marine Corps); there is a separate set of root name servers for this domain.
net	Networking organizations and Internet providers (for example, `hiwaay.net` for HiWAAY Information Systems); many commercial organizations have registered names under this domain too.
org	Noncommercial organizations (for example, `fidonet.org` for FidoNet).
au	Australia.
uk	United Kingdom.
ca	Canada.
us	United States.
jp	Japan.

Each of these nodes then branches out into another set of domains, and they combine to form what we refer to as *domain names*, such as `microsoft.com`. A domain name identifies the domain's position in the logical DNS hierarchy in relation to its parent domain by separating each branch of the tree with a dot. Figure 5.2 shows a few of the top-level domains, where the Microsoft domain fits, and a host called Tigger within the `microsoft.com` domain. If someone wanted to contact that host, they would use the *fully qualified domain name (FQDN)*, `tigger.microsoft.com`.

FIGURE 5.2   The DNS hierarchy

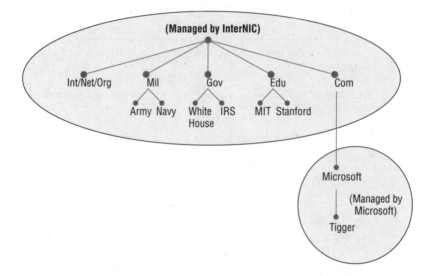

An FQDN includes the trailing dot (.) to indicate the root node, but it's commonly left off in practice.

As previously stated, one of the strengths of DNS is the ability to delegate control over portions of the DNS namespace to multiple organizations. For example, the Internet Corporation for Assigned Names and Numbers (ICANN) assigns the control over TLDs to one or more organizations. In turn, those organizations delegate portions of the DNS namespace to other organizations. For example, when you register a domain name, let's call it example.com, you control the DNS for the portion of the DNS namespace within example.com. The registrar controlling the .com TLD has delegated control over the example.com node in the DNS tree. No other node can be named example directly below the .com within the DNS database.

Within the portion of the domain namespace that you control (example.com), you could create host and other records (more on these later). You could also further subdivide example.com and delegate control over those divisions to other organizations or departments. These divisions are called *subdomains*. For example, you might create subdomains named for the cities in which the company has branch offices and then delegate control over those subdomains to the branch offices. The subdomains might be named losangeles .example.com, chicago.example.com, portsmouth.example.com, and so on.

Each domain (or delegated subdomain) is associated with DNS name servers. In other words, for every node in the DNS, one or more servers can give an authoritative answer to queries about that domain. At the root of the domain namespace are the root servers, which I'll cover later in the chapter.

Domain names and hostnames must contain only characters a to z, A to Z, 0 to 9, and − (hyphen). Other common and useful characters, such as the & (ampersand), / (slash), . (period), and _ (underscore) characters, are not allowed. This is in conflict with NetBIOS's naming restrictions. However, you'll find that Windows Server 2022 is smart enough to take a NetBIOS name, like Server_1, and turn it into a legal DNS name, like server1 .example.com.

DNS servers work together to resolve hierarchical names. If a server already has information about a name, it simply fulfills the query for the client. Otherwise, it queries other DNS servers for the appropriate information. The system works well because it distributes the authority over separate parts of the DNS structure to specific servers. A DNS zone is a portion of the DNS namespace over which a specific DNS server has authority. (DNS zone types are discussed in detail later in this chapter.)

Within a given DNS zone, resource records (RRs) contain the hosts and other database information that make up the data for the zone. For example, an RR might contain the host entry for www.example.com, pointing it to the IP address 192.168.1.10.

Understanding Servers, Clients, and Resolvers

You will need to know a few terms and concepts in order to manage a DNS server. Understanding these terms will make it easier to understand how the Windows Server 2022 DNS server works:

DNS Server   Any computer providing domain name services is a *DNS name server*. No matter where the server resides in the DNS namespace, it's still a DNS name server. For example, 13 root name servers at the top of the DNS tree are responsible for delegating the TLDs. The *root servers* provide referrals to name servers for the TLDs, which in turn provides referrals to an authoritative name server for a given domain.

 The Berkeley Internet Name Domain (BIND) was originally the only software available for running the root servers on the Internet. However, a few years ago the organizations responsible for the root servers undertook an effort to diversify the software running on these important machines. Today, root servers run multiple types of name server software. BIND is still primarily on Unix-based machines, and it is also the most popular for Internet providers. None of the root servers run Windows DNS.

Any DNS server implementation supporting Service Location Resource Records (see RFC 2782) and Dynamic Updates (RFC 2136) is sufficient to provide the name service for any operating system running Windows 2003 software and newer.

DNS Client   A *DNS client* is any machine that issues queries to a DNS server. The client hostname may or may not be registered in a DNS database. Clients issue DNS requests through processes called *resolvers*. You'll sometimes see the terms *client* and *resolver* used synonymously.

Resolver   *Resolvers* are software processes, sometimes implemented in software libraries, which handles the actual process of finding the answers to queries for DNS data. The resolver is also built into many larger pieces of software so that external libraries don't have to be called to make and process DNS queries. Resolvers can be what you'd consider client computers or other DNS servers attempting to resolve an answer on behalf of a client (for example, Internet Explorer).

Query   A *query* is a request for information sent to a DNS server. Three types of queries can be made to a DNS server: recursive, inverse, and iterative. I'll discuss the differences between these query types in the section "DNS Queries" a bit later in the chapter.

Understanding the DNS Process

To help you understand the DNS process, I will start by covering the differences between Dynamic DNS and Non-dynamic DNS. During this discussion, you will learn how Dynamic DNS populates the DNS database. You'll also see how to implement security for Dynamic DNS. I will then talk about the workings of different types of DNS queries. Finally, I will discuss caching and time to live (TTL). You'll learn how to determine the best setting for your organization.

Dynamic DNS and Non-dynamic DNS

To understand Dynamic DNS and Non-dynamic DNS, you must go back in time (here is where the TV screen always used to get wavy). Many years ago when we all worked on NT 3.51 and NT 4.0, most networks used Windows Internet Name Service (WINS) to do their TCP/IP name resolution. Windows versions 95/98 and NT 4.0 Professional were all built on the idea of using WINS. This worked out well for administrators because WINS was dynamic (which meant that once it was installed, it automatically built its own database). Back then, there was no such thing as Dynamic DNS; administrators had to enter DNS records into the server manually. This is important to know even today. If you have clients still running any of these older operating systems (95/98 or NT 4), these clients cannot use Dynamic DNS.

Now let's move forward in time to the release of Windows Server 2000. Microsoft announced that DNS was going to be the name resolution method of choice. Many administrators (me included) did not look forward to the switch. Because there was no such thing as Dynamic DNS, most administrators had nightmares about manually entering records. However, luckily for us, when Microsoft released Windows Server 2000, DNS had the ability to operate dynamically. Now when you're setting up Windows Server 2022 DNS, you can choose what type of dynamic update you would like to use, if any. Let's talk about why you would want to choose one over the other.

The *Dynamic DNS (DDNS) standard*, described in RFC 2136, allows DNS clients to update information in the DNS database files. For example, a Windows Server 2022 DHCP server can automatically tell a DDNS server which IP addresses it has assigned to what machines. Windows 2000 (and higher) and Windows 7 (and higher) DHCP clients can do this too. For security reasons, however, it's better to let the DHCP server do it. The result: IP addresses and DNS records stay in sync so that you can use DNS and DHCP together seamlessly. Because DDNS is a proposed Internet standard, you can even use the Windows Server 2022 DDNS-aware parts with Unix/Linux-based DNS servers.

Non-dynamic DNS (NDDNS) does not automatically populate the DNS database. The client systems do not have the ability to update to DNS. If you decide to use Non-dynamic DNS, you will need to populate the DNS database manually. Non-dynamic DNS is a reasonable choice if your organization is small to midsized and you do not want extra network traffic (clients updating to the DNS server) or if you need to enter the computer's TCP/IP information manually because of strict security measures.

Dynamic DNS has the ability to be secure, and the chances are slim that a rogue system (a computer that does not belong in your DNS database) could update to a secure DNS server. Nevertheless, some organizations have to follow stricter security measures and are not allowed to have dynamic updates.

The major downside to entering records into DNS manually occurs when the organization is using the *Dynamic Host Configuration Protocol (DHCP)*. When using DHCP, it is possible for users to end up with different TCP/IP addresses every day. This means that you have to update DNS manually each day to keep it accurate.

If you choose to allow Dynamic DNS, you need to decide how you want to set it up. When setting up dynamic updates on your DNS server, you have three choices (see Figure 5.3).

FIGURE 5.3 Setting the Dynamic Updates option

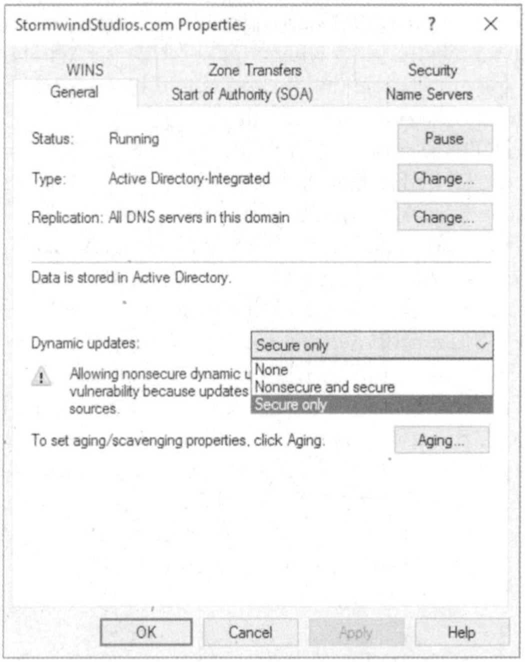

None   This means your DNS server is Non-dynamic.

Nonsecure and Secure   This means that any machine (even if it does not have a domain account) can register with DNS. Using this setting could allow rogue systems to enter records into your DNS server.

Secure Only   This means that only machines with accounts in Active Directory can register with DNS. Before DNS registers any account in its database, it checks Active Directory to make sure that account is an authorized domain computer.

How Dynamic DNS Populates the DNS Database

TCP/IP is the protocol used for network communications on a Microsoft Windows Server 2022 network. Users have two ways to receive a TCP/IP number:

- Static (you manually enter the TCP/IP information)
- Dynamic (using DHCP)

When you set up TCP/IP, DNS can also be configured.

Once a client gets the address of the DNS server, if that client is allowed to update with DNS, the client sends a registration to DNS or requests DHCP to send the registration. DNS then does one of two things, depending on which Dynamic Updates option is specified:

- Check with Active Directory to see if that computer has an account (Secure Only updates) and, if it does, enter the record into the database.

- Enter the record into its database (nonsecure and secure updates).

What if you have clients that cannot update DNS? Well, there is a solution—DHCP. In the DNS tab of the IPv4 Properties window, check the option labeled "Dynamically update DNS records for DHCP clients that do not request updates (for example, clients running Windows NT 4.0)," which is shown in Figure 5.4.

FIGURE 5.4 DHCP settings for DNS

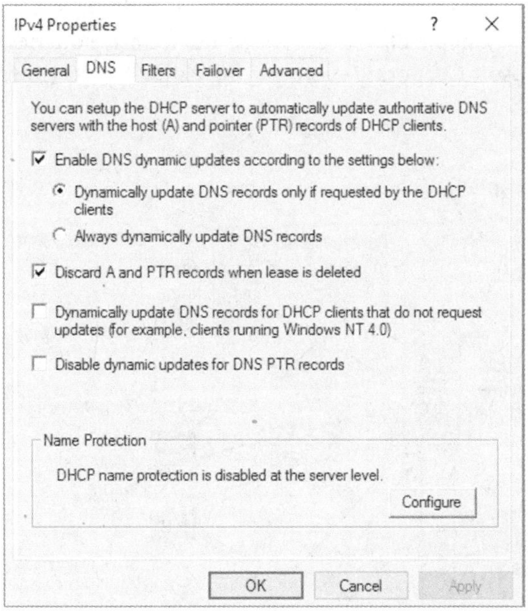

DHCP, along with Dynamic DNS clients, allows an organization to update its DNS database dynamically without the time and effort of having an administrator manually enter DNS records.

DNS Queries

As stated earlier, a client can make three types of queries to a DNS server: recursive, inverse, and iterative. Remember that the client of a DNS server can be a resolver (what you'd normally call a client) or another DNS server.

Iterative Queries

Iterative queries are the easiest to understand: a client asks the DNS server for an answer, and the server returns the best answer. This information likely comes from the server's cache. The server never sends out an additional query in response to an iterative query. If the server doesn't know the answer, it may direct the client to another server through a referral.

Recursive Queries

In a *recursive query*, the client sends a query to a name server, asking it to respond either with the requested answer or with an error message. The error states one of two things:

- The server can't come up with the right answer.

- The domain name doesn't exist.

In a recursive query, the name server isn't allowed to just refer the client to some other name server. Most resolvers use recursive queries. In addition, if your DNS server uses a forwarder, the requests sent by your server to the forwarder will be recursive queries.

Figure 5.5 shows an example of both recursive and iterative queries. In this example, a client within the Microsoft Corporation is querying its DNS server for the IP address for www.whitehouse.gov.

FIGURE 5.5   A sample DNS query

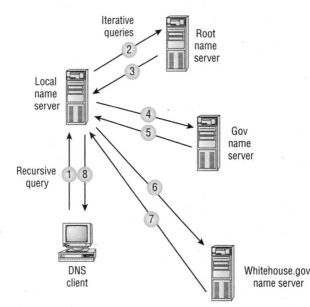

Here's what happens to resolve the request:

1. The resolver sends a recursive DNS query to its local DNS server asking for the IP address of www.whitehouse.gov. The local name server is responsible for resolving the name, and it cannot refer the resolver to another name server.

2. The local name server checks its zones, and it finds no zones corresponding to the requested domain name.

3. The root name server has authority for the root domain and will reply with the IP address of a name server for the .gov top-level domain.

4. The local name server sends an iterative query for www.whitehouse.gov to the Gov name server.

5. The Gov name server replies with the IP address of the name server servicing the whitehouse.gov domain.

6. The local name server sends an iterative query for www.whitehouse.gov to the whitehouse.gov name server.

7. The whitehouse.gov name server replies with the IP address corresponding to www.whitehouse.gov.

8. The local name server sends the IP address of www.whitehouse.gov back to the original resolver.

Inverse Queries

Inverse queries use pointer (PTR) records. Instead of supplying a name and then asking for an IP address, the client first provides the IP address and then asks for the name. Because there's no direct correlation in the DNS namespace between a domain name and its associated IP address, this search would be fruitless without the use of the in-addr.arpa domain. Nodes in the in-addr.arpa domain are named after the numbers in the dotted-octet representation of IP addresses. However, because IP addresses get more specific from left to right and domain names get less specific from left to right, the order of IP address octets must be reversed when building the in-addr.arpa tree. With this arrangement, administration of the lower limbs of the DNS in-addr.arpa tree can be given to companies as they are assigned their Class A, B, or C subnet address or delegated even further down thanks to Variable Length Subnet Masking (VLSM).

Once the domain tree is built into the DNS database, a special PTR record is added to associate the IP addresses with the corresponding hostnames. In other words, to find a hostname for the IP address 206.131.234.1, the resolver would query the DNS server for a PTR record for 1.234.131.206.in-addr.arpa. If this IP address is outside the local domain, the DNS server will start at the root and sequentially resolve the domain nodes until arriving at 234.131.206.in-addr.arpa, which would contain the PTR record for the desired host.

Caching and Time to Live

When a name server is processing a recursive query, it may be required to send out several queries to find the definitive answer. Name servers, acting as resolvers, are allowed to cache all of the received information during this process; each record contains information called *time to live (TTL)*. The TTL specifies how long the record will be held in the local cache until it must be resolved again. If a query comes in that can be satisfied by this cached data, the TTL that's returned with it equals the current amount of time left before the data is flushed.

There is also a negative cache TTL. The *negative cache TTL* is used when an authoritative server responds to a query indicating that the record queried doesn't exist, and it indicates the amount of time that this negative answer may be held. Negative caching is quite helpful in preventing repeated queries for names that don't exist.

The administrator for the DNS zone sets TTL values for the entire zone. The value can be the same across the zone, or the administrator can set a separate TTL for each RR within the zone. Client resolvers also have data caches and honor the TTL value so that they know when to flush. Users also have the ability to manually flush the DNS cache by running the `Ipconfig /flushDNS` command.

Introducing DNS Database Zones

As mentioned earlier in this chapter, a DNS zone is a portion of the DNS namespace over which a specific DNS server has authority. Within a given DNS zone, there are resource records that define the hosts and other types of information that make up the database for the zone. You can choose from several different zone types. Understanding the characteristics of each will help you choose which is right for your organization.

> **NOTE** The DNS zones discussed in this book are all Microsoft Windows Server 2022 zones. Non-Windows (for example, Unix) systems set up their DNS zones differently.

In the following sections, I will discuss the different zone types and their characteristics.

Understanding Primary Zones

When you're learning about zone types, things can get a bit confusing. But it's really not difficult to understand how they work and why you would want to choose one type of zone over another. Zones are databases that store records. By choosing one zone type over another, you are basically just choosing how the database works and how it will be stored on the server.

The primary zone is responsible for maintaining all of the records for the DNS zone. It contains the primary copy of the DNS database. All record updates occur on the primary zone. You will want to create and add primary zones whenever you create a new DNS domain.

There are two types of primary zones:

- Primary zone
- Primary zone with Active Directory Integration (Active Directory DNS)

 From this point forward, I refer to a primary zone with Active Directory Integration as an *Active Directory DNS*. When I use the term *primary zone,* Active Directory is not included.

To install DNS as a primary zone, first you must install DNS using the Server Manager MMC. Once DNS is installed and running, you create a new zone and specify it as a primary zone.

 The process of installing DNS and its zones will be discussed later in this chapter. In addition, there will be step-by-step exercises to walk you through how to install these components.

Primary zones have advantages and disadvantages. Knowing the characteristics of a primary zone will help you decide when you need the zone and when it fits into your organization.

Local Database

Primary DNS zones get stored locally in a file (with the suffix .dns) on the server. This allows you to store a primary zone on a domain controller or a member server. In addition, by loading DNS onto a member server, you can help a small organization conserve resources. Such an organization may not have the resources to load DNS on an Active Directory domain controller.

Unfortunately, the local database has many disadvantages:

Lack of Fault Tolerance Think of a primary zone as a contact list on your smartphone. All of the contacts in the list are the records in your database. The problem is that if you lose your phone or the phone breaks, you lose your contact list. Until your phone gets fixed or you swap out your phone card, the contacts may become unavailable.

It works the same way with a primary zone. If the server goes down or you lose the hard drive, DNS records on that machine are unreachable. You can install a secondary zone (explained in the next section), and that provides temporary fault tolerance. Unfortunately, if the primary zone is down for an extended period of time, the secondary server's information will no longer be valid.

Additional Network Traffic Let's imagine that you are looking for a contact number for John Smith. John Smith is not listed in your cell phone directory, but he is listed in your partner's cell phone. You have to contact your partner to get the listing. You cannot directly access your partner's cell contacts.

When a resolver sends a request to DNS to get the TCP/IP address for Jsmith (in this case Jsmith is a computer name) and the DNS server does not have an answer, it does not have the ability to check the other server's database directly to get an answer. Thus, it forwards the request to another DNS. When DNS servers are replicating zone databases with other DNS servers, this causes additional network traffic.

No Security   Staying with the cell phone example, let's say that you call your partner looking for John Smith's phone number. When your partner gives you the phone number over your wireless phone, someone with a scanner can pick up your conversation. Unfortunately, wireless telephone calls are not very secure.

Now a resolver asks a primary zone for the Jsmith TCP/IP address. If someone on the network has a packet sniffer, they can steal the information in the DNS packets being sent over the network. The packets are not secure unless you implement some form of secondary security. Also, the DNS server has the ability to be dynamic. A primary zone accepts all updates from DNS servers. You cannot set it to accept secure updates only.

Understanding Secondary Zones

In Windows Server 2022 DNS, you have the ability to use secondary DNS zones. Secondary zones are noneditable copies of the DNS database. You use them for *load balancing* (also referred to as *load sharing*), which is a way of managing network overloads on a single server. A secondary zone gets its database from a primary zone.

A *secondary zone* contains a database with all of the same information as the primary zone, and it can be used to resolve DNS requests. Secondary zones have the following advantages:

- A secondary zone provides fault tolerance, so if the primary zone server becomes unavailable, name resolution can still occur using the secondary zone server.

- Secondary DNS servers can also increase network performance by offloading some of the traffic that would otherwise go to the primary server.

Secondary servers are often placed within the parts of an organization that have high-speed network access. This prevents DNS queries from having to run across slow WAN connections. For example, if there are two remote offices within the `stormwind.com` organization, you may want to place a secondary DNS server in each remote office. This way, when clients require name resolution, they will contact the nearest server for this IP address information, thus preventing unnecessary WAN traffic.

Having too many secondary zone servers can actually cause an increase in network traffic because of replication (especially if DNS changes are fairly frequent). Therefore, you should always weigh the benefits and drawbacks and properly plan for secondary zone servers.

Configure Zone Delegation

One advantage of DNS is the ability of turning a namespace into one or more zones. These zones can be replicated to each other or other DNS servers. As an administrator, you must decide when you want to break your DNS into multiple zones. When considering this option, there are a few things to think about:

- You want the management of your DNS namespace to be delegated by another location or department in your organization.

- You want to load-balance your traffic among multiple servers by turning a large zone into many smaller zones. This will help improve performance and create redundancy among your DNS servers.

- You have remote offices opening up, and you want to expand your DNS namespace.

  To create a new zone delegation, complete the following steps:

1. Open the DNS console.

2. In the console tree, right-click the applicable subdomain and then click New Delegation.

3. Follow the instructions provided in the New Delegation Wizard to finish creating the newly delegated domain.

Understanding Active Directory Integrated DNS

Windows Server 2000 introduced *Active Directory Integrated DNS* to the world. This zone type was unique, and it was a separate choice during setup. In Windows Server 2003, this zone type became an add-on to a primary zone. In Windows Server 2022, it works the same way. After choosing to set up a primary zone, you select the Store The Zone In Active Directory option (see Figure 5.6).

FIGURE 5.6 Setting up an Active Directory Integrated zone

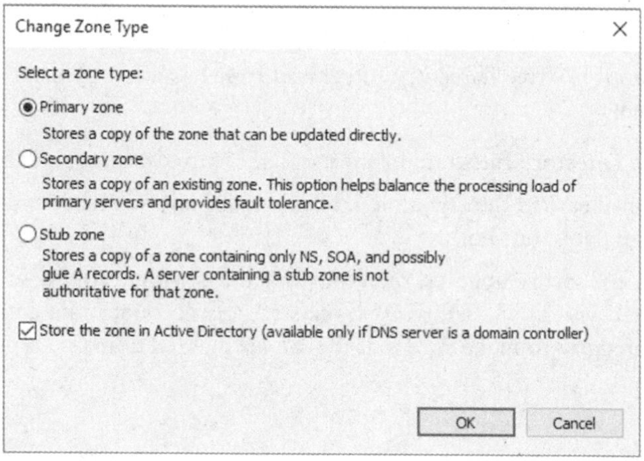

Disadvantages of Active Directory Integrated DNS

The main disadvantage of Active Directory Integrated DNS is that it has to reside on a domain controller because the DNS database is stored in Active Directory. As a result, you cannot load this zone type on a member server, and small organizations might not have the resources to set up a dedicated domain controller.

Advantages of Active Directory Integrated DNS

The advantages of using an Active Directory Integrated DNS zone well outweigh the disadvantages just discussed. The following are some of the major advantages to an Active Directory Integrated DNS zone:

Full Fault Tolerance   Think of an Active Directory Integrated zone as a database on your server that stores contact information for all your clients. If you need to retrieve John Smith's phone number, as long as it was entered, you can look it up on the software.

If John Smith's phone number was stored only on your computer and your computer stopped working, no one could access John Smith's phone number. But since John Smith's phone number is stored in a database to which everyone has access, if your computer stops working, other users can still retrieve John Smith's phone number.

An Active Directory Integrated zone works the same way. Since the DNS database is stored in Active Directory, all Active Directory DNS servers can have access to the same data. If one server goes down or you lose a hard drive, all other Active Directory DNS servers can still retrieve DNS records.

No Additional Network Traffic   As previously discussed, an Active Directory Integrated zone is stored in Active Directory. Since all records are now stored in Active Directory, when a resolver needs a TCP/IP address for Jsmith, any Active Directory DNS server can access Jsmith's address and respond to the resolver.

When you choose an Active Directory Integrated zone, DNS zone data can be replicated automatically to other DNS servers during the normal Active Directory replication process.

DNS Security   An Active Directory Integrated zone has a few security advantages over a primary zone:

- An Active Directory Integrated zone can use secure dynamic updates.

- As explained earlier, the Dynamic DNS standard allows secure-only updates or dynamic updates, not both.

- If you choose secure updates, then only machines with accounts in Active Directory can register with DNS. Before DNS registers any account in its database, it checks Active Directory to make sure that it is an authorized domain computer.

- An Active Directory Integrated zone stores and replicates its database through Active Directory replication. Because of this, the data gets encrypted as it is sent from one DNS server to another.

Background Zone Loading   Background zone loading (discussed in more detail later in this chapter) allows an Active Directory Integrated DNS zone to load in the background. As a result, a DNS server can service client requests while the zone is still loading into memory.

Understanding Stub Zones

Stub zones work a lot like secondary zones—the database is a noneditable copy of a primary zone. The difference is that the stub zone's database contains only the information necessary (three record types) to identify the authoritative DNS servers for a zone (see Figure 5.7). You should not use stub zones to replace secondary zones, nor should you use them for redundancy and load balancing.

FIGURE 5.7   DNS stub zone type

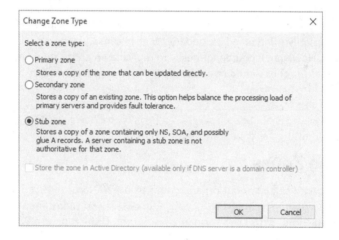

 Stub zone databases contain only three record types: name server (NS), start of authority (SOA), and glue host (A) records. Understanding these records will help you on the Microsoft certification exams. Microsoft asks many questions about stub zones on all DNS-related exams.

When to Use Stub Zones

Stub zones become particularly useful in a couple of different scenarios. Consider what happens when two large companies merge: example.com and example.net. In most cases, the DNS zone information from both companies must be available to every employee. You could set up a new zone on each side that acts as a secondary for the other side's primary zone, but administrators tend to be very protective of their DNS databases and probably wouldn't agree to this plan.

A better solution is to add to each side a stub zone that points to the primary server on the other side. When a client in example.com (which you help administer) makes a request for a name in example.net, the stub zone on the example.com DNS server would send the client to the primary DNS server for example.net without actually resolving the name. At this point, it would be up to example.net's primary server to resolve the name.

An added benefit is that, even if the administrators over at example.net change their configuration, you won't have to do anything because the changes will automatically replicate to the stub zone, just as they would for a secondary server.

Stub zones can also be useful when you administer two domains across a slow connection. Let's change the previous example a bit and assume that you have full control over example.com and example.net but they connect through a 56 Kbps line. In this case, you wouldn't necessarily mind using secondary zones because you personally administer the entire network. However, it could get messy to replicate an entire zone file across that slow line. Instead, stub zones would refer clients to the appropriate primary server at the other site.

GlobalName Zones

Earlier in this chapter, I talked about organizations using WINS to resolve NetBIOS names (also referred to as *computer names*) to TCP/IP addresses. Even today, many organizations still use WINS along with DNS for name resolution. Unfortunately, WINS is slowly becoming obsolete.

To help organizations move forward with an all-DNS network, Microsoft Windows Server 2022 DNS supports *GlobalName zones*. These use single-label names (DNS names that do not contain a suffix such as .com, .net, and so on). GlobalName zones are not intended to support peer-to-peer networks and workstation name resolution, and they don't support dynamic DNS updates.

GlobalName zones are designed to be used with servers. Because GlobalName zones are not dynamic, you have to enter the records into the zone database manually. In most organizations, the servers have static TCP/IP addresses, and this works well with the GlobalName zone design. GlobalName zones are usually used to map single-label CNAME (alias) resource records to an FQDN.

Zone Transfers and Replication

DNS is such an important part of the network that you should not just use a single DNS server. With a single DNS server, you also have a single point of failure and in fact, many domain registrars encourage the use of more than two name servers for a domain. Secondary servers or multiple primary Active Directory Integrated servers play an integral role in providing DNS information for an entire domain.

As previously stated, secondary DNS servers receive their zone databases through zone transfers. When you configure a secondary server for the first time, you must specify the primary server that is authoritative for the zone and will send the zone transfer. The primary server must also permit the secondary server to request the zone transfer.

Zone transfers occur in one of two ways: *full zone transfers (AXFR)* and *incremental zone transfers (IXFR)*.

When a new secondary server is configured for the first time, it receives a full zone transfer from the primary DNS server. The full zone transfer contains all of the information in the DNS database. Some DNS implementations always receive full zone transfers.

After the secondary server receives its first full zone transfer, subsequent zone transfers are incremental. The primary name server compares its zone version number with that of the secondary server, and it sends only the changes that have been made in the interim. This significantly reduces network traffic generated by zone transfers.

The secondary server typically initiates zone transfers when the refresh interval time for the zone expires or when the secondary or stub server boots. Alternatively, you can configure notify lists on the primary server that send a message to the secondary or stub servers whenever any changes to the zone database occur.

When you consider your DNS strategy, you must carefully consider the layout of your network. If you have a single domain with offices in separate cities, you want to reduce the number of zone transfers across the potentially slow or expensive WAN links, although this is becoming less of a concern because of continuous increases in bandwidth.

Active Directory Integrated zones do away with traditional zone transfers altogether with other DNS integrated zones. Instead, they replicate across Active Directory with all of the other AD information. This replication is secure and encrypted because it uses the Active Directory security. AD Integrated zones can still do database transfers to DNS servers that are set up as a secondary zone.

How DNS Notify Works

Windows Server 2022 supports DNS Notify. *DNS Notify* is a mechanism that allows the process of initiating notifications to secondary servers when zone changes occur (RFC 1996). DNS Notify uses a push mechanism for communicating to a select set of secondary zone servers when their zone information is updated. (DNS Notify does not allow you to configure a notify list for a stub zone.)

After being notified of the changes, secondary servers can then start a pull zone transfer and update their local copies of the database.

Many different mechanisms use the push/pull relationship. Normally, one object pushes information to another, and the second object pulls the information from the first. Most applications push replication on a change value and pull it on a time value. For example, a system can push replication after 10 updates, or it can be pulled every 30 minutes.

To configure the DNS Notify process, you create a list of secondary servers to notify. List the IP address of the server in the primary master's Notify dialog box (see Figure 5.8). The Notify dialog box is located on the Zone Transfers tab, which is located in the zone Properties dialog box (see Figure 5.9).

FIGURE 5.8   DNS Notify dialog box

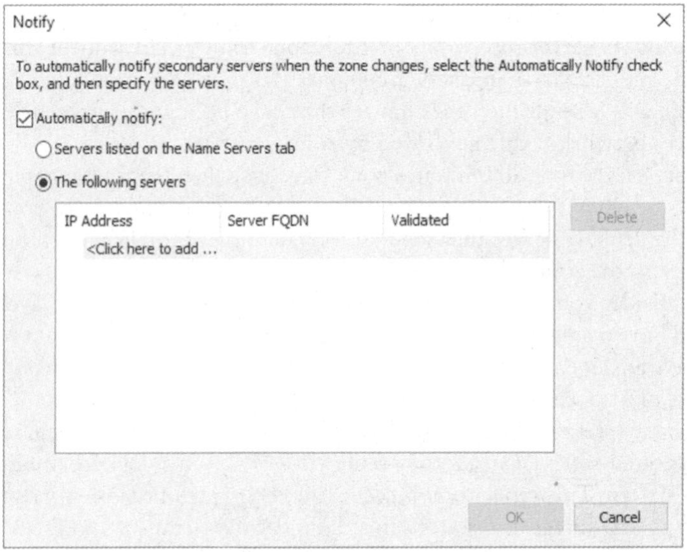

Notify   ✕

To automatically notify secondary servers when the zone changes, select the Automatically Notify check box, and then specify the servers.

☑ Automatically notify:

  ○ Servers listed on the Name Servers tab

  ◉ The following servers

IP Address	Server FQDN	Validated	Delete
<Click here to add ...			

                                                        OK   Cancel

FIGURE 5.9 DNS Zone Transfers tab

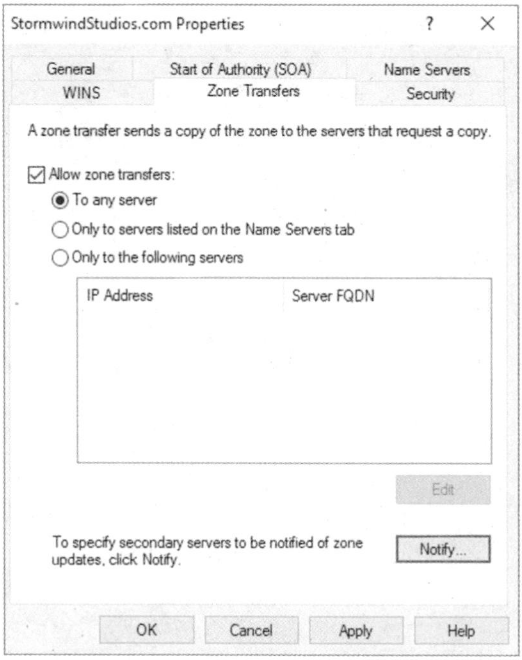

Configuring Stub Zone Transfers with Zone Replication

In the preceding section, I talked about how to configure secondary server zone transfers. What if you wanted to configure settings for stub zone transfers? This is where zone replication scope comes in.

Only Active Directory–integrated primary and stub zones can configure their replication scope. Secondary servers do not have this ability.

You can configure zone replication scope configurations in two ways. You can set configuration options through the DNS snap-in or by using a command-line tool called DNSCmd.

To configure zone replication scope through the DNS snap-in, follow these steps:

1. Click Start ➢ Administrative Tools ➢ DNS.

2. Right-click the zone that you want to set up.

3. Choose Properties.

4. In the Properties dialog box, click the Change button next to Replication (see Figure 5.10).

5. Choose the replication scope that fits your organization.

FIGURE 5.10   DNS zone replication scope

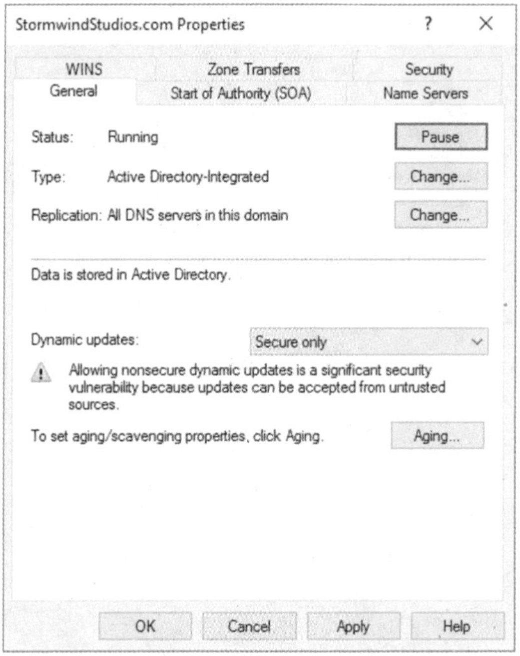

Advantages of DNS in Windows Server 2022

DNS in Microsoft Windows Server 2022 has some great advantages over many other versions of Microsoft DNS. Here are some of the improvements of DNS in Windows Server 2022 (some of these became available in previous versions of Windows Server):

- Background zone loading
- Support for TCP/IP version 6 (IPv6)
- Read-only domain controllers
- GlobalName zone
- DNS socket pools
- DNS cache locking
- Response Rate Limiting (RRL)
- Unknown Record support

- IPv6 root hints
- DNS Security Extensions (DNSSEC)
- DNS devolution
- Record weighting
- Netmask ordering
- DnsUpdateProxy group
- DNS Policies

Background Zone Loading

If an organization had to restart a DNS server with an extremely large Active Directory Integrated DNS zones database in the past, DNS had a common problem with an Active Directory Integrated DNS zone. After the DNS restart, it could take hours for DNS data to be retrieved from Active Directory. During this time, the DNS server was unable to service any client requests.

Microsoft Windows Server 2008 DNS addressed this problem by implementing background zone loading, and Windows Server 2022 has taken it a step further. As the DNS restarts, the Active Directory zone data populates the database in the background. This allows the DNS server to service client requests for data from other zones almost immediately after a restart.

Background zone loading accomplishes this task by loading the DNS zone using separate threads. This allows a DNS server to service requests while still loading the rest of the zone. If a client sends a request to the DNS server for a computer that has not yet loaded into memory, the DNS server retrieves the data from Active Directory and updates the record.

Support for IPv6 Addresses

Over the past few years, the Internet has starting running into a problem that was not foreseen when it was first created—it started running out of TCP/IP addresses. As you probably know, when the Internet was created, it was used for government and academic purposes only. Then, seemingly overnight, it grew to be the information superhighway. Nowadays, asking someone for their email address is almost more common as asking for their phone number.

Version 4 (IPv4) was the common version of TCP/IP. The release of TCP/IP version 6 (IPv6) has solved the lack-of-IP-addresses problem. IPv4 addresses are 32 bits long, but IPv6 addresses are 128 bits in length. The longer lengths allow for a much greater number of globally unique TCP/IP addresses.

Microsoft Windows Server 2022 DNS has built-in support to accommodate both IPv4 and IPv6 address records (DNS records are explained later in this chapter). DHCP can also issue IPv6 addresses, which lets administrators allow DHCP to register the client with DNS, or the IPv6 client can register their address with the DNS server.

Support for Read-Only Domain Controllers

Windows Server 2008 introduced a new type of domain controller called the *read-only domain controller (RODC)*. This is a full copy of the Active Directory database without the ability to write to Active Directory. The RODC gives an organization the ability to install a domain controller in a location (onsite or offsite) where security is a concern.

Microsoft Windows Server 2022 DNS has implemented a type of zone to help support an RODC. A primary read-only zone allows a DNS server to receive a copy of the application partition (including ForestDNSZones and DomainDNSZones) that DNS uses. This allows DNS to support an RODC because DNS now has a full copy of all DNS zones stored in Active Directory.

A primary, read-only zone is just what it says—a read-only zone; so to make any changes to it, you have to change the primary zones server. Read-only zones cannot have any changes made directly to the read-only server.

DNS Socket Pools

If your server is running Windows Server 2022, you will be able to take advantage of DNS socket pools. *DNS socket pools* allow source port randomization to protect against DNS cache-poisoning attacks.

If you choose to use source port randomization, when the DNS service starts, the DNS server will randomly pick a source port from a pool of available sockets. This is an advantage because instead of DNS using a well-known source port when issuing queries, the DNS server uses a random port selected from the socket pool. This helps guard against attacks because a hacker must correctly access the source port of the DNS query. The socket pool is automatically enabled in DNS with the default settings.

When using the DNS socket pool, the default size of the DNS socket pool is 2,500. When configuring the socket pool, you have the ability to choose a size value from 0 to 10,000. The larger the value, the greater the protection you will have against DNS spoofing attacks. If you decide to configure your socket pool size with a zero value, only a single socket for remote DNS queries will be used.

DNS Cache Locking

Windows Server 2022 *DNS cache locking* allows cached DNS records to remain safe for the duration of the record's time to live (TTL) value. This means that the cached DNS records cannot be overwritten or changed. Because of this DNS feature, it's tougher for hackers to perform cache-poisoning attacks against your DNS server.

DNS administrators can set how long a record will remain safe in cache. The configuration is based on a percent value. For example, if you set your cache locking value to 50 percent, then the cached records cannot be overwritten until half of the TTL has been reached. DNS cache locking is set to 100 percent by default. This means that the cached records never get overwritten.

Response Rate Limiting

Response Rate Limiting (RRL) allows you to help prevent the possibility of hackers using your corporate DNS servers to initiate a denial-of-service (DoS) attack on your corporate DNS clients.

You have the ability to configure your RRL settings so that they can control how requests are responded to by DNS servers when these servers receive multiple requests by the same clients. When you configure these settings, it helps prevent hackers from sending a DoS attack using your corporate DNS servers. When configuring RRL, you can manipulate the following settings:

Responses Per Second   This setting allows you to set the maximum number of times the same response will be given to a client per second.

Errors Per Second   This setting allows you to set the maximum number of times an error response will be sent to the same client per second.

Window   This setting allows you to set the number of requests that are made by a client. This setting sets the number of seconds for which responses to a client will be suspended if too many requests are made.

Leak Rate   This setting allows you to set how often the DNS server will respond to a query during the suspended time responses. For example, if the DNS server suspends a response to a client for 20 seconds and the leak rate is 10, then the server will still respond to one query for every 10 queries sent. This will ensure that the appropriate clients get responses even when the DNS server is applying response rate limiting.

TC Rate   You can set this setting to inform clients who are trying to connect using TCP when responses to the client are suspended. For example, if the TC rate is 3 and the DNS server suspends responses to a client, the server will issue a request for TCP connection for every three queries. You want to set the value of the TC rate lower than the leak rate. This gives clients the option to connect using TCP before the leak rate applies.

Maximum Responses   This setting allows you to set the maximum number of responses a DNS server will issue to a client while responses are suspended.

White List Domains   You can set the list of domains that are to be excluded from RRL settings.

White List Subnets   You can set the list of subnets that are to be excluded from RRL settings.

White List Server Interfaces   You can set the list of DNS server interfaces that are to be excluded from RRL settings.

Unknown Record Support

There are times when a DNS server does not recognize the RDATA format of a resource record. These resource records are known as *Unknown Records*.

Windows Server 2022 now supports Unknown Records (RFC 3597). This now means that you can add these unsupported record types into the Windows DNS server zone. You can add these records using the binary on-wire supported format.

Windows caching resolvers already have the ability to support these unknown record types, but DNS servers do not do any processing of these unknown records. What happens is after you add the unknown record types to the DNS zone, the DNS servers will respond back to the clients when queries are received.

IPv6 Root Hints

Windows Server 2022 DNS now supports root hints as published by the IANA. DNS name queries now have the ability to use IPv6 root servers for completing name resolution.

DNS Security Extensions

One major issue that you must always look at is keeping your DNS safe. Think about it: DNS is a database of computer names and IP addresses. As a hacker, if I control DNS, I can control your company. In organizations that do not support extra security like IPsec, DNS security is even more important. This is where *Domain Name System Security Extensions (DNSSEC)* can help.

Windows Server 2022 can use a suite of extensions that will help add security to DNS, and that suite is called DNSSEC, which was introduced in Windows Server 2008 R2. The DNSSEC protocol allows your DNS servers to be secure by validating DNS responses. DNSSEC secures your DNS resource records by accompanying the records with a digital signature.

To allow your DNS resource records to receive digital signatures, DNSSEC is applied to your DNS server by a procedure called *zone signing*. This process begins when a DNS resolver initiates a DNS query for a resource record in a signed DNS zone. When a response is returned, a digital signature (RRSIG) accompanies the response, and this allows the response to be verified. If the verification is successful, then the DNS resolver knows that the data has not been modified or tampered with in any way.

Once you implement a zone with DNSSEC, all of the records that are contained within that zone get individually signed. Since all of the records in the zone get individually signed, this gives you the ability to add, modify, or delete records without re-signing the entire zone. The only requirement is to re-sign any updated records.

DNS-Based Authentication of Named Entities

Another RFC that deals with DNS security is RFC 6698. RFC 6698 explains DNS-Based Authentication of Named Entities (DANE). DANE is a protocol that is based on Transport

Layer Security Authentication (TLSA). The TLSA records then provide information to DNS clients telling the clients which CA server they should expect their certificate from. By knowing your CA, hackers can't corrupt your DNS cache. Man in the middle On-path attackers can change your cache to point you to their websites. DANE stops these types of attacks. DANE support is now included with Windows Server 2022.

Trust Anchors

Trust anchors are an important part of the DNSSEC process because trust anchors allow the DNS servers to validate the DNSKEY resource records. *Trust anchors* are preconfigured public keys that are linked to a DNS zone. For a DNS server to perform validation, one or more trust anchors must be configured. If you are running an Active Directory Integrated zone, trust anchors can be stored in the Active Directory Domain Services directory partition of the forest. If you decide to store the trust anchors in the directory partition, then all DNS servers that reside on a domain controller get a copy of this trust anchor. On DNS servers that reside on stand-alone servers, trust anchors are stored in a file called `TrustAnchors.dns`.

If your servers are running Windows Server 2022, then you can view trust anchors in the DNS Manager Console tree in the Trust Points container. You can also use Windows PowerShell or `Dnscmd.exe` to view trust anchors. Windows PowerShell is the recommended command-line method for viewing trust anchors. The following line is a PowerShell command to view the trust anchors for `Contoso.com`:

```
get-dnsservertrustanchor sec.contoso.com
```

DNSSEC Clients

Windows 7, Windows 8/8.1, Windows 10/11, Windows Server 2008/2008 R2, and Windows Server 2012/R2, Windows Server 2016, Windows Server 2019, and Server 2022 are all DNS clients that receive a response to a DNS query, examine the response, and then evaluate whether the response has been validated by a DNS server. The DNS client itself is nonvalidating, and the DNS client relies on the local DNS server to indicate that validation was successful. If the server doesn't perform validation, then the DNS client service can be configured to return no results.

DNS Devolution

Using *DNS devolution*, if a client computer is a member of a child namespace, the client computer will be able to access resources in the parent namespace without the need to explicitly provide the fully qualified domain name of the resource. DNS devolution removes the leftmost label of the namespace to get to the parent suffix. DNS devolution allows the DNS resolver to create the new FQDNs. DNS devolution works by appending the single-label, unqualified domain name with the parent suffix of the primary DNS suffix name.

Record Weighting

Weighting DNS records will allow you to place a value on DNS SRV records. Clients will then randomly choose SRV records proportional to the weight value assigned.

Netmask Ordering

If round-robin is enabled, when a client requests name resolution, the first address entered in the database is returned to the resolver, and it is then sent to the end of the list. The next time a client attempts to resolve the name, the DNS server returns the second name in the database (which is now the first name) and then sends it to the end of the list, and so on. Round-robin is enabled by default.

Netmask ordering is a part of the round-robin process. When you configure netmask ordering, the DNS server will detect the subnet of the querying client. The DNS server will then return a host address available for the same subnet. Netmask ordering is enabled through the DNS Manager console on the Advanced tab of the server Properties dialog box.

DnsUpdateProxy Group

As mentioned previously, the DHCP server can be configured to register host (A) and pointer (PTR) resource records dynamically on behalf of DHCP clients. Because of this, the DNS server can end up with stale resources. To help solve this issue, you can use the built-in security group called DnsUpdateProxy.

To use the DnsUpdateProxy group, you must first create a dedicated user account and configure the DHCP servers with its credentials. This will protect against the creation of unsecured records. Also, when you create the dedicated user account, members of the DnsUpdateProxy group will be able to register records in zones that allow only secured dynamic updates. Multiple DHCP servers can use the same credentials of one dedicated user account.

DNS Policies

One of the best advantages to Windows Server 2022 DNS is the ability to set up DNS policies. You can set up policies based on location, time of day, deployment types, queries, application load balancing, and more. The following are just some of the items that you can configure:

Application Load Balancing   There are many times in a corporate environment when you have multiple copies of the same application running in different locations. Application load balancing allows DNS to pass client requests for the same applications (even when they are in different locations) to multiple servers hosting that application. This allows DNS to give an application load balancing.

Location-Based Traffic Management   You can set DNS to work off locations and help direct users to resources that are closer to their location. You can set up DNS policies so that a DNS server will respond to a DNS client's query based on geographic location of the client and the IP address of the nearest requested resource.

Split-Brain DNS   Another DNS policy that you can set up is the ability to have DNS split zones. Split zones allow a DNS server to respond to a client based on whether the clients are internal or external clients. Active Directory zones or stand-alone DNS servers can be configured as split-brain DNS servers.

Filtering   You now have the ability to set up policies to create query filters that are based on criteria that you supply. Query filters allow you to set up the DNS server to send a custom response based on a specific type of DNS query and/or DNS client.

Forensics   You also have the ability to set up a DNS honeypot. A honeypot allows a DNS server to redirect a malicious DNS client to an IP address that does not exist.

Time of Day–Based Redirection   You can set up a DNS policy to distribute application traffic between different locations. DNS will be able to do this because the policy that you set for an application will be based on the time of day. So for example, when its 1:00 p.m., a server that has a copy of the application gets all client requests, and at 7:00 p.m., a different server that has a copy of the application gets all of the client requests.

Now that you have learned about some of the features of Windows Server 2022 DNS, let's take a look at some of the DNS record types.

Introducing DNS Record Types

No matter where your zone information is stored, you can rest assured that it contains a variety of DNS information. Although the DNS snap-in makes it unlikely that you'll ever need to edit these files by hand, it's good to know exactly what data is contained there.

As stated previously, zone files consist of a number of resource records. You need to know about several types of resource records to manage your DNS servers effectively. They are discussed in this section.

Start of Authority (SOA) Records

The first record in a database file is the *start of authority (SOA) record*. The SOA defines the general parameters for the DNS zone, including the identity of the authoritative server for the zone.

The SOA appears in the following format:

```
@ IN SOA primary_mastercontact_e-mailserial_number
refresh_timeretry_timeexpiration_timetime_to_live
```

Here is a sample SOA from the domain example.com:

```
@ IN SOA win2k3r2.example.com. hostmaster.example.com. (
                        5              ; serial number
                        900            ; refresh
                        600            ; retry
                        86400          ; expire
                        3600        ) ; default TTL
```

Table 5.2 lists the attributes stored in the SOA record.

TABLE 5.2 The SOA record structure

Field	Meaning
Current zone	The current zone for the SOA. This can be represented by an @ symbol to indicate the current zone or by naming the zone itself. In the example, the current zone is example.com. The trailing dot (.com.) indicates the zone's place relative to the root of the DNS.
Class	This will almost always be the letters *IN* for the Internet class.
Type of record	The type of record follows. In this case, it's SOA.
Primary master	The primary master for the zone on which this file is maintained.
Contact email	The Internet email address for the person responsible for this domain's database file. There is no @ symbol in this contact email address because @ is a special character in zone files. The contact email address is separated by a single dot (.). So, the email address of root@example.com would be represented by root.example.com in a zone file.
Serial number	This is the "version number" of this database file. It increases each time the database file is changed.
Refresh time	The amount of time (in seconds) that a secondary server will wait between checks to its master server to see whether the database file has changed and a zone transfer should be requested.
Retry time	The amount of time (in seconds) that a secondary server will wait before retrying a failed zone transfer.
Expiration time	The amount of time (in seconds) that a secondary server will spend trying to download a zone. Once this time limit expires, the old zone information will be discarded.
Time to live	The amount of time (in seconds) that another DNS server is allowed to cache any resource records from this database file. This is the value that is sent out with all query responses from this zone file when the individual resource record doesn't contain an overriding value.

Name Server Records

Name server (NS) records list the name servers for a domain. This record allows other name servers to look up names in your domain. A zone file may contain more than one name server record. The format of these records is simple:

```
example.com.    IN      NS      Hostname.example.com
```

Table 5.3 explains the attributes stored in the NS record.

TABLE 5.3 The NS record structure

Field	Meaning
Name	The domain that will be serviced by this name server. In this case I used `example.com`.
AddressClass	Internet (IN).
RecordType	Name server (NS).
Name Server Name	The FQDN of the server responsible for the domain.

 Any domain name in the database file that is not terminated with a period will have the root domain appended to the end. For example, an entry that just has the name *sales* will be expanded by adding the root domain to the end, whereas the entry `sales.example.com.` won't be expanded.

Host Record

A *host record* (also called an *A record* for IPv4 and *AAAA record* for IPv6) is used to associate statically a host's name to its IP addresses. The format is pretty simple:

```
host_nameoptional_TTL IN  A   IP_Address
```

Here's an example from my DNS database:

```
www  IN  A  192.168.0.204
SMTP IN  A  192.168.3.144
```

The A or AAAA record ties a hostname (which is part of an FQDN) to a specific IP address. This makes these records suitable for use when you have devices with statically assigned IP addresses. In this case, you create these records manually using the DNS snap-in. As it turns out, if you enable DDNS, your DHCP server can create these for you. This automatic creation is what enables DDNS to work.

Notice that an optional TTL field is available for each resource record in the DNS. This value is used to set a TTL that is different from the default TTL for the domain. For example, if you wanted a 60-second TTL for the www A or AAAA record, it would look like this:

```
www 60 IN  A  192.168.0.204
```

Alias Record

Closely related to the host record is the *alias record*, or *canonical name (CNAME) record*. The syntax of an alias record is as follows:

```
aliasoptional_TTL  IN  CNAME  hostname
```

Aliases are used to point more than one DNS record toward a host for which an A record already exists. For example, if the hostname of your web server was actually chaos, you would likely have an A record such as this:

```
chaos IN A 192.168.1.10
```

Then you could make an alias or CNAME for the record so that www.example.com would point to chaos:

```
www IN CNAME chaos.example.com.
```

Note the trailing dot (.) on the end of the CNAME record. This means the root domain is not appended to the entry.

Pointer Record

A or AAAA records are probably the most visible component of the DNS database because Internet users depend on them to turn FQDNs like www.microsoft.com into the IP addresses that browsers and other components require to find Internet resources. However, the host record has a lesser-known but still important twin: the *pointer (PTR) record*. The format of a PTR record appears as follows:

```
reversed_address.in-addr.arpa. optional_TTL IN PTR targeted_domain_name
```

The A or AAAA record maps a hostname to an IP address, and the PTR record does just the opposite—mapping an IP address to a hostname through the use of the in-addr.arpa zone.

The PTR record is necessary because IP addresses begin with the least-specific portion first (the network) and end with the most-specific portion (the host), whereas hostnames begin with the most-specific portion at the beginning and the least-specific portion at the end.

Consider the example 192.168.1.10 with a subnet mask 255.255.255.0. The portion 192.168.1 defines the network and the final .10 defines the host, or the most specific portion of the address. DNS is just the opposite: The hostname www.example.com. defines the most-specific portion, www, at the beginning and then traverses the DNS tree to the least-specific part, the dot (.), at the root of the tree.

Reverse DNS records, therefore, need to be represented in this most-specific-to-least-specific manner. The PTR record for mapping 192.168.1.10 to www.example.com would look like this:

```
10.1.168.192.in-addr.arpa. IN PTR www.example.com.
```

Now a DNS query for that record can follow the logical DNS hierarchy from the root of the DNS tree all the way to the most specific portion.

Mail Exchanger Record

The *mail exchanger (MX) record* is used to specify which servers accept mail for this domain. Each MX record contains two parameters—a preference and a mail server, as shown in the following example:

```
domain IN MX preference mailserver_host
```

The MX record uses the preference value to specify which server should be used if more than one MX record is present. The preference value is a number. The lower the number, the more preferred the server. Here's an example:

```
example.com.    IN  MX  0  mail.example.com.
example.com.    IN  MX  10 backupmail.example.com.
```

In the example, mail.example.com is the default mail server for the domain. If that server goes down for any reason, the backupmail.example.com mail server is used by emailers.

Service Record

Windows Server 2022 depends on some other services, like the Lightweight Directory Access Protocol (LDAP) and Kerberos. Using a service record, which is another type of DNS record, a Windows 2000, XP, Vista, Windows 7, Windows 8 / 8.1, or Windows 10/11 client can query DNS servers for the location of a domain controller. This makes it much easier (for both the client and the administrator) to manage and distribute logon traffic in large-scale networks. For this approach to work, Microsoft has to have some way to register the presence of a service in DNS. Enter the service (SRV) record.

Service (SRV) records tie together the location of a service (like a domain controller) with information about how to contact the service. SRV records provide seven items of information. Let's review an example to help clarify this powerful concept. (Table 5.4 explains the fields in the following example.)

```
ldap.tcp.example.com.  86400 IN SRV  10  100  389  hsv.example.com
ldap.tcp.example.com.  86400 IN SRV  20  100  389  msy.example.com
```

TABLE 5.4   The SRV record structure

Field	Meaning
Domain name	Domain for which this record is valid (`ldap.tcp.example.com.`).
TTL	Time to live (86,400 seconds).
Class	This field is always `IN`, which stands for Internet.
Record type	Type of record (`SRV`).
Priority	Specifies a preference, similar to the Preference field in an MX record. The SRV record with the lowest priority is used first (`10`).
Weight	Service records with equal priority are chosen according to their weight (`100`).
Port number	The port where the server is listening for this service (`389`).
Target	The FQDN of the host computer (`hsv.example.com` and `msy.example.com`).

You can define other types of service records. If your applications support them, they can query DNS to find the services they need.

Configuring DNS

In this section, you'll begin to learn about the actual DNS server. You will start by installing DNS. Then I will talk about different zone configuration options and what they mean. Finally, you'll complete an exercise that covers configuring Dynamic DNS, delegating zones, and manually entering records.

Installing DNS

If DNS is already installed onto your server, you can skip this exercise. But if you have not installed DNS, let's start by installing DNS. Installing DNS is an important part of running a network. Exercise 5.1 walks you through the installation of a DNS server.

If you are using a Dynamic TCP/IP address, please change your TCP/IP number to static.

EXERCISE 5.1

Installing and Configuring the DNS Service

1. Open Server Manager.

2. On the Server Manager dashboard, click the Add Roles And Features link.

3. If a Before You Begin screen appears, click Next.

4. On the Selection type page, choose role-based or feature-based installation and click Next.

5. Click the Select A Server From The Server Pool radio button and select the server in the Server Pool section. Click Next.

6. Click the DNS Server Item in the Server Role list. If a pop-up window appears telling you that you need to add additional features, click the Add Features button. Click Next to continue.

7. On the Add Features page, just click Next.

8. Click Next on the DNS Server information screen.

9. On the Confirm Installation screen, select the Restart The Destination Server Automatically If Required option and then click the Install button.

10. At the Installation progress screen, click Close after the DNS server is installed.

11. Close Server Manager.

Load Balancing with Round-Robin

Like other DNS implementations, the Windows Server 2022 implementation of DNS supports load balancing through the use of round-robin. Load balancing distributes the network load among multiple network hosts if they are available. You set up round-robin load balancing by creating multiple resource records with the same hostname but different IP addresses for multiple computers. Depending on the options that you select, the DNS server responds with the addresses of one of the host computers.

If round-robin is enabled, when a client requests name resolution, the first address entered in the database is returned to the resolver and is then sent to the end of the list. The next time a client attempts to resolve the name, the DNS server returns the second name in the database (which is now the first name) and then sends it to the end of the list, and so on. Round-robin is enabled by default.

Configuring a Caching-Only Server

Although all DNS name servers cache queries that they have resolved, caching-only servers are DNS name servers that only perform queries, cache the answers, and return the results. They are not authoritative for any domains, and the information that they contain is limited to what has been cached while resolving queries. Accordingly, they don't have any zone files, and they don't participate in zone transfers. When a caching-only server is first started, it has no information in its cache; the cache is gradually built over time.

Caching-only servers are easy to configure. After installing the DNS service, simply make sure the root hints are configured properly. One advantage to Windows Server 2022 is the ability to also support IPv6 root hints.

1. Right-click your DNS server and choose the Properties command.

2. When the Properties dialog box appears, switch to the Root Hints tab (see Figure 5.11).

3. If your server is connected to the Internet, you should see a list of root hints for the root servers maintained by ICANN and the Internet Assigned Numbers Authority (IANA). If not, click the Add button to add root hints as defined in the cache.dns file.

FIGURE 5.11   The Root Hints tab of the DNS server's Properties dialog box

You can obtain current cache.dns files on the Internet by using a search engine. Just search for **cache.dns** and download one. (I always try to get cache·dns files from a university or a company that manages domain names.)

Setting Zone Properties

There are six tabs on the Properties dialog box for a forward or reverse lookup zone. You only use the Security tab to control who can change properties and to make dynamic updates to records on that zone. The other tabs are discussed in the following subsections.

Secondary zones don't have a Security tab, and their SOA tab shows you the contents of the master SOA record, which you can't change.

General Tab

The General tab includes the following:

- The Status indicator and the associated Pause button let you see and control whether this zone can be used to answer queries. When the zone is running, the server can use it to answer client queries; when it's paused, the server won't answer any queries it gets for that particular zone.

- The Type indicator and its Change button allow you to select the zone type. The options are Standard Primary, Standard Secondary, and AD-Integrated. (See "Introducing DNS Database Zones" earlier in this chapter.) As you change the type, the controls you see below the horizontal dividing line change too. For primary zones, you'll see a field that lets you select the zone filename; for secondary zones, you'll get controls that allow you to specify the IP addresses of the primary servers. But the most interesting controls are the ones you see for AD Integrated zones. When you change to the AD Integrated zones, you have the ability to make the dynamic zones Secure Only.

- The Replication indicator and its Change button allow you to change the replication scope if the zone is stored in Active Directory. You can choose to replicate the zone data to any of the following:

  - All DNS servers in the Active Directory forest

  - All DNS servers in a specified domain

  - All domain controllers in the Active Directory domain (required if you use Windows 2000 domain controllers in your domain)

  - All domain controllers specified in the replication scope of the application directory partition

- The Dynamic Updates field gives you a way to specify whether you want to support Dynamic DNS updates from compatible DHCP servers. As you learned earlier in the section "Dynamic DNS and Non-dynamic DNS," the DHCP server or DHCP client must know about and support Dynamic DNS in order to use it, but the DNS server has to participate too. You can turn dynamic updates on or off, or you can require that updates be secured.

Start Of Authority (SOA) Tab

The following options in the Start Of Authority (SOA) tab, shown in Figure 5.12, control the contents of the SOA record for this zone.

FIGURE 5.12   The Start Of Authority (SOA) tab of the zone Properties dialog box

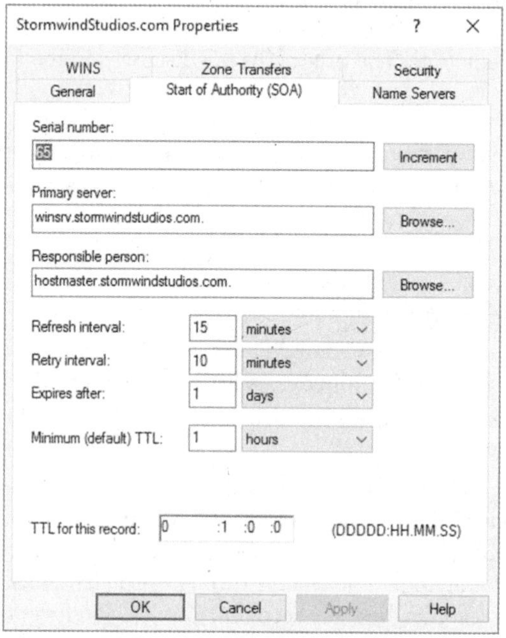

- The Serial Number field indicates which version of the SOA record the server currently holds. Every time you change another field, you should increment the serial number so that other servers will notice the change and get a copy of the updated record.

- The Primary Server and Responsible Person fields indicate the location of the primary name server for this zone and the email address of the administrator responsible for the maintenance of this zone, respectively. The standard username for this is hostmaster.

- The Refresh Interval field controls how often any secondary zones of this zone must contact the primary zone server and get any changes that have been posted since the last update.

- The Retry Interval field controls how long secondary servers will wait after a zone transfer fails before they try again. They'll keep trying at the interval you specify (which should be shorter than the refresh interval) until they eventually succeed in transferring zone data.

- The Expires After field tells the secondary servers when to throw away zone data. The default of 1 day (24 hours) means that a secondary server that hasn't gotten an update in 24 hours will delete its local copy of the zone data.

- The Minimum (Default) TTL field sets the default TTL for all RRs created in the zone. You can assign specific TTLs to individual records if you want.

- The TTL For This Record field controls the TTL for the SOA record itself.

Name Servers Tab

The *name server (NS) record* for a zone indicates which name servers are authoritative for the zone. That normally means the zone primary server and any secondary servers you've configured for the zone. (Remember, secondary servers are authoritative read-only copies of the zone.) You edit the NS record for a zone using the Name Servers tab (see Figure 5.13). The tab shows you which servers are currently listed, and you use the Add, Edit, and Remove buttons to specify which name servers you want included in the zone's NS record.

FIGURE 5.13   The Name Servers tab of the zone Properties dialog box

WINS Tab

The WINS tab allows you to control whether this zone uses WINS forward lookups or not. These lookups pass on queries that DNS can't resolve to WINS for action. This is a useful setup if you're still using WINS on your network. You must explicitly turn this option on with the Use WINS Forward Lookup check box in the WINS tab for a particular zone.

Zone Transfers Tab

Zone transfers are necessary and useful because they're the mechanism used to propagate zone data between primary and secondary servers. For primary servers (whether AD Integrated or not), you can specify whether your servers will allow zone transfers and, if so, to whom.

You can use the following controls on the Zone Transfers tab to configure these settings per zone:

- The Allow Zone Transfers option controls whether the server answers zone transfer requests for this zone at all—when it's not selected, no zone data is transferred. The Allow Zone Transfers selections are as follows:

  - To Any Server allows any server anywhere on the Internet to request a copy of your zone data.

  - Only To Servers Listed On The Name Servers Tab (the default) limits transfers to servers you specify. This is a more secure setting than To Any Server because it limits transfers to other servers for the same zone.

  - Only To The Following Servers allows you to specify exactly which servers are allowed to request zone transfers. This list can be larger or smaller than the list specified on the Name Servers tab.

- The Notify button is for setting up automatic notification triggers that are sent to secondary servers for this zone. Those triggers signal the secondary servers that changes have occurred on the primary server so that the secondary servers can request updates sooner than their normally scheduled interval. The options in the Notify dialog box are similar to those in the Zone Transfers tab. You can enable automatic notification and then choose either Servers Listed On The Name Servers Tab or The Following Servers.

Configuring Zones for Dynamic Updates

In Exercise 5.2, you will create and then modify the properties of a forward lookup zone. In addition, you'll configure the zone to allow dynamic updates.

EXERCISE 5.2

Configuring a Zone for Dynamic Updates

1. Open the DNS management snap-in by selecting Server Manager. Once in Server Manager, click DNS on the left side. In the Servers window (center screen), right-click your server name and choose DNS Manager.

2. Click the DNS server to expand it and then click the Forward Lookup Zones folder. Right-click the Forward Lookup Zones folder and choose New Zone.

3. At the New Zone Welcome screen, click Next.

4. At the Zone Type screen, choose the Primary Zone option. If your DNS server is also a domain controller, do not select the option to store the zone in Active Directory. Click Next when you are ready.

5. Enter a new zone name in the Zone Name field and click Next. (I used my last name—Panek.com.)

6. Leave the default zone filename and click Next.

7. Select the Do Not Allow Dynamic Updates radio button and click Next.

8. Click Finish to end the wizard.

9. Right-click the zone you just created and choose the Properties command.

10. Click the down arrow next to Dynamic Updates. Notice that there are only two options (None and Nonsecure And Secure). The Secure Only option is not available because you are not using Active Directory Integrated. Make sure Nonsecure And Secure is chosen.

11. Click OK to close the Properties box.

12. Close the DNS management snap-in.

13. Close the Server Manager snap-in.

Delegating Zones for DNS

DNS provides the ability to divide the namespace into one or more zones, which can then be stored, distributed, and replicated to other DNS servers. When deciding whether to divide your DNS namespace to make additional zones, consider the following reasons to use additional zones:

- A need to delegate management of part of your DNS namespace to another location or department within your organization

- A need to divide one large zone into smaller zones for distributing traffic loads among multiple servers, for improving DNS name-resolution performance, or for creating a more fault-tolerant DNS environment

- A need to extend the namespace by adding numerous subdomains at once, such as to accommodate the opening of a new branch or site

Each newly delegated zone requires a primary DNS server just as a regular DNS zone does. When delegating zones within your namespace, be aware that for each new zone you create, you need to place delegation records in other zones that point to the authoritative DNS servers for the new zone. This is necessary both to transfer authority and to provide correct referral to other DNS servers and clients of the new servers being made authoritative for the new zone.

In Exercise 5.3, you'll create a delegated subdomain of the domain you created in Exercise 5.2. Note that the name of the server to which you want to delegate the subdomain must be stored in an A or CNAME record in the parent domain.

EXERCISE 5.3

Creating a Delegated DNS Zone

1. Open the DNS management snap-in by selecting Server Manager. Once in Server Manager, click DNS on the left side. In the Servers window (center screen), right-click your server name and choose DNS Manager.

2. Expand the DNS server and locate the zone you created in Exercise 5.2.

3. Right-click the zone and choose the New Delegation command.

4. The New Delegation Wizard appears. Click Next to dismiss the initial wizard page.

5. Enter **ns1** (or whatever other name you like) in the Delegated Domain field of the Delegated Domain Name page. This is the name of the domain for which you want to delegate authority to another DNS server. It should be a subdomain of the primary domain (for example, to delegate authority for farmington.example.net, you'd enter **farmington** in the Delegated Domain field). Click Next to complete this step.

6. When the Name Servers page appears, click the Add button to add the names and IP addresses of the servers that will be hosting the newly delegated zone. For the purpose of this exercise, enter the server name you used in Exercise 5.2. Click the Resolve button to resolve this domain name's IP address automatically into the IP address field. Click OK when you are finished. Click Next to continue with the wizard.

7. Click the Finish button. The New Delegation Wizard disappears, and you'll see the new zone you just created appear beneath the zone you selected in step 3. The newly delegated zone's folder icon is drawn in gray to indicate that control of the zone is delegated.

DNS Forwarding

If a DNS server does not have an answer to a DNS request, it may be necessary to send that request to another DNS server. This is called *DNS forwarding*. You need to understand the two main types of forwarding:

External Forwarding   When a DNS server forwards an external DNS request to a DNS server outside of your organization, this is considered *external forwarding*. For example, a resolver requests the host www.microsoft.com. Most likely, your internal DNS server is not going to have Microsoft's web address in its DNS database. So, your DNS server is going to send the request to an external DNS (most likely your ISP) or use the setup root hints.

Conditional Forwarding   *Conditional forwarding* is a lot like external forwarding except that you are going to forward requests to specific DNS servers based on a condition. Usually this is an excellent setup for internal DNS resolution. For example, let's say that you have two companies, `stormwind.com` and `stormtest.com`. If a request comes in for `Stormwind.com`, it gets forwarded to the Stormwind DNS server, and any requests for `Stormtest.com` will get forwarded to the Stormtest DNS server. Requests are forwarded to a specific DNS server depending on the condition that you set up.

Manually Creating DNS Records

From time to time you may find it necessary to add resource records manually to your Windows Server 2022 DNS servers. Although Dynamic DNS frees you from the need to fiddle with A and PTR records for clients and other such entries, you still have to create other resource types (including MX records, required for the proper flow of SMTP email) manually. You can manually create A, PTR, MX, SRV, and many other record types.

There are only two important things to remember for manually creating DNS records:

- You must right-click the zone and choose either the New Record command or the Other New Records command.

- You must know how to fill in the fields of whatever record type you're using.

    For example, to create an MX record, you need three pieces of information (the domain, the mail server, and the priority). To create an SRV record, however, you need several more pieces of information.

In Exercise 5.4, you will manually create an MX record for a mailtest server in the zone you created in Exercise 5.2.

EXERCISE 5.4

Manually Creating DNS RRs

1. Open the DNS management snap-in by selecting Server Manager. Once in Server Manager, click DNS on the left side. In the Servers window (center screen), right-click your server name and choose DNS Manager.

2. Expand your DNS server, right-click its zone, and choose New Host (A record).

3. Enter **mailtest** in the Name field. Enter a TCP/IP number in the IP Address field. (You can use any number for this exercise, such as, for example, 192.168.1.254.) Click the Add Host button.

4. A dialog box appears stating that the host record was created successfully. Click OK. Click Done.

5. Right-click your zone name and choose New Mail Exchanger (MX).

6. Enter **mailtest** in the Host Or Child Domain field and enter **mailtest.yourDomain**
   .com (or whatever domain name you used in Exercise 5.2) in the Fully-Qualified
   Domain Name (FQDN) Of Mail Server field and then click OK. Notice that the new
   record is already visible.

7. Next create an alias (or CNAME) record to point to the mail server. (It is assumed that
   you already have an A record for mailtest in your zone.) Right-click your zone and
   choose New Alias (CNAME).

8. Type **mail** into the Alias Name field.

9. Type **mailtest.yourDomain.com** into the Fully-Qualified Domain Name (FQDN)
   For Target Host field.

10. Click OK.

11. Close the DNS management snap-in.

DNS Aging and Scavenging

When using dynamic updates, computers (or DHCP) will register a resource record with
DNS. These records get removed when a computer is shut down properly. A major problem
in the industry is that laptops are frequently removed from the network without a proper
shutdown. Therefore, their resource records continue to live in the DNS database.

Windows Server 2022 DNS supports two features called *DNS aging* and *DNS scavenging*. These features are used to clean up and remove stale resource records. DNS zone or
DNS server aging and scavenging flag old resource records that have not been updated in
a certain amount of time (determined by the scavenging interval). These stale records will
be scavenged at the next cleanup interval. DNS uses time stamps on the resource records to
determine how long they have been listed in the DNS database.

By default, DNS aging and scavenging are disabled by default. Microsoft states that these
features should only be enabled if you have users that are not logging off the network properly. If your users are all using desktops or if your users log off the network properly every
day, you should keep these features disabled.

The issue that you can run into if this feature is enabled and DNS deletes records that
should not be deleted, then that can stop users from access resources on the network because
their DNS records have been deleted improperly.

If you decide that you want to enable DNS aging and scavenging, you must enable these
features on both at the DNS server and on the zone.

DNS aging and scavenging is done by using time stamps. Time stamps are a date and time
value that is used by the DNS server. The date and time is used to determine removal of the
resource record when it performs the aging and scavenging operations.

DNS PowerShell Commands

When talking about PowerShell commands for DNS, I must let you know that there are dozens of commands that you can use to configure and maintain a DNS server. Before I show you the table of DNS PowerShell commands, let's look at two commands first.

When we install DNS onto a server, we can use PowerShell to do the install. But when we are talking about Nano server, the PowerShell commands are a bit different.

Let's first look at how you install DNS on a regular Windows server using PowerShell. The following command is used to install DNS on a Windows Server:

```
Install-WindowsFeature DNS -IncludeManagementTools
```

Now let's take a look at the PowerShell command for installing DNS on a Nano server. The following commands are used to install DNS on a Nano server. The first command downloads DNS to the Nano server, and the second command installs it on the server:

```
Install-NanoServerPackage Microsoft-NanoServer-DNS-Package -Culture en-us
Enable-WindowsOptionalFeature -Online -FeatureName DNS-Server-Full-Role
```

Nano servers have no GUI interface and all installations have to be done using remote tools or PowerShell commands. There are dozens of possible PowerShell commands. Nano servers are excellent servers to use as DNS servers. Just be sure that you know what roles can be installed onto a Nano server and which roles can't be installed on a Nano server (like DHCP).

In Table 5.5, I will show you just some of the possible PowerShell commands that are available for DNS.

 For a complete list of DNS PowerShell commands, please visit Microsoft's website at https://docs.microsoft.com/en-us/ powershell/module/dnsserver/?view=windowsserver2019-ps.

TABLE 5.5 PowerShell commands for DNS

PowerShell command	Description
Add-DnsServerClientSubnet	This command allows you to add a client subnet to a DNS server.
Add-DnsServerConditionalForwarderZone	You can use this command to add a conditional forwarder to a DNS server.
Add-DnsServerForwarder	This command allows you to add forwarders to a DNS server.
Add-DnsServerPrimaryZone	You can use this command to add a primary zone to a DNS server.

TABLE 5.5   PowerShell commands for DNS *(Continued)*

PowerShell command	Description
Add-DnsServerQueryResolutionPolicy	This command allows you to add a query resolution policy to DNS.
Add-DnsServerResourceRecord	You can use this command to add a resource record to a DNS zone.
Add-DnsServerResourceRecordA	This command allows you to add an A record to a DNS zone.
Add-DnsServerResourceRecordAAAA	This command allows you to add an AAAA record to a DNS zone.
Add-DnsServerResourceRecordCName	This command allows you to add a CNAME record to a DNS zone.
Add-DnsServerResourceRecordDnsKey	You can use this command to add a DNSKEY record to a DNS zone.
Add-DnsServerResourceRecordDS	This command allows you to add a DS record to a DNS zone.
Add-DnsServerResourceRecordMX	This command allows you to add an MX record to a DNS zone.
Add-DnsServerResourceRecordPtr	This command allows you to add a PTR record to a DNS zone.
Add-DnsServerSecondaryZone	You can use this command to add a secondary zone.
Add-DnsServerSigningKey	This command adds a KSK or ZSK to a signed zone.
Add-DnsServerStubZone	This command adds a stub zone to a DNS server.
Add-DnsServerTrustAnchor	You can use this command to add a trust anchor to a DNS server.
Add-DnsServerZoneDelegation	This command allows you to add a new delegated DNS zone to an existing zone.
Clear-DnsServerCache	You use this command to clear resource records from a DNS cache.

PowerShell command	Description
ConvertTo-DnsServerPrimaryZone	This command converts a zone to a primary zone.
Get-DnsServer	This command retrieves configuration information for a DNS server.
Get-DnsServerDsSetting	This command allows you to gather information about DNS Active Directory settings.
Get-DnsServerRootHint	You use this command to view root hints on a DNS server.
Get-DnsServerScavenging	You use this command to view DNS aging and scavenging settings.
Get-DnsServerSetting	This command allows you to view DNS server settings.
Get-DnsServerSigningKey	This command allows you to view zone signing keys.
Import-DnsServerResourceRecordDS	This command allows you to import DNS resource record from a file.
Import-DnsServerRootHint	This command imports root hints from a DNS server.
Remove-DnsServerZone	You use this command to remove a DNS zone from a server.
Resume-DnsServerZone	This command allows you to resume resolution on a suspended zone.
Set-DnsServer	You can use this command to set the DNS server configuration.
Set-DnsServerRootHint	This command allows you to replace a server's root hints.
Set-DnsServerSetting	You can use this command to change DNS server settings.
Test-DnsServer	This command allows you to test a functioning DNS server.

Summary

DNS was designed to be a robust, scalable, and high-performance system for resolving friendly names to TCP/IP host addresses. This chapter presented an overview of the basics of DNS and how DNS names are generated. You then looked at the many new features available in the Microsoft Windows Server 2022 version of DNS, and you learned how to install, configure, and manage the necessary services. Microsoft's DNS is based on a widely accepted set of industry standards. Because of this, Microsoft's DNS can work with both Windows- and non-Windows-based networks.

Exam Essentials

Understand the purpose of DNS.   DNS is a standard set of protocols that defines a mechanism for querying and updating address information in the database, a mechanism for replicating the information in the database among servers, and a schema of the database.

Understand the different parts of the DNS database.   The SOA record defines the general parameters for the DNS zone, including who is the authoritative server. NS records list the name servers for a domain; they allow other name servers to look up names in your domain. A host record (also called an address record or an A record) statically associates a host's name with its IP addresses. Pointer records (PTRs) map an IP address to a hostname, making it possible to do reverse lookups. Alias records allow you to use more than one name to point to a single host. The MX record tells you which servers can accept mail bound for a domain. SRV records tie together the location of a service (like a domain controller) with information about how to contact the service.

Know how DNS resolves names.   With iterative queries, a client asks the DNS server for an answer, and the client, or resolver, returns the best kind of answer it has. In a recursive query, the client sends a query to one name server, asking it to respond either with the requested answer or with an error. The error states either that the server can't come up with the right answer or that the domain name doesn't exist. With inverse queries, instead of supplying a name and then asking for an IP address, the client first provides the IP address and then asks for the name.

Understand the differences among DNS servers, clients, and resolvers.   Any computer providing domain name services is a DNS server. A DNS client is any machine issuing queries to a DNS server. A resolver handles the process of mapping a symbolic name to an actual network address.

Know how to install and configure DNS.   DNS can be installed before, during, or after installing the Active Directory service. When you install the DNS server, the DNS snap-in is installed too. Configuring a DNS server ranges from easy to difficult, depending on what you're trying to make it do. In the simplest configuration, for a caching-only server, you don't have to do anything except to make sure that the server's root hints are set correctly. You can also configure a root server, a normal forward lookup server, and a reverse lookup server.

Know how to create new forward and reverse lookup zones.   You can use the New Zone Wizard to create a new forward or reverse lookup zone. The process is basically the same for both types, but the specific steps and wizard pages differ somewhat. The wizard walks you through the steps, such as specifying a name for the zone (in the case of forward lookup zones) or the network ID portion of the network that the zone covers (in the case of reverse lookup zones).

Know how to configure zones for dynamic updates.   The DNS service allows dynamic updates to be enabled or disabled on a per-zone basis at each server. This is easily done in the DNS snap-in.

Know how to delegate zones for DNS.   DNS provides the ability to divide the namespace into one or more zones; these can then be stored, distributed, and replicated to other DNS servers. When delegating zones within your namespace, be aware that for each new zone you create, you need delegation records in other zones that point to the authoritative DNS servers for the new zone.

Understand the tools that are available for monitoring and troubleshooting DNS.   You can use the DNS snap-in to do some basic server testing and monitoring. More important, you use the snap-in to monitor and set logging options. Windows Server 2022 automatically logs DNS events in the event log under a distinct DNS server heading. `Nslookup` offers the ability to perform query testing of DNS servers and to obtain detailed responses at the command prompt. You can use the command-line tool `ipconfig` to view your DNS client settings, to view and reset cached information used locally for resolving DNS name queries, and to register the resource records for a dynamic update client. Finally, you can configure the DNS server to create a log file that records queries, notification messages, dynamic updates, and various other DNS information.

Review Questions

1. You are the network administrator for the ABC Company. Your network consists of two DNS servers named *DNS1* and *DNS2*. The users who are configured to use DNS2 complain because they are unable to connect to Internet websites. The following table shows the configuration of both servers.

DNS1	DNS2
_msdcs.abc.comabc.com	.(root)_msdcs.abc.comabc.com

   The users connected to DNS2 need to be able to access the Internet. What needs to be done?

   A. Build a new Active Directory Integrated zone on DNS2.

   B. Delete the .(root) zone from DNS2, and configure conditional forwarding on DNS2.

   C. Delete the current cache.dns file.

   D. Update your cache.dns file and root hints.

2. You are the network administrator for a large company that has one main site and one branch office. Your company has a single Active Directory forest, ABC.com. You have a single domain controller (ServerA) in the main site that has the DNS role installed. ServerA is configured as a primary DNS zone. You have decided to place a domain controller (ServerB) in the remote site and implement the DNS role on that server. You want to configure DNS so that, if the WAN link fails, users in both sites can still update records and resolve any DNS queries. How should you configure the DNS servers?

   A. Configure ServerB as a secondary DNS server. Set replication to occur every 5 minutes.

   B. Configure ServerB as a stub zone.

   C. Configure ServerB as an Active Directory Integrated zone, and convert ServerA to an Active Directory Integrated zone.

   D. Convert ServerA to an Active Directory Integrated zone, and configure ServerB as a secondary zone.

3. You are the network administrator for a midsized computer company. You have a single Active Directory forest, and your DNS servers are configured as Active Directory Integrated zones. When you look at the DNS records in Active Directory, you notice that there are many records for computers that do not exist on your domain. You want to make sure only domain computers register with your DNS servers. What should you do to resolve this issue?

   A. Set dynamic updates to None.

   B. Set dynamic updates to Nonsecure And Secure.

   C. Set dynamic updates to Domain Users Only.

   D. Set dynamic updates to Secure Only.

4. Your company consists of a single Active Directory forest. You have a Windows Server 2022 domain controller that also has the DNS role installed. You also have a Unix-based DNS server at the same location. You need to configure your Windows DNS server to allow zone transfers to the Unix-based DNS server. What should you do?

    A. Enable BIND secondaries.

    B. Configure the Unix machine as a stub zone.

    C. Convert the DNS server to Active Directory Integrated.

    D. Configure the Microsoft DNS server to forward all requests to the Unix DNS server.

5. You are the network administrator for Stormwind Corporation. Stormwind has two trees in its Active Directory forest, `Stormwind.com` and `abc.com`. Company policy does not allow DNS zone transfers between the two trees. You need to make sure that when anyone in `abc.com` tries to access the `Stormwind.com` domain, all names are resolved from the `Stormwind.com` DNS server. What should you do?

    A. Create a new secondary zone in `abc.com` for `Stormwind.com`.

    B. Configure conditional forwarding on the `abc.com` DNS server for `Stormwind.com`.

    C. Create a new secondary zone in `Stormwind.com` for `abc.com`.

    D. Configure conditional forwarding on the `Stormwind.com` DNS server for `abc.com`.

6. You are the network administrator for your organization. A new company policy states that all inbound DNS queries need to be recorded. What can you do to verify that the IT department is compliant with this new policy?

    A. Enable Server Auditing – Object Access.

    B. Enable DNS debug logging.

    C. Enable server database query logging.

    D. Enable DNS Auditing – Object Access.

7. You are the network administrator for a small company with two DNS servers: DNS1 and DNS2. Both DNS servers reside on domain controllers. DNS1 is set up as a standard primary zone, and DNS2 is set up as a secondary zone. A new security policy was written stating that all DNS zone transfers must be encrypted. How can you implement the new security policy?

    A. Enable the Secure Only setting on DNS1.

    B. Enable the Secure Only setting on DNS2.

    C. Configure Secure Only on the Zone Transfers tab for both servers.

    D. Delete the secondary zone on DNS2. Convert both DNS servers to use Active Directory Integrated zones.

8. You are responsible for DNS in your organization. You look at the DNS database and see a large number of older records on the server. These records are no longer valid. What should you do?

    A. In the zone properties, enable Zone Aging and Scavenging.

    B. In the server properties, enable Zone Aging and Scavenging.

    C. Manually delete all the old records.

    D. Set Dynamic Updates to None.

9. Your IT team has been informed by the compliance team that they need copies of the DNS Active Directory Integrated zones for security reasons. You need to give the Compliance department a copy of the DNS zone. How should you accomplish this goal?

    A. Run dnscmd /zonecopy.

    B. Run dnscmd /zoneinfo.

    C. Run dnscmd /zoneexport.

    D. Run dnscmd /zonefile.

10. You are the network administrator for a Windows Server 2022 network. You have multiple remote locations connected to your main office by slow satellite links. You want to install DNS into these offices so that clients can locate authoritative DNS servers in the main location. What type of DNS servers should be installed in the remote locations?

    A. Primary DNS zones

    B. Secondary DNS zones

    C. Active Directory Integrated zones

    D. Stub zones

11. You assign two DNS server addresses as part of the options for a scope. Later you find a client workstation that isn't using those addresses. What's the most likely cause?

    A. The client didn't get the option information as part of its lease.

    B. The client has been manually configured with a different set of DNS servers.

    C. The client has a reserved IP address in the address pool.

    D. There's a bug in the DHCP server service.

12. You are the network administrator for your company. After configuring a new computer and connecting it to the network, you discover that you cannot access any of the computers on the remote subnet by IP address. You can access some of the computers on the local subnet by IP address. What is the most likely problem?

    A. Incorrectly defined IP address

    B. Incorrectly defined subnet mask

    C. Incorrectly defined default gateway

    D. Incorrectly defined DNS server

13. A user cannot access a server in the domain. After troubleshooting, you determine that the user cannot access the server by name but can access the server by IP address. What is the most likely problem?

    A. Incorrectly defined IP address

    B. Incorrectly defined subnet mask

    C. Incorrectly defined DHCP server

    D. Incorrectly defined DNS server

14. You have a Windows client machine that needs to have a static TCP/IP address. You assign the IP address to the machine and you now want to register the computer with DNS. How can you do this from the Windows client machine?

   A. `ipconfig /renewdns`

   B. `ipconfig /flushdns`

   C. `ipconfig /dns`

   D. `ipconfig /registerdns`

15. You are the administrator for your company network. Your network has a DNS server that contained corrupted data. You fix the issues on the server. One of the users in the network is complaining that they are still unable to access Internet resources. You check to see whether things are working on another computer on the same subnet. What command should you run to fix the issue?

   A. You should run the `DNS /flushdns` command.

   B. You should run the `ipconfig /flush` command.

   C. You should run the `ipconfig /flushdns` command.

   D. You should run the `ping /flush` command.

16. You are the administrator for your company network. A user is using a computer running a Windows client. When this user connects to the corporate network, they are unable to access the internal company servers but can access the servers on the Internet. You run the `ipconfig /all` command and receive the following:

```
Connection-specific DNS Suffix . :
Description . . . . . . . . . . : Ethernet 1
Physical Address . . . . . . . : 00-50-B6-7B-E4-81
DHCP Enabled . . . . . . . . . : Yes
Autoconfiguration Enabled . . . : Yes
Link-local IPv6 Address . . . . : fe80::5d56:3419:eB3b:3c46%17 (Preferred)
IPv4 Address . . . . . . . . . : 192.168.0.121(Preferred)
Subnet Mask . . . . . . . . . : 255.255.255.0
Lease Obtained . . . . . . . . : Friday, August 5, 2022 11:38:12 AM
Lease Expires . . . . . . . . : Friday, August 5, 2022 11:38:12 PM
Default Gateway . . . . . . . . : 192.168.0.1
DHCP Server . . . . . . . . . : 192.168.0.2
DHCPv6 IAID . . . . . . . . . : 536891574
DHCPv6 Client DUID . . . . . . : 00-01-00-01-22-AC-5F-64-00-50-B6-7B-E4-81
DNS Servers . . . . . . . . . : 131.107.10.60
        192.168.0.3
NetBIOS over Tcpip . . . . . . : Enabled
```

You send a ping request and can ping the default gateway, the DNS servers, and the DHCP server successfully. What configuration could be causing the issue?

A. The issue is with the default gateway address.

B. The issue is with the DNS servers.

C. The issue is with the IPv4 address.

D. The issue is with the subnet mask.

17. You need to configure your Windows DNS server to allow zone transfers to the Unix-based DNS server. What should you do?

A. Enable BIND secondaries.

B. Configure the Unix machine as a stub zone.

C. Convert the DNS server to Active Directory Integrated.

D. Configure the Microsoft DNS server to forward all requests to the Unix DNS server.

18. You have two DNS servers: DNSA and DNSB. Both DNS servers reside on domain controllers. DNSA is set up as a standard primary zone, and DNSB is set up as a secondary zone. All DNS zone transfers must be encrypted. How can you implement the new security policy?

A. Enable the Secure Only setting on DNSA.

B. Enable the Secure Only setting on DNSB.

C. Configure Secure Only on the Zone Transfers tab for both servers.

D. Delete the secondary zone on DNSB. Convert both DNS servers to use Active Directory Integrated zones.

19. You notice that in your DNS database you see a number of older records on the server. These records are no longer valid. What should you do?

A. In the zone properties, enable Zone Aging and Scavenging.

B. In the server properties, enable Zone Aging and Scavenging.

C. Manually delete all the old records.

D. Set Dynamic Updates to None.

20. How do you give an administrator a copy of the DNS zone?

A. Run dnscmd /zonecopy.

B. Run dnscmd /zoneinfo.

C. Run dnscmd /zoneexport.

D. Run dnscmd /zonefile.

Chapter

6

Configuring DHCP and IPAM

THE FOLLOWING AZ-800 EXAM OBJECTIVES ARE COVERED IN THIS CHAPTER:

✓ **Manage IP addressing in on-premises and hybrid scenarios**

   ▪ Implement and manage IPAM

   ▪ Implement and configure the DHCP server role (on-premises only)

   ▪ Resolve IP address issues in hybrid environments

   ▪ Create and manage scopes

   ▪ Create and manage IP reservations

   ▪ Implement DHCP high availability

In this chapter, I will show you the various methods of setting up an IP address network. If you want systems to be able to share network resources, the computers must all talk the same type of language. This is where DHCP comes into play.

DHCP allows your users to get the required information so that they can properly communicate on the network. This chapter shows you how to install and configure DHCP. I'll also discuss the advantages of using DHCP and how DHCP can save you hours of configuration time.

This book covers how to work with and configure protocols and services like TCP/IP, DNS, and DHCP (in this chapter). I'll show you a tool that allows you to manage and manipulate these services and protocols from one application.

You'll also learn how you can use the IP Address Management (IPAM) tool to manage and configure all of your TCP/IP services. I'll show you how you can use this application to do your entire TCP/IP configuration from one location.

Understanding DHCP

When you're setting up a network, the computers need to communicate with each other using the same type of computer language. This is referred to as a *protocol*. TCP/IP is the priority protocol for Windows Server 2022. For all of your machines to work using TCP/IP, each system must have its own unique IP address. There are two ways to have clients and servers get TCP/IP addresses:

- You can manually assign the addresses.
- The addresses can be assigned automatically.

Manually assigning addresses is a fairly simple process. You go to each of the machines on the network and assign TCP/IP addresses. The problem with this method arises when the network becomes midsized or larger. Think if you had to individually assign 4,000 TCP/IP addresses, subnet masks, default gateways, and all other configuration options needed to run your network.

DHCP's job is to centralize the process of IP address and option assignment. You can configure a DHCP server with a range of addresses (called a *pool*) and other configuration information and let it assign all of the IP parameters—addresses, default gateways, DNS server addresses, and so on.

One of the nice advantages of DHCP is that you can install DHCP onto a Server Core server. DHCP is one of the roles that can be deployed onto a Server Core server. As of this writing, DHCP was not supported on a Nano server. So, you can't load DHCP on a Windows Server 2022 Nano server.

 DHCP is defined by a series of Request for Comments documents, notably 2131 and 2132.

Introducing the DORA Process

An easy way to remember how DHCP works is to learn the acronym DORA. *DORA* stands for Discover, Offer, Request, and Acknowledge. In brief, here is DHCP's DORA process:

1. *Discover:* When IP networking starts up on a DHCP-enabled client, a special message called a `DHCPDISCOVER` is broadcast within the local physical subnet.

2. *Offer:* Any DHCP server that hears the request checks its internal database and replies with a message called a `DHCPOFFER`, which contains an available IP address.

   The contents of this message depend on how the DHCP server is configured—there are numerous options aside from an IP address that you can specify to pass to the client on a Windows Server DHCP server.

3. *Request:* The client receives one or more `DHCPOFFER`s (depending on how many DHCP servers exist on the local subnet), chooses an address from one of the offers, and sends a `DHCPREQUEST` message to the server to signal acceptance of the `DHCPOFFER`.

   This message might also request additional configuration parameters.

   Other DHCP servers that sent offers take the request message as an acknowledgment that the client didn't accept their offer.

4. *Acknowledge:* When the DHCP server receives the `DHCPREQUEST`, it marks the IP address as being in use (i.e., usually, though it's not required). Then it sends a `DHCPACK` to the client.

   The acknowledgment message might contain requested configuration parameters.

   If the server is unable to accept the `DHCPREQUEST` for any reason, it sends a `DHCPNAK` message. If a client receives a `DHCPNAK`, it begins the configuration process over again.

5. When the client accepts the IP offer, the address is assigned to the client for a specified period of time, called a *lease*. After receiving the `DHCPACK` message, the client performs a final check on the parameters (sometimes it sends an ARP request for the offered IP address) and makes note of the duration of the lease. The client is now configured. If the client detects that the address is already in use, it sends a `DHCPDECLINE`.

If the DHCP server has given out all the IP addresses in its pool, it won't make an offer. If no other servers make an offer, the client's IP network initialization will fail, and the client will use Automatic Private IP Addressing (APIPA).

DHCP Lease Renewal

No matter how long the lease period, the client sends a new lease request message directly to the DHCP server when the lease period is half over (give or take some randomness required by RFC 2131). This period goes by the name *T1* (not to be confused with the T1 type of network connection). If the server hears the request message and there's no reason to reject it, it sends a `DHCPACK` to the client. This resets the lease period.

If the DHCP server isn't available, the client realizes that the lease can't be renewed. The client continues to use the address, and once 87.5 percent of the lease period has elapsed (again, give or take some randomness), the client sends out another renewal request. This interval is known as *T2*. At that point, any DHCP server that hears the renewal can respond to this *DHCP request message* (which is a request for a lease renewal) with a `DHCPACK` and renew the lease. If at any time during this process the client gets a negative `DHCPNACK` message, it must stop using its IP address immediately and start the leasing process over from the beginning by requesting a new lease.

When a client initializes its IP networking, it always attempts to renew its old address. If the client has time left on the lease, it continues to use the lease until its end. If the client is unable to get a new lease by that time, the client will swap over to using an APIPA address and that client would only be able to talk to the local segment with other computers using an APIPA address.

DHCP Lease Release

Although leases can be renewed repeatedly, at some point they might run out. Furthermore, the lease process is "at will." In other words, the client or server can cancel the lease before it ends. In addition, if the client doesn't succeed in renewing the lease before it expires, the client loses its lease and reverts to APIPA. This release process is important for reclaiming extinct IP addresses used by systems that have moved or switched to a non-DHCP address.

Advantages and Disadvantages of DHCP

DHCP was designed from the start to simplify network management. It has some significant advantages, but it also has some drawbacks.

Advantages of DHCP

The following are advantages of DHCP:

- Configuration of large and even midsized networks is much simpler. If a DNS server address or some other change is necessary to the client, you don't have to touch each device in the network physically to reconfigure it with the new settings.

- Once you enter the IP configuration information in one place—the server—it's automatically propagated to clients, eliminating the risk that a user will misconfigure some parameters and require you to fix them.

- IP addresses are conserved because DHCP assigns them only when requested.

- IP configuration becomes almost completely automatic. In most cases, you can plug in a new system (or move one) and then watch as it receives a configuration from the server. For example, when you install new network changes, such as a gateway or DNS server, the client configuration is done at only one location—the DHCP server.

- It allows a preboot execution environment (PXE) client to get a TCP/IP address from DHCP. PXE clients (also called Microsoft Windows Deployment Services [WDS] clients) can get an IP address without needing to have an operating system installed. This allows WDS clients to connect to a WDS server through the TCP/IP protocol and download an operating system remotely.

Disadvantages of DHCP

Unfortunately, there are a few drawbacks with DHCP:

- DHCP can become a single point of failure for your network. If you have only one DHCP server and it's not available, clients can't request or renew leases.

- If the DHCP server contains incorrect information, the misinformation will automatically be delivered to all of your DHCP clients.

- If you want to use DHCP on a multisegmented network, you must put either a DHCP server or a relay agent on each segment, or you must ensure that your router can forward Bootstrap Protocol (BOOTP) broadcasts.

Ipconfig Lease Options

The ipconfig command is useful for working with network settings. Its /renew and /release switches make it particularly handy for DHCP clients. These switches allow you to request renewal of, or give up, your machine's existing address lease. You can do the same thing by toggling the Obtain An IP Address Automatically button in the Internet Protocol (TCP/IP) Properties dialog box, but the command-line option is useful especially when you're setting up a new network.

For example, I spend about a third of my time teaching MCSA or MCSE classes, usually in temporary classrooms set up at conferences, hotels, and so on. Laptops are used in these classes, with one brawny one set up as a DNS/DHCP/DC server. Occasionally, a client will lose its DHCP lease (or not get one, perhaps because a cable has come loose). The quickest way to fix it is to pop open a command-line window and type **ipconfig /renew**.

You can configure DHCP to assign options only to certain classes. *Classes*, defined by an administrator, are groups of computers that require identical DHCP options. The /setclassid*classID* switch of ipconfig is the only way to assign a machine to a class. More specifically, the switches do the following:

ipconfig /renew Instructs the DHCP client to request a lease renewal. If the client already has a lease, it requests a renewal from the server that issued the current lease. This is equivalent to what happens when the client reaches the half-life of its lease. Alternatively, if the client doesn't currently have a lease, it is equivalent to what happens when you boot a DHCP client for the first time.

ipconfig /release Forces the client to give up its lease immediately by sending the server a DHCP release notification. The server updates its status information and marks the client's old IP address as "available," leaving the client with no address bound to its network interface. When you use this command, most of the time it will be immediately followed by ipconfig/renew. The combination releases the existing lease and gets a new one, probably with a different address. (It's also a handy way to force your client to get a new set of settings from the server before the lease expiration time.)

ipconfig /setclassidclassID Sets a new class ID for the client. You will see how to configure class options later in the section "Setting Scope Options for IPv4." For now, you should know that the only way to add a client machine to a class is to use this command. Note that you need to renew the client lease for the class assignment to take effect.

If you have multiple network adapters in a single machine, you can provide the name of the adapter (or adapters) upon which you want the command to work, including an asterisk (*) as a wildcard. For example, one of my servers has two network cards: an Intel EtherExpress (ELNK1) and a generic 100 Mbps card. If I want to renew DHCP settings for both adapters, I can type **ipconfig /renew** *. If I just want to renew the Intel EtherExpress card, I can type **ipconfig /renew ELNK1**.

Understanding Scope Details

By now you should have a good grasp of what a lease is and how it works. To learn how to configure your servers to hand out those leases, however, you need to have a complete understanding of some additional topics: scopes, superscopes, exclusions, reservations, address pool, and relay agents.

Scope

Let's start with the concept of a *scope*, which is a contiguous range of addresses. There's usually one scope per physical subnet, and a scope can cover a Class A, Class B, or Class C network address or a TCP/IP v6 address. DHCP uses scopes as the basis for managing and assigning IP addressing information.

Each scope has a set of parameters, or scope options, that you can configure. *Scope options* control what data is delivered to DHCP clients when they're completing the DHCP negotiation process with a particular server. For example, the DNS server name, default gateway, and default network time server are all separate options that can be assigned. These settings are called *option types*. You can use any of the types provided with Windows Server 2022, or you can specify your own.

Superscope

A *superscope* enables the DHCP server to provide addresses from more than one scope to clients on the same physical subnet. This is helpful when clients within the same subnet have more than one IP network and thus need IPs from more than one address pool. Microsoft's

DHCP snap-in allows you to manage IP address assignment in the superscope, though you must still configure other scope options individually for each child scope.

Exclusions and Reservations

The scope defines what IP addresses could potentially be assigned, but you can influence the assignment process in two additional ways by specifying exclusions and reservations:

Exclusions   These are IP addresses within the range that you never want automatically assigned. These excluded addresses are off-limits to DHCP. You'll typically use exclusions to tag any addresses that you never want the DHCP server to assign at all. You might use exclusions to set aside addresses that you want to assign permanently to servers that play a vital role in your organization.

Reservations   These are IP addresses within the range for which you want a permanent DHCP lease. They essentially reserve a particular IP address for a particular device. The device still goes through the DHCP process (i.e., its lease expires and it asks for a new one), but it always obtains the same addressing information from the DHCP server.

Exclusions are useful for addresses that you don't want to participate in DHCP at all. *Reservations* are helpful for situations in which you want a client to get the same settings each time they obtain an address.

An address cannot be simultaneously reserved and excluded. Be aware of this fact for the exam, possibly relating to a troubleshooting question.

🌐 Real World Scenario

Using Reservations and Exclusions

Deciding when to assign a reservation or exclusion can sometimes be confusing. In practice, you'll find that certain computers in the network greatly benefit by having static IP network information. Servers such as DNS servers, the DHCP server itself, SMTP servers, and other low-level infrastructure servers are good candidates for static assignment. There are usually so few of these servers that the administrator is not overburdened if a change in network settings requires going out to reconfigure each individually. Even in large installations, I find it preferable to manage these vital servers by hand rather than rely on DHCP.

Reservations are also appropriate for application servers and other special but nonvital infrastructure servers. With a reservation in DHCP, the client device will still go through the DHCP process but will always obtain the same addressing information from the DHCP server. The premise behind this strategy is that these nonvital servers can withstand a short outage if DHCP settings change or if the DHCP server fails.

Address Pool

The range of IP addresses that the DHCP server can assign is called its *address pool*. For example, let's say you set up a new DHCP scope covering the 192.168.1 subnet. That gives you 254 usable IP addresses in the pool. After adding an exclusion from 192.168.1.241 to 192.168.1.254, you're left with 240 (254 – 14) IP addresses in the pool. That means (in theory, at least) that you can service 240 unique clients at a time before you run out of IP addresses.

DHCP Relay Agent

By design, DHCP is intended to work with clients and servers on a single IP network. But RFC 1542 sets out how BOOTP (on which DHCP is based) should work in circumstances in which the client and server are on different IP networks. If no DHCP server is available on the client's network, you can use a DHCP relay agent to forward DHCP broadcasts from the client's network to the DHCP server. The relay agent acts like a radio repeater, listening for DHCP client requests and retransmitting them through the router to the server.

Installing and Authorizing DHCP

Installing DHCP is easy using the Windows Server 2022/2012 R2 installation mechanism. Unlike some other services discussed in this book, the installation process installs just the service and its associated snap-in, starting it when the installation is complete. At that point, it's not delivering any DHCP service, but you don't have to reboot.

Installing DHCP

Exercise 6.1 shows you how to install a DHCP Server using Server Manager. This exercise was completed on a Windows Server 2022 Member Server since Active Directory is not installed yet.

EXERCISE 6.1

Installing the DHCP Service

1. Choose Server Manager by clicking the Server Manager icon on the Taskbar.

2. Click Add Roles And Features.

3. Choose role-based or feature-based installation and click Next.

4. Choose your server and click Next.

5. Choose DHCP (as shown in Figure 6.1) and click Next.

FIGURE 6.1   Choosing DHCP

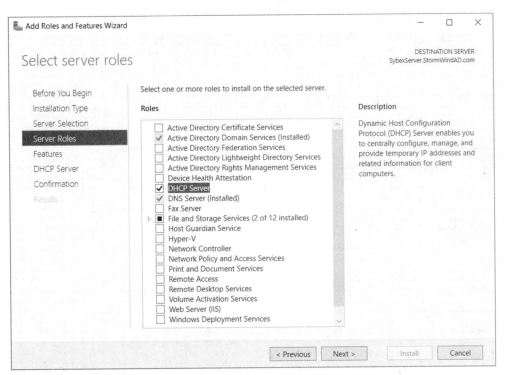

6.   At the Features screen, click Next.

7.   Click Next at the DHCP screen.

8.   At the DHCP confirmation screen, click the Install button.

9.   When the installation is complete, click the Close button.

10.   On the left side, click the DHCP link.

11.   Click the More link next to Configuration Required For DHCP Server.

12.   Under Action, click Complete DHCP Configuration.

13.   At the DHCP Description page, click Commit.

14.   Click Close at the Summary screen.

15.   Close Server Manager.

Introducing the DHCP Snap-In

When you install the DHCP server, the DHCP snap-in is also installed. You can open it by selecting Administrative Tools ➢ DHCP. Figure 6.2 shows the DHCP management snap-in option.

FIGURE 6.2 Admin Tools screen

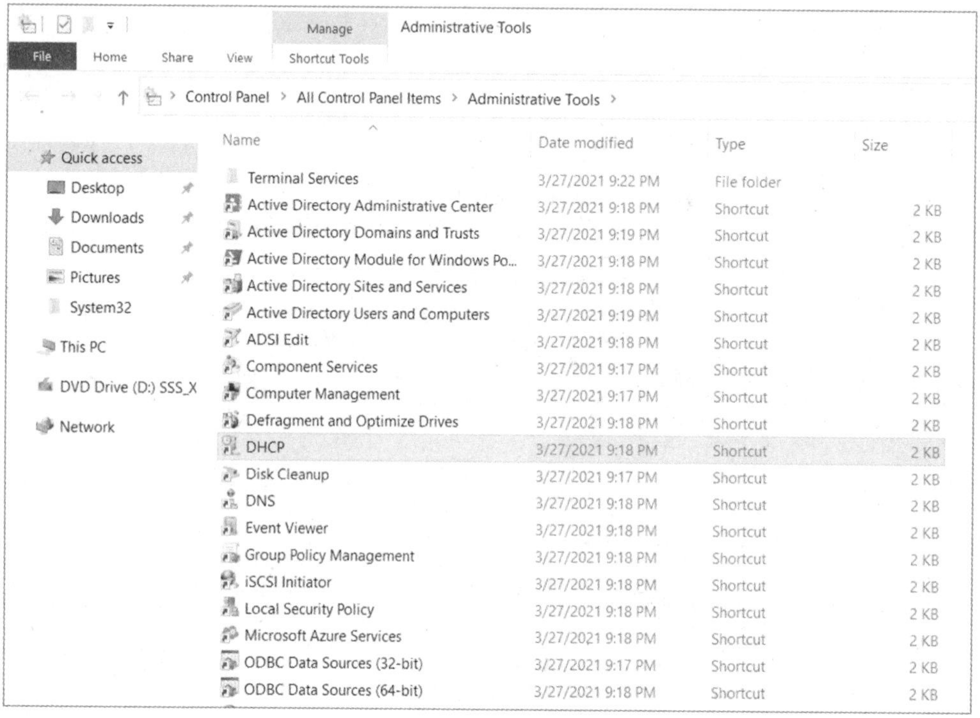

As you can see, the snap-in follows the standard MMC model. The left pane displays IPv4 and IPv6 sections and which servers are available; you can connect to servers other than the one to which you're already connected. A `Server Options` folder contains options that are specific to a particular DHCP server. Each server contains subordinate items grouped into folders. Each scope has a folder named after the scope's IP address range. Within each scope, four subordinate views show you interesting things about the scope, such as the following:

- The Address Pool view shows what the address pool looks like.

- The Address Leases view shows one entry for each current lease. Each lease shows the computer name to which the lease was issued, the corresponding IP address, and the current lease expiration time.

- The Reservations view shows the IP addresses that are reserved and which devices hold them.

- The Scope Options view lists the set of options you've defined for this scope.

Authorizing DHCP for Active Directory

Authorization creates an Active Directory object representing the new server. It helps keep unauthorized servers off your network. Unauthorized servers can cause two kinds of problems. They may hand out bogus leases, or they may fraudulently deny renewal requests from legitimate clients.

When you install a DHCP server using Windows Server 2022 and Active Directory is present on your network, the server won't be allowed to provide DHCP services to clients until it has been authorized. If you install DHCP on a member server in an Active Directory domain or on a stand-alone server, you'll have to authorize the server manually. When you authorize a server, you're adding its IP address to the Active Directory object that contains the IP addresses of all authorized DHCP servers.

At start time, each DHCP server queries the directory, looking for its IP address on the "authorized" list. If it can't find the list or if it can't find its IP address on the list, the DHCP service fails to start. Instead, it adds a message to the event log, indicating that it couldn't service client requests because the server wasn't authorized.

Exercise 6.2 and Exercise 6.3 show you how to authorize and unauthorize a DHCP server onto a network with Active Directory. If you installed DHCP onto a network with a domain, you can complete the following two exercises, but if you are still on a stand-alone server, you *cannot* do these exercises. Also, if you install the DHCP server on a domain controller, as of this writing, the DHCP server will auto-authorize. These steps are here to show you how to do it after you have Active Directory on your network or you install DHCP onto a member server.

EXERCISE 6.2

Authorizing a DHCP Server

1. From Administrative Tools, choose DHCP to open the DHCP snap-in.

2. Right-click the server you want to authorize and choose the Authorize command (see Figure 6.3).

EXERCISE 6.2 *(continued)*

FIGURE 6.3   Choosing Authorize

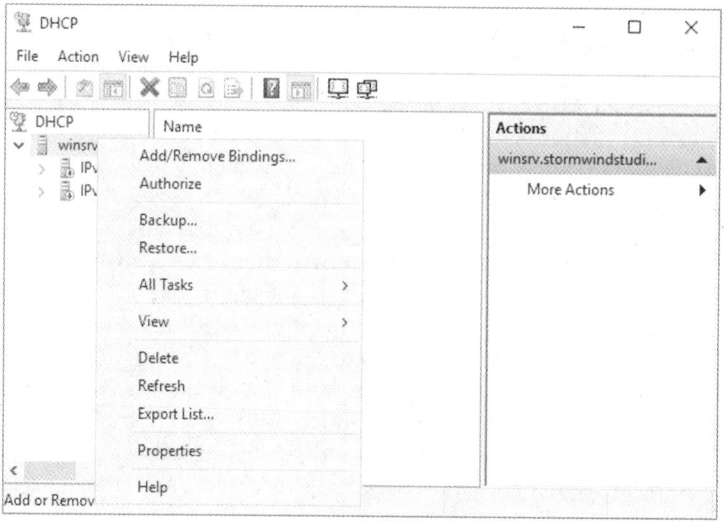

3. Wait a few seconds and then press F5. This will refresh the server. You should see that the red down arrows are now green.

EXERCISE 6.3

Unauthorizing a DHCP Server

1. From Administrative Tools, choose DHCP to open the DHCP snap-in.

2. Right-click the server you want to authorize and choose the Unauthorize command (as shown in Figure 6.4).

FIGURE 6.4   Choosing Unauthorize

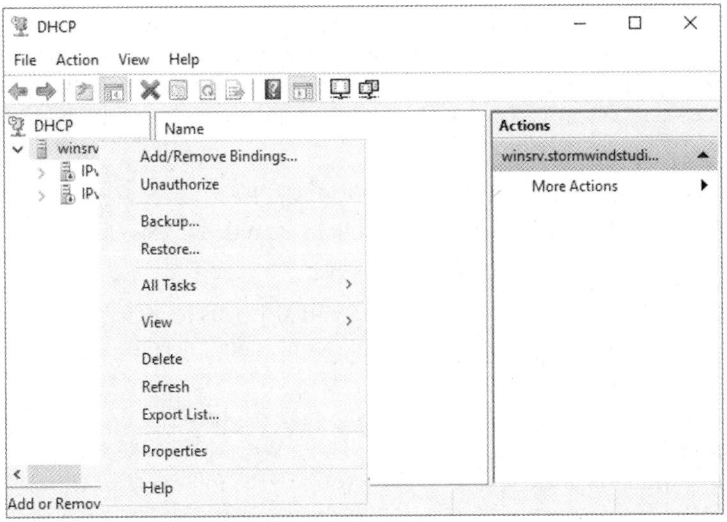

3. Wait a few seconds and then press F5. This will refresh the server. You should see that the green arrows are now red.

4. Now let's reauthorize the server. Right-click the server and choose the Authorize command. Wait a few seconds and press F5.

Creating and Managing DHCP Scopes

You can use any number of DHCP servers on a single physical network if you divide the range of addresses that you want assigned into multiple scopes. Each scope contains a number of useful pieces of data, but before you can understand them, you need to know some additional terminology.

You can perform the following management tasks on DHCP scopes:

- Create a scope
- Configure scope properties
- Configure reservations and exclusions
- Set scope options
- Activate and deactivate scopes
- Create a superscope
- Create a multicast scope
- Integrate Dynamic DNS and DHCP

I will cover each task in the following sections.

Creating a New Scope in IPv4

Like many other things in Windows Server 2022, a wizard drives the process of creating a new scope. You will most likely create a scope while installing DHCP, but you may need to create more than one. The overall process is simple, as long as you know beforehand what the wizard is going to ask. If you think about what defines a scope, you'll be well prepared. You need to know the following:

- The IP address range for the scope you want to create.

- Which IP addresses, if any, you want to exclude from the address pool.

- Which IP addresses, if any, you want to reserve.

- Values for the DHCP options you want to set, if any. This item isn't strictly necessary for creating a scope. However, to create a useful scope, you'll need to have some options to specify for the clients.

To create a scope, under the server name, right-click the IPv4 option in the DHCP snap-in, and use the Action ➤ New Scope command. This starts the New Scope Wizard (see Figure 6.5). You will look at each page of the wizard in the following sections.

FIGURE 6.5   Welcome page of the New Scope Wizard

Setting the Screen Name

The Scope Name page allows you to enter a name and description for your scope. These will be displayed by the DHCP snap-in.

It's a good idea to pick sensible names for your scopes so that other administrators will be able to figure out the purpose of the scope. For example, the name DHCP is likely not very helpful, whereas a name like 1st Floor Subnet is more descriptive and can help in troubleshooting.

Defining the IP Address Range

The IP Address Range page (see Figure 6.6) is where you enter the start and end IP addresses for your range. The wizard does minimal checking on the addresses you enter, and it automatically calculates the appropriate subnet mask for the range. You can modify the subnet mask if you know what you're doing.

FIGURE 6.6 IP Address Range page of the New Scope Wizard

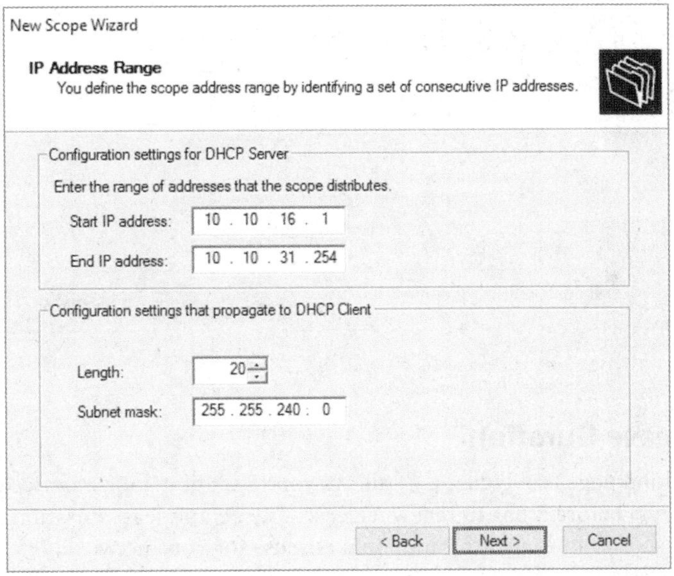

New Scope Wizard

IP Address Range
You define the scope address range by identifying a set of consecutive IP addresses.

Configuration settings for DHCP Server

Enter the range of addresses that the scope distributes.

Start IP address: 10 . 10 . 16 . 1

End IP address: 10 . 10 . 31 . 254

Configuration settings that propagate to DHCP Client

Length: 20

Subnet mask: 255 . 255 . 240 . 0

< Back   Next >   Cancel

Adding Exclusions and Delay

The Add Exclusions And Delay page (see Figure 6.7) allows you to create exclusion ranges. Exclusions are TCP/IP numbers that are in the pool, but they do not get issued to clients. To exclude one address, put it in the Start IP Address field. To exclude a range, also fill in the End IP Address field. The delay setting is a time duration by which the server will delay the transmission of a DHCPOFFER message.

Although you can always add exclusions later, it's best to include them when you create the scope so that no excluded addresses are ever passed out to clients.

FIGURE 6.7   Add Exclusions And Delay page of the New Scope Wizard

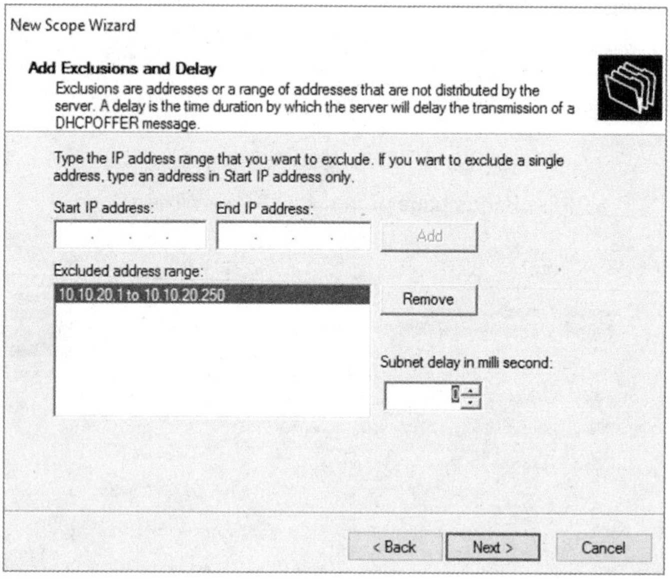

New Scope Wizard

Add Exclusions and Delay
Exclusions are addresses or a range of addresses that are not distributed by the server. A delay is the time duration by which the server will delay the transmission of a DHCPOFFER message.

Type the IP address range that you want to exclude. If you want to exclude a single address, type an address in Start IP address only.

Start IP address: End IP address: Add

Excluded address range:
10.10.20.1 to 10.10.20.250   Remove

Subnet delay in milli second:
0

< Back   Next >   Cancel

Setting a Lease Duration

The Lease Duration page (see Figure 6.8) allows you to set how long a device gets to use an assigned IP address before it has to renew its lease. The default lease duration is 8 days. You may find that a shorter or longer duration makes sense for your network. If your network is highly dynamic, with lots of arrivals, departures, and moving computers, set a shorter lease duration; if it's less active, make it longer.

FIGURE 6.8   Lease Duration page of the New Scope Wizard

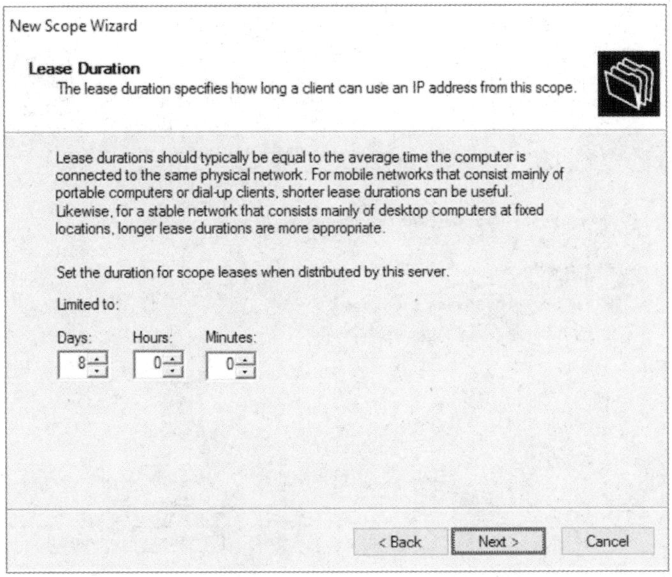

New Scope Wizard

Lease Duration
The lease duration specifies how long a client can use an IP address from this scope.

Lease durations should typically be equal to the average time the computer is connected to the same physical network. For mobile networks that consist mainly of portable computers or dial-up clients, shorter lease durations can be useful. Likewise, for a stable network that consists mainly of desktop computers at fixed locations, longer lease durations are more appropriate.

Set the duration for scope leases when distributed by this server.

Limited to:

Days: Hours: Minutes:
  8   0   0

< Back   Next >   Cancel

Remember that renewal attempts begin when approximately half of the lease period is over (give or take a random interval) or when a system restarts, so don't set them too short. For example, leases that are set too short can cause renewal traffic in the middle of the workday and this can cause network delays while all the machines try to renew their addresses.

Configuring Basic DHCP Options

The Configure DHCP Options page (see Figure 6.9) allows you to choose whether you want to set up basic DHCP options such as default gateway and DNS settings. The options are described in the following sections. If you choose not to configure options, you can always do so later. However, you should not activate the scope until you've configured the options you want assigned.

FIGURE 6.9   Configure DHCP Options page of the New Scope Wizard

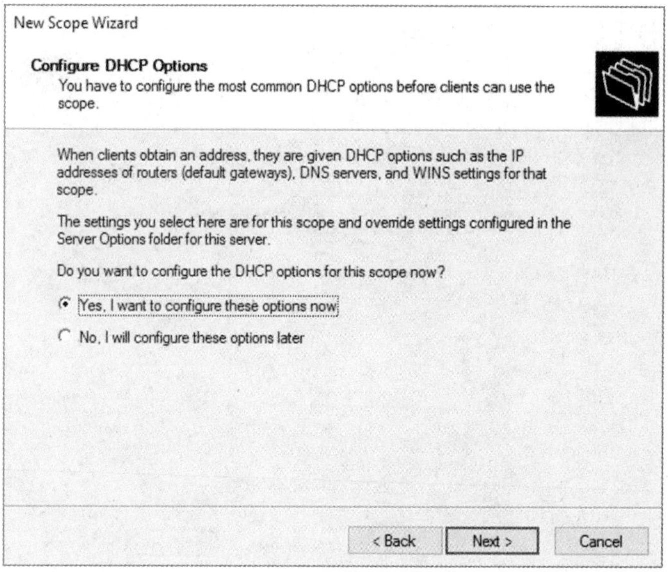

Configuring a Router

The first option configuration page is the Router (Default Gateway) page (see Figure 6.10), in which you enter the IP addresses of one or more routers (more commonly referred to as *default gateways*) that you want to use for outbound traffic. After entering the IP addresses of the routers, use the Up and Down buttons to order the addresses. Clients will use the routers in the order specified when attempting to send outgoing packets.

FIGURE 6.10 Router (Default Gateway) page of the New Scope Wizard

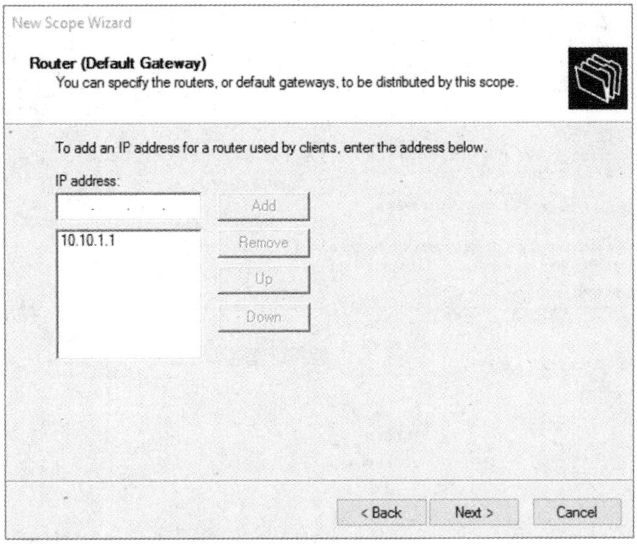

Providing DNS Settings

On the Domain Name And DNS Servers page (see Figure 6.11), you specify the set of DNS servers and the parent domain you want passed down to DHCP clients. Normally, you'll want to specify at least one DNS server by filling in its DNS name or IP address. You can also specify the domain suffix that you want clients to use as the base domain for all connections that aren't fully qualified. For example, if your clients are used to navigating based on server name alone rather than the fully qualified domain name (FQDN) of `server.willpanek.com`, then you'll want to place your domain here.

FIGURE 6.11 Domain Name And DNS Servers page of the New Scope Wizard

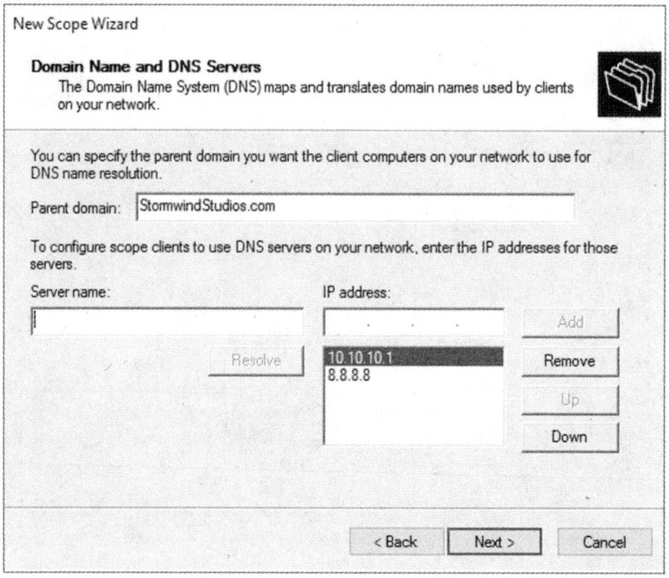

Providing WINS Settings

If you're still using Windows Internet Name Service (WINS) on your network, you can configure DHCP so that it passes WINS server addresses to your Windows clients. (If you want the Windows clients to honor it, you'll also need to define the WINS/NBT Node Type option for the scope.) As on the DNS server page, on the WINS Servers page (see Figure 6.12) you can enter the addresses of several servers and move them into the order in which you want clients to try them. You can enter the DNS or NetBIOS name of each server, or you can enter an IP address.

FIGURE 6.12   WINS Servers page of the New Scope Wizard

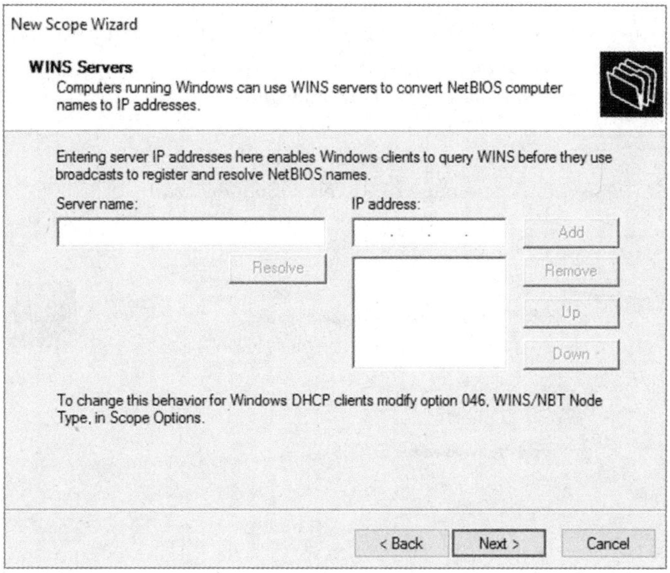

New Scope Wizard

WINS Servers
Computers running Windows can use WINS servers to convert NetBIOS computer
names to IP addresses.

Entering server IP addresses here enables Windows clients to query WINS before they use
broadcasts to register and resolve NetBIOS names.

Server name: IP address:

[   ]   [.   .   .]   Add

                        Resolve   [   ]   Remove

                                                                           Up

                                                                           Down

To change this behavior for Windows DHCP clients modify option 046, WINS/NBT Node
Type, in Scope Options.

                                    < Back   Next >   Cancel

Here are some of the more common options you can set on a DHCP server:

003 Router   Used to provide a list of available routers or default gateways on the same subnet.

006 DNS Servers   Used to provide a list of DNS servers.

015 DNS Domain Name   Used to provide the DNS suffix.

028 Broadcast Address   Used to configure the broadcast address, if different than the default, based on the subnet mask.

44 WINS/NBNS Servers   Used to configure the IP addresses of WINS servers.

46 WINS/NBT Node Type   Used to configure the preferred NetBIOS name resolution method. There are four settings for node type:

B Node (0x1)   Broadcast for NetBIOS resolution

P Node (0x2)   Peer-to-peer (WINS) server for NetBIOS resolution

M Node (0x4)   Mixed node (does a B node and then a P node)

H Node (0x8)   Hybrid node (does a P node and then a B node)

051 Lease   Used to configure a special lease duration.

Activating the Scope

The Activate Scope page (see Figure 6.13) gives you the option to activate the scope immediately after creating it. By default, the wizard assumes that you want the scope activated unless you select the No, I Will Activate This Scope Later radio button, in which case the scope will remain dormant until you activate it manually.

FIGURE 6.13   Activate Scope page of the New Scope Wizard

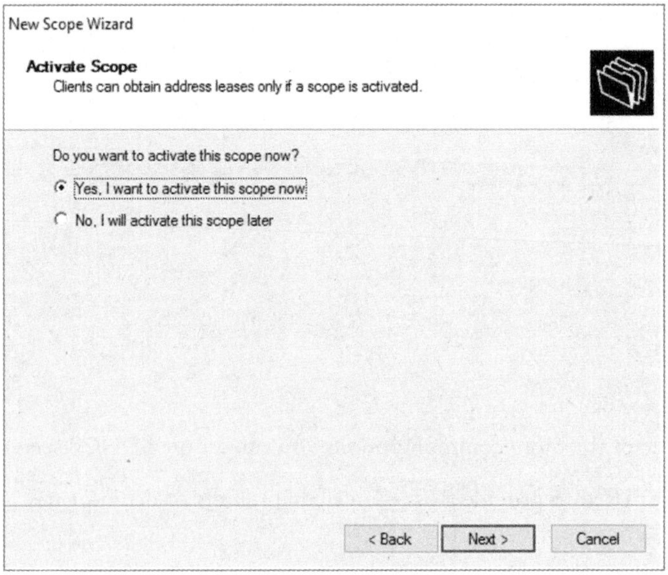

New Scope Wizard

Activate Scope
Clients can obtain address leases only if a scope is activated.

Do you want to activate this scope now?

◉ Yes, I want to activate this scope now

○ No, I will activate this scope later

`< Back`   `Next >`   `Cancel`

WARNING   Be sure to verify that there are no other DHCP servers assigned to the address range you choose!

In Exercise 6.4, you will create a new scope for the 192.168.0.x private Class C network. First you need to complete Exercise 6.1 before beginning this exercise.

EXERCISE 6.4

Creating a New Scope

1. Open the DHCP snap-in by selecting Administrative Tools ➢ DHCP.

2. Right-click the IPv4 folder and choose New Scope. The New Scope Wizard appears.

3. Click the Next button on the welcome page.

4. Enter a name and a description for your new scope and click the Next button.

5. On the IP Address Range page, enter **192.168.0.2** as the start IP address for the scope and **192.168.0.250** as the end IP address. Leave the subnet mask controls alone (though when creating a scope on a production network, you might need to change them). Click Next.

6. On the Add Exclusions And Delay page, click Next without adding any excluded addresses or delays.

7. On the Lease Duration page, set the lease duration to 3 days and click Next.

8. On the Configure DHCP Options page, click Next to indicate you want to configure default options for this scope.

9. On the Router (Default Gateway) page, enter **192.168.0.1** for the router IP address and then click the Add button. Once the address is added, click Next.

10. On the Domain Name And DNS Servers page, enter the IP address of a DNS server on your network in the IP Address field (for example, you might enter **192.168.0.251**) and click the Add button. Click Next.

11. On the WINS Servers page, click Next to leave the WINS options unset.

12. On the Activate Scope page, if your network is currently using the 192.168.0.*x* range, select Yes, I Want To Activate This Scope Now. Click Next.

13. When the wizard's summary page appears, click Finish to create the scope.

Creating a New Scope in IPv6

Now that you've seen how to create a new scope in IPv4, I'll go through the steps to create a new scope in IPv6.

To create a scope, right-click the IPv6 option in the DHCP snap-in under the server name and select the Action ➤ New Scope command. This starts the New Scope Wizard. Just as with creating a scope in IPv4, the welcome page of the wizard tells you that you've launched the New Scope Wizard. You will look at each page of the wizard in the following sections.

Setting the Screen Name

The Scope Name page (see Figure 6.14) allows you to enter a name and description for your scope. These will be displayed by the DHCP snap-in.

FIGURE 6.14   IPv6 Scope Name page of the New Scope Wizard

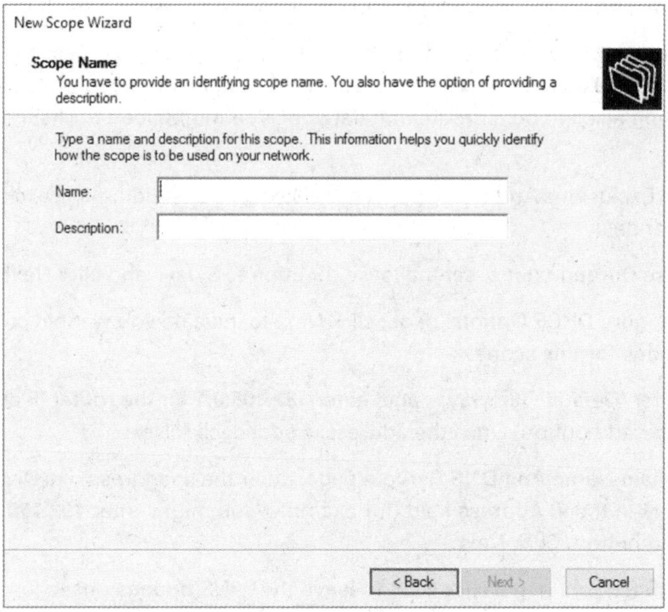

New Scope Wizard

Scope Name
You have to provide an identifying scope name. You also have the option of providing a
description.

Type a name and description for this scope. This information helps you quickly identify
how the scope is to be used on your network.

Name:

Description:

< Back   Next >   Cancel

It's a good idea to pick a sensible name for your scopes so that other
administrators will be able to figure out what the scope is used for.

Scope Prefix

The Scope Prefix page (see Figure 6.15) gets you started creating the IPv6 scope. IPv6 has
three types of addresses, which can be categorized by type and scope:

FIGURE 6.15   Scope Prefix page of the New Scope Wizard

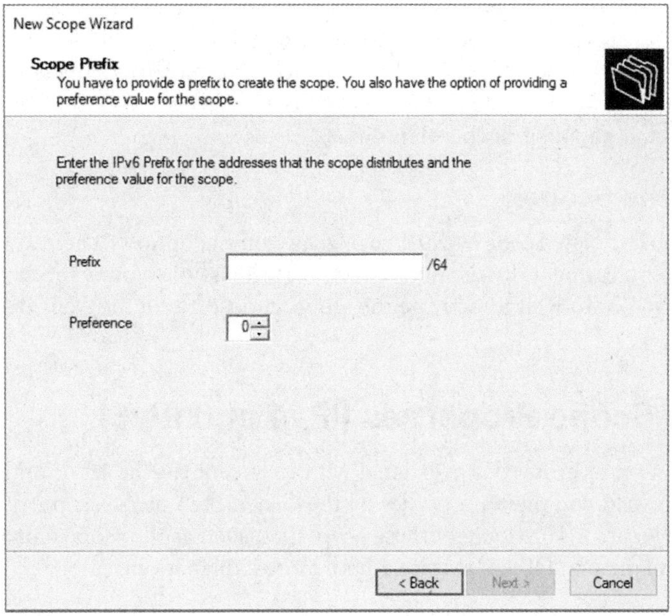

New Scope Wizard

Scope Prefix
You have to provide a prefix to create the scope. You also have the option of providing a
preference value for the scope.

Enter the IPv6 Prefix for the addresses that the scope distributes and the
preference value for the scope.

Prefix   /64

Preference   0

< Back   Next >   Cancel

Unicast Addresses   *One-to-one*. A packet from one host is delivered to another host.
The following are some examples of IPv6 unicast:

- The unicast prefix for site-local addresses is `FEC0::/48`.

- The unicast prefix for link-local addresses is `FE80::/64`.

The 6to4 address allows communication between two hosts running both IPv4
and IPv6. The way to calculate the 6to4 address is by combining the global prefix
`2002::/16` with the 32 bits of a public IPv4 address of the host. This gives you a 48-bit
prefix. 6to4 is described in RFC 3056.

Multicast Addresses   *One-to-many*. A packet from one host is delivered to multiple
hosts (but not everyone). The prefix for multicast addresses is `FF00::/8`.

Anycast Addresses   A packet from one host is delivered to the nearest of multiple hosts
(in terms of routing distance).

Adding Exclusions

As with the IPv4 New Scope Wizard, the Add Exclusions page allows you to create exclusion
ranges. *Exclusions* are TCP/IP numbers that are in the pool but do not get issued to clients.
To exclude one address, put it in the Start IPv6 Address field. To exclude a range, also fill in
the End IPv6 Address field.

Setting a Lease Duration

The Scope Lease page allows you to set how long a device gets to use an assigned IP address before it has to renew its lease. You can set two different lease durations. The section labeled Non Temporary Address (IANA) is the lease time for your more permanent hosts (such as printers and server towers). The one labeled Temporary Address (IATA) is for hosts that might disconnect at any time, such as laptops.

Activating the Scope

The Completing The New Scope Wizard page gives you the option to activate the scope immediately after creating it. By default, the wizard will assume you want the scope activated. If you want to wait to activate the scope, choose No in the Activate Scope Now box.

Changing Scope Properties (IPv4 and IPv6)

Each scope has a set of properties associated with it. Except for the set of options assigned by the scope, you can find these properties on the General tab of the scope's Properties dialog box (see Figure 6.16). Some of these properties, such as the scope name and description, are self-explanatory. Others require a little more explanation:

FIGURE 6.16 General tab of the scope's Properties dialog box for an IPv4 scope

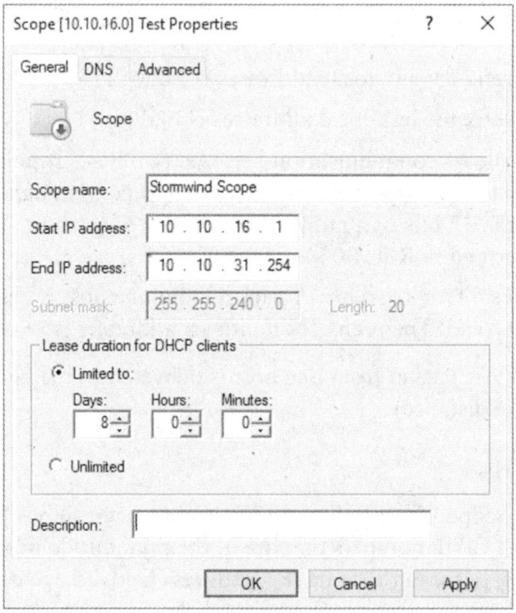

- The Start IP Address and End IP Address fields allow you to set the range of the scope.

- For IPv4 scopes, the settings in the section Lease Duration For DHCP Clients control how long leases in this scope are valid.

  The IPv6 Scope dialog box includes a Lease tab where you set the lease properties.

> When you make changes to these properties, they have no effect on existing leases. For example, say you create a scope from 172.30.1.1 to 172.30.1.199. You use that scope for a while and then edit its properties to reduce the range from 172.30.1.1 to 172.30.1.150. If a client has been assigned the address 172.30.1.180, which was part of the scope before you changed it, the client will retain that address until the lease expires but will not be able to renew it.

Changing Server Properties

Just as each scope has its own set of properties, so too does the server itself. You access the server properties by right-clicking the IPv4 or IPv6 object within the DHCP Management Console and selecting Properties.

IPv4 Server Properties

Figure 6.17 shows the IPv4 Properties dialog box.

FIGURE 6.17   The General tab of the IPv4 Properties dialog box for the server

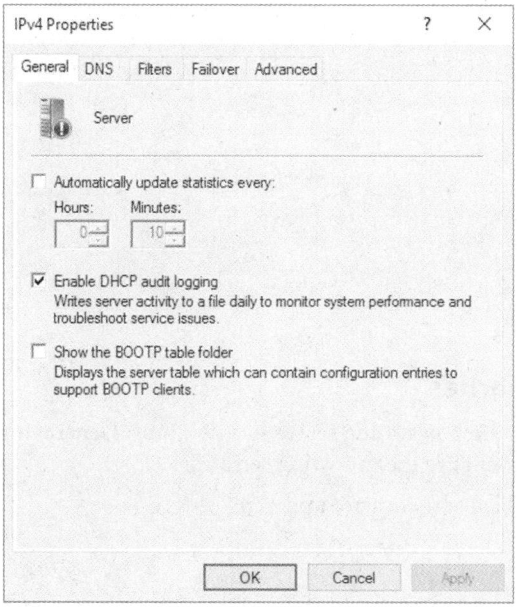

The IPv4 Properties dialog box has five tabs: General, DNS, Filters, Failover, and Advanced. The Advanced tab, shown in Figure 6.18, contains the following configuration parameters:

- Conflict Detection Attempts specifies how many ICMP echo requests (pings) the server sends for an address it is about to offer. The default is 0. Conflict detection is a way to verify that the DHCP server is not issuing IP addresses that are already being used on the network.

- Audit Log File Path is where you enter the location for log files.

- Change Server Connection Bindings allows you to choose which of the network adapters will be used by the DHCP server for both IPv4 and IPv6 addresses.

- DNS Dynamic Update Registration Credentials allows you to put in user credentials so that DHCP can update DNS if DNS is using Secure Only dynamic updates.

FIGURE 6.18   Advanced tab of the IPv4 Properties dialog box for the server

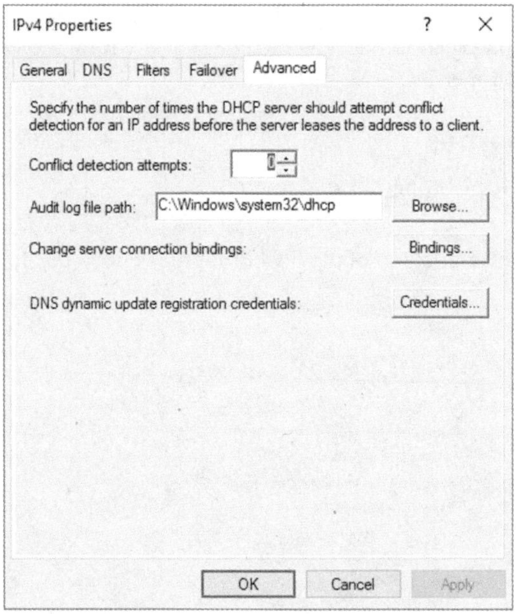

IPv6 Server Properties

The IPv6 Properties dialog box for the server has two tabs: General and Advanced. On the General tab, you can configure the following settings:

- Frequency with which statistics are updated

- DHCP auditing

The Advanced tab allows you to configure the following settings:

- Database path for the audit log file path.
- Connection bindings.
- Registration credentials for Dynamic DNS. The registration credential is the user account that DHCP will use to register clients with Active Directory.

Managing Reservations and Exclusions

After defining the address pool for your scope, the next step is to create reservations and exclusions, which reduce the size of the pool. In the following sections, you will learn how to add and remove exclusions and reservations.

Adding and Removing Exclusions

When you want to exclude an entire range of IP addresses, you need to add that range as an exclusion. Ordinarily, you'll want to do this before you enable a scope because that prevents any of the IP addresses you want excluded from being leased before you have a chance to exclude them. In fact, you can't create an exclusion that includes a leased address—you have to get rid of the lease first.

Adding an Exclusion Range

Here's how to add an exclusion range:

1. Open the DHCP snap-in and find the scope to which you want to add an exclusion (either IPv4 or IPv6).
2. Expand the scope so that you can see its Address Pool item for IPv4 or the Exclusion section for IPv6.
3. Right-click the Address Pool or Exclusion section and choose the New Exclusion Range command.
4. When the Add Exclusion dialog box appears, enter the IP addresses you want to exclude. To exclude a single address, type it in the Start IP Address field. To exclude a range of addresses, also fill in the End IP Address field.
5. Click the Add button to add the exclusion.

When you add exclusions, they appear in the Address Pool node, which is under the Scope section for IPv4 and under the Exclusion section of IPv6.

Removing an Exclusion Range

To remove an exclusion, just right-click it and choose the Delete command. After confirming your command, the snap-in removes the excluded range and the addresses become immediately available for issuance.

Adding and Removing Reservations

Adding a reservation is simple as long as you have the MAC address of the device for which you want to create a reservation. Because reservations belong to a single scope, you create and remove them within the Reservations node beneath each scope.

Adding a Reservation

To add a reservation, perform the following tasks:

1.   Right-click the scope and select New Reservation.

     This displays the New Reservation dialog box, shown in Figure 6.19.

FIGURE 6.19   New Reservation dialog boxes for IPv4 and IPv6

2.   Enter the IP address and MAC address or ID for the reservation.

> To find the MAC address of the local computer, use the `ipconfig` command. To find the MAC address of a remote machine, use the `nbtstat-acomputername` command.

3.   If you want, you can also enter a name and description.

4.   For IPv4, in the Supported Types section, choose whether the reservation will be made by DHCP only, BOOTP only (useful for remote-access devices), or both.

Removing a Reservation

To remove a reservation, right-click it and select Delete. This removes the reservation but does nothing to the client device.

 There's no way to change a reservation once it has been created. If you want to change any of the associated settings, you'll have to delete and re-create the reservation.

Setting Scope Options for IPv4

Once you've installed a server, authorized it in Active Directory, and fixed up the address pool, the next step is to set scope options that you want sent out to clients, such as router (that is, default gateway) and DNS server addresses. You must configure the options you want sent out before you activate a scope. If you don't, clients may register in the scope without getting any options, rendering them virtually useless. Thus, configure the scope options, along with the IP address and subnet mask that you configured earlier in this chapter.

In the following sections, you will learn how to configure and assign scope options on the DHCP server.

Understanding Option Assignment

You can control which DHCP options are doled out to clients in five (slightly overlapping) ways:

Predefined Options   *Predefined options* are templates that are available in the Server, Scope, or Client Options dialog box.

Server Options   *Server options* are assigned to all scopes and clients of a particular server. That means if there's some setting you want all clients of a DHCP server to have, no matter what scope they're in, this is where you assign it. Specific options (those that are set at the class, scope, or client level) will override server-level options. That gives you an escape valve; it's a better idea, though, to be careful about which options you assign if your server manages multiple scopes.

Scope Options   If you want a particular option value assigned only to those clients in a certain subnet, you should assign it as a *scope option*. For example, it's common to specify different routers for different physical subnets; if you have two scopes corresponding to different subnets, each scope would probably have a separate value for the router option.

Class Options   You can assign different options to clients of different types, that is, *class options*. For example, Windows 2000, XP, Vista, Windows 7, Windows 8/8.1, Windows 10/11, Server 2003/2003 R2, Server 2008/ 2008 R2, Server 2012/2012 R2, Windows Server 2016, Server 2019, and Server 2022 machines recognize a number of

DHCP options that Windows 98, Windows NT, and macOS machines ignore, and vice versa. By defining a Windows 2000 or newer class (using the `ipconfig /setclassid` command you saw earlier), you could assign those options only to machines that report themselves as being in that class.

Client Options   If a client is using DHCP reservations, you can assign certain options to that specific client. You attach *client options* to a particular reservation. Client options override scope, server, and class options. The only way to override a client option is to configure the client manually. The DHCP server manages client options.

Client options override class options, class options override scope options, and scope options override server options.

Assigning Options

You can use the DHCP snap-in to assign options at the scope, server, reserved address, or class level. The mechanism you use to assign these options is the same for each; the only difference is where you set the options.

When you create an option assignment, remember that it applies to all the clients in the server or the scope from that point forward. Option assignments aren't retroactive, and they don't migrate from one scope to another.

Creating and Assigning a New Option

To create a new option and have it assigned, follow these steps:

1. Select the scope or server where you want the option assigned.

2. Select the corresponding Options node and choose Action ➤ Configure Options.

    To set options for a reserved client, right-click its entry in the Reservations node and select Configure Options.

    Then you'll see the Scope Options dialog box, which lists all the options that you might want to configure.

3. To select an individual option, check the box next to it and then use the controls in the Data Entry control group to enter the value you want associated with the option.

4. Continue to add options until you've specified all the ones you want attached to the server or scope. Then click OK.

Configuring the DHCP Server for Classes

Now it is time for you to learn how to configure the DHCP server to recognize your customized classes and configure options for them. In Exercise 6.5, you will create a new user class and configure options for the new class. Before you begin, make sure that the computers you want to use in the class have been configured with the `ipconfig /setclassid` command.

EXERCISE 6.5

Configuring User Class Options

1. Open the DHCP snap-in by selecting Administrative Tools ➢ DHCP.

2. Right-click the IPv4 item and select Define User Classes.

3. Click the Add button in the DHCP User Classes dialog box.

4. In the New Class dialog box, enter a descriptive name for the class in the Display Name field. Enter a class ID in the ID field. (Typically, you will enter the class ID in the ASCII portion of the ID field.) When you have finished, click OK.

5. The new class appears in the DHCP User Classes dialog box. Click the Close button to return to the DHCP snap-in.

6. Right-click the Scope Options node and select Configure Options.

7. Click the Advanced tab. Select the class you defined in step 4 from the User Class pop-up menu.

8. Configure the options you want to set for the class. Click OK when you have finished. Notice that the options you configured (and the class with which they are associated) appear in the right pane of the DHCP window.

About the Default Routing and Remote Access Predefined User Class

Windows Server 2022 includes a predefined user class called the *Default Routing and Remote Access class*. This class includes options important to clients connecting to Routing and Remote Access, notably the 051 Lease option.

 Be sure to know that the 051 Lease option is included within this class and that it can be used to assign a shorter lease duration for clients connecting to routing and remote access.

Activating and Deactivating Scopes

When you've completed the steps in Exercise 6.4 and you're ready to unleash your new scope so that it can be used to make client assignments, the final required step is activating the scope. When you activate a scope, you're just telling the server that it's OK to start handing out addresses from that scope's address pool. As soon as you activate a scope, addresses from its pool may be assigned to clients. Of course, this is a necessary precondition to getting any use out of your scope.

If you later want to stop using a scope, you can, but be aware that it's a permanent change. When you deactivate a scope, DHCP tells all clients registered with the scope that they need to release their leases immediately and renew them someplace else—the equivalent of a landlord who evicts tenants when the building is condemned!

WARNING   Don't deactivate a scope unless you want clients to stop using it immediately.

Creating a Superscope for IPv4

A *superscope* allows the DHCP server to provide multiple logical subnet addresses to DHCP clients on a single physical network. You create superscopes with the New Superscope command, which triggers the New Superscope Wizard.

NOTE   You can have only one superscope per server.

The steps in Exercise 6.6 take you through the process of creating a superscope.

EXERCISE 6.6

Creating a Superscope

1. Open the DHCP snap-in by selecting Administrative Tools ➤ DHCP.

2. Follow the instructions in Exercise 6.4 to create two scopes: one for 192.168.0.2 through 192.168.0.127 and one for 192.168.1.12 through 192.168.1.127.

3. Right-click IPv4 and choose the New Superscope command. The New Superscope Wizard appears. Click the Next button.

4. On the Superscope Name page, name your superscope and click Next.

5. The Select Scopes page appears, listing all scopes on the current server. Select the two scopes you created in step 2 and then click Next.

6. The wizard's summary page appears. Click Finish to create your scope.

7. Verify that your new superscope appears in the DHCP snap-in.

Deleting a Superscope

You can delete a superscope by right-clicking it and choosing the Delete command. A superscope is just an administrative convenience, so you can safely delete one at any time—it doesn't affect the "real" scopes that make up the superscope.

Adding a Scope to a Superscope

To add a scope to an existing superscope, find the scope you want to add, right-click it, and choose Action ➤ Add To Superscope. A dialog box appears, listing all of the superscopes known to this server. Pick the one to which you want the current scope appended and click the OK button.

Removing a Scope from a Superscope

To remove a scope from a superscope, open the superscope and right-click the target scope. The pop-up menu provides a Remove From Superscope command that will do the deed.

Activating and Deactivating Superscopes

Just as with regular scopes, you can activate and deactivate superscopes. The same restrictions and guidelines apply. You must activate a superscope before it can be used, and you must not deactivate it until you want all of your clients to lose their existing leases and be forced to request new ones.

To activate or deactivate a superscope, right-click the superscope name and select Activate or Deactivate, respectively, from the pop-up menu.

Creating IPv4 Multicast Scopes

Multicasting occurs when one machine communicates to a network of subscribed computers rather than specifically addressing each computer on the destination network. It's much more efficient to multicast a video or audio stream to multiple destinations than it is to unicast it to the same number of clients, and the increased demand for multicast-friendly network hardware has resulted in some head scratching about how to automate the multicast configuration.

In the following sections, you will learn about MADCAP, the protocol that controls multicasting, and about how to build and configure a multicast scope.

Understanding the Multicast Address Dynamic Client Allocation Protocol

DHCP is usually used to assign IP configuration information for *unicast* (or one-to-one) network communications. With multicast, there's a separate type of address space assigned from 224.0.0.0 through 239.255.255.255. Addresses in this space are known as *Class D addresses*, or simply *multicast addresses*. Clients can participate in a multicast just by knowing (and using) the multicast address for the content they want to receive. However, multicast clients also need to have an ordinary IP address.

How do clients know what address to use? Ordinary DHCP won't help because it's designed to assign IP addresses and option information to one client at a time. Realizing this, the Internet Engineering Task Force (IETF) defined a new protocol: *Multicast Address Dynamic Client Allocation Protocol (MADCAP)*. MADCAP provides an analog to DHCP but for multicast use. A MADCAP server issues leases for multicast addresses only. MADCAP clients can request a multicast lease when they want to participate in a multicast.

DHCP and MADCAP have some important differences. First you have to realize that the two are totally separate. A single server can be a DHCP server, a MADCAP server, or both; no implied or actual relation exists between the two. Likewise, clients can use DHCP and/or MADCAP at the same time—the only requirement is that every MADCAP client has to get a unicast IP address from somewhere.

Remember that DHCP can assign options as part of the lease process but MADCAP cannot. The only thing MADCAP does is dynamically assign multicast addresses.

Building Multicast Scopes

Most of the steps you go through when creating a multicast scope are identical to those required for an ordinary unicast scope. Exercise 6.7 highlights the differences.

Creating a New Multicast Scope

1. Open the DHCP snap-in by selecting Administrative Tools ➢ DHCP.

2. Right-click IPv4 and choose New Multicast Scope. The New Multicast Scope Wizard appears. Click the Next button on the welcome page.

3. In the Multicast Scope Name page, name your multicast scope (and add a description if you'd like). Click Next.

4. The IP Address Range page appears. Enter a start IP address of **224.0.0.0** and an end IP address of **224.255.0.0**. Adjust the TTL to 1 to make sure that no multicast packets escape your local network segment. Click Next when you're finished.

5. The Add Exclusions page appears; click Next.

6. The Lease Duration page appears. Since multicast addresses are used for video and audio, you'd ordinarily leave multicast scope assignments in place somewhat longer than you would with a regular unicast scope, so the default lease length is 30 days (instead of 8 days for a unicast scope). Click Next.

7. The wizard asks you if you want to activate the scope now. Click the No radio button and then the Next button.

8. The wizard's summary page appears; click Finish to create your scope.

9. Verify that your new multicast scope appears in the DHCP snap-in.

Setting Multicast Scope Properties

Once you create a multicast scope, you can adjust its properties by right-clicking the scope name and selecting Properties.

The Multicast Scope Properties dialog box has two tabs. The General tab allows you to change the scope's name, its start and end addresses, its Time To Live (TTL) value, its lease duration, and its description—in essence, all the settings you provided when you created it in the first place.

The Lifetime tab allows you to limit how long your multicast scope will be active. By default, a newly created multicast scope will live forever, but if you're creating a scope to provide MADCAP assignments for a single event (or a set of events of limited duration), you can specify an expiration time for the scope. When that time is reached, the scope disappears from the server but not before making all of its clients give up their multicast address leases. This is a nice way to make sure that the lease cleans up after itself when you're finished with it.

Integrating Dynamic DNS and IPv4 DHCP

DHCP integration with Dynamic DNS is a simple concept but powerful in action. By setting up this integration, you can pass addresses to DHCP clients while still maintaining the integrity of your DNS services.

The DNS server can be updated in two ways. One way is for the DHCP client to tell the DNS server its address. Another way is for the DHCP server to tell the DNS server when it registers a new client.

Neither of these updates will take place, however, unless you configure the DNS server to use Dynamic DNS. You can make this change in two ways:

- If you change it at the scope level, it will apply only to the scope.

- If you change it at the server level, it will apply to all scopes and superscopes served by the server.

Which of these options you choose depends on how widely you want to support Dynamic DNS; most of the sites I visit have enabled DNS updates at the server level.

To update the settings at either the server or the scope level, you need to open the scope or server properties by right-clicking the appropriate object and choosing Properties. The DNS tab of the Properties dialog box (see Figure 6.20) includes the following options:

FIGURE 6.20   DNS tab of the scope's IPv4 Properties dialog box

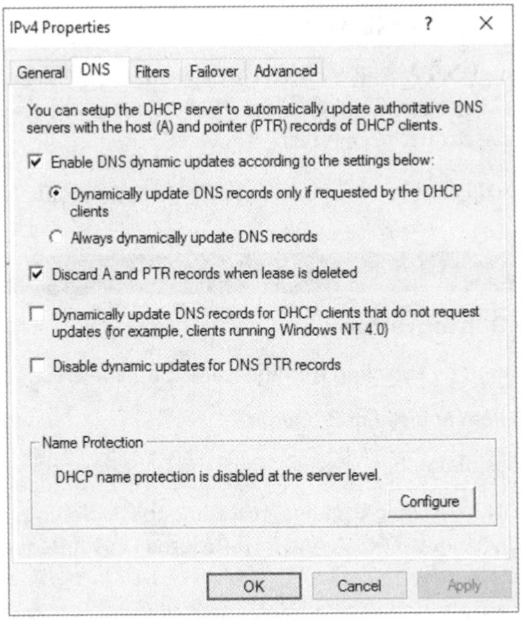

Enable DNS Dynamic Updates According To The Settings Below   This option controls whether this DHCP server will attempt to register lease information with a DNS server. It must be selected to enable Dynamic DNS.

Dynamically Update DNS A And PTR Records Only If Requested By The DHCP Clients   This radio button (which is on by default) tells the DHCP server to register the update only if the DHCP client asks for DNS registration. When this button is active, DHCP clients that aren't hip to DDNS won't have their DNS records updated. However, Windows 7, Windows 8/8.1, Windows 10/11, Server 2003/2003 R2 and above DHCP clients are smart enough to ask for the updates.

Always Dynamically Update DNS A And PTR Records   This option forces the DHCP server to register any client to which it issues a lease. This setting may add DNS registrations for DHCP-enabled devices that don't really need them, such as print servers. However, it allows other clients (such as macOS, Windows NT, and Linux machines) to have their DNS information automatically updated.

Discard A And PTR Records When Lease Is Deleted   This option has a long name but a simple function. When a DHCP lease expires, what should happen to the DNS registration? Obviously, it would be nice if the DNS record associated with a lease vanished when the lease expired. When this option is selected (as it is by default), that's exactly what happens. If you deselect this option, your DNS will contain entries for expired leases that are no longer valid. When a particular IP address is reissued on a new lease, the DNS will be updated, but in between leases you'll have incorrect data in your DNS—something that's always best to avoid.

Dynamically Update DNS A And PTR Records For DHCP Clients That Do Not Request Updates   This option lets you handle these older clients graciously by making the updates using a separate mechanism.

In Exercise 6.8, you will enable a scope to participate in Dynamic DNS updates.

EXERCISE 6.8

Enabling DHCP-DNS Integration

1. Open the DHCP snap-in by selecting Administrative Tools ➤ DHCP.

2. Right-click the IPv4 item and select Properties.

3. The Server Properties dialog box appears. Click the DNS tab.

4. Verify that Enable DNS Dynamic Updates According To The Settings Below is selected and that Dynamically Update DNS A And PTR Records Only If Requested By The DHCP Clients is also selected.

5. Verify that the Discard A And PTR Records When Lease Is Deleted option is selected. If it's not, then select it.

6. Click OK to apply your changes and close the Server Properties dialog box.

Using DHCP Failover Architecture

DHCP can become a single point of failure within a network if there is only one DHCP server. If that server becomes unavailable, clients will not be able to obtain new leases or renew existing leases. For this reason, you should have more than one DHCP server in the network. However, more than one DHCP server can create problems if they both are configured to use the same scope or set of addresses. Microsoft recommends the 80/20 rule for redundancy of DHCP services in a network.

Implementing the 80/20 rule calls for one DHCP server to make approximately 80 percent of the addresses for a given subnet available through DHCP while another server makes the remaining 20 percent of the addresses available. For example, with a /24 network of 254 addresses, say 192.168.1.1 to 192.168.1.254, you might have Server 1 offer 192.168.1.10 to 192.168.1.210 while Server 2 offers 192.168.1.211 to 192.168.254.

DHCP Load Sharing

Load sharing is the normal default way that you use multiple DHCP servers (as explained earlier). Both servers cover the same subnets (remember that a DHCP server can handle multiple subnets at the same time) simultaneously, and both servers assign IP addresses and options to clients on the assigned subnets. The client requests are load balanced and shared between the two servers.

This is a good option for a company that has multiple DHCP servers in the same physical location. The DHCP servers are set up in a failover relationship at the same site, and both servers respond to all DHCP client requests from the subnets to which they are associated. The DHCP server administrator can set the load distribution ratio between the multiple DHCP servers.

DHCP Hot Standby

When thinking of a DHCP hot standby setup, think of the old server failover cluster. You have two servers where one server does all of the work and the other server is a standby server in the event that the first server crashes or goes down.

In a DHCP hot standby situation, the two DHCP servers operate in a failover relationship where one server acts as an active server and is responsible for leasing IP addresses to all clients in a scope or subnet. The secondary DHCP server assumes the standby role, and it is ready to go in the event that the primary DHCP server becomes unavailable. If the primary server becomes unavailable, the secondary DHCP server is given the role of the primary DHCP server and takes over all the responsibilities of the primary DHCP server.

This failover situation is best suited to DHCP deployments where a company has DHCP servers in multiple locations.

Working with the DHCP Database Files

DHCP uses a set of database files to maintain its knowledge of scopes, superscopes, and client leases. These files, which live in the *systemroot*\System32\DHCP folder, are always open when the DHCP service is running. DHCP servers use Joint Engine Technology (JET) databases to maintain their records.

> You shouldn't modify or alter the DHCP database files when the service is running.

The primary database file is dhcp.mdb—it has all of the scope data in it.
The following files are also part of the DHCP database:

Dhcp.tmp This is a backup copy of the database file created during reindexing of the database. You normally won't see this file, but if the service fails during reindexing, it may not remove the file when it should.

J50.log This file (plus a number of files named J50*xxxxx*.log, where *xxxxx* stands for 00001, 00002, 00003, and so on) is a log file that stores changes before they're written to the database. The DHCP database engine can recover some changes from these files when it restarts.

J50.chk This is a checkpoint file that tells the DHCP engine which log files it still needs to recover.

In the following sections, you will see how to manipulate the DHCP database files.

Removing the Database Files

If you're convinced that your database is corrupted because the lease information that you see doesn't match what's on the network, the easiest repair mechanism is to remove the database files and start over with an empty database.

> If you think the database is corrupted because the DHCP service fails at startup, you should check the event log.

To start over, follow these steps:

1. Stop the DHCP service by typing **net stop dhcpserver** at the command prompt.
2. Remove all the files from the *systemroot*\system32\DHCP folder.
3. Restart the service (at the command prompt, type **net start dhcpserver**).
4. Reconcile the scope.

Changing the Database Backup Interval

By default, the DHCP service backs up its databases every 60 minutes. You can adjust this setting by editing the Backup Interval value under `HKEY_LOCAL_MACHINE\SYSTEM\CurrentControlSet\Services\DHCPServer\Parameters`. This allows you to make backups either more frequently (if your database changes a lot or if you seem to have ongoing corruption problems) or less often (if everything seems to be on an even keel).

Moving the DHCP Database Files

You may find that you need to dismantle or change the role of your DHCP server and offload the DHCP functions to another computer. Rather than spend the time re-creating the DHCP database on the new machine by hand, you can copy the database files and use them directly. This is especially helpful if you have a complicated DHCP database with lots of reservations and option assignments.

By copying the files, you also minimize the amount of human error that could be introduced by reentering the information by hand.

Compacting the DHCP Database Files

There may be a time when you need to compact the DHCP database. Microsoft has a utility called `jetpack.exe` that allows you to compact the JET database. Microsoft JET databases are used for WINS and DHCP databases. If you wanted to use the `jetpack` command, the proper syntax is

```
JETPACK.EXE <database name><temp database name>
```

After you compact the database, you rename the temp database to `dhcp.mdb`.

Working with Advanced DHCP Configuration Options

DHCP makes the life of an administrator easy when it comes to managing the IP addresses of devices within an organization. Could you imagine having to keep track of each device and that device's IP manually? With Windows Server 2022's DHCP high availability and load balancing options available, life gets even easier. This section will cover how to implement advanced DHCP solutions in detail.

Implement DHCPv6

In Windows Server 2022, you can create and manage both IPv4 and IPv6 DHCP scopes for your organization. Even though they are managed separately, they have the same capabilities of being able to configure reservations, exclusions, and other DHCP options. Unlike an IPv4 client, a DHCPv6 client uses a device unique identifier (DUID) instead of a MAC address to get an IP address from the DHCP server.

DHCPv6 supports both stateful address configuration and stateless address configuration. An easy way to think of the difference between a stateful configuration and a stateless configuration is that, with a stateful configuration, the DHCPv6 client receives its IPv6 address and its additional DHCP options from the DHCPv6 server. With a stateless configuration, the IPv6 client can automatically assign itself an IPv6 address without ever having to communicate with the DHCPv6 server. The stateless configuration process is also known as DHCPv6 *autoconfiguration*. Exercise 6.9 will walk you through the process of creating and activating a new DHCPv6 scope.

EXERCISE 6.9

Creating and Activating a New DHCPv6 Scope

1. Open the DHCP Management Console.

2. Right-click IPv6 and choose the New Scope command. The New Scope Wizard appears. Click the Next button.

3. On the Welcome To The New Scope Wizard page, click Next.

4. On the Scope Name page, provide a name and description for your new DHCPv6 scope. Click Next.

5. On the Scope Prefix page, input the corresponding prefix for your organization's IPv6 network settings. In the event that you have more than one DHCPv6 server, you can set a preference value that will indicate your server priority. The lower the preference value, the higher the server priority. Click Next.

6. On the Add Exclusions page of the wizard, you can configure either a single IP exclusion or a range of IPs to exclude from obtaining an address automatically. Exclusions should include any device or range of devices that have been manually set with a static IP on that particular scope. Click Next.

7. Keep the default selections on the Scope Lease page. Click Next.

8. Make sure the Activate Scope Now radio button is toggled to Yes. Click Finish to complete the creation and activation of your new DHCPv6 scope.

9. Verify that your new scope appears in the DHCP Management Console to complete this exercise.

Configure High Availability for DHCP, Including DHCP Failover and Split Scopes

DHCP failover provides load balancing and redundancy for DHCP services, enabling you to deploy a highly resilient DHCP service for your organization. The idea is to share your DHCP IPV4 scopes between two Windows Server 2022 servers so that if one of the failover partners goes down, then the other failover partner will continue providing DHCP services throughout the environment. DHCP failover supports large-scale DHCP deployments without the challenges of a split-scope DHCP environment.

Here are a few of the benefits that DHCP failover provides:

Multisite   DHCP failover supports a deployment architecture that includes multiple sites. DHCP failover partner servers do not need to be located at the same physical site.

Flexibility   DHCP failover can be configured to provide redundancy in hot standby mode, or with load balancing mode, client requests can be distributed between two DHCP servers.

Seamless   DHCP servers share lease information, allowing one server to assume the responsibility for servicing clients if the other server is unavailable. DHCP clients can keep the same IP address when a lease is renewed, even if a different DHCP server issues the lease.

Simplicity   A wizard is provided to create DHCP failover relationships between DHCP servers. The wizard automatically replicates scopes and settings from the primary server to the failover partner.

Configuring DHCP Failover

One of the nice things about DHCP failover is that the configured scope is replicated between both clustered DHCP nodes whether or not you are running the cluster in hot standby or load balancing mode. If one server fails, the other can manage the entire pool of IP addresses on behalf of the environment. Exercise 6.10 provides a step-by-step DHCP failover configuration in Windows Server 2022.

EXERCISE 6.10

Configuring DHCP Failover

1. Open the DHCP Management Console.

2. Right-click IPv4 and choose the Configure Failover command to launch the Configure Failover Wizard. Click Next on the Introduction page.

3. On the Specify The Partner Server To Use For Failover page, select your partner DHCP server from the drop-down menu or by browsing the Add Server directory. Click Next.

4. On the Create A New Failover Relationship page, provide a relationship name, select the Load Balance mode from the drop-down, and provide a shared secret password that will be used to authenticate the DHCP failover relationship between the two servers in the failover cluster. Click Next.

5. Review your configuration settings and click the Finish button to configure your new DHCP failover configuration. Click Close upon successful completion.

6. After the wizard successfully completes on the primary DHCP server, verify that the new failover scope has been created and activated on the secondary DHCP server in the DHCP Management Console to complete this exercise.

You can always go back in and change the properties of the failover scope if you want. Test both hot standby and load balancing modes to decide which deployment configuration option best suits your organization's needs. Expect to see exam scenarios discussing both DHCP failover configuration modes and the differences between them.

DHCP Split Scopes

Even though you have the capabilities of DHCP failover in Windows Server 2022, for exam purposes you will need to understand how DHCP split scopes work. Split scopes are configurable only on IPv4 IP addresses and cannot be configured on IPv6 scopes. The idea of DHCP split scopes is to have two stand-alone DHCP servers that are individually responsible for only a percentage of the IP addresses on a particular subnet.

For example, DHCP Server 1 would be responsible for 70 percent of the IP addresses, and DHCP Server 2 would be responsible for the other 30 percent of IP addresses. The two DHCP servers in a split-scope configuration do not share any lease information between one another, and they do not take over for one another in the event that one of the two DHCP servers fails. As you can see, a split-scope configuration is less fault tolerant than a full DHCP failover configuration. However, a split-scope configuration does split the load of DHCP leases and renewals between two servers, providing a basic level of native load balancing in a Windows Server 2022 environment.

DHCP Allow and Deny Filtering

One of the nice things about DHCP is that you can use allow or deny filtering to control which devices get an IP address and which devices do not on your network. DHCP filtering is controlled by recording a client's MAC address in a list and then enabling either the Allow or Deny filter. One thing to keep in mind about DHCP filtering is that by enabling the allow list, you automatically deny DHCP addresses to any client computer not on the list. In Exercise 6.11, you will configure DHCP filtering by adding a client machine to the Deny filter by MAC address.

EXERCISE 6.11

Configuring DHCP Filtering

1. Open the DHCP Management Console.

2. Expand IPv4 until you reach the Deny filter object in your DHCP hierarchy.

3. Right-click the Deny filter object and select New Filter.

4. Enter the MAC address of the device you want to exclude from your network, provide a description such as Unwanted Device, click Add, and then click Close.

5. Right-click the Deny filter and select Enable to complete this exercise.

One of the good things about these filters is that you can move devices from one filter to the other quite easily at any time by right-clicking the device in the list and selecting either Move To Allow or Move To Deny. Test both Allow and Deny filters thoroughly while preparing for the exam. You will most likely see multiple scenarios surrounding DHCP filtering.

Configure DHCP Name Protection

DHCP name protection is an additional configuration option that you should consider when working DHCP within your environment. Name protection protects a DHCP leased machine's name from being overwritten by another machine with the same name during DNS dynamic updates so that you can configure a Windows 2022 DHCP server to verify and update the DNS records of a client machine during the lease renewal process. If the DHCP server detects that a machine's DNS A and PTR records already exist in the environment when a DHCP update occurs, then that DHCP update will fail on that client machine, making sure not to overwrite the existing server name. There are just a few simple steps needed in order to configure DHCP name protection. Exercise 6.12 will walk you through these steps.

EXERCISE 6.12

Enabling DHCP Name Protection

1. Open the DHCP Management Console.

2. Right-click IPv4 and select Properties.

3. The Server Properties dialog box appears. Click the DNS tab.

4. Verify that Enable DNS Dynamic Updates According To The Settings Below is selected, and verify that the radio button labeled Dynamically Update DNS A And PTR Records Only If Requested By The DHCP Clients is selected.

5. Verify that Discard A And PTR Records When Lease Is Deleted is selected. If it's not, then select it.

6. Click Configure under Name Protection, and select Enable Name Protection.

7. Click OK twice to complete this exercise.

Understanding IPAM

One of the great features of Windows Server 2022 is the *IP Address Management (IPAM)* utility. IPAM is a built-in utility that allows you to discover, monitor, audit, and manage the TCP/IP schema used on your network. IPAM provides you with the ability to observe and administer the servers that are running the Dynamic Host Configuration Protocol (DHCP) and the Domain Name System (DNS). IPAM includes some of the following advantages:

Automatic IP Address Infrastructure Discovery   IPAM has the ability to discover automatically the domain's DHCP servers, DNS servers, and domain controllers. IPAM can do the discovery for any of the domains you specify. You also have the ability to enable or disable management of these servers using the IPAM utility.

Management of DHCP and DNS Services   IPAM gives you the capability to monitor and manage Microsoft DHCP and DNS servers across an entire network using the IPAM console. IPAM allows you to configure things as easy as adding a resource record to DNS or as complex as configuring DHCP policies and failover servers.

Custom IP Address Management   You now have the ability to customize the display of IP addresses and tracking and utilization data. IPAM allows the IP address space to be organized into IP address blocks, IP address ranges, and individual IP addresses. To help you organize the IP address space further, built-in or user-defined fields are also assigned to the IP addresses.

Multiple Active Directory Forest Support   You can manage Multiple Active Directory Forests using IPAM as long as there is a two-way trust between the two forests. There may be times when an organization needs to have multiple forests in their structure or when a company purchases another company. Once both forests are connected by a trust, you can manage both companies IP services through one application.

Purge Utilization Data   You now have the ability to reduce the size of the IPAM database. This is done by purging the IP address utilization data older than the date that you specify.

Auditing and Tracking of IP Address   IPAM allows you to track and audit IP addresses through the use of the IPAM console. IPAM allows IP addresses to be tracked using DHCP lease events and user logon events. These events are collected from the Network Policy Server (NPS) servers, domain controllers, and DHCP servers. You can track IP data by following the IP address, client ID, hostname, or username.

PowerShell Support   Windows Server 2022 now allows you to manage access scopes on IPAM objects using PowerShell commands.

As an administrator, you should understand a few things before installing the IPAM feature. There are three main methods to deploy an IPAM server:

Distributed   This method allows an IPAM server deployment at every site in an enterprise network.

Centralized   This method allows only one IPAM server in an enterprise network.

Hybrid   This method uses a central IPAM server deployment along with dedicated IPAM servers at each site in the enterprise network.

Installing IPAM

Now that I have started explaining what IPAM can do for your organization, the next step is to install IPAM. When you are thinking of installing IPAM, there are a few considerations that you must think about. So, let's start with looking at the hardware and software requirements needed for IPAM.

IPAM Hardware and Software Requirements

So, let's start with the main requirement. IPAM must be loaded onto a Windows Server. Since this is a Windows Server 2022 book, I would recommend that you use Windows Server 2022. But you can load IPAM onto a Windows Server 2008 or higher system.

You can also load an IPAM client (this allows you to remotely operate IPAM) onto any Windows 7 or higher system. Before the IPAM client can be used, you must first install the Remote Server Administration Tools (RSAT). You need to make sure that you install the proper version of RSAT based on the version of Windows that you have installed.

Your network needs to be a domain. Workgroup networks are not supported by IPAM. So the server that you decide to install IPAM onto needs to be part of a domain, but it can't be a domain controller. Domain controllers are servers that are part of a domain and have a copy of the Active Directory database. When you install IPAM, you *have* to load it on a member server.

IPAM will work on both an IPv4 and IPv6 network. The member server that you install IPAM onto must be able to see and connect to the other servers on your network. If the IPAM server is not able to access the other servers (like Microsoft DNS and Microsoft DHCP), the IPAM server will not be able to help monitor and maintain these servers.

One of the advantages of IPAM is that the IPAM server will automatically discover other servers on your network. Server discovery requires the IPAM server to be able to access at least one domain controller and an authoritative DNS server.

Microsoft's best practices are to place the IPAM server onto its own server. You should *not* put the IPAM server on a server with other network services like DNS or DHCP. For example, DHCP server discovery will be automatically disabled if you install IPAM and DHCP onto the same server.

This makes IPAM a good candidate for virtual machines or containers. By using a virtual machine or container for the IPAM installation, you don't give up all of the hardware resources of a powerful server for just one feature. Some other IPAM specifications and features are as follows:

- Server discovery for IPAM is limited to a single Active Directory forest.

- IPAM can manage DNS and DHCP servers belonging to a different AD forest as long as a two-way trust relationship is set up between your forest and the other forest. The servers in the other forest will need to be manually entered into IPAM.

- IPAM only works with Microsoft servers (domain controllers, DHCP, DNS, and NPS) using Windows Server 2008 and above.

- IPAM only supports Microsoft-based systems. IPAM does not support non-Microsoft network devices.

- IPAM only supports Windows Internal Databases (WID) or SQL Server. Other database engines are not supported.

- Windows Server 2022 IPAM now supports /31, /32, and /128 subnets.

- Windows Server 2022 IPAM now supports DNS resource records, conditional forwarders, and DNS zone management for both primary zones and primary zones with Active Directory integrated.

- You can now purge IP address utilization data, thus reducing the size of the IPAM database.

So let's go ahead and install the IPAM feature. Exercise 6.13 will show you how. You will install and configure the IPAM feature using Server Manager. Remember, this exercise has to be done on a member server.

EXERCISE 6.13

Installing the IPAM Feature

1. Open Server Manager.

2. Click the number 2 link, Add Roles And Features. If the Before You Begin screen appears, just click Next.

3. Choose a role-based or feature-based installation and click Next.

4. Select your server and click Next.

5. On the Roles screen, just click Next.

6. On the Features screen, click the box for the IP Address Management (IPAM) server (see Figure 6.21). Click the Add Features button when the box appears. Click Next.

FIGURE 6.21 Choosing the IPAM feature

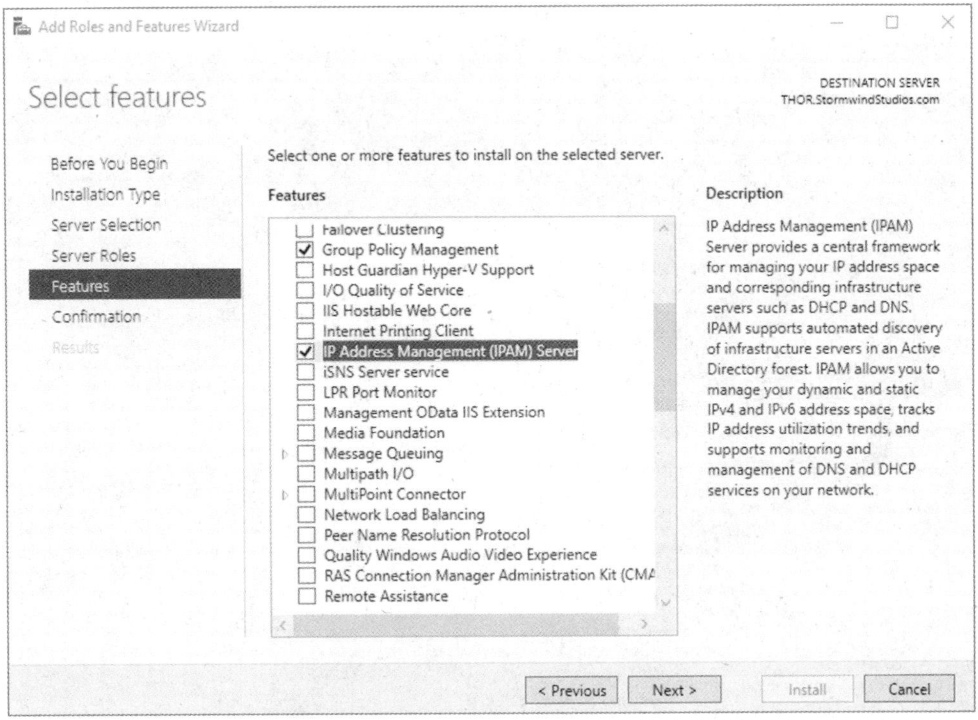

7. At the Confirmation screen, make sure the option Restart The Destination Server Automatically If Required is selected (see Figure 6.22) and then click the Install button.

EXERCISE 6.13 *(continued)*

FIGURE 6.22 Confirmation screen

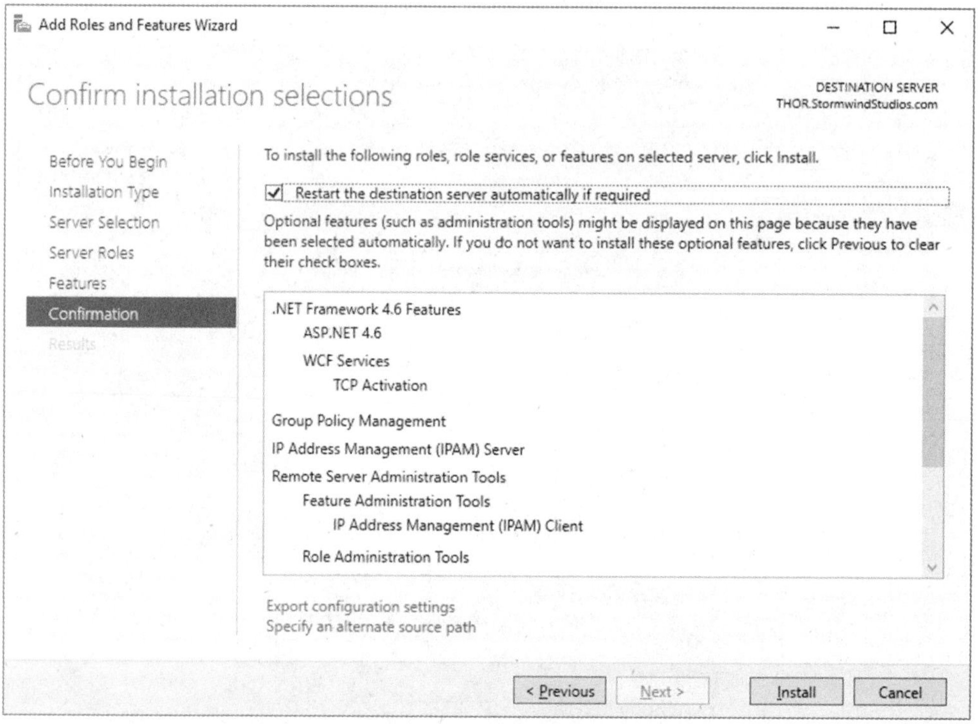

8. Once the installation is complete, click the Close button. Close Server Manager.
9. In the Add Servers dialog box, click the DNS tab. In the search box, type the name of your DNS server and click the magnifying glass.
10. Under Name, double-click the server name. The server will be added to the right-side box. Click OK. Close Server Manager.

Provision IPAM Manually or by Using Group Policy

When setting up an IPAM server, you must determine how the IPAM server will communicate with your other servers. This is called IPAM provisioning. IPAM provisioning can be set up two ways: manually or by using GPOs.

IPAM will try to locate your DNS servers, DHCP servers, and domain controllers as long as those servers are within the searching scope that you have configured. You can configure whether the servers (DNS, DHCP, and domain controllers) are managed by IPAM or unmanaged. Please note that this will work only with Microsoft products; it won't find Infoblox or Unix-based DNS/DHCP.

If you want your servers to be managed by IPAM, you must make sure you set up the network and the servers properly. For example, you will need to configure the security settings and firewall ports properly on the servers (DNS, DHCP, and domain controllers) in order to allow IPAM to access these servers and perform its configuration and monitoring.

Once you have decided to use the Group Policy provisioning method, you will be required to create a GPO name prefix in the provisioning wizard (I use IPAM1 in Exercise 6.2). Once you have set up the GPO name prefix, the provisioning wizard will show you the names of the GPOs that you will need to create. You will be required to either manually create or automatically create (using PowerShell) the GPOs for the different servers.

If you decide to manually create the GPOs, you will need to open the Group Policy Management console and then create a GPO for each of the different server types that IPAM will manage. This is a more difficult way to create the GPOs. It is easier to create the provisioned GPOs automatically.

To create these provisioned GPOs automatically, you will need to use the `Invoke-IpamGpoProvisioning` cmdlet at an elevated Windows PowerShell prompt. The following is an example of the `Invoke-IpamGpoProvisioning` command. In this example, the IPAM server is named `IPAMServer`. The name of our domain is `StormWindStudios.com` and the GPO Prefix name will be `IPAM1`. As you will see in the command, I added a `-Force` switch to the end of the command. This switch forces the PowerShell command to run without asking the user for confirmation.

```
Invoke-IpamGPOProvioning -Domain StormWindStudios.com -GpoPrefixName IPAM1 -
IpamServerFqdn IPAMServer.StormWindStudios.com -Force
```

After you run the `Invoke-IpamGpoProvisioning` command, new GPOs will be created based on your network setup. For example, I am running a domain controller and NPS together. So the GPOs may look like the following;

```
<GPO-prefix>_DHCP
```

```
<GPO-prefix>_DNS
```

```
<GPO-prefix>_DC_NPS
```

The created GPOs will all have the GPO Prefix name that you used in the `Invoke-IpamGpoProvisioning` command. For example, I used `IPAM1` in the previous `Invoke-IpamGPOProvisioning` command. So my actual GPOs look like the following:

```
IPAM1_DHCP
```

```
IPAM1_DNS
```

```
IPAM1_DC_NPS
```

In order for IPAM to automatically manage these servers, you must create these GPOs. After the GPOs are created, IPAM will be able to manage these servers through the IPAM console. When an IPAM server no longer manages these servers (servers will be shown as unmanaged), the GPOs can be removed.

The IPAM server needs to be able to manipulate the GPOs directly. To ensure that IPAM can manage the GPOs directly, you must make sure that the GPO security filtering includes the IPAM servers. If the IPAM servers are not added to the security filtering for the GPOs, the IPAM server will not be able to manage these other servers (DNS, DHCP, and NPS).

In Exercise 6.14, I will walk you through the process of provisioning your IPAM server. I will also show you how to create the GPOs needed for the IPAM provisioning, and then I will show you how to add the IPAM servers to the GPOs security filter. To complete this exercise properly, you will need to log into the IPAM Server with a domain admin account or higher.

EXERCISE 6.14

Provisioning an IPAM server

1. Open Server Manager

2. Click the IPAM link on the left side. This opens the IPAM Overview page.

3. Click number 2, Provision The IPAM Server (see Figure 6.23).

FIGURE 6.23   IPAM Overview screen

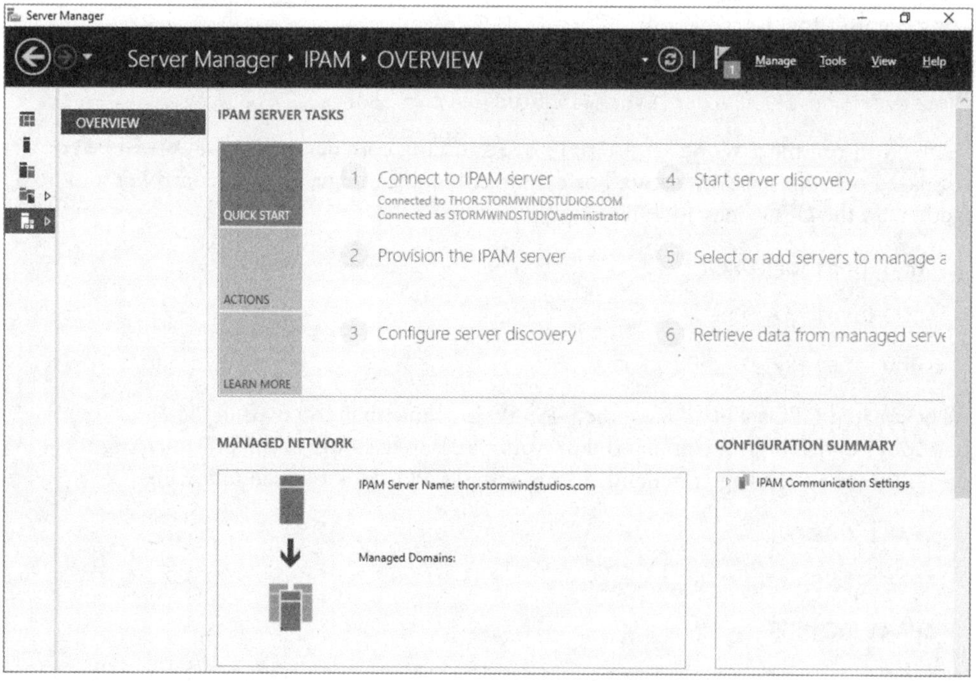

4. Click Next at the Before You Begin screen.

5. At the Configure Database screen, you will need to set up a database for IPAM. You can either use the Windows Internal Database (WID) or a Microsoft SQL Server. If you choose to use a WID (I am using a WID in this exercise), you will need to put in a location for the database storage. Make your database selection on the Configure Database screen and click Next.

6. At the Select Provisioning Method screen, choose GPO and enter a GPO suffix name. I used IPAM1 for the GPO suffix name (see Figure 6.24).

FIGURE 6.24   Select Provisioning Method

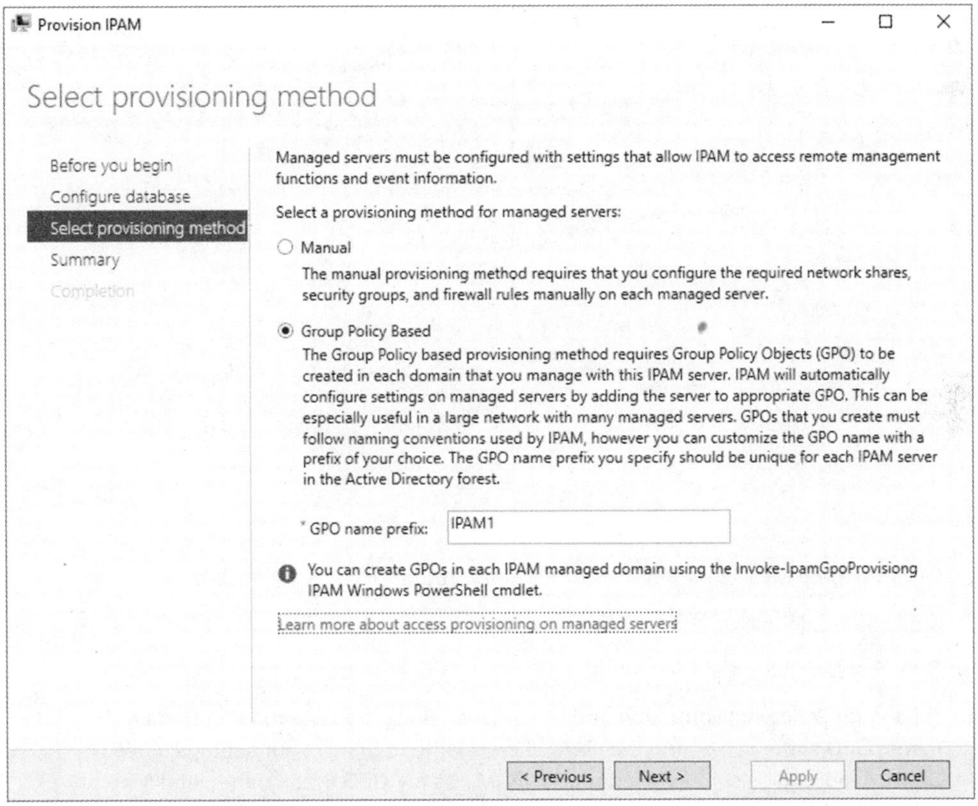

7. At the Summary screen, enter the names of the GPOs that you need to create (see Figure 6.25). Click the Apply button.

EXERCISE 6.14 *(continued)*

FIGURE 6.25 GPOs needed

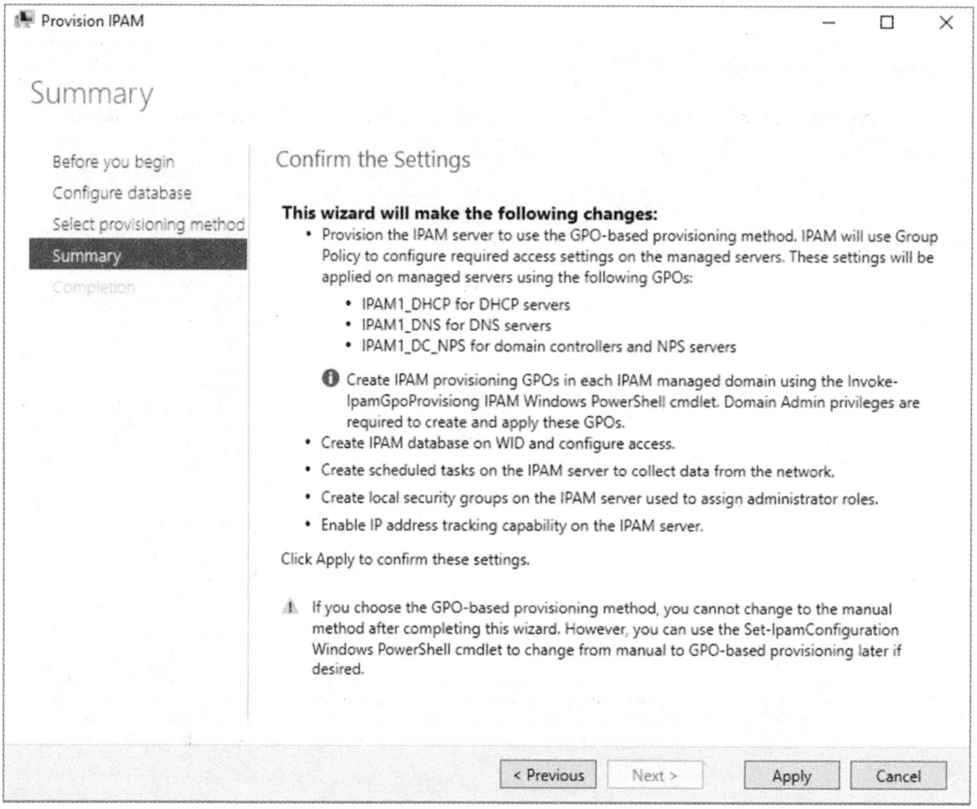

8. Once the process is completed, click the Close button.
9. Close Server Manager.
10. Open PowerShell.
11. Type in the following command and press Enter. Be sure to change the domain name, GPO suffix name, and the IPAM server name to match your settings. I used StormWindStudios.com as my domain, IPAM1 as my GPO Prefix name, and Mercury as my IPAM server name.

```
Invoke-IpamGPOProvisioning -Domain StormwindStudios.com
-GPOPrefixName IPAM1 -
IpamServerFqdn Mercury.StormwindStudios.com -Force
```

12. You will be asked to confirm the installation of the GPOs. This is normally asked three times. When asked to confirm, click Y and press Enter for all three.
13. After the command has finished, close PowerShell.

14. On your domain controller, open the Group Policy Management console.

15. Under Forest, expand domains and expand the name of your domain. You should now see the three new GPOs (see Figure 6.26).

FIGURE 6.26   New GPOs

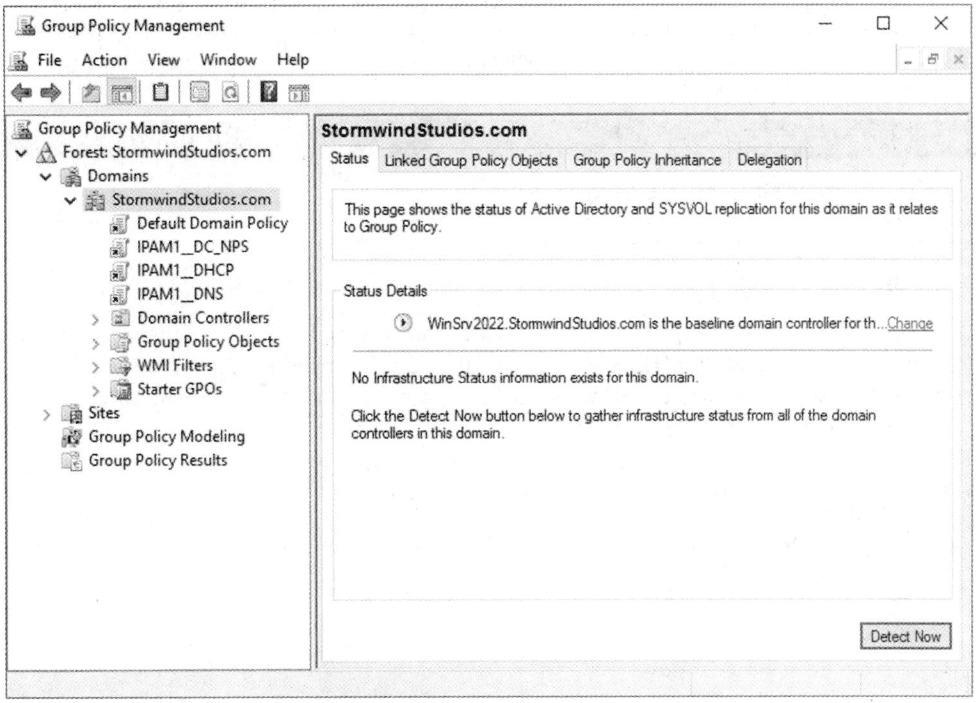

16. Click the GPO that you want to configure. For example, if you are adding a managed DHCP server, click the GPO name ending in _DHCP.

17. On the Scope tab, in the Security Filtering section, click the Add button.

18. In the Select User, Computer, Or Group window, click the Object Types button.

19. Select the Computers option, and then click OK.

20. In the section Enter The Object Name To Select, type the name of the IPAM server and click the Check Names button. If the name is proper, the server name will become underlined. Click OK.

21. Repeat steps 16–20 for the other IPAM GPOs. Only do these steps for every server that you currently have. For example, if you only have a DHCP and a DNS server, perform these steps for just those two servers.

22. When finished, close the Group Policy Management console.

Configure Server Discovery

Once you have successfully installed and provisioned the IPAM feature on your Windows Server 2022 machine, you can begin server discovery. One of the great things about IPAM is that you can define multiple domains within the same forest to be managed by a single IPAM server.

Once initiated, server discovery will automatically search for all the machines running on the specified domain. Administrator privileges are required for the domain against which you are running server discovery. Exercise 6.15 will walk you through the server discovery process.

Configuring IPAM Server Discovery

1. Open Server Manager and select IPAM.

2. On the IPAM Overview page, select option 3, Configure Server Discovery.

3. On the Configure Server Discovery page, select and add the forest and domains you want to discover and click OK. When you add the domain, it should appear under the Select The Server Roles To Discover section and Domain Controller, DNS, and DHCP should be checked (see Figure 6.27).

FIGURE 6.27 Configuring Server Discovery

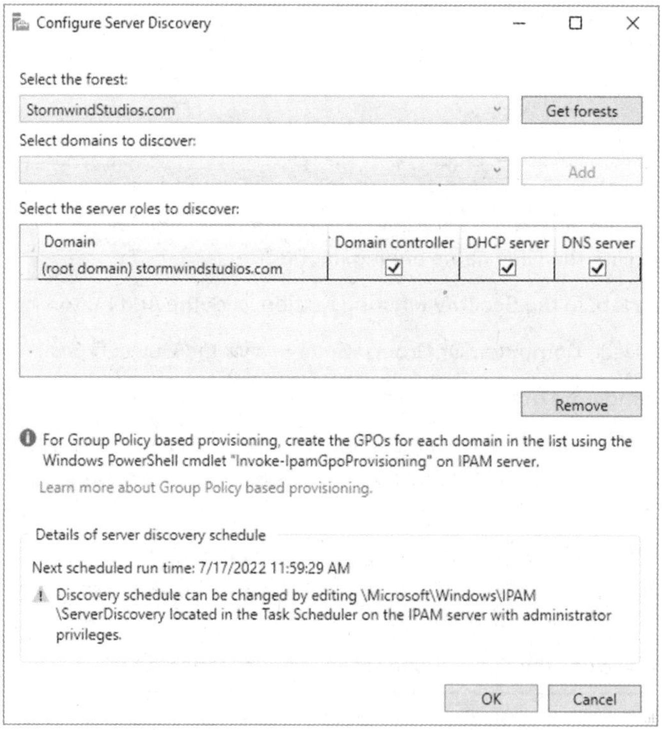

4. On the IPAM Overview page, select option 4, Start Server Discovery. The task will run in the background. You will receive notification once server discovery has completed.

5. On the IPAM home page, select Server Inventory to review the now-completed server discovery of the requested domain (see Figure 6.28). This may take a few minutes and you may need to refresh Server Manager.

6. Close Server Manager.

FIGURE 6.28 Server Inventory screen

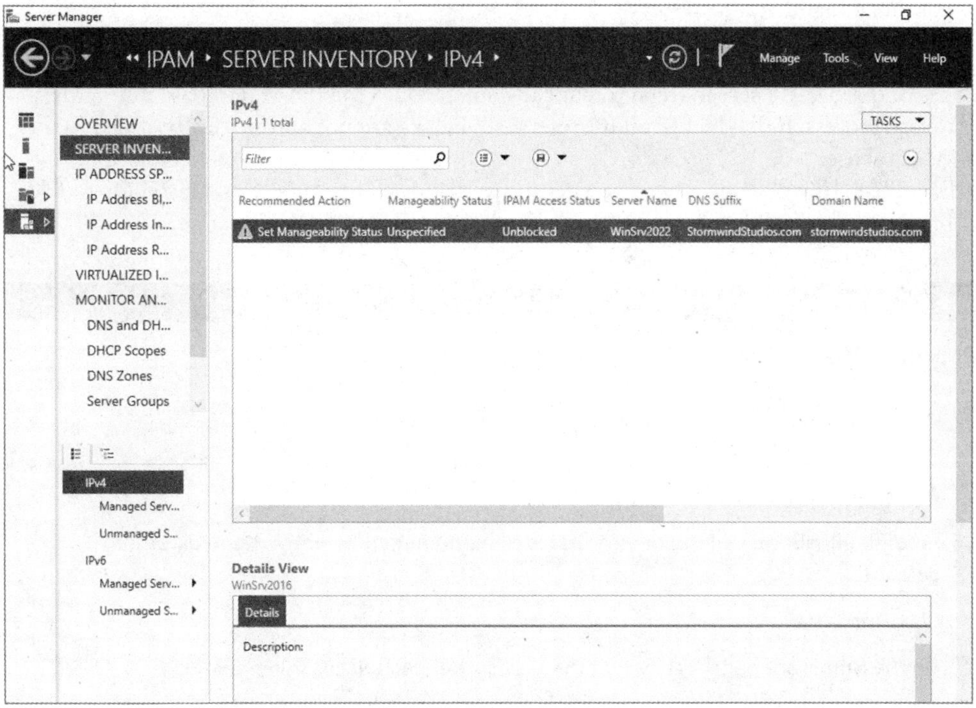

Create and Manage IP Blocks and Ranges

In IPAM, IP address space is divided into addresses, ranges, and blocks. Blocks are groups of ranges, and ranges are groups of IPs. Here you will find a breakdown of each IP Management space found within IPAM:

IP Addresses Individual IP addresses map to a single IP address range. When you map an IP address to a range, it enables actions to be taken on a range that affect all IP addresses in the range, such as adding, updating, or deleting IP address fields.

IP Address Ranges   IP address ranges are smaller chunks of IP addresses that typically correspond to a DHCP scope. IP address ranges are contained within, or "mapped to," IP address blocks. IP address ranges cannot map to multiple IP address blocks and ranges that map to the same block cannot overlap.

IP Address Blocks   IP address blocks are large chunks of IP addresses that are used to organize address space at a high level. For example, you might use one IP address block for all private IP addresses in your organization and another block for public IP addresses. You can think of IP address blocks as containers that hold IP address ranges. IP address blocks are not deployed and managed on the network like IP address ranges or individual IP addresses.

When you have an IPAM managed DHCP server, the IP address ranges found within the scopes of that DHCP server are automatically entered into the IPAM database during the discovery process. Individual IP addresses and IP blocks are not automatically added to the IPAM database.

Exercise 6.16 will demonstrate how to add an IP address manually and also how to add an IP address block. I will be adding the IP address of my DNS/DHCP server.

EXERCISE 6.16

Manually Add IPAM IP Address and Blocks

1. Open Server Manager and select IPAM.

2. Select IP Address Blocks.

3. Right-click IPv4 and select Add IP Address.

4. Enter the IP address of the device that is to be managed by IPAM. Keep all other defaults.

5. Click Apply.

6. On the Summary page, verify that the task completed successfully. Click OK.

7. Your new IP address is now managed by IPAM. You can now both create and delete DHCP reservations and DNS records for this IP address space from inside the IPAM management console.

8. Right-click IPv4 and select Add IP Address Block.

9. Fill in the following field and click OK:

    Network ID: 10.10.16.0

    Leave all other fields at their defaults.

10. Close Server Manager.

Auditing IPAM

One of the nicest advantages to IPAM is the ability to audit the different services that you are monitoring. In today's complex IT world, we all have many different servers and applications that we are running to get our job done. We use Microsoft products and non-Microsoft products to accomplish the tasks that help our end users do their jobs more efficiently.

One of the issues that we have because of using all of these different servers and applications is knowing how they all operate and making sure that we are keeping these products operating at maximum performance. As an IT member today, you have to be a jack of all trades when it comes to networking technologies. This is where auditing really comes into play. Being able to audit a server, services, or applications allows us to make sure that we are running these products the way they should be run.

Once you decide that you are going to be using IPAM for all of your IP-based services, you now also need a single application to monitor all of these services. IPAM allows you to audit the changes performed on the DNS and DHCP servers, audit the IPAM address usage trail, audit DHCP lease events, and audit user logon events (to name just a few). This is very easy to do since we are using the same IPAM console that we have used for everything else IPAM related. That's the nice advantage. Normally if you want to audit these services, you have to open a different application. With IPAM, the auditing is located in the same console as the rest of the IPAM services.

IPAM allows you to audit all of the IPAM events using the Event Catalog (see Figure 6.29), or you can audit events just for the individual services like DHCP (see Figure 6.30).

FIGURE 6.29   Event Catalog

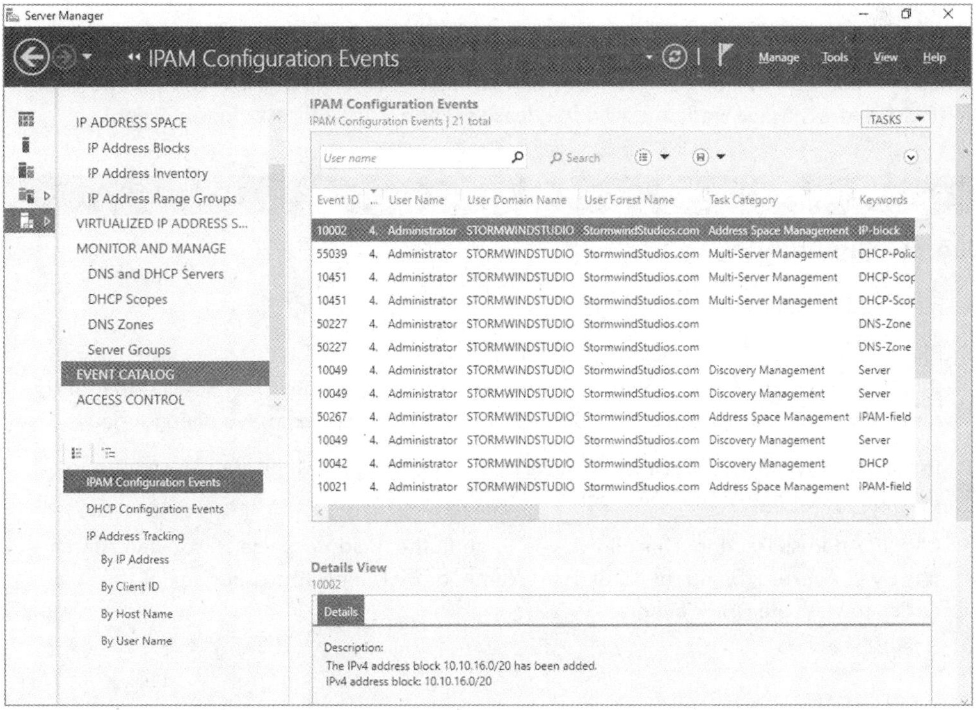

FIGURE 6.30 DHCP Event Catalog

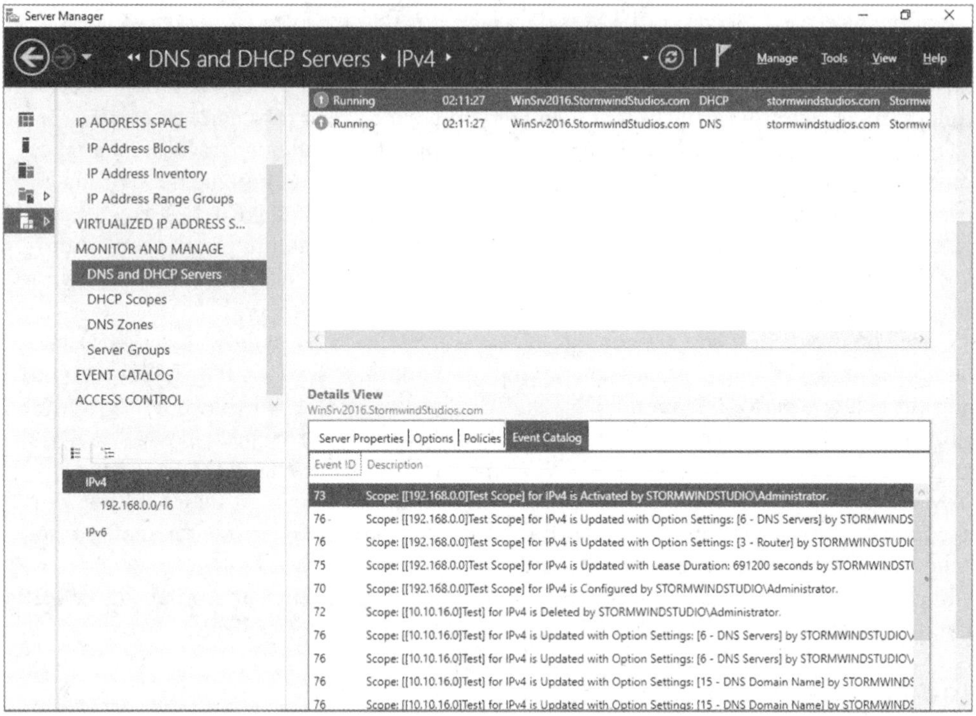

In Exercise 6.17 you'll learn how to configure auditing for IPAM using Server Manager. I will show you how to audit the changes performed on the DNS and DHCP servers, audit the IPAM address usage trail, audit DHCP lease events, and audit user logon events.

EXERCISE 6.17

Configuring Auditing

1. Open Server Manager.

2. Click IPAM.

3. Click Event Catalog in the navigation window. On the right side under IPAM Configuration Event, you will see all of the IPAM configuration events that have been logged.

4. In the lower window, click DHCP Configuration Events. This will display any configuration changes made to the DHCP servers.

5. Click IP Address Tracking. This allows you to audit the IP address usage. You can search this By IP Address, By Client ID, By Host Name, or By User Name. Click any of the categories to view the DHCP events.

6. In the Monitor And Manage section, click DNS And DHCP Servers. In the right-hand window, click either of the two servers and then click Event Catalog under Details View (see Figure 6.31). This allows you to monitor DNS and DHCP events independently. You can look at DHCP lease events or look at DNS zone events. It just depends on which server you are monitoring.

FIGURE 6.31   DNS Event Catalog

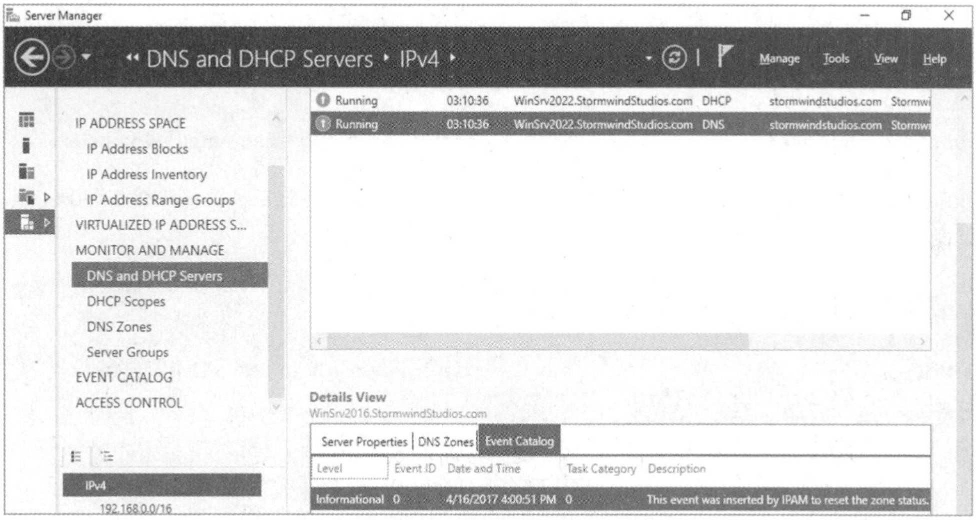

7. In the Monitor And Manage section, you can choose any server that you want to monitor, including your domain controllers. Just select the server and then click Event Catalog under Details View. You can search domain controllers for user logon information, or you can choose NPS and see policy changes that were performed.

8. Once you have finished looking at all the different servers you have in IPAM, close Server Manager.

PowerShell Commands

When talking about PowerShell commands for DHCP, I must let you know that there are dozens of commands that you can use to configure and maintain a DHCP server. Table 6.1 shows just some of the possible PowerShell commands that are available for DHCP.

The following table lists just some of the PowerShell commands available for DHCP. To see the complete list, visit Microsoft's website at https://docs.microsoft.com/en-us/powershell/module/dhcpserver/?view=windowsserver2019-ps.

TABLE 6.1   DHCP PowerShell commands

Command	Description
Add-DhcpServerInDC	This command allows you to authorize the DHCP server services in Active Directory.
Add-DhcpServerv4Class	This command allows you to add an IPv4 vendor or user class.
Add-DhcpServerv4ExclusionRange	You can use this command to add an exclusion range to an IPv4 scope.
Add-DhcpServerv4Failover	You can use this command to add an IPv4 failover.
Add-DhcpServerv4Lease	This command allows you to add a new IPv4 address lease.
Add-DhcpServerv4MulticastScope	You use this command to add a multicast scope server.
Add-DhcpServerv4OptionDefinition	This command allows you to add a DHCPv4 option definition.
Add-DhcpServerv4Policy	You can use this command to add a new policy to either the server or scope level.
Add-DhcpServerv4Reservation	This command allows you to reserve a client IPv4 address in the scope.
Add-DhcpServerv4Scope	This command adds an IPv4 scope.
Add-DhcpServerv6Class	This command allows you to add an IPv6 vendor or user class.
Add-DhcpServerv6ExclusionRange	You can use this command to add an exclusion range to an IPv6 scope.
Add-DhcpServerv6Lease	This command allows you to add a new IPv6 address lease.
Add-DhcpServerv6OptionDefinition	This command allows you to add a DHCPv6 option definition.
Add-DhcpServerv6Reservation	This command allows you to reserve a client IPv6 address in the scope.
Add-DhcpServerv6Scope	This command adds an IPv6 scope.

Command	Description
Backup-DhcpServer	You can use this command to back up the DHCP database.
Export-DhcpServer	This command allows you to export the DHCP server configuration and lease data.
Get-DhcpServerAuditLog	This command shows you the audit log for the DHCP configuration.
Get-DhcpServerDatabase	You can use this command to view the configuration parameters of the DHCP database.
Get-DhcpServerSetting	This command allows you to view the configuration parameters of the DHCP database.
Get-DhcpServerv4Class	You use this command to view the IPv4 vendor or user class settings.
Set-DhcpServerDatabase	This command allows you to modify configuration settings of the DHCP database.
Set-DhcpServerDnsCredential	You can set the credentials of the DHCP Server service, which help register or deregister client records.
Set-DhcpServerSetting	This command allows you to configure the server-level settings.
Set-DhcpServerv4Class	This command allows you to configure the IPv4 vendor class or user class settings.
Set-DhcpServerv4Failover	This command allows you to configure the settings for an existing failover relationship.
Set-DhcpServerv4Policy	You can use this command to configure the settings of a DHCP policy.
Set-DhcpServerv4Reservation	This command allows you to configure an IPv4 reservation.
Set-DhcpServerv4Scope	You can use this command to configure the settings of an existing IPv4 scope.
Set-DhcpServerv6Reservation	This command allows you to configure an IPv4 reservation.
Set-DhcpServerv6Scope	You can use this command to configure the settings of an existing IPv6 scope.

Table 6.2 shows some of the possible PowerShell commands for IPAM.

For a complete list of IPAM PowerShell commands, please visit Microsoft's website at https://technet.microsoft.com/en-us/itpro/powershell/windows/ipamserver/ipamserver.

TABLE 6.2 PowerShell commands for IPAM

Command	Description
Add-IpamAddress	This command allows you to add an IP address to IPAM.
Add-IpamAddressSpace	This command allows you to add an address space to IPAM.
Add-IpamBlock	You can use this command to add an IP address block to IPAM.
Add-IpamCustomField	This command is used to add a custom field to IPAM.
Add-IpamCustomValue	You can use this command to add an IPAM value to a custom field.
Add-IpamDiscoveryDomain	This command allows you to add a new domain in which IPAM discovers infrastructure servers.
Add-IpamRange	You can use this command to add an IP address range to an IPAM server.
Disable-IpamCapability	This command allows you to disable an IPAM optional capability.
Enable-IpamCapability	This command allows you to enable an IPAM optional capability.
Export-IpamAddress	You can use this command to export IP addresses from an IPAM server.
Export-IpamRange	You can use this command to export all of the IP address ranges.
Export-IpamSubnet	This command allows you to export the subnets of an IP address.

Command	Description
Find-IpamFreeAddress	This command will show you the available subnets for allocation, given an IP block, prefix length, and number of requested subnets.
Get-IpamAddress	This command shows you a requested IP addresses from IPAM.
Get-IpamAddressSpace	This command shows you address spaces in IPAM.
Get-IpamBlock	This command shows you a set of address blocks from IPAM.
Get-IpamDatabase	You can use this command to view the IPAM database configuration settings.
Get-IpamDhcpScope	You can use this command to view DHCP scopes on an IPAM server.
Get-IpamDhcpServer	This command allows you to view DHCP server information from IPAM database.
Get-IpamDnsResourceRecord	You can use this command to view DNS resource records in an IPAM database.
Get-IpamDnsServer	This command allows you to view DNS server information from IPAM database.
Get-IpamDnsZone	This command allows you to view DNS zone information from IPAM database.
Get-IpamIpAddressAuditEvent	You can use this command to view IP address audit events in IPAM.
Import-IpamAddress	This command allows you to import an IP address into the IPAM server.
Import-IpamRange	This command allows you to import an IP address range into the IPAM server.
Import-IpamSubnet	This command allows you to import an IP address subnet into the IPAM server.
Invoke-IpamGpoProvisioning	You can create and links IPAM Group Policy Objects (GPOs) for provisioning.

TABLE 6.2 PowerShell commands for IPAM *(Continued)*

Command	Description
Move-IpamDatabase	This command allows you to move an IPAM database to a SQL server database.
Remove-IpamAddress	You use this command on an IPAM server to remove a set of IP addresses.
Remove-IpamAddressSpace	You use this command on an IPAM server to remove a set of IP address spaces.
Set-IpamAccessScope	This command allows you to set up an IPAM access scope.
Set-IpamAddress	You can use this command to configure an IP address in IPAM.
Set-IpamAddressSpace	You can use this command to configure an IP address space in IPAM.
Set-IpamBlock	You can use this command to configure an IP address block in IPAM.
Set-IpamConfiguration	You can adjust the configuration of a computer that hosts the IPAM server.
Set-IpamDatabase	This command allows you to change the settings on how IPAM connects to the IPAM database.
Set-IpamDiscoveryDomain	You use this command to change the IPAM discovery configuration.
Set-IpamRange	This command is used to modify an existing IP address range.
Set-IpamSubnet	This command is used to modify an existing IP subnet.
Update-IpamServer	You can use this command to update the IPAM server after an operating system upgrade.

Summary

In this chapter, I explained how DHCP can help your company by issuing all of the TCP/IP settings to your corporate clients. There are two ways to set up a TCP/IP network: manually or automatic. Manually means that you need to set up the TCP/IP for each client. Automatic means that your corporate clients get their TCP/IP settings from DHCP.

This chapter covered the DHCP lease process as it relates to TCP/IP configuration information for clients. The following stages were covered: IP discovery, IP lease offer, IP lease selection, and IP lease acknowledgment. I showed you how to install and configure the DHCP server on Windows Server 2022 and how to create and manage DHCP scopes and scope options.

I also discussed the authorization of DHCP servers within Active Directory and scopes for IPv4 and IPv6, and then I showed you how to create them. I also covered superscopes as well as managing client leases with their options.

In this chapter, I showed you how to install and configure IPAM. I explained how you need to set up the required GPOs using PowerShell and the different types of role-based administration IPAM allows.

Understanding how DHCP, DNS, and IPAM all work together is essential for ensuring success when taking the exam. Focus your attention on completing the exercises found within the chapter and learning the ins and outs of managing TCP/IP services using IPAM administration.

Exam Essentials

Know how to install and authorize a DHCP server.   You install the DHCP service using the Add/Remove Windows Components Wizard. You authorize the DHCP server using the DHCP snap-in. When you authorize a server, you're actually adding its IP address to the Active Directory object that contains a list of the IP addresses of all authorized DHCP servers.

Know how to create a DHCP scope.   You use the New Scope Wizard to create a new scope for both IPv4 and IPv6. Before you start, you'll need to know the IP address range for the scope you want to create; which IP addresses, if any, you want to exclude from the address pool; which IP addresses, if any, you want to reserve; and the values for the DHCP options you want to set, if any.

Understand how relay agents help with multiple physical network segments.   A question about relay agents on the exam may appear to be a DHCP-related question. Relay agents assist DHCP message propagation across network or router boundaries where such messages ordinarily wouldn't pass.

Understand the difference between exclusions and reservations.   When you want to exclude an entire range of IP addresses, you need to add that range as an exclusion. Any IP addresses within the range for which you want a permanent DHCP lease are known as reservations. Remember that exclusions are TCP/IP numbers in a pool that do not get issued and reservations are numbers in a TCP/IP pool that get issued only to the same client each time.

Understand DHCP failover.   DHCP failover (and load sharing) is one of the hottest features in Windows Server 2022. It is easy to deploy, and it provides an added level of redundancy when compared to using a DHCP split-scope configuration.

Know how to configure DHCP name protection.   DHCP name protection protects DNS Host A records from being overwritten by other client's Host A records during DNS dynamic updates. DHCP name protection is configured using the DHCP Management Console.

Understand IP address management.   IPAM allows you to track and audit IP addresses through the use of the IPAM console. IPAM allows IP addresses to be tracked using DHCP lease events and user logon events.

Know how to provision IPAM and configure server discovery.   IPAM is managed and monitored in Server Manager. Know that there are two separate provisioning models—manual and GPO—and know how to configure each. Know how to configure IPAM server discovery.

Review Questions

1. You are the network administrator for a midsized computer company. You have a single Active Directory forest, and you have a requirement to implement DHCP for the organization. You need to ensure that your DHCP deployment configuration is both fault-tolerant and redundant. Out of the options provided, which is the most reliable DHCP configuration that you could implement?

    A. DHCP split scope

    B. DHCP multicast scope

    C. DHCP failover

    D. DHCP super scope

2. You are the network administrator for your organization. You need to configure the settings of an existing IPv4 scope. What PowerShell cmdlet would you use?

    A. `Set-DhcpServerScope`

    B. `Set-Serverv4Scope`

    C. `Set-DhcpServerv4Scope`

    D. `Set-DhcpScope`

3. You have decided to split the DHCP scope between two DHCP servers. What is the recommended split that Microsoft states that you should use?

    A. 50/50

    B. 60/40

    C. 70/30

    D. 80/20

4. You are the network administrator for an organization with two servers. The servers are named Server1 and Server2. Server2 is a DHCP server. You want Server1 to help lease addresses for Server2. You add the DHCP role to Server1. What should you do next?

    A. In the DHCP console, run the Configure Failover wizard.

    B. In the DHCP console, run the Configure Zone Wizard.

    C. On Server2, set the DHCP role to enabled.

    D. On Server1, start the Share Zone Information Wizard.

5. True or False: You can load DHCP on a Nano server.

    A. True

    B. False

6. You are the network administrator for a large training company. You have been asked to set up the default gateway setting using DHCP. Which option would you configure?

A. 003 Router

B. 006 DNS

C. 015 DNS Domain Name

D. 028 Broadcast Address

7. You are the network administrator for your organization. Your DHCP server (Server1) has a scope of 10.10.16.0 to 10.10.16.254 with a subnet mask of /20. You need to ensure that all of the client computers obtain an IP address from Server1. What PowerShell cmdlet would you use?

A. `Reconcile-DHCPServerv4IPRecord`

B. `Get-Serverv4Scope`

C. `Get- DHCPServerv4IPRecord`

D. `Set-DhcpServerv4Scope`

8. You are the network administrator for a large training company. You have been asked to set up the DNS setting of all you clients using DHCP. Which option would you configure?

A. 003 Router

B. 006 DNS

C. 015 DNS Domain Name

D. 028 Broadcast Address

9. Your network contains two servers named ServerA and ServerB that run Windows Server 2022. ServerA is a DHCP server that is configured to have a scope named Scope1. ServerB is configured to obtain an IP address automatically. In the scope on ServerA, you create a reservation named ServerB_Reservation for ServerB. A technician replaces the network adapter on ServerB. You need to make sure that ServerB can obtain the same IP address as it did before the network card got replaced. What should you modify on Server1?

A. The Advanced settings of ServerB_Reservation

B. The MAC address of ServerB_Reservation

C. The Network Access Protection settings of Scope1

D. The Name Protection settings of Scope1

10. You are the network administrator for a large training company. You have one DHCP server called DHCP1. DHCP1 has an IPv4 scope named Scope1. Users report that when they boot up their systems, it takes a long time to access the network. After auditing your network, you notice that it takes a long time for computers to receive their IP addresses from DHCP because the DHCP server sends out five pings before issuing the IP address to the client machine. How do you reduce the amount of time it takes for computers to receive their IP addresses?

A. Run the DHCP Configuration Wizard.

B. Create a new IPv4 filter.

C. Modify the Conflict Detection Attempts setting.

D. Modify the Ethernet properties of DHCP1.

11. You are the network administrator for your company. You need to use a PowerShell command to configure an IP address block in IPAM. What command do you use?

    A. `Set-IpamIP`

    B. `Set-IpamBlock`

    C. `Set-IPBlock`

    D. `Set-IPAddressBlock`

12. You are the network administrator for your company. You need to use a PowerShell command to add an IP address range to an IPAM server. What command do you use?

    A. `Get-IpRange`

    B. `Set-IpRange`

    C. `Add-IpamRange`

    D. `Set-IPBlock`

13. You are the administrator for StormWind Studios online training company. You need to change the IPAM discovery configuration. What PowerShell command do you use?

    A. `Get-IpamDiscovery`

    B. `Get-IpamDiscoveryDomain`

    C. `Set-IpamDiscovery`

    D. `Set-IpamDiscoveryDomain`

14. You are the network administrator for a large training company. You need to view the DNS zone information from the IPAM database. What PowerShell command do you use?

    A. `Get-IpamDnsZone`

    B. `Add-IpamDnsZone`

    C. `Set-IpamDnsZone`

    D. `View-IpamDnsZone`

15. You are the administrator for StormWind Studios. You are installing and configuring IPAM. You have already installed IPAM and now you need to set up the GPOs for IPAM provisioning. What PowerShell command creates the provisioned GPOs needed for IPAM to function properly?

    A. `Get-IpamGpoProvisioning`

    B. `Add-IpamGpoProvisioning`

    C. `Invoke-IpamGpoProvisioning`

    D. `Set-IpamGpoProvisioning`

16. You are the infrastructure team lead for a high-tech hardware development company. You need to delegate some of the team's IPAM administration responsibilities between team members. You decide that Noelle will be managing IPAM address spaces, but she will not be managing IP address tracking and auditing. Which IPAM security group would best fit Noelle's new responsibilities?

    A. IPAM Administrators

    B. IPAM Users

    C. IPAM ASM Administrators

    D. IPAM MSM Administrators

17. You are the network administrator for a large communications company. You have recently decided to implement IPAM within your organization with the release of Windows Server 2022. You want to set up your IPAM infrastructure so that one primary server can manage your entire enterprise. Which IPAM deployment method would fulfill this requirement?

    A. Isolated

    B. Centralized

    C. Hybrid

    D. Distributed

18. You are the network administrator for your organization. You need to view the DNS server information from the IPAM database. What PowerShell command would you use?

    A. `View-IpamDnsServer`

    B. `Get-IpamDnsServer`

    C. `View-DnsServer`

    D. `Get-DnsServer`

19. You are the lead network administrator for a web hosting company. You have recently made the decision to implement IPAM within your organization. You have already installed and provisioned the IPAM feature on your dedicated Windows Server 2022 server. What is the next logical step in your IPAM deployment?

    A. Create a new IP block.

    B. Delegate IPAM administration.

    C. Configure server discovery.

    D. Create a new IP range.

20. You are a systems administrator for the Stellacon Corporation. Because of the unusual growth of TCP/IP devices on your corporate network over the last year, you need to scale out your IPAM database capabilities. You are currently using a Windows Internal Database (WID) for your IPAM infrastructure, and you want to migrate your IPAM database to a Microsoft SQL Server. Which PowerShell cmdlet would you use to verify current IPAM database configuration settings?

    A. `Move-IpamDatabase`

    B. `Show-IpamDatabaseConfig`

    C. `Show-IpamStatistics`

    D. `Get-IpamMigrationSettings`

Understanding Active Directory

THE FOLLOWING AZ-800 EXAM OBJECTIVES ARE COVERED IN THIS CHAPTER:

✓ **Deploy and manage AD DS domain controllers**

- Deploy and manage domain controllers on-premises
- Deploy and manage domain controllers in Azure
- Deploy Read-Only Domain Controllers (RODCs)
- Troubleshoot flexible single master operations (FSMO) roles

✓ **Configure and manage multi-site, multi-domain, and multi-forest environments**

- Configure and manage forest and domain trusts
- Configure and manage AD DS sites
- Configure and manage AD DS replication

✓ **Create and manage AD DS security principals**

- Create and manage AD DS users and groups
- Manage users and groups in multi-domain and multi-forest scenarios
- Implement group managed service accounts (gMSAs)
- Join Windows Servers to AD DS, Azure AD DS, and Azure AD

THE FOLLOWING AZ-801 EXAM OBJECTIVES ARE COVERED IN THIS CHAPTER:

✓ **Secure a hybrid Active Directory (AD) infrastructure**

- Configure password policies
- Enable password block lists

- Manage protected users
- Manage account security on a Read-Only Domain Controller (RODC)
- Harden domain controllers
- Configure authentication policies silos
- Restrict access to domain controllers
- Configure account security
- Manage AD built-in administrative groups
- Manage AD delegation

✓ **Migrate an AD DS infrastructure to Windows Server 2022 AD DS**

- Migrate AD DS objects, including users, groups and Group Policies, using Active Directory Migration Tool
- Migrate to a new Active Directory forest
- Upgrade an existing forest

One of the most important tasks that you will complete on a network is setting up your domain. To set up your domain properly, you must know how to install and configure your domain controllers.

Once you understand how to plan properly for your domain environment, you will learn how to install Active Directory, which you will accomplish by promoting a Windows Server 2022 computer to a domain controller. We will look at the difference between setting up Active Directory on a Server Core machine versus Windows Server 2022 with the Desktop Experience.

I will also discuss a feature in Windows Server 2022 called a *read-only domain controller (RODC)*, and I will show you how to install Active Directory using Windows PowerShell.

For these exercises, I assume you are creating a Windows Server 2022 machine in a test environment and not on a live network.

Verifying the Filesystem

When you're planning your Active Directory deployment, the filesystem that the operating system uses is an important concern for two reasons. First, the filesystem can provide the ultimate level of security for all the information stored on the server itself. Second, it is responsible for managing and tracking all of this data. The Windows Server 2022 platform supports three filesystems:

- File Allocation Table 32 (FAT32)
- Windows NT File System (NTFS)
- Resilient File System (ReFS)

Although ReFS was new to Windows Server 2012, NTFS has been around for many years, and NTFS in Windows Server 2022 has been improved for better performance.

If you have been working with servers for many years, you may have noticed a few changes to the server filesystem choices. For example, in Windows Server 2003, you could choose between FAT, FAT32, and NTFS. In Windows Server 2022, you could choose between FAT32, NTFS, and ReFS (see Figure 7.1).

FIGURE 7.1 Format options on Windows Server 2022

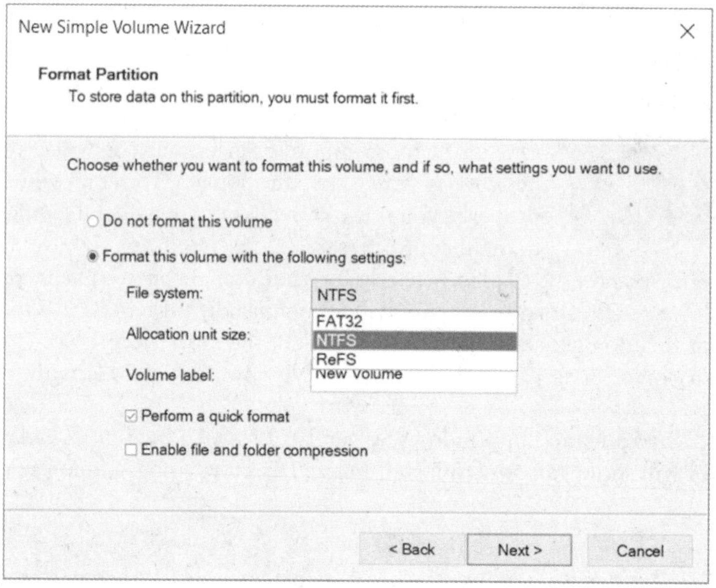

Resilient File System (ReFS)

Windows Server 2022 includes a filesystem called *Resilient File System (ReFS)*. ReFS was created to help Windows Server maximize the availability of data and online operation. ReFS allows the Windows Server 2022 system to continue to function despite some errors that would normally cause data to be lost or the system to go down. ReFS uses data integrity to protect your data from errors and also to make sure that all of your important data is online when that data is needed.

One of the issues that IT members have had to face over the years is the problem of rapidly growing data sizes. As we continue to rely more and more on computers, our data continues to get larger and larger. This is where ReFS can help an IT department. ReFS was designed specifically with the issues of scalability and performance in mind, which resulted in some of the following ReFS features:

Availability   If your hard disk becomes corrupted, ReFS has the ability to implement a salvage strategy that removes the data that has been corrupted. This feature allows the healthy data to continue to be available while the unhealthy data is removed. All of this can be done without taking the hard disk offline.

Scalability   One of the main advantages of ReFS is the ability to support volume sizes up to 2^{78} bytes using 16 KB cluster sizes, while Windows stack addressing allows 2^{64} bytes. ReFS also supports file sizes of $2^{64}-1$ bytes, 2^{64} files in a directory, and the same number of directories in a volume.

Robust Disk Updating   ReFS uses a disk updating system referred to as an *allocate-on-write transactional model* (also known as *copy on write*). This model helps to avoid many hard disk issues while data is written to the disk because ReFS updates data using disk writes to multiple locations in an atomic manner instead of updating data in place.

Data Integrity   ReFS uses a check-summed system to verify that all data that is being written and stored is accurate and reliable. ReFS always uses allocate-on-write for updates to the data, and it uses checksums to detect disk corruption.

Application Compatibility   ReFS allows for most NTFS features and also supports the Win32 API. Because of this, ReFS is compatible with most Windows applications.

NTFS

Let's start with some of the features of NTFS. There are many benefits to using NTFS, including support for the following:

Disk Quotas   To restrict the amount of disk space used by users on the network, you can establish *disk quotas*. By default, Windows Server 2022 supports disk quota restrictions at the volume level. That is, you can restrict the amount of storage space that a specific user uses on a single disk volume. Third-party solutions that allow more granular quota settings are also available.

Filesystem Encryption   One of the fundamental problems with network operating systems (NOSs) is that system administrators are often given full permission to view all files and data stored on hard disks, which can be a security and privacy concern. In some cases, this is necessary. For example, to perform backup, recovery, and disk management functions, at least one user must have all permissions. Windows Server 2022 and NTFS address these issues by allowing for *filesystem encryption*. Encryption essentially scrambles all of the data stored within files before they are written to the disk. When an authorized user requests the files, they are transparently decrypted and provided. By using encryption, you can prevent the data from being used in case it is stolen or intercepted by an unauthorized user—even a system administrator.

Dynamic Volumes   Protecting against disk failures is an important concern for production servers. Although earlier versions of Windows NT supported various levels of Redundant Array of Independent Disks (RAID) technology, software-based solutions had some shortcomings. Perhaps the most significant was that administrators needed to perform server reboots to change RAID configurations. Also, you could not make some configuration changes without completely reinstalling the operating system. With Windows Server 2022 support for *dynamic volumes*, you can change RAID and other disk configuration settings without needing to reboot or reinstall the server. The result is greater data protection, increased scalability, and increased uptime. Dynamic volumes are also included with ReFS.

Mounted Drives   By using *mounted drives*, you can map a local disk drive to an NTFS directory name. This helps you organize disk space on servers and increase manageability. By using mounted drives, you can mount the C:\Users directory to an actual physical disk. If that disk becomes full, you can copy all of the files to another, larger drive without changing the directory pathname or reconfiguring applications.

Remote Storage   System administrators often notice that as soon as they add more space, they must plan the next upgrade. One way to recover disk space is to move infrequently used files to external hard drives. However, backing up and restoring these files can be quite difficult and time-consuming. You can use the *remote storage* features supported by NTFS to off-load seldom-used data automatically to a backup system or other devices. The files, however, remain available to users. If a user requests an archived file, Windows Server 2022 can automatically restore the file from a remote storage device and make it available. Using remote storage like this frees up system administrators' time and allows them to focus on tasks other than micromanaging disk space.

Self-Healing NTFS   In previous versions of the Windows Server operating system, if you had to fix a corrupted NTFS volume, you used a tool called Chkdsk.exe. The disadvantage of this tool is that the Windows Server's availability was disrupted. If this server was your domain controller, that could stop domain logon authentication.

To help protect the Windows Server 2022 NTFS filesystem, Microsoft now uses a feature called self-healing NTFS. *Self-healing NTFS* attempts to fix corrupted NTFS filesystems without taking them offline. Self-healing NTFS allows an NTFS filesystem to be corrected without running Chkdsk.exe. New features added to the NTFS kernel code allow disk inconsistencies to be corrected without system downtime.

Security   NTFS allows you to configure not only folder-level security but also file-level security. NTFS security is one of the biggest reasons most companies use NTFS. ReFS also allows folder- and file-level security.

Setting Up the NTFS Partition

Although the features mentioned in the previous section likely compel most system administrators to use NTFS, additional reasons make using it mandatory. The most important reason is that the Active Directory data store must reside on an NTFS partition. Therefore, before you begin installing Active Directory, make sure you have at least one NTFS partition available. Also, be sure you have a reasonable amount of disk space available (at least 4 GB). Because the size of the Active Directory data store will grow as you add objects to it, also be sure that you have adequate space for the future.

Exercise 7.1 shows you how to use the administrative tools to view and modify disk configuration.

WARNING Before you make any disk configuration changes, be sure you completely understand their potential effects; then perform the test in a lab environment and make sure you have good, verifiable backups handy. Changing partition sizes and adding and removing partitions can result in a total loss of all information on one or more partitions.

If you want to convert an existing partition from FAT or FAT32 to NTFS, you need to use the CONVERT command. For example, the following command converts the C: partition from FAT to NTFS:

```
CONVERT c: /fs:ntfs
```

EXERCISE 7.1

Viewing the Disk Configurations

1. Right-click on the Start button and then choose Computer Management.

2. Under Storage, click Disk Management (see Figure 7.2).

FIGURE 7.2 Disk Management

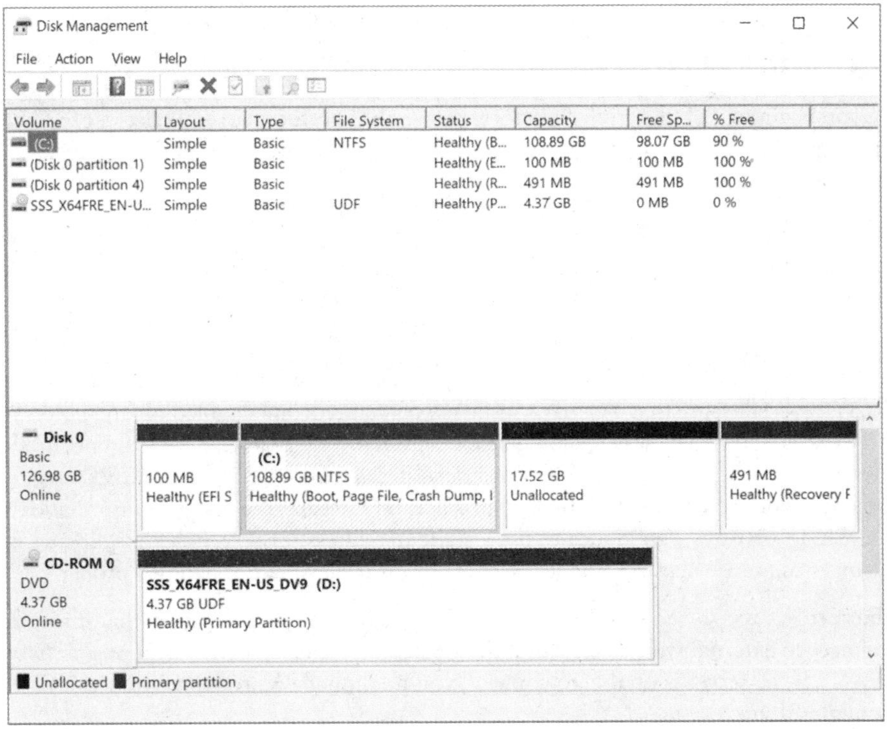

Volume	Layout	Type	File System	Status	Capacity	Free Sp...	% Free	
▬ (C:)	Simple	Basic	NTFS	Healthy (B...	108.89 GB	98.07 GB	90 %	
▬ (Disk 0 partition 1)	Simple	Basic		Healthy (E...	100 MB	100 MB	100 %	
▬ (Disk 0 partition 4)	Simple	Basic		Healthy (R...	491 MB	491 MB	100 %	
SSS_X64FRE_EN-U...	Simple	Basic	UDF	Healthy (P...	4.37 GB	0 MB	0 %	

▬ Disk 0
Basic
126.98 GB
Online

| 100 MB | (C:) 108.89 GB NTFS | 17.52 GB | 491 MB |
| Healthy (EFI S | Healthy (Boot, Page File, Crash Dump, | Unallocated | Healthy (Recovery F |

◎ CD-ROM 0
DVD
4.37 GB
Online

SSS_X64FRE_EN-US_DV9 (D:)
4.37 GB UDF
Healthy (Primary Partition)

■ Unallocated ■ Primary partition

The Disk Management program shows you the logical and physical disks that are currently configured on your system.

3. Use the View menu to choose various depictions of the physical and logical drives in your system.

4. To see the available options for modifying partition settings, right-click any of the disks or partitions. This step is optional.

5. Close Computer Management.

Verifying Network Connectivity

Although a Windows Server 2022 computer can be used by itself without connecting to a network, you will not harness much of the potential of the operating system without network connectivity. Because the fundamental purpose of a network operating system is to provide resources to users, you must verify network connectivity.

Basic Connectivity Tests

Before you begin to install Active Directory, you should perform several checks of your current configuration to ensure that the server is configured properly on the network. You should test the following:

Network Adapter   At least one network adapter should be installed and properly configured on your server. A quick way to verify that a network adapter is properly installed is to use the Computer Management administrative tool. Under Device Manager, Network Adapters branch, you should have at least one network adapter listed. If you don't, click the Add Hardware icon in Control Panel to configure hardware.

TCP/IP   Make sure that TCP/IP is installed, configured, and enabled on any necessary network adapters. The server should also be given a valid IP address and subnet mask. Optionally, you may need to configure a default gateway, DNS servers, WINS servers, and other network settings. If you are using DHCP, be sure that the assigned information is correct. It is always a good idea to use a static IP address for servers because IP address changes can cause network connectivity problems if they are not handled properly.

Internet Access   If the server should have access to the Internet, verify that it is able to connect to external web servers and other machines outside of the local area network (LAN). If the server is unable to connect, you might have a problem with the TCP/IP configuration.

LAN Access   The server should be able to view other servers and workstations on the network. If other machines are not visible, make sure that the network and TCP/IP configurations are correct for your environment.

Client Access   Network client computers should be able to connect to your server and view any shared resources. A simple way to test connectivity is to create a share and test whether other machines are able to see files and folders within it. If clients cannot access the machine, make sure that both the client and the server are configured properly.

Wide Area Network Access   If you're working in a distributed environment, you should ensure that you have access to any remote sites or users who will need to connect to this machine. Usually, this is a simple test that can be performed by a network administrator.

Tools and Techniques for Testing Network Configuration

In some cases, verifying network access can be quite simple. You might have some internal and external network resources with which to test. In other cases, it might be more complicated. You can use several tools and techniques to verify that your network configuration is correct.

Using the ipconfig Utility   By typing **ipconfig/all** at the command prompt, you can view information about the TCP/IP settings of a computer. Figure 7.3 shows the types of information you'll receive.

FIGURE 7.3   Viewing TCP/IP information with the ipconfig utility

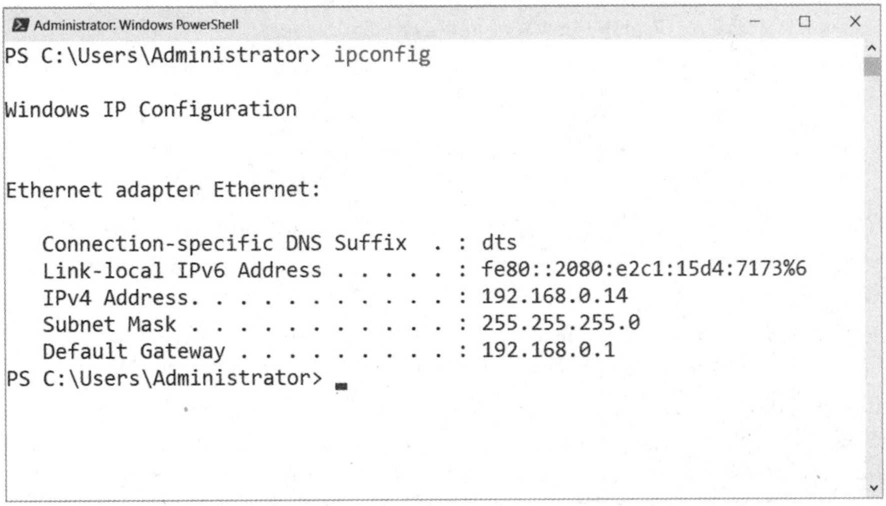

```
PS C:\Users\Administrator> ipconfig

Windows IP Configuration


Ethernet adapter Ethernet:

   Connection-specific DNS Suffix  . : dts
   Link-local IPv6 Address . . . . . : fe80::2080:e2c1:15d4:7173%6
   IPv4 Address. . . . . . . . . . . : 192.168.0.14
   Subnet Mask . . . . . . . . . . . : 255.255.255.0
   Default Gateway . . . . . . . . . : 192.168.0.1
PS C:\Users\Administrator>
```

Using the ping Command   The `ping` command was designed to test connectivity to other computers. You can use the command simply by typing **ping** and then an IP address or hostname at the command line. The following are some steps for testing connectivity using the `ping` command:

Ping Other Computers on the Same Subnet   You should start by pinging a known active IP address on the network to check for a response. If you receive one, then you have connectivity to the network.

Next check to see whether you can ping another machine using its hostname. If this works, then local name resolution works properly.

Ping Computers on Different Subnets   To ensure that routing is set up properly, you should attempt to ping computers that are on other subnets (if any exist) on your network. If this test fails, try pinging the default gateway. Any errors may indicate a problem in the network configuration or a problem with a router.

When You Don't Receive a Response

Some firewalls, routers, or servers on your network or on the Internet might prevent you from receiving a successful response from a `ping` command. This is usually for security reasons (malicious users might attempt to disrupt network traffic using excessive pings as well as redirects and smurf attacks). If you don't receive a response, don't assume that the service is not available. Instead, try to verify connectivity in other ways. For example, you can use the TRACERT command to demonstrate connectivity beyond your subnet, even if other routers ignore Internet Control Message Protocol (ICMP) responses. Because the display of a second router implies connectivity, the path to an ultimate destination shows success even if it doesn't display the actual names and addresses.

Using the tracert Command   The `tracert` command works just like the `ping` command except that `tracert` shows you every hop along the way. So if one router or switch is down, the `tracert` command will show you where the trace stops.

Browsing the Network   To ensure that you have access to other computers on the network, be sure that they can be viewed by clicking Network. This verifies that your name resolution parameters are set up correctly and that other computers are accessible. Also, try connecting to resources (such as file shares or printers) on other machines.

Browsing the Internet   You can quickly verify whether your server has access to the Internet by visiting a known website, such as www.microsoft.com. Success ensures that you have access outside of your network. If you do not have access to the web, you might need to verify your proxy server settings (if applicable) and your DNS server settings.

By performing these simple tests, you can ensure that you have a properly configured network connection and that other network resources are available.

Understanding Active Directory

The first thing that you need to understand about Active Directory is that Active Directory is just a database. When you think about Active Directory this way, it makes Active Directory easier to understand and not such a scary proposition.

Now, even though it's just a database, it's one of the most important databases that you will ever set up. This is a database that controls all the objects in your network.

The first step when setting up Active Directory is to understand the different ways you can set it up. During the installation process, you need to understand the difference between a domain, a tree, and a forest. These options will be asked during the Active Directory setup. If you choose the wrong option, you may set up your network incorrectly. So, this is where we need to start.

Domains

There is one question that I frequently get from new IT people or people who work for a company. What is a domain? Most IT people have heard this term, but it can be a difficult thing to explain to people.

Domains are *logical* groupings of objects. You may hear people say that a domain is a logical grouping of security objects. But this is not really true because not all objects in a domain are security objects.

So why did I stress the word *logical*? Domains are logical groupings and not physical groupings. For example, Microsoft.com is worldwide. Their network has offices all of the world. They are not all located in the same physical location. That's why domains are logical. They can stretch across multiple geographic locations.

When you are reading one of my books or reading about domains on Microsoft's website, you will notice that domains are represented by a triangle. So, when you are seeing a drawing of a domain, the triangle represents that single domain.

When you name your first domain, for example, `StormWindAD.net`, you are establishing a tree. So, let's look at how trees work.

Trees

Trees are one or more domains that follow the same contiguous namespace. For example, I have a domain called `StormWindAD.net`. If I decide to create a child domain called Florida, the full name of that domain name is `Florida.StormWindAD.net`.

Think about when you were born. When my parents named me William, I took on my parents' last name. So, I became William Panek. Domains in a tree work in the same way. When you create a child domain, its takes on the name of the parent.

We can even take it a step further. Let's create another child domain under `Florida` called `Orlando`. The full name would be `Orlando.Florida.StormWindAD.net`. This allows you to set up child domains for any reason if you need them.

I have worked with companies that create child domains based on geographic location, department names, or even the resources held in the domain. This gives you a lot of flexibility on how you set up your network.

Most small to mid-sized companies will only have a single tree in their Active Directory structure. But there may be times that you want to create a second tree. For example, say StormWind buys out `WillPanek.com`. StormWind may choose to create a second tree with the parent name of `WillPanek.com`.

Now we have two trees: `StormWindAD.net` and `WillPanek.com`. All of the child domains will follow the parent name of whichever tree they are created in.

Forests

So now that you understand trees, let's talk about forests. Let's take a look at the example I gave you in the previous section. We have two trees: `StormWindAD.com` and `WillPanek.com`. These two trees are part of the same Active Directory. This is our forest.

A forest is one or more trees that are part of the same Active Directory structure. So, if you have only one tree, you still have a forest (one or more trees). If I have three trees in my Active Directory, all three are part of the same forest.

Now don't get me wrong. You can have multiple forests in a company. For example, if `StormWindAD.net` buys out `WillPanek.com` but `StormWind` does not want the `WillPanek` network to be part of their Active Directory forest, they can leave it as two separate forests.

The downside to this is that forests do *not* work together by default. Most companies have their own forest, and you would not want your network to automatically work with someone else's network. That's not a partnership—that's just hacking.

So, if you own two separate forests, you will need to do extra work to make them work together. This can be done in many different ways, but it will require extra work.

This is why it is so important to understand what domains, trees, and forests do—because if I set up a network and I set each company department as their own forest, none of my departments will be able to work with each other unless I do a lot of work to make it happen.

During the Active Directory installation, you will have the option to do the following:

- Add an additional domain controller to an existing domain
- Add a new domain to an existing tree
- Add a new tree to an existing forest
- Add a new forest

So, it is important to understand each of these components so that you set up your Active Directory network properly for your organization.

Understanding Domain and Forest Functionality

Windows Server 2022 Active Directory uses a concept called *domain and forest functionality*. The functional level that you choose during the Active Directory installation determines which features your domain can use. Since Windows Server 2022 is built on the Windows Server 2016 frame, the highest function level you can choose is Windows Server 2016.

About the Domain Functional Level

Windows Server 2022 will support the following domain functional levels:

- Windows Server 2008
- Windows Server 2008 R2
- Windows Server 2012
- Windows Server 2012 R2
- Windows Server 2016

Which function level you use depends on the domain controllers you have installed on your network. This is an important fact to remember. You can use any version of Windows Server as long as those servers are member servers only. You can only use domain controllers as low as your function level.

For example, if the domain function level is Windows Server 2012 R2, then all domain controllers must be running Windows Server 2012 R2 or higher. You can have Windows Server 2008 R2 member servers, but all of your domain controllers need to be at least 2012 R2.

Windows Server 2022 no longer supports the Windows Server 2003 function levels. With Windows Server 2003 no longer supported, the Windows Server 2003 function levels have been removed.

Table 7.1 shows the features available in Windows Server 2008, Windows Server 2008 R2, Windows Server 2012, Windows Server 2012 R2, and Windows Server 2016 domain function levels.

TABLE 7.1 Comparing domain functional levels

Domain functional feature	Windows Server 2008	Windows Server 2008 R2	Windows Server 2012	Windows Server 2012 R2	Windows Server 2016
Privileged access management	Disabled	Disabled	Disabled	Enabled	Enabled
Authentication assurance	Disabled	Enabled	Enabled	Enabled	Enabled
Fine-grained password policies	Enabled	Enabled	Enabled	Enabled	Enabled
Last interactive logon information	Enabled	Enabled	Enabled	Enabled	Enabled
Advanced Encryption Services (AES 128 and 256) support for the Kerberos protocol	Enabled	Enabled	Enabled	Enabled	Enabled
Distributed Filesystem replication support for Sysvol	Enabled	Enabled	Enabled	Enabled	Enabled
Read-only domain controller (RODC)	Enabled	Enabled	Enabled	Enabled	Enabled
Ability to redirect the Users and Computers containers	Enabled	Enabled	Enabled	Enabled	Enabled
Ability to rename domain controllers	Enabled	Enabled	Enabled	Enabled	Enabled
Logon time stamp updates	Enabled	Enabled	Enabled	Enabled	Enabled
Kerberos KDC key version numbers	Enabled	Enabled	Enabled	Enabled	Enabled
Passwords for InetOrgPerson objects	Enabled	Enabled	Enabled	Enabled	Enabled
Converts NT groups to domain local and global groups	Enabled	Enabled	Enabled	Enabled	Enabled

Domain functional feature	Windows Server 2008	Windows Server 2008 R2	Windows Server 2012	Windows Server 2012 R2	Windows Server 2016
SID history	Enabled	Enabled	Enabled	Enabled	Enabled
Group nesting	Enabled	Enabled	Enabled	Enabled	Enabled
Universal groups	Enabled	Enabled	Enabled	Enabled	Enabled

About Forest Functionality

Windows Server 2022 forest functionality applies to all of the domains in a forest. All domains have to be upgraded to Windows Server 2016/2019/2022 before the forest can be upgraded to Windows Server 2016.

There are five levels of forest functionality:

- Windows Server 2008
- Windows Server 2008 R2
- Windows Server 2012
- Windows Server 2012 R2
- Windows Server 2016

Windows Server 2008, Windows Server 2008 R2, Windows Server 2012, Windows Server 2012 R2, and Windows Server 2022 have many of the same forest features. Some of these features are described in the following list:

Global Catalog Replication Enhancements When you add a new attribute to the global catalog, only those changes are replicated to other global catalogs in the forest. This can significantly reduce the amount of network traffic generated by replication.

Defunct Schema Classes and Attributes You can never permanently remove classes and attributes from the Active Directory schema. However, you can mark them as defunct so that they cannot be used. With Windows Server 2003, Windows Server 2008/2008 R2, Windows Server 2012/2012 R2, Windows Server 2016, Windows Server 2019, and Windows Server 2022 forest functionality, you can redefine the defunct schema attribute so that it occupies a new role in the schema.

Forest Trusts Previously, system administrators had no easy way of granting permission on resources in different forests. Windows Server 2003, Windows Server 2008/2008 R2, Windows Server 2012/2012 R2, Windows Server 2016, Windows Server 2019, and

Windows Server 2022 resolve some of these difficulties by allowing trust relationships between separate Active Directory forests. Forest trusts act much like domain trusts, except that they extend to every domain in two forests. Note that all forest trusts are intransitive.

Linked Value Replication   Windows Server 2003, Windows Server 2008/2008 R2, Windows Server 2012/2012 R2, Windows Server 2016, Windows Server 2019, and Windows Server 2022 use a concept called *linked value replication*. With linked value replication, only the user record that has been changed is replicated (not the entire group). This can significantly reduce network traffic associated with replication.

Renaming Domains   Although the Active Directory domain structure was originally designed to be flexible, there were several limitations. Because of mergers, acquisitions, corporate reorganizations, and other business changes, you may need to rename domains. In Windows Server 2008/2008 R2, Windows Server 2012/2012 R2, and Windows Server 2016/2019/2022, you can change the DNS and NetBIOS names for any domain. Note that this operation is not as simple as just issuing a `rename` command. Instead, there's a specific process that you must follow to make sure the operation is successful. Fortunately, when you properly follow the procedure, Microsoft supports domain renaming even though not all applications support it.

Other Features   Windows Server 2008 and higher also support the following features:

- Improved replication algorithms and dynamic auxiliary classes are designed to increase performance, scalability, and reliability.

- *Active Directory Federation Services (AD FS)*, also known as *Trustbridge*, handles federated identity management. *Federated identity management* is a standards-based information technology process that enables distributed identification, authentication, and authorization across organizational and platform boundaries. The ADFS solution in Windows Server 2008, Windows Server 2008 R2, Windows Server 2012, Windows Server 2012 R2, and Windows Server 2016/2019/2022 helps you address these challenges by enabling organizations to share a user's identity information securely.

- *Active Directory Lightweight Directory Services (AD LDS)* was developed for organizations that require flexible support for directory-enabled applications. AD LDS, which uses the Lightweight Directory Access Protocol (LDAP), is a directory service that adds flexibility and helps organizations avoid increased infrastructure costs.

- Active Directory Recycle Bin (Windows Server 2008 R2 Forest level or higher) provides you with the ability to restore deleted objects in their entirety while AD DS is running. Before this, if you deleted an Active Directory object, you needed to recover it from a backup. Now you can recover the object from the AD recycle bin.

Many of the concepts related to domain and forest functional features are covered in greater detail later in this book.

Planning the Domain Structure

Once you have verified the technical configuration of your server for Active Directory, it's time to verify the Active Directory configuration for your organization. Since the content of this chapter focuses on installing the first domain in your environment, you really need to know only the following information prior to beginning setup:

- The DNS name of the domain
- The computer name or the NetBIOS name of the server (which will be used by previous versions of Windows to access server resources)
- In which domain function level the domain will operate
- Whether other DNS servers are available on the network
- What type of and how many DNS servers are available on the network

However, if you will be installing additional domain controllers in your environment or will be attaching to an existing Active Directory structure, you should also have the following information:

- If this domain controller will join an existing domain, you should know the name of that domain. You will also either require a password for a member of the Enterprise Administrators group for that domain or have someone with those permissions create a domain account before promotion.
- You should know whether the new domain will join an existing tree and, if so, the name of the tree it will join.
- You should know the name of a forest to which this domain will connect (if applicable).

Installing Active Directory

Installing Active Directory is an easy and straightforward process as long as you plan adequately and make the necessary decisions beforehand. There are many ways that you can install Active Directory. You can install Active Directory by using the Windows Server 2022 installation disk (Install from Media [IFM]), using Server Manager, or using Windows PowerShell. But before you can do the actual installation, you must first make sure that your network is ready for the installation.

In the following sections, you'll look at the benefits and required steps to install the first domain controller in a given environment.

Improved Active Directory Features

As with any new version of Windows Server, Microsoft has made some improvements to Active Directory. The following improvements have been made to Windows Server 2016/2019/2022 Active Directory:

Privileged Access Management Privileged access management (PAM) allows you to alleviate security concerns about the Active Directory environment. Some of these security issues include credential theft techniques (pass-the-hash and spear phishing) along with other types of similar attacks. PAM allows you to create new access solutions that can be configured by using Microsoft Identity Manager (MIM).

Azure AD Join Azure Active Directory Join allows you to set up an Office 365–based Azure network and then easily join your end users systems to that domain.

Microsoft Passport Microsoft Passport allows your users to set up a key-based authentication that allows your users to authenticate by using more than just their password (biometrics or PIN numbers). Your users can then log on to their systems using a biometric or PIN number that is linked to a certificate or an asymmetrical key pair.

Read-Only Domain Controllers

Windows Server 2022 supports another type of domain controller called the *read-only domain controller (RODC)*. This is a full copy of the Active Directory database without the ability to write to Active Directory. The RODC gives an organization the ability to install a domain controller in a location (onsite or offsite) where security is a concern.

RODCs need to get their Active Directory database from another domain controller. If there are no domain controllers set up yet for a domain, RODCs will not be available (the option will be grayed out). Implementing an RODC is the same as adding another domain controller to a domain. The installation is exactly the same except that when you get to the screen to choose domain controller options, you check the box for RODC. Again, this is *only* available if there are other domain controllers already in the domain.

Adprep

When you are adding a new user to Active Directory, you fill in the fields First Name, Last Name, and so on. These fields are called *attributes*. The problem is that when you go to install Windows Server 2022, its version of Active Directory has newer attributes than the previous versions of Active Directory. Thus, you need to set up your current version of Active Directory so that it can accept the installation of Windows Server 2022 Active Directory. This is why you use Adprep. Adprep is required to run in order to add the first Windows Server 2022 domain controller to an existing domain or forest.

You need to run **Adprep /forestprep** to add the first Windows Server 2022 domain controller to an existing forest. The command must be run by an administrator who is a member of the Enterprise Admins group, the Schema Admins group, and the Domain Admins group of the domain that hosts the schema master.

You need to run **Adprep /domainprep** to add the first Windows Server 2022 domain controller to an existing domain. Again, to achieve this command, you must be a member of the Domain Admins group of the domain where you are installing the Windows Server 2022 domain controller.

You must run **Adprep /rodcprep** to add the first Windows Server 2022 RODC to an existing forest. To run this command, you must be a member of the Enterprise Admins group.

One feature of Windows Server 2022 Active Directory installation process is that, if needed, Adprep will automatically be executed during the normal Active Directory Domain Services installation.

Active Directory Prerequisites

Before you install Active Directory into your network, you must first make sure that your network and the server meet some minimum requirements. Table 7.2 will show you the requirements needed for Active Directory.

TABLE 7.2   Active Directory requirements

Requirement	Description
Adprep	When adding the first Windows Server 2022 domain controller to an existing Active Directory domain, Adprep commands run automatically as needed.
Credentials	When installing a new AD DS forest, the administrator must be set to local Administrator on the first server. To install an additional domain controller in an existing domain, you need to be a member of the Domain Admins group.
DNS	Domain Name System needs to be installed for Active Directory to function properly. You can install DNS during the Active Directory installation.
NTFS	The Windows Server 2022 drives that store the database, log files, and SYSVOL folder must be placed on a volume that is formatted with the NTFS filesystem.
RODCs	Read-only domain controllers can be installed as long as another domain controller (Windows Server 2008 or newer) already exists on the domain.
TCP/IP	You must configure the appropriate TCP/IP settings on your domain, and you must configure the DNS server addresses.

The Installation Process

Windows Server 2022 computers are configured as either member servers (if they are joined to a domain) or stand-alone servers (if they are part of a workgroup). The process of converting a server to a domain controller is known as *promotion*. Through the use of a simple and intuitive wizard in Server Manager, you can quickly configure servers to be domain controllers after installation. You also have the ability to promote domain controllers using Windows PowerShell.

The first step in installing Active Directory is promoting a Windows Server 2022 computer to a domain controller. The first domain controller in an environment serves as the starting point for the forest, trees, domains, and the operations master roles.

Exercise 7.2 shows the steps you need to follow to promote an existing Windows Server 2022 computer to a domain controller. To complete the steps in this exercise, you must have already installed and configured a Windows Server 2022 computer. You also need a DNS server that supports SRV records. If you do not have a DNS server available, the Active Directory Installation Wizard automatically configures one for you.

EXERCISE 7.2

Promoting a Domain Controller

1. Install the Active Directory Domain Services by clicking the Add Roles And Features link in Server Manager's Dashboard view.

2. At the Before You Begin screen, click Next.

3. The Select Installation Type screen will be next. Make sure that the Role-Based radio button is selected and click Next.

4. At the Select Destination Server screen, choose the local machine. Click Next.

5. At the Select Server Roles screen, select the option Active Directory Domain Services.

6. A pop-up menu will appear asking you to install additional features. Click the Add Features button.

7. Click Next.

8. At the Select Features screen, accept the defaults and click Next.

9. Click Next at the information screen.

10. Click the Install button at the Confirmation Installation screen. The Installation Progress screen will show you how the installation is progressing.

11. After the installation is complete, click the Close button.

12. On the left side window, click the AD DS link.

13. Click the More link (see Figure 7.4) next to Configuration Required For Active Directory Domain Services.

FIGURE 7.4 Clicking More

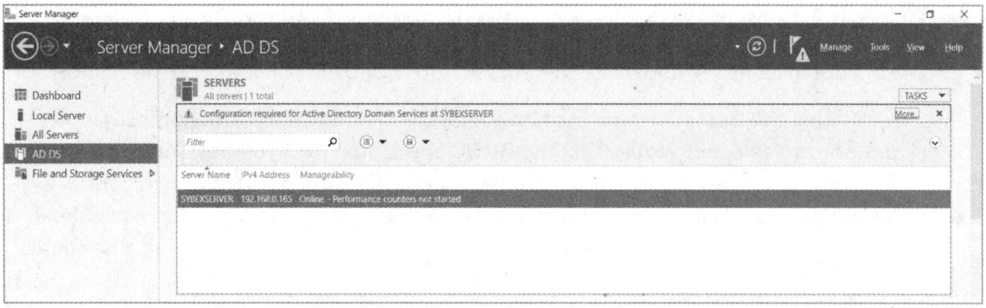

14. In the Post-Deployment Configuration section, click the Promote This Server To A Domain Controller link.

15. At this point, you will configure this domain controller. You are going to install a new domain controller in a new domain in a new forest. At the Deployment Configuration screen, choose the Add A New Forest radio button. You then need to add a root domain name. In this exercise, I will use `StormWindAD.com` (see Figure 7.5). Click Next.

FIGURE 7.5 Deployment Configuration screen

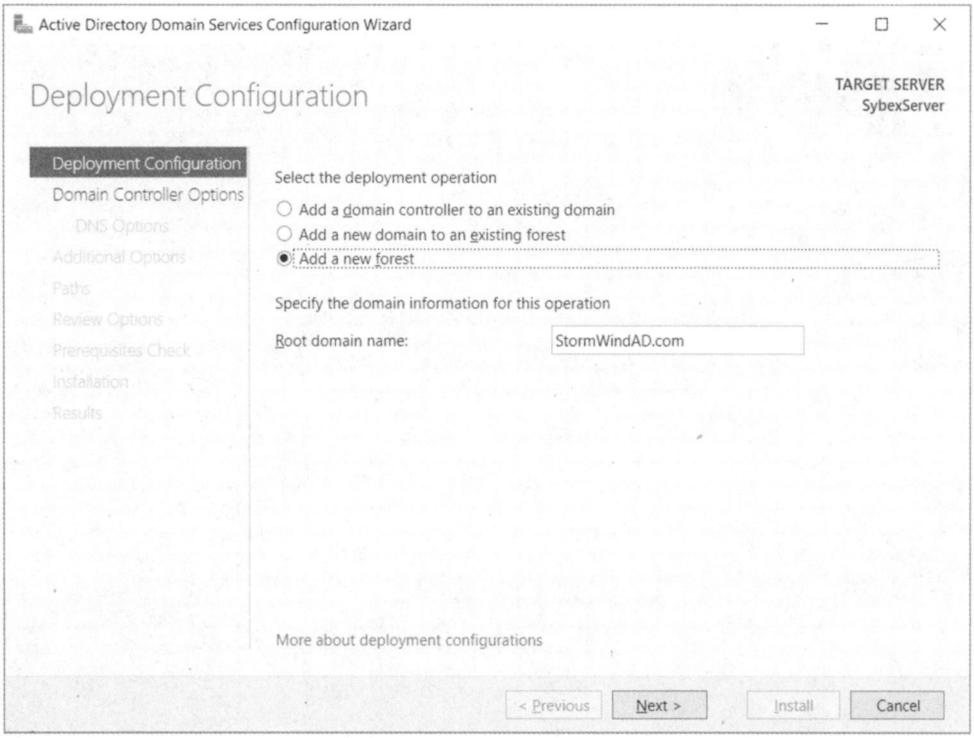

EXERCISE 7.2 *(continued)*

16. At the Domain Controller Options screen, set the following options (see Figure 7.6):
    - Functional levels: Windows Server 2012 R2 (for both; we will upgrade them later).
    - Verify that the Domain Name System (DNS) Server and Global Catalog (GC) options are selected. Notice that the RODC check box is grayed out. This is because RODCs need to get their Active Directory database from another domain controller. Since this is the first domain controller in the forest, RODCs are not possible. If you need an RODC, complete the previous steps on a member server in a domain where domain controllers already exist.

    Password: **P@ssw0rd** (do not use P@ssw0rd for a live server)

    Then click Next.

FIGURE 7.6 Domain Controller options

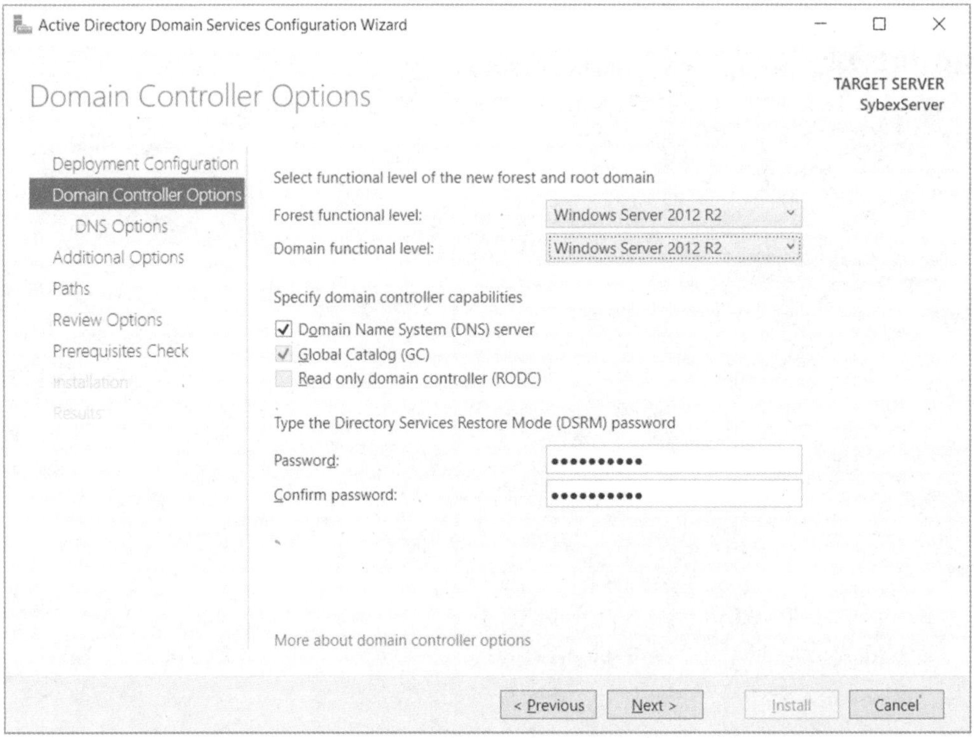

17. At the DNS screen, click Next.

18. At the Additional Options screen, accept the default NetBIOS domain name and click Next.

19. At the Paths screen, accept the default file locations and click Next.

20. At the Review Options screen (see Figure 7.7), verify your settings and click Next. At this screen, there is also a View Script button. Click it if you want to grab a PowerShell script based on the features you have just set up.

FIGURE 7.7   Review Options screen

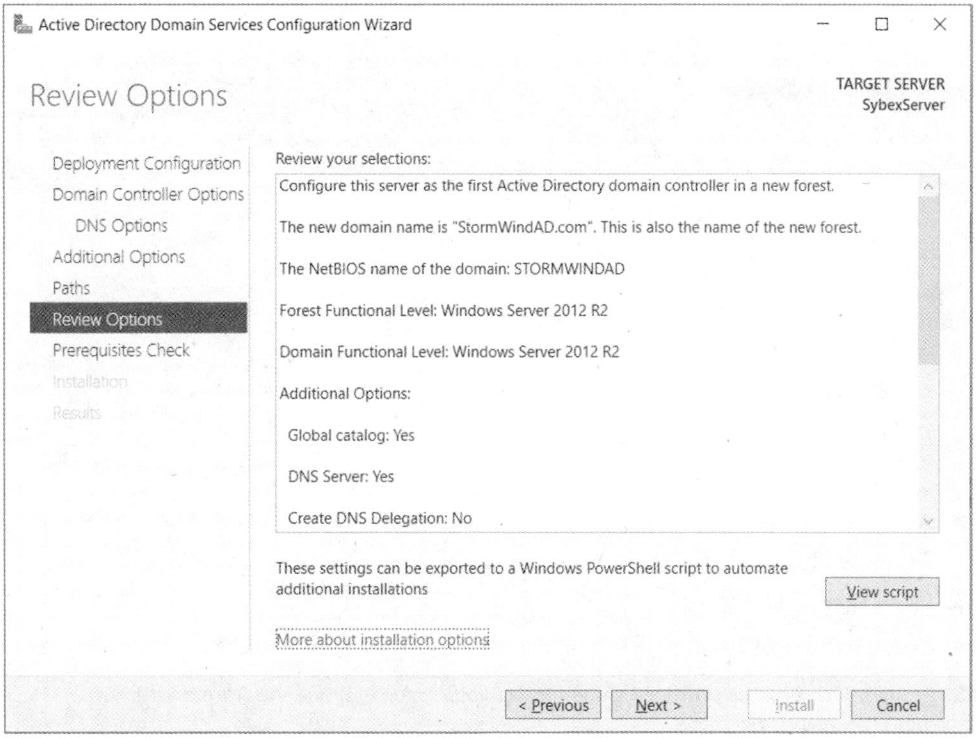

21. At the Prerequisites Check screen, click the Install button (as long as there are no errors). Warnings are OK just as long as there are no errors (see Figure 7.8).

EXERCISE 7.2 *(continued)*

FIGURE 7.8 Prerequisites Check screen

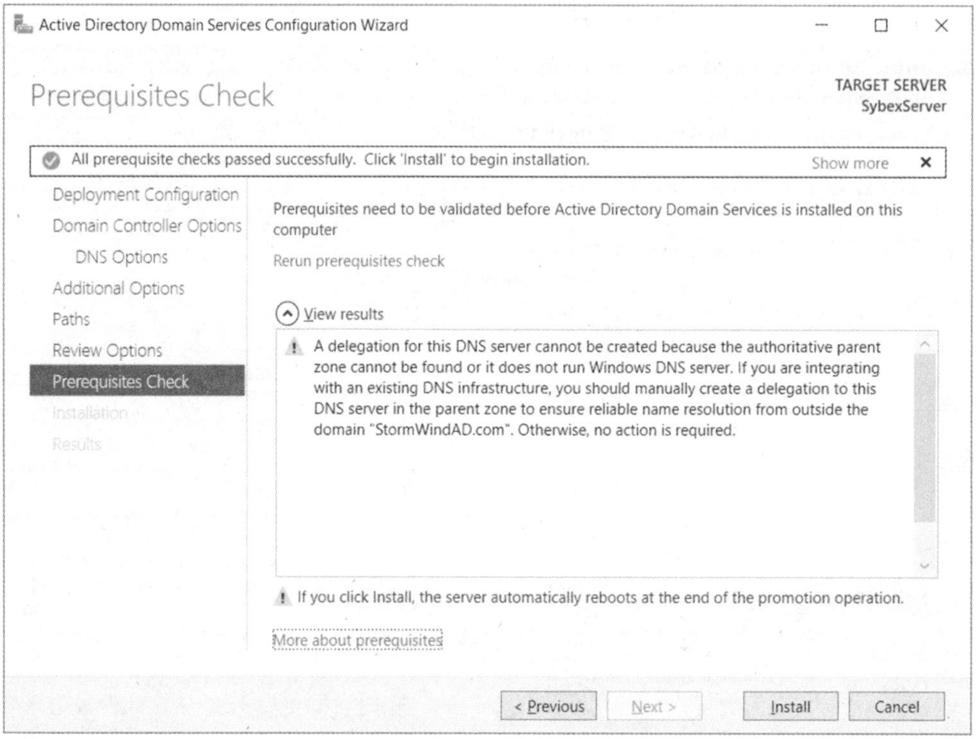

22. After the installation completes, the machine will automatically reboot. Log in as the administrator.
23. Close Server Manager.
24. Click the Start button on the keyboard and choose Administrative Tools.
25. You should see new MMC snap-ins for Active Directory. Close the Administrative Tools window.

In Exercise 7.3, you will learn how to install Active Directory on a Server Core installation. You will use Windows Server 2022 Datacenter Server Core. Before actually installing AD DS, you will learn how to configure the computer name, the time, your password, and a static TCP/IP address, and then you will install DNS.

Exercise 7.3 will have you install Active Directory onto a Datacenter Server Core server using Microsoft PowerShell. If you need to install Active Directory onto any Windows Server 2022 server using PowerShell, use the same steps.

EXERCISE 7.3

Installing AD DS on Server Core Using PowerShell

1. At the Server Core command prompt, type **cd\windows\system32** and press Enter.

2. Type **timedate.cpl** and set your date, local time zone, and time. Click OK.

3. Type **Netsh** and press Enter.

4. Type **Interface** and press Enter.

5. Type **IPv4** and press Enter.

6. Type **Show IP** and press Enter. This will show you the current TCP/IP address and the interface with which the TCP/IP address is associated.

7. As you can see, interface 12 is my Ethernet interface. To change this interface, type the following command and press Enter:

    ```
    Set address name="12" source=static address=192.168.0.165 mask=255.255.255.0
    gateway=192.168.0.1
    ```

    I used 192.168.0.x for my address. You can replace the address, mask, and gateway based on your local settings.

8. Type **Show IP** and press Enter. You should see that the new address is now manual and set to the IP address you set.

9. Type **Exit** and press Enter.

10. Type **Net User Administrator *** and press Enter.

11. Type your password and then confirm the password. I used P@ssw0rd for my password.

12. Type the following command and press Enter:

    ```
    Netdom renamecomputer %computername% /newname:ServerA
    ```

13. Type **Y** and press Enter.

14. Type **Shutdown /R /T 0** and press Enter. This will reboot the machine. After the reboot, log back into the system.

15. Type **PowerShell** and press Enter.

16. At the PowerShell prompt, type **Add-WindowsFeature DNS** and press Enter. This will add DNS to the server.

17. At the PowerShell prompt, type **Add-WindowsFeature AD-Domain-Services** and press Enter.

18. At the PowerShell prompt, type **Import-Module ADDSDeployment**.

19. At the PowerShell prompt, type **Install-ADDSForest**.

EXERCISE 7.3 *(continued)*

20. Type your domain name and press Enter. I used Sybex.com.

21. Next you will be asked for your Safe mode administrator password. Type **P@ssw0rd** and then confirm it.

22. Type **Y** and press Enter. Active Directory will install, and the machine will automatically reboot.

Now that we have installed Active Directory onto two different types of systems, let's take a look at how to install an RODC. In Exercise 7.4 I will show you how to add an RODC to a domain. To do this exercise, you need another domain controller in the domain.

EXERCISE 7.4

Creating an RODC Server

1. Install Active Directory Domain Services by clicking the Add Roles And Features link in Server Manager's Dashboard view.

2. At the Before You Begin screen, click Next.

3. The Select Installation Type screen will be next. Make sure that the Role-Based radio button is selected and click Next.

4. At the Select Destination Server screen, choose the local machine. Click Next.

5. At the Select Server Roles screen, select the option Active Directory Domain Services.

6. A pop-up menu will appear asking you to install additional features. Click the Add Features button.

7. Click Next.

8. At the Select Features screen, accept the defaults and click Next.

9. Click Next at the information screen.

10. Click the Install button at the Confirmation Installation screen. The Installation Progress screen will show you how the installation is progressing.

11. After the installation is complete, click the Close button.

12. In the left window, click the AD DS link.

13. Click the More link next to Configuration Required For Active Directory Domain Services.

14. In the Post-Deployment Configuration section, click the Promote This Server To A Domain Controller link.

15. At this point, you will configure this domain controller. You are going to install a new domain controller in an existing domain. At the Deployment Configuration screen, choose Add A Domain Controller To An existing Domain. You then need to add the name of another domain controller in that domain.

16. At the Domain Controller Options screen, set the following options:

- Verify that the RODC check box is selected.

- Password: **P@ssw0rd**

Then click Next.

17. At the Paths screen, accept the default file locations and click Next.

18. At the Review Options screen, verify your settings and click Next. At this screen, there is a View Script button. This button allows you to grab a PowerShell script based on the features you have just set up.

19. At the Prerequisites Check screen, click the Install button (as long as there are no errors). Warnings are OK just as long as there are no errors.

20. After the installation completes, the machine will automatically reboot. Log in as the administrator.

21. Close Server Manager.

Installing Additional Domain Controllers by Using Install from Media

There may be times when you need to install additional domain controllers without having a lot of additional replication traffic. When you can install a domain controller without the need of additional replication traffic, the installation is much quicker. This is the perfect time to install an additional domain controller by using the install from media (IFM) method.

Windows Server 2022 allows you to install a domain controller using the IFM method by using the Ntdsutil or PowerShell utilities. With the Ntdsutil or PowerShell utility, you can create installation media for an additional domain controller in a domain. One issue that you must remember is that any objects that were created, modified, or deleted since the IFM was created must be replicated. Creating the IFM as close (time-wise) as the installation of the domain controller guarantees that all objects will be created at the time the domain controller is installed.

One other way that you can create the IFM is by restoring a backup of a similar domain controller in the same domain to another location.

Verifying Active Directory Installation

Once you have installed and configured Active Directory, you'll want to verify that you have done so properly. In this section, we'll look at methods for doing this.

Using Event Viewer

The first (and perhaps most informative) way to verify the operations of Active Directory is to query information stored in the Windows Server 2022 event log. You can do this using the Windows Server 2022 Event Viewer. Exercise 7.5 walks you through this procedure. Entries seen with the Event Viewer include errors, warnings, and informational messages.

To complete the steps in Exercise 7.5, you must have configured the local machine as a domain controller.

EXERCISE 7.5

Viewing the Active Directory Event Log

1. Open Administrative tools by pressing the Windows Key and choosing Administrative Tools.

2. Open the Event Viewer snap-in from the Administrative Tools program group.

3. In the left pane, under Applications And Services Logs, select Directory Service.

4. In the right pane, you can sort information by clicking column headings. For example, you can click the Source column to sort by the service or process that reported the event.

5. Double-click an event in the list to see the details for that item. Note that you can click the Copy button to copy the event information to the Clipboard. You can then paste the data into a document for later reference. Also, you can move between items using the up and down arrows. Click OK when you have finished viewing an event.

6. Filter an event list by right-clicking the Directory Service item in the left pane and selecting Filter Current Log. Note that filtering does not remove entries from the event logs—it only restricts their display.

7. To verify Active Directory installation, look for events related to the proper startup of Active Directory, such as Event ID 1000 (Active Directory Startup Complete) and 1394 (Attempts To Update The Active Directory Database Are Succeeding). Also, be sure to examine any error or warning messages because they could indicate problems with DNS or other necessary services.

8. When you've finished viewing information in the Event Viewer, close the application.

Gaining Insight Through Event Viewer

Despite its simple user interface and somewhat limited GUI functionality, the Event Viewer tool can be your best ally in isolating and troubleshooting problems with Windows Server 2022. The Event Viewer allows you to view information that is stored in various log files that are maintained by the operating system. This includes information from the following logs:

Application   Stores messages generated by programs running on your system. For example, SQL Server 2012 might report the completion of a database backup job within the Application log.

Security   Contains security-related information as defined by your auditing settings. For example, you could see when users have logged onto the system or when particularly sensitive files have been accessed.

System   Contains operating system-related information and messages. Common messages might include a service startup failure or information about when the operating system was last rebooted.

Directory Service   Stores messages and events related to how Active Directory functions. For example, you might find details related to replication here.

DNS Server   Contains details about the operations of the DNS service. This log is useful for troubleshooting replication or name-resolution problems.

Other Log Files   Contain various features of Windows Server 2022 and the applications that may run on this operating system, which can create additional types of logs. These files allow you to view more information about other applications or services through the familiar Event Viewer tool.

Additionally, developers can easily send custom information from their programs to the Application log. Having all of this information in one place really makes it easy to analyze operating system and application messages. Also, many third-party tools and utilities are available for analyzing log files.

Although the Event Viewer GUI does a reasonably good job of letting you find the information you need, you might want to extract information to analyze other systems or applications. One especially useful feature of the Event Viewer is its ability to save a log file in various formats. You can access this feature by clicking Action ➢ Save As. You'll be given the option of saving in various formats, including tab- and comma-delimited text files. You can then open these files in other applications (such as Microsoft Excel) for additional data analysis.

Overall, in the real world, the Event Viewer can be an excellent resource for monitoring and troubleshooting your important servers and workstations.

In addition to providing information about the status of events related to Active Directory, the Event Viewer shows you useful information about other system services and applications. You should routinely use this tool.

Using Active Directory Administrative Tools

After a server has been promoted to a domain controller, you will see that various tools are added to the Administrative Tools program group, including the following:

Active Directory Administrative Center   This is a *Microsoft Management Console (MMC)* snap-in that allows you to accomplish many Active Directory tasks from one central location. This MMC snap-in allows you to manage your directory services objects, including doing the following tasks:

- Reset user passwords
- Create or manage user accounts
- Create or manage groups
- Create or manage computer accounts
- Create or manage organizational units (OUs) and containers
- Connect to one or several domains or domain controllers in the same instance of Active Directory Administrative Center
- Filter Active Directory data

Active Directory Domains and Trusts   Use this tool to view and change information related to the various domains in an Active Directory environment. This MMC snap-in also allows you to set up shortcut trusts.

Active Directory Sites and Services   Use this tool to create and manage Active Directory sites and services to map to an organization's physical network infrastructure.

Active Directory Users and Computers   User and computer management is fundamental for an Active Directory environment. The Active Directory Users and Computers tool allows you to set machine- and user-specific settings across the domain. This tool is discussed throughout this book.

Active Directory Module for Windows PowerShell   *Windows PowerShell* is a command-line shell and scripting language. The Active Directory Module for Windows PowerShell is a group of cmdlets used to manage your Active Directory domains, Active Directory Lightweight Directory Services (AD LDS) configuration sets, and Active Directory Database Mounting Tool instances in a single, self-contained package. The Active Directory Module for Windows PowerShell is a normal PowerShell window. The only difference is that the Active Directory PowerShell module is preloaded when you choose the Active Directory Module for Windows PowerShell.

A good way to make sure that Active Directory is accessible and functioning properly is to run the Active Directory Users and Computers tool. When you open the tool, you should see a configuration similar to that shown in Figure 7.9. Specifically, you should make sure the name of the domain you created appears in the list. You should also click the Domain Controllers folder and make sure that the name of your local server appears in the right pane. If your configuration passes these two checks, Active Directory is present and configured.

FIGURE 7.9   Viewing Active Directory information using the Active Directory Users and Computers tool

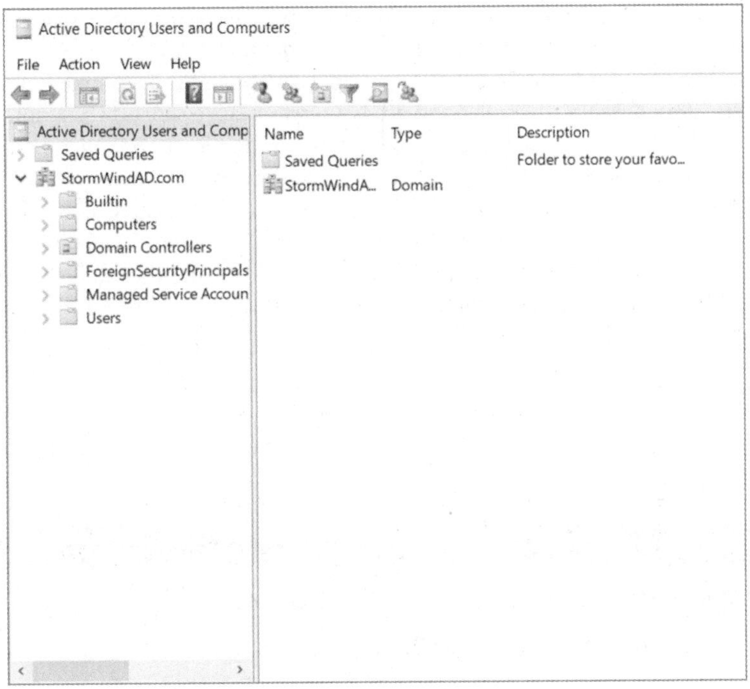

Testing from Clients

The best test of any solution is simply to verify that it works the way you had intended in your environment. When it comes to using Active Directory, a good test is to ensure that clients can view and access the various resources presented by Windows Server 2022 domain controllers. In the following subsections, we'll look at several ways to verify that Active Directory is functioning properly.

Verifying Client Connectivity

If you are unable to see the recently promoted server on the network, there is likely a network configuration error. If only one or a few clients are unable to see the machine, the problem is probably related to client-side configuration. To fix this, make sure that the client computers have the appropriate TCP/IP configuration (including DNS server settings) and that they can see other computers on the network.

If the new domain controller is unavailable from any of the other client computers, you should verify the proper startup of Active Directory using the methods mentioned earlier in this chapter. If Active Directory has been started, ensure that the DNS settings are correct. Finally, test network connectivity between the server and the clients by accessing the network or by using the ping command.

Joining a Domain

If Active Directory has been properly configured, clients and other servers should be able to join the domain. Exercise 7.6 outlines the steps you need to take to join a Windows 7, Windows 8/8.1, or Windows 10/11 computer to the domain.

To complete this exercise, you must have already installed and properly configured at least one Active Directory domain controller and a DNS server that supports SRV records in your environment. In addition to the domain controller, you need at least one other computer, not configured as a domain controller, running one of the following operating systems: Windows 7, Windows 8, Windows 8.1, Windows 10, Windows Server 2008, Windows Server 2008 R2, Windows Server 2012, Windows Server 2012 R2, or Windows Server 2016/2019/2022.

Once clients are able to join the domain successfully, they should be able to view Active Directory resources using the Network icon. This test validates the proper functioning of Active Directory and ensures that you have connectivity with client computers.

 Exercise 7.6 is being done from a Windows 10 Enterprise computer.

EXERCISE 7.6

Joining a Computer to an Active Directory Domain

1. Right-click the Start menu and choose System.

2. Go to the section called Computer Name. On the right side, click the Change Settings link.

3. Next to the section To Rename This Computer Or Change Its Domain Or Workgroup, click the Change button.

4. In the Member Of section, choose the Domain option. Type the name of the Active Directory domain that this computer should join. Click OK.

5. When prompted for the username and password of an account that has permission to join computers to the domain, enter the information for an administrator of the domain. Click OK to commit the changes. If you successfully joined the domain, you will see a dialog box welcoming you to the new domain.

6. You will be notified that you must reboot the computer before the changes take place. Select Yes when prompted to reboot.

Creating and Configuring Application Data Partitions

Organizations store many different kinds of information in various places. For the IT departments that support this information, it can be difficult to ensure that the right information is available when and where it is needed. Windows Server 2022 uses a feature called *application data partitions*, which allows system administrators and application developers to store custom information within Active Directory. The idea behind application data partitions is that since you already have a directory service that can replicate all kinds of information, you might as well use it to keep track of your own information.

Developing distributed applications that can, for example, synchronize information across an enterprise is not a trivial task. You have to come up with a way to transfer data between remote sites (some of which are located across the world), and you have to ensure that the data is properly replicated. By storing application information in Active Directory, you can take advantage of its storage mechanism and replication topology. Application-related information stored on domain controllers benefits from having fault-tolerance features and availability.

Consider the following simple example to understand how this can work. Suppose your organization has developed a customer Sales Tracking and Inventory application. The company needs to make the information that is stored by this application available to all of its branch offices and users located throughout the world. However, the goal is to do this with the least amount of IT administrative effort. Assuming that Active Directory has already been deployed throughout the organization, developers can build support into the application for storing data within Active Directory. They can then rely on Active Directory to store and synchronize the information among various sites. When users request updated data from the application, the application can obtain this information from the nearest domain controller that hosts a replica of the Sales Tracking and Inventory data.

Other types of applications can also benefit greatly from the use of application data partitions. Now that you have a good understanding of the nature of application data partitions, let's take a look at how you can create and manage them using Windows Server 2022 and Active Directory.

Creating Application Data Partitions

By default, after you create an Active Directory environment, you will not have any customer application data partitions. Therefore, the first step in making this functionality available is to create a new application data partition. You can use several tools to do this:

> **Third-Party Applications or Application-Specific Tools**   Generally, if you are planning to install an application that can store information in the Active Directory database, you'll receive some method of administering and configuring that data along with the application. For example, the setup process for the application might assist you in the steps you need to take to set up a new application data partition and to create the necessary structures for storing data.

Creating and managing application data partitions are advanced Active Directory–related functions. Be sure that you have a solid understanding of the Active Directory schema, Active Directory replication, LDAP, and your applications' needs before you attempt to create new application data partitions in a live environment.

Active Directory Service Interfaces   ADSI is a set of programmable objects that can be accessed through languages such as Visual Basic Scripting Edition (VBScript), Visual C#, Visual Basic .NET, and many other language technologies that support the Component Object Model (COM) standard. Through the use of ADSI, developers can create, access, and update data stored in Active Directory and in any application data partitions.

The LDP Tool   You can view and modify the contents of the Active Directory schema using LDAP-based queries. The LDP tool allows you to view information about application data partitions.

`Ldp.exe` is a graphical user interface (GUI) tool that allows you to configure Lightweight Directory Access Protocol (LDAP) directory service. You have the ability to use the LDP tool to administer an Active Directory Lightweight Directory Services (AD LDS) instance. To use the LDP tool, you must be an administrator or equivalent.

`Ntdsutil`   The `ntdsutil` command is the main method by which system administrators create and manage application data partitions on their Windows Server 2022 domain controllers. The specific `ntdsutil` commands are covered later in this chapter.

 Creating and managing application data partitions can be fairly complex. Such a project's success depends on the quality of the architecture design. This is a good example of where IT staff and application developers must cooperate to ensure that data is stored effectively and that it is replicated efficiently.

You can create an application data partition in one of three different locations within an Active Directory forest:

- As a new tree in an Active Directory forest
- As a child of an Active Directory domain partition

  For example, you can create an Accounting application data partition within the `Finance.MyCompany.com` domain.

- As a child of another application data partition

  This method allows you to create a hierarchy of application data partitions.

As you might expect, you must be a member of the Enterprise Admins or Domain Admins group to be able to create application data partitions. Alternatively, you can be delegated the appropriate permissions to create new partitions.

Now that you have a good idea of the basic ways in which you can create application data partitions, let's look at how replicas (copies of application data partition information) are handled.

Managing Replicas

A *replica* is a copy of any data stored within Active Directory. Unlike the basic information that is stored in Active Directory, application partitions cannot contain security principals. Also, not all domain controllers automatically contain copies of the data stored in an application data partition. You can define which domain controllers host copies of the application data. This is an important feature because, if replicas are used effectively, you can find a good balance between replication traffic and data consistency. For example, suppose that three of your organization's 30 locations require up-to-date accounting-related information. You might choose to replicate the data only to domain controllers located in the places that require the data. Limiting replication of this data reduces network traffic.

Replication is the process by which replicas are kept up-to-date. Application data can be stored and updated on designated servers in the same way basic Active Directory information (such as users and groups) is synchronized between domain controllers. Application data partition replicas are managed using the *Knowledge Consistency Checker (KCC)*, which ensures that the designated domain controllers receive updated replica information. Additionally, the KCC uses all Active Directory sites and connection objects that you create to determine the best method to handle replication.

Removing Replicas

When you perform a *demotion* on a domain controller, that server can no longer host an application data partition. If a domain controller contains a replica of application data partition information, you must remove the replica from the domain controller before you demote it. If a domain controller is the machine that hosts a replica of the application data partition, then the entire application data partition is removed and will be permanently lost. Generally, you want to do this only after you're absolutely sure that your organization no longer needs access to the data stored in the application data partition.

Using *ntdsutil* to Manage Application Data Partitions

The primary method by which system administrators create and manage application data partitions is through the ntdsutil command. You can launch this tool simply by entering **ntdsutil** at a command prompt. The ntdsutil command is both interactive and context sensitive. That is, once you launch the utility, you'll see an ntdsutil command prompt. At this prompt, you can enter various commands that set your context within the application. For example, if you enter the domain management command, you'll be able to use domain-related commands. Several operations also require you to connect to a domain, a domain controller, or an Active Directory object before you perform a command.

 For complete details on using ntdsutil, see the Windows Server 2022 Help and Support Center.

Table 7.3 describes the domain management commands supported by `ntdsutil`. You can access this information by typing the following sequence of commands at a command prompt:

```
ntdsutil
domain management
Help
```

TABLE 7.3   ntdsutil domain management commands

ntdsutil domain management command	Purpose
Help or ?	Displays information about the commands that are available within the Domain Management menu of the `ntdsutil` command.
Connection or Connections	Allows you to connect to a specific domain controller. This will set the context for further operations that are performed on specific domain controllers.
Create NC *PartitionDistinguishedName DNSName*	Creates a new application directory partition.
Delete NC *PartitionDistinguishedName*	Removes an application data partition.
List NC Information *PartitionDistinguishedName*	Shows information about the specified application data partition.
List NC Replicas *PartitionDistinguishedName*	Returns information about all replicas for the specific application data partition.
Precreate *PartitionDistinguished NameServerDNSName*	Pre-creates cross-reference application data partition objects. This allows the specified DNS server to host a copy of the application data partition.
Remove NC Replica *PartitionDistinguishedName DCDNSName*	Removes a replica from the specified domain controller.
Select Operation Target	Selects the naming context that will be used for other operations.
Set NC Reference Domain *PartitionDistinguishedName DomainDistinguishedName*	Specifies the reference domain for an application data partition.
Set NC Replicate NotificationDelay *PartitionDistinguishedName FirstDCNotificationDelay OtherDCNotificationDelay*	Defines settings for how often replication will occur for the specified application data partition.

The ntdsutil commands are all case insensitive. Mixed case was used in the table to make them easier to read. NC in commands stands for "naming context," referring to the fact that this is a partition of the Active Directory schema.

Configuring DNS Integration with Active Directory

There are many benefits to integrating Active Directory and DNS services:

- You can configure and manage replication along with other Active Directory components.

- You can automate much of the maintenance of DNS resource records through the use of dynamic updates.

- You will be able to set specific security options on the various properties of the DNS service.

Exercise 7.7 shows the steps that you must take to ensure that these integration features are enabled. You'll look at the various DNS functions that are specific to interoperability with Active Directory.

Before you begin this exercise, make sure that the local machine is configured as an Active Directory domain controller and that DNS services have been properly configured. If you instructed the Active Directory Installation Wizard to configure DNS automatically, many of the settings mentioned in this section may already be enabled. However, you should verify the configuration and be familiar with how the options can be set manually.

EXERCISE 7.7

Configuring DNS Integration with Active Directory

1. Open Administrative Tools by pressing the Windows Key and choosing Administrative Tools.

2. Open the DNS snap-in from the Administrative Tools program group.

3. Right-click the icon for the local DNS server and select Properties. Click the Security tab. Notice that you can now specify which users and groups have access to modify the configuration of the DNS server. Make any necessary changes and click OK.

4. Expand the local server branch and the Forward Lookup Zones folder.

5. Right-click the name of the Active Directory domain you created and select Properties.

EXERCISE 7.7 *(continued)*

6. On the General tab (see Figure 7.10), verify that the type is Active Directory–Integrated and that the Data Is Stored In Active Directory message is displayed. If this option is not currently selected, you can change it by clicking the Change button next to Type and choosing the Store The Zone In Active Directory check box on the bottom.

FIGURE 7.10 General tab of DNS zone properties

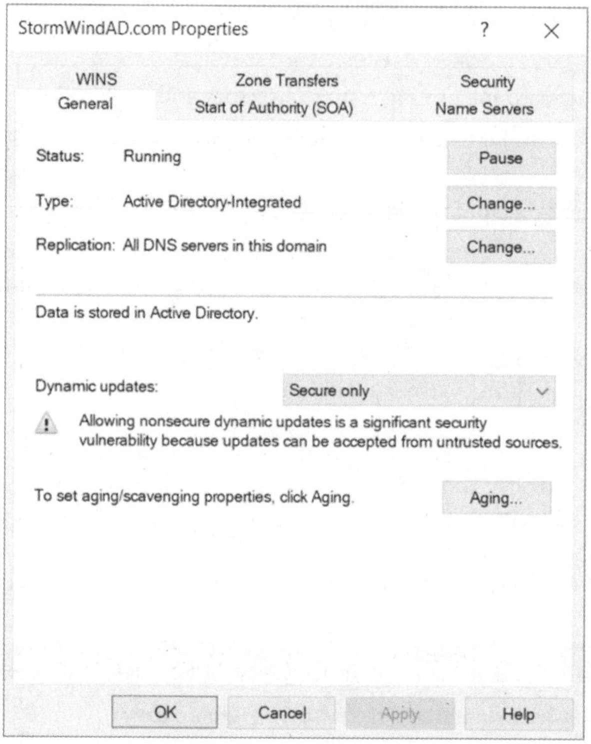

7. Verify that the Dynamic Updates option is set to Secure Only. This ensures that all updates to the DNS resource records database are made through authenticated Active Directory accounts and processes.

   The other options are Nonsecure And Secure (accepts all updates) and None (to disallow dynamic updates).

8. Finally, notice that you can define the security permissions at the zone level by clicking the Security tab. Make any necessary changes and click OK.

Active Directory Object Overview

Now that we have installed Active Directory, it's time for us to look at creating Active Directory objects.

Understanding Security Principals

Security principals are Active Directory objects that are assigned *security identifiers (SIDs)*. An SID is a unique identifier that is used to manage any object to which permissions can be assigned. Security principals are assigned permissions to perform certain actions and access certain network resources.

The following basic types of Active Directory objects serve as security principals:

User Accounts   User accounts identify individual users on your network by including information such as the user's name and their password. User accounts are the fundamental unit of security administration.

Groups   There are two main types of groups: security groups and distribution groups. Both types can contain user accounts. You use security groups to ease the management of security permissions. They use distribution groups, on the other hand, solely to send email. Distribution groups are not security principals.

Computer Accounts   Computer accounts identify which client computers are members of particular domains. Because these computers participate in the Active Directory database, you can manage security settings that affect the computer. You use computer accounts to determine whether a computer can join a domain and for authentication purposes. As you'll see later in this chapter, you can also place restrictions on certain computer settings to increase security. These settings apply to the computer and, therefore, also apply to any user who is using it (regardless of the permissions granted to the user account).

Note that other objects—such as OUs—do not function as security principals. What this means is that you can apply certain settings (such as Group Policy) on all of the objects within an OU; however, you cannot specifically set permissions with respect to the OU itself. The purpose of OUs is to organize other Active Directory objects logically based on business needs, add a needed level of control for security, and create an easier way to delegate.

You can manage security by performing the following actions with security principals:

- You can assign them permissions to access various network resources.
- You can give them user rights.
- You can track their actions through auditing (covered later in this chapter).

The major types of security principals—user accounts, groups, and computer accounts—form the basis of the Active Directory security architecture. As a system administrator, you will likely spend a portion of your time managing permissions for these objects.

It is important to understand that, since a unique SID defines each security principal, deleting a security principal is an irreversible process. For example, if you delete a user account and then later re-create one with the same name, you'll need to reassign permissions and group membership settings for the new account. Once a user account is deleted, its SID is deleted. This is why you should always consider disabling accounts instead of deleting them.

An Overview of OUs

An *organizational unit (OU)* is a logical group of Active Directory objects, just as the name implies. OUs serve as containers (see Figure 7.11) within which Active Directory objects can be created, but they do not form part of the DNS namespace. They are used solely to create organization within a domain.

FIGURE 7.11   Active Directory OUs

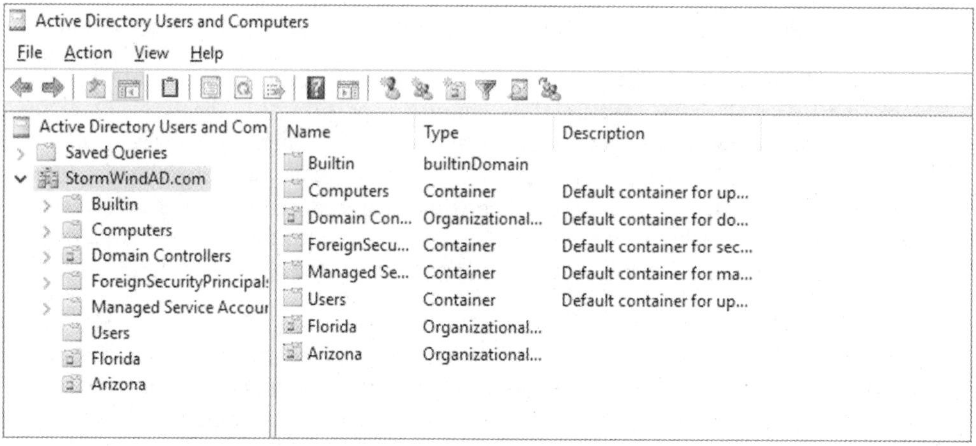

Name	Type	Description
Builtin	builtinDomain	
Computers	Container	Default container for up...
Domain Con...	Organizational...	Default container for do...
ForeignSecu...	Container	Default container for sec...
Managed Se...	Container	Default container for ma...
Users	Container	Default container for up...
Florida	Organizational...	
Arizona	Organizational...	

Active Directory Users and Computers
File   Action   View   Help

Active Directory Users and Com
> Saved Queries
∨ StormWindAD.com
  > Builtin
  > Computers
  > Domain Controllers
  > ForeignSecurityPrincipals
  > Managed Service Accounts
    Users
    Florida
    Arizona

OUs can contain the following types of Active Directory objects:

- Users
- Groups
- Computers
- Shared Folder objects
- Contacts
- Printers

- `InetOrgPerson` objects
- Microsoft Message Queuing (MSMQ) Queue aliases
- Other OUs

Perhaps the most useful feature of OUs is that they can contain other OU objects. As a result, you can hierarchically group resources and objects according to business practices. The OU structure is extremely flexible and, as you will see later in this chapter, can easily be rearranged to reflect business reorganizations.

Another advantage of OUs is that each can have its own set of policies. You can create individual and unique Group Policy Objects (GPOs) for each OU. GPOs are rules or policies that can apply to all of the objects within the OU.

Each type of object has its own purpose within the organization of Active Directory domains. Later in this chapter, we'll look at the specifics of User, Computer, Group, and Shared Folder objects. For now, let's focus on the purpose and benefits of using OUs.

The Purpose of OUs

OUs are mainly used to organize the objects within Active Directory. Before you dive into the details of OUs, however, you must understand how OUs, users, and groups interact. Most important, you should understand that OUs are simply containers that you can use to group various objects logically. They are not, however, groups in the classical sense. That is, they are not used for assigning security permissions. Another way of stating this is that the user accounts, computer accounts, and group accounts that are contained in OUs are considered security principals whereas the OUs themselves are not.

OUs do not take the place of standard user and group permissions. A good general practice is to assign users to groups and then place the groups within OUs. This approach enhances the benefits of setting security permissions and of using the OU hierarchy for making settings.

An OU contains objects only from within the domain in which it resides. As you'll see in the section "Delegating Administrative Control" later in this chapter, the OU is the finest level of granularity used for Group Policies and other administrative settings.

Benefits of OUs

There are many benefits to using OUs throughout your network environment:

- OUs are the smallest unit to which you can assign directory permissions.
- You can easily change the OU structure, and it is more flexible than the domain structure.
- The OU structure can support many different levels of hierarchy.
- Child objects can inherit OU settings.
- You can set Group Policy settings on OUs.
- You can easily delegate the administration of OUs and the objects within them to the appropriate users and groups.

Now that you have a good idea of why you should use OUs, let's take a look at some general practices you can use to plan the OU structure.

Planning the OU Structure

One of the key benefits of Active Directory is the way in which it can bring organization to complex network environments. Before you can begin to implement OUs in various configurations, you must plan a structure that is compatible with business and technical needs. Next, you'll learn about several factors that you should consider when planning for the structure of OUs.

Logical Grouping of Resources

The fundamental purpose of using OUs is to group resources (which exist within Active Directory) hierarchically. Fortunately, hierarchical groups are quite intuitive and widely used in most businesses. For example, a typical manufacturing business might divide its various operations into different departments as follows:

- Sales
- Marketing
- Engineering
- Research and Development
- Support
- Information Technology (IT)

Each of these departments usually has its own goals and mission. To make the business competitive, individuals within each of the departments are assigned to various roles. The following role types might be used:

- Managers
- Clerical staff
- Technical staff
- Planners

Each of these roles usually entails specific job responsibilities. For example, managers should provide direction to general staff members. Note that the very nature of these roles suggests that employees may fill many different positions. That is, one employee might be a manager in one department and a member of the technical staff in another. In the modern workplace, such situations are quite common.

All of this information helps you plan how to use OUs. First, the structure of OUs within a given network environment should map well to the business's needs, including the political and logical structure of the organization as well as its technical needs. Figure 7.12 shows how a business organization might be mapped to the OU structure within an Active Directory domain.

FIGURE 7.12   Mapping a business organization to an OU structure

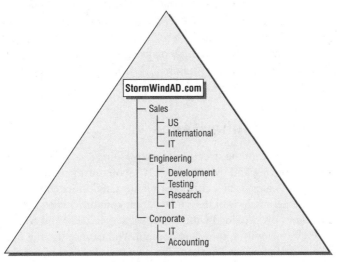

StormWindAD.com Domain

When naming OUs for your organization, you should keep several considerations and limitations in mind:

Keep the names and descriptions simple.   The purpose of OUs is to make administering and using resources simple. Therefore, it's always a good idea to keep the names of your objects simple and descriptive. Sometimes, finding a balance between these two goals can be a challenge. For example, although a printer name like "The LaserJet located near Bob's cube" might seem descriptive, it is certainly difficult to type. Also, imagine the naming changes that you might have to make if Bob moves (or leaves the company)!

Pay attention to limitations.   The maximum length for the name of an OU is 64 characters. In most cases, this should adequately describe the OU. Remember, the name of an OU does not have to describe the object uniquely because the OU is generally referenced only as part of the overall hierarchy. For example, you can choose to create an OU named "IT" within two different parent OUs. Even though the OUs have the same name, users and administrators are able to distinguish between them based on their complete pathname.

Pay attention to the hierarchical consistency.   The fundamental basis of an OU structure is its position in a hierarchy. From a design standpoint, this means you cannot have two OUs with the same name at the same level. However, you can have OUs with the same name at different levels. For example, you could create an OU named "Corporate" within the North America OU and another one within the South America OU. This is because the fully qualified domain name includes information about the hierarchy. When you try to access resources in a Corporate OU, you must specify which Corporate OU you mean.

For example, if you create a North America OU, the Canada OU should logically fit under it. If you decide that you want to separate the North America and Canada OUs into completely different containers, then you might want to use other, more appropriate names. For example, you could change North America to "U.S." Users and administrators depend on the hierarchy of OUs within the domain, so make sure that it remains logically consistent.

Based on these considerations, you should have a good idea of how best to organize the OU structure for your domain.

Understanding OU Inheritance

When you rearrange OUs within the structure of Active Directory, you can change several settings. When they are moving and reorganizing OUs, you must pay careful attention to automatic and unforeseen changes in security permissions and other configuration options. By default, OUs inherit the permissions of their new parent container when they are moved.

By using the built-in tools provided with Windows Server 2022 and Active Directory, you can move or copy OUs only within the same domain. You cannot use the Active Directory Users and Computers tool to move OUs between domains. To do this, use the *Active Directory Migration Tool (ADMT)*. This is one of the many Active Directory support tools.

Delegating Administrative Control

I already mentioned that OUs are the smallest component within a domain to which administrative permissions and Group Policies can be assigned by administrators. Now you'll take a look specifically at how administrative control is set on OUs.

Businesses generally have a division of labor that handles all of the tasks involved in keeping the company's networks humming. Network operating systems (NOSs), however, often make it difficult to assign just the right permissions; in other words, they do not support very granular permission assignments. Sometimes, fine granularity is necessary to ensure that only the right permissions are assigned. A good general rule of thumb is to provide users and administrators with the minimum permissions they require to do their jobs. This way, you can ensure that accidental, malicious, and otherwise unwanted changes do not occur.

In the world of Active Directory, you delegate to define responsibilities for OU administrators. As a system administrator, you will occasionally be tasked with having to delegate responsibility to others—you can't do it all, although sometimes administrators believe that they can. You understand the old IT logic of doing all of the tasks yourself for job security, but this can actually make you look worse.

     You can delegate control only at the OU level and not at the object level within the OU.

If you do find yourself in a role where you need to delegate, remember that Windows Server 2022 was designed to offer you the ability to do so. In its simplest definition, *delegation* allows a higher administrative authority to grant specific administrative rights for containers and subtrees to individuals and groups. What this essentially does is eliminate the need for domain administrators with sweeping authority over large segments of the user population. You can break up this control over branches within your tree, within each OU you create.

 To understand delegation and rights, you should first understand the concept of *access control entries (ACEs)*. ACEs grant specific administrative rights on objects in a container to a user or group. A container's access control list (ACL) is used to store ACEs.

When you are considering implementing delegation, keep these two concerns in mind:

Parent-Child Relationships   The OU hierarchy you create will be important when you consider the maintainability of security permissions. OUs can exist in a parent-child relationship, which means that permissions and group policies set on OUs higher up in the hierarchy (parents) can interact with objects in lower-level OUs (children). When it comes to delegating permissions, this is extremely important. You can allow child containers to inherit the permissions set on parent containers automatically. For example, if the North America division of your organization contains 12 other OUs, you could delegate permissions to all of them at once (saving time and reducing the likelihood of human error) by placing security permissions on the North America division. This feature can greatly ease administration, especially in larger organizations, but it is also a reminder of the importance of properly planning the OU structure within a domain.

Inheritance Settings   Now that you've seen how you can use parent-child relationships for administration, you should consider *inheritance*, the process in which child objects take on the permissions of a parent container. When you set permissions on a parent container, all of the child objects are configured to inherit the same permissions. You can override this behavior, however, if business rules do not lend themselves well to inheritance.

Applying Group Policies

One of the strengths of the Windows operating system is that it offers users a great deal of power and flexibility. From installing new software to adding device drivers, users can make many changes to their workstation configurations. However, this level of flexibility is also a potential problem. For instance, inexperienced users might inadvertently change settings, causing problems that can require many hours to fix.

In many cases (and especially in business environments), users require only a subset of the complete functionality the operating system provides. In the past, however, the difficulty associated with implementing and managing security and policy settings has led to lax security policies. Some of the reasons for this are technical—it can be tedious and difficult to implement and manage security restrictions. Other problems have been political—users and management might feel that they should have full permissions on their local machines, despite the potential problems this might cause.

That's where the idea of Group Policies comes in. *Group Policies* are collections of rules that you can apply to objects within Active Directory. Specifically, Group Policy settings are assigned at the site, domain, and OU levels, and they can apply to user accounts and computer accounts. For example, you can use Group Policies to configure the following settings:

- Restricting users from installing new programs
- Disallowing the use of Control Panel
- Limiting choices for display and desktop settings

Creating OUs

Now that we've looked at several ways in which OUs can be used to bring organization to the objects within Active Directory, it's time to examine how you can create and manage them.

Through the use of the *Active Directory Users and Computers administrative tool*, also called the *MMC (Microsoft Management Console)*, you can quickly and easily add, move, and change OUs. This graphical tool makes it easy to visualize and create the various levels of hierarchy an organization requires.

Figure 7.13 shows a geographically based OU structure that a multinational company might use. Note that the organization is based in North America and that it has a corporate office located there. In general, the other offices are much smaller than the corporate office located in North America.

FIGURE 7.13   A geographically based OU structure

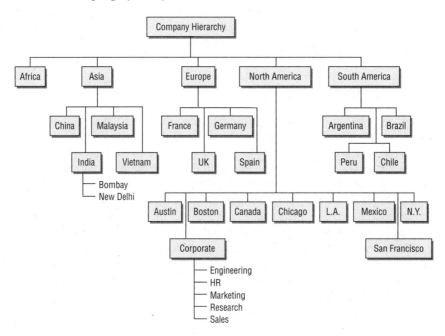

It's important to note that this OU structure could have been designed in several different ways. For example, I could have chosen to group all of the offices located in the United States within an OU named "U.S." However, because of the large size of these offices, I chose to place these objects at the same level as the Canada and Mexico OUs. This prevents an unnecessarily deep OU hierarchy while still logically grouping the offices.

One nice feature when creating an OU is the ability to protect the OU from being accidentally deleted. When you create an OU, you can select the Protect Container From Accidental Deletion option. This option prevents an administrator from deleting the OU. To delete the OU, you must go into the advanced view of the OU and deselect the option.

Exercise 7.8 walks you through the process of creating several OUs for a multinational business. You'll be using this OU structure in later exercises within this chapter.

To perform the exercises included in this chapter, you must have administrative access to a Windows Server 2022 domain controller.

EXERCISE 7.8

Creating an OU Structure

1. Open Active Directory Users and Computers by clicking Start ➢ Administrative Tools ➢ Active Directory Users And Computers.

2. Right-click the name of the local domain and choose New ➢ Organizational Unit.

3. Type **North America** for the name of the first OU (see Figure 7.14). Deselect the option Protect Container From Accidental Deletion and click OK to create this object.

FIGURE 7.14 New OU dialog box

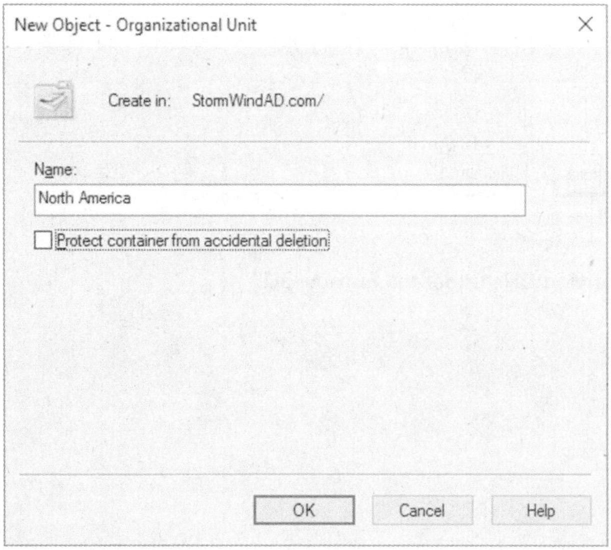

New Object - Organizational Unit	×
Create in: StormWindAD.com/	
Name:	
North America	
☐ Protect container from accidental deletion	
OK Cancel Help	

4. Create the following top-level OUs by right-clicking the name of the domain and choosing New ➤ Organizational Unit. Also make sure to deselect the Protect Container From Accidental Deletion option for all OUs in these exercises because you'll be deleting some of these OUs in later ones.

    Africa

    Asia

    Europe

    South America

    Note that the order in which you create the OUs is not important. In this exercise, you are simply using a method that emphasizes the hierarchical relationship.

5. Create the following second-level OUs within the North America OU by right-clicking the North America OU and selecting New ➤ Organizational Unit:

    Austin

    Boston

    Canada

    Chicago

    Corporate

    Los Angeles

    Mexico

    New York

    San Francisco

6. Create the following OUs under the Asia OU:

    China

    India

    Malaysia

    Vietnam

7. Create the following OUs under the Europe OU:

    France

    Germany

    Spain

    UK

8. Create the following OUs under the South America OU:

    Argentina

    Brazil

    Chile

    Peru

9. Create the following third-level OUs under the India OU by right-clicking India within the Asia OU and selecting New ➢ Organizational Unit:

    Bombay

    New Delhi

10. Within the North America Corporate OU, create the following OUs:

    Engineering

    HR

    Marketing

    Research

    Sales

11. When you have completed creating the OUs, close Active Directory.

Managing OUs

Managing network environments would still be challenging, even if things rarely changed. However, in the real world, business units, departments, and employee roles change frequently. As business and technical needs change, so should the structure of Active Directory.

Fortunately, changing the structure of OUs within a domain is a relatively simple process. In the following sections, you'll look at ways to delegate control of OUs and make other changes.

Moving, Deleting, and Renaming OUs

The process of moving, deleting, and renaming OUs is a simple one. Exercise 7.9 shows how you can easily modify and reorganize OUs to reflect changes in the business organization. The specific scenario covered in this exercise includes the following changes:

- The Research and Engineering departments have been combined to form a department known as Research and Development (RD).

- The Sales department has been moved from the Corporate headquarters office to the New York office.

- The Marketing department has been moved from the Corporate headquarters office to the Chicago office.

This exercise assumes you have already completed the steps in Exercise 7.8.

EXERCISE 7.9

Modifying OU Structure

1. Open Active Directory Users and Computers by clicking Start ≻ Administrative Tools ≻ Active Directory Users And Computers.

2. Right-click the Engineering OU (located within North America ≻ Corporate) and click Delete. When you are prompted for confirmation, click Yes. Note that if this OU contained objects, they would have all been automatically deleted as well.

3. Right-click the Research OU and select Rename. Type **RD** to change the name of the OU and press Enter.

4. Right-click the Sales OU and select Move. In the Move dialog box, expand the North America branch and click the New York OU. Click OK to move the OU.

5. You will use an alternate method to move the Marketing OU. Drag the Marketing OU and drop it onto the Chicago OU.

6. When you have finished, close the Active Directory Users and Computers administrative tool.

Administering Properties of OUs

Although OUs are primarily created for organizational purposes within the Active Directory environment, they have several settings that you can modify. To modify the properties of an OU using Active Directory Users and Computers, right-click the name of any OU and select Properties. When you do, the OU Properties dialog box appears. In the example shown in Figure 7.15, you'll see the options on the General tab.

FIGURE 7.15 The General tab of the OU's Properties dialog box

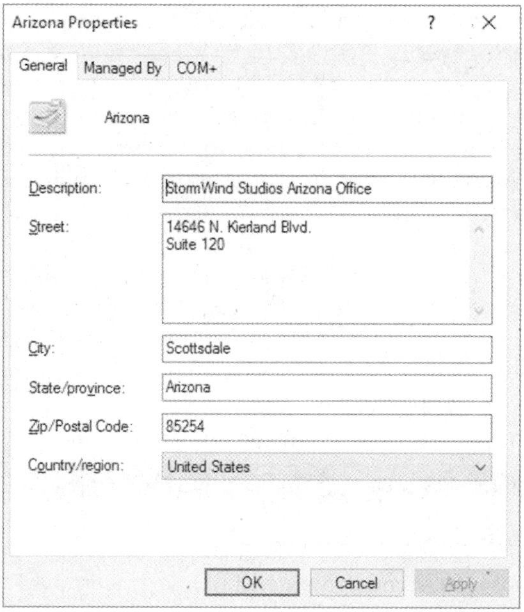

In any organization, it helps to know who is responsible for managing an OU. You can set this information on the Managed By tab (see Figure 7.16). The information specified on this tab is convenient because it is automatically pulled from the contact information on a user record. You should consider always having a contact for each OU within your organization so that other system administrators know whom to contact if they need to make any changes.

FIGURE 7.16 The Managed By tab of the OU's Properties dialog box

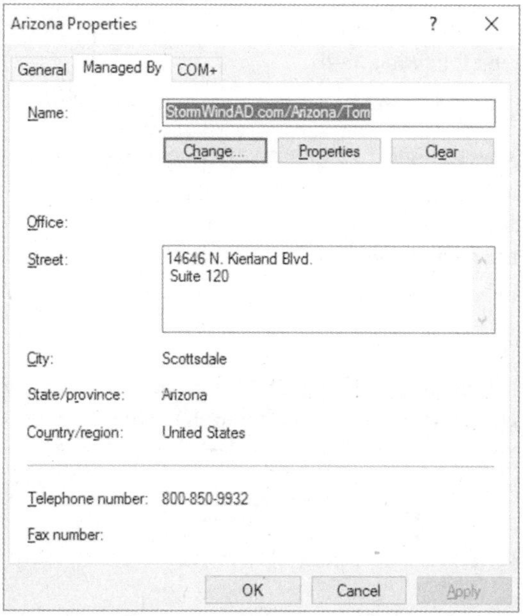

Delegating Control of OUs

In simple environments, one or a few system administrators may be responsible for managing all of the settings within Active Directory. For example, a single system administrator could manage all users within all OUs in the environment. In larger organizations, however, roles and responsibilities may be divided among many different individuals. A typical situation is one in which a system administrator is responsible for objects within only a few OUs in an Active Directory domain. Alternatively, one system administrator might manage User and Group objects while another is responsible for managing file and print services.

Fortunately, using the Active Directory Users and Computers tool, you can quickly and easily ensure that specific users receive only the permissions they need. In Exercise 7.10, you will use the Delegation Of Control Wizard to assign permissions to individuals. To complete these steps successfully, first you must have created the objects in the previous exercises of this chapter.

EXERCISE 7.10

Using the Delegation Of Control Wizard

1. Open Active Directory Users and Computers by clicking Start ➢ Administrative Tools ➢ Active Directory Users And Computers.

2. Right-click the Corporate OU within the North America OU and select Delegate Control. This starts the Delegation Of Control Wizard. Click Next to begin configuring security settings.

3. On the Users Or Groups page, click the Add button. In the Enter The Object Names To Select field, enter **Account Operators** and click the Check Names button. Click OK. Click Next to continue.

4. In the Tasks To Delegate page, select Delegate The Following Common Tasks and place a check mark next to the following items:

    Create, Delete, And Manage User Accounts

    Reset User Passwords And Force Password Change At Next Logon

    Read All User Information

    Create, Delete, And Manage Groups

    Modify The Membership Of A Group

5. Click Next to continue.

6. The Completing The Delegation Of Control Wizard page then provides a summary of the operations you have selected. To implement the changes, click Finish.

Although the common tasks available through the wizard are sufficient for many delegation operations, you may have cases in which you want more control. For example, you might want to give a particular system administrator permission to modify only Computer objects. Exercise 7.11 uses the Delegation Of Control Wizard to assign more granular permissions. To complete these steps successfully, you must have completed the previous exercises in this chapter.

EXERCISE 7.11

Delegating Custom Tasks

1. Open Active Directory Users and Computers by clicking Start ≻ Administrative Tools ≻ Active Directory Users And Computers.

2. Right-click the Corporate OU within the North America OU and select Delegate Control. This starts the Delegation Of Control Wizard. Click Next to begin making security settings.

3. In the Users Or Groups page, click the Add button. In the Enter The Object Names To Select field, enter **Server Operators** and click the Check Names button. Click OK and then click Next to continue.

4. In the Tasks To Delegate page, select the Create A Custom Task To Delegate radio button and click Next to continue.

5. In the Active Directory Object Type page, select Only The Following Objects In The Folder and place a check mark next to the following items. (You will have to scroll down to see them all.)

   User Objects

   Computer Objects

   Contact Objects

   Group Objects

   Organizational Unit Objects

   Printer Objects

6. Click Next to continue.

7. On the Permissions page, select the General option and make sure the other options are not selected. Note that if the various objects within your Active Directory schema had property-specific settings, you would see those options here. Place a check mark next to the following items:

   Create All Child Objects

   Read All Properties

   Write All Properties

This gives the members of the Server Operators group the ability to create new objects within the Corporate OU and the permissions to read and write all properties for these objects.

8. Click Next to continue.

9. The Completing The Delegation Of Control Wizard page provides a summary of the operations you have selected. To implement the changes, click Finish.

Creating and Managing Active Directory Objects

Now that you are familiar with the task of creating OUs, you should find creating and managing other Active Directory objects quite simple. This section will examine the details.

Overview of Active Directory Objects

When you install and configure a domain controller, Active Directory sets up an organizational structure for you, and you can create and manage several types of objects.

Active Directory Organization

When you are looking at your Active Directory structure, you will see objects that look like folders in Windows Explorer. These objects are containers, or *organizational units (OUs)*. The difference is that an OU is a container to which you can link a GPO. Normal containers cannot have a GPO linked to them. That's what makes an OU a special container.

By default, after you install and configure a domain controller, you will see the following organizational sections within the Active Directory Users and Computers tool (they look like folders):

Built-In   The *Built-In container* includes all of the standard groups that are installed by default when you promote a domain controller. You can use these groups to administer the servers in your environment. Examples include the Administrators group, Backup Operators group, and Print Operators group.

Computers   By default, the *Computers container* contains a list of the workstations in your domain. From here, you can manage all of the computers in your domain.

Domain Controllers   The *Domain Controllers OU* includes a list of all the domain controllers for the domain.

Foreign Security Principals   In environments that have more than one domain, you may need to grant permissions to users who reside in multiple domains. Generally, you manage this using Active Directory trees and forests. However, in some cases, you may want to provide resources to users who belong to domains that are not part of the forest.

Active Directory uses the concept of foreign security principals to allow permissions to be assigned to users who are not part of an Active Directory forest. This process is automatic and does not require the intervention of system administrators. You can then add the foreign security principals to domain local groups for which, in turn, you can grant permissions for resources within the domain. You can view a list of foreign security principals by using the Active Directory Users and Computers tool.

Foreign security principals containers are any objects to which security can be assigned and that are not part of the current domain. Security principals are Active Directory objects to which permissions can be applied, and they can be used to manage permissions in Active Directory.

Managed Service Accounts   The Managed Service Accounts container is a Windows Server 2022 container. Service accounts are accounts created to run specific services such as Exchange and SQL Server. Having a Managed Service Accounts container allows you to control the service accounts better and thus allows for better service account security. To create Managed Service Accounts, you must use the `New-ADServiceAccount` PowerShell command.

Users   The *Users container* includes all the security accounts that are part of the domain. When you first install the domain controller, there will be several groups in this container. For example, the Domain Admins group and the administrator account are created in this container.

You want to be sure to protect the administrator account. You should rename the admin account and make sure the password is complex. Protected admin accounts can make your network safer. Every hacker knows that there is an administrator account on the server by default. Be sure to make your network safer by protecting the admin account.

Active Directory Objects

You can create and manage several different types of Active Directory objects. The following are specific object types:

Computer   *Computer objects* represent workstations that are part of the Active Directory domain. All computers within a domain share the same security database, including user and group information. Computer objects are useful for managing security permissions and enforcing Group Policy restrictions.

Contact *Contact objects* are usually used in OUs to specify the main administrative contact. Contacts are not security principals like users. They are used to specify information about individuals outside the organization.

Group *Group objects* are logical collections of users primarily for assigning security permissions to resources. When managing users, you should place them into groups and then assign permissions to the group. This allows for flexible management without the need to set permissions for individual users.

InetOrgPerson The InetOrgPerson *object* is an Active Directory object that defines attributes of users in Lightweight Directory Access Protocol (LDAP) and X.500 directories.

MSIMaging-PSPs MSIMaging-PSPs is a container for all Enterprise Scan Post Scan Process objects.

MSMQ Queue Alias An *MSMQ Queue Alias object* is an Active Directory object for the MSMQ-Custom-Recipient class type. The Microsoft Message Queuing (MSMQ) Queue Alias object associates an Active Directory path and a user-defined alias with a public, private, or direct single-element format name. This allows a queue alias to be used to reference a queue that might not be listed in Active Directory Domain Services (AD DS).

Organizational Unit An *OU object* is created to build a hierarchy within the Active Directory domain. It is the smallest unit that can be used to create administrative groupings, and it can be used to assign group policies. Generally, the OU structure within a domain reflects a company's business organization.

Printer *Printer objects* map to printers.

Shared Folder *Shared Folder objects* map to server shares. They are used to organize the various file resources that may be available on file/print servers. Often, Shared Folder objects are used to give logical names to specific file collections. For example, you might create separate shared folders for common applications, user data, and shared public files.

User A *User object* is the fundamental security principal on which Active Directory is based. User accounts contain information about individuals as well as password and other permission information.

Creating Objects Using the Active Directory Users and Computers Tool

Exercise 7.12 walks you through the steps necessary to create various objects within an Active Directory domain. In this exercise, you create some basic Active Directory objects. To complete this exercise, you must have access to at least one Active Directory domain controller, and you should have also completed the previous exercises in this chapter.

EXERCISE 7.12

Creating Active Directory Objects

1. Open Active Directory Users and Computers by clicking Start ➢ Administrative Tools ➢ Active Directory Users And Computers.

2. Expand the current domain to list the objects currently contained within it. For this exercise, you will use the second- and third-level OUs contained within the North America top-level OU.

3. Right-click the Corporate OU and select New ➢ User. Fill in the following information:

    First Name: **Maria**

    Initial: **D**

    Last Name: **President**

    Full Name: (leave as default)

    User Logon Name: **mdpresident** (leave default domain)

    Click Next to continue.

4. Enter **P@ssw0rd** for the password for this user and then confirm it. Note that you can also make changes to password settings here. Click Next.

5. You will see a summary of the user information. Click Finish to create the new user.

6. Click the RD container and create another user in that container with the following information:

    First Name: **John**

    Initial: **Q**

    Last Name: **Adams**

    Full Name: (leave as default)

    User Logon Name: **jqadams** (leave default domain)

    Click Next to continue.

7. Assign the password **P@ssw0rd**. Click Next and then click Finish to create the user.

8. Right-click the RD OU and select New ➢ Contact. Use the following information to fill in the properties of the Contact object:

    First Name: **Jane**

    Initials: **R**

    Last Name: **Admin**

    Display Name: **jradmin**

    Click OK to create the new Contact object.

EXERCISE 7.12 *(continued)*

9. Right-click the RD OU and select New ➤ Shared Folder. Enter **Software** for the name and **\\server1\applications** for the network path (also known as the Universal Naming Convention [UNC] path). Note that you can create the object even though this resource (the physical server) does not exist. Click OK to create the Shared Folder object.

10. Right-click the HR OU and select New ➤ Group. Type **All Users** for the group name. Do not change the value in the Group Name (Pre–Windows 2000) field. For Group Scope, select Global, and for Group Type, select Security. To create the group, click OK.

11. Right-click the Sales OU and select New ➤ Computer. Type **Workstation1** for the name of the computer. Notice that the pre–Windows 2000 name is automatically populated and that, by default, the members of the Domain Admins group are the only ones who can add this computer to the domain. Select the Assign This Computer Account As A Pre-Windows 2000 Computer option and then click OK to create the Computer object.

12. Close the Active Directory Users and Computers tool.

Configuring the User Principal Name

When you log into a domain, your logon name looks like an email address (for example, wpanek@willpanek.com). This is called your *user principal name (UPN)*. A UPN is the username followed by the @ sign and the domain name. At the time the user account is created, the UPN suffix is generated by default. The UPN is created as *userName@DomainName*, but you can alter or change the default UPN. If your forest has multiple domains and you need to change the UPN to a different domain, you have that ability. To change the UPN suffix, in Active Directory Users and Computers, choose a user and go into their properties. Select the Attribute Editor tab. Scroll down to the userPrincipalName attribute and make your changes. These changes then get replicated to the Global Catalog.

> **NOTE** If your organization has multiple forests set up by a trust, you can't change the UPN to a domain in the other forest. Global Catalogs are used to log on users. Because UPNs get replicated to the local forest Global Catalog servers, you cannot log onto other forests using the UPN.

Using Templates

Now we're going to dive into user templates. *User templates* allow an Active Directory administrator to create a default account (for example, template_sales) and use that account to create all of the other users who match it (all the salespeople).

If you are creating multiple accounts, this can save you a lot of time and resources. For example, if you need to add 35 new salespeople to your company, you'll create one template for sales and use a copy of that template for all of the other new accounts. This saves you the trouble of filling out many of the same fields over and over again. When you copy a template, some of the information does *not* get copied over. This is because it is user-specific information. Here are some of the fields that do not get copied over from a template:

- Name
- Logon Name
- Password
- Email
- Phone Numbers
- Description
- Office
- Web Page

Many of the important fields such as Member Of (groups to which the user belongs), Profile Path, Department, and Company all get copied over. There is one important item that needs to be done when creating a template: the template account needs to be disabled after creation. You do not want anyone using this account to access your network. In Exercise 7.13, you will create a template to use for your Sales department.

EXERCISE 7.13

Creating a User Template

1. Open Active Directory Users and Computers by clicking Start ➤ Administrative Tools ➤ Active Directory Users And Computers.

2. Expand the current domain to list the objects contained within it. For this exercise, you will use the Sales OU. Right-click the Sales OU and choose New ➤ User.

3. Use the following properties:

    First Name: **Sales**

    Last Name: **Template**

    Username: **sales_template**

    Password: **P@ssw0rd**

4. Click Next and then click Finish.

5. In the right window, double-click the Sales Template user to open the properties.

6. On the General tab, complete the following items:

    Description: **Template Account**

    Office: **Corporate**

    Telephone: **999-999-9999**

    Email: **Salet@abc.com**

    Web: **www.abc.com**

7. Click the Profile tab. In the Profile Path field, type **\\ServerA\%username%**.

8. On the Members Of tab, click the Add button. At the Enter The Object Name To Select box, type **Administrator** and click the Check Names button. (Normally you would not add salespeople to the Administrators group, but you are doing so just for this exercise.) Click OK.

9. Click the Account tab. Scroll down in the Account Options box and select the Account Is Disabled option.

10. Click OK in the user's Properties window to go back to the Sales OU.

11. Right-click the Sales Template account and choose Copy.

12. Enter the following information:

> First Name: **Jenny**
>
> Last Name: **Sales**
>
> Username: **jsales**
>
> Password: **P@ssw0rd**

Deselect the Account Is Disabled option.

13. In the right window, double-click the Jenny Sales user to open the properties.

14. Take a look at the Members Of tab, the General tab, and the Profile tab, and you will see that some of the fields are prefilled (including the Administrators group).

15. Close Jenny Sales Properties and exit Active Directory Users and Computers.

Importing Objects from a File

In Exercise 7.13, you created an account using the Active Directory Users and Computers tool. But what if you need to bulk import accounts? There are two main applications for doing bulk imports of accounts: the ldifde.exe utility and the csvde.exe utility. Both utilities import accounts from files.

The ldifde.exe utility imports from line-delimited files. It allows you to export and import data, thus allowing batch operations such as Add, Modify, and Delete to be performed in Active Directory. Windows Server 2022 includes ldifde.exe to help support batch operations.

The csvde.exe utility performs the same export functions as ldifde.exe, but csvde.exe uses a comma-separated value file format. The csvde.exe utility does not allow you to modify or delete objects. It only supports adding objects to Active Directory.

Active Directory Migration Tool

Another tool that administrators have used in the past is *Active Directory Migration Tool (ADMT)*. ADMT allows you to migrate users, groups, and computers from a previous version of the server to a current version of the server.

Administrators also used ADMT to migrate users, groups, and computers between Active Directory domains in different forests (interforest migration) and between Active Directory domains in the same forest (intraforest migration).

As of this writing, Microsoft had not yet released a new version of ADMT that is supported by Windows Server 2022. The reason I even mention it in this book is because Microsoft may be releasing a version of it soon and I wanted you to understand what it can do. Continue to check the Microsoft website to see whether a new version has been released.

Offline Domain Join of a Computer

Offline domain join gives you the ability to preprovision computer accounts in the domain to prepare operating systems for deployments. At startup, computers can then join the domain without the need to contact a domain controller. This helps reduce the time it takes to deploy computers in a datacenter.

Let's say your datacenter needs to have multiple virtual machines deployed. This is where offline domain join can be useful. Upon initial startup after the operating system is installed, offline domain join allows the virtual machines to join the domain automatically. No additional steps or restarts are needed.

The following are some of the benefits of using offline domain join:

- There is no additional network traffic for Active Directory state changes.

- There is no additional network traffic for computer state changes to the domain controller.

- Changes for both the Active Directory state and the computer state can be completed at a different times.

Managing Object Properties

Once you've created the necessary Active Directory objects, you'll probably need to make changes to their default properties. In addition to the settings you made when you were creating Active Directory objects, you can configure several more properties. You can also access object properties by right clicking any object and selecting Properties from the pop-up menu.

Each object type contains a unique set of properties.

User Object Properties

The following list describes some of the properties of a User object (see Figure 7.17):

FIGURE 7.17 User Properties

General General account information about this user

Address Physical location information about this user

Account User logon name and other account restrictions, such as workstation restrictions and logon hours

Profile Information about the user's roaming profile settings

Telephones Telephone contact information for the user

Organization The user's title, department, and company information

Member Of Group membership information for the user

Dial-In Remote Access Service (RAS) permissions for the user

Environment Logon and other network settings for the user

Sessions Session limits, including maximum session time and idle session settings

Remote Control Remote control options for this user's session

Remote Desktop Services Profile   Information about the user's profile for use with Remote Desktop Services

Personal Virtual Desktop   Allows you to assign a user a specific virtual machine to use as a personal virtual desktop

COM+   Specifies a COM+ partition set for the user

Computer Object Properties

Computer objects have different properties than User objects. Computer objects refer to the systems that clients are operating to be part of a domain. The following list describes some Computer object properties:

General   Information about the name of the computer, the role of the computer, and its description

(You can enable an option to allow the Local System account of this machine to request services from other servers. This is useful if the machine is a trusted and secure computer.)

Operating System   The name, version, and service pack information for the operating system running on the computer

Member Of   Active Directory groups of which this Computer object is a member

Delegation   Allows you to set services that work on behalf of another user

Location   A description of the computer's physical location

Managed By   Information about the User or Contact object that is responsible for managing this computer

Dial-In   Sets dial-in options for the computer

Setting Properties for Active Directory Objects

Now that you have seen the various properties that can be set for the Active Directory objects, let's complete an exercise on how to configure some of these properties. Exercise 7.14 walks you through how to set various properties for Active Directory objects. To complete the steps in this exercise, first you must have completed Exercise 7.12.

Although it may seem a bit tedious, it's always a good idea to enter as much information as you know about Active Directory objects when you create them. Although the name Printer1 may be meaningful to you, users will appreciate the additional information, such as location, when they are searching for objects.

EXERCISE 7.14

Managing Object Properties

1. Open Active Directory Users and Computers by clicking Start ➢ Administrative Tools ➢ Active Directory Users And Computers.

2. Expand the name of the domain and select the RD container. Right-click the John Q. Adams user account and select Properties.

3. Here you will see the various Properties tabs for the User account. Make some configuration changes based on your personal preferences. Click OK to continue.

4. Select the HR OU. Right-click the All Users group and click Properties. In the All Users Properties dialog box, you will be able to modify the membership of the group.

   Click the Members tab and then click Add. Add the Maria D. President and John Q. Admin user accounts to the group. Click OK to save the settings and then click OK to accept the group modifications.

5. Select the Sales OU. Right-click the Workstation1 Computer object. Notice that you can choose to disable the account or reset it (to allow another computer to join the domain under that same name). From the context menu, choose Properties. You'll see the properties for the Computer object.

   Examine the various options and make changes based on your personal preference. After you have examined the available options, click OK to continue.

6. Select the Corporate OU. Right-click the Maria D. President user account and choose Reset Password. You will be prompted to enter a new password, and then you'll be asked to confirm it. Note that you can also force the user to change this password upon the next logon, and you can also unlock the user's account from here. For this exercise, do not enter a new password; just click Cancel.

7. Close the Active Directory Users and Computers tool.

By now, you have probably noticed that Active Directory objects have a lot of common options. For example, Group and Computer objects both have a Managed By tab.

Windows Server 2022 allows you to manage many User objects at once. For instance, you can select several User objects by holding down the Shift or Ctrl key while selecting. You can then right-click any one of the selected objects and select Properties to display the properties that are available for multiple users. Notice that not every user property is available because some properties are unique to each user. You can configure the Description field for multiple object selections that include both users and nonusers, such as computers and groups.

> An important thing to think about when it comes to accounts is the difference between disabling an account and deleting an account. When you delete an account, the security ID (SID) gets deleted. Even if you later create an account with the same username, it will have a different SID number, and therefore it will be a different account. It is sometimes better to disable an account and place it into a nonactive OU called *Disabled*. This way, if you ever need to reaccess the account, you can do so.

Another object management task is the process of deprovisioning. *Deprovisioning* is the management of Active Directory objects in the container. When you remove an object from an Active Directory container, the deprovisioning process removes the object and synchronizes the container to stay current.

Understanding Groups

Now that you know how to create user accounts, it's time to learn how to create group accounts. As an instructor, I am always amazed when students (who work in the IT field) have no idea why they should use groups. This is something every organization should be using.

To illustrate their usefulness, let's say you have a Sales department user by the name of wpanek. Your organization has 100 resources shared on the network for users to access. Because wpanek is part of the Sales department, he has access to 50 of the resources. The Marketing department uses the other 50. If the organization is not using groups and wpanek moves from Sales to Marketing, how many changes do you have to make? The answer is 100. You have to move him out of the 50 resources he currently can use and place his account into the 50 new resources that he now needs.

Now let's say that you use groups. The Sales group has access to 50 resources, and the Marketing group has access to the other 50. If wpanek moves from Sales to Marketing, you need to make only two changes. You just have to take wpanek out of the Sales group and place him in the Marketing group. Once this is done, wpanek can access everything he needs to do his job.

Group Properties

Now that you understand why you should use groups, let's go over setting up groups and their properties (see Figure 7.18). When you are creating groups, it helps to understand some of the options that you need to use.

FIGURE 7.18   New Group dialog box

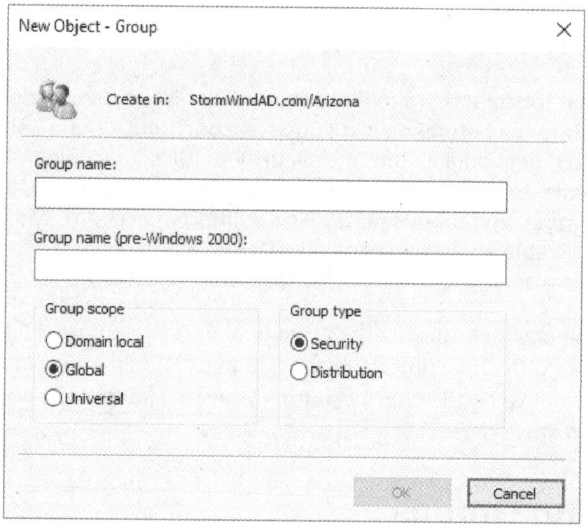

Group Type   You can choose from two group types: security groups and distribution groups.

> **Security Groups**   These groups can have rights and permissions placed on them. For example, if you want to give a certain group of users access to a particular printer but you want to control what they are allowed to do with this printer, you'd create a security group and then apply certain rights and permissions to this group.
>
> Security groups can also receive emails. If someone sent an email to the group, all users within that group would receive it (as long as they have a mail system that allows for mail-enabled groups, like Exchange).
>
> **Distribution Groups**   These groups are used for email *only* (as long as they have a mail system that allows for mail-enabled groups, like Exchange). You cannot place permissions and rights for objects on this group type.

Group Scope   When it comes to group scopes, you have three choices:

> **Domain Local Groups**   Domain local groups are groups that remain in the domain in which they were created. You use these groups to grant permissions within a single domain. For example, if you create a domain local group named HPLaser, you cannot use that group in any other domain, and it has to reside in the domain in which you created it.
>
> **Global Groups**   Global groups can contain other groups and accounts from the domain in which the group is created. In addition, you can give them permissions in any domain in the forest.

Universal Groups   Universal groups can include other groups and accounts from any domain in the domain tree or forest. You can give universal groups permissions in any domain in the domain tree or forest.

Creating Group Strategies

When you are creating a group strategy, think of this acronym that Microsoft likes to use in the exam: AGDLP (or AGLP). This acronym stands for a series of actions you should perform. Here is how it expands:

A   Accounts (Create your user accounts.)

G   Global groups (Put user accounts into global groups.)

DL   Domain local groups (Put global groups into domain local groups.)

P   Permissions (Assign permissions such as Deny or Apply on the domain local group.)

Another acronym that stands for a strategy you can use is AGUDLP (or AULP). Here is how it expands:

A   Accounts (Create your user accounts.)

G   Global groups (Put user accounts into global groups.)

U   Universal groups (Put the global groups into universal groups.)

DL   Domain local groups (Put universal groups into domain local groups.)

P   Permissions (Place permissions on the local group.)

Creating a Group

To create a new group, open the Active Directory Users and Computers snap-in. Click the OU where the group is going to reside. Right-click and choose New and then Group. After you create the group, select the Members tab and click Add. Add the users you want to reside in that group, and that's all there is to it.

Filtering and Advanced Active Directory Features

The Active Directory Users and Computers tool has a couple of other features that come in quite handy when you are managing many objects. You can access the Filter Options dialog box by clicking the View menu in the MMC and choosing Filter Options. You'll see a dialog box similar to the one shown in Figure 7.19. Here you can choose to filter objects by their specific types within the display. For example, if you are an administrator who works primarily with user accounts and groups, you can select those specific items by placing check marks in the list. In addition, you can create more complex filters by clicking Create Custom. Doing so provides you with an interface that looks similar to that of the Find command.

FIGURE 7.19   The Filter Options dialog box

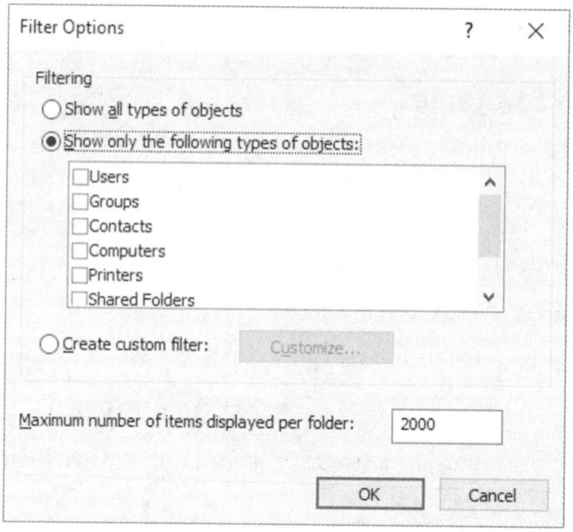

Another option in the Active Directory Users and Computers tool is to view advanced options. You can enable the advanced options by choosing Advanced Features in the View menu. This adds some top-level folders to the list under the name of the domain. Let's take a look at a couple of the new top-level folders.

The `System` folder (shown in Figure 7.20) provides additional features that you can configure to work with Active Directory. You can configure settings for the Distributed File System (DFS), IP Security (IPsec) policies, the File Replication Service (FRS), and more. In addition to the `System` folder, you'll see the `LostAndFound` folder. This folder contains any files that may not have been replicated properly between domain controllers. You should check this folder periodically for any files so that you can decide whether you need to move them or copy them to other locations.

FIGURE 7.20   Advanced Features in the System folder of the Active Directory Users and Computers tool

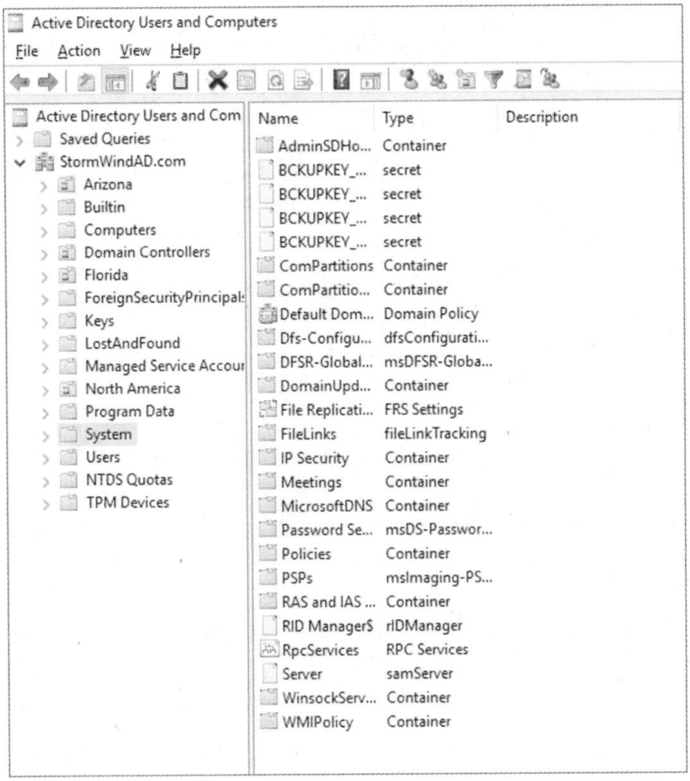

As you can see, managing Active Directory objects is generally a simple task. The Active Directory Users and Computers tool allows you to configure several objects. Let's move on to look at one more common administration function: moving objects.

Moving, Renaming, and Deleting Active Directory Objects

One of the extremely useful features of the Active Directory Users and Computers tool is its ability to move users and resources easily.

Exercise 7.15 walks you through the process of moving Active Directory objects. In this exercise, you will make several changes to the organization of Active Directory objects. To complete this exercise, first you must have completed Exercise 7.12.

EXERCISE 7.15

Moving Active Directory Objects

1. Open Active Directory Users and Computers by clicking Start ➢ Administrative Tools ➢ Active Directory Users And Computers.

2. Expand the name of the domain.

3. Select the Sales OU (under the New York OU), right-click Workstation1, and select Move. A dialog box appears. Select the RD OU and click OK to move the Computer object to that container.

4. Click the RD OU and verify that Workstation1 was moved.

5. Close the Active Directory Users and Computers tool.

In addition to moving objects within Active Directory, you can easily rename them by right-clicking an object and selecting Rename. Note that this option does not apply to all objects. You can remove objects from Active Directory by right-clicking them and choosing Delete.

Resetting an Existing Computer Account

Every computer on the domain establishes a discrete channel of communication with the domain controller at logon time. The domain controller stores a randomly selected password (different from the user password) for authentication across the channel. The password is updated every 30 days.

Sometimes the computer's password and the domain controller's password don't match, and communication between the two machines fails. Without the ability to reset the computer account, you wouldn't be able to connect the machine to the domain. Fortunately, you can use the Active Directory Users and Computers tool to reestablish the connection.

Exercise 7.16 shows you how to reset an existing computer account. You should have completed the previous exercises in this chapter before you begin this one.

EXERCISE 7.16

Resetting an Existing Computer Account

1. Open Active Directory Users and Computers by clicking Start ➢ Administrative Tools ➢ Active Directory Users And Computers.

2. Expand the name of the domain.

3. Click the RD OU and then right-click the Workstation1 computer account.

4. Select Reset Account from the context menu. Click Yes to confirm your selection. Click OK at the success prompt.

5. When you reset the account, you break the connection between the computer and the domain. So, after performing this exercise, reconnect the computer to the domain if you want it to continue working on the network.

Throughout this book, I have shown you the PowerShell way of doing a task shown previously using an MMC snap-in. Well, this is going to be no different.

This example shows you how to reset the secure connection between the local computer and the domain to which it is joined using a PowerShell command. In this example, the domain controller that performs the operation is specified as `StormDC1.StormWindAD.com`. To execute this PowerShell command, you must run this command on the local computer:

```
Test-ComputerSecureChannel -Repair -Server StormDC1.StormWindAD.com
```

Understanding Dynamic Access Control

One of the advantages of Windows Server 2022 is the ability to apply data governance to your file server. This will help control who has access to information and auditing. You get these advantages through the use of *Dynamic Access Control (DAC)*. DAC allows you to identify data by using data classifications (both automatic and manual) and then control access to these files based on these classifications.

DAC also gives you the ability to control file access by using a central access policy. This central access policy will also allow you to set up audit access to files for reporting and forensic investigation.

DAC allows you to set up Active Directory Rights Management Service encryption for Microsoft Office documents. For example, you can set up encryption for any documents that contain financial information.

DAC gives you the flexibility to configure file access and auditing to domain-based file servers. To do this, DAC controls claims in the authentication token, resource properties, and conditional expressions within permission and auditing entries.

You have the ability to give users access to files and folders based on Active Directory attributes. For example, a user named Dana is given access to the file server share because in the user's Active Directory (department attribute) properties, the value contains the value Sales.

Managing Security and Permissions

Now that you understand the basic issues, terms, and Active Directory objects that pertain to security, it's time to look at how you can apply this information to secure your network resources. The general practice for managing security is to assign users to groups and then grant permissions and logon parameters to the groups so that they can access certain resources.

For management ease and to implement a hierarchical structure, you can place groups within OUs. You can also assign Group Policy settings to all of the objects contained within an OU. By using this method, you can combine the benefits of a hierarchical structure (through OUs) with the use of security principals.

The primary tool you use to manage security permissions for users, groups, and computers is the Active Directory Users and Computers tool. Using this tool, you can create and manage Active Directory objects and organize them based on your business needs. Common tasks for many system administrators might include the following:

- Resetting a user's password (for example, in cases where they forget their password)

- Creating new user accounts (when, for instance, a new employee joins the company)

- Modifying group memberships based on changes in job requirements and functions

- Disabling user accounts (when, for example, users will be out of the office for long periods of time and will not require network resource access)

Once you've properly grouped your users, you need to set the actual permissions that affect the objects within Active Directory. The actual permissions that are available vary based on the type of object. Table 7.4 provides an example of some of the permissions that you can apply to various Active Directory objects and an explanation of what each permission does.

TABLE 7.4   Permissions of Active Directory objects

Permission	Explanation
Control Access	Changes security permissions on the object
Create Child	Creates objects within an OU (such as other OUs)
Delete Child	Deletes child objects within an OU
Delete Tree	Deletes an OU and the objects within it
List Contents	Views objects within an OU
List Object	Views a list of the objects within an OU
Read	Views properties of an object (such as a username)
Write	Modifies properties of an object

Configure Password Policies

All administrator and user accounts that have been created and maintained in Azure AD have a password policy applied. With a password policy you can prohibit weak passwords and set parameters that will lock out an account after a specified number of failed login attempts. Table 7.5 comes directly from Microsoft's website and shows the Azure AD password policy requirements that will apply to all passwords that are created, changed, or reset in Azure AD.

TABLE 7.5 Azure AD password policy requirements

Property	Requirements
Characters allowed	Uppercase characters (A–Z) Lowercase characters (a–z) Numbers (0–9) Symbols: @ # $ % ^ & * - _ ! + = [ ] { } | \ : ' , . ? / ` ~ " ( ) ; < > blank space
Characters not allowed	Unicode characters
Password length	Passwords require A minimum of eight characters A maximum of 256 characters
Password complexity	Passwords require three out of four of the following categories: Uppercase characters Lowercase characters Numbers Symbols
Password not recently used	When a user changes or resets their password, the new password can't be the same as the current or recently used passwords.
Password isn't banned by Azure AD Password Protection	The password can't be on the global list of banned passwords for Azure AD Password Protection, or on the customizable list of banned passwords specific to your organization.

In Azure Active Directory Domain Services (Azure AD DS) you can define fine-grained password policies (FGPPs) to manage user security. These FGPPs can control account lockout settings or minimum password length and complexity. A default FGPP is created and applied to all users in an Azure AD DS managed domain. In a managed domain, policies are distributed through group association and any changes made will be applied when the user next logs on. Also, depending on how the user account was created, password policies may perform a bit differently. There are two ways that a user account can be created in Azure AD DS:

- The account can be synchronized in from Azure AD. This includes cloud-only user accounts created directly in Azure, and hybrid user accounts synchronized from an on-premises AD DS environment using Azure AD Connect.

- The account can be manually created in a managed domain; they don't exist in Azure AD.

All users will have the following account lockout policies applied by default:

- Account lockout duration: 30
- Number of failed logon attempts allowed: 5
- Reset failed logon attempts count after: 2 minutes
- Maximum password age (lifetime): 90 days

For user accounts that were created manually in a managed domain, there are a few more password settings that are also applied to the default policy. These settings do not apply to user accounts that are synchronized in from Azure AD, as a user can't update their password directly in Azure AD DS. These additional password settings are

- Minimum password length (characters): 7
- Passwords must meet complexity requirements

You can also create a custom password policy to meet your corporate needs. Custom password policies are applied to groups in a managed domain. This configuration will override the default policy. To create a custom password policy in a managed domain, you must be signed in to a user account that's a member of the AAD DC Administrators group.

To create a custom password policy, follow these steps:

1. From the Start screen, select Administrative Tools.

2. Select Active Directory Administrative Center from the list of administrative tools to create and manage OUs.

3. In the left pane, choose your domain.

4. Open the System container, then the Password Settings Container. A built-in password policy for the managed domain is shown. You cannot change the built-in policy. Instead, create a custom password policy to override the default policy.

5. In the Tasks panel on the right, select New and then Password Settings.

6. In the Create Password Settings dialog box, enter a name for the policy.

7. When multiple password policies exist, the policy with the highest precedence is applied to a user. The lower the number, the higher the priority. The default password policy has a priority of 200. Set the precedence for your custom password policy to be lower than the default.

8. Edit the password policy settings. Account lockout settings apply to all users, but only take effect within the managed domain and not in Azure AD itself.

9. Uncheck Protect from accidental deletion. If this option is selected, you can't save the FGPP.

10. In the Directly Applies To section, click the Add button. In the Select Users or Groups dialog box, click the Locations button.

11. Password policies can only be applied to groups. In the Locations dialog box, expand the domain name and then select an OU. If you have a custom OU that contains a group of users you wish to apply, select that OU.

12. Type the name of the group you wish to apply the policy to, then click Check Names to validate that the group exists.

13. With the name of the group you selected now displayed in Directly Applies To section, click OK to save your custom password policy.

Enable Password Block Lists

Azure AD Password Protection can detect and block known weak passwords and their variants, and you can also block additional weak passwords that you set by creating a custom banned password list. Azure AD Password Protection has a default global banned password list that is automatically applied to all users in your Azure AD tenant.

The Azure AD Identity Protection team constantly analyzes Azure AD security telemetry data to look for passwords that are commonly used, compromised, or weak. When the team finds these types of passwords, they are added to the global banned password list. Then, if a password is changed or reset for an Azure AD tenant user, the current version of the global banned password list is used to validate the strength of the password. This validation check ensures stronger passwords for all Azure AD customers. The global banned password list is applied automatically to all users in an Azure AD tenant and cannot be disabled.

You can further improve security by creating a custom banned password list. The custom banned password list works with the global banned password list. The custom banned password list is limited to a maximum of 1,000 terms and is not designed to block large lists of passwords. You can add additional entries to the custom banned password list at any time. Organizational-specific terms can be added to the custom banned password list, such as:

- Abbreviations that have specific company meaning

- Brand names

- Company-specific internal terms

- Locations, such as company headquarters

- Months and weekdays with your company's local languages

- Product names

If a user tries to reset a password to something that's on the global or custom banned password list, they see one of the following error messages:

- Unfortunately, your password contains a word, phrase, or pattern that makes your password easily guessable. Please try again with a different password.

- Unfortunately, you can't use that password because it contains words or characters that have been blocked by your administrator. Please try again with a different password.

To configure a custom banned password list, perform the following:

1. Sign into the Azure portal using an account with global administrator permissions.

2. Search for and select Azure Active Directory, then choose Security from the menu on the left-hand side.

3. Under the Manage menu, select Authentication Methods, then Password Protection.

4. Set the option for Enforce Custom List to Yes.

5. Add strings to the Custom Banned Password list, one string per line. The following considerations and limitations apply to the custom banned password list:

   - The custom banned password list can contain up to 1,000 terms.

   - The custom banned password list is case-insensitive.

   - The custom banned password list considers common character substitution, such as *o* and *0*, or *a* and *@*.

   - The minimum string length is four characters, and the maximum is 16 characters.

6. Leave the option Enable Password Protection On Windows Server Active Directory set to No.

7. To enable the custom banned passwords and your entries, click Save. It may take several hours for updates to the custom banned password list to be applied.

Manage Protected Users

The Protected Users security group was introduced in Windows Server 2012 R2 domain controllers and was designed to help protect against credential theft attacks. By default, members of the Protected Users security group are nonconfigurable and the only way to modify the protections for an account is to remove the account from the security group. You should never add accounts for services and computers to the Protected Users group; if you do, then authentication will fail and you will receive the error "the user name or password is incorrect.".

To add users to the Protected Users group, you can use Active Directory Administrative Center (ADAC), Active Directory Users and Computers (ADUC), or Windows PowerShell. In Active Directory, this group is located in the default Users container. Using PowerShell, you can review the Protected Users security group by using the cmdlet `Get-ADGroup -Identity "Protected Users"`. To add, use the `Add-ADGroupMember` cmdlet.

It's important to note that if members of the Enterprise Admins group or the Domain Admins group are added to the Protected Users group, it is possible for those accounts to be locked out. You should never add all highly privileged accounts to the Protected Users group.

Publishing Active Directory Objects

One of the main goals of Active Directory is to make resources easy to find. Two of the most commonly used resources in a networked environment are server file shares and printers. These are so common, in fact, that most organizations have dedicated file and print servers. When it comes to managing these types of resources, Active Directory makes it easy to determine which files and printers are available to users.

With that being said, let's take a look at how Active Directory manages to publish shared folders and printers.

Making Active Directory Objects Available to Users

An important aspect of managing Active Directory objects is that a system administrator can control which objects users can see. The act of making an Active Directory object available is known as *publishing*. The two main types of publishable objects are Printer objects and Shared Folder objects.

The general process for creating server shares and shared printers has remained unchanged from previous versions of Windows: you create the various objects (a printer or a filesystem folder) and then enable them for sharing. To make these resources available via Active Directory, however, there's an additional step: you must publish the resources. Once an object has been published in Active Directory, clients will be able to use it.

When you publish objects in Active Directory, you should know the server name and share name of the resource. When you use Active Directory objects, you can change the resource to which the object points, without having to reconfigure or even notify clients. For example, if you move a share from one server to another, all you need to do is to update the Shared Folder object's properties to point to the new location. Active Directory clients still refer to the resource with the same path and name that they used before.

Publishing Printers

Printers can be published easily within Active Directory. This makes them available to users in your domain.

Exercise 7.17 walks you through the steps you need to take to share and publish a Printer object by having you create and share a printer. To complete the printer installation, you need access to the Windows Server 2022 installation media (via the hard disk, a network share, or the CD-ROM drive).

EXERCISE 7.17

Creating and Publishing a Printer

1. Click the Windows Key on the keyboard and select Control Panel.

2. Click Devices And Printers ➢ Add A Printer. This starts the Add Printer Wizard. Then click the Next button.

3. On the Choose A Local Or Network Printer page, select Add A Local Printer. This should automatically take you to the next page. If it doesn't, click Next.

4. On the Choose A Printer Port page, select Use An Existing Port. From the drop-down list beside that option, make sure LPT1: (Printer Port) is selected. Click Next.

5. On the Install The Printer Driver page, select Generic for the manufacturer. For the printer, highlight Generic/Text Only. Click Next.

6. On the Type A Printer Name page, type **Text Printer**. Deselect the Set As The Default Printer option and then click Next.

7.   The Installing Printer screen appears. After the system is finished, the Printer Sharing page appears. Make sure the option "Share this printer so that others on your network can find and use it" is selected, and accept the default share name of Text Printer.

8.   In the Location section, type **Building 203**, and in the Comment section, add the following comment: **This is a text-only Printer**. Click Next.

9.   On the You've Successfully Added Text Printer page, click Finish.

10.   Next you need to verify that the printer will be listed in Active Directory. Right-click the Text Printer icon and select Printer Properties.

11.   Select the Sharing tab and make sure that the List In The Directory option is selected. Note that you can also add additional printer drivers for other operating systems using this tab. Click OK to accept the settings.

Note that when you create and share a printer this way, an Active Directory Printer object is not displayed within the Active Directory Users and Computers tool. The printer is actually associated with the Computer object to which it is connected.

Publishing Shared Folders

Now that you've created and published a printer, you'll see how the same thing can be done to shared folders.

Exercise 7.18 walks through the steps required to create a folder, share it, and then publish it in Active Directory. This exercise assumes you are using the C: partition; however, you may want to change this based on your server configuration. This exercise assumes you have completed Exercise 7.12.

Creating and Publishing a Shared Folder

1.   Create a new folder in the root directory of your C: partition and name it **Test Share**. To do this, click the File Explorer link on the toolbar.

2.   Right-click the Test Share folder. Choose Share With ➢ Specific People.

3. In the File Sharing dialog box, enter the names of users with whom you want to share this folder. In the upper box, enter **Everyone** and then click Add. Note that Everyone appears in the lower box. Click in the Permission Level column next to Everyone and choose Read/Write from the pop-up menu. Then click Share.

4. You'll see a message that your folder has been shared. Click Done.

5. Click the Windows Key on the keyboard and choose Administrative Tools.

6. Open the Active Directory Users and Computers tool. Expand the current domain and right-click the RD OU. Select New ➤ Shared Folder.

7. In the New Object – Shared Folder dialog box, type **Shared Folder Test** for the name of the folder. Then type the UNC path to the share (for example, **\\server1\Test Share**). Click OK to create the share.

Once you have created and published the Shared Folder object, clients can use the My Network Places icon to find it. The Shared Folder object will be organized based on the OU in which you created it. When you use publication, you can see how this makes it easy to manage shared folders.

PowerShell for Active Directory

Table 7.6 will show you just some of the available PowerShell commands for maintaining Active Directory. These PowerShell commands can help you do everything from unlocking disabled accounts to resetting passwords.

TABLE 7.6 PowerShell commands for Active Directory

Command	Explanation
Add-ADComputerServiceAccount	This command allows you to add service accounts to Active Directory.
Add-ADGroupMember	This command allows you to add users to an Active Directory group.
Disable-ADAccount	You can use this command to disable an Active Directory account.
Enable-ADAccount	You can use this command to enable an Active Directory account.
Get-ADComputer	This command allows you to view one or more Active Directory computers.
Get-ADDomain	You can use this command to view an Active Directory domain.
Get-ADFineGrainedPasswordPolicy	This command allows you to view the Active Directory fine-grained password policies.
Get-ADGroup	You can use this command to view Active Directory groups.
Get-ADGroupMember	This command allows you to view the users in an Active Directory group.
Get-ADServiceAccount	You can use this command to view the Active Directory service accounts.
Get-ADUser	This command allows you to view one or more Active Directory users.
New-ADComputer	You can use this command to create a new Active Directory computer.
New-ADGroup	You can use this command to create a new Active Directory group.
New-ADServiceAccount	This command is the *only* way that you can create a new Managed Service Account.
New-ADUser	You can use this command to create a new Active Directory user.

Command	Explanation
`Set-ADAccountPassword`	This command allows you to modify the password of an Active Directory account.
`Unlock-ADAccount`	You can use this command to unlock an Active Directory account.

Summary

This chapter covered the basics of implementing an Active Directory forest and domain structure, creating and configuring application data partitions, and setting the functional level of your domain and forest.

You are now familiar with how you can implement Active Directory. We carefully examined all of the necessary steps and conditions that you need to follow to install Active Directory on your network. First you need to prepare for the Domain Name System because Active Directory cannot be installed without the support of a DNS server.

You also need to verify that the computer you upgrade to a domain controller meets some basic filesystem and network connectivity requirements so that Active Directory can run smoothly and efficiently in your organization. These are some of the most common things you will have to do when you deploy Active Directory.

The chapter also covered the concept of domain functional levels, which essentially determine the kinds of domain controllers you can use in your environment.

You also learned how to install Active Directory, which you accomplish by promoting a Windows Server 2022 computer to a domain controller using Server Manager. You also learned how to verify the installation by testing Active Directory from a client computer.

This chapter covered the fundamentals of administering Active Directory. The most important part of administering Active Directory is learning about how to work with OUs. Therefore, you should be aware of the purpose of OUs; that is, they help you organize and manage the directory. For instance, think of administrative control. If you wanted to delegate rights to another administrator (such as a sales manager), you could delegate that authority to that user within the Sales OU. As the system administrator, you would retain the rights to the castle.

We also looked at how to design an OU structure from an example. The example showed you how to design a proper OU layout. You can also create, organize, and reorganize OUs if need be.

In addition, you took a look at groups and group strategies. There are different types of groups (domain local, global, and universal groups), and you should know when each group is available and when to use each group.

Finally, this chapter covered how to use the Active Directory Users and Computers tool to manage Active Directory objects. If you're responsible for day-to-day system administration, there's a good chance that you are already familiar with this tool; if not, you should be after reading this chapter. Using this tool, you learned how to work with Active Directory objects such as User, Computer, and Group objects.

Exam Essentials

Know the prerequisites for promoting a server to a domain controller.   You should understand the tasks that you must complete before you attempt to upgrade a server to a domain controller. Also, you should have a good idea of the information you need in order to complete the domain controller promotion process.

Understand the steps of the Active Directory Installation Wizard.   When you run the Active Directory Installation Wizard, you'll be presented with many different choices. You should understand the effects of the various options provided in each step of the wizard.

Be familiar with the tools that you will use to administer Active Directory.   Three main administrative tools are installed when you promote a Windows Server 2022 to a domain controller. Be sure that you know which tools to use for which types of tasks.

Understand the purpose of application data partitions.   The idea behind application data partitions is that since you already have a directory service that can replicate all kinds of security information, you can also use it to keep track of application data. The main benefit of storing application information in Active Directory is that you can take advantage of its storage mechanism and replication topology. Application-related information stored on domain controllers benefits from having fault-tolerance features and availability.

Understand the purpose of OUs.   OUs are used to create a hierarchical, logical organization for objects within an Active Directory domain.

Understand the concept of inheritance.   By default, child OUs inherit permissions and Group Policy assignments set for parent OUs. However, these settings can be overridden for more granular control of security.

Know groups and group strategies.   You can use three groups: domain local, global, and universal. Understand the group strategies and when they apply.

Understand how Active Directory objects work.   Active Directory objects represent some piece of information about components within a domain. The objects themselves have attributes that describe details about them.

Review Questions

1. You are the system administrator of a large organization that has recently implemented Windows Server 2022. You have a few remote sites that do not have very tight security. You have decided to implement read-only domain controllers (RODCs). What forest and function levels does the network need for you to do the install? (Choose all that apply.)

   A. Windows Server 2022

   B. Windows Server 2008 R2

   C. Windows Server 2012 R2

   D. Windows Server 2008

2. What is the maximum number of domains that a Windows Server 2022 computer configured as a domain controller may participate in at one time?

   A. Zero

   B. One

   C. Two

   D. Any number of domains

3. A system administrator is trying to determine which filesystem to use for a server that will become a Windows Server 2022 file server and domain controller. The company has the following requirements:

   - The filesystem must allow for file-level security from within Windows 2016 Server.

   - The filesystem must make efficient use of space on large partitions.

   - The domain controller Sysvol must be stored on the partition.

   Which of the following filesystems meets these requirements?

   A. FAT

   B. FAT32

   C. HPFS

   D. NTFS

4. For security reasons, you have decided that you must convert the system partition on your removable drive from the FAT32 filesystem to NTFS. Which of the following steps must you take in order to convert the filesystem? (Choose two.)

   A. Run the command CONVERT /FS:NTFS from the command prompt.

   B. Rerun Windows Server 2022 Setup and choose to convert the partition to NTFS during the reinstallation.

   C. Boot Windows Server 2022 Setup from the installation CD-ROM and choose Rebuild Filesystem.

   D. Reboot the computer.

5. Windows Server 2022 requires the use of which of the following protocols or services in order to support Active Directory? (Choose two.)

A. DHCP

B. TCP/IP

C. NetBEUI

D. IPX/SPX

E. DNS

6. You are promoting a Windows Server 2022 computer to an Active Directory domain controller for test purposes. The new domain controller will be added to an existing domain. While you are using the Active Directory Installation Wizard, you receive an error message that prevents the server from being promoted. Which of the following might be the cause of the problem? (Choose all that apply.)

A. The system does not contain an NTFS partition on which the Sysvol directory can be created.

B. You do not have a Windows Server 2022 DNS server on the network.

C. The TCP/IP configuration on the new server is incorrect.

D. The domain has reached its maximum number of domain controllers.

7. Your network contains a single Active Directory domain. The domain contains five Windows Server 2008 R2 domain controllers. You plan to install a new Windows Server 2022 domain controller. Which two actions would you need to perform? (Each correct answer presents part of the solution. Choose two.)

A. Run `adprep.exe /rodcprep` at the command line.

B. Run `adprep.exe /forestprep` at the command line.

C. Run `adprep.exe /domainprep` at the command line.

D. From Active Directory Domains and Trusts, raise the functional level of the domain.

E. From Active Directory Users and Computers, prestage the RODC computer account.

8. You are the network administrator for a large company that creates widgets. Management asks you to implement a new Windows Server 2022 system. You need to implement federated identity management. Which of the following will help you do this?

A. Active Directory Federation Services

B. Active Directory DNS Services

C. Active Directory IIS Services

D. Active Directory IAS Services

9. You are the system administrator responsible for your company's infrastructure. You think you have an issue with name resolution, and you need to verify that you are using the correct hostname. You want to test DNS on the local system and need to see whether the hostname server-1 resolves to the IP address 10.1.1.1. Which of the following actions provides a solution to the problem?

A. Add a DNS server to your local subnet.

B. Add the mapping for the hostname server-1 to the IP address 10.1.1.1 in the local system's HOSTS file.

C. Add an A record to your local WINS server.

D. Add an MX record to your local DNS server.

10. You have one Active Directory forest in your organization that contains one domain named `WillPanek.com`. You have two domain controllers configured with the DNS role installed. There are two Active Directory Integrated zones named `WillPanek.com` and `WillPanekAD.com`. One of your IT members (who is not an administrator) needs to be able to modify the `WillPanek.com` DNS server, but you need to prevent this user from modifying the `WillPanekAD.com` SOA record. How do you accomplish this?

A. Modify the permissions of the `WillPanek.com` zone from the DNS Manager snap-in.

B. Modify the permissions of the `WillPanekAd.com` zone from the DNS Manager snap-in.

C. Run the Delegation Of Control Wizard in Active Directory.

D. Run the Delegation Of Control Wizard in the DNS snap-in.

11. You are the administrator of an organization with a single Active Directory domain. A user who left the company returns after 16 weeks. The user tries to log onto their old computer and receives an error stating that authentication has failed. The user's account has been enabled. You need to ensure that the user is able to log onto the domain using that computer. What do you do?

A. Reset the computer account in Active Directory. Disjoin the computer from the domain and then rejoin the computer to the domain.

B. Run the `ADadd` command to rejoin the computer account.

C. Run the MMC utility on the user's computer, and add the Domain Computers snap-in.

D. Re-create the user account and reconnect the user account to the computer account.

12. You are the administrator of an organization with a single Active Directory domain. One of your senior executives tries to log onto a machine and receives the error "This user account has expired. Ask your administrator to reactivate your account." You need to make sure that this doesn't happen again to this user. What do you do?

A. Configure the domain policy to disable account lockouts.

B. Configure the password policy to extend the maximum password age to 0.

C. Modify the user's properties to set the Account Never Expires setting.

D. Modify the user's properties to extend the maximum password age to 0.

13. You need to create a new user account using the command prompt. Which command would you use?

A. `dsmodify`

B. `dscreate`

C. `dsnew`

D. `dsadd`

14. Maria is a user who belongs to the Sales distribution global group. She is not able to access the laser printer that is shared on the network. The Sales global group has full access to the laser printer. How do you fix the problem?

    A. Change the group type to a security group.

    B. Add the Sales global group to the Administrators group.

    C. Add the Sales global group to the Printer Operators group.

    D. Change the Sales group to a local group.

15. You are a domain administrator for a large domain. Recently, you have been asked to make changes to some of the permissions related to OUs within the domain. To restrict security for the Texas OU further, you remove some permissions at that level. Later, a junior system administrator mentions that she is no longer able to make changes to objects within the Austin OU (which is located within the Texas OU). Assuming that no other changes have been made to Active Directory permissions, which of the following characteristics of OUs might have caused the change in permissions?

    A. Inheritance

    B. Group Policy

    C. Delegation

    D. Object properties

16. Isabel, a system administrator, created a new Active Directory domain in an environment that already contains two trees. During the promotion of the domain controller, she chose to create a new Active Directory forest. Isabel is a member of the Enterprise Administrators group and has full permissions over all domains. During the organization's migration to Active Directory, many updates were made to the information stored within the domains. Recently, users and other system administrators have complained about not being able to find specific Active Directory objects in one or more domains (although the objects exist in others). To investigate the problem, Isabel wants to check for any objects that have not been properly replicated among domain controllers. If possible, she would like to restore these objects to their proper place within the relevant Active Directory domains.

Which two of the following actions should she perform to be able to view the relevant information? (Choose two.)

    A. Change Active Directory permissions to allow object information to be viewed in all domains.

    B. Select the Advanced Features item in the View menu.

    C. Promote a member server in each domain to a domain controller.

    D. Rebuild all domain controllers from the latest backups.

    E. Examine the contents of the LostAndFound folder using the Active Directory Users and Computers tool.

17. You are a consultant hired to evaluate an organization's Active Directory domain. The domain contains more than 200,000 objects and hundreds of OUs. You begin examining the objects within the domain, but you find that the loading of the contents of specific OUs takes a long time. Furthermore, the list of objects can be large. You want to do the following:

- Use the built-in Active Directory administrative tools and avoid the use of third-party tools or utilities.

- Limit the list of objects within an OU to only the type of objects that you're examining (for example, only Computer objects).

- Prevent any changes to the Active Directory domain or any of the objects within it.

Which one of the following actions meets these requirements?

A. Use the Filter option in the Active Directory Users and Computers tool to restrict the display of objects.

B. Use the Delegation of Control Wizard to give yourself permissions over only a certain type of object.

C. Implement a new naming convention for objects within an OU and then sort the results using this new naming convention.

D. Use the Active Directory Domains and Trusts tool to view information from only selected domain controllers.

E. Edit the domain Group Policy settings to allow yourself to view only the objects of interest.

18. You are the administrator for a small organization with four servers. You have one file server named StormSrvA that runs Windows Server 2022. You have a junior administrator who needs to do backups on this server. You need to ensure that the junior admin can use Windows Server Backup to create a complete backup of StormSrvA. What should you configure to allow the junior admin to do the backups?

A. The local groups by using Computer Management

B. A task by using Authorization Manager

C. The User Rights Assignment by using the Local Group Policy Editor

D. The Role Assignment by using Authorization Manager

19. Miguel is a junior-level system administrator, and he has basic knowledge about working with Active Directory. As his supervisor, you have asked Miguel to make several security-related changes to OUs within the company's Active Directory domain. You instruct Miguel to use the basic functionality provided in the Delegation Of Control Wizard. Which of the following operations are represented as common tasks within the Delegation Of Control Wizard? (Choose all that apply.)

A. Reset passwords on user accounts.

B. Manage Group Policy links.

C. Modify the membership of a group.

D. Create, delete, and manage groups.

20. You are the primary system administrator for a large Active Directory domain. Recently, you have hired another system administrator and you intend to offload some of your responsibilities to them. This system administrator will be responsible for handling help desk calls and for basic user account management. You want to allow the new employee to have permissions to reset passwords for all users within a specific OU. However, for security reasons, it's important that the user not be able to make permissions changes for objects within other OUs in the domain. Which of the following is the best way to do this?

    A. Create a special administration account within the OU and grant it full permissions for all objects within Active Directory.

    B. Move the user's login account into the OU that the new employee is to administer.

    C. Move the user's login account to an OU that contains the OU (that is, the parent OU of the one that the new employee is to administer).

    D. Use the Delegation Of Control Wizard to assign the necessary permissions on the OU that the new employee is to administer.

Chapter

8

Understanding Group Policies

THE FOLLOWING AZ-800 EXAM OBJECTIVES ARE COVERED IN THIS CHAPTER:

✓ **Manage Windows Server by using domain-based Group Policies**

- Implement Group Policy in AD DS
- Implement Group Policy Preferences in AD DS
- Implement Group Policy in Azure AD DS

For many years, making changes to computer or user environments was a time-consuming process. If you wanted to install a service pack or a piece of software, unless you had a third-party utility you had to use the *sneakernet* (that is, you had to walk from one computer to another with a disk containing the software).

Installing any type of software or companywide security change was one of the biggest challenges faced by system administrators. It was difficult enough just to deploy and manage workstations throughout the environment. Combine this with the fact that users were generally able to make system configuration changes to their own machines; it quickly became a management nightmare!

For example, consider the case of users who change system settings. Relatively minor changes, such as modifying TCP/IP or desktop settings, could cause hours of support headaches. Now multiply these (or other common) problems by hundreds (or even thousands) of end users. Clearly, system administrators needed to have a secure way to limit the options available to users of client operating systems.

How do you prevent problems such as these from occurring in a Windows Server 2022 environment? Fortunately, there's a readily available solution delivered with the base operating system that's easy to implement. Two of the most important system administration features in Windows Server 2022 and Active Directory are *Group Policy* and *security policy*. By using *Group Policy objects (GPOs)*, administrators can quickly and easily define restrictions on common actions and then apply them at the site, domain, or organizational unit (OU) level. In this chapter, you will see how group and security policies work.

Introducing Group Policy

One of the strengths of Windows-based operating systems is their flexibility. End users and system administrators can configure many different options to suit the network environment and their personal tastes. However, this flexibility comes at a price—generally, end users on a network should not change many of these options. For example, TCP/IP configuration and security policies should remain consistent for all client computers. In fact, end users don't need to be able to change these types of settings in the first place because many of them do not understand the purpose of these settings.

Windows Server 2022 *Group Policies* are designed to provide system administrators with the ability to customize end-user settings and to place restrictions on the types of actions that users can perform. Group Policies can be easily created by system administrators and then later applied to one or more users or computers within the environment. Although they ultimately do affect Registry settings, it is much easier to configure and apply settings through the use of Group Policy than it is to make changes to the Registry manually. To make management easy, Microsoft has set up Windows Server 2022 so that Group Policy settings are all managed from within the Microsoft Management Console (MMC) in the Group Policy Management Console (GPMC).

Group Policies have several potential uses. I'll cover the use of Group Policies for software deployment, and I'll also focus on the technical background of Group Policies and how they apply to general configuration management.

Let's begin by looking at how Group Policies function.

Understanding Group Policy Settings

Group Policy settings are based on *Group Policy administrative templates*. These templates provide a list of user-friendly configuration options and specify the system settings to which they apply. For example, an option for a user or computer that reads Require A Specific Desktop Wallpaper Setting would map to a key in the Registry that maintains this value. When the option is set, the appropriate change is made in the Registry of the affected users and computers.

By default, Windows Server 2022 comes with several administrative template files that you can use to manage common settings. Additionally, system administrators and application developers can create their own administrative template files to set options for specific functionality.

Most Group Policy items have three different settings options (see Figure 8.1):

Enabled   Specifies that a setting for this GPO has been configured. Some settings require values or options to be set.

Disabled   Specifies that this option is disabled for client computers. Note that disabling an option *is* a setting. That is, it specifies that the system administrator wants to disallow certain functionality.

Not Configured   Specifies that these settings have been neither enabled nor disabled. Not Configured is the default option for most settings. It simply states that this group policy will not specify an option and that other policy settings may take precedence.

FIGURE 8.1 Group Policy configuration settings

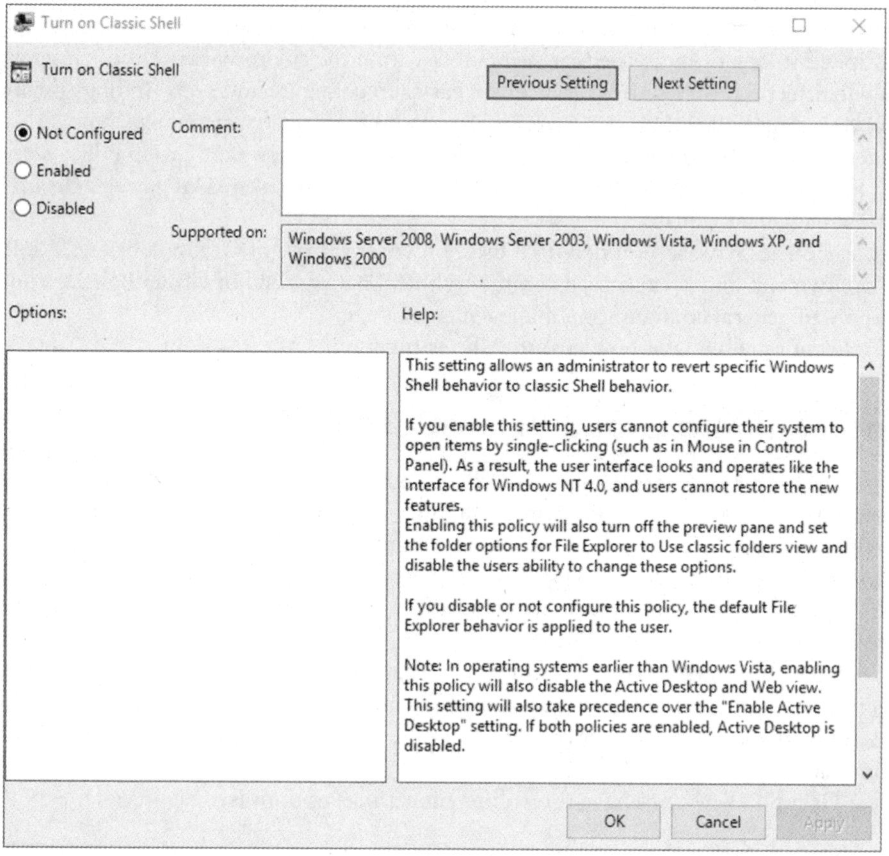

The specific options available (and their effects) will depend on the setting. Often, you will need additional information. For example, when setting the Account Lockout policy, you must specify how many bad login attempts may be made before the account is locked out. With this in mind, let's look at the types of user and computer settings that can be managed.

Group Policy settings can apply to two types of Active Directory objects: User objects and Computer objects. Because both users and computers can be placed into groups and organized within OUs, this type of configuration simplifies the management of hundreds, or even thousands, of computers.

The main options you can configure within user and computer Group Policies are as follows:

Software Settings The *Software Settings* options apply to specific applications and software that might be installed on the computer. You can use these settings to make new applications available to end users and to control the default configuration for these applications.

Windows Settings   The *Windows Settings* options allow you to customize the behavior of the Windows operating system. The specific options that are available here are divided into two types: user and computer. User-specific settings let you configure your Internet browser (including the default home page and other settings). Computer settings include security options, such as Account Policy and Event Log options.

Administrative Templates   *Administrative templates* are used to configure user and computer settings further. In addition to the default options available, you can create your own administrative templates with custom options.

Group Policy Preferences   The Windows Server 2022 operating system includes *Group Policy preferences (GPPs)*, which give you more than 20 Group Policy extensions. These extensions, in turn, give you a vast range of configurable settings within a Group Policy Object. Included in the Group Policy preference extensions are settings for folder options, mapped drives, printers, the Registry, local users and groups, scheduled tasks, services, and the Start Menu.

Besides providing easier management, Group Policy preferences give you the ability to deploy settings for client computers without restricting the users from changing the settings. This gives you the flexibility needed to decide which settings to enforce and which not to enforce.

Figure 8.2 shows some of the options you can configure with Group Policy.

FIGURE 8.2   Group Policy options

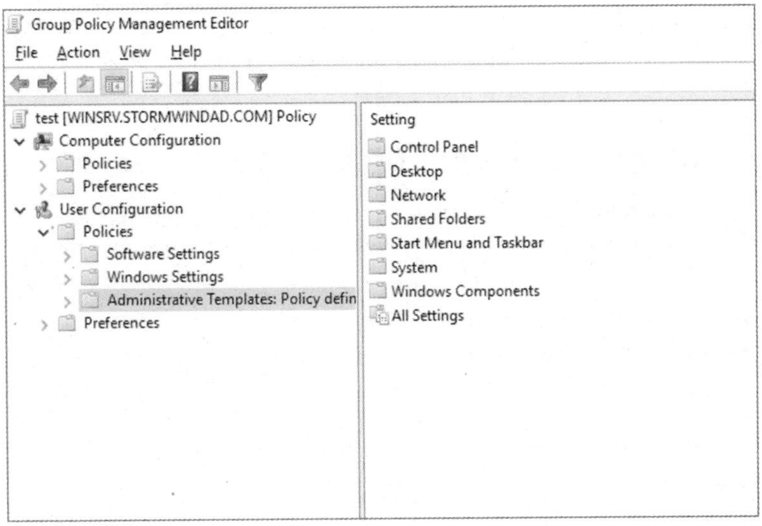

ADMX Central Store   Another consideration in GPO settings is whether to set up an *ADMX Central Store*. GPO administrative template files are saved as ADMX (with the file extension `.admx`) files and AMXL (with the file extension `.amxl`) for the supported languages. To get the most benefit out of using administrative templates, you should create an ADMX Central Store.

You create the Central Store in the `SYSVOL` folder on a domain controller. The Central Store is a repository for all your administrative templates, and the Group Policy tools check it. The Group Policy tools then use any ADMX files that they find in the Central Store. These files then replicate to all domain controllers in the domain.

If you want your clients to be able to edit domain-based GPOs by using the ADMX files that are stored in the ADMX Central Store, you must be using Windows 7 or above and Server 2008 or above.

Security Template   *Security templates* are used to configure security settings through a GPO. Some of the security settings that can be configured are settings for account policies, local policies, event logs, restricted groups, system services, and the Registry.

Starter GPOs   *Starter Group Policy Objects* give you the ability to store a collection of administrative template policy settings in a single object. You can then import and export starter GPOs to distribute the GPOs easily to other environments. When a GPO is created from a starter GPO, as with any template, the new GPO receives the settings and values that were defined from the administrative template policy in the starter GPO.

Group Policy settings do not take effect immediately. You must run the gpupdate command at the command prompt or wait for the regular update cycle in order for the policy changes to take effect.

The Security Settings Section of the GPO

One of the most important sections of a GPO is the Security Settings section. The Security Settings section, under the Windows Settings section, allows you to secure many aspects of the computer and user policies. The following are some of the configurable options for the Security Settings section:

Computer Section Only of the GPO

- Account Policies
- Local Policies
- Event Policies
- Restricted Groups
- System Services

- Registry
- File System
- Wired Network
- Windows Firewall With Advanced Security
- Network List Manager Policies
- Wireless Networks
- Network Access Protection
- Application Control Policies
- IP Security Policies
- Advanced Audit Policy Configuration

Computer and User Sections of the GPO
- Public Key Policies
- Software Restriction Policy

Restricted Groups

The *Restricted Groups* settings allow you to control group membership by using a GPO. The group membership I am referring to is the normal Active Directory groups (domain local, global, and universal). The settings offer two configurable properties: Members and Members Of.

The users on the Members list do not belong to the restricted group. The users on the Members Of list do belong to the restricted group. When you configure a Restricted Group policy, members of the restricted group that are not on the Members list are removed. Users who are on the Members list who are not currently a member of the restricted group are added.

Software Restriction Policy

Software restriction policies allow you to identify software and to control its ability to run on the user's local computer, organizational unit, domain, or site. This prevents users from installing unauthorized software. Software Restriction Policy is discussed in greater detail later in this chapter in the section "Implementing Software Deployment."

Client-Side Extensions

In Windows Server, Group Policies are designed using both server-side and client-side extensions (CSEs). The server-side elements include a user interface for creating each Group Policy Object (GPO). When a Windows client system logs into the Active Directory network, the client-side extensions (normally a series of DLL files) receive their GPOs and the GPOs make changes to the Windows client systems.

Within GPOs, there are computer policies that exist for each CSE. The policies normally include a maximum of three options: Allow Processing Across A Slow Network Connection, Do Not Apply During Periodic Background Processing, and Process Even If The Group Policy Objects Have Not Changed.

Group Policy Objects

So far, I have discussed what Group Policies are designed to do. Now it's time to drill down to determine exactly how you can set up and configure them.

To make them easier to manage, Group Policies may be placed in *Group Policy Objects (GPOs)*. GPOs act as containers for the settings made within Group Policy files, which simplifies the management of settings. For example, as a system administrator, you might have different policies for users and computers in different departments. Based on these requirements, you could create a GPO for members of the Sales department and another for members of the Engineering department. Then you could apply the GPOs to the OU for each department. Another important concept you need to understand is that Group Policy settings are hierarchical—that is, you can apply Group Policy settings at four different levels. These levels determine the GPO processing priority.

Local Every Windows operating system computer has one Group Policy object that is stored locally. This GPO functions for both the computer and user Group Policy processing.

Sites At the highest level, you can configure GPOs to apply to entire sites within an Active Directory environment. These settings apply to all of the domains and servers that are part of a site. Group Policy settings managed at the site level may apply to more than one domain within the same forest. Therefore, they are useful when you want to make settings that apply to all of the domains within an Active Directory tree or forest.

Domains Domains are the third level to which you can assign GPOs. GPO settings placed at the domain level will apply to all of the User and Computer objects within the domain. Usually, you make master settings at the domain level.

Organizational Units The most granular level of settings for GPOs is the OU level. By configuring Group Policy options for OUs, you can take advantage of the hierarchical structure of Active Directory. If the OU structure is planned well, you will find it easy to make logical GPO assignments for various business units at the OU level.

Based on the business need and the organization of the Active Directory environment, you might decide to set up Group Policy settings at any of these four levels. Because the settings are cumulative by default, a User object might receive policy settings from the site level, from the domain level, and from the OUs in which it is contained.

 You can also apply Group Policy settings to the local computer (in which case Active Directory is not used at all), but this limits the manageability of the Group Policy settings.

Group Policy Inheritance

In most cases, Group Policy settings are cumulative. For example, a GPO at the domain level might specify that all users within the domain must change their password every 60 days, and a GPO at the OU level might specify the default desktop background for all users and computers within that OU. In this case, both settings apply, so users within the OU are forced to change their password every 60 days and have the default Desktop setting.

What happens if there's a conflict in the settings? For example, suppose you create a scenario where a GPO at the site level specifies that users are to use red wallpaper and another GPO at the OU level specifies that they must use green wallpaper. The users at the OU layer would have green wallpaper by default. Although hypothetical, this raises an important point about *inheritance*. By default, the settings at the most specific level (in this case, the OU that contains the User object) override those at more general levels. As a friend of mine from Microsoft always says, "Last one to apply wins."

Although the default behavior is for settings to be cumulative and inherited, you can modify this behavior. You can set two main options at the various levels to which GPOs might apply.

Block Policy Inheritance   The *Block Policy Inheritance* option specifies that Group Policy settings for an object are not inherited from its parents. You might use this, for example, when a child OU requires completely different settings from a parent OU. Note, however, that you should manage blocking policy inheritance carefully because this option allows other system administrators to override the settings made at higher levels.

Force Policy Inheritance   The *Enforced option* (sometimes referred as *No Override*) can be placed on a parent object, and it ensures that all lower-level objects inherit these settings. In some cases, you want to ensure that Group Policy inheritance is not blocked at other levels. For example, suppose it is corporate policy that all network accounts are locked out after five incorrect password attempts. In this case, you would not want lower-level system administrators to override the option with other settings.

You generally use this option when they want to enforce a specific setting globally. For example, if a password expiration policy should apply to all users and computers within a domain, a GPO with the *Force Policy Inheritance* option enabled could be created at the domain level.

You must consider one final case: If a conflict exists between the computer and user settings, the user settings take effect. If, for instance, a system administrator applies a default desktop setting for the Computer policy and a different default desktop setting for the User policy, the one they specify in the User policy takes effect. This is because the user settings are more specific, and they allow system administrators to make changes for individual users regardless of the computer they're using.

Planning a Group Policy Strategy

Through the use of Group Policy settings, you can control many different aspects of your network environment. As you'll see throughout this chapter, you can use GPOs to configure user settings and computer configurations. Windows Server 2022 includes many different administrative tools for performing these tasks. However, it's important to keep in mind that, as with many aspects of using Active Directory, a successful Group Policy strategy involves planning.

Because there are thousands of possible Group Policy settings and many different ways to implement them, you should start by determining the business and technical needs of your organization. For example, you should first group your users based on their work functions. You might find, for example, that users in remote branch offices require particular network configuration options. In that case, you might implement Group Policy settings best at the site level. In another instance, you might find that certain departments have varying requirements for disk quota settings. In this case, it would probably make the most sense to apply GPOs to the appropriate department OUs within the domain.

The overall goal should be to reduce complexity (e.g., by reducing the overall number of GPOs and GPO links) while still meeting the needs of your users. By taking into account the various needs of your users and the parts of your organization, you can often determine a logical and efficient method of creating and applying GPOs. Although it's rare that you'll come across a right or wrong method of implementing Group Policy settings, you will usually encounter some that are either better or worse than others.

By implementing a logical and consistent set of policies, you'll also be well prepared to troubleshoot any problems that might come up or to adapt to your organization's changing requirements. Later in this chapter, you'll learn about some specific methods for determining effective Group Policy settings before you apply them.

Implementing Group Policy

Now that I've covered the basic layout and structure of group policies and how they work, let's look at how you can implement them in an Active Directory environment. In the following sections, you'll start by creating GPOs. Then you'll apply these GPOs to specific Active Directory objects, and you'll take a look at how to use administrative templates.

Creating GPOs

In older versions of server like, Windows Server 2000 and Windows Server 2003, you could create GPOs from many different locations. For example, you could use Active Directory Users and Computers to create GPOs on your OUs along with other GPO tools. In Windows

Server 2022, things are simpler. You can create GPOs for OUs in only one location: the Group Policy Management Console (GPMC). You have your choice of three applications for setting up policies on your Windows Server 2022 computers.

Local Computer Policy Tool   This administrative tool allows you to quickly access the Group Policy settings that are available for the local computer. These options apply to the local machine and to users who access it. You must be a member of the local Administrators group to access and make changes to these settings.

Administrators may need the ability to work on multiple local group policy objects (MLGPOs) at the same time. To do this, you would complete the following steps. (You can't configure MLGPOs on domain controllers.)

1.   Open the MMC by typing **MMC** in the Run command box.

2.   Click File and then click Add/Remove Snap-in.

3.   From the available snap-ins list, choose Group Policy Object Editor and click Add.

4.   In the Select Group Policy Object dialog box, click the Browse button.

5.   Select the Users tab in the Browse For The Group Policy Object dialog box.

6.   Click the user or group for which you want to create or edit a local Group Policy and click OK.

7.   Click Finish and then click OK.

8.   Configure the multiple policy settings.

Group Policy Management Console   You must use the GPMC to manage Group Policy deployment. The GPMC provides a single solution for managing all Group Policy–related tasks, and it is also best suited to handle enterprise-level tasks, such as forest-related work.

The GPMC allows you to manage Group Policy and GPOs all from one easy-to-use console whether their enterprise solution spans multiple domains and sites within one or more forests or is local to one site. The GPMC adds flexibility, manageability, and functionality. Using this console, you can also perform other functions, such as backup and restore, importing, and copying.

Auditpol.exe   `Auditpol.exe` is a command-line utility that works with Windows 7 or above and Windows Server 2008 and above. You have the ability to display information about policies and also to perform some functions to manipulate audit policies. Table 8.1 shows some of the switches available for `auditpol.exe`.

TABLE 8.1   Auditpol.exe switches

Switch	Description
/?	This is the Auditpol.exe help command.
/get	This allows you to display the current audit policy.
/set	This allows you to set a policy.
/list	This displays selectable policy elements.
/backup	This allows you to save the audit policy to a file.
/restore	This restores a policy from previous backup.
/clear	This clears the audit policy.
/remove	This removes all per-user audit policy settings and disables all system audit policy settings.
/ResourceSACL	This configures the Global Resource SACL.

WARNING   You should be careful when making Group Policy settings because certain options might prevent the proper use of systems on your network. Always test Group Policy settings on a small group of users before you deploy them throughout your organization. You'll probably find that some settings need to be changed to be effective.

Exercise 8.1 walks you through the process of installing the Group Policy Management MMC snap-in for editing Group Policy settings and creating a GPO.

EXERCISE 8.1

Creating a Group Policy Object Using the GPMC

1. Click the Windows button and choose Administrative Tools ➤ Group Policy Management. The Group Policy Management tool opens.

2. Expand the Forest, Domains, *your domain name,* and North America containers. Right-click the Corporate OU and then choose Create A GPO In This Domain, And Link It Here.

3. When the New GPO dialog box appears, type **Warning Box** in the Name field. Click OK.

4. The New GPO will be listed on the right side of the Group Policy Management window. Right-click the GPO and choose Edit.

5. In the Group Policy Management Editor, expand the following: Computer Configuration ➢ Policies ➢ Windows Settings ➢ Security Settings ➢ Local Policies ➢ Security Options. On the right side, scroll down and double-click Interactive Logon: Message Text For Users Attempting To Log On.

6. Select the option Define This Policy Setting In The Template. In the text box, type **Unauthorized use of this machine is prohibited** and then click OK. Close the GPO and return to the GPMC main screen.

7. Under the domain name (in the GPMC), right-click Group Policy Objects and click New.

8. When the New GPO dialog box appears, type **Unlinked Test GPO** in the Name field. Click OK.

9. On the right side, the new GPO will appear. Right-click Unlinked Test GPO and click Edit.

10. Under the User Configuration section, click Policies ➢ Administrative Templates ➢ Desktop. On the right side, double-click Hide And Disable All Items On The Desktop and then click Enabled. Click OK and then close the GPMC.

Note that Group Policy changes may not take effect until the next user logs in (some settings may even require that the machine be rebooted). That is, users who are currently working on the system will not see the effects of the changes until they log off and log in again. GPOs are reapplied every 90 minutes with a 30-minute offset. In other words, users who are logged in will have their policies reapplied every 60 to 120 minutes. Not all settings are reapplied (for example, software settings and password policies).

Linking Existing GPOs to Active Directory

Creating a GPO is the first step in assigning Group Policies. The second step is to link the GPO to a specific Active Directory object. As mentioned earlier in this chapter, GPOs can be linked to sites, domains, and OUs.

Exercise 8.2 walks you through the steps that you must take to assign an existing GPO to an OU within the local domain. In this exercise, you will link the Test Domain Policy GPO to an OU. To complete the steps in this exercise, you must have completed Exercise 8.1.

EXERCISE 8.2

Linking Existing GPOs to Active Directory

1. Open the Group Policy Management Console.

2. Expand the Forest and Domain containers and right-click the Africa OU.

3. Choose Link An Existing GPO.

4. The Select GPO dialog box appears. Click Unlinked Test GPO and click OK.

5. Close the Group Policy Management Console.

Note that the GPMC tool offers a lot of flexibility in assigning GPOs. You can create new GPOs, add multiple GPOs, edit them directly, change priority settings, remove links, and delete GPOs, all from within this interface. In general, creating new GPOs using the GPMC tool is the quickest and easiest way to create the settings you need.

To test the Group Policy settings, you can simply create a user account within the Africa OU that you used in Exercise 8.2. Then, using another computer that is a member of the same domain, you can log on as the newly created user.

Forcing a GPO to Update

There will be times when you need a GPO to get processed immediately. If you are testing a GPO, you will not want to wait for the GPO to process in its own time or you may not want to have to log off the domain and log back onto the domain just to get the GPO processed.

Windows Server 2022 has changed how GPOs get processed. In a Windows Server 2022 domain, when a user logs onto the domain, the latest version of the Group Policy gets downloaded from the domain controller, and it writes that policy to the local store.

If you have your GPOs set up and running in synchronous mode, then the next time the computer restarts, it will use the most recently downloaded GPO from the local store and not download the GPO from the domain. This is a new feature in Windows Server 2022, and it helps to reduce the time it takes to log onto the domain because the GPO doesn't need to be downloaded each time.

So, now that you understand how GPOs get processed in Windows Server 2022, let's look at a few different ways that you can force a GPO to get processed immediately.

Forcing the GPO from the Server

Windows Server 2022 has an MMC called Group Policy Management Console (GPMC), and by using this MMC, you can remotely refresh an organizational unit (OU) and force the GPO on all users and computers within that OU. The GPMC remote refresh automatically updates all settings, including security settings, which are configured in the GPO that is linked to the OU. In the OU's context menu, you can choose to refresh remotely the OU and the GPOs associated with that OU. When you remotely refresh an OU, the following steps occur:

1. Windows Server 2022 does an Active Directory query, and that query returns a list of all users and computers that belong to the OU.

2. Windows Management Instrumentation (WMI) queries all users and computers that are currently logged into the domain and creates a list that will be used.

3. Using the list that was created in step 2, a remote scheduled task is created, and a GPUpdate.exe /force is executed on all of the users and computers that are logged into the domain. The remote scheduled task is then scheduled to execute with a 10-minute random delay to help decrease the load on network traffic.

 When you are using the GPMC to force a GPO update, you do not have the ability to change the 10-minute random delay, but if you force the GPO through the use of PowerShell, you have the ability to set the delay.

Another way that you can force a GPO to update immediately is to use Windows PowerShell. By using the PowerShell command Invoke-GPUpdate cmdlet, you can not only force the GPO but also set the parameters to be more granular.

Forcing the GPO from the Client

As an administrator, you have the ability also to force a GPO onto a client machine on which you may be working. The GPUpdate.exe command allows you to run a GPO on a client machine. The GPUpdate command will run on all Windows client machines from Windows Vista to Windows Server 2022. Table 8.2 shows some of the GPUpdate switches you can use.

TABLE 8.2   GPUpdate.exe switches

Switch	Description
/target:{Computer | User}	Updates only the User or Computer policy settings for the computer or user specified.
/force	Forces the GPO to reapply all policy settings. By default, only policy settings that have changed are applied.
/wait:<VALUE>	Determines the number of seconds that the system will wait after a policy is processed before returning to the command prompt.
/logoff	The domain user account will automatically log off the computer after the Group Policy settings are updated.
/boot	The computer will automatically restart after the Group Policy settings are applied.
/sync	This switch forces the next available foreground policy application to be done synchronously. Foreground policies are applied when the computer boots up and the user logs in.
/?	Displays help at the command prompt.

Managing Group Policy

Now that you have implemented GPOs and applied them to sites, domains, and OUs within Active Directory, it's time to look at some ways to manage them. In the following sections, you'll look at how multiple GPOs can interact with one another and ways that you can provide security for GPO management. Using these features is an important part of working with Active Directory, and if you properly plan Group Policy, you can greatly reduce the time the help desk spends troubleshooting common problems.

Managing GPOs

One of the benefits of GPOs is that they're modular and can apply to many different objects and levels within Active Directory. This can also be one of the drawbacks of GPOs if they're not managed properly. A common administrative function related to using GPOs is finding all of the Active Directory links for each of these objects. You can do this when you are viewing the Linked Group Policy Objects tab of the site, domain, or OU in the GPMC (shown in Figure 8.3).

FIGURE 8.3   Viewing GPO links to an Active Directory OU

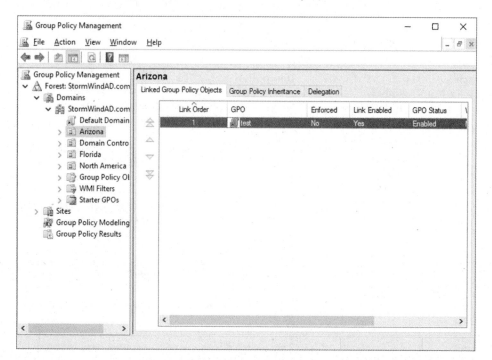

In addition to the common action of delegating permissions on OUs, you can set permissions regarding the modification of GPOs. The best way to accomplish this is to add users to the Group Policy Creator/Owners built-in security group. The members of this group are able to modify security policy.

Windows Management Instrumentation

Windows Management Instrumentation (WMI) scripts are used to gather information or to help GPOs deploy better. The best way to explain this is to give an example. Let's say you wanted to deploy Microsoft Office 2016 to everyone in the company. You would first set up a GPO to deploy the Office package (explained later in the section "Deploying Software Through a GPO").

You can then place a WMI script on the GPO stating that only computers with 10 GB of hard disk space actually deploy Office. Now if a computer has 10 GB of free space, the Office GPO would get installed. If the computer does not have the 10 GB of hard disk space, the GPO will not deploy. You can use WMI scripts to check for computer information such as MAC addresses. WMI is a powerful tool because if you know how to write scripts, the possibilities are endless. The following script is a sample of a WMI script that is checking for at least 10 GB of free space on the C: partition/volume:

```
Select * from Win32_LogicalDisk where FreeSpace > 10737418240 AND Caption = "C:"
```

Security Filtering of a Group Policy

Another method of securing access to GPOs is to set permissions on the GPOs themselves. You can do this by opening the GPMC, selecting the GPO, and clicking the Advanced button in the Delegation tab. The Unlinked Test GPO Security Settings dialog box appears (see Figure 8.4).

FIGURE 8.4   A GPO's Security Settings dialog box

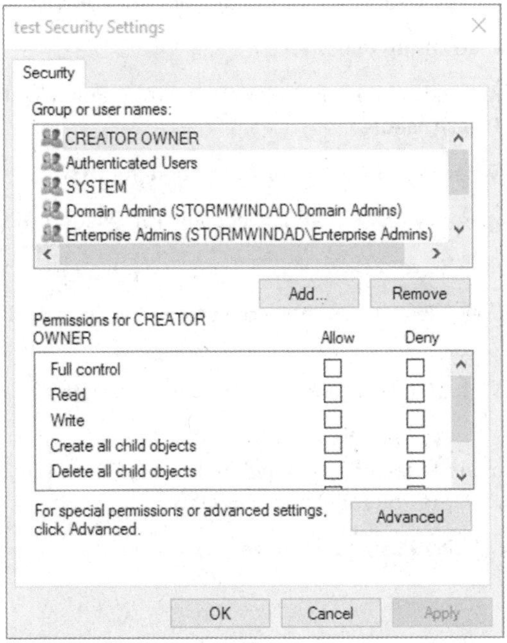

The following permissions options are available:

- Full Control
- Read
- Write
- Create All Child Objects
- Delete All Child Objects
- Apply Group Policy

You might have to scroll the Permissions window to see the Apply Group Policy item. Of these, the Apply Group Policy setting is particularly important because you use it to filter the scope of the GPO. *Filtering* is the process by which selected security groups are included or excluded from the effects of the GPOs. To specify that the settings should apply to a GPO, you should select the Allow check box for both the Apply Group Policy setting and the Read setting. These settings will be applied only if the security group is also contained within a site, domain, or OU to which the GPO is linked. To disable GPO access for a group, choose Deny for both of these settings. Finally, if you do not want to specify either Allow or Deny, leave both boxes blank. This is effectively the same as having no setting.

In Exercise 8.3, you will filter Group Policy using security groups. To complete the steps in this exercise, you must have completed Exercises 8.1 and 8.2.

EXERCISE 8.3

Filtering Group Policy Using Security Groups

1. Open the Active Directory Users and Computers administrative tool.

2. Create a new OU called **Group Policy Test**.

3. Create two new global security groups within the Group Policy Test OU and name them **PolicyEnabled** and **PolicyDisabled**.

4. Exit Active Directory Users and Computers and open the GPMC.

5. Right-click the Group Policy Test OU and select Link An Existing GPO.

6. Choose Unlinked Test GPO and click OK.

7. Expand the Group Policy Test OU so that you can see the GPO (Unlinked Test GPO) underneath the OU.

8. Click the Delegation tab and then click the Advanced button in the lower-right corner of the window.

9. Click the Add button and type **PolicyEnabled** in the Enter The Object Names To Select field. Click the Check Names button. Then click OK.

10. Add a group named **PolicyDisabled** in the same way.

11. Highlight the PolicyEnabled group and select Allow for the Read and Apply Group Policy permissions. This ensures that users in the PolicyEnabled group will be affected by this policy.

12. Highlight the PolicyDisabled group and select Deny for the Read and Apply Group Policy permissions. This ensures that users in the PolicyDisabled group will not be affected by this policy.

13. Click OK. You will see a message stating that you are choosing to use the Deny permission and that the Deny permission takes precedence over the Allow entries. Click the Yes button to continue.

14. When you have finished, close the GPMC tool.

Delegating Administrative Control of GPOs

So far, you have learned about how to use Group Policy to manage user and computer settings. What you haven't done yet is to determine who can modify GPOs. It's important to establish the appropriate security on GPOs themselves for two reasons.

- If the security settings aren't set properly, users and system administrators can easily override them. This defeats the purpose of having the GPOs in the first place.

- Having many different system administrators creating and modifying GPOs can become extremely difficult to manage. When problems arise, the hierarchical nature of GPO inheritance can make it difficult to pinpoint the problem.

Fortunately, through the use of delegation, determining security permissions for GPOs is a simple task. Exercise 8.4 walks you through the steps that you must take to grant the appropriate permissions to a user account. Specifically, the process involves delegating the ability to manage Group Policy links on an Active Directory object (such as an OU). To complete this exercise, you must have completed Exercises 8.1 and 8.2.

EXERCISE 8.4

Delegating Administrative Control of Group Policy

1. Open the Active Directory Users and Computers tool.

2. Expand the local domain and create a user named **Policy Admin** within the Group Policy Test OU.

3. Exit Active Directory Users and Computers and open the GPMC.

4. Click the Group Policy Test OU and select the Delegation tab.

5. Click the Add button. In the field Enter The Object Name To Select, type **Policy Admin** and click the Check Names button.

6. The Add Group Or User dialog box appears. In the Permissions drop-down list, make sure that the item labeled Edit Settings, Delete, Modify Security is chosen. Click OK.

7. At this point you should be looking at the Group Policy Test Delegation window. Click the Advanced button in the lower-right corner.

8. Highlight the Policy Admin account and check the Allow Full Control box. This user now has full control of these OUs and all child OUs and GPOs for these OUs. Click OK.

If you just want to give this user individual rights, then, in the Properties window (step 8), click the Advanced button and then the Effective Permissions tab. This is where you can also choose a user and give them only the rights that you want them to have.

9. When you have finished, close the GPMC tool.

Understanding Delegation

Although I have talked about delegation throughout the book, it's important to discuss it again in the context of OUs, Group Policy, and Active Directory.

Once configured, Active Directory administrative delegation allows you to delegate tasks (usually administration related) to specific user accounts or groups. What this means is that if you don't manage it all, the user accounts (or groups) you choose will be able to manage their portions of the tree.

It's important to be aware of the benefits of Active Directory Delegation (AD Delegation). *AD Delegation* will help you manage the assignment of administrative control over objects in Active Directory, such as users, groups, computers, printers, domains, and sites. AD Delegation is used to create more administrators, which essentially saves time.

For example, let's say you have a company whose IT department is small and situated in a central location. The central location connects three other smaller remote sites. These sites do not each warrant a full-time IT person, but the manager on staff (for example) at each remote site can become an administrator for their portion of the tree. If that manager administers the user accounts for the staff at the remote site, this reduces the burden on the system administrator of doing trivial administrative work, such as unlocking user accounts or changing passwords, and thus it reduces costs.

Controlling Inheritance and Filtering Group Policy

Controlling inheritance is an important function when you are managing GPOs. Earlier in this chapter, you learned that, by default, GPO settings flow from higher-level Active Directory objects to lower-level ones. For example, the effective set of Group Policy settings for a user might be based on GPOs assigned at the site level, at the domain level, and in the OU hierarchy. In general, this is probably the behavior you would want.

In some cases, however, you might want to block Group Policy inheritance. You can accomplish this easily by selecting the object to which a GPO has been linked. Right-click the object and choose Block Inheritance. By enabling this option, you are effectively specifying that this object starts with a clean slate; that is, no other Group Policy settings will apply to the contents of this Active Directory site, domain, or OU.

You can also force inheritance. By setting the Enforced option, you can prevent other system administrators from making changes to default policies. You can set the Enforced option by right-clicking the GPO and choosing Enforced (see Figure 8.5).

FIGURE 8.5   Setting the Enforced GPO option

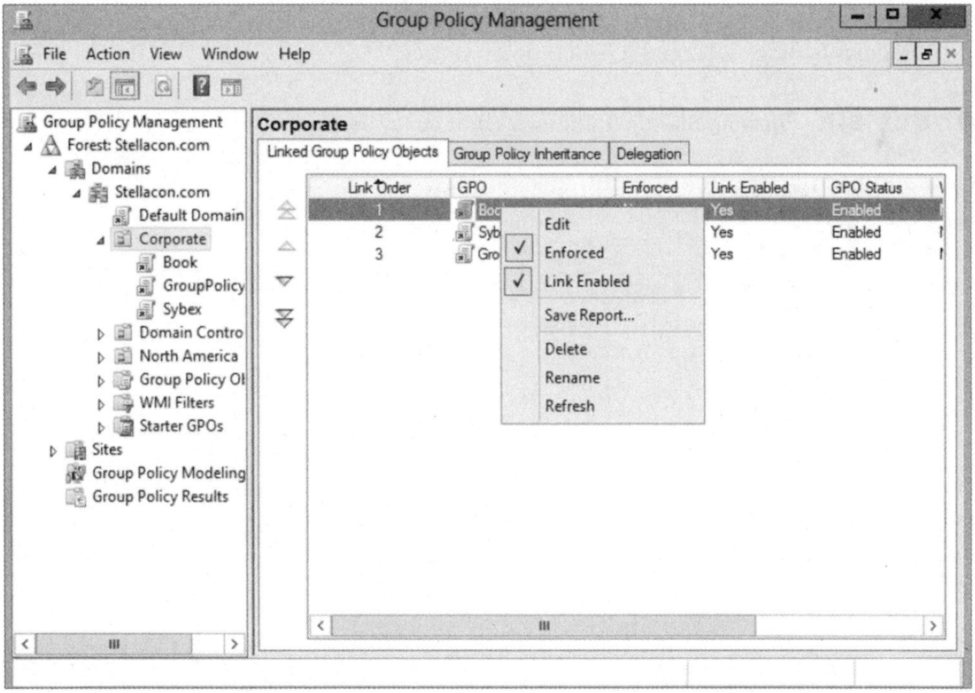

Assigning Script Policies

You might want to make several changes and implement certain settings that would apply while the computer is starting up or the user is logging on. Perhaps the most common operation that logon scripts perform is mapping network drives. Although users can manually map network drives, providing this functionality within login scripts ensures that mappings stay consistent and that users only need to remember the drive letters for their resources.

Script policies are specific options that are part of Group Policy settings for users and computers. These settings direct the operating system to the specific files that should be processed during the startup/shutdown or logon/logoff processes. You can create the scripts by using the *Windows Script Host (WSH)* or with standard batch file commands. WSH allows developers and system administrators to create scripts quickly and easily using Visual Basic Scripting Edition (VBScript) or JScript (Microsoft's implementation of JavaScript). Additionally, WSH can be expanded to accommodate other common scripting languages.

To set script policy options, you simply edit the Group Policy settings. As shown in Figure 8.6, there are two main areas for setting script policy settings:

Startup/Shutdown Scripts   These settings are located within the Computer Configuration ➤ Windows Settings ➤ Scripts (Startup/Shutdown) object.

Logon/Logoff Scripts   These settings are located within the User Configuration ➤ Windows Settings ➤ Scripts (Logon/Logoff) object.

FIGURE 8.6   Viewing Startup/Shutdown script policy settings

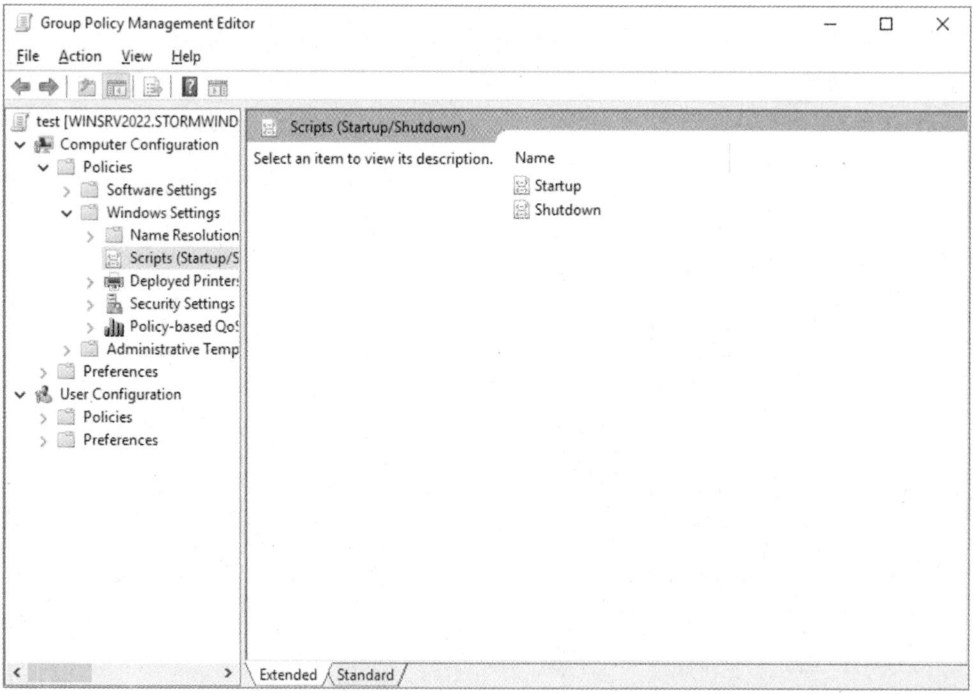

To assign scripts, simply double-click the setting and its Properties dialog box appears. For instance, if you double-click the Startup setting, the Startup Properties dialog box appears (see Figure 8.7). To add a script filename, click the Add button. When you do, you will be asked to provide the name of the script file (such as `MapNetworkDrives.vbs` or `ResetEnvironment.bat`).

FIGURE 8.7   Setting scripting options

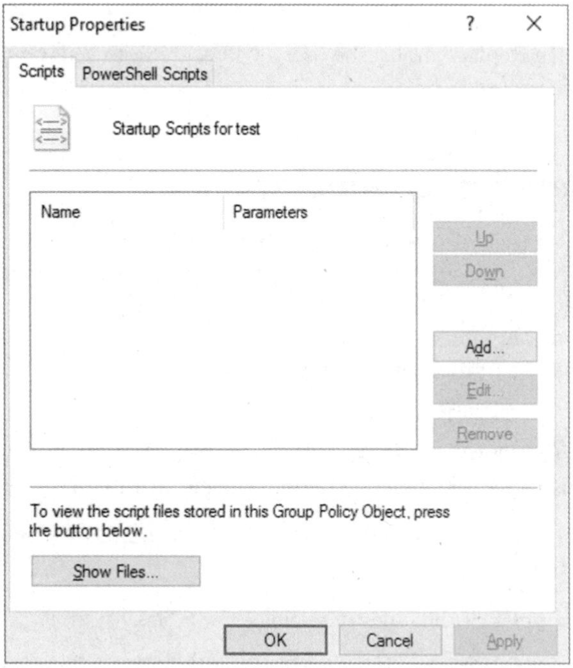

Note that you can change the order in which the scripts are run by using the Up and Down buttons. The Show Files button opens the directory folder in which you should store the Logon script files. To ensure that the files are replicated to all domain controllers, you should be sure you place the files within the SYSVOL share.

Understanding the Loopback Policy

There may be times when the user settings of a Group Policy Object should be applied to a computer based on its location instead of the User object. Usually, the user Group Policy processing dictates that the GPOs be applied in order during computer startup based on the computers located in their organizational unit. User GPOs, on the other hand, are applied in order during logon, regardless of the computer to which they log on.

In some situations, this processing order may not be appropriate. A good example is a kiosk machine. You would not want applications that have been assigned or published to a user to be installed when the user is logged on to the kiosk machine. *Loopback Policy* allows two ways to retrieve the list of GPOs for any user when they are using a specific computer in an OU.

Merge Mode   The GPOs for the computer are added to the end of the GPOs for the user. Because of this, the computer's GPOs have higher precedence than the user's GPOs.

Replace Mode   In Replace mode, the user's GPOs are not used. Only the GPOs of the Computer object are used.

Managing Network Configuration

Group Policies are also useful in network configuration. Although you can handle network settings at the protocol level using many different methods, such as Dynamic Host Configuration Protocol (DHCP), Group Policy allows you to set which functions and operations are available to users and computers.

Figure 8.8 shows some of the features that are available for managing Group Policy settings. The paths to these settings are as follows:

Computer Network Options   These settings are located within the Computer Configuration ➤ Administrative Templates ➤ Network ➤ Network Connections folder.

User Network Options   These settings are located within User Configuration ➤ Administrative Templates ➤ Network.

Here are some examples of the types of settings available:

- The ability to allow or disallow the modification of network settings.

  In many environments, the improper changing of network configurations and protocol settings is a common cause of help desk calls.

- The ability to allow or disallow the creation of Remote Access Service (RAS) connections.

FIGURE 8.8   Viewing Group Policy User network configuration options

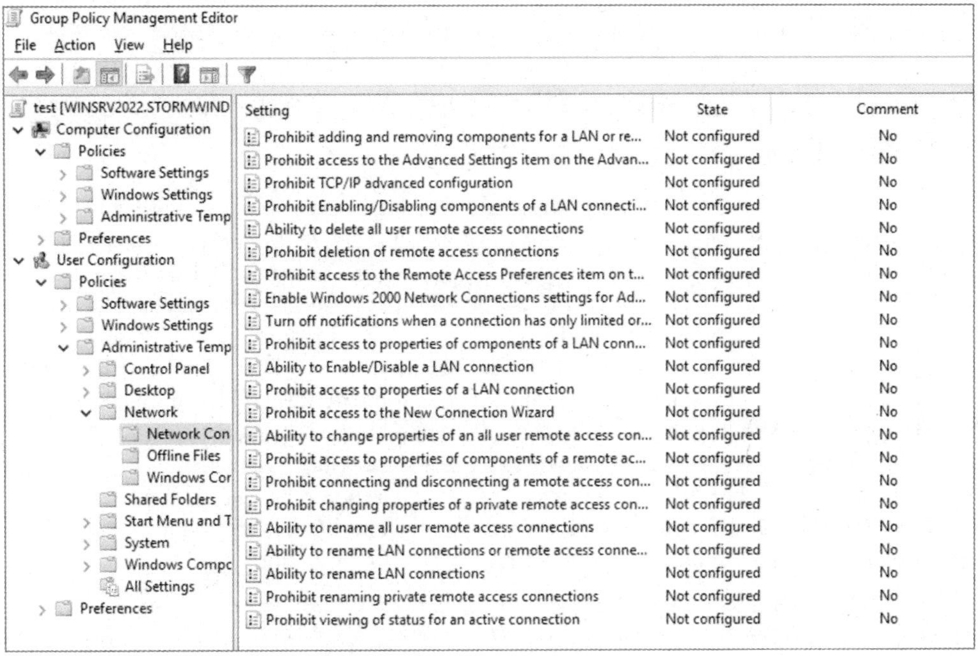

This option is useful, especially in larger networked environments, because the use of modems and other WAN devices can pose a security threat to the network.

- The ability to set offline files and folders options.

  This is especially useful for keeping files synchronized for traveling users, and it is commonly configured for laptops.

Each setting includes detailed instructions in the description area of the GPO Editor window. By using these configuration options, you can maintain consistency for users and computers and avoid many of the most common troubleshooting calls.

Configuring Network Settings

In Windows Server 2022, you can set a lot of user and network settings by using GPOs. Some of the different settings that can be configured are configure printer preferences, defining network drive mappings, configuring power options, setting custom Registry settings, manipulating Control Panel settings, configuring Microsoft Edge settings, settings for file and folder deployment, setting up shortcut deployments, and configuring item-level targeting.

To configure any of these settings, open the Group Policy Management Console and choose the GPO you want to edit. Once you start editing, you can configure any of these network settings.

Automatically Enrolling User and Computer Certificates in Group Policy

You can also use Group Policy to enroll user and computer certificates automatically, making the entire certificate process transparent to your end users. Before proceeding, you should understand what certificates are and why they are an important part of network security.

Think of a digital certificate as a carrying case for a public key. A certificate can contain both a public and a private key and a set of attributes, including the key holder's name and email address. These attributes specify something about the holder: their identity, what they're allowed to do with the certificate, and so on. The attributes and the public key are bound together because the certificate is digitally signed by the entity that issued it. Anyone who wants to verify the certificate's contents can verify the issuer's signature.

Certificates are one part of what security experts call a *public-key infrastructure (PKI)*. A PKI has several different components that you can mix and match to achieve the desired results. Microsoft's PKI implementation offers the following functions:

Certificate Authorities   CAs issue certificates, revoke certificates they've issued, and publish certificates for their clients. Big CAs like Thawte and VeriSign do this for millions of users. If you want, you can also set up your own CA for each department or workgroup in your organization. Each CA is responsible for choosing which attributes it will include in a certificate and what mechanism it will use to verify those attributes before it issues the certificate.

Certificate Publishers   They make certificates publicly available, inside or outside an organization. This allows widespread availability of the critical material needed to support the entire PKI.

PKI-Savvy Applications   These allow you and your users to do useful things with certificates, such as encrypt email or network connections. Ideally, the user shouldn't have to know (or even be aware of) what the application is doing—everything should work seamlessly and automatically. The best-known examples of PKI-savvy applications are web browsers such as Internet Explorer and Firefox and email applications such as Outlook.

Certificate Templates   These act like rubber stamps. By specifying a particular template as the model you want to use for a newly issued certificate, you're actually telling the CA which optional attributes to add to the certificate as well as implicitly telling it how to fill some of the mandatory attributes. Templates greatly simplify the process of issuing certificates because they keep you from having to memorize the names of all of the attributes you may potentially want to put in a certificate.

Learn More About PKI

When discussing certificates, it's also important to mention PKI and its definition. The exam doesn't go deeply into PKI, but I recommend you do some extra research on your own because it is an important technology and shouldn't be overlooked. PKI is actually a simple concept with a lot of moving parts. When broken down to its bare essentials, PKI is nothing more than a server and workstations utilizing a software service to add security to your infrastructure. When you use PKI, you are adding a layer of protection. The auto-enrollment Settings policy determines whether users and/or computers are automatically enrolled for the appropriate certificates when necessary. By default, this policy is enabled if a certificate server is installed, but you can make changes to the settings, as shown in Exercise 8.5.

In Exercise 8.5, you will learn how to configure automatic certificate enrollment in Group Policy. You must have first completed the other exercises in this chapter in order to proceed with Exercise 8.5.

EXERCISE 8.5

Configuring Automatic Certificate Enrollment in Group Policy

1. Open the Group Policy Management Console tool.

2. Right-click the North America OU that you created in the previous exercises in this book.

3. Select Create A GPO In This Domain And Link It Here and name it **Test CA**. Click OK.

4. Right-click the Test CA GPO and choose Edit.

5. Open Computer Configuration ➢ Policies ➢ Windows Settings ➢ Security Settings ➢ Public Key Policies.

6. Double-click Certificate Services Client – Auto-Enrollment in the right pane.

7. The Certificate Services Client – Auto-Enrollment Properties dialog box will appear. For now, don't change anything—just become familiar with the settings in this dialog box. Click OK to close it.

Redirecting Folders

Another set of Group Policy settings that you will learn about are the *folder redirection settings*. Group Policy provides a means for redirecting the Documents, Desktop, and

Start Menu folders, as well as cached application data, to network locations. Folder redirection is particularly useful for the following reasons:

- When they are using roaming user profiles, a user's Documents folder is copied to the local machine each time they log on. This requires high bandwidth consumption and time if the Documents folder is large. If you redirect the Documents folder, it stays in the redirected location, and the user opens and saves files directly to that location.

- Documents are always available no matter where the user logs on.

- Data in the shared location can be backed up during the normal backup cycle without user intervention.

- Data can be redirected to a more robust server-side administered disk that is less prone to physical and user errors.

When you decide to redirect folders, you have two options:

- *Basic* redirection redirects everyone's folders to the same location (but each user gets their own folder within that location).

- *Advanced* redirection redirects folders to different locations based on group membership. For instance, you could configure the Engineers group to redirect their folders to //Engineering1/Documents/ and the Marketing group to //Marketing1/ Documents/. Again, individual users still get their own folder within the redirected location.

To configure folder redirection, follow the steps in Exercise 8.6. You must have completed the other exercises in this chapter to proceed with this exercise.

EXERCISE 8.6

Configuring Folder Redirection in Group Policy

1. Open the GPMC tool.

2. Open the North America OU and then edit the Test CA GPO.

3. Open User Configuration ➢ Policies ➢ Windows Settings ➢ Folder Redirection ➢ Documents.

4. Right-click Documents, and select Properties.

5. On the Target tab of the Documents Properties dialog box, choose the Basic – Redirect Everyone's Folder To The Same Location selection from the Settings drop-down list.

6. Leave the default option for the Target Folder Location drop-down list and specify a network path in the Root Path field.

7. Click the Settings tab. All of the default settings are self-explanatory and should typically be left at the default setting. Click OK when you have finished.

Folder Redirection Facts

Try not to mix up the concepts of *folder redirection* and *offline folders*, especially in a world with ever-increasing numbers of mobile users. Folder redirection and offline folders are different features.

Windows Server 2022 folder redirection works as follows: The system uses a pointer that moves the folders you want to a location you specify. Users do not see any of this—it is transparent to them. One problem with folder redirection is that it does not work for mobile users (users who will be offline and who will not have access to files they may need).

Offline folders, however, are copies of folders that were local to you. Files are now available locally to you on the system you have with you. They are also located back on the server where they are stored. The next time you log in, the folders are synchronized so that both folders contain the latest data. This is a perfect feature for mobile users, whereas folder redirection provides no benefit for the mobile user.

Managing GPOs with Windows PowerShell Group Policy Cmdlets

As stated earlier in this book, *Windows PowerShell* is a Windows command-line shell and scripting language. Windows PowerShell can also help you automate many of the same tasks that you perform using the Group Policy Management Console.

Windows Server 2022 helps you perform many of the Group Policy tasks by providing dozens of cmdlets. Each of these cmdlets is a simple, single-function command-line tool.

The Windows PowerShell Group Policy cmdlets can help you perform some of the following tasks for domain-based Group Policy objects:

- Maintain, create, remove, back up, and import GPOs

- Create, update, and remove GPO links to Active Directory containers

- Set Active Directory OUs and domain permissions and inheritance flags

- Configure Group Policy Registry settings

- Create and edit starter GPOs

The requirement for Windows PowerShell Group Policy cmdlets is Windows Server 2022 on either a domain controller or a member server that has the GPMC installed. Windows 7 or above also gives you the ability to use Windows PowerShell Group Policy cmdlets if you have Remote Server Administration Tools (RSAT) installed. RSAT includes the GPMC and its cmdlets. PowerShell is also a requirement.

Item-Level Targeting

You have the ability to apply individual preference items only to selected users or computers using a GPO feature called item-level targeting. *Item-level targeting* allows you to select specific items that the GPO will look at and then apply that GPO only to the specific users or computers. You have the ability to include multiple preference items, and you can customize each item for specific users or computers to use.

The target item has a value that belongs to it, and the value can be either true or false. You can get even more granular by using the operation command of AND or OR while building this GPO, and this will allow you to combine the targeted items with the preceding one. Once all of the conditions are executed, if the final value is false, then the GPO is not applied. If the final value is true, the GPO is applied to the users or computers that were previously determined. You have the ability to item-target the following items:

- Battery Present Targeting
- Computer Name Targeting
- CPU Speed Targeting
- Date Match Targeting
- Disk Space Targeting
- Domain Targeting
- Environment Variable Targeting
- File Match Targeting
- IP Address Range Targeting
- Language Targeting
- LDAP Query Targeting
- MAC Address Range Targeting
- MSI Query Targeting
- Network Connection Targeting
- Operating System Targeting
- Organizational Unit Targeting
- PCMCIA Present Targeting
- Portable Computer Targeting
- Processing Mode Targeting
- RAM Targeting
- Registry Match Targeting
- Security Group Targeting
- Site Targeting
- Terminal Session Targeting
- Time Range Targeting

- User Targeting
- WMI Query Targeting

You can easily set up item-level targeting by following these steps:

1. Open the Group Policy Management Console. Select the GPO that will contain the new preferences by right-clicking the GPO and then choosing Edit.

2. In the console tree under Computer Configuration or User Configuration, expand the Preferences folder and then browse to the preference extension.

3. Double-click the node for the preference extension, right-click the preference item, and click Properties.

4. In the Properties dialog box, select the Common tab.

5. Select Item-Level Targeting and then click Targeting.

6. Click New Item. If you are configuring multiple targeted items, from the Item Option menu choose the logical operation (AND or OR). Then click OK when finished.

7. Click OK in the Properties dialog box, and you are all set.

Back Up, Restore, Import, Copy, and Migration Tables

One of the biggest advantages of using the Group Policy Management Console is that it is a one-stop shopping utility. You can do everything you need to do for GPOs in one location. The GPMC not only allows you to create and link a GPO but also lets you back up, restore, import, copy, and use migration tables.

Backing Up a GPO

Since this book is about Windows Server 2022 and everything you should do to set up the server properly, then you most likely already understand what backups can do for you.

The reason administrators back up data is in the event of a crash or major error that requires us to reload data to the server. Backups should be done daily on all data that is important to your organization. Backups can be done by using Windows Server 2022's backup utility, or you can purchase third-party software/hardware to back up your data.

I am an IT director, and data recoverability is one of the most critical items that I deal with on a daily basis. I use a third-party hardware device from a company called Unitrends. This is just one of many companies that helps protect an organization's data.

This hardware device does hourly backups for all of my servers. One of the nice features of the Unitrends box is that it backs up onto the hardware device and then sends my data to the cloud automatically for an offsite backup. This way, if I need to recover just one piece of data, I can grab it off the hardware device. But if I have a major issue, such as a fire that destroys the entire server room, I have an offsite backup from which I can retrieve my data.

It's the same for GPOs. You need to make sure you back up your GPOs in the event of an issue that requires you to do a reload. To back up your GPOs manually, you can go into the GPMC MMC and, under Group Policy Objects, you can right-click and choose Backup All or right-click the specific GPO and choose Backup.

Restoring a GPO

There may be times when you have to restore a GPO that was previously backed up. There are normally two reasons why you have to restore a GPO—you accidentally deleted the GPO, or you need to restore the GPO to a previous state. (This normally happens if you make changes and they cause an issue.) Restoring a GPO is simple:

1. Open the Group Policy Management Console.

2. In the console tree, right-click Group Policy Objects and choose Manage Backups.

3. Select the backup you want to restore and click the Restore button.

Importing or Copying GPOs

As an administrator, you may you need to import or copy a GPO from one domain to another domain. You do this so that the second domain has the same settings as the first domain.

You can use the import or copy-to-transfer settings from one GPO to another GPO within the same domain, to a GPO in another domain in the same forest, or to a GPO in a domain in a different forest.

Importing or copying a GPO is an easy process. To do this, complete the following steps:

1. Open the Group Policy Management Console.

2. In the console tree, right-click Group Policy Objects and choose either Import Settings or Copy.

Migration Tables

One issue that we run into when copying or moving a GPO from one system to another is that when some GPOs are built, they are domain specific. Doing so can be a problem when the GPOs are moved to a system in another domain. This is where migration tables can help you out. *Migration tables* tell you how domain-specific settings should be treated when the GPO is moved from the domain in which it was created to another domain.

Migration tables are files that are used to map previous domain information (such as users and groups) to the new domain's object-specific data. Migration tables have mapping entries that map the old data to the new data.

Migration tables store their mapping data in an XML format, and the migration tables have their own file extension, `.migtable`. If you want to create a migration table, you can use the *Migration Table Editor (MTE)*. The MTE is an easy-to-use utility for configuring or just viewing migration tables.

It does not matter if you decide to copy or import a GPO; migration tables apply to any of the settings within the GPO. However, if you copy a GPO instead of move it, you have the option of bringing the Discretionary Access Control List (DACL) option over with the copy.

If you are looking at using migration tables, there are three settings that you can configure:

Do Not Use A Migration Table   If you choose this option, the GPO is copied over exactly as is. All security objects and UNC paths are copied over without any modification.

Use A Migration Table   If you choose this option, the GPO has all of the options that can be in the migration table mapped.

Use A Migration Table Exclusively   If you choose this option, all security principals and UNC path information in the GPO are chosen. If any of this information is not included in the migration table, the operation will fail.

To open the Migration Table Editor, perform the following steps:

1. Open the Group Policy Management Console.
2. In the console tree, right-click Group Policy Objects and choose Open Migration Table Editor.

Resetting the Default GPO

There may be a time when you need to reset the default GPO to its original settings. This is easy to do as long as you understand how to use the DCGPOFix command-line utility. This command-line utility does just what it spells—it fixes the domain controller's GPO. To use this command, use the following syntax:

```
DCGPOFix [/ignoreschema] [/target: {Domain | DC | Both}] [/?]
```

Let's take a look at the switches in the previous command. The /ignoreschema switch ignores the current version of the Active Directory schema. The reason you use this switch is because this command works only on the same schema version as the Windows version in which the command was shipped. By using this switch, you don't need to worry about what schema you have on the system.

The next switch is [/target: {Domain | DC | Both}]. This switch specifies the GPO you are going to restore. You have the ability to restore the Default Domain Policy GPO, the Default Domain Controllers GPO, or both. The final switch, /?, displays the help for this command.

Summary

In this chapter, you examined Active Directory's solution to a common headache for many systems administrators: policy settings. Specifically, I discussed topics that covered Group Policy.

I covered the fundamentals of Group Policy, including its fundamental purpose. You can use Group Policy to enforce granular permissions for users in an Active Directory environment. Group Policies can restrict and modify the actions allowed for users and computers within the Active Directory environment.

Certain Group Policy settings may apply to users, computers, or both. Computer settings affect all users who access the machines to which the policy applies. User settings affect users regardless of the machines to which they log on.

You learned that you can link Group Policy objects to Active Directory sites, domains, or OUs. This link determines to which objects the policies apply. GPO links can interact through inheritance and filtering to result in an effective set of policies.

The chapter covered inheritance and how GPOs filter down. I showed you how to use the Enforced option on a GPO issued from a parent and how to block a GPO from a child.

You can also use administrative templates to simplify the creation of GPOs. There are some basic default templates that come with Windows Server 2022. In addition, you can delegate control over GPOs in order to distribute administrative responsibilities. Delegation is an important concept because it allows for distributed administration.

You can also deploy software using GPOs. This feature can save time and increase productivity throughout the entire software management life cycle by automating software installation and removal on client computers. The Windows Installer offers a more robust method for managing installation and removal, and applications that support it can take advantage of new Active Directory features. Make sure you are comfortable using the Windows Installer.

You learned about publishing applications via Active Directory and the difference between publishing and assigning applications. You can assign some applications to users and computers so that they are always available. You can also publish them to users so that the user can install them with minimal effort when required.

You also learned how to prepare for software deployment. Before your users can take advantage of automated software installation, you must set up an installation share and provide the appropriate permissions.

The final portion of the chapter covered the Resultant Set of Policy (RSoP) tool, which you can use in logging mode or planning mode to determine exactly which set of policies applies to users, computers, OUs, domains, and sites.

Exam Essentials

Understand the purpose of Group Policy. You use Group Policy to enforce granular permissions for users in an Active Directory environment.

Understand user and computer settings. Certain Group Policy settings may apply to users, computers, or both. Computer settings affect all users that access the machines to which the policy applies. User settings affect users, regardless of which machines they log on to.

Know the interactions between Group Policy Objects and Active Directory. GPOs can be linked to Active Directory objects. This link determines to which objects the policies apply.

Understand filtering and inheritance interactions between GPOs. For ease of administration, GPOs can interact via inheritance and filtering. It is important to understand these interactions when you are implementing and troubleshooting Group Policy.

Know how Group Policy settings can affect script policies and network settings.   You can use special sets of GPOs to manage network configuration settings.

Understand how delegation of administration can be used in an Active Directory environment.   Delegation is an important concept because it allows for distributed administration.

Know how to use the Resultant Set of Policy (RSoP) tool to troubleshoot and plan Group Policy.   Windows Server 2022 includes the RSoP feature, which you can run in logging mode or planning mode to determine exactly which set of policies applies to users, computers, OUs, domains, and sites.

Understand the difference between publishing and assigning applications.   Some applications can be assigned to users and computers so that they are always available. Applications can be published to users so that the user may install the application with a minimal amount of effort when it is required.

Know how to configure application settings using Active Directory and Group Policy.   Using standard Windows Server 2016 administrative tools, you can create an application policy that meets your requirements. You can use automatic, on-demand installation of applications as well as many other features.

Review Questions

1. The process of assigning permissions to set Group Policy for objects within an OU is known as:

   A. Promotion

   B. Inheritance

   C. Delegation

   D. Filtering

2. Which of the following statements is true regarding the actions that occur when a software package is removed from a GPO that is linked to an OU?

   A. The application will be automatically uninstalled for all users within the OU.

   B. Current application installations will be unaffected by the change.

   C. The system administrator may determine the effect.

   D. The current user may determine the effect.

3. You are the network administrator for your organization. You are working on creating a new GPO for the sales OU. You want the GPO to take effect immediately. Which command would you use?

   A. GPForce

   B. GPUpdate

   C. GPResult

   D. GPExecute

4. You are the network administrator for your organization. You are working on creating a new GPO for the Marketing OU. You want the GPO to take effect immediately, and you need to use Windows PowerShell. Which PowerShell cmdlet command would you use?

   A. Invoke-GPUpdate

   B. Invoke-GPForce

   C. Invoke-GPResult

   D. Invoke-GPExecute

5. You are the network administrator, and you have decided to set up a GPO with item-level targeting. Which of the following is *not* an option for item-level targeting?

   A. Battery Present Targeting

   B. Computer Name Targeting

   C. CPU Speed Targeting

   D. DVD Present Targeting

6. Your network contains an Active Directory Domain Services (AD DS) domain. You have a Group Policy Object (GPO) named GPO1 that contains Group Policy preferences. You plan to link GPO1 to the domain. You need to ensure that the preferences in GPO1 apply only to domain member servers and *not* to domain controllers or client computers. All the other Group Policy settings in GPO1 must apply to all the computers. The solution must minimize administrative effort. Which type of item level targeting should you use?

A. Domain

B. Operating System

C. Security Group

D. Environment Variable

7. You work for an organization with a single Windows Server 2022 Active Directory domain. The domain has OUs for Sales, Marketing, Admin, R&D, and Finance. You need the users in the Finance OU only to get Microsoft Office 2016 installed automatically onto their computers. You create a GPO named OfficeApp. What is the next step in getting all of the Finance users Office 2016?

A. Edit the GPO and assign the Office application to the user's account. Link the GPO to the Finance OU.

B. Edit the GPO, and assign the Office application to the user's account. Link the GPO to the domain.

C. Edit the GPO, and assign the Office application to the computer account. Link the GPO to the domain.

D. Edit the GPO, and assign the Office application to the computer account. Link the GPO to the Finance OU.

8. You are hired as a consultant to the ABC Company. The owner of the company complains that she continues to have desktop wallpaper that she did not choose. When you speak with the IT team, you find out that a former employee created 20 GPOs and they have not been able to figure out which GPO is changing the owner's desktop wallpaper. How can you resolve this issue?

A. Run the RSoP utility against all forest computer accounts.

B. Run the RSoP utility against the owner's computer account.

C. Run the RSoP utility against the owner's user account.

D. Run the RSoP utility against all domain computer accounts.

9. You are the network administrator for a large organization that has multiple sites and multiple OUs. You have a site named SalesSite that is for the sales building across the street. In the domain, there is an OU for all salespeople called Sales. You set up a GPO for the SalesSite, and you need to be sure that it applies to the Sales OU. The Sales OU GPOs cannot override the SalesSite GPO. What do you do?

A. On the GPO, disable the Block Child Inheritance setting.

B. On the GPO, set the Enforce setting.

C. On the GPO, set the priorities to 1.

D. On the Sales OU, configure the Inherit Parent Policy settings.

10. You are the administrator for an organization that has multiple locations. You are running Windows Server 2022, and you have only one domain with multiple OUs set up for each location. One of your locations, Boston, is connected to the main location by a 256 Kbps ISDN line. You configure a GPO to assign a sales application to all computers in the entire domain. You have to be sure that Boston users receive the GPO properly. What should you do?

    A. Disable the Slow Link Detection setting in the GPO.

    B. Link the GPO to the Boston OU.

    C. Change the properties of the GPO to publish the application to the Boston OU.

    D. Have the users in Boston run the `GPResult/force` command.

11. You are the network administrator for a large organization that uses Windows Server 2022 domain controllers and DNS servers. All of your client machines currently have the Windows XP operating system. You want to be able to have client computers edit the domain-based GPOs by using the ADMX files that are located in the ADMX Central Store. How do you accomplish this task? (Choose all that apply.)

    A. Upgrade your clients to Windows 8.

    B. Upgrade your clients to Windows 10.

    C. Add the client machines to the ADMX edit utility.

    D. In the ADMX store, choose the box Allow All Client Privileges.

12. You work for an organization with a single Windows Server 2022 Active Directory domain. The domain has OUs for Sales, Marketing, Admin, R&D, and Finance. You need only the users in the Finance OU to get Windows Office 2016 installed automatically onto their computers. You create a GPO named OfficeApp. What is the next step in getting all of the Finance users Office 2016?

    A. Edit the GPO, and assign the Office application to the user's account. Link the GPO to the Finance OU.

    B. Edit the GPO, and assign the Office application to the user's account. Link the GPO to the domain.

    C. Edit the GPO, and assign the Office application to the computer account. Link the GPO to the domain.

    D. Edit the GPO, and assign the Office application to the computer account. Link the GPO to the Finance OU.

13. To disable GPO settings for a specific security group, which of the following permissions should you use?

    A. Deny Write

    B. Allow Write

    C. Enable Apply Group Policy

    D. Deny Apply Group Policy

14. GPOs assigned at which of the following level(s) will override GPO settings at the domain level?

A. OU

B. Site

C. Domain

D. Both OU and site

15. A system administrator wants to ensure that only the GPOs set at the OU level affect the Group Policy settings for objects within the OU. Which option can they use to do this (assuming that all other GPO settings are the defaults)?

A. The Enforced option

B. The Block Policy Inheritance option

C. The Disable option

D. The Deny permission

16. A system administrator is planning to implement Group Policy Objects in a new Windows Server 2022 Active Directory environment. In order to meet the needs of the organization, he decides to implement a hierarchical system of Group Policy settings. At which of the following levels is he able to assign Group Policy settings? (Choose all that apply.)

A. Sites

B. Domains

C. Organizational units

D. Local system

17. Ann is a system administrator for a medium-sized Active Directory environment. She has determined that several new applications that will be deployed throughout the organization use Registry-based settings. She would like to do the following:

- Control these Registry settings using Group Policy

- Create a standard set of options for these applications and allow other system administrators to modify them using the standard Active Directory tools

Which of the following options can she use to meet these requirements? (Choose all that apply.)

A. Implement the inheritance functionality of GPOs.

B. Implement delegation of specific objects within Active Directory.

C. Implement the No Override functionality of GPOs.

D. Create administrative templates.

E. Provide administrative templates to the system administrators who are responsible for creating Group Policy for the applications.

Chapter

9

Introduction to Microsoft Azure

So far, I have explained how to set up and build a Windows Server on an on-site domain. Now it's time for us to look at how to integrate your on-site domain to the cloud.

Before we actually connect the network to the cloud, it's important to understand how the cloud works and the different types of cloud setups that you can choose from.

In this chapter, I will explain the types of cloud setups available as well as the terminology that you will need to understand so that we can build our cloud network.

This chapter does not have any exam objectives directly related to this chapter. But the concepts in this chapter are very important to understand so that as you move forward in the next chapters, you understand the terms and concepts to help you design the proper cloud environment. But there are questions on the exam about the various types of services (e.g., IaaS, PaaS, and SaaS) and what they do. So even though there are no objectives listed, you will get questions about these topics.

Understanding Cloud Concepts

The cloud is one of the fastest growing areas of IT over the past few years. I want to make sure that you first understand what the *cloud* actually is. Simply put, it means that you are loading your data or network on someone else's network. That doesn't mean that the cloud is not a good thing. For many companies, the cloud allows them to use network components that they could never use in the past.

Cloud Advantages

The cloud can offer companies of any size a lot of benefits. Let's take a look at some of those benefits:

High Availability (HA)   The capability of an application to remain running in a healthy state, without any substantial downtime, is known as high availability (HA). When an application is in a healthy state, it is responsive by allowing users to connect and interact with it.

Scalability   The increase or decrease of a service or resource at any particular time, regardless of the demand, is called scalability. Adding additional resources to an existing server is called *vertical scaling*, or *scaling up*.

Elasticity   This is a cloud service that automatically scales resources as needed. Elasticity is the ability to automatically increase or decrease computer processing, memory, and storage resources to meet the current demand. It is usually measured by system monitoring tools. With cloud elasticity, a business can avoid paying for resources that aren't being used, and they don't have to worry about purchasing new equipment or maintaining current systems.

Cloud Agility   Being able to quickly change your infrastructure lets you adapt to changing business requirements. Cloud agility is all about giving the corporation the ability to develop, test, and launch applications as needed and to do so quickly.

Fault Tolerance   Fault tolerance is a way to make sure that you are not too badly impacted if/when something unexpected happens. The cloud services architecture has redundancy built right in. With fault tolerance, if one component fails, then another backup component steps up to the plate and takes over.

Disaster Recovery   Disaster recovery is a blend of strategies and services for backing up data, applications, and other resources to a public cloud or dedicated service providers. If a disaster occurs, the affected source can be restored and you can resume normal operations. Disaster recovery means that the cloud infrastructure can replicate application resources in an unaffected region so that the data is safe and the application availability isn't compromised.

Understanding CapEx vs. OpEx

When deciding if the cloud is a good fit for your company, you need to think about money. Obviously, money makes the IT world go around. When considering building a network, you need to take into account the money it will cost for you to build an onsite network. You may decide it's more beneficial to use the cloud.

To make this decision, you must consider the cost of buying, building, and maintaining an onsite network compared to using an online network. This means you must understand the difference between capital expenditures (CapEx) and operational expenditures (OpEx).

Capital Expenditures

Capital expenditures (CapEx) is when a company spends money on their physical assets up-front. This cost, over the life of the equipment, will depreciate. For example, if you pay in advance to acquire, upgrade, and/or support physical assets, then you can deduct these expenses from your tax bill. Here are some items that are considered CapEx:

Server Costs   Server costs include the cost of supporting your servers as well as any hardware needed to support them. It's important to remember that when buying servers, you will want to incorporate fault tolerance and redundancy. Server costs can include adding redundant and uninterruptible power supplies and server clustering, among other factors. If a server needs to be added or replaced, this becomes an up-front cost that can affect the corporate cash flow.

Storage Costs   Storage costs include the costs that are associated with all storage hardware components and the support of those components. Depending on the level of redundancy and fault tolerance used, storage can get costly. If you are part of a larger organization, you may want to create storage tiers where your most critical applications use the fault-tolerant storage devices and your lower-priority data uses a less expensive storage device.

Network Costs   Networking costs include all of your onsite hardware components. These costs can include routers, switches, access points, any cables, the wide area network (WAN), and Internet connections.

Backup and Archive Costs   Backup and archive costs are the costs associated with backing up your data. Copying and archiving data also falls into this category. There may be up-front costs as well, such as the cost of purchasing hardware or backup tapes.

Organization Continuity and Disaster Recovery Costs   Organization continuity and disaster recovery costs are the costs associated with how you plan to recover from a disaster so that you can continue working without interruptions. These costs can include the creation of a disaster recovery site or the purchase of backup generators.

Datacenter Infrastructure Costs   Datacenter infrastructure costs are any costs associated with building and construction equipment. These costs may incur operational expenses. These expenses can include building maintenance; heating, ventilation, and air conditioning (HVAC); and electricity, among others.

Technical Personnel   While not typically a capital expenditure, you need to take into account the costs associated with the personnel that are needed to maintain your on-premises datacenters as well as your disaster recovery site.

Operational Expenditure (OpEx)

Operational expenditures (OpEx) are the costs of products and services that are being used at this moment. These expenses can be deducted from your tax bill within the same year. You are paying as you go. Here are some items that are considered OpEx:

Leasing Software and Customized Features   Leasing software and customized features are considered a pay-per-use model. Ensuring that your users do not misappropriate services or that provisioned accounts are being used properly requires that you actively manage your subscriptions. Billing will start as soon as you start using those resources. If the resources are not used, you will want to deprovision them in order to decrease costs.

Scaling Charges Based on Usage and Demand   Scaling charges are based on usage and demand. They can be billed in a number of different ways. Billing can be based on the number of users or the CPU usage times. Billing can also be based on the I/O operations per second (IOPS), allotted RAM, or the amount of storage used.

Billing at the User or Organization Level   Billing at the user or organization level can be based on the pay-per-use model; this is also called your *subscription*. The subscription is the billing method. You will be billed for the services used. This is typically a recurring expense. You can scale your resources to meet your corporate needs.

Understanding Different Cloud Concepts

Many IT people don't know that, when we are talking about the cloud, there are different types of cloud options. You need to become familiar with the various types of cloud environments so that you can choose the best option for your organization.

Public Cloud

Microsoft describes the public cloud as

> . . . computing services offered by third-party providers over the public Internet, making them available to anyone who wants to use or purchase them. They may be free or sold on-demand, allowing customers to pay only per usage for the CPU cycles, storage, or bandwidth they consume.
>
> Source: `https://azure.microsoft.com/en-us/resources/cloud-computing-dictionary/what-is-a-public-cloud`

Public clouds are the most common way to deploy cloud resources. An example of a public cloud is Microsoft Azure. Public clouds can save you from the costs associated with having to buy, manage, and maintain onsite hardware and application resources. Public clouds have the following advantages:

High Reliability   To ensure against failures, a wide array of servers is available.

Lower Costs   There is no need to purchase any hardware or software. You have to pay only for the services you use.

Near-Unlimited Scalability   To meet your corporate needs, on-demand resources are available.

No Maintenance   You will have no associated maintenance costs. Your service provider handles all the maintenance needed.

Private Cloud

Microsoft describes the private cloud as "computing services offered either over the Internet or a private internal network and only to select users instead of the general public" (`https://azure.microsoft.com/en-gb/resources/cloud-computing-dictionary/what-is-a-private-cloud`). A private cloud can also be called an internal or corporate cloud. A private cloud can be located physically at your company's onsite datacenter, or it can be hosted by a third-party service provider.

Cloud services can be delivered in a private cloud in two models. One of these models is known as infrastructure-as-a-service (IaaS). IaaS allows you to use infrastructure resources such as compute, network, and storage as a service. The other model is platform-as-a-service (PaaS), which lets you deliver a wide range of applications. Private clouds can also be merged with public clouds to create what is known as a *hybrid* cloud (see the following section). Private clouds have the following advantages:

Flexibility   You can customize the cloud environment to meet your corporate requirements.

High Scalability   Private clouds offer scalability and efficiency.

Improved Security   Since resources are not shared with others, private clouds provide a higher level of control and security.

Hybrid-Based Networks

A hybrid cloud combines both a private cloud and a public cloud and allows data and applications to be shared between them. This ability provides additional deployment options and more flexibility. Hybrid clouds have the following advantages:

Cost Effective   Hybrid clouds are on a pay-as-you-go model. You are renting the hardware and paying for the resources that you've used.

Current   The cloud providers maintain all the computer hardware and software.

Elasticity   Depending on demand or workload, you can add or remove resources automatically to meet your needs. You may notice that there are times when you use more resources; this option will allow you to shift those resources depending on the demand.

Global   The cloud providers have datacenters located all over the world to implement performance, redundancy, and compliance requirements.

Low Latency   Low latency is the capability of a computing system or network to provide responses with the least delay. A cloud service that helps users quickly access an Internet Azure resource provides for faster and more reliable access.

Reliable   The cloud providers provide the backup, disaster recovery, and replication services. The service level agreement (SLA) that you chose for your Azure subscription will determine the amount of acceptable downtime from Microsoft.

Scalable   Depending on demand or workload, you can increase or decrease the resources and services used.

Secure   The cloud providers provide better security by implementing a broad set of policies, technologies, controls, and expert technical skills.

Understanding the Difference between IaaS, PaaS, and SaaS

Organizational networks are more than just building the physical network and adding servers. Networks contain many different components. Let's take a look at some of these components and how you can use the cloud to use and support them.

Infrastructure-as-a-Service (IaaS)

Infrastructure-as-a-service (IaaS) is a cloud computing service that provides on demand compute, storage, and networking resources on a pay-as-you-go basis over the Internet.

Using an IaaS solution will help you reduce maintenance of your onsite datacenters and can help with the expense of hardware costs. It also allows you the flexibility to scale your resources depending on demand. You only pay for what you use.

IaaS Advantages

The following are the advantages of IaaS:

Eliminates Capital Expense and Reduces Ongoing Cost   IaaS avoids the up-front expenses of setting up and managing an onsite datacenter.

Enhanced Security   With the appropriate SLA in place, your cloud service provider can provide better security for your applications and data than if you were to maintain it onsite.

Helps Innovate and Get New Apps to the Users Faster   With IaaS, once you've launched a new product, the necessary computing infrastructure can be ready in a few minutes or hours, rather than in days or weeks. This allows you to deliver your apps much faster.

Improved Business Continuity and Disaster Recovery   With the appropriate SLA in place, IaaS can help reduce the cost of achieving high availability, business continuity, and disaster recovery.

Increased Scale and Performance of IT Workloads   IaaS allows you to scale globally and will adjust to changes in resource demand.

Increased Stability, Reliability, and Support   With IaaS, since the provider maintains all the hardware and software, there is no need for you to upgrade software/hardware or to troubleshoot any equipment issues. IaaS frees up your team to allow them to focus on your business rather than on IT infrastructure issues. You still have to handle operating system issues, maintenance, and monitoring. You won't need to worry about the physical hardware.

Reduced Capital Expenditures and Optimized Costs   IaaS eliminates the costs associated with managing and configuring an onsite datacenter. When you're migrating to the cloud, IaaS makes it extremely cost-effective. IaaS providers use the pay-as-you-go subscription model.

Platform-as-a-Service (PaaS)

According to Microsoft, "platform as a service (PaaS) is a complete development and deployment environment in the cloud, with resources that enable you to deliver everything from simple cloud-based apps to sophisticated, cloud-enabled enterprise applications" (`https://azure.microsoft.com/en-us/resources/cloud-computing-dictionary/what-is-paas`). You can purchase the required resources from a cloud service provider on a pay-as-you-go basis and then access those resources via a secure Internet connection.

PaaS includes infrastructure, such as servers, storage, and networking. It also consists of the middleware, development tools, business intelligence (BI) services, database management systems, and more.

PaaS allows you to avoid the costs of buying and managing software licenses. Basically, you manage the applications and services that they developed, and the cloud service provider manages all other aspects.

Platform-as-a-Service (PaaS) Advantages

The following are the advantages of PaaS:

Adds Development Capabilities Without Adding Staff   PaaS can provide your development team with new capabilities without the need to hire new staff.

Cuts Coding Time   You can reduce the time it takes to code new applications by using pre-coded application components that are built into the platform. These include workflow, directory services, security features, search, and more.

Easily Develop for Multiple Platforms   Service providers can offer you development options for multiple platforms. These can include computers, mobile devices, and browsers to make cross-platform applications easier to develop.

Efficiently Manage the Application Life Cycle   PaaS provides all of the capabilities needed to support the complete web application life cycle. The life cycle includes building, testing, deploying, managing, and updating within the same integrated environment.

Supports Geographically Distributed Development Teams   Since the development environment is accessed over the Internet, PaaS makes it easier for development teams to work together on projects, even when in remote locations.

Uses Sophisticated Tools Affordably   Since PaaS is a pay-as-you-go model, it makes it possible to use advanced development software and business intelligence (BI) as well as analytics tools that you typically could not afford to purchase.

Software-as-a-Service (SaaS)

Over the Internet, software-as-a-service (SaaS) allows users to connect to and use cloud-based applications. SaaS provides a software solution that is purchased on a pay-as-you-go basis from a cloud service provider. Basically, you are renting the use of an application and users connect to it over the Internet. Common examples are email, calendaring, and office tools (such as Microsoft Office 365).

All of the core infrastructure, middleware, application software, and application data are located in the service provider's datacenter. The service provider maintains all the hardware and software.

SaaS allows a company to get up and running quickly with few up-front costs. When employing an SaaS solution, you will be responsible for configuring the SaaS solution. Then, everything else is managed by the cloud provider.

Software-as-a-Service (SaaS) Advantages

The following are the advantages of SaaS:

Access App Data from Anywhere Since the data is stored in the cloud, your users can access the information from any Internet-connected computer or mobile device. Since the application data is stored in the cloud, no data is lost if a user's computer or device fails.

Gain Access to Sophisticated Applications To provide SaaS applications to users, there is no need to purchase, install, update, or maintain any hardware, middleware, or software.

Mobilize Your Workforce Easily Users can access SaaS applications and data from any Internet-connected computer or mobile device. There is also no need to hire additional staff to maintain the applications.

Pay Only for What You Use You will save money since the SaaS service will automatically scale up and down depending on your usage levels.

Use Free Client Software Users can run most SaaS applications using their web browser without the need to download or install any software.

Compare and Contrast the Service Types

Table 9.1 shows you all of the different components and how IaaS, PaaS, and SaaS can be used in the cloud. Table 9.1 also shows the benefits of each of these components when deciding to use the cloud.

TABLE 9.1 IaaS, PaaS, and SaaS benefits and features

Feature	IaaS	PaaS	SaaS
Up-front Costs	No up-front costs. Pay only for what is consumed.	No up-front costs. Pay only for what is consumed.	No up-front costs. Users pay for a subscription, usually on a monthly or annual basis.
User Ownership	User is responsible for the purchase, installation, configuration, and management of their own software, operating systems, middleware, and applications.	User is responsible for the development of their own applications. But they are not responsible for managing the server or infrastructure.	Users just use the application software. Users are not responsible for the maintenance or management of that software.
Cloud Provider Ownership	The cloud provider is responsible for making sure that the cloud infrastructure is available for the users. This includes the virtual machines, storage, and networking.	The cloud provider is responsible for the operating system management, network, and service configurations. Cloud providers deliver a complete managed platform on which to run the application.	The cloud provider is responsible for the provision, management, and maintenance of the application software.

Understanding Azure Benefits

Before you decide to use Azure in your organization, you must determine whether it's a good choice for your environment. Azure is a consumption-based model. This means that the more services you use in Azure, the more it will cost your organization.

But this can be a benefit for your organization. You only pay for what you use. So, your organization can move the entire network to the cloud or only move certain components to help save money.

Therefore, it's important that you understand the benefits and services that you get from using Azure. That's where we will begin. Let's take a look at some of the Azure benefits.

Azure Benefits

Microsoft Azure offers an organization many benefits. Choosing the options that are right for your organization will depend on your organization's budget and circumstances. Azure can offer your organization many advantages, but we will look at just some of the main ones.

Application Development Speed

When people think of the cloud and speed, they may think about how much lag they may encounter or how quickly they can access their information.

But when talking about the speed of Microsoft Azure, we're referring to how well Azure performs. Azure allows your teams to quickly produce, test, and deploy applications. Azure allows you to upgrade service plans or add new features quickly. You can rapidly recover data and use artificial intelligence (AI) and machine learning (ML) to process vast amounts of data, to analyze that data, and to receive recommendations.

Azure provides automated solutions to quickly speed up development of applications and also provides real-time solutions. Azure provides templates and prebuilt tools to build applications in minimal time. You don't have to create applications from scratch.

Enhanced Flexibility

Another benefit of Microsoft Azure is the enhanced flexibility. Azure has three features with enhanced flexibility:

Flexible Service Levels   Azure provides flexible scalability services to its cloud storage so users can safely and easily access it. Companies only pay for what they use, making it easier to change tiers to maximize your budget.

Flexible Storage Locations   Microsoft has over 40 datacenters around the world for you to use. This allows you to back up your data in more than one location.

Flexible Coding Languages   Azure uses many familiar coding tools, such as ASP, .NET, Visual Studio, Visual Basic, C, and C++. These coding tools allow you to develop applications in a language you may be more comfortable with.

Integrated Delivery Pipeline

Azure has a broad integrated delivery pipeline. This end-to-end solution ranges from the development of an application to its deployment. Azure ensures flexibility because all the tools are embedded in the same environment.

Disaster Recovery

Azure covers all aspects of disaster recovery to quickly resolve issues such as backups and virtual systems testing.

Azure can help shield critical data and applications by offering an end-to-end backup and disaster recovery solution that can be integrated with your on-premise backup solutions:

Backups   Azure provides a backup solution that can be used by enabling the Data Recovery option. You will be provided with the option to either use Azure Backup on-premises or on the cloud. You no longer need to have your own servers to keep your data safe, and accessing backups on the cloud takes much less time than using traditional methods of tapes and onsite servers.

Virtual Systems Testing   Azure provides testing capabilities that allow you to test your application before launching it. You can run dev-test copies without disturbing users. This allows you to test new versions of applications using your existing live data to allow for a smooth transition. Azure provides a wide range of connections to increase performance and usage by using environments such as virtual private networks, delivery nodes, clear caches, and ExpressRoute networks.

Security

Security is extremely important. Azure can help safeguard your backup environment by using built-in security tools for hybrid and cloud environments. Azure also provides compliance by using wide-range security and privacy regulations. It aids with security by using a single sign-on feature that can be utilized by all users.

Microsoft uses a multitude of compliance certificates, including Family Educational Rights and Privacy Act (FERPA), General Data Protection Regulation (GDPR), Health Insurance Portability and Accountability Act (HIPAA), and IRS. You can also protect your data by using multifactor authentication, strict password requirements, and training.

Azure will send out notifications when you need to upgrade or enable a new protection feature. One feature included with Azure is Key Vault. This feature will safeguard cryptographic keys and other secrets that are used by cloud applications and services.

With Microsoft's Defender for Cloud (previously called Azure Security Center) you can assess the security posture of your cloud resources and threat protection. You can even assess your security standings, which will give you a secure score that rates you on your actions and provide tips to make your environment more secure.

Defender for Cloud fills three vital requirements when managing the security of your resources either in the cloud or on-premises:

Continuous Assessment   Allows you to understand your current security posture by providing a secure score. This score tells you your current security situation. The higher the score, the lower the risk level.

Defend   This will detect and resolve threats to your resources and services. This will provide security alerts. Defender for Cloud will detect threats to your resources and workloads. These alerts will appear in the Azure portal or can be emailed.

Secure   Harden all connected resources and services. This will offer security recommendations to improve your posture.

Understanding the Azure Dashboards

Microsoft Azure can support a number of dashboards in the Azure portal. Each dashboard will include tiles showing data from different Azure resources across different resource groups and subscriptions. You can also create different dashboards for different teams or clone an existing one.

In the Azure portal, dashboards are a focused and organized view of your cloud resources. You can use dashboards as a workspace where you can monitor resources and launch tasks. The Azure portal provides a default dashboard as a starting point.

Using the Azure Dashboard

Dashboards provide a focused view of the resources in your subscription. When you first use Azure, you will be provided with a default dashboard. You can customize this dashboard to allow you to view only those resources that are most important to you. Changes that you make to the default view will affect your experience only. You can create other dashboards for your own use, or publish customized dashboards to be shared with other users within your organization.

Each user can create up to 100 private dashboards. If you publish and share the dashboard, it will be implemented as an Azure resource in your subscription and will not count toward this limit.

Exercise 9.1 will show you how to create a new private dashboard using an assigned name. All dashboards are private when they are created, but you can choose to publish and share the dashboard with other users.

EXERCISE 9.1

Creating a New Dashboard

1. Sign into the Azure portal: `http://portal.azure.com`.

2. From the Azure portal menu, select Dashboard (see Figure 9.1). The default view may be already set.

FIGURE 9.1 Azure Dashboard

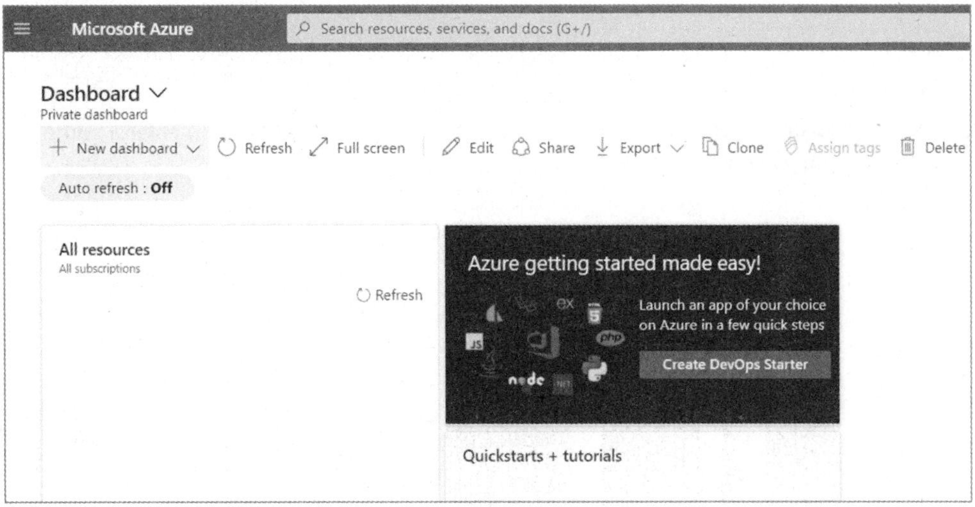

EXERCISE 9.1 ***(continued)***

3. Select New Dashboard, then select Blank Dashboard (see Figure 9.2). This will open the Tile Gallery. Here you can select tiles and arrange those tiles onto an empty grid to design it how you'd like.

FIGURE 9.2 New Azure dashboard

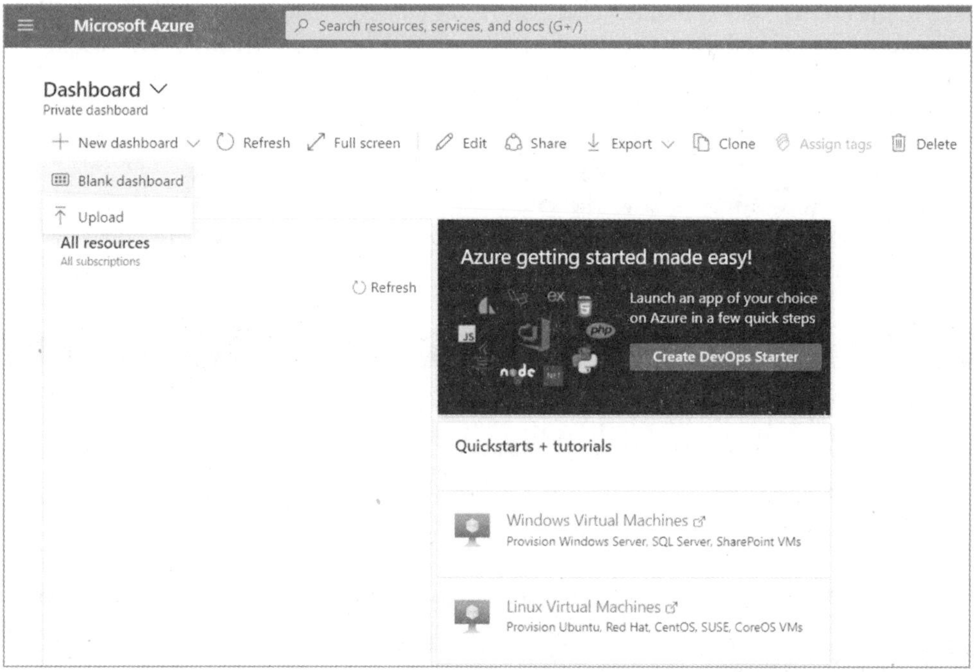

4. Select the My Dashboard text (see Figure 9.3) in the dashboard label and enter a name to identify the custom dashboard.

FIGURE 9.3   Naming the new Azure dashboard

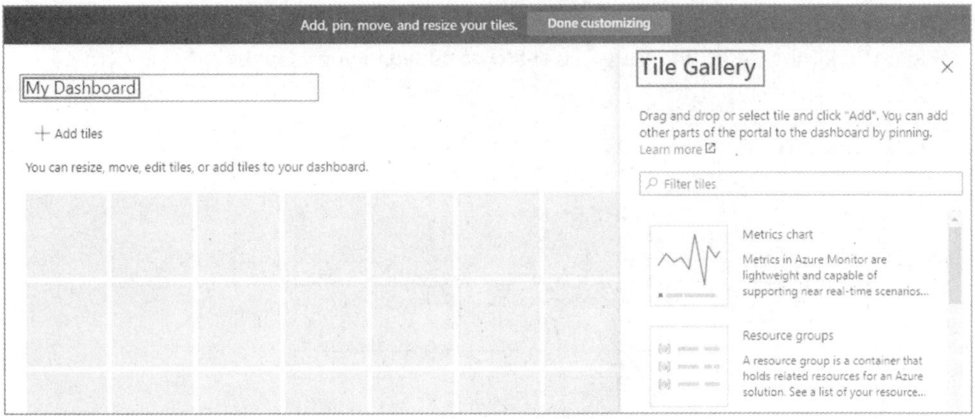

5. To save the dashboard as is, on the page header, select Done Customizing.

The dashboard view will now show your new dashboard. Select the arrow next to the dashboard name to see your available dashboards. The list might include dashboards that other users have created and shared.

Next, you can edit a dashboard. This will give you the ability to add, resize, and arrange the tiles to suit your needs. Exercise 9.2 will show you how to add tiles to a dashboard from the Tile Gallery.

EXERCISE 9.2

Adding Tiles from the Tile Gallery

1. Select Edit from the dashboard's page header (see Figure 9.4).

FIGURE 9.4   Edit Dashboard

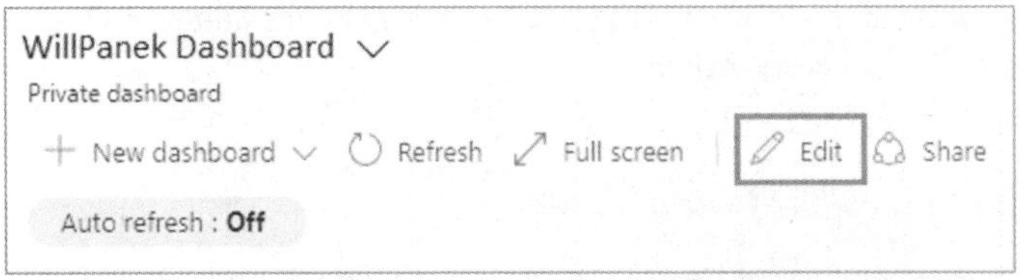

EXERCISE 9.2 *(continued)*

2. Browse the Tile Gallery to find a certain tile, or you can use the search field (see Figure 9.5). Then, select the tile you want to be added to your dashboard.

FIGURE 9.5 Tile Gallery

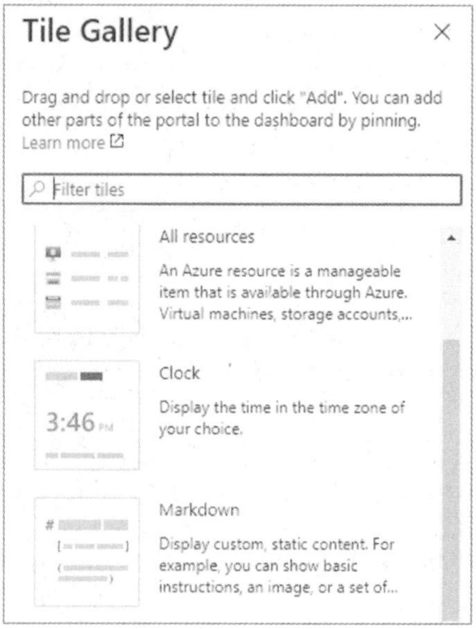

3. Click Add to add the tile to the dashboard with a default size and location, or you can drag the tile to the grid and place it where you want.
4. If desired, resize or rearrange your tiles.
5. To save your changes, click Save in the page header (see Figure 9.6). You can also choose to preview the changes without saving by selecting the Preview button. This allows you to see how filters affect your tiles. From the preview screen, if you like the changes you've made, you can select Save to keep the changes. If you do not care for the changes, you can click Discard to remove them, or click Edit to go back to the editing options and make further changes.

FIGURE 9.6 Save the Tile Gallery

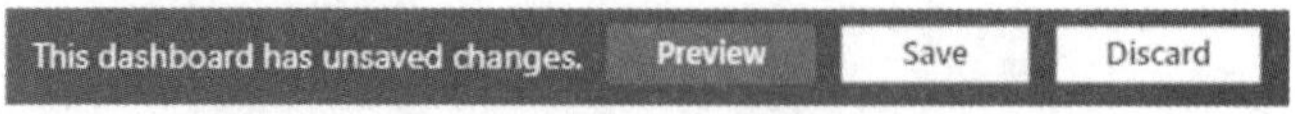

Pin Content from a Resource Group Page

Another way that you can add tiles to your dashboard is by adding them directly from a Resource Group page (see Figure 9.7). Many resource pages have a pin icon on the page header. This means that you can pin the tile to the source page. Figure 9.7 shows what the pin looks like.

FIGURE 9.7 Resource Group page

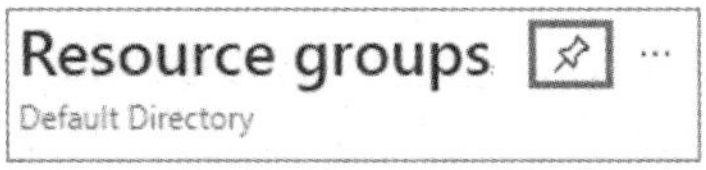

If you click this icon, you can then pin the tile to an existing private or shared dashboard (see Figure 9.8). By selecting Create New, you can create a new dashboard that will include the pin.

FIGURE 9.8 Pin To Dashboard

Copy a Tile to a New Dashboard

You also have the ability to reuse a tile and use it on another dashboard. You can copy it from one dashboard to another. To do this, open the menu in the upper-right corner and then choose Copy, as shown in Figure 9.9.

FIGURE 9.9 Copying a Tile

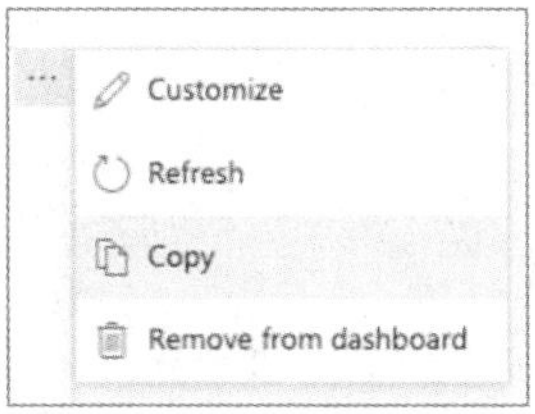

You can then select whether you want to copy the tile to an existing private or shared dashboard or create a copy of the tile within the dashboard you are currently working on. You will also have the ability to create a new dashboard that will include a copy of the tile by clicking Create New.

Exercise 9.3 shows you the steps for changing the size of a tile or rearranging tiles on a dashboard.

EXERCISE 9.3

Resizing or Rearranging Tiles

1. Select Edit from the page header.

2. Then, select the menu in the upper-right corner of a tile. The Configure Tile Size window will appear on right-hand side (see Figure 9.10). Tiles that support any size also include a "handle" in the lower-right corner that lets you drag the tile to the size you want.

FIGURE 9.10   Configuring tile size

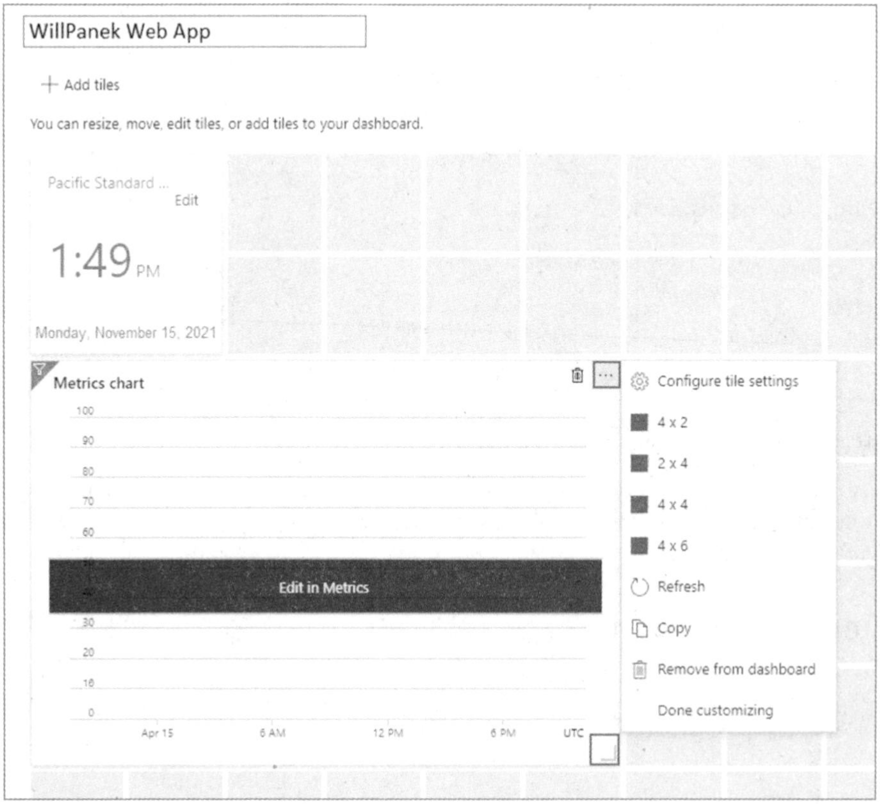

3. To arrange your dashboard, select a tile and drag it to a new location on the grid.

Set and Override Dashboard Filters

Near the top of the dashboard, you will see several options where you can set the Auto Refresh and Time settings for the data displayed on the dashboard (see Figure 9.11). There are other options to add additional filters.

FIGURE 9.11 Auto Refresh and Time Settings

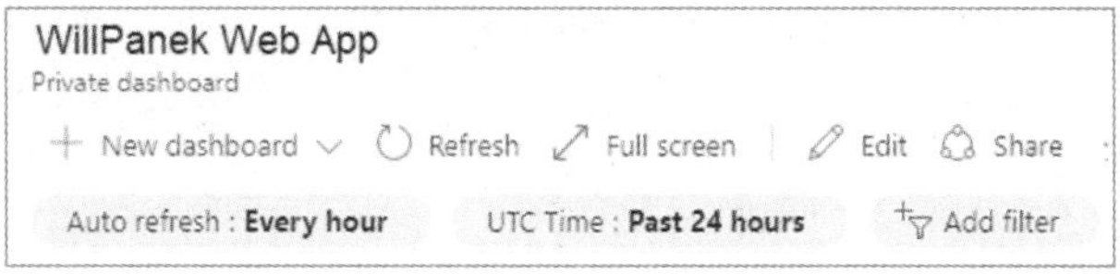

By default, the data will be refreshed hourly. To change this, click Auto Refresh and choose a new interval to refresh. Once you have made your selection, click Apply. The default time is set to UTC Time, showing the data for the past 24 hours. To modify this, click the button and choose a new time range, time granularity, and/or time zone, then click Apply.

If you'd like to apply additional filters, select Add Filters. The options you see will vary depending on the tiles on your dashboard. Select the filter you'd like to use and the filter will then be applied to your data. If you'd like to remove the filter, click the X in its button.

Tiles that support filtering will have a filter icon in the top-left corner, as shown in Figure 9.12. If you set filters for a particular tile, the left corner of that tile displays a double filter icon, which indicates that the data has its own applied filters.

FIGURE 9.12 Filter icon

Modify Tile Settings

There may be times when a tile is not configured to show you exactly the information you want. You can configure tiles to show the required information. You can override the dashboard's default time settings and filters by customizing the tile data.

Data that is displayed on the dashboard shows current activity and based on the global filters that are set for that tile. But some tiles allow you to choose a different time span to display. To do this, follow the steps in Exercise 9.4.

EXERCISE 9.4

Customizing the Time Span for a Tile

1. Select Customize tile data from the menu in the right-hand corner (as shown in Figure 9.13) or click the Filter icon in the upper-left corner of the tile.

FIGURE 9.13   Configure Tile Settings

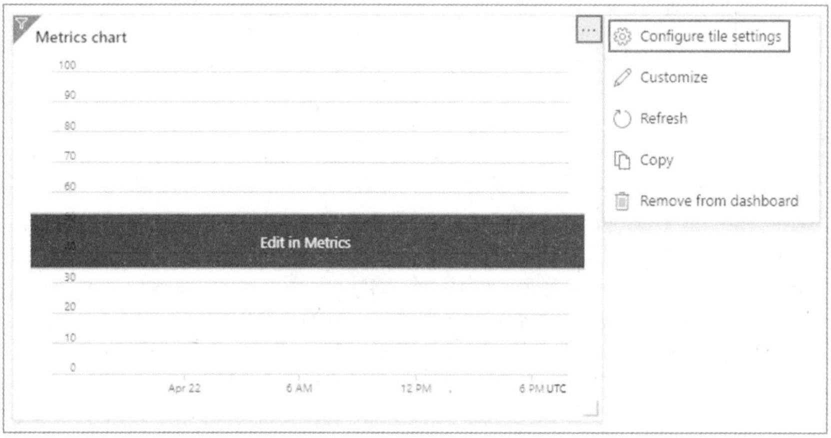

2. Select the option Override The Dashboard Time Settings At The Tile Level (as shown in Figure 9.14).

FIGURE 9.14   Override The Dashboard

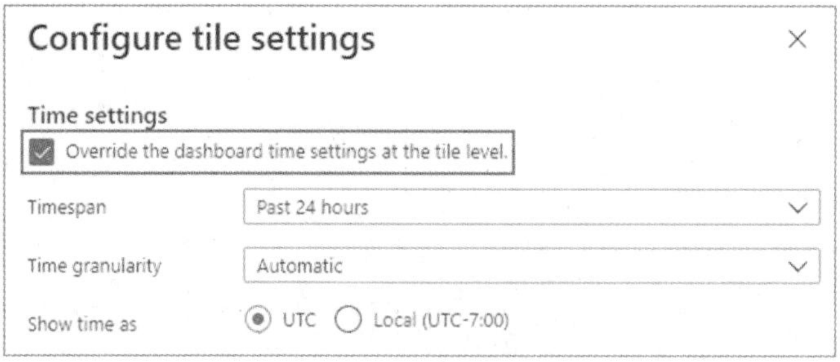

3. Next, choose the time span you'd like to display for the tile. You can select from the past 30 minutes to the past 30 days. You can also select a custom range.

4. Next, choose the time granularity that you'd like to display. You can select anywhere from one-minute intervals to one-month.

5. When done, click Apply.

Change the Title and Subtitle of a Tile

You may decide that you want to change the name of a tile; some tiles give you that ability. From the menu, select Configure Tile Settings (as shown in Figure 9.15).

FIGURE 9.15   Configure Tile Settings

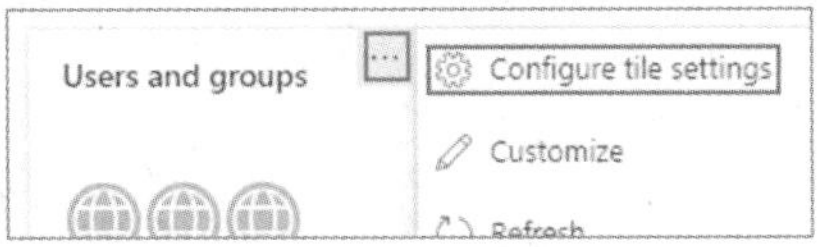

After you choose Configure Tile Settings, you can then make any changes that you want to make and click Apply, as shown in Figure 9.16.

FIGURE 9.16   Configure Tile Settings

Configure tile settings   ✕

Edit title
Title *

My new title   ✓

Subtitle

My new subtitle

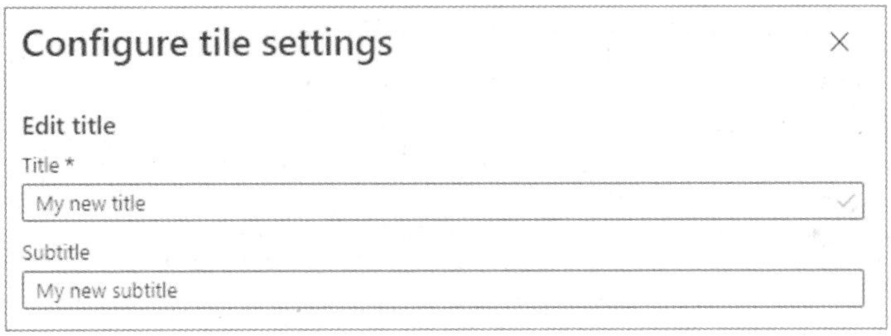

Delete a Tile

If you decide that you no longer want to have a tile on your dashboard, you can remove it (as shown in Figure 9.17). There are a couple ways to remove a tile from the dashboard:

- In the upper-right corner of the tile, open the menu. Then choose Remove From Dashboard.
- Click the Edit icon to go into the customization mode. Then, hover the cursor over the upper-right corner of the tile and click the Delete icon.

FIGURE 9.17   Remove From Dashboard settings

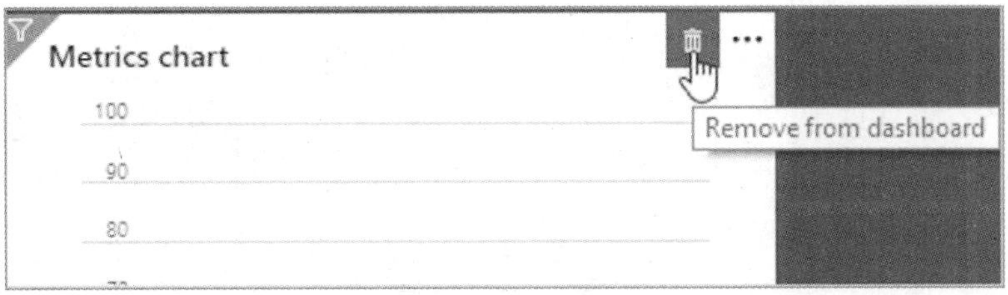

Metrics chart   🗑 ···

100

90   Remove from dashboard

80

Cloning a Dashboard

As an administrator, you also have the ability to clone a dashboard, which allows you to quickly enable a new dashboard. You are basically using an existing dashboard as a template.

In Exercise 9.5, I will show you the steps needed to clone a dashboard.

EXERCISE 9.5

Cloning a Dashboard

1. Ensure that the dashboard view is the dashboard you want to clone.

2. Click the Clone icon in the page header.

3. A copy of the dashboard, which will be named *Clone of <your dashboard name>,* will open in edit mode. Then, continue to configure the dashboard how you'd like, rename it, and apply the changes.

Publish, Sharing, and Deleting a Dashboard

By default, whenever you create a dashboard, it will be private. As the administrator who creates the dashboard, you will be the only person who can view that dashboard unless you publish and share it. If you would like to share your dashboard with other users and allow those users to open it, you need to share the dashboard.

Exercise 9.6 will show you how to publish and share a dashboard with other administrators or users.

EXERCISE 9.6

Opening a Shared Dashboard

1. Click the arrow next to the dashboard name you want to select.

2. Then, select the dashboard from the list that is displayed. If the dashboard you want to open isn't listed:

    a. Click Browse All Dashboards (see Figure 9.18).

FIGURE 9.18   Browse All Dashboards

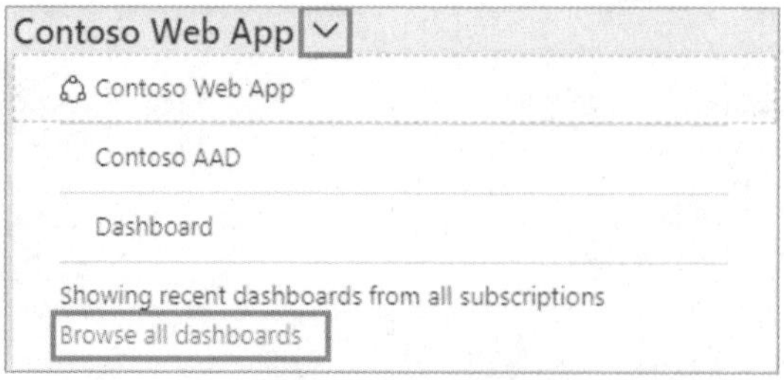

b. In the Type field, select Shared Dashboards.

c. You can then select one or more subscriptions. To filter dashboards by name, just enter text.

d. Select a dashboard from the list of shared dashboards.

You have the ability to delete a private or shared dashboard. Exercise 9.7 will show you how to delete a dashboard.

Deleting a Dashboard

1. Select the dashboard you want to delete from the list.

2. On the page header, click the Delete icon.

3. For a private dashboard, click OK (as shown in Figure 9.19) in the confirmation box. For a shared dashboard, in the confirmation box, select the option "This published dashboard will no longer be viewable by others." Then, click OK.

FIGURE 9.19 Delete the Dashboard

You can recover a deleted dashboard within 14 days of the delete as long as you are an Azure Global Administrator and you deleted the published dashboard in the Azure portal.

Configuring the Azure Portal Settings

As an Azure administrator, you also have the ability to modify the default settings of the Azure portal. Most of the settings that you can change can be found in the Settings menu (shown as a spoke), which is at the top-right of the global pane header, as shown in Figure 9.20.

FIGURE 9.20 Azure Portal Settings

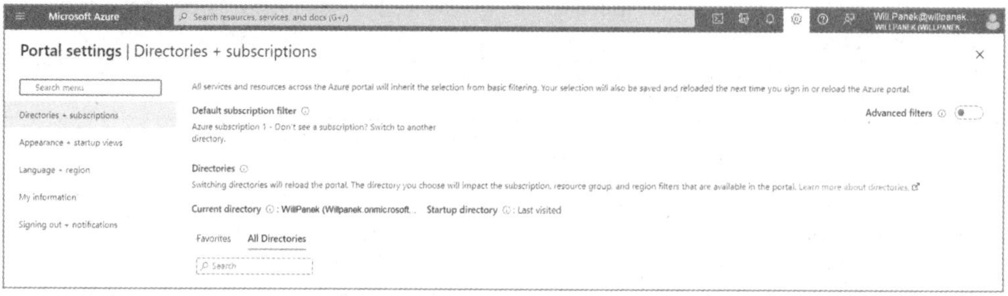

You'll see several options. These settings include Directories + Subscriptions, Appearance + Startup Views, Language + Region, My Information, and Signing Out + Notifications.

Directories + Subscriptions

As an Azure administrator, you have the ability to manage your directories and set subscription filters by using the Directories + Subscriptions pane. The Startup directory will show you the default directory that you will see when you are signed into the Azure portal. If you want to choose a different startup directory, then go to the Appearance + Startup Views page (this will be covered in the next section).

Select All Directories if you want to see a complete list of directories that you have access to. If you want to select a directory as a favorite, then click the star icon to the left of the name. Any directory that has been marked a favorite will be listed in the Favorites section.

If you want to switch to a different directory, select the directory that you want and then click the Switch button next to it, as shown in Figure 9.21.

FIGURE 9.21 Switching directories

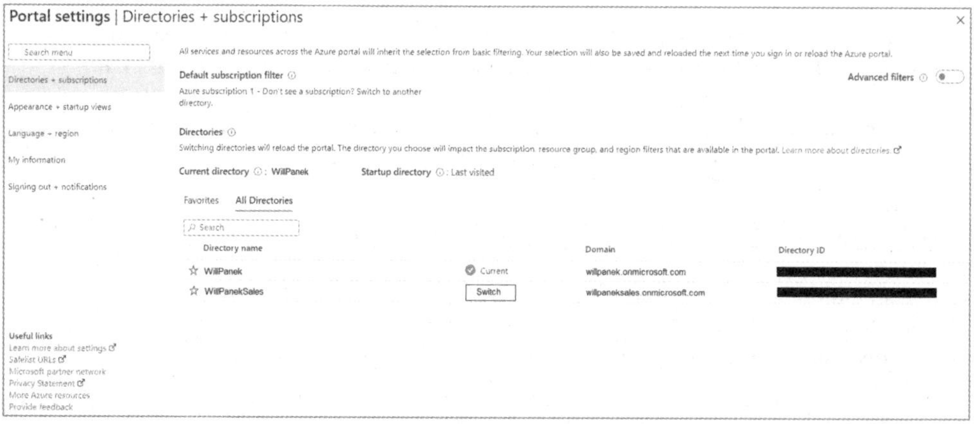

You can also select the subscriptions that are filtered by default when you sign onto the Azure portal using the Directories + Subscriptions page. Select Advanced Filters (as shown in Figure 9.22) if you wish to customize filters. You will see a confirmation pop-up before continuing. You can then create, modify, or delete subscription filters on the Advanced Filters page (as shown in Figure 9.23).

FIGURE 9.22 Enable Advance Filters

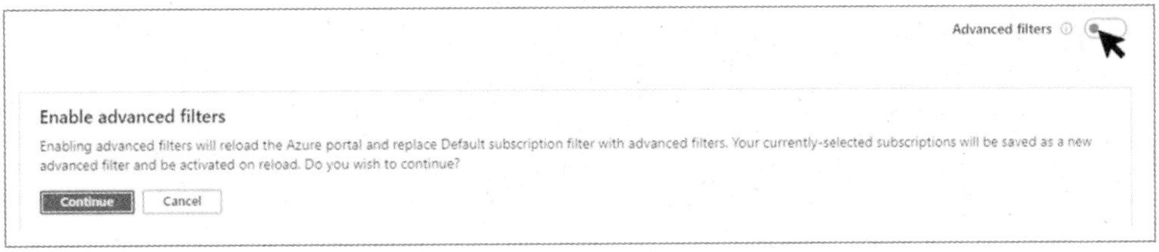

FIGURE 9.23 Advanced Filters page

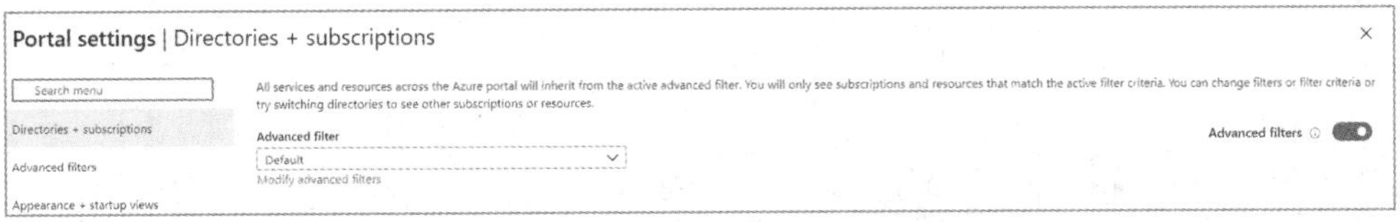

To create a new filter, click the Create A Filter option (shown in Figure 9.24). You can create up to 10 filters, each with a unique name that is between 8 and 50 characters long and contains only letters, numbers, and hyphens.

FIGURE 9.24 Create A Filter

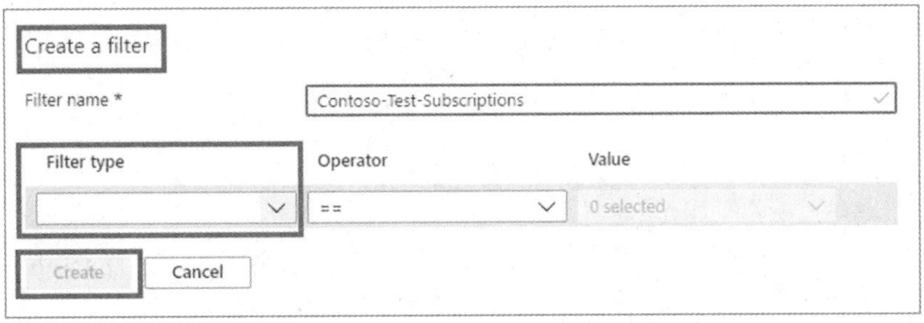

Once you have named the filter, you will need to enter at least one condition. From the Filter Type field, select Subscription Name, Subscription ID, or Subscription State and then select an operator and enter a value (see Figure 9.25).

FIGURE 9.25   Operator Value screen

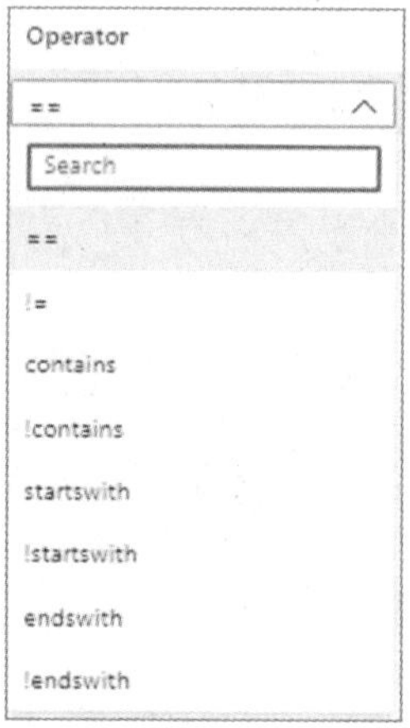

You can also create, modify, and delete filters. To create a filter, select Create. The filter will appear in the Active Filters list. If you want to modify or rename an existing filter, click the pencil icon next to the filter. Make your changes and then click Apply. To delete a filter, click the Delete icon (trash can) next to the filter. You cannot delete the default filter or any filter that is currently being used.

Appearance + Startup Views

The Appearance + Startup Views pane has two sections: the Appearance section and the Startup Views section (shown in Figure 9.26). The Appearance section allows you to change menu behavior and the color theme, and specify whether you'd like to use a high-contrast theme. The Startup Views section allows you to set up the options for what you see when you first log into the Azure portal.

FIGURE 9.26   Appearance + Startup Views screen

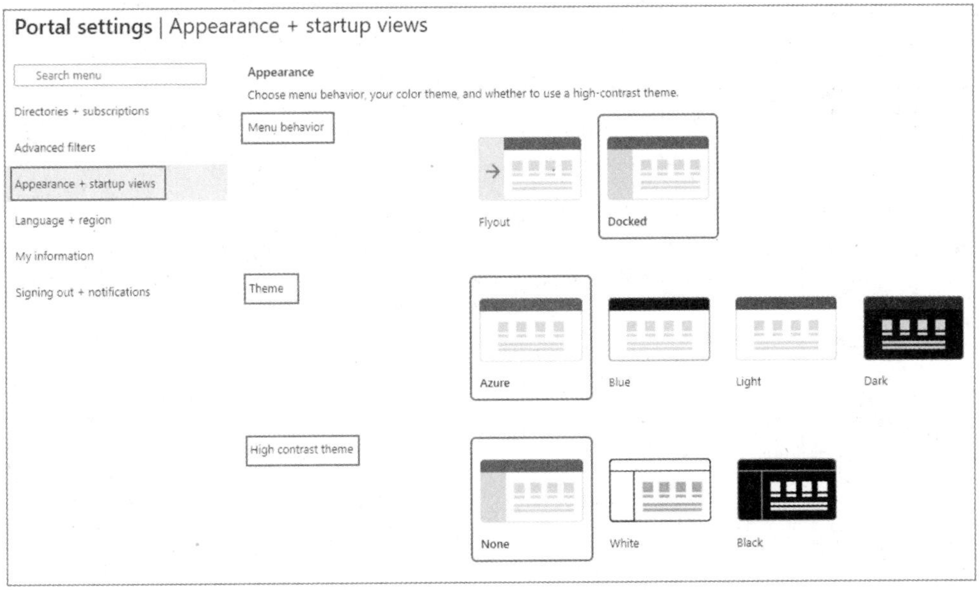

The Menu Behavior section allows you to change how the default Azure portal menu acts. You can choose from a flyout or a docked position:

- Flyout means that the menu will be hidden. To see the menu, you will need to click the menu icon in the upper-left corner. You will click this option to both open and close the menu.

- Docked means that the menu remains visible. You do have the option to collapse the menu if you'd like.

The theme you select will affect both the background and font colors when in the Azure portal. You can choose one of the four preset color themes in the Theme section. To select a color theme, just choose the color thumbnail. The High Contrast Theme section allows you to choose a theme that can make the Azure portal easier to read. This can be helpful if a user has a visual impairment.

The Startup Views section allows you to choose to see the home page or the dashboard when you log into the Azure portal:

- **Home:** This option will display the home page. The home page includes shortcuts to Azure services, recently used resources, and useful links to tools, documentation, and more.

- **Dashboard:** This option will display your most recently used dashboard.

You can also choose your startup directory views (as shown in Figure 9.27) when you log into the Azure portal. You can either sign into your last visited directory or you can select a directory.

FIGURE 9.27 Startup Views screen

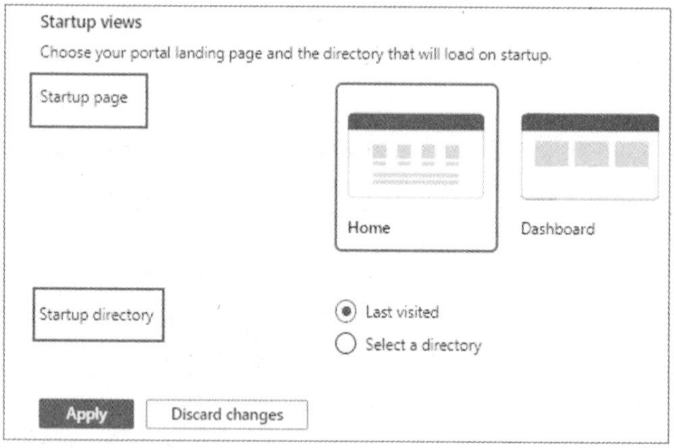

Language + Region

The Language + Region pane (shown in Figure 9.28) has two sections that you can configure: Language and Regional Format. This will affect how data such as currency will be displayed in the Azure portal.

FIGURE 9.28 Language + Region pane

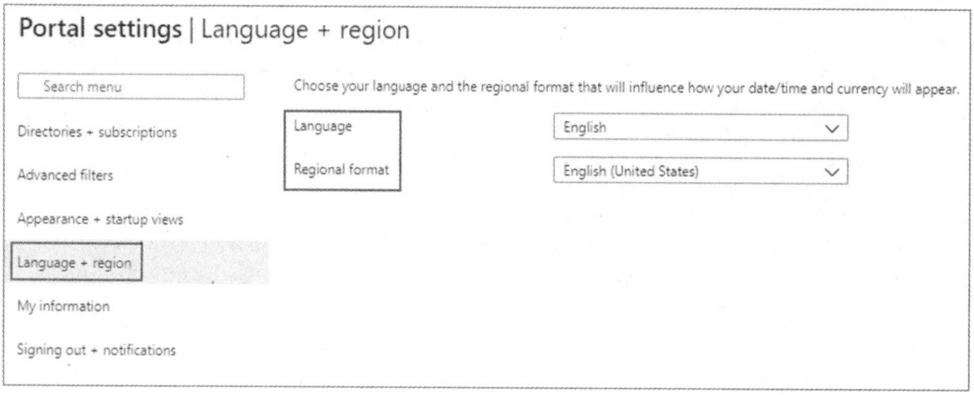

To change the language, use the Language drop-down list to choose from the list of available languages. Use the Regional Format drop-down list to choose the regional format. When you are done, click Apply.

My Information

The My Information page allows you to update your information such as your email address (see Figure 9.29). Near the top of the page, you also have the options to export, restore, or delete settings.

FIGURE 9.29   My Information pane

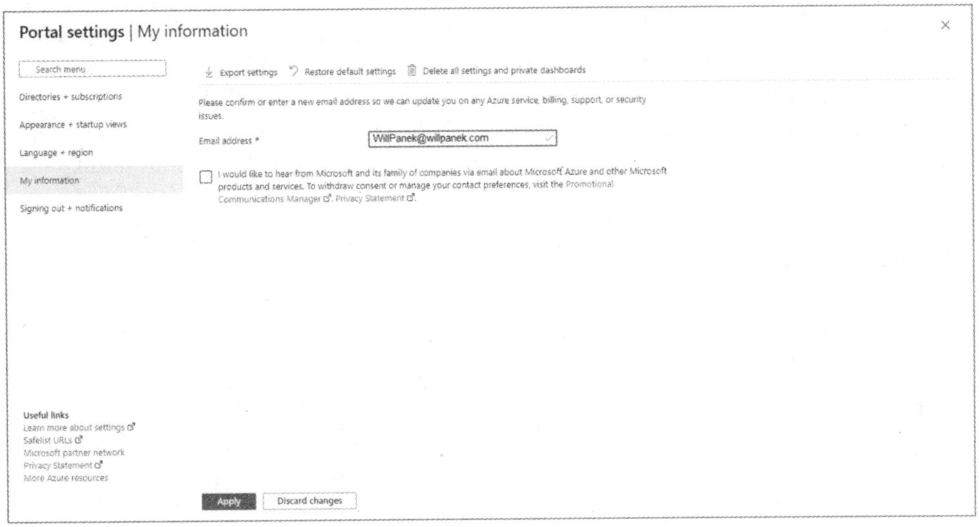

Export allows you to export user settings, such as private dashboards, user settings such as favorite subscriptions or directories, and themes and other custom settings. To export portal settings, click Export Settings. This creates a JSON file that contains the user settings data.

To restore default settings, click Restore Default Settings. You will be asked to confirm the action. You also have the ability to delete user settings and dashboards by clicking Delete All Settings And Dashboards. You will be asked to confirm this action.

Signing Out + Notifications

The Signing Out + Notifications pane (shown in Figure 9.30) allows you to manage pop-up notifications and session timeouts.

FIGURE 9.30 Signing Out + Notifications pane

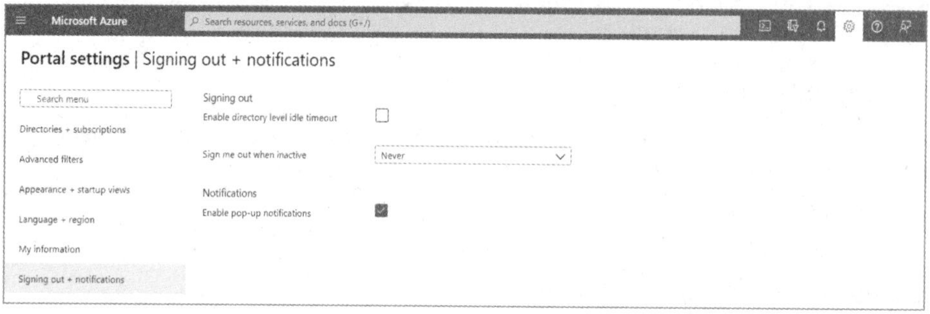

The Signing Out section (shown in Figure 9.31) helps protect resources from unauthorized access. After a user has been idle for a given period of time, they will be automatically signed out of the Azure portal. You can change the duration by using the Hour and Minutes boxes and clicking Apply. Note that an administrator in the Global Administrator role can override the idle time by enforcing a maximum idle time. This inactivity timeout setting will be applied at the directory level.

FIGURE 9.31 Inactive Signing Out settings

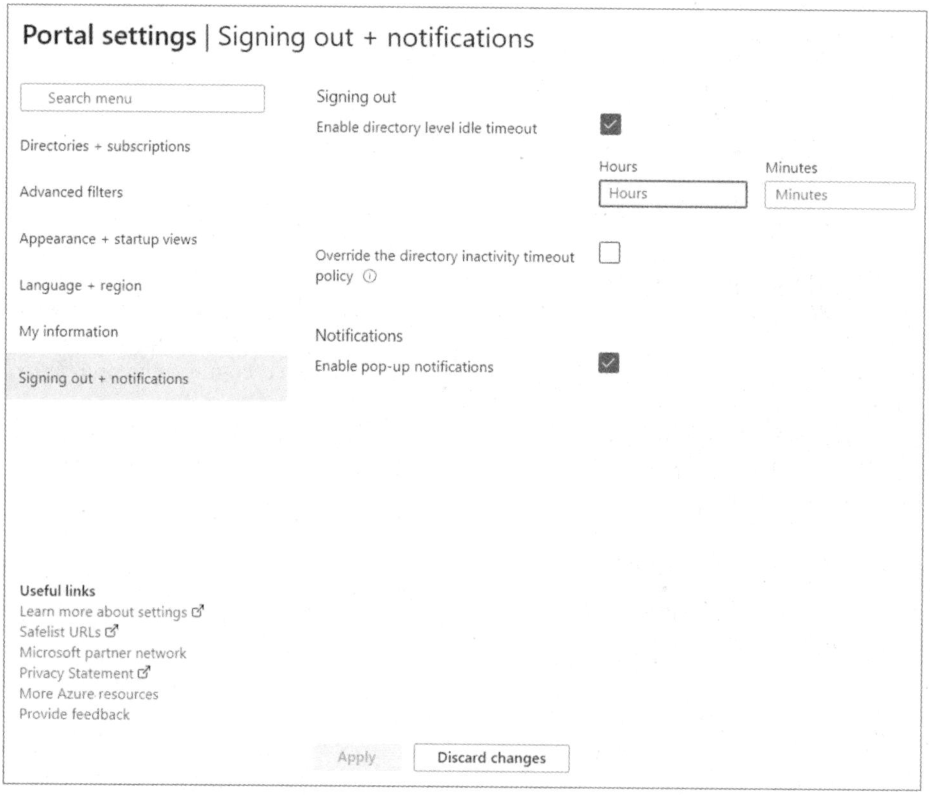

Notifications are system messages that relate to your current session. If pop-up notifications are turned on, the messages will display briefly in the top corner of the screen. To enable pop-up notifications, select the Enable Pop-Up Notifications option.

Summary

In this chapter, I explained the basics of using cloud-based resources like IaaS, PaaS, and SaaS. We then explored the various components of Azure, and I discussed some of the benefits and features of Azure.

I then introduced you to the Azure dashboard. We went through many of the different sections that are included in the Azure dashboard.

As I noted earlier, this chapter did not cover specific exam objectives, but the exam will include questions about the different types of services (e.g., IaaS, PaaS, & SaaS) and what they do. So even though there are no objectives listed, you will get questions about these topics.

Exam Essentials

Understand the features of Azure AD.   Make sure that you understand the features and benefits of using Azure. This is important not only for taking the Microsoft exams, but it is also important to determine if Azure is the correct choice for your organization.

Understand the basic cloud concepts.   This is very important for many reasons. First, and most obvious, is to understand what Azure can do and not do when it comes to the Microsoft exam. Second, you need to make sure that Azure can handle all the services that your organization is trying to achieve. It is essential to understand how IaaS, PaaS, and SaaS can help your organization. Knowing the benefits of these cloud concepts will ensure that you make the right decision for your organization.

Know how to use the Azure dashboard.   You need to understand the Azure dashboard and where you set the different components for Azure. You also need to know how to access other dashboards (like the Azure AD Identity Protection dashboard) so that you can properly navigate Azure AD and its features.

Review Questions

1. When you are implementing a software-as-a-service (SaaS) solution, as the administrator you are responsible for configuring high availability. What would you need to do to achieve this goal?

   A. No change is needed.

   B. Define scalability rules.

   C. Install the SaaS solution.

   D. Configure the SaaS solution.

2. You need to choose a cloud option. Your organization requires that the physical hosts in its infrastructure be managed by the cloud provider. Which cloud option achieves this goal?

   A. No change is needed.

   B. Private cloud

   C. Public cloud

   D. A Hyper-V host

3. You deploy a new Azure resource. The resource becomes unavailable for an extended period due to an Azure service outage. How does Microsoft compensate an organization for an outage?

   A. No change is needed. .

   B. Automatically migrates the resource to another subscription

   C. Automatically credits your account

   D. Sends you a coupon code that you can redeem for Azure credits

4. Your company hosts an accounting named App1 that is used by all the customers of the company. App1 has low usage during the first three weeks of each month and very high usage during the last week of each month. Which benefit of Azure Cloud Services supports cost management for this type of usage pattern?

   A. High availability

   B. High latency

   C. Elasticity

   D. Load balancing

5. Your company is planning to migrate a web application to Azure. The web application is accessed by external users. You need to recommend a cloud deployment solution to minimize the amount of administrative effort used to build and manage the web application. What should you include in the recommendation?

   A. Software-as-a-service (SaaS)

   B. Platform-as-a-service (PaaS)

   C. Infrastructure-as-a-service (IaaS)

   D. Database-as-a-service (DaaS)

6. Your company is planning to install a new VM on Azure. What option would you include in the recommendation for adding a new VM?

   A. Software-as-a-service (SaaS)

   B. Platform-as-a-service (PaaS)

   C. Infrastructure-as-a-service (IaaS)

   D. Database-as-a-service (DaaS)

7. You have an on-premises network that contains 100 servers. You need to recommend a cloud solution that provides additional resources to your users. The solution must minimize capital and operational expenditure costs. What should you include in the recommendation?

   A. A complete migration to the public cloud

   B. An additional datacenter

   C. A private cloud

   D. A hybrid cloud

8. What is guaranteed in an Azure service level agreement (SLA)?

   A. Uptime

   B. Feature availability

   C. Bandwidth

   D. Performance

9. Your company is planning to install O365 from Azure. What service would you include in the recommendation for deploying O365?

   A. Software-as-a-service (SaaS)

   B. Platform-as-a-service (PaaS)

   C. Infrastructure-as-a-service (IaaS)

   D. Database-as-a-service (DaaS)

10. Your company HR department runs employee reports at the beginning of every month. These reports can take up to 7 days to complete. HR reports high usage during the first week of each month and very low usage during the last three weeks of each month. Which benefit of Azure Cloud Services supports cost management for this type of usage pattern?

    A. High availability

    B. High latency

    C. Elasticity

    D. Load balancing

Chapter

10

Understanding Azure Active Directory

THE FOLLOWING AZ-800 EXAM OBJECTIVES ARE COVERED IN THIS CHAPTER:

✓ **Implement and manage hybrid identities**

- Implement Azure AD Connect

- Manage Azure AD Connect Synchronization

- Implement Azure AD Connect cloud sync

- Integrate Azure AD, AD DS, and Azure AD DS

- Manage Azure AD DS

- Manage Azure AD Connect Health

- Manage authentication in on-premises and hybrid environments

- Configure and manage AD DS passwords

✓ **Implement on-premises and hybrid network connectivity**

- Implement site-to-site virtual private network (VPN)

In this chapter, it is time for us to dive into the world of Azure Active Directory. Azure Active Directory is a cloud-based identity and access management service. The Azure environment is controlled by the Azure Resource Manager. It can be controlled by templates, PowerShell, the Azure portal, CLI, and APIs. Azure AD controls access to resources using RBAC and conditional access.

This is a very important topic because if you set up Azure Active Directory incorrectly, you may stop users from properly accessing the Azure environment, but even more important, you may give access to people who should not have access.

In this chapter, I will show you how to connect your onsite domain to Azure using Azure AD Connect. I will also show you how to set up and manage this connection. You'll also learn how to set up authentication methods, use multifactor authentication, and reset passwords.

Understanding Azure Active Directory

So now that you understand how to install Active Directory on your onsite network, it's time to see how to configure your Azure Active Directory (Azure AD). One big misconception is that Azure AD is set up and configured the same way that your onsite Active Directory is set up. The advantage of Azure AD is that there is no installation unless you decide to add another instance of Azure AD to your tenant. As soon as you set up your Azure subscription, Azure AD is ready to go.

So, before we begin setting up your Azure AD, let's take a look at some of the features that Azure AD delivers. The following features are just some of the features available in Azure AD:

Simple Deployment   You can easily set up Azure AD for your Azure AD directory. Managed users include cloud-only user accounts and user accounts synchronized from an on-premises directory.

Azure Devices   You have the ability to easily join computers to the Azure network. You can even set up Azure so that the Windows clients can automatically join the Azure environment.

Setting Domain Names   You have the ability to create custom domain names (for example, WillPanek.com) that are either verified or unverified with the Azure AD Custom Domain Name Wizard. You can also create domain names using the Microsoft suffix of onmicrosoft.com. If you want, you can create an Azure name of WillPanek .onmicrosoft.com. You have a lot of flexibility when creating Azure names for your organization.

Group Policy Support   You have the ability to create and use built-in GPOs for both the user and computer containers. This gives you the ability to enforce company compliances for security policies. You can create custom GPOs that can be assigned to organizational units (OUs), and this in turn will help you manage and enforce company policies.

For example, you can set up a GPO so that your users will use folder redirection. Folder redirection allows a user to place a file in one folder but it gets redirected to another (this includes OneDrive).

To use a Group Policy to redirect OneDrive, you need the OneDrive sync to be at least build 18.111.0603.0004 or later. You can see the OneDrive build number on the About tab of the OneDrive settings.

> The Group Policy object (GPO) for "OneDrive Known Folder Move" won't work if you have already set up a Windows Folder Redirection policy to redirect a user's Documents, Pictures, or Desktop folders to a storage location other than OneDrive. If you have done this, you must first remove the Redirection GPO that has already been created. The redirection for OneDrive doesn't affect the Music and Videos folders, so you can keep them redirected with the Windows GPO that is already created.

Azure AD Integration   One of the nice advantages of Azure is that you do not need to manage or configure Azure AD replication. Azure user accounts, group membership, or even user hashes are automatically replicated between your onsite Active Directory and Azure AD. Azure AD tenant information is automatically replicated and synchronized to your onsite or Azure AD environments.

DNS Support   You have the ability to set up, configure, and integrate DNS with your Azure network. DNS is a hostname resolution service, and Azure allows you to easily configure DNS with many of the same DNS administration tools that you are familiar with.

High Availability   One of the most important requirements for any IT department is the ability to keep their network up and running. Some organizations require minimum downtime requirements. This means that your organization can only be down for a certain amount of time per year. Azure AD offers an organization the ability to set up high availability for your Azure environment.

This feature guarantees higher service resiliency and uptime. With built-in health monitoring, Azure offers automatic failure recovery by spinning up a new instance to take over for any failed instances. This feature provides automatic and continued services for your organization's Azure network.

Management Tools Support You have the ability to use the same tools that you are familiar with for managing your current domains. You can use the Active Directory Administrative Center and Active Directory PowerShell utilities when managing your Azure AD.

Azure AD Questions and Answers

The following section contains questions and answers about features and functionality of Azure AD. This section was taken directly from Microsoft's website (http://docs .microsoft.com/en-us/azure/active-directory-domain-services/faqs). I recommend that you visit this page often for updates about features and services.

Q. Can I create multiple managed domains for a single Azure AD directory?

Answer: No. You can only create a single managed domain serviced by Azure AD Domain Services for a single Azure AD directory.

Q. Can I enable Azure AD Domain Services in an Azure Resource Manager virtual network?

Answer: Yes. Azure AD Domain Services can be enabled in an Azure Resource Manager virtual network. Classic Azure virtual networks are no longer supported for creating new managed domains.

Q. Can I migrate my existing managed domain from a classic virtual network to a Resource Manager virtual network?

Answer: Not currently. Microsoft will deliver a mechanism to migrate your existing managed domain from a classic virtual network to a Resource Manager virtual network in the future.

Q. Can I enable Azure AD Domain Services in an Azure CSP (Cloud Solution Provider) subscription?

Answer: Yes.

Q. Can I enable Azure AD Domain Services in a federated Azure AD directory? I do not synchronize password hashes to Azure AD. Can I enable Azure AD Domain Services for this directory?

Answer: No. Azure AD Domain Services needs access to the password hashes of user accounts, to authenticate users via NTLM or Kerberos. In a federated directory, password hashes are not stored in the Azure AD directory. Therefore, Azure AD Domain Services does not work with such Azure AD directories.

Q. Can I make Azure AD Domain Services available in multiple virtual networks within my subscription?

Answer: The service itself does not directly support this scenario. Your managed domain is available in only one virtual network at a time. However, you may configure connectivity between multiple virtual networks to expose Azure AD Domain Services to other virtual networks.

Q. Can I enable Azure AD Domain Services using PowerShell?

Answer: Yes. Enable Azure AD Domain Services using PowerShell.

Q. Can I enable Azure AD Domain Services using a Resource Manager Template?

Answer: No, it is not currently possible to enable Azure AD Domain Services using a template. Instead use PowerShell.

Q. Can I add domain controllers to an Azure AD Domain Services managed domain?

Answer: No. The domain provided by Azure AD Domain Services is a managed domain. You do not need to provision, configure, or otherwise manage domain controllers for this domain—these management activities are provided as a service by Microsoft. Therefore, you cannot add additional domain controllers (read-write or read-only) for the managed domain.

Q. Can guest users invited to my directory use Azure AD Domain Services?

Answer: No. Guest users invited to your Azure AD directory using the Azure AD B2B invite process are synchronized into your Azure AD Domain Services managed domain. However, passwords for these users are not stored in your Azure AD directory.

Q. Can I connect to the domain controller for my managed domain using Remote Desktop?

Answer: No. You do not have permissions to connect to domain controllers for the managed domain via Remote Desktop. Members of the 'AAD DC Administrators' group can administer the managed domain using AD administration tools such as the Active Directory Administration Center (ADAC) or AD PowerShell. These tools are installed using the 'Remote Server Administration Tools' feature on a Windows server joined to the managed domain.

Q. I've enabled Azure AD Domain Services. What user account do I use to domain join machines to this domain?

Answer: Members of the administrative group 'AAD DC Administrators' can domain-join machines. Additionally, members of this group are granted remote desktop access to machines that have been joined to the domain.

Q. Do I have domain administrator privileges for the managed domain provided by Azure AD Domain Services?

Answer: No. You are not granted administrative privileges on the managed domain. Both 'Domain Administrator' and 'Enterprise Administrator' privileges are not available for you to use within the domain. Members of the domain administrator or enterprise administrator groups in your on-premises Active Directory are also not granted domain/enterprise administrator privileges on the managed domain.

Q. Can I modify group memberships using LDAP or other AD administrative tools on managed domains?

Answer: No. Group memberships cannot be modified on domains serviced by Azure AD Domain Services. The same applies for user attributes. You may however change group memberships or user attributes either in Azure AD or on your on-premises domain. Such changes are automatically synchronized to Azure AD Domain Services.

Q. How long does it take for changes I make to my Azure AD directory to be visible in my managed domain?

Answer: Changes made in your Azure AD directory using either the Azure AD UI or Power-Shell are synchronized to your managed domain. This synchronization process runs in the background. Once initial synchronization is complete, it typically takes about 20 minutes for changes made in Azure AD to be reflected in your managed domain.

Q. Can I extend the schema of the managed domain provided by Azure AD Domain Services?

Answer: No. The schema is administered by Microsoft for the managed domain. Schema extensions are not supported by Azure AD Domain Services.

Q. Can I modify or add DNS records in my managed domain?

Answer: Yes. Members of the 'AAD DC Administrators' group are granted 'DNS Administrator' privileges, to modify DNS records in the managed domain. They can use the DNS Manager console on a machine running Windows Server joined to the managed domain, to manage DNS. To use the DNS Manager console, install 'DNS Server Tools', which is part of the 'Remote Server Administration Tools' optional feature on the server. More information on utilities for administering, monitoring, and troubleshooting DNS is available on TechNet.

Q. What is the password lifetime policy on a managed domain?

Answer: The default password lifetime on an Azure AD Domain Services managed domain is 90 days. This password lifetime is not synchronized with the password lifetime configured in Azure AD. Therefore, you may have a situation where users' passwords expire in your managed domain, but are still valid in Azure AD. In such scenarios, users need to change their password in Azure AD and the new password will synchronize to your managed domain. Additionally, the 'password-does-not-expire' and 'user-must-change-password-at-next-logon' attributes for user accounts are not synchronized to your managed domain.

Q. Does Azure AD Domain Services provide AD account lockout protection?

Answer: Yes. Five invalid password attempts within 2 minutes on the managed domain cause a user account to be locked out for 30 minutes. After 30 minutes, the user account is automatically unlocked. Invalid password attempts on the managed domain do not lock out the user account in Azure AD. The user account is locked out only within your Azure AD Domain Services managed domain.

Q. Can I failover Azure AD Domain Services to another region for a DR event?

Answer: No. Azure AD Domain Services does not currently provide a geo-redundant deployment model. It is limited to a single virtual network in an Azure region. If you want to utilize multiple Azure regions, you need to run your Active Directory Domain Controllers on Azure IaaS VMs.

Q. Can I get Azure AD Domain Services as part of Enterprise Mobility Suite (EMS)? Do I need Azure AD Premium to use Azure AD Domain Services?

Answer: No. Azure AD Domain Services is a pay-as-you-go Azure service and is not part of EMS. Azure AD Domain Services can be used with all editions of Azure AD (Free, Basic, and, Premium). You are billed on an hourly basis, depending on usage.

Managing Azure AD

So, now that we have looked at some of the features of Azure AD along with the common questions and answers about Azure AD, it's time to go through the Azure AD dashboard. Figure 10.1 shows the Azure AD dashboard (you access this dashboard by choosing Azure AD from the left menu of the main dashboard). Let's take a look at some of the different options on the left side, starting with Overview.

FIGURE 10.1   Viewing the Azure AD dashboard

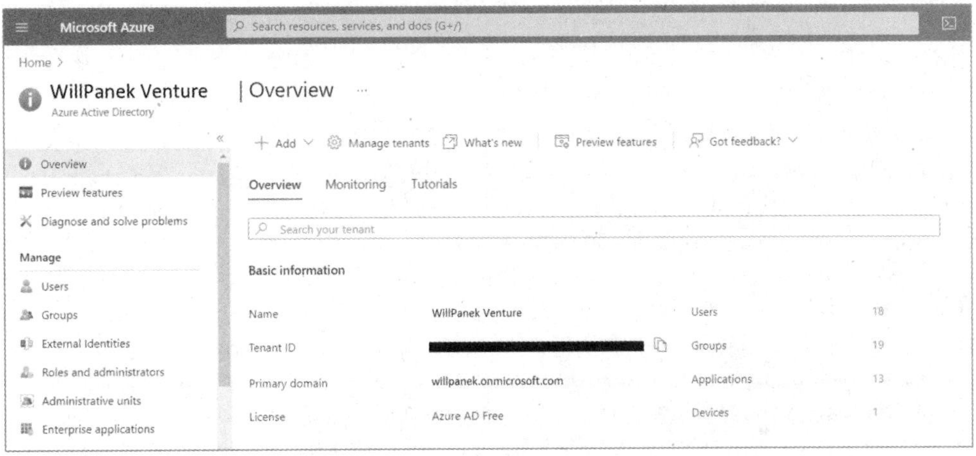

Overview

The Overview section of the Azure AD Dashboard is the figure you are looking at in Figure 10.1. The first thing you will notice in the center of the screen is the default Azure AD directory and the number of users on Azure.

On the left-hand side, you can add Users, Groups, External Identities, Roles and Administrators, Administrative Units, Enterprise Applications, Devices, App Registrations, Identity Governance, Application Proxy, Licenses, Azure AD Connect, and other Azure AD options.

Users

The Users section (under Manage) on the left side allows you to view all of your current Azure AD user accounts (see Figure 10.2). In the Users section, you can create new users and new guest users, reset passwords, delete users, multifactor authentication, refresh your screen, or set up your columns.

Another task that can be created in the Users section is the ability to manipulate the user's settings. The User Settings link allows you to set up how the user can launch and view applications, how the user can register applications, and if the user can access the Azure AD administrative portal. Administrators can also manage external users and access panel control from the Settings section.

FIGURE 10.2 The Users section

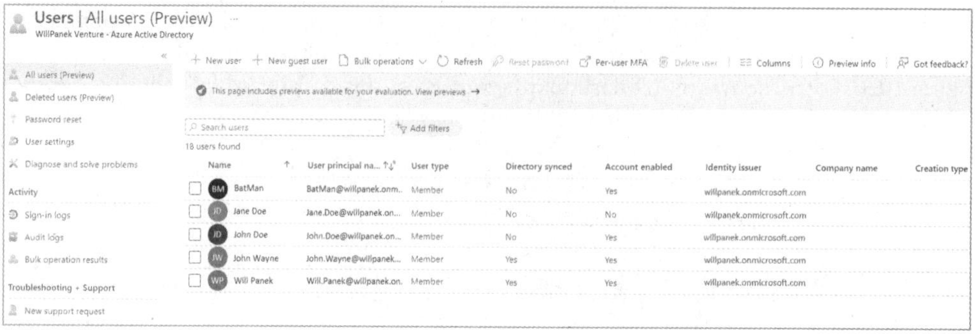

The Users section also allows you to see how often the user is logging into Azure (this allows you to perform an access review), and you can also get audit information about the user account. Finally, in the Users section, you can also troubleshoot user issues and open a support ticket with Microsoft for additional help.

Groups

The Groups section allows you to create and manage groups (see Figure 10.3). In the Groups section, you can create new groups, manage group settings for all groups, manage group membership, and delete groups. You can also do auditing on groups along with trouble-shooting group issues or opening a support ticket with Microsoft for additional help.

FIGURE 10.3 Groups section

External Identities

The External Identities section allows you to work with user accounts from other organizations. The Organizational Relationship section also allows you to invite users who already own an Azure Active Directory account or a Microsoft account. If they have one of these account types already set up, they can automatically sign in without any further configuration from an administrator.

In the Settings section of External Identities (see Figure 10.4), you can specify what guest accounts can do in Azure. For example, you can decide if guest user access is limited or if users can invite other users to use your organization's Azure network. Finally, you can set up collaboration restrictions (which domains you can invite users from) for your guest user accounts.

FIGURE 10.4 Settings section of External Identities

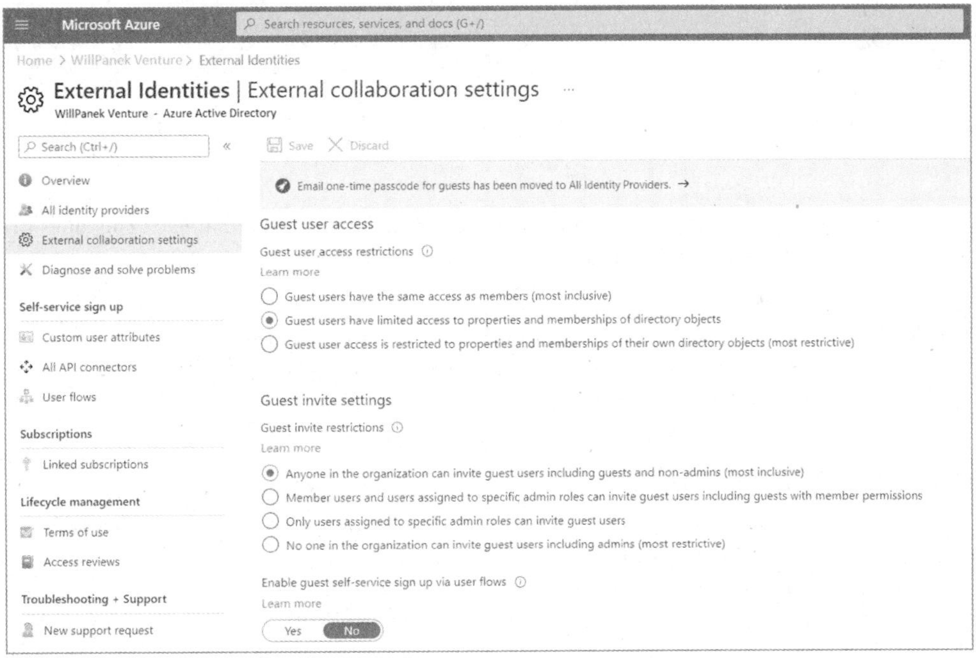

The Lifecycle Management section of External Identities lets you establish terms of use agreements while also allowing you to set up auditing of your guest users. Finally, you can troubleshoot issues or open a support ticket with Microsoft for additional help.

Roles and Administrators

The Roles and Administrators section (shown in Figure 10.5) allows you to see just some of the available Azure AD roles and what each role does.

FIGURE 10.5   Roles and Administrators Section

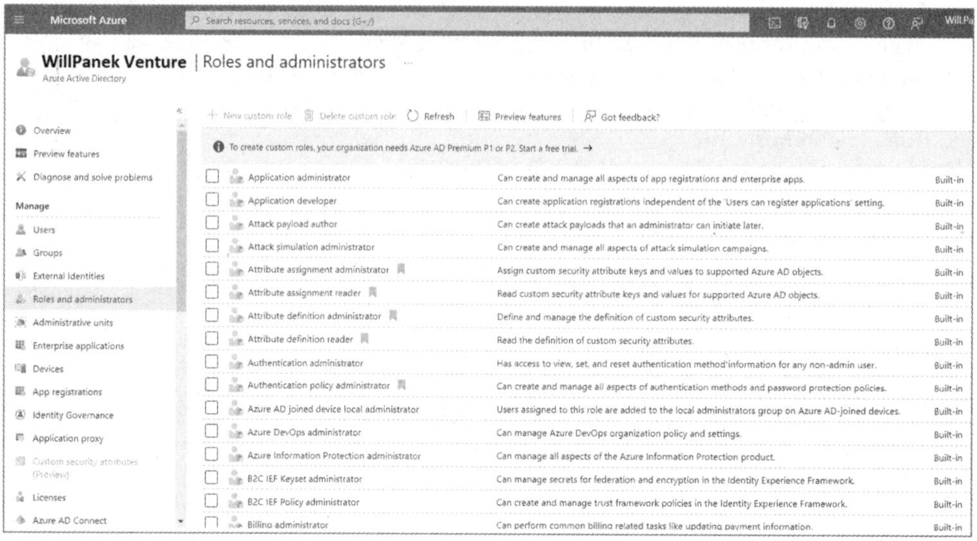

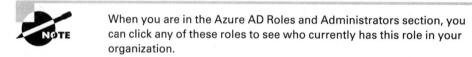

Table 10.1 shows some of the various roles that are available and what each role does in Azure AD. This table was taken directly from Microsoft's website.

> **NOTE** When you are in the Azure AD Roles and Administrators section, you can click any of these roles to see who currently has this role in your organization.

TABLE 10.1   Azure roles

Role	Description
Application Administrator	Can create and manage all aspects of app registrations and enterprise apps.
Application Developer	Can create application registrations independent of the 'Users can register applications' setting.
Attack Payload Author	Can create attack payloads that an administrator can initiate later.
Attack Simulation Administrator	Can create and manage all aspects of attack simulation campaigns.
Authentication Administrator	Can access view, set, and reset authentication method information for any non-admin user.

Role	Description
Authentication Policy Administrator	Can create and manage the authentication methods policy, tenant-wide MFA settings, password protection policy, and verifiable credentials.
Azure AD Joined Device Local Administrator	Users assigned to this role are added to the local administrators group on Azure AD-joined devices.
Azure DevOps Administrator	Can manage Azure DevOps organization policy and settings.
Azure Information Protection Administrator	Can manage all aspects of the Azure Information Protection product.
B2C IEF Keyset Administrator	Can manage secrets for federation and encryption in the Identity Experience Framework (IEF).
B2C IEF Policy Administrator	Can create and manage trust framework policies in the Identity Experience Framework (IEF).
Billing Administrator	Can perform common billing related tasks like updating payment information.
Cloud App Security Administrator	Can manage all aspects of the Cloud App Security product.
Cloud Application Administrator	Can create and manage all aspects of app registrations and enterprise apps except App Proxy.
Cloud Device Administrator	Limited access to manage devices in Azure AD.
Compliance Administrator	Can read and manage compliance configuration and reports in Azure AD and Microsoft 365.
Compliance Data Administrator	Creates and manages compliance content.
Conditional Access Administrator	Can manage Conditional Access capabilities.
Customer LockBox Access Approver	Can approve Microsoft support requests to access customer organizational data.

TABLE 10.1 Azure roles *(continued)*

Role	Description
Desktop Analytics Administrator	Can access and manage Desktop management tools and services.
Directory Readers	Can read basic directory information. Commonly used to grant directory read access to applications and guests.
Directory Synchronization Accounts	Only used by Azure AD Connect service.
Directory Writers	Can read and write basic directory information. For granting access to applications, not intended for users.
Domain Name Administrator	Can manage domain names in cloud and on-premises.
Dynamics 365 Administrator	Can manage all aspects of the Dynamics 365 product.
Edge Administrator	Manage all aspects of Microsoft Edge.
Exchange Administrator	Can manage all aspects of the Exchange product.
Exchange Recipient Administrator	Can create or update Exchange Online recipients within the Exchange Online organization.
External ID User Flow Administrator	Can create and manage all aspects of user flows.
External ID User Flow Attribute Administrator	Can create and manage the attribute schema available to all user flows.
External Identity Provider Administrator	Can configure identity providers for use in direct federation.
Global Administrator	Can manage all aspects of Azure AD and Microsoft services that use Azure AD identities.
Global Reader	Can read everything that a Global Administrator can, but not update anything.

Role	Description
Groups Administrator	Members of this role can create/manage groups, create/manage groups settings like naming and expiration policies, and view groups activity and audit reports.
Guest Inviter	Can invite guest users independent of the 'members can invite guests' setting.
Helpdesk Administrator	Can reset passwords for non-administrators and Helpdesk Administrators.
Hybrid Identity Administrator	Can manage AD to Azure AD cloud provisioning, Azure AD Connect, and federation settings.
Identity Governance Administrator	Manage access using Azure AD for identity governance scenarios.
Insights Administrator	Has administrative access in the Microsoft 365 Insights app.
Insights Business Leader	Can view and share dashboards and insights via the Microsoft 365 Insights app.
Intune Administrator	Can manage all aspects of the Intune product.
Kaizala Administrator	Can manage settings for Microsoft Kaizala.
Knowledge Administrator	Can configure knowledge, learning, and other intelligent features.
Knowledge Manager	Can organize, create, manage, and promote topics and knowledge.
License Administrator	Can manage product licenses on users and groups.
Message Center Privacy Reader	Can read security messages and updates in Office 365 Message Center only.
Message Center Reader	Can read messages and updates for their organization in Office 365 Message Center only.
Modern Commerce User	Can manage commercial purchases for a company, department, or team.
Network Administrator	Can manage network locations and review enterprise network design insights for Microsoft 365 Software as a Service applications.

TABLE 10.1   Azure roles *(continued)*

Role	Description
Office Apps Administrator	Can manage Office apps cloud services, including policy and settings management, and manage the ability to select, unselect, and publish 'what's new' feature content to end-user's devices.
Partner Tier1 Support	Do not use - not intended for general use.
Partner Tier2 Support	Do not use - not intended for general use.
Password Administrator	Can reset passwords for non-administrators and Password Administrators.
Power BI Administrator	Can manage all aspects of the Power BI product.
Power Platform Administrator	Can create and manage all aspects of Microsoft Dynamics 365, Power Apps, and Power Automate.
Printer Administrator	Can manage all aspects of printers and printer connectors.
Printer Technician	Can register and unregister printers and update printer status.
Privileged Authentication Administrator	Can access view, set, and reset authentication method information for any user (admin or non-admin).
Privileged Role Administrator	Can manage role assignments in Azure AD, and all aspects of Privileged Identity Management.
Reports Reader	Can read sign-in and audit reports.
Search Administrator	Can create and manage all aspects of Microsoft Search settings.
Search Editor	Can create and manage the editorial content such as bookmarks, Q and As, locations, floorplan.
Security Administrator	Can read security information and reports, and manage configuration in Azure AD and Office 365.
Security Operator	Creates and manages security events.
Security Reader	Can read security information and reports in Azure AD and Office 365.
Service Support Administrator	Can read service health information and manage support tickets.

Role	Description
SharePoint Administrator	Can manage all aspects of the SharePoint service.
Skype for Business Administrator	Can manage all aspects of the Skype for Business product.
Teams Administrator	Can manage the Microsoft Teams service.
Teams Communications Administrator	Can manage calling and meetings features within the Microsoft Teams service.
Teams Communications Support Engineer	Can troubleshoot communications issues within Teams using advanced tools.
Teams Communications Support Specialist	Can troubleshoot communications issues within Teams using basic tools.
Teams Devices Administrator	Can perform management related tasks on Teams certified devices.
Usage Summary Reports Reader	Can see only tenant level aggregates in Microsoft 365 Usage Analytics and Productivity Score.
User Administrator	Can manage all aspects of users and groups, including resetting passwords for limited admins.
Windows 365 Administrator	Can provision and manage all aspects of Cloud PCs.
Windows Update Deployment Administrator	Create and manage all aspects of Windows Update deployments through the Windows Update for Business deployment service.

Enterprise Applications

The Enterprise Applications section allows you to view, set up, and configure your organization's enterprise applications. You can also set up an application proxy within the Enterprise Applications section. An application proxy allows you to provide single sign-on (SSO) and secure remote access for web applications hosted on your on-premises network.

The Enterprise Applications section also lets you set up user settings for your enterprise applications. These settings include users giving consent to applications accessing data on their company networks, users adding applications to their Access panel, and whether users can only see Micrsoft 365 in the M365 portal.

In the Enterprise Applications section, you can also set up Conditional Access (setting up application policies), see who has logged into the applications, and set up auditing. You can also troubleshoot application issues or open a support ticket with Microsoft for additional help.

Devices

The Devices section allows you to specify which devices can access Azure AD. You can also configure device settings and device roaming settings (Enterprise State Roaming). You can do auditing and troubleshooting from the Devices section.

In the Devices section, you also have the ability to set up BitLocker keys. You can view and copy BitLocker keys so that users have the ability to recover encrypted drives. BitLocker keys are only available for Windows devices that have been encrypted using BitLocker, and those keys are stored in Azure AD.

Administrators can find these BitLocker keys when they view a device's details by selecting Show Recovery Key to generate an audit log. You can find the BitLocker keys in the Key-Management category of the audit log.

Licenses

The Licenses section allows you to view purchased licensing for additional Azure AD components. If you purchase additional Azure AD components (e.g., Azure Active Directory Premium P2 or Enterprise Mobility + Security E5), those additional components will show up in the Licenses section. You can also see if there are any licensing issues in this section.

The Licenses section also allows you to view additional components that are available and what those components do. You can also view auditing and perform troubleshooting from this section.

Azure AD Connect

Azure AD Connect (see Figure 10.6) lets you integrate your Azure AD with your Windows Server AD or another directory on your network. One of the nice advantages of Azure AD Connect is that you can download and install Azure AD Connect by using the Azure Active Directory Connect Download link. As you can see in Figure 10.6, Azure AD and my domain have already been connected by using seamless single sign-on.

Azure AD Connect helps you integrate your on-premises Active Directory with Azure AD. This allows your users to be more productive by giving those users access to both cloud and on-premises resources by using a common user account for accessing both networks. By using Azure AD Connect, users and organizations can take advantage of the following features:

- Users can have a common hybrid identity that allows them to access onsite or cloud-based services that use both Windows Server Active Directory and Azure AD.

- You can provide conditional access based on your device and user identity, network location, application resource, and multifactor authentication.

FIGURE 10.6   Azure AD Connect section

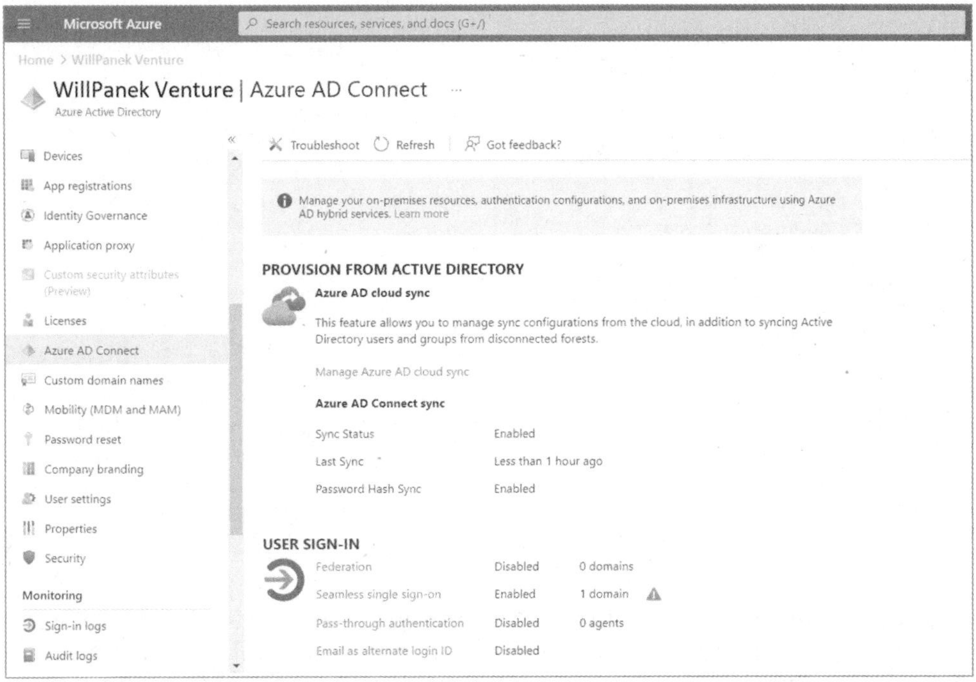

- Users can use this common identity in Azure AD, Microsoft 365, Intune, SaaS apps, and third-party applications.
- Developers can create applications that use the common identity model, thus integrating applications into onsite Active Directory or cloud-based Azure applications.

To use Azure AD Connect, your onsite network must be using Windows Server 2008 or higher.

Use the Azure AD Connect section to set up how your users will seamlessly pass between both networks. You can set up seamless connections by using a Federation server (including AD Federation Server), seamless single sign-on, or pass-through authentication.

Custom Domain Names

The Custom Domain Names section allows you to add and verify new domain names (see Figure 10.7). When you first build your Azure subscription, your new Azure AD tenant comes with an initial domain name (e.g., `willpanek.onmicrosoft.com`).

You can't change or delete the initial domain name that is created but you do have the ability to add your organization's domain names to the list of supported names. Adding custom domain names allows you to create usernames that are familiar to your users, such as `wpanek@willpanek.com`.

FIGURE 10.7 Custom Domain Names section

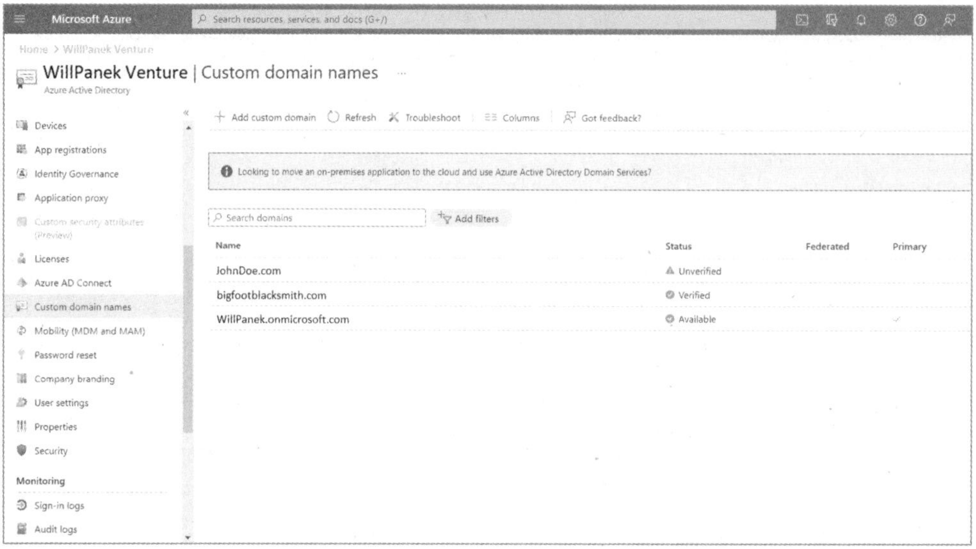

After you register your custom domain name, you can make sure it's valid in Azure AD. As you can see in Figure 10.7, JohnDoe.com has not been verified. You can verify a custom domain name by clicking the domain name to open a screen where you can verify the custom domain name.

After creating a DNS TXT or MX record, you can click the Verify button to have Azure verify the custom domain name. These DNS records must be created either on your web server's DNS server (ISP or hosting company) or on your onsite DNS server if you are hosting your own website. This step ensures that your company owns the custom name that you are trying to register.

Mobility (MDM and MAM)

One feature that many organizations have started to implement is the ability for their employees to bring in their own devices (Bring Your Own Device [BYOD]) to work.

Also, many organizations have started issuing devices such as tablets to their employees, and many companies do not mind if you use those devices for personal use. To address this, Microsoft has implemented mobility into their Azure AD networks. Click the Device Settings link to connect devices (either personal or corporate) to your corporate Azure AD network.

Once these devices are connected to Azure, you can control them by using Microsoft Intune and Microsoft Intune Enrollment utilities (as shown in Figure 10.8). As of this writing, Microsoft has begun using Microsoft Endpoint Manager for Intune. But as you can see, Intune is still being shown as one of the utilities.

FIGURE 10.8   Mobility (MDM and MAM) screen

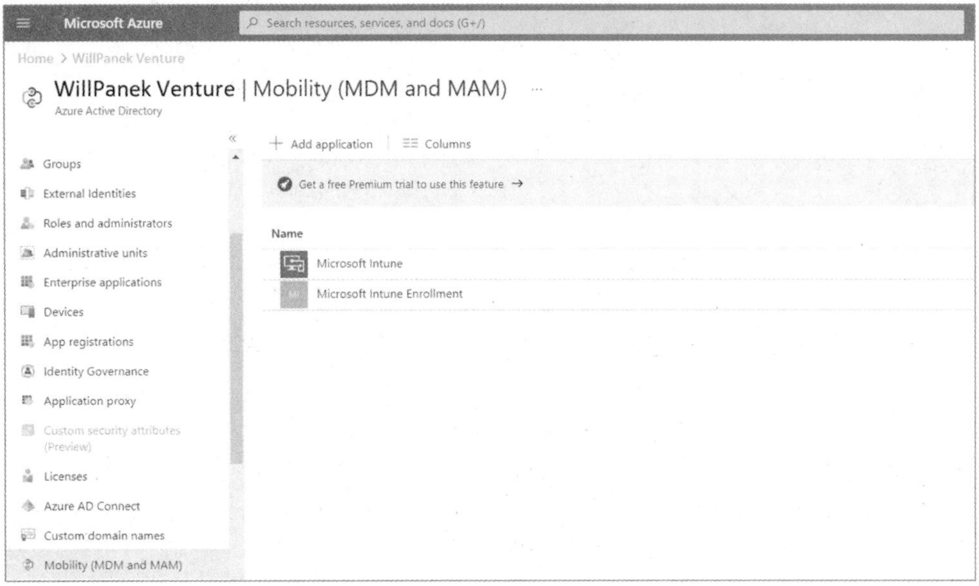

When a user connects their personal device to a corporate network, the user should understand that corporate policies may affect their devices and settings.

Password Reset

The Password Reset section allows you to specify whether you want to enable self-service password resets (SSPRs). If you decide to enable this feature, users will be able to reset their own passwords or unlock their accounts.

You can allow all accounts to use SSPRs (see Figure 10.9), or you can choose certain groups that will have the ability to use SSPRs.

In the Password Reset section, you can also choose to use authentication methods. Authentication methods allow an organization to verify that the user is who they say they are. Methods for this include verification by mobile app notification, mobile app code, email, mobile phone, office phone, or security question. You can choose between using a single verification or using multiple verifications.

You can also require registrations when a user logs into Azure AD and set up password resets so that a user is notified if their password changes. You can also be notified when administrator passwords are reset. Also in the Password Reset section, you can choose to enable a custom help desk link (under the Customization link) for users.

FIGURE 10.9   Setting the self-service password reset

You can specify that password changes be replicated back (password writeback) to an Active Directory network by configuring on-premises integration. Password writeback, when enabled in Azure AD Connect and SSPR, allows users who change or reset their password in Azure to have those passwords updated back to the on-premises Active Directory domain environment as well.

Finally, you can perform auditing and troubleshooting from the Password Reset section.

Company Branding

The Company Branding section allows you to set up custom text and graphics that your users will see when they sign into Azure AD. This allows your organization to set up their logo and custom color schemes. Organizations can provide a consistent look and feel for their users when they sign into their Azure AD pages.

Properties

The Properties section allows you to change settings, including Tenant Name, Notification Language, Tenant ID, Technical Contact Email, Global Privacy Contact, Privacy Statement URL, and Access Management Person For Azure.

Security

The Security section gives you an overview of your security policies and security issues. Security is a big part of Azure AD because unlike an onsite network, the Azure AD network can be accessed from anywhere in the world. So, making sure your Azure AD security is strong is a very important task for any Azure administrator.

Azure AD offers a wide range of security features to protect your organization. Some of these features are as follows:

- Azure AD Conditional Access
- Azure AD Identity Protection
- Microsoft Defender for Cloud
- Identity Secure Score
- Named locations
- Authentication methods
- Multifactor Authentication (MFA)

NOTE All of the Azure Security settings will be covered in greater detail throughout the rest of this book.

Conditional Access

The Conditional Access section (see Figure 10.10) allows you to configure security policies. When it comes to Azure, one of the biggest concerns for organizations is cloud-based security. Azure allows users to access their networks from anywhere in the world and from almost any device. Because of this, just securing resource access is not enough. This is where Conditional Access policies come into play.

FIGURE 10.10 Conditional Access Policies section

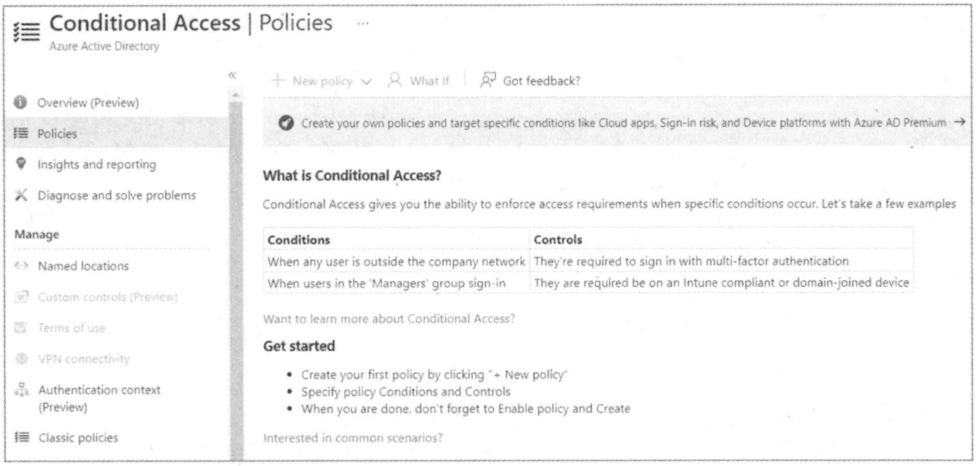
Conditional Access | Policies
Azure Active Directory
New policy
What If
Got feedback?
Overview (Preview)
Policies
Insights and reporting
Diagnose and solve problems
Manage
Named locations
Custom controls (Preview)
Terms of use
VPN connectivity
Authentication context (Preview)
Classic policies
Create your own policies and target specific conditions like Cloud apps, Sign-in risk, and Device platforms with Azure AD Premium
What is Conditional Access?
Conditional Access gives you the ability to enforce access requirements when specific conditions occur. Let's take a few examples
Conditions
Controls
When any user is outside the company network
They're required to sign in with multi-factor authentication
When users in the 'Managers' group sign-in
They are required be on an Intune compliant or domain-joined device
Want to learn more about Conditional Access?
Get started
Create your first policy by clicking "+ New policy"
Specify policy Conditions and Controls
When you are done, don't forget to Enable policy and Create
Interested in common scenarios?

Conditional Access policies allow an organization to set how resources are accessed using access control decisions (who has access to resources) through Azure AD. Setting up Conditional Access policies allows your organization to have automated access control decisions based on the policies that your organization sets. Some of the situations that Conditional Access policies can help with are sign-in risk, network location risk, device management, and client applications.

Identity Secure Score

The Identity Secure Score section lets you view your Azure AD Identity Security score. The Identity Secure score is an indicator of how aligned Azure AD is with Microsoft's best practice recommendations for your organization's security setup.

The Identity Secure Score is an integer number, and the higher the number, the better your security settings align with Microsoft's recommendations. The score helps your organization objectively measure their identity security position, plan for identity security improvements, and review the successful implementation of your organization's improvements.

On this Identity Secure Score dashboard, you will be able to view your organization's score, comparison graph, trend graph, and a list of identity security best practices.

So, the way this works is that Azure views your security configuration every 48 hours. It then takes what it sees and compares your organization's settings against Microsoft's best practices. Based on that evaluation, your organization's security score is calculated. Based on that security score, you can adjust your security settings and policies to make improvements.

Configuring Objects

Now that we have looked at some of the different sections within Azure AD, let's see how to create objects such as users and groups.

User accounts allow employees to log into the Azure network. In Exercise 10.1, I will show you how to create a user account in Azure AD.

EXERCISE 10.1

Creating an Azure AD User Account

1. Log into the Azure dashboard.

2. Click the Azure Active Directory link.

3. Under Manage, click the Users link.

4. Click the link +New User.

5. Type the name of your user and a username. For this exercise, I used George Washington as my user's name and GWashington@wpanek.onmicrosoft.com as the username.

6. Click Profile and enter the user's name and job information. Click OK when you're done filling out the profile information.

7. We are not going to add this user to a group yet. Make sure the Directory role is set to User.

8. Click the Show Password box to see the temporary password assigned. Then click the Create button.

9. You should now see your user account. If you would like to change any user information, double-click the user account and make changes. Be sure to save any changes that are made.

In Exercise 10.2, I will show you how to create a group in Azure AD.

EXERCISE 10.2

Creating an Azure AD Group Account

1. Log into the Azure dashboard.

2. Click the Azure Active Directory link.

3. Under Manage, click the Groups link.

4. Click the link +New Group.

5. From the Group Type pull-down, choose Security. Security groups are the group type you use when you want the group to be assigned to resources. Microsoft 365 groups allow users to collaborate with other users by giving them access to a shared mailbox, calendar, files, SharePoint site, and more.

6. In the Group Name field, type the name of your group. I used Marketing for my group name.

7. In the Group Description field, type a description for your group.

8. From the Membership Type pull-down, choose Assigned. Assigned groups allow you to add specific users to the group and to have unique permissions. Dynamic user groups allow you to use dynamic group rules to automatically add and remove members. Dynamic device groups let you use dynamic group rules to automatically add and remove devices.

9. Click the Create button.

Self-Service Password Reset

As stated before, the Password Reset section allows you to specify if you want to enable self-service password resets (SSPRs). If you decide to enable this feature, users will be able to reset their own passwords or unlock their accounts.

You can choose from three SSPR options: None, Selected, and All Users. If you choose None, then no one can reset their own passwords. You can also select the option Selected to choose which users can reset their password, or you can choose All Users, which will allow all users to reset their passwords. To set up SSPR, you must meet the following prerequisites:

- An Azure AD tenant subscription with the minimum of at least one trial license enabled
- Global Administrator account that can be used to enable SSPR
- A non-administrator test account with a password that you know
- A pilot group account to test with the non-administrator test account (the user account needs to be a member of this group)

In Exercise 10.3, I will show you how to configure the Self-Service Password Reset option in Azure AD. To complete this exercise, you must have created a user (Exercise 10.1) and a group (Exercise 10.2).

EXERCISE 10.3

Setting up Self-Service Password Reset

1. From your existing Azure AD tenant, click the Azure Active Directory.

2. Select Password Reset.

3. From the Properties page, under the option Self Service Password Reset Enabled, choose the Selected option.

4. From Select Group, choose your pilot group.

5. Click Save.

6. On the Authentication Methods page, make the following choices and then click Save:

    Number of methods required to reset: 1

    Methods available to users:

    Mobile phone

    Office phone

7. On the Registration page, make the following choices:

    Require users to register when they sign in: Yes

    Set the number of days before users are asked to reconfirm their authentication information: 365

In Exercise 10.4, you'll learn how to test the Self-Service Password Reset option. To complete this exercise, you must have completed the previous exercise (Exercise 10.3). This test must be done with a normal user account. You can't run this test using your account.

EXERCISE 10.4

Testing the Self-Service Password Reset

1. Open a new browser window in InPrivate or incognito mode, and browse to `https://aka.ms/ssprsetup`.

2. Sign in as a non-administrator test user and register your authentication phone.

3. Once complete, click the Looks Good button and close the browser window.

4. Open a new browser window in InPrivate or incognito mode and browse to `https://aka.ms/sspr`.

5. Enter your non-administrator test user's User ID, type the characters in the CAPTCHA, and then click Next.

6. Follow the verification steps to reset your password

Creating a Hybrid Network

One nice feature of using both an onsite and an Azure network is that Microsoft has many different tools to help you connect both networks. Connecting both networks is important so that users can seamlessly move between the two networks.

Microsoft's identity solutions extend your organization's onsite network with the Azure network features. These solutions create a common user identity for authentication and authorization to all resources. The advantage is that users can access these resources no matter where they reside. This is what Microsoft refers to as *hybrid identity*.

To properly set up your hybrid identity, you can use one of the following authentication methods. Which one you decide to go with depends on your environment scenario.

- Password hash synchronization (PHS)

- Pass-through authentication (PTA)

- Federation

So, what is the real advantage of setting up both networks using one of these methods? When you choose one of the authentication methods, you are providing your users with *single sign-on (SSO)* capabilities. Single sign-on allows your users to sign in once but have access to resources on both networks. This is what gives your users seamless access to all resources. Let's take a look at some of the available identity solutions.

Password Hash Synchronization with Azure AD

One of the hybrid identity sign-in methods that you can use is called *password hash synchronization*. Azure AD and your onsite Active Directory synchronize with each other by using a hash value. The hash value is created based on the user's password. This way the two systems can stay in sync with each other. Azure AD Connect is also required for this setup to function properly.

Password hash synchronization is a feature that is part of the Azure AD Connect sync, and it allows you to log into Azure AD applications like M365. The advantage is that your users log into their account using their onsite username and password. This helps users because it reduces the number of usernames and passwords that they need to know.

Another advantage to your organization is that you can use password hash synchronization as a backup sign-on method if your organization decides to use Federation services with Active Directory Federation Services (AD FS). To set up password hash synchronization, your environment needs to implement the following;

- Azure AD Connect
- Directory synchronization between your on-site Active Directory and your Azure AD instance
- Have password hash synchronization enabled

Azure Active Directory Pass-Through Authentication

Another option for allowing your users to sign into both onsite and cloud-based applications using the same passwords is *Azure AD Pass-Through Authentication*. Organizations can use Azure AD Pass-Through Authentication instead of using Azure AD Password Hash Synchronization. The benefits to using Azure AD Pass-Through Authentication include the ability to enforce onsite Active Directory security and password policies.

This option will help your organization with costs because your IT support desk will not be inundated by users' calls trying to remember their different passwords. This will help lower your IT department budget for total cost of ownership (TCO). Fewer calls to support means fewer support people needed. Some of the key benefits to using Azure AD Pass-Through Authentication are as follows:

- Better user experience
  - Users can use the same account password to sign into both your Azure AD and onsite AD networks.
  - Users don't need to talk to IT as often to reset passwords for multiple accounts.
  - Azure AD allows your users to do their own password management using the Self-Service Password Management tools.
- Easy deployment
  - There is no need to deploy a large infrastructure onsite. The Azure AD network can handle most of your networking services.
  - Less budgeting is needed for onsite IT departments. Since your Azure AD and your onsite AD can easily integrate with each other, there is no need for large IT departments onsite.

- Security
    - One nice advantage is that onsite passwords will never be stored in the Azure cloud.
    - Users' accounts are protected using Azure AD Conditional Access policies. These policies include multifactor authentication (MFA), filtering for brute-force password attacks, and stopping legacy authentication.
    - The Azure agent will only allow outbound connections from within your network. The advantage of this means that you are not required to load an agent on your perimeter network.
    - With the use of certificate-based authentication, organizations get secure connections between the Azure agent and Azure AD.
- Highly available
    - By installing additional Azure agents onto onsite servers, you can get high availability of Azure sign-in requests.

Federation with Azure AD

To understand what Federation can do for your organization, you must first understand trusts. *Federation* services (including Active Directory Federation Services [AD FS]) are just trusts on steroids. Understanding what a trust can do for your organization will help you understand why we use Federation.

Understanding Trusts

Trust relationships make it easier to share security information and network resources between domains. Standard transitive two-way trusts are automatically created between the domains in a tree and between each of the trees in a forest. When configuring trusts, you need to consider two main characteristics:

Transitive Trusts   By default, Active Directory trusts are *transitive trusts*. The simplest way to understand transitive relationships is through this example: If Domain A trusts Domain B and Domain B trusts Domain C, then Domain A implicitly trusts Domain C. If you need to apply a tighter level of security, trusts can be configured as intransitive.

One-Way vs. Two-Way   Trusts can be configured as one-way or two-way relationships. The default operation is to create *two-way trusts* or *bidirectional trusts*. This makes it easier to manage trust relationships by reducing the trusts you must create. In some cases, however, you might decide against two-way trusts. In one-way relationships, the trusting domain allows resources to be shared with the trusted domain but not the other way around.

When domains are added together to form trees and forests, an automatic transitive two-way trust is created between them. Although the default trust relationships work well for most organizations, there are some reasons you might want to manage trusts manually:

- You may want to remove trusts between domains if you are absolutely sure you do not want resources to be shared between domains.

- Because of security concerns, you may need to keep resources isolated.

In addition to the default trust types, you can configure the following types of special trusts:

External Trusts   You use *external trusts* to provide access to resources that cannot use a forest trust. In some cases, external trusts could be your only option. External trusts are always nontransitive, but they can be established in a one-way or a two-way configuration.

Default SID Filtering on External Trusts   When you set up an external trust, remember that it is possible for hackers to compromise a domain controller in a trusted domain. If this trust is compromised, a hacker can use the security identifier (SID) history attribute to associate SIDs with new user accounts, granting themselves unauthorized rights (this is called an *elevation-of-privileges attack*). To help prevent this type of attack, Windows Server 2022 automatically enables SID filter quarantining on all external trusts. SID filtering allows the domain controllers in the trusting domain (the domain with the resources) to remove all SID history attributes that are not members of the trusted domain.

Realm Trusts   *Realm trusts* are similar to external trusts. You use them to connect to a non-Windows domain that uses Kerberos authentication. Realm trusts can be transitive or nontransitive, one-way or two-way.

Cross-Forest Trusts   *Cross-forest trusts* are used to share resources between forests. They have been used since Windows Server 2000 domains and cannot be nontransitive, but you can establish them in a one-way or a two-way configuration. Authentication requests in either forest can reach the other forest in a two-way cross-forest trust. If you want one forest to trust another forest, you must set it (at a minimum) to at least the forest function level of Windows Server 2003.

Selective Authentication vs. Forest-wide Authentication   Forest-wide authentication on a forest trust means that users of the trusted forest can access all the resources of the trusting forest as long as they have the appropriate permissions. Selective authentication means that users cannot authenticate to a domain controller or resource server in the trusting forest unless they are explicitly allowed to do so.

Shortcut Trusts   In some cases, you may actually want to create direct trusts between two domains that implicitly trust each other. Such a trust is sometimes referred to as a *shortcut trust,* and it can improve the speed at which resources are accessed across many different domains. Let's say you have a forest, as shown in Figure 10.11.

FIGURE 10.11   Example of a forest

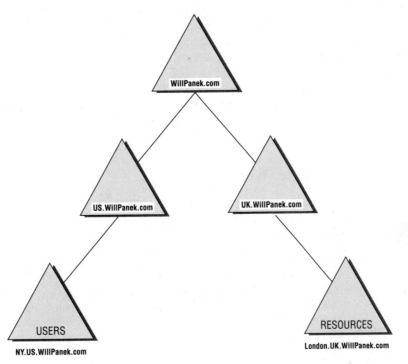

Users in the NY.us.WillPanek.com domain can access resources in the London
.uk.WillPanek.com domain, but the users must authenticate using the parent domains
to gain access (NY.us.WillPanek.com to us.WillPanek.com to WillPanek.com to
uk.WillPanek.com to finally reach London.uk.WillPanek.com). This process can be
slow. You can set up a one-way trust from London.uk.WillPanek.com (trusting domain) to
NY.us.WillPanek.com (trusted domain) so that the users can access the resources directly.

> Perhaps the most important aspect to remember regarding trusts is that
> creating them only *allows* you to share resources between domains. The
> trust does not grant any permissions between domains by itself. Once
> a trust has been established, however, system administrators can easily
> assign the necessary permissions.

Understanding Federation

So now that you understand trusts, it's easier to understand Federation because Federation is
just a group of domains that have an established trust. These domains can be between sites
or between separate organizations.

Remember, even though it's your company on Azure, Azure is owned by Microsoft. So, you are technically setting up a trust between your company and Microsoft's network (onmicrosoft.com).

When you set up Federation, you can set the trust level to whatever your organization needs for its users. You do not need to just give open access to everyone. Also, Federation is just the mechanism to allow access across the trust. You still need to set up users' permissions to your resources.

When you use Federation to set up authentication and authorization between your onsite network and Azure AD, all user authentications happen onsite. This gives your organization better levels of access control.

Common Identity Scenarios

Table 10.2 was taken directly from Microsoft's website, and it shows some of the common hybrid identity and access management scenarios along with their recommendations as to which hybrid identity option would be suitable for each.

In Table 10.2, the three headers are abbreviated. Column 2, PHS and SSO, stands for password hash synchronization with single sign-on. Column 3, PTA and SSO, stands for pass-through authentication and single sign-on. Finally, Column 4 stands for Federated single sign-on using Active Directory Federation Services.

TABLE 10.2   Common Identity Scenarios and Recommendations

Scenario	PHS and SSO	PTA and SSO	AD FS
Sync new user, contact, and group accounts created in my on-premises Active Directory to the cloud automatically.	X	X	X
Set up my tenant for Microsoft 365 hybrid scenarios	X	X	X
Enable my users to sign in and access cloud services using their on-premises password	X	X	X
Implement single sign-on using corporate credentials	X	X	X
Ensure no password hashes are stored in the cloud		X	X
Enable cloud multifactor authentication solutions		X	X
Enable on-premises multifactor authentication solutions			X
Support smartcard authentication for my users			X
Display password expiry notifications in the Office Portal and on the Windows 10/11 desktop			X

Azure AD Connect

Once you decide that you want your onsite network to be integrated with Azure AD, you need to install a component that allows both versions of Active Directory to work together. This component is called Azure AD Connect.

Azure AD Connect is a Microsoft utility that allows you to set up a hybrid design between Azure AD and your onsite AD. It provides the following features:

- Password hash synchronization
- Pass-through authentication
- Federation integration
- Synchronization
- Health Monitoring

Azure AD Connect Health Monitoring

Azure AD Connect Health Monitoring is a way that you can monitor your onsite identity infrastructure and maintain a constant connection to all of your Azure services.

To access the Azure AD Connect Health information, you must connect to the Azure AD Connect Health portal. The portal can be used to view alerts, usage information, performance monitoring, and other key information. The portal gives you a one-stop shop for all of your Azure AD Connect monitoring.

Creating and Verifying a Custom Domain Name

Once you have decided to create a hybrid network between your onsite domain and Azure, you must add your domain name to Azure. Once you add the Custom Domain Name in Azure, you have to create either a DNS .TXT record or an MX record.

Once you open the Azure portal, click Azure Active Directory. From the left-side menu, choose Custom Domain Name. Click the Add button and enter the name of your domain. Once you do this, Azure will show you the settings for either creating a TXT or an MX record. Open your domain DNS and create the TXT file. It's preferred that you create a TXT record in DNS. Use an MX record only if your DNS server does not allow TXT records.

After you open your domain DNS server, create a new TXT record. Copy the information from Azure into your new TXT record. After the TXT record is created on your DNS server, in Azure click Verify to verify the Custom Domain Name. Once the verification process happens, you can continue with Azure AD Connect.

Be aware that the verification process can take 24–48 hours. So, make sure this is done well before you connect the two networks.

Installing Azure AD Connect

Before you can install Azure AD Connect, you need to make sure that your infrastructure and your Azure network have met some prerequisites. The following is a list of requirements for installing Azure AD Connect:

- Azure AD.

- Onsite Active Directory.

- Azure AD Connect server.

- If you plan to use the feature password writeback, the domain controllers must be on Windows Server 2016 or later.

- SQL Server database used by Azure AD Connect.

- Azure AD Global Administrator account.

- Enterprise Administrator account.

- Connectivity between networks.

- PowerShell and .NET 4.6.2 or higher Framework setup

- Enabled TLS 1.2 for Azure AD Connect

In Exercise 10.5, you'll learn how to download and install Azure AD Connect. To complete this exercise, you must have an onsite version of AD that can be connected to Azure.

EXERCISE 10.5

Azure AD Connect

1. Go to the Azure AD Connect download page: www.microsoft.com/en-us/download/details.aspx?id=47594

2. Click the Download button.

3. When the download box appears, choose to download the AzureADConnect.msi file to a network location. Once the download is complete, close the download box.

4. Log into the server (where you wish to install Azure AD Connect) as the local administrator.

5. Navigate to the AzureADConnect.msi file and double-click the file to start the installation.

6. On the Welcome screen, select the box to agree to the license terms and then click Continue.

7. On the Express Settings page, click Use Express Settings.

8. On the Connect To Azure AD page, enter the Azure global administrator's username and password and then click Next.

9. The Connect To AD DS page will appear; enter the username and password for an onsite enterprise admin and then click Next.

10. The Azure AD sign-in configuration page will appear. Review every domain marked Not Added and Not Verified. Make sure domains are verified in Azure AD. Once the domains are verified in Azure, click the Refresh symbol. If you need to verify your domains, go into Azure Active Directory, and then select Custom Domain Names. Enter the domain names for your onsite domain.

11. On the Ready To Configure page, click Install.

12. When the installation completes, click Exit.

13. After the installation has completed, you will need to sign off and sign in again before you can use or set up any other services.

Azure VPN Gateway

As I have stated throughout this book, most (if not all) companies will have both an onsite network and an Azure network. Because of this, you will need to know how to connect both networks. This is where you would use a site-to-site VPN gateway connection.

Site-to-site VPN gateway connections allow you to connect both networks together over a secure IPsec/IKE VPN tunnel. To make this type of connection between networks, you need to have a VPN device located onsite. This VPN device will require a public IP address on the external side (the side facing the Internet) of the device.

To use a site-to-site VPN connection, you must meet the following requirements:

- Compatible VPN device that you can configure to connect to the external device .

- An external public IP address for that VPN device.

- Knowledge of your onsite IP configuration and subnetting. None of your onsite IP subnets can overlap your Azure virtual network subnets.

Example Values for Site-to-Site VPN Connection

To help IT people better understand and configure site-to-site VPN connections, Microsoft released example values on their website. These example values can be used to set up a test environment, or they can be used to help you better understand what values are needed to set up a site-to-site VPN connection.

Site-to-Site VPN Connection Examples

The following examples were taken directly from Microsoft's website, https://docs.microsoft.com/en-us/azure/vpn-gateway/vpn-gateway-howto-site-to-site-resource-manager-portal.

- VNet Name: TestVNet1
- Address Space: 10.1.0.0/16
- Subscription: The subscription you want to use
- Resource Group: TestRG1
- Location: East US
- Subnet: FrontEnd: 10.1.0.0/24, BackEnd: 10.1.1.0/24 (optional for this exercise)
- Gateway Subnet name: GatewaySubnet (this will autofill in the portal)
- Gateway Subnet address range: 10.1.255.0/27
- DNS Server: 8.8.8.8 - Optional. The IP address of your DNS server
- Virtual Network Gateway Name: VNet1GW
- Public IP: VNet1GWIP
- VPN Type: Route-based
- Connection Type: Site-to-site (IPsec)
- Gateway Type: VPN
- Local Network Gateway Name: Site1
- Connection Name: VNet1toSite1
- Shared key: For this example, we use abc123. But you can use whatever is compatible with your VPN hardware. The important thing is that the values match on both sides of the connection.

Creating the VPN Gateway

Now that understand why you would need a VPN gateway, let's look at what it takes to create one. Since every VPN device is different, I will show you how to create the actual site-to-site VPN connection in Exercise 10.6. You need to have someone create the connection on the VPN device.

EXERCISE 10.6

Creating the Site-to-Site VPN connection

1. Log into the Azure dashboard.

2. On the left side of the portal page, click + Create A Resource and then type **Virtual Network Gateway** in the search box. In the Results section, click Virtual Network Gateway.

3. On the Virtual Network Gateway page, click the Create button.

4. On the Create Virtual Network Gateway page, enter the values for your virtual network gateway settings:

- **Name:** This is the name of your gateway object.

- **Gateway type:** Select VPN. VPN gateways use the VPN type.

- **VPN type:** Choose the VPN type that fits your configuration. Route-based VPNs are the most common type.

- **SKU:** Select your gateway SKU. This will depend on the VPN type you select.

- **Enable active-active mode:** If you are creating an active-active gateway configuration, select this check box. If you are not creating an active-active gateway configuration, leave this check box unselected.

- **Location:** Choose your appropriate geographical location.

- **Virtual network:** Choose the virtual network you want for this gateway. You can choose the virtual network we created earlier in this book.

- **Gateway subnet address range:** This setting will only be seen if you did not already create a gateway subnet for your virtual network. If you did create a valid gateway subnet, this setting will not appear.

- **Public IP address:** This setting specifies the public IP address that gets associated to the VPN gateway. Make sure Create New is the selected radio button and type a name for your public IP address.

- **BGP ASN:** Unless your configuration specifically requires BGP ASN, leave this configuration's check box unselected. If BGP ASN is required, the default setting for ASN is 65515. You can change this if needed.

5. Click Create. The settings will be validated and you'll see the *Deploying Virtual network gateway* message on the dashboard. This process can take up to 45 minutes. Refresh your portal page to see the current status.

Creating the Local Network Gateway

The next step is creating the local network gateway. The local network gateway refers to your onsite network. What you need to do is give your onsite network a name that Azure can use to access that network.

After you name the onsite network on Azure, you then have to tell Azure what IP address to use to access the onsite VPN device. You also have to specify the IP address prefix (that is located on your onsite location) that will be used to route traffic through the VPN gateway and to the VPN device.

In Exercise 10.7, I will show you how to set up the local network gateway. To complete this exercise, you need to know the IP address information for your onsite test or live network.

EXERCISE 10.7

Creating the Local Network Gateway

1. Log into the Azure dashboard.

2. On the left side of the portal page, click + Create A Resource and then type **Local network gateway** in the search box. In the Results section, click Virtual Network Gateway.

3. On the Local Network Gateway page, click Create.

4. On the Create Local Network Gateway page, enter the values for your virtual network gateway settings:

   - **Name:** Specify the name of your local network gateway.

   - **IP address:** This is the public IP address of the VPN device.

   - **Address Space:** This is the IP address ranges for the local network.

   - **Configure BGP settings:** Use this setting when configuring BGP. Otherwise, don't select this check box.

   - **Subscription:** Verify that your current Azure subscription is showing.

   - **Resource Group:** You can create a new resource group or choose one that you have already created.

   - **Location:** Choose your appropriate geographical location.

5. Click Create.

Once you have finished creating the VPN connection, you must configure your company's VPN device. As stated earlier, site-to-site connections require a VPN device. Once the VPN device is configured properly, your site-to-site communications are completed.

Understanding ExpressRoute

ExpressRoute allows you to set up another way to connect your two networks. ExpressRoute allows you to connect your internal network to your external network using a private connection provided by your connection provider. Using ExpressRoute allows you to connect your internal network with any or all of the different Microsoft networks, including Azure, Microsoft 365, and Dynamics 365.

Since the connection is through your connection provider and not the Internet, ExpressRoute is a much faster, more reliable, better security, and lower-latency connection over the Internet.

Planning Azure AD Authentication Options

Azure AD is a centralized identity provider in the cloud, and authentication is the process of verifying that you are who you say you are. It helps protect a user's identity and also simplifies the login experience. The Microsoft identity platform makes it easy to authorize and authenticate by providing identity as a service.

In Azure AD, authentication entails more than just verifying a username and password. Azure AD authentication includes the components that will be used to increase security and to reduce the need for contacting the help desk for assistance. These components include the following:

- Azure AD Multifactor Authentication
- Hybrid integration to enforce password protection policies for an on-premises environment
- Hybrid integration to write password changes back to on-premises environment
- Passwordless authentication
- Self-service password reset

Azure AD Multifactor Authentication

Azure AD Multifactor Authentication allows you to choose a variety of authentication methods during sign-in, such as receiving a phone call or receiving a verification code or a text message (as seen in Figure 10.12).

By requiring a second form of authentication, you will be increasing your security. If you only use passwords to authenticate a user, this practice can potentially open doors for an attacker.

Azure AD Multifactor Authentication works by requiring two or more of the following:

- Something you know, such as a password
- Something you have, such as a trusted device, like a phone or hardware key, that cannot be easily duplicated
- Something you are, such as biometrics like a fingerprint or face scan

Password Protection

By default, Azure AD blocks weak passwords. An example of a weak password is Password1. Weak and known passwords are added to a global banned password list that is enforced and updated automatically. Therefore, if a user tries to use one of the passwords on the list, they will get a notification that they need to create a password that is more secure.

FIGURE 10.12 Multifactor authentication methods

To boost your security, you can also define a custom password protection policy that will use filters to block different variations of passwords such as those containing names or locations.

You can also incorporate Azure AD password protection with an on-premises AD environment to create hybrid security. An on-premises component will get the global banned password list and the custom password protection policy and then the domain controllers will use both to process password change events. This will ensure that strong passwords will be enforced regardless of how a user changes their passwords.

Passwordless Authentication

Passwordless authentication is an authentication method that will allow your users to obtain access without answering any security questions or entering a password. This eliminates the requirement of a user to create and remember passwords.

To strengthen security, expand on the user's experience, and to help reduce operation expenses, passwordless authentication can be used with multifactor authentication (MFA) and single sign-on (SSO) solutions.

When signing in using the passwordless authentication method, the credentials are provided by using approaches such as a fingerprint using biometrics with Windows Hello for Business or a FIDO2 security key. An attacker cannot easily duplicate these forms of authentication.

Self-Service Password Reset (SSPR)

Self-service password reset allows a user to change or reset their password without any assistance from the help desk or the administrator. If a user gets locked out of their account or cannot remember their password, they can simply follow prompts to get themselves back into the system. This ability reduces the number of help desk service calls and prevents loss of employee productivity.

SSPR allows users to:

Change Their Password   This is used when the user knows their password and wants to change it.

Reset Their Password   This is used when the user cannot sign in, because they forgot their password and want to reset it.

Unlock Their Account   This is used when the user cannot sign in because the account is now locked and they want to unlock it.

To Enable Self-Service Password Reset

Azure AD allows you to set SSPR to None, Selected, or All Users (see Figure 10.13). Using the Azure portal, you can enable only one Azure AD group for SSPR.

1. Using an account with global administrator permissions, sign into the Azure portal.

2. Search for and select Azure Active Directory, then select Password Reset from the menu on the left side.

3. From the Properties page, under the option Self-Service Password Reset Enabled, choose Selected.

4. If your group isn't visible, choose No Groups Selected, browse for and select your Azure AD group, and then choose Select.

5. To enable SSPR for the select users, select Save.

Azure AD Connect Sync: Understand and Customize Synchronization

Objects and credentials, from an on-premises AD DS domain, can be synchronized to Azure AD using Azure AD Connect in a hybrid environment. Once those objects are synchronized to Azure AD, the automatic background sync then makes those objects and credentials available to applications using the managed domain.

A main component of Azure AD Connect is the Azure Active Directory Connect synchronization services (Azure AD Connect sync). Azure AD Connect Sync handles all the operations that pertain to synchronizing identity data between your on-premises environment and Azure AD. Azure AD Connect sync replaces DirSync, Azure AD Sync, and Forefront Identity Manager.

FIGURE 10.13 Enable Self-Service Password Reset

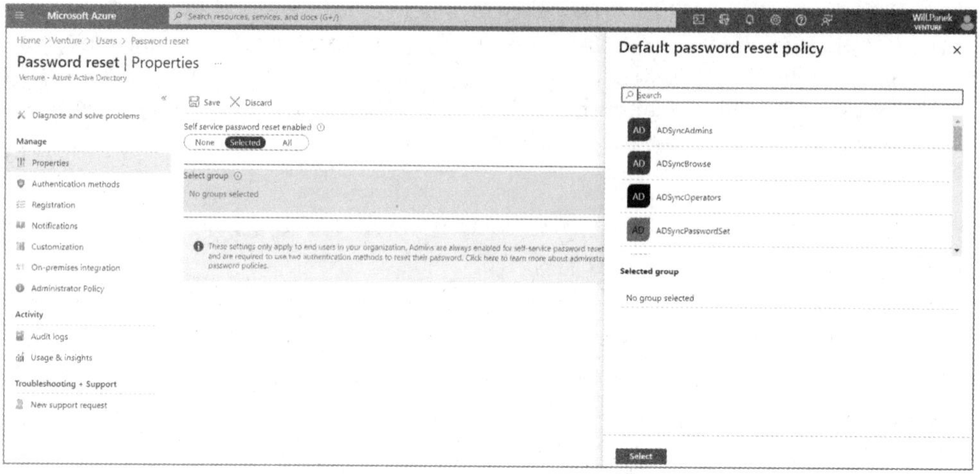

The Azure AD Connect sync service consists of two components:

- The on-premises Azure AD Connect sync component, also called Sync Engine
- The service side in Azure AD called Azure AD Connect sync service

These settings are configured by the Azure AD Module for Windows PowerShell. To see the configuration in your Azure AD directory, run **Get-MsolDirSyncFeatures** (as shown in Figure 10.14).

FIGURE 10.14 Running Get-MsolDirSyncFeatures

```
PS C:\> Connect-MsolService
PS C:\> Get-MsolDirSyncFeatures

ExtensionData                       DirSyncFeature                     Enabled
-------------                       --------------                     -------
System.Runtime.Serialization.Extensi... DeviceWriteback                   False
System.Runtime.Serialization.Extensi... DirectoryExtensions               True
System.Runtime.Serialization.Extensi... DuplicateProxyAddressResiliency   True
System.Runtime.Serialization.Extensi... DuplicateUPNResiliency            True
System.Runtime.Serialization.Extensi... EnableSoftMatchOnUpn              False
System.Runtime.Serialization.Extensi... PasswordSync                      True
System.Runtime.Serialization.Extensi... SynchronizeUpnForManagedUsers     False
System.Runtime.Serialization.Extensi... UnifiedGroupWriteback             True
System.Runtime.Serialization.Extensi... UserWriteback                     True
```

Many of these settings can only be changed by Azure AD Connect. The following settings can be configured by Set-MsolDirSyncFeature:

- **EnableSoftMatchOnUpn:** Allows objects to join on userPrincipalName in addition to the primary SMTP address
- **SynchronizeUpnForManagedUsers:** Allows the Sync Engine to update the user PrincipalName attribute for managed/licensed (non-Federated) users.

Once you have enabled a feature, it cannot be disabled again. Table 10.3 shows you the settings configured by Azure AD Connect that cannot be modified by `Set-MsolDirSyncFeature`.

TABLE 10.3 Settings configured by Azure AD Connect

DirSync feature	Note
DeviceWriteback	Azure AD Connect: Enables device writeback
DirectoryExtensions	Azure AD Connect sync: Directory extensions
DuplicateProxyAddress Resiliency DuplicateUPNResiliency	Allows an attribute to be quarantined when it is a duplicate of another object rather than failing the entire object during export
Password Hash Sync	Implement password hash synchronization with Azure AD Connect sync
Pass-through Authentication	User sign-in with Azure Active Directory Pass-through Authentication
UnifiedGroupWriteback	Group writeback
UserWriteback	Not currently supported

Using PowerShell Commands

Table 10.4 contains some of the PowerShell commands available for Azure AD. You must be using a newer version of PowerShell on your onsite servers or client machines. If you run into any issues trying to run these commands, please check out a newer version of Microsoft PowerShell on Microsoft's website.

TABLE 10.4 PowerShell commands for Azure AD

Command	Description
Add-AzureADAdministrativeUnit Member	This command allows you to add an administrative unit member.
Add-AzureADApplicationPolicy	You can use this command to add an application policy.

TABLE 10.4   PowerShell commands for Azure AD *(continued)*

Command	Description
Add-AzureADScopedRoleMembership	This command allows you to add a scoped role membership to an administrative unit.
Add-AzureADServicePrincipalPolicy	You can use this command to add a service principal policy.
Get-AzureADAdministrativeUnit	This command allows you to view an administrative unit.
Get-AzureADAdministrativeUnit Member	You can use this command to view a member of an administrative unit.
Get-AzureADApplicationPolicy	This command allows you to view an application policy.
Get-AzureADDirectorySetting	You can use this command to view a directory setting.
Get-AzureADDirectorySetting Template	This command allows you to view a directory setting template.
Get-AzureADObjectSetting	You can use this command to view an object setting.
Get-AzureADPolicy	This command allows you to view a policy.
Get-AzureADPolicyAppliedObject	You can use this command to view the objects to which a policy is applied.
Get-AzureADScopedRoleMembership	This command allows you to view a scoped role membership from an administrative unit.
Get-AzureADServicePrincipalPolicy	You can use this command to view the service principal policy.
New-AzureADAdministrativeUnit	This command allows you to create an administrative unit.
New-AzureADDirectorySetting	You can use this command to create a directory settings object.
New-AzureADObjectSetting	This command allows you to create a settings object.

Command	Description
New-AzureADPolicy	You can use this command to create a policy.
Remove-AzureADAdministrativeUnit	This command allows you to remove an administrative unit.
Remove-AzureADAdministrativeUnit Member	You can use this command to remove an administrative unit member.
Remove-AzureADDirectorySetting	This command allows you to delete a directory setting in Azure Active Directory.
Remove-AzureADObjectSetting	You can use this command to delete settings in Azure Active Directory.
Remove-AzureADPolicy	This command allows you to delete a policy.
Remove-AzureADScopedRoleMembership	You can use this command to remove a scoped role membership.
Set-AzureADDirectorySetting	This command updates a directory setting in Azure Active Directory.
Set-AzureADObjectSetting	This command allows you to update object settings.
Set-AzureADPolicy	You can use this command to update a policy.
Get-AzureADApplicationProxy ConnectorGroupMembers	This command retrieves the members of an Application Proxy connector group.

Summary

This chapter covered the basics of implementing Azure AD. I showed you all of the benefits and features of Azure AD in addition to the common questions and answers about Azure AD directly from Microsoft's website.

You were introduced to the Azure AD dashboard and many of its different sections. I showed you how to create an Azure AD users account and an Azure AD group. I then talked about the Azure AD Password Reset option and how to configure that feature.

This chapter also covered the benefits of using the Azure AD Identity Protection feature, and I showed you how to add that feature to your subscription. You learned how to configure Identity Protection and set up an email address so that you can receive alerts.

You saw how you can set up a hybrid network and the importance of setting up an onsite network along with your Azure AD network.

This chapter then covered the various authentication methods and what each method can do for you. I also explained Azure AD Connect and how it can link your onsite AD with Azure AD.

I explained the benefits of using site-to-site VPN gateway connections. I showed you the requirements and how to set up and configure the components needed for site-to-site VPN gateway connections.

Exam Essentials

Understand the difference between Active Directory and Azure AD.   Make sure you understand the features and benefits of using Azure AD. Not only is this important for taking the Microsoft exams, but it is also important to determine if Azure AD is the correct choice for your organization.

Understand the Q&As of Azure AD.   This is very important for a couple of reasons. First, and most obvious, for the Microsoft exam you need to understand what Azure AD can and cannot do. Second, you need to make sure that Azure AD can handle all the services your organization is trying to provide.

Be able to use the Azure AD dashboard.   You need to be able to use the Azure AD dashboard and know how to configure the various components for Azure AD. You also need to know how to access other dashboards (like the Azure AD Identity Protection dashboard) so that you can properly navigate Azure AD and its features.

Know how to set up and configure password resets.   You should understand what the process is for password resets and how to configure different authentication methods. Understand how to verify the users by using text messages or emails for verification.

Understand Azure AD Identity Protection.   Know how to add Azure AD Identity Protection to your Azure subscription. Make sure you know how to configure the different policies and how to set alerts for an Azure administrator.

Understand Azure AD Connect.   Understand why we use Azure AD Connect. Azure AD Connect allows you to connect your onsite AD with Azure AD. This allows your user accounts and passwords to be replicated.

Be familiar with site-to-site VPN gateway connections.   Know and understand what site-to-site VPN gateways can do for your company. Site-to-site VPN gateway connections allow you to connect both of your networks over a secure IPsec/IKE VPN tunnel.

Know the Azure AD PowerShell commands.   Microsoft announced that all of their Microsoft exams would start asking questions about using PowerShell. This is going to be true for all chapters in this book, so make sure you understand the basic Azure AD PowerShell commands.

Review Questions

1. You are the system administrator of a large organization that has recently decided to add an Azure AD subscription. Your boss has asked you about Azure security and making sure that user logins are secure. What feature can you explain to your boss to ease their concerns?

   A. Azure AD User Security

   B. Azure AD Identity Protection

   C. Azure AD Security add-on

   D. Azure Identity Protection

2. You want to create a new Azure AD policy for your users. What PowerShell command would you use to accomplish this task?

   A. `New-AzurePolicy`

   B. `New-AzureActiveDirectoryPolicy`

   C. `Set-AzurePolicy`

   D. `New-AzureADPolicy`

3. You want to look at an Azure AD policy for your users. What PowerShell command would you use to accomplish this task?

   A. `Get-AzureADPolicy`

   B. `Get-AzurePolicy`

   C. `View-AzurePolicy`

   D. `View-AzureADPolicy`

4. You are the administrator for a large organization that has subscribed to a new Azure AD subscription. You want your users to be able to reset passwords themselves. What Azure AD feature allows this to happen?

   A. User-enabled password resets

   B. Azure password reset feature

   C. Self-service password reset

   D. Password reset service

5. You are the new Azure AD Global Administrator for your organization. Your company wants to set up a way to integrate their onsite AD with Azure AD. What tool can you use to do this?

   A. Site-to-site VPN gateway connectors

   B. Azure AD Connect

   C. Azure AD Replication

   D. Active Directory Replicator

6.   You want to look at an Azure AD application policy for your users' applications. What PowerShell command would you use to accomplish this task?

   A.   `Add-AzureADPolicy`

   B.   `Add-AzureADApplicationPolicy`

   C.   `Create-AzurePolicy`

   D.   `Install-AzureADPolicy`

7.   You want to change an Azure Active Directory policy for your users. What PowerShell command would you use to accomplish this task?

   A.   `New-AzureADPolicy`

   B.   `Edit-AzureADPolicy`

   C.   `New-AzurePolicy`

   D.   `Set-AzureADPolicy`

8.   You are the new Azure AD Global Administrator for your organization. Your company has an Azure AD domain name of `ContosoAzure.onmicrosoft.com`. Your bosses want you to change the default domain name to `Contoso.onmicrosoft.com`. How can you change the initial domain name?

   A.   Use the Custom Domain Names section of Azure AD and change the name.

   B.   In Azure AD, go to default directories and change the domain name.

   C.   Use PowerShell to change the default domain name.

   D.   This can't be done.

9.   You are the new Azure AD Global Administrator for your organization. Your company has an Azure AD domain name of `ContosoAzure.onmicrosoft.com`. Your bosses want you to add a new domain name for `Contoso.onmicrosoft.com`. How can you add the new domain name to your existing domain?

   A.   Use the Custom Domain Names section of Azure AD and change the name.

   B.   In Azure AD, go to default directories and add the domain name.

   C.   Use the Azure Administrative Center to add the new domain name.

   D.   This can't be done.

10.   You want to view your Azure AD directory settings for your Azure AD subscription. What PowerShell command would you use to accomplish this task?

   A.   `View-AzureADDirectorySetting`

   B.   `Get-AzureADDirectorySetting`

   C.   `Add-AzureADDirectorySetting`

   D.   `Set-AzureADDirectorySetting`

11. You are the administrator for your company network. You want to look at an Azure AD application policy for your users' applications. What PowerShell command should you use?

    A. Add-AzureADPolicy

    B. Get-AzureADApplicationPolicy

    C. Create-AzurePolicy

    D. Install-AzureADPolicy

12. You are the administrator for your company network. You have 20 Windows client computers that are joined to Azure AD. You have a Microsoft 365 subscription. You are planning to replace these computers with new computers that also run Windows 10/11. The new computers will be joined to Azure AD. What should you configure if you need to ensure that the desktop background, the Favorites, and the browsing history are available on the new computers?

    A. You should configure Enterprise State Roaming.

    B. You should configure Folder Redirection.

    C. You should configure system settings.

    D. You should configure roaming user profiles.

13. You are the administrator for your company network. You and a colleague are discussing different authentication methods. Which one of the following tools allows for the use of security questions?

    A. Azure AD Self-Service Password Reset (SSPR).

    B. Azure Multifactor Authentication (Azure MFA).

    C. Password Manager (PassMgr).

    D. This can't be done.

14. You are the administrator for your company network. You have an Azure AD tenant. All corporate devices are enrolled. You have a web-based application that uses Azure AD to authenticate. What should you configure if you need to prompt all users of the application to agree to the protection of corporate data when they access the app from both corporate and noncorporate devices?

    A. You should configure notifications in Device Compliance.

    B. You should configure Terms and Conditions in Device Enrollment.

    C. You should configure Terms of Use in Conditional Access.

    D. You should configure an Endpoint Protection Profile in Device Configuration.

15. You are the administrator for your company network. You need to ensure that when managers join Azure AD that their computers are enrolled automatically into Mobile Device Management (MDM). What tool should you use to do this?

    A. The Configuration Manager console

    B. The Group Policy Management Editor

    C. The Azure portal

    D. The Microsoft Intune portal

16. You are the administrator for your company network. You and a colleague are discussing conditional access policies and how to set one up. One section of the conditional access policy controls the who, what, and where of the conditional access policy. What section is being discussed?

   A. Access Controls

   B. Admission Control

   C. Assignments

   D. Tasks

17. You are the administrator for your company network. You and a colleague are discussing a feature used by Azure AD to bring together signals, to make decisions, and to enforce organizational policies. What is this tool called?

   A. Conditional access

   B. Device access

   C. Microsoft Cloud App Security (MCAS)

   D. Microsoft Empowerment

18. You are the administrator for your company network. You and a colleague are discussing the ability of Windows 10/11 Azure AD users to roam their profile data between multiple devices, allowing the user and app settings to sync between the devices regardless of where the user is located. What is this called?

   A. Azure Readiness Roaming

   B. Enterprise State Roaming

   C. Mandatory User Profile

   D. Roaming User Profile

19. You are the administrator for your company network. You and a colleague are discussing a tool that allows an organization to automate the detection and remediation of identity-based risks. What is this tool called?

   A. Azure AD User Security

   B. Azure AD Identity Protection

   C. Azure AD Security add-on

   D. Azure Identity Protection

20. You are the administrator for your company network. You and a colleague are discussing roles and permissions. You are using Azure AD and you want to assign permissions to users for maintaining conditional access. What role should you assign to the users if you'd like them to be able to view, create, modify, and delete conditional access policies?

   A. The Application Administrator role

   B. The Compliance Administrator role

   C. The Conditional Access Administrator role

   D. The Conditional Admission Administrator role

Chapter

11

Configuring Storage

THE FOLLOWING AZ-800 EXAM OBJECTIVES ARE COVERED IN THIS CHAPTER:

✓ **Configure Windows Server storage**

- ▪ Configure disks and volumes
- ▪ Configure and manage Storage Spaces
- ▪ Configure and manage Storage Replica
- ▪ Configure Data Deduplication
- ▪ Configure SMB Direct
- ▪ Configure Storage Quality of Service (QoS)
- ▪ Configure file systems

✓ **Configure and manage Windows Server file shares**

- ▪ Configure Windows Server file share access
- ▪ Configure File Screens
- ▪ Configure FSRM quotas
- ▪ Configure BranchCache
- ▪ Implement and configure Distributed File System (DFS)

THE FOLLOWING AZ-801 EXAM OBJECTIVES ARE COVERED IN THIS CHAPTER:

✓ **Secure Windows Server storage**

- ▪ Manage Windows BitLocker Drive Encryption (BitLocker)
- ▪ Manage and recover encrypted volumes
- ▪ Enable storage encryption by using Azure Disk Encryption
- ▪ Manage disk encryption keys for IaaS virtual machines

This chapter explains how to set up your servers so that your network users have something to access. Before you can set up a server, you have to determine its purpose. Is it going to be a print server, a file storage server, a remote access server, or a domain controller?

After you have decided how the machine is going to help your network, you must implement your decision. In this chapter, I'll show you how to set up a print server and a file server. In addition, I will discuss how to set up permissions and security for these servers and how you can limit the amount of space your users can have on a server.

I will show you how to set up and use data duplication. I will explain the benefits of duplication and how to use data duplication for backups. I will also show you how to monitor the data that is being duplicated.

I will talk about using the File Server Resource Manager. This is a utility that allows you to manage and configure file servers. This includes setting up how much space your users will get on the file servers. I will also show you how to set up and manage encrypted files using the Encrypting File System (EFS).

I will then introduce you to the Distributed File System (DFS) setup. You'll learn how to install and set up a DFS namespace. I will then show you how to add shared folders to the DFS structure.

Understanding Filesystems

When we begin the discussion about understanding Windows filesystems, we have to first think about how the Windows Server 2022 machine will be used. There are four supported filesystems: FAT, FAT32, NTFS, and ReFS. FAT and FAT32 partitions may not always be an available option. As you can see in Figure 11.1, all four filesystems are available because the partition is under 4 GB.

FAT has a maximum partition size of 4 GB and FAT32 has a max partition size of 32 GB. In Figure 11.1, since it's a 3 GB partition, all four options are available. But since most drives today are much larger than 32 GB, we will continue our focus on just NTFS and ReFS.

When you're planning your Active Directory deployment, the filesystem that the operating system uses is an important concern for two reasons. First, the filesystem can provide the ultimate level of security for all the information stored on the server itself. Second, it is responsible for managing and tracking all this data. The Windows Server 2022 platform supports two main filesystems:

- Windows NT File System (NTFS)
- Resilient File System (ReFS)

FIGURE 11.1   Format options on Windows Server 2022

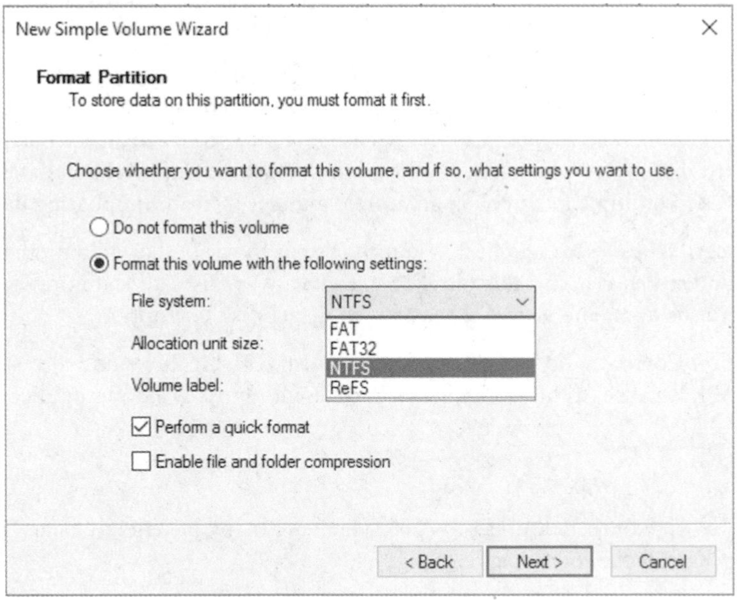

New Simple Volume Wizard   ✕

Format Partition
To store data on this partition, you must format it first.

Choose whether you want to format this volume, and if so, what settings you want to use.

○ Do not format this volume

◉ Format this volume with the following settings:

File system: NTFS ⌄

Allocation unit size: FAT
FAT32
NTFS
Volume label: ReFS

☑ Perform a quick format

☐ Enable file and folder compression

< Back   Next >   Cancel

Although ReFS was new to Windows Server 2012, NTFS has been around for many years, and NTFS in Windows Server 2022 has been improved for better performance.

Resilient File System (ReFS)

Windows Server 2022 includes a filesystem called *Resilient File System (ReFS)*. ReFS was created to help Windows Server 2022 maximize the availability of data and online operation. ReFS allows the Windows Server 2022 system to continue to function despite some errors that would normally cause data to be lost or the system to go down. ReFS uses data integrity to protect your data from errors and also to make sure that all of your important data is online when that data is needed.

One of the issues that IT members have had to face over the years is the problem of rapidly growing data sizes. As we continue to rely more and more on computers, our data continues to get larger and larger. This is where ReFS can help an IT department. ReFS was designed specifically with the issues of scalability and performance in mind, which resulted in some of the following ReFS features:

Availability   If your hard disk becomes corrupted, ReFS has the ability to implement a salvage strategy that removes the data that has been corrupted. This feature allows the healthy data to continue to be available while the unhealthy data is removed. All of this can be done without taking the hard disk offline.

Scalability   One of the main advantages of ReFS is the ability to support volume sizes up to 2^78 bytes using 16 KB cluster sizes, while Windows stack addressing allows 2^64 bytes. ReFS also supports file sizes of 2^64-1 bytes, 2^64 files in a directory, and the same number of directories in a volume.

Robust Disk Updating   ReFS uses a disk updating system referred to as an *allocate-on-write transactional model* (also known as *copy on write*). This model helps to avoid many hard disk issues while data is written to the disk because ReFS updates data using disk writes to multiple locations in an atomic manner instead of updating data in place.

Data Integrity   ReFS uses a check-summed system to verify that all data that is being written and stored is accurate and reliable. ReFS always uses allocate-on-write for updates to the data, and it uses checksums to detect disk corruption.

Application Compatibility   ReFS allows for most NTFS features and also supports the Win32 API. Because of this, ReFS is compatible with most Windows applications.

NTFS

Let's start with some of the features of NTFS. There are many benefits to using NTFS, including support for the following:

Disk Quotas   To restrict the amount of disk space used by users on the network, you can establish *disk quotas*. By default, Windows Server 2022 supports disk quota restrictions at the volume level. That is, you can restrict the amount of storage space that a specific user uses on a single disk volume. Third-party solutions that allow more granular quota settings are also available.

File System Encryption   One of the fundamental problems with network operating systems (NOSs) is that system administrators are often given full permission to view all files and data stored on hard disks, which can be a security and privacy concern. In some cases, this is necessary. For example, to perform backup, recovery, and disk management functions, at least one user must have all permissions. Windows Server 2022 and NTFS address these issues by allowing for *filesystem encryption*. Encryption essentially scrambles all of the data stored within files before they are written to the disk. When an authorized user requests the files, they are transparently decrypted and provided. By using encryption, you can prevent the data from being used in case it is stolen or intercepted by an unauthorized user—even a system administrator.

Dynamic Volumes   Protecting against disk failures is an important concern for production servers. Although earlier versions of Windows NT supported various levels of Redundant Array of Independent Disks (RAID) technology, software-based solutions had some shortcomings. Perhaps the most significant was that administrators needed to perform server reboots to change RAID configurations. Also, you could not make some configuration changes without completely reinstalling the operating system. With Windows Server 2022 support for *dynamic volumes*, you can change RAID and other disk configuration settings without needing to reboot or reinstall the server. The result is greater data protection, increased scalability, and increased uptime. Dynamic volumes are also included with ReFS.

Mounted Drives   By using *mounted drives*, you can map a local disk drive to an NTFS directory name. This helps you organize disk space on servers and increase manageability. By using mounted drives, you can mount the `C:\Users` directory to an actual physical disk. If that disk becomes full, you can copy all of the files to another, larger drive without changing the directory pathname or reconfiguring applications.

Remote Storage   System administrators often notice that as soon as they add more space, they must plan the next upgrade. One way to recover disk space is to move infrequently used files to external hard drives. However, backing up and restoring these files can be quite difficult and time-consuming. You can use the *remote storage* features supported by NTFS to off-load seldom-used data automatically to a backup system or other devices. The files, however, remain available to users. If a user requests an archived file, Windows Server 2022 can automatically restore the file from a remote storage device and make it available. Using remote storage like this frees up system administrators' time and allows them to focus on tasks other than micromanaging disk space.

Self-healing NTFS   In previous versions of the Windows Server operating system, if you had to fix a corrupted NTFS volume, you used a tool called `Chkdsk.exe`. The disadvantage of this tool is that the Windows Server's availability was disrupted. If this server was your domain controller, that could stop domain logon authentication.

To help protect the Windows Server 2022 NTFS file system, Microsoft now uses a feature called self-healing NTFS. *Self-healing NTFS* attempts to fix corrupted NTFS file systems without taking them offline. Self-healing NTFS allows an NTFS file system to be corrected without running the `Chkdsk.exe` utility. New features added to the NTFS kernel code allow disk inconsistencies to be corrected without system downtime.

Security   NTFS allows you to configure not only folder-level security but also file-level security. NTFS security is one of the biggest reasons most companies use NTFS. ReFS also allows folder- and file-level security.

Setting Up the NTFS Partition

Although the features mentioned in the previous section likely compel most system administrators to use NTFS, additional reasons make using it mandatory. The most important reason is that the Active Directory data store must reside on an NTFS partition. Therefore, before you begin installing Active Directory, make sure you have at least one NTFS partition available. Also, be sure you have a reasonable amount of disk space available (at least 4GB). Because the size of the Active Directory data store will grow as you add objects to it, also be sure that you have adequate space for the future.

Exercise 11.1 shows you how to use the administrative tools to view and modify disk configuration.

WARNING Before you make any disk configuration changes, be sure you completely understand their potential effects; then perform the test in a lab environment and make sure you have good, verifiable backups handy. Changing partition sizes and adding and removing partitions can result in a total loss of all information on one or more partitions.

If you want to convert an existing partition from FAT or FAT32 to NTFS, you need to use the CONVERT command-line utility. For example, the following command converts the C: partition from FAT to NTFS:

```
CONVERT c: /fs:ntfs
```

EXERCISE 11.1

Viewing Disk Configurations

1. Right click the Start button and then choose Disk Management (shown in Figure 11.2).

FIGURE 11.2 Computer Management

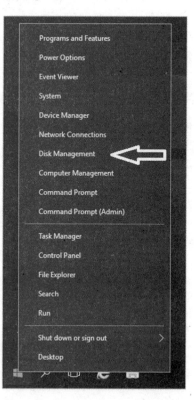

The Disk Management program shows you the logical and physical disks that are currently configured on your system. Note that information about the size of each partition is also displayed (in the Capacity column).

2. To see the available options for modifying partition settings, right-click any of the disks or partitions and choose Properties. This step is optional.

3. Close Computer Management.

Storage in Windows Server 2022

As an IT administrator, you'll need to ask many questions before you start setting up a server. What type of disks should be used? What type of RAID sets should be made? What type of hardware platform should be purchased? These are all questions you must ask when planning for storage in a Windows Server 2022 server. In the following sections, I will answer these questions so that you can make the best decisions for storage in your network's environment.

Initializing Disks

To begin, I must discuss how to add disk drives to a server. Once a disk drive has been physically installed, it must be initialized by selecting the type of partition. Different types of partition styles are used to initialize disks: *Master Boot Record (MBR)* and *GUID Partition Table (GPT)*.

MBR has a partition table that indicates where the partitions are located on the disk drive, and with this particular partition style, only volumes up to 2 TB (2,048 GB) are supported. An MBR drive can have up to four primary partitions or can have three primary partitions and one extended partition that can be divided into unlimited logical drives.

Windows Server 2022 can only boot off an MBR disk unless it is based on the Extensible Firmware Interface (EFI); then it can boot from GPT. An Itanium server is an example of an EFI-based system. GPT is not constrained by the same limitations as MBR. In fact, a GPT disk drive can support volumes of up to 18EB (18,874,368 million terabytes) and 128 partitions. As a result, GPT is recommended for disks larger than 2TB or disks used on Itanium-based computers. Exercise 11.2 demonstrates the process of initializing additional disk drives to an active computer running Windows Server 2022. If you're not adding a new drive, then stop after step 4. I am completing this exercise using Computer Management, but you also can do this exercise using Server Manager.

EXERCISE 11.2

Initializing Disk Drives

1. Open Computer Management under Administrative Tools.

2. Select Disk Management.

3. After disk drives have been installed, right-click Disk Management and select Rescan Disks.

4. A pop-up box appears indicating that the server is scanning for new disks. If you did not add a new disk, go to step 9.

5. After the server has completed the scan, the new disk appears as Unknown.

6. Right-click the Unknown disk, and select Initialize Disk.

7. A pop-up box appears asking for the partition style. For this exercise, choose MBR.

8. Click OK.

9. Close Computer Management.

The disk will now appear online as a basic disk with unallocated space.

Configuring Basic and Dynamic Disks

Windows Server 2022 supports two types of disk configurations: basic and dynamic. Basic disks are divided into partitions and can be used with previous versions of Windows. Dynamic disks are divided into volumes and can be used with Windows 2000 Server and newer releases.

When a disk is initialized, it is automatically created as a basic disk, but when a new fault-tolerant (RAID) volume set is created, the disks in the set are converted to dynamic disks. Fault-tolerance features and the ability to modify disks without having to reboot the server are what distinguish dynamic disks from basic disks.

 Fault tolerance (RAID) is discussed in detail later in this chapter in the "Redundant Array of Independent Disks" section.

A basic disk can simply be converted to a dynamic disk without loss of data. When a basic disk is converted, the partitions are automatically changed to the appropriate volumes. However, converting a dynamic disk back to a basic disk is not as simple. First, all the data on the dynamic disk must be backed up or moved. Then, all the volumes on the dynamic disk have to be deleted. The dynamic disk can then be converted to a basic disk. Partitions and logical drives can be created, and the data can be restored.

The following are actions that can be performed on basic disks:

- Formatting partitions
- Marking partitions as active
- Creating and deleting primary and extended partitions
- Creating and deleting logical drives
- Converting from a basic disk to a dynamic disk

The following are actions that can be performed on dynamic disks:

- Creating and deleting simple, striped, spanned, mirrored, or RAID-5 volumes
- Removing or breaking a mirrored volume
- Extending simple or spanned volumes
- Repairing mirrored or RAID-5 volumes
- Converting from a dynamic disk to a basic disk after deleting all volumes

In Exercise 11.3, you'll convert a basic disk to a dynamic disk.

EXERCISE 11.3

Converting a Basic Disk to a Dynamic Disk

1. Open Computer Management under Administrative Tools.

2. Select Disk Management.

3. Right-click a basic disk that you want to convert and select Convert To Dynamic Disk, as shown in Figure 11.3.

EXERCISE 11.3 *(continued)*

FIGURE 11.3 Converting a disk

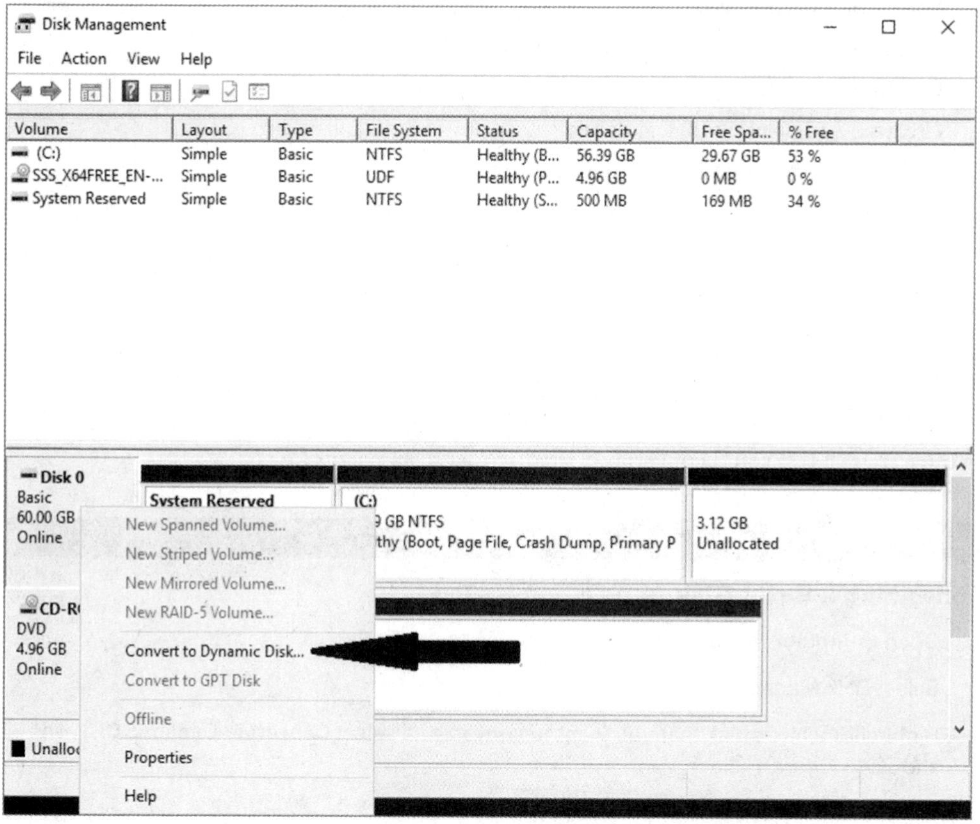

4. The Convert To Dynamic Disk dialog box appears. From here, select all of the disks that you want to convert to dynamic disks. In this exercise, only one disk will be converted.

5. Click OK.

6. The Convert To Dynamic Disk dialog box changes to the Disks To Convert dialog box and shows the disk/disks that will be converted to dynamic disks.

7. Click Convert.

8. Disk Management will warn that if you convert the disk to dynamic, you will not be able to start the installed operating system from any volume on the disk (except the current boot volume). Click Yes.

9. Close Computer Management.

The converted disk will now show as Dynamic in Disk Management.

Managing Volumes

A *volume set* is created from volumes that span multiple drives by using the free space from those drives to construct what will appear to be a single drive. The following list includes the various types of volume sets and their definitions:

- *Simple volume* uses only one disk or a portion of a disk.

- *Spanned volume* is a simple volume that spans multiple disks, with a maximum of 32. Use a spanned volume if the volume needs are too great for a single disk.

- *Striped volume* stores data in stripes across two or more disks. A striped volume gives you fast access to data but is not fault tolerant, nor can it be extended or mirrored. If one disk in the striped set fails, the entire volume fails.

- *Mirrored volume* duplicates data across two disks. This type of volume is fault tolerant because if one drive fails, the data on the other disk is unaffected.

- *RAID-5 volume* stores data in stripes across three or more disks. This type of volume is fault tolerant because if a drive fails, the data can be re-created from the parity off of the remaining disk drives. Operating system files and boot files cannot reside on the RAID-5 disks.

Exercise 11.4 illustrates the procedure for creating a volume set.

EXERCISE 11.4

Creating a Volume Set

1. Open Computer Management under Administrative Tools.

2. Select Disk Management.

3. Select and right-click a disk that has unallocated space. If there are no disk drives available for a particular volume set, that volume set will be grayed out as a selectable option. In this exercise, you'll choose a spanned volume set, but the process after the volume set selection is the same regardless of which kind you choose. The only thing that differs is the number of disk drives chosen.

4. The Welcome page of the New Spanned Volume Wizard appears and explains the type of volume set chosen. Click Next.

5. The Select Disks page appears. Select the disk that will be included with the volume set and click Add. Repeat this process until all of the desired disks have been added. Click Next.

6. The Assign Drive Letter Or Path page appears. From here you can select the desired drive letter for the volume, mount the volume in an empty NTFS folder, or choose not to assign a drive letter. The new volume is labeled as E. Click Next.

7. The Format Volume page appears. Choose to format the new volume. Click Next.

8.   Click Finish.

9.   If the disks have not been converted to dynamic, you will be asked to convert the disks. Click Yes.

The new volume will appear as a healthy spanned dynamic volume with the new available disk space of the new volume set.

Storage Spaces in Windows Server 2022

Windows Server 2022 includes a technology called *Storage Spaces*. Windows Server 2022 allows an administrator to virtualize storage by grouping disks into storage pools. These storage pools can then be turned into virtual disks called *storage spaces*.

The Storage Spaces technology allows an administrator to have a highly available, scalable, low-cost, and flexible solution for both physical and virtual installations. Storage Spaces allow you to set up this advantage on either a single server or in scalable ultimode mode. So, before going any further, let's look at these two terms that you must understand.

Storage Pools   *Storage pools* are a group of physical disks that allows an administrator to delegate administration, expand disk sizes, and group disks together.

Storage Spaces   *Storage spaces* allow an administrator to take free space from storage pools and create virtual disks called storage spaces. Storage spaces give administrators the ability to have precise control, resiliency, and storage tiers.

Storage spaces and storage pools can be managed by an administrator through the use of the Windows Storage Management API, Server Manager, or Windows PowerShell.

One of the advantages of using the Storage Spaces technology is the ability to set up resiliency. There are three types of Storage Space resiliency: mirror, parity, and simple (no resiliency).

   Fault tolerance (RAID) is discussed in detail in the "Redundant Array of Independent Disks" section.

Now that you understand what storage spaces and storage pools do, let's take a look at some of the other advantages of using these features in Windows Server 2022.

Availability   One advantage to the Storage Spaces technology is the ability to fully integrate the storage space with failover clustering. This advantage allows administrators to achieve service deployments that are continuously available. Administrators have the ability to set up storage pools to be clustered across multiple nodes within a single cluster.

Tiered Storage   The Storage Spaces technology allows virtual disks to be created with a two-tier storage setup. For data that is used often, you have an SSD tier; for data that is not used often, you use an HDD tier. The Storage Spaces technology will automatically transfer data at a subfile level between the two different tiers based on how often the data is used. Because of tiered storage, performance is greatly increased for data that is used most often, and data that is not used often still gets the advantage of being stored on a low-cost storage option.

Delegation   One advantage of using storage pools is that administrators have the ability to control access by using access control lists (ACLs). What is nice about this advantage is that each storage pool can have its own unique access control lists. Storage pools are fully integrated with Active Directory Domain Services.

Redundant Array of Independent Disks

The ability to support drive sets and arrays using *Redundant Array of Independent Disks (RAID)* technology is built into Windows Server 2022. RAID can be used to enhance data performance, or it can be used to provide fault tolerance to maintain data integrity in case of a hard disk failure. Windows Server 2022 supports three types of RAID technologies: RAID-0, RAID-1, and RAID-5.

RAID-0 (Disk Striping)   *Disk striping* is using two or more volumes on independent disks created as a single striped set. There can be a maximum of 32 disks. In a striped set, data is divided into blocks that are distributed sequentially across all of the drives in the set. With RAID-0 disk striping, you get very fast read and write performance because multiple blocks of data can be accessed from multiple drives simultaneously. However, RAID-0 does not offer the ability to maintain data integrity during a single disk failure. In other words, RAID-0 is not fault tolerant; a single disk event will cause the entire striped set to be lost, and it will have to be re-created through some type of recovery process, such as a tape backup.

RAID-1 (Disk Mirroring)   *Disk mirroring* is two logical volumes on two separate identical disks created as a duplicate disk set. Data is written on two disks at the same time; that way, in the event of a disk failure, data integrity is maintained and available. Although this fault tolerance gives administrators data redundancy, it comes with a price because it diminishes the amount of available storage space by half. For example, if an administrator wants to create a 300 GB mirrored set, they would have to install two 300 GB hard drives into the server, thus doubling the cost for the same available space.

RAID-5 Volume (Disk Striping with Parity)   With a RAID-5 volume, you have the ability to use a minimum of three disks and a maximum of 32 disks. RAID-5 volumes allow data to be striped across all of the disks with an additional block of error-correction called parity. *Parity* is used to reconstruct the data in the event of a disk failure. RAID-5 has slower write performance than the other RAID types because the OS must calculate the parity information for each stripe that is written, but the read performance is equivalent to a stripe set, RAID-0, because the parity information is not read. Like RAID-1, RAID-5 comes with additional cost considerations. For every RAID-5 set, roughly an entire hard disk is consumed for storing the parity information. For example, a minimum RAID-5 set requires three hard disks, and if those disks are 300 GB each, approximately 600 GB of disk space is available to the OS and 300 GB is consumed by parity information, which equates to 33.3 percent of the available space. Similarly, in a five-disk RAID-5 set of 300 GB disks, approximately 1,200 GB of disk space is available to the OS, which means that 20 percent of the total available space is consumed by the parity information. The words *roughly* and *approximately* are used when calculating disk space because a 300 GB disk will really be only about 279 GB of space. This is because vendors define a gigabyte as 1 billion bytes, but the OS defines it as 2^{30} (1,073,741,824) bytes. Also, remember that file systems and volume managers have overhead as well.

Software RAID is a nice option for a small company, but hardware RAID is definitely a better option if the money is available.

Table 11.1 breaks down the various aspects of the supported RAID types in Window Server 2022.

TABLE 11.1   Supported RAID-level properties in Windows Server 2022

RAID Level	RAID Type	Fault Tolerant	Advantages	Minimum Number of Disks	Maximum Number of Disks
0	Disk striping	No	Fast reads and writes	2	32
1	Disk mirroring	Yes	Data redundancy and faster writes than RAID-5	2	2
5	Disk striping with parity	Yes	Data redundancy with less overhead and faster reads than RAID-1	3	32

Creating RAID Sets

Now that you understand the concepts of RAID and how to use it, you can look at the creation of RAID sets in Windows Server 2022. The process of creating a RAID set is the same as the process for creating a simple or spanned volume set, except for the minimum disk requirements associated with each RAID type.

Creating a mirrored volume set is basically the same as creating a volume set except that you will select New Mirrored Volume. It is after the disk select wizard appears that you'll begin to see the difference. Since a new mirrored volume is being created, the volume requires two disks.

During the disk select process, if only one disk is selected, the Next button will be unavailable because the disk minimum has not been met. Refer to Figure 11.4 to view the Select Disks page of the New Mirrored Volume Wizard during the creation of a new mirrored volume, and notice that the Next button is not available.

FIGURE 11.4   Select Disks page of the New Mirrored Volume Wizard

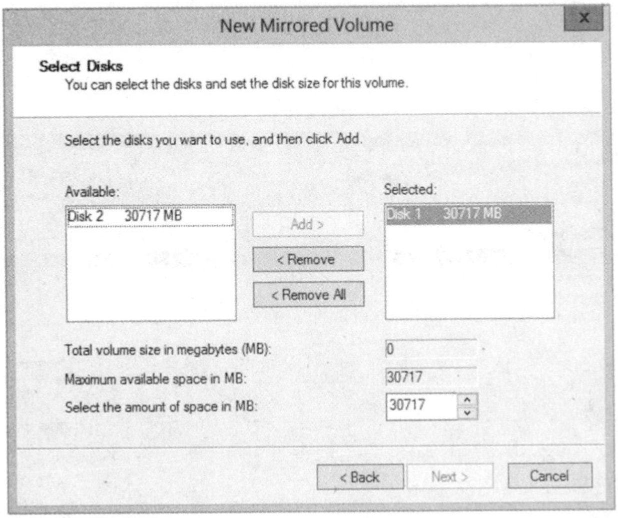

To complete the process, you must select a second disk by highlighting the appropriate disk and adding it to the volume set. Once the second disk has been added, the Next button is available to complete the mirrored volume set creation.

A drive letter will have to be assigned, and the volume will need to be formatted. The new mirrored volume set will appear in Disk Management. In Figure 11.5, notice that the capacity of the volume equals one disk even though two disks have been selected.

To create a RAID-5 volume set, you use the same process that you use to create a mirrored volume set. The only difference is that a RAID-5 volume set requires that a minimum of three disks be selected to complete the volume creation. The process is simple: Select New RAID-5 Volume, select the three disks that will be used in the volume set, assign a drive letter, and format the volume.

FIGURE 11.5 Newly created mirrored volume set

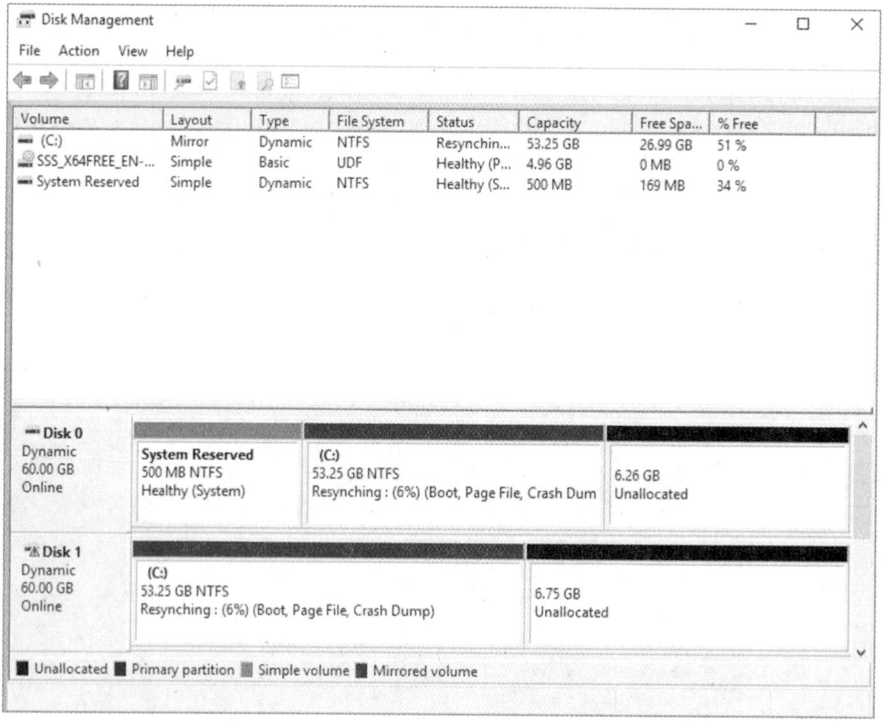

Mount Points

With the ever-increasing demands of storage, mount points are used to surpass the limitation of 26 drive letters and to join two volumes into a folder on a separate physical disk drive. A *mount point* allows you to configure a volume to be accessed from a folder on another existing disk.

Through Disk Management, a mount point folder can be assigned to a drive instead of using a drive letter, and it can be used on basic or dynamic volumes that are formatted with NTFS. However, mount point folders can be created only on empty folders within a volume. Additionally, mount point folder paths cannot be modified; they can be removed only once they have been created. Exercise 11.5 shows the steps to create a mount point.

EXERCISE 11.5

Creating Mount Points

1. Right-click the Start button and select Disk Management.

2. Right-click the volume where the mount point folder will be assigned, and select Change Drive Letter And Paths.

3. Click Add.

4. Either type the path to an empty folder on an NTFS volume or click Browse to select or make a new folder for the mount point.

When you explore the drive, you'll see the new folder created. Notice that the icon indicates that it is a mount point.

Microsoft MPIO

Multipath I/O (MPIO) is associated with high availability because a computer will be able to use a solution with redundant physical paths connected to a storage device. Thus, if one path fails, an application will continue to run because it can access the data across the other path.

The MPIO software provides the functionality needed for the computer to take advantage of the redundant storage paths. MPIO solutions can also load-balance data traffic across both paths to the storage device, virtually eliminating bandwidth bottlenecks to the computer. What allows MPIO to provide this functionality is the new native *Microsoft Device Specific Module (Microsoft DSM)*. The Microsoft DSM is a driver that communicates with storage devices—iSCSI, Fibre Channel, or SAS—and it provides the chosen load-balancing policies. Windows Server 2022 supports the following load-balancing policies:

Failover   In a failover configuration, there is no load balancing. There is a primary path that is established for all requests and subsequent standby paths. If the primary path fails, one of the standby paths will be used.

Failback   This is similar to failover in that it has primary and standby paths. However, with failback you designate a preferred path that will handle all process requests until it fails, after which the standby path will become active until the primary reestablishes a connection and automatically regains control.

Round Robin   In a round-robin configuration, all available paths will be active and will be used to distribute I/O in a balanced round-robin fashion.

Round Robin with a Subset of Paths   In this configuration, a specific set of paths will be designated as a primary set and another as standby paths. All I/O will use the primary set of paths in a round-robin fashion until all of the sets fail. Only at this time will the standby paths become active.

Dynamic Least Queue Depth   In a dynamic least queue depth configuration, I/O will route to the path with the least number of outstanding requests.

Weighted Path   In a weighted path configuration, paths are assigned a numbered weight. I/O requests will use the path with the least weight—the higher the number, the lower the priority.

Exercise 11.6 demonstrates the process of installing the Microsoft MPIO feature for Windows Server 2022.

EXERCISE 11.6

Installing Microsoft MPIO

1. Choose Server Manager by clicking the Server Manager icon on the Taskbar.

2. Click number 2, Add Roles And Features.

3. Choose role-based or feature-based installation and click Next.

4. Choose your server and click Next.

5. Click Next on the Roles screen.

6. On the Select Features screen, choose the Multipath I/O check box (see Figure 11.6). Click Next.

FIGURE 11.6 Multipath I/O

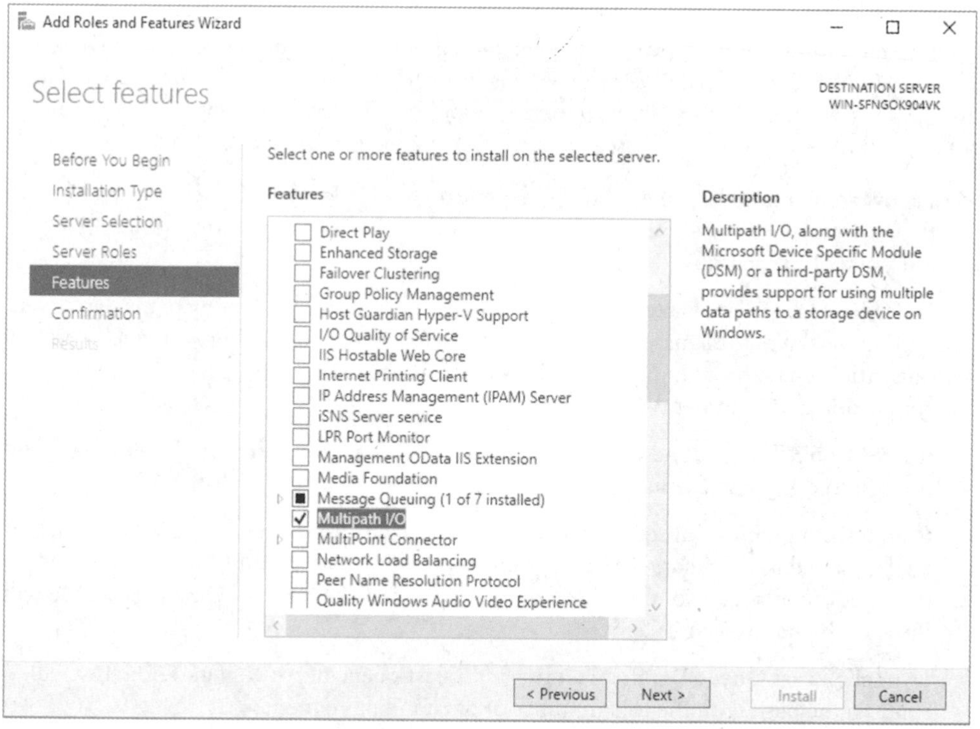

7. On the Confirm Installation Selections page, verify that Multipath I/O is the feature that will be installed. Click Install.

8. After the installation completes, the Installation Results page appears stating that the server must be rebooted to finish the installation process.

9. Click Close.

10. Restart the system.

Typically, most storage arrays work with the Microsoft DSM. However, some hardware vendors require DSM software that is specific to their products. Third-party DSM software is installed through the MPIO utility as follows:

1. Open Administrative Tools ⇨ MPIO.

2. Select the DSM Install tab.

3. Add the path of the INF file and click Install.

Configuring iSCSI Target

Internet Small Computer System Interface (iSCSI) is an interconnect protocol used to establish and manage a connection between a computer (initiator) and a storage device (target). It does this by using a connection through TCP port 3260, which allows it to be used over a LAN, a WAN, or the Internet. Each initiator is identified by its iSCSI Qualified Name (iqn), and it is used to establish its connection to an iSCSI target.

iSCSI was developed to allow block-level access to a storage device over a network. This is different from using a network attached storage (NAS) device that connects through the use of Common Internet File System (CIFS) or Network File System (NFS).

Block-level access is important to many applications that require direct access to storage. Microsoft Exchange and Microsoft SQL are examples of applications that require direct access to storage.

By being able to leverage the existing network infrastructure, iSCSI was also developed as an alternative to Fibre Channel storage by alleviating the additional hardware costs associated with a Fibre Channel storage solution.

iSCSI also has another advantage over Fibre Channel in that it can provide security for the storage devices. iSCSI can use Challenge Handshake Authentication Protocol (CHAP or MS-CHAP) for authentication and Internet Protocol Security (Ipsec) for encryption. Windows Server 2022 is able to connect an iSCSI storage device out of the box with no additional software needing to be installed. This is because the Microsoft iSCSI initiator is built into the operating system.

Windows Server 2022 supports two different ways to initiate an iSCSI session.

- Through the native Microsoft iSCSI software initiator that resides on Windows Server 2022

- Using a hardware iSCSI host bus adapter (HBA) that is installed in the computer

Both the Microsoft iSCSI software initiator and iSCSI HBA present an iSCSI qualified name that identifies the host initiator. When the Microsoft iSCSI software initiator is
used, the CPU utilization may be as much as 30 percent higher than on a computer with a
hardware iSCSI HBA. This is because all of the iSCSI process requests are handled within
the operating system. Using a hardware iSCSI HBA, process requests can be offloaded to the
adapter, thus freeing the CPU overhead associated with the Microsoft iSCSI software initiator. However, iSCSI HBAs can be expensive, whereas the Microsoft iSCSI software initiator
is free.

It is worthwhile to install the Microsoft iSCSI software initiator and perform load testing to see how much overhead the computer will have prior to purchasing an iSCSI HBA or
HBAs, depending on the redundancy level. Exercise 11.7 explains how to install and configure an iSCSI connection.

EXERCISE 11.7

Configuring iSCSI Storage Connection

1. Right-click the Start button ➤ Control Panel ➤ Administrative Tools ➤ iSCSI Initiator.

2. If a dialog box appears, click Yes to start the service.

3. Click the Discovery tab.

4. In the Target Portals portion of the page, click Discover Portal.

5. Enter the IP address of the target portal and click OK.

6. The IP address of the target portal appears in the Target Portals box.

7. Click OK.

Internet Storage Name Service

Internet Storage Name Service (iSNS) allows for central registration of an iSCSI environment
because it automatically discovers available targets on the network. The purpose of iSNS is
to help find available targets on a large iSCSI network.

The Microsoft iSCSI initiator includes an iSNS client that is used to register with the
iSNS. The iSNS feature maintains a database of clients that it has registered either through
DCHP discovery or through manual registration. iSNS DHCP is available after the installation of the service, and it is used to allow iSNS clients to discover the location of the
iSNS. However, if iSNS DHCP is not configured, iSNS clients must be registered manually
with the `iscsicli` command.

To execute the command, launch a command prompt on a computer hosting the Microsoft
iSCSI and type **`iscsicli addisnsserver server_name`**, where **`server_name`** is the name of
the computer hosting iSNS. Exercise 11.8 walks you through the steps required to install the
iSNS feature on Windows Server 2022, and then it explains the different tabs in iSNS.

EXERCISE 11.8

Installing the iSNS Feature

1. Choose Server Manager by clicking the Server Manager icon on the Taskbar.

2. Click number 2 ➢ Add Roles And Features.

3. Choose role-based or featured-based installation and click Next.

4. Choose your server and click Next.

5. Click Next on the Roles screen.

6. On the Select Features screen, choose the iSNS Server Service check box. Click Next.

7. On the Confirmation screen, click the Install button.

8. Click the Close button. Close Server Manager and reboot.

9. Log in and open the iSNS server under Administrative Tools.

10. Click the General tab. This tab displays the list of registered initiators and targets. In addition to their iSCSI qualified name, it lists storage node type (Target or Initiator), alias string, and entity identifier (the Fully Qualified Domain Name [FQDN] of the machine hosting the iSNS client).

11. Click the Discovery Domains tab. The purpose of Discovery Domains is to provide a way to separate and group nodes. This is similar to zoning in Fibre Channel. The following options are available on the Discovery Domains tab:

    - *Create* is used to create a new discovery domain.

    - *Refresh* is used to repopulate the Discovery Domain drop-down list.

    - *Delete* is used to delete the currently selected discovery domain.

    - *Add* is used to add nodes that are already registered in iSNS to the currently selected discovery domain.

    - *Add New* is used to add nodes by entering the iSCSI Qualified Name (iQN) of the node. These nodes do not have to be currently registered.

    - *Remove Used* is used to remove selected nodes from the discovery domain.

12. Click the Discovery Domain Sets tab (see Figure 11.7). The purpose of discovery domain sets is to separate further discovery domains. Discovery domains can be enabled or disabled, giving administrators the ability to restrict further the visibility of all initiators and targets. The options on the Discovery Domain Sets tab are as follows:

    - The *Enable* check box is used to indicate the status of the discovery domain sets and to turn them off and on.

    - *Create* is used to create new discovery domain sets.

EXERCISE 11.8 *(continued)*

- *Refresh* is used to repopulate the Discovery Domain Sets drop-down list.
- *Delete* is used to delete the currently selected discovery domain set.
- *Add* is used to add discovery domains to the currently selected discovery domain set.
- *Remove* is used to remove selected nodes from the discovery domain sets.

FIGURE 11.7 Discovery Domain Tab

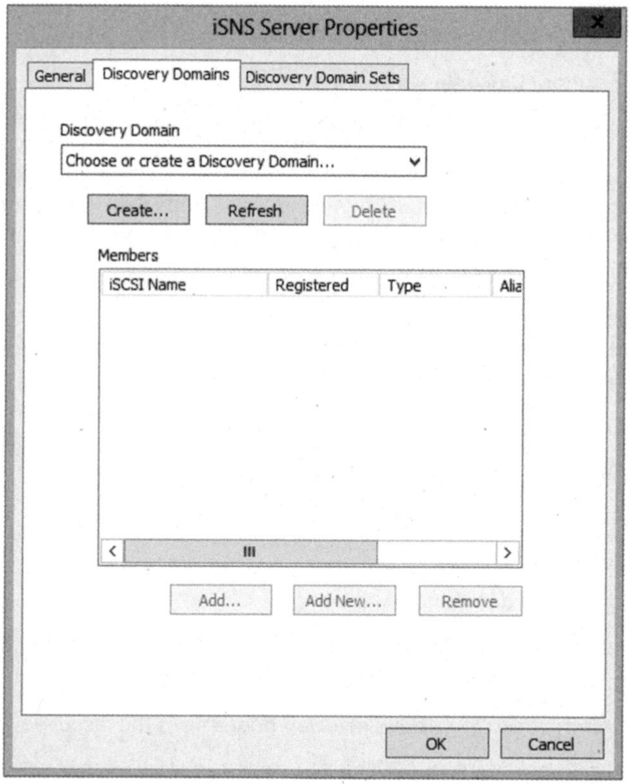

13. Close the iSNS server.

Implement Thin Provisioning and Trim

Thin provisioning and trim can be useful features that allow organizations to get the most out of their storage arrays. These solutions apply directly to a virtualized environment using virtual disks that are thin provisioned.

Thin provisioning is a way of providing what is known as just-in-time allocations. Blocks of data are written to disk only as they are used instead of zeroing out all of the blocks of data that have been allocated to the virtual disk configuration. Thin provisioning is tricky to manage properly because you could easily find yourself in a position where you have an over-provisioned environment because of over-allocation.

For example, you have 100 VMs that are all provisioned with 40 GB thin-provisioned virtual disks. Each VM is currently utilizing only 20 GB of the total 40 GB that has been allocated. The problem is that you have only 2 TB worth of storage. Without realizing it, you've over-provisioned your environment by 200 percent because of thin provisioning.

This is where trim comes in to help us manage thin provisioning. *Trim* automatically reclaims free space that is not being used. In addition to trim, Windows Server 2022 provides standardized notifications that will alert administrators when certain storage thresholds are crossed.

Fibre Channel

Fibre Channel storage devices are similar to iSCSI storage devices in that they both allow block-level access to their data sets and can provide MPIO policies with the proper hardware configurations. However, Fibre Channel requires a Fibre Channel HBA, fiber-optic cables, and Fibre Channel switches to connect to a storage device.

A *World Wide Name (WWN)* from the Fibre Channel HBA is used from the host and device so that they can communicate directly with each other, similar to using a NIC's MAC address. In other words, a logical unit number (LUN) is presented from a Fibre Channel storage device to the WWN of the host's HBA. Fibre Channel has been the preferred method of storage because of the available connection bandwidth between the storage and the host.

Fibre Channel devices support 1Gb/s, 2Gb/s, and 4Gb/s connections, and they soon will support 8Gb/s connections, but now that 10Gb/s Ethernet networks are becoming more prevalent in many datacenters, iSCSI can be a suitable alternative. It is important to consider that 10Gb/s network switches can be more expensive than comparable Fibre Channel switches.

N-Port Identification Virtualization (NPIV) is a Fibre Channel facility allowing multiple n-port IDs to share a single physical N-Port. This allows multiple Fibre Channel initiators to occupy a single physical port. By using a single port, this eases hardware requirements in storage area network (SAN) design.

Network Attached Storage

The concept of a *network attached storage (NAS)* solution is that it is a low-cost device for storing data and serving files through the use of an Ethernet LAN connection. A NAS device accesses data at the file level via a communication protocol such as NFS, CIFS, or even

HTTP, which is different from iSCSI or FC Fibre Channel storage devices that access the data at the block level. NAS devices are best used in file-storing applications, and they do not require a storage expert to install and maintain the device. In most cases, the only setup that is required is an IP address and an Ethernet connection.

Virtual Disk Service

Virtual Disk Service (VDS) was created to ease the administrative efforts involved in managing all of the various types of storage devices. Many storage hardware providers used their own applications for installation and management, and this made administering all of these various devices very cumbersome.

VDS is a set of application programming interfaces (APIs) that provides a centralized interface for managing all of the various storage devices. The native VDS API enables the management of disks and volumes at an OS level, and hardware vendor-supplied APIs manage the storage devices at a RAID level. These are known as software and hardware providers.

A *software provider* is host based, and it interacts with Plug and Play Manager because each disk is discovered and operates on volumes, disks, and disk partitions. VDS includes two software providers: basic and dynamic. The basic software provider manages basic disks with no fault tolerance, whereas the dynamic software providers manage dynamic disks with fault management. A hardware provider translates the VDS APIs into instructions specific to the storage hardware. This is how storage management applications are able to communicate with the storage hardware to create LUNs or Fibre Channel HBAs to view the WWN. The following are Windows Server 2022 storage management applications that use VDS:

- The *Disk Management snap-in* is an application that allows you to configure and manage the disk drives on the host computer. You have already seen this application in use when you initialized disks and created volume sets.

- DiskPart is a command-line utility that configures and manages disks, volumes, and partitions on the host computer. It can also be used to script many of the storage management commands. DiskPart is a robust tool that you should study on your own because it is beyond the scope of this book. Figure 11.8 shows the various commands and their function in the DiskPart utility.

- DiskRAID is also a scriptable command-line utility that configures and manages hardware RAID storage systems. However, at least one VDS hardware provider must be installed for DiskRAID to be functional. DiskRAID is another useful utility that you should study on your own because it's beyond the scope of this book.

Understanding Data Center Bridging

I think the easiest way to understanding Data Center Bridging (DCB) is to understand NIC bridging. Many of us who have used laptops have used both the Wireless and Wired networks at the same time. This is bridging network adapter cards to work as one. Well, Data Center Bridging is the same thing but just done on a larger scale.

FIGURE 11.8   DiskPart commands

```
Administrator: Command Prompt - diskpart

DISKPART> help

Microsoft DiskPart

ACTIVE       - Mark the selected partition as active.
ADD          - Add a mirror to a simple volume.
ASSIGN       - Assign a drive letter or mount point to the selected volume.
ATTRIBUTES   - Manipulate volume or disk attributes.
ATTACH       - Attaches a virtual disk file.
AUTOMOUNT    - Enable and disable automatic mounting of basic volumes.
BREAK        - Break a mirror set.
CLEAN        - Clear the configuration information, or all information, off the
               disk.
COMPACT      - Attempts to reduce the physical size of the file.
CONVERT      - Convert between different disk formats.
CREATE       - Create a volume, partition or virtual disk.
DELETE       - Delete an object.
DETAIL       - Provide details about an object.
DETACH       - Detaches a virtual disk file.
EXIT         - Exit DiskPart.
EXTEND       - Extend a volume.
EXPAND       - Expands the maximum size available on a virtual disk.
FILESYSTEMS  - Display current and supported file systems on the volume.
FORMAT       - Format the volume or partition.
GPT          - Assign attributes to the selected GPT partition.
HELP         - Display a list of commands.
IMPORT       - Import a disk group.
INACTIVE     - Mark the selected partition as inactive.
LIST         - Display a list of objects.
MERGE        - Merges a child disk with its parents.
ONLINE       - Online an object that is currently marked as offline.
OFFLINE      - Offline an object that is currently marked as online.
RECOVER      - Refreshes the state of all disks in the selected pack.
               Attempts recovery on disks in the invalid pack, and
               resynchronizes mirrored volumes and RAID5 volumes
               that have stale plex or parity data.
REM          - Does nothing. This is used to comment scripts.
REMOVE       - Remove a drive letter or mount point assignment.
REPAIR       - Repair a RAID-5 volume with a failed member.
RESCAN       - Rescan the computer looking for disks and volumes.
RETAIN       - Place a retained partition under a simple volume.
SAN          - Display or set the SAN policy for the currently booted OS.
SELECT       - Shift the focus to an object.
SETID        - Change the partition type.
SHRINK       - Reduce the size of the selected volume.
UNIQUEID     - Displays or sets the GUID partition table (GPT) identifier or
               master boot record (MBR) signature of a disk.

DISKPART>
```

The Institute of Electrical and Electronic Engineers (IEEE) created a suite of standards called Data Center Bridging. DCB allows the same ethernet infrastructure to work throughout the data center. This means that all of the network servers, clusters, and data center will share the same ethernet infrastructure. DCB works through the use of hardware based bandwidth allocation. This means that the hardware controls the flow of data through DCB.

DCB is nice because when you setup the hardware based flow control, you can determine which type of traffic gets a higher priority to the allocated bandwidth. This can be very useful for data that bypasses the operating system and accesses the network adapters directly (like virtualization can). DCB can work with different types of network adapters including Remote Direct Memory Access (RDMA) over Converged Ethernet, Internet Small Computer System Interface (iSCSI), or Fiber Channel over Ethernet (fCoE).

The reason that the IEEE has developed the DCB standard is because many third party and hardware manufacturers do not work together well. By having an industry standard of hardware based flow control protocol, many IT data centers can use DCB to make different vendors work together. Also, Windows Server 2022 makes it very easy to deploy and manage DCB. There are a couple of requirements that are needed when deploying DCB through Windows Server 2022;

- The Ethernet adapters installed into the Windows Server 2022 systems must be DCB compatible.

- The Hardware switches that are deployed to your infrastructure must also be DCB compatible.

DCB can be installed onto a Windows Server two ways; through Server Manager or through PowerShell. Here are the steps for both ways.

Installing DCB using PowerShell

If you would like to install and use DCB through PowerShell, you need to complete the following Steps;

1. Click the Start button, then right-click the Windows PowerShell ➤ More ➤ Run as Administrator.

2. In the Windows PowerShell console, enter the following command followed by the Enter Key:

   `Install-WindowsFeature "data-center-bridging".`

Installing DCB using Server Manager

If you would like to install and use DCB through Server Manager, you need to complete the following Steps:

1. On the Windows Server 2022 system, open Server Manager.

2. Click the Add Roles and Features link.

3. At the Before You Begin screen, click Next.

4. At the Select installation type screen, choose Role-based or feature-based installation and then click Next.

5. The Select destination server screen will be next. Make sure the server that you want to install DCB on is selected and then click Next.

6. On the Select server roles screen, just click Next.

7. On the Select features screen, check the box for Data Center Bridging. If a dialog box appears asking to install additional features, click the Add Feature button. Then click Next.

8. At the Confirmation screen, verify that everything is OK and then click the Install button.

Configuring Permissions

Before I dive into how permissions work, let's first talk about how clients and servers talk to each other. In the Microsoft Windows world, clients and servers talk to each other using the Server Message Block (SMB) protocol. So we'll start our discussion there.

Understanding SMB

The Server Message Block (SMB) is a network sharing protocol that allows Windows machines (either client- or server-based operating systems) that are running applications to read and write data to files. SMB also allows systems to request services or resources that are running on remote servers. The one advantage to SMB is that it doesn't matter what network protocol you are using (TCP/IP, etc.); SMB runs on top of the network protocol that is being used on your corporate infrastructure.

It's important to understand what protocols work with client- and server-based systems because it can affect your network's performance. For example, when Microsoft released Windows Server 2012, it released SMB 3.0. The issue that many users had was that SMB 3.0 was not compatible with Apple-based systems. So if you were running macOS on your network and upgraded to Windows Server 2012, your Apple-based systems would not communicate properly. This issue was eventually resolved, but this is why it's important to understand that SMB file sharing is used between Windows client and server systems.

I will show you how to use PowerShell for configuring SMB shares in the section "Windows PowerShell." For a complete list of SMB PowerShell commands, visit Microsoft's website at https://technet.microsoft .com/en-us/library/jj635726(v=wps.630).aspx.

Now that you understand how Windows clients and servers communicate with each other, let's now look at how we can protect the files and folders that clients access. You can add security to a folder in two ways: NTFS Security or Shared Permissions. But when it comes to securing files, you can secure files in only one way: NTFS Security. So let's investigate these methods and see how they work independently and then together.

Understanding NTFS

NTFS is an option that you have when you are formatting a hard drive. You can format a hard drive for a Microsoft operating system in three ways:

- File Allocation Table (FAT) is supported in older operating systems only (Server 2003, Server 2000, XP, and so on).
- FAT32 is supported in Windows Server 2022.
- NTFS is supported in Windows Server 2022.

NTFS has many advantages over FAT and FAT32. They include the following:

Compression Compression helps compact files or folders to allow for more efficient use of hard drive space. For example, a file that usually takes up 20 MB of space might use only 13 MB after compression. To enable compression, just open the Advanced Attributes dialog box for a folder and select Compress Contents To Save Disk Space (see Figure 11.9).

FIGURE 11.9 Setting up compression on a folder

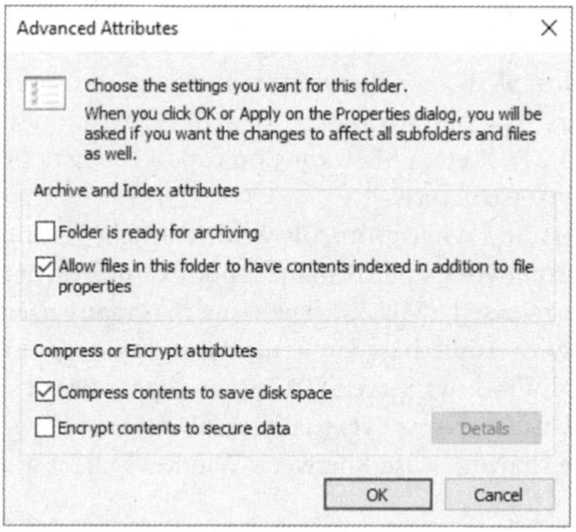

Advanced Attributes dialog box showing Archive and Index attributes, Compress or Encrypt attributes sections with Compress contents to save disk space checked.

Quotas *Quotas* allow you to limit how much hard drive space users can have on a server. Quotas are discussed in greater detail in the section "Configuring Disk Quotas."

Encryption *Encrypting File System (EFS)* allows a user or administrator to secure files or folders by using encryption. Encryption employs the user's security identification (SID) number to secure the file or folder. To implement encryption, open the Advanced Attributes dialog box for a folder and check Encrypt Contents To Secure Data (see Figure 11.10).

If files are encrypted using EFS and you have to unencrypt the files, there are two ways to do this. First, you can log in using the user's account (the account that encrypted the files) and unencrypt the files. Second, you can become a recovery agent and manually unencrypt the files.

If you use EFS, it's best not to delete users immediately when they leave a company. Administrators have the ability to recover encrypted files, but it is much easier to gain access to the user's encrypted files by logging in as the user who left the company and deselecting the encryption option.

FIGURE 11.10   Setting up encryption on a folder

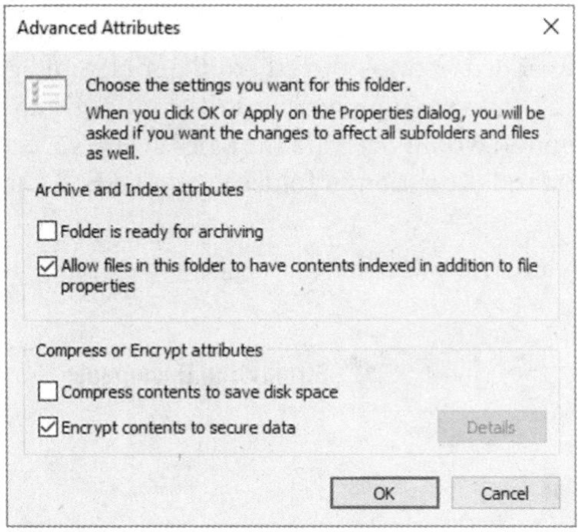

Advanced Attributes   ×

    Choose the settings you want for this folder.

    When you click OK or Apply on the Properties dialog, you will be
    asked if you want the changes to affect all subfolders and files
    as well.

Archive and Index attributes

☐ Folder is ready for archiving

☑ Allow files in this folder to have contents indexed in addition to file
   properties

Compress or Encrypt attributes

☐ Compress contents to save disk space

☑ Encrypt contents to secure data   Details

OK   Cancel

Security   One of the biggest advantages of NTFS is security. Security is one of the most important aspects of an IT administrator's job. An advantage of NTFS security is that the security can be placed on individual files and folders. It does not matter whether you are local to the share (in front of the machine where the data is stored) or remote to the share (coming across the network to access the data); the security is always in place with NTFS.

The default security permission is Users = Read on new folders or shares.

NTFS security is *additive*. In other words, if you are a member of three groups (Marketing, Sales, and R&D) and these three groups have different security settings, you get the highest level of permissions. For example, let's say you have a user by the name of wpanek who belongs to all three groups (Marketing, Sales, and R&D). Figure 11.11 shows this user's permissions. The Marketing group has Read and Execute permissions to the StormWind Documents folder. The Sales group has Read and Write, and the R&D group has Full Control. Since wpanek is a member of all three groups, wpanek would get Full Control (the highest level).

FIGURE 11.11   Security settings on the StormWind Documents folder

StromWind Documents

Marketing	Sales	R&D
RX	RW	FC

The only time this does not apply is with the Deny permission. Deny overrides any other group setting. Taking the same example, if Sales has Deny permission for the StormWind Documents folder, the user wpanek would be denied access to that folder. The only way around this Deny is if you added wpanek directly to the folder and gave him individual permissions (see Figure 11.12). Individual permissions override a group Deny. In this example, the individual right of wpanek would override the Sales group's Deny. The user's security permission for the StormWind Documents folder would be Full Control.

FIGURE 11.12   Individual permissions

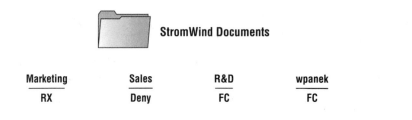

Marketing	Sales	R&D	wpanek
RX	Deny	FC	FC

Give users only the permissions necessary to do their jobs. Do not give them higher levels than they need.

Understanding Shared Permissions

When you set up a folder to be shared, you have the ability to assign that folder's permissions. *Shared permissions* can be placed only on the folder and not on individual files. Files have the ability to inherit their permissions from the parent folder.

Shared folder permissions are in effect only when users are remote to the shared data. In other words, if computer A shares a folder called Test Share and assigns that folder shared permissions, those permissions would apply only if you connected to that share from a machine other than computer A. If you were sitting in front of computer A, the shared permissions would not apply.

Like NTFS permissions (discussed in the previous section), shared permissions are additive, so users receive the highest level of permissions granted by the groups of which they are members.

Also, as with NTFS permissions, the Deny permission (see Figure 11.13) overrides any group permission, and an individual permission overrides a group Deny.

The default shared permission is Administrators = Full Control. The shared permissions going from lowest to highest are Read, Change, Full Control, and Deny. Table 11.2 compares the two different types of permissions and security.

FIGURE 11.13 Setting up permissions on a shared folder

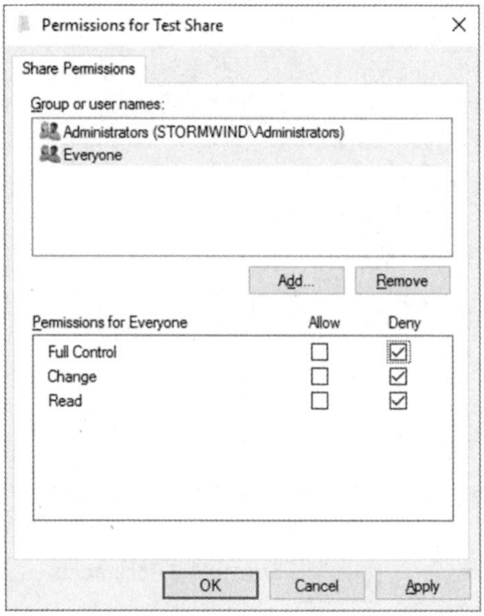

TABLE 11.2 NTFS security vs. shared permissions

Description	NTFS	Shared
Folder-level security.	Yes	Yes
File-level security.	Yes	No
In effect when local to the data.	Yes	No
In effect when remote to the data.	Yes	Yes
Permissions are additive.	Yes	Yes
Group Deny overrides all other group settings.	Yes	Yes
Individual settings override group settings.	Yes	Yes

How NTFS Security and Shared Permissions Work Together

When you set up a shared folder, you need to set up shared permissions on that folder. If you're using NTFS, you will also need to set up NTFS security on the folder. Since both shared permissions and NTFS security are in effect when the user is remote, what happens when the two conflict?

These are the two basic rules of thumb:

- The local permission is the NTFS permission.

- The remote permission is the more restrictive set of permissions between NTFS and shared.

This is easy to do as long as you do it in steps. Let's look at Figure 11.14 and walk through the process of figuring out what wpanek has for rights.

FIGURE 11.14   NTFS security and shared permissions example

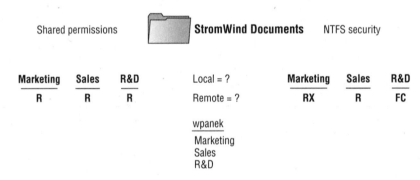

As you can see, wpanek belongs to three groups (Marketing, Sales, and R&D), and all three groups have settings for the StormWind Documents folder. In the figure, you will notice that there are two questions: Remote = ? and Local = ? That's what you need to figure out—what are wpanek's effective permissions when he is sitting at the computer that shares the folder, and what are his effective permissions when he connects to the folder from another computer (remotely)? To figure this out, follow these steps:

1. Add up the permissions on each side separately.

   Remember, permissions and security are *additive*. You get the highest permission. So, if you look at each side, the highest shared permission is the Read permission. The NTFS security side should add up to equal Full Control. Thus, now you have Read permission on shared and Full Control on NTFS.

2. Determine the local permissions.

Shared permissions do not apply when you are local to the data. Only NTFS would apply. Thus, the local permission would be Full Control.

3. Determine the remote permissions.

Remember, the remote permission is the most restrictive set of permissions between NTFS and shared. Since Read is more restrictive than Full Control, the remote permission would be Read.

Let's try another. Look at Figure 11.15, and see whether you can come up with wpanek's local and remote permissions.

FIGURE 11.15   NTFS security and shared permissions

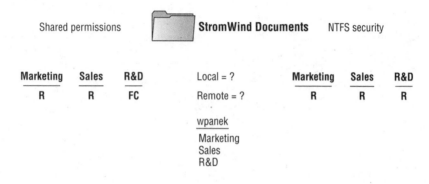

Your answer should match the following:

Local = Read

Remote = Read

Remember, first you add up each side to get the highest level of rights. NTFS would be Read, and shared would be Full Control. The local permission is always just NTFS (shared does not apply to local permissions), and remote permission is whichever permission (NTFS or shared) is the most restrictive (which would be Read on the NTFS side).

Exercise 11.9 walks you through the process of setting both NTFS and shared permissions. This exercise assumes that you have Active Directory installed on the server and you have some groups created. If you do not, go to Computer Management (right-click Start ↺ Computer Management) and under Local Users and Groups, create a new group that can be used in this exercise.

EXERCISE 11.9

Configuring Shared and NTFS Settings

1. Create a new folder in the root directory of your C: partition and name it **Test Share**.

2. Right-click the Test Share folder you created and choose Properties.

3. Click the Sharing tab and then click the Advanced Sharing button. Select Share This Folder. Make sure the share name is Test Share (see Figure 11.16).

FIGURE 11.16   Advanced Sharing

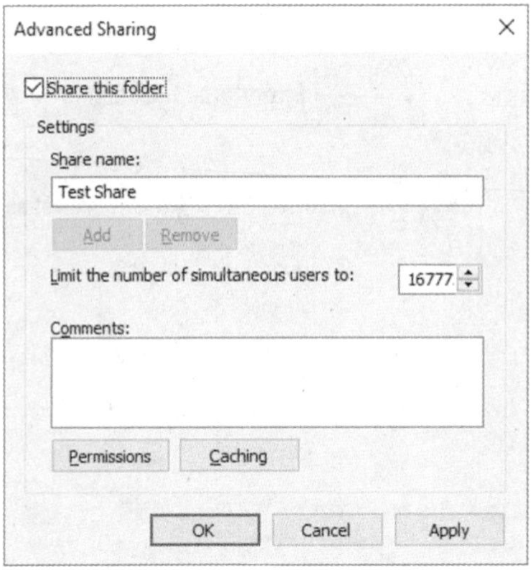

4. Click the Permissions button. Click Add. When the Select User page appears, choose a group from Active Directory or from the local group you created. (I used the Sales group.) Once you find your group, click OK.

5. The Permissions dialog box appears. With your group highlighted, click the Allow check box next to Full Control and click OK. (All of the other Allow check boxes will automatically become checked.)

6. On the Advanced Sharing page, click OK. Now click the Security tab. (This allows you to set the NTFS security settings.)

7. Click the Edit button. That takes you to the Permissions page. Now click Add. When the Select User page appears, choose a group from Active Directory. (I used the Everyone group.) Once you find your group, click OK.

8. The Permissions dialog box appears. With your group highlighted, click the Allow check box next to Modify, and click OK. (All of the check boxes below Modify will automatically become checked.)

9. Click Close.

Understanding NFS Shares

The NFS role service and feature set gives IT administrators the ability to integrate a Windows Server–based environment with Unix-based operating systems. Most corporate environments today consist of a mixed operating system infrastructure to some extent. Using a Windows NFS file server, you can configure file shares for use by multiple operating systems throughout the environment.

Windows Server 2022 takes those capabilities even further by enabling you to integrate with platforms such as ESXi. ESXi is vMware's exclusive operating system–independent hypervisor. ESXi is referred to as a *bare-metal* operating system because once it is installed on server virtualization hardware, guest virtual machines can be installed without requiring the use of any other underlying operating system. With Windows Server 2022, you can use an NFS share efficiently as an ESXi data store to house all of your guest virtual machines. Let's take a look at configuring an NFS data store in Exercise 11.10.

For this exercise, you will need the following:

- A Windows Server 2022 server
- A vMware ESXi 6.7 server

EXERCISE 11.10

Configuring the NFS Data Store

1. Open Server Manager on your Windows Server 2022 machine.

2. Launch the Add Roles And Features Wizard from the dashboard.

3. Install the Server For NFS role on the server. A reboot is not required.

4. Create a new folder on your server named **NFS_Datastore**, right-click and select Properties, and then navigate to the NFS Sharing tab.

5. Click the Manage NFS Sharing button to open the NFS Advanced Sharing page and then select Share This Folder. Notice how enabling the share also enables the share's default settings. The share settings let you configure share authentication and user access further if the need arises. The default settings will work just fine for this exercise.

EXERCISE 11.10 *(continued)*

6. Click the Permissions tab to open the NFS Share Permissions page. This is where you will configure the type of access that will be allowed by machines accessing this NFS data store. By default, the NFS share permissions are set to Read-Only and do not include root access. For this exercise, you will need to change the type of access to Read-Write and select the option to allow root access.

7. Click OK to close the NFS Share Permissions page and then click Apply and OK on the NFS Advanced Sharing page. Your new NFS share is now built, ready to be presented as an NFS data store to a vMware ESXi host. Be sure to record the network path displayed on the NFS Sharing tab of the share's Properties page. You will need that information to perform a proper mount on the ESXi host.

8. Switch to your ESXi host and launch the Add Storage Wizard from the Configuration tab.

9. On the Select Storage Type page of the wizard, select the Network File System storage type; click Next to continue to the Locate Network File System page.

10. On this page of the wizard, you will fill in the server and folder information for the NFS share that you will be using as a vSphere data store. Using the information recorded from step 7, properly fill out the server and folder fields and then name your new data store.

11. Click Next to continue to the Ready To Complete page of the wizard. Review the information and click Finish. Once the Create NAS data store task completes on the ESXi host, you are ready to use your Windows Server 2022 shared folder as a vSphere ESXi data store.

The previous exercise shows how versatile Windows Server 2022 shares can be. The same principles can be applied to making Windows Server shares available to other Unix-based operating systems such as ESXi.

I will show you how to use Windows PowerShell for configuring NFS shares in the section "Windows PowerShell." If you would like to see a more complete list of NFS PowerShell commands, please visit Microsoft's website at https://technet.microsoft.com/en-us/library/jj603081(v=wps.630).aspx.

Configuring Disk Quotas

In this chapter so far, you have seen how to set up a share and publish it to Active Directory. You've also learned how to set up permissions and security and how NTFS and shared permissions work with each other. It's time to learn how to limit users' hard drive space on the servers.

Disk quotas give administrators the ability to limit how much storage space a user can have on a hard drive. Disk quotas are an advantage of using NTFS over FAT32. If you decide to use FAT32 on a volume or partition, quotas will not be available.

You have a few options available to you when you set up disk quotas. You can set up disk quotas based on volume or on users:

> A good rule of thumb is to set up an umbrella quota policy that covers the entire volume and then let individual users exceed the umbrella as needed.

Setting Quotas by Volume   One way to set up disk quotas is by setting the quota by volume, on a per-volume basis. This means that if you have a hard drive with C:, D:, and E: volumes, you would have to set up three individual quotas—one for each volume. This is your umbrella. This is where you set up an entire disk quota based on the volume for all users.

Setting Quotas by User   You have the ability to set up quotas on volumes by user. Here is where you would individually let users have independent quotas that exceed your umbrella quota.

Specifying Quota Entries   You use quota entries to configure the volume and user quotas. You do this on the Quotas tab of the volume's Properties dialog box. (See Exercise 11.10.)

Creating Quota Templates   Quota templates are predefined ways to set up quotas. Templates allow you to set up disk quotas without needing to create a disk quota from scratch. One advantage of using a template is that when you want to set up disk quotas on multiple volumes (C:, D:, and E:) on the same hard drive, you do not need to re-create the quota on each volume.

Exercise 11.11 will show you how to set up an umbrella quota for all users and then have an individual account in your Active Directory exceed this quota.

EXERCISE 11.11

Configuring Disk Quotas

1.   Open Windows Explorer.

2.   Right-click the local disk (C:) and choose Properties.

3.   Click the Quotas tab.

4.   Select the Enable Quota Management and the Deny Disk Space To Users Exceeding Quota Limit options.

5.   Select the Limit Disk Space To option and enter **1000MB** in the box.

6. Enter **750MB** in the Set Warning Level To boxes.

7. Click the Apply button. If a warning box appears, click OK. This warning is just inform-ing you that the disk may need to be rescanned for the quota.

8. Now that you have set up an umbrella quota to cover everyone, you'll set up a quota that exceeds the umbrella. Click the Quota Entries button.

9. The Quotas Entries For (C:) window appears. You will see some users already listed. These are users who are already using space on the volume. From the Quota menu at the top, choose New Quota Entry.

   Notice the N/A entry in the Percent Used column. This belongs to the administrator account, which by default has no limit.

10. On the Select User page, choose a user that you want to allow to exceed the quota (for this example, I used the wpanek account). Click OK.

11. In the Add New Quota Entry dialog box, select the Do Not Limit Disk Usage option and click OK.

12. You will notice that the new user has no limit. Close the disk quota tool.

Understanding Data Duplication

Data deduplication involves finding and removing duplicate data within the company net-work without compromising its integrity. The object is to store more data in less space by segmenting files into small chunks, identifying duplicate chunks, and maintaining a single copy of each chunk.

Data duplication allows redundant copies of data chunks and then it references those multiple copies into a single copy. The data is first compressed and then the data is config-ured into a filesystem container in the System Volume Information folder.

After the data duplication is completed, the data files will no longer be stored as independent files. The data files are replaced with markers that direct the computer system to the data blocks within the data store. Because the duplicate files are now migrated into a single data point, the data is only stored once and thus saves space on the servers.

When the files are then accessed, the data blocks are transparently reassembled to fulfill the data request. This is all done without the users or applications having any knowledge that the data has been transformed into a single spot. This is a nice advantage to administra-tors because they do not have to worry that the data will be impacted in any negative way by using data duplication.

To enable data duplication, you enable a volume for duplication and then the data is automatically optimized. After this happens, the volume will contain the following;

Optimized Files   The volume will contain files that are optimized and that means that these files will have pointers to map the data to its respective areas of the chunk store.

Unoptimized Files   Some files will not meet the standards for data duplication. These files will remain as Unoptimized files. For example, encrypted files are not eligible to be optimized. So these encrypted files will remain Unoptimized on the volume.

Chunk Store   This is the location where the data duplicated files will be stored and optimized.

Free Space   Because data files are optimized and require less space, your volumes will have additional free space that you can use for users or applications.

Backup and Restoring Deduplicated Volumes

One issue that every administrator has faced in their career has to do with how we are going to protect our data by using backups. Backups are a million-dollar industry because every backup company knows the importance of protecting your data. Well, the issue that we, as IT administrators, deal with is backup space.

This is where data duplication can help us out. Because the files are optimized, the files will require less space used on backups. This doesn't matter if it's cloud-based or tape-based backups. The backups will use less space and this in turn will allow us to retain the data longer without requiring more space. Also, because the data is optimized (thus being smaller), the backups will be quicker and if any restores are needed, they will also be faster.

Any backup system that uses block-based backup applications should work without any modifications to the backup systems. File-based backups may be an issue because they normally copy the files in their original data form. If you are using file-based backups, you must have enough backup space available to handle the files in their original form.

If your organization is using the Windows Server 2022 backup software, your backups will have the ability to back up the files as optimized files and no other changes will be needed. Since many of us don't use Windows Backup, make sure your backup can handle data duplication if you are planning on using it.

If you decide to use Windows backup, the following steps will help you backup and restore data duplicated files.

1. You will need to install Windows Server Backup on the machines running data duplication. This can be done through Server Manager or by running the following PowerShell command:

    ```
    Add-WindowsFeature -name Windows-Server-Backup
    ```

2. You can then run a backup by using the following PowerShell command (this command is backing up the E: volume to the F: drive):

```
wbadmin start backup -include:E: -backuptarget:F:
```

3. You will then want to get the version ID of the backup you just created. You can do this by running the following command:

```
wbadmin get versions
```

4. After you run the `wbadmin get versions` command, you will be given the date and time of the backup. This will be needed if you are going to do a restore. The following is an example of the output: `04/24/2017-14:30`. To restore the volume you would run the following command:

```
Wbadmin start recovery -version:04/24/2017-14:30 -itemtype:Volume -
items:E: -recoveryTarget:E:
```

To restore just a part of a volume or folder, you would run the following command (for example, the `E:\wPanek` folder):

```
Wbadmin start recovery -version:04/24/2017-14:30 -itemtype:File -
items:E:\wPanek  -recursive
```

Installing and Enabling Data Deduplication

To install data duplication, you have two ways to choose from. You can install data duplication through Server Manager or through PowerShell. Let's take a look at each way.

To install data deduplication by using Server Manager:

1. On the Windows Server 2022 system, open Server Manager.

2. Click the Add Roles And Features link.

3. At the Before You Begin screen, click Next.

4. At the Select Installation Type screen, choose role-based or feature-based installation and then click Next.

5. Choose the server where you want to install Data Duplication and click Next.

6. On the Select Server Roles screen, select File and Storage Services ➤ File And iSCSI Services and then select the Data Deduplication option (shown in Figure 11.17). Click Next.

7. Click Next at the Selected Features screen.

8. Click the Install button once you've confirmed that all options are correct.

9. Once completed, close Server Manager.

FIGURE 11.17   Selecting Data Deduplication

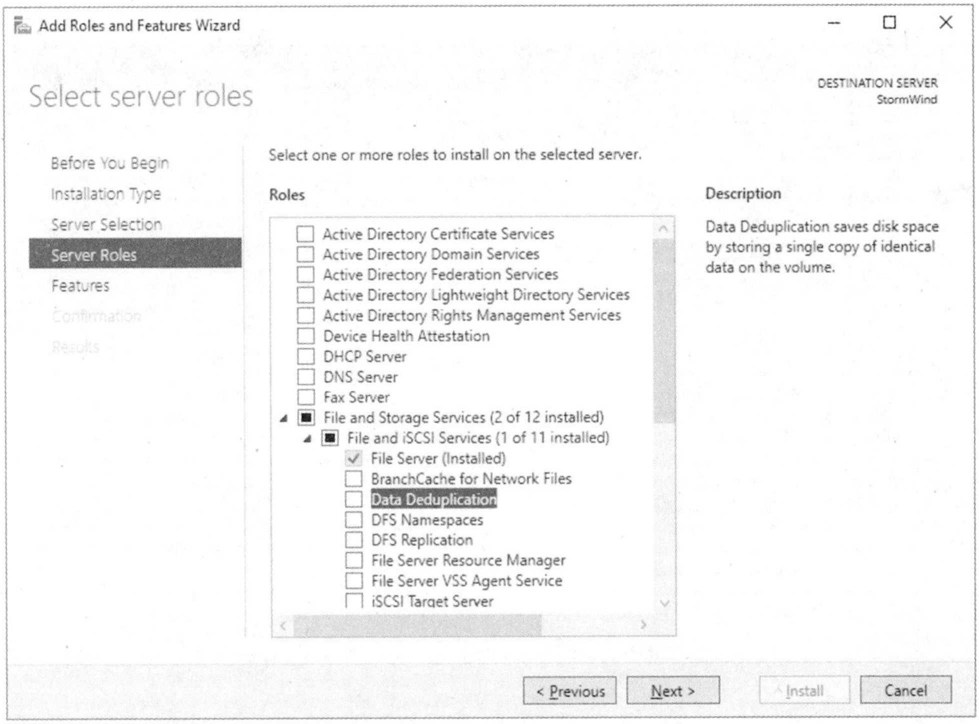

To install data deduplication by using PowerShell:

1. Click the Start button, then click Windows PowerShell ➤ More ➤ Run As Administrator.

2. In the Windows PowerShell console, enter the following commands (one at a time) followed by the Enter key:

```
Import-Module ServerManager
Add-WindowsFeature -name FS-Data-Deduplication
Import-Module Deduplication
```

After you have installed data duplication, you must then enable it on the servers. To enable data duplication in Server Manager, you would need to complete the following steps:

1. In Server Manager, click File And Storage Services.

2. Click Volumes. On right side, click the volume where you want to set up Data Duplication. Right-click the volume and choose Configure Data Deduplication (see Figure 11.18).

FIGURE 11.18 Enabling Data Deduplication

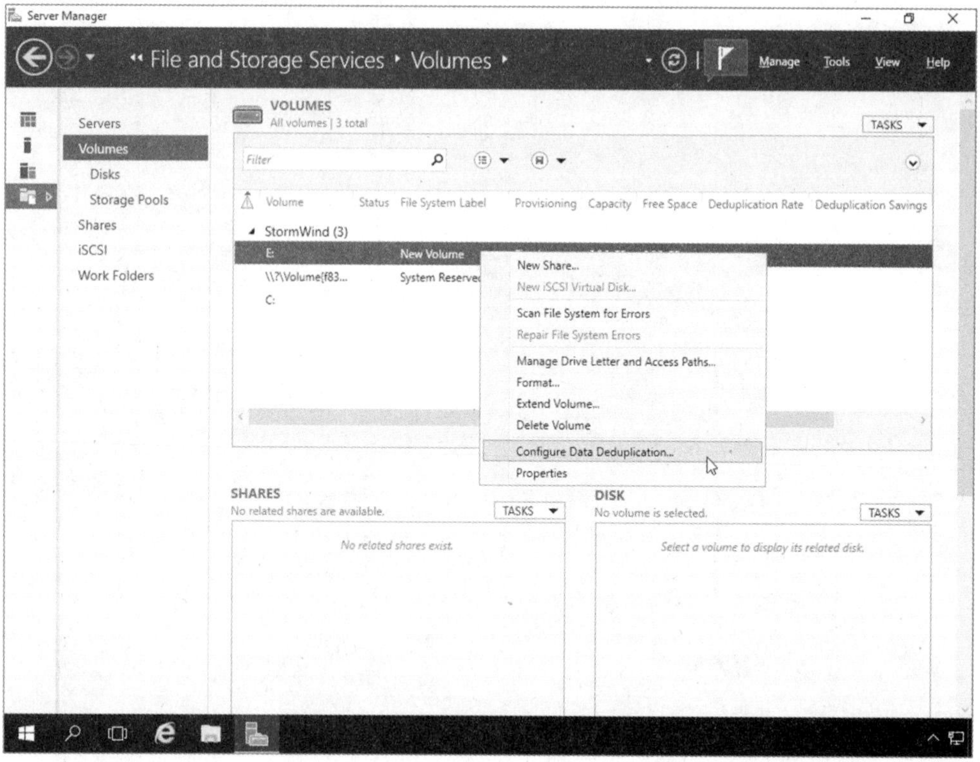

3. The New Volume Deduplication Settings Wizard will start. From the Data Deduplication pull-down, choose General Purpose File Server (shown in Figure 11.19). Enter the number of days that should elapse from the date of file creation until files are deduplicated (I used 3 days), enter the extensions of any file types that should not be duplicated (I used **.exe**), and then click Add to browse to any folders with files that should not be deduplicated (I included **\test share**). Click OK once completed. You can also set a deduplication schedule by clicking the Set Deduplication Schedule button.

Monitoring Data Deduplication

Finally, after data deduplication is installed and configured, you will want to monitor the progress of the data deduplication jobs. To do this, you can run the following PowerShell commands (these commands will show you the status of the duplication process):

```
Get-DedupStatus
Get-DedupVolume
```

FIGURE 11.19   Data Deduplication setup

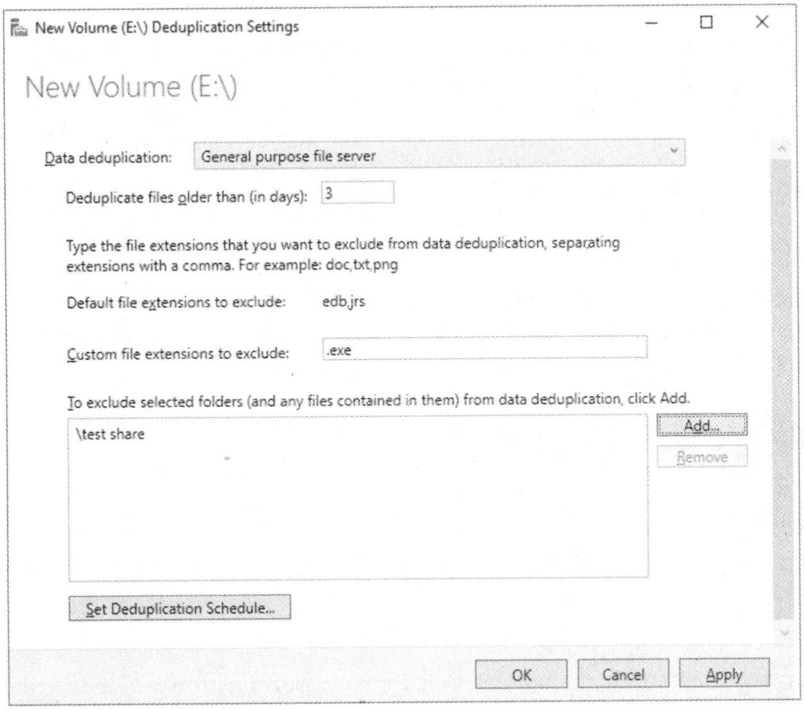

Configuring File Server Resource Manager

As an administrator, when you need to control and manage the amount and type of data stored on your servers, Microsoft delivers the tools to help you do just that. The *File Server Resource Manager (FSRM)* is a suite of tools that allows you to place quotas on folders or volumes, filter file types, and create detailed storage reports. These tools allow you to properly plan and implement policies on data as needed.

FSRM Features

Many of the advantages of using FSRM come from all of the included features, which allow you to manage the data that is stored on your file servers. Some of the advantages included with FSRM are as follows:

Configure File Management Tasks   FSRM allows you to apply a policy or action to data files. Some of the actions that can be performed include the ability to encrypt files or run a custom command.

Configure Quotas   Quotas give you the ability to limit how much disk space a user can use on a file server. You can limit space to an entire volume or to specific folders.

File Classification Infrastructure   You can set file classifications and then manage the data more effectively by using these classifications. Classifying files, and then setting policies to those classifications, allows you to set policies on those classifications. These policies include restricting file access, file encryption, and file expirations.

Configure File Screens   You can set file screening on a server and limit the types of files that are being stored on that server. For example, you can set a file screen on a server so that any file ending in .bmp gets rejected.

Configure Reports   You can create reports that show you how data is classified and accessed. You also have the ability to see which users are trying to save unauthorized file extensions.

Installing the FSRM Role Service

Installing FSRM is easy when using either Server Manager or PowerShell. To install using Server Manager, you go into Add Roles And Features and choose File And Storage Services ➤ File Services ➤ File Server Resource Manager. To install FSRM using PowerShell, you use the following command:

```
Install-WindowsFeature -Name FS-Resource-Manager -IncludeManagementTools
```

Configuring FSRM using the Windows GUI version is straightforward, but setting up FSRM using PowerShell is a bit more challenging. Table 11.3 describes some of the PowerShell commands for FSRM.

TABLE 11.3   PowerShell commands for FSRM

PowerShell Cmdlet	Description
Get-FsrmAutoQuota	Gets auto-apply quotas on a server
Get-FsrmClassification	Gets the status of the running file classification
Get-FsrmClassificationRule	Gets classification rules
Get-FsrmFileGroup	Gets file groups
Get-FsrmFileScreen	Gets file screens
Get-FsrmFileScreenException	Gets file screen exceptions
Get-FsrmQuota	Gets quotas on the server

PowerShell Cmdlet	Description
Get-FsrmSetting	Gets the current FSRM settings
Get-FsrmStorageReport	Gets storage reports
New-FsrmAutoQuota	Creates an auto-apply quota
New-FsrmFileGroup	Creates a file group
New-FsrmFileScreen	Creates a file screen
New-FsrmQuota	Creates an FSRM quota
New-FsrmQuotaTemplate	Creates a quota template
Remove-FsrmClassificationRule	Removes classification rules
Remove-FsrmFileScreen	Removes a file screen
Remove-FsrmQuota	Removes an FSRM quota from the server
Set-FsrmFileScreen	Changes the configuration settings of a file screen
Set-FsrmQuota	Changes the configuration settings for an FSRM quota

Configure File and Disk Encryption

Hardware and software encryption are some of the most important actions you can take as an administrator. You must make sure that if anyone steals hardware from your company or from your server rooms that the data they are stealing is secured and cannot be used. This is where BitLocker can help.

Using BitLocker Drive Encryption

To prevent individuals from stealing your computer and viewing personal and sensitive data found on your hard disk, some editions of Windows come with a new feature called *Bit-Locker Drive Encryption*. BitLocker encrypts the entire system drive. New files added to this drive are encrypted automatically, and files moved from this drive to another drive or computers are decrypted automatically.

Windows Server 2022 includes BitLocker Drive Encryption, and only the operating system drive (usually C:) or internal hard drives can be encrypted with BitLocker. Files on other types of drives must be encrypted using BitLocker To Go. BitLocker To Go allows you to put BitLocker on removable media such as external hard disks or USB drives.

BitLocker Recovery Password

The BitLocker recovery password is important. Do not lose it, or you may not be able to unlock the drive. Even if you do not have a Trusted Platform Module (TPM), be sure to keep your recovery password in case your USB drive becomes lost or corrupted.

BitLocker uses a *Trusted Platform Module (TPM)* version 1.2 or newer to store the security key. A TPM is a chip that is found in newer computers. If you do not have a computer with a TPM, you can store the key on a removable USB drive. The USB drive will be required each time you start the computer so that the system drive can be decrypted.

If the TPM discovers a potential security risk, such as a disk error or changes made to the BIOS, hardware, system files, or startup components, the system drive will not be unlocked until you enter the 48-digit BitLocker recovery password or use a USB drive with a recovery key as a recovery agent.

BitLocker must be set up either within the Local Group Policy editor or through the BitLocker icon in Control Panel. One advantage of using BitLocker is that you can prevent any unencrypted data from being copied onto a removable disk, thus protecting the computer.

BitLocker requires that you have a hard disk with at least two partitions, both formatted with NTFS. One partition will be the system partition that will be encrypted. The other partition will be the active partition that is used to start the computer. This partition will remain unencrypted.

Features of BitLocker

As with any version of Windows, Microsoft continues to improve on the technologies used in Windows Server 2022 and Windows 10/11. The following subsections cover some of the features of BitLocker.

BitLocker Provisioning

In previous versions of BitLocker (Windows Vista and Windows 7), BitLocker provisioning (system and data volumes) was completed during the post installation of the BitLocker utility. BitLocker provisioning was done through either the command-line interface (CLI) or Control Panel. In the Windows 8+ /Windows Server 2022 version of BitLocker, you can choose to provision BitLocker before the operating system is even installed.

You can enable BitLocker prior to the operating system deployment from the Windows Preinstallation Environment (WinPE). BitLocker is applied to the formatted volume, and BitLocker encrypts the volume prior to running the Windows setup process.

If you want to check the status of BitLocker on a particular volume, you can view the status of the drive either in the BitLocker Control Panel applet or in Windows Explorer.

Used Disk Space–Only Encryption

Windows 7 BitLocker requires that all data and free space on the drive must be encrypted. Because of this requirement, the encryption process can take a long time on larger volumes. In Windows 10+ BitLocker, you have the ability to encrypt either the entire volume or just the space being used. When you choose the Used Disk Space Only option, only the section of the drive that contains data will be encrypted. Because of this, encryption is completed much faster.

Standard User PIN and Password Change

One issue that BitLocker has had in the past is that you need to be an administrator to configure BitLocker on operating system drives. This could become an issue in a large organization because deploying TPM + PIN to a large number of computers can be challenging.

Even with the new operating system changes, administrative privileges are still needed to configure BitLocker, but now your users have the ability to change the BitLocker PIN for the operating system or change the password on the data volumes.

When a user gets to choose their own PIN and password, they normally choose something that has meaning to them and something that is easy to remember. That is a good and a bad thing at the same time. It's a good thing because when your users choose their own PIN and password, they normally don't need to write it down—they just know it. It's a bad thing because if anyone knows the user well, they can have an easier time figuring out the person's PIN and password. Even when you allow your users to choose their own PIN and password, make sure you set a GPO to require password complexity.

Network Unlock

One of the features of BitLocker is Network Unlock. *Network Unlock* allows you to easily manage desktops and servers that are configured to use BitLocker. Network Unlock allows you to configure BitLocker to automatically unlock an encrypted hard drive during a system reboot when that hard drive is connected to your trusted corporate environment. For this to function properly on a machine, there has to be a DHCP driver implementation in the system's firmware.

If your operating system volume is also protected by the TPM + PIN protection, you have to be sure to enter the PIN at the time of the reboot. This protection can actually make using Network Unlock more difficult to use, but they can be used in combination.

Support for Encrypted Hard Drives for Windows

One of the new advantages of using BitLocker is *Full Volume Encryption (FVE)*. BitLocker provides built-in encryption for Windows data files and Windows operating system files. The advantage of this type of encryption is that encrypted hard drives that use *Full Disk Encryption (FDE)* get each block of the physical disk space encrypted. Because each physical block gets encrypted, it offers much better encryption. The only downside to this is that because each physical block is encrypted, it degrades the hard drive speed somewhat. So, as an administrator, you have to decide whether you want better speed or better security on your hard disk.

In Exercise 11.12, you will enable BitLocker on the Windows Server 2022 system.

EXERCISE 11.12

Enabling BitLocker in Windows Server 2022

1. Open Server Manager by clicking the Server Manager icon or running **server manager.exe**.

2. Select Add Roles And Features from the dashboard.

3. Select Next in the Before You Begin pane (if shown).

4. Select role-based or feature-based installation and click Next to continue.

5. Select the Select A Server From The Server Pool option and click Next.

6. At the Select Server Roles screen, click Next.

7. At the Select Features screen, click the BitLocker Drive Encryption check box. When the Add Roles and Features dialog box appears, click the Add Features button. Then click Next.

8. Click the Install button in the Confirmation pane of the Add Roles And Features Wizard to begin BitLocker feature installation. The BitLocker feature requires a restart to complete. Selecting the Restart The Destination Server Automatically If Required option in the Confirmation pane will force a restart of the computer after installation is complete.

9. If the Restart The Destination Server Automatically If Required option is not selected, the Results pane of the Add Roles And Features Wizard will display the success or failure of the BitLocker feature installation. If required, a notification of additional action necessary to complete the feature installation, such as the restart of the computer, will be displayed in the results text.

You also can install BitLocker by using the Windows PowerShell utility. To install BitLocker, use the following PowerShell commands:

```
Install-WindowsFeature BitLocker -IncludeAllSubFeature -
IncludeManagementTools -Restart
```

Using EFS Drive Encryption

If you have been in the computer industry long enough, you may remember the days when only servers used NTFS. Years ago, most client systems used FAT or FAT32, but NTFS had some key benefits over FAT/FAT32. The main advantages were NTFS security, quotas, compression, and encryption. Encryption is available on a system because you are using a file structure (for example, NTFS) that allows encryption. Windows Server 2022 NTFS allows you to use these four advantages, including encryption.

Encrypting File System (EFS) allows a user or administrator to secure files or folders by using encryption. Encryption employs the user's security identification (SID) number to secure the file or folder. Encryption is the strongest protection that Windows provides to help you keep your information secure. Some key features of EFS are as follows:

- Encrypting is simple; just select a check box in the file or folder's properties to turn it on.

- You have control over who can read the files.

- Files are encrypted when you close them but are automatically ready to use when you open them.

- If you change your mind about encrypting a file, clear the check box in the file's properties.

To implement encryption, open the Advanced Attributes dialog box for a folder and check the Encrypt Contents To Secure Data option.

If files are encrypted using EFS and you have to unencrypt the files, there are two ways you can do this. You can log in using the user's account (the account that encrypted the files) and unencrypt the files using the cipher command. Alternatively, you can become a recovery agent and manually unencrypt the files.

If you use EFS, it's best not to delete users immediately when they leave a company. You have the ability to recover encrypted files, but it is much easier to gain access to the user's encrypted files by logging in as the user who left the company and deselecting the encryption option.

Using the *cipher* Command

The cipher command is useful when it comes to EFS. Cipher is a command-line utility that allows you to change and/or configure EFS. When it comes to using the cipher command, you should be aware of a few things:

- You can decrypt files by running **Cipher.exe** in the command prompt window (advanced users).

- You can use Cipher to modify an EFS-encrypted file.

- You can use Cipher to import EFS certificates and keys.

- You can also use Cipher to back up EFS certificates and keys.

Let's take a look at some of the switches that you can use with cipher. Table 11.4 describes many of the cipher switches you can use. This table comes from Microsoft's Tech-Net site. Microsoft continues to add and improve switches, so make sure you check Microsoft's website to see whether there are any changes.

TABLE 11.4   Using the cipher switches

cipher switch	Description
/e	This switch allows you to encrypt specified folders. With this folder encrypted, any files added to this folder will automatically be encrypted.
/d	This switch allows you to decrypt specified folders.
/s: dir	With this switch, the operation you are running will be performed in the specified folder and all subfolders.
/i	By default, when an error occurs, cipher automatically halts. By using this switch, cipher will continue to operate even after errors occur.
/f	The force switch (/f) will encrypt or decrypt all of the specified objects, even if the files have been modified by using encryption previously. Cipher, by default, does not touch files that have been encrypted or decrypted previously.
/q	This switch shows you a report about the most critical information of the EFS object.
/h	Normally, system or hidden files are not touched by encryption. By using this switch, you can display files with hidden or system attributes.
/k	This switch will create a new file encryption key based on the user currently running the cipher command.
/?	This shows the cipher help command.

Configuring Distributed File System

One problem that network administrators have is deciding how to share folders and communicating to end users how to find the shares. For example, if you share a folder called StormWind Documents on server A, how do you make sure your users will find the folder and the files within it? The users have to know the server name and the share name. This can be a huge problem if you have hundreds of shares on multiple servers. If you want to have multiple copies of the folder called StormWind Documents for fault tolerance and load balancing, the problem becomes even more complicated.

Distributed File System (DFS) in Windows Server 2022 offers a simplified way for users to access geographically dispersed files. DFS allows you to set up a tree structure of virtual directories that allows users to connect to shared folders throughout the entire network.

You have the ability to take shared folders that are located on different servers and transparently connect them to one or more DFS namespaces—virtual trees of shared folders throughout an organization. The advantage of using DFS is that if one of the folders becomes unavailable, DFS has failover capability that will allow your users to connect to the data on a different server.

You can use the DFS tools to choose which shared folders will appear in the namespace and also to decide how the names of these shared folders will show up in the virtual tree listing.

Advantages of DFS

One of the advantages of DFS is that when a user views this virtual tree, the shared folders appear to be located on a single machine. These are some of the other advantages of DFS:

Simplified Data Migration   DFS gives you the ability to move data from one location to another without the user needing to know the physical location of the data. Because the users do not need to know the physical location of the shared data, you can simply move data from one location to another.

Security Integration   You do not need to configure additional security for the DFS shared folders. The shared folders use the NTFS and shared folder permissions that you have already assigned when the share was set up.

Access-Based Enumeration (ABE)   This DFS feature (disabled by default) displays only the files and folders that a user has permissions to access. If a user does not have access to a folder, Windows hides the folder from the user's DFS view. This feature is not active if the user is viewing the files and folders locally.

Types of DFS

The following are types of DFS:

DFS Replication (DFSR)   You have the ability to manage replication scheduling and bandwidth throttling using the DFS management console. Replication is the process of sharing data between multiple machines. Replicated shared folders allow you to balance the load and have fault tolerance. DFS also has read-only replication folders.

DFS Namespace   The DFS Namespace service is the virtual tree listing in the DFS server. You can set up multiple namespaces on the DFS, allowing for multiple virtual trees within DFS. The DFS Namespace service was once known as *Distributed File System* in Windows 2000 Server and Windows Server 2003 (in case you still use Server 2003).

In Exercise 11.13, you will install the DFS Namespace service on the file server. You need to start the installation using the Server Manager MMC.

EXERCISE 11.13

Installing the DFS Namespace Service

1. Open Server Manager by clicking the Server Manager icon or running **server manager.exe**.

2. Select Add Roles And Features from the dashboard.

3. Select Next in the Before You Begin pane (if shown).

4. Select Role-Based or Feature-Based installation and click Next to continue.

5. Select the Select A Server From The Server Pool option and click Next.

6. On the Select Server Roles screen, expand File And Storage Services and select the DFS Namespace and DFS Replication options (see Figure 11.20). Then click Next. If a dialog box appears, click the Add Features button.

FIGURE 11.20 Select Server Roles

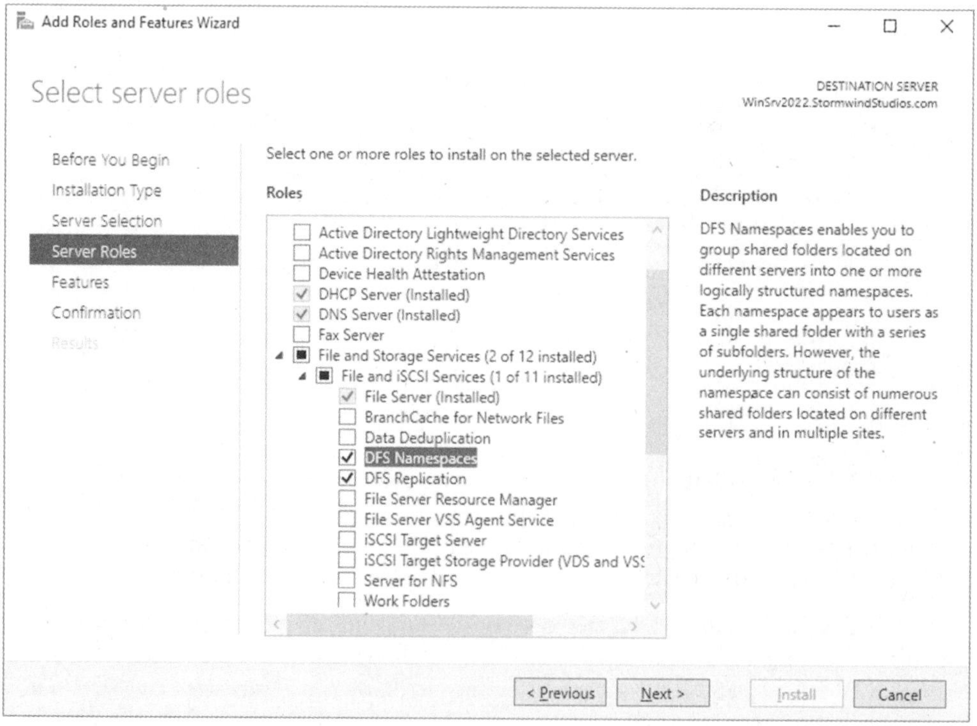

7. At the Select Features screen, click Next.

8. At the Confirmation screen, click the Install button.

9. After the installation is complete, click the Close button.

10. Close Server Manager.

Once you have installed DFS, it's time to learn how to manage DFS with the DFS Management MMC. The DFS Management console (see Figure 11.21) gives you one place to do all of your DFS configurations. The DFS Management console allows you to set up DFS Replication and DFS Namespace. Another task you can do in the DFS Management console is add a folder target—a folder that you add to the DFS namespace (the virtual tree) for all your users to share.

FIGURE 11.21   DFS Management console

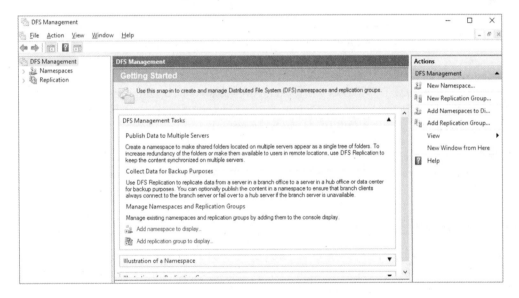

Database Cloning

For the first time ever in DFS, Windows Server 2022 includes a new DFS database cloning function. This new feature allows you to accelerate replication when creating folders, servers, or recovery systems. You will now have the ability to extract the DFS database from a single DFS server and then clone that database to multiple DFS servers.

You can use PowerShell and the `Export-DfsrClone` cmdlet to export the volume that contains the DFS database and configuration XML file settings. When you execute this PowerShell cmdlet, a trigger is engaged that exports the DFS service, and the system will not proceed until the service is completed. You then use the PowerShell cmdlet `Import-DfsrClone` to import the data to a specific volume. The service will then validate that the replication was transferred completely.

Recovering a DFS Database

Windows Server 2022 DFS database recovery is a feature that allows DFS to detect a corrupted database, thus allowing DFS to rebuild the database automatically and continue with normal operations of DFS replication. One advantage to this is that when DFS detects and fixes a corrupted database, it does so with no file conflicts.

Before the introduction of this feature, if a DFS database were determined to be corrupted, DFS Replication would delete the database and start again with an initial nonauthoritative sync process. This would cause newer file versions to be overwritten by older data, causing real data loss.

DFS in Windows Server 2022 uses local files and an update sequence number (USN) to fix a corrupted database, ensuring no loss of data.

Optimizing DFS

Windows Server 2022 DFS allows you to configure variable file staging sizes on individual DFS servers. This allows you to set a minimum file size for a file to stage. This increases the staging size of files, and that in turn increases the performance of the replication.

Prior to Windows Server 2022, DFS Replication used a hard-coded 256 KB file size to determine staging requirements. If a file size were larger than 256 KB, that file would be staged before it replicated. The more file staging that you have, the longer replication takes on a DFS system.

Remote Differential Compression

One issue that can arise occurs when files are changed. There has to be some mechanism that helps files stay accurate. That's where the *Remote Differential Compression (RDC)* feature comes into play. RDC is a group of APIs that programs can use to determine whether files have changed. Once RDC determines that there has been a change, RDC then helps to detect which portions of the files contain the changes. RDC has the ability to detect insertions, removals, and rearrangements of data in files. This feature becomes helpful with limited-bandwidth networks when they replicate changes.

To install the RDC feature, use Server Manager and then run the Add Features Wizard, or type the following command at an elevated command prompt:

```
Servermanagercmd -Install Rdc
```

Now that I have shown you how to install DFS and how DFS works, let's go ahead and set up DFS. In Exercise 11.14, I will show you how to configure a DFS Namespace and how to add a shared folder to DFS.

EXERCISE 11.14

Setting Up a DFS Namespace

1. Open DFS Management (Start ➤ Administrative Tools ➤ DFS Management).

2. Right-click Namespaces (see Figure 11.22) and choose New Namespace.

FIGURE 11.22 Adding a namespace

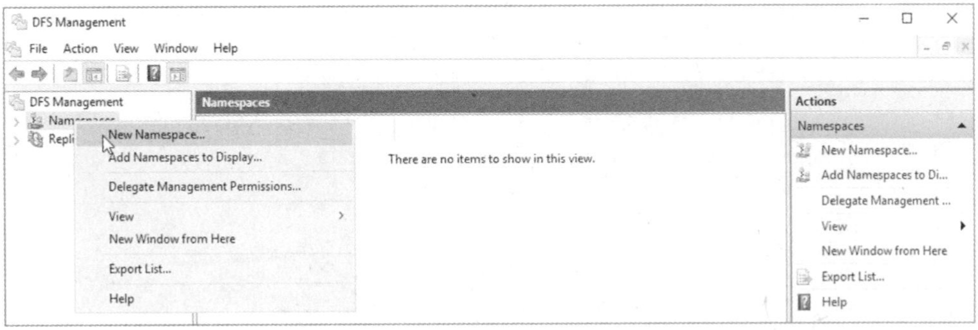

3. In the Server box, enter the name of the server that will host this namespace (I am using the DFS server). Click Next.

4. At the Namespace screen, enter the namespace you want (see Figure 11.23) to use and click Next.

EXERCISE 11.14 *(continued)*

FIGURE 11.23 Entering a Namespace

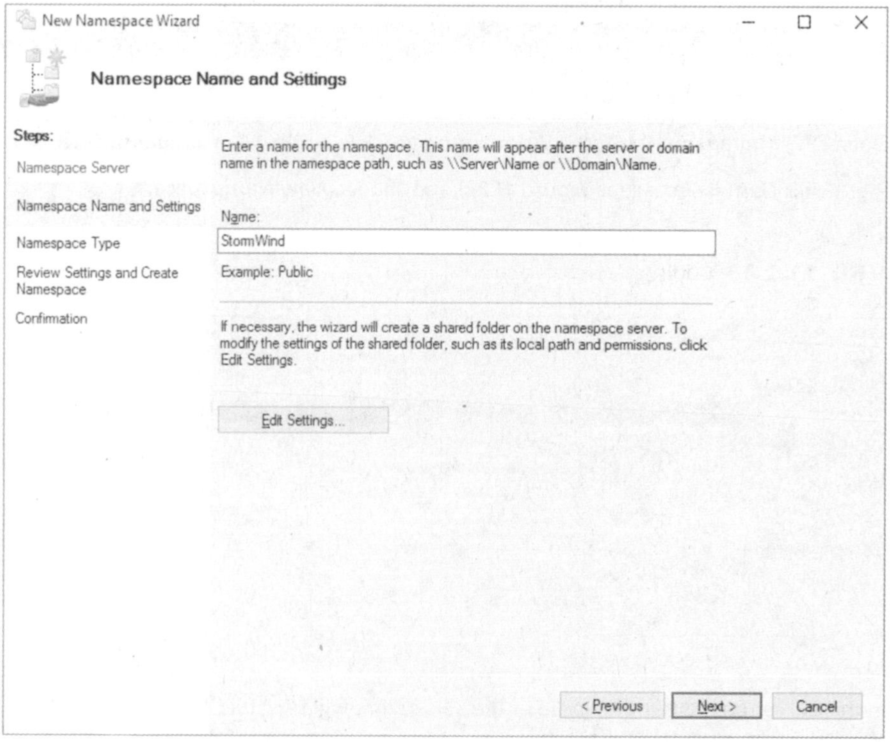

5. On the Namespace Type screen, choose Stand-Alone or Domain Based and click Next. I am using a Stand-Alone DFS.
6. At the Review screen, click Create.
7. Click the Close button. Leave DFS open.
8. Go to Windows Explorer by pressing the Windows Key+E.
9. Create a new folder called **Home** and share the folder.
10. In DFS under the Actions section (right-hand side), choose New Folder (see Figure 11.24).

FIGURE 11.24 New Folder

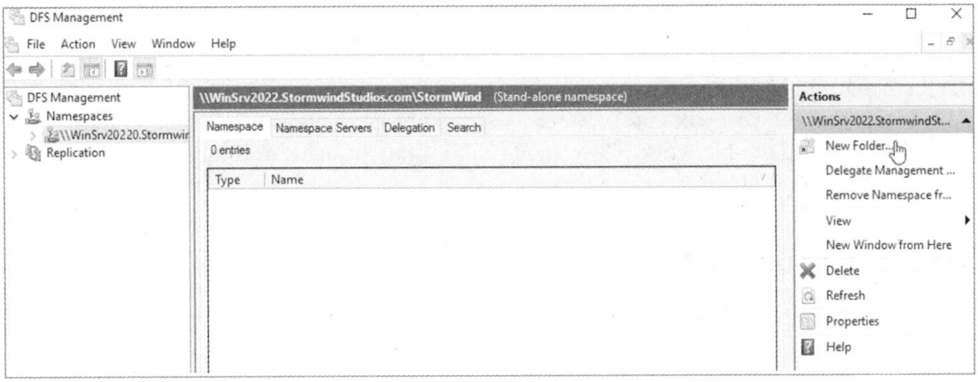

11. When the New Folder screen appears, type the name for this folder and then click Add.

12. Add the shared Home folder and click OK.

13. After you have entered a name and put in the Home folder (see Figure 11.25), click OK.

FIGURE 11.25 Home folder

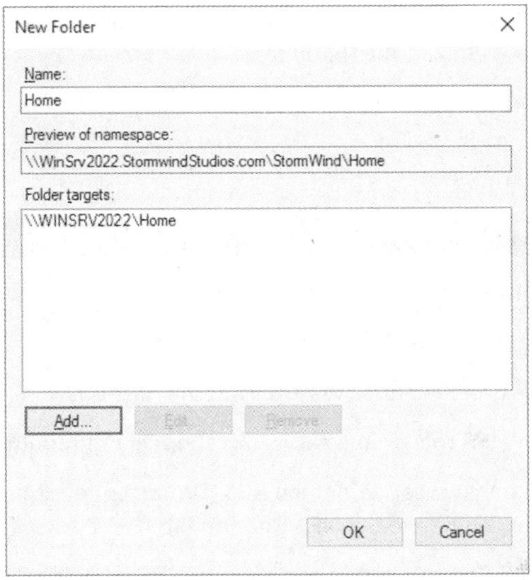

14. The namespace has been created and you have added a shared folder to the namespace. Add any of your other shared folders and then close DFS.

Configure Advanced File Services

Windows Server has come a long way in terms of its file and storage capabilities. I have talked quite a bit about the new features and functionality provided in Windows Server 2022. In this section, you will take a closer look at some of the advanced configuration options available in the Network File System (NFS), BranchCache, and the File Server Resource Manager (FSRM).

Configure the NFS Data Store

The NFS role service and feature set gives IT administrators the ability to integrate a Windows Server–based environment with Unix-based operating systems. Most corporate environments today consist of a mixed operating system infrastructure to some extent. Using a Windows NFS file server, you can configure file shares for use by multiple operating systems throughout the environment.

Windows Server 2022 takes those capabilities even further by enabling you to integrate with platforms such as ESXi. ESXi is vMware's exclusive operating system–independent hypervisor. ESXi is referred to as a *bare-metal* operating system because once it is installed on server virtualization hardware, guest virtual machines can be installed without requiring the use of any other underlying operating system. With Windows Server 2022, you can use an NFS share efficiently as an ESXi data store to house all of your guest virtual machines. Let's take a look at configuring an NFS data store in Exercise 11.15.

For this exercise, you will need the following:

- A Windows Server 2022 server
- A vMware ESXi 5 server

EXERCISE 11.15

Configure the NFS Data Store

1. Open Server Manager on your Windows Server 2022 machine.

2. Launch the Add Roles And Features Wizard from the dashboard.

3. Install the Server for NFS role on the server. A reboot is not required.

4. Create a new folder on your server named NFS_Datastore, right-click and select Properties, and then navigate to the NFS Sharing tab.

5. Click the Manage NFS Sharing button to open the NFS Advanced Sharing page and then check the Share This Folder box. Notice how enabling the share also enables the share's default settings. The share settings let you configure share authentication and user access further if the need arises. The default settings will work just fine for this exercise.

6. Click the Permissions tab to open the NFS Share Permissions page. This is where you will configure the type of access that will be allowed by machines accessing this NFS data store. By default, the NFS share permissions are set to Read-Only and do not include root access. For this exercise, you will need to change the type of access to Read-Write and check the box to allow root access.

7. Click OK to close the NFS Share Permissions page and then click Apply and OK on the NFS Advanced Sharing page. Your new NFS share is now built, ready to be presented as an NFS data store to a VMware ESXi host. Be sure to record the network path displayed on the NFS Sharing tab of the share's Properties page. You will need that information to perform a proper mount on the ESXi host.

8. Switch to your ESXi host and launch the Add Storage Wizard from the Configuration tab.

9. On the Select Storage Type page of the wizard, select the Network File System storage type; click Next to continue to the Locate Network File System page.

10. On this page of the wizard, you will fill in the server and folder information for the NFS share that you will be using as a vSphere data store. Using the information recorded from step 7, properly fill out the server and folder fields and then name your new data store.

11. Click Next to continue to the Ready To Complete page of the wizard. Review the information and click Finish. Once the Create NAS data store task completes on the ESXi host, you are ready to use your Windows Server 2022 shared folder as a vSphere ESXi data store.

The previous exercise shows how versatile Windows Server 2022 shares can be. The same principles can be applied to making Windows Server shares available to other Unix-based operating systems such as ESXi. Now that you have configured an NFS data store, let's take a look at what BranchCache has to offer.

Configure BranchCache

BranchCache is a technology that was introduced with Windows Server 2008 R2 and Windows 7. BranchCache allows an organization with slower links between offices to cache data so that downloads between offices do not have to occur each time a file is accessed.

For example, John comes into work and logs into the network. John accesses the corporate website and downloads a media file that takes four minutes to download. With BranchCache enabled, when Judy comes into work, connects to the corporate website, and tries to download the same media file, the file will be cached from the previous download and Judy will have immediate access to the file.

You can set up two types of BranchCache configurations:

Distributed Cache Mode   In the distributed cache mode configuration, all Windows client machines cache the files locally on the client machines. Thus, in the previous example, after John downloaded the media file, Judy would receive the cached media file from John's Windows 7 version or above (except for home versions).

Hosted Mode   In the hosted mode configuration, the cache files are cached on a local (within the site) Windows Server 2022 machine. So, in the previous example, after John downloads the media file, the cached file would be placed on a Windows Server 2022 machine by default, and all other users (Judy) would download the media file from the Windows Server 2022 machine.

Distributed Cache Mode Requirements

If you decide to install BranchCache in the distributed cache mode configuration, a hosted cache server running Windows Server 2022 is not required at the branch office. To set up distributed cache mode, the client machines must be running Windows 7 or above (except for home versions).

The Windows client machines would download the data files from the content computer at the main branch office, and then these machines become the local cache servers. To set up distributed cache mode, you must install a content computer (the computer that will hold the original content) at the main office first. After the content server is installed, physical connections (WAN or VPN connections) between the sites and branch offices must be established.

Client computers running Windows 7 Enterprise or higher (from versions listed above) have BranchCache installed by default. However, you must enable and configure Branch-Cache and configure firewall exceptions. Complete Exercise 11.16 to configure BranchCache firewall rule exceptions.

EXERCISE 11.16

Configuring BranchCache Firewall Exceptions

1. On a domain controller, open the Group Policy Management Console.

2. In the Group Policy Management Console, expand the following path: Forest ➤ Domains ➤ Group Policy Objects. Make sure the domain you choose contains the BranchCache Windows 7/Windows 8 client computer accounts that you want to configure.

3. In the Group Policy Management Console, right-click Group Policy Objects and select New. Name the policy **BranchCache Client** and click OK. Right-click BranchCache Client and click Edit. The Group Policy Management Editor console opens.

In the Group Policy Management Editor console, expand the following path:
   Computer Configuration ➤ Policies ➤ Windows Settings ➤ Security Settings ➤ Windows
   Firewall With Advanced Security ➤ Windows Firewall With Advanced Security – LDAP ➤
   Inbound Rules.

5. Right-click Inbound Rules and then click New Rule. The New Inbound Rule
   Wizard opens.

6. On the Rule Type screen, click Predefined, expand the list of choices, and then click
   BranchCache – Content Retrieval (Uses HTTP). Click Next.

7. On the Predefined Rules screen, click Next.

8. On the Action screen, ensure that Allow The Connection is selected and then click
   Finish. You must select Allow The Connection for the BranchCache client to be able to
   receive traffic on this port.

9. To create the WS-Discovery firewall exception, right-click Inbound Rules and click New
   Rule. The New Inbound Rule Wizard opens.

10. On the Rule Type screen, click Predefined, expand the list of choices, and then click
   BranchCache – Peer Discovery (Uses WSD). Click Next.

11. On the Predefined Rules screen, click Next.

12. On the Action screen, ensure that Allow The Connection is selected and then
   click Finish.

13. In the Group Policy Management Editor console, right-click Outbound Rules and then
   click New Rule. The New Outbound Rule Wizard opens.

14. On the Rule Type screen, click Predefined, expand the list of choices, and then click
   BranchCache – Content Retrieval (Uses HTTP). Click Next.

15. On the Predefined Rules screen, click Next.

16. On the Action screen, make sure that Allow The Connection is selected and then
   click Finish.

17. Create the WS-Discovery firewall exception by right-clicking Outbound Rules and then
   clicking New Rule. The New Outbound Rule Wizard opens.

18. On the Rule Type screen, click Predefined, expand the list of choices, and then click
   BranchCache – Peer Discovery (Uses WSD). Click Next.

19. On the Predefined Rules screen, click Next.

20. On the Action screen, make sure that Allow The Connection is selected and then click
   Finish. Close the Group Policy Management console.

Now that you have looked at the distributed cache mode configuration, let's take a look at the hosted mode configuration.

Hosted Mode Requirements

To set up a hosted mode BranchCache configuration, you must first set up a Windows Server 2022 hosted cache server at the main and branch offices. You also need to be running Windows 7 or above (except for home versions) at the branch offices.

The Windows client machines download the data from the main cache server, and then the hosted cache servers at the branch offices obtain a copy of the downloaded data for other users to access.

Your network infrastructure must also allow for physical connections between the main office and the branch offices. These connections can be VPNs or some type of WAN links. After these requirements are met, your cache server must obtain a server certificate so that the client computers in the branch offices can positively identify the cache servers.

Exercise 11.17 walks you through the process of installing the BranchCache feature on a Windows Server 2022 machine. To begin this exercise, you must be logged into the Windows Server 2022 machine as an administrator.

EXERCISE 11.17

Installing BranchCache on Windows Server 2022

1. Open Server Manager by clicking the Server Manager icon or by running **server manager.exe**.

2. Select Add Roles And Features.

3. Click Next in the Before You Begin pane (if shown).

4. Select role-based or feature-based installation and click Next to continue.

5. Select the Select A Server From The Server Pool option and click Next.

6. At the Select Server Roles screen, click Next.

7. At the Select Features screen, click the check box for BranchCache (see Figure 11.26). Then click Next.

FIGURE 11.26   BranchCache option

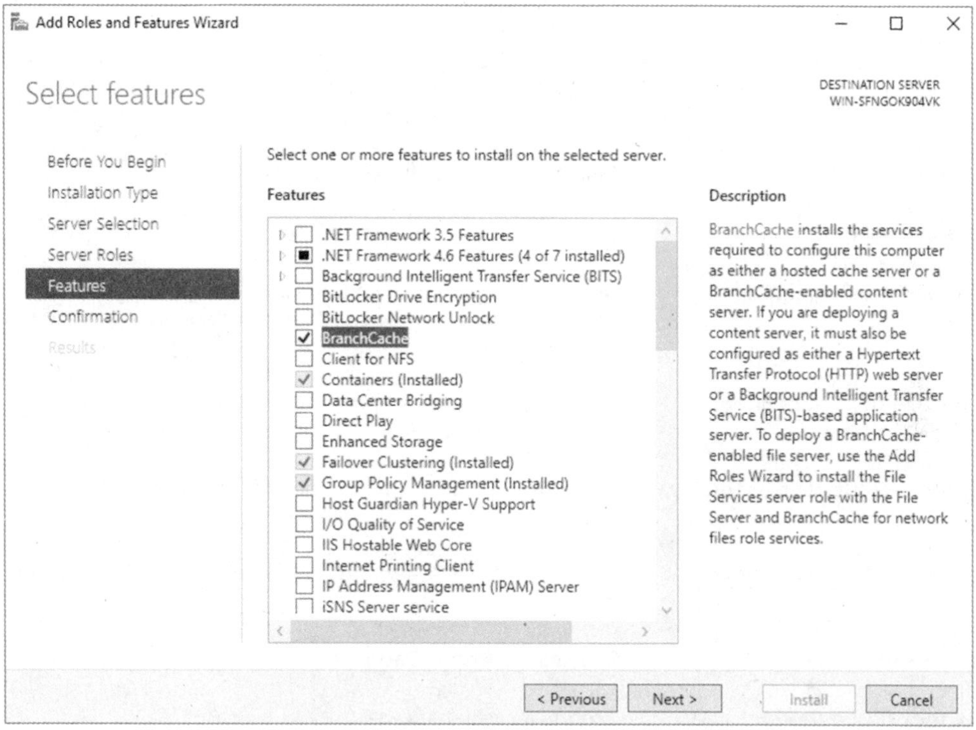

8. Check the Restart The Destination Server If Required option and then click Install. If a dialog box appears about restarting, click Yes. The system should restart.

9. After the system restarts, log in as the administrator.

Make sure to repeat this exercise on all branch office cache servers. One of the requirements for BranchCache is a physical connection between the main office and the branch offices.

BranchCache and PowerShell

As stated throughout this book, PowerShell is a command-line shell and scripting tool. BranchCache has many different PowerShell cmdlets that allow you to configure and maintain the BranchCache feature. Table 11.5 shows just some of the different PowerShell cmdlets for BranchCache.

TABLE 11.5 PowerShell cmdlets for BranchCache

Cmdlet	Description
Add-BCDataCacheExtension	Increases the amount of cache storage space that is available on a hosted cache server by adding a new cache file
Clear-BCCache	Deletes all data in all data and hash files
Disable-BC	Disables the BranchCache service
Disable-BCDowngrading	Disables downgrading so that client computers that are running Windows 10 do not request Windows 7/8 specific versions of content information from content servers
Enable-BCDistributed	Enables BranchCache and configures a computer to operate in distributed cache mode
Enable-BCHostedClient	Configures BranchCache to operate in hosted cache client mode
Enable-BCHostedServer	Configures BranchCache to operate in hosted cache server mode
Enable-BCLocal	Enables the BranchCache service in local caching mode
Export-BCCachePackage	Exports a cache package
Export-BCSecretKey	Exports a secret key to a file
Get-BCClientConfiguration	Gets the current BranchCache client computer settings
Get-BCContentServer Configuration	Gets the current BranchCache content server settings
Get-BCDataCache	Gets the BranchCache data cache
Get-BCStatus	Gets a set of objects that provide BranchCache status and configuration information
Import-BCCachePackage	Imports a cache package into BranchCache
Import-BCSecretKey	Imports the cryptographic key that BranchCache uses for generating segment secrets
Set-BCAuthentication	Specifies the BranchCache computer authentication mode

Cmdlet	Description
Set-BCCache	Modifies the cache file configuration
Set-BCSecretKey	Sets the cryptographic key used in the generation of segment secrets

Enhanced Features in Windows Server 2022 BranchCache

Microsoft continues to improve on many of the features of Windows Server, and Branch-Cache is no different. Microsoft has improved BranchCache in Windows Server 2022 and Windows 10/11. The following list includes some of the enhanced features:

Office sizes and the number of branch offices are not limited.   Windows Server 2022 BranchCache allows any number of offices along with any number of users once you deploy hosted cache mode with multiple hosted cache servers.

There are no requirements for a Group Policy Object (GPO) for each office location, streamlining deployment.   All that is required to deploy BranchCache is a single GPO that contains a small number of settings.

Client computer configuration is easy.   You have the ability to configure their clients through the use of a GPO. If this is done, client configuration will automatically be configured through the GPO, and if a client can't find a hosted cache server, the client will automatically self-configure as a hosted cache mode client.

BranchCache is deeply integrated with the Windows file server.   BranchCache is automatically integrated with Windows file server technology. Because of this, the process of finding duplicate pieces in independent files is greatly improved.

Duplicate content is stored and downloaded only once.   BranchCache stores only one instance of the content on a hosted cache server or content server, and because of this, you get greater disk storage savings. Since client computers at the remote offices download only one instance of any content, your network saves on additional WAN bandwidth.

Small changes to large files produce bandwidth savings.   One advantage of Branch-Cache is the file server chunking system that helps divide files and web pages into smaller parts. Now when a file is changed, only the part of that file that has been changed gets replicated. This allows BranchCache to use lower bandwidth requirements.

Offline content creation improves performance.   When BranchCache is deployed as content or file servers, the data is calculated offline before a client even has the chance to request it. Because of this, the systems get faster performance and bandwidth.

Cache encryption is enabled automatically.   BranchCache stores its cached data as encrypted data. This guarantees data security without the need to encrypt the entire drive.

Summary

In this chapter, I discussed file servers and how they can be effective on your network. I also discussed sharing folders for users to access, and then I discussed how to publish those shared folders to Active Directory.

You learned about NTFS security versus shared folder permissions and how to limit users' hard drive space by setting up disk quotas. The chapter also covered the Encrypting File System (EFS) and how users can encrypt and compress files.

I also discussed how configuring file and storage solutions can be highly effective within your organization. You now have a better understanding of how Windows Server 2022 can provide you with extended functionality for effectively controlling corporate data.

I talked about Data Deduplication and how it can help protect your corporate data and also provide a backup solution.

This chapter took you through the use of many server tools and utilities such as DFS and encryption. Distributed File System allows you to set up a tree structure of virtual directories that lets users connect to a shared folder anywhere throughout the entire network.

You also learned about EFS and how to use Cipher to modify or configure EFS in a command window. Cipher is the best way to change encrypted directories and files.

Exam Essentials

Know storage technologies.   Understand how to use the Fibre Channel, iSCSI, and NAS storage technologies. Know how to configure an iSCSI initiator and how to establish a connection to a target. Practice configuring tiered storage and using thin provisioning and trim.

Know how to configure NTFS security.   One of the major advantages of using NTFS over FAT32 is access to additional security features. NTFS allows you to put security at the file and folder layers. NTFS security is in effect whether the user is remote or local to the computer with the data.

Know how to configure shared permissions.   Shared permissions allow you to determine the access a user will receive when connecting to a shared folder. Shared permissions are allowed only at the folder layer and are in effect only when the user is remote to the computer with the shared data.

Understand how NTFS and shared permissions work together.   NTFS and shared permissions are individually additive—you get the highest level of security and permissions within each type. NTFS is always in effect, and it is the only security available locally. Shared permissions are in effect only when connecting remotely to access the shared data. When the two types of permissions meet, the most restrictive set of permissions applies.

Know how to configure disk quotas.   Disk quotas allow an organization to determine the amount of disk space that users can have on a volume of a server. You can set up disk quotas based on volumes or by users. Each volume must have its own separate set of disk quotas.

Understand data deduplication.   Know that data deduplication involves finding and removing duplicate data within the company network without compromising its integrity. Understand that the goal is to store more data in less space by segmenting files into small chunks, identifying duplicate chunks, and maintaining a single copy of each chunk.

Know how to configure DFS.   Distributed File System in Windows Server 2022 offers a simplified way for users to access geographically dispersed files. The DFS Namespace service allows you to set up a tree structure of virtual directories that lets users connect to shared folders throughout the entire network.

Understand EFS and Cipher.   Users can encrypt their directories and files by using EFS. Understand how Cipher can help you configure or modify an EFS object while in the command prompt.

Review Questions

1. What is the default TCP port for iSCSI?

   A. 3260

   B. 1433

   C. 21

   D. 3389

2. You have a Windows Server 2022 Hyper-V host named Jupiter. You want to deploy several shielded virtual machines on Jupiter. You deploy a Host Guardian on a new server. You need to view the process of the shielded virtual machines installation. What should you run to see the progress of the shielded VM?

   A. `Get-ShieldedVMProvisioningStatus` cmdlet

   B. `Diskpart` command

   C. `Set-VHD` cmdlet

   D. `Set-VM` cmdlet

3. You are the administrator of a mid-sized network. You have a Hyper-V host that runs Windows Server 2022. The host contains a virtual machine named Virtual1. Virtual1 has resource metering enabled. You need to use resource metering to track the amount of network traffic that Virtual1 sends to the 10.10.16.0/20 network. Which cmdlet would you run?

   A. `Add-VMNetworkAdapteiAd`

   B. `Set-VMNetworkAdapter`

   C. `New-VMResourcePool`

   D. `Set-VMNetworkAdapterRoutingDomamMapping`

4. You are the administrator for an organization that has started using Hyper-V. You have a Hyper-V host named Server1 that runs Windows Server 2022. Server1 contains a virtual machine named Earth. You need to make sure that you can use nested virtualization on Earth. What should you run on Server1?

   A. `Mount-VHD` cmdlet

   B. `Diskpart` command

   C. `Set-VMProcessor` cmdlet

   D. `Set-VM` cmdlet

5. You need to ensure that VM1 and VM2 can communicate with each other only. The solution must prevent VM1 and VM2 from communicating with Server1. Which cmdlet should you use?

   A. `Set-NetNeighbor`

   B. `Remove-VMSwitchTeamMember`

   C. `Set-VMSwitch`

   D. `Enable-VMSwitchExtension`

6. You are the admin for a mid-sized company. You have a Hyper-V host named Server1 that runs Windows Server 2022. Server1 has a dynamically expanding virtual hard disk (VHD) file that is 950 GB. The VHD currently contains around 450 GB of free space. You want to reduce the amount of disk space used by the VHD. What command should you run?

A. `Mount-VHD` cmdlet

B. `Diskpart` command

C. `Set-VHD` cmdlet

D. `Optimize-VHD` cmdlet

7. You have a Nano Server named Nano1. Which cmdlet should you use to identify whether the DNS Server role is installed on Nano1?

A. `Find-ServerPackage`

B. `Get-Package`

C. `Find-Package`

D. `Get-WindowsOptionalFeature`

8. You are working on a Windows Server 2022 Datacenter Server system. You need to view which roles and services are installed on the machine. Which PowerShell cmdlet can you use to see this?

A. `Get-event`

B. `New-event`

C. `Trace-command`

D. `Get-WindowsFeature`

9. What command would be used to register an iSCSI initiator manually to an iSNS server?

A. `iscsicli refreshisnsserver server_name`

B. `iscsicli listisnsservers server_name`

C. `iscsicli removeisnsserver server_name`

D. `iscsicli addisnsserver server_name`

10. You are an administrator who has set up two Hyper-V servers named Server1 (Windows Server 2022) and Server2 (Windows Server 2012 R2). Each Hyper-V server has multiple network cards. Each network card is connected to a different TCP/IP subnet. Server1 contains a dedicated migration network. Server2 contains a virtual machine named VM1. You plan to perform a live migration of VM1 to Server1. You need to ensure that Server1 uses all of the available networks to perform the live migration of VM1. What should you run to complete this task?

A. `Mount-VHD` cmdlet

B. `Diskpart` command

C. `Set-VHD` cmdlet

D. `Set-VMHost` cmdlet

11. Your company has decided to implement a Windows 2022 server. The company IT manager before you always used FAT32 as the system partition. Your company wants to know whether it should move to NTFS. Which of the following are some advantages of NTFS? (Choose all that apply.)

    A. Security

    B. Quotas

    C. Compression

    D. Encryption

12. You are the administrator of your network, which consists of two Windows Server 2022 systems. One of the servers is a domain controller, and the other server is a file server for data storage. The hard drive of the file server is starting to fill up. You do not have the ability to install another hard drive, so you decide to limit the amount of space everyone gets on the hard drive. What do you need to implement to solve your problem?

    A. Disk spacing

    B. Disk quotas

    C. Disk hardening

    D. Disk limitations

13. A system administrator is trying to determine which filesystem to use for a server that will become a Windows Server 2022 file server and domain controller. The company has the following requirements:

    ▪ The filesystem must allow for file-level security from within Windows 2022 Server.

    ▪ The filesystem must make efficient use of space on large partitions.

    ▪ The domain controller SYSVOL must be stored on the partition.

    Which of the following filesystems meets these requirements?

    A. FAT

    B. FAT32

    C. HPFS

    D. NTFS

14. You are an IT administrator who manages an environment that runs multiple Windows Server 2022 servers from multiple site locations across the United States. Your Windows Server 2022 machines use iSCSI storage. Other administrators report it is difficult to locate available iSCSI resources on the network. You need to make sure other administrators can easily access iSCSI resources using a centralized repository. What feature should you deploy?

    A. The iSCSI Target Storage Provider feature

    B. The Windows Standards-Based Storage Management feature

    C. The iSCSI Target Server role feature

    D. The iSNS Server service feature

15. You are the IT manager for your company. You have been asked to give the Admin group the rights to read, change, and assign permissions to documents in the StormWind Documents folder. The following table shows the current permissions on the StormWind Documents shared folder:

Group/User	NTFS	Shared
Sales	Read	Change
Marketing	Modify	Change
R&D	Deny	Full Control
Finance	Read	Read
Admin	Change	Change

What do you need to do to give the Admin group the rights to do their job? (Choose all that apply.)

A. Give Sales Full Control to shared permissions.

B. Give Full Control to NTFS security.

C. Give Admin Full Control to shared permissions.

D. Give Finance Modify to NTFS security.

E. Give Admin Full Control to NTFS security.

16. Will, the IT manager for your company, has been asked to give Moe the rights to read and change documents in the StormWind Documents folder. The following table shows the current permissions on the shared folder:

Group/User	NTFS	Shared
Sales	Read	Change
Marketing	Modify	Change
R&D	Deny	Full Control
Finance	Read	Read
Tylor	Read	Change

Moe is a member of the Sales and Finance groups. When Moe accesses the StormWind Documents folder, he can read all the files, but the system won't let him change or delete files. What does Will need to do to give Moe the minimum amount of rights to do his job?

A. Give Sales Full Control to shared permissions.

B. Give Moe Full Control to NTFS security.

C. Give Finance Change to shared permissions.

D. Give Finance Modify to NTFS security.

E. Give Moe Modify to NTFS security.

17. For security reasons, you have decided that you must convert the system partition on your removable drive from the FAT32 filesystem to NTFS. Which of the following steps must you take in order to convert the filesystem? (Choose two.)

    A. Run the command `CONVERT /FS:NTFS` from the command prompt.

    B. Rerun Windows Server 2022 Setup, and choose to convert the partition to NTFS during the reinstallation.

    C. Boot Windows Server 2022 Setup from the installation CD-ROM, and choose Rebuild File System.

    D. Reboot the computer.

18. You are the administrator of your network, which consists of two Windows Server 2022 systems. One of the servers is a domain controller, and the other server is a file server for data storage. The hard drive of the file server is starting to fill up. You do not have the ability to install another hard drive, so you decide to shrink the data on the file server. What do you need to implement to solve your problem?

    A. Disk spacing

    B. Disk compression

    C. Disk hardening

    D. Disk limitations

19. You are the administrator of a large organization. Four weeks ago you have built a new Windows Server 2022 Datacenter Server. You can't remember all of the roles and features that you previously installed. You need to view which roles and features are installed on the machine. Which PowerShell cmdlet can you use to see this?

    A. `Get-event`

    B. `New-event`

    C. `Trace-command`

    D. `Get-WindowsFeature`

20. What is the default TCP port for RDP?

    A. 3260

    B. 1433

    C. 21

    D. 3389

Chapter

12

Building an Azure Infrastructure

THE FOLLOWING AZ-800 EXAM OBJECTIVES ARE COVERED IN THIS CHAPTER:

✓ **Create and manage containers**

- ▪ Create Windows Server container images
- ▪ Manage Windows Server container images
- ▪ Configure Container networking
- ▪ Manage container instances

✓ **Manage Azure Virtual Machines that run Windows Server**

- ▪ Manage data disks
- ▪ Resize Azure Virtual Machines
- ▪ Configure continuous delivery for Azure Virtual Machines
- ▪ Configure connections to VMs
- ▪ Manage Azure Virtual Machines network configuration

✓ **Implement on-premises and hybrid network connectivity**

- ▪ Implement and manage the Remote Access role
- ▪ Implement and manage Azure Network Adapter
- ▪ Implement and manage Azure Extended Network
- ▪ Implement and manage Network Policy Server role
- ▪ Implement Web Application Proxy
- ▪ Implement Azure Relay
- ▪ Implement Azure Virtual WAN
- ▪ Implement Azure AD Application Proxy

✓ **Manage Windows Servers and workloads by using Azure services**

- ▪ Manage Windows Servers by using Azure Arc
- ▪ Assign Azure Policy Guest Configuration
- ▪ Deploy Azure services using Azure VM extensions on non-Azure machines

As I said in the introduction of Chapter 2, "Understanding Hyper-V," one of the greatest advancements in servers over the last decade has been the ability to have one physical server but run multiple servers on top of that one physical box. This is known as *virtualization*.

In this chapter, I will talk about building an Azure infrastructure. We'll start by talking about a smaller type of virtual environment called a *container*. I will then talk about using the various Azure components that allow you to build and secure your Azure infrastructure.

Azure allows an organization of any size to act and compete with other organizations of any size. A small company can choose an Azure subscription and create and build an infrastructure of any size.

For large organizations, an administrator can consolidate multiple physical servers onto an Azure tenant. This can save the organization time and money by using fewer physical boxes onsite but still having all the virtual servers needed to run their entire business.

In this chapter, you will also get a solid understanding of what is important in building an Azure infrastructure, and the different components and virtual machines that can be added directly to your Azure tenant.

Introduction to Containers

Windows containers are independent and isolated environments that run an operating system. These isolated environments allow you to place an application into its own container, thus not affecting any other applications or containers.

Think of containers as virtual environments that are used to run independent applications. They load much faster than virtual machines, and you can run as many containers as needed for all of the applications that you run.

One of the nice advantages of using Windows containers is that the containers can be managed the same way you manage an operating system. A container works the same way as a newly installed physical or virtual machine. So, once you know how to configure these containers, management is much easier than configuring a physical machine.

There are two different types of Windows containers:

Windows Server Containers This container allows you to isolate applications so they can run in their own space and not affect other applications. The question that you may be asking is, why not use a virtual machine? Well, the advantage of Windows Server containers is that they are already prebuilt and you don't need all the other services that a virtual machine would need to run. So Windows containers are smaller, faster, and more efficient when isolating applications. In a Windows Server container, the kernel is shared between all the different Windows containers.

Hyper-V Containers Hyper-V containers and Windows containers work the same way. The difference between the two is that Hyper-V containers run within a virtual machine and the Windows containers don't need to run in a Hyper-V environment. In a Hyper-V container, the container host's kernel is not shared between the other Hyper-V containers.

Container Terminology

As with any new technology, it is important to understand the terminology that goes along with that new technology. The first thing that you may have noticed is that a container works a lot like a virtual machine. Just like a virtual machine, the container has a running operating system within the container.

The container, which has a filesystem, can also be accessed through the network the same way you access a virtual machine. The advantage is that a container is a more efficient operating system. But to truly understand how containers work, you need to understand all of the components that allow containers to function properly:

Container Host This component can be on a physical or virtual machine, and it's the component that is configured with the Windows container feature. So the Windows container sits on top of the container host.

Container OS Image This component provides the operating system to the container. Containers are made up of multiple images that are stacked on top of each other.

Container Image This is the component that contains all the layers of the container. So the container image contains the operating system, the application, and all the services required to make that application function properly.

Container Registry This component is the heart and brain of the container. The container images are kept within the container's registry. The advantage of doing containers this way is that you can download other registries to automatically add other applications or services quickly.

Docker Daemon This is the component that runs the Docker application. The Docker daemon is automatically installed after you complete the installation of the Docker application.

Dockerfile This component is used to create the container images. The advantage of using the Dockerfile is that you can automate how containers are created. Dockerfiles are batches of instructions (within a text file) and commands that are called on when an image is assembled.

Docker Hub Repositories   This component is a location where all of your images are stored. By having a central location for stored images, the images can be used among coworkers and customers, or for the entire IT community. There are Docker hub repositories on the Internet where you can grab and use images for your organization.

Install and Configure Server Containers

So now that we have talked about the different components of a container, it's time to look at installing containers on your Windows Server 2022 system. When it comes to Microsoft, it doesn't matter if we are installing containers on a GUI-based system or non-GUI-based system. We are going to install the components needed by using Windows PowerShell.

But before we can look at installing and using containers, I need to show you what is required on the Windows Server 2022 system. So, the first step in using containers is looking at what we need on our network and computers for containers to run properly.

Requirements

Now that you have decided to work with containers, you must make sure that your network meets the minimum requirements to install and work with Windows containers:

- The Windows container feature is available on Windows Server 2022, Windows Server (Semi-Annual Channel), Windows Server 2019, Windows Server 2016, and Windows 10 Professional and Enterprise Editions (version 1607 and later).

- The Hyper-V role must be installed before running Hyper-V isolation.

- Windows Server Container hosts must have Windows installed to C:. This restriction does not apply if only Hyper-V isolated containers will be deployed.

Here are the requirements if you are going to be running virtualization with containers:

- For systems running the Hyper-V containers, the Hyper-V role must be installed on the system.

- If you are going to run a Windows container host from a Hyper-V virtual machine (and also hosting Hyper-V containers), you will need to enable nested virtualization. Nested virtualization also has some requirements:

- Operating system that allows nested virtualization (Windows Server 2022).

- Minimum of 4 GB of RAM available to the virtualized Hyper-V host.

- The processor needs to use Intel VT-x (this is only available for Intel processors).

- Two virtual processors for the container host VM.

Supported Images for Windows Containers

When I talk about setting up containers and you are getting ready to start using containers, there is one major requirement that we need to consider. The operating system on the host machine must be the same operating system that is used in the Windows container. If you install a different operating system in the Windows container, the container may load but you will most likely start to see errors, and there is no guarantee that you'll be able to use all the container's functionalities.

So, it is very important to make sure that the version of Windows Server 2022 that you install onto the host system is the same version that you run in the Windows container. One nice advantage to using Windows is that you can check what version of Windows you are using. To do so, enter the system's Registry (Regedit.exe) and search for the following Registry key (see Figure 12.1):

HKEY_LOCAL_MACHINE\Software\Microsoft\Windows NT\CurrentVersion.

FIGURE 12.1   Regedit version

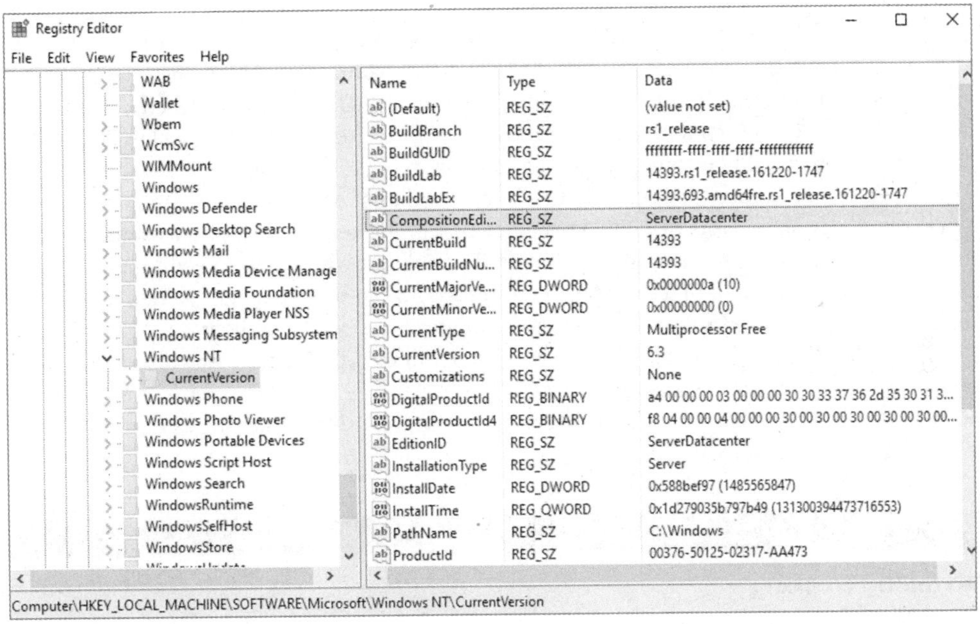

The host operating system that you are going to run will determine what operating systems you can run in the Windows Server container or Hyper-V container. Not all operating systems are available depending on the host OS image. Table 12.1 shows you all of the supported configurations for each host operating system.

TABLE 12.1 Supported base images

Host operating system	Windows Server container	Hyper-V container
Windows Server 2022 with Desktop	Server Core/Nano Server	Server Core/Nano Server
Windows Server 2022 Core	Server Core/Nano Server	Server Core/Nano Server
Nano Server	Nano Server	Server Core/Nano Server
Windows 10/11 (Pro/Enterprise)	Not Available	Server Core/Nano Server

Installing Docker

So the first step in setting up our Windows containers is to install Docker. Docker is the software package that allows you to create and manipulate containers and images.

Docker is the software package that you install and the Docker daemon is the application that you use to do your configuration and management. After you install Docker, the Docker daemon is automatically installed and configured with default settings.

Docker is a third-party application that Microsoft has started using for containers. The Docker application consists of a Docker engine and a Docker client (Docker daemon). So the first thing that we need to do is install Docker. To begin, download and install the Docker application. Another item that needs to be completed when installing and using Docker is making sure that all of the current Microsoft updates have been installed.

In Exercise 12.1, you'll learn how to download and install Docker. I will also show you how to get your Windows updates. The steps in this exercise install Docker to a Windows Server 2022 (with GUI) Datacenter operating system, but this installation can be done on a Nano Server or a server with no GUI.

EXERCISE 12.1

Installing Docker

1. Open an elevated command prompt by clicking the Start button and right-clicking on Windows PowerShell ➤ More ➤ Run As Administrator.

2. At the PowerShell prompt, type **Sconfig**. This will bring up the Server Configuration menu (see Figure 12.2). Choose option 6 by entering 6 and pressing the Enter key to update Windows Server 2022.

FIGURE 12.2 Server Configuration screen

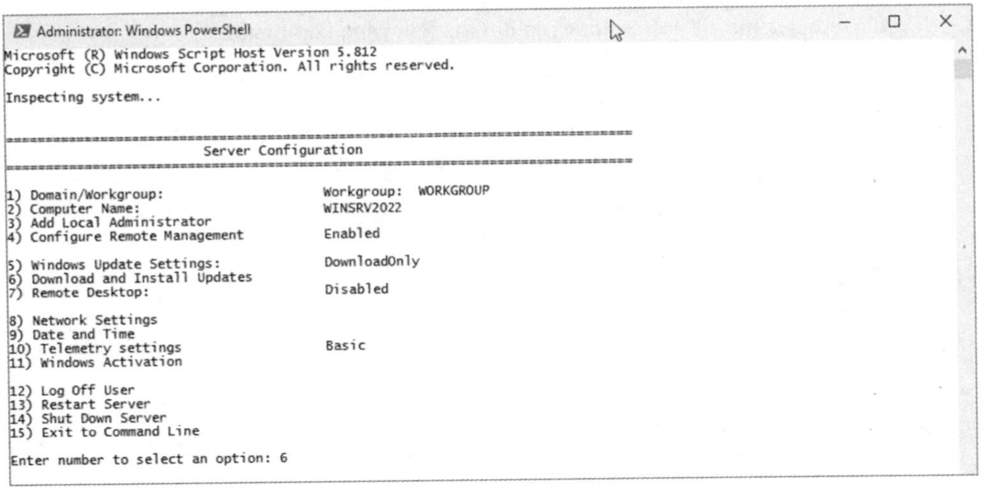

```
Administrator: Windows PowerShell                                    —   □   ×
Microsoft (R) Windows Script Host Version 5.812
Copyright (C) Microsoft Corporation. All rights reserved.

Inspecting system...


===================================================================
                        Server Configuration
===================================================================

1) Domain/Workgroup:               Workgroup:  WORKGROUP
2) Computer Name:                   WINSRV2022
3) Add Local Administrator
4) Configure Remote Management      Enabled

5) Windows Update Settings:         DownloadOnly
6) Download and Install Updates
7) Remote Desktop:                  Disabled

8) Network Settings
9) Date and Time
10) Telemetry settings              Basic
11) Windows Activation

12) Log Off User
13) Restart Server
14) Shut Down Server
15) Exit to Command Line

Enter number to select an option: 6
```

3. A screen should appear asking if you want to install All Updates or Recommended Updates only. Choose A for All Updates and press Enter. If there are any updates available, click A for installing all updates and press Enter. The updates will be downloaded and installed.

4. If there were no updates, go to step 6. After all updates have been installed, choose option 13 to restart the server. You'll see a message asking if you are sure you want to reboot. Click Yes.

5. Log in and restart PowerShell with administrative rights.

6. At the PowerShell prompt, type the following command and press Enter to download the Docker software:

   ```
   Install-Module -Name DockerMsftProvider -Repository PSGallery -Force
   ```

7. If you get a message that the NuGet provider needs to be installed (see Figure 12.3), choose Y and press Enter. If this message doesn't appear, go to step 9.

FIGURE 12.3 Install NuGet

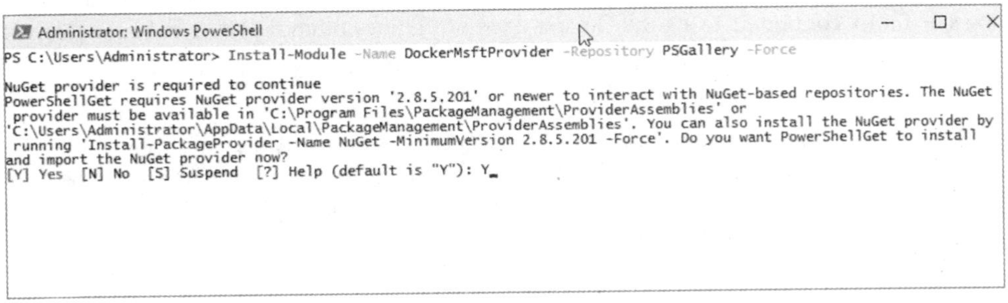

```
Administrator: Windows PowerShell                                    —   □   ×
PS C:\Users\Administrator> Install-Module -Name DockerMsftProvider -Repository PSGallery -Force

NuGet provider is required to continue
PowerShellGet requires NuGet provider version '2.8.5.201' or newer to interact with NuGet-based repositories. The NuGet
provider must be available in 'C:\Program Files\PackageManagement\ProviderAssemblies' or
'C:\Users\Administrator\AppData\Local\PackageManagement\ProviderAssemblies'. You can also install the NuGet provider by
running 'Install-PackageProvider -Name NuGet -MinimumVersion 2.8.5.201 -Force'. Do you want PowerShellGet to install
and import the NuGet provider now?
[Y] Yes  [N] No  [S] Suspend  [?] Help (default is "Y"): Y_
```

8. If you needed to install NuGet, then reenter the following command:

```
Install-Module -Name DockerMsftProvider -Repository PSGallery -Force
```

9. Now that we have downloaded Docker, it's time to install it. At the PowerShell prompt, type the following command (see Figure 12.4) and press Enter.

```
Install-Package -Name docker -ProviderName DockerMsftProvider
```

FIGURE 12.4 Install Docker

```
Administrator: Windows PowerShell                                    —  □  ×
PS C:\Users\Administrator> Install-Module -Name DockerMsftProvider -Repository PSGallery -Force

NuGet provider is required to continue
PowerShellGet requires NuGet provider version '2.8.5.201' or newer to interact with NuGet-based repositories. The NuGet
provider must be available in 'C:\Program Files\PackageManagement\ProviderAssemblies' or
'C:\Users\Administrator\AppData\Local\PackageManagement\ProviderAssemblies'. You can also install the NuGet provider by
running 'Install-PackageProvider -Name NuGet -MinimumVersion 2.8.5.201 -Force'. Do you want PowerShellGet to install
and import the NuGet provider now?
[Y] Yes  [N] No  [S] Suspend  [?] Help (default is "Y"): Y
PS C:\Users\Administrator> Install-Module -Name DockerMsftProvider -Repository PSGallery -Force
PS C:\Users\Administrator> Install-Package -Name docker -ProviderName DockerMsftProvider_
```

10. A message will appear stating that the package is not trusted and asking if you want to install software from DockerDefault. Click Y and press Enter.

11. Now that Docker is installed, let's check for updates again and then reboot. Type **Sconfig** and choose option 6. Click A for All Updates. If there are any updates, click A for installing All Updates.

12. After the updates complete, you will return to the Server Configuration screen. Choose option 13. Click Yes to reboot.

13. Log into the server.

Docker is now downloaded and installed onto the Windows Server 2022 machine. The next step is to work with Docker to install and configure containers.

When using Docker, there are some switches that you can use. Table 12.2 shows some of the Docker switches and what each switch does. You'll use these commands to manage Windows or Linux containers using the Docker daemon. These commands can be run in PowerShell or at an elevated command prompt.

Table 12.2 is just a partial list of Docker commands. To see a more complete list, go to Microsoft's website at https://docs.docker.com/engine/reference/run. In the left-hand window, the entire list is under Engine (Docker) CLI.

TABLE 12.2   Docker PowerShell and command-line commands

Command	Description
docker attach	This command allows you to attach to a running container.
docker build	Using this command allows you to build an image from a Docker file.
docker checkpoint	You can use this command to manage a Docker checkpoint.
docker commit	This command allows you to debug and build a new image.
docker container	This command allows you to manage containers.
docker cp	Using this command allows you to copy files and folders between the container and the local computer system.
docker create	This command gives you the ability to create a new container.
docker deploy	You can use this command to create and modify a stack.
docker diff	This command allows you to view changes to files or directories in the container's filesystem.
docker events	This command allows you to see a server's events in real time.
docker exec	You can use this command to run a new command in an existing container.
docker image	This command (along with its options) allows you to manage your images.
docker info	Using this command allows you to view system information of the Docker installation.
docker kill	This command allows you to terminate running containers.
docker login	You can use this command to log into the Docker registry of a server.
docker pause	This command allows you to pause all processes within a container.
docker port	Use this command to view the port mappings for a container.
docker ps	This command allows you to view all the containers.
docker pull	You can use this command to pull an image from a registry.

TABLE 12.2 Docker PowerShell and command-line commands *(Continued)*

Command	Description
docker push	This command allows you to push an image to a registry.
docker rename	This command allows you to rename a container.
docker restart	Using this command allows you to restart a container.
docker rm	You can use this command to remove a container.
docker run	Using this command (along with the options), you can add to or override the image settings set by a developer.
docker save	This command allows you to save images to an archive.
docker search	This command allows you to search the Docker Hub for images.
docker start	This command allows you to start a stopped container.
docker stop	This command allows you to stop a running container.
docker update	You can use this command to update the configuration of a container.
docker version	This command allows you to view the Docker version information.

After Docker is installed, you may want to configure the Docker daemon to specify how Docker will start and stop after a system restart or when the system needs to reboot. If you want to set a restart policy, use the -restart flag with the Docker run command.

Table 12.3 shows you all the various restart policies that you can set on a container.

TABLE 12.3 Docker restart policies

Policy	Result
no	This setting will not automatically restart the container. This is the default setting for a container.
on-failure [:max-retries]	This setting will restart the container only if the container has a non-zero exit status. Also, you have the ability to limit the number of restart retries that the Docker daemon will attempt.
always	This setting will always restart the container. When the setting is set to always, Docker will try to restart the container indefinitely. The container will also always start on daemon startup.
unless-stopped	This setting will always restart the container unless the container was stopped before the restart.

Install and Configure Windows Containers

So now that you have installed Docker on your Windows Server 2022 system, let's take a look at how to install and configure containers.

In Exercise 12.2, you'll learn how to make sure your Docker service is started. I will then show you how to install a base operating system image onto your host and how to create Windows Server containers.

There are dozens of premade Docker images. You can look at all of the various Docker components at the Docker Store. Go to https://store.docker.com to see all the available Docker downloads (including premade images).

EXERCISE 12.2

Installing a Base Operating System

1. Open the Services MMC by clicking Start ➤ Windows Administrative Tools ➤ Services.

2. Scroll down until you see Docker. Make sure that the Docker Service has started (see Figure 12.5). If it hasn't started, right-click Docker and choose Start.

FIGURE 12.5   Checking that Docker Service has started

Name	Description	Status	Startup Type	Log On As
Device Install Service	Enables a c...		Manual (Trig...	Local Syste...
Device Management Enroll...	Performs D...		Manual	Local Syste...
Device Setup Manager	Enables the ...		Manual (Trig...	Local Syste...
DevQuery Background Disc...	Enables app...		Manual (Trig...	Local Syste...
DHCP Client	Registers an...	Running	Automatic	Local Service
Diagnostic Policy Service	The Diagno...	Running	Automatic (D...	Local Service
Diagnostic Service Host	The Diagno...		Manual	Local Service
Diagnostic System Host	The Diagno...		Manual	Local Syste...
Distributed Link Tracking Cl...	Maintains li...	Running	Automatic	Local Syste...
Distributed Transaction Coo...	Coordinates...	Running	Automatic (D...	Network S...
dmwappushsvc	WAP Push ...		Manual (Trig...	Local Syste...
DNS Client	The DNS Cli...	Running	Automatic (T...	Network S...
Docker		Running	Automatic	Local Syste...
Downloaded Maps Manager	Windows se...		Automatic (D...	Network S...
Embedded Mode	The Embed...		Manual (Trig...	Local Syste...
Encrypting File System (EFS)	Provides th...		Manual (Trig...	Local Syste...
Enterprise App Managemen...	Enables ent...		Manual	Local Syste...
Extensible Authentication P...	The Extensi...		Manual	Local Syste...
Function Discovery Provide...	The FDPHO...		Manual	Local Service
Function Discovery Resourc...	Publishes th...		Manual	Local Service
Geolocation Service	This service ...	Running	Manual (Trig...	Local Syste...
Group Policy Client	The service ...	Running	Automatic (T...	Local Syste...
Host Network Service	Provides su...	Running	Manual	Local Syste...

EXERCISE 12.2 *(continued)*

3. Close Services.

4. Open PowerShell with administrative privileges by clicking Start and right-clicking Windows PowerShell, then choosing More ⟡ Run As Administrator.

5. Now we are going to see if any containers are running. To do this, type **docker info** in PowerShell and press Enter. You will see a report (see Figure 12.6) that will show you if you have any containers running.

FIGURE 12.6 Docker Info

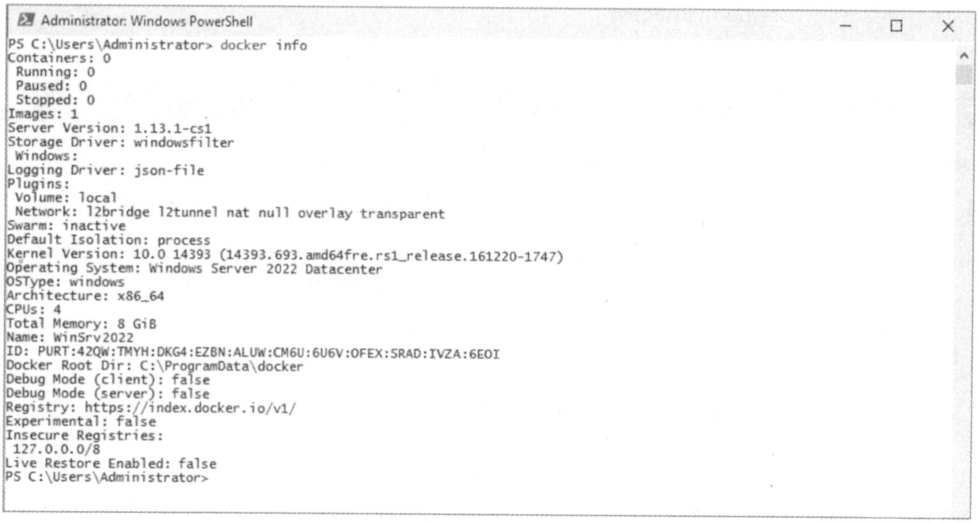

```
Administrator: Windows PowerShell                                      —   □   ×
PS C:\Users\Administrator> docker info
Containers: 0
 Running: 0
 Paused: 0
 Stopped: 0
Images: 1
Server Version: 1.13.1-cs1
Storage Driver: windowsfilter
 Windows:
Logging Driver: json-file
Plugins:
 Volume: local
 Network: l2bridge l2tunnel nat null overlay transparent
Swarm: inactive
Default Isolation: process
Kernel Version: 10.0 14393 (14393.693.amd64fre.rs1_release.161220-1747)
Operating System: Windows Server 2022 Datacenter
OSType: windows
Architecture: x86_64
CPUs: 4
Total Memory: 8 GiB
Name: WinSrv2022
ID: PURT:4ZQW:TMYH:DKG4:EZBN:ALUW:CM6U:6U6V:OFEX:SRAD:IVZA:6EOI
Docker Root Dir: C:\ProgramData\docker
Debug Mode (client): false
Debug Mode (server): false
Registry: https://index.docker.io/v1/
Experimental: false
Insecure Registries:
 127.0.0.0/8
Live Restore Enabled: false
PS C:\Users\Administrator>
```

6. So now we are going to install a container image for either Microsoft Nano Server or Windows Server Core from the online package repository. To begin, type one of the following commands into PowerShell (choose the command for the operating system that you want):

```
Docker pull microsoft/nanoserver
docker pull microsoft/windowsservercore
```

7. After your container is installed, restart the Docker service. Type the following command into PowerShell:

```
Restart-Service docker
```

8. Now let's take a look at your Docker information again by typing **docker info** at the PowerShell prompt. As you can see, we now have an image that we didn't have before (see Figure 12.7).

FIGURE 12.7   Checking Docker information

9. To see all the images that you have on your system, at the PowerShell prompt type **docker images** (see Figure 12.8).

FIGURE 12.8   Docker images

10. So now that you have seen how to grab a base image from docker, let's create a Windows Server container with Nano Server installed. At the PowerShell prompt, type the following command:

```
docker run microsoft/dotnet-samples:dotnetapp-nanoserver
```

11. If the installation worked properly, you should see what looks like to be a small alien on your screen (see Figure 12.9). Type **docker info** at the PowerShell prompt and you will see that you now have a container. You will also notice that you have two images now: the one you downloaded earlier and the one you just downloaded.

FIGURE 12.9   Container created

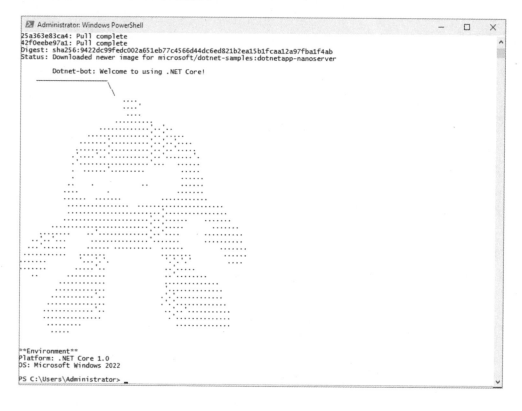

12. Close PowerShell.

Now that you've seen how to download an image to the systems repository, let's turn an image into a container. To do so, you need to just use the **docker run** command to get the image into a container. Also there may be a time when you need to remove an image from a container. You can do so using the **docker rm** command.

But first you need to know which image you want to put into a container. Exercise 12.3 will show you how to see your images and then how to add an image to a container. To complete Exercise 12.3, you must have completed Exercise 12.2.

EXERCISE 12.3

Adding an Image to a Container

1. Open a PowerShell window with administrative rights.

2. Type **docker info** at the PowerShell prompt. You should only have one container at this time.

3. Next we need see what images are in our repository. To do this, type **docker images** in the PowerShell window. This will show you your Docker images (see Figure 12.10).

FIGURE 12.10 Docker images

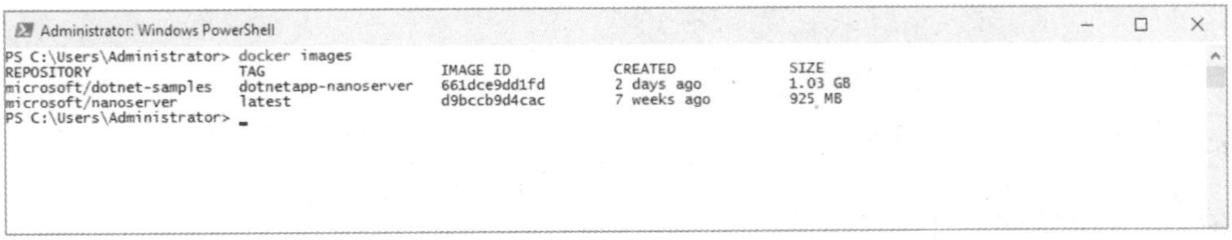

```
Administrator: Windows PowerShell                                              —  □  ×
PS C:\Users\Administrator> docker images
REPOSITORY                 TAG                    IMAGE ID        CREATED         SIZE
microsoft/dotnet-samples   dotnetapp-nanoserver   661dce9dd1fd    2 days ago      1.03 GB
microsoft/nanoserver       latest                 d9bccb9d4cac    7 weeks ago     925 MB
PS C:\Users\Administrator> _
```

4. We need the Image ID from the Nano Server or Server Core that we downloaded in Exercise 12.2. The Image ID for my Nano Server is d9bccb9d4cac. We will use this ID to turn the image into a container. Type the following at a PowerShell prompt (your Image ID will be different) and press Enter (see Figure 12.11):

   docker run d9bccb9d4cac

FIGURE 12.11 Docker run command

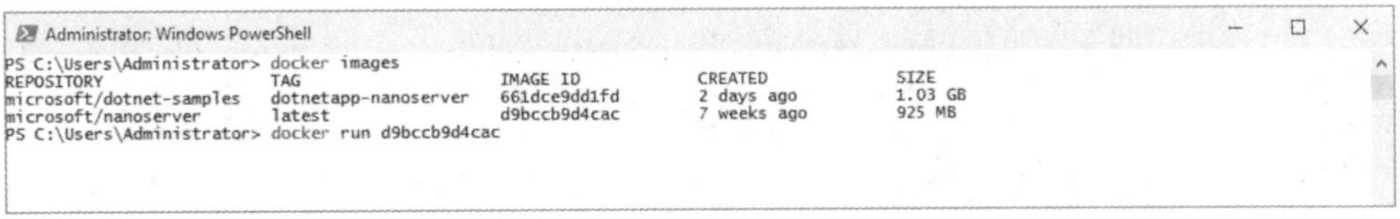

```
Administrator: Windows PowerShell                                              —  □  ×
PS C:\Users\Administrator> docker images
REPOSITORY                 TAG                    IMAGE ID        CREATED         SIZE
microsoft/dotnet-samples   dotnetapp-nanoserver   661dce9dd1fd    2 days ago      1.03 GB
microsoft/nanoserver       latest                 d9bccb9d4cac    7 weeks ago     925 MB
PS C:\Users\Administrator> docker run d9bccb9d4cac
```

5. Type **docker info** at the PowerShell prompt. You should now have two containers instead of just one (see Figure 12.12).

FIGURE 12.12 docker info command

6. Close PowerShell.

Tagging an Image

You can change the tags associated with the images. Many administrators use tag names as version names so that they can keep track of the various images on their machine.

Having tags that you create allows you to easily access the images later by their tag names. To tag an image, you use the **-t** parameter. So to tag an image as WillPanekImage, you'd use the following:

```
docker build -t WillPanekImage
```

Uninstall an Operating System Image

One of the maintenance issues that many IT administrators must deal with is hard drive space. As you are downloading and using images, there may be a time when you need to remove images from your server that are no longer being used.

If you continue to download and use multiple images files, make sure that every once in a while you look at all of your images and delete any that are no longer valid or no longer in use.

Exercise 12.4 will show you how to remove an image file from your host system. To complete this exercise, make sure that you have completed the earlier exercises in this chapter.

EXERCISE 12.4

Uninstalling an Image

1. Open a PowerShell window with administrative rights.

2. Type **docker images** and get the ID number of the Nano Server image.

3. Type **docker rm *d9bccb9d4cac*** (replace *d9bccb9d4cac* with your ID number).

4. Type **docker images**. The image is now gone.

5. Close PowerShell.

Creating New Images Using Dockerfiles

One nice advantage of using Docker is that you can go to Docker's website and look at the different images that are available. There are images for operating systems, applications, and software.

But what if you can't find an image that you need? Well, then you can build your own images using Dockerfiles. When you install Docker, the Docker engine includes tools that the IT department can use to create Dockerfiles. Dockerfiles are just text files that are manually created, and they are compiled and turned into an image file.

If your organization decides that they want to build their own Dockerfiles, then they will get some benefits while doing just that. Some of the advantages of building your own Dockerfiles are as follows:

- You can store images as code.

- You can re-create images rapidly that can then be used for maintenance and upgrade cycles.

- You can customize your Dockerfiles to reflect your organization's needs.

The Docker installation includes components that you can use to create your own Dockerfiles. These two Docker components are the Docker engine and the compiler (docker build command).

If you have ever built INI files or even a host file, then you understand how building a file can work. As with many programming codes or INI files, you can use the pound sign (#) to show comments in the file. This is very useful.

Many years ago, before I got into networking, I was a programmer. One thing that most programmers hate is when you look at someone else's coding and you have no idea what they were doing. When a coder takes the time to put in comments so that anyone can follow them and work on the code, it makes following that coder a thousand times easier. This is what the comments in the Dockerfile do. Use the pound sign (#) for making comments and state exactly why each line is included so that someone following you understands what the code is doing, or if someone is trying to learn what you do.

Let's take a look at an example of a Dockerfile:

```
# Sample Dockerfile for WillPanek
# We will be using Windows Server Core as our base image.
FROM microsoft/windowsservercore
# Uses dism.exe to install the DNS role.
RUN dism.exe /online /enable-feature /all /featurename: : DNS-Server-Full-
Role /NoRestart
# Sets a command or process that will run each time a container is run from
the new image.
CMD [ "cmd" ]
```

Let's break down some of the different sections that you can configure. Table 12.4 shows some of the configuration settings that you can use.

TABLE 12.4 Dockerfile commands

Command	Description
Add	This setting will copy new files, directories or remote file URLs from a source (<src>) location to the filesystem of the image destination <dest>.
CMD	This setting specifies the default commands that will be executed when deploying the container image.
Copy	This setting will copy new files or directories from a source (<src>) location to the filesystem of the image destination <dest>.
Escape	This setting is used to escape characters in a line and to escape a newline. Normally the Escape command is followed by the character that will represent a new line. For example: escape=\. This means that when a \ (backslash) is in the file, it will represent a new line.
ENV	This setting allows you to add an environmental variable.
Expose	This setting tells Docker that the container is listening on the specified network ports during runtime.
From	This setting shows the location of the container image that will be used during the image creation process.
Label	This setting adds metadata to an image.
Onbuild	This setting allows you to set a trigger that gets executed when the image is used as the base for another build.

Command	Description
Run	This setting specifies what commands are to be run in the Dockerfile process. These commands can include software installation and file, directory, and environment creation.
User	This setting allows you to set up a user's account that will be used during the runtime.
Volume	This setting allows you to create a mount point and externally mounted volumes from host systems or other containers.
Workdir	This setting allows you to set the working directory that will be used during the runtime.

Understanding Hyper-V Containers

So far in this chapter we have discussed Windows containers, but now we are going to look at Hyper-V containers. As I stated earlier, Windows containers share the system's kernel between all containers and the host. Hyper-V containers are different because each Hyper-V container uses its own instance of the Windows kernel. Since Hyper-V containers use their own instance of the Windows kernel, you can use different versions of Windows between the host system and the image version.

Also, the Windows host system needs to have the Microsoft Hyper-V role installed. Windows Server 2022 and Windows 10/11 Professional and Enterprise (Anniversary Editions) both allow you to create containers in Hyper-V.

The one nice feature is that both container types, Windows containers and Hyper-V containers, are created, managed, and function the exact same way. The only difference is that the Hyper-V containers have better isolation from the kernel.

When you are working with Hyper-V containers in Docker, the settings are identical to managing Windows Server containers. The one difference that you want to include in the Hyper-V container is using the --isolation=hyperv parameter. The following is an example of the docker command with the Hyper-V parameters:

```
docker run -it --isolation=hyperv microsoft/nanoserver cmd
```

Managing Container Networking

A feature included with building containers is the ability to access the servers and data within the container the same way you would on a normal network server or Hyper-V server. Once you have installed Docker, there will be two networks that are created automatically. You can see these networks by typing **docker network ls** in PowerShell (see Figure 12.13) or at an elevated command prompt.

FIGURE 12.13 Docker network

```
Administrator: Windows PowerShell                                          —  □  ×
Windows PowerShell
PS C:\Users\Administrator> docker network ls
NETWORK ID        NAME              DRIVER        SCOPE
3cb894810795      nat               nat           local
2fdbb2f60f2b      none              null          local
PS C:\Users\Administrator>
```

If you would like to get even more details about a specific network (see Figure 12.14), after you run the `docker network ls` command, grab the Network ID number. Then type the following PowerShell command followed by the Network ID number (my Network ID is 3cb894810795):

```
Docker network inspect 3cb894810795
```

FIGURE 12.14 More Docker network details

```
PS C:\Users\Administrator> docker network ls
NETWORK ID        NAME              DRIVER            SCOPE
3cb894810795      nat               nat               local
2fdbb2f60f2b      none              null              local
PS C:\Users\Administrator> docker network inspect 3cb894810795
[
    {
        "Name": "nat",
        "Id": "3cb89481079578852381b299f54067313fdf3472909174193ca9e742f3fa6f9d",
        "Created": "2017-02-28T16:12:41.1703268-05:00",
        "Scope": "local",
        "Driver": "nat",
        "EnableIPv6": false,
        "IPAM": {
            "Driver": "windows",
            "Options": null,
            "Config": [
                {
                    "Subnet": "172.28.144.0/20",
                    "Gateway": "172.28.144.1"
                }
            ]
        },
        "Internal": false,
        "Attachable": false,
        "Containers": {},
        "Options": {
            "com.docker.network.windowsshim.hnsid": "2444fc7a-0048-4480-b769-11b2ee5242f9",
            "com.docker.network.windowsshim.networkname": "nat"
        },
        "Labels": {}
    }
]
PS C:\Users\Administrator>
```

One nice thing about working with networks within containers is that these two networks are always available to you even when you choose only one to be part of your container. You can specify which network you want your container to run on by using the **--Network** flag.

When you create a container, the host network adds the container onto the host's network stack. There are very few reasons you would even need to manage or manipulate the container's network. The only network that you may need to work with is the bridge network. The Docker default bridge is created as soon as you install the Docker engine. It creates your bridge network, and its name is `bridge`.

Using Docker Hub Repository

Another nice advantage of using containers is that there are hundreds of images that you can use. Docker has a public database of images that you can access. The Docker Hub repository has images for Microsoft, Unix, Linux, and hundreds more. If you want to see what a vendor has out on the repository, just type **docker search vendorname**. To see what Microsoft has for you in the repository, type **docker search Microsoft** (see Figure 12.15).

FIGURE 12.15   docker search Microsoft command

```
Administrator: Windows PowerShell                                                    —    □    ×
PS C:\Users\Administrator> docker search Microsoft
NAME                                    DESCRIPTION                                  STARS    OFFICIAL    AUTOMATED
microsoft/aspnet                        ASP.NET is an open source server-side Web ... 560                  [OK]
microsoft/dotnet                        Official images for .NET Core for Linux an... 452                  [OK]
mono                                    Mono is an open source implementation of M... 220      [OK]
microsoft/mssql-server-linux            Official images for Microsoft SQL Server o... 182
microsoft/nanoserver                    Windows Server 2016 Nano Server base OS im... 139
microsoft/windowsservercore             Windows Server 2016 Server Core base OS im... 132
microsoft/aspnetcore                    Official images for running compiled ASP.N... 101                  [OK]
microsoft/iis                           Internet Information Services (IIS) instal... 94
microsoft/azure-cli                     Docker image for Microsoft Azure Command L... 77                   [OK]
microsoft/mssql-server-windows-express  Official Microsoft SQL Server Express Edit... 55
microsoft/mssql-server-windows          Official images for Microsoft SQL Server f... 31
microsoft/aspnetcore-build              Official images for building ASP.NET Core ... 25                   [OK]
microsoft/powershell                    Official PowerShell Core releases from htt... 25                   [OK]
microsoft/oms                           Monitor your containers using the Operatio... 17                   [OK]
microsoft/vsts-agent                    Official images for the Visual Studio Team... 16
microsoft/dotnet-samples                .NET Core Docker Samples                      13                   [OK]
microsoft/powershell-nightly            Nightly builds of PowerShell Core for CI     6                    [OK]
microsoft/cntk                          CNTK images from github.com/Microsoft/CNTK... 6                    [OK]
microsoft/applicationinsights           Application Insights for Docker helps you ... 4                    [OK]
microsoft/dotnet-nightly                Preview bits of the .NET Core CLI            3                    [OK]
berlius/microsoft-malmo                 Microsoft-malmo - artificial intelligence    1
microsoft/aspnetcore-build-nightly      Images to build preview versions of ASP.NE... 1                    [OK]
renerchen/microsoft                                                                  0
dreher/microsoft                        Microsoft Test Repo                          0
cvugrinec/microsoft-prep70533                                                        0
PS C:\Users\Administrator>
```

You can set up a private repository so that coworkers can share and use the images that you create. After you create your images using the Docker daemon, you can push those images to your corporate Docker Hub repository. You can add users and accounts to the Docker Hub to verify that only your organization's users are accessing the images.

If you are building images and placing those images on GitHub or Bitbucket, you can use the automatic build repository that is included with the Docker Hub service.

When you are ready to start uploading corporate images to the Docker Hub, create a Docker Hub user account (`https://cloud.docker.com`). After you have created your account, click the Create menu and choose Create Repository.

You will then be asked to enter a Docker ID namespace for your organization. The repository name must be unique, and it can be up to 255 characters. The namespace will only allow letters, numbers, or the dash (-) and underscore (_). You are then asked to enter a short description (100 characters or less) and a dull description. Click Create and you are finished.

After your repository is created, you can push images to the repository by putting in the name of your image, your Docker Hub username, the repository name that you created earlier, and the image tag. The following is an example of the docker push command:

```
docker push <hub-user>/<repo-name>:<tag>
```

Using Microsoft Azure for Images

Azure containers allow you to easily create, configure, and manage your virtual machine containers. The Azure Container Service uses open source scheduling and management tools. By using open source tools, the Azure Container Service connects you with thousands of other users who are also designing, building, and maintaining container images.

Azure administrators have the ability to manage containers at scale with a managed Kubernetes container management and orchestration service that integrates with Azure Active Directory.

Azure includes the Azure Kubernetes Service (AKS). AKS allows you to quickly and easily start developing and deploying cloud-native apps in Azure, datacenters, or at the edge with built-in code-to-cloud pipelines and guardrails.

AKS gives you the ability to have a unified management and governance system for onsite, edge, and multicloud Kubernetes clusters. You can interoperate with Azure security, identity, cost management, and migration services.

The Azure Container Service uses the Docker format, but it is also compatible with Marathon, DC/OS, Kubernetes, or Docker Swarm. Because the Azure Container Service works with all of these different formats, you can work with thousands of applications and images. But since this is Microsoft Azure's platform, you get all of the security benefits and features that Azure has to offer.

To set up the Azure Container Service, you must first set up an Azure Container Service cluster through the Azure portal. Once you have entered the portal, use the Azure Resource Manager template for Docker Swarm, DC/OS, and Kubernetes, or use the Azure CLI.

Table 12.5 shows which Azure service you need depending on the container that you want to install. This table was taken directly from Microsoft's website. For more information, please visit https://azure.microsoft.com/en-us/products/category/containers.

TABLE 12.5   Azure service and container options

Goal	Azure Option to Use
Deploy and scale containers on managed Kubernetes	Azure Kubernetes Service (AKS)
Deploy and scale containers on managed Red Hat OpenShift	Azure Red Hat OpenShift
Build and deploy modern apps and microservices using serverless containers	Azure Container Apps
Execute event-driven, serverless code with an end-to-end development experience	Azure Functions
Run containerized web apps on Windows and Linux	Web App for Containers
Launch containers with hypervisor isolation	Azure Container Instances
Deploy and operate always-on, scalable, distributed apps	Azure Service Fabric
Build, store, secure, and replicate container images and artifacts	Azure Container Registry

Using PowerShell for Containers

Table 12.6 contains just some of the PowerShell commands available for using containers and Docker.

TABLE 12.6   PowerShell commands

PowerShell command	Description
Add-ContainerNetworkAdapter	This command allows you to add a virtual network adapter to a container.
Connect-ContainerNetworkAdapter	You can use this command to connect a virtual network adapter to a virtual switch.
Disconnect-ContainerNetworkAdapter	This command allows you to disconnect a virtual network adapter from a virtual switch.
Export-ContainerImage	You can use this command to export a container image to a file.

TABLE 12.6   PowerShell commands *(Continued)*

PowerShell command	Description
Get-Container	This command allows you to view information about containers.
Get-ContainerHost	This command allows you to view information about the host.
Get-ContainerImage	You can use this command to view local container images.
Get-ContainerNetworkAdapter	You can use this command to view the virtual network adapter of a container.
Import-ContainerImage	You can use this command to import a container image from a file.
Install-ContainerOSImage	This command allows you to install the operating system image to a base container.
Install-Module	You can use this command to download a module from an online gallery. This module can then be installed on the local computer.
Install-Package	You can use this command to install a software package on a computer.
Install-PackageProvider	This command allows you to install a Package Management package provider.
Move-ContainerImageRepository	You can use this command to move the local container image repository.
New-Container	This command allows you to create a container image from an existing container.
Remove-Container	You can use this command to delete a container.
Remove-ContainerImage	This command allows you to remove a container image.
Remove-ContainerNetworkAdapter	This command allows you to removes a virtual network adapter from a container.
Restart-Computer	You can use this command to restart a local and remote computer.

PowerShell command	Description
Set-ContainerNetworkAdapter	You can use this command to configure the features of the virtual network adapter within a container.
Start-Container	You can use this command to start a container.
Stop-Container	You can use this command to stop a container.
Test-ContainerImage	This command allows you to test for issues with a container image.
Uninstall-ContainerOSImage	You can use this command to uninstall the container operating system image.

Azure Virtual Machine Configuration

This section explains how to create and manage Azure virtual machines. Setting up an Azure virtual machine is much easier than setting up a server in Hyper-V. When you build a new virtual machine in Hyper-V, you create the virtual machine and then you install the guest operating system. So, if I wanted to create a new Windows Server 2022 VM, I would create the new virtual machine in Hyper-V. Once that is done, I would start the VM and install Windows Server 2022.

When you choose the guest operating system in Azure, the operating system is automatically created after you set your option—no need to install the actual server software. Azure builds the VM exactly as you want it built. You choose the disk size, management options, networking options, advanced options, and then choose to create the VM. Microsoft will give you all the information that you need so that you can remote into the VM. Once you are logged into the VM, you can then work on the server the same way you work on any other VM.

Creating a Virtual Machine in Azure

There's one very important thing to consider when building virtual machines or anything in Azure: Azure is a consumption-based model. This means the more you use, the more you pay. Be careful. As you are building the VM and see all the available options, be sure to choose only what you need.

When you're working in Azure, you're going to feel like a kid in a candy store. Everything they offer looks good and they always try to make you think that you need the extras. But for every extra option that you choose, your monthly charges increase.

Exercise 12.5 will walk you through the process of building a new VM in Azure. We will build a new VM with Windows Server 2022 Datacenter as the guest operating system. The creation process is simple, as Exercise 12.5 demonstrates. If there are any fields that you are not sure about setting, click the information icon (the small circle with an I in the center). This will explain what that option does for your setup.

EXERCISE 12.5

Creating an Azure Virtual Machine

1. Log into the Azure portal at `https://portal.azure.com`.

2. Choose Deploy A Virtual Machine, as shown in Figure 12.16.

FIGURE 12.16 Deploy a virtual machine

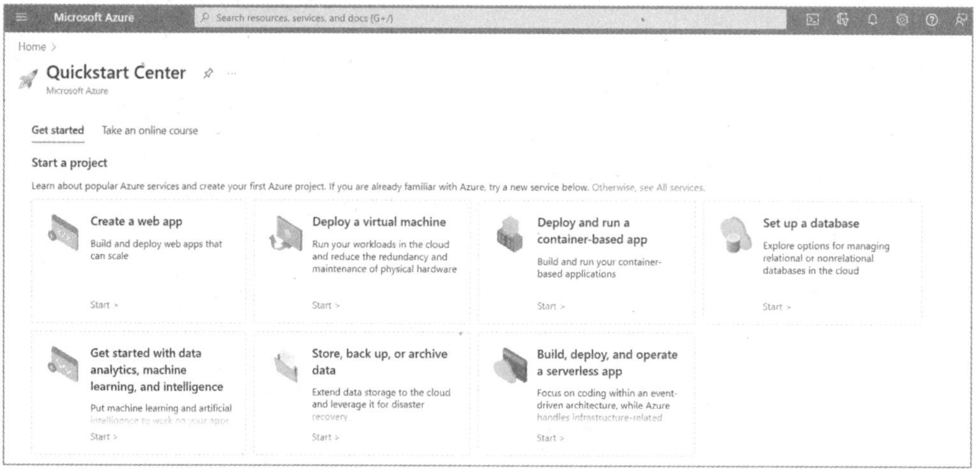

3. We are going to create a new Windows VM. Click the Create button under Create A Windows Virtual Machine (see Figure 12.17).

FIGURE 12.17   Create the Windows VM

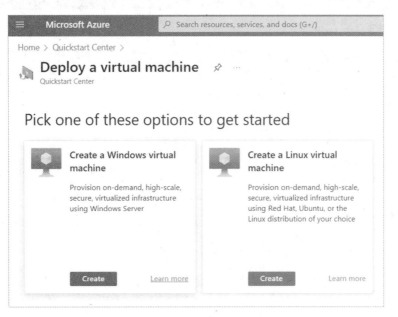

4. The Create A Virtual Machine screen opens. On this screen (see Figure 12.18), we can choose which subscription we will add to this VM. You also name your virtual machine (I used WinSrv2022 as my VM name), choose your region, image (the operating system you want to use), admin username and password, and other information. Fill in all the fields and the region. Once all the fields are completed, we can create the VM or we can choose the components for the VM (disks, network, etc.) that we want to set up. We are going to go through each screen, but I will leave the defaults for the rest of my options. Click the Next: Disks button.

EXERCISE 12.5 ***(continued)***

FIGURE 12.18 Create A Virtual Machine page

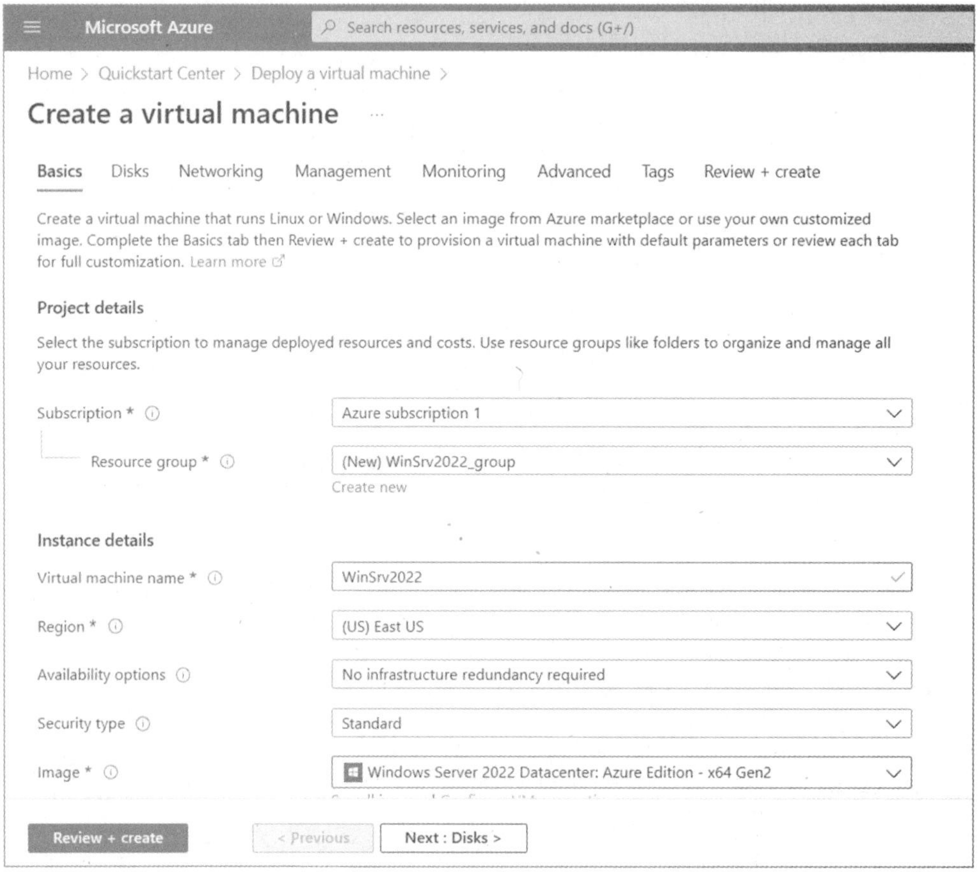

5. On the Disks page (shown in Figure 12.19), review the disk information. Make any changes for your VM. I am leaving the defaults. After you choose your disk options, click Next: Networking.

FIGURE 12.19   VM Disks page

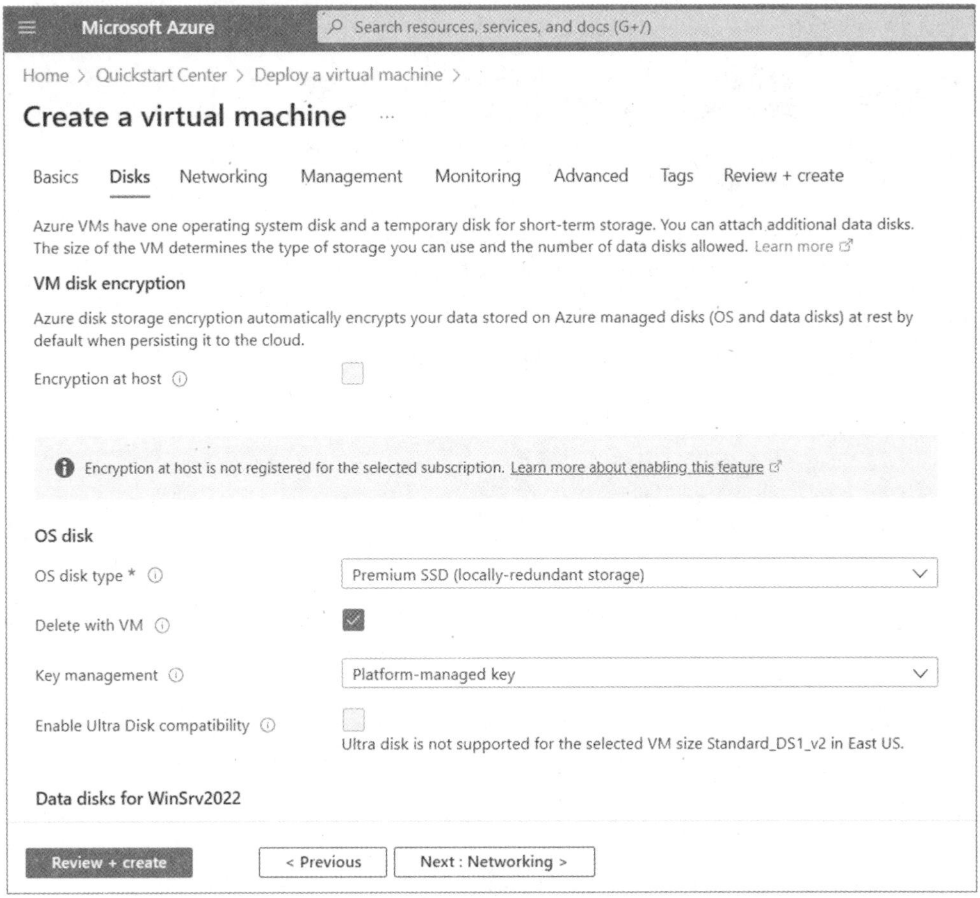

6. On the Networking page (see Figure 12.20), you can choose your virtual network, IP address, NIC security, and any ports that can connect to this VM. Once you have made your choices, click Next: Management.

EXERCISE 12.5 *(continued)*

FIGURE 12.20 Networking page

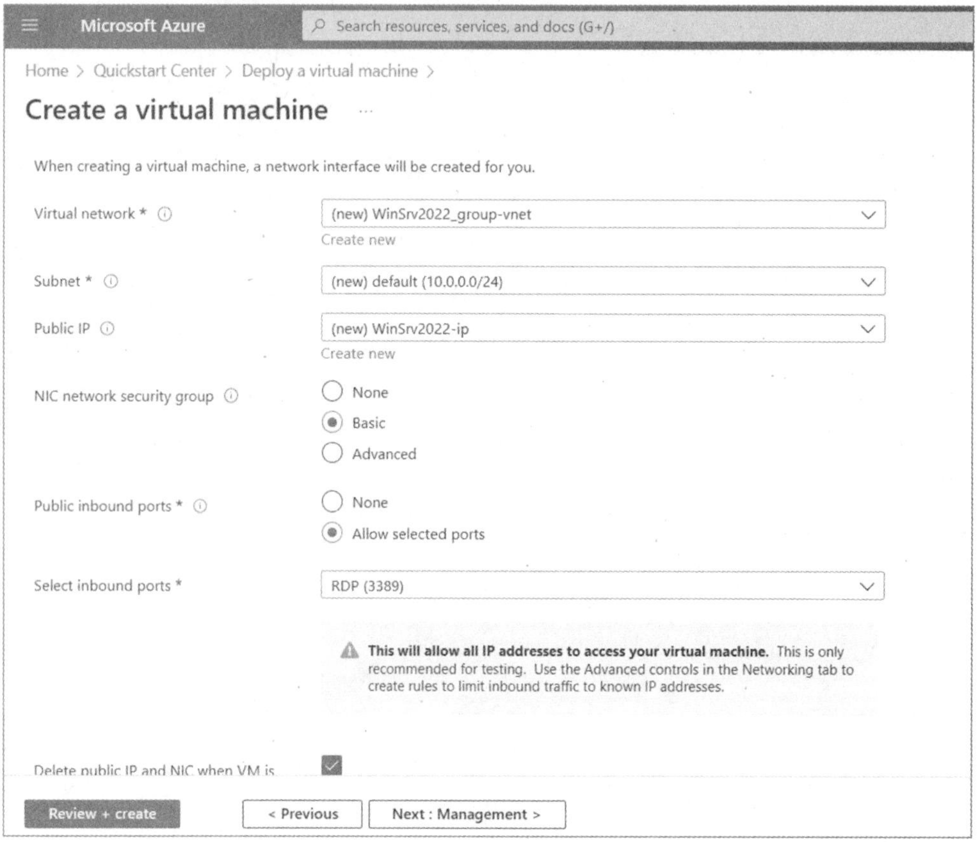

7. On the Management page, choose the options that you want set for your VM and then click Next: Monitoring.
8. On the Monitoring page, you can choose to set up alert rules and diagnostic data (see Figure 12.21). Make any changes that you wish and then click Next: Advanced.

FIGURE 12.21   Monitoring page

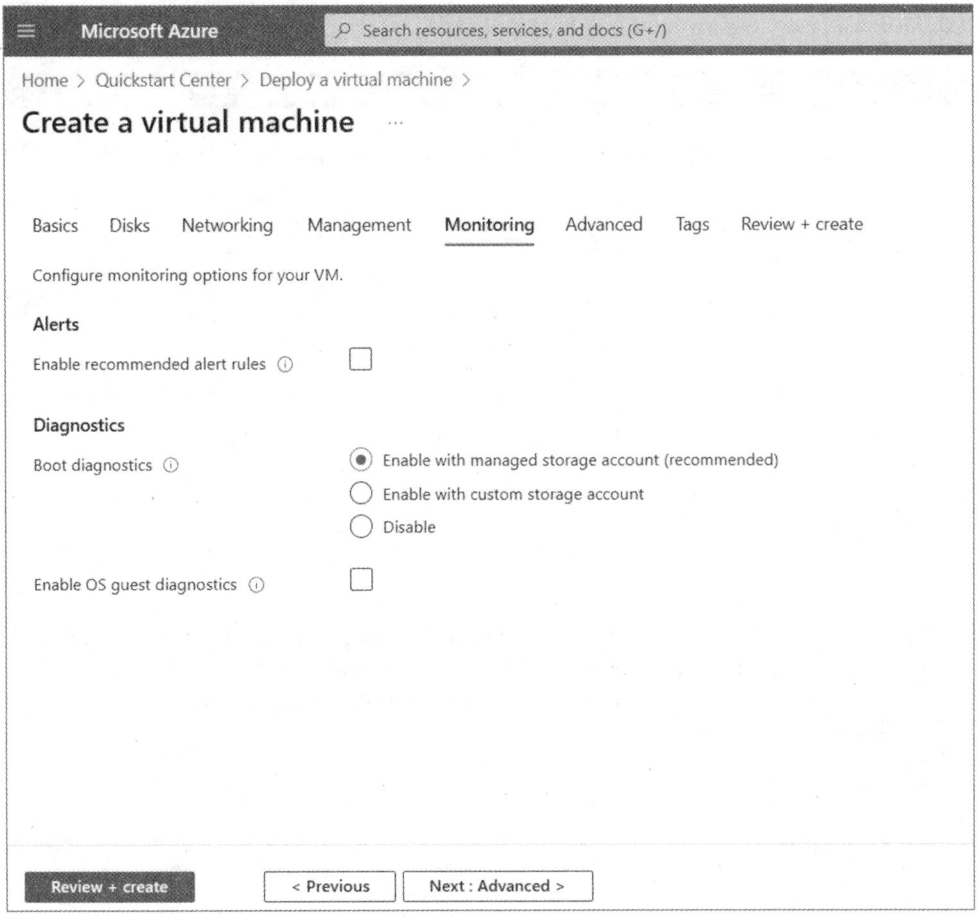

9. On the Advanced page, you can choose if you want any applications automatically installed, scripts, user settings for accessing the VM, and other VM settings. Choose any additional options and then click Next: Tags.

10. The Tags page will appear. Tags are user-defined key-value pairs that can be directly placed on a resource or a resource group. Azure currently supports up to 50 tags per resource and resource group. Tags may be placed on a resource at the time of creation or added to an existing resource. Once you choose your Tags options, click the Next: Review And Create button.

11. On the Review and Create page, review all the options that you chose. If everything is correct, click Create. The VM will be created (as shown in Figure 12.22).

EXERCISE 12.5 *(continued)*

FIGURE 12.22 Deployment Is In Progress page

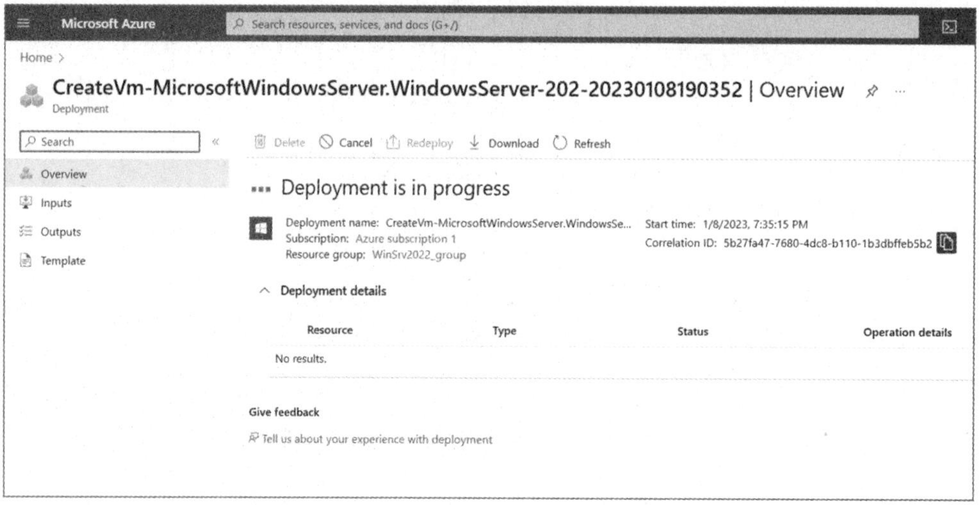

12. Once the VM is created, you will see a screen stating that your deployment is complete (as shown in Figure 12.23). Click the Go To Resource button. The VM is built and ready to start. You can start the VM, connect to the guest operating system, and start your server.

FIGURE 12.23 Your Deployment Is Complete

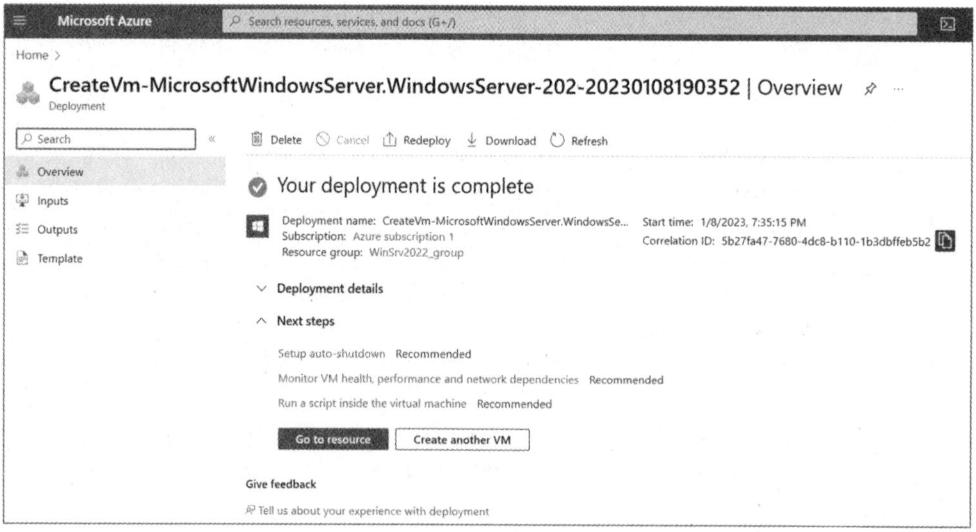

After the virtual machine is created, you will be shown the information for your new Azure virtual server (see Figure 12.24). Make sure you copy or print this information. As part of the information presented, you will be given an IP address so that you can use options like Remote Desktop to make the connection. I will be deleting this VM but I still used **xxxx** over my private information for this VM.

FIGURE 12.24   VM information

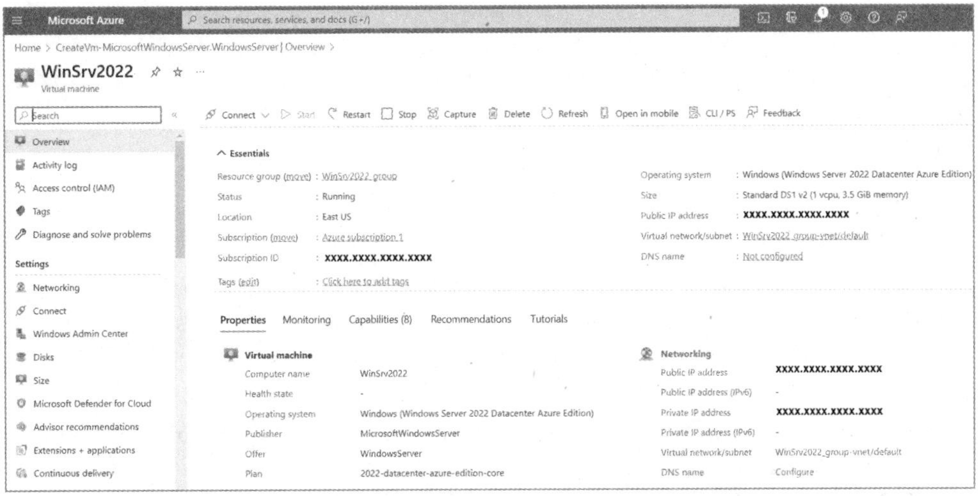

Configure Azure VM Settings

In this section, you will get an overview of just some of the available Azure virtual machine settings. You can configure all of these settings by using the Azure portal, PowerShell, Azure CLI, or the Windows Admin Center.

The Azure Virtual Machine Settings page includes the following settings:

Networking   The Networking section (shown in Figure 12.25) allows you to set up and configure the Inbound Rules, Outbound Rules, Application Security Groups, and Load Balancing settings. Setting Inbound and Outbound rules can help protect your network by stopping unauthorized traffic.

FIGURE 12.25   VM Networking settings

Connect   The Connect section allows you to configure which protocols that you want to use to connect to the virtual machine. Here you can specify the protocols (RDP, SSH, and Bastion) that you want to use to connect to the VM.

Windows Admin Center   The Windows Admin Center is a utility that allows you to manage servers, clients, clustering, and Azure VMs. The Windows Admin Center can be deployed in two different ways.

You can download the Windows Admin Center for free directly from Microsoft and then install it onto a server or a Windows client (Windows 10/11).

Also, Azure allows you to use the Windows Admin Center directly from Azure. There is no need to install the Windows Admin Center into Azure. By clicking the Windows Admin Center link, you can configure your settings and connect to your servers.

Disks   The Disks setting section allows you to create and manage your virtual machine hard drives. The Disks settings let you attach an existing or create a new virtual hard disk. You can also click the Additional Settings link to configure the virtual hard disk encryption.

Size   One of the best advantages of using Azure is the ability to quickly and easily change the size of your VM based on the needs for CPU, network, or disk performance (see Figure 12.26). Remember, the more resources that you add to the VM, the more it's going to cost your organization.

FIGURE 12.26   VM Size settings

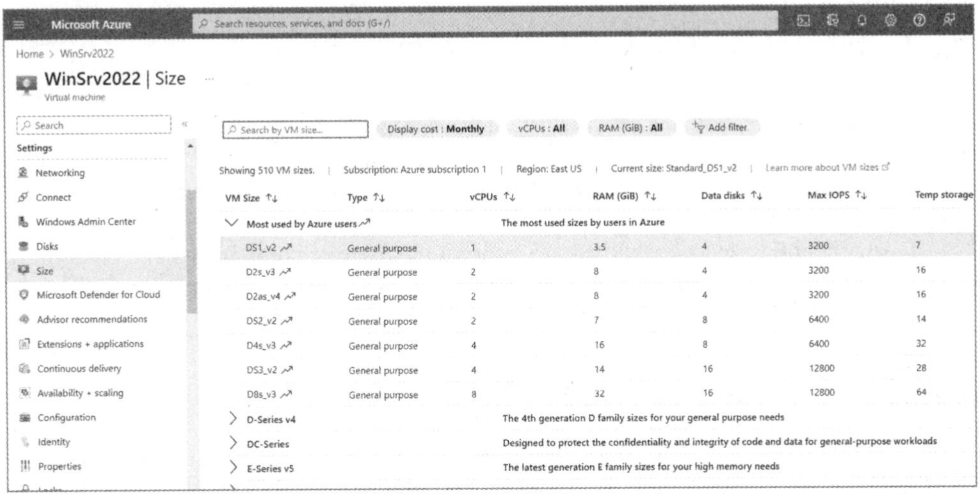

VM Size ↑↓	Type ↑↓	vCPUs ↑↓	RAM (GiB) ↑↓	Data disks ↑↓	Max IOPS ↑↓	Temp storage
∨ Most used by Azure users ↗			The most used sizes by users in Azure			
DS1_v2 ↗	General purpose	1	3.5	4	3200	7
D2s_v3 ↗	General purpose	2	8	4	3200	16
D2as_v4 ↗	General purpose	2	8	4	3200	16
DS2_v2 ↗	General purpose	2	7	8	6400	14
D4s_v3 ↗	General purpose	4	16	8	6400	32
DS3_v2 ↗	General purpose	4	14	16	12800	28
D8s_v3 ↗	General purpose	8	32	16	12800	64
⟩ D-Series v4		The 4th generation D family sizes for your general purpose needs				
⟩ DC-Series		Designed to protect the confidentiality and integrity of code and data for general-purpose workloads				
⟩ E-Series v5		The latest generation E family sizes for your high memory needs				

Microsoft Defender for Cloud   Microsoft Defender for Cloud constantly examines the configuration of your virtual machines to identify possible security vulnerabilities and recommends actions to help solve the issues.

Advisor Recommendations   The Azure VM Advisor delivers relevant best practices so that an administrator can improve reliability, security, and performance, and reduce costs. You can target a specific server, resource, resource group, or subscription to verify that the servers and services are running to get the best performance. Access the Advisor through the Azure portal, the Azure CLI, or the Advisor API.

Extensions + Applications   Azure Virtual Machine Extensions are smaller applications that run on Azure VMs. Azure Virtual Machine Extensions allow post-deployment configuration and automation of the Azure VMs. Azure has many different extensions that allow you to set up configuring, monitoring, security, and utility applications. You just need to provide mandatory parameters. You can view the available extensions by choosing a VM, then selecting Extensions from the left menu.

Azure VM extensions can be managed using the Azure CLI, PowerShell, Resource Manager templates, and the Azure portal. To try an extension, go to the Azure portal, select the Custom Script Extension, then pass in a command or script to run the extension.

> If you have any issues installing Azure Virtual Machine Extensions, please check out Microsoft's website: learn.microsoft.com/en-us/azure/virtual-machines/extensions/troubleshoot.

Understanding Additional Infrastructure Components

As I have previously stated, one of Azure's best advantages is the ability to create and manage a network in the cloud. You need another server to run as a file server? Just create and configure another Azure VM on the spot. There's no need to purchase or set up any new equipment and no need to front thousands of dollars for new equipment.

Just as with an onsite network, there are other infrastructure components and roles that you need to install to help ensure that your network is accessible by your employees but not accessible to hackers.

Additional Azure Services and Roles

In today's networking world, there are two main ways to set up a network. You can purchase physical equipment and build your network or you can build your network as a virtual network. Azure Virtual WAN is a networking service that brings many networking, security, and routing functionalities together to provide a single operational interface.

Building a network is like building a house. You don't have a house if all you do is pour a foundation. For a house to be a livable home, you need to install doors, windows, plumbing, and electricity.

When you build a network, just running cabling throughout the office does not give you a network. It's not a network until you install your servers, set up your shares, create your users, set roles and permissions, and install additional components.

These types of components can include things like using firewalls, routers, proxy, or NAT services, along with other components. One of the advantages of using Azure is that all of these components can be set up and used in the Azure Virtual WAN.

Let's explore some of the additional Azure services and roles that you can add to your cloud network.

 Depending on your organization, not all of these services are required. Also, your organization may need to use some Azure services that are not listed here. To learn more about all of the available Azure services and components, please visit Microsoft's website at http://azure .microsoft.com/en-us/products.

Using the Remote Access Role

The DirectAccess Remote Client Management deployment uses DirectAccess to maintain clients over the Internet. Windows Server 2022 took the best of Windows Server 2016 and Windows Server 2012 and combined DirectAccess and Routing and Remote Access Service (RRAS) VPN into a single Remote Access role.

The Remote Access Role is installed and uninstalled by using Windows PowerShell or from the Server Manager console (on VMs or Servers). The Remote Access role consists of two components:

- **DirectAccess and Routing and Remote Access Services (RRAS) VPN:** DirectAccess and VPN are managed in the Remote Access Management console.

- **RRAS:** Features are managed in the Routing and Remote Access console.

The Remote Access server role is dependent on the following features:

- **Web Server (IIS):** Required to configure the network location server and default web probe

- **Windows internal database:** Used for local accounting on the Remote Access server

If your organization is looking at implanting DirectAccess, I recommend that you visit Microsoft's website at http://learn.microsoft.com/en-us/windows-server/remote/remote-access/ras/manage-remote-access.

Using the Azure Network Adapter

One advantage of using Azure is the ability for your end users or clients to access your cloud-based network from anywhere in the world. Basically, if you have Internet access and the proper permissions, you can access the Azure network.

Azure allows you to set up and use the Azure Network Adapter. The Azure Network Adapter lets you connect remotely to your virtual network. You can access your Azure network from any remote location, such as a remote office, hotel, or any location with Internet access.

You can also configure and use the Azure Network Adapter instead of a site-to-site VPN. This can be very useful when you need to connect only a few servers to the virtual network. Azure Network Adapter connections don't require a VPN device or even a public-facing IP address.

If you want to allow access to a virtual network, setting up an Azure Network Adapter requires the following components:

- An account connected to at least one active Azure subscription
- A current virtual network
- Internet access between your Azure virtual network and the servers that you want to connect
- Current version of the Windows Admin Center that has the ability to connect to Azure

To configure an Azure Network Adapter, in the Windows Admin Center, choose Networks under Tools, and then follow these steps:

1. Open the Windows Admin Center.

2. Choose the VMs that you want to add to the Azure Network Adapter.

3. Under Tools, select Networks.

4. Select Add Azure Network Adapter.

5. In the Add Azure Network Adapter pane, configure the options that you want to use and then click Create.

If your Azure setup doesn't have an Azure Virtual Network Gateway, the Windows Admin Center will automatically create a gateway for you. The actual setup can take up to 25–30 minutes, so be sure to plan the deployment carefully. Give yourself enough time to ensure that everything is ready before you start trying to make connections. Once the connection is complete, you will be able to access the virtual machines directly.

Understanding Azure Extended Network

As a director of IT, trainer, and consultant for over 30 years, I can tell you that one of the hardest things for IT people to learn is the Internet Protocol (IP). Configuring and maintaining an IP network can be confusing to many IT people. But IP is not a hard topic to learn once someone shows you how easy it is to configure.

One part of IP that can be difficult is the practice of subnetting a network. To understand using an Azure Extended Network, you must first understand subnetting. Think of IP subnetting as a large open warehouse. The warehouse is wide open (no walls or doors inside the warehouse). This is an example of setting up an IP network where everyone is on the same IP network. There are no segmented offices or rooms. Everyone works in the same open warehouse together.

Say the company has decided that they want to separate the warehouse into conference rooms. Each conference room will be used only by the department (sales, marketing, etc.) that owns that room. So, you build your walls and segment the warehouse into multiple conference rooms. Each room is assigned to a specific group of people based on their department. Users have to work in their conference room only. They can access any other room, but they work in their department's conference room. This is an example of subnetting a network.

When an IP network is not subnetted, every user on the network is part of the same IP network. If I decide that I need to subnet my network, I will install routers and turn the large network into a bunch of smaller networks. This is called subnetting.

As I stated earlier, building a subnetted network is not easy for most IT people. Now, let's take it to the next level. Think about building a network and subnetting that network; now you need to add Azure as part of your IP network. This adds a whole new level of issues that you can run into. This is where Azure Extended Network comes into play. Azure Extended Network allows you to extend an onsite subnet to an Azure cloud network. That way, onsite virtual machines retain their original onsite private IP addresses when migrating to Azure.

Azure Extended Network lets you extend the onsite network to Azure by using a bidirectional VXLAN tunnel. You set the VXLAN tunnel between two Windows Server 2022 VMs. The 2022 VMs act as a virtual appliance, with one VM running onsite and the other VM running in Azure. Each VM also needs to be connected to the subnet that you want to extend. Every subnet that you are going to extend requires one pair of appliances. Multiple subnets can be extended using multiple VM pairs.

Extended networks are not something that is required or even recommended unless you are having a very specific issue migrating servers to Azure. Once you decide that your organization is migrating to Azure, you may run into a situation where an onsite server/VM needs to keep its original IP address. The Azure network may not use the same IP scheme that you had configured onsite.

Extended Network for Azure should only be configured and used for machines that cannot have their IP address changed when migrating to Azure. If possible, it is always better to change the IP address and connect it to the subnet that exists in Azure.

Azure Extended Networks allow you to configure up to 250 IP addresses. You can anticipate a combined throughput of about 700 Mbps. This throughput will also depend on the virtual machine components. One of the variables that can affect throughput is CPU speed of the VMs that are being used as the Azure virtual appliances.

Using the Web Application Proxy

In my career, I have had the pleasure to work with a lot of new IT people. One thing that I like to stress to new IT people is that even the IT department has clients. For many corporate employees, they have clients that they are responsible for. For example, salespeople are responsible for working with the customers of the company.

But it's the same in IT. Our customers are our employees. The better our network works, the more our customers (our end users) can do and the easier we can make their job. One of the tasks that we can set up to help our end users is single sign-on (SSO). SSO allows your users to log into one network and automatically get access to another network. For example, SSO allows our users to log into one network (onsite) and have access to the Azure cloud network without having to enter a new username or password.

Azure Active Directory's Application Proxy provides secure remote access to web applications that are located on your local onsite network. Because of SSO, users can sign into Azure AD and then they will have access to both cloud-based and onsite applications. This is possible through an external URL or an internal application portal.

Azure AD, along with an Azure Application Proxy, allows users to access onsite web applications from a remote client. Application Proxy uses an Azure Application Proxy service that runs in the cloud and an Application Proxy connector that runs on an onsite server. The process requires that you use Azure AD, the Application Proxy service, and the Application Proxy connector. All three components work together to securely pass the user's sign-on token from Azure AD to the onsite web application.

Application Proxy was designed to allow Azure users to access onsite web applications. It is designed to work with the following:

- Web applications that use Integrated Windows authentication
- Web applications that use form-based or header-based access
- Web APIs that you want to expose to rich applications on different devices
- Applications hosted behind a Remote Desktop Gateway
- Rich client apps that are integrated with the Microsoft Authentication Library (MSAL)

Application Proxy is an excellent option for giving remote users access to internal onsite resources. It allows your users to connect remotely to web applications without the need of a VPN or reverse proxy. It is not intended for internal users on the corporate network. Internal onsite users should already have access to the onsite web applications. If onsite users use Application Proxy, it can cause performance issues, so only remote users who are connected to the Azure network should use it.

Understanding the Azure Relay Service

In today's fast-moving technology world, one of the issues that we all must face is security and the threat of cyberattacks, ransomware, and all other types of malware. One major factor that we must all consider when building a network is security.

The Azure Relay Service allows you to securely execute services that run in your corporate network to the public cloud. You can configure the Azure Relay Service without opening a port on your firewall or without making intrusive changes to your corporate network infrastructure. The service supports multiple scenarios between onsite services and the applications that run in the cloud or in another onsite environment.

The Azure Relay Service is different from other network technologies such as VPN. You can configure the Azure Relay Service to a single application endpoint on a single machine.

If your IT department decides to install a VPN for all of its users, the IT department has to make sure the network is properly configured for VPN access. Also, anyone who has VPN access can use that access to connect to part of or the entire network.

The Azure Relay Service does not require changing the physical network. You can set up the service to communicate to a single address. Here are the steps that are used in the Azure Relay Service:

1. Using an outbound port, an on-premises service can connect to the relay service directly.
2. The Azure Relay Service creates a bidirectional socket for communication tied to a particular address.
3. The client can then communicate with the onsite service by sending traffic to the Azure Relay Service targeting that address.
4. The Azure Relay Service then relays the data to the onsite service through the bidirectional socket dedicated to the client. The client doesn't need a direct connection to the onsite service.

Using Azure Arc

One really nice advantage of Azure is the ability to use, or not use, any of the available services and tools. Most cloud-based networks are consumption based. The more services that you use, the more you pay. But for many companies, not all features or services will be needed when setting up your Azure network. This is the category that Azure Arc falls under.

Azure Arc is an Azure service that may greatly help your company, especially if your company creates and uses applications that you build internally. For any organization that develops their own software or services, Azure Arc can be a great feature. It allows a company of any size to easily secure, develop, and operate infrastructure, apps, and Azure services from anywhere. Azure Arc helps you extend the Azure platform so that you can build applications and services with the flexibility to run across datacenters, at the edge, and in multicloud environments. This allows your developers to build cloud-based applications with a consistent development, operations, and security model.

 If your organization uses developers and you would like more information about using Azure Arc, please feel free to check out Microsoft's website: https://azure.microsoft.com/en-us/products/azure-arc.

Summary

In this chapter, you learned about Windows containers. Windows containers are brand-new technology to Windows Server 2022 or some versions of Windows 10/11. You learned how to install, configure, and maintain your Windows containers. We also discussed the components needed to work with containers.

I then showed you some exercises for configuring Windows Server 2022 containers and how to download and work with image files. These image files can be used to create Windows and Hyper-V containers.

I also showed you how to build and configure Azure virtual machines. Setting up a virtual network can be less expensive and an easy way for a company of any size to quickly and easily build an entire network in the cloud.

Finally, I explained various services and roles that you can use to help secure and access your virtual network and your onsite network.

Exam Essentials

Understand Windows containers. Windows containers work a lot like virtual machines except that when you build a virtual machine, you need all of the services that make that VM run properly. Windows containers are fast operating system builds that allow you to run applications in their own environment.

Know the PowerShell commands used for containers. The Microsoft exams are going to focus on PowerShell commands. Make sure you know the PowerShell commands that are used for Docker and containers.

Understand Docker technology. Understand that Docker is the technology that is used to manage and maintain Windows containers. There are preset images on Docker that you can pull down and run. Microsoft also has preset Docker images that you can use and manipulate.

Know the different docker switches. Know how docker switches are used. Know that you run docker switches in PowerShell or at an elevated command prompt.

Understand virtual networks and virtual hard disks. Virtual networks and hard disks are the two most tested topics. You definitely should know the types of virtual networks available (external, internal only, and private virtual network) as well as all types of virtual hard disks (dynamically expanding, fixed size, differential, and physical or pass-through). You should be able to apply the correct one when needed. Be familiar with the Edit Virtual Hard Disk Wizard, which is a good source for exam questions.

Know how to create and manage Azure virtual machines. You should be able to explain how to create an Azure virtual machine, what options are available to install an operating system in a virtual machine, and how to install any additional Hyper-V components on a virtual machine.

Review Questions

1. You are the network administrator for a company that has decided to start using Windows containers. You download the wrong image from Docker. What command allows you to delete an image?

   A. docker del

   B. docker rm

   C. docker kill

   D. docker dl

2. You are the network administrator for a company that has decided to start using Windows containers. You want to create a new container. What command should you use?

   A. docker create

   B. docker build container

   C. docker new

   D. docker build

3. You are the network administrator for a company that has decided to start using Windows containers. You have built a number of containers. What PowerShell command allows you to view them?

   A. docker view

   B. docker see

   C. View-Container

   D. Get-Container

4. You are the network administrator for a company that has decided to start using Windows containers. You have created some images. What command allows you to see your images?

   A. docker images

   B. docker info

   C. docker view

   D. docker see

5. You are the administrator for an organization that has started using containers. You need to build and use a Dockerfile. You want to compile and create an image using the Dockerfile. What command do you use?

   A. Docker run

   B. Docker rm

   C. Docker build

   D. Docker compile

6. You are the administrator for an organization that has started using containers. You need to build and use a Dockerfile. You want to execute commands within the Dockerfile. What command should you use?

   A. Docker run

   B. Docker rm

   C. Docker build

   D. Docker compile

7. You are the network administrator for a company that has decided to start using Windows containers. You want to delete a container. What PowerShell command allows you to do that?

   A. docker delete

   B. docker kill container

   C. Remove-Container

   D. Delete-docker-Container

8. You are the administrator for an organization that has started using containers. You need to build a new image using Windows Server Core. What command would you use to get a Windows Server Core image?

   A. Docker run microsoft/windowsservercore

   B. docker pull microsoft/windowsservercore

   C. Docker build microsoft/windowsservercore

   D. Docker get microsoft/windowsservercore

9. You have a Windows Server 2022 server named Server1. Server1 has the Web Server (IIS) server role installed. Server1 hosts an ASP.NET Core web app named WebApp1 and the app's source files. You install Docker on Server1. You want to ensure that you can deploy WebApp1 to an Azure App Service web app from the Azure Container Registry. Which three actions should you perform in sequence? (Choose three.)

   A. Run the docker push command.

   B. Run the docker run command.

   C. Run the docker build command.

   D. Create a Dockerfile.

   E. Run the docker pull command.

10. How do you add another virtual disk to an Azure virtual machine?

    A. Use the Virtual Hard Disk Wizard.

    B. Use the Edit Virtual Hard Disk Wizard.

    C. Choose Disks from the VM options.

    D. Use the New Virtual Machine Wizard.

Chapter

13

Managing Data in a Hybrid Network

THE FOLLOWING AZ-801 EXAM OBJECTIVES ARE COVERED IN THIS CHAPTER:

✓ **Implement and manage Storage Spaces Direct**

- Create a failover cluster using Storage Spaces Direct
- Upgrade a Storage Spaces Direct node
- Implement networking for Storage Spaces Direct
- Configure Storage Spaces Direct

✓ **Implement as**

- Implement a failover cluster on-premises, hybrid, or cloud-only
- Create a Windows failover cluster
- Stretch cluster across datacenter or Azure regions
- Configure storage for failover clustering
- Modify quorum options
- Configure network adapters for failover clustering
- Configure cluster workload options
- Configure cluster sets
- Configure Scale-Out File servers
- Create an Azure witness
- Configure a floating IP address for the cluster
- Implement load balancing for the failover cluster

✓ Manage failover clustering

- Implement cluster-aware updating
- Recover a failed cluster node
- Upgrade a node to Windows Server 2022
- Failover workloads between nodes
- Install Windows updates on cluster nodes
- Manage failover clusters using Windows Admin Center

In this chapter, I will introduce you to some of the techniques and components of high availability. You'll learn how to set up high availability using network load balancing (NLB). We'll discuss why you would choose to use NLB over using a failover cluster and which applications or servers work better with NLB. I will also show you how to use PowerShell for NLB.

You'll also learn how to keep your Hyper-V servers up and running by implementing high availability and disaster recovery options in Hyper-V. Finally, I'll explain how clustering can be used for high availability.

Components of High Availability

High availability is a buzzword that many application and hardware vendors like to throw around to get you to purchase their products. Many different options are available to achieve high availability, and there also seems to be a number of definitions and variations that help vendors sell their products as high availability solutions.

When it comes right down to it, however, high availability simply means providing services with maximum uptime by avoiding unplanned downtime. Often, *disaster recovery (DR)* is also closely lumped into discussions of high availability, but DR encompasses the business and technical processes used to recover once a disaster has happened.

Defining a high availability plan usually starts with a *service level agreement (SLA)*. At its most basic, an SLA defines the services and metrics that must be met for the availability and performance of an application or service. Often, an SLA is created for an IT department or service provider to deliver a specific level of service. An example of this might be an SLA for a Microsoft Exchange server. The SLA for an Exchange server might have uptime metrics on how much time during the month the mailboxes need to be available to end users, or it might define performance metrics for the amount of time it takes for email messages to be delivered.

When determining what goes into an SLA, two other factors need to be considered. However, you will often see them discussed only in the context of disaster recovery, even though they are important for designing a highly available solution. These factors are the *recovery point objective (RPO)* and the *recovery time objective (RTO)*.

An RTO is the length of time an application can be unavailable before service must be restored to meet the SLA. For example, a single component failure would have an RTO of less than five minutes, and a full-site failure might have an RTO of three hours. An RPO is essentially the amount of data that must be restored in the event of a failure. For example, in a single server or component failure, the RPO would be 0, but in a site failure, the RPO might allow for up to 20 minutes of lost data.

SLAs, on the other hand, are usually expressed in percentages of the time the application is available. These percentages are also often referred to by the number of nines the percentage includes. So, if someone told you that you need to make sure that the router has a rating of five 9s, that would mean that the router could only be down for 5.26 minutes a year. Table 13.1 shows you some of the different nines rating and what each rating allows for downtime.

TABLE 13.1   Availability percentages

Availability rating	Allowed unplanned downtime/year
99 (two nines) percent	3.65 days
99.9 (three nines) percent	8.76 hours
99.99 (four nines) percent	52.56 minutes
99.999 (five nines) percent	5.26 minutes
99.9999 (six nines) percent	31.5 seconds
99.99999 (seven nines) percent	3.15 seconds

Two important factors that affect an SLA are the *mean time between failure (MTBF)* and the *mean time to recovery (MTTR)*. To be able to reduce the amount of unplanned downtime, the time between failures must be increased, and the time it takes to recover must be reduced. Modifying these two factors will be addressed in the next several sections of this chapter.

Achieving High Availability

Windows Server 2022 is the most secure and reliable Windows version to date. It also is the most stable, mature, and capable of any version of Windows. Although similar claims have been made for previous versions of Windows Server, you can rest assured that Windows Server 2022 is much better than previous versions for a variety of reasons.

An honest look at the feature set and real-world use should prove that this latest version of Windows provides the most suitable foundation for creating a highly available solution. However, more than just good software is needed to be able to offer high availability for applications.

In today's technology world, there are many ways to set up and manage a high availability network. Since the AZ-800 and AZ-801 exams cover both onsite servers and Azure, we will talk about setting up high availability using these two methods. Many third-party companies offer high availability solutions, but we will focus on onsite and Azure setups.

High Availability Foundation

Just as a house needs a good foundation, a highly available Windows server needs a stable and reliable hardware platform on which to run. Although Windows Server 2022 will technically run on desktop-class hardware, high availability is more easily achieved with server-class hardware. What differentiates desktop-class from server-class hardware? *Server-class hardware* has more management and monitoring features built into it so that the health of the hardware can be monitored and maintained.

Another big difference is that server-class hardware has redundancy options. Server-class hardware often has options to protect from drive failures, such as RAID controllers, and to protect against power supply failures, such as multiple power supplies. Enterprise-class servers have even more protection.

More needs to be done than just installing Windows Server 2022 to ensure that the applications remain running with the best availability possible. Just as a house needs maintenance and upkeep to keep the structure in proper repair, so too does a server. In the case of a highly available server, this means *patch management*.

Installing Patches

Microsoft releases monthly updates to fix security problems with its software, both for operating system fixes and for applications. To ensure that your highly available applications are immune to known vulnerabilities, these patches need to be applied in a timely manner during a scheduled maintenance window. Also, to address stability and performance issues, updates and service packs are released regularly for many applications, such as Microsoft SQL Server, Exchange Server, and SharePoint Portal Server. Many companies have a set schedule—daily, weekly, or monthly—to apply these patches and updates after they are tested and approved.

Desired Configuration Manager (DCM), an option in Microsoft Configuration Manager, is a great tool for helping to validate that your cluster nodes are patched. It can leverage the SCCM client to collect installed patches and help reporting within the enterprise on compliancy with desired system states based on the software installed.

To continue with the house analogy, if you were planning to have the master bath remodeled, would you rather hire a college student on spring break looking to make some extra money to do the job or a seasoned artisan? Of course, you would want someone with experience and a proven record of accomplishment to remodel your master bath.

Likewise, with any work that needs to be done on your highly available applications, it's best to hire only decidedly qualified individuals. This is why obtaining a Microsoft certification is definitely an excellent start to becoming qualified to configure a highly available server properly. There is no substitute for real-life and hands-on experience.

Working with highly available configurations in a lab and in production will help you know not only what configurations are available but also how the changes should be made.

For example, it may be possible to use failover clustering for a DNS server, but in practice DNS replication may be easier to support and require less expensive hardware in order to provide high availability. This is something you would know only if you had enough experience to make this decision.

As with your house, once you have a firm and stable foundation built by skilled artisans and a maintenance plan has been put into place, you need to ascertain what more is needed. If you can't achieve enough uptime with proper server configuration and mature operational processes, a cluster may be needed.

Windows Server 2022 provides two types of high availability: *failover clustering* and *network load balancing (NLB)*. Failover clustering is used for applications and services such as SQL Server and Exchange Server. Network load balancing is used for network-based services such as web and FTP servers.

Understanding Network Load Balancing

This section discusses onsite network load balancing (NLB). Performing NLB using Azure will be discussed later in this chapter. So, the first thing we have to discuss is why you would choose to use NLB. NLB lets you configure two or more servers as a single virtual cluster. It's designed for high availability and scalability of Internet server applications. This means that Windows Server 2022 NLB is designed to work with web servers, FTP servers, firewalls, proxy servers, and virtual private networks (VPNs).

You can use NLB for other mission-critical servers, but you can also use failover clusters on many of these servers. So, after reading this and the next chapter ("Hybrid Data and Servers"), hopefully you will be able to choose the appropriate high availability server setup for your network and applications.

NLB is a form of clustering where the nodes are highly available for a network-based service. This is typically a port listener configuration where a farm of, say, Microsoft Internet Information Services servers all listen on ports 80 and 443 for incoming web traffic from client endpoints. These nodes, while not fully clustered in a technical sense, are load balanced, where each node handles some of the distributed network traffic.

The NLB feature uses the TCP/IP networking protocol to distribute traffic. For web and other necessary servers, NLB can provide performance and consistency when two or more computers are combined into a single virtual cluster.

Hosts are servers that make up an NLB cluster. Each host runs its own individual copy of the server applications. The incoming client requests are distributed by NLB to each of the hosts in the cluster. You can configure the load so that it is handled by each host. Hosts can be added to the cluster to increase the load. If NLB has all traffic directed to a specific single host, then it is called a default host.

With the use of NLB, all the computers in a cluster can use the same set of IP addresses while each host maintains its own exclusive IP address. When a host fails for load-balanced applications, the computers still in operation will receive the workload automatically. When the down computer is ready to rejoin the cluster, it comes back online and will regain its share of the workload. This allows the rest of the computers in the cluster to handle less traffic.

NLB is beneficial in that stateless applications (e.g., web servers) and are available with little downtime, and it allows for scalability. Scalability is the capability of a system, network, or process to handle a growing amount of work, or its potential to be enlarged in order to accommodate growth. Scalability, when used for NLB clusters, is the ability to add one or more systems to an existing cluster when the need arises. You can do the following with NLB to support scalability:

- A single cluster can support up to 32 computers.

- Handle multiple server load requests from across multiple hosts in a cluster.

- For single TCP/IP services, balance-load requests across the NLB cluster.

- As the workload grows, you can add hosts to the NLB cluster without failure.

- When the workload declines, you can remove hosts from the cluster.

- Allow higher performance and lower overhead by using a pipelined implementation. Pipelining allows requests to be sent to the NLB cluster without waiting for a response.

- Use NLB Manager or Windows PowerShell cmdlets to manage and configure NLB clusters and hosts from a single computer.

- Determine port rules for each website. Port rules allow you to configure which ports are going to be enabled or disabled. Ports are doorways that applications can use to access resources. For example, DNS traffic uses port 53 for all DNS traffic. Here are some of the more common port numbers:

  - FTP uses ports 20/21.

  - Secure Shell uses port 22.

  - SMTP (mail) uses port 25.

  - DNS uses port 53.

  - HTTP uses port 80.

  - POPv3 uses port 110.

  - HTTPS uses port 443.

- Determine load balancing behavior using port management rules for an IP port or group of ports.

- Use an optional, single-host rule that will direct all client requests to a single host. NLB will route client requests to a specific host that is running particular applications.

- Allow certain IP ports to block unwanted network access.

- When operating in multicast mode, enable Internet Group Management Protocol (IGMP) support on the cluster host. This will control switch port flooding (when all incoming network packets are sent to all ports on the switch).

- Use Windows PowerShell to start, stop, and control NLB actions remotely.

- Check NLB events using Windows Event Log. All NLB actions and cluster changes are logged in the Event Log.

NLB Requirements

The following are NLB cluster hardware requirements:

- All hosts must be on the same subnet.

- For each host, there is no limitation to the number of network adapters.

- All network adapters must be multicast or unicast within the cluster. Mixed environments, within a single cluster, are *not* supported.

- If using unicast mode, the network adapter used to handle client-to-cluster traffic must support media access control (MAC) address changing.

   NLB cluster software requirements are as follows:

- The adapter on which NLB is enabled can only support TCP/IP.

- Must have a static IP address on the servers in the cluster.

Installing NLB Nodes

You can install NLB nodes like any other server build. You can install NLB by using either Server Manager or the Windows PowerShell commands for NLB.

   First make sure that all NLB servers have the most current updates, provisioned with appropriate resources (typically with multiple network interface cards for capacity and responsiveness), and monitored for health and reliability. In Exercise 13.1, I will walk you through the installation of your NLB nodes.

EXERCISE 13.1

Installing NLB Nodes

1. Once you have multiple hosts ready for the installation of NLB, run the Add Roles And Features Wizard and select Network Load Balancing in the Features area of the wizard. If the Add Features dialog box appears, click Add Features.

2. Click Next. At the Confirmation screen, click the Install button. After the installation is finished, click the Close button and then close Server Manager.

3. Check that the wizard has placed the Network Load Balancing Manager in your Start menu under Windows Administrative Tools (see Figure 13.1).

FIGURE 13.1   Network Load Balancing

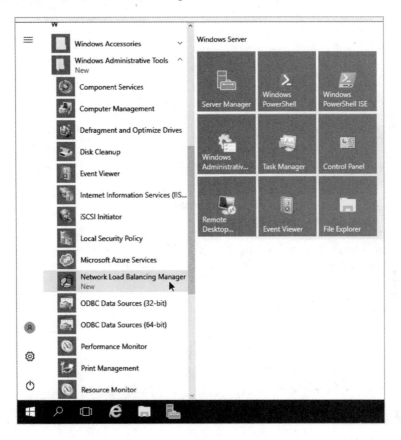

4. Right-click Network Load Balancing Clusters and select New Cluster (see Figure 13.2).

EXERCISE 13.1 *(continued)*

FIGURE 13.2 New Cluster

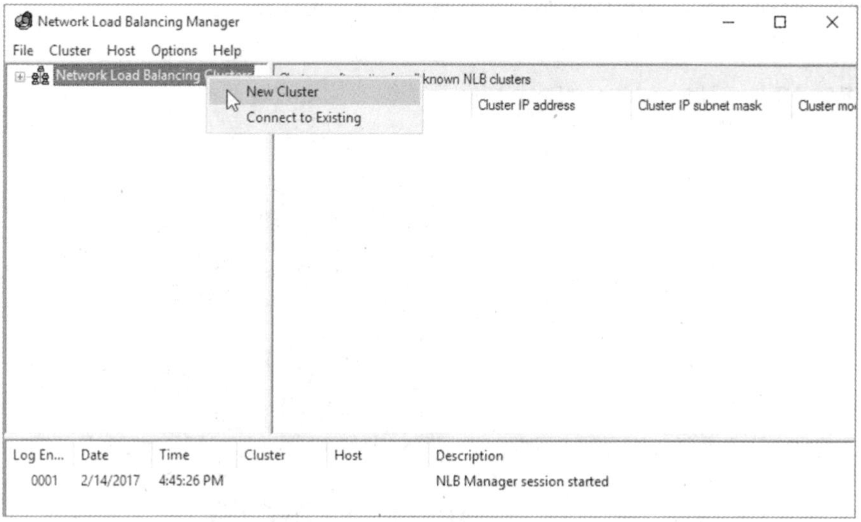

5. You are then presented with the New Cluster: Connect Wizard, where you can specify the name of one of your hosts. Type the name of one of your cluster nodes and click Connect (see Figure 13.3). After the connection is made, the TCP/IP address will be shown. Click Next.

FIGURE 13.3 Hostname setup

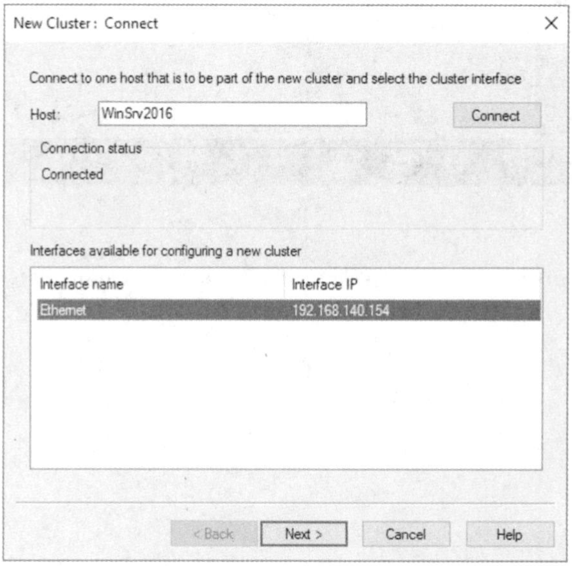

6. If you see a DHCP dialog box, disable DHCP on this adapter. Click OK.

7. The next page reveals a prompt to add any additional IPs and assign a priority level. You can do all this later, so click Next. If you see a No Dedicated IP Addresses dialog box, click Yes.

8. The next wizard page is where you specify the cluster IP address. This is the address that the endpoints or clients or users of the NLB cluster will contact. Typically, the network team will assign a cluster IP address for this use (see Figure 13.4). Click OK, then click Next.

FIGURE 13.4 Add IP Address

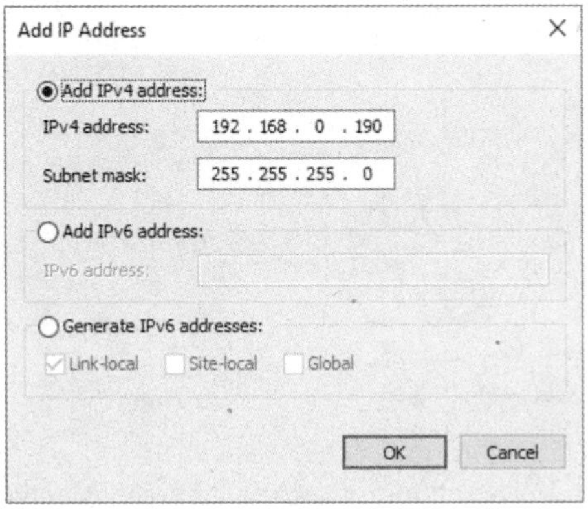

9. On the next page, configure the Cluster operation mode (see Figure 13.5) and specify a Full Internet Name.

FIGURE 13.5   Cluster parameters

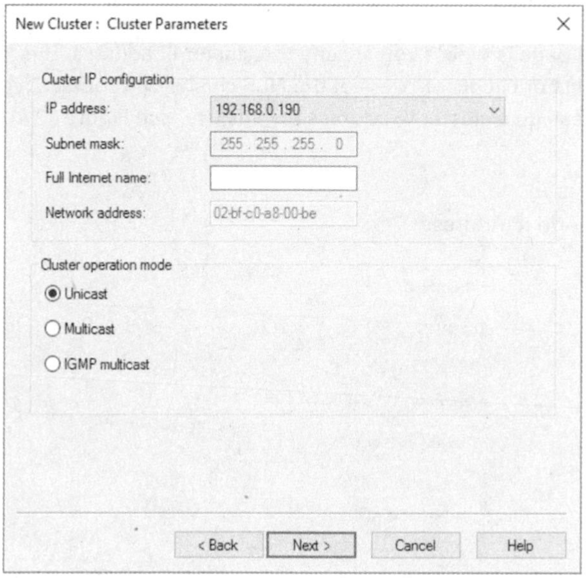

With regard to the cluster operation modes, the differences between them are as follows:

Unicast

The cluster adapters for all nodes are assigned the same MAC address.

The outgoing MAC address for each packet is modified based on priority to prevent upstream switches from discovering that all nodes have the same MAC address.

Communication between cluster nodes (other than heartbeat and other administrative NLB traffic) is not possible unless there are additional adapters (because all nodes have the same MAC address).

Depending on load, this configuration can cause switch flooding since all inbound packets are sent to all ports on the switch.

Multicast

The cluster adapters for all nodes are assigned their own MAC unicast address.

The cluster adapters for all nodes are assigned a multicast MAC address (derived from the IP of the cluster).

Non-NLB network traffic between cluster nodes works fine since they all have their own MAC address.

IGMP Multicast

This is much like multicast, but the MAC traffic goes only to the switch ports of the NLB cluster, preventing switch flooding.

10. After you select the appropriate settings, the next page is where port rules (see Figure 13.6) are configured. By default, it is set up to be wide open. Most implementations will limit NLB ports to just the ports needed for the application. For example, a web server would need port 80 enabled. It is also in this area where you can configure filtering mode.

FIGURE 13.6 Port Rules

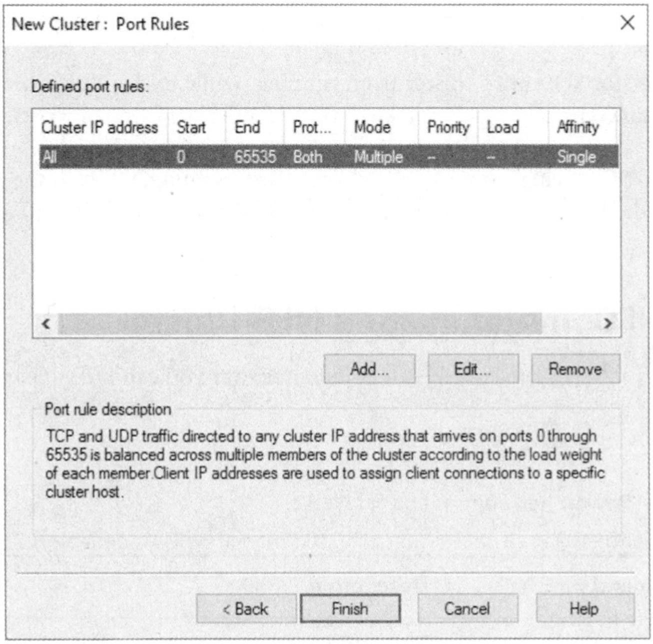

The affinity sets a client's preference to a particular NLB host. It is not recommended to set affinity to None when UDP is an expected traffic type.

11. Click the Finish button. Close the NLB Manager.

If you decide that you want to install NLB using Windows PowerShell commands, open an elevated Windows PowerShell prompt and type the following command:

```
Install-WindowsFeature NLB -IncludeManagementTools
```

Upgrading an NLB Cluster

Upgrading an NLB cluster is a fairly straightforward process. The first thing that you have to do is stop the NLB cluster. There are two ways to do so:

- Use the stop command to stop the cluster immediately. This also means that any current connections to the NLB cluster are killed.

- Use the drainstop command. The cluster stops after answering all of the current NLB connections. So the current NLB connections are finished but no new connections to that node are accepted.

So, to do your upgrade, you should execute a stop or drainstop on the NLB cluster node that you want to upgrade or to remove existing connections to the application on the local host. After the NLB cluster is stopped, you then perform an in-place upgrade in a rolling manner.

If you want to stop the entire cluster from running, while in the NLB manager (type **NLBmgr** in the Run command), right-click the cluster, point to Control Hosts, and then choose Stop.

If you want to stop a single node in the cluster from running, while in the NLB manager (type **NLBmgr** in the Run command), right-click the node, point to Control Hosts, and then choose Stop.

PowerShell Commands for a NLB Cluster

Table 13.2 shows some of the PowerShell commands that you can use to manage the NLB cluster.

TABLE 13.2   PowerShell commands for NLB

PowerShell command	Description
Add-NlbClusterNode	This command adds a new node to the NLB cluster.
Add-NlbClusterNodeDip	This command adds a dedicated IP address to a cluster.
Add-NlbClusterPortRule	This command adds a new port rule to a cluster.
Add-NlbClusterVip	This command adds a virtual IP address to a cluster.
Disable-NlbClusterPortRule	This command disables a port rule on a Network Load Balancing (NLB) cluster.
Enable-NlbClusterPortRule	This command enables a port rule on a cluster.

PowerShell command	Description
Get-NlbCluster	This command allows you to view information about the Network Load Balancing (NLB) cluster.
Get-NlbClusterDriverInfo	This command allows you to see information about the NLB drivers on a machine.
Get-NlbClusterNode	This command gets the information about the cluster object.
Get-NlbClusterPortRule	This command gets the port rule objects.
New-NlbCluster	This command creates a cluster on the specified interface.
New-NlbClusterIpv6Address	This command generates IPv6 addresses to create cluster virtual IP addresses.
Remove-NlbCluster	This command deletes a cluster.
Remove-NlbClusterNode	This command removes a node from a cluster.
Remove-NlbClusterPortRule	This command deletes a port rule from a cluster.
Resume-NlbCluster	This command resumes all nodes in the cluster.
Set-NlbCluster	This command allows you to edit the configuration of an NLB cluster.
Set-NlbClusterNode	This command allows you to edit the NLB cluster node settings.
Set-NlbClusterPortRule	This command allows you to edit the NLB port rules.
Start-NlbCluster	This command will start all of the nodes in a cluster.
Start-NlbClusterNode	This command will start one of the nodes in a cluster.
Stop-NlbCluster	This command stops all nodes in the cluster.
Stop-NlbClusterNode	This command will stop one of the nodes in a cluster.

Load Balancing with Azure

If you are using Azure for your network, then Azure has a number of tools that will help you with load balancing as well. As of this writing, Azure has the following tools available for load balancing:

Azure Traffic Manager   ADNS-based traffic load balancer that will spread traffic to services across global Azure regions by using DNS-based traffic routing methods. It prioritizes user access, helps to make sure that data sovereignty is adhered to, and for app upgrades and maintenance can adjust traffic. Azure Traffic Manager supports HTTP, HTTPS, HTTP/2, TCP, UDP, Layer 7, and global apps.

Azure Load Balancer   A network-layer load balancer that improves network performance and availability of your applications by using low-latency Layer 4 load balancing capabilities. Azure Load Balancer can balance traffic between virtual machines inside your virtual networks and across multitiered hybrid apps. It supports TCP, UDP, Layer 4, and global/regional apps.

Azure Application Gateway   An application delivery controller as a service that turns web front-ends into highly available apps by using Layer 7 load balancing capabilities by securely distributing regional apps. It supports HTTP, HTTPS, HTTP/2, Layer 7, regional apps, web application firewall, and SSL/TLS offloading.

Azure Front Door   Microsoft's cloud content delivery network (CDN) that safeguards the delivery of global apps by delivering real-time performance by using the Microsoft global edge network. The Microsoft global edge network is one of the biggest backbone networks in the world. Azure Front Door provides access between your apps' static and dynamic web content and your users around the world. It supports HTTP, HTTPS, HTTP/2, Layer 7, global apps, web application firewall, and SSL/TLS offloading.

Azure also has a service selection tool that can help you choose the best Azure cloud load-balancing service for your needs by answering a few questions regarding your app, workloads, and performance requirements. To access the tool, log into your Azure portal at `https://portal.azure.com/#blade/Microsoft_Azure_Network/ LoadBalancingHubMenuBlade/overview` and answer a few questions.

Azure Load Balancer

Since we have been discussing network load balancing, I want to delve a bit deeper into Azure's network load balancing tool called Azure Load Balancer. Azure Load Balancer has three different SKUs that you can choose from: Basic, Standard, and Gateway. Each is designed for specific scenarios and each has differences in scale, features, and pricing.

Azure Load Balancer operates at Layer 4 of the Open Systems Interconnection (OSI) model and distributes inbound flows that enter at the load balancer's front-end to backend pool instances and supports both inbound and outbound scenarios. As with some other

Azure tools, there is a cost associated with using Azure Load Balancer. For more information on pricing, check out Microsoft's website at `https://azure.microsoft.com/en-us/pricing/details/load-balancer/#purchase-options`.

With Azure Load Balancer you can create either a public (external) load balancer or an internal (private) load balancer. A public load balancer can provide outbound connections for VMs inside your virtual network and are used to load-balance Internet traffic to the VMs. These connections work by converting their private IP addresses to public IP addresses. An internal (or private) load balancer can route traffic from the public to resources within your network and are used to load-balance traffic inside a virtual network. It can be accessed only from private resources that are internal to the network.

Azure Load Balancer works across virtual machines, virtual machine scale sets, and IP addresses. There are three SKUs that you can choose from:

Standard Load Balancer   Designed for load-balancing network layer traffic when high performance and super-low latency are required. It routes traffic within and across regions, and to availability zones for high resiliency.

Basic Load Balancer   Designed for small-scale applications that do not need high-availability or redundancy. Not compatible with availability zones.

Gateway Load Balancer   Designed to help deploy, scale, and manage third-party virtual appliances. Provides one gateway for distributing traffic across multiple virtual appliances. You can scale them up or down, depending on demand.

For step-by-step instructions on how to create a public (external) load balancer using the Azure portal, check out Microsoft's website at `https://learn.microsoft.com/en-us/azure/load-balancer/quickstart-load-balancer-standard-public-portal`.

Configure a Floating IP Address for the Cluster

Some application scenarios may require or suggest that the same port be used by several applications on a single VM in the backend pool. Some examples of common port reuse are clustering for high availability and network virtual appliances. You will need to enable Floating IP in the rule definition if you want to reuse the backend port across multiple rules. When it's enabled, Azure will change the IP address mapping to the front-end IP address of the load balancer front end instead of the backend's IP address, which allows for greater flexibility.

You can configure a Floating IP on a Load Balancer rule by using a number of tools such as the Azure portal, REST API, CLI, or PowerShell. You must also configure the virtual machine's Guest OS in order to use a Floating IP. To work properly, the Guest OS for the VM must be configured to receive all traffic bound for the front-end IP and port of the load balancer.

Achieving High Availability with Hyper-V

One of the nice advantages of using Hyper-V is the ability to run an operating server within another server. Virtualization allows you to run multiple servers on top of a single Hyper-V server. But we need to make sure that these servers stay up and running.

That is where Hyper-V high availability comes into play. Ensuring that your Hyper-V servers are going to continue to run even if there is a hardware issue is an important step in guaranteeing the success of your network. There are many ways to achieve that. One is to set up clustering and another is to set up Hyper-V high availability without clustering. Setting up reliability without clustering requires that your Hyper-V servers have replica copies that can automatically start up if the virtual machine errors out. This is referred to as live migration and replica servers.

Implementing a Hyper-V Replica

Hyper-V Replica is an important part of the Hyper-V role. It replicates the Hyper-V virtual machines from the primary site to the replica secondary sites simultaneously.

Once you enable Hyper-V Replica for a particular virtual machine on the primary Hyper-V host server, the Hyper-V replica will begin to create an exact copy of the virtual machine for the secondary site. After this replication, Hyper-V Replica creates a log file for the virtual machine VHDs. This log file is rerun in reverse order to the replica VHD. This is done using replication frequency. The log files and reverse order helps ensure that the latest changes are stored and copied asynchronously. If there is an issue with the replication frequency, you will receive an alert.

On the virtual machine, you can establish resynchronization settings. You can do this manually, automatically, or automatically on an explicit schedule. To fix constant synchronization issues, you may choose to set up automatic resynchronization.

Hyper-V Replica will aid in a disaster recovery strategy by replicating virtual machines from one host to other while keeping workloads accessible. Hyper-V Replica can create a copy of a running virtual machine to a replica offline virtual machine.

Hyper-V Hosts

With replication over a WAN link, the primary and secondary host servers can be located in the same physical location or at different geographical locations. Hyper-V hosts can be stand-alone, clustered, or a combination of both. Hyper-V hosts are not dependent on Active Directory, and there is no need to be domain members.

Replication and Change Tracking

When you enable Hyper-V Replica on a virtual machine, an identical copy of that VM is created on a secondary host server. Once this happens, the Hyper-V Replica will create a log file that will track changes made on a virtual machine VHD. The log file is rerun in reverse order to the replica VHD. This is based on the replication frequency settings, and it ensures that the latest changes are created and replicated asynchronously. This can be done over HTTP or HTTPS.

Extended (Chained) Replication

Extended (Chained) Replication allows you to replicate a virtual machine from a primary host to a secondary host and then replicate the secondary host to a third host. It is not possible to replicate from the primary host directly to the second and third hosts.

Extended (Chained) Replication aids in disaster recovery in that you can recover from both the primary and extended replica. Extended Replication will also help if the primary and secondary locations go offline. It must be noted that the extended replica does not support application-consistent replication and it must use the same VHD that the secondary replica uses.

Setting the Affinity

NLB allows you to configure three types of affinity settings to help response times between NLB clients. Each affinity setting determines a method of distributing NLB client requests. There are three different affinity settings:

No Affinity (None)   If you set the affinity to No Affinity (None), NLB will not assign a NLB client with any specific member. When a request is sent to the NLB, the requests are balanced among all the nodes. No Affinity provides greater performance, but there may be issues with clients establishing sessions. This happens because the request may be load-balanced between NLB nodes and session information may not be present.

Single Affinity   Setting the cluster affinity to Single (this is the default setting) will send all traffic from a specific IP address to a single cluster node. This will keep a client on a specific node where the client should not have to authenticate again. Setting the affinity mode to Single would remove the authentication problem but would not distribute the load to other servers unless the initial server was down. Setting the affinity to Single allows a client's IP address to always connect to the same NLB node. This setting allows clients using an intranet to get the best performance.

Class C Affinity   When setting the affinity to Class C, NLB links clients with a specific member based on the Class C part of the client's IP address. This allows you to set up NLB so that clients from the same Class C address range can access the same NLB member. This affinity is best for NLB clusters using the Internet.

Failover

If the primary or the secondary (extended) host server locations goes offline, you can manually initiate failover. Failover is not automatic. There are several different types of manually initiating failover:

Test Failover   Use Test Failover to verify that the replica virtual machine can successfully start in the secondary site. It will create a copy test virtual machine during failover and does not affect standard replication. After the test failover, if you select Failover on the replica test virtual machine, the test failover will be deleted.

Planned Failover   Use Planned Failover during scheduled downtime. You will have to turn off the primary machine before performing a planned failover. Once the machine fails over, the Hyper-V Replica will start replicating changes back to the primary server. The changes are tracked and sent to ensure that no data is lost. Once the planned failover is complete, the reverse replication begins so that the primary virtual machine become the secondary, and vice versa. This ensures that the hosts are synchronized.

Unplanned Failover   Use Unplanned Failover during unforeseen outages. Unplanned failover is started on the replica virtual machine. This should only be used if the primary machine goes offline. A check will confirm whether the primary machine is running. If you have recovery history enabled, then it is possible to recover to an earlier point in time. During failover, you should ensure that the recovery point is acceptable and then finish the failover to ensure that recovery points are combined.

Virtual Machine Advanced Features

One nice feature of virtual machines is the ability to set up advanced features. In the Advanced Features section (see Figure 13.7), there are multiple settings that you can configure.

FIGURE 13.7   VM Advanced Features

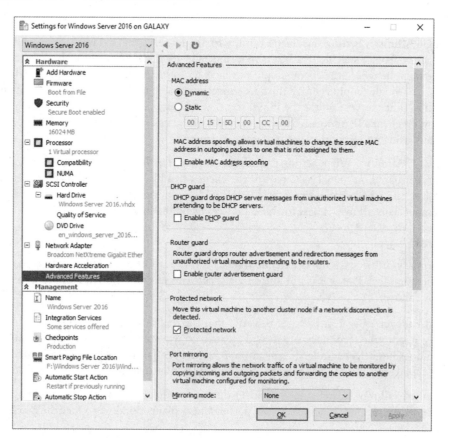

MAC Addressing   The first thing that you can configure in the Advanced Features section is setting a MAC address. The MAC address is a physical address that is associated to the NIC adapter. You can set the MAC address to Dynamic (it creates its own MAC addresses) or Static (this is where you can set a MAC address).

You also have the ability to do MAC spoofing. This is where a VM can change the source MAC address in outgoing packets to one that is not assigned to the NIC adapters.

DHCP Guard   DHCP Guard drops DHCP server messages from unauthorized virtual machines pretending to be a DHCP server. So what does this mean to you? If a server tries to pretend to be a DHCP server, your virtual machine will drop any messages that are sent by that DHCP server.

Router Guard   Router Guard drops router advertisement and redirection messages from unauthorized virtual machines pretending to be routers. It works almost the same way DHCP Guard works. If an unauthorized router tries to send messages to a virtual machine, that VM will not accept those messages.

Protected Network   You can set Network Health Detection at the virtual machine level for a Hyper-V host cluster. This is configured as a Protected Network. When you select the Protected Network check box, the virtual machine will be moved to another cluster node if a network disconnection is detected. If the health of a network connection is showing as disconnected, the VM will be automatically moved.

Port Mirroring   Port mirroring allows the network traffic of a virtual machine to be monitored by copying incoming and outgoing packets and forwarding the copies to another virtual machine configured for monitoring.

NIC Teaming   NIC Teaming gives you the ability to allow multiple network adapters on a system to be placed into a team. You can establish NIC Teaming in the guest operating system to aggregate bandwidth and provide redundancy. This is useful if teaming is not configured in the management operating system.

Device Naming   Device naming causes the name of the network adapter to be propagated into supported guest operating systems.

VM Checkpoints

One thing that you may want to set up on your Hyper-V server is recovery points or checkpoints. A checkpoint is a snapshot in time from when you can recover a virtual machine. It's like taking a picture of the virtual machine and using that picture to recover the VM. You can create multiple checkpoints of a VM and then recover back to any of those checkpoints if there is an issue. Using a more recent recovery point will result in less data lost. Checkpoints can be accessed from up to 24 hours ago.

If you want to enable these checkpoints in time for Hyper-V, you just need to follow these steps:

1. In Hyper-V Manager, right-click the virtual machine and choose Settings.

2. In the Management section, select Checkpoints.

3. To enable checkpoints for a VM, select Enable Checkpoints. If you want to disable checkpoints, just clear the check box.

4. Click Apply. Once you are finished, click OK and close Hyper-V Manager.

Software Load Balancing

Windows Server 2022 Hyper-V also allows you to distribute virtual network traffic using software load balancing (SLB). SLB allows you to have multiple servers hosting the same virtual networking workload in a multitenant environment. That way, you can set up high availability.

Using SLB allows you to load-balance virtual machines on the same Hyper-V server. Let's take a look at how SLB works. SLB is possible because it sets up a virtual IP address (VIP) that is automatically mapped to the dynamic IP addresses (DIP) of the virtual machines. The DIP addresses are the IP addresses of the virtual machines that are part of the load-balancing setup.

So, when someone tries to access the resources in the load-balancing setup, they access it by using the VIP address. The VIP request then gets sent to the DIP address of the virtual machines. So, users use the single VIP address, and that address gets sent to the load-balancing virtual machines.

Understanding Live Migration

Before we can implement live migration, you should understand what live migration does for Hyper-V. Hyper-V live migration transfers a running virtual machine from one physical server to another. The real nice advantage is that during the move of the virtual machine, there is no impact on the network's users. The virtual machine will continue to operate even during the move. This is different from using Hyper-V Quick Migration. Quick Migration required a pause in the Hyper-V VM while it's being moved.

Live migration lets you move virtual machines between servers. This is very useful when a Hyper-V server starts having issues. For example, if a Hyper-V machine is starting to have hardware issues, you can move the virtual machines from that Hyper-V server to another server that is running properly.

When setting up VM migrations, you have a few options. You can live-migrate a VM, Quick Migrate a VM, or just move a VM. As stated before, live migration requires no interruption of the VM. Quick Migration requires that you first pause the VM, then save the VM, then move the VM, and finally restart the VM. Moving a virtual machine means that you are going to copy a VM from one Hyper-V server to another while the virtual machine is turned off.

So, if you decide to use live migrations, there are a few things you should understand before setting it up. Let's take a look at some of the settings you can configure.

Configure CredSSP or Kerberos authentication

When you choose to use live migrations, one of the settings you configure is the type of authentication you can use. Choosing the authentication type is a feature listed under the Advanced Features of live migration. You can choose two types of authentication (as shown in Figure 13.8): Kerberos or Credential Security Support Provider (CredSSP).

FIGURE 13.8   Advanced Features for a live migration

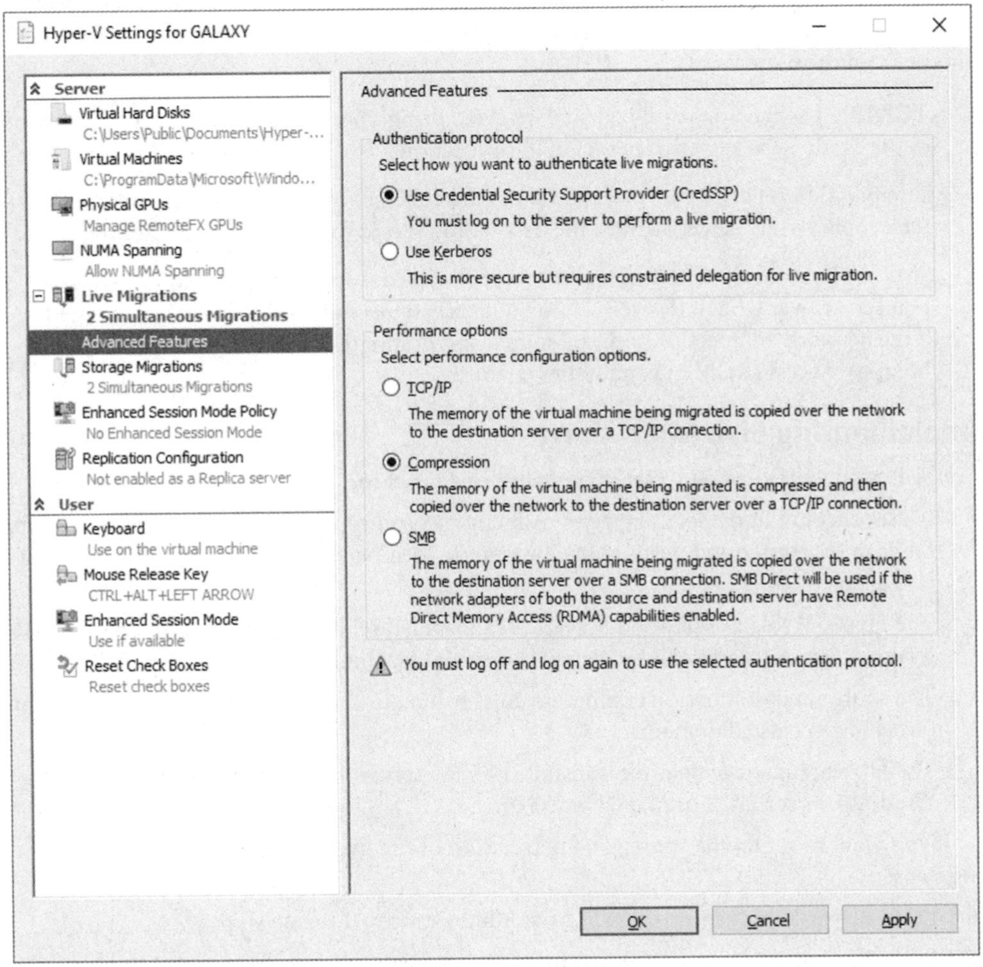

Authentication is choosing which protocol you will use to guarantee that live migration traffic between the source and destination servers is verified. Let's take a look at both options:

Credential Security Support Provider (CredSSP)   This option allows you to set up better security but requires constrained delegation for live migration. You have the ability to sign in to the source server by using a local console session, a Remote Desktop session, or a remote Windows PowerShell session.

Kerberos   This option lets you avoid having to sign into the server but requires constrained delegation to be set up.

Another section that you configure in the Advanced Features is Performance. This section allows you to choose how the network traffic for live migrations will be configured. You can choose from three options:

TCP/IP   The memory of the virtual machine being migrated is copied over the network to the destination server over a TCP/IP connection.

Compression   The memory of the virtual machine being migrated is compressed and then copied over the network to the destination server over a TCP/IP connection.

SMB   The memory of the virtual machine is copied over the network to the destination server over a SMB (Server Message Block) connection. SMB Direct will be used if the network adapters of both the source and destination server have Remote Direct Memory Access (RDMA) capabilities enabled.

Implementing Live Migration

You will need the following to set up nonclustered hosts for live migration:

- A user account in the local Hyper-V Administrators group or the Administrators group on both the source and destination computers. Membership in the Domain Administrators group.

- The Hyper-V role in Windows Server 2022 installed on both the source and destination servers. Live migration can be done if the virtual machine is at least version 5.

- The source and destination computers must belong to the same Active Directory domain or belong to trusted domains.

- The Hyper-V management tools installed on the server. The computer must be running Windows Server 2022 or Windows 10/11.

If you want to set up the source and destination of the live migration, use the following steps:

1. Open Hyper-V Manager. (Click Start ➤ Administrative Tools ➤ Hyper-V Manager.)

2. In the navigation pane, select one of the servers. Right-click the server and choose Hyper-V Settings ➤ Live Migrations.

3. In the Live Migrations pane, select Enable Incoming And Outgoing Live Migrations.

4. In the section Simultaneous Live Migrations, specify the number of simultaneous live migrations (the default is 2).

5. Under Incoming Live Migrations, accept any network for live migrations or specify the IP address you want to use for live migration. If you want to use an IP address, click the Add button and type the IP address information. Click OK when you're finished.

6. For Kerberos and performance options, expand Live Migrations (click the plus sign next to Live Migrations) and then select Advanced Features:
   - Under Authentication Protocol, select Use CredSSP or Use Kerberos.
   - Under Performance options, select performance configuration options (either TCP/IP, Compression, or SMB).

7. Click OK.

8. If you have another server that you want to set up for live migrations, select the server and repeat the steps.

Implement Shared Nothing Live Migration

Administrators can now live-migrate virtual machines even if the Hyper-V host is not part of a cluster. Before using live migrate without a Windows cluster, you have to configure the servers. Choose Kerberos or Credential Security Support Provider (CredSSP) to authenticate the live migration.

To trigger a Shared Nothing Live Migration remotely, you'll need to enable Kerberos constrained delegation, which you configure on the Delegation tab of Active Directory Users and Computers for each computer taking part in the Shared Nothing Live Migration.

Implementing Storage Migration

Hyper-V supports moving virtual machine storage without downtime by allowing you to move storage while the virtual machine is running. You do this by using Hyper-V Manager or Windows PowerShell. You can add storage to a Hyper-V cluster or a stand-alone computer, and then move VMs to the new storage while the virtual machines continue to run. You can move virtual machine storage between physical storage devices to respond to a decrease in performance that results from bottlenecks.

Storage Migration Requirements

To use the Hyper-V functionality of moving virtual machine storage, you must meet these prerequisites:

- One or more installations of Windows Server 2022 with the Hyper-V role installed
- A server that is capable of running Hyper-V
- Virtual machines that are configured to use only virtual hard disks for storage

Storage Migration lets you move the virtual hard disks of a virtual machine while the virtual hard disks are still able to be used by the running virtual machine (see Figure 13.9).

When you move a running virtual machine's virtual hard disks, Hyper-V performs the following steps:

1. Disk reads and writes use the source virtual hard disk.

2. When reads and writes occur on the source virtual hard disk, the disk data is copied to the new destination virtual hard disk.

3. Once the initial disk copy is complete, the disk writes are mirrored to both the source and destination virtual hard disks while outstanding disk changes are replicated.

4. After the source and destination virtual hard disks are entirely synchronized, the virtual machine changes over to using the destination virtual hard disk.

5. The source virtual hard disk is deleted.

FIGURE 13.9 Storage Migration settings

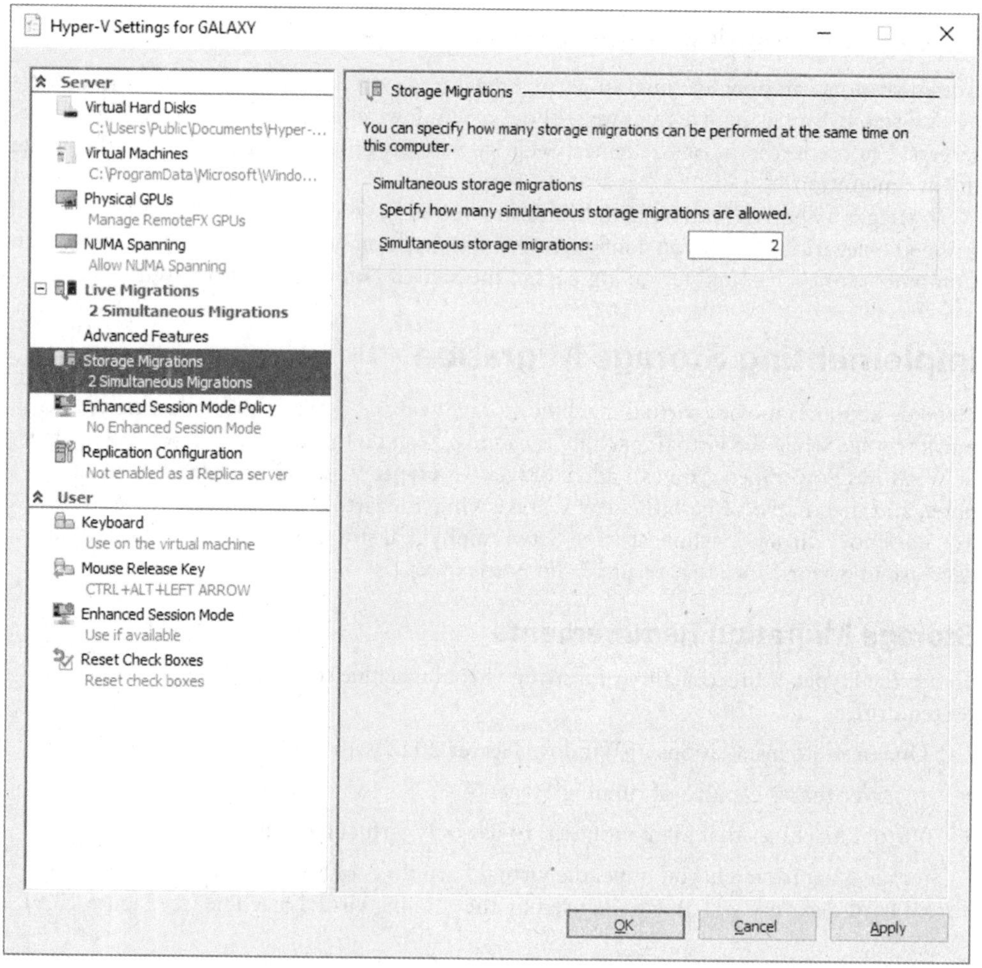

Achieving High Availability with Clustering

Taking high availability to the next level for enterprise services often means creating a cluster. Normally you have two types of clusters: failover clusters or high-performance clusters.

In a failover cluster, all of the clustered application or service resources are assigned to one node or server in the cluster. If that node goes offline for any reason, the cluster continues to operate on a second node. When setting up a failover cluster, you can set the cluster up to be a straight failover cluster or a load-balancing cluster. Both options normally use two nodes. Normal failover clusters have a primary server (active server) and a backup server (passive server). If the primary server goes offline, the secondary server takes over. On a load-balancing failover cluster, both nodes handle requests from clients. If one of the nodes goes offline, the other node picks up the slack from the offline node.

High availability clusters normally have multiple nodes all connected to the same cluster. Because all of the clustered nodes work at the same time, you are getting the best performance along with the data protection of a cluster. The disadvantage of this type of cluster is that it normally requires more nodes as part of the cluster.

Commonly clustered applications are SQL Server and Exchange Server; commonly clustered services are File and Print. Since the differences between a clustered application and a clustered service are primarily related to the number of functions or features, for simplicity's sake I will refer to both as *clustered applications*. Most often, clustered resources are a Hyper-V virtual machine in Azure or on an onsite domain.

If there is a failure of a clustered node or if the clustered node is taken offline for maintenance, the clustered application can continue to run on other cluster nodes. The client requests are automatically redirected to the next available cluster node to minimize the impact of the down clustered node.

How does clustering improve availability? By increasing the number of server nodes available on which the application or virtual machine can run, you can move the application or virtual machine to a healthy server if there is a problem, if maintenance needs to be completed on the hardware or the operating system, or if patches need to be applied. The clustered application that's moved will have to restart on the new server regardless of whether the move was intentional. This is why the term *highly available* is used instead of *fault tolerant*.

Virtual machines, however, can be moved from one node to another using live migration. Live migration is where one or more virtual machines are intentionally moved from one node to another with their current memory state intact through the cluster network with no indicators to the virtual machine consumer that the virtual machine has moved from one server to another. However, in the event of a cluster node or virtual machine failure, the virtual machine will still fail and will then be brought online again on another healthy cluster node.

Figure 13.10 shows an example of SQL Server running on the first node of a Windows Server 2022 failover cluster.

FIGURE 13.10   Using failover clustering to cluster SQL Server

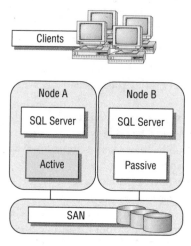

The clustered SQL Server in Figure 13.11 can be failed over to another node in the cluster and still service database requests. However, the database will be restarted.

FIGURE 13.11   Failing the SQL Server service to another node

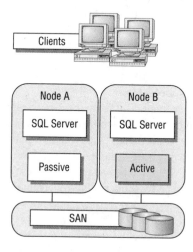

Failover Clustering Requirements

The Failover Clustering feature is available in the Datacenter, Standard, and Hyper-V editions of Windows Server 2022.

To be able to configure a failover cluster, you must have the required components. A single failover cluster can have up to 64 nodes when using Windows Server 2022, and the clustered service or application must support that number of nodes.

Before creating a failover cluster, make sure that all the hardware involved meets the cluster requirements. To be supported by Microsoft, all hardware must be certified for Windows Server 2022, and the complete failover cluster solution must pass all tests in the Validate A Configuration Wizard. Although the exact hardware will depend on the clustered application, a few requirements are standard:

- Server components must be marked with the "Certified for Windows Server 2022" logo.
- Although not explicitly required, server hardware should match and contain the same or similar components.
- All of the Validate A Configuration Wizard tests must pass.

The requirements for failover clustering storage have changed from previous versions of Windows. For example, Parallel SCSI is no longer a supported storage technology for any of the clustered disks. There are, however, additional requirements that need to be met for the storage components:

- Disks available for the cluster must be Fibre Channel, iSCSI, or Serial Attached SCSI.
- Each cluster node must have a dedicated network interface card for iSCSI connectivity. The network interface card you use for iSCSI should not be used for network communication.
- Multipath software must be based on Microsoft's Multipath I/O (MPIO).
- Storage drivers must be based on `storport.sys`.
- Drivers and firmware for the storage controllers on each server node in the cluster should be identical.
- Storage components must be marked with the "Certified for Windows Server 2022" logo.

In addition, there are network requirements that must be met for failover clustering:

- Cluster nodes should be connected to multiple networks for communication redundancy.
- Network adapters should be the same make, use the same driver, and have the firmware version in each cluster node.
- Network components must be marked with the "Certified for Windows Server 2022" logo.

There are two types of network connections in a failover cluster. These should have adequate redundancy because total failure of either could cause loss of functionality of the cluster. The two types are as follows:

Public Network   This is the network through which clients are able to connect to the clustered service application.

Private Network   This is the network used by the nodes to communicate with each other.

To provide redundancy for these two network types, you would need to add more network adapters to the node and configure them to connect to the networks.

In previous versions of Windows Server, support was given only when the entire cluster configuration was tested and listed on the Hardware Compatibility List. The tested configuration listed the server and storage configuration down to the firmware and driver versions. This proved to be difficult and expensive from both a vendor and a consumer perspective to deploy supported Windows clusters.

When problems did arise and Microsoft support was needed, it caused undue troubleshooting complexity as well. With Windows Server 2022 failover clustering and simplified requirements, including the "Certified for Windows Server 2022" logo program and the Validate A Configuration Wizard, it all but eliminates the guesswork of getting the cluster components configured in a way that follows best practices and allows Microsoft support to assist you easily when needed.

Workgroup and Multidomain Clusters

One nice new advantage of using Windows Server 2022 is the ability to set up a cluster on systems not part of the same domain. Windows Server 2022 allows you to set up a cluster without using Active Directory dependencies. You can create clusters in the following situations:

Single-Domain Cluster   All nodes in a cluster are part of the same domain.

Multidomain Cluster   Nodes in a cluster are part of a different domain.

Workgroup Cluster   Nodes are member servers and part of a workgroup.

Site-Aware, Stretched, or Geographically Dispersed Clusters (Geoclustering)

One nice advantage of Windows Server 2022 clustering is that you can set up site-aware failover clusters. Using site-aware clustering, you can expand clustered nodes to different geographic locations (sites). Site-aware failover clusters allow you to set up clusters in remote locations for failover, placement policies, Cross-Site Heartbeating, and quorum placement.

One of the issues with previous clusters was the heartbeat. The cluster heartbeat is a signal sent between servers so that they know the machines are up and running. Servers send heartbeats, and if after five nonresponsive heartbeats, the cluster assumes that the node was offline. So, if you had nodes in remote locations, the heartbeats would not get the response they needed.

But now Windows Server 2022 includes Cross-Site Heartbeating, which allows you to set up delays so that remote nodes can answer the heartbeat in time. Use the following two PowerShell commands to specify the delay necessary for Cross-Site Heartbeating:

```
(Get-Cluster).CrossSiteDelay = <value>
(Get-Cluster).CrossSiteThreshold = <value>
```

The first PowerShell command (`CrossSiteDelay`) is what is used to set the amount of time between each heartbeat sent to nodes. This value is done in milliseconds (the default is 1000).

The second PowerShell command (`CrossSiteThreshold`) is the value that you set for the number of missed heartbeats (the default is 20) before the node is considered offline.

One issue you may face is if you have multiple sites or if the cluster is geographically dispersed. If the failover cluster does not have a shared common disk, data replication between nodes might not pass the cluster validation "storage" tests.

Setting up a cluster in a site-aware, stretched, or geocluster (these terms can be used interchangeably) configuration is a common practice. As long as the cluster solution does not require external storage to fail over, it will not need to pass the storage test to function properly.

Cluster Quorum

When a group of people set out to accomplish a single task or goal, a method for settling disagreements and for making decisions is required. In the case of a cluster, the goal is to provide a highly available service in spite of failures. When a problem occurs and a cluster node loses communication with the other nodes because of a network error, the functioning nodes are supposed to try to bring the redundant service back online.

How, though, is it determined which node should bring the clustered service back online? If all the nodes are functional despite the network communications issue, each one might try. Just like a group of people with their own ideas, a method must be put in place to determine which idea, or node, to grant control of the cluster. Windows Server 2022 failover clustering, like other clustering technologies, requires that a quorum exist between the cluster nodes before a cluster becomes available.

A *quorum* is a consensus of the status of each of the nodes in the cluster. Quorum must be achieved in order for a clustered application to come online by obtaining a majority of the votes available (see Figure 13.12). Windows Server 2022 has four models, or methods, for determining quorum and for adjusting the number and types of votes available:

- Node majority (no witness)
- Node majority with witness (disk or file share)
- Node and file share majority
- No majority (disk witness only)

FIGURE 13.12   Majority needed

When a majority of the nodes are communicating, the cluster is functional.

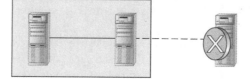

When a majority of the nodes are not communicating, the cluster stops.

Witness Configuration

Most administrators follow some basic rules. For example, when you configure a quorum, the voting components in the cluster should be an odd number. For example, if I set up a quorum for five elements and I lose one element, I continue to work. If I lose two elements, I continue to work. If I lose three elements, the cluster stops—as soon as it hits half plus 1, the cluster stops. This works well with an odd number.

If the cluster contains an even number of voting elements, you should then configure a disk witness or a file share witness. The advantage of using a witness (disk or file share) is that the cluster will continue to run even if half of the cluster nodes simultaneously go down or are disconnected. Configuring a disk witness is possible only if the storage vendor supports read-write access from all sites to the replicated storage.

One of the advantages of Windows Server 2022 is the advanced quorum configuration option. This option allows you to assign or remove quorum votes on a per-node basis. You now have the ability to remove votes from nodes in certain configurations. For example, if your organization uses a site-aware cluster, you may choose to remove votes from the nodes in the backup site. This way, those backup nodes would not affect your quorum calculations.

There are different ways that you can set up quorum witnesses. Here are some of the options that you can choose from:

Configuring a Disk Witness   Choose the quorum disk witness if all nodes can see the disks. To set up this disk witness, the cluster must be able to see the dedicated LUN. The LUN needs to store a copy of the cluster database, and it's most useful for clusters that are using shared storage. The following list is just some of the requirements when setting up a disk witness:

- The LUN needs to be at least 512 MB minimum.
- The disk must be dedicated to cluster use only.

- Must pass disk storage validation tests.
- The disk can't be used as a Cluster Shared Volume (CSV).
- You must use a single volume for Basic disks.
- No drive letter is needed.
- The drive must be formatted using NTFS or ReFS.
- Can be used with hardware RAID.
- Should not be used with antivirus or backup software.

Configuring a File Share Witness   You should use the file share witness when you need to think about multisite disaster recovery and the file server must be using the SMB file share.

The following list is just some of the requirements when setting up a file share witness:

- Minimum of 5 MB of free space.
- File share must be dedicated to the cluster and not used to store user data or application data.

Configuring a Cloud Witness   The Windows Server 2022 cloud witness is a new type of failover cluster quorum witness that leverages Azure as the intercession point. The cloud witness gets a vote just like any other quorum witness. You can set up the cloud witness as a quorum witness using the Configure A Cluster Quorum Wizard.

Dynamic Quorum Management

Windows Server 2022 provides *dynamic quorum management*, which automatically manages the vote assignment to nodes. With this feature enabled, votes are automatically added or removed from nodes when that node either joins or leaves a cluster. In Windows Server 2022, dynamic quorum management is enabled by default.

Validating a Cluster Configuration

Configuring a failover cluster in Windows Server 2022 is much simpler than in previous versions of Windows Server. Before a cluster can be configured, run the Validate A Configuration Wizard to verify that your hardware is configured in a fashion that is supportable. Before you can run the Validate A Configuration Wizard, however, the Failover Clustering feature needs to be installed using Server Manager. The account that is used to create a cluster must have administrative rights on each of the cluster nodes and have permission to create a cluster name object in Active Directory. Follow these steps:

1. Ensure that you meet the hardware and software perquisites.
2. Install the Failover Clustering feature on each server.
3. Log in with the appropriate user ID and run the Validate A Configuration Wizard.

4. Create a cluster.

5. Install and cluster applications and services.

To install the Failover Clustering feature on a cluster node, follow the steps outlined in Exercise 13.2.

EXERCISE 13.2

Installing the Failover Cluster Feature

1. Press the Windows Key and select Administrative Tools ➤ Server Manager.

2. Select number 2, Add Roles And Features.

3. At the Select Installation Type screen, choose a role-based or feature-based installation.

4. At the Select Destination Server screen, choose Select A Server From The Server Pool and click Next.

5. At the Select Server Roles screen, click Next.

6. At the Select Features screen, click the Failover Clustering (see Figure 13.13) check box. If the Add Features dialog box appears, click the Add Features button. Click Next.

FIGURE 13.13   Failover Cluster feature

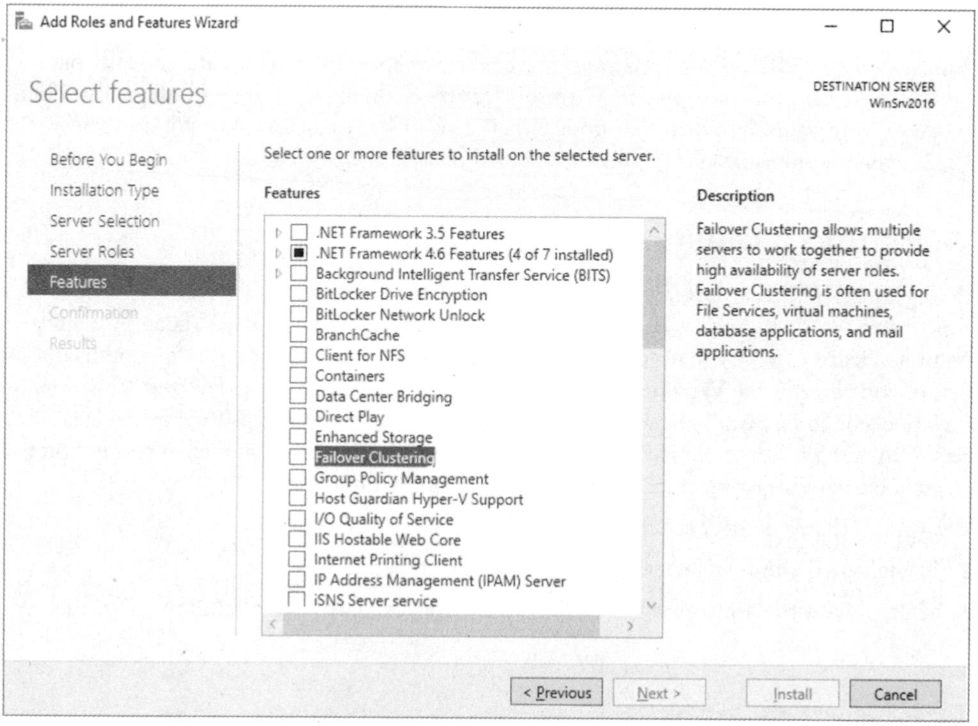

7. At the confirmation screen (see Figure 13.14), click the Install button.

FIGURE 13.14 Confirmation screen

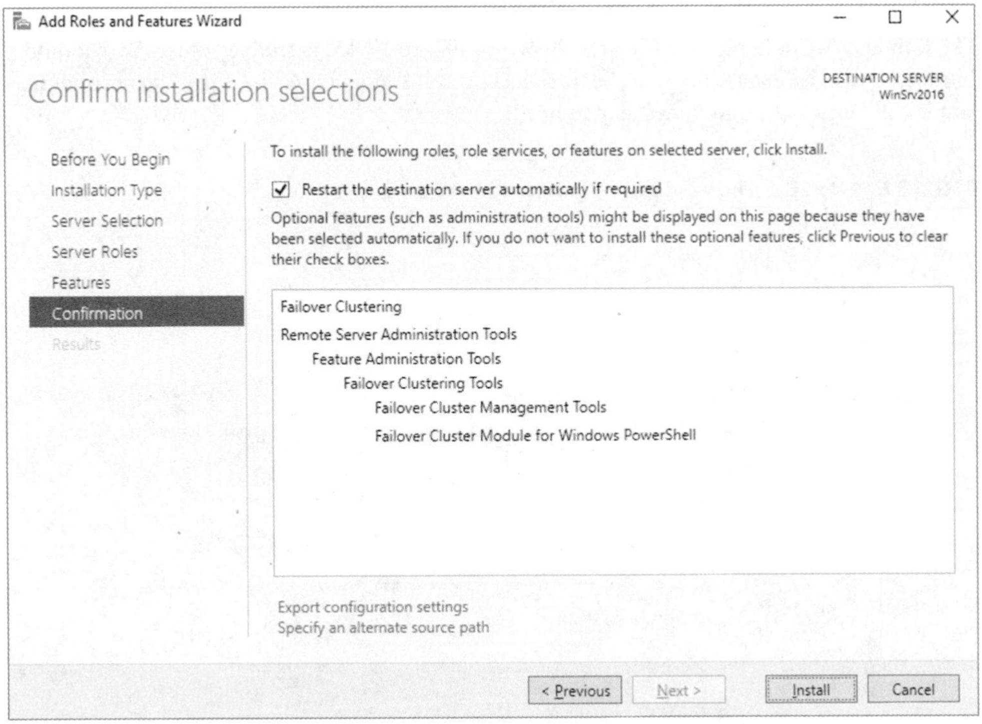

8. Once the installation is complete, click Close.

9. Close Server Manager.

Using the Validate A Configuration Wizard before creating a cluster is highly recommended. This wizard validates that the hardware and the software for the potential cluster nodes are in a supported configuration. Even if the configuration passes the tests, take care to review all warnings and informational messages so that they can be addressed or documented before you create the cluster.

Running the Validate A Configuration Wizard does the following:

- Conducts four types of tests (software and hardware inventory, network, storage, and system configuration)

- Confirms that the hardware and software settings are supportable by Microsoft support staff

You should run the Validate A Configuration Wizard before creating a cluster or after making any major hardware or software changes to the cluster. Doing this will help you identify any misconfigurations that could cause problems with the failover cluster.

Running the Validate A Configuration Wizard

The Validate A Configuration Wizard, shown in Figure 13.15, is simple to use. You should run it after the Failover Clustering feature has been installed on each of the cluster nodes, and it can be run as many times as you need.

FIGURE 13.15   The Validate A Configuration Wizard

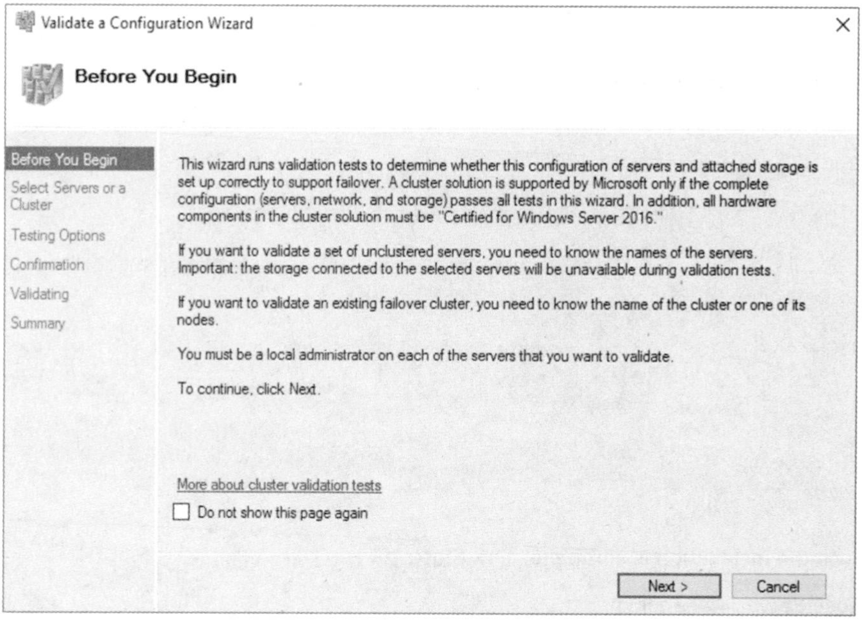

![Validate a Configuration Wizard - Before You Begin screen]

When you are troubleshooting cluster problems or have changed the configuration of the cluster hardware, it is a good idea to run the Validate A Configuration Wizard again to help pinpoint potential cluster configuration problems.

If you already have a cluster configured and want to run the Validate A Configuration Wizard, you can do so; however, you will not be able to run all the storage tests without taking the clustered resources offline. You will be prompted either to skip the disruptive tests or to take the clustered resources offline so that the tests can complete.

Exercise 13.3 shows the steps for running the Validate A Configuration Wizard successfully on clusters named NODEA and NODEB, which are not yet clustered.

I am using servers called NODEA and NODEB in the exercises. You need to replace these two nodes with your own two servers to complete these steps.

EXERCISE 13.3

Running the Validate A Configuration Wizard

1. Press the Windows Key and select Administrative Tools ➢ Failover Cluster Management.

2. In the Actions pane (right side of screen), click Validate Configuration.

3. At the Before You Begin screen, click Next.

4. Type **First Server Name** (this is your server's name) in the Enter Name field and click Add.

5. Type **Second Server Name** (this is the second server's name) in the Enter Name field and click Add.

6. Click Next.

7. Leave Run All Tests (Recommended) selected and click Next.

8. You will see tests being run (see Figure 13.16). Let the test complete, review the report in the Summary window, and then click Finish.

FIGURE 13.16   Summary window

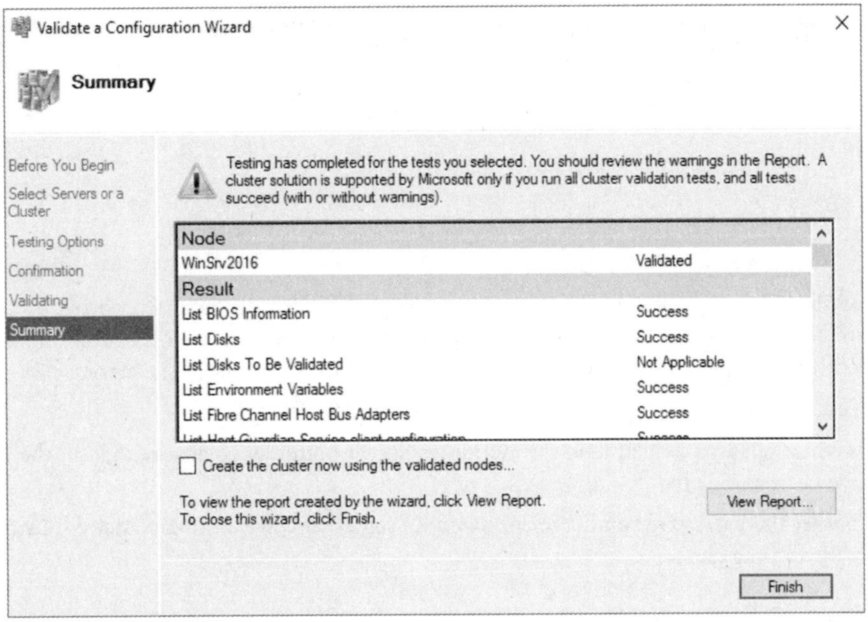

Validate a Configuration Wizard	✕

Summary

Before You Begin
Select Servers or a Cluster
Testing Options
Confirmation
Validating
Summary

⚠ Testing has completed for the tests you selected. You should review the warnings in the Report. A cluster solution is supported by Microsoft only if you run all cluster validation tests, and all tests succeed (with or without warnings).

Node	
WinSrv2016	Validated
Result	
List BIOS Information	Success
List Disks	Success
List Disks To Be Validated	Not Applicable
List Environment Variables	Success
List Fibre Channel Host Bus Adapters	Success
List Host Guardian Service client configuration	Success

☐ Create the cluster now using the validated nodes...

To view the report created by the wizard, click View Report.
To close this wizard, click Finish.

[View Report...]

[Finish]

9. Close the Failover Cluster Wizard.

Addressing Problems Reported by the Validate A Configuration Wizard

After the Validate A Configuration Wizard has run, it will display the results, as shown in Figure 13.17. You can review this report in detail later using a web browser. The report is named with the date and time the wizard was run, and it is stored in %windir%\cluster\ Reports.

FIGURE 13.17 Validate A Configuration Wizard results

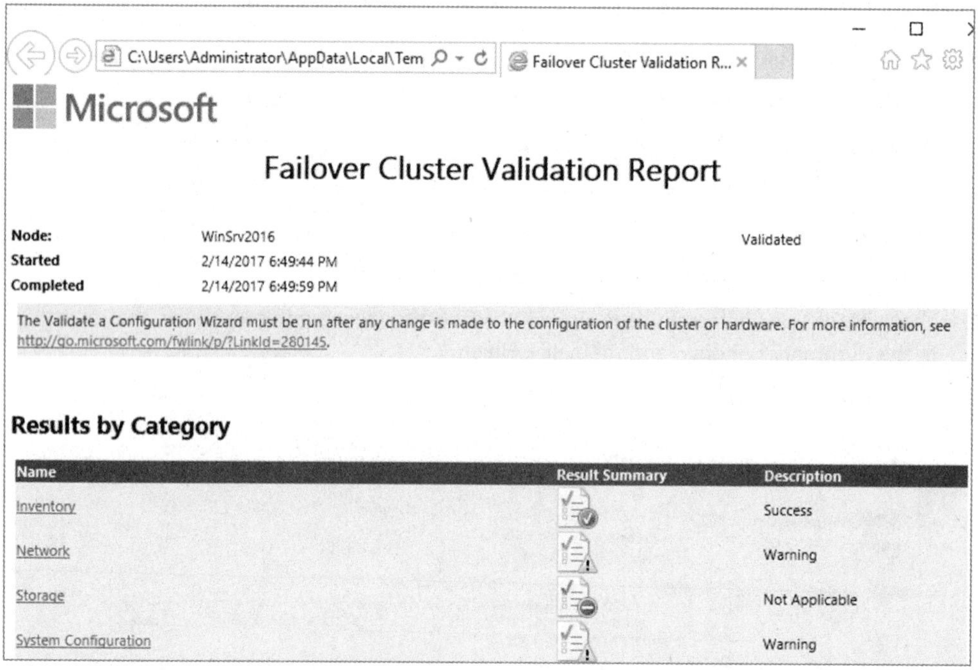

How should errors listed in the report be addressed? Often, the errors reported by the Validate A Configuration Wizard are self-explanatory; however, sometimes additional help is required. The following three guidelines should help you troubleshoot the errors:

- Read all of the errors because multiple errors may be related.
- Use the checklists available in the Windows Server help files to ensure that all the steps have been completed.
- Contact the hardware vendor for updated drivers, firmware, and guidance for using the hardware in a cluster.

Creating a Cluster

After you have successfully validated a configuration and the cluster hardware is in a supportable state, you can create a cluster. The process for creating a cluster is straightforward and similar to running the Validate A Configuration Wizard. To create a cluster with two servers, follow the instructions in Exercise 13.4.

EXERCISE 13.4

Creating a Cluster

1. Open the Failover Cluster Management MMC.

2. In the Management section of the center pane, select Create A Cluster.

3. Read the Before You Begin information and click Next.

4. In the Enter Server Name box, type **Your Server** and then click Add.

5. Again, in the Enter Server Name box, type **Your Second Server** and then click Add. Click Next.

6. At the Validation screen, choose No for this exercise and then click Next.

7. In the Access Point For Administering The Cluster section, enter **Cluster1** for the cluster name.

8. Type an IP address and then click Next. This IP address will be the IP address of the cluster.

9. In the Confirmation dialog box, verify the information and then click Next.

10. On the Summary page, click Finish.

Working with Cluster Nodes

Once a cluster is created, a couple of actions are available. First, you can add another node to the cluster by using the Add Node Wizard from the Failover Cluster Management Actions pane. At this point, you also have the option to pause a node, which prevents resources from being failed over or moved to the node. You typically would pause a node when the node is involved in maintenance or troubleshooting. After a node is paused, it must be resumed to allow resources to be run on it again.

Another action available to perform on a node at this time is *evict*. Eviction is an irreversible process. Once you evict the node, it must be re-added to the cluster. You would evict a node when it is damaged beyond repair or is no longer needed in the cluster. If you evict a damaged node, you can repair or rebuild it and then add it back to the cluster using the Add Node Wizard.

Clustering Roles, Services, and Applications

Once the cluster is created, applications, services, and roles can be clustered. Windows Server 2022 includes a number of built-in roles and features that can be clustered (see Figure 13.18):

FIGURE 13.18 High availability roles

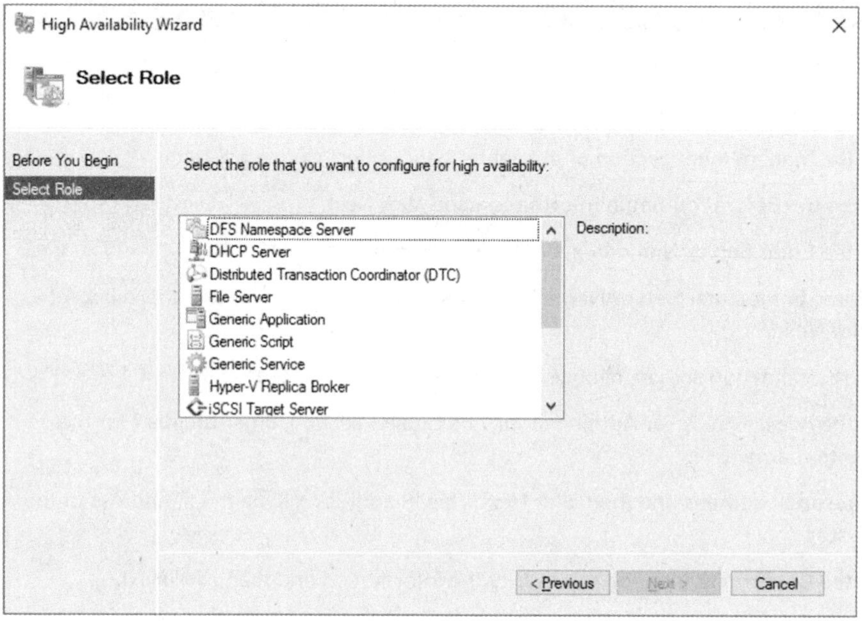

- DFS Namespace Server
- DHCP Server
- Distributed Transaction Coordinator (DTC)
- File Server
- Generic Application
- Generic Script
- Generic Service
- Hyper-V Replica Broker
- iSCSI Target Server
- iSNS Server
- Message Queuing

- Other Server

- Virtual Machine

In addition, other common services and applications can be clustered on Windows Server 2022 clusters:

- Enterprise database services, such as Microsoft SQL Server

- Enterprise messaging services, such as Microsoft Exchange Server

To cluster a role or feature such as Print Services, the first step is to install the role or feature on each node of the cluster. The next step is to use the Configure A Service Or Application Wizard in the Failover Cluster Management tool. Exercise 13.5 shows you how to cluster the Print Services role once an appropriate disk has been presented to the cluster. To complete this exercise, you must have created a cluster.

EXERCISE 13.5

Clustering the Print Services Role

1. Open the Failover Cluster Management MMC.

2. In the console tree, click the arrow next to the cluster name to expand the items underneath it.

3. Right-click Roles and choose Configure Role.

4. Click Next on the Before You Begin page.

5. Click Other Server on the Select Role screen and then click Next.

6. Type the name of the print server, such as **Print1**, and type the IP address that will be used to access the print service, such as **80.0.0.34**. Then click Next.

7. At the Select Storage page, just click Next.

8. Click Next at the Confirmation page.

9. After the wizard runs and the Summary page appears, you can view a report of the tasks the wizard performed by clicking View Report.

10. Close the report and click Finish.

The built-in roles and features all are configured in a similar fashion. Other applications, such as Microsoft Exchange Server 2016, have specialized cluster configuration routines that are outside the scope of these exams. Applications that are not developed to be clustered can also be clustered using the Generic Application, Generic Script, or Generic Service option in the Configure A Service Or Application Wizard, as shown in Figure 13.19.

FIGURE 13.19 Configuring a generic application

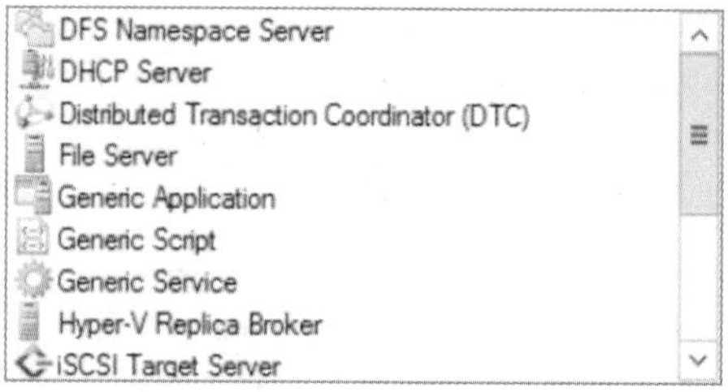

DFS Namespace Server
DHCP Server
Distributed Transaction Coordinator (DTC)
File Server
Generic Application
Generic Script
Generic Service
Hyper-V Replica Broker
iSCSI Target Server

Clustered Application Settings

Windows Server 2022 has options that let fine-tune the failover process to meet the needs of your business. I'll cover these options in the next few sections.

Failover occurs when a clustered application or service moves from one node to another. The process can be triggered automatically because of a failure or server maintenance or can be done manually by an administrator. The failover process works like this:

1. The cluster service takes all of the resources in the role offline in the order set in the dependency hierarchy.

2. The cluster service transfers the role to the node that is listed next on the application's list of preferred host nodes.

3. The cluster service attempts to bring all of the role's resources online, starting at the bottom of the dependency hierarchy.

These steps can change depending on the use of live migration.

In a cluster that is hosting multiple applications, it may be important to set specific nodes to be primarily responsible for each clustered application. This can be helpful from a troubleshooting perspective since a specific node is targeted for hosting service. To set a preferred node and an order of preference for failover, use the General tab in the Properties dialog box of the clustered application.

Also, the order of failover is set in this same dialog box by moving the order in which the nodes are listed. If NODEA should be the primary node and NODEC should be the server that the application fails to first, NODEA should be listed first and selected as the preferred owner. NODEC should be listed second, and the remaining cluster nodes should be listed after NODEC.

A number of failover settings can be configured for the clustered service. The failover settings control the number of times a clustered application can fail in a period of time before the cluster stops trying to restart it. Typically, if a clustered application fails a number of times, some sort of manual intervention will be required to return the application to a stable state.

Specifying the maximum number of failures will keep the application from trying to restart until it is manually brought back online after the problem has been resolved. This is beneficial because if the application continues to be brought online and then fails, it may show as being functional to the monitoring system, even though it continues to fail. After the application is put in a failed state, the monitoring system will not be able to contact the application and should report it as being offline.

Failback settings control whether and when a clustered application would fail back to the preferred cluster node once it becomes available. The default setting is Prevent Failback. If failback is allowed, two additional options are available, either to fail back immediately after the preferred node is available or to fail back within a specified time.

The time is specified in the 24-hour format. If you want to allow failback between 10 p.m. and 11 p.m., set the failback time to be between 22 and 23. Setting a failback time to off-hours is an excellent way to ensure that your clustered applications are running on the designated nodes and automatically scheduling the failover process for a time when it will impact the fewest users.

One tool that is valuable in determining how resources affect other resources is the dependency walker. The *dependency walker* visualizes the dependency hierarchy created for an application or service. Using this tool can help when you're troubleshooting why specific resources are causing failures and allow you to visualize the current configuration better and adjust it to meet business needs. Exercise 13.6 will show you how to run the dependency viewer.

EXERCISE 13.6

Using the Dependency Viewer

1. Open the Failover Cluster Management MMC.

2. In the console tree, click the arrow to expand the cluster.

3. Click Roles.

4. Under the Roles section in the center of the screen, click one of the roles (such as Print1).

5. Right-click the role and under More Actions click Show Dependency Report.

6. Review the dependency report.

7. Close the Dependency Report and close the Failover Cluster Manager.

Exercise 13.5 generated a dependency report that shows how the print service is dependent on a network name and a clustered disk resource. The network name is then dependent on an IP address.

Resource Properties

Resources are physical or logical objects, such as a file share or IP address, that the failover cluster manages. They may be a service or application available to clients, or they may be part of the cluster. Resources include physical hardware devices such as disks and logical items such as network names. They are the smallest configurable unit in a cluster and can run on only a single node in a cluster at a time.

Like clustered applications, resources have a number of properties available for meeting business requirements for high availability. This section covers resource dependencies and policies.

Dependencies can be set on individual resources and control how resources are brought online and offline. Simply put, a dependent resource is brought online after the resources that it depends on, and it is taken offline before those resources. As shown in Figure 13.20, dependencies can be set on a specific resource, such as the generic application.

FIGURE 13.20   Resource dependencies

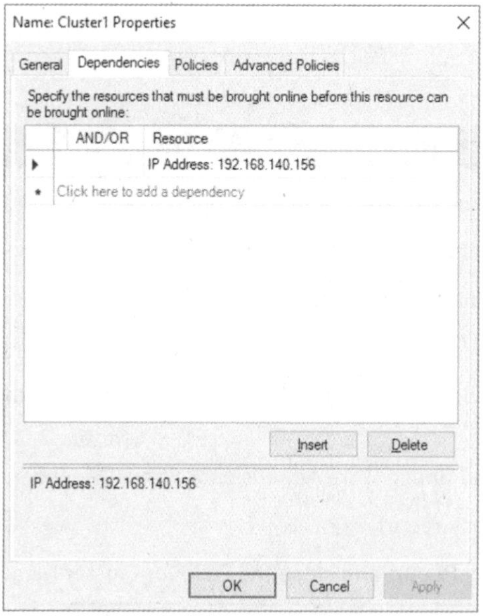

Resource policies are settings that control how resources respond when a failure occurs and how resources are monitored for failures. Figure 13.21 shows the Policies tab of a resource's Properties dialog box.

FIGURE 13.21   Resource policies

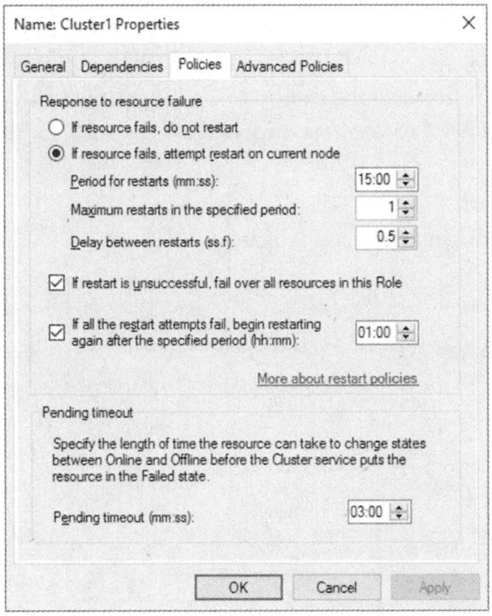

You set configuration options on the Policies tab for how a resource should respond in the event of a failure. The options available are as follows:

If Resource Fails, Do Not Restart   This option, as it would lead you to believe, leaves the failed resource offline.

If Resource Fails, Attempt Restart On Current Node   With this option set, the resource tries to restart if it fails on the node on which it is currently running. There are two additional options if this is selected so that the number of restarts can be limited. They set the number of times the resource should restart on the current node in a specified length of time. For example, if you specify 5 for Maximum Restarts In The Specified Period and 10:00 (mm:ss) for Period For Restarts, the cluster service will try to restart the resource five times during that 10-minute period. After the fifth restart, the cluster service will no longer attempt to restart the service on the active node.

If Restart Is Unsuccessful, Fail Over All Resources In This Service Or Application   If this option is selected, when the cluster service is no longer trying to restart the resource on the active node, it will fail the entire service or application to another cluster node.

If you wanted to leave the application or service with a failed resource on the current node, you would clear this check box.

If All The Restart Attempts Fail, Begin Restarting Again After The Specified Period (hh:mm)   If this option is selected, the cluster service will restart the resource at a specified interval if all previous attempts have failed.

Pending Timeout   This option is used to set the amount of time in minutes and seconds that the cluster service should wait for this resource to respond to a change in states. If a resource takes longer than the cluster expects to change states, the cluster will mark it as having failed. If a resource consistently takes longer than this and the problem cannot be resolved, you may need to increase this value. Figure 13.22 shows the Advanced Policies tab.

FIGURE 13.22   Resource Advanced Policies

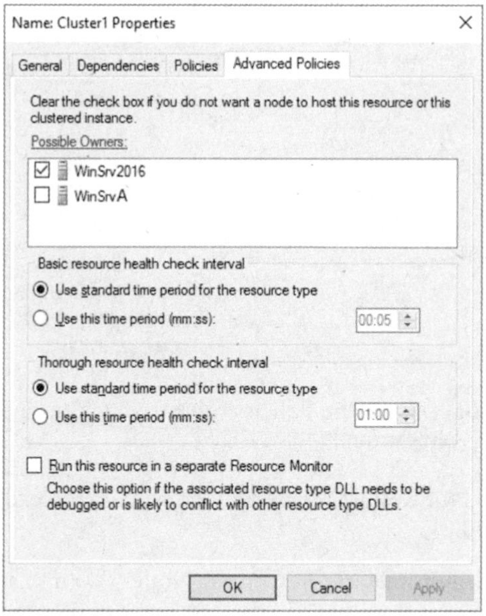

The options available on the Advanced Policies tab are as follows:

Possible Owners   This option allows you to remove specific cluster nodes from running this resource. Using this option is valuable when there are issues with a resource on a particular node and you want to keep the applications from failing over to that node until the problem can be repaired.

Basic Resource Health Check Interval   This option allows you to customize the health check interval for this resource.

Thorough Resource Health Check Interval   This option allows you to customize the thorough health check interval for this resource.

Run This Resource In A Separate Resource Monitor   If the resource needs to be debugged by a support engineer or if the resource conflicts with other resources, you may select this option.

Windows Server 2022 Clustering Features

Many features are included in the Windows Server 2022 release for clustering. It is a rich feature set of high availability with greatly improved flexibility based on the needs of IT organizations. The new features relate to quorum behavior, virtual machine hosting, Active Directory–detached clusters, and a new dashboard.

Windows PowerShell Cmdlets for Failover Clusters   As I have explained throughout this book, PowerShell is a command-line shell and scripting tool. Windows Server 2022 clustering has new cmdlets that provide powerful ways to script cluster configuration and management tasks. Windows PowerShell cmdlets have now replaced the `Cluster.exe` command-line interface.

Cluster Shared Volumes   *Cluster Shared Volumes (CSV)* allows for the configuration of clustered virtual machines. CSV allows you to do the following:

- Reduce the number of LUNs (disks) required for your virtual machines.
- Make better use of disk space. Any VHD file on that LUN can use the free space on a CSV volume.
- More easily track the paths to VHD files and other files used by virtual machines.
- Use a few CSV volumes to create a configuration that supports many clustered virtual machines.

CSV volumes also are used for the Scale-Out-File-Server cluster role.

Management of Large-Scale Clusters   One advantage of Windows Server 2022 clusters is the ability for Server Manager to discover and manage the nodes in a cluster. By starting the Failover Cluster Manager from Server Manager, you can do remote multiserver management and role and feature installation. You can also manage a cluster from one convenient location.

Management and Mobility of Clustered Virtual Machines   Microsoft, as well as the industry as a whole, is moving toward the cloud and virtualization. With that in mind, you can now configure settings such as prioritizing the starting or placement of virtual machines in the clustered workloads. This lets you allocate resources efficiently to your cluster.

Cluster-Aware Updating   One issue that every administrator has dealt with is updating a system or application while it is running. For example, if you are running Microsoft Exchange and you want to do an Exchange update, when do you take the server offline to do the update? It always seems that someone is on the system 24 hours a day. Well, Windows Server 2022 clustering has a solution. *Cluster-Aware Updating (CAU)* is an automated feature that allows system updates to be applied automatically while the cluster remains available during the entire update process.

Cluster Node Fairness   The Virtual Machine Load Balancing feature is new to Windows Server 2022. This new load-balancing feature helps optimize the nodes in a cluster. When an organization builds a virtual machine cluster, there will be times when that cluster needs to have maintenance and certain virtual machines will be taken offline. When this happens, an unbalanced cluster (this is when some nodes are hosting VMs more often than others) may occur. This is where the VM Load Balancing feature (Node Fairness) helps the cluster. The Balancer will redistribute VMs from an over-balanced node to an under-balanced node. To set up Node Fairness, use the PowerShell command `(Get-Cluster).AutoBalancerLevel = <value>`. The value input is 1, 2, or 3. 1 is equivalent to the Low setting (move the host when showing more than 80 percent loaded), 2 is equivalent to Medium (move the host when more than 70 percent loaded) and 3 is equivalent to High (average nodes and move the host when showing more than 5 percent above the average).

Cluster Operating System Rolling Upgrade   One of the problems that many IT people face is the issue with downtime while their servers get upgraded to a new operating system. Windows Server 2022 includes a new feature called Cluster Operating System Rolling Upgrade. This new feature lets you upgrade a Hyper-V or Scale-Out File Server cluster from Windows Server 2012 R2 to Windows Server 2022 without stopping the servers.

Scale-Out File Server for Application Data   By using *Microsoft Storage Spaces,* you can create a highly available clustered file share that uses SMB 3.0 and CSV to provide scalable access to data.

Scale-out file servers are useful for storing the following application data:

- Hyper-V virtual machine storage
- SQL Server database files

Be aware that scale-out file servers are not useful at all for typical file share data because they benefit only from applications that require a persistent connection to their storage.

Shared Virtual Hard Disks   In the previous versions of Windows, Failover Cluster nodes running as virtual machines had to use iSCSI or virtual HBAs to connect directly to SAN-based storage. With Windows Server 2022, you can set your Hyper-V virtualized cluster to use a shared VHDX virtual disk. Shared virtual hard disks can reside on the following:

- A scale-out file server failover cluster
- Cluster CSV volumes

Shared virtual hard disks are extremely useful in providing highly available shared storage for the following virtualized workloads:

- SQL Server
- Virtual Machine Manager
- Exchange Server

Virtual Machine Drain on Shutdown   When needing to perform maintenance on a Hyper-V failover cluster, you may have a lot of virtual machines on one node of a cluster. Inevitably, you will need to restart a cluster node for updates or shut it down for maintenance.

In previous versions of Windows, virtual machines running on the cluster would save their state, and then the cluster node would shut down. Windows Server 2022 helps alleviate this issue by automatically draining the virtual machines running on a node before it shuts down or restarts. Windows does this by attempting to live-migrate all virtual machines on the cluster node to other nodes in the cluster when at all possible.

This feature is turned on by default, but you can disable it using PowerShell.

Active Directory–Detached Clusters   Previous versions of Windows Failover Clustering have depended on Active Directory to provide computer objects for the cluster name object as well as virtual computer objects. With Active Directory–detached failover clusters, communication to the cluster-form clients will use NTLM authentication rather than the normal Kerberos authentication. This is useful in maintaining high availability should a person accidentally delete a virtual computer object in Active Directory that a clustered resource depends on for Kerberos authentication.

Dynamic Witness   Earlier in this chapter, I mentioned the dynamic quorum model and how votes were dynamically adjusted based on the number of nodes in a cluster. In Windows Server 2022, there is a new feature called *dynamic witness* that is enabled by default when the cluster is configured to use a dynamic quorum. Since it is preferred to have an odd number of votes at any one time in a cluster, the dynamic witness will turn on or off the witness vote in order to ensure that there are an odd number of votes in the cluster.

Tie Breaker For 50% Node Split   Like the *dynamic witness* feature just described, the Tie Breaker For 50% Node Split option in Windows Server 2022 dynamically adjusts cluster node votes in order to maintain an odd number of votes in a cluster where no witness is being used. This is useful for a cluster in a site-aware, stretched, or geocluster configuration.

Global Update Manager Mode   Since the first release of Microsoft Cluster Services appearing in Windows NT 4.0 Enterprise, all nodes in a cluster maintain a local database that keeps a copy of the cluster configuration. The *Global Update Manager (GUM)* is a component of the cluster that ensures that before a change is marked as being committed for the entire cluster, all nodes have received and committed that change to their local cluster database. If one or more nodes do not report back or commit a change, the cluster node is kicked out of being a member of the cluster. Another issue that can occur is that for various clustered applications, such as SQL and Exchange, their performance can be negatively impacted by the time it takes the GUM to coordinate with all the nodes of a cluster for any changes. The GUM is only as fast as the slowest node in the cluster.

With Windows Server 2022, a new feature was added to Failover Clustering called *Global Update Manager mode*. This feature allows you to configure the GUM readwrite modes manually in order to greatly speed up the processing of changes by the GUM and to improve the performance of certain clustered resources.

Turn Off IPsec Encryption For Inter-node Cluster Communications   In network environments where IPsec is used, slow Group Policy updates and other issues can cause Active Directory Domain Services to be temporarily unavailable to cluster nodes. If the cluster intracluster communications protocol uses IPsec encryption, then these delays could cause cluster nodes to drop out of the cluster for failure to communicate in a timely manner with the rest of the nodes in the cluster. Windows Server 2022 provides a way to turn off IPsec encryption on the cluster communication network.

Cluster Dashboard   Starting with Windows Server 2012, Failover Clustering supports up to 64 nodes in a cluster. Keeping track of the status and resources on all of these nodes can be an administrative headache! Managing more than one failover cluster and determining what a certain cluster hosts can be painful as well. Fortunately, in Windows Server 2022, the *Failover Cluster Manager*'s main dashboard has been updated to make it easier to see the status and health of multiple clusters.

Hyper-V Replica Broker   Starting with Windows Server 2012, Hyper-V supported continuous replication of virtual machines to another server or cluster for disaster recovery purposes. The Hyper-V Recovery Broker allows virtual machines in a cluster to be replicated. The Hyper-V Recovery Broker keeps track of which cluster nodes virtual machines are residing on and ensures that replication is maintained.

Hyper-V Manager Integration into Failover Cluster Manager   In Windows Server 2022, the Hyper-V Management Console is integrated with Failover Cluster Manager for managing virtual machines that are clustered. Normal Hyper-V operations such as configuring, exporting, importing, configuring replication, stopping, starting, and livemigrating virtual machines are supported directly through Failover Cluster Manager.

Virtual Machine Monitoring   Starting with Windows Server 2012, Failover Clustering supports Virtual Machine Monitoring for Windows Server virtual machines. Virtual Machine Monitoring monitors administrator-selected Windows services running within a virtual machine and will automatically restart a service if it should fail. If the service does not start for the configured number of restart attempts, the virtual machine will fail over to another node and then restart. For example, you can configure Failover Clustering to monitor the Print Spooler service on a Windows Server 2022 virtual machine. If the Print Spooler service goes offline, then the cluster will attempt to restart the Print Spooler service within the virtual machine. If the service still fails, Failover Clustering will move the virtual machine to another node.

Configure Cluster Sets

A cluster set is a group of multiple failover clusters that are clustered together. You can increase the number of server nodes in a single software-defined datacenter (SDDC) cloud by orders of magnitude by configuring cluster sets.

Benefits of Cluster Sets

There are a number of benefits of cluster sets, such as the following:

- Support is increased on the SDDC cloud scale for running highly available VMs by joining several smaller clusters into a single larger one. This allows you to migrate VMs across the cluster set.
- Increases resiliency by having multiple clusters in a cluster set will give you better resiliency than if you were using a single cluster in case a node goes down.
- You can manage the failover cluster life cycle, including onboarding and retiring clusters, without affecting tenant VM availability.
- Flexibility of the VMs across individual clusters and offers a unified storage namespace.
- Can change the compute-to-storage workload ratio in your hyper-converged environment.
- Live migration of VMs between clusters.

Requirements and Limitations of Cluster Sets

There are some requirements and limitations for using cluster sets:

- All member clusters must be in the same Active Directory (AD) forest.
- Virtual machines can't be live-migrated between different operating systems, so member servers must run the same operating system version.
- For live migration, identical processor hardware is needed for all member servers between clusters to occur. If not, then you must select CPU Processor Compatibility in the virtual machines' settings.
- Cluster set VMs must be manually live-migrated across clusters. They cannot fail over automatically.
- Storage Replica must be used between member clusters for storage resiliency in case of cluster failures.
- Storage Spaces Direct doesn't function across member clusters. Storage Spaces Direct applies to a single cluster, with each cluster having its own storage pool.

Cluster Set Architecture

There are a number of elements within a cluster set:

Management Cluster   This hosts the highly available management plane and the namespace referral Scale-Out File Server (SOFS) for the cluster set.

Cluster Set Namespace Referral SOFS   This is a namespace for the cluster set. It is used with an SOFS server role running on the management cluster.

Cluster Set Master   The cluster set master (CS-Master) resource is highly available and resilient to individual member cluster or management cluster node failures. The CS-Master handles and coordinates the communication between member clusters.

Member Cluster   Runs the VM and Storage Spaces Direct workloads.

Cluster Set Worker   The cluster set worker (CS-Worker) responds to requests by the CS-Master, including VM placement and doing resource inventory. There is one CS-Worker instance per member cluster.

Fault Domain   A group of hardware and software that could fail together. Fault domain boundaries are based on datacenter topology, networking architecture, and other considerations.

Availability Set   Used to configure the redundancy of clustered workloads across fault domains by grouping and deploying workloads.

Creating Cluster Sets

In order to create cluster sets, you must first configure a management client and install the failover cluster tools on the server. Then, the member clusters need to be created. I discussed creating failover clusters earlier in the chapter. You should create a separate management cluster that will oversee the member clusters.

Once the failover clusters are created, you will then run a series of PowerShell commands to create the cluster set. If you wish to see an example of creating a cluster set step by step, please visit the Microsoft website at https://learn.microsoft.com/en-us/windows-server/failover-clustering/cluster-set#create-a-cluster-set.

Here are some of the PowerShell commands that you can use to create a new cluster set:

New-ClusterSet   Creates a new cluster set

Add-ClusterSetMember   Adds members to a cluster set

Get-ClusterSetMember   Lists the nodes and properties of each node

Get-ClusterSet   Lists the member clusters and management cluster nodes

Get-ClusterSetNode   Lists all the nodes for the cluster set

Get-SmbShare   Lists the SMB shares on the cluster set

Get-ClusterSetog   Lists information pertaining to one or more nodes in a cluster set

Azure Stack HCI

Azure Stack HCI is a hyperconverged infrastructure (HCI) cluster solution that hosts virtualized Windows and Linux workloads and their storage in a hybrid environment. It merges your on-premises infrastructure with Azure cloud services. Azure Stack HCI is delivered as an Azure service and billed to an Azure subscription. It is priced on a per-core basis on your on-premises server. When you first download the Azure Stack HCI, you get a free 60-day trial. After the trial, the price is $10 per physical core per month. To download the Azure Stack HCI software, go to Microsoft's website at `https://azure.microsoft.com/en-us/contact/azure-stack-hci`.

Azure Stack HCI is intended to be used as a virtualization host, so most apps and server roles must run inside of VMs. You can also manage your clusters using the Windows Admin Center and PowerShell. Each Azure Stack HCI cluster consists of between 1 and 16 physical validated servers.

By using Azure Stack HCI and Windows Admin Center, you can create a hyperconverged cluster that uses Storage Spaces Direct with the option to stretch the cluster across sites and use automatic failover. For clusters stretched across sites you need at least four severs (two in each site) with at least one 1 Gb connection between the sites (a 25 Gb RDMA connection is preferred).

Create a Cluster using the Windows Admin Center

To create a simple two-node, single-site cluster, perform the following steps:

1. In Windows Admin Center, under All Connections, select Add.

2. In the Add Resources panel, under Windows Server Cluster, select Create New.

3. Under Choose Cluster Type, select Azure Stack HCI.

4. Under Select Server Locations, select All Servers In One Site.

5. Click Create. You will now see the Create Cluster Wizard. If the Credential Security Service Provider (CredSSP) pop-up appears, select Yes to temporarily enable it.

The Create Cluster Wizard has five sections, each with its own steps:

Get Started   This section allows you to check for any prerequisites, add servers, join a domain, install required features and updates, and restart the servers.

Networking   This section will verify that the correct networking adapters are enabled and will disable any unused adapters. From here you can select management adapters, set up a virtual switch configuration, and define the network by supplying IP addresses.

Clustering   This section will validate that the servers have a consistent configuration and are suitable for clustering, and then you will create the actual cluster.

Storage   This section will clean and check drives, validate storage, and enable Storage Spaces Direct.

SDN   This section is optional and you will only be using it if you set up software-defined networking (SDN) for your clusters.

To add and connect to an Azure Stack HCI cluster using the Windows Admin Center, you can add a cluster to manage from the main overview page by performing the following steps:

1. Click + Add under All Connections.

2. Choose Add A Windows Server Cluster.

3. Type the name of the cluster you want to manage and click Add. The cluster will be added to the connection list on the overview page.

4. Under All Connections, click the name of the cluster you just added. Windows Admin Center will start Cluster Manager and take you directly to the Windows Admin Center dashboard for that cluster.

Create an Azure Witness

Microsoft Cloud Witness is a high-availability feature for failover clusters that uses storage in Azure so that clusters will continue to work if there is an onsite outage. It is a type of failover cluster quorum witness that uses Azure. I briefly discussed Cloud Witness earlier in the chapter, but now I want to go over how to create a cloud witness using Azure.

A cloud witness uses Azure Blob Storage to read/write a blob file, which is then used as an arbitration point. I will be discussing Azure Blob Storage in greater detail later in this chapter. There are several benefits of using a Cloud Witness in Azure:

- Built-in Cloud Witness resource type.

- Cost is minimal to the Storage Account since only a small amount of data is written per blob file. The blob file is updated only when a cluster node's state changes.

- No need for third separate datacenter because it uses Microsoft Azure.

- Same Azure Storage account can be used for multiple clusters (one blob file per cluster; cluster unique ID used as a blob filename).

- Uses standard available Azure Blob Storage (no extra maintenance overhead of virtual machines hosted in public cloud).

The cloud witness feature can benefit organizations that have clusters across multiple sites or that are running small Hyper-V clusters in remote offices. You must have an Azure storage account in order to use a cloud witness. You add the Azure account information when configuring the cloud witness portion of a failover cluster quorum. The cluster nodes must have access to the Internet and open HTTPS ports to use the Azure account.

There are a number of ways which you can set up a cloud witness. Let's take a look at some of them.

Set Up a Cloud Witness for a Cluster Using the Windows Admin Center

If one of your servers in a cluster goes offline, you will want to make sure that you have a witness resource assigned. That way, it does not cause the other nodes to become unavailable. To set up a cloud witness using the Windows Admin Center, perform the following steps:

1. In Windows Admin Center, select Cluster Manager from the top drop-down menu.
2. Under Cluster Connections, select the cluster.
3. Under Tools, select Settings.
4. In the right pane, select Witness.
5. For Witness Type, select File Share Witness.
6. Specify a file share path such as `\servername.domain.com\Witness$` and supply credentials if needed.
7. Click Save.

Set Up a Cloud Witness for a Cluster Using Azure

You can also use an Azure cloud witness if all the server nodes in the cluster have a reliable Internet connection. To set up a cloud witness as a quorum witness for your cluster, you must first create an Azure Storage Account to use as a cloud witness, and then configure the cloud witness as a quorum witness for your cluster.

To create an Azure Storage Account, perform the following steps:

1. Sign into the Azure portal.
2. From the Hub menu, select New ➤ Data + Storage ➤ Storage Account.
3. On the Create A Storage Account page, do the following:

   a. Enter a name for your storage account. The name must be between 3 and 24 characters in length and may contain numbers and lowercase letters only. The storage account name must also be unique within Azure.

   b. For Account Kind, select General Purpose. You cannot use a blob storage account for a cloud witness.

   c. For Performance, select Standard. You cannot use Azure Premium Storage for a cloud witness.

   d. For Replication, select Locally-Redundant Storage (LRS) or Zone-Redundant Storage (ZRS) as applicable.

When you create an Azure Storage Account, two access keys are automatically generated. They are the Primary Access key and the Secondary Access key. For a first-time creation of a cloud witness you will want to use the Primary Access key. To view your storage access keys, go to the Azure portal, navigate to your storage account, click All Settings, and then click Access Keys to view, copy, and regenerate your account access keys.

Configure Cloud Witness as a Quorum Witness

To configure a cloud witness as a quorum witness, perform the following steps:

1. Launch Failover Cluster Manager.
2. Right-click the cluster and choose More Actions ➤ Configure Cluster Quorum Settings. This will start the Configure Cluster Quorum Wizard.

3. On the Select Quorum Configurations page, choose Select The Quorum Witness.

4. On the Select Quorum Witness page, select Configure A Cloud Witness.

5. On the Configure Cloud Witness page, enter the following information (as shown in Figure 13.23):

   a. Azure Storage Account Name (Required).

   b. Access Key corresponding to the Storage Account (Required).

   c. If you plan on using a different Azure service endpoint (for example, the Microsoft Azure service in China), then update the endpoint server name (Optional).

FIGURE 13.23   Configure Cloud Witness

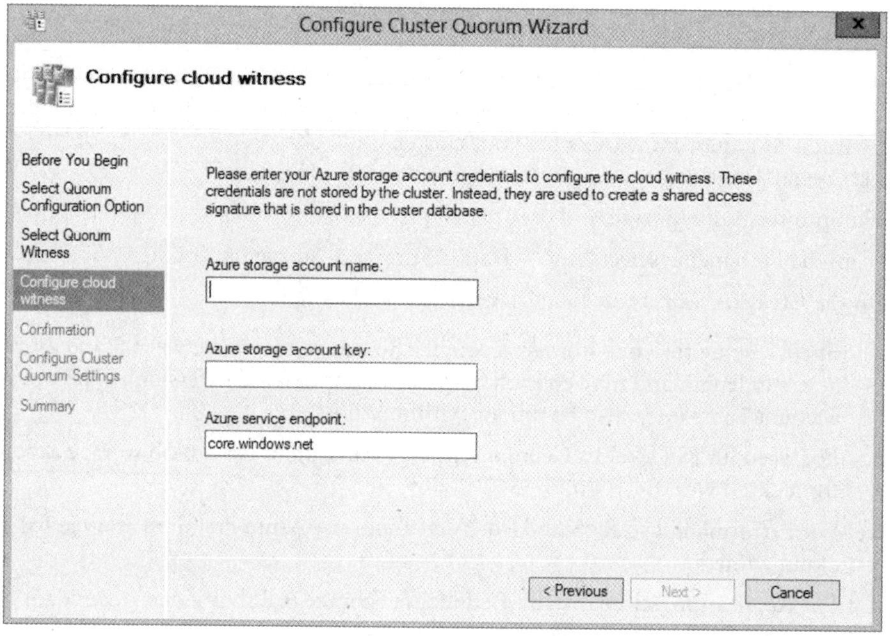

6. Once the cloud witness has been successfully configured, you can view the newly created witness resource in the Failover Cluster Manager snap-in.

Azure Blob Storage

Microsoft's object storage solution for the cloud is called Azure Blob Storage. Blob Storage is designed for storing large amounts of unstructured data, which is data that doesn't adhere to any particular data model or definition, such as text or binary data.

Blob Storage is used for these purposes:

- Serving images or documents directly to a browser
- Storing data for analysis by an on-premises or Azure-hosted service.
- Storing data for backup and restore, disaster recovery, and archiving
- Storing files for distributed access
- Streaming video and audio
- Writing to log files

From anywhere in the world, your user and client apps can access objects in Blob Storage using the Internet (HTTP/HTTPS). Items in Blob Storage can be accessed using the Azure Storage REST API, Azure PowerShell, Azure CLI, or an Azure Storage client library. You can also connect to Blob Storage securely by using SSH File Transfer Protocol (SFTP) and mount Blob Storage containers by using the Network File System (NFS) 3.0 protocol.

Blob Storage offers three types of resources:

- The storage account
- A container in the storage account
- A blob in a container

The storage account is a unique namespace in Azure for your data. Every object that you store in Azure Storage has an address that includes your unique account name. The combination of both the account name and the Blob Storage endpoint becomes the base address for the objects placed in your storage account. For example, if your storage account is named wpanekstorageaccount, then the default endpoint for your Blob Storage would be http://wpanekstorageaccount.blob.core.windows.net.

There are several different types of storage accounts that are supported for Blob Storage:

General-Purpose v2   This is a Standard storage account type for blobs, file shares, queues, and tables. This is the recommended storage type for most scenarios that use Blob Storage or another Azure Storage service.

Block Blob   This is a Premium storage account type for block blobs and append blobs. This is the recommended storage type for scenarios with high transaction rates, that use smaller objects, or that requires low storage latency.

Page Blob   This is a Premium storage account type for page blobs only. Page blobs are made up of 512-byte pages up to 8 TB in total size and are designed for frequent random read/write operations.

A container in the storage account organizes a set of blobs. It is similar to a directory in a filesystem but can contain an unlimited number of containers and store an unlimited number of blobs.

When naming a container, follow these rules:

- Can be between 3 and 63 characters long

- Must start with a letter or number, and can contain only lowercase letters, numbers, and the dash (-) character

- Cannot have two or more consecutive dash characters

A blob in a container can support three types of blobs: block blobs, append blobs, and page blobs. Block blobs store text and binary data. They consist of blocks of data that can be individually managed and can store up to approximately 190.7 tebibytes (TiB). Append blobs consist of blocks much like block blobs but are optimized for append operations. This type of blob is best used for scenarios such as logging data from virtual machines. Page blobs store random access files up to 8 TiB in size. Page blobs store virtual hard drive (VHD) files and serve as disks for Azure virtual machines.

When naming a blob, follow these rules:

- Can contain any combination of characters.

- Must be at least one character long and cannot be more than 1,024 characters long. They are also case-sensitive.

- Reserved URL characters must be properly escaped.

- Cannot exceed 254 path segments. A path segment is the string between consecutive delimiter characters (e.g., the forward slash, /) that corresponds to the name of a virtual directory. Microsoft notes that you should also avoid blob names that end with a dot (.), a forward slash (/), or a sequence or combination of the two. No path segments should end with a dot (.).

Using the Windows Admin Center to Create and Manage Failover Clusters

You can also use the Windows Admin Center to manage failover clusters. The Windows Admin Center is a locally deployed, browser-based app that is used to manage Windows servers, clusters, hyper-converged infrastructure, as well as Windows client computers. You can download the Windows Admin Center from Microsoft's website at www .microsoft.com/en-us/evalcenter/download-windows-admin-center.

Using the Windows Admin Center, you can create failover clusters, as well as view and manage cluster resources, storage, network, nodes, roles, virtual machines, and virtual switches.

To add a cluster to Windows Admin Center, perform the following steps:

1. Click + Add under All Connections.

2. Choose to add server clusters.

3. Type the name of the cluster and, if prompted, any required credentials. You will have the option to add the cluster nodes as individual server connections in Windows Admin Center.

4. Click Add to finish. The new cluster will now be added to the connection list on the Overview page. To connect to the cluster, just click it.

For failover cluster connections, there are a number of tools available in the Windows Admin Center:

Overview   Here you can view failover cluster details and manage cluster resources.

Disks   Here you can view cluster shared disks and volumes.

Networks   Here you can view networks in the cluster.

Nodes   Here you can view and manage cluster nodes.

Roles   Here you can manage cluster roles or create an empty role.

Updates   Here you can manage Cluster-Aware Updates (requires CredSSP).

Virtual Machines   Here you can view and manage virtual machines.

Virtual Switches   Here you can view and manage virtual switches.

PowerShell Commands for Clustering

Table 13.3 contains just some of the PowerShell commands that you can use to configure and manage Windows Server 2022 clustering.

TABLE 13.3   Windows Server 2022 clustering PowerShell commands

PowerShell command	Description
Add-ClusterDisk	This command allows you to add a new disk to a failover cluster. The disk's LUN must be visible to all cluster nodes.
Add-ClusterFileServerRole	This command allows you to create a clustered file server.
Add-ClusterGenericApplicationRole	This command allows you to configure high availability for an application that is normally not designed for clustering.
Add-ClusterGroup	This command allows you to add a resource group to the failover cluster.
Add-ClusterNode	This command allows an admin to add a node to a failover cluster.
Add-ClusterResource	This command allows you to add a resource to a failover cluster.

TABLE 13.3 Windows Server 2022 clustering PowerShell commands *(Continued)*

PowerShell command	Description
Add-ClusterResourceDependency	This command allows an admin to add a resource dependency to a failover cluster.
Add-ClusterServerRole	This command allows you to add the cluster server role to a server.
Block-ClusterAccess	This command allows you to block the specified users from accessing a cluster.
Get-Cluster	This command shows you the information about a failover clusters.
Get-ClusterAccess	This command shows you the permissions for a failover clusters.
Get-ClusterNode	This command shows you the information about the servers in a failover clusters.
Get-ClusterQuorum	This command shows you the information about the cluster quorum in a clusters.
New-Cluster	This command allows you to create a new failover cluster.
Remove-Cluster	This command allows you to remove a failover cluster.
Remove-ClusterAccess	This command allows you to remove a user's access from the cluster.
Remove-ClusterNode	This command allows you to remove a node from a failover cluster.
Start-Cluster	This command allows you to start the Cluster service on all nodes.
Stop-Cluster	This command allows you to stop the Cluster service on all nodes.
Stop-ClusterNode	This command stops the Cluster service on a node.
Test-Cluster	This command allows you to complete validation tests for a cluster.

Storage Spaces

With Windows Server 2012, Microsoft introduced the Storage Spaces feature. With Windows Server 2016, Microsoft released a similar feature called Storage Spaces Direct. Storage Spaces Direct will be covered in the next section of this chapter. Storage Spaces can be used with the Windows client and with Windows Server. It can be used to help protect your data from drive failures and is very similar to RAID (Redundant Array of Independent Disks). Storage Spaces can be used to group two or more drives together into a storage pool. You need at least two extra drives (in addition to the drive where Windows is installed). These drives can be internal or external hard drives, or solid-state drives. You can use a variety of types of drives with Storage Spaces, including USB, SATA, and SAS drives.

There are several ways that you can use Storage Spaces. You can use it on a Windows client machine; on a stand-alone server with all storage in a single server; on a clustered server using Storage Spaces Direct with local, direct-attached storage in each cluster node; or on a clustered server with one or more shared SAS storage enclosures holding all drives.

You must first create one or more storage pools in order to create a storage space. A storage pool is a collection of physical disks. Then from within the storage pool you can create one or more virtual disks. The virtual disks are also known as storage spaces. These storage spaces will appear as regular disks within the operating system, and you can then create formatted volumes. A storage space cannot be used to host the Windows operating system. Storage spaces will usually contain two copies of your data; that way, if a drive fails, you will still retain your data. If you start to run low on space, you can just add more drives to the storage pool.

Storage Spaces Resiliency Layouts

There are three types of resiliency layouts for Storage Spaces:

Simple   This is for increased performance, but the downfall is that your files are not protected from drive failure. Simple spaces require at least two drives.

Mirrored   This is for increased performance and will protect your files from drive failure by keeping multiple copies of your data.

- Two-way mirrors will make two copies of your files and can tolerate one drive failure and requires at least two drives.
- Three-way mirrors can tolerate two drive failures and requires at least five drives.

Parity   This is for increased performance and will protect your files from drive failure by keeping multiple copies. To protect from a single drive failure, Parity requires at least three drives and at least seven drives in order to protect from two drive failures.

Storage Spaces Provisioning Types

Provisioning means to make something available. There are two provisioning types that you can choose from:

Thin   Space is allocated on an as-needed basis. This will optimize how the available storage is used. But you will need to monitor how much disk space is available because thin provisioning allows you to overallocate storage.

Fixed   Storage capacity is immediately assigned when the virtual disk is created. Fixed provisioning will use the storage pool space that is equal to the virtual disk size.

Create Storage Spaces

To create a storage space on a Windows client, perform the following:

1. Add or connect the drives that you want to group together with Storage Spaces.

2. Go to the taskbar, type **Storage Spaces** in the search box, and select Storage Spaces from the list of search results.

3. Select Create A New Pool And Storage Space, as shown in Figure 13.24.

4. Select the drives you want to add to the new storage space, and then click Create Pool.

5. Give the drive a name and letter, and then choose a layout. Two-Way Mirror, Three-Way Mirror, and Parity can help protect the files in the storage space from drive failure.

6. Enter the maximum size the storage space can reach, and then click Create Storage Space.

FIGURE 13.24   Create A New Pool And Storage Space option

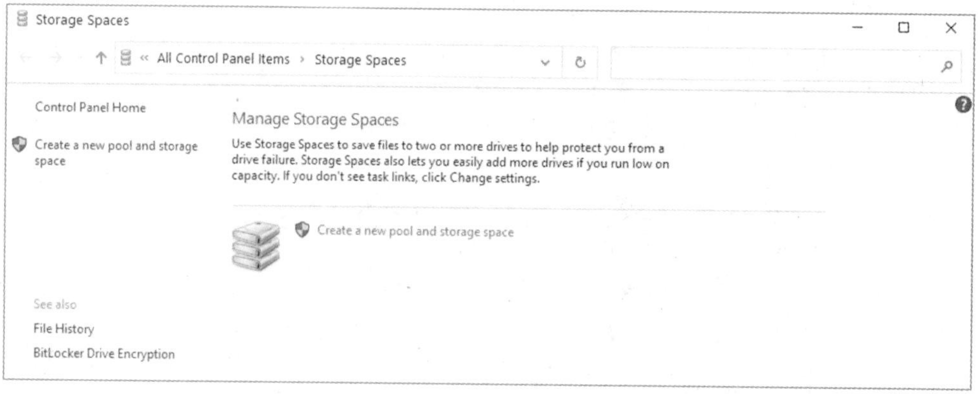

To create a storage space on a stand-alone server, you'll follow three steps:

- Step 1: Create a storage pool: Group available physical disks into one or more storage pools.

- Step 2: Create a virtual disk: Select how the data is laid out across the physical disks.
- Step 3: Create a volume.

Step 1: To create a storage pool:

1. In the Server Manager navigation pane, select File And Storage Services.
2. Select the Storage Pools page from the navigation pane.
3. Under Storage Pools, select the Tasks list, and then select New Storage Pool. The New Storage Pool Wizard will open.
4. Click Next on the Before You Begin page.
5. On the Specify A Storage Pool Name And Subsystem page, enter a name for the storage pool and an optional description. Select the group of available physical disks you want to use, and then click Next.
6. On the Select Physical Disks For The Storage Pool page, select the check box next to each physical disk that you want to include in the storage pool. To designate one or more disks as hot spares, under Allocation, click the drop-down arrow, then choose Hot Spare. Click Next.
7. On the Confirm Selections page, verify that the settings are correct, and then click Create.
8. On the View Results page, verify that all tasks completed, and then click Close.
9. Finally, verify that your newly created storage pool is listed under Storage Pools.

Step 2: To create a virtual disk:

1. If the New Virtual Disk Wizard is not already open, on the Storage Pools page in Server Manager, under Storage Pools, select the desired storage pool.
2. Under Virtual Disks, select the Tasks list, and then select New Virtual Disk. The New Virtual Disk Wizard will open.
3. On the Before You Begin page, click Next.
4. On the Select The Storage Pool page, select the desired storage pool, and then click Next.
5. On the Specify The Virtual Disk Name page, enter a name and optional description, then click Next.
6. On the Select The Storage Layout page, select the desired layout, then click Next.
7. If you chose Mirror as the storage layout, the Configure The Resiliency Settings page will appear. Select either Two-Way or Three-Way Mirror.
8. On the Specify The Provisioning Type page, select your desired provisioning type, then click Next.
9. On the Specify The Size Of The Virtual Disk page (depending on the provisioning type selected), enter the size required and then click Next.

10. On the Confirm Selections page, verify that the settings are correct, and then click Create.

11. On the View Results page, verify that all tasks completed, and then click Close.

<u>Step 3:</u> **To create a volume:**

1. If the New Volume Wizard is not already open, in Server Manager, on the Storage Pools page under Virtual Disks, right-click the desired virtual disk, and then select New Volume. This will open the New Volume Wizard.

2. On the Before You Begin page, click Next.

3. On the Select The Server And Disk page, in the Server area, select the server where you want to provision the volume, and in the Disk area, select the virtual disk where you want to create the volume. Then, click Next.

4. Then, on the Specify The Size Of The Volume page, enter a volume size, specify the units (MB, GB, or TB), and then click Next.

5. On the Assign To A Drive Letter Or Folder page, configure the desired option, and then click Next.

6. On the Select File System Settings page, in the File System list, select either NTFS or ReFS. Then, in the Allocation Unit Size list, either leave the setting at Default or set the allocation unit size. You also have the option to assign a volume name, if you wish, by entering a name in the Volume Label box. Then, click Next.

7. On the Confirm Selections page, verify that the settings are correct, and then click Create.

8. On the View Results page, verify that all tasks completed, and then click Close.

9. You can now verify that the volume has been created. In Server Manager, select the Volumes page. The volume is listed under the server where it was created. You can also verify that the volume is in Windows Explorer.

Implementing Storage Spaces Direct

Storage Spaces Direct uses local-attached drives on servers to create highly available storage at a minimal cost of traditional storage devices (SAN or NAS). Storage Spaces Direct uses regular hard drives that are connected to a single node of the failover cluster, and these disks can be used as storage for the cluster.

To understand how Storage Spaces Direct truly works, I think it is better to first understand some other technology terms for Windows Server 2022. When an IT administrator takes a bunch of physical disks and puts them together, it is called a storage pool. Storage spaces are virtual disks that are created from storage pools. Storage Spaces Direct is the evolution of Storage Spaces.

Many of the same features are used in Windows Server 2022 like Failover Clustering, Cluster Shared Volumes, and SMB.

Storage Spaces Direct uses disks that are connected to one node of a failover cluster and allows for the creation of pools using those disks by Storage Spaces. Storage Spaces Direct streamlines deployment by using converged or hyper-converged architecture.

Virtual disks (spaces) that are constructed on a pool will have their mirrors or parity (redundant data) span across the disks using different nodes of the cluster. Since replicas of the data are spread across the disks, this allows for access to data in the event a node fails or is going down for maintenance.

You can implement Storage Spaces Direct in virtual machines, with each VM configured with two or more virtual disks connected to the VM's SCSI Controller. Each node of the cluster running inside the virtual machine can connect to its own disks, but using Storage Spaces Direct allows all the disks to be part of the storage pool that spans the entire cluster node. For the redundant data (mirror or parity spaces) to be spread across the nodes, Storage Spaces Direct uses SMB3 as the protocol transport.

Networking Hardware   To communicate between servers Storage Spaces Direct uses SMB3, including SMB Direct and SMB Multichannel over Ethernet. It is recommended that you use 10+Gbe with Remote-Direct Memory Access (RDMA), or either Internet Wide Area RDMA Protocol (iWARP) or RDMA over Converged Ethernet (RoCE).

Storage Hardware   2–16 servers with locally attached SATA, SAS, or NVMe drives.

- Must have at least two solid-state drives on each server and at least four additional drives.
- SATA and SAS device should be following a Host Bus Adapter (HBA) and SAS expander.

Failover Clustering   To connect the servers, Windows Server 2022 uses the built-in clustering feature.

Software Storage Bus   Storage Spaces Direct has a new feature called Software Storage Bus. This allows all the servers to see all of each other's local drives by spanning the cluster and establishing a software-defined storage structure.

Storage Bus Layer Cache   The Software Storage Bus joins the fastest drives available to the slower drives to provide server-side read/write caching that speeds up the I/O and boosts data.

Storage Pool   The storage pool is the collection of drives that form the storage space. It is created automatically and all qualified drives are discovered and added. You should use the default settings on one pool per cluster.

Storage Spaces   Storage Spaces offers fault tolerance to virtual disk using mirroring, erasure coding, or both. Think of it as distributed, software-defined RAID using the drives in the pool. These virtual disks normally have resiliency when two synchronized drives or servers fail.

Resilient File System (ReFS)   The Resilient File System (ReFS) is Microsoft's latest file-system and was designed to maximize data availability, efficiently scale to large datasets across varied workloads, and provide data integrity. It includes improving the VHDX file operations such as creating, expanding, checkpoint merging, and built-in checksums to distinguish and fix bit errors. ReFS also introduced real-time tiers, based on usage, which will rotate data between "hot" and "cold" storage tiers.

Cluster Shared Volumes   The Cluster Shared Volumes (CSV) filesystem unites all the ReFS volumes into a single namespace available through any server. This namespace allows every server and every volume to look and act like it's mounted locally.

Scale-Out File Server   This option is necessary in converged deployments only. It offers remote file access by using the SMB3 protocol to clients over the network. It essentially turns Storage Spaces Direct into network-attached storage (NAS).

> To see step-by-step instructions on configuring and deploying Storage Spaces Direct, visit Microsoft's website at https://learn.microsoft.com/en-us/windows-server/storage/storage-spaces/deploy-storage-spaces-direct.

The Benefits of Storage Spaces Direct

The following are just some of the benefits of using Storage Spaces Direct with Windows Server 2022:

Simplicity   In less than 15 minutes, you can go from a standard server running Windows Server 2022 to creating a Storage Spaces Direct cluster. It's just the click of a check box if you're using System Center.

Unrivaled Performance   Storage Spaces Direct exceeds 150,000 mixed 4k random IOPS per server with reliability, low latency, built-in read/write cache, and support for NVMe drives that are mounted directly on the PCIe bus.

Fault Tolerance   Constantly available built-in resiliency that will handle drives, servers, or component failures. Chassis and rack fault tolerance can also be configured for larger deployments. There are no complex management steps needed when hardware fails. Simply change it out for another one and the software will fix itself.

Resource Efficiency   Greater resource efficiency with Erasure coding delivering up to 2.4× more storage. Using Local Reconstruction Codes and ReFS, real-time tiers extend to hard disk drives and mixed hot/cold workloads, all while reducing CPU usage to give the resources back to the virtual machines where they are needed.

Manageability   Keep excessively active virtual machines in order by using Storage QoS Controls with minimum and maximum per-VM IOPS limits. Continuously monitor and alert by using the built-in Health Service. There are also new APIs that make it easier to collect cluster-wide performance statistics and capacity metrics.

Scalability   For multiple petabytes of storage per cluster, you can increase up to 16 servers and add over 400 drives. To scale out, you just have to add drives or add more servers. Storage Spaces Direct will automatically add the new drives and begin using them.

Deployment Options

When using Windows Server 2022 and installing Storage Spaces Direct, you can choose between two deployment options:

Converged   In converged, there are separate clusters for each storage and compute. The converged deployment option, also called *disaggregated*, puts a Scale-Out File Server (SoFS) on top of Storage Spaces Direct to provide NAS over SMB3 file shares. This allows for scaling computer/workloads separately from the storage cluster. This is essential when working with large-scale deployments such as Hyper-V infrastructure-as-a-service (IaaS).

Hyper-Converged   In hyper-converged, there is only one cluster for storage and compute. The hyper-converged deployment option runs the Hyper-V virtual machines or SQL Server databases directly on the servers delivering the storage, storing files on the local volumes. This removes the need to configure file server access and permissions. It also reduces the hardware costs associated for small-to-medium business or remote office/branch office deployments.

Requirements to Set Up Storage Spaces Direct

To set up Storage Spaces Direct properly, you must make sure that all your hardware components meet the minimum requirements. Table 13.4 was taken directly from Microsoft's website and contains Microsoft's recommendations for proper configuration of Storage Spaces Direct. To see the entire list of recommendations, please visit Microsoft's website at `https://learn.microsoft.com/en-us/windows-server/storage/storage-spaces/storage-spaces-direct-hardware-requirements`.

TABLE 13.4   Storage Spaces Direct requirements

Component	Requirements
Servers	Minimum of 2 servers, maximum of 16 servers.
	All servers should be the same make and model.
	Requires Windows Server Datacenter Edition. You can use the Server Core installation option, or Server with Desktop Experience.
CPU	Minimum of Intel Nehalem or later compatible processor, or AMD EPYC or later compatible processor.
Memory	4 GB of RAM per terabyte (TB) of cache drive capacity on each server to store Storage Spaces Direct metadata.
	Any memory used by Windows Server, VMs, and other apps or workloads.
Boot	Any boot device supported by Windows Server, which now includes SATADOM.
	RAID 1 mirror is not required, but is supported for boot.
	Recommended: 200 GB minimum size.
Networking	Minimum interconnect for small scale 2-3 node: 10 Gbps network interface card (NIC), or faster.
	Recommends two or more network connections from each node for redundancy and performance.
	Recommended interconnect for high performance, at scale, or deployments of 4+:
	NICs that are remote-direct memory access (RDMA) capable, iWARP (recommended) or RoCE.
	Recommends two or more network connections from each node for redundancy and performance.
	25 Gbps NIC or faster.
	Switched or switchless node interconnects:
	Switched: Network switches must be properly configured to handle the bandwidth and networking type. If using RDMA that implements the RoCE protocol, network device and switch configuration is even more important.
	Switchless: Nodes can be interconnected using direct connections, avoiding using a switch. It's required that every node have a direct connection with every other node of the cluster.
Drives	Use local-attached SATA, SAS, or NVMe drives.
	Every drive must be physically connected to only one server.
	All servers must have the same drive types.
	Recommended: All servers have the same drive configuration.
	SSDs must have power-loss protection, i.e., they are enterprise-grade.
	Recommended: SSDs used for cache have high endurance, providing minimum of 5 drive-writes-per-day (DWPD).
	Add capacity drives in multiples of the number of NVMe or SSD cache devices.
	Not supported: Multi-path IO (MPIO) or physically connecting drives via multiple paths.

Component	Requirements
Host-bus adapter (HBA)	Simple pass-through SAS HBA for both SAS and SATA drives. SCSI Enclosure Services (SES) for SAS and SATA drives. Any direct-attached storage enclosures must present Unique ID. Not supported: RAID HBA controllers or SAN (Fibre Channel, iSCSI, FCoE) devices.

Configuring Storage Spaces Direct

To configure Storage Spaces Direct, follow these steps:

 The steps to configure Storage Spaces Direct involve a large number of PowerShell commands. Microsoft includes a number of scripts that you can copy from their website that will assist in performing these steps. For more information, visit https://learn.microsoft.com/en-us/windows-server/storage/storage-spaces/deploy-storage-spaces-direct#step-3-configure-storage-spaces-direct. Microsoft recommends that these scripts not be run remotely by using a PowerShell session; instead, they should be run in a local PowerShell session on the management system using administrative permissions.

Clean the drives.   Before you can enable Storage Spaces Direct, make sure that the drives are empty and that there are no old partitions or other data.

Validate the cluster.   For this step you will run a cluster validation tool using the Test-Cluster PowerShell command that will ensure that the server nodes are properly configured to create a cluster by using Storage Spaces Direct.

Create the cluster.   For this step you will create a cluster using the New-Cluster PowerShell command, including the nodes that you previously validated. Just note that it may take some time for the DNS entry to be replicated for this cluster.

Configure a cluster witness.   For this step Microsoft recommends that you configure a witness for the cluster. I discussed how to create a cluster witness earlier in this chapter.

Enable Storage Spaces Direct.   For this step you will use the Enable-ClusterStorage SpacesDirect PowerShell cmdlet, which will put the storage system into the Storage Spaces Direct mode and automatically create the pool, configure the Storage Spaces Direct caches, and create two tiers as default tiers called Capacity and Performance. This command may take several minutes to complete. When done, the system will be ready for you to create the volumes.

Create volumes.   For this step you will use the New-Volume PowerShell cmdlet. This command will create the virtual disk, partitions, format the disk, and create a volume with the same name. It will also add the volume to the cluster shared volume (CSV).

Enable the CSV cache (optional). If you wish, you can enable the CSV cache to use system memory (RAM) as a write-through block-level cache of read operations that aren't already cached by the Windows cache manager. By enabling this, you will reduce the amount of memory available to run VMs on a hyper-converged cluster.

Deploy virtual machines for hyper-converged deployments. For this step, if you have deployed a hyper-converged cluster, then you will want to provision the VMs on the Storage Spaces Direct cluster.

Upgrade a Storage Spaces Direct Node

To upgrade a Storage Spaces Direct cluster, you have four options available. Each option has its own pros and cons, so choose a method that best suits your needs.

The first option is an in-place upgrade while the VMs are running on each server in the cluster. With this option, there will be no downtime for the VMs, but you must wait for storage jobs (mirror repair) to finish after each server is upgraded.

The second option is a clean OS installation while the VMs are running on each server in the cluster. Again, with this option there will be no downtime for the VMs, but you must wait for storage jobs (mirror repair) to finish after each server is upgraded. You also need to set up each server and all its apps and roles again. Microsoft recommends this option over an in-place upgrade.

The third option is an in-place upgrade while the VMs are stopped on each server in the cluster. There's no downtime for the VMs, but you do *not* have to wait for storage jobs (mirror repair) to finish.

The fourth option is a clean OS installation while the VMs are stopped on each server in the cluster. there's no downtime for the VMs, but you do *not* have to wait for storage jobs (mirror repair) to finish. Microsoft recommends this option over an in-place upgrade.

Before you proceed with an upgrade, make sure that you have backups available just in case an issue arises during the upgrade process. Also, ensure that your hardware vendor has a BIOS, firmware, and drivers for your servers to support Windows Server 2022.

Manage and Monitor Storage Spaces Direct

You can use the following tools to manage and monitor Storage Spaces Direct:

- Windows Admin Center
- Server Manager & Failover Cluster Manager
- Windows PowerShell
- System Center Virtual Machine Manager (SCVMM) and Operations Manager

Storage Spaces Direct Using Windows PowerShell

Table 13.5 contains just some of the PowerShell commands that you can use to configure and manage Storage Spaces Direct.

TABLE 13.5   Storage Spaces Direct PowerShell commands

PowerShell command	Description
Disable-NetQosFlowControl	This command allows you to turn off flow control.
Enable-ClusterStorageSpacesDirect	This command enables Storage Spaces Direct.
Enable-NetAdapterQos	This command allows you to apply network QoS policies to the target adapters.
Enable-NetAdapterRDMA	This command allows you to enable remote direct memory access (RDMA) on a network adapter.
Enable-NetQosFlowControl	This command allows you to turn on flow control.
Enable-ClusterStorageSpacesDirect	This command allows you to enable highly available Storage Spaces that use directly attached storage, Storage Spaces Direct (S2D), on a cluster.
Get-ClusterAvailableDisk	This command allows you to view the information about the disks that can support failover clustering and are visible to all nodes. But these disks are not yet part of the set of clustered disks.
Get-ClusterParameter	This command allows you to view detailed information about an object in a failover cluster. Use this command to manage private properties for a cluster object.
Get-NetAdapter	This command will retrieve a list of the network adapters.
Get-StoragePool	This command allows you to see a specific storage pool, or a set of StoragePool objects.
Get-StorageTier	This command allows you to see storage tiers on Windows Storage subsystems. Use this command to see Storage Spaces Direct default tier templates called Performance and Capacity.
New-Cluster	This command creates a new cluster.
New-NetQosPolicy	This command allows you to create a new network QoS policy.
New-NetQosTrafficClass	This command allows you to create a traffic class (like SMB).

TABLE 13.5 Storage Spaces Direct PowerShell commands *(Continued)*

PowerShell command	Description
New-Volume	This command creates a new volume.
Set-Item	This command allows you to configure the trusted hosts to all hosts.
Test-Cluster	This command allows you to test a set of servers for use as a Storage Spaces Direct cluster.
Update-StorageProviderCache	This command allows you to update the cache of the service for a particular provider and associated child objects.

PowerShell Commands for Hyper-V High Availability

When configuring Hyper-V high availability, you may want to set up some of the components using PowerShell. Table 13.6 shows you some of the available PowerShell commands available for setting up Hyper-V high availability.

TABLE 13.6 PowerShell commands for high availability

PowerShell command	Description
Complete-VMFailover	This command helps finish a virtual machine's failover process on the Replica server.
Disable-VMMigration	This command allows you to disable virtual machine migration on a virtual machine host.
Enable-VMMigration	This command allows you to enable virtual machine migration on a virtual machine host.
Enable-VMReplication	This command lets you enable replication of a virtual machine.
Get-VMMigrationNetwork	This command shows you the virtual machine networks used for migration.
Get-VMReplication	This command shows you the replication settings for a virtual machine.

PowerShell command	Description
Get-VMReplicationAuthorizationEntry	This command shows you the authorization entries of a Replica server.
Get-VMReplicationServer	This command shows you the replication and authentication settings of a Replica server.
Import-VMInitialReplication	This command imports initial replication files for a Replica virtual machine when using external media.
Measure-VMReplication	This command shows you the replication statistics and information associated with a virtual machine.
New-VMReplicationAuthorizationEntry	This command allows you to create an authorization entry to replicate data to a specified Replica server.
Remove-VMMigrationNetwork	This command allows you to remove a network from use in migration.
Remove-VMReplication	This command removes the replication from a specific virtual machine.
Reset-VMReplicationStatistics	This command allows you to reset the replication statistics of a virtual machine.
Resume-VMReplication	This command allows you to resume virtual machine replication after an error, a pause, a suspension, or a resynchronization.
Set-VMProcessor	This command allows you to configure which processors are used for a virtual machine.
Set-VMReplication	This command allows you to modify the replication settings of a virtual machine.
Set-VMReplicationServer	This command allows an admin to configure a host as a Replica server.
Start-VMInitialReplication	This command starts replication of a virtual machine.
Stop-VMReplication	This command stops replication of a virtual machine.
Suspend-VMReplication	This command suspends replication of a virtual machine.
Test-VMReplicationConnection	This command allows you to test the connection of a primary server and a Replica server.

Summary

High availability is more than just clustering. It is achieved through improved hardware, software, and processes. This chapter focused on how to configure failover clustering and network load balancing in order to achieve high availability and scalability.

High availability should be approached through proper hardware configuration, training, and operational discipline. Failover clustering provides a highly available base for many applications, such as databases and mail servers.

Network load-balanced clusters are used to provide high availability and scalability for network-based applications, such as VPNs and web servers. Network load-balanced clusters can be configured with any edition of Windows Server 2022 except for the Windows Server 2022 Hyper-V Edition.

You can also set up high availability on Windows Server 2022 Hyper-V without using clustering. You can also set up live migrations on Hyper-V virtual machines. Live migration allows you to move a virtual machine from one server to another without any impact on the users. This can be very useful if you have a Hyper-V server that is starting to show hardware issues. You can move the virtual machine from the server with issues to a server without any issues.

Exam Essentials

Know the hardware requirements for network load balancing (NLB).   Network load balancing has distinct hardware requirements.

Know the PowerShell commands for NLB.   Make sure you know the PowerShell commands for NLB. Understand which command is used to create, manage, and stop NLB clusters.

Understand live migration.   Understand how live migrations work and why we use them. Live migrations allow you to move a virtual machine from one server to another without any impact on the users.

Know PowerShell for VM replication.   Make sure you know the different PowerShell commands for virtual machine replication. Understand which commands are used to create, manage, and stop VM replication.

Know how to implement and manage Storage Spaces and Storage Spaces Direct.   Know how to configure Storage Spaces Direct and how to create a failover cluster by using Storage Spaces Direct. Know the difference between Storage Spaces and Storages Spaces Direct. Understand how to upgrade a Storage Spaces Direct node and how to implement networking.

Understand how to implement a Windows Server failover cluster.   Know how to implement failover clusters on-premises, hybrid, and cloud infrastructures and know how to create failover clusters. Understand how to stretch clusters and configure storage. Be able to modify quorum options and configure network adapters. Know how to work with cluster workload options and how to configure cluster sets and Scale-Out File Servers. Understand Floating IPs, and be able to implement load balancing. Understand Blob Storage.

Know how to manage failover clustering.   Understand how to implement cluster-aware updating and how to recover a failed cluster node. Know how to upgrade a node to Windows Server 2022 and how to manage failover workloads between nodes. Know how to install Windows Updates on cluster nodes and how to manage failover clusters by using the Windows Admin Center.

Review Questions

1. You are the administrator for a mid-sized organization. You have been asked by the owner to set up an NLB cluster. You want to use PowerShell to do this. What cmdlet should you use?

   A. `New-NlbCluster`

   B. `Create-NlbCluster`

   C. `Setup-NlbCluster`

   D. `Set-NlbCluster`

2. You and a colleague are discussing Azure and the tools that it has that can help you with load balancing. One of the tools is a network-layer load balancer that improves network performance and availability of your applications. What is this tool called?

   A. Azure Application Gateway

   B. Azure Front Door

   C. Azure Load Balancer

   D. Azure Traffic Manager

3. What is the maximum number of nodes that can participate in a Windows Server 2022 NLB single cluster?

   A. 32

   B. 4

   C. 16

   D. 64

4. Which of the following actions should be performed against an NLB cluster node if maintenance needs to be performed while not terminating current connections?

   A. `evict`

   B. `drainstop`

   C. `pause`

   D. `stop`

5. Which of the following actions should be performed against an NLB cluster node if maintenance needs to be performed and all connections must be terminated immediately?

   A. `evict`

   B. `drainstop`

   C. `pause`

   D. `stop`

6. You are the network administrator for your organization and you want to stop virtual machine replication. What PowerShell cmdlet should you use?

   A. `Stop-VMReplication`

   B. `Terminate-VMReplication`

   C. `Kill-VMReplication`

   D. `Drainstop-VMReplication`

7. You are the network administrator for a company that has a Windows Server 2022 Hyper-V failover cluster. This cluster contains two nodes named ServerA and ServerB. On ServerA, you create a virtual machine named VirtualMachineA by using Hyper-V Manage. You need to configure VirtualMachineA to move to ServerB automatically if ServerA becomes unavailable. What should you do?

   A. In the Failover Cluster Manager, run the Configure Role actions.

   B. In the Hyper-V Manager, click VirtualMachineA and click Enable Replication.

   C. In the Hyper-V Manager click ServerA and modify the Hyper-V settings.

   D. Using Windows PowerShell, run the `Enable-VMReplication` cmdlet.

8. To configure an NLB cluster with unicast, what is the minimum number of network adapters required in each node?

   A. One

   B. Two

   C. Three

   D. Six

9. Users who are connecting to an NLB cluster have been complaining that after using the site for a few minutes they are prompted to log in using their username. What should you do to fix the problem and retain scalability?

   A. Create a port rule to allow only ports 80 and 443.

   B. Set the cluster affinity to None.

   C. Set the filtering mode to Single Host.

   D. Set the cluster affinity to Single.

10. Users who are connecting to an NLB cluster through the Internet are complaining that they keep connecting to different NLB nodes in different locations. You want to keep Internet users connecting to the same NLB members each time they connect. What should you do to fix the problem?

   A. Create a port rule to allow only ports 80 and 443.

   B. Set the cluster affinity to None.

   C. Set the cluster affinity to Class C.

   D. Set the cluster affinity to Single.

11. You have a failover cluster named FailoverCluster1 that has the following configurations:

- Number of nodes: 6
- Quorum: Dynamic quorum
- Witness: File share, Dynamic witness

While maintaining the quorum, what is the maximum number of nodes that can fail simultaneously?

A. 1

B. 2

C. 3

D. 4

12. Your company uses Storage Spaces Direct. What should you use if you want to view the available storage in a Storage Space Direct storage pool?

A. System Configuration

B. File Server Resource Manager (FSRM)

C. Get-StorageFileServer cmdlet

D. Failover Cluster Manager

13. You are the administrator for a mid-sized organization. You have been asked by the owner to view the information about an NLB cluster. You want to use PowerShell to view the cluster. What command should you use?

A. Get-NlbCluster

B. Create-NlbCluster

C. Setup-NlbCluster

D. Set-NlbCluster

14. You have a failover cluster named Failover1 that contains two nodes named Svr1 and Svr2. Failover1 is configured to use a file share witness. You are planning on configuring Failover1 to use a cloud witness. What storage account type should you configure if you need to configure Azure Storage accounts for the cloud witness?

A. Premium Block Blobs

B. Premium File Shares

C. Premium Page Blobs

D. Standard

15. You have a failover cluster named Failover1 that contains two nodes named Svr1 and Svr2. Failover1 is configured to use a file share witness. You are planning on configuring Failover1 to use a cloud witness. What authentication method should you configure if you need to configure Azure Storage accounts for the cloud witness?

A. Access Key

B. Shared Access Signature (SAS)

    C.   System-Assigned Managed Identity in Azure AD

    D.   User-Assigned Managed Identity in Azure AD

16. You are the administrator for a mid-sized organization. You have been asked by the owner to change the Hyper-V replication settings. You want to use PowerShell to change the settings. What cmdlet should you use?

    A.   `Set-VMReplication`

    B.   `Get-VMReplication`

    C.   `Setup-VMReplication`

    D.   `Create-VMReplication`

17. You need to distribute an application evenly among your virtual machines. The virtual machines are configured in a multitenant setup across multiple Hyper-V VMs. What can you do in this environment?

    A.   Windows Server Network Load Balancing (NLB) nodes

    B.   Application Load Balancing (ALB) nodes

    C.   RAS Load Balancing (RLB) nodes.

    D.   Software Load Balancing (SLB) nodes

18. You have three servers named Server1, Server2, and Server3 that run Windows Server and have the Hyper-V server role installed. You are planning to create a hyper-converged cluster to host Hyper-V virtual machines. What three actions should you perform if you need to ensure that you can store VMs in Storage Spaces Direct? (Choose three).

    A.   Add a Scale-Out File Server for application role.

    B.   Create a Distributed File System (DFS) namespace.

    C.   Create a failover cluster.

    D.   Create a file share.

    E.   Create a volume.

    F.   Enable Storage Spaces Direct.

19. You are planning to deploy Storage Spaces Direct on Windows Server. As a part of the process, you have already deployed the Windows Server and configured the network. Now, the next step is to configure Storage Spaces Direct. Given these options, choose the substeps that are recommended in order to configure Storage Spaces Direct.

    A.   Clean your drives to ensure that the drives are empty.

    B.   Configure a cluster witness.

    C.   Enable Storage Spaces Direct.

    D.   Create the volumes.

    E.   Deploy virtual machines for hyper-converged deployments.

    F.   All of these.

20. You and a colleague are discussing working with cluster nodes. One of the actions you can perform is an irreversible process. What is this action called?

   A. Add another node.

   B. Evict a node.

   C. Pause a node.

   D. Stop a node.

Chapter

14

Hybrid Data and Servers

THE FOLLOWING AZ-800 EXAM OBJECTIVES ARE COVERED IN THIS CHAPTER:

✓ **Configure and manage Azure File Sync**

- Create Azure File Sync Service
- Create Sync Groups
- Create Cloud Endpoints
- Register servers
- Create Server Endpoints
- Configure Cloud Tiering
- Monitor File Sync
- Migrate DFS to Azure File Sync

THE FOLLOWING AZ-801 EXAM OBJECTIVES ARE COVERED IN THIS CHAPTER:

✓ **Migrate on-premises storage to on-premises servers or Azure**

- Transfer data and share
- Cut over to a new server by using Storage Migration Service (SMS)
- Use Storage Migration Service to migrate to Azure VMs
- Migrate to Azure file shares

✓ **Migrate on-premises Servers to Azure**

  ▪ Deploy and configure Azure Migrate appliance

  ▪ Migrate VM workloads to Azure IaaS

  ▪ Migrate physical workloads to Azure IaaS

  ▪ Migrate by using Azure Migrate

✓ **Migrate workloads from previous versions to Windows Server 2022**

  ▪ Migrate IIS

  ▪ Migrate Hyper-V hosts

  ▪ Migrate RDS host servers

  ▪ Migrate DHCP

  ▪ Migrate print servers

This chapter explores the benefits of using Microsoft Endpoint and the tools and applications that will help IT administrators manage their software and applications.

We'll discuss Windows Autopilot and how you can use it to deploy operating systems to new or repurposed machines. It is truly a zero-touch installation.

You'll learn how to migrate data and servers from onsite (on-premises) servers to Azure. I will show you how to keep the data accurate between multiple servers. Finally, I will show you how to migrate your servers to Azure.

Let's begin with a look at the benefits and features of Microsoft Endpoint Manager.

Using Microsoft Endpoint Manager

Microsoft Endpoint Manager is used for maintaining, monitoring, and protecting your end users and endpoints. Whether you are using the cloud or using an on-premises networks, Microsoft Endpoint Manager will help keep your data safe and secure. It consists of the tools and services that you can use to monitor and maintain your endpoints. Endpoints include:

- Apps
- Desktop computers
- Embedded devices
- Mobile devices
- Servers
- Shared devices
- Virtual machines

Microsoft Endpoint Manager includes a variety of services:

- Azure Active Directory (Azure AD)
- Co-management
- Configuration Manager
- Desktop Analytics
- Endpoint Manager Admin Center
- Microsoft Intune
- Windows Autopilot

Endpoint Manager uses Azure Active Directory (Azure AD) to identify devices, groups, multifactor authentication (MFA), and users.

Co-management is used to join an already existent on-premises Configuration Manager asset to the cloud by using either Intune or another Microsoft 365 cloud service. As an administrator, you will determine which service will be the management authority.

Desktop Analytics is a cloud-based service that works in conjunction with Configuration Manager. It helps you make important decisions regarding the update readiness of a Windows client. Desktop Analytics looks at the data from your company along with data collected from millions of other devices that are connected to the Microsoft cloud to help provide information on apps, security updates, and more. Desktop Analytics is used to keep Windows 10 devices current.

The Endpoint Manager Admin Center is a comprehensive website that you can use to manage devices and create policies. It is where you can locate the Microsoft Intune service, as well as other device management–related settings.

Microsoft Intune is a cloud-based mobile device management (MDM) and mobile application management (MAM) provider that you use for apps and devices. Using the cloud, Intune can create and check for compliance, deploy apps, and change features and settings on a variety of devices.

Windows Autopilot is used to streamline the way devices get deployed, reset, and repurposed by using a deployment method that requires no interaction from the IT department. Autopilot is used to preconfigure devices and to automatically enroll devices in Intune. Your users simply unbox the device and turn it on, and Windows Autopilot will configure it from the cloud using just a few steps.

What deployment method should you use? This is a question that is often asked. There really is no right or wrong answer. Use what works best for you and your organization and consider what you wish to accomplish. You can start with Windows Autopilot if you are continually provisioning new devices, or you can use Intune if you add rules and control settings for your apps, devices, and users.

Endpoint Manager can be thought of in three separate parts:

Cloud   All your data is stored in Azure. This method provides you with the benefits of mobility on the cloud as well as the security advantages that are provided by Azure.

On-premises   If you aren't ready to use the cloud, then you can keep your existing systems in house. All hardware and software applications are hosted onsite.

Hybrid   These environments use a combination of both cloud and on-premises solutions.

There are a number of benefits to using Microsoft Endpoint Manager to manage and protect your endpoints. You can:

- Confirm that user devices are configured and protected according to corporate policies.
- Confirm that your corporate security rules are in place.
- Ensure that corporate services are available to your end users and on all of their devices.
- Ensure that your company is using correct credentials in order to access and share corporate information.
- Protect the apps and devices that access your resources.
- Protect the data that your users are accessing.

If you have Microsoft Endpoint Configuration Manager and Microsoft Intune, then you already have Microsoft Endpoint Manager. These are all now one management system.

Using Mobile Device Management

Mobile device management (MDM) is basically a way in which administrators can manage mobile devices. It refers to a set of functions and features that regulate the use of mobile devices to make sure they are compliant with corporate policies.

MDM allows you to maintain, secure, and enforce mobile endpoint policies. You can use it to set up Windows 10/11 policies that can incorporate a wide variety of scenarios, such as the ability to control a user's access to the Windows Store or the ability to access the corporate VPN.

To help you manage corporate security policies and business applications, Windows 10 and Windows 11 provide an enterprise management solution that consists of two parts:

- The enrollment client, which enrolls and configures the device to communicate with the enterprise management server
- The management client, which synchronizes with the management server to check for updates and apply policies

MDM administers mobile devices without joining them to an on-premises Active Directory Domain Service (AD DS). In order to manage a device using MDM, implement MDM by using an MDM authority and MDM clients. Microsoft offers two MDM authority solutions:

- Basic Mobility and Security (Microsoft 365)
- Microsoft Intune

Once the device is enrolled, you can still implement policies and profiles to manage the device. Each of these solutions use Microsoft 365 Endpoint Manager for administering the MDM solutions. They each manage enrolled devices, but they provide distinct capabilities.

MDM client functionality is included with the Windows 10/11 operating system. MDM includes the delivery of applications, settings, and data to devices that are enrolled to MDM. Windows 10/11 devices can be enrolled in MDM by any of these methods:

- Being enrolled into Azure AD (if Azure AD and MDM are configured)
- Using Group Policies in a hybrid environment
- Using a provisioning package
- Using the Settings app
- Manually configuring

MDM authority, such as Intune, can provide these capabilities:

Application Management   You can install apps and manage settings by using both MDM and Mobile Application Management (MAM).

Configuring Devices   You can use profiles and policies to configure devices, control what users can access, and set device settings to comply with corporate policies.

Device Enrollment   MDM can only manage supported devices that have been enrolled. In order to manage a device, the device can either include the MDM client functionality, such as Windows 10, or you must install a Company Portal app (for example, on Android or iOS devices).

Monitoring and Reporting   With the MDM management tool, you can get a notification if a device is having an issue or if a policy was not properly applied. Enrolled devices can also be added to groups. You can also configure Windows Autopilot device deployment by using Intune.

Selective Delete Data   Should a device ever get lost or stolen, or if a user leaves your company, you can wipe the corporate data is that is on the device. A wipe is basically just erasing the data from the hard disk on the device. You have the option to either wipe all the data on the device or perform a selective wipe, which will leave the user's personal data on the device intact.

Even if a device isn't a member of the domain, the device can be managed by MDM. If you have a Windows 10/11 device that is a member of the domain, then you can manage it by using Group Policy and MDM simultaneously. With Windows 10 version 1803 and newer, you can specify whether a Group Policy setting or an MDM policy setting will take precedence if there is a conflict.

You can manage the following Windows 10/11 configuration areas by using MDM:

- Application management
- Device configuration and security
- Enrollment
- Inventory
- Remote assistance
- Unenrollment

Application management benefits include:

- Custom Windows Store
- Business Store Portal (BSP) app deployments; license reclaim
- Enterprise app management
- Line-of-business (LOB) app management
- Win32 (MSI) app management
- App inventory (LOB/Store apps)
- App allow/deny lists using AppLocker
- Windows Information Protection (WIP)

Device configuration and security benefits include:

- Device update control
- Email provisioning
- Enterprise Wi-Fi
- Extended set of policies for client certificate management
- Kiosk, Start screen, Start Menu configuration, and control
- MDM push
- VPN management

Enrollment benefits include:

- Azure AD integration
- Bulk enrollment
- Converged protocol
- Provisioning
- Simple bootstrap

Inventory benefits include additional device inventory.
Remote Assistance benefits include:

- Enhanced inventory for compliance decisions
- Full device wipe
- Remote lock, PIN reset, ring and find

Unenrollment benefits include:

- Removal of enterprise configuration (apps, certs, profiles, policies) and enterprise-encrypted data (with EDP)
- Unenrollment with alerts

Policy Settings Using Basic Mobility and Security (Microsoft 365)

In Microsoft 365, the Basic Mobility and Security service provides a built-in MDM solution that provides the core device management features.

The Basic Mobility and Security service is hosted by the Intune service and contains a subset of Intune services. Even though it has some of the features used by Intune, according to Microsoft, it's not an "Intune-lite" solution.

You can use Basic Mobility and Security to manage many types of mobile devices. Each person must have an applicable Microsoft 365 license, and their device must be enrolled in

Basic Mobility and Security. Once the devices are enrolled, you can manage, block access to, and even wipe the devices.

When you create policies or profiles, they can only be deployed by assigning them to groups of users. You can't directly assign a policy to a specific user or to an individual device. The user will receive an enrollment message on their device, and once they have completed the enrollment, then their device will be constrained by the policies that you set. Then, using the MDM management tool, you can monitor the policy deployment.

Using Basic Mobility and Security, you can manage these mobile devices settings:

Organizationwide Device Access Settings   You can specify whether you want to allow or deny access to Exchange mail for devices that are not supported by Basic Mobility and Security and which groups should be excluded from access control.

Device Security Policies   You can use these policies to protect devices from unauthorized access. These policies include password settings, encryption settings, managing email profile settings, and settings that control the use of device features, such as Bluetooth and videoconferencing.

Many MDM solutions help protect organizational data by making sure that users and devices meet specific requirements. These are known as compliance policies and act as the rules and settings that users and devices must meet in order to be compliant. When you pair them with Conditional Access requirements, you can deny users and devices that do not meet your rules. You can use some of these policies to help affect the entire Microsoft 365 experience:

Compliance   Microsoft uses the default compliance rules that are built into Configuration Manager for mobile devices, but also offers configuration items (CIs) and built-in compliance rules whose values are based on Microsoft's digital security requirements. Microsoft has created a configuration baseline for those CIs and targeted the configuration baseline to mobile devices.

Messaging   The default policies for Exchange align policy settings between Exchange ActiveSync (EAS) and MDM.

Security   The default policies enforce Microsoft corporate compliance settings on mobile devices, such as password policy and encryption settings.

Policy Settings Using Microsoft Intune

Microsoft Intune is a cloud-based service that focuses on MDM and MAM. With Intune, you can control how your mobile devices are used. It also allows you to configure specific policies that control applications using MAM.

Intune allows you to control how mobiles devices are used whether it's a corporate owned or a personal device. On personal devices, Intune can help ensure that corporate data is protected, and it can also isolate the corporate data from personal data. Intune allows you to manage multiple devices per person, regardless of the different platforms that are run on the different devices. In Intune, users will see a dialog box that tells them about the policies. They can then select to allow or cancel device enrollment.

 You cannot start using Basic Mobility and Security if you are already using Microsoft Intune.

You can manage the same settings in Microsoft Intune as in Basic Mobility and Security as well as other settings:

- Application deployment, configuration policies, and protection policies
- Conditional Access
- Device compliance policies
- Device configuration policies
- Device enrollment and restrictions
- Software updates, which include Windows 10/11 update rings and update policies for iOS

While Basic Mobility and Security is part of the Microsoft 365 plans, Microsoft Intune is a stand-alone product included with certain Microsoft 365 plans. Table 14.1 identifies which plans provide the MDM solution.

TABLE 14.1 Microsoft 365 plans

Plan	Basic Mobility and Security	Microsoft Intune
Microsoft 365 Apps	Yes	No
Microsoft 365 Business Basic	Yes	No
Microsoft 365 Business Standard	Yes	No
Office 365 E1	Yes	No
Office 365 E3	Yes	No
Office 365 E5	Yes	No
Microsoft 365 Business Premium	Yes	Yes
Microsoft 365 Firstline 3	Yes	Yes
Microsoft 365 Enterprise E3	Yes	Yes
Microsoft 365 Enterprise E5	Yes	Yes

TABLE 14.1   Microsoft 365 plans *(Continued)*

Plan	Basic Mobility and Security	Microsoft Intune
Microsoft 365 Education A1	Yes	Yes
Microsoft 365 Education A3	Yes	Yes
Microsoft 365 Education A5	Yes	Yes
Microsoft Intune	No	Yes
Enterprise Mobility & Security E3	No	Yes
Enterprise Mobility & Security E5	No	Yes

Understanding AutoPilot

Windows Autopilot is a set of programs that helps simplify and streamline bulk deployment, setup, and configuration of devices. Autopilot allows you to truly have a zero-touch installation of the Windows client operating system. You can use Autopilot to reset, repurpose, and recover devices, reducing the time spent on deploying, managing, and retiring devices.

Autopilot allows you to:

- Auto-enroll devices into MDM services.
- Automatically join devices to Azure AD or Active Directory (via Hybrid Azure AD Join).
- Create and auto-assign devices to configuration groups based on a device's profile.
- Customize out-of-box-experience (OOBE) content specific to your organization.

You can use Autopilot to set up and preconfigure new Windows devices for your organization, right out of the box, without having to build an image or infrastructure to manage. Users go through the process by themselves, without making any decisions and without the need to involve an IT administrator.

With Autopilot Reset, existing devices can be quickly prepared for a new user. The Reset capability can also be used if a device needs to be fixed in order to bring the device back to a working state.

You can provide new devices to your end users without the need to build, maintain, and apply custom operating system images to the devices by using Microsoft Intune and Autopilot. Once deployed, Windows devices can be managed by tools such as Microsoft Intune, Windows Update for Business, Configuration Manager, and other similar tools.

Autopilot allows you to get a list of device IDs from a manufacturer. You enter the device IDs into your Azure environment. You assign a device profile to that machine and that's it.

Once the user logs on to the Internet, the machine automatically recognizes that it is part of your organization and the installation is completed—without any IT intervention.

Autopilot Benefits

Administrators used to spend hours upon hours building and customizing images that would later be used to deploy devices. But with Autopilot, you do not need to reimage or manually set up new devices before giving them to your end users.

Devices can be shipped to your users directly from the vendor. It only takes a few simple actions to make the device ready to use. The end user just connects to the network and verifies their credentials. Beyond that, everything else is automated by Autopilot. Here are some of the key benefits:

Easy Device Setup Users connect their devices to the Internet and answer some quick setup questions, and Autopilot installs all preconfigured user, device, and app policies.

Increased Employee Satisfaction Devices configured with Autopilot provide users with an easy login experience that reduces the need for tech support.

Saves Time and Resources Instead of setting up devices, you can create a customized OOBE of preconfigured apps and settings, and then deploy them to users' devices using the cloud.

Ability to Use the Device Anywhere Devices configured using Autopilot can be shipped anywhere and set up wherever. The user only needs an Internet connection.

Autopilot Prerequisites

Autopilot relies on specific capabilities that are available in Windows 10/11, Azure AD, and MDM services. Let's take a look at the requirements for Autopilot.

Software Requirements

In order to use Autopilot, a supported version of Windows 11 or Windows 10 semiannual channel is required.

Networking Requirements

The network requirements depend on various Internet-based services. Access to these services must be provided for Autopilot to function properly:

- Ensure DNS name resolution for Internet DNS names
- Allow access to all hosts through ports 80 (HTTP), 443 (HTTPS), and 123 (UDP/NTP)

Licensing Requirements

Autopilot depends on specific capabilities available in Windows 10/11 and Azure AD and an MDM service such as Microsoft Intune. One of the following subscriptions is required:

- Microsoft 365 Business Premium subscription
- Microsoft 365 F1 or F3 subscription
- Microsoft 365 Academic A1, A3, or A5 subscription
- Microsoft 365 Enterprise E3 or E5 subscription, which include all Windows 10, Microsoft 365, and Enterprise Mobility and Security (EM+S) features (Azure AD and Intune)
- Enterprise Mobility + Security E3 or E5 subscription
- Intune for Education subscription
- Azure Active Directory Premium P1 or P2 and Microsoft Intune subscription (or an alternative MDM service)

According to Microsoft, the following subscriptions are also recommended, but not required:

- Microsoft 365 Apps for Enterprise (formerly Office 365 Pro Plus)
- Windows Subscription Activation, to automatically upgrade devices from Windows 10 Pro to Windows 10 Enterprise

Configuration Requirements

Before Autopilot can be used to support common Autopilot scenarios, the following configuration tasks must be done:

- Configure Azure AD automatic enrollment.
- Configure Azure AD custom branding.
- Enable Windows Subscription Activation.

Some scenarios have other requirements. There are typically two tasks that should be done:

- **Device registration:** Devices must be added to Autopilot to support most Autopilot scenarios.
- **Profile configuration:** Once devices have been added to Autopilot, a profile of settings must be applied to each device.

Autopilot Profiles

Autopilot profiles control how Windows is installed on user devices. The profiles contain settings that are automatically set and optional settings that you can configure manually. Automatically set options include the following:

Skip Cortana, OneDrive, And OEM Registration   This option will skip the installation of apps such as Cortana and OneDrive.

Sign-in Experience With Your Company Brand   If you have an "Add your company branding to Microsoft 365 Sign-In page," then the device will get that experience when signing in.

MDM Auto-enrollment With Configured AAD Accounts   The user identity will be managed by Azure AD. The user will log in using their Microsoft 365 Business Premium credentials.

Manually set options include:

Skip Privacy Settings (Off by Default)   If this is set to On, the user will not see the license agreement for the device and Windows when they first sign in.

Don't Allow The User To Become The Local Admin   If this is set to On, the user will not be able to install any personal apps.

Deployment Scenarios

You have several ways to deploy Autopilot:

- User-driven mode
- Self-deploying mode
- Windows Autopilot Reset
- Pre-provisioning
- Support for existing devices

User-Driven Mode

Autopilot user-driven mode allows you to configure new Windows devices to automatically transform them from their factory state to a ready-to-use state. This process doesn't require that an administrator even touch the device. The devices can be shipped or distributed to the end user directly with the following instructions:

1. Unbox the device, plug it in, and turn it on.
2. Choose a language, locale, and keyboard.
3. Connect the device to a wireless or wired network with Internet access.
4. Specify your corporate email address and password.

The rest of the process is automated. The device will automatically:

1. Join the organization.
2. Enroll in Intune (or another MDM service).
3. Get configured as defined by your company.

Self-Deploying Mode

Self-deployment mode is very similar to user-driven mode. This mode allows you to deploy a device with little to no user interaction. For devices with an Ethernet connection, no user interaction is required. However, for devices connected using Wi-Fi, the user must only:

- Choose the language, locale, and keyboard
- Make a network connection

Self-deploying mode provides the following:

- Joins the device to Azure Active Directory
- Enrolls the device in Intune (or another MDM service) using Azure AD for automatic MDM enrollment
- Makes sure that all policies, applications, certificates, and networking profiles are provisioned on the device
- Uses the Enrollment Status Page to prevent access until the device is fully provisioned

Self-deploying mode does not support Active Directory Join or Hybrid Azure AD Join. All devices will be joined to Azure AD.

Windows Autopilot Reset

Takes the device back to a business-ready state by:

- Removing personal files, apps, and settings
- Reapplying a device's original settings
- Setting the region, language, and keyboard to the original values
- Maintaining the device's identity connection to Azure AD
- Maintaining the device's management connection to Intune

The Autopilot Reset process automatically keeps information from the existing device:

- Wi-Fi connection details
- Provisioning packages previously applied
- A provisioning package present on a USB drive when the reset process is started
- Azure AD device membership and MDM enrollment information

When Autopilot Reset is used on a device, the device's primary user will be removed and the next person who signs in after the reset will become the new primary user.

Autopilot Reset does not support Hybrid Azure AD joined devices; a full device wipe will be required. Once a hybrid device goes through a full device reset, it may take up to 24 hours for it to be ready to be deployed.

Pre-provisioning

This was once referred to as the Autopilot White Glove feature, but it has been renamed to Windows Autopilot for pre-provisioned deployment. The provisioning process is split with the time-consuming portions being done by the IT administrators, partners, or OEMs (this is called the technician flow). The end user just needs to perform a few necessary settings and policies and then they can begin using their device (this is called the user flow). Autopilot for pre-provisioned deployment supports two distinct scenarios:

User-Driven Deployments with Azure AD Join   The device will be joined to an Azure AD tenant.

User-Driven Deployments with Hybrid Azure AD Join   The device will be joined to an on-premises Active Directory domain and separately registered with Azure AD.

Each scenario consists of two parts: a technician flow and a user flow.

Support for Existing Devices

Autopilot for existing devices only supports user-driven Azure AD and Hybrid Azure AD profiles. Self-deploying and pre-provisioning profiles are not supported.

Windows Autopilot Devices

Devices that have been registered with the Autopilot service are displayed in the Admin Center, as shown in Figure 14.1, under Devices ➤ Enroll Devices ➤ Windows Enrollment ➤ Windows Autopilot Deployment Program ➤ Devices.

FIGURE 14.1   Autopilot deployment

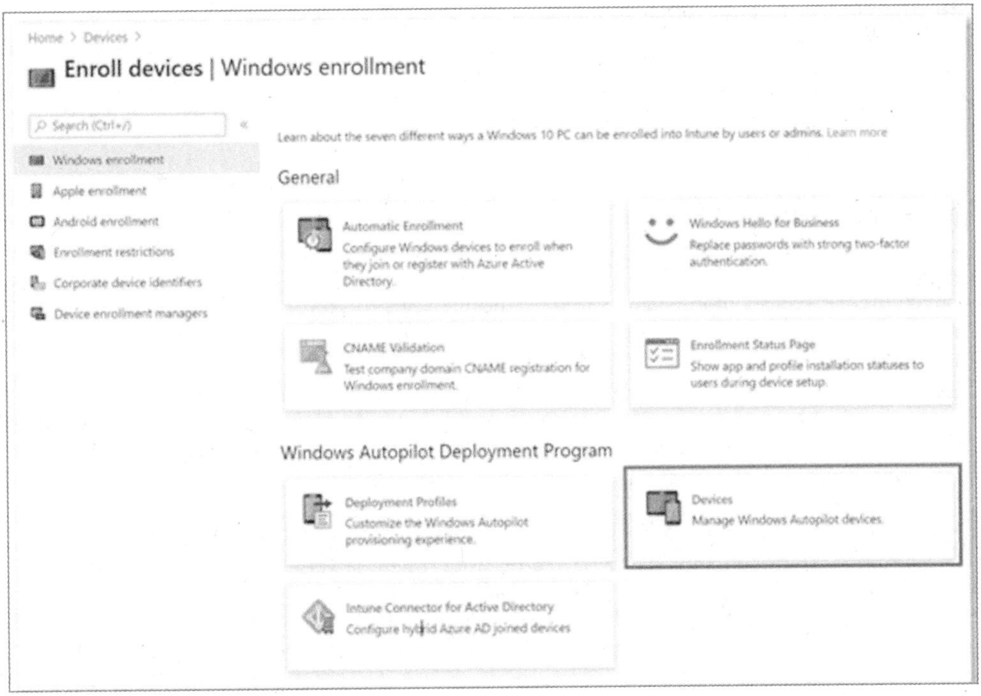

Devices that are listed in Intune under Devices ➤ Windows | Windows Devices are not the same as Windows Autopilot devices (Devices ➤ Enroll Devices ➤ Windows Enrollment ➤ Windows Autopilot Deployment Program | Devices).

Windows Autopilot devices are added to the list of Windows devices when both of the following are complete:

- The Autopilot registration process is successful.

- A licensed user has signed in on the device.

Planning for Secure Applications Data on Devices

AS YOU PLAN AND PREPARE THE SECURE APPLICATIONS DATA ON DEVICES, KEEP IN MIND THE FOLLOWING:

Configuring Managed Apps for Mobile Application Management

Sometimes the assumption is made that MDM is the same as MAM. However, that is not necessarily the case. MDM is more about controlling devices whereas MAM is concerned with your company applications and data.

MAM is software that protects and enables you to control company applications on your end users' devices. It allows you to apply and enforce policies on apps and limit the sharing of corporate data. It also allows you to separate corporate from personal data on these devices.

MAM Basics

Intune MAM refers to the suite of Intune management features that allow you to publish, push, configure, secure, monitor, and update mobile apps to your users. It allows you to manage and protect your company data within an application. Intune MAM supports two configurations:

Intune MDM + MAM   You can manage apps using MAM on devices that are enrolled with Intune MDM. Users should use Intune in the Microsoft Endpoint Manager admin center.

Unenrolled Devices with MAM Managed Applications   You can manage corporate data and accounts in apps using MAM on unenrolled devices or devices enrolled with third-party enterprise mobility management (EMM) providers. Users should use Intune in the Microsoft Endpoint Manager admin center.

Most app-related information can be found in the Apps workload. You can find this by signing into the Microsoft Endpoint Manager admin center and selecting Apps. The apps workload provides links to access common app information and functionality. The top of the App workload navigation menu provides commonly used app details:

Overview   Allows you to view the tenant name, MDM authority, tenant location, account status, app installation status, and app protection policy status.

All Apps   Displays a list of all available apps and their statuses.

Monitor Apps   There are a few options under this section:

> **App Licenses**   You can view, assign, and monitor volume-purchased apps from the app stores.
>
> **Discovered Apps**   You can view apps that were assigned by Intune or installed on a device.
>
> **App Install Status**   You can view the status of an app assignment that you created.
>
> **App Protection Status**   You can view the status of an app protection policy for a selected user.

By Platform   You can select these platforms to view the available apps by platform: Windows, iOS, macOS, and Android.

Policy   There are a few options under this section:

> **App Protection Policies**   Choose this option to associate settings with an app and help protect the company data it uses.
>
> **App Configuration Policies**   Choose this option to supply settings that might be required when a user runs an app.
>
> **iOS App Provisioning Profiles**   iOS apps include a provisioning profile and code that is signed by a certificate. When the certificate expires, the app can no longer be run. Intune gives you the tools to assign a new provisioning profile policy to devices that have apps that are nearing expiration.
>
> **S Mode Supplemental Policies**   Choose this option to authorize additional applications to run on your managed S mode devices.
>
> **Policies for Office apps**   Choose this option to create mobile app management policies for Office mobile apps that connect to Microsoft 365 services.
>
> **Policy Sets**   Choose this option to create an assignable collection of apps, policies, and other management objects that you have built.

Other   There are a few options under this section:

> **App Selective Wipe**   Choose this option to remove only corporate data from a selected user's device.
>
> **App Categories**   You can add, pin, and delete app category names.
>
> **E-books**   Some app stores give you the ability to purchase multiple licenses for an app or books that you want to use in your company.

Help and Support   Choose this to troubleshoot, request support, or view Intune status.

Add an App Using Intune

This is an example of how to use Intune to add and assign an app for your corporate users. You will first want to sign in to the Microsoft Endpoint Manager admin center as a global administrator or an Intune Service administrator.

Perform these steps to add an app to Intune:

1. Sign in to Microsoft Endpoint Manager admin center and select Apps ≻ All Apps ≻ Add.
2. From the App Type drop-down list, select Windows 10.
3. Click Select. The Add App steps are displayed.
4. Confirm the default details in the App Suite Information step and click Next.
5. Confirm the default settings in the App Settings step and click Next.
6. Select the group assignments for the app.
7. Click Next to display the Review + Create page. Review the values and settings you entered for the app.
8. When you are done, click Create to add the app to Intune.

Assign the App to a Group

Once you have added an app using Microsoft Intune, you can assign the app to additional groups of users or devices.

Perform these steps to assign an app to a group:

1. In Intune, select Apps ≻ All Apps.
2. Select the app that you want to assign.
3. Click Properties. Next to Assignments click Edit.
4. Click Add Group in the Required section. The Select Group pane is displayed.

5. Find the group that you want to add and click Select at the bottom of the pane.

6. Click Review + Save ≻ Save to assign the group.

You now have assigned the app to an additional group.

Install the App on the Enrolled Device

Your end users must install and use the Company Portal app to install an app that is available in Intune. Here are the steps:

1. Log into the enrolled Windows 10 Desktop device. The device must be enrolled with Intune and must be signed in using an account contained in the group that was assigned to the app.

2. From the Start Menu, open the Microsoft Store. Then, find the Company Portal app and install it.

3. Launch the Company Portal app.

4. Click the app that you added using Intune.

5. Click Install.

Protecting Enterprise Data Using Windows Information Protection

Information protection in today's cybersecurity settings consists of four parts:

- **Device Protection:** Protect system and data when a device is lost or stolen.

- **Data Separation:** Containment and data separation.

- **Leak Protection:** Prevent unauthorized users and apps from accessing and leaking data.

- **Sharing Protection:** Protect data when shared with others, or shared outside of corporate devices and control.

Windows Information Protection (WIP) helps protect corporate data in a world that is increasingly becoming a Bring Your Own Device (BYOD) environment. Since many organizations are allowing employees to connect their own devices to their network, the possibility of corporate data being compromised because of non-corporate programs running on these personal devices is increasing. WIP helps protect information by separating corporate applications and corporate data from being disclosed by personal devices and personal applications.

WIP was previously known as Enterprise Data Protection (EDP). WIP is a built-in Windows 10/11 feature that allows you to maintain and monitor company data separate from any personal data that is on a user's device.

WIP aids in protecting against possible data leaks and protects enterprise apps and data on both enterprise-owned and personal devices without interfering with the user's experience while on the corporate network. Users do not need to open any special apps or enter into any specific modes in order for WIP to work. Users just use apps that they are used to and WIP will provide the data protection.

Besides separating corporate and personal data, WIP can also determine which users and apps have access to particular data and can determine what users are allowed to do with that corporate data. For example, you have the ability to stop a user from copying corporate data from an approved app and pasting that data into another unapproved app.

The WIP Intune policy maintains a list of protected apps, corporate network locations, the levels of protection granted, and the encryption settings. WIP provides the following:

- Allows you to track issues and find corrective actions by using audit reports.

- Integrates with existing management systems to deploy, configure, and manage WIPs. Management systems can include Microsoft Intune, Microsoft Configuration Manager (MCM), or an MDM.

- Provides added protection for present line-of-business apps without needing to update any apps.

- Provides the capability to remove corporate data from Intune MDM–enrolled devices while, at the same time, not touching the personal data on a device.

- Separates personal data from corporate data, without the need for the user to change apps or settings.

You can set a WIP policy with a different level of protection and management modes. There are four protection and management modes (see Figure 14.2):

- **Block:** Prevents users from engaging in unauthorized actions, such as copying and pasting corporate data. WIP searches for unacceptable data sharing and will stop the user from performing any further.

- **Override:** Alerts users whenever they try to execute an unauthorized action. The user can ignore the warning and proceed with the unauthorized action; however, WIP will log the event in its audit log where you can review it later.

- **Silent:** Will run in the background, tracking the user's actions with no indicator of an unauthorized action and logging any inappropriate data sharing. However, if an action is blocked, the action will be prevented as usual.

- **Off:** WIP is disabled and provides no protection or auditing.

FIGURE 14.2   Configure Windows Information Protection Settings

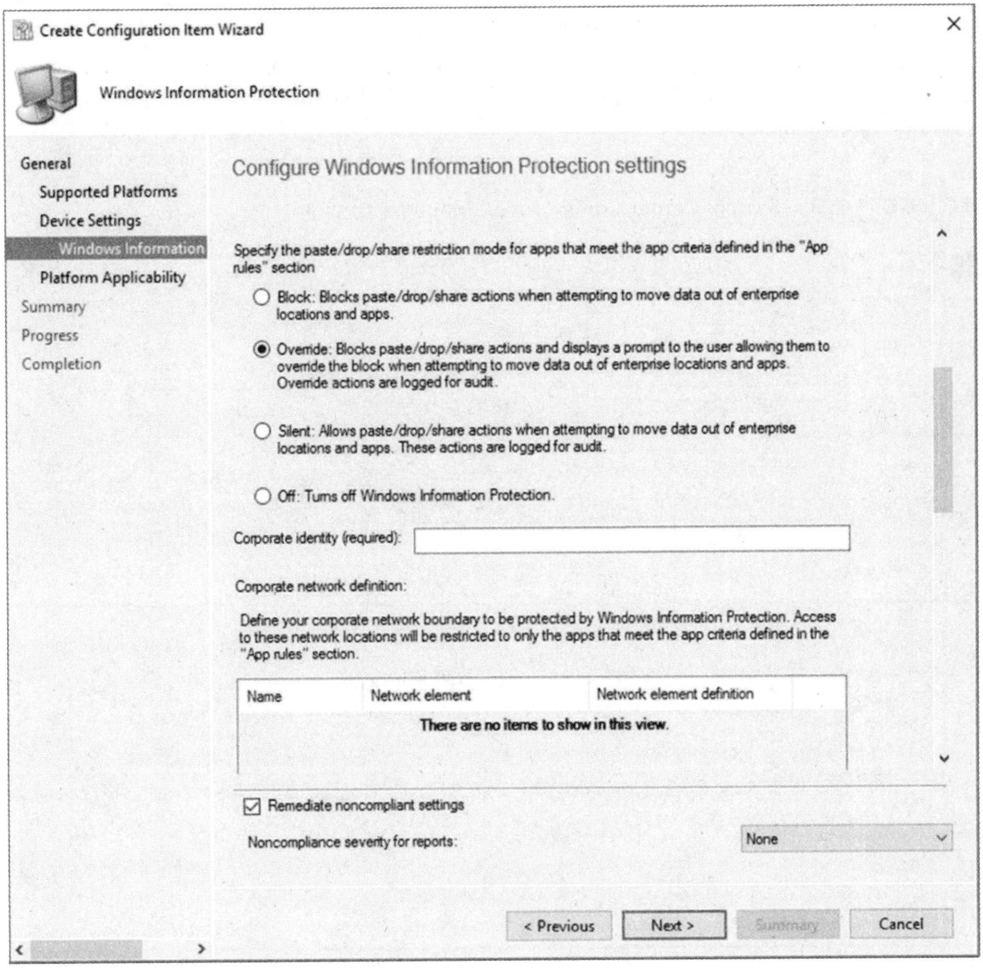

🖳 Create Configuration Item Wizard	×

🖥️ **Windows Information Protection**

General	**Configure Windows Information Protection settings**
Supported Platforms	
Device Settings	
Windows Information	Specify the paste/drop/share restriction mode for apps that meet the app criteria defined in the "App rules" section
Platform Applicability	
Summary	○ Block: Blocks paste/drop/share actions when attempting to move data out of enterprise locations and apps.
Progress	◉ Override: Blocks paste/drop/share actions and displays a prompt to the user allowing them to override the block when attempting to move data out of enterprise locations and apps. Override actions are logged for audit.
Completion	

Specify the paste/drop/share restriction mode for apps that meet the app criteria defined in the "App rules" section

- ○ Block: Blocks paste/drop/share actions when attempting to move data out of enterprise locations and apps.
- ◉ Override: Blocks paste/drop/share actions and displays a prompt to the user allowing them to override the block when attempting to move data out of enterprise locations and apps. Override actions are logged for audit.
- ○ Silent: Allows paste/drop/share actions when attempting to move data out of enterprise locations and apps. These actions are logged for audit.
- ○ Off: Turns off Windows Information Protection.

Corporate identity (required):

Corporate network definition:

Define your corporate network boundary to be protected by Windows Information Protection. Access to these network locations will be restricted to only the apps that meet the app criteria defined in the "App rules" section.

Name	Network element	Network element definition
	There are no items to show in this view.	

☑ Remediate noncompliant settings

Noncompliance severity for reports: None

< Previous   Next >   Summary   Cancel

It's not recommended, but you can turn off WIP. This can be done without data loss to the devices that were managed by WIP. WIP can be turned back on, but the previously applied decryption and policy information will not be automatically reapplied.

WIP uses Microsoft Configuration Manager (MCM) to design and implement WIP policies. Once you have set up SCCM, you must create a configuration item for WIP; this is the WIP policy.

Creating a Configuration Item for WIP

To create a configuration item for WIP, follow these steps:

1. Open the SCCM console, click the Assets And Compliance node, expand the Overview node, expand the Compliance Settings node, and then expand the Configuration Items node (see Figure 14.3).

FIGURE 14.3 System Center Configuration Manager console

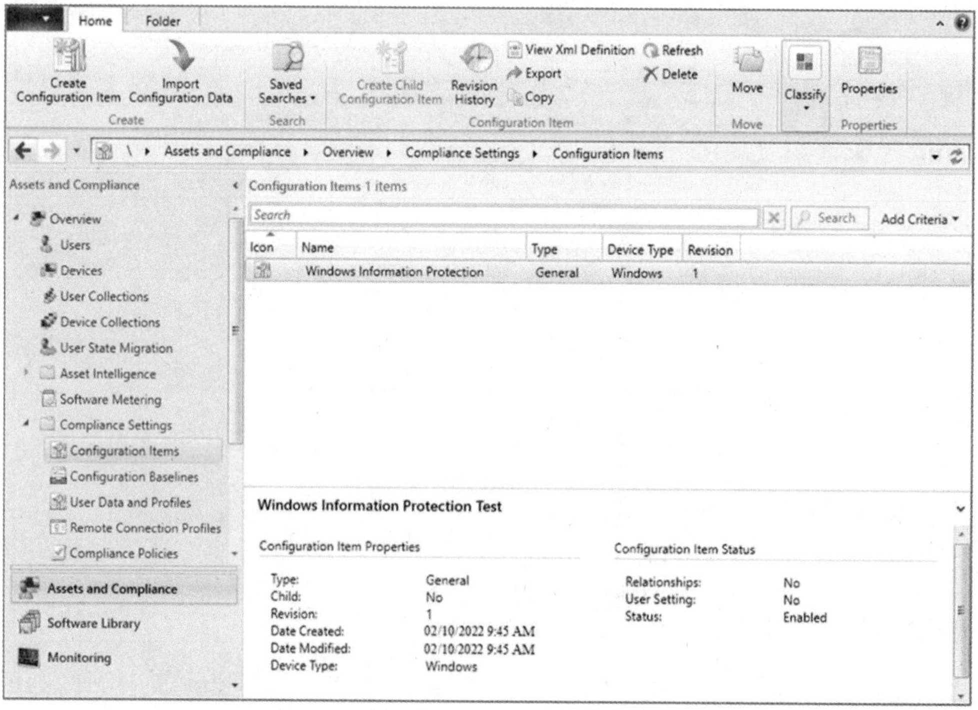

2. Click the Create Configuration Item button. The Create Configuration Item Wizard will start (see Figure 14.4).

FIGURE 14.4 Create Configuration Item Wizard

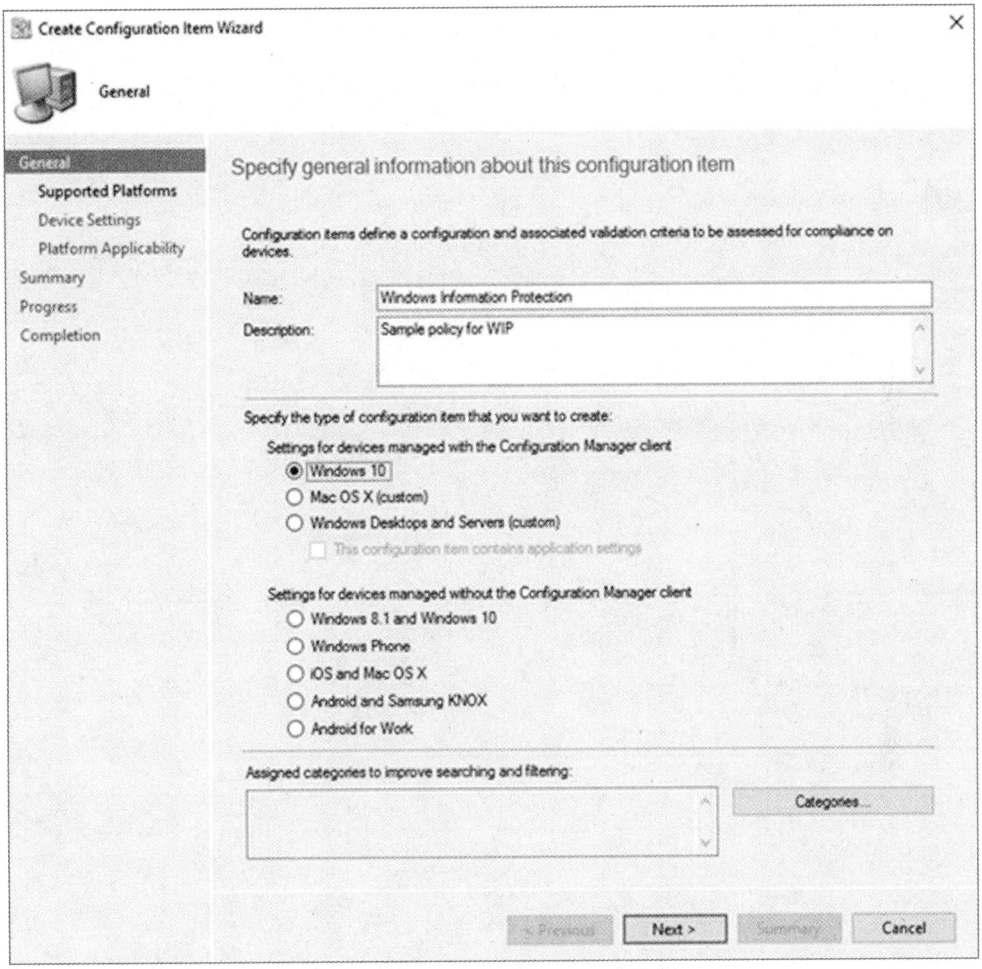

3. On the General Information page, type a name (required) and a description (optional) for the policy into the Name and Description boxes.

4. In the Specify The Type Of Configuration Item That You Want To Create area, select the option that represents whether you'd like to use SCCM for device management, and then click Next. The options are as follows:

   - Settings For Devices Managed With The Configuration Manager Client: Windows 10

   - Settings For Devices Managed Without The Configuration Manager Client: Windows 8.1 and Windows 10

5. On the Supported Platforms page (see Figure 14.5), click the Windows 10 box, and then click Next.

FIGURE 14.5   Create Configuration Item Wizard – Supported Platforms

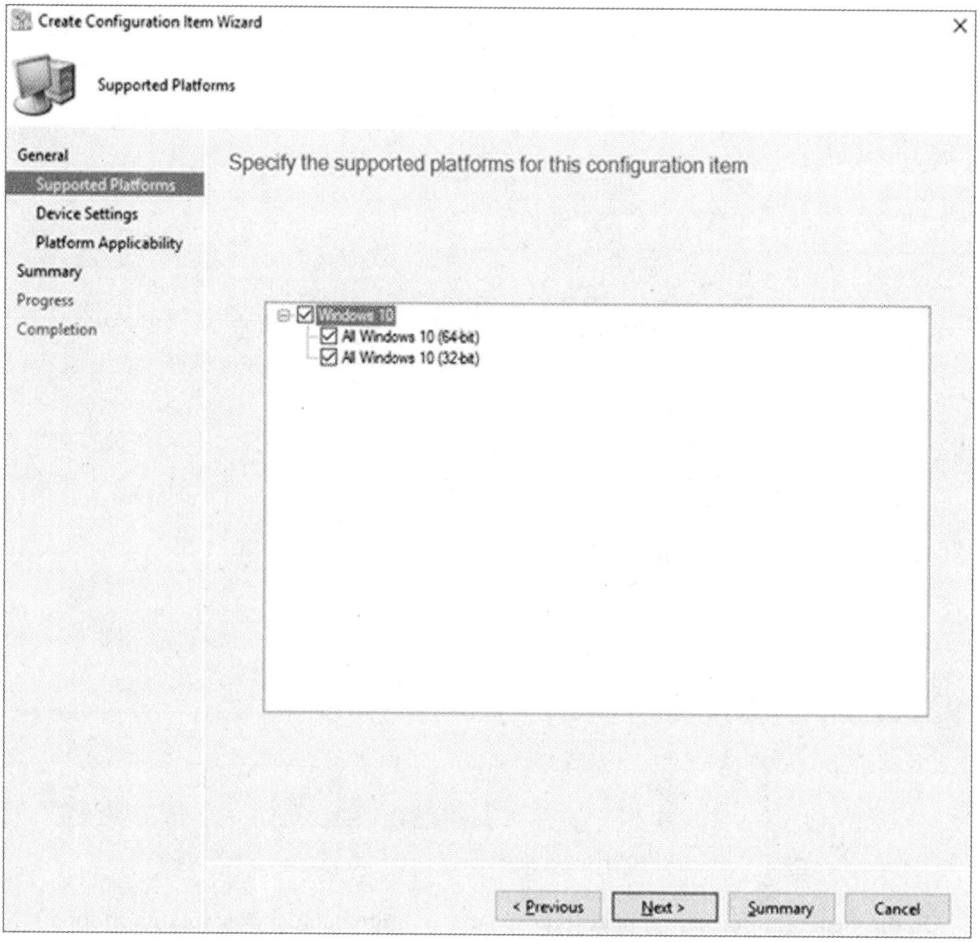

6. On the Device Settings page (see Figure 14.6), click Windows Information Protection, and then click Next.

FIGURE 14.6   Create Configuration Item Wizard – Device Settings

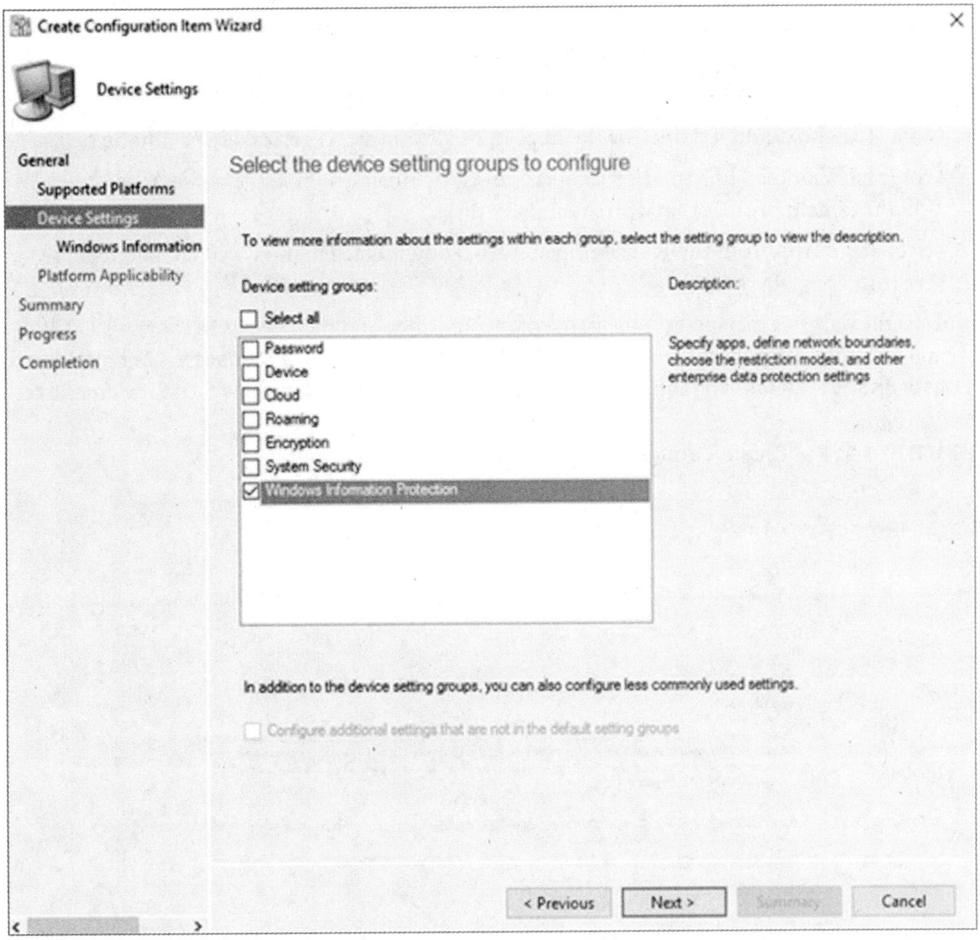

7.   The Configure Windows Information Protection settings page appears, where you can configure a policy for the company.

When you create a process in SCCM, you can choose the apps that will be granted access to corporate data via WIP. Apps on the list can protect and restrict data from being copied or moved to unapproved apps.

The steps to add app rules are based on the type of rule template that is being applied. You can add the following:

- Store app (known as a Universal Windows Platform [UWP] app)
- Signed Windows desktop app
- AppLocker policy file

In the following sections, we will be adding Microsoft OneNote, which is a store app, to the App Rules list.

Adding a Microsoft Store Application

There may be times when you need to add a Microsoft Store application to the App Rules list. The following steps will show you how to complete this task:

1. In the App Rules area (see Figure 14.7), click Add. The Add App Rule box appears.

2. In the Title box, add a name for the app. In this example, it's **Microsoft OneNote**.

3. From the Windows Information Protection Mode drop-down list, choose Allow to turn WIP on to help protect that app's company data.

4. Select Store App from the Rule Template drop-down list. The box will change to show the store app rule options.

5. Type the name of the app and the name of its publisher, and then click OK. For this UWP app example, the publisher is **CN=Microsoft Corporation, O=Microsoft Corporation, L=Redmond, S=Washington, C=US** and the product name is **Microsoft.Office.OneNote**.

FIGURE 14.7 Create Configuration Item Wizard – Add App Rule

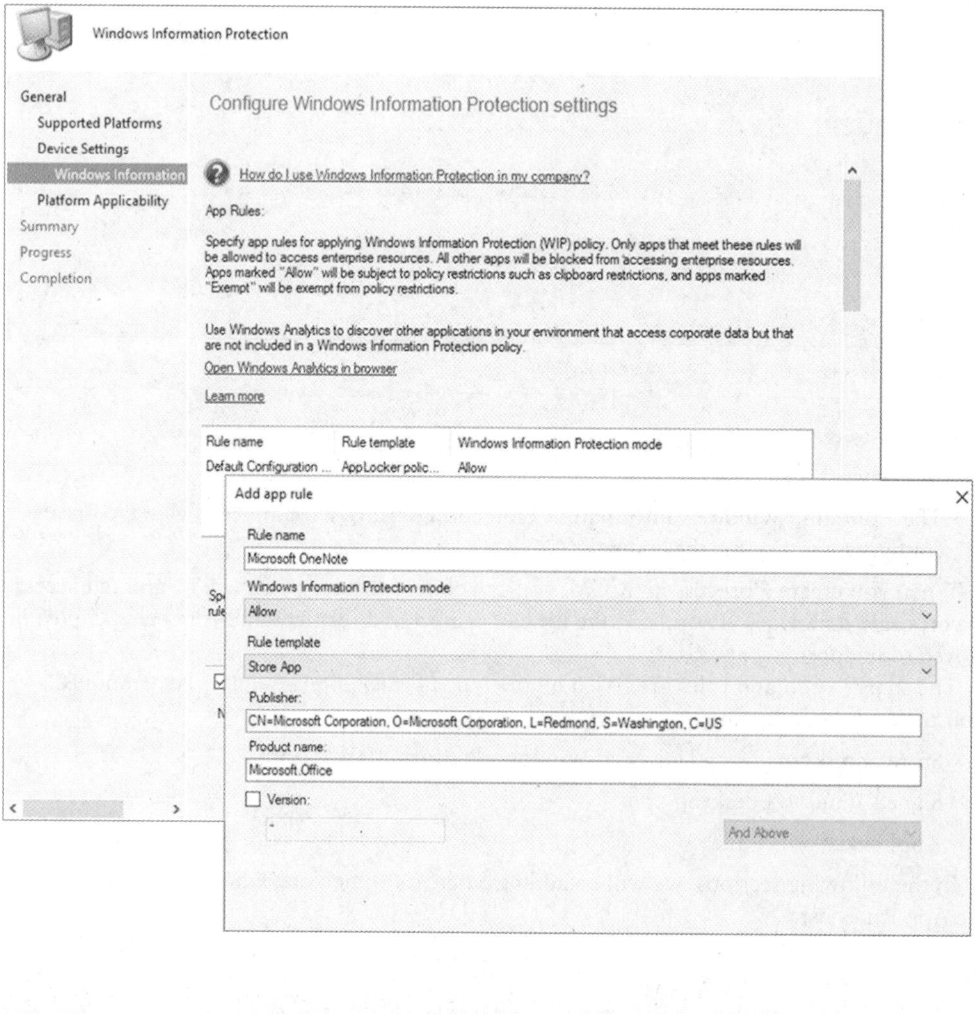

6. After configuring the policy, you can review all of the settings by looking at the Summary screen. Click Summary to review the policy choices and then click Next to finish and save the policy.

WIP File Behavior

Files and apps can be categorized as either work or personal. Where you get the file and where you save new files determines whether files are protected by WIP.

When working with existing files:

- If you get a file from a corporate location, it will automatically be WIP-protected.
- If you get it from a personal location, it will not be WIP-protected.

When saving new files:

- If you save it to a corporate location, it will be WIP-protected.
- If you save it to a personal location, it will not be WIP-protected.

Enlightened apps also provide the option when saving a file to specify whether it's corporate-related or personal. However, if you store a work file to a personal location, WIP gives you the option of saving it as a personal file or saving it at a different location.

Determine the Enterprise Context of an App

You can check the context of an app on your machine by using Windows Task Manager. But you must first activate the Enterprise Context column in Task Manager. To activate the column, perform the following:

1. Open Task Manager and, if you aren't already in the detail view, click More Details.

2. Select the Details tab.

3. Right-click in the column heading area and then click Select Columns.

4. Scroll down, select the Enterprise Context option, and then click OK to close the box. The Enterprise Context column will now be visible in Task Manager.

The Enterprise Context column displays what each app can do with your corporate data:

Domain   If your domain is displayed, the app is running in corporate-related mode and protects the content the app is currently accessing.

Personal   If Personal is displayed, the app is running in personal mode and can't touch any work data or resources.

Exempt   If Exempt is displayed, the app is running in trusted mode and WIP policies are bypassed.

Monitor WIP Events

A device protected by WIP will generate different events that are saved to the event log on the local machine. WIP will create audit events in the following situations:

- A user changes the File ownership for a file from corporate to personal data.

- Data is marked as corporate data but shared to a personal app or web page. Can be shared through copy and paste, drag and drop, sharing a contact, uploading to a personal web page, or if the user grants a personal app temporary access to a protected file.

- An app has custom audit events.

You can use Windows Event Forwarding to collect the WIP audit events and then view those events using Event Viewer.

Changing File Ownership

It is possible to change the file ownership using Windows Explorer. You simply check File Ownership and change it from Personal to Work, or vice versa. When you perform this operation, it will be saved to the event log.

Configure Intune Application Protection Policies for Devices

App protection policies (APPs) are sets of rules that ensure a company's data remains safe or contained in a managed app. A policy can be a rule that is enforced if a user tries to access or move the data, or it can be a set of actions that are monitored when a user is using the app. A managed app is an app that has APPs applied to it and that can be managed by Intune. APPs can apply to apps running on devices that may or may not be managed by Intune.

You can use Intune APP separate of any MDM solution. This allows you to protect corporate data with or without enrolling devices in a device management solution. You can restrict access to corporate resources by applying app-level policies.

APPs can be configured for apps that run on devices that are:

- **Enrolled in Microsoft Intune:** These devices are typically corporate owned.

- **Enrolled in a third-party MDM solution:** These devices are typically corporate owned.

- **Not enrolled in any MDM solution:** These devices are typically owned by the user and the devices are not managed or enrolled in Intune or other MDM solutions.

There are a number of benefits when using APP:

Corporate data is protected at the app level.   Since MAM does not require device management, you can protect corporate data on both managed and unmanaged devices.

End-user productivity is not affected and policies do not apply when using the app in a personal context.   The policies are applied only in a work context, which gives you the ability to protect corporate data without touching personal data.

App protection policies make sure that the app-layer protections are in place.   This means you can:

- Require a PIN to open an app in a work context
- Control the sharing of data between apps
- Prevent the saving of company app data to a personal storage location

MDM, in addition to MAM, makes sure that the device is protected.   This means you can require a PIN to access the device, or you can deploy managed apps to the device.

The choices available in APP allow you to customize the protection to meet your specific needs. To help you prioritize mobile client endpoint hardening, Microsoft has introduced taxonomy for its APP data protection framework for iOS and Android mobile app management.

The APP data protection framework is organized into three different configuration levels, with each level building off the previous level:

Enterprise Basic Data Protection (Level 1)   Ensures that apps are protected with a PIN and encrypted and performs selective wipe operations.

Enterprise Enhanced Data Protection (Level 2)   Introduces APP data leakage prevention mechanisms and minimum OS requirements. This is the configuration that is applicable to most mobile users accessing work or school data.

Enterprise High Data Protection (Level 3)   Introduces advanced data protection mechanisms, enhanced PIN configuration, and APP Mobile Threat Defense. This configuration is desirable for users who are accessing high-risk data.

Create an App Protection Policy

The following steps will walk you through the process of creating an APP:

1. In Intune, select Apps ➤ App Protection Policies ➤ Create Policy ➤ Windows 10.
2. Enter the following details:
   - Name: The name of this app protection policy.
   - Description [Optional]: The description of this app protection policy.
   - Enrollment state:
3. Under Protected Apps, click Add. The Add Apps pane is displayed.
4. Choose the apps that must adhere to this policy and click OK.
5. Click Next to display the Required settings.

6. Click Allow Overrides to set the Windows Information Protection mode. Selecting this option will block enterprise data from leaving the protected app.

7. Click Next to display the Advanced settings.

8. Click Next to display the Assignments.

9. Click Select Groups To Include, click the group, and click Select.

10. Click Next to display the Review + Create step.

11. Click Create to create your policy.

Change Existing Policies

You can also edit an existing policy and apply it to the targeted users. But you need to be aware that when you make changes to an existing policy, any user who is already signed into the apps will not see the changes for an 8-hour period. In order to see the effects of changes immediately, the end user must sign out of the app and then sign back in.

To change policy settings:

1. In the App Protection Policies pane, select the policy you wish to modify.

2. In the Intune App Protection pane, click Properties.

3. Next to the section corresponding to the settings you want to change, click Edit. Then change the settings to new values.

4. Click Review + Create to review the updated settings for this policy.

5. Click Save to save your changes. Repeat the process to select a settings area and modify and then save your changes until all your changes are complete. You can then close the Properties pane in Intune App Protection.

Migrating Data

Up to this point, this chapter has explained how to get software and applications deployed using Azure and Endpoint Manager. Besides knowing how to use Azure to deploy applications and operating systems, it is also important to understand how to move applications and data from an on-premises network to Azure.

Cloud migration gives you the ability of moving applications and data from one location (onsite, another cloud provider, etc.) to a public cloud provider's server. There are many benefits, such as lowering IT costs, improving performance, using Azure security, and having the ability to increase or decrease your Azure network on the fly.

Some of the more commonly migrated workloads to Azure are IIS, SQL Server, Linux, SAP, and Windows Server. But you can migrate almost any data or applications to gain the cloud-based features. Many organizations have started migrating all of their servers to Azure. That can include Hyper-V hosts, Remote Desktop Services (RDS), Migrating Dynamic

Host Configuration Protocol (DHCP), IIS, and print servers. IT departments that still use mainframes can even migrate to the cloud. Two of the more commonly used mainframes are IBM and Unisys.

When you're migrating workloads, there are two main ways to achieve the migration. One method, called Lift and Shift, allows you to migrate these workloads without making any changes to them. The second main way to migrate data is to do an update, called *refactoring*, of the workload. The advantage of refactoring is the ability for you to optimize performance and reliability.

Migrating Onsite Storage

Once your organization has decided to move to the cloud, the first step is to plan out which servers, services, or applications that you want to move into the cloud. That is one of the advantages to a hybrid cloud setup. Not all servers, services, or applications need to be migrated to the cloud.

Many companies decide to leave some of their resources in their onsite server room and many companies decide to move all resources to the cloud. It's very important to understand that there is no right or wrong way to create a hybrid network. Depending on your company and the company needs, this will help you determine which resources are best left onsite and which resources should be in the cloud.

Hybrid clouds can also be a very good option to ensure that your data is backed up and secure in the cloud. Being able to retrieve data in the event of a server crash or major disaster is one of the most important tasks that we have in IT. Using a hybrid cloud environment for data backups is an excellent way to ensure that you are protecting your company from any type of major issue or crash.

Azure Data Share

Azure Data Share allows an organization to securely share data with multiple partners and customers. Organizations that choose to share their data are completely in control of the data that they have decided to share. Azure Data Share gives an organization a simple way to manage and monitor the data that they have decided to share.

In today's ever-changing Internet world, data is viewed as a crucial strategic asset that many organizations need to share with their customers and partners simply and securely. For many of us, if we currently want to share data with people outside of our organization, we have to use third-party utilities and tools like email or an FTP server.

The problem with using utilities like FTP is that it's hard to track the data and to know exactly who is accessing it. Also, unless an organization uses their own FTP server, it can be very expensive, especially if your users all use their own favorite FTP sites.

Data Share allows an organization to easily share their data and manage the data shares all in one place. Organizations have the ability to control how their data is handled by setting up specific terms of use for sharing the data. Before anyone can access the shared data, they must accept the organization's terms before being able to receive the data.

Organizations that decide to use Data Share can specify the interval at which their data will receive updates. Access to new updates can be revoked at any time by the organization that is sharing the data.

> **NOTE**
>
> The following three examples of using Azure Data Share were taken directly from Microsoft's website. Microsoft likes to ask exam questions using examples that they provide from their website. So, I wanted to include these examples just in case you see one of them on the exam.

Many different types of industries can use Azure Data Share. For example, a business may want to share their recent point-of-sales data with their suppliers. Using Azure Data Share, a business can set up a data share containing point-of-sales data for all of their suppliers and share sales on an hourly or daily basis.

Azure Data Share can also be used to establish a data marketplace for a specific organization—for example, a government or a research institution that regularly shares anonymized data about population growth with third parties.

Another use case for Azure Data Share is establishing a data consortium. For example, many different research institutions can share data with a single trusted body. Data is analyzed, aggregated, or processed using Azure analytics tools and then shared with interested parties.

Snapshot-Based Sharing

One of the options that you have when sharing data is called *snapshot-based sharing*. When I explain snapshot-based sharing, I like to talk a little bit about doing backups.

One issue that we can run into when backing up data can happen when you try to back up an open database or file. Most backups cannot back up files or databases if the data is currently open. For example, Exchange runs 24 hours a day, 365 days a year. It makes backing up Exchange a bit more challenging.

So to help solve these types of backup issues, most backups work with the Volume Shadow Service (VSS) to create the backups of open files. The way it works is that the backup software takes a snapshot of the open database or file and it backs up that snapshot.

With snapshot-based sharing, your company's data moves from the original data provider's Azure subscription and then is placed into the consumer's Azure subscription. Once your company decides to use Azure Data Share, you will then provision a data share and invite recipients to access that data share. The recipients receive an invitation to your data share through email. Once the recipient accepts the invitation, they can initiate a full snapshot of the data that is being shared with them. This data is received by the consumer and that data is placed into the consumer's storage account. The consumers have the ability to receive updates for the data that is shared with them so that they always have the latest version of the data.

Companies can offer consumers incremental updates to the data shared with them through a snapshot schedule. Snapshot schedules can be set up on an hourly or a daily basis.

Once a consumer accepts the data share, they can subscribe to a snapshot schedule that works for both organizations.

In-place Sharing

Azure Data Share in-place sharing allows companies to share their data without the need to copy the data to another location. The data can be accessed from its original location.

After establishing a connection through the use of an invitation, a representational link is created between the company's source data store and the other company's target data store. Companies that receive the data can access that data in real time using their own data store. This allows any changes to the source data store to be available to the data consumer immediately. In-place sharing is currently available for Azure Data Explorer.

Using Storage Migration Service

Anyone who has been in the IT field long enough knows that there are times when we have to move data from one device to another. Maybe you are replacing an older server for a new server or adding some type of data storage device (like a SAN or NAS). Being able to build, configure, and use a new server is like taking a child to a toy store. Nothing beats setting up new, better, and more secure server. But one task that many of us don't look forward to is moving all the data from the older server to the newer server.

You can now use Storage Migration Service to easily migrate data to a Windows Server or to an Azure subscription. Storage Migration Service gives you a graphical utility that will do an inventory of data on Windows, Linux, and NetApp CIFS servers. Using that inventory, Storage Migration Service will help transfer the data to newer servers or to Azure virtual machines.

Storage Migration Service will also give you the option to transfer the identity of a server to the destination server. This will allow applications and users to access their data without needing to change links or paths of the data's location.

Storage Migration Service is designed to help any company by completing the following:

- Inventory multiple servers and the data that is stored on each server.

- Quickly transfer files, file shares, and security configuration from the source servers.

- Optionally, you can take over the identity of the source servers (also known as *cutting over*) so that users and applications don't have to change anything to access the existing data.

- Manage one or more migrations using the Windows Admin Center user interface.

The Storage Migration Service uses a three-step process to function properly:

1. Servers are inventoried to collect information about their files and configuration.

2. The data is then transferred (copied) from the source servers to the destination servers.

3. Converts over to the new servers.

Once your company has decided to use Storage Migration Service, you need to configure the following:

- Files and data (that need to be migrated) from a source server or failover cluster.

- For best performance, a destination server running Windows Server 2022 or Windows Server 2019. Previous versions of Windows Server (2012 R2/2016) work but they will be about 50 percent slower.

- To help control the migrated data, an orchestrator server running Windows Server 2022. If your organization is migrating only a few servers and at least one of the servers is running Windows Server 2019 or higher, that server can also act as the orchestrator. If your organization is migrating a lot of servers, Microsoft recommends using a separate orchestrator server.

- The current version of Windows Admin Center to run the Storage Migration Service user interface. Windows Admin Center also works along with the latest Storage Migration Service tool (extension). The Windows Admin Center must be at least version 2103.

Microsoft recommends that the orchestrator and destination computers have a minimum of at least two cores or two vCPUs. Microsoft also recommends that the machines have at least 2 GB of RAM. The faster the CPU and the more RAM your servers have, the faster your inventory and transfer operations will complete.

You should set up a migration administrator account on the source/destination computers and the orchestrator computer. The administrator account can be a local or domain account. The one exception is in the case of a non-domain computer. In this case, you need to use a local user account for that non-domain system.

The orchestrator server needs to have inbound firewall rules enabled to allow File and Printer Sharing (SMB-In). The source and destination computers must also have firewall rules enabled inbound for the following:

- File and Printer Sharing (SMB-In)

- Netlogon Service (NP-In)

- Windows Management Instrumentation (DCOM-In)

- Windows Management Instrumentation (WMI-In)

If your company's computers belong to an Active Directory domain, they should all be on the same forest. The destination server must also be in the same domain as the source server if you want to transfer the source's domain name to the destination when cutting over. When cutting over, technically the cutover will work across domains. But the fully qualified domain name of the destination will be different from the source.

The source server must run one of the following operating systems:

- Windows Server, Semi-Annual Channel

- Windows Server 2022

- Windows Server 2019
- Windows Server 2016
- Windows Server 2012 R2
- Windows Server 2012
- Windows Server 2008 R2
- Windows Server 2008
- Windows Server 2003 R2
- Windows Server 2003
- Windows Small Business Server 2003 R2
- Windows Small Business Server 2008
- Windows Small Business Server 2011
- Windows Server 2012 Essentials
- Windows Server 2012 R2 Essentials
- Windows Server 2016 Essentials
- Windows Server 2019 Essentials
- Windows Storage Server 2008
- Windows Storage Server 2008 R2
- Windows Storage Server 2012
- Windows Storage Server 2012 R2
- Windows Storage Server 2016

The destination server must run one of the following:

- Windows Server, Semi-Annual Channel
- Windows Server 2022
- Windows Server 2019
- Windows Server 2016
- Windows Server 2012 R2

Stand-alone and clustered servers can be used as destination servers. If you choose to use a stand-alone/cluster server, you cannot run the Azure Stack HCI or use a non-Microsoft clustering add-on. The Storage Migration Service will not support Azure Files as a destination server. But the Storage Migration Service will fully support servers that are running the Azure File Sync agent with cloud tiering.

Cloud Tiering

Cloud tiering is an optional feature that an Azure administrator can enable for Azure File Sync. When enabled, cloud tiering helps decrease the amount of local storage that is required while still maintaining the performance of the on-site file server.

When cloud tiering is enabled, Azure File Sync only stores frequently accessed files, referred to as *hot*, on your local server. Files that are infrequently accessed, referred to as *cold*, are split into namespace (file and folder structure) and file content. So once cloud tiering is enabled, the namespace is then stored locally and the file content is stored in the Azure file share in the cloud. When a user accesses a tiered file, Azure File Sync quickly recalls the file from the file share in Azure.

When enabling cloud tiering, you can set up two policy types: the volume free space policy and the date policy. The volume free space policy tells Azure File Sync to tier cool files to the cloud once a certain amount of space is used up on your local disk. With the date policy, cool files are tiered to the cloud if they haven't been accessed for a set number of days.

The Windows Admin Center incorporates Azure IaaS deployments into the Storage Migration Service. This can help save an IT department a lot of time and money. Normally, you build new servers and VMs by hand using the Azure portal. By using the Windows Admin Center, you can deploy the Azure IaaS VM while also configuring its storage. The Windows Admin Center also allows you to configure the Azure VM so that it is joined to your domain and all roles are installed, and then it will also set up your distributed system.

The following features are available when running the Storage Migration Server orchestrator on Windows Server 2022:

- Migrate local users and groups to the new server
- Migrate storage from failover clusters, migrate to failover clusters, and migrate between stand-alone servers and failover clusters
- Migrate storage from a Linux server that uses Samba
- More easily sync migrated shares into Azure by using Azure File Sync
- Migrate to new networks such as Azure
- Migrate NetApp CIFS servers from NetApp FAS arrays to Windows servers and clusters

Understanding Azure Migrate Appliance

One nice advantage to using Azure is all the different tools and utilities that you can use to make some of your daily tasks easier. The more ways that you can monitor and maintain your networks, the better it is for your organization. Monitoring can not only help you discover issues, but it has also helped me catch people doing bad things on our network.

The Azure Migrate appliance is a lightweight appliance that is used by the Azure Migrate Discovery and Assessment tool. The Azure Migrate Discovery and Assessment tool is used to help discover and assess physical or virtual servers on your network. The Azure Migrate Appliance is also used in the migration and modernization tool.

The Azure Migrate appliance offers an organization the following:

- The appliance is deployed on-premises as a physical server or a virtualized server.

- The appliance discovers onsite servers and constantly sends server metadata and performance data to Azure Migrate.

- Appliance discovery is agentless. Nothing is installed on the discovered servers.

The Azure Migrate Appliance can be deployed using one of these methods:

- The appliance can be deployed using a template for servers running in VMware or Hyper-V environment.

- If you do not want to use a template, you can deploy the appliance for the VMware or Hyper-V environment using a PowerShell installer script.

- In Azure Government, you should deploy the appliance using a PowerShell installer script.

- For physical or virtualized servers on-premises or any other cloud, you should deploy the appliance using a PowerShell installer script.

Data that's collected by using the Azure Migrate appliance is stored in the Azure location that you created when building the project.

Summary

In this chapter, you saw how to use Endpoint Manager to deploy applications and operating systems. I talked about the ability to deploy operating systems by using Autopilot. After looking at easy ways to deploy applications and software, I showed you how to migrate servers and data from an onsite network to Azure.

Knowing how to easily deploy applications to your users is just one step. We need to ensure that the servers and applications that we are deploying in Azure are properly created or migrated from the onsite network to Azure.

Finally, we looked at migrating data from onsite to Azure and how to migrate data from multiple locations. Once you decide to move to Azure, you need to determine which servers, VMs, applications, and services should be migrated to the cloud.

Exam Essentials

Understand MDM.   Mobile device management (MDM) allows you to manage and configure Windows devices. Should a device ever get lost or stolen, or if a user leaves your company, you can wipe the corporate data that is on the device.

Know how to use Autopilot.   Autopilot allows you to install operating systems quickly and easily on new or repurposed machines without IT personnel having to build each machine. Autopilot allows you to get a list of device IDs from the manufacturer, and the device IDs are entered into your Azure environment. You assign a device profile to that machine and that's it. Once the user logs on to the Internet, the machine automatically recognizes that it is part of your organization and the installation is completed, without any IT intervention.

Understand how to use Migration.   Once you decide to move to Azure, you need to decide which servers and application will be hosted in the cloud. Then, you can use the different migration methods to transfer your data.

Review Questions

1. Choose the valid policies that can be set to inform Azure File Sync when cool files should be tiered while enabling cloud tiering. (Choose two.)

   A. Date policy

   B. Cost policy

   C. Volume free space policy

   D. Disk space policy

   E. Read policy

2. You have two file servers named Server1 and Server2 that run Windows Server. Server1 contains a shared folder named Data. Data contains 10 TB of data. You plan to decommission Server1. You need to migrate the files from Data to a new shared folder on Server2. The solution must meet the following requirements:

   - Ensure that share, file, and folder permissions are copied.

   - After the initial copy occurs, ensure that changes in \\Server1\Data can be synced to the destination without initiating a full copy.

   - Minimize administrative effort.

   What should you use?

   A. xcopy

   B. Storage Replica

   C. Storage Migration Service

   D. AzCopy

3. You have three servers named Server 1, Server 2, and Server 3. Server1 and Server3 run Windows Server and have the Hyper-V server rote installed. Server 1 hosts an Azure Migrate appliance named Migrate1. You plan to migrate virtual machines to Azure. You need to ensure that any new virtual machines created on Server 1, Server2, and Server3 are available in Azure Migrate. What should you do?

   A. On Migrate1, add a discovery source.

   B. On the DNS server used by Migrate 1, create a GlobalName zone.

   C. On Migrate1, set the Startup Type of the Computer Browser service to Automatic.

   D. On the network that has Migrate1 deployed, deploy a WINS server.

4. You have two servers that run Windows Server as shown here:

Name	Location	Domain/Workgroup
Server1	On-Premises	Domain
Server2	Azure VM	Workgroup

You need to copy the contents of volume E from Server1 to Server2. The solution must meet the following requirements:

- Ensure that files in use are copied.
- Minimize administrative effort.

What should you use?

A. Storage Migration Service

B. Azure File Sync

C. Azure Backup

D. Storage Replica

5. Your on-premises network has a 200-Mbps connection to Azure and contains a server named Server1 that stores 70 TB of data files. You have an Azure Storage account named Storage1. You plan to migrate the data files from Server1 to a blob storage container in Storage1. Testing shows that copying the data files by using AzCopy will take approximately 35 days. You need to minimize how long it will take to migrate the data to Azure. What should you use?

A. Storage Migration Service

B. Azure Storage Explorer

C. Azure Data Box

D. Azure File Sync

6. You are planning the data share migration to support the on-premises migration plan. What should you use to perform the migration?

A. File Server Resource Manager (FSRM)

B. Microsoft File Server Migration Toolkit

C. Windows Server Migration Tools

D. Storage Migration Service

7. You are the network administrator for StormWind Studios. Your network contains an Active Directory domain. The domain contains 300 computers that run Windows 10/11. You have both an onsite Active Directory network and Azure AD with Microsoft Intune. You need to automatically register all the existing computers to the Azure AD network and also enroll all of the computers in Intune. What should you use?

A. Use a DNS Autodiscover address record.

B. Use a Windows Autopilot deployment profile.

C. Use an Autodiscover service connection point (SCP).

D. Set up a Group Policy Object (GPO).

8. You are the administrator for your company network. You use Windows Autopilot to configure the computer settings of computers that are issued to employees. An employee has been using an issued Windows client computer and then leaves the company. You'd like to transfer that computer to a new user. You need to make sure that when the new user first starts the computer, they will be prompted to select the language settings and to agree to the license agreement. What should you do?

    A. You should create a new Windows Autopilot self-deploying deployment profile.

    B. You should create a new Windows Autopilot user-driven deployment profile.

    C. You should perform a local Windows Autopilot Reset.

    D. You should perform a remote Windows Autopilot Reset.

9. You have computers that run Windows 10 Pro. The computers are joined to Azure AD and enrolled in Microsoft Intune for Mobile Device Management (MDM). You need to upgrade the computers to Windows 10 Enterprise. What should you configure in Intune?

    A. A device enrollment policy

    B. A device cleanup rule

    C. A device compliance policy

    D. A Windows Autopilot device profile

10. You are the administrator for your company network. You and a colleague are discussing the different deployment scenarios and the categories into which certain scenarios fall. You are discussing Subscription Activation. Which category does this fall into with regard to deployment scenarios?

    A. Contemporary deployment category

    B. Dynamic deployment category

    C. Modern deployment category

    D. Traditional deployment category

11. You are the administrator for your company network. The network has an Active Directory domain. The domain contains several thousand Windows client computers. You implement hybrid Azure AD and Microsoft Intune. You have to register all of the existing computers automatically to Azure AD and enroll the computers in Intune. What should you do while using the least amount of administrative effort?

    A. Configure an Autodiscover address record.

    B. Configure an Autodiscover service connection point (SCP).

    C. Configure a Group Policy object (GPO).

    D. Configure a Windows Autopilot deployment profile.

12. You are the administrator for your company network. You have several computers that are running Windows 10/11 and have been configured using Windows Autopilot. A user performs the following tasks on one of the computers:

    - Creates a VPN connection to the corporate network

    - Installs a Microsoft Store app named App1

    - Connects to a Wi-Fi network

You perform a Windows Autopilot Reset on the computer. What will be the state of App1 on the computer when the user signs in?

A.   The app will be reinstalled at sign-in.

B.   The app will be removed.

C.   The app will be retained.

D.   Nothing will happen; it can't be done.

13. You are the administrator for your company network. You have a hybrid Azure AD tenant. You configure a Windows Autopilot deployment profile. The deployment profile is configured as follows:

Name: Autopilot1

Convert all targeted devices to Autopilot: No

Deployment Mode: User-Driven

Join to Azure AD as: Azure AD joined

You want to apply the profile to a new computer. What should you do first?

A.   Assign a user to a specific Autopilot device.

B.   Enroll the device in Microsoft Intune.

C.   Import a CSV file into Windows Autopilot.

D.   Join the device to Azure AD.

14. You are the administrator for your company network. There is a Microsoft tool that allows a Windows client computer to be set up with all applications and operating systems automatically without any administrator intervention. What is it called?

A.   Deployment Image Servicing and Management (DISM)

B.   Windows 10 Admin setup

C.   Windows Autopilot

D.   Windows Internal Database (WID) Server

15. You are the administrator for your company network. You and a colleague are discussing files that can be used with the User State Migration Tool (USMT). What file extension is used with the migration files?

A.   `.csv`

B.   `.docx`

C.   `.txt`

D.   `.xml`

Chapter

15

Implementing Security

THE FOLLOWING AZ-801 EXAM OBJECTIVES ARE COVERED IN THIS CHAPTER:

✓ **Secure Windows Server operating system**

- Configure and manage exploit protection
- Configure and manage Windows Defender Application Control
- Configure and manage Microsoft Defender for Endpoint
- Configure and manage Windows Defender Credential Guard
- Configure SmartScreen
- Implement operating system security by using Group Policies

✓ **Secure Windows Server networking**

- Manage Windows Defender Firewall
- Implement domain isolation
- Implement connection security rules

In this chapter, you'll learn how to defend your Windows systems by using the built-in Windows Security. I will show you how to protect your Windows client and server devices by using the Windows Defender Firewall. The Windows Defender Firewall can help protect your client systems from being illegally breached, but when you're building a network, it should *not* be your only firewall. Your network connection to the Internet should also be protected by some type of firewall, but that is an entirely different course (depending on your firewall type).

You'll learn how to use Azure to protect your network. Azure offers organizations multiple ways to protect devices and data by using tools like Microsoft Defender Application Guard, Microsoft Defender for Endpoint, and Microsoft Defender Antivirus.

So, let's get started by looking at protecting your Windows devices by using Windows Security.

Managing Windows Security

Without showing my age, I have been in the computer industry for over 30 years. When I first got into networking, security basically was just protecting files from unauthorized access from people in your own organization. Today, that is completely changed. We still have to make sure that our servers and data is protected from unauthorized employee access, but we also have to spend much of our time protecting our networks from outside threats.

Unfortunately, there is no magic pill or solution to stop these external threats. Even if you decide that you want to completely disconnect your network from the Internet, your organization can still be attacked. One of the main reasons is because of our end users. In today's technology world, most of our users have devices that they use at home and also on their corporate network.

So, when we talk about network security, it's not just a single thing that we can do to protect our network. To truly protect our networks, we need to use multiple layers of security. This not only includes tools and devices that we can put on our physical network like hardware-based firewalls and intrusion detection systems, but also tools that we can add to our devices to help keep them secure.

Microsoft Windows devices (client and server based) include built-in Windows Security (see Figure 15.1), such as antivirus protection. Windows devices are automatically protected from the very moment that your users start using Windows. Windows Security is always scanning the system for viruses, malware (malicious software), and security dangers.

Not only does Windows provide real-time protection, but Microsoft also continually releases operating system updates to make sure that your corporate devices stay safe and that the devices are protected from any new threats.

FIGURE 15.1   Windows Security

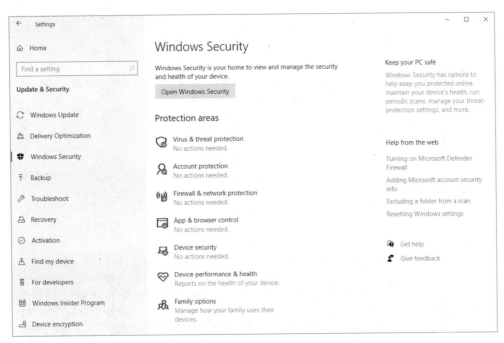

Windows Security Basics

Windows Security is built into Windows and includes an antivirus program called Microsoft Defender Antivirus. In early versions of Server, Windows Security was called Microsoft Defender Security Center. Windows Security is where the tools that protect a device and data can be found. This is one of many ways that you can protect your system.

Windows Security (see Figure 15.2) is a built-in Windows application that protects your system from viruses and spyware. It is included free with the operating system, and once you turn your operating system on, Windows Security starts automatically protecting your system.

FIGURE 15.2   Security At A Glance

Windows Security has multiple options to help protect your system. Let's take a look at some of these options. I am going to show the options that are available on a Windows 10/11 client system. Windows Server 2022 only has the following options: Virus and Threat Protection, Firewall and Network Protection, App & Browser Control, and Device Security. The reason that I am covering the client-side options is because it is important to configure both the Server Firewall protection and the Client Firewall protection to ensure that your network has multiple layers of security. The options include the following:

Virus and Threat Protection   Windows will automatically monitor for threats that can impact your device, run scans on your system, and get updates to help protect against any new threats. Windows has an antivirus built in, and it will get automatic updates when your Windows systems get updated.

Account Protection   You can configure the user's sign-in options and account settings. These settings are included while using Windows 10/11.

Firewall and Network Protection   Windows includes a Windows Defender Firewall that allows you to help prevent unauthorized users or malicious software from accessing your computer.

App and Browser Control   You can configure update settings for Microsoft Defender SmartScreen and this helps protect your Windows devices against potentially dangerous applications, downloads, files, and websites. This gives you the ability to control exploit protection and customize settings that will help protect your Windows devices.

Device Security   Device Security allows you to use built-in security options to defend your organization's Windows devices from malicious software attacks.

Device Performance and Health   Windows allows you to view the status information about the device's performance health. This helps you keep your organization's devices clean and up to date with the latest version of Windows. These settings are included while using Windows 10/11.

Family Options   The Family Options feature in Windows Security is not a feature that most administrators will configure in a corporate environment. These options provide tools to help manage children's computer access. Parents can use Family Options to help keep their children's devices clean and up to date with the latest version of Windows and to protect their children when they are on the Internet. These settings are included while using Windows 10/11.

You may notice status icons on the protection areas; these indicate the level of safety:

- Green indicates that there aren't any recommended actions that need to be taken right now.

- Yellow indicates that there is a safety recommendation.

- Red indicates that there is a warning that something needs immediate attention.

In Exercise 15.1, I will show you how to run an advanced virus and threat scan on your Windows device.

<hr>

EXERCISE 15.1

Running an Advanced Scan

1. In Windows 10, click Start ➤ Settings ➤ Update & Security ➤ Windows Security and then choose Virus & Threat Protection.

   In Windows 11, click Start ➤ Settings ➤ Privacy & Security ➤ Windows Security and then choose Virus & Threat Protection.

2. Under Current Threats, select Scan Options (or in early versions of Windows 10, under Threat History, select Run A New Advanced Scan).

3. Make sure the Full Scan radio button is selected and click the Scan Now button.

   In the Scan Options menu (see Figure 15.3), you will see a list of four different types of scans you can perform:

   Quick Scan   Scans folders on your device where threats are usually found, such as the Downloads and Windows folders. This usually only takes a few minutes to finish.

   Full Scan   This scan scans all files on your computer and all running programs. The scan may take longer to complete than other scans.

   Custom Scan   If you select this option, Windows Security will ask you for a specific file or folder location that you want to scan.

EXERCISE 15.1 *(continued)*

Microsoft Defender Offline Scan This option restarts your computer and scans system files and programs while they are not running; this can be handy if there is malware running on the computer that may interfere with the scan.

FIGURE 15.3 Scan Options

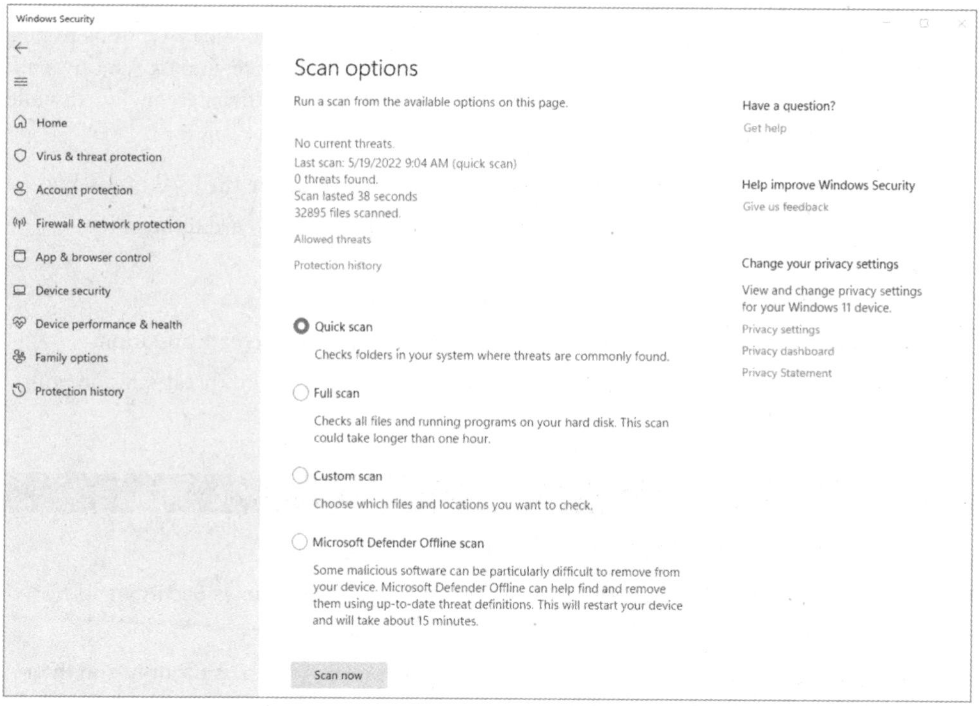

4. The scan will take a while. After the scan finishes, close the Defender Security Center.

Now that you understand how to work with the Windows Security Center, let's take a look at how to configure your firewall within that Security Center.

Configuring Windows Defender Firewall

Windows Defender Firewall, which is included with Windows, helps prevent unauthorized users or malicious software from accessing your computer. Windows Defender Firewall does not allow unsolicited traffic, which is traffic that was not sent in response to a request, to pass through the firewall. It also allows or blocks connections to and from other computers on a network. Windows Defender Firewall is sometimes referred to as Windows Defender for short, but it should not be confused with Microsoft Defender Antivirus software.

Understanding the Windows Defender Firewall Basics

The Windows Defender Firewall is the same app in Windows 10/11, but how you access them is a bit different. The only difference is the rounded corners that Windows 11 uses. Both Windows 10/11 use Control Panel to access the Windows Defender Firewall. In Windows 10, you configure Windows Defender Firewall by clicking Start ➢ Windows System ➢ Control Panel ➢ Large Icons View ➢ Windows Defender Firewall.

In Windows 11, the easiest way to access Control Panel is by searching for the app. Then select, Large Icons View ➢ Windows Defender Firewall.

You can then decide what firewall options you want to set (as shown in Figure 15.4) like changing firewall notifications, turning the Windows Defender Firewall on or off, restoring defaults, setting advanced settings, and troubleshooting.

FIGURE 15.4   Windows Defender Firewall settings

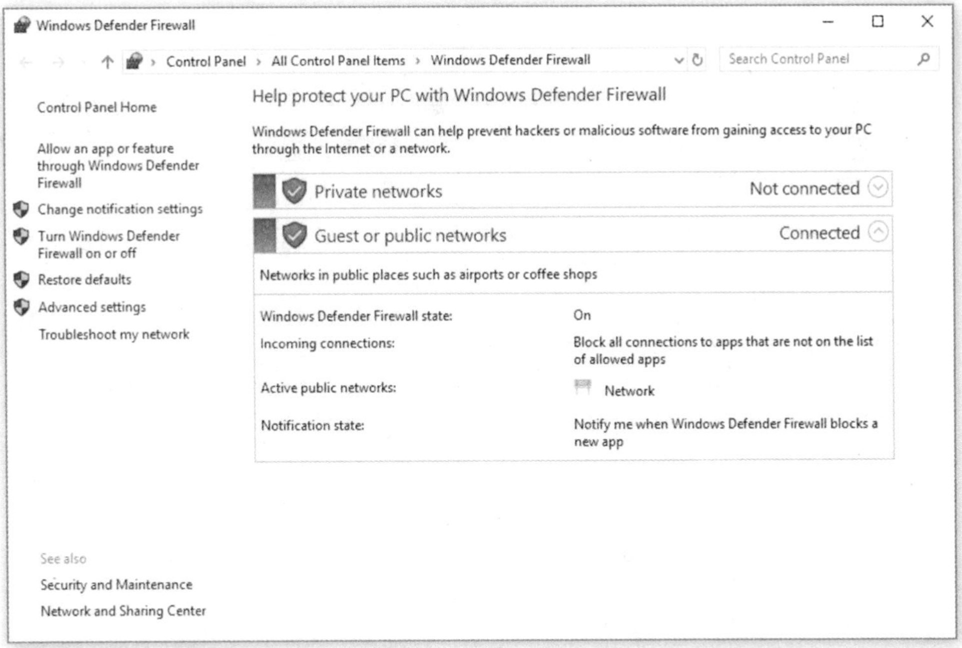

The Windows Firewall settings screen allows you to turn Windows Firewall on or off for both private and public networks. The On setting will block incoming sources, and the Turn Off Windows Firewall setting will allow incoming sources to connect.

There is also a check box for Block All Incoming Connections. This feature allows you to connect to networks that are not secure. When Block All Incoming Connections is selected, all incoming connections (even ones allowed in the Allowed Apps list) will be blocked by Windows Firewall.

> Be aware that sometimes a third-party security solution that you have installed on your device may take control of your firewall settings.

Windows Defender Firewall with Advanced Security

You can configure more advanced settings by configuring Windows Firewall with Advanced Security (WFAS) by using the Advanced Settings link (on the left-hand side) in the Windows Defender Firewall app. The Windows Defender Firewall with Advanced Security screen appears, as shown in Figure 15.5.

FIGURE 15.5   Windows Defender Firewall with Advanced Security

The scope pane to the left shows that you can set up specific inbound and outbound rules, connection security rules, and monitoring rules. The central area shows an overview of the firewall's status when no rule is selected in the left pane. When a rule is selected, the central area shows the rule's settings. The right pane shows the same actions as the Actions menu on the top. These are just shortcuts to the different actions that can be performed in Windows Defender Firewall. Let's take a more detailed look at some of the elements available.

Inbound and Outbound Rules

Inbound and outbound rules consist of many preconfigured rules that can be enabled or disabled. Obviously, inbound rules (see Figure 15.6) monitor inbound traffic, and outbound rules monitor outbound traffic. By default, many are disabled. Double-clicking a rule will bring up its Properties dialog box (Figure 15.7).

FIGURE 15.6   Inbound rules

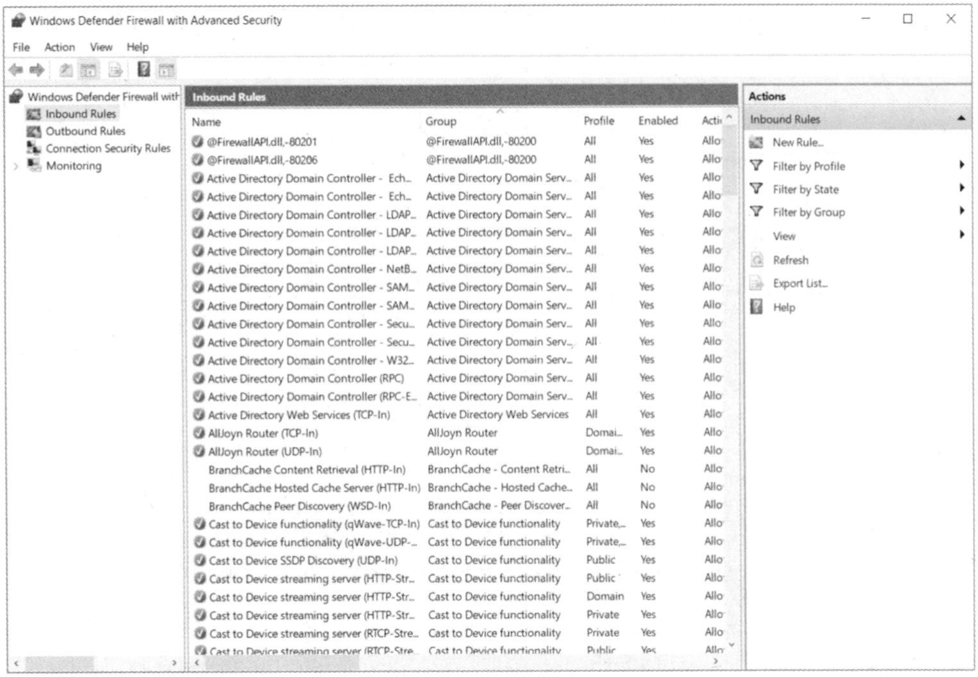

FIGURE 15.7   An inbound rule's Properties dialog box

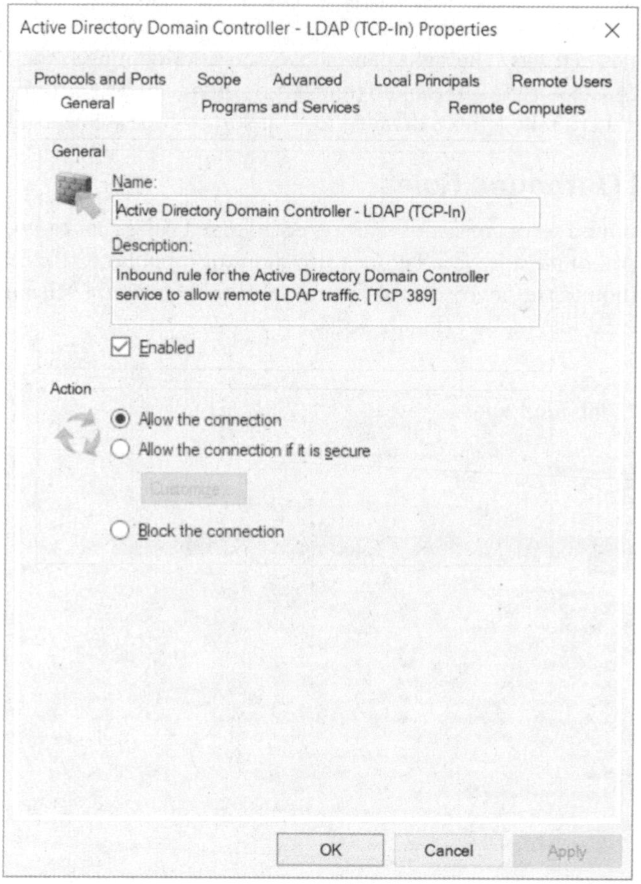

You can filter the rules to make them easier to view. Filtering can be based on the profile the rule affects, on whether the rule is enabled or disabled, or on the rule group. You can filter a rule by clicking which filter type you want to use in the right pane or by clicking the Actions menu on the top of the screen.

If you can't find a rule that is appropriate for your needs, you can create a new rule by right-clicking Inbound Rules or Outbound Rules in the scope pane and then selecting New Rule. The New Inbound (or Outbound) Rule Wizard will launch, and you will be asked whether you want to create a rule based on a particular program, protocol or port, pre-defined category, or custom settings.

As you are setting up the firewall rules, you have the ability to configure authenticated exceptions. No matter how well your system security is set up, there are almost always times when computers on your network can't use IPsec. This is when you set up authenticated exceptions. It's important to understand that when you set up these authenticated exceptions, you are reducing the security of the network because it allows computers to send unprotected IPsec network traffic. So, make sure that the computers that are added to the authenticated exceptions list are managed and trusted computers only.

Table 15.1 shows you some of the most common port numbers and what those port numbers are used for.

TABLE 15.1 Common port numbers

Port number	Associated application or service
20	FTP Data
21	FTP Control
22	Secure Shell (SSH)
23	Telnet
25	SMTP
53	DNS
67/68	DHCP/BOOTP
80	HTTP
102	Microsoft Exchange Server
110	POP3
443	HHTPS (HTTP with SSL)

Complete Exercise 15.2 to create a new inbound rule that will allow only encrypted TCP traffic.

EXERCISE 15.2

Creating a New Inbound Rule

1. Open Control Panel and select Large Icons View ➢ Windows Defender Firewall.

2. Click Advanced Settings on the left side.

3. Right-click Inbound Rules and select New Rule.

4. Select a rule type. For this exercise, select Custom so that you can see all the options available to you. Then click Next.

5. On the Program page, choose All Programs. Then click Next.

6. Select the protocol type as well as the local and remote port numbers that are affected by this rule. For this exercise, choose TCP, and ensure that All Ports is selected for both Local Port and Remote Port. Click Next to continue.

7. On the Scope page, choose Any IP Address for both Local and Remote. Then click Next.

8. On the Action page, select Allow The Connection Only If It Is Secure. Click Next.

9. On the Users page, you can experiment with these options if you want by entering users to both sections. Once you click one of the check boxes, the Add and Remove buttons become available. Click Next to continue.

10. On the Computers page, you can choose what computers you will authorize or allow through this rule (exceptions). Again, you can experiment with these options if you want. Click Next to continue.

11. On the Profiles page, select which profiles will be affected by this rule. Select one or more profiles and click Next.

12. Give your profile a name and description, and then click Finish. Your custom rule will appear in the list of inbound rules, and the rule will be enabled.

13. Double-click your newly created rule. Notice that you can change the options that you previously configured.

14. Delete the rule by right-clicking it and choosing Delete. A dialog box will appear asking if you are sure. Click Yes.

15. Close the Windows Firewall.

Connection Security Rules

Connection security rules are used to configure how and when authentication occurs. These rules do not specifically allow connections; that's the job of inbound and outbound rules. You can configure the following connection security rules:

Isolation   To restrict a connection based on authentication criteria

Authentication Exemption   To specify computers that are exempt from authentication requirements

Server-to-Server   To authenticate connections between computers

Tunnel   To authenticate connections between gateway computers

Custom   Use custom to create a customized connection security rule

Monitoring

The Monitoring section shows detailed information about the firewall configurations for the Domain Profile, Private Profile, and Public Profile settings. These network location profiles determine what settings are enforced for private networks, public networks, and networks connected to a domain.

Real World Scenario

Use More Than Just Windows Defender Firewall

When doing consulting, it always concerns me when I see small to midsized companies using Windows Defender Firewall and no other protection. Windows Defender Firewall should be your *last* line of defense. You need to make sure that you have good hardware firewalls that separate your network from the world.

Also watch Windows Defender Firewall when it comes to printing. I have run into many situations where a printer that needs to communicate with the operating system has issues when Windows Defender Firewall is enabled. If this happens, make sure that the printer is allowed in the Allowed Programs section.

Datacenter Firewall

Firewalls allow you to set up policies on who or what can be allowed past the firewall. For example, if you want to allow DNS traffic to pass through the firewall, you would enable port 53. If you want the traffic to leave the firewall, you would configure port 53 outbound. If you want to have the traffic enter into the company, you would configure inbound.

Datacenter Firewalls were introduced with Windows Server 2022 network layer, stateful, multitenant firewalls. Network administrators that work with virtual network tenants can install and then configure firewall policies. These firewall policies can help protect their virtual networks from unwanted traffic from Internet and intranet networks.

The Datacenter Firewall allows you to set up granular access control lists (ACLs). This way, you can apply firewall policies at the VM interface level or at the subnet level. To create ACLs on the Datacenter Firewall, use Windows PowerShell. The following is an example of the PowerShell command that is used to assign the ACL to the `AccessControlList` property of the network interface.

```
$nic.properties.ipconfigurations[0].properties.AccessControlList = $acl
```

Windows Server 2022 Datacenter Firewalls give you the following tenant benefits:

- You have the ability to define firewall rules that help protect Internet-facing workloads on virtual networks.
- You can define firewall rules to protect data between virtual machines on the same layer 2 or different layer 2 virtual subnets.
- You can define firewall rules to protect and isolate network traffic between tenants on a virtual network from a service provider.

So now that we have taken a look at Windows Defender Firewall, let's now look at protecting your Windows devices by using Microsoft Defender.

Managing Security

Another way that you can help defend your corporate devices is by using Microsoft Defender. Microsoft Defender has many different tools that allow you to control and protect your company's Windows devices.

Earlier in the chapter, I talked about using Windows Security. Now we are going to look at using Microsoft Defender for Endpoint.

Implementing Microsoft Defender for Endpoint

When talking about Microsoft Defender, it can be a little confusing to people. The reason for this is that Windows 10/11 comes with Microsoft Defender and Azure also now comes with Microsoft Defender. So, when IT people are discussing Defender, it's important that they specify which version they are talking about. We'll discuss Azure's version of Microsoft Defender and the benefits that it provides to organizations.

Microsoft Defender for Identity (previously called Azure Advanced Threat Protection) allows organizations to monitor domain controller traffic whereas Microsoft Defender for Endpoint (previously called Microsoft Defender Advanced Threat Protection) allows organizations to monitor endpoints (for example, users' devices). Organizations can use both of these defenses together for the best possible protection, and both can be managed by using a single Azure interface.

When deciding to integrate Microsoft Defender for Identity and Microsoft Defender for Endpoint together, you get the benefits of both systems working together. Some of these benefits are as follows:

Endpoint Behavioral Sensors   Endpoint behavioral sensors are sensors that are built into the Windows 10/11 operating system, and these sensors gather and process behavioral data for things like the Registry, files, processors, and communications. This data is then sent to the Microsoft Defender for Endpoint.

Microsoft Defender for Identity Sensors and Stand-Alone Sensors   These sensors can be placed directly onto your domain controllers, or they can be set up to port mirror directly from your domain controller to Microsoft Defender for Identity. These sensors have the ability to collect and parse traffic for multiple protocols that work with authentication or authorization, or just for informational gathering.

Threat Intelligence   Threat intelligence consists of multiple Microsoft tools, security groups, and third-party threat defending partners. Threat intelligence allows Microsoft Defender for Endpoint to properly recognize tools and activities that hackers use and then report alerts when those tools or activities are observed.

Cloud Security Analytics   Cloud security analytics uses multiple detection signals and Microsoft insights to detect and recommend protection against advanced threats.

Microsoft Defender for Identity uses several technologies to detect suspicious behavior during all phases of a cyber-based attack. These phases include:

Investigation Phase (Reconnaissance)   This is the phase where hackers gather information on a target organization. This phase can include information gathering by using Internet investigation, dumpster diving, etc.

Scanning Phase   This phase is when an attacker tries to scan for vulnerabilities. These can be port scanners (looking for open ports to access), vulnerability scanning (looking for known vulnerabilities), and network scanning (looking at network components like routers and firewalls).

Access Phase   This is the phase when hackers try to gain access to your network based on the investigation and scanning phases.

Maintaining Access Phase   This is the phase when hackers try to put back doors or software in place so that they can continue to gain access to your network.

Clearing Their Tracks Phase   Hackers who are any good will try to clear their tracks so that no one knows they were there. In this phase, hackers will try to delete logs and any evidence that the hack even took place.

Microsoft Defender for Endpoint uses Microsoft technologies and expertise to help detect and stop the different phases of a hacker. Microsoft has put in advanced methods to detect hacking before the hacks take place. Microsoft Defender for Endpoint provides several benefits, as shown in Figure 15.8.

FIGURE 15.8   Microsoft Defender for Endpoint

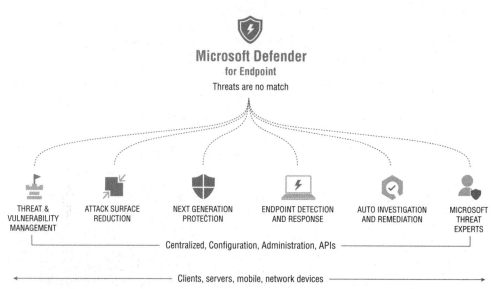

As of this writing, Microsoft Defender for Endpoint is available in two plans, Defender for Endpoint Plan 1 and Plan 2. A new add-on called Microsoft Defender Vulnerability Management is available for Plan 2. These plans provide you with advanced threat protection, with antivirus and antimalware protection, ransomware mitigation, and more. They also provide centralized management and reporting.

This information in Table 15.2 was taken directly from Microsoft's website.

TABLE 15.2   Comparison of Microsoft's endpoint security plans

Plan	What's included
Defender for Endpoint Plan 1	Next-generation protection (includes antimalware and antivirus)
	Attack surface reduction
	Manual response actions
	Centralized management
	Security reports
	APIs
	Support for Windows 1011, iOS, Android OS, and macOS devices

Plan	What's included
Defender for Endpoint Plan 2	All of the Defender for Endpoint Plan 1 capabilities, plus: Device discovery Device inventory Core Defender Vulnerability Management capabilities Threat Analytics Automated investigation and response Advanced hunting Endpoint detection and response Microsoft Threat Experts Support for Windows (client and server) and non-Windows platforms (macOS, iOS, Android, and Linux)
Defender Vulnerability Management add-on	More Defender Vulnerability Management capabilities for Defender for Endpoint Plan 2: Security baselines assessment Block vulnerable applications Browser extensions Digital certificate assessment Network share analysis Support for Windows (client and server) and non-Windows platforms (macOS, iOS, Android, and Linux)

Microsoft Defender for Endpoint Plan 1 is available as a stand-alone subscription for commercial and education customers and is also included as part of Microsoft 365 E3/A3. Microsoft Defender for Endpoint Plan 2, which was previously called Microsoft Defender for Endpoint, is available as a stand-alone subscription. It's also included as part of the following plans:

- Windows 11 Enterprise E5/A5
- Windows 10 Enterprise E5/A5
- Microsoft 365 E5/A5/G5 (which includes Windows 10 or Windows 11 Enterprise E5)
- Microsoft 365 E5/A5/G5/F5 Security
- Microsoft 365 F5 Security & Compliance

Planning Your Microsoft Defender for Endpoint Deployment

When planning your Microsoft Defender for Endpoint deployment, you want to plan it so that you can get the most out of its security capabilities to protect your environment from cyberattacks. Figure 15.9 provides guidance on how to identify your environment architecture, select the best type of deployment tool, and guides you on how to configure your required capabilities. For more information regarding planning your Microsoft Defender for Endpoint deployment, check out Microsoft's website at `https://learn.microsoft.com/en-us/microsoft-365/security/defender-endpoint/deployment-strategy?view=o365-worldwide`.

FIGURE 15.9   Planning your Microsoft Defender for Endpoint deployment

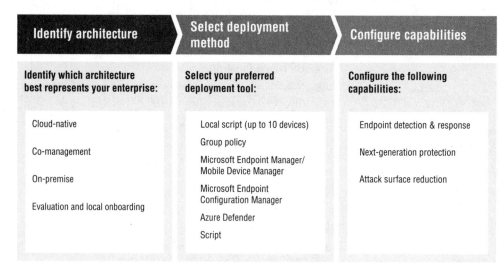

Because every environment is different, some tools may be better suited to meet your deployment needs. Because there are so many different ways to plan your deployment, I want to share an extremely helpful web page that can assist with the planning phase. This web page allows you to download a variety of PDFs that cover the multitude of ways to plan your deployment. The information included with the guides provide information on prerequisites, design, and configuration options. So, check out Microsoft's website at `https://docs.microsoft.com/en-us/microsoft-365/security/defender-endpoint/deployment-strategy`.

Microsoft Defender for Endpoint Deployment

Once you plan your Microsoft Defender for Endpoint deployment, the next phase will be the actual deployment phase. The deployment phase has its own phases that include:

▪ **Phase 1 – Prepare:** Determine what should be considered, such as stakeholder approvals, environment considerations, access permissions, and adoption order of capabilities.

▪ **Phase 2 – Setup:** The initial steps needed so you can access the portal, such as licensing validation, tenant configuration using the setup wizard, and network configuration.

▪ **Phase 3 – Onboard:** Depending on the operating system and deployment method, you can use one of the tools in Table 15.3 to onboard devices to Defender for Endpoint.

Table 15.3 lists the available tools based on the endpoint that you need to onboard. The information in Table 15.3 was taken directly from Microsoft's website.

TABLE 15.3   Onboarding tool options

Endpoint	Tool options
Windows	Local script (up to 10 devices)
	Group Policy
	Microsoft Endpoint Manager/Mobile Device Manager
	Microsoft Endpoint Configuration Manager
	VDI scripts
	Integration with Microsoft Defender for Cloud
macOS	Local scripts
	Microsoft Endpoint Manager
	JAMF Pro
	Mobile Device Management
Linux Server	Local script
	Puppet
	Ansible
iOS	Microsoft Endpoint Manager
Android	Microsoft Endpoint Manager

As you can see in Table 15.3, there are a number of ways to onboard devices to Defender for Endpoint depending on the operating system and deployment method. You can use the onboarding wizard to help guide you through the process. You will go through the onboarding section of the Defender for Endpoint portal to onboard any of the supported devices. Depending on the device, you will be provided with instructions and package files to meet your needs for the device chosen.

Monitoring Microsoft Defender for Endpoint

You can view information on device compliance and onboarding by using the Microsoft Endpoint Manager admin center. To monitor the state of devices that have a Microsoft Defender for Endpoint compliance policy, perform the following steps:

1. Sign into the Microsoft Endpoint Manager admin center at `https://endpoint .microsoft.com`.

2. Select Devices ➤ Monitor ➤ Policy Compliance.

3. Locate the Microsoft Defender for Endpoint policy that you want from the list and check to see which devices are compliant or noncompliant.

You can also take a look at the operational report for noncompliant devices by going to Devices ➤ Monitor ➤ Noncompliant Devices. If you want to learn the onboarding status of your Intune-managed devices, you can select Endpoint Security ➤ Microsoft Defender For Endpoint. Here you can also onboard more devices to Microsoft Defender for Endpoint by creating a device configuration profile.

Endpoint Detection and Response

Microsoft Defender for Endpoint provides you with near-real-time detection and response capabilities. This allows you to take actions quickly if a threat is encountered. If a threat is detected, then an alert will be created. Microsoft Defender for Endpoint collects process information, network activity, user login activity, Registry and filesystem changes, and more, which is kept for six months.

To view threats, you can use the Security Operations dashboard. Here you will see an overview of threats that have been detected and when response actions are required. The dashboard shows you an overview of the following, as you can see in Figure 15.10:

- Active alerts
- Devices at risk
- Sensor health
- Service health
- Daily devices reporting
- Active automated investigations
- Automated investigations statistics
- Users at risk
- Suspicious activities

FIGURE 15.10 Security Operations dashboard

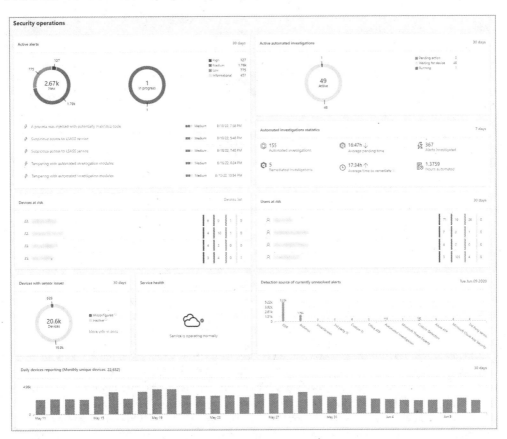

From the dashboard, you can quickly explore and investigate alerts and devices to see if there are any threats or suspicious activity. The dashboard also has tiles that you can click that will provide more information on your overall health state.

If you click Active Alerts, you can view the overall number of active alerts for the past 30 days. Alerts are grouped into New and In Progress, as shown in Figure 15.11.

FIGURE 15.11   Active Alerts

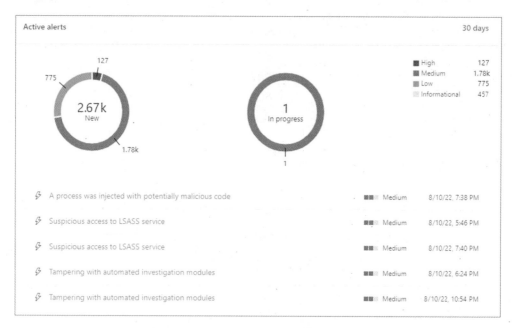

You can click the number inside each alert ring to see that category's queue (New or In Progress). Each will be sorted by their alert severity levels. The Alerts queue will show you a list of alerts that have been flagged from devices on your network. By default, the queue displays any alerts that were seen in the last 30 days, with the most recent alert being at the top of the list. Each row will include an alert severity category and a brief description. If you click an alert, you will see a detailed view. From the Alerts Queue page, you can customize the alerts view to suit your needs. On the top navigation, you can:

- Add or remove columns
- Apply filters
- Display the alerts for a particular duration (1 Day, 3 Days, 1 Week, 30 Days, and 6 Months)
- Export the alerts list to Microsoft Excel
- Manage alerts

You will also notice that the Alerts Queue page displays the severity levels by color, as shown in Figure 15.12:

- **High (Red):** These alerts indicate a high risk because of the severity of damage they can inflict on devices.

- **Medium (Orange):** These alerts indicate endpoint detection and response behaviors that might be a part of an advanced persistent threat (APT) such as Registry changes or the execution of a suspicious file.

- **Low (Yellow):** These alerts may be associated with malware attacks, such as logs being cleared. These threats do not indicate that there was an attack, but it's best to investigate.

- **Informational (Gray):** These alerts may not be considered harmful but could indicate a security issue.

FIGURE 15.12   Alerts Queue page

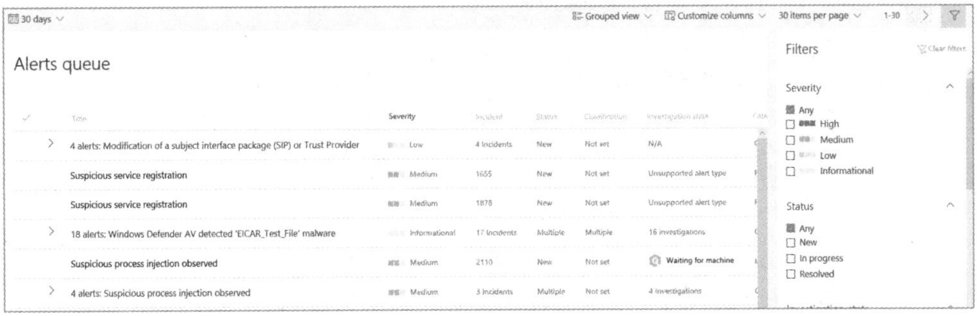

Also on the Security Operations dashboard, if you look at the Devices At Risk tile, this will show you a list of devices that have the most active alerts. For each device, the total number of alerts is shown in a circle next to the device name and then further categorized by severity level. To view more details about a device, just click the name of the device. When you select a device to investigate, you will see a device summary page, as shown in Figure 15.13. On the summary page you will see the following:

Device Details   This provides information such as the domain, OS, and health state of the device.

Response Actions   These are tasks you can perform for the given device.

Tabs (Overview, Alerts, Timeline, Security Recommendations, Software Inventory, Discovered Vulnerabilities, Missing KBs)   These tabs provide security and threat prevention information.

Cards (Active Alerts, Logged On Users, Security Assessment, Device Health Status)   Cards display an overview of alerts related to the device and their risk level.

FIGURE 15.13 Device Summary

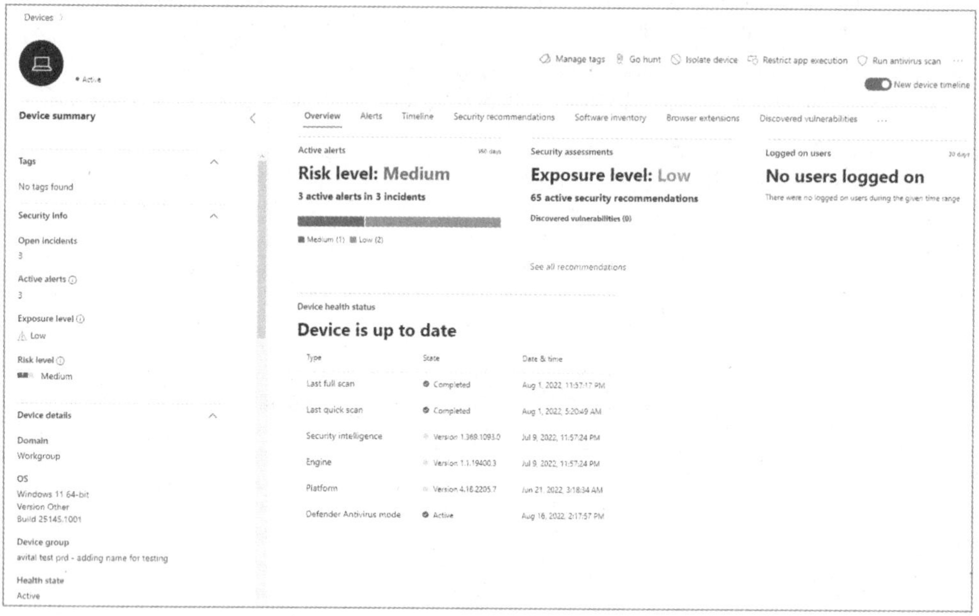

On the Device Summary page, there are also a number of response actions that you can take, as shown in Figure 15.14. These actions include:

- Manage Tags
- Initiate Automated Investigation
- Initiate Live Response Session
- Collect Investigation Package
- Run Antivirus Scan
- Remove App Restrictions
- Isolate Device
- Consult A Threat Expert
- Action Center

FIGURE 15.14 Response actions

On the Security Operations dashboard, if you look at the Devices With Sensor Issues tile, this will give you information on a device's ability to provide sensor data to the Microsoft Defender for Endpoint service. It shows how many devices require attention and helps you identify devices that may have problems, as shown in Figure 15.15.

FIGURE 15.15   Devices With Sensor Issues tile

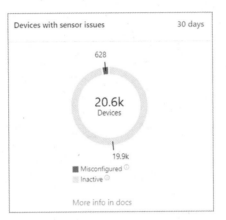

Here you will see two different status indicators:

- **Misconfigured:** This is the number of devices that may have configuration errors that need to be corrected.
- **Inactive:** This is the number of devices that have stopped reporting to the Microsoft Defender for Endpoint service for more than seven days within the past month.

The Service Health tile shows whether the service is active or if there are issues, as shown in Figure 15.16.

FIGURE 15.16   Service Health tile

If you click this tile, it will open the Service Health page, which shows the health state of each cloud service in a table format, as shown in Figure 15.17.

FIGURE 15.17 Service Health page

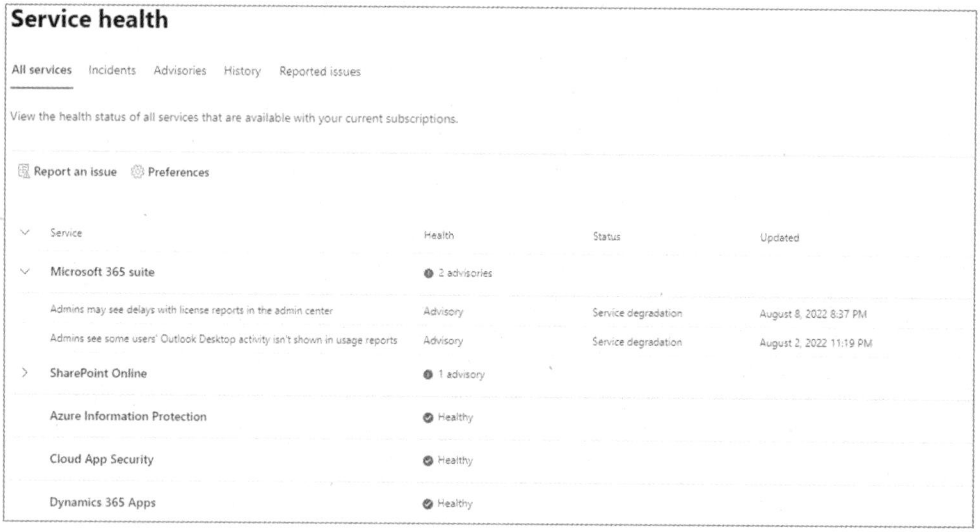

Service health
All services
Incidents
Advisories
History
Reported issues
View the health status of all services that are available with your current subscriptions.
Report an issue
Preferences
Service
Health
Status
Updated
Microsoft 365 suite
2 advisories
Admins may see delays with license reports in the admin center
Advisory
Service degradation
August 8, 2022 8:37 PM
Admins see some users' Outlook Desktop activity isn't shown in usage reports
Advisory
Service degradation
August 2, 2022 11:19 PM
SharePoint Online
1 advisory
Azure Information Protection
Healthy
Cloud App Security
Healthy
Dynamics 365 Apps
Healthy

The default view is the All Services tab, which shows all services, their current health state, and any active incidents or advisories. An icon and status in the Health column indicate the state of each service.

On the Security Operations dashboard, if you look at the Daily Devices Reporting tile (as shown in Figure 15.18), it will show you a bar graph that shows the number of devices that are reporting within the last 30 days. You can hover over an individual bar on the graph to see the exact number of devices reporting that day.

FIGURE 15.18 Daily Devices Reporting tile

Daily devices reporting (Monthly unique devices: 22,652)
30 days
4.98k
0
May 11
May 15
May 19
May 23
May 27
May 31
Jun 4
Jun 8

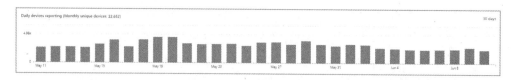

If you look at the Active Automated Investigations tile (shown in Figure 15.19), it will show you the number of automated investigations from the last 30 days. The number of investigations are categorized into Pending Action, Waiting For Device, and Running.

FIGURE 15.19   Active Automated Investigations tile

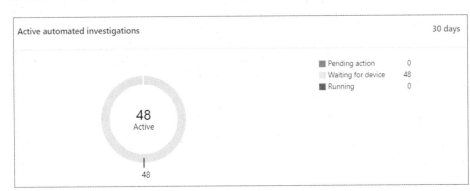

The Automated Investigations Statistics tile (shown in Figure 15.20) shows statistics pertaining to automated investigations within the past seven days.

FIGURE 15.20   Automated Investigations Statistics tile

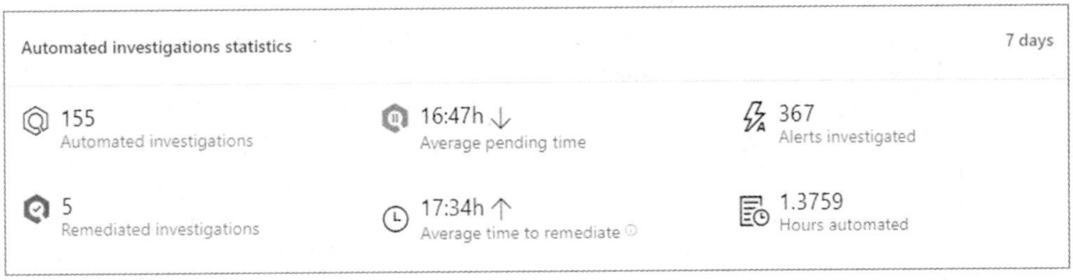

This tile shows you:

- The number of completed investigations
- The number of successfully remediated investigations
- The average pending time it takes for an investigation to be initiated
- The average time it takes to remediate an alert
- The number of alerts investigated
- The number of hours of automation saved from a typical manual investigation

You can click Automated Investigations, Remediated Investigations, and Alerts Investigated to navigate to the Investigations page.

On the Security Operations dashboard, if you look at the Users At Risk tile (shown in Figure 15.21), it will show you a list of user accounts that have the most active alerts and the number of alerts seen on high, medium, or low alerts.

FIGURE 15.21   Users at Risk tile

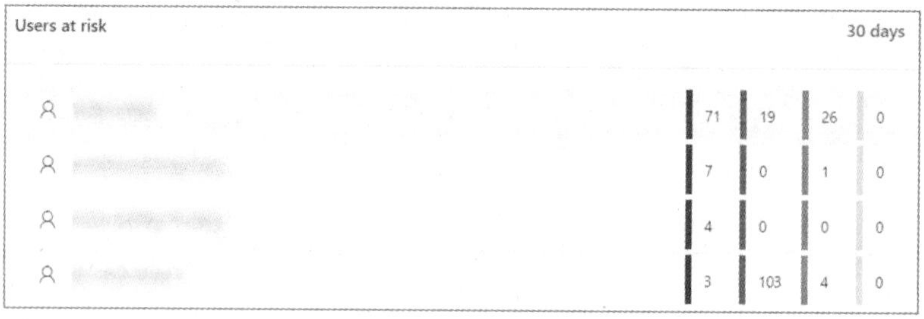

Users at risk	30 days
👤	71 19 26 0
👤	7 0 1 0
👤	4 0 0 0
👤	3 103 4 0

By selecting a user account, you can see more details about that user, as shown in Figure 15.22:

- User account details, Microsoft Defender for Identity alerts, and logged-on devices, role, logon type, and other details
- Overview of the incidents and the user's devices
- Alerts related to this user
- Observed in organization (devices logged on to)

FIGURE 15.22   User account details

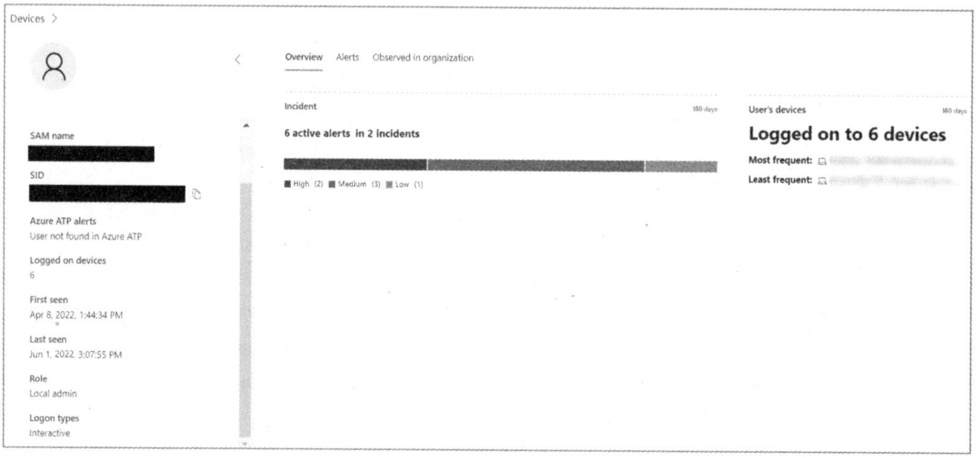

Endpoint Security

Endpoints are the devices that connect to a computer network. Endpoints include desktops, laptops, tablets, mobile devices, servers, IoT devices, virtual machines, and more. Endpoint security helps to protect these endpoints from cyberattacks by using a wide variety of services and solutions. The first endpoint security tools were the traditional antivirus and anti-malware software. Now, endpoint security has expanded to include more advanced cloud solutions. Some of the more common endpoint security risks are as follows:

Device Loss   This is when a device is physically lost, allowing an attacker to access important corporate information.

Drive-by Downloads   This type of attack uses the automated download of software to a device without the user's knowledge or consent.

Malware Ads   These attacks use online ads to spread malware and hack into systems.

Outdated Patches   If devices are not updated regularly, then this may expose vulnerabilities that will allow an attacker to break into a device and steal information.

Phishing   This attack is a form of social engineering attack that tricks the target into sharing sensitive information.

Ransomware   This is a malware attack that will hold the target's information or system hostage until the attacker is paid to release it.

Endpoint Security Best Practices

To help protect against cyberattacks, there are some best practices that you can follow. One of the most important things you can do is educate your users. When it comes to endpoint security, you are the first line of defense. Keep your users up to date on security and compliance training. Keep track of devices that are connected to your network, and make sure that your endpoints have the most current updates and patches. You can add another layer of protection to devices and information by encrypting your endpoints. You can implement strong passwords by using complex passwords, enforcing regular password updates, and prohibiting users from using old passwords.

Microsoft Defender for Endpoint was designed to help enterprise networks prevent, detect, investigate, and respond to advanced threats. It is a cloud-powered endpoint security solution that will help protect against ransomware, file-less malware, and other attacks on Windows, macOS, Linux, Android, and iOS.

Managing Endpoint Security in Microsoft Intune

You can use Intune to configure device security to manage security tasks for devices by using the Endpoint security node. Endpoint security policies are created to help you reduce risks and focus on device security. The Endpoint Security node (as shown in Figure 15.23) is where you will find the tools that you can use to keep your devices secure. You will be able to perform the following:

Create Compliance Policies   You can set up device and user requirements using compliance policies. These are the rules that devices and users must meet to be considered compliant.

Deploy Security Baselines   Intune includes security baselines for Windows devices and a list of applications, such as Microsoft Defender for Endpoint and Microsoft Edge. The security baselines are preconfigured groups of Windows settings that help you apply a recommended configuration. We will discuss security baselines more in the next section.

Integrate Intune with Your Microsoft Defender for Endpoint Team   By integrating the two, you can access security tasks. Security tasks help your security team identify devices that may be at risk and include steps on how to correct any issues.

Manage Security Configurations   Endpoint security policies focus on device security such as antivirus, disk encryption, firewalls, and more through the use of Microsoft Defender for Endpoint.

Review Managed Device Statuses   You can use the All Devices section to see whether devices are in compliance, and if they're not, you can use this section to see how to resolve issues for the devices that are not in compliance.

FIGURE 15.23   Endpoint Security Overview

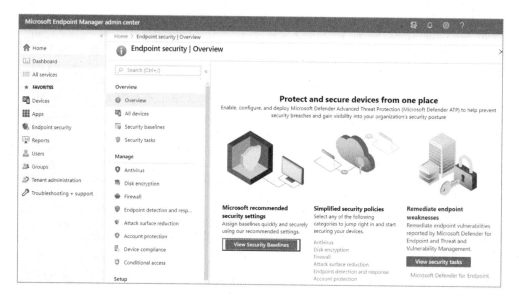

Managing Security Baselines

In Intune, security baselines are preconfigured groups of settings that are best practice recommendations from the Microsoft security teams for that product. These recommendations protect your users and devices. Intune supports security baselines for Windows 10/11 device settings, Microsoft Edge, Microsoft Defender for Endpoint Protection, and more. Security baselines are supported for devices that run Windows 10 version 1809 and later, and Windows 11.

Prior to deploying security baselines, you can customize them in order to enforce only the settings and values you want. Because in most situations, the default settings of a security baseline are the most restrictive, you want to ensure that the default settings do not interfere with other policy settings you have established already. When you create a security baseline profile in Intune, you are creating a template that consists of multiple device configuration profiles. In Intune, security baselines are deployed to groups of users or devices.

To access security baselines, go to the Microsoft Endpoint Manager admin center ➤ Endpoint Security ➤ Security Baselines (as shown in Figure 15.24). You will then see a list of all the available baselines. The list will show you the name of the baseline template, how many profiles you have that use that type of baseline, how many versions of the baseline type are available, and the last published date that shows when the latest version of the baseline template became available.

FIGURE 15.24   Security baselines

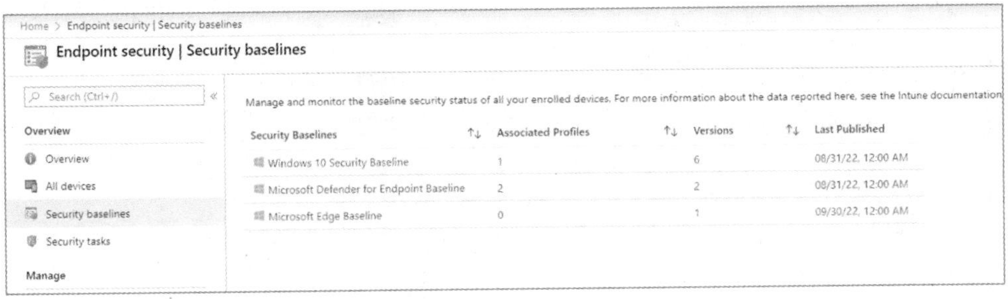

In order to manage security baselines in Intune, you must have an account with the Policy and Profile Manager built-in role, and you may have to have an active subscription to additional services, such as Microsoft Defender for Endpoint.

Some common tasks when working with security baselines include creating a profile, changing the version, and removing a baseline assignment. To create a profile, follow these steps:

1. Sign into the Microsoft Endpoint Manager admin center at `https://endpoint.microsoft.com`.

2. Select Endpoint Security ➤ Security Baselines to view the list of available baselines (as shown in Figure 12.3 earlier).

3. Select the baseline you want to use and then click Create Profile.

4. On the Basics tab, specify the name and description. The description is optional but I recommend that you include it. Then click Next to go to the next tab.

5. On the Configuration Settings tab, view the available baseline settings you can select. You can expand a group to view the settings in that group, and the default values for those settings in the baseline (as shown in Figure 15.25).

FIGURE 15.25   Security Baselines: Configuration Settings

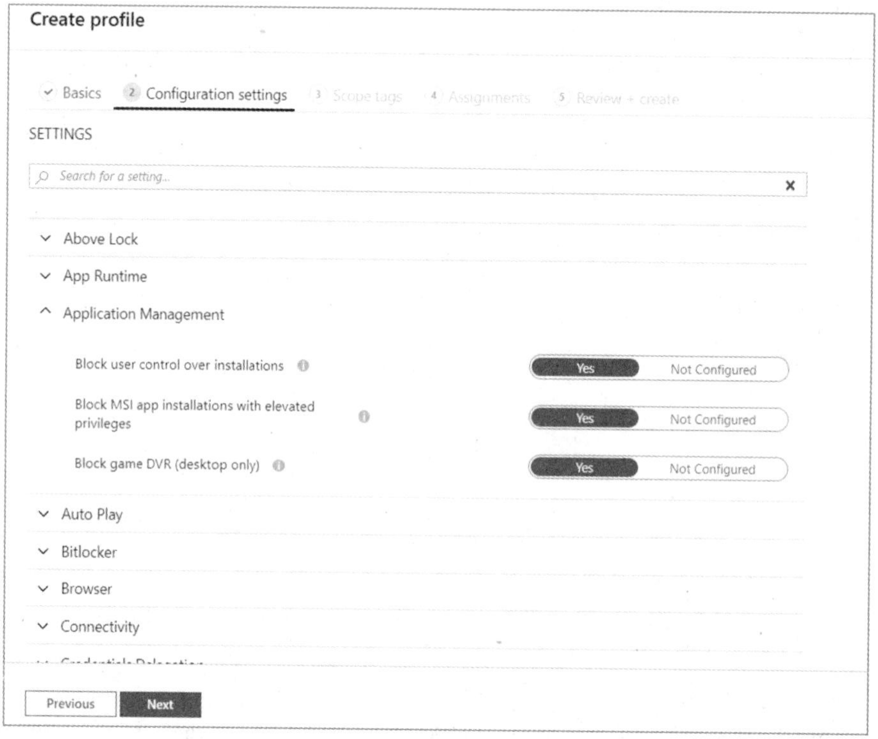

6. On the Scope Tags tab, click Select Scope Tags to open the Select Tags pane, where you can assign scope tags to the profile.

7. On the Assignments tab, click Select Groups To Include and then assign the baseline to one or more groups.

8. When you are ready to deploy the baseline, select the Review + Create tab and review the details for the baseline. Click Create to save and deploy the profile. As soon as the profile is created, it will be pushed to the assigned group and immediately applied.

Once a profile has been created, you can edit it by going to Endpoint Security ➤ Security Baselines, selecting the baseline type that you configured, and then selecting Profiles. Then, select the profile from the list of available profiles, and click Properties. You can edit settings from all the available configuration tabs, and click Review + Save to commit your changes.

Changing the Baseline Version for a Profile

There may be times where you need to change the baseline version for a profile. Perform the following steps to change the baseline version:

1. Sign into the Microsoft Endpoint Manager admin center at `https://endpoint.microsoft.com`.

2. Select Endpoint Security ≻ Security Baselines and then select the tile for the baseline type that has the profile you want to change.

3. Next, click Profiles, select the check box for the profile you want to edit, and then select Change Version, as shown in Figure 15.26.

FIGURE 15.26   Selecting Change Version

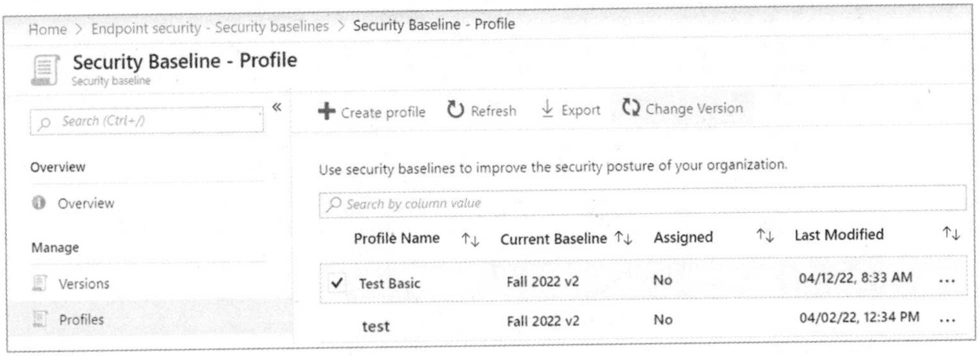

4. In the Change Version pane, open the Select A Security Baseline To Update To drop-down list, and select the version you want to use.

5. Click Review Update to download a CSV file that will display the differences between the profiles. Review the file so that you know which settings are new or removed, and what the default values for these settings are in the updated profile. When ready, continue to the next step.

6. Select one of the two options for Select A Method To Update The Profile:

   ■ Accept Baseline Changes But Keep My Existing Setting Customizations: This option keeps the customizations you made to the baseline profile and applies them to the new version you've chosen to use.

   ■ Accept Baseline Changes And Discard Existing Setting Customizations: This option overwrites your original profile completely. The updated profile will use the default values for all settings.

7. Finally, click Submit. The profile updates to the selected baseline version, and after the conversion is complete, the baseline immediately redeploys to assigned groups.

Managing Device Security Using Policies

You can use the security policies that are located under the Manage section in the Endpoint Security node to configure device security, as shown in Figure 15.27.

FIGURE 15.27 Endpoint Security – Manage section

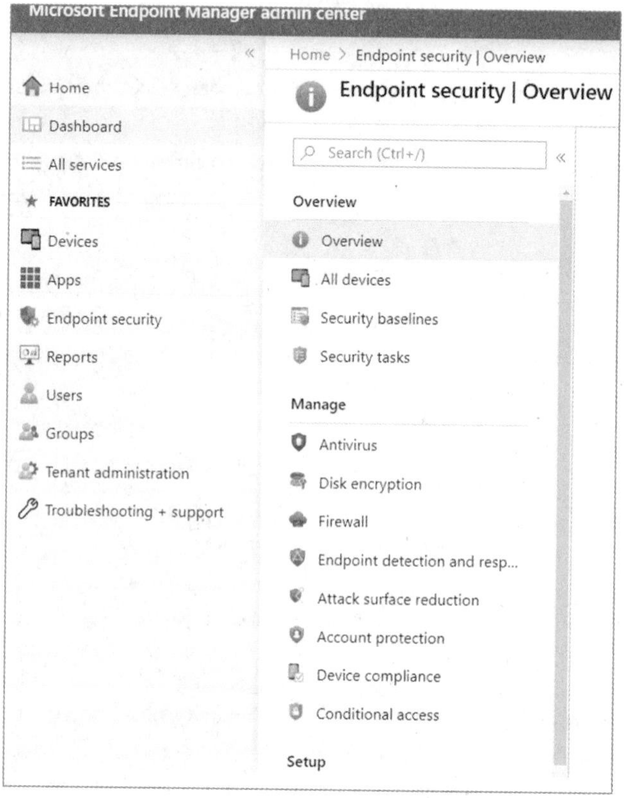

Endpoint security policies are one of several ways in which Intune is used to configure device settings. Each endpoint security profile focuses on a specific subset of device settings and is used to configure one particular aspect. It's important to note that in Intune, security baselines, device configuration policies, and endpoint security policies are all treated equally as sources of device configuration settings, and a settings conflict can happen when a device receives multiple configuration settings from different sources. Here are some of the items you can manage, along with a brief description of each:

▪ **Antivirus:** These policies help you focus on managing antivirus settings for managed devices.

▪ **Disk Encryption:** This focuses on only the settings that are relevant for a device's built-in encryption method, such as FileVault or BitLocker.

- **Firewall:** Use this section to configure the built-in firewall for devices that run macOS and Windows 10/11.

- **Endpoint Detection And Response (EDR):** These policies are used when you integrate Microsoft Defender for Endpoint with Intune. The policies are used to manage EDR settings and to onboard devices to Microsoft Defender for Endpoint.

- **Attack Surface Reduction:** When Defender antivirus is in use on your Windows 10/11 devices, use this to manage those settings.

- **Account Protection:** This is used to help you protect the identity and accounts of your users. The account protection policy focuses on the settings for Windows Hello and Credential Guard.

Also found under Manage are device compliance and conditional access policies. These policy types aren't focused security policies for configuring endpoints but are important tools for managing devices and access to your company resources.

To create an endpoint security policy, perform the following steps:

1. Sign into the Microsoft Endpoint Manager admin center at `https://endpoint.microsoft.com`.

2. Select Endpoint Security, select the type of policy you want to configure, and then click Create Policy. Choose from the following policy types:

   - Antivirus

   - Disk encryption

   - Firewall

   - Endpoint detection and response

   - Attack surface reduction

   - Account protection

3. Enter the following properties:

   - **Platform:** Choose the platform that you are creating the policy for. The available options will vary depend on the policy type you select.

   - **Profile:** Choose from the available profiles for the selected platform.

4. Click Create.

5. On the Basics page, enter a name and description for the profile, then click Next.

6. On the Configuration Settings page, expand each group of settings, and configure the settings you want to manage. When done, click Next.

7. On the Scope Tags page, choose Select Scope Tags to open the Select Tags pane, where you can assign scope tags to the profile. Click Next to continue.

8. On the Assignments page, select the groups you want to receive the profile and then click Next.

9. On the Review + Create page, when you're done, click Create.

Duplicating a Policy

There may be times when you need to create another endpoint security policy that is nearly identical to another except for one small difference. Suppose you want to assign similar policies but to different groups. Instead of creating a new policy from scratch, you can simply duplicate the policy and then edit it to fit your requirements. When you create a duplicate of a policy, it will come with all the original configuration settings and scope tags, but it will not have any assignments and you will have to assign it a new name. You can duplicate the following types of endpoint security policies:

- Account protection
- Antivirus
- Attack surface reduction
- Disk encryption
- Endpoint detection and response
- Firewall

To duplicate an endpoint security policy, perform the following steps:

1. Sign into the Microsoft Endpoint Manager admin center at `https://endpoint.microsoft.com`.

2. Select the policy that you want to copy. Next, click Duplicate or click the ellipsis (. . .) to the right of the policy and select Duplicate.

3. Give the policy a new name and then click Save.

Then you can edit the policy to suit your needs. To edit an endpoint security policy, perform the following steps:

1. Select the new policy and then select Properties.

2. Select Settings to expand a list of the configuration settings in the policy to review the current configuration, then click Edit for each category to modify the policy. Select each tab and make your changes. The tabs are:

   - Basics
   - Assignments
   - Scope Tags
   - Configuration Settings

3. Edits to one category must be saved before you can edit other categories. You do this by clicking Save.

Troubleshooting an Endpoint Security Baseline

There may be times when you have deployed an endpoint security baseline but the deployment status is showing an error. What should you do? Microsoft has provided you with the tools you need to troubleshoot the error. To figure out what the error might be, perform the following steps:

1. In Intune, select Security Baselines, select a baseline, and click Profiles.

2. Under Monitor, select a profile and then select Per-Setting Status.

3. A table will show you all the settings along with a status of each. Select the Error or the Conflict column to see the setting causing the error.

Understanding Microsoft Defender Application Guard

One of the biggest issues that we have in IT is the Internet. It's a world gamechanger and a company gamechanger. But that also means it's an IT gamechanger. We in IT have to rethink how we protect our networks, and that's because of the Internet.

Years ago, hackers had to use phone lines, and that helped prevent a lot of hacker wannabes. Phone lines were easy to track, and it could be expensive for a young hacker to spend a lot of money on phone calls—especially if they were unsuccessful with their hacks.

Today, anyone can hack from anywhere because of the World Wide Web, and they pay only a monthly fee for Internet access. So, we must rethink how we protect our data and our companies. This is where Application Guard can help us.

Application Guard was specifically designed for Windows 10/11 and Microsoft Edge. Application Guard works with Microsoft Edge to isolate untrusted websites, thus protecting your organization's network and data while your users are working on the Internet.

As an enterprise administrator, you can pick which websites are defined as trusted sites. These sites can be internal websites, external websites, company websites, and cloud-based organizations. If a site is not on the trusted list, it is then considered untrusted and automatically isolated when a user visits the site.

When a user accesses a website that is not on the trusted list, Microsoft Edge will be automatically opened in an isolated Hyper-V-enabled container. This container will be a separate environment from the host operating system, and this will help protect untrusted websites from causing damage to the Windows client system. Also, since the website will be isolated, any type of attack will not affect the corporate network or its data.

Microsoft Defender Application Guard is disabled by default. It works in two modes: Standalone or Enterprise. Standalone mode allows a noncorporate user to use Microsoft Defender Application Guard without any administrator-configured policies. Enterprise mode is used in an enterprise environment and can be configured automatically by the enterprise administrator.

For you to use Microsoft Defender Application Guard, your environment must meet a few hardware requirements. These include the following:

- **64-bit CPU:** A 64-bit computer with minimum four cores (logical processors) is required for hypervisor and virtualization-based security (VBS).

- **CPU virtualization extensions:** Extended page tables, also called Second-Level Address Translation (SLAT), and either one of these virtualization extensions for VBS: VT-x (Intel) or AMD-V.

- **Hardware memory:** Microsoft requires a minimum of 8 GB of RAM.

- **Hard disk:** 5 GB of free space, solid-state disk (SSD) recommended.
- **Input/Output Memory Management Unit (IOMMU) support:** Not required but recommended.

Microsoft Defender Application Guard Standalone Mode

If a user wants to use Standalone mode on Windows client or Windows Server, they need to be using either Windows 10 Enterprise edition (version 1709 or higher) or Windows 10 Pro edition (version 1803 or higher). The user must install Application Guard manually on their Windows device and then they need to manually start Microsoft Edge in Application Guard while they are browsing untrusted sites.

Exercise 15.3 will show you how to install Microsoft Defender Application Guard using the Windows Control Panel.

EXERCISE 15.3

Installing Microsoft Defender Application Guard

1. Right-click Start and choose Windows System ➢ Control Panel ➢ Large Icon View ➢ Programs And Features.

2. Click the link Turn Windows Features On Or Off.

3. Scroll down and check the box for Microsoft Defender Application Guard (shown in Figure 15.28), and then click OK.

FIGURE 15.28   Installing Microsoft Defender Application Guard

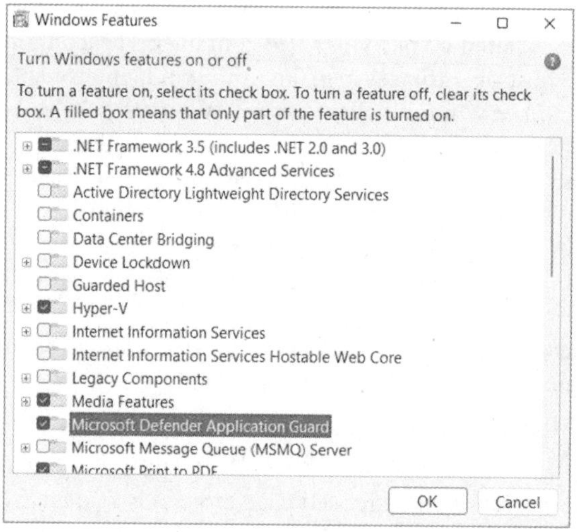

4. After Microsoft Defender Application Guard installs, close Control Panel.

You can also install Microsoft Defender Application Guard by using PowerShell. To do this, you need to right-click on PowerShell and choose the top option, Run As Administrator (see Figure 15.29).

FIGURE 15.29   Opening PowerShell as an administrator

Once you are in the PowerShell window, run the following PowerShell command and then restart the Windows client device:

```
Enable-WindowsOptionalFeature -online -FeatureName
Windows-Defender-ApplicationGuard
```

You can also install Microsoft Defender Application Guard using Intune. To do so, perform the following steps:

1. Go to the Microsoft Endpoint admin center at `https://endpoint.microsoft.com` and sign in.

2. Choose Devices ➢ Configuration Profiles ➢ + Create Profile, and do the following:

   a. In the Platform list, select Windows 10 and later.

   b. In the Profile list, select Endpoint Protection.

   c. Click Create.

3. Specify the following settings for the profile:

   - Name and description

   - In the Select A Category To Configure Settings section, choose Microsoft Defender Application Guard.

   - In the Application Guard list, click Enabled for Edge.

   - Choose your preferences for Clipboard Behavior, External Content, and the remaining settings.

4. Click OK, and then click OK again.

5. Review your settings, and then click Create.

6. Click Assignments, and then do the following:

   a. On the Include tab, from the Assign To list, choose an option.

   b. If you have any devices or users you want to exclude from this endpoint protection profile, specify them on the Exclude tab.

   c. Click Save.

After the profile is created, any devices to which the policy should apply will have Microsoft Defender Application Guard enabled. However, your users may have to restart their devices in order for protection to begin.

In Exercise 15.4, I will show you how to use Windows Defender Application Guard in Standalone mode. I will be using Windows and Microsoft Edge for this exercise. To complete this exercise, you must complete Exercise 15.3 and install Microsoft Defender Application Guard on your Windows device.

EXERCISE 15.4

Using Microsoft Defender Application Guard

1. Open Microsoft Edge.

2. From the options menu, choose New Application Guard Window (see Figure 15.30).

FIGURE 15.30   New Application Guard Window option

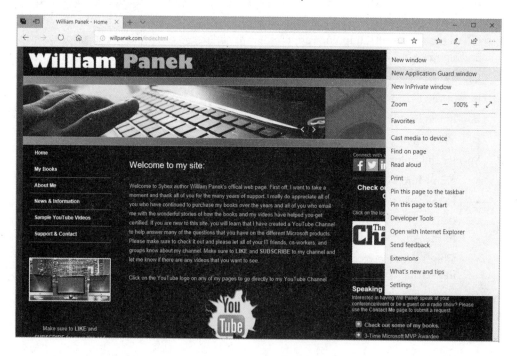

3. You will need to wait for Application Guard to set up the isolated environment (see Figure 15.31). This may take a few moments.

FIGURE 15.31   Application Guard starting screen

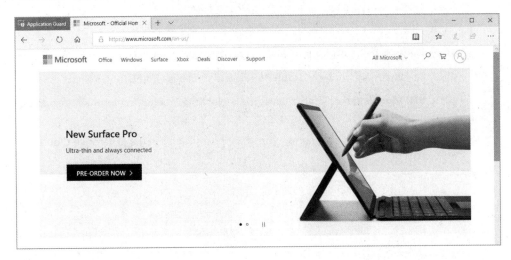

4. As you can see in Figure 15.32, we opened Microsoft's website in Application Guard mode, and you can see that in the upper-left corner of the window. Close Edge.

FIGURE 15.32   Microsoft's website in Application Guard mode

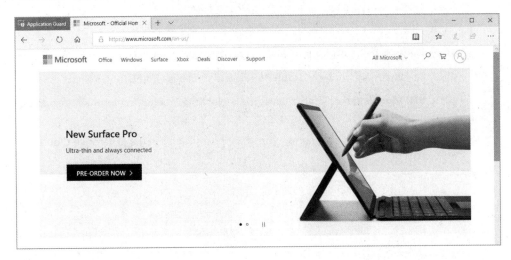

Microsoft Defender Application Guard Enterprise Mode

Microsoft Defender Application Guard in the enterprise environment is not much different for the user as in Standalone mode. The main difference is that the enterprise administrator configures the Microsoft Defender Application Guard application. The enterprise administrator sets up and configures the application. When a user accesses an untrusted website, Microsoft Defender Application Guard automatically starts.

So, let's take a look at some of the enterprise-based systems that will benefit from Microsoft Defender Application Guard:

Enterprise Desktops and Laptops Enterprise desktops are machines that are joined to your domain and managed by your company's administrators. Enterprise administrators can configure Microsoft Defender Application Guard through Configuration Manager or Microsoft Intune.

Bring Your Own Device (BYOD) Laptops Normally organizations that allow users to use their own devices for company business need to follow company rules. So, these devices are normally managed by the enterprise administrators through Intune. If a user wants to use a personal device but they don't want to follow corporate rules, most companies won't allow the use of the personal device.

In Exercise 15.5, I will show you how to use Microsoft Defender Application Guard in Enterprise mode. Before your organization can use Application Guard in Enterprise mode, you must install Windows Enterprise edition (version 1709 or higher) on your corporate network or the needed functionality will not work.

EXERCISE 15.5

Microsoft Defender Application Guard Enterprise

1. Install Application Guard using one of the methods listed earlier.

2. Restart the device, and then start Microsoft Edge.

3. Set up the Network Isolation settings in Group Policy as shown in Figure 15.33:

   a. Click the Windows icon, type **Group Policy**, and then click Edit Group Policy.

   b. Go to the Administrative Templates\Network\Network Isolation\Enterprise Resource Domains Hosted In The Cloud setting.

   c. For the purposes of this scenario, type .microsoft.com in the Enterprise Cloud Resources box.

FIGURE 15.33   Network Isolation GPO

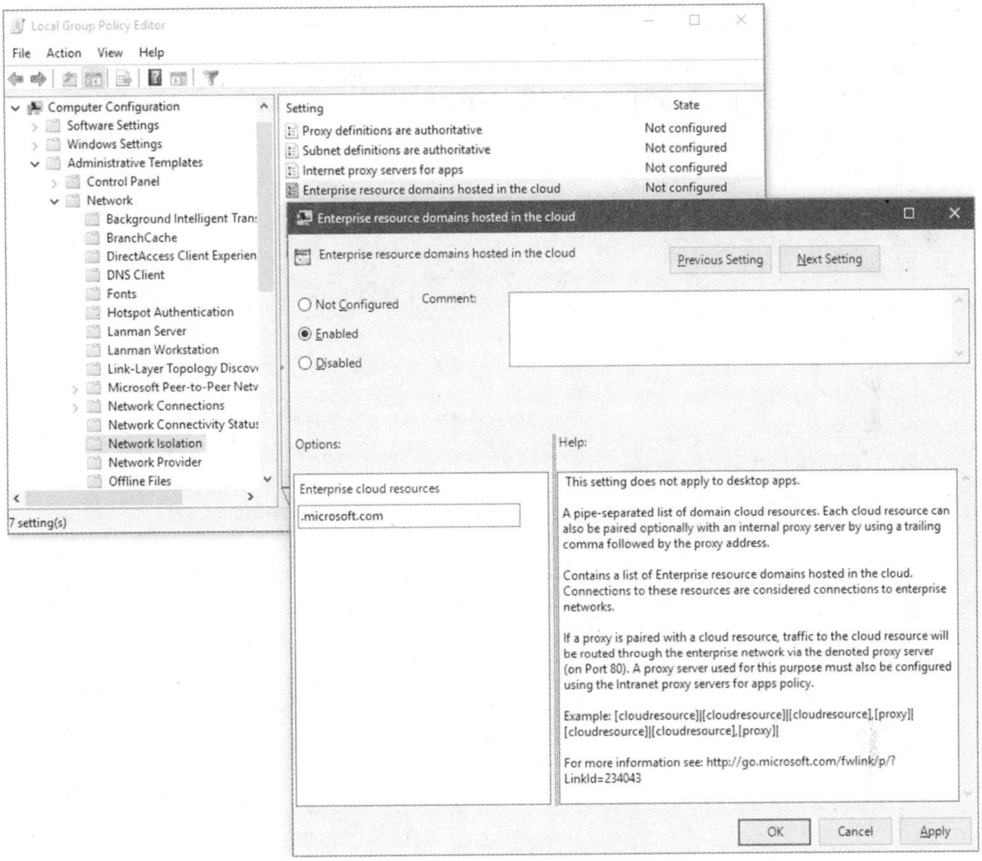

4. Go to the Administrative Templates\Network\Network Isolation\Domains Categorized As Both Work And Personal setting. Enter the websites that you trust in the Neutral Resources box, as shown in Figure 15.34.

EXERCISE 15.5 *(continued)*

FIGURE 15.34 Domains Categorized As Both Work And Personal setting

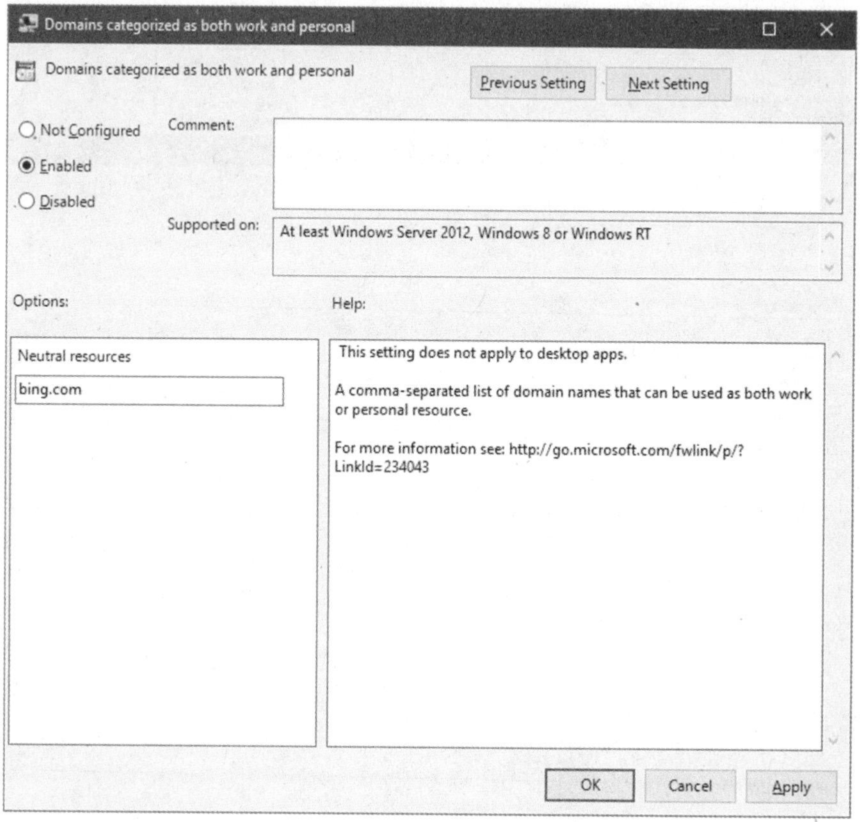

5. Go to the Computer Configuration\Administrative Templates\Windows Components\Microsoft Defender Application Guard\Turn On Microsoft Defender Application Guard In Enterprise Mode setting.
6. Click the Enabled radio button, choose Option 1 (see Figure 15.35), and click OK.

FIGURE 15.35   Turn On Microsoft Defender Application Guard In Enterprise Mode setting

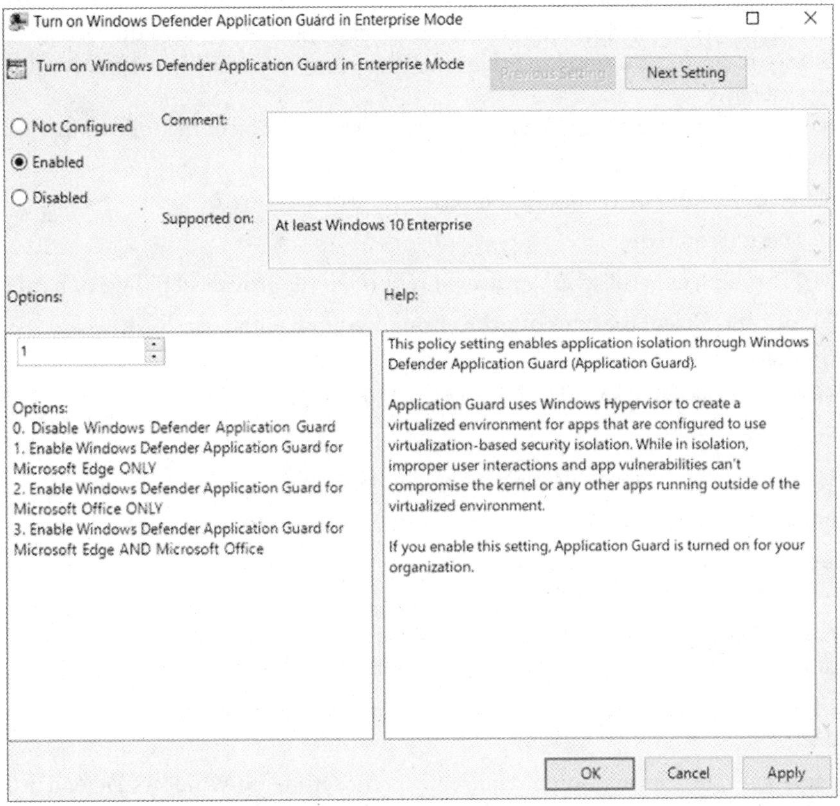

7. Close the GPO editor.

Understanding Windows Defender Credential Guard

Windows Server 2022 and Windows Enterprise use a security measure called Windows Defender Credential Guard. Windows Defender Credential Guard is a virtualization-based security service to help isolate critical files so that only system software that is privileged can access those critical files.

Once the feature is enabled, a Windows client machine that is part of Active Directory or Azure AD will have the system's credentials protected by Windows Defender Credential Guard.

After you enable Windows Defender Credential Guard, the Local Security Authority (LSA) process in the operating system works with a new component called the isolated LSA. The isolated process stores and protects the system's critical data.

Once data is stored by the isolated LSA process, the system then uses the virtualization-based security to protect the data and that data is no longer accessible to the rest of the operating system.

To enable Windows Defender Credential Guard, you must meet the following requirements:

- Machine must support virtualization-based security (required)
- Secure boot (required)
- TPM 1.2 or 2.0, either discrete or firmware (preferred; provides binding to hardware)
- UEFI lock (preferred; prevents attacker from disabling with a simple Registry key change)

The virtualization-based security requires the following:

- 64-bit CPU
- CPU virtualization extensions plus extended page tables
- Windows hypervisor (does not require Hyper-V Windows Feature to be installed)

If you want to use Windows Defender Credential Guard in a Hyper-V virtual machine, the following requirements need to be met:

- Windows 10 (version 1607 or higher) or Windows Server 2016 or higher and the system must have Hyper-V with Input Output Memory Management Unit (IOMMU).
- The Hyper-V virtual machine must be set as Generation 2 and virtual TPM needs to be enabled.

Once you have met the minimum requirements for setting up Windows Defender Credential Guard, you can enable it with any of the following methods:

- Using Group Policy
- Modifying the Registry
- Using the Hypervisor-Protected Code Integrity (HVCI)
- Using the Windows Defender Credential Guard hardware readiness tool

In Exercise 15.6, I will show you how to enable Windows Defender Credential Guard using a Group Policy Object (GPO).

EXERCISE 15.6

Enabling Windows Defender Credential Guard Using a GPO

1. Open the Group Policy Management editor on a Windows Server machine.

2. Create a new GPO, click the GPO, and choose Edit.

3. Go to Computer Configuration ➤ Administrative Templates ➤ System ➤ Device Guard.

4. Select Turn On Virtualization Based Security and then choose the Enabled option (see Figure 15.36).

FIGURE 15.36   Turn On Virtualization Based Security setting

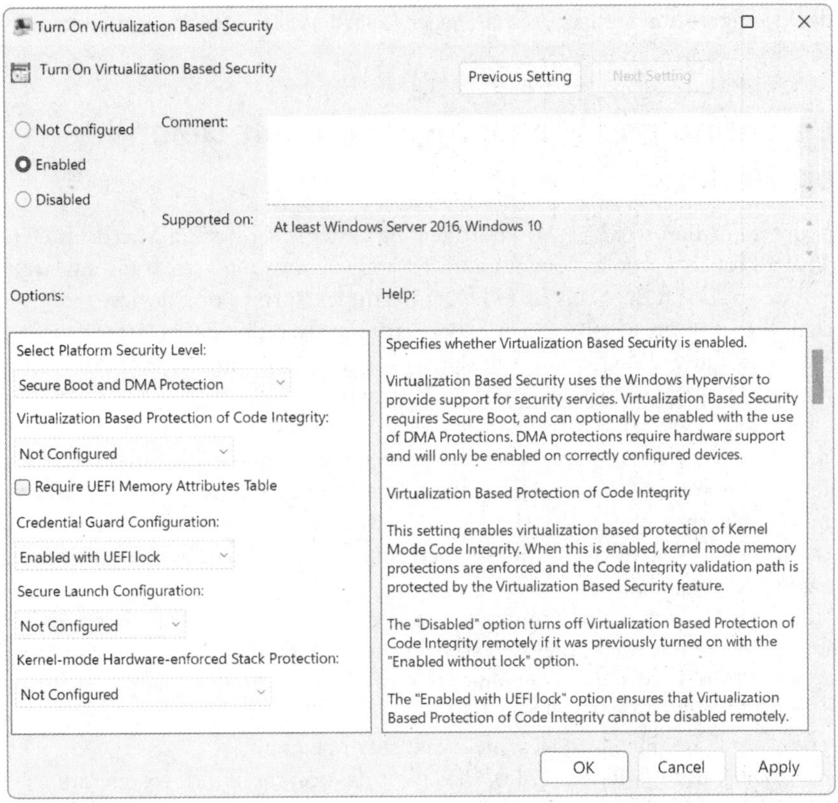

5. In the Select Platform Security Level box, choose Secure Boot or Secure Boot And DMA Protection.

6. In the Credential Guard Configuration box, select Enabled With UEFI Lock, and then click OK. (If you want to be able to turn off Windows Defender Credential Guard remotely, choose Enabled Without Lock.)

7. In the Secure Launch Configuration box, choose Not Configured, Enabled, or Disabled.

8. Click OK and then close the Group Policy Management Console.

9. To enforce processing of the Group Policy, run **gpupdate/force**.

You can also enable Windows Defender Credential Guard by using Microsoft Endpoint Manager. To do so, perform the following steps:

1. From the Microsoft Endpoint Manager admin center, select Devices.

2. Select Configuration Profiles.

3. Select Create Profile ➤ Windows 10 And Later ➤ Settings Catalog ➤ + Create.

4. Under Configuration Settings, select Device Guard as the category and add your required settings.

Implementing and Managing Microsoft Defender Exploit Guard

Another way that Microsoft has started protecting systems is by using Microsoft Defender Exploit Guard. It helps protect your Windows system against malware, ransomware, and other types of attacks. It does this by reducing the attack surface of a device.

So, what does it mean when someone says that they are reducing the attack surface of a system? The way I always explain it is in this way. I am a huge hockey fan. When I lived in New Jersey, and I used to go to dozens of hockey games.

Now think of a hockey net (or soccer net) as the Windows system. During one of the hockey intermissions (when the players get a break), they would bring out a piece of plexiglass and on the bottom of the plexiglass, there was an opening just a bit bigger than a hockey puck. Then they would give someone a stick and a puck and allow them to shoot at the net from the center of the ice. If the puck went in, they would win a car or money or whatever the prize was that night.

Now think of the open net as Windows. You can have a great goaltender (your firewall) but if someone is good enough, they can still get the puck by the goaltender. Now think of the plexiglass. The only way that someone can score is by getting the puck in that tiny little opening. This is an example of a reduced attack surface. The goaltender doesn't need to protect the entire net. They just need to protect that tiny opening.

Microsoft Defender Exploit Guard is your plexiglass on the Windows operating system. By protecting common ways that hackers exploit the system, the hackers now have to get into the system by using that tiny little opening.

Microsoft Defender Exploit Guard helps protect your system from common malware hacks that use executable files and scripts that attack applications like Microsoft Office (e.g., Outlook). Microsoft Defender Exploit Guard also looks for suspicious scripts or behavior that is not normal on the Windows system.

One of the common hacks today is ransomware. This is when a hacker takes over your system and requests a ransom to release your files. During this time, the hackers are holding your documents hostage until you pay. Once Microsoft Defender Exploit Guard is enabled, folders and files are assessed to determine if the files are safe or harmful from ransomware threats.

There are numerous ways to turn on Microsoft Defender Exploit Guard—you can use any of the following tools:

- Windows Security app
- Mobile Device Management (MDM) using Microsoft Intune
- Microsoft Endpoint Manager
- Microsoft Endpoint Configuration Manager
- Group Policy
- PowerShell

You can configure and deploy Configuration Manager policies that manage all four components of Microsoft Defender Exploit Guard. These components include:

- Attack surface reduction
- Controlled folder access
- Exploit protection
- Network protection

In Exercise 15.7, I will show you how to enable Microsoft Defender Exploit Guard using Intune.

EXERCISE 15.7

Enabling Microsoft Defender Exploit Guard Using Intune

1. Open Settings by clicking the Start button and then clicking the Settings (spoke) icon.

2. Select Update And Security.

3. Select Windows Security and click Virus And Threat Protection.

4. Click Ransomware Protection and make sure the setting is turned on (see Figure 15.37).

FIGURE 15.37 Turning on the Ransomware setting

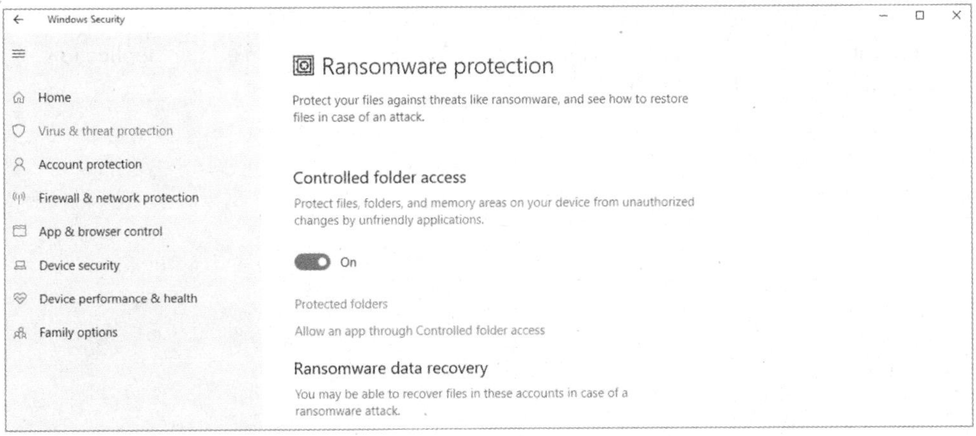

EXERCISE 15.7 *(continued)*

5. Click Protected Folders to see what folders are currently protected (Figure 15.38). You can click + Add A Protected Folder to add additional folders.

FIGURE 15.38 Protected Folders screen

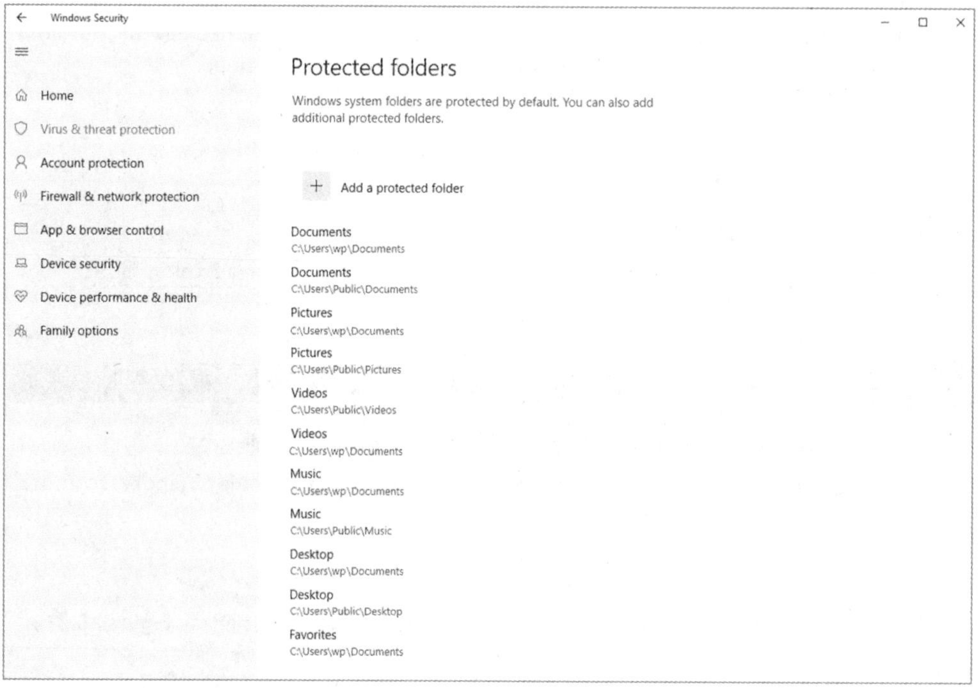

6. If you would like an application to have access, you can click the link Allow An App Through Controlled Folder Access. Once you click the link, you can add an application that will be allowed access (see Figure 15.39).

FIGURE 15.39 Allow An App Through Controlled Folder Access screen

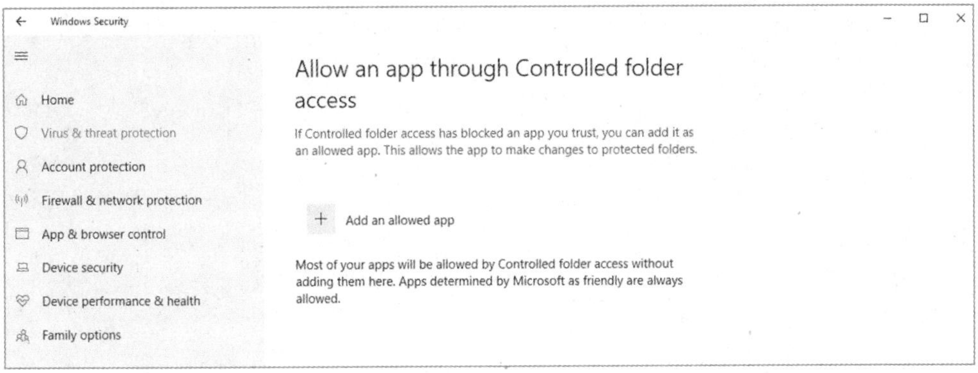

Windows Security
Allow an app through Controlled folder access
If Controlled folder access has blocked an app you trust, you can add it as an allowed app. This allows the app to make changes to protected folders.
Add an allowed app
Most of your apps will be allowed by Controlled folder access without adding them here. Apps determined by Microsoft as friendly are always allowed.
Home
Virus & threat protection
Account protection
Firewall & network protection
App & browser control
Device security
Device performance & health
Family options

7. Close the Security Center (reboot if you made any changes).

Once Microsoft Defender Exploit Guard is enabled, when the Windows client system suspects that a file is a danger, the Windows system will display a Virus & Threat Protection screen (see Figure 15.40). This protection is completed in real time as the Windows system is operating.

FIGURE 15.40 Virus & Threat Protection warning

Virus & threat protection
Unauthorized changes blocked
Controlled Folder Access blocked C:\Users \cber.exe from making changes to the Desktop

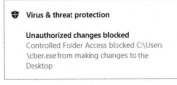

Another part of controlling application exploitation is when users try to get applications from the web and Microsoft Store. You have the ability to set up and use Microsoft Defender SmartScreen (see Figure 15.41).

FIGURE 15.41   Microsoft Defender SmartScreen

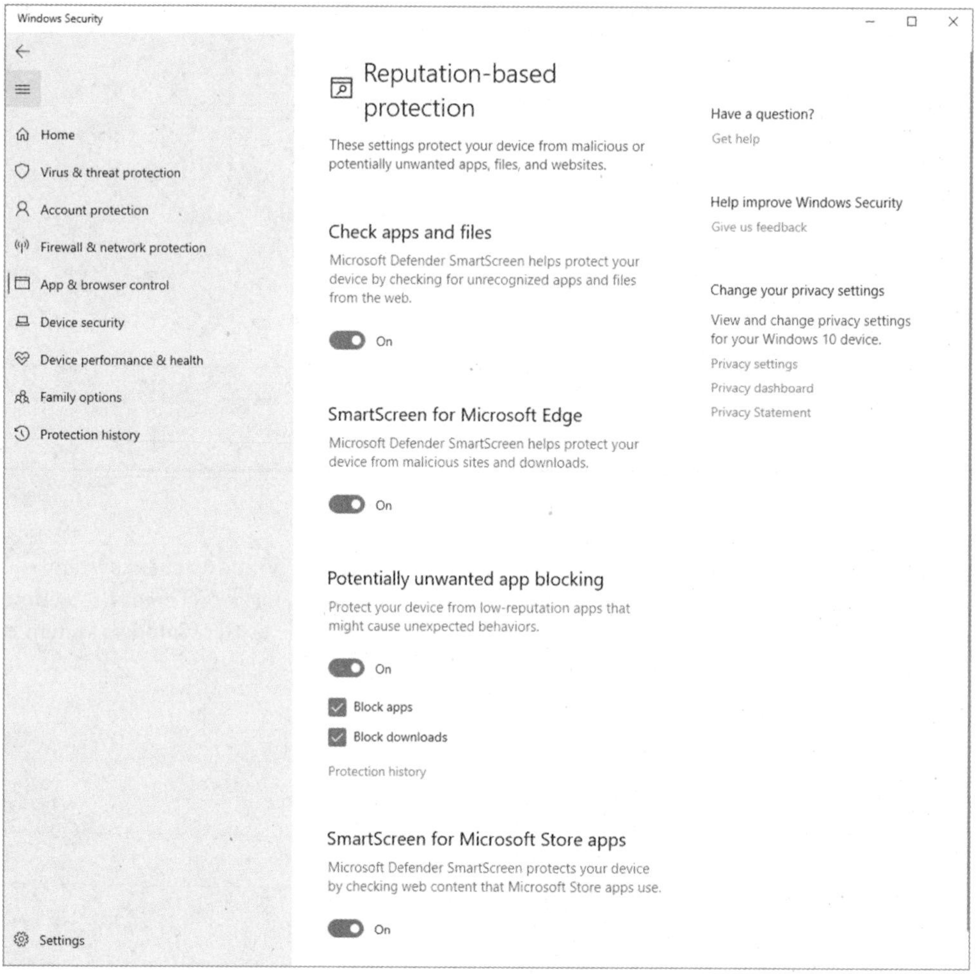

Microsoft Defender SmartScreen helps you protect your employees when they try to visit websites that have previously been reported as phishing or malware websites. Microsoft Defender SmartScreen also helps protect Windows if an employee tries to download potentially malicious files.

SmartScreen allows Windows to determine if a downloaded application or an application installer may be potentially malicious:

- SmartScreen checks to see if downloaded files are on a list of known malicious software sites or if programs that are being downloaded are known to be unsafe. If any file or program is on these lists, SmartScreen will prompt the user with a warning to let that user know that the data or site might be malicious.

- When a user downloads a file or program that isn't on the list, SmartScreen will show the user a warning prompt to advise caution.

Another way that your organization can help stop users from downloading applications that are possibly harmful is by using Windows Defender Application Control.

Using Windows Defender Application Control

So now that we have discussed how to protect the system and system files, let's talk about protecting applications. When an application runs, it has the ability to access data with the same access to data that a user has. Because of this, Microsoft has created Windows Defender Application Control (WDAC) to help stop attacks of data through the use of applications.

For many years, if a user had local admin rights and they wanted to install an application onto a corporate machine, they just did it. Users just assume that applications that they buy or download is trustworthy.

You can now use Windows Defender Application Control to ensure that only applications that you explicitly allow can run on your Windows computers. It allows you to control applications, and this is a big advantage over just using antivirus software. By stopping applications from running unless you explicitly allow the application is just another layer of protection that organizations can use in their war against data theft.

For many years, top-level security analysts have stated that application control is one of the best ways to address the many threats that executable-based malware uses against companies. Now, you can add another layer of security by listing what applications can specifically run on your Windows corporate systems.

If you want to create policies to use with Windows Defender Application Control, you must meet the following system requirements:

- Windows 10/11 Enterprise
- Windows Server 2016 and higher

There are several ways to deploy Windows Defender Application Control policies to manage endpoints, including:

- Deploying using a mobile device management (MDM) solution, such as Intune
- Deploying using Microsoft Endpoint Configuration Manager
- Deploying via script
- Deploying via Group Policy

Once Windows Defender Application Control is set up, you can create and configure policies by using GPOs or Intune.

Summary

This chapter discussed Windows Security, the tools that help protect a device and its data. This is one of many ways that you can protect your system.

We discussed Windows Firewall and using Windows Firewall with Advanced Security. Windows Firewall helps prevent unauthorized users from connecting to the client operating system. Windows Firewall is an extra line of defense, but it should not replace a perimeter firewall for your network.

We then explored working with Microsoft Defender for Endpoint. We described the plans available and the deployment steps. We also discussed the numerous ways that you can onboard devices to Defender for Endpoint, which vary depending on the operating system and deployment method you are using.

You learned how to monitor your devices using Microsoft Defender for Endpoint and how you can view information about device compliance and onboarding by using the Microsoft Endpoint Manager admin center.

We discussed Endpoint Protection and what endpoints are. Endpoint security helps you protect your endpoints from cyberattacks by using a wide variety of services and solutions.

Then we covered endpoint security using Intune and creating and monitoring security baselines. In Intune, security baselines are preconfigured groups of settings that are recommended best practices from the Microsoft security teams for that product.

We also discussed Endpoint Detection and Response by using the Security Operations dashboard to view a wide variety of tiles such as Active Alerts, Devices At Risk, Devices With Sensor Issues, Service Health, and Daily Devices Reporting. We explored the response actions you can take.

You then learned about Microsoft Defender Application Guard, specifically designed for Windows 10/11 and Microsoft Edge. Application Guard works with Edge to isolate untrusted websites, thus protecting your organization's network and data while users are working on the Internet.

Then we focused on Windows Defender Credential Guard, a virtualization-based security service to help isolate critical files so that only system software that is privileged can access those critical files.

You learned how to use Microsoft Defender Exploit Guard to protect your Windows 10/11 system against malware, ransomware, and other types of attacks. Microsoft Defender Exploit Guard does this by reducing the attack surface of a device.

Finally, you learned how to use Windows Defender Application Control to control applications and stop them from running unless you explicitly allow it.

Exam Essentials

Know how to run scans with Windows Security.   Know how to set up and run virus scans using Windows Security.

Know how to configure Windows Firewall.   Know how to set up and maintain Windows Firewall with Advanced Security. Know that you can set up inbound and outbound rules by using Windows Firewall. Know how to allow or deny applications by using Windows Firewall.

Know how to use Microsoft Defender for Endpoint.   Know what Microsoft Defender for Endpoint can do for you as well as how to onboard devices into Microsoft Defender for Endpoint. Also, know how to monitor Microsoft Defender for Endpoint as well as how to investigate and respond to threats using the Security Operations dashboard and response actions.

Know how to plan and implement Endpoint Protection.   Know and understand what endpoints are and how to plan endpoint security.

Understand Endpoint Security.   Know how to create and manage configuration policies for Endpoint Security, including antivirus, encryption, firewall, endpoint detection and response, and attack surface reduction.

Know how to use security baselines in Intune.   Know what security baselines are and how to implement and manage them in Intune.

Understand how to use Microsoft Defender Application Guard.   Understand how Application Guard works with Edge to isolate untrusted websites and how to set up Standalone and Enterprise modes.

Understand how to use Windows Defender Credential Guard.   Know how Windows Defender Credential Guard uses virtualization-based security to help isolate critical files so that only system software with privileges can access those critical files.

Understand how to use Microsoft Defender Exploit Guard.   Know how Microsoft Defender Exploit Guard helps protect your Windows client system against malware, ransomware, and other types of attacks.

Know how to use Windows Defender Application Control.   Understand how Windows Defender Application Control allows you to control which applications are allowed on a Windows client system.

Review Questions

1. You are the administrator for an organization with 275 computers that all run Windows 10/11. These computers are all joined to Azure AD and all computers are enrolled in Intune. You need to make sure that only approved applications are allowed to run on all of these computers. What should you implement to ensure this?

    A.   Windows Defender Credential Guard

    B.   Microsoft Defender Exploit Guard

    C.   Microsoft Defender Application Guard

    D.   Microsoft Defender Antivirus

2. You are the administrator for a large organization and all your computers run Windows 10/11. These computers are all joined to Azure AD and all computers are enrolled in Intune. You need to ensure that all applications installed on the Windows client systems are only applications that are approved by the IT department. What should you implement to ensure this?

    A.   Microsoft Defender Application Guard

    B.   Windows Defender Credential Guard

    C.   Microsoft Defender Exploit Guard

    D.   Microsoft Defender Antivirus

3. You are the administrator for an organization where all computers run Windows 10/11. You need to make sure that critical files are isolated so that only system software with privileges can access those critical files. What should you implement to ensure this?

    A.   Windows Defender Credential Guard

    B.   Microsoft Defender Exploit Guard

    C.   Windows Defender Application Control

    D.   Microsoft Defender Antivirus

4. You are the administrator for your company network. You and a colleague are discussing enabling Windows Defender Credential Guard by using Intune. When enabling Windows Defender Credential Guard using Intune, what profile type should you use?

    A.   The Endpoint Protection profile type

    B.   The Administrative Templates profile type

    C.   The Identity Protection (Windows) profile type

    D.   The Device Restrictions profile type

5. You are the administrator for your company network. You want to enable Windows Defender Credential Guard on computers that are running Windows 10/11. What should you install on these computers?

   A. Containers

   B. A guarded host

   C. Hyper-V

   D. Microsoft Defender Application Guard

6. You are the IT manager for `WillPanek.com`. The company has an Active Directory domain and a cloud-based Azure Active Directory. You need to protect your systems from common malware hacks that use executable files and scripts that attack applications like Microsoft Office (e.g., Outlook). What do you need to do to accomplish this?

   A. Windows Defender Credential Guard

   B. Microsoft Defender Exploit Guard

   C. Microsoft Defender Application Guard

   D. Windows Defender Firewall with Advanced Security

7. You are the administrator for your company network. You and a colleague are discussing Microsoft Defender Application Guard. You know that there are a few hardware requirements that must be met to be able to use this feature. What is the minimum amount of RAM that Microsoft recommends to use Microsoft Defender Application Guard?

   A. 2 GB

   B. 4 GB

   C. 8 GB

   D. 12 GB

8. You are the administrator for StormWind Studios. You are trying to set up your Windows Defender Firewall to allow DNS inbound and outbound rules. Which port number would you set up?

   A. Port 20

   B. Port 25

   C. Port 53

   D. Port 80

9. You and a colleague are discussing how to implement Microsoft Defender for Endpoint. You have the following devices:

   ▪ Device 1: Window 10 Pro machine that is not a domain member

   ▪ Device 2: Windows 10 Enterprise machine that is a domain member

   ▪ Device 3: Windows 11 Pro machine that is a domain member

   ▪ Device 4: Mac OS X machine that is not a domain member

Which devices can be onboarded to Microsoft Defender for Endpoint using Microsoft Endpoint Configuration Manager?

A. Device 3 only

B. Device 1, Device 2, and Device 3 only

C. Device 1, Device 2, Device 3, and Device 4

D. Device 2 and Device 3 only

10. You are the administrator for your company network. You and a colleague are discussing Microsoft Defender for Endpoint and its built-in features and capabilities. Once this capability is put in place, it will detect, investigate, and respond to advanced threats. What is the name of this Microsoft Defender for Endpoint capability?

A. Attack Surface Reduction

B. Endpoint Detection and Response

C. Next Generation Protection

D. Threat & Vulnerability Management

11. You are the administrator for your company network. You and a colleague are discussing Microsoft Defender Antivirus. You know that there are a number of scan options available with Microsoft Defender Antivirus. You want to perform a scan that will scan the most likely areas on a hard disk that spyware, malware, and viruses are commonly known to infect. What scan option is being discussed?

A. A custom scan

B. A full scan

C. A quick scan

D. A Microsoft Defender offline scan

12. You are the administrator for your company network. You and a colleague are discussing Windows Security. One section of Windows Security covers the Microsoft Defender SmartScreen settings and Exploit Protection mitigations. What section is being discussed?

A. Account Protection

B. App & Browser Control

C. Device Security

D. Virus & Threat Protection

13. You are the administrator for your company network. You and a colleague are discussing setting up security baselines by using Intune. Which Intune built-in role account can create the security baselines?

A. Application Manager

B. Help Desk Operator

C. Policy and Profile Manager

D. Read Only Operator

14. You are the administrator for your company network. You and a colleague are discussing endpoint security risks. One of these risks is when an attack uses an automated download of software to a device without the user's consent. What risk type are you discussing?

A. Drive-by downloads

B. Malware ads

C. Phishing

D. Ransomware

15. You are the administrator for your company network. You and a colleague are discussing Microsoft Defender Application Guard. You know that it is turned off by default, and you want to install it using Control Panel. Where in Control Panel do you install it?

A. Ease of Access

B. Network and Internet

C. Programs and Features

D. System and Security

16. You are the administrator for your company network. You and a colleague are discussing Microsoft Defender Application Guard. You know that you can configure the mode used by Microsoft Defender Application Guard. What mode allows users to manage their own device settings?

A. Enterprise mode

B. Readiness mode

C. Standalone mode

D. User mode

17. You are the administrator for your company network. You and a colleague are discussing Microsoft Defender for Endpoint and the Security Operations dashboard. One of the tiles shows you a list of devices that have the most active alerts. What is the name of this tile?

A. Active Alerts

B. Devices At Risk

C. Sensor Health

D. Service Health

18. You are the administrator for your company network. You and a colleague are discussing Microsoft Defender Exploit Guard components. One of the components consists of rules that help prevent attack vectors that are applied by scripts, email, and Office-based malware. What is being discussed?

A. Attack surface reduction rules

B. Controlled folder access

C. Exploit protection

D. Network protection

19. You are the network administrator for a small organization. Your organization has implemented Windows 10/11 on all client machines. You want to implement another line of security on the Windows client machine so that unauthorized users can't access the machines. What can you implement?

A. Windows Data Protection

B. Windows Encryption Protection

C. Windows Defender Firewall

D. Windows Secure Data Protocol

20. You are the administrator for your company network. You and a colleague are discussing the ways to enable Windows Defender Credential Guard. Windows Defender Credential Guard can be enabled by using Group Policy, the Registry, or the Hypervisor-Protected Code Integrity (HVCI) and the Windows Defender Credential Guard hardware readiness tool. You decide that you'd like to enable it using Group Policy. What setting in Group Policy should you enable?

A. Deploy Windows Defender Application Control

B. Install Windows Defender Application Control

C. Turn On Virtualization Based Security

D. Turn Off Virtualization Based Security

Chapter

16

Understanding Monitoring

THE FOLLOWING AZ-800 EXAM OBJECTIVES ARE COVERED IN THIS CHAPTER:

✓ **Manage Windows Servers in a hybrid environment**

- Deploy a Windows Admin Center gateway server

- Configure a target machine for Windows Admin Center

- Configure PowerShell Remoting

- Configure CredSSP or Kerberos delegation for second hop remoting

- Configure JEA for PowerShell Remoting

THE FOLLOWING AZ-801 EXAM OBJECTIVES ARE COVERED IN THIS CHAPTER:

✓ **Monitor Windows Server by using Windows Server tools and Azure services**

- Monitor Windows Server by using Performance Monitor

- Create and configure Data Collector Sets

- Monitor servers and configure alerts by using Windows Admin Center

- Monitor by using System Insights

- Manage event logs

- Deploy Log Analytics agents

- Collect performance counters to Azure

- Create alerts

- Monitor Azure Virtual Machines by using Azure diagnostics extension

- Monitor Azure Virtual Machines performance by using VM insights

A very important task of an IT team is to keep the network up and running quickly and efficiently. Keeping your network running at its peak performance is one way to make sure your end users continue to use the network and its resources without problems or interruptions.

Sometimes, performance optimization can feel like a luxury, especially if you can't get your domain controllers to the point where they are actually performing the services for which you intended them, such as servicing printers or allowing users to share and work on files. The Windows Server 2022 operating system has been specifically designed to provide high-availability services solely intended to keep your mission-critical applications and data accessible, even in times of disaster.

The most common cause of such problems is a hardware configuration issue. Poorly written device drivers and unsupported hardware can cause problems with system stability. Failed hardware components (such as system memory) may do so as well. Memory chips can be faulty, electrostatic discharge can ruin them, and other hardware issues can occur. No matter what, a problem with your memory chip spells disaster for your server.

Third-party hardware vendors usually provide utility programs with their computers that can be used for performing hardware diagnostics on machines to help you find problems. These utilities are a good first step in resolving intermittent server crashes. When these utility programs are used in combination with the troubleshooting tips provided in this and other chapters of this book, you should be able to pinpoint most network-related problems that might occur.

In this chapter, I'll cover the tools and methods used for measuring performance and troubleshooting failures in Windows Server 2022. Before you dive into the technical details, however, you should thoroughly understand what you're trying to accomplish and how you'll meet this goal.

Knowing How to Locate and Isolate Problems

In a book such as this, it would be almost impossible to cover everything that could go wrong with your Windows Server 2022 system. This book covers many of the most common issues that you might come across, but almost anything is possible. Make sure you focus on the methodology used and the steps required to locate and isolate a problem—even if you are not 100 percent sure about the cause of the problem. Use online resources to help you locate and troubleshoot the problem, but don't believe everything you read (some things that are posted online can be wrong or misleading).

Test your changes in a lab environment, and try to read multiple sources. Always use Microsoft Support (`http://support.microsoft.com`) as one of your sources because this site is most likely the right source for information. You won't be able to find and fix everything, but knowing where to find critical information that will help you in your efforts never hurts. One of the tools that many of us in the industry use is Microsoft TechNet. The full version of TechNet (a paid subscription) is a resource that will help you find and fix many real-world issues.

Overview of Windows Server 2022 Performance Monitoring

The first step in any performance optimization strategy is to measure performance accurately and consistently. The insight that you'll gain from monitoring factors such as network and system utilization will be extremely useful when you measure the effects of any changes.

The overall performance monitoring process usually involves the following steps:

1. Establish a baseline of current performance.
2. Identify the bottlenecks.
3. Plan for and implement changes.
4. Measure the effects of the changes.
5. Repeat the process based on business needs.

Note that the performance optimization process is never really finished because you can always try to gain more performance from your system by modifying settings and applying other well-known tweaks.

Before you get discouraged, realize that you'll reach some level of performance that you and your network and system users consider acceptable and that it's not worth the additional effort it will take to optimize performance any further. Also note that as your network and system load increases (more users or users doing more), so too will the need to reiterate this process. By continuing to monitor, measure, and optimize, you will keep ahead of the pack and keep your end users happy.

Now that you have an idea of the overall process, let's focus on how changes should be made. It's important to keep in mind the following ideas when monitoring performance:

Plan changes carefully.   Here's a rule of thumb that you should always try to follow: An hour of planning can save a week of work. When you are working in an easy-to-use GUI-based operating system like Windows Server 2022, it's tempting to remove a check mark here or there and then retest the performance. You should resist the urge to do this because some changes can cause large decreases in performance or can impact functionality. Before you make haphazard changes (especially on production servers), take the time to learn about, plan for, and test your changes. Plan for outages and testing accordingly.

Use a test environment.   Test in a test lab that simulates a production environment. Do not make changes on production environments without first giving warning. Ideally, change production environments in off-hours when fewer network and system users will be affected. Making haphazard changes in a production environment can cause serious problems. These problems will likely outweigh any benefits that you may receive from making performance tweaks.

Make only one change at a time.   The golden rule of scientific experiments is that you should always keep track of as many variables as possible. When the topic is server optimization, this roughly translates into making only one change at a time.

One of the problems with making multiple system changes is that although you may have improved overall performance, it's hard to determine exactly *which* change created the positive effects. It's also possible, for example, that changing one parameter increased performance greatly while changing another decreased it only slightly. Although the overall result was an increase in performance, you should identify the second, performance-reducing option so that the same mistake is not made again. To reduce the chance of obtaining misleading results, always try to make only one change at a time.

The main reason to make one change at a time, however, is that if you do make a mistake or create an unexpected issue, you can easily "back out" of the change. If you make two or three changes at the same time and are not sure which one created the problem, you will have to undo all of the changes and then make one alteration at a time to find the problem. If you make only one change at a time and follow that methodology every time, you won't find yourself in this situation.

It's important to remember that many changes (such as Registry changes) take place immediately; they do not need to be applied explicitly. Once the change is made, it's live. Be careful to plan your changes wisely.

Ensure consistency in measurements. When you are monitoring performance, consistency is extremely important. You should strive to have repeatable and accurate measurements. Controlling variables, such as system load at various times during the day, can help.

Assume, for instance, that you want to measure the number of transactions that you can simulate on the accounting database server within an hour. The results would be widely different if you ran the test during the month-end accounting close than if you ran the test on a Sunday morning. By running the same tests when the server is under a relatively static load, you will be able to get more accurate measurements.

Maintain a performance history. In the introduction to this chapter, I mentioned that the performance optimization cycle is a continuous improvement process. Because many changes may be made over time, it is important to keep track of the changes that have been made and the results you have experienced. Documenting this knowledge will help solve similar problems if they arise. I understand that many IT professionals do not like to document, but documentation can make life much easier in the long run.

As you can see, you need to keep a lot of factors in mind when optimizing performance. Although this might seem like a lot to digest and remember, do not fear. As a system administrator, you will learn some of the rules you need to know to keep your system running optimally. Fortunately, the tools included with Windows Server 2022 can help you organize the process and take measurements. Now that you have a good overview of the process, let's move on to look at the tools that can be used to set it in motion.

Using Windows Server 2022 Performance Tools

Because performance monitoring and optimization are vital functions in network environments of any size, Windows Server 2022 includes several performance-related tools.

Introducing Performance Monitor

The first and most useful tool is the Windows Server 2022 *Performance Monitor*, which was designed to allow users and system administrators to monitor performance statistics for various operating system parameters. Specifically, you can collect, store, and analyze information about CPU, memory, disk, and network resources using this tool, and these are only a handful of the things that you can monitor. By collecting and analyzing performance values, you can identify many potential problems.

You can use the Performance Monitor in the following ways:

Performance Monitor ActiveX Control   The Windows Server 2022 Performance Monitor is an ActiveX control that you can place within other applications. Examples of applications that can host the Performance Monitor control include web browsers and client programs such as Microsoft Word or Microsoft Excel. This functionality can make it easy for applications developers and system administrators to incorporate the Performance Monitor into their own tools and applications.

Performance Monitor MMC   For more common performance monitoring functions, you'll want to use the built-in Microsoft Management Console (MMC) version of the Performance Monitor.

System Stability Index   The *System Stability Index* is a numerical value from 1 (least stable) to 10 (most stable) that represents the stability of your network. Performance Monitor calculates and creates the System Stability Index. You can view a graph of this index value. The graph can help you identify when your network started encountering problems. The System Stability Index also offers side-by-side comparisons. You can view when system changes occurred (installing applications, devices, or drivers) and when system problems started to occur. This way, you can determine whether any system changes caused the problems that you are encountering.

Data Collector Sets   Windows Server 2022 Performance Monitor includes the Data Collector Set. This tool works with performance logs, telling Performance Monitor where the logs are stored and when the log needs to run. The Data Collector Sets also define the credentials used to run the set.

To access the Performance Monitor MMC, you open Administrative Tools and then choose Performance Monitor. This launches the Performance MMC and loads and initializes Performance Monitor with a handful of default counters.

You can choose from many different methods of monitoring performance when you are using Performance Monitor. A couple of examples are listed here:

- You can look at a snapshot of current activity for a few of the most important counters. This allows you to find areas of potential bottlenecks and monitor the load on your servers at a certain point in time.

- You can save information to a log file for historical reporting and later analysis. This type of information is useful, for example, if you want to compare the load on your servers from three months ago to the current load.

You'll get to take a closer look at this method and many others as you examine Performance Monitor in more detail.

In the following sections, you'll learn about the basics of working with the Windows Server 2022 Performance Monitor and other performance tools. Then you'll apply these tools and techniques when you monitor the performance of your network.

Your Performance Monitor grows as your system grows, and whenever you add services to Windows Server 2022 (such as installing Exchange Server), you also add to what you can monitor. You should make sure that, as you install services, you take a look at what it is you can monitor.

Deciding What to Monitor

The first step in monitoring performance is to decide *what* you want to monitor. In Windows Server 2022, the operating system and related services include hundreds of performance statistics that you can track easily. For example, you may want to monitor IPsec by monitoring connection security rules. This is just one of many items that can be monitored. All performance statistics fall into three main categories that you can choose to measure:

Performance Objects   A *performance object* within Performance Monitor is a collection of various performance statistics that you can monitor. Performance objects are based on various areas of system resources. For example, there are performance objects for the processor and memory as well as for specific services such as web services.

Counters   *Counters* are the actual parameters measured by Performance Monitor. They are specific items that are grouped within performance objects. For example, within the Processor performance object, there is a counter for % Processor Time. This counter displays one type of detailed information about the Processor performance object (specifically, the amount of total CPU time all of the processes on the system are using). Another set of counters you can use will allow you to monitor print servers.

Instances   Some counters will have instances. An *instance* further identifies which performance parameter the counter is measuring. A simple example is a server with two CPUs. If you decide you want to monitor processor usage (using the Processor performance object)—specifically, utilization (the % Total Utilization counter)—you must still specify *which* CPU(s) you want to measure. In this example, you would have the choice of monitoring either of the two CPUs or a total value for both (using the Total instance).

 One important thing that you want to watch when monitoring objects and counters is the average number. For example, there will be times when your CPU is at 100%. This doesn't mean that you need to buy a newer CPU or add an additional CPU. The number that you want to watch is the average CPU usage. If that is over 80% on average, then your CPU can't handle the workload of the server. If the Hard Page Faults per second average more than 5 per second, you don't have enough RAM. Make sure to watch the averages and not just what's happening at this moment.

To specify which performance objects, counters, and instances you want to monitor, you add them to Performance Monitor using the Add Counters dialog box. Figure 16.1 shows the various options that are available when you add new counters to monitor using Performance Monitor.

FIGURE 16.1   Adding a new Performance Monitor counter

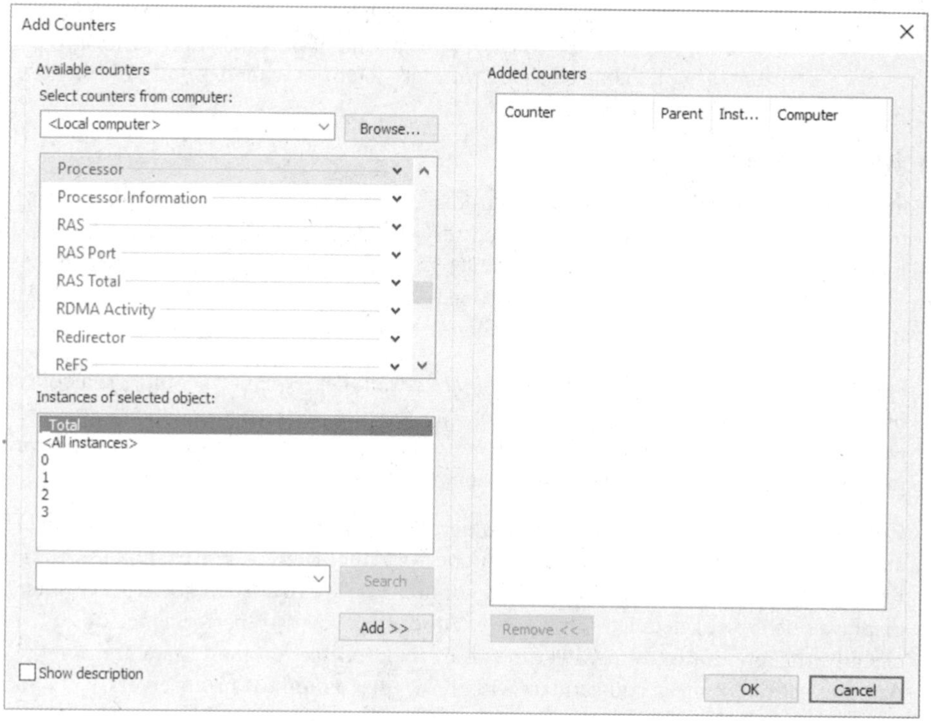

The items that you will be able to monitor will be based on your hardware and software configuration. For example, if you have not installed and configured the IIS, the options available within the Web Server performance object will not be available. Or, if you have multiple network adapters or CPUs in the server, you will have the option of viewing each instance separately or as part of the total value.

Viewing Performance Information   The Windows Server 2022 Performance Monitor was designed to show information in a clear and easy-to-understand format. Performance objects, counters, and instances may be displayed in each of three views. This flexibility allows you to define quickly and easily the information they want to see once and then choose how it will be displayed based on specific needs. Most likely, you will use only one view, but it's helpful to know what other views are available depending on what it is you are trying to assess.

You can use the following main views to review statistics and information on performance:

Line View   The Line view (also referred to as the Graph view) is the default display that is presented when you first access the Windows Server 2022 Performance Monitor. The chart displays values using the vertical axis and displays time using the horizontal axis. This view is useful if you want to display values over a period of time or see the changes in these values over that time period. Each point that is plotted on the graph is based on an average value calculated during the sample interval for the measurement being made. For example, you may notice overall CPU utilization starting at a low value at the beginning of the chart and then becoming much higher during later measurements. This indicates that the server has become busier (specifically, with CPU-intensive processes). Figure 16.2 provides an example of the Graph view.

FIGURE 16.2   Viewing information in Performance Monitor Line view

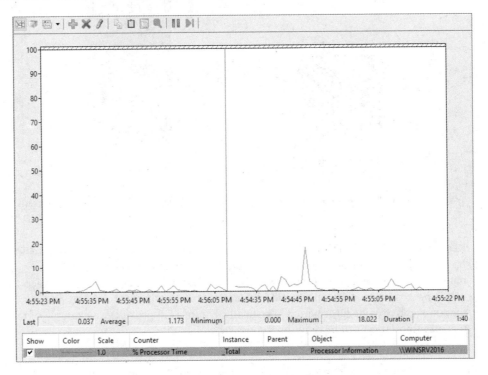

Histogram View   The *Histogram view* shows performance statistics and information using a set of relative bar charts. This view is useful if you want to see a snapshot of the latest value for a given counter. For example, if you were interested in viewing a snapshot of current system performance statistics during each refresh interval, the length of each of the bars in the display would give you a visual representation of each value. It would also allow you to compare measurements visually relative to each other. You can set the histogram to display an average measurement as well as minimum and maximum thresholds. Figure 16.3 shows a typical Histogram view.

FIGURE 16.3   Viewing information in Performance Monitor Histogram view

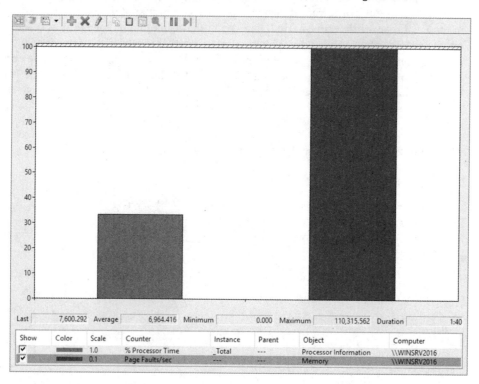

Show	Color	Scale	Counter	Instance	Parent	Object	Computer
✓		1.0	% Processor Time	_Total	---	Processor Information	\\WINSRV2016
✓		0.1	Page Faults/sec	---	---	Memory	\\WINSRV2016

Last 7,600.292 Average 6,964.416 Minimum 0.000 Maximum 110,315.562 Duration 1:40

Report View   Like the Histogram view, the *Report view* shows performance statistics based on the latest measurement. You can see an average measurement as well as minimum and maximum thresholds. This view is most useful for determining exact values because it provides information in numeric terms, whereas the Chart and Histogram views provide information graphically. Figure 16.4 provides an example of the type of information you'll see in the Report view.

FIGURE 16.4   Viewing information in Performance Monitor Report view

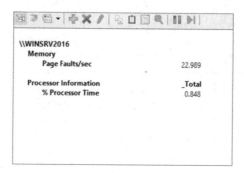

Managing Performance Monitor Properties

You can specify additional settings for viewing performance information within the properties of Performance Monitor. You can access these options by clicking the Properties button in the Taskbar or by right-clicking the Performance Monitor display and selecting Properties. You can change these additional settings by using the following tabs:

General Tab   On the General tab (shown in Figure 16.5), you can specify several options that relate to Performance Monitor views:

FIGURE 16.5   General tab of the Performance Monitor Properties dialog box

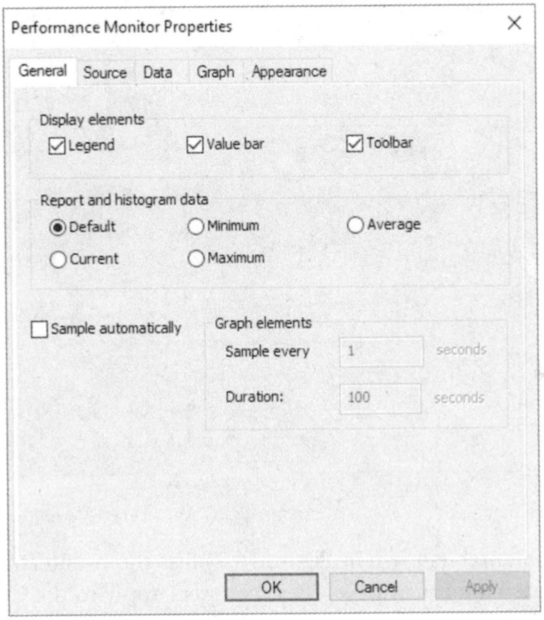

- You can enable or disable legends (which display information about the various counters), the value bar, and the toolbar.
- For the Report and Histogram views, you can choose which type of information is displayed. The options are Default, Current, Minimum, Maximum, and Average. What you see with each of these options depends on the type of data being collected. These options are not available for the Graph view because the Graph view displays an average value over a period of time (the sample interval).
- You can also choose the graph elements. By default, the display will be set to update every second. If you want to update less often, you should increase the number of seconds between updates.

Source Tab On the Source tab (shown in Figure 16.6), you can specify the source for the performance information you want to view. Options include current activity (the default setting) or data from a log file. If you choose to analyze information from a log file, you can also specify the time range for which you want to view statistics. We'll cover these selections in the next section.

FIGURE 16.6 Source tab of the Performance Monitor Properties dialog box

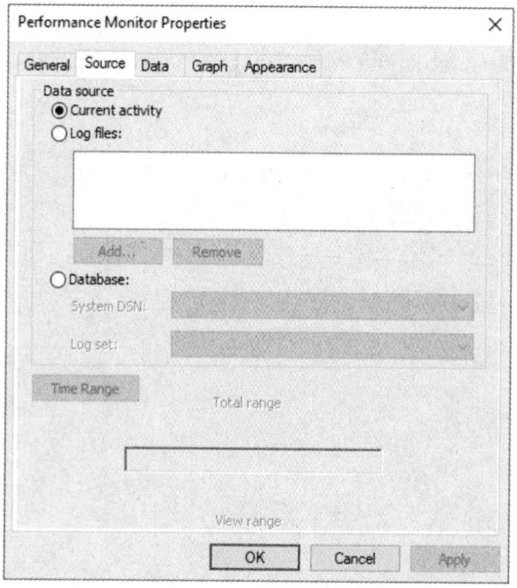

Data Tab The Data tab (shown in Figure 16.7) lists the counters that have been added to the Performance Monitor display. These counters apply to the Chart, Histogram, and Report views. Using this interface, you can also add or remove any of the counters and change the properties, such as the width, style, and color of the line and the scale used for display.

FIGURE 16.7   The Data tab of the Performance Monitor Properties dialog box

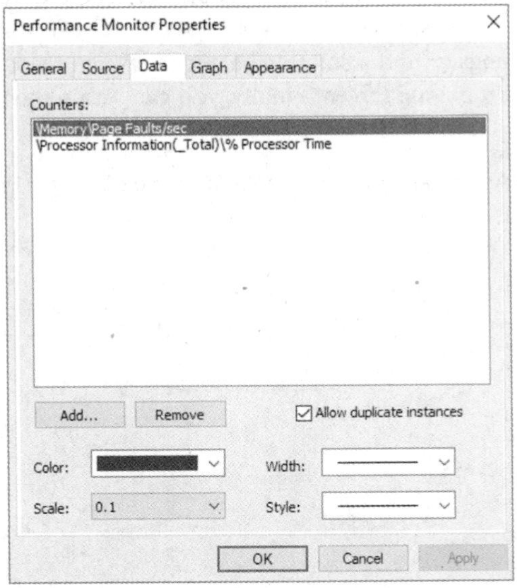

Graph Tab   On the Graph tab (shown in Figure 16.8), you can specify certain options that will allow you to customize the display of Performance Monitor views. First you can specify what type of view you want to see (Line, Histogram, or Report). Then you can add a title for the graph, specify a label for the vertical axis, choose to display grids, and specify the vertical scale range.

FIGURE 16.8   The Graph tab of the Performance Monitor Properties dialog box

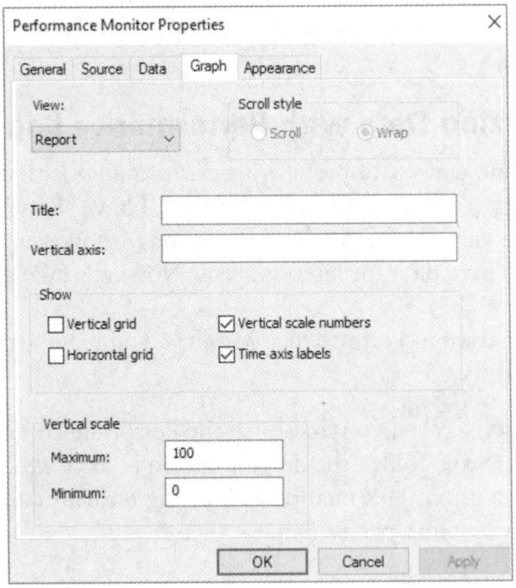

Appearance Tab   Using the Appearance tab (see Figure 16.9), you can specify the colors for the areas of the display, such as the background and foreground. You can also specify the fonts that are used to display counter values in Performance Monitor views. You can change settings to find a suitable balance between readability and the amount of information shown on one screen. Finally, you can set up the properties for a border.

FIGURE 16.9   The Appearance tab of the Performance Monitor Properties dialog box

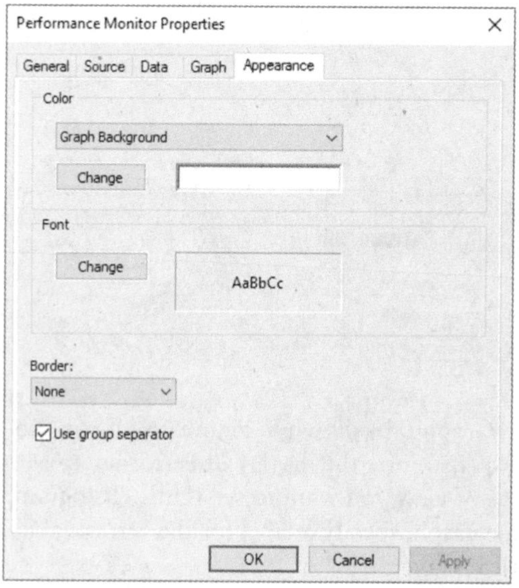

Now that you have an idea of the types of information Performance Monitor tracks and how this data is displayed, let's take a look at another feature—saving and analyzing performance data.

Saving and Analyzing Data with Performance Logs and Alerts

One of the most important aspects of monitoring performance is that it should be done over a given period of time (referred to as a *baseline*). So far, I have shown you how you can use Performance Monitor to view statistics in real time. I have, however, also alluded to using Performance Monitor to save data for later analysis. Now let's take a look at how you can do this.

When viewing information in Performance Monitor, you have two main options with respect to the data on display:

View Current Activity   When you first open the Performance icon from the Administrative Tools folder, the default option is to view data obtained from current system information. This method of viewing measures and displays various real-time statistics on the system's performance.

View Log File Data   This option allows you to view information that was previously saved to a log file. Although the performance objects, counters, and instances may appear to be the same as those viewed using the View Current Activity option, the information itself was actually captured at a previous point in time and stored into a log file.

Log files for the View Log File Data option are created in the Performance Logs And Alerts section of the Windows Server 2022 Performance tool.

Three items allow you to customize how the data is collected in the log files:

Counter Logs   *Counter logs* record performance statistics based on the various performance objects, counters, and instances available in Performance Monitor. The values are updated based on a time interval setting and are saved to a file for later analysis.

Circular Logging   In *circular logging*, the data that is stored within a file is overwritten as new data is entered into the log. This is a useful method of logging if you want to record information only for a certain time frame (e.g., the past four hours). Circular logging also conserves disk space by ensuring that the performance log file will not continue to grow over certain limits.

Linear Logging   In *linear logging*, data is never deleted from the log files, and new information is added to the end of the log file. The result is a log file that continually grows. The benefit is that all historical information is retained.

Now that you have an idea of the types of functions that are supported by the Windows Server 2022 Performance tools, you can learn how you can apply this information to the task at hand—monitoring and troubleshooting your Windows network.

🌐 Real World Scenario

Real-World Performance Monitoring

In our daily jobs as system engineers and administrators, we come across systems that are in need of our help . . . and may even ask for it. You, of course, check your Event Viewer and Performance Monitor and perform other tasks that help you troubleshoot. But what is really the most common problem that occurs? From my experience, I'd say that you suffer performance problems many times if your Windows Server 2022 operating system is installed on a subpar system. Either the server hardware isn't enterprise class or the minimum hardware requirements weren't addressed. Most production servers suffer from slow response times, lagging, and so on, because money wasn't spent where it should have been in the first place—on the server's hardware requirements.

In Exercise 16.1, I will show you how to use Performance Monitor. I will also show you how to add objects and counters and then view those items in the Line view.

EXERCISE 16.1

Using Performance Monitor

1. Right-click the Start Menu and choose Run. Type **Perfmon.exe** and press the Enter key.

2. On the left-hand side under Monitoring Tools, click Performance Monitor.

3. In the center window, click the green plus sign. This will allow you to add a counter.

4. Under Available Counters, make sure Local Computer is chosen. Then expand Processor and choose % Processor Time. Click the Add button. Click OK.

5. Choose any other counters that you want to watch. If you would like to change the view, use the pull-down arrow next to the green plus sign.

6. Close Performance Monitor when you're done.

Using Other Monitoring Tools

Performance Monitor allows you to monitor different parameters of the Windows Server 2022 operating system and associated services and applications. However, you can also use two other tools to monitor performance in Windows Server 2022: Task Manager and Event Viewer. Both of these tools are useful for monitoring different areas of overall system performance and for examining details related to specific system events. In the following sections, you'll take a quick look at these tools and how you can best use them.

Microsoft Message Analyzer

Although Performance Monitor is a great tool for viewing overall network performance statistics, it isn't equipped for packet-level analysis and doesn't give you much insight into what types of network traffic are traveling on the wire. That's where the Microsoft Message Analyzer (MMA) tool comes in.

The Microsoft Message Analyzer Agent is available for use with Windows 7, Windows 8, Windows 10, Windows Server 2008 R2, Windows Server 2012, Windows Server 2012 R2, Windows Server 2016, Windows Server 2019, and Windows Server 2022. The agent allows you to track network packets. When you install the Microsoft Message Analyzer Agent, you will also be able to access the Network Segment System Monitor counter.

On Windows Server 2022 computers, you'll see the Microsoft Message Analyzer icon appear in the Administrative Tools program group. You can use the Microsoft Message Analyzer tool to capture data as it travels on your network.

> The full version of Microsoft Message Analyzer is available at Microsoft's download server. For more information, see www.microsoft.com/downloads.

Once you have captured the data of interest, you can save it to a capture file or further analyze it using Microsoft Message Analyzer. Experienced network and system administrators can use this information to determine how applications are communicating and the types of data that are being passed via the network.

> For the exam, you don't need to understand the detailed information that Microsoft Message Analyzer displays, but you should be aware of the types of information that you can view and when you should use Microsoft Message Analyzer.

Task Manager

Performance Monitor is designed to allow you to keep track of specific aspects of system performance over time. But what do you do if you want to get a quick snapshot of what the local system is doing? Creating a System Monitor chart, adding counters, and choosing a view is overkill. Fortunately, the Windows Server 2022 Task Manager has been designed to provide a quick overview of important system performance statistics without requiring any configuration. Better yet, it's always readily available.

You can easily access Task Manager in several ways:

- Right-click the Windows taskbar and then click Task Manager.
- Press Windows Key+R.
- Press Ctrl+Alt+Del and then select Task Manager.
- Press Ctrl+Shift+Esc.

Each of these methods allows you to access a snapshot of the current system performance quickly.

Once you access Task Manager, you will see the following five tabs:

Processes Tab The Processes tab shows you all the processes that are currently running on the local computer. By default, you'll be able to view how much CPU time and memory a particular process is using. By clicking any of the columns, you can quickly sort by the data values in that particular column. This is useful, for example, if you want to find out which processes are using the most memory on your server.

By accessing the performance objects in the View menu, you can add columns to the Processes tab. Figure 16.10 shows a list of the current processes running on a Windows Server 2022 computer.

FIGURE 16.10   Viewing process statistics and information using Task Manager

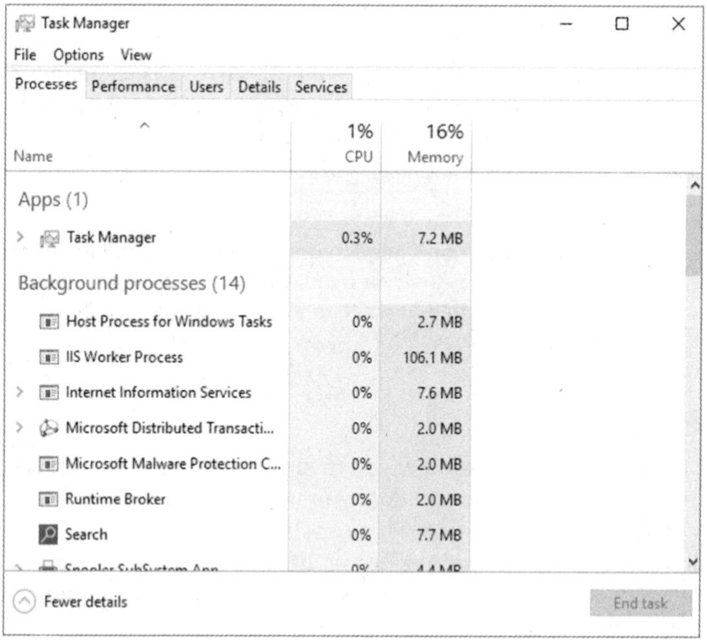

Performance Tab   One of the problems with using Performance Monitor to get a quick snapshot of system performance is that you have to add counters to a chart. Most system administrators are too busy to take the time to do this when all they need is basic CPU and memory information. That's where the Performance tab of Task Manager comes in. Using the Performance tab, you can view details about how memory is allocated on the computer and how much of the CPU is used (see Figure 16.11).

FIGURE 16.11   Viewing CPU and memory performance information using Task Manager

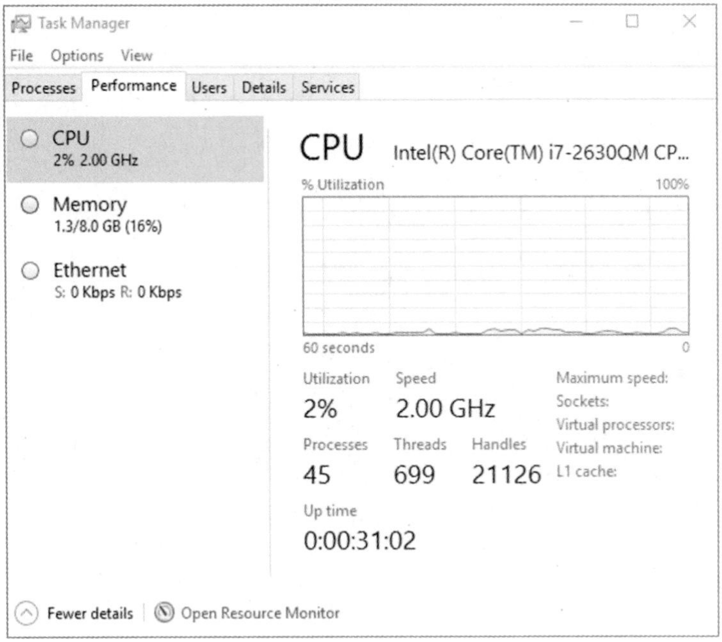

Users Tab   The Users tab (see Figure 16.12) lists the currently active user accounts. This is particularly helpful if you want to see who is online and quickly log off or disconnect users. You can also view all of the services and applications that are being used by that user. As you can see in Figure 16.12, the Administrator account has a lot of services that are running on this system.

FIGURE 16.12 Viewing user information using Task Manager

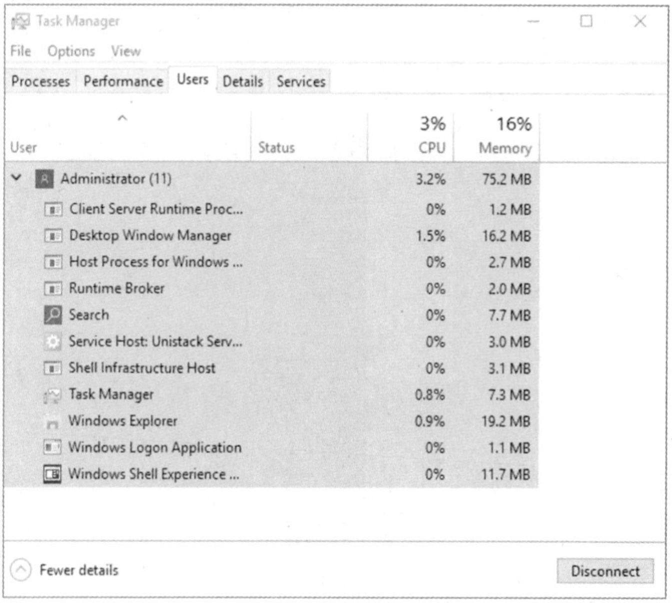

Details Tab The Details tab (see Figure 16.13) shows you what applications are currently running on the system. From this location, you can stop an application from running by right-clicking the application and choosing Stop. You also have the ability to set your affinity level here. By setting the affinity, you can choose which applications will use which processors on your system.

FIGURE 16.13   Viewing applications that are currently running using Task Manager

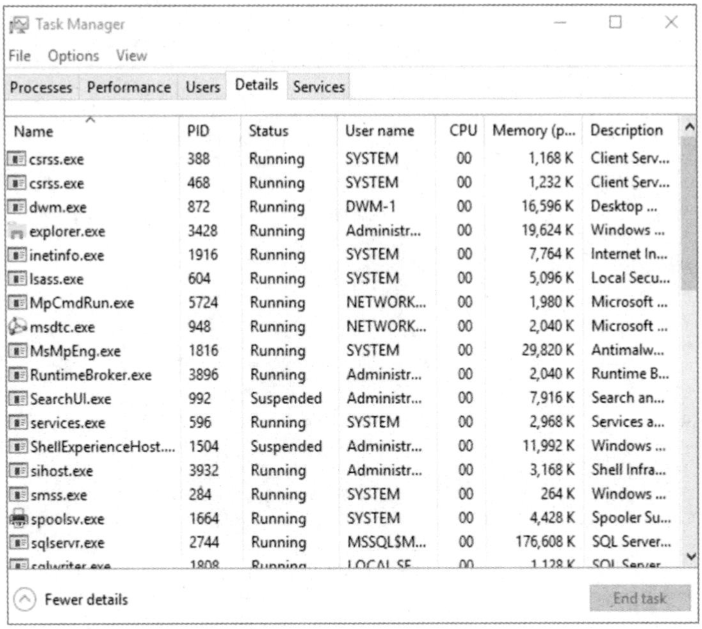

Task Manager

File   Options   View

Processes   Performance   Users   **Details**   Services

Name	PID	Status	User name	CPU	Memory (p...	Description
csrss.exe	388	Running	SYSTEM	00	1,168 K	Client Serv...
csrss.exe	468	Running	SYSTEM	00	1,232 K	Client Serv...
dwm.exe	872	Running	DWM-1	00	16,596 K	Desktop ...
explorer.exe	3428	Running	Administr...	00	19,624 K	Windows ...
inetinfo.exe	1916	Running	SYSTEM	00	7,764 K	Internet In...
lsass.exe	604	Running	SYSTEM	00	5,096 K	Local Secu...
MpCmdRun.exe	5724	Running	NETWORK...	00	1,980 K	Microsoft ...
msdtc.exe	948	Running	NETWORK...	00	2,040 K	Microsoft ...
MsMpEng.exe	1816	Running	SYSTEM	00	29,820 K	Antimalw...
RuntimeBroker.exe	3896	Running	Administr...	00	2,040 K	Runtime B...
SearchUI.exe	992	Suspended	Administr...	00	7,916 K	Search an...
services.exe	596	Running	SYSTEM	00	2,968 K	Services a...
ShellExperienceHost....	1504	Suspended	Administr...	00	11,992 K	Windows ...
sihost.exe	3932	Running	Administr...	00	3,168 K	Shell Infra...
smss.exe	284	Running	SYSTEM	00	264 K	Windows ...
spoolsv.exe	1664	Running	SYSTEM	00	4,428 K	Spooler Su...
sqlservr.exe	2744	Running	MSSQL$M...	00	176,608 K	SQL Server...
sqlwriter.exe	1808	Running	LOCAL SE...	00	1,128 K	SQL Server...

Fewer details   End task

Services Tab   The Services tab (see Figure 16.14) shows you what services are currently running on the system. From this location, you can stop a service from running by right-clicking the service and choosing Stop. The Open Services link launches the Services MMC.

FIGURE 16.14   Viewing services information using Task Manager

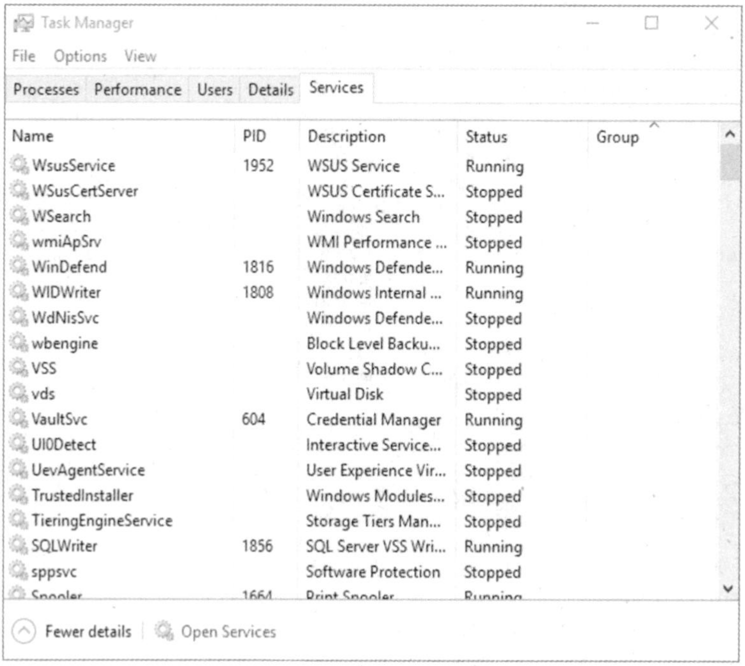

Task Manager				— ☐ ✕
File Options View				
Processes Performance Users Details **Services**				
Name	PID	Description	Status	Group ^ ^
WsusService	1952	WSUS Service	Running	
WSusCertServer		WSUS Certificate S...	Stopped	
WSearch		Windows Search	Stopped	
wmiApSrv		WMI Performance ...	Stopped	
WinDefend	1816	Windows Defende...	Running	
WIDWriter	1808	Windows Internal ...	Running	
WdNisSvc		Windows Defende...	Stopped	
wbengine		Block Level Backu...	Stopped	
VSS		Volume Shadow C...	Stopped	
vds		Virtual Disk	Stopped	
VaultSvc	604	Credential Manager	Running	
UI0Detect		Interactive Service...	Stopped	
UevAgentService		User Experience Vir...	Stopped	
TrustedInstaller		Windows Modules...	Stopped	
TieringEngineService		Storage Tiers Man...	Stopped	
SQLWriter	1856	SQL Server VSS Wri...	Running	
sppsvc		Software Protection	Stopped	
Spooler	1664	Print Spooler	Running	
⌄ Fewer details	Open Services				

The Task Manager tabs can be different on Windows Client machines. For example, Windows 7 has six tabs and Windows 10 has seven tabs.

As you can see, Task Manager is useful for providing important information about the system quickly. Once you get used to using Task Manager, you won't be able to get by without it!

Make sure that you use Task Manager and familiarize yourself with all that it can do; you can end processes that have become intermittent, kill applications that may hang the system, view NIC performance, and so on. In addition, you can access this tool quickly to get an idea of what could be causing you problems. Event Viewer and Performance Monitor are both great tools for getting granular information on potential problems.

Event Viewer

Event Viewer is also useful for monitoring network information. Specifically, you can use the logs to view any information, warnings, or alerts related to the proper functioning of the network. You can access Event Viewer by selecting Administrative Tools ➤ Event Viewer. Clicking any of the items in the left pane displays the various events that have been logged for each item. Figure 16.15 shows the contents of the Directory Service log.

Each event is preceded by a blue *i* icon. That icon designates that these events are informational and do not indicate problems with the network. Rather, they record benign events such as Active Directory startup or a domain controller finding a global catalog server.

FIGURE 16.15   Event Viewer

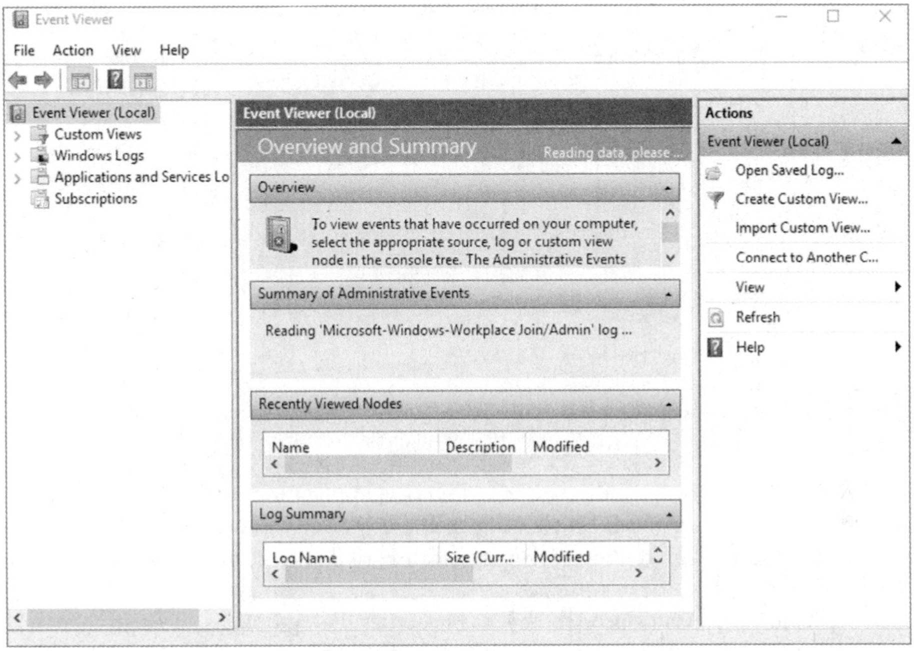

A yellow warning icon or a red error icon, both of which are shown in Figure 16.16, indicate problematic or potentially problematic events. Warnings usually indicate a problem that wouldn't prevent a service from running but might cause undesired effects with the service in question. For example, I was configuring a site with some fictional domain controllers and IP addresses. My local domain controller's IP address wasn't associated with any of the sites, and Event Viewer generated a warning. In this case, the local domain controller could still function as a domain controller, but the site configuration could produce undesirable results.

FIGURE 16.16 Information, errors, and warnings in Event Viewer

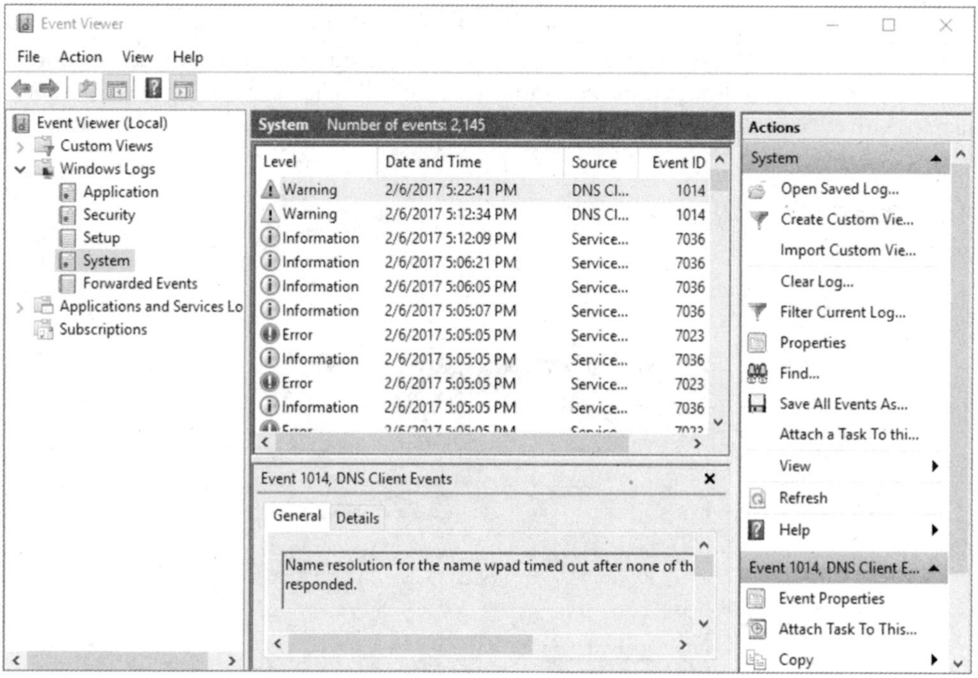

Error events almost always indicate a failed service, application, or function. For instance, if the dynamic registration of a DNS client fails, Event Viewer will generate an error. As you can see, errors are more severe than warnings because, in this case, the DNS client cannot participate in DNS at all.

Double-clicking any event opens the Event Properties dialog box, as shown in Figure 16.17, which displays a detailed description of the event.

FIGURE 16.17   An Event Properties dialog box

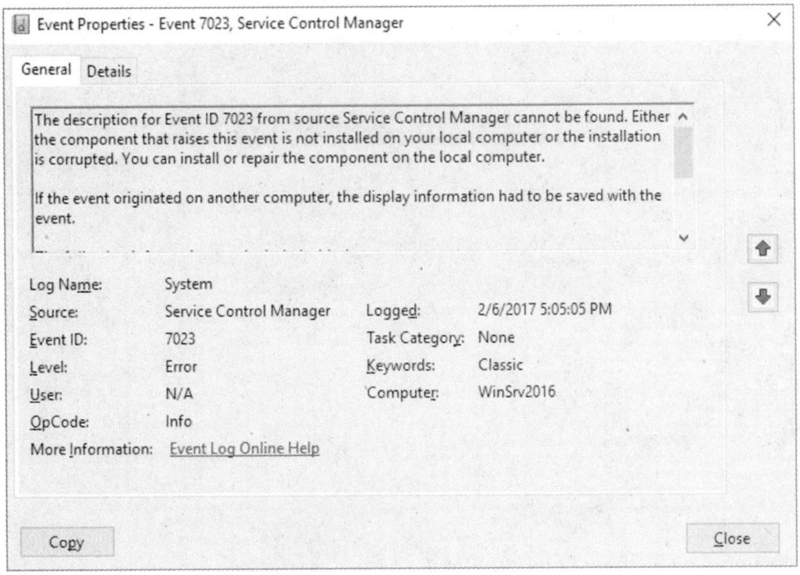

Event Viewer can display thousands of different events, so it would be impossible to list them all here. The important points of which you should be aware are the following:

- Information events are always benign.
- Warnings indicate noncritical problems.
- Errors indicate show-stopping events.

Let's discuss some of the logs and the ways you can view data.

Applications and Services   The *applications and services logs* are part of Event Viewer where applications (for example, Exchange) and services (DNS) log their events. DFS events would be logged in this part of Event Viewer. An important log in this section is the DNS Server log (see Figure 16.18). This is where all of your DNS events get stored.

FIGURE 16.18 The applications and services DNS Server log

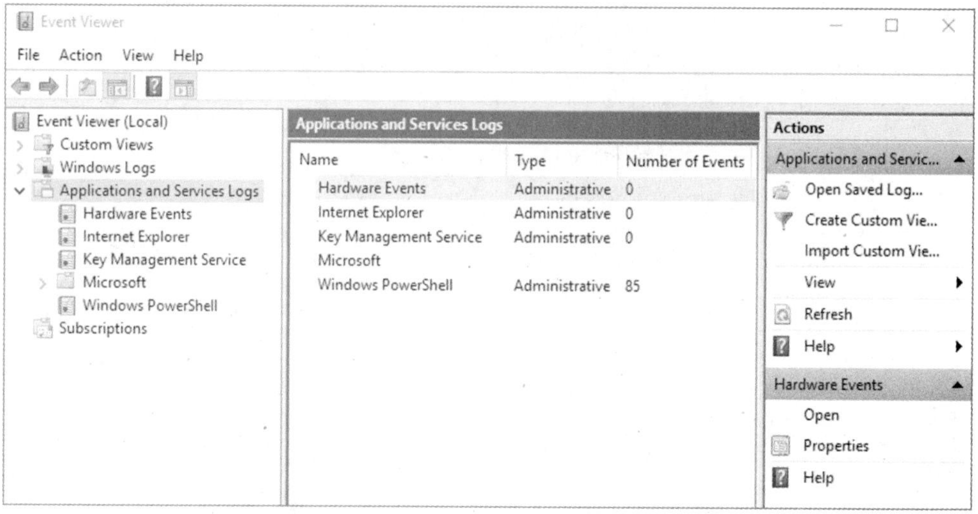

Custom Views *Custom views* allow you to filter events (see Figure 16.19) to create your own customized look. You can filter events by event level (critical, error, warning, and so on), by logs and by source. You also have the ability to view events occurring within a specific timeframe. This allows you to look only at the events that are important to you.

FIGURE 16.19 Create Custom View dialog box

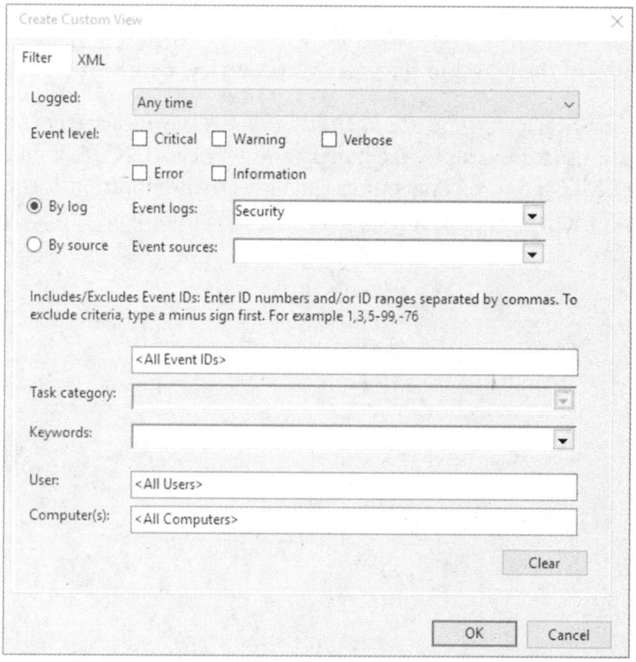

Subscriptions   *Subscriptions* allow a user to receive alerts about events that you predefine. In the Subscription Properties dialog box (see Figure 16.20), you can define what type of events you want notifications about and the notification method. The Subscriptions section is an advanced alerting service to help you watch for events.

FIGURE 16.20   Subscription Properties dialog box

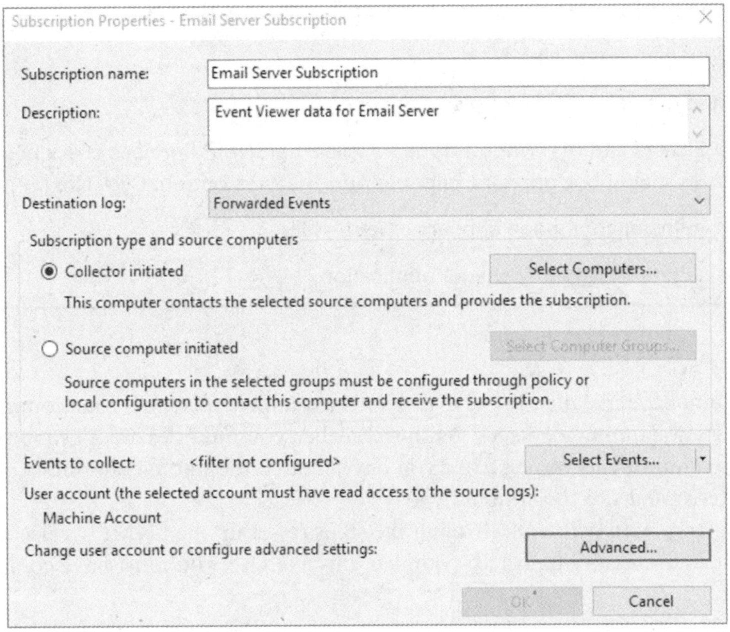

Simple Network Management Protocol

The *Simple Network Management Protocol (SNMP)* is a TCP/IP protocol monitor. The SNMP service creates trap messages that are then sent to a trap destination. One way you might use SNMP is to trap messages that don't contain an appropriate hostname for a particular service.

When you set up SNMP, you set up communities. *Communities* are groupings of computers that help monitor each other.

Windows Server 2022 includes SNMP with the operating system. To install the service, you must use Server Manager. In Exercise 16.2, you will walk through the process of installing the SNMP service.

EXERCISE 16.2

Installing SNMP

1. Open Server Manager.

2. Click option number 2, Add Roles And Features. If you see the Before You Begin screen, just click Next.

3. Choose role-based or feature-based installation and click Next.

4. Choose your server and click Next.

5. Click Next at the Select Server Roles screen.

6. When the Select Features window appears, click the SNMP Services check box. If an Add Features dialog box appears, click the Add Features button. Click Next.

7. The Confirm Installation page appears. Click Install.

8. Click Close. Exit the Server Manager application.

Now that you have installed the SNMP service, you have to set up your community so that you can start trapping messages. As stated earlier, communities are a grouping of computers to help monitor each other. After you have created the initial community, you can add other computer systems to the community.

In Exercise 16.3, you will walk through the steps to set up the SNMP service and also set up your first community name. To complete this exercise, you must have completed Exercise 16.2.

EXERCISE 16.3

Configuring SNMP

1. Open Computer Management by pressing the keyboard's Windows Key and selecting Administrative Tools ➢ Computer Management.

2. Expand Services And Applications. Click Services. In the right pane, double-click SNMP Service.

3. The SNMP Service Properties window will open. Click the Traps tab. In the Community Name box, enter **Community1**. Click the Add To List button.

4. Click the General tab. Click the Start button to start the service. Click OK.

5. Close Computer Management.

Using Resource Monitor

The Resource Monitor is another utility that allows you to view some of the resources on your server. You can access the Resource Monitor by going into the Administrative tools and choosing Resource Monitor or by typing **Resmon.exe** in the Run box.

Resource Monitor is a method of viewing Performance Monitoring data in a quick to view format. One advantage to using the Resource Monitor is that you can choose items that are affecting the systems performance and the view will change to show that item along with the totals.

As seen in Figure 16.21, you can use Resource Monitor to watch the system's CPU, Memory, Disk, and Network. There are five tabs that show you the different components. Figure 16.21 shows the Overview tab. The Overview tab allows you to watch all four hardware components in one window. Now let's take a look at each tab (which represents a component).

FIGURE 16.21   Resource Monitor

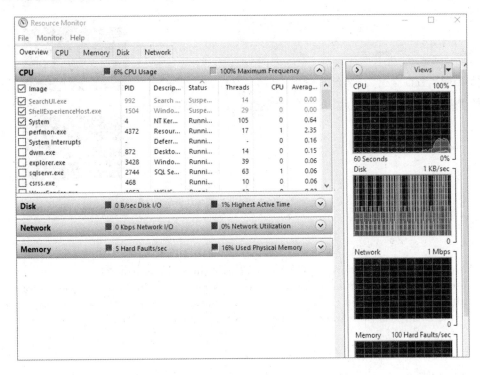

CPU The CPU tab (shown in Figure 16.22) will show you the total percentage of the CPU being used in a green color, and it will show you the Maximum Frequency of the CPU in blue.

FIGURE 16.22 Resource Monitor CPU tab

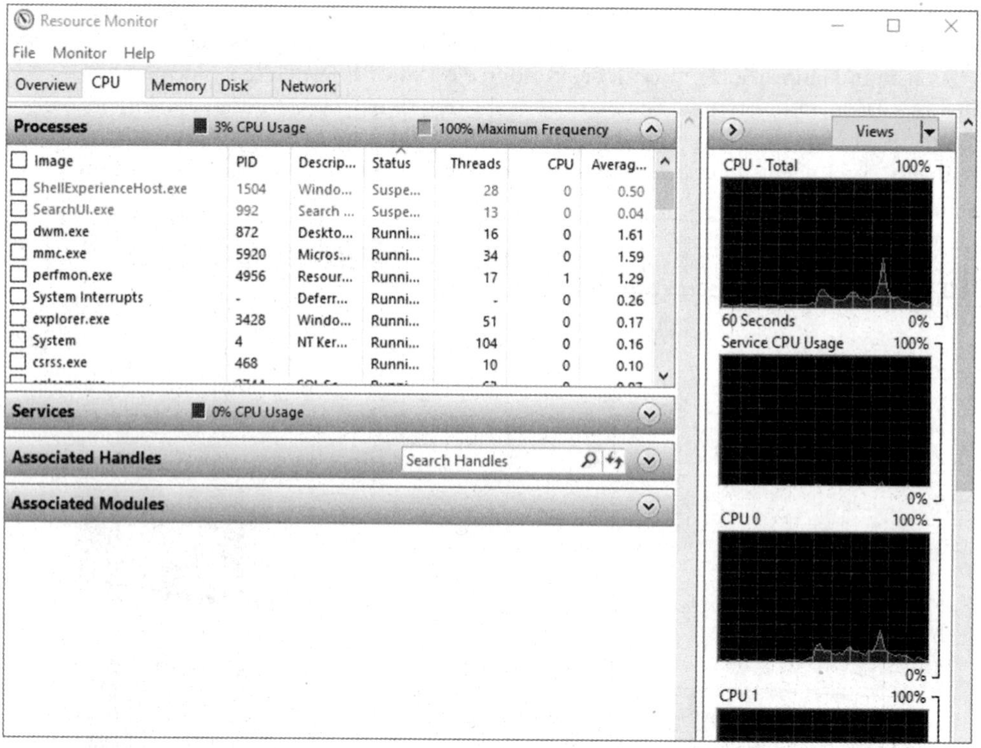

Memory This tab (shown in Figure 16.23) will show you how much memory is being used. When looking at the Resource Overview Memory window, there are two colors that you need to monitor. The current physical memory that is being used will be shown in the color green. The Standby Memory is shown in the color blue.

FIGURE 16.23   Resource Monitor Memory tab

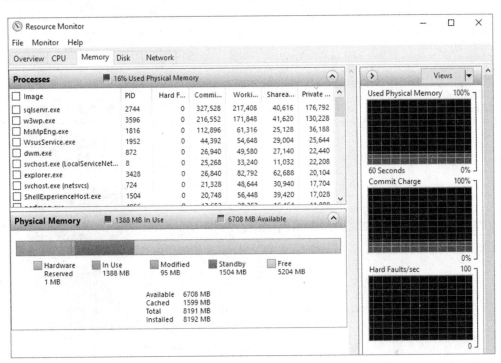

Disk   The Disk tab (shown in Figure 16.24) will show you the total current Input/
Output in the color green and it will show you the highest activity time. The current
disk activity will be shown in green and the highest activity in blue.

FIGURE 16.24   Resource Monitor Disk tab

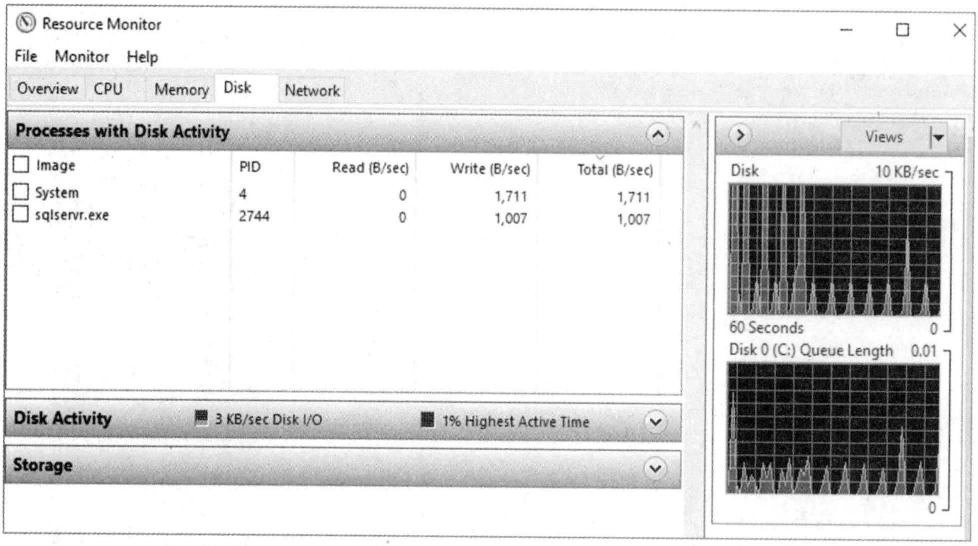

Network   The Network tab (shown in Figure 16.25) shows you how the network traffic is operating. The window will show you the percentage of network capacity and the total current network traffic.

FIGURE 16.25   Resource Monitor Network tab

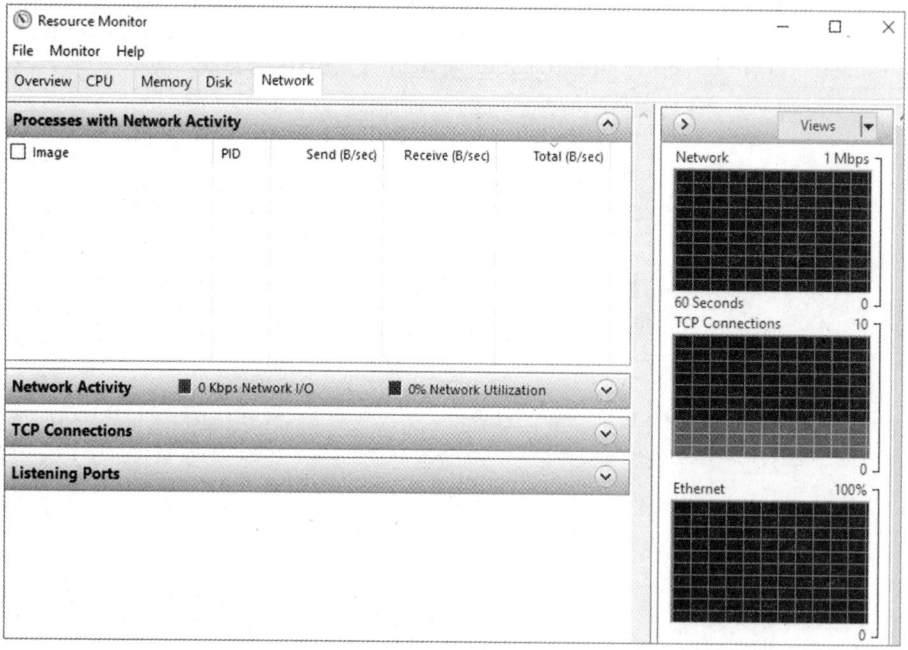

Windows Admin Center

The Windows Admin Center runs in a web browser and manages Windows Server 2022, Windows Server 2019, Windows Server 2016, Windows Server 2012 R2, Windows Server 2012, Windows 11, Windows 10, Azure Stack HCI, and more through the Windows Admin Center gateway that is installed on Windows Server or a domain-joined Windows 10/11 machine, or by using your Azure portal. It is a free product and can be downloaded from the Microsoft Evaluation Center at `www.microsoft.com/en-us/evalcenter/ evaluate-windows-admin-center`.

It should be noted that the Windows Admin Center complements System Center and should not be used as a replacement. The gateway manages the servers by using Remote PowerShell and WMI over WinRM. The gateway is included with the Windows Admin Center download.

There are a few benefits to using the Windows Admin Center:

Simplifies Server Management   It allows you to manage your servers and clusters with current versions of familiar tools such as Server Manager.

Works with Hybrid Solutions   It integrates with Azure to help you connect your on-premises servers to cloud services.

Streamlines Hyperconverged Management   Windows Admin Center can streamline the management of Azure Stack HCI or Windows Server hyperconverged clusters. It allows you to use simplified workloads to create and manage VMs, Storage Spaces Direct volumes, software-defined networking, and more.

The Windows Admin Center will operate only on Google Chrome and Microsoft Edge browsers. While the Windows Admin Center runs in a browser, it does not require Internet access to operate.

The Windows Admin Center dashboard shows the performance of a cluster and resource utilization on a server. It can run Remote Desktop, Event Viewer, and File Explorer, as well as handle a variety of administrative tasks, such as:

- Certificate management
- Firewall administration
- Local user and group setups
- Network setting monitoring
- Process management
- Registry edits
- Roles and features control
- Storage handling
- Virtual switch and Hyper-V VM administration
- Windows services management
- Windows Update management

As of this writing, the Windows Admin Center cannot manage certain roles, such as Active Directory, Dynamic Host Configuration Protocol (DHCP), Domain Name System (DNS), and Internet Information Services (IIS). The Windows Admin Center also comes with a PowerShell console that allows you to run scripts.

The Windows Admin Center uses role-based access control to restrict features from certain users. Windows Admin Center supports three roles:

Administrator   This role allows the user to access most of the Windows Admin Center tools without the need for PowerShell or Remote Desktop access.

Hyper-V Administrators   This role allows the user to only adjust Hyper-V VMs and switches.

Readers   This role only allows users to see server settings and information, without making any changes.

Deploy a Windows Admin Center Gateway Server

The Windows Admin Center has a number of different installation options that are available. The installation types include:

Local Client   On a local Windows 10 client that has connectivity to the managed servers. Operating system includes Windows 10/11.

Gateway Server   On a designated gateway server; can access the Windows Admin Center from any client browser that has connectivity to the gateway server. Operating systems include Windows Server Semi-Annual Channel, Windows Server 2016, Windows Server 2019, and Windows Server 2022.

Managed Server   On a managed server to remotely manage the server or a cluster in which it's a member node. Operating systems include Windows Server Semi-Annual Channel, Windows Server 2016, Windows Server 2019, and Windows Server 2022.

Failover Cluster   Windows Admin Center is deployed in a failover cluster to enable high availability of the gateway service. Operating systems include Windows Server Semi-Annual Channel, Windows Server 2016, Windows Server 2019, and Windows Server 2022.

Installing Windows Admin Center on a domain controller is not supported.

There are some Server versions that need additional preparation before they are ready to manage with Windows Admin Center. These include:

- Windows Server 2012 and 2012 R2
- Microsoft Hyper-V Server 2016
- Microsoft Hyper-V Server 2012 R2

Some of the prerequisites for preparing to run Windows Admin Center on these server versions include, but are not limited to:

- Enabling Remote Management
- Enabling File Server Role
- Enabling Hyper-V Module for PowerShell

For more information, check out Microsoft's website at

```
https://learn.microsoft.com/en-us/windows-server/manage/
windows-admin-center/deploy/prepare-environment
```

Windows Admin Center settings consist of user-level and gateway-level settings. Any changes to a user-level setting will affect only the current user's profile and changes to a gateway-level setting will affect all users who use that Windows Admin Center gateway. User-level settings include several tabs:

Account Tab   You can see the credentials that were used to authenticate to Windows Admin Center.

Personalization Tab   You can change your user interface theme.

Language/Region Tab   You can change the language and region formats that are displayed.

Suggestions Tab   You can review suggestions about Azure services and features.

Advanced Tab   Gives Windows Admin Center extension developers more capabilities.

General Tab   You can set the session to expire after a certain amount of time inactive.

Gateway settings include several tabs:

Extensions Tab   Only gateway administrators can see and change the setting in this tab. Any changes made here change the gateway configuration and will affect all users who use that particular gateway. Administrators can install, uninstall, or update gateway extensions.

Access Tab   You can configure who is allowed to access the Windows Admin Center gateway. You can also include an identity provider that is used to authenticate users.

Azure Tab   You can register the gateway with Azure to enable Azure integration features.

Shared Connections Tab   This tab allows you to configure a list of connections that will be shared across all the users of the Windows Admin Center gateway.

WebSocket Validation Tab   You can validate their WebSocket connections and customize condition settings.

The Windows Admin Center gateway service has several roles who can access the Windows Admin Center gateway service:

Gateway Users   Can connect to the Windows Admin Center gateway service to control the servers through that gateway, but they cannot change the authentication mechanism or the permissions used to access the gateway.

Gateway Administrators   Can configure user access and how those users are authenticated by the gateway. Only gateway administrators are able to view and configure the Access settings in Windows Admin Center.

Windows Admin Center CredSSP   This is an additional role specific to the management of the Credential Security Support Provider protocol (CredSSP). Administrators are registered with the Windows Admin Center CredSSP endpoint and have permissions to carry out predefined CredSSP operations. This is useful when installing Windows Admin Center in desktop mode, where by default, only the user account that installed Windows Admin Center is given these permissions.

Enabling PowerShell Remoting

PowerShell is one way to remotely configure and maintain Windows 10/11. It is becoming more and more popular as newer versions of Windows get released. You need to make sure that your Windows systems (including Windows 10/11) can accept remote PowerShell commands. If this feature is not already enabled on your system, you can enable it by running the **Enable-PSRemoting** cmdlet. To enable remote PowerShell commands, you must be an administrator when running the cmdlet. After PowerShell is enabled, you can then enter a PowerShell session on the Windows 10/11 system by using **New-PSSession**. To exit the PowerShell session when completed, run the **Exit-PSSession** cmdlet.

Many PowerShell commands do not require an active PowerShell session when running commands remotely (as long as remote commands are enabled). If you are running a PowerShell command that has the computer name in the command, you can specify the Windows client machine in the command. For example, the following PowerShell command shows the computer name (our Windows client systems are named Computer01 and Computer02):

```
Restart-Computer -ComputerName "Computer01," "Computer02," "localhost"
```

Now that you can connect and run commands on a remote Windows client system, you can also run scripts on Windows 10/11. After you write a PowerShell script (a file that ends in .ps1) for Windows 10/11, you can then run that command remotely by using the **Invoke-Command** cmdlet. The following example is running a PowerShell script on a Windows client machine named Computer01:

```
Invoke-Command -ComputerName Computer01 -FilePath c:\Scripts\DataCollect.ps1
```

If you would like to see additional commands and information about PowerShell remote connections, visit Microsoft's website:

```
http://docs.microsoft.com/en-us/powershell/scripting/
learn/remoting/running-remote-commands?view=powershell-6
```

Configure CredSSP or Kerberos Delegation for Second-Hop Remoting

So, what is second-hop remoting? It's when you are in a PowerShell Remoting session and you attempt to access a resource that is outside of that remote computer, as shown in Figure 16.26.

FIGURE 16.26 Second-hop remoting

You log into Server1. Then from that server you start a remote PowerShell session to connect to Server2. You run a command on Server2 that tries to access a resource on Server3. However, even though you have already authenticated to the remote session by supplying your username and password, you may get an Access Denied message when attempting to access the resources on Server3.

There are several ways to address this issue. I will be discussing CredSSP, Kerberos constrained delegation, and Just Enough Administration (JEA).

Credential Security Support Provider (CredSSP)

Credential Security Support Provider (CredSSP) is used for authentication issues. It stores the credential information onto the remote server. In our example, that would be on Server2. It provides an encrypted Transport Layer Security Protocol channel. But there are some pros and cons with using it. CredSSP has some security vulnerabilities in that it may open up your network to credential attacks and if that remote system is hacked, then the attacker may have access to your credentials. By default, CredSSP is disabled on both server and client computers and should only be used in trusted networks. CredSSP works on all servers with Windows Server 2008 or later, and it does require that both the client and server roles be configured and it will not work with the Protected Users group.

In order for CredSSP to work, you must first identify which servers can be entrusted. To specify those servers, you will want to modify the settings in the Group Policy Editor MMC snap-in. The settings that control delegation can be found under Computer Configuration | Administrative Templates | System | Credentials Delegation.

The following types of credentials that control delegation can be found in the Group policy settings:

Default Credentials   These are the credentials that are acquired when the user first logs on to Windows.

Fresh Credentials   These are the credentials that the user is prompted for when starting an application.

Saved Credentials   These are the credentials that are saved by using Credential Manager.

Kerberos-Constrained Delegation (KCD)

To make the second hop, you can use legacy-constrained delegation (not resource-based) by configuring Kerberos-constrained delegation (KCD) with the option Use Any Authentication Protocol to allow the protocol transition. KCD is an authentication protocol that you can set up for delegating client credentials for specific service accounts. If you are planning on using SharePoint 2019 Analysis Services and Power Pivot data, you will need to configure KCD. KCD allows a service account to impersonate another service account, and this allows access to specific resources.

Again, as with everything, there are some pros and cons to using KCD. KCD does not require any special coding and the credentials are not stored. However, to configure it requires Domain Administrator access, and it doesn't support the second hop for WinRM. It must be configured on the Active Directory object of the remote server (in our example, Server2) and it cannot cross domains or forests, so it's limited to one domain. KCD requires rights to update objects and service principal names (SPNs). Also, the remote server (in our example, Server2) can acquire a Kerberos ticket to Server3 on behalf of the user without user intervention.

Configure Just Enough Administration (JEA) for PowerShell Remoting

Just Enough Administration (JEA) lets you restrict what commands you can run during a PowerShell session. It can be used to help solve the second-hop issue. It can provide the best security; however, it requires more configuration. JEA is a security technology that enables delegated administration for anything managed by PowerShell. With JEA, you can:

- Reduce the number of administrators using virtual accounts or group-managed service accounts to perform actions on behalf of users.

- Limit what users can do by specifying which cmdlets, functions, and external commands they can run.

- Know what your users are doing by using transcripts and logs that show you what commands a user executed during their session.

Again, there are pros and cons with using JEA. When using a virtual account, there is no password maintenance. JEA requires Windows Management Framework (WMF) 5.0 or later, and it requires configuration on every intermediate server (in our example, Server2). You need to make sure that PowerShell Remoting is enabled and properly secured prior to using JEA.

If you just want to test your JEA configuration or perform simple tasks, you can use JEA in the same way as a regular PowerShell remoting session. For complex remoting tasks, Microsoft recommends using implicit remoting. Implicit remoting allows users to operate with the data objects locally. For more information on using JEA with implicit remoting, check out Microsoft's website at `https://learn.microsoft.com/en-us/powershell/scripting/learn/remoting/jea/using-jea?view=powershell-7.3#using-jea-with-implicit-remoting`.

To use JEA interactively, you need the following:

- The name of the computer that you are connecting to (can be the local machine)
- The name of the JEA endpoint registered on that computer
- The credentials that have access to the JEA endpoint on that computer

Once you have this information, you can start a JEA session by using the `New-PSSession` or the `Enter-PSSession` cmdlet. Here is an example:

```
$nonAdminCred = Get-Credential
Enter-PSSession -ComputerName localhost -ConfigurationName JEAMaintenance
-Credential $nonAdminCred
```

When the PowerShell prompt changes to `[localhost]: PS>` you are now interacting with the remote JEA session. You can run `Get-Command` to see which commands are available.

Azure Monitor

The Windows Admin Center allows you to expand your on-premises environments by working with hybrid Azure services. Windows Admin Center works with Azure Monitor to collect events and performance counters from a Windows server. You can run analytics and reporting in Azure and then take actions if a certain condition is detected.

Azure Monitor is software-as-a-service (SaaS). All of the supporting infrastructure runs in Azure and is handled by Microsoft. Azure Monitor was created to perform analytics, diagnostics, and monitoring. The core components of the infrastructure, such as collectors, metrics and logs store, and analytics, are run by Microsoft (see Figure 16.27).

Many of the following figures were taken directly from Microsoft's website. Since many of the figures point out specific issues, most of the figures were taken from Microsoft's website to demonstrate those points. For more information on Azure Monitor, please check out Microsoft's website at `https://learn.microsoft.com/en-us/azure/azure-monitor`.

FIGURE 16.27   Azure Monitor dashboard

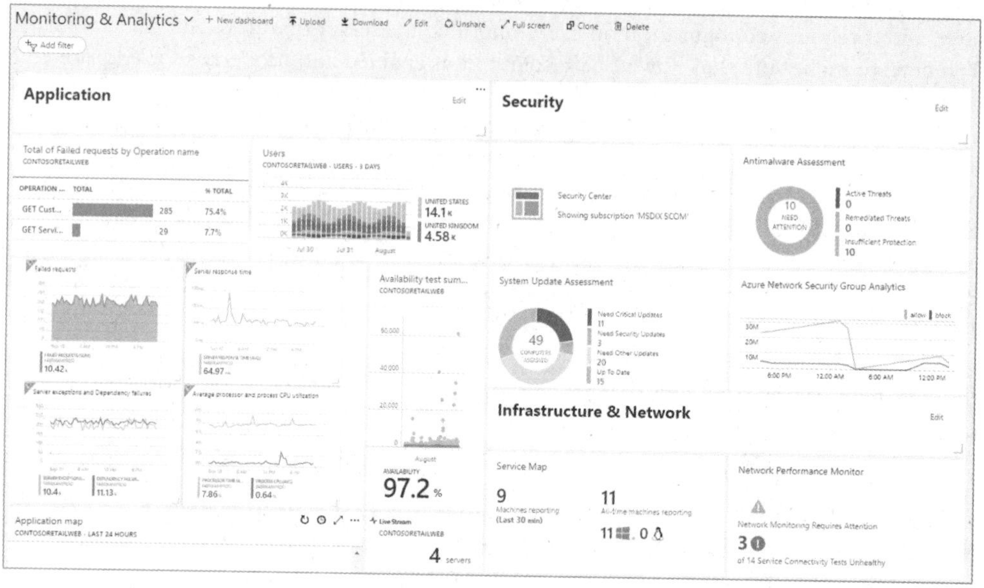

Here are a few things that you can do with Azure Monitor:

- With Application Insights, you can detect and diagnose issues across applications and dependencies.

- With VMs and Azure Monitor for Containers, you can compare infrastructure issues.

- By using Log Analytics for troubleshooting and deep diagnostics, you can monitor data.

- By using smart alerts and automated actions, you can support operations at scale.

- By using Azure dashboards and workbooks, you can create visualizations.

Figure 16.28 provides a view of how Azure Monitor works. In the middle are the two fundamental types of data used by Azure Monitor; these are the data stores for metrics and logs. On the left side are the sources that populate the data stores. On the right side are the various functions that Azure Monitor can perform with this collected data.

FIGURE 16.28   How Azure Monitor works

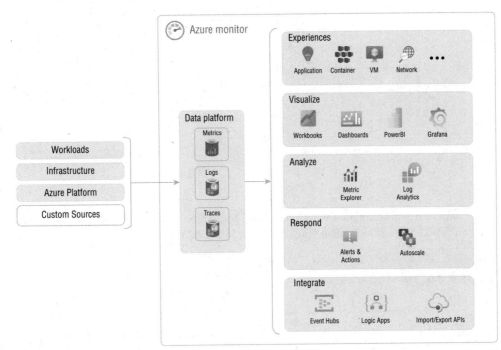

All the data that is collected by Azure Monitor fits into one of two fundamental types:

- *Metrics* are numerical values that express a piece of the system at a specific point in time. They are capable of supporting real-time scenarios.

- *Logs* contain other kinds of data, which is arranged into records with different sets of properties for each type.

Data collected by Azure Monitor will appear on the right-hand side of the Overview page in the Azure portal. You may notice several charts that display the performance metrics. Click any of the graphs to open the data in Metrics Explorer, shown in Figure 16.29, so that you can chart the values of various metrics over a given period of time. You can also view the charts or pin them to a dashboard to view them with other visualizations.

FIGURE 16.29   Metrics Explorer

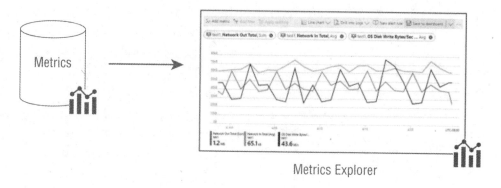

Metrics Explorer

Log data that is accumulated with Azure Monitor can be analyzed by using queries. You can create and test queries by using Log Analytics in the Azure portal (see Figure 16.30).

FIGURE 16.30   Log Analytics

Log Analytics

Azure Monitor collects data from a wide variety of sources, including data collected from the following tiers:

- **Application monitoring data:** Data about the performance and functionality of the code written, regardless of its platform

- **Guest operating system monitoring data:** Data about the operating system on which the application is running

- **Azure resource monitoring data:** Data about the operation of an Azure resource

- **Azure subscription monitoring data:** Data about the operation and management of an Azure subscription, including data on the health and operation of Azure itself

- **Azure tenant monitoring data:** Data about the operation of tenant-level Azure services, such as Azure Active Directory

- **Azure resource change data:** Data about changes within your Azure resources and how to address and triage incidents and issues

Azure Monitor starts collecting data as soon as you create an Azure subscription and start adding resources. The Activity log records when resources were created or modified, and the Metrics will show how the resources are performing.

Using the Data Collector API, Azure Monitor can collect log data from any REST client, which will allow you to create custom monitoring scenarios.

Azure Monitor includes several features and tools that can provide helpful insights into your applications and other resources. These features include Application Insights, Azure Monitor for Containers, and VM Insights.

Application Insights

Application Insights monitors the availability, performance, and usage of web applications that are hosted either in the cloud or on-premises. It uses Azure Monitor to provide insight into an application's operations and to diagnose problems without waiting for a user to report it. Application Insights includes connection points to several different development tools and can integrate with Visual Studio to support DevOps processes (see Figure 16.31).

FIGURE 16.31   Application Insights

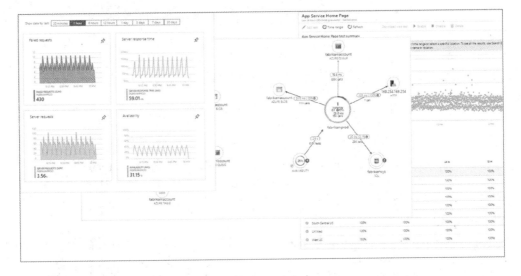

Container Insights

Container Insights is a feature intended to monitor the performance of container workloads. It shows performance visibility by collecting memory and processor metrics from controllers, nodes, and containers. Container logs are also collected (see Figure 16.32).

FIGURE 16.32   Container Insights

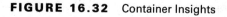

Container Insights monitors the performance and health of Azure Kubernetes Services or Azure Container Instances. It also collects container logs and inventory data about containers and their images.

VM Insights

VM Insights monitors Azure virtual machines (VMs) by analyzing the performance and health of the Windows and Linux VMs. This includes support for monitoring performance and application dependencies for VMs hosted on-premises or on another cloud provider (see Figure 16.33).

FIGURE 16.33   VM Insights

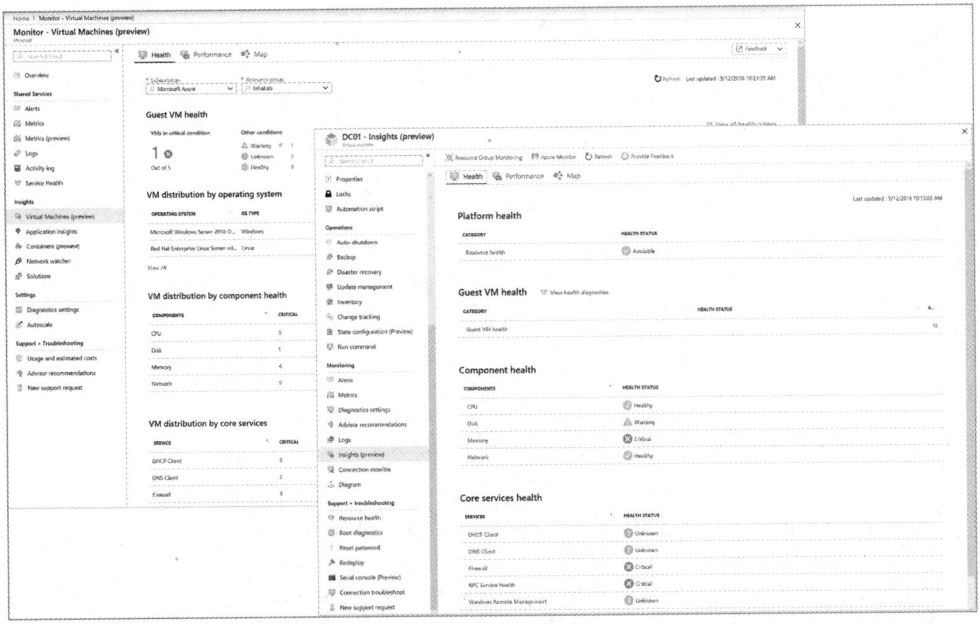

VM Insights delivers health monitoring for the guest Azure VMs when you're monitoring Windows and Linux virtual machines. It evaluates the health of major operating system components to determine the current health state. When it determines the guest VM is experiencing an issue, it will generate an alert.

In addition to monitoring data, Azure Monitor allows you to perform other functions to meet your needs:

- **Alerts:** Inform you of critical conditions and can attempt to take corrective action. Alert rules (see Figure 16.34) provide near-real-time alerting based on metric numeric values, while rules based on logs allow for complex logic across data from numerous sources. Alert rules use action groups, which contain unique sets of recipients and actions that can be shared across multiple rules.

FIGURE 16.34   Alerts

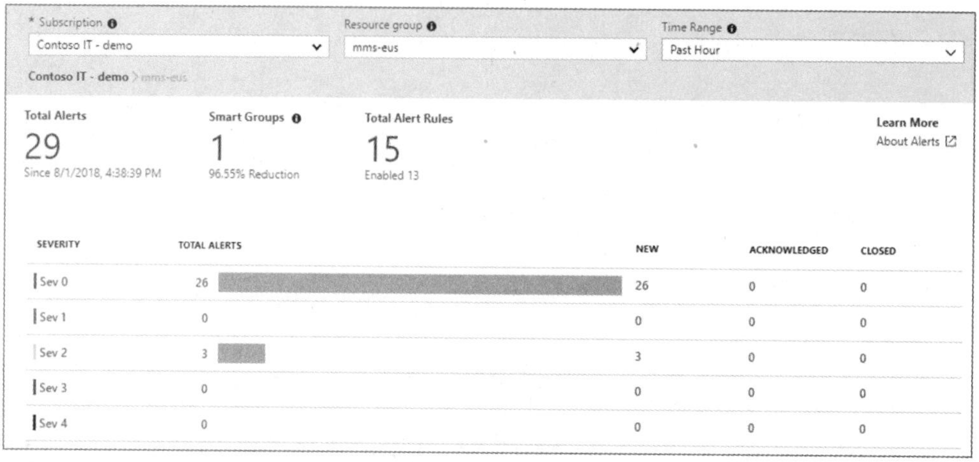

* Subscription ❶		Resource group ❶		Time Range ❶
Contoso IT - demo ▾		mms-eus ▾		Past Hour ▾

Contoso IT - demo › mms-eus

Total Alerts	Smart Groups ❶	Total Alert Rules		Learn More
29	**1**	**15**		About Alerts ⬏
Since 8/1/2018, 4:38:39 PM	96.55% Reduction	Enabled 13		

SEVERITY	TOTAL ALERTS		NEW	ACKNOWLEDGED	CLOSED
Sev 0	26		26	0	0
Sev 1	0		0	0	0
Sev 2	3		3	0	0
Sev 3	0		0	0	0
Sev 4	0		0	0	0

- **Autoscale:** Allows you to have just the right amount of resources needed in order to handle application workload. Azure Monitor allows you to create rules that use metrics collected to determine when resources will be added automatically to handle increases in workload and can save money by removing idle resources. You can specify a minimum and maximum number of instances and the logic for when to increase or decrease resources (see Figure 16.35).

FIGURE 16.35   Autoscale

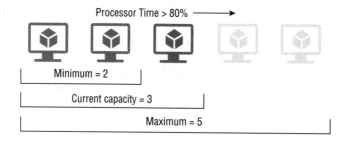

- **Azure dashboards:** Allow you to join different kinds of data, including metrics and logs, into a single pane in the Azure portal (see Figure 16.36).

FIGURE 16.36   Azure Monitor dashboard

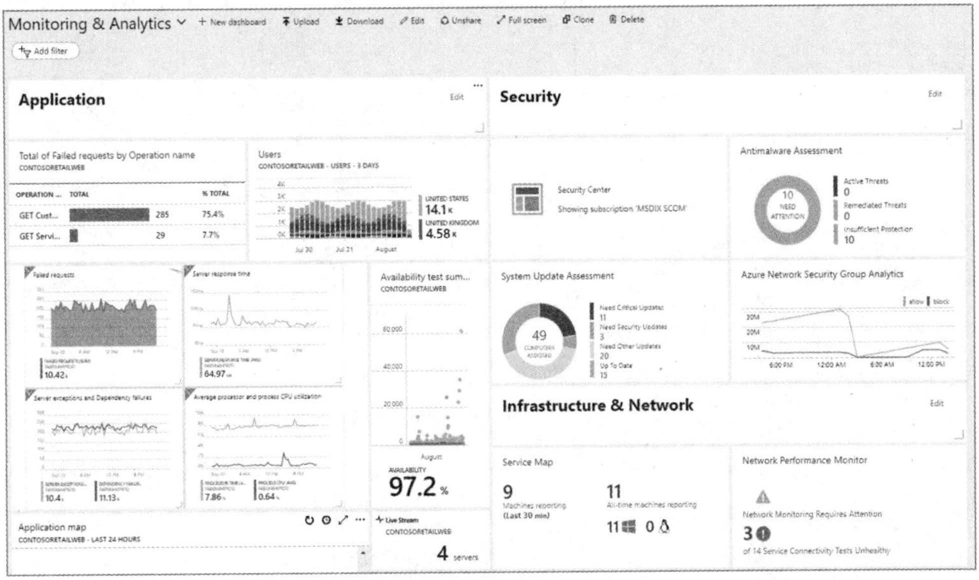

- **Workbooks:** Provide an area for data analysis with the ability to create visual reports (see Figure 16.37). Workbooks can use multiple data sources across Azure and combine them into one unified experience. You can use the workbooks that are provided with Insights, or you can create your own using a template.

FIGURE 16.37 Workbooks

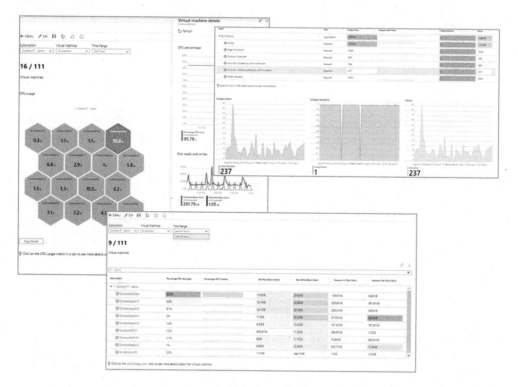

- **Power BI:** A business analytics service that provides interactive visualizations across a wide variety of data sources and makes data available to others either within or outside the organization. You can configure Power BI to import log data automatically from Azure Monitor (see Figure 16.38).

FIGURE 16.38   Power BI

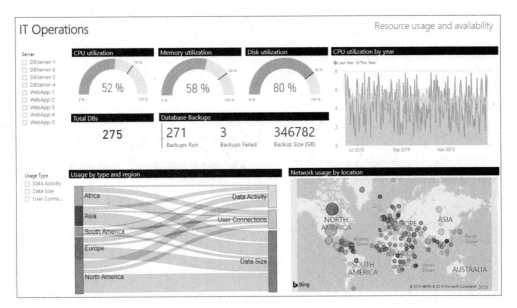

Using Azure Monitor, you can also import and export data to create custom solutions that use your monitoring data to suit your needs:

Azure Event Hubs   A streaming platform and event breakdown service that transforms and stores data using any real-time analytics provider. Use Event Hubs to stream Azure Monitor data to partner SIEM and monitoring tools.

Logic Apps   A service that allows the automation of tasks and processes using work-flows that combine different systems and services. Activities are available that read and write metrics and logs in Azure Monitor, which allows you to build workflows integrating with a variety of other systems.

Multiple APIs   These are available to read and write metrics and logs to and from Azure Monitor, as well as access generated alerts. You can also use them to configure and retrieve alerts.

System Insights

System Insights is a feature in Windows Server 2019/2022 that uses predictive analytics to analyze previous usage trends and predict future resource usage.

You can manage System Insights by using a Windows Admin Center extension or by using PowerShell. System Insights lets you configure each predictive capability separately in order to meet your needs. Using the Windows Admin Center dashboard allows you to view System Insights to display the four default capabilities as shown in Figure 16.39:

- CPU capacity forecasting
- Networking capacity forecasting
- Total storage consumption forecasting
- Volume consumption forecasting

FIGURE 16.39 System Insights on the Window Admin Center dashboard

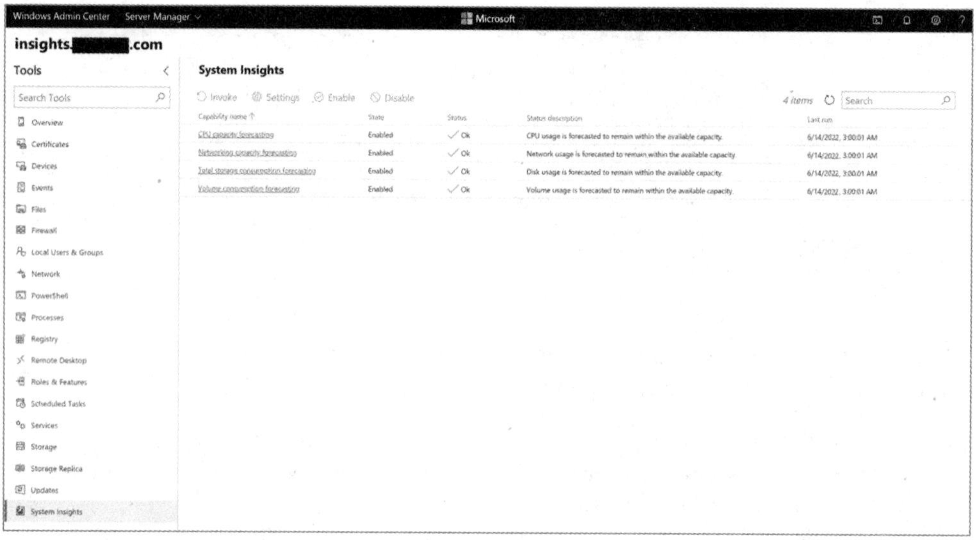

System Insights runs locally on Windows Server, where all of the data is collected, preserved, and analyzed and then predictions and forecasts are made. It collects and stores up to a year's worth of data. If you want to keep your data when upgrading the operating system, make sure that you use an in-place upgrade to retain that information. System Insights is available on any Windows Server 2019/2022 instance and runs on both host and guest machines, on any hypervisor, and in any cloud.

You can install System Insights by using the extension within Windows Admin Center, using Server Manager by adding the System Insights feature, or by using PowerShell using the following cmdlet:

```
Add-WindowsFeature System-Insights -IncludeManagementTools
```

For a complete list of cmdlets and parameters that can be used with System Insights using PowerShell, check out Microsoft's website at http://learn.microsoft.com/en-us/powershell/module/systeminsights/?view=windowsserver2022-ps.

Each capability can be either enabled or disabled. When you disable a capability, it will prevent that capability from being invoked. Invoked means that the capability will present an output that explains the results of the analysis or prediction. All capabilities are enabled by default. By selecting a capability in Windows Admin Center, you can modify the settings by selecting either the Enable or the Disable button.

Each capability will display an output that shows the status and status description. The status description provides an explanation for the given status. The capability statuses are:

Ok   Everything looks good.

Warning   No immediate attention required, but you should take a look.

Critical   You should take a look soon.

Error   An unknown problem caused the capability to fail.

None   No prediction was made. This could be due to a lack of data or any other capability-specific reason for not making a prediction.

Summary

This chapter began with a discussion of server optimization and reliability, including many tools that can help you monitor and manage your systems and the basics of troubleshooting your network in times of disaster.

Monitoring performance on servers is imperative to rooting out any issues that may affect your network. If your systems are not running at their best, your end users may experience issues such as latency, or worse, you may experience corruption in your network data. Either way, it's important to know how to monitor the performance of your servers. We also looked at ways you can optimize the operations of your servers to ensure that your end users experience adequate performance.

You also examined how to use the various performance-related tools that are included with Windows Server 2022. Tools such as Performance Monitor, Task Manager, Resource Monitor, Windows Admin Center, and Event Viewer can help you diagnose and troubleshoot system performance issues. These tools will help you find typical problems related to memory, disk space, and any other hardware-related issues you may experience.

Knowing how to use tools to troubleshoot and test your systems is imperative, not only to passing the exams but also to performing your duties at work. To have a smoothly running network environment, it is vital that you understand the issues related to the reliability and performance of your network servers and domain controllers.

Exam Essentials

Understand the methodology behind troubleshooting performance.   By following a set of steps that involves making measurements and finding bottlenecks, you can systematically troubleshoot performance problems.

Be familiar with the features and capabilities of the Windows Server 2022 Performance Monitor tool for troubleshooting performance problems.   The Performance Monitor administrative tool is a powerful method for collecting data about all areas of system performance. Through the use of performance objects, counters, and instances, you can choose to collect and record only the data of interest and use this information for pinpointing performance problems.

Know the importance of common performance counters.   Several important performance-related counters deal with general system performance. Know the importance of monitoring memory, print server, CPU, and network usage on a busy server.

Understand the role of other troubleshooting tools.   Windows Task Manager, SNMP, and Event Viewer can all be used to diagnose and troubleshoot configuration- and performance-related issues.

Understand how to troubleshoot common sources of server reliability problems.   Windows Server 2022 has been designed to be a stable, robust, and reliable operating system. Should you experience intermittent failures, you should know how to troubleshoot device drivers and buggy system-level software.

Know how to work with the Windows Admin Center and working with System Insights.   Windows Admin Center is a locally deployed, browser-based management tool that lets you manage your Windows Servers with no Azure or cloud dependency. It gives you full control over all aspects of your server infrastructure and is helpful for managing servers on private networks that are not connected to the Internet. I discussed how to use the Windows Admin Center to deploy a gateway server and how to configure a target machine as well as work with System Insights.

Know how to configure PowerShell Remoting, configure JEA for PowerShell Remoting, and work with second-hop remoting.   PowerShell remoting allows you to run any Windows PowerShell command on one or more remote computers. I discussed how to configure PowerShell Remoting and work with second-hop remoting using CredSSP, Kerberos delegation, and Just Enough Administration (JEA) for PowerShell.

Review Questions

1. You need to stop an application from running in Task Manager. Which tab would you use to stop an application from running?

    A. Performance

    B. Users

    C. Options

    D. Details

2. Your network has two computers named Computer1 and Computer2 that run Windows client. On Computer1, you need to run the `Invoke-Command` cmdlet to execute several PowerShell commands on Computer2. What should you do first?

    A. Add Computer1 to the Remote Management Users group on Computer2.

    B. Configure the Trusted For Delegation setting for the computer account of Computer2 from Active Directory.

    C. Run the `Enable-PSRemoting` cmdlet on Computer2.

    D. Run the `New-PSSession` cmdlet on Computer1.

3. You are the network administrator for your company. You want to look at some of the resources on the network. Specifically you want to watch the CPU and Memory. Which tool can you use to get the most detailed information about the resources?

    A. Performance Monitor

    B. System Hardware Monitor

    C. Event Viewer

    D. Server Manager

4. What command-line command would you type to start Performance Monitor?

    A. `Netmon.exe`

    B. `Perfmon.exe`

    C. `Performon.exe`

    D. `Resmon.exe`

5. You need to view which users are running applications on a server. Which application can you use to see what users are currently connected to the server?

    A. System Information

    B. Resource Monitor

    C. Performance Monitor

    D. Task Manager

6. You are the network administrator for a large organization. You need to watch some of the main components on a server. These include the Memory, CPU, Network, and Disk. What utility can you use to get a quick overview of these four components?

A. System Monitor

B. Resource Monitor

C. System Configuration

D. Event Viewer

7. What command-line command would you type to start Resource Monitor?

A. Netmon.exe

B. Perfmon.exe

C. Performon.exe

D. Resmon.exe

8. You have been hired as a consultant to research a network-related problem at a small organization. The environment supports many custom-developed applications that are not well documented. A manager suspects that some computers on the network are generating excessive traffic and bogging down the network. You want to do the following:

- Determine which computers are causing the problems.

- Record and examine network packets that are coming to/from specific machines.

- View data related only to specific types of network packets.

What tool should you use to accomplish all of the requirements?

A. Task Manager

B. Performance Monitor

C. Event Viewer

D. Microsoft Message Analyzer

9. You and a colleague are discussing a tool that was created to perform analytics, diagnostics, and monitoring. What is the name of this tool?

A. Azure Monitor

B. Azure Observer

C. Log Analytics

D. Log Analyzer

10. You need to disconnect a user running applications on a server. Which application can you use to disconnect a user currently connected to the server?

A. System Information

B. Resource Monitor

C. Performance Monitor

D. Task Manager

11. What are the four items that the Resource Monitor can watch? (Choose all that apply.)

    A. CPU

    B. Memory

    C. Disk

    D. Network

12. You are the administrator on your network. You have a user who has an application that keeps locking up. What utility can the user use to kill the application?

    A. Performance Monitor

    B. Task Manager

    C. Resource Monitor

    D. Event Viewer

13. You and a colleague are discussing a PowerShell Remoting session and the term used when attempting to access a resource that is outside of that remote computer. What is this known as?

    A. Single-hop remoting

    B. Second-hop remoting

    C. Jump remoting

    D. This cannot be done.

14. You are the network admin for your company. One of your users has called you and asked you to tell them how to start Resource Monitor. What command-line command would you tell them to type to start Resource Monitor?

    A. `Netmon.exe`

    B. `Perfmon.exe`

    C. `Performon.exe`

    D. `Resmon.exe`

15. You are the network admin for your company. One of your users has called you and asked you to tell them how to start Performance Monitor. What command-line command would you tell them to type to start Performance Monitor?

    A. `Netmon.exe`

    B. `Perfmon.exe`

    C. `Performon.exe`

    D. `Resmon.exe`

16. You are the network administrator for your company. You want to look at the CPU and Memory of one of your Windows 2016 servers. Which tool can you use to get the most detailed information about the CPU and Memory?

    A. Performance Monitor

    B. System Hardware Monitor

C. Event Viewer

D. Server Manager

17. You are the security administrator for your company. You see that a hacker has gained access to your network. You need to disconnect the hacker on a server. Which application can you use to disconnect the hacker currently connected to the server?

A. System Information

B. Resource Monitor

C. Performance Monitor

D. Task Manager

18. You and a colleague are discussing the installation options that are available for the Windows Admin Center. One of the installation types is a designated machine that can access the Windows Admin Center from any client browser that has connectivity to it. What is this installation type known as?

A. Failover cluster

B. Gateway server

C. Local client

D. Managed Server

19. You need to set the priority of an application that is running on the server. Which tab in Task Manager would you use to see the application's priority?

A. Performance

B. Users

C. Options

D. Details

20. You need to use Task Manager to see what the processor's affinity settings are. Which tab would you use to see the processor's affinity settings?

A. Performance

B. Users

C. Options

D. Details

Understanding Disaster Recovery

THE FOLLOWING AZ-801 EXAM OBJECTIVES ARE COVERED IN THIS CHAPTER:

✓ **Identify and remediate Windows Server security issues by using Azure Services**

- Monitor on-premises servers and Azure IaaS VMs by using Microsoft Sentinel
- Identify and remediate security issues on-premises servers and Azure IaaS VMs by using Microsoft Defender for Cloud

✓ **Manage backup and recovery for Windows Server**

- Back up and restore files and folders to Azure Recovery Services Vault
- Install and manage Azure Backup Server
- Back up and recover using Azure Backup Server
- Manage backups in Azure Recovery Services Vault
- Create a backup policy
- Configure backup for Azure VM using the built-in backup agent
- Recover VM using temporary snapshots
- Recover VMs to new Azure VMs
- Restore a VM

✓ **Implement disaster recovery by using Azure Site Recovery**

- Configure Azure Site Recovery networking
- Configure Site Recovery for on-premises VMs
- Configure a recovery plan
- Configure Site Recovery for Azure VMs
- Implement VM replication to secondary datacenter or Azure region
- Configure Azure Site Recovery policies

One of the most important tasks that an administrator has is to protect their network data. You, as an administrator, need to have a recovery plan in place in case of failure of your company's Azure and Windows systems.

The best way to protect any data is to make sure that the data can be restored in the event of a system failure or disaster. In this chapter, I will talk about ways to protect your data and your systems by using Azure.

Azure has a number of tools available to help identify and remediate security issues. I will briefly discuss some of them, and I will delve into how to identify and remediate Windows Server security issues by using Azure services such as Microsoft Sentinel and Microsoft Defender for Cloud.

I will discuss how to manage backup and recovery and how to back up and restore files and folders by using Azure Recovery Services Vault and Azure Backup Server. I will cover creating a backup policy and using the built-in backup agent. Then, I will discuss ways in which to recover and restore a VM.

Finally, I will discuss how to implement disaster recovery by using the Azure Site Recovery tool to recover networking and on-premises VMs, as well as how to create a recovery plan and policies.

Introduction to Azure Security

As of this writing, the Azure cloud platform has more than 200 products and services to choose from. With these tools you can create, run, and manage applications across on-premises networks or multiple clouds. Azure also has a wide variety of security tools and features that allow you to customize security in order to meet your company's security needs and make it possible to create secure solutions by using the Azure subscription platform.

Azure security has a number of built-in tools that can be organized into six different functional areas. I will discuss some of the tools and features. This is not a complete list. These functional areas include Applications, Compute, Identity and Access, Networking, Operations, and Storage.

Applications

This section will discuss some of the tools and features that are available for application security. I will briefly discuss some of these tools/features and what each is capable of.

Authentication and Authorization in Azure App Service

This feature allows users to sign into applications without having to change the code on the application backend. It can protect your apps and work with data on a per-user basis.

Layered Security Architecture

App developers can create a layered security approach to provide different levels of network access for each application tier. So, on an Azure Virtual Network (VNet) subnet that contains an App Service Environment, developers can use network security groups (NSGs) to restrict public access to applications.

Web Application Firewall

The Web Application Firewall (WAF) in the Azure Application Gateway can help protect web applications from common web-based attacks. WAF is preconfigured with protection from threats that have been listed as the top 10 common vulnerabilities by the Open Web Application Security Project (OWASP).

Web Server and Application Diagnostics

For both the web server and web applications, the App Service web app can provide diagnostics for logging information. These are categorized into two different diagnostics, one for the web server and one for applications. Information pertaining to application pools, worker processes, sites, application domains, and running requests can be seen in real time.

Compute

This section will discuss some of the tools and features that are available for compute security. I will briefly discuss some of these tools/features and what each is capable of.

Antimalware and Antivirus

With Azure IaaS, you can use antimalware software from a wide variety of security vendors to protect your VMs. Microsoft Antimalware for Azure Cloud Services and Virtual Machines can help you identify and remove viruses, spyware, and other threats as well as allow you to configure alerts. It can be deployed by using Microsoft Defender for Cloud, which I will be discussing in greater detail later in this chapter.

Azure Confidential Computing

Azure confidential computing lets you keep your data encrypted all the time by using Remote Attestation. Remote Attestation will verify that the VM has securely booted and is properly configured prior to unlocking your data.

Azure Site Recovery

Azure Site Recovery can help with replication, failover, and the recovery of workloads and apps from a secondary location if your primary location fails. I will be discussing Azure Site Recovery in greater detail later in this chapter.

Hardware Security Module

The Azure Key Vault can protect and manage the security of your critical secrets and keys by storing them. Permissions and access to these protected items are managed using Azure AD.

Virtual Machine Backup

Azure Backup can protect your application data. It will automatically allocate and manage your backup storage. You only pay for the storage you use since Azure Backup uses a pay-as-you-use model. I will be discussing Azure Backup in greater detail later in this chapter.

Virtual Networking

Azure requires VMs to be connected to VNet since VMs need network connectivity. A VNet allows many types of Azure resources to communicate securely with other VNets, the Internet, and on-premises networks. Each VNet is isolated to make sure that network traffic in your deployments is not accessible to other Azure customers.

VM Disk Encryption

You can encrypt your IaaS VM disks using Azure Disk Encryption for Linux VMs or Azure Disk Encryption for Windows VMs. Azure Disk Encryption for Windows VMs applies the Windows BitLocker feature while the Azure Disk Encryption for Linux VMs applies the DM-Crypt feature to provide volume encryption for the operating system and the data disks. This works with your Azure Key Vault subscription.

Identity and Access Management

This section will discuss some of the tools and features that are available for identity and access management. I will briefly discuss some of these tools/features and what each is capable of.

Secure Apps and Data

There are a number of tools/features that can secure applications and data, such as the following:

- Azure AD is a cloud-based identity and access management service that helps protect access to data in applications on-premises and in the cloud. It also helps with the management of users and groups. You can add other paid features by using the Basic, Premium P1, or Premium P2 edition.

- Cloud App Discovery allows you to identify cloud applications that are being used by your employees. It is a Premium feature of Azure AD.
- Azure Active Directory Identity Protection is a security tool that detects identity-based risks. It can provide a consolidated view of risk detections and possible vulnerabilities.
- Azure Active Directory Domain Services (Azure AD DS) allows you to add Azure VMs to a domain without having to deploy domain controllers. To access resources, your users sign in to the VMs by using their corporate AD credentials.
- Azure Active Directory B2C (Azure AD B2C) is a customer identity access management (CIAM) solution that allows your customers to sign in to all your apps using their existing social media accounts, or you can create new stand-alone credentials.
- Azure AD joined allows you to expand cloud capabilities to Windows 10/11 devices for centralized management. Allows users to connect to the corporate cloud using Azure AD, which will simplify access to apps and resources.

Secure Identity

Microsoft uses numerous security practices and technologies in order to help manage identity and access:

- Azure role-based access control (Azure RBAC) allows access to Azure resources. It is an authorization system that is incorporated into the Azure Resource Manager. Use Azure RBAC to grant access to cloud resources depending on the user's assigned role.
- Integrated identity management (hybrid identity) allows you to create a single user identity that will be used for authentication and authorization for all your resources across on-premises datacenters and cloud resources.
- Microsoft Authenticator is an app that allows for two-factor authentication to provide added security to your online accounts. It works with both Azure AD and Microsoft accounts.
- Multifactor authentication (MFA) is an authentication method used to gain access to either on-premises or cloud resources. It requires your users to provide two or more verification factors in order to gain access.
- Password policy enforcement allows you to configure password policies by using Group Policy settings. Using password policies allows you to set the length and complexity requirements, failed lockout attempts, and more.
- Token-based authentication is a protocol where your users will verify their identity and, in return, get a unique access token through Azure AD.

Networking

This section will discuss some of the tools and features that are available for Azure network security. I will briefly discuss some of these tools and features and what each is capable of.

Application Gateway

Microsoft Azure Application Gateway is a web traffic load balancer that enables you to manage traffic to your web applications. It offers an Application Delivery Controller (ADC) as a service for your application by providing numerous Layer 7 load-balancing capabilities.

Azure DNS

The Domain Name System (DNS) translates a website or service name to its IP address. Azure DNS is a hosting service for DNS domains. It provides name resolution by using the Azure infrastructure. You can manage your DNS records by using the same credentials, APIs, tools, and billing as your other Azure services by hosting your domains in Azure.

Azure Firewall

Azure Firewall is a cloud-based network security service that protects your Azure VNet resources. It provides threat protection for your cloud workloads that are running in Azure. Azure Firewall is offered in two SKUs: Standard and Premium.

Azure Load Balancer

Azure Load Balancer is a Layer 4 (TCP, UDP) load balancer that distributes incoming traffic among healthy instances that are defined in a load-balanced set. You can configure Azure Load Balancer for the following:

- Public load balancing, which will load-balance all incoming Internet traffic to VMs.

- Internal load balancing, which will load-balance traffic between VMs in a virtual network, between VMs in cloud services, or between on-premises computers and VMs in a cross-premises virtual network.

- Forward external traffic to a specific virtual machine

Azure Monitor Logs Network Security Groups (NSGs)

You can enable Event and Rule counter diagnostic log categories for NSGs. The Event log category will consist of entries for which NSG rules have been applied to the VMs and instance roles by using MAC addresses. The status for these rules will be collected every 60 seconds. The Rule counter diagnostic log category will consist of entries for how many times each NSG rule is applied.

Azure Private Link

Azure Private Link provides a private connection from a virtual network to Azure platform-as-a-service (PaaS), customer-owned, or Microsoft partner services. It secures the connection between endpoints in Azure by preventing data exposure to the public Internet. Traffic from your virtual network to the Azure service will stay on the Azure backbone network.

Azure Virtual Network (VNet)

An Azure virtual network (VNet) is basically your network in the cloud. VNet is similar to your on-premises network that you'd operate in your own datacenter. You control the IP address blocks, DNS settings, security policies, and route tables within this network.

ExpressRoute

ExpressRoute is an Azure service that lets you create private connections using a dedicated WAN link that allows you to extend your on-premises networks into the Microsoft cloud over a dedicated private connection. ExpressRoute connections do not go over the public Internet.

Internal DNS

By using the management portal or the network configuration file, you can manage the list of DNS servers that are used on your VNet. You can add up to 12 DNS servers for each VNet.

Microsoft Defender for Cloud

Microsoft Defender for Cloud analyzes the security state of your Azure resources for network security best practices. It will identify possible security vulnerabilities and create recommendations.

Network Access Control (NAC)

Network access control (NAC) is a security solution that limits connectivity to and from specific devices or subnets. It ensures that your VMs and services are only accessible to the users and devices that are allowed.

Network Security Group

A network security group (NSG) contains the security rules that allow or deny inbound/outbound network traffic to or from Azure resources. They are used to control traffic moving between subnets within a VNet and traffic between a VNet and the Internet.

Route Control and Forced Tunneling

Route Control is the ability to control the routing behavior on your VNet. You can configure user-defined routes that will allow you to customize inbound and outbound paths to ensure the most secure route possible. Forced tunneling is a mechanism that you can use to make sure that your services are not allowed to initiate a connection to devices on the Internet. Forced tunneling is commonly used to force outbound traffic to the Internet to go through on-premises security proxies and firewalls.

Traffic Manager

Azure Traffic Manager is a DNS-based traffic load balancer that allows you to distribute traffic to your public-facing applications across the global Azure regions. Service endpoints supported include Azure VMs, web apps, and cloud services. Traffic Manager uses Domain Name System (DNS) to direct client requests to the most appropriate endpoint depending on a traffic-routing method and the health of the endpoints.

VPN Gateway

A VPN gateway is a type of virtual network gateway that sends encrypted traffic across a public connection. In order to send network traffic between your VNet and your on-premises site, you need to create a VPN gateway for your VNet.

Web Application Firewall (WAF)

Web Application Firewall (WAF) is an Azure Application Gateway feature that provides protection to web applications that use the application gateway for standard Application Delivery Control (ADC) functions. It helps protect web applications by filtering and monitoring HTTP traffic between a web application and the Internet.

Operations

This section will discuss some of the tools that are available for security operations. I will briefly discuss some of these tools and features and what each is capable of.

Application Insights

Application Insights is an extension of Azure Monitor and provides Application Performance Monitoring (APM) features for web developers. APM tools are useful for monitoring applications from development, testing, all the way into production. With Application Insights, you can monitor your live web applications and detect performance issues. It has analytic tools that help you diagnose problems and create charts and tables.

Azure Advisor

Azure Advisor is an Azure service that will provide recommendations depending on the configuration of your deployed Azure services. It is a personalized cloud consultant that helps optimize your Azure deployments by analyzing your resource configurations and usage telemetry.

Azure Monitor

Azure Monitor collects, analyzes, and acts on telemetry data from your cloud and hybrid environments. You can use Azure Monitor to alert you of security-related events that are generated in your Azure Monitor logs. Azure Monitor logs let you see the metrics for your entire environment in one location. The logs are a useful tool in forensic and security analysis.

Azure Resource Manager

Azure Resource Manager is the Azure deployment and management service that consists of a management layer that allows you to create, update, and delete resources in your Azure account. You can set access controls, locks, and tags, in order to secure your resources after deployment.

Microsoft Defender for Cloud

Microsoft Defender for Cloud helps prevent, detect, and respond to threats to your Azure resources. It provides a single dashboard that shows you alerts and recommendations.

I will be going into more detail on Microsoft Defender for Cloud later in this chapter.

Microsoft Sentinel

Microsoft Sentinel is a cloud-native solution that is scalable and that provides:

- Security information and event management (SIEM)
- Security orchestration, automation, and response (SOAR)

It provides security analytics and threat intelligence as well as providing attack detection, threat visibility, proactive hunting, and threat response.

I will be going into more detail regarding Microsoft Sentinel later in this chapter.

Storage

This section will discuss some of the tools that are available for storage operations. I will briefly discuss some of these tools and features and what each is capable of.

Azure Role-Based Access Control (Azure RBAC)

Azure RBAC is an authorization system built into Azure Resource Manager that provides access management to Azure resources. It helps you manage who has access to resources and what they can do with those resources. Access is based on the security principles of need to know and least privilege.

Enabling Browser-Based Clients Using CORS

Cross-Origin Resource Sharing (CORS) is a browser mechanism that allows a server to specify the origins such as domain, scheme, or port, other than its own from which a browser should permit loading resources. The User Agent sends extra headers to ensure that any JavaScript code loaded from a certain domain is allowed to access resources located at another domain.

Encryption at Rest

Encryption at rest is a cybersecurity practice that will encrypt stored data to prevent unauthorized access. There are three Azure storage security features that provide encryption at rest:

Azure Disk Encryption for Linux VMs and Azure Disk Encryption for Windows VMs   Allow you to encrypt the operating system and data disks that are used by an IaaS VM.

Client-Side Encryption   The cybersecurity practice of encrypting data on the sender's side prior to being transmitted to a server such as a cloud storage service.

Storage Service Encryption (SSE)   Allows you to request that the storage service will automatically encrypt data when writing it to Azure Storage and decrypt it prior to its retrieval.

Encryption in Transit

Encryption in transit is a cybersecurity practice of protecting data when it's transmitted across networks. With Azure Storage, you can secure data by using transport-level encryption, wire encryption, or client-side encryption.

Shared Access Signature (SAS)

A shared access signature (SAS) is a Uniform Resource Identifier (URI) that allows restricted access rights to Azure Storage resources. You can allow a user to access objects in your storage account by setting permissions for a specified period and with a specified set of permissions. You can grant these permissions without having to share your account access keys.

Storage Analytics

For a storage account, Azure Storage Analytics performs logging and provides metrics data. This data can be used to trace requests, analyze trends, and diagnose problems with your storage account. Storage Analytics logs consist of detailed information pertaining to successful and failed requests to a storage service.

Now that I've briefly covered some of the tools and features of Azure security, let's delve more into using Microsoft Sentinel.

Microsoft Sentinel

Microsoft Sentinel was previously known as Azure Sentinel. It is a cloud-native solution that is scalable and that provides security information and event management (SIEM) and security orchestration, automation, and response (SOAR). It provides security analytics and threat intelligence as well as attack detection, threat visibility, proactive hunting, and threat response. To get started with Microsoft Sentinel, you need to have an Azure subscription.

Microsoft Sentinel collects data for users, devices, applications, and infrastructure, both on-premises and in multiple clouds. By using Microsoft's analytics and threat intelligence, you can detect threats and minimize false positives. You can investigate threats using artificial intelligence (AI) to hunt for suspicious activity as well as respond quickly to incidents.

Onboarding Global Prerequisites for Using Microsoft Sentinel

There are a few global prerequisites that must be met in order to onboard Microsoft Sentinel. First, you must have an active Azure subscription. You also need to have a Log Analytics workspace. To ensure that you can use all features and functionality of Microsoft Sentinel, you must raise the retention to 90 days. There are several permissions that must be met in order to work with Microsoft Sentinel. You need to have contributor permissions to the subscription where the Microsoft Sentinel workspace resides, you need either contributor or reader permissions on the resource group that the workspace belongs to, and you may need other permissions in order to connect to specific data sources.

Microsoft Sentinel Pricing

Microsoft Sentinel is billed depending on the volume of data analyzed in Microsoft Sentinel and how much is stored in Azure Monitor Log Analytics workspace. Data can be separated into Analytics Logs and Basic Logs:

- **Analytic Logs:** Support all data types covering full analytics, alerts, and no query limits. Analytics Logs can be monitored with scheduled alerts and analytics. There are two ways to pay for the Microsoft Sentinel Service: Pay-As-You-Go and Commitment Tiers.

- **Pay-As-You-Go:** You are billed per gigabyte (GB) for the volume of data used for security analysis in Microsoft Sentinel and stored in the Azure Monitor Log Analytics workspace.

- **Commitment Tiers:** You are billed on a fixed price depending on your selected tier. You can select different pricing tiers for Microsoft Sentinel and Azure Monitor Log Analytics depending on your specific needs.

- **Basic Logs:** Typically verbose and contain high-volume and low-security value data without the full capabilities of analytics logs.

To see the entire pricing matrix for Microsoft Sentinel, please check out Microsoft's website at `https://azure.microsoft.com/en-us/pricing/details/microsoft-sentinel`.

To onboard Microsoft Sentinel, you must first enable it and then set up data connectors. The data connectors will be used to monitor and protect the environment.

Enable Microsoft Sentinel

To enable Microsoft Sentinel:

1. Sign into the Azure portal at `https://portal.azure.com`.

2. Search for and select Microsoft Sentinel (as shown in Figure 17.1).

FIGURE 17.1   Selecting Microsoft Sentinel in Azure

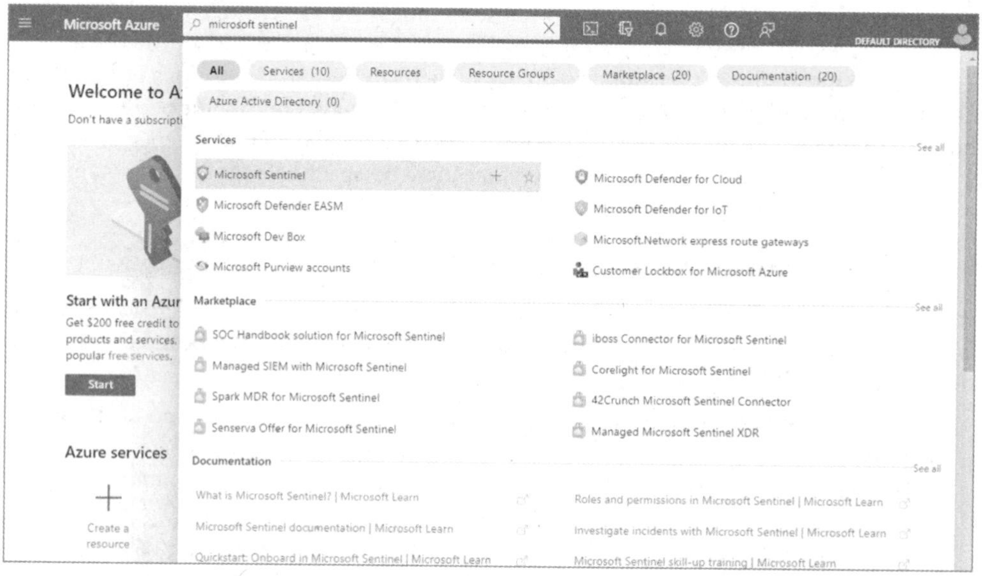

3. Click Add.

4. Select the workspace you want to use or you can create a new one (see Figure 17.2). You can run Microsoft Sentinel on more than one workspace, but the data is isolated to a single workspace.

FIGURE 17.2   Choosing a workspace

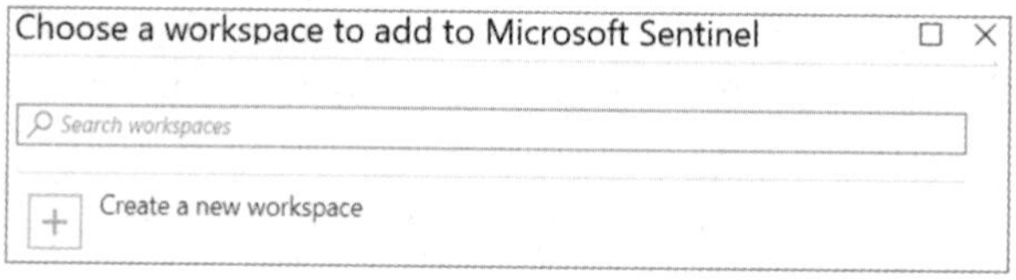

5. Select Add Microsoft Sentinel.

Microsoft Sentinel does not support moving the workspace to another resource groups or subscription once it's deployed. If you have already moved the workspace, you need to disable all active rules under Analytics and reenable them after 5 minutes. Microsoft states that this may be effective in most cases but that moving the workspace is not supported.

The next step is to set up your data connectors.

Set Up Data Connectors

Once Microsoft Sentinel is onboarded, you can use data connectors to start obtaining your information. Microsoft Sentinel comes with numerous out-of-the-box connectors for Microsoft services, which you can then integrate in real time.

Microsoft Sentinel obtains the data from services and apps by connecting to the service and then forwarding the events and logs to Microsoft Sentinel. For physical and virtual machines, you can install the Log Analytics agent or for firewalls and proxies, you can install the Log Analytics agent on a Linux Syslog server, and the agent will collect the log files and forward them onto Microsoft Sentinel.

To set up data connectors, perform the following:

1. From the main menu, select Data Connectors. This opens the data connectors gallery, as shown in Figure 17.3.

FIGURE 17.3   Microsoft Sentinel data connectors gallery

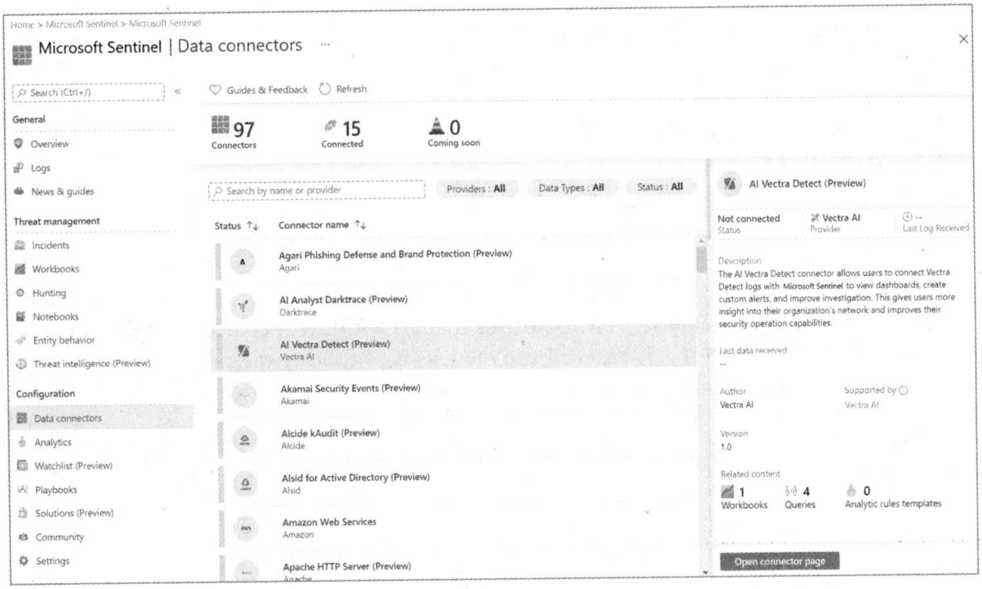

2. Select your desired data connector, and then click the Open Connector Page button.

3. The Connector page shows instructions for configuring the connector and any other instructions that may be necessary. Follow the installation instructions. Once connected, you will see a summary of the data in the Data Received graph and the connectivity status of the data types, as shown in Figure 17.4.

FIGURE 17.4   Microsoft Sentinel data received

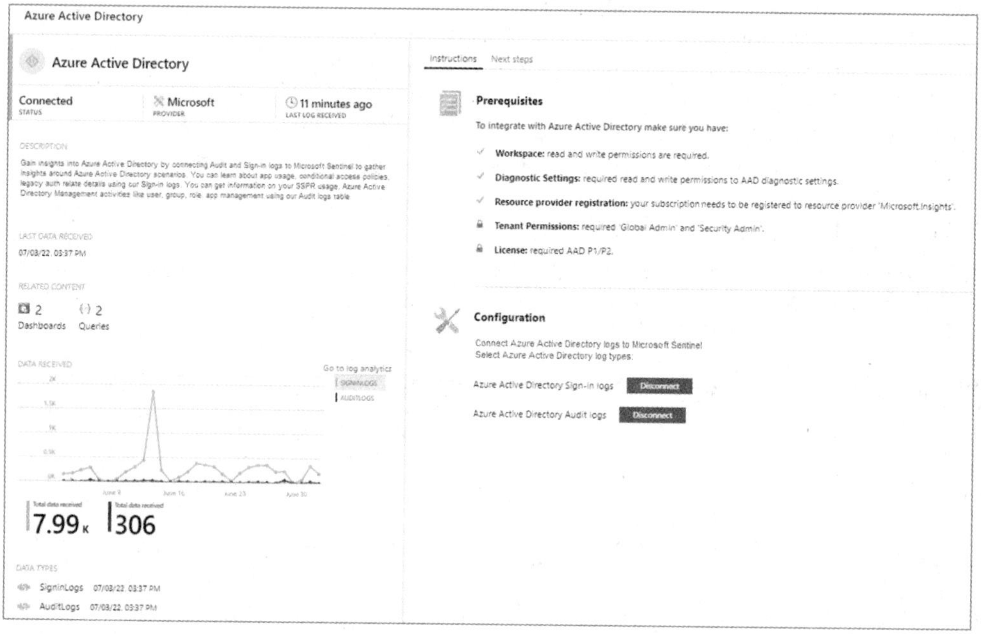

4. The Next Steps tab on the Connector page shows all the relevant built-in workbooks, sample queries, and analytics rule templates that go with the specified the data connector, as shown in Figure 17.5. You can use these as is or modify them—either way, you can immediately obtain insights across your data.

FIGURE 17.5   Microsoft Sentinel Next Steps tab

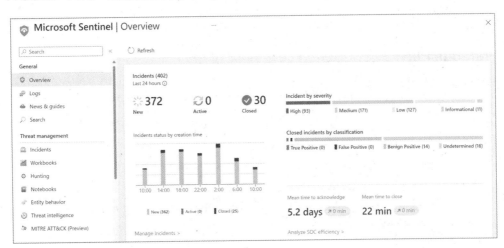

Once done, your data will start streaming into Microsoft Sentinel and you can start working with it.

To see what is happening with your environment, take a look at the Overview dashboard. In the Azure portal, select Microsoft Sentinel and then select the workspace you want to monitor, as shown in Figure 17.6.

FIGURE 17.6   Microsoft Sentinel Overview dashboard

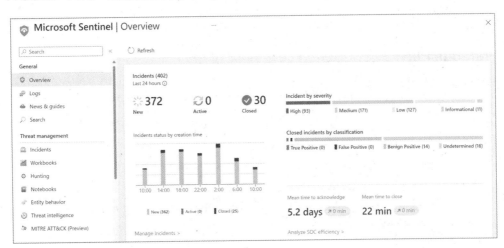

Now, let's take a look at how to identify and remediate security issues using Microsoft Defender for Cloud.

Microsoft Defender for Cloud

Microsoft Defender for Cloud helps you find and fix security vulnerabilities, block malicious activity by applying access and application controls, detect threats by using analytics, and if you are under attack, helps you respond. Microsoft Defender for Cloud has two main pillars for cloud security: Cloud Security Posture Management (CSPM) and Cloud Workload Protection Platform (CWPP).

Microsoft Defender for Cloud covers three important needs so that you can manage the security of workloads and resources both in the cloud and on-premises:

Continuously Assess   This allows you to know your security posture and identify and track vulnerabilities. It will provide you with a secure score, vulnerability assessments, assess inventory, regulatory compliance, and file integrity monitoring.

Secure   This allows you to harden resources and services using Azure Security Benchmarks and AWS Security Best Practices. It will provide you with security recommendations, just-in-time VM access, adaptive network hardening, and adaptive application control. It will provide you with step-by-step actions that need to be taken in order to protect your workloads from known security risks.

Defend   This allows you to detect and resolve threats to your resources and services. It will provide you with Microsoft Defender, security alerts, and integration with Microsoft Sentinel.

Pricing

Microsoft Defender for Cloud is free for the first 30 days, and the free features provide only limited security for your Azure resources only. Any usage beyond 30 days will be automatically charged. For more information on pricing, check out Microsoft's website at `http://azure.microsoft.com/en-us/pricing/details/defender-for-cloud`.

Prerequisites

In order to use Microsoft Defender for Cloud, you need to have an Azure subscription. You will only be able to see the information for resources that you have been assigned the Owner, Contributor, or Reader role for the subscription or for the resource group the resource is in.

To Enable Microsoft Defender for Cloud

To enable Microsoft Defender for Cloud, perform the following:

1. Sign into the Azure portal at `https://portal.azure.com`.

2. From the portal's menu, select Microsoft Defender for Cloud. The Overview page will open, as shown in Figure 17.7.

FIGURE 17.7 Microsoft Defender for Cloud Overview page

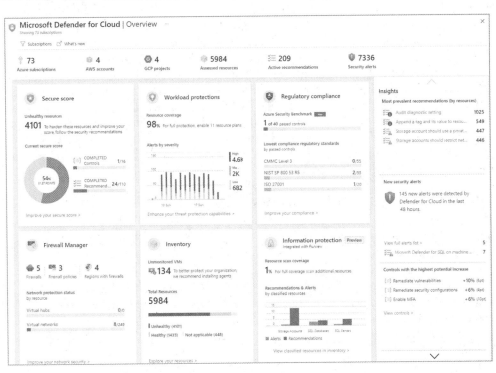

The Overview page is an interactive dashboard that provides a look at the security posture of your workloads and shows security alerts, coverage information, and more. You can select any section on the page to get more information. You can also view and filter the list of subscriptions by selecting the Subscriptions menu item. After launching Microsoft Defender for Cloud the first time, you will see a secure score, a list of hardening recommendations, which will show you ways in which you can improve the security of your connected resources, and an inventory of all the resources being assessed, along with a security posture of each one.

With Cloud Security Posture Management (CSPM), you can remediate security issues and improve your security posture using Microsoft Defender for Cloud. The CSPM posture management feature provides hardening assistance to help you enhance your security and visibility. As I mentioned earlier, Microsoft Defender for Cloud constantly measures your resources, subscriptions, and company for security issues and shows your security posture in secure score. The score will tell you your current security situation, the higher the score, the lower the identified risk level. CSPM has two different options that you can use: a free option and a premium option. Microsoft recommends enabling the premium option so that you can have full coverage and benefits.

There is a graph-based algorithm that scans the cloud security graph; this is called an attack path analysis. This will show you possible paths that an attacker may use to breach your workload. The attack path analysis will expose the paths and make recommendations on how to best remediate the problems to prevent the breach.

Many Azure services are monitored and protected without needing any deployment on Microsoft Defender for Cloud because it's an Azure-native service. However, you can add resources that are on-premises or in other public clouds. For Azure machines the deployment is directly managed, but for hybrid and multicloud environments, plans may be extended to non-Azure machines by using Azure Arc. Azure Arc is a bridge that expands the Azure platform in order to help build applications and services that have the flexibility to run across different platforms such as working on new and existing hardware, virtualization and Kubernetes platforms, IoT devices, and integrated systems.

Manage and Respond to Security Alerts

Microsoft Defender for Cloud gathers, evaluates, and integrates log data from your Azure resources such as firewalls and endpoint agents to detect threats and reduce false positives. With Microsoft Defender for Cloud's enhanced security features enabled, you can have Advanced Detection, which triggers security alerts.

Security alerts are the notifications that are produced by Microsoft Defender for Cloud and Defender for Cloud plans when threats are recognized in your cloud, hybrid, or on-premises environment.

Now, let's take a look at how you can manage your security alerts using Microsoft Defender for Cloud.

Manage Your Security Alerts

To manage your security alerts on Microsoft Defender for Cloud, perform the following:

1. From Defender for Cloud's overview page, at the top of the page, select the Security Alerts tile. You can also click the link on the sidebar. The Security Alerts page will open.

2. From here you can filter the alerts list by selecting any of the relevant filters. You can also add additional filters using the Add Filter option.

Respond to Security Alerts

You can now respond to security alerts. To do so, follow these steps:

1. From the Security Alerts list, select an alert. A side pane will open that will show you a description of the alert and all the resources that are affected.

2. Select View Full Details to view more information. You will see two separate panes: the left pane and the right pane. On the left pane, it will show you the title, severity, status, activity time, description of the suspicious activity, and the affected resource. On the right pane you will have two tabs: Alert Details and Take Action. The Alert details tab will show you information to help you investigate the issue such as the IP addresses,

files, and processes. The Take Action tab allows you to take further actions regarding the security alert, such as the following:

- **Inspect Resource Context:** Sends you to the resource's activity logs that support the security alert.

- **Mitigate The Threat:** Provides manual remediation steps for this security alert.

- **Prevent Future Attacks:** Offers security recommendations to help you reduce the attack surface, increase security posture, and thus prevent future attacks.

- **Trigger Automated Response:** Provides the option to trigger a logic app as a response to this security alert.

- **Suppress Similar Alerts:** Gives you the option to suppress future alerts with similar characteristics if the alert isn't relevant for your organization.

For a complete list of the security alerts you may receive from Microsoft Defender for Cloud and any Microsoft Defender plans that you have enabled, check out Microsoft's website at `https://learn.microsoft.com/en-us/azure/defender-for-cloud/alerts-reference#alerts-windows`.

Azure Logic Apps

For incident response, security programs consist of several workflows. Automation can improve security by making sure that steps are performed in a timely manner, that they are consistent, and that they match your predefined requirements. Microsoft Defender for Cloud has a workflow automation feature that can trigger Logic Apps on items such as security alerts and recommendations, and if there are any changes to regulatory compliance.

Azure Logic Apps is a platform-on-the-cloud service that allows you to create and run automated workflows with little to no coding. You can use the Visual Designer or you can pick from the prebuilt operations. Here are a few things that you can do with Azure Logic Apps:

- Move uploaded files from an SFTP or FTP server to Azure Storage.

- Route and process customer orders across on-premises systems and cloud services.

- Schedule and send email notifications using Microsoft 365 if a specific event happens.

Create a Logic App

Now, let's take a look at how to create a Logic App and define when it should automatically run. To do this, perform the following:

1. Sign in to the Azure portal at `https://portal.azure.com`.

2. From the portal's menu, select Microsoft Defender for Cloud; the Overview page will open.

3. From Defender for Cloud's sidebar, select Workflow Automation. Then, from this page you can create new automation rules and enable, disable, or delete existing ones.

4. To define a new workflow, select Add Workflow Automation. This will open the Options pane for your new automation. Here you can enter the following:

   - In the General section, enter information such as a Name, Description, Subscription, and Resource group.

   - In the Trigger Conditions section, complete fields such as Defender For Cloud Data Type, Alert Name Contains, and Alert Severity.

   - The Actions section is where you will configure the Logic App to be triggered. You can select the Logic Apps page to begin the Logic App creation process. This will take you to the Azure Logic Apps – Create Logic App page.

5. Select (+) Add.

6. Fill out all of the required fields and select Review + Create.

   You will get a message that the deployment is in progress. Wait for the Deployment Complete notification to appear, and then select Go To Resource from the notification.

7. Review the information you entered and click Create. In your new logic app, you can choose from built-in, predefined templates from the Security category, or you can define a custom flow of events to occur when this process is triggered. The Logic App Designer supports these Microsoft Defender for Cloud triggers:

   - **When A Microsoft Defender For Cloud Recommendation Is Created Or Triggered:** If your logic app relies on a recommendation that gets deprecated or replaced, your automation will stop working and you'll need to update the trigger.

   - **When A Defender For Cloud Alert Is Created Or Triggered:** You can customize the trigger so that it relates only to alerts with the severity levels that you are interested in.

   - **A Defender For Cloud Regulatory Compliance Assessment Is Created Or Triggered:** Trigger automations based on updates to regulatory compliance assessments.

8. Once you have defined your logic app, return to the workflow automation definition pane (Add Workflow Automation). Click Refresh.

9. Select your logic app and save the automation.

Vulnerability Scanner for Azure and Hybrid Machines

An essential component of all security programs is the identification and analysis of vulnerabilities. Microsoft Defender for Cloud consistently checks your connected machines to make sure that they are running vulnerability assessment tools. Microsoft Defender for Cloud includes vulnerability scanning at no extra charge. This scanner is powered by Qualys.

If a machine is found that is not running a vulnerability assessment solution, Microsoft Defender for Cloud will generate a security recommendation that states "Machines should have a vulnerability assessment solution." Use this recommendation to deploy the vulnerability assessment solution to your Azure VMs and Azure Arc–enabled hybrid machines.

How the vulnerability scanner extension works:

1. Deploy—Microsoft Defender for Cloud monitors your machines and provides recommendations on how to deploy the extension.

2. Gather information—The extension collects artifacts and sends them for analysis.

3. Analyze—Qualys's cloud service conducts the vulnerability assessment and sends its findings to Microsoft Defender for Cloud.

4. Report—The findings are listed in Microsoft Defender for Cloud.

Deploy the Integrated Scanner to Your Azure and Hybrid Machines

To deploy the integrated scanner to your Azure and hybrid machines, perform the following:

1. From the Azure portal, open Microsoft Defender for Cloud.

2. From Microsoft Defender for Cloud's menu, open the Recommendations page.

3. Select the recommendation "Machines should have a vulnerability assessment solution." Machines will appear in one or more of the following groups:

   - **Healthy Resources:** Microsoft Defender for Cloud has detected a vulnerability assessment solution running on the machines.

   - **Unhealthy Resources:** A vulnerability scanner extension can be deployed to the machines.

   - **Not Applicable Resources:** The vulnerability scanner extension is not supported on the machines.

4. From the list of unhealthy machines, select the ones to receive a vulnerability assessment solution and click Remediate.

5. Choose the recommended option "Deploy integrated vulnerability scanner" and click Proceed.

6. You'll be asked again for further confirmation. Click Remediate. It will only take a few minutes for the scanner extension to be installed on the selected machines and scanning will start as soon as the extension is deployed. Scans will run every 12 hours (this time interval cannot be changed).

Manage Backup and Recovery for Windows Server

Organizations can protect against data loss by using the practice of backup and recovery. A backup creates a copy of data that can be recovered in the event of a failure. Recovery involves restoring lost or damaged data to the original location from a backup.

Azure provides several different tools and services for backup and recovery. I am going to discuss three of these:

- **Azure Backup:** An Azure-based service that can back up and restore your data in the Microsoft cloud

- **Azure Backup Server:** Allows you to protect application workloads such as Hyper-V VMs, Microsoft SQL Server, SharePoint Server, Microsoft Exchange, and Windows clients by using a single console

- **Azure Recovery Services Vault:** A management entity that stores recovery points that are created over time and that provides an interface to perform backup-related functions

Azure Backup and Azure Site Recovery use a centralized management interface, known as the Backup Center, to make it easier to create policies to protect, monitor, and manage enterprise workloads across hybrid and cloud networks. This will be discussed in greater detail later in this chapter.

I am going to start by discussing Azure Backup.

Azure Backup

Azure Backup is an Azure-based service that you can use to back up and restore your data in the Microsoft cloud. By isolating backup data from original data and using accidental delete protection and multifactor authentication, you can protect your data from deletion and ransomware. You can manage and monitor Azure Backup by using the Backup Center. Azure Backup can be used on a pay-as-you-go basis to protect your workloads deployed in Azure, multicloud, and hybrid cloud deployments.

There are a number of items that you can back up using Azure Backup:

Azure Blobs   You can back up the overview of operational backup for Azure Blobs.

Azure Database for PostgreSQL Servers   You can back up Azure PostgreSQL databases and retain the backups for up to 10 years.

Azure Files Shares   You can back up the Azure File shares to a storage account.

Azure Managed Disks   You can back up the Azure Managed Disks.

Azure VMs   You can back up the entire Windows/Linux VMs (using backup extensions) or back up files, folders, and system state using the Microsoft Azure Recovery Services (MARS) agent.

On-premises   You can back up files, folders, and system state using the MARS agent. Or you can use the System Center Data Protection Manager (DPM) or Microsoft Azure Backup Server (MABS) agent to protect on-premises VMs (Hyper-V and VMware) and other on-premises workloads.

SQL Server in Azure VMs   You can back up the SQL Server databases running on Azure VMs.

Azure Backup Pricing

The size of the data you have backed up will determine the price. For VMs, the size calculation is based on the actual size of VM. This is the sum of all data in the VM, excluding temporary storage. When you back up files and folders, it's the size of the configured files and folders. When you back up a SQL Server, the size of the configured databases determine the size. For more information about pricing, please go to Microsoft's website at `https://azure.microsoft.com/en-us/pricing/details/backup`.

Azure Backup Key Benefits

There are a number of benefits to working with Azure Backup:

Automatic Storage Management   Hybrid environments often require heterogeneous storage—some on-premises and some in the cloud—but with Azure Backup, there is no charge for using on-premises storage devices. Azure Backup automatically allocates and manages backup storage, and it uses a pay-as-you-use model so that you pay only for the storage you use.

Backs Up Azure IaaS VMs   Delivers independent and isolated backups to help protect against accidental deletion. The backups are stored in a Recovery Services Vault (which will be discussed in greater detail a bit later in this chapter).

Centralized Monitoring and Management   Provides built-in monitoring and alerting capabilities in a Recovery Services vault. By using Azure Monitor, you can also increase the scale of your monitoring and reporting.

App-Consistent Backups   Application-consistent backup means that a recovery point has all the needed data to restore the backup copy quickly.

Keeps Data Secure   Provides solutions for securing data in transit and at rest.

Multiple Storage Options   Offers three types of replication options in order to keep your storage/data highly available:

Geo-redundant Storage (GRS)   The default and recommended replication option. GRS replicates your data to a secondary region, which is typically hundreds of miles away from the primary location of the source data. GRS provides a higher level of durability for your data, even if there's a regional outage, and it costs more than LRS.

Locally Redundant Storage (LRS)   Replicates your data by creating three copies and places them within a storage scale unit in a datacenter. All copies exist in the same region. LRS is a low-cost option for protecting your data from local hardware failures.

Zone-Redundant Storage (ZRS)   Replicates your data in availability zones; guarantees data residency and resiliency in the same region. ZRS has no downtime.

Offload On-premises Backup   Provides an easy solution for backing up your on-premises resources to the cloud. It is also scalable.

Retain Short and Long-Term Data   Use Recovery Services Vaults for short-term and long-term data retention.

Unlimited Data Transfer   There is no limit to the amount of inbound or outbound data you can transfer, and no charge for the data that's transferred. Outbound data refers to data that is transferred from a Recovery Services Vault during a restore operation.

Microsoft Azure Recovery Services (MARS) Agent

To back up and recover files, folders, volumes, or system state data from an on-premises computer to Azure, Azure Backup uses the Microsoft Azure Recovery Services (MARS) agent. MARS is also called the Azure Backup agent.

The main approach for backing up Azure VMs is to use an Azure Backup extension on the VM. This extension will back up the entire VM. But if you are looking to only back up certain files and folders on the VM, then install the MARS agent on the VM.

You can run the MARS agent:

Directly on on-premises Windows machines. These machines can back up directly to a Recovery Services Vault in Azure.

On Azure VMs that run Windows with the Azure VM backup extension. The agent will back up specific files and folders on the VM.

On a Microsoft Azure Backup Server (MABS) instance or a System Center Data Protection Manager (DPM) server. The machines and workloads will back up to MABS or DPM. Then, MABS or DPM will use the MARS agent to back up to a vault in Azure.

I will cover downloading and installing the MARS agent in greater detail when I discuss creating a Recovery Services Vault in the next section.

Azure Recovery Services Vault

A Recovery Services Vault is basically an Azure storage entity that holds data. It stores recovery points that have been created over a period of time, and provides an interface used to perform backup-related procedures, including performing on-demand backups, restores, and creating backup policies.

You can use Recovery Services Vaults to hold backup data for a number of Azure services such as IaaS VMs (Linux or Windows) and SQL Server in Azure VMs.

Backup Using the Recovery Services Vault

I will be covering these steps in greater detail; however, this is a brief overview on the steps needed to back up items using the Recovery Services Vault:

1. From the Azure portal, create a Recovery Services Vault, and from the Backup Goals section, select Files, Folders, and the System State.

2. Download the Recovery Services Vault credentials and agent installer to an on-premises machine.

3. Install the agent and use the downloaded vault credentials to register the machine to the Recovery Services Vault.

4. From the agent console on the client, configure the backup to specify what you want to back up, schedule the backup, and configure the retention policy (how long the backups should be retained in Azure).

Create a Recovery Services Vault

To create a Recovery Services Vault, perform the following:

1. Sign in to the Azure portal at `https://portal.azure.com`.

2. Search for Backup Center, and then go to the Backup Center dashboard.

3. On the Overview pane, as shown in Figure 17.8, select + Vault.

FIGURE 17.8   Backup Center Overview page

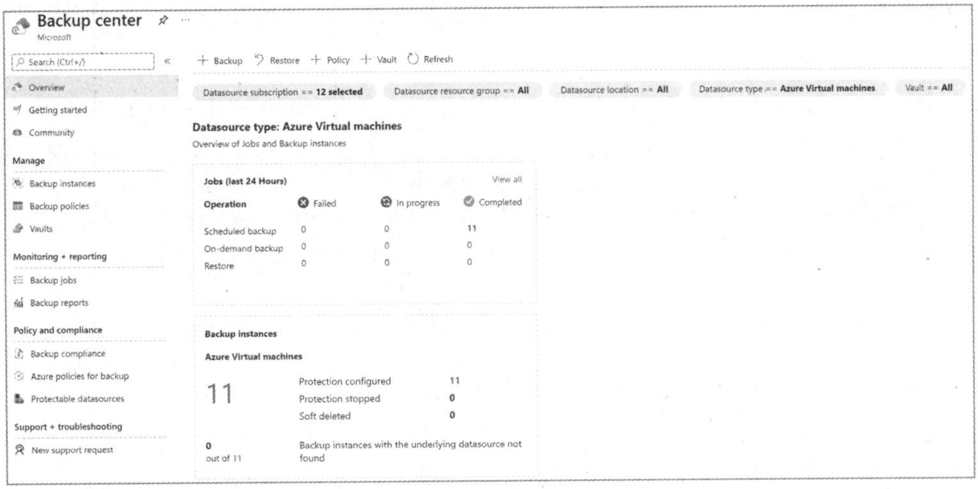

4. Select the Recovery Services Vault radio button and click the Continue button, as shown in Figure 17.9.

FIGURE 17.9 Start: Create Vault page

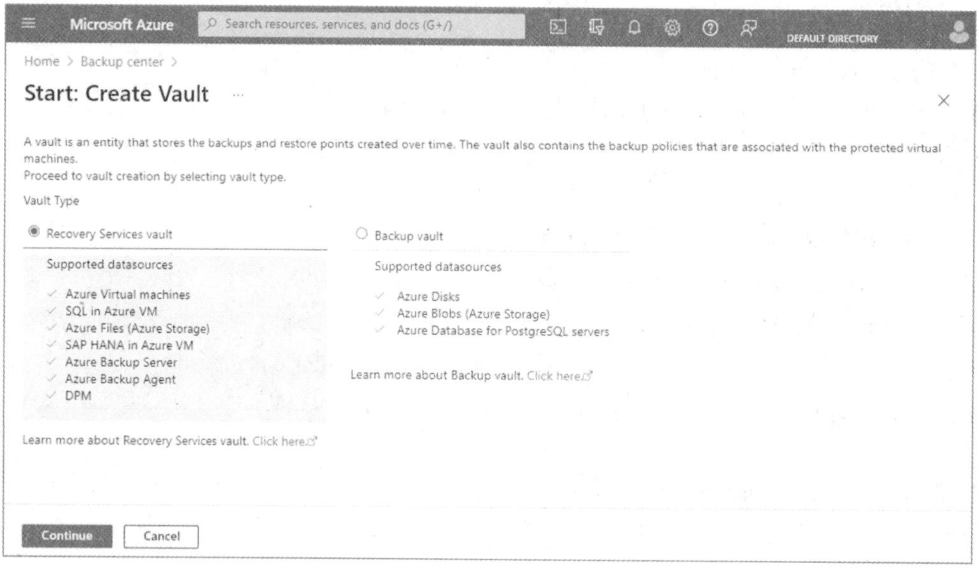

5. On the Create Recovery Services Vault – *Basic tab, as shown in Figure 17.10, enter the following values:

Subscription—Select the subscription you want to use. If you are a member of only one subscription, then you'll see that name. If you are unsure, use the default option.

Resource Group—Use an existing resource group or create a new one. To create a new resource group, click Create New, and then enter the name.

Vault Name—Enter a name to identify the vault. The name must be unique to the Azure subscription. The name must be between 2 to 50 characters, must start with a letter, and consist of only of letters, numbers, and hyphens.

Region—Select the geographic region for the vault. The vault must be in the same region as the data source.

FIGURE 17.10   Create Recovery Services Vault – *Basics Tab

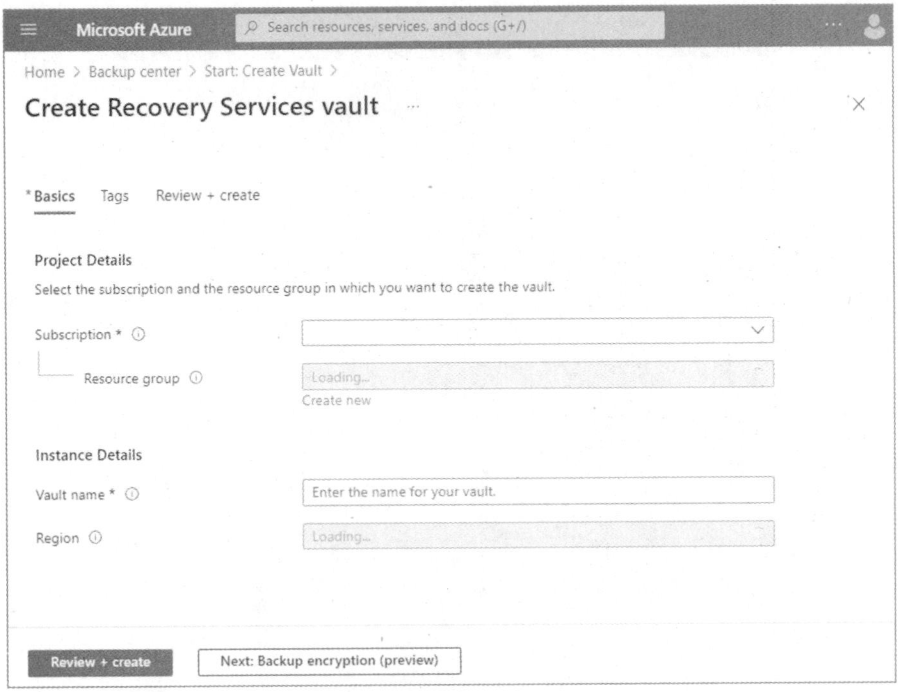

6.   After entering the values, click the Review + Create button.

7.   Click Create to finish creating the Recovery Services Vault.

It may take a while for the Recovery Services Vault to be created. You can monitor the status notifications in the Notifications area at the upper right. After the vault is created, it will appear in the list of Recovery Services Vaults. If the vault does not appear, click Refresh.

Download the MARS Agent

There are a couple different ways to download the MARS agent. One way is to go to Microsoft's website at `https://aka.ms/azurebackup_agent`. The download will start automatically.

Another way is to open the Recovery Services Vault to start a backup:

1.   Sign into the Azure portal using your Azure subscription.

2.   In the portal, select All Services.

3.   In the All Services dialog box, type **Recovery Services**.

4.   From the list of vaults, select a vault to open its Overview dashboard.

5.   In the vault, under Getting Started, select Backup, as shown in Figure 17.11.

FIGURE 17.11   Getting Started With Backup

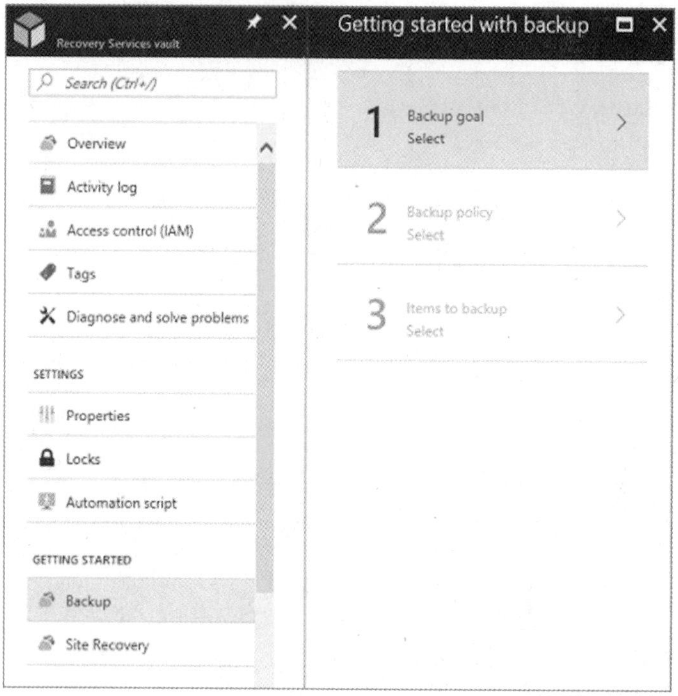

6. Under Where Is Your Workload Running?, select On-premises. Select this option even if you want to install the MARS agent on an Azure VM.

7. Under What Do You Want To Back Up?, select Files And Folders, as shown in Figure 17.12. A number of options are available, but some of them are only supported if you are running a secondary backup server.

FIGURE 17.12 Backup Goal window

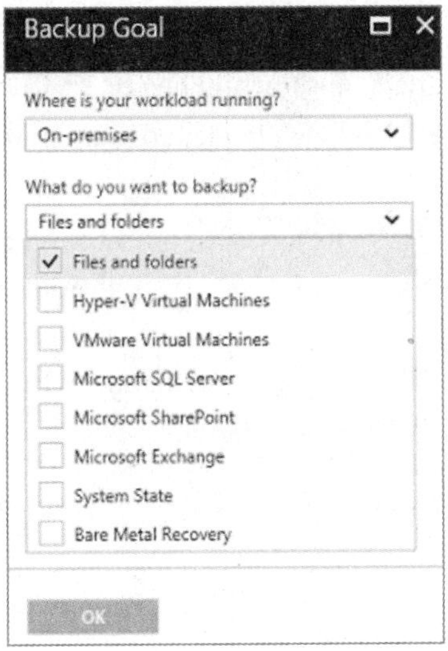

8. For Prepare Infrastructure, under Install Recovery Services Agent, select Download Agent For Windows Server (or For Windows Client), as shown in Figure 17.13. Click OK.

FIGURE 17.13 Prepare Infrastructure window

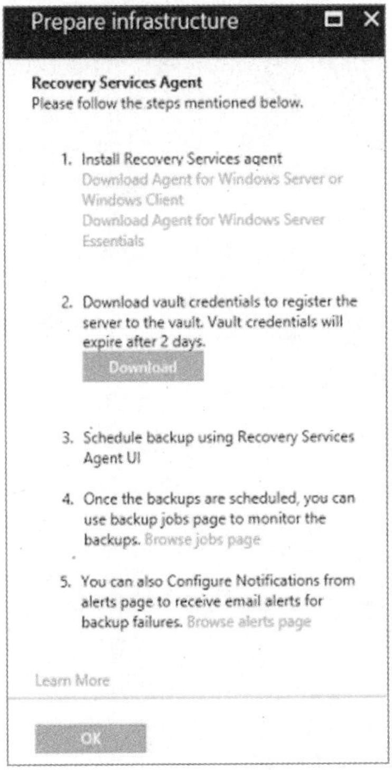

9. From the Download menu, select Save. By default, the **MARSagentinstaller.exe** file is saved to your Downloads folder.

10. Select Already Downloaded or Using The Latest Recovery Services Agent, and then download the vault credentials, as shown in Figure 17.13.

11. When done, click OK. The file is downloaded to your Downloads folder.

Install and Register the MARS Agent

To install and register the MARS agent, perform the following steps:

1. Run **MARSagentinstaller.exe** on the machines that you want to back up.

2. In the MARS Agent Setup Wizard, select Installation Settings. Choose where you want to install the agent, and then select a location for the cache. Then, click Next, as shown in Figure 17.14. Azure Backup uses the cache to store data snapshots before sending them to Azure. The cache location should have free space equal to at least 5 percent of the size of the data that will be backed up.

FIGURE 17.14   MARS Agent Setup Wizard

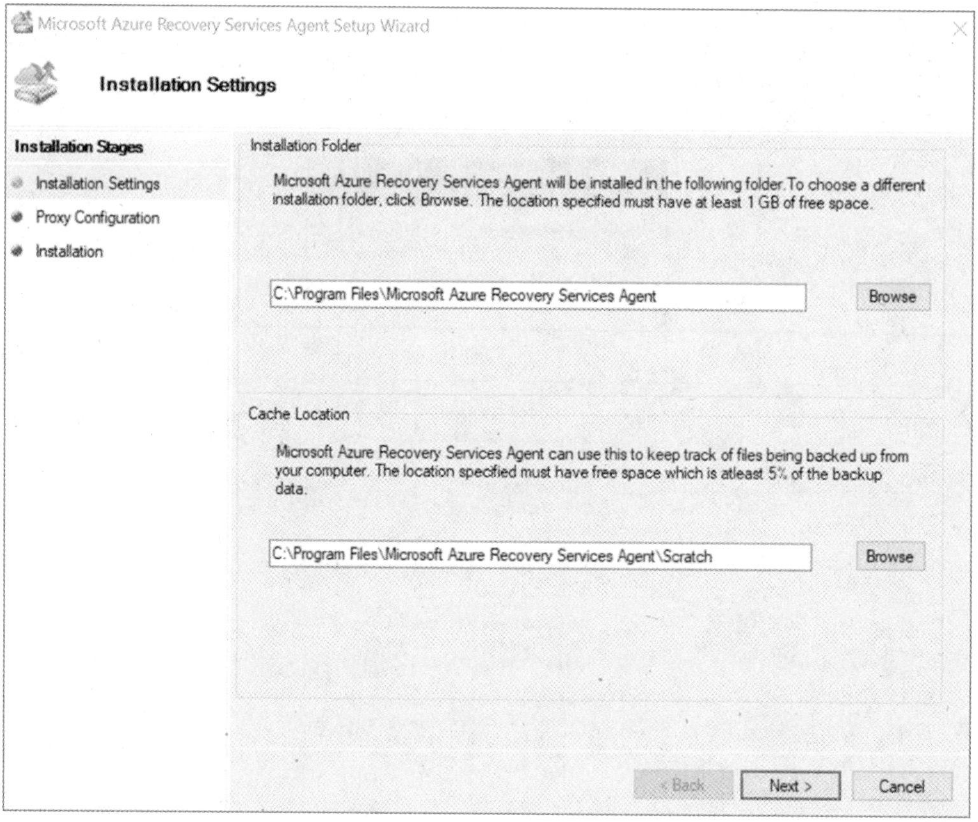

3. On the Proxy Configuration page, specify how the agent will connect to the Internet. Then, click Next, as shown in Figure 17.15.

FIGURE 17.15   Proxy Configuration page

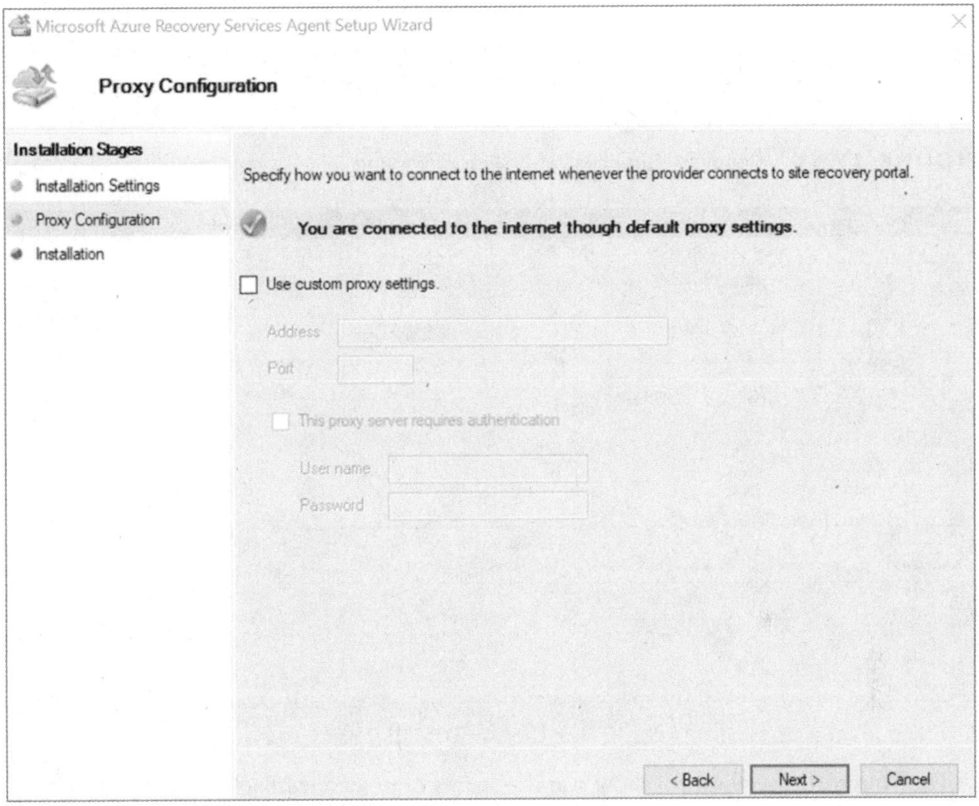

4. On the Installation page, review the prerequisites, and then click Install.

5. After the agent is installed, select Proceed To Registration. The Register Server Wizard will open.

6. In Register Server Wizard, select Vault Identification and browse to and select the credentials file that you created earlier. Then, click Next.

7. On the Encryption Setting page, specify a passphrase that will be used to encrypt and decrypt backups for the machine. If you lose or forget this passphrase, Microsoft cannot help you recover the backup data, so save the passphrase in a secure location.

8. When done, click Finish. The agent is now installed, and your machine is registered to the vault. You can now configure and schedule backups.

Monitor and Manage Recovery Services Vaults

When you open a Recovery Services Vault from the list, the Overview dashboard for the selected vault will open, as shown in Figure 17.16. To monitor alerts or to view the management data regarding a Recovery Services Vault, open the vault to view the Overview dashboard. The dashboard provides a number of details regarding the vault. The tiles will show you items such as the status of critical and warning alerts, in-progress and failed backup jobs, and the amount of backup storage used. If you back up Azure VMs to the vault, the Backup Pre-Check Status tile will show any critical or warning items.

FIGURE 17.16   Recovery Services Vault Overview page

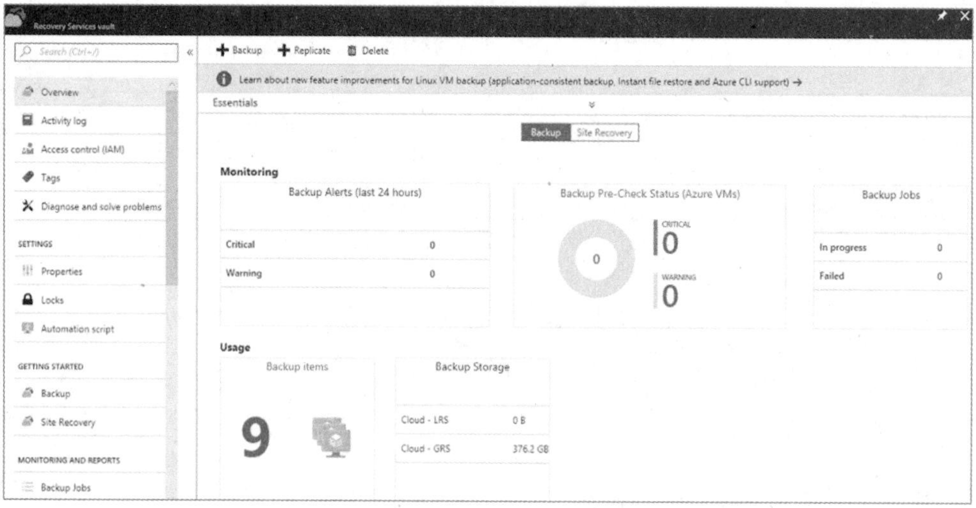

The Monitoring section will show you the results of predefined Backup Alerts and Backup Jobs queries. It provides up-to-date information on Critical and Warning alerts for Backup Jobs (in the last 24 hours), Backup Pre-check Status (Azure VMs), Backup Jobs in progress, and jobs that have failed (in the last 24 hours), as shown in Figure 17.17.

FIGURE 17.17   Recovery Services Vault Monitoring section

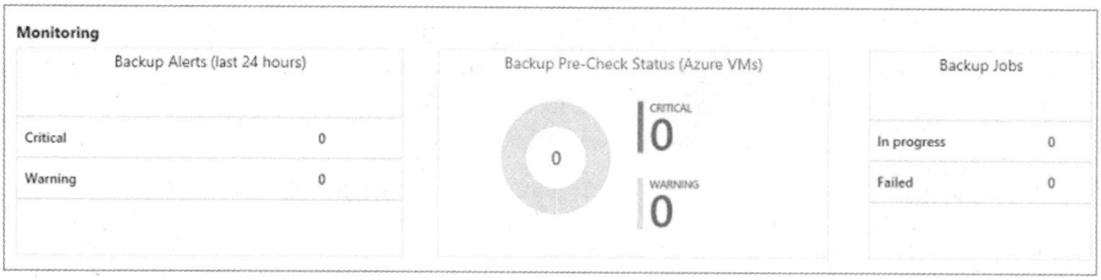

The Usage tiles will show the number of backup items configured for the vault, and the amount of used backup storage separated by LRS and GRS, as shown in Figure 17.18.

FIGURE 17.18   Recovery Services Vault Usage section

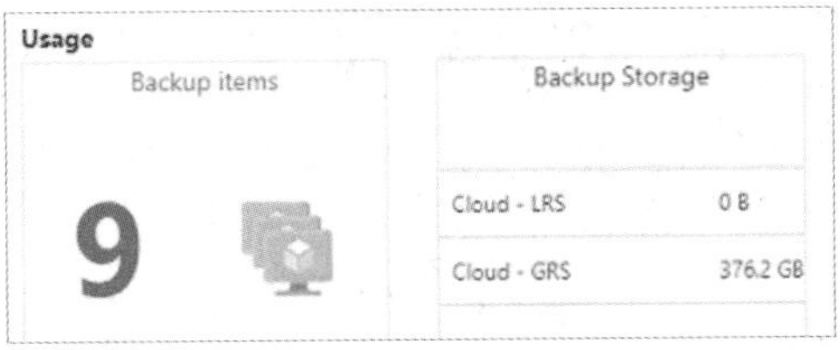

To Manage Backup Alerts

To open the Backup Alerts menu, in the Recovery Services Vault menu (on the left-hand side), under Monitoring And Reports, select Backup Alerts. The Backup Alerts report will list all the alerts for the vault. By default, the Backup Alerts report tracks eight items about each alert:

- Alert
- Backup Item
- Protected Server
- Severity
- Duration
- Creation Time
- Status
- Latest Occurrence Time

The Backup Alerts report will list all the alerts for the vault and display an alert severity. There are three different alert levels:

Critical   You will see this alert when backup jobs or recovery jobs fail, and when you stop protection on a server but retain the data.

Warning   You will see this alert when backup jobs finish with warnings.

Informational   Currently, no informational alerts are generated by the Azure Backup service.

Azure Backup Center

As I mentioned earlier, both Azure Backup and Azure Site Recovery use a centralized management interface, known as the Backup Center, to make it easier to create policies to protect, monitor, and manage enterprise workloads across hybrid and cloud networks. I also discussed using the Azure Backup Center to create an Azure Recovery Services Vault earlier in this chapter.

Azure Backup Center is currently supported for the following:

- Azure Blobs backup

- Azure Database for PostgreSQL Server backup

- Azure Files backup

- Azure Managed Disks backup

- Azure to Azure disaster recovery

- Azure VM backup

- SAP HANA on Azure VM backup

- SQL in Azure VM backup

- VMware and Physical to Azure disaster recovery

Here are some actions that you can perform by using the Backup Center:

- Configure backup for your data sources

- Create a new backup policy

- Create a new vault

- Restore a backup instance

- Stop backup for a backup instance

- Trigger an on-demand backup for a backup instance

To get started using Backup Center, search for Backup Center in the Azure portal and navigate to the Backup Center dashboard. The dashboard will open an Overview blade, as shown in Figure 17.8 earlier.

The Overview blade has two tiles: Jobs and Backup Instances. The Jobs tile will show you a list of all backup- and restore-related jobs that were started in the past 24 hours. You will see a status of completed, failed, or in-progress. Selecting any of the numbers in the tile will show you more information pertaining to that particular job. The Backup Instances tile will show you a list of all the backup instances as well as all of the replicated items. Selecting any of the numbers in the tile will show you more information such as the data source type and protection state.

I will be covering a few of the things you can do using the Backup Center.

Configure Backup to a Recovery Services Vault

To configure a backup to a Recovery Services Vault, perform the following:

1. Navigate to the Backup Center and select + Backup from the top of the Overview tab.

2. Select the type of data source that you want to back up, as shown in Figure 17.19.

FIGURE 17.19   Initiate: Configure Backup

Home > Backup Center >

Initiate: Configure Backup 🖨

Datasource type	Azure Virtual machines ⌄
Vault type	Recovery Services Vault ⌄
Vault *	Select a Vault
	Select

ⓘ Selected vault is maintained in **Recovery Services Vault**, you will be redirected to Recovery Services Vault for configuring backup. Learn more.

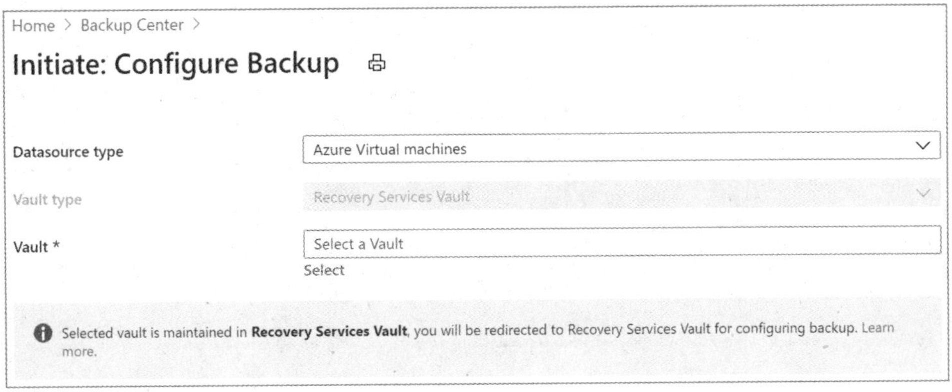

3. Choose a Recovery Services Vault and then click Proceed. This will direct you to the backup configuration experience that is identical to the one reachable from a Recovery Services Vault.

Configure Backup to a Backup Vault

To configure a backup to a Backup Vault, perform the following:

1. Navigate to the Backup Center and select + Backup at the top of the Overview tab.

2. Select the type of data source that you want to back up, as shown in Figure 17.20.

FIGURE 17.20   Initiate: Configure Backup

Home > Backup Center >

Initiate: Configure Backup 🖨

Datasource type	Azure Database for PostgreSQL servers ⌄
Vault type	Backup Vault ⌄

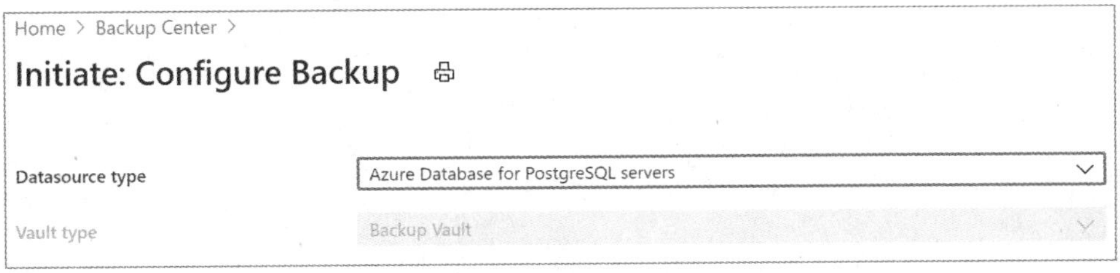

3. Click Proceed. This will direct you to the backup configuration experience that is identical to the one reachable from a Backup Vault.

Restore a Backup Instance from a Recovery Services Vault

To restore a backup instance from a Recovery Services Vault, perform the following:

1. Navigate to the Backup Center and select Restore from the top of the Overview tab.

2. Select the type of data source that you want to restore, as shown in Figure 17.21.

FIGURE 17.21   Initiate: Restore

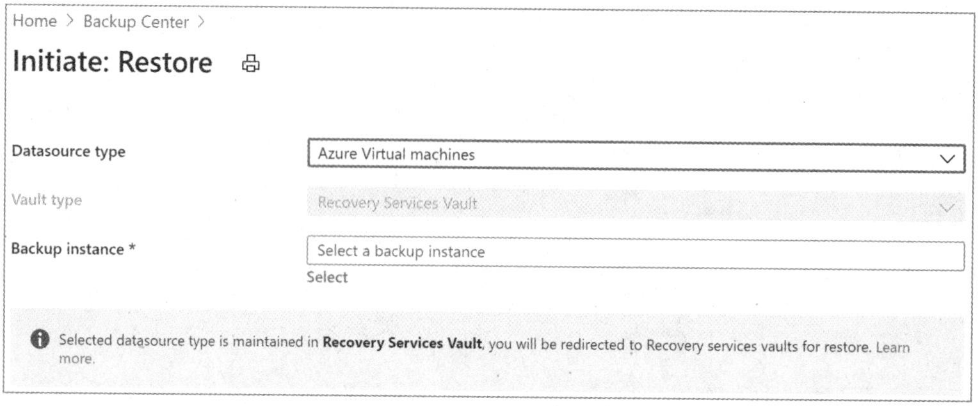

3. Choose a backup instance and then click Proceed. This will direct you to the restore settings experience that is identical to the one reachable from a Recovery Services Vault.

Restore a Backup Instance from a Backup Vault

To restore a backup instance from a Backup Vault, perform the following:

1. Navigate to the Backup Center and select Restore from the top of the Overview tab.

2. Select the type of data source that you want to restore, as shown in Figure 17.22.

FIGURE 17.22   Initiate: Restore

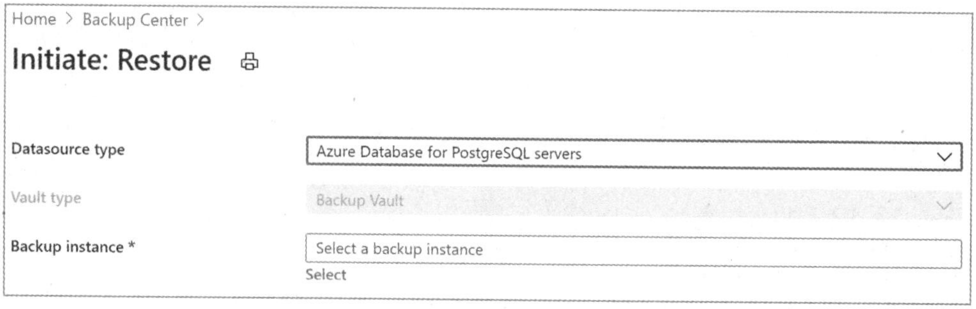

3. Choose a backup instance and then click Proceed. This will direct you to the restore settings experience that is identical to the one reachable from a Recovery Services Vault.

Create a New Backup Policy to Back Up to a Recovery Services Vault

To create a new backup policy to back up to a Recovery Services Vault, perform the following:

1. Navigate to the Backup Center and select + Policy from the top of the Overview tab.
2. Select the type of data source that you want to backup, as shown in Figure 17.23.

FIGURE 17.23   Initiate: Create Policy

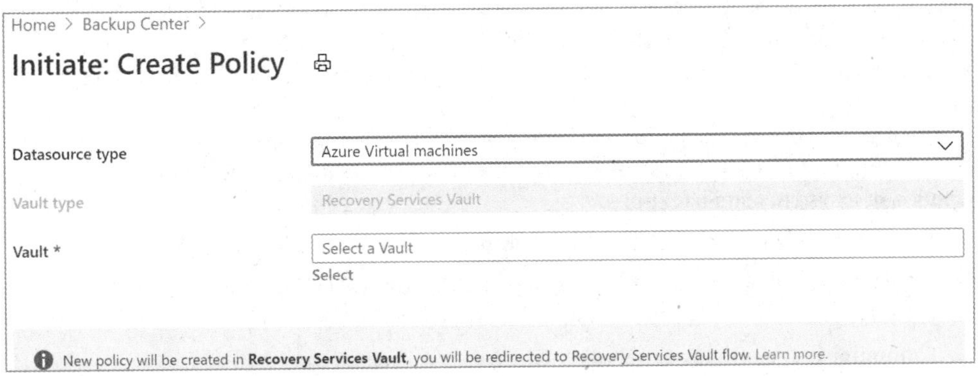

3. Choose a Recovery Services Vault and then click Proceed. This will direct you to the policy creation experience that is identical to the one reachable from a Recovery Services Vault.

Create a New Backup Policy to Back Up to a Backup Vault

To create a new backup policy to back up to a Backup Vault, perform the following:

1. Navigate to the Backup Center and select + Policy from the top of the Overview tab.
2. Select the type of data source that you want to back up, as shown in Figure 17.24.

FIGURE 17.24   Initiate: Create Policy

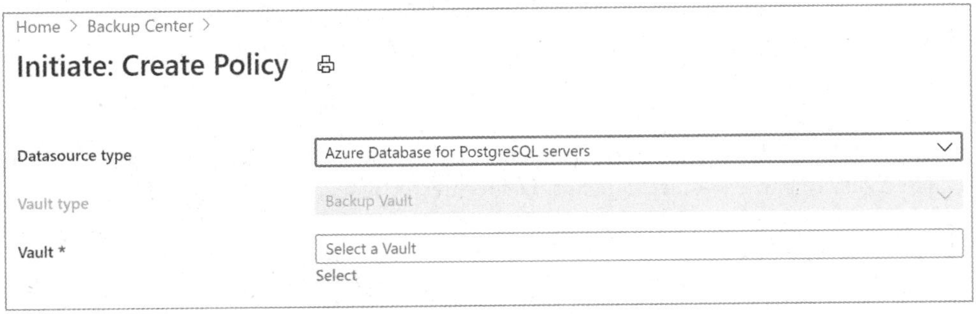

3. Click Proceed. This will direct you to the policy creation experience that is identical to the one reachable from a Backup Vault.

Azure Backup Server

Microsoft Azure Backup Server (MABS), also called Azure Backup Server, is a server product that you can use to protect application workloads such as Hyper-V VMs, Microsoft SQL Server, SharePoint Server, Microsoft Exchange, and Windows clients using a single console. With Azure Backup Server, you can back up your on-premises workloads, and if MABS is deployed in Azure, you can also back up your Azure VMs. You can also set up the machines on your on-premise or Azure VMs to back up to MABS, which will then back up your data to a Recovery Services Vault in the Azure Cloud.

Azure Backup Server backs up system state and provides bare-metal recovery (BMR) protection.

System State Backup backs up operating system files. This backup allows you to recover when a computer starts, but system files and the Registry are lost. The following elements are included in a system state backup:

- **Domain member:** Boot files, COM+ class registration database, Registry

- **Domain controller:** Windows Server Active Directory (NTDS), boot files, COM+ class registration database, Registry, system volume (SYSVOL)

- **Computer that runs cluster services:** Cluster server metadata

- **Computer that runs certificate services:** Certificate data

Bare-Metal Backup backs up operating system files and all data on critical volumes, except for user data. By definition, a BMR backup includes a system state backup. BMR provides protection when a computer will not start and you have to recover everything.

In order to start working with MABS, you need to set up a Windows Server, either on-premises or in Azure. Installing Azure Backup Server is not supported on Windows Server Core or Microsoft Hyper-V Server. You will always want to join MABS to a domain and move an existing MABS machine to a new domain afterward if deployment is not supported. The Azure Backup Server must be registered with a Recovery Services Vault. There are a few other rules when working with MABS.

For a server on-premises:

- The Azure Backup Server must be located on-premises and be connected to the domain.

- MABS can run on a Hyper-V VM, a VMware VM, or a physical host.

- Microsoft recommends at least a minimum of two cores and 8 GB of RAM for the server.

- The supported operating systems for the on-premises server are Windows Server 2019/2022, 64-bit, Standard, Datacenter, or Essentials or Windows Server 2016 with the latest service packs, 64-bit, Standard, Datacenter, or Essentials.

For a server in Azure:

- The Azure Backup Server must be located in Azure, running as an Azure VM, and be connected to the domain.
- Microsoft recommends that you start with a gallery image of Windows Server 2016 Datacenter or Windows Server 2019/2022 Datacenter.
- The recommended minimum requirements for the server VM should be Standard_A4_v2 with four cores and 8 GB of RAM.

MABS is designed to run on a single, dedicated server and cannot be installed on any of the following:

- A domain controller
- A computer that has the Application Server role installed
- A computer that is a System Center Operations Manager management server
- A computer that has Exchange Server running
- A computer that is a node of a cluster

How to Install MABS

Your MABS server must be a member of your AD domain prior to starting the installation process. Then, the first step is creating an Azure Recovery Services Vault, which I discussed earlier in this chapter. All the steps to creating an Azure Recovery Services Vault are the same as I outlined earlier, but when you get to the Backup Goal pane, from the Where Is Your Workload Running? drop-down menu, select On-Premises and from the What Do You Want To Back Up? drop-down menu, select the workloads you want to protect using Azure Backup Server, Then click OK, as shown in Figure 17.25.

FIGURE 17.25   Backup Goal

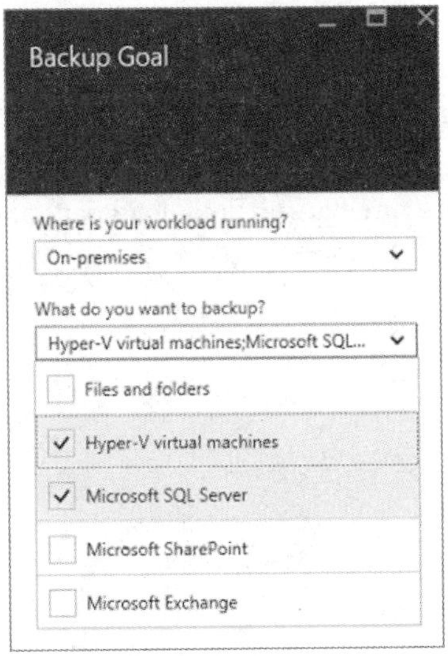

The Getting Started With Backup Wizard will switch the Prepare Infrastructure option to back up workloads to Azure. When the Prepare Infrastructure pane that opens, click the Download links for Install Azure Backup Server and Download Vault Credentials. You will use the vault credentials that were created during the registration of Azure Backup Server to the Recovery Services Vault. The links take you to the Download Center, where you can download the software package, as shown in Figure 17.26.

FIGURE 17.26   Prepare Infrastructure

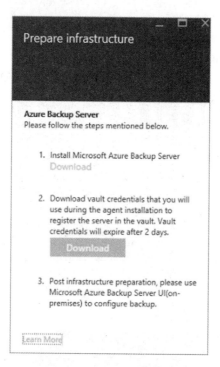

Next, select all the files and click Next, as shown in Figure 17.27. Download all the files coming in from the Microsoft Azure Backup download page and put all the files in the same folder.

FIGURE 17.27 Choose the Download You Want

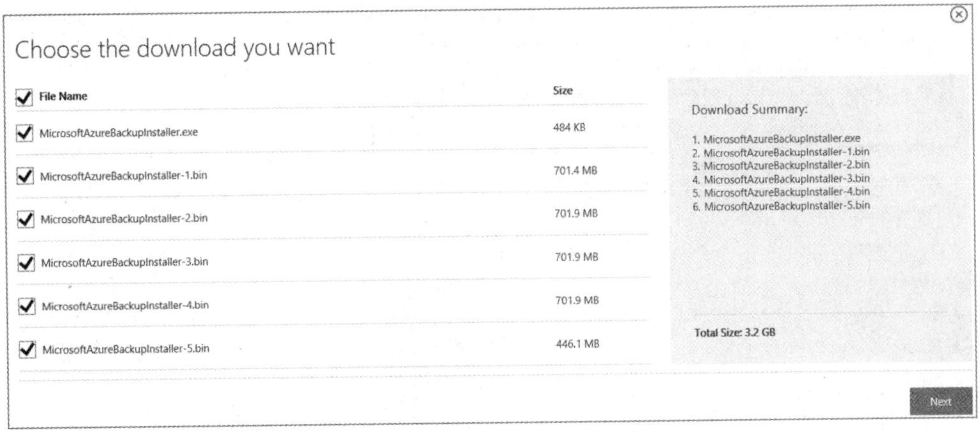

Extracting the Software Package

After all the files have been downloaded, click `MicrosoftAzureBackupInstaller.exe`. This will start the Microsoft Azure Backup Setup Wizard. Continue through the wizard and click the Extract button. You need at least 4 GB of free space to extract the setup files. When done, check the box to launch the extracted `setup.exe` to begin installing Microsoft Azure Backup Server and click the Finish button.

Installing the Software Package

To install the software package, perform the following:

1. Select Microsoft Azure Backup to launch the setup wizard.

2. On the Welcome screen, click Next. This takes you to the Prerequisite Checks section, as shown in Figure 17.28. On this screen, click Check to determine if the hardware and software prerequisites for Azure Backup Server have been met. If all prerequisites are met successfully, you'll see a message indicating that the machine meets the requirements. Click Next.

FIGURE 17.28   Microsoft Azure Backup Setup – Prerequisite Checks

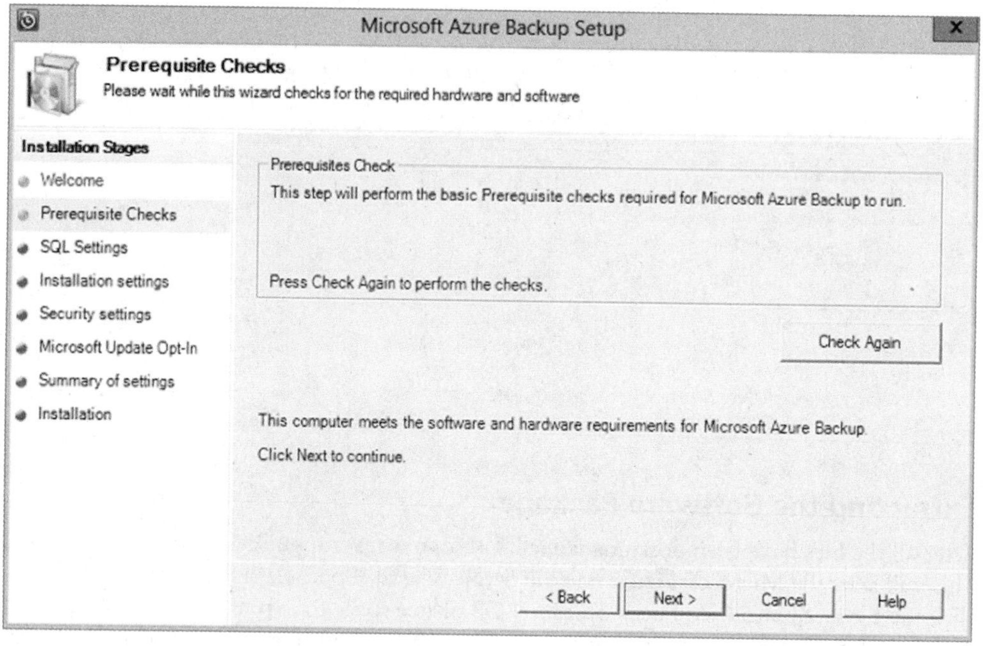

3. The Azure Backup Server installation package comes with the SQL Server binaries. On the SQL Settings page, when starting a new Azure Backup Server installation, select the option Install New Instance Of SQL Server With This Setup and click the Check And Install button. Once the prerequisites are successfully installed, click Next.

4. On the Installation Settings page, select a location for the installation and click Next.

5. On the Security Settings page, type a password and then click Next.

6. On the Microsoft Update Opt-In page, select whether you want to use Microsoft Update to check for updates and click Next.

7. On the Summary of Settings page, review your settings and click Install.

8. The installation happens in phases. In the first phase, the MARS Agent is installed on the server. The wizard also checks for Internet connectivity. If available, you can continue with the installation. If not, you need to provide proxy details to connect to the Internet.

9. The next step is to configure the Microsoft Azure Recovery Services (MARS) Agent. We discussed how to do this earlier in this chapter. In the Register Server Wizard, supply the Vault Identification information, Encryption Settings, and Server Registration.

10. Once registration of the MABS finishes, the setup wizard will proceed with the installation and configuration of SQL Server and the Azure Backup Server components.

11. When the installation is done, a desktop icon will be created. To launch, double-click the desktop icon.

Install and Update the Data Protection Manager (DPM) Protection Agent

MABS comes with the System Center Data Protection Manager (DPM), which is a software package that provides data protection and data recovery in Microsoft Windows environments. MABS uses the DPM protection agent. Here are the steps to install the protection agent for client computers:

1. In the Backup Server Administrator Console, select Management ➤ Agents.

2. In the display pane, select the client computers that you want to update the protection agent on.

3. To install updated protection agents on the selected computers, in the Actions pane, click Update.

4. If a client computer isn't connected to the network, the Agent Status column will show an Update Pending status. Once connected to the network, the status will show Updating.

Restore Files to Windows Server Using the MARS Agent

You can use the Recover Data wizard in the MARS Agent to restore data. I discussed the MARS Agent earlier in this chapter. You can restore data to the same machine where the backup was taken or you can restore to a different machine.

You can use the Instant Restore feature to mount a writeable recovery point snapshot as a recovery volume. Then, you can select the files that you want to restore and copy the files to the local machine.

Use Instant Restore to Recover Data to the Same Machine

If you accidentally delete a file and you want to restore it to the same machine, perform the following steps to recover the file. This restore has to be on the same machine where the backup was taken.

1. Open the Microsoft Azure Backup snap-in. If you don't know where the snap-in was installed, just search the computer or server for Microsoft Azure Backup.

2. Click Recover Data to start the wizard, as shown in Figure 17.29.

FIGURE 17.29 Microsoft Azure Backup Actions

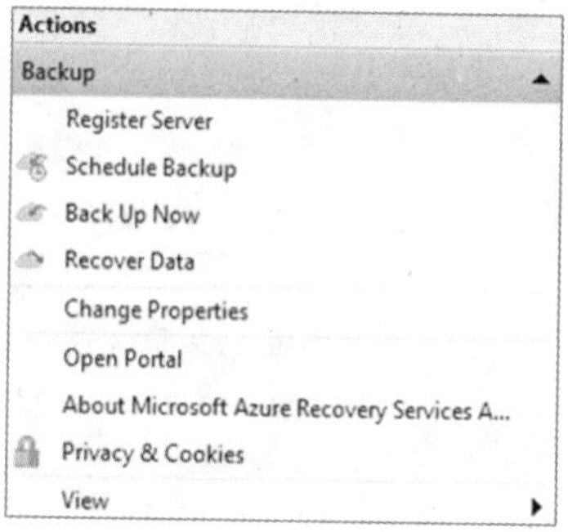

3. On the Getting Started page, to restore the data to the same server or computer, select This Server (*<server name>*) and then click Next, as shown in Figure 17.30.

FIGURE 17.30 Recover Data Wizard – Getting Started

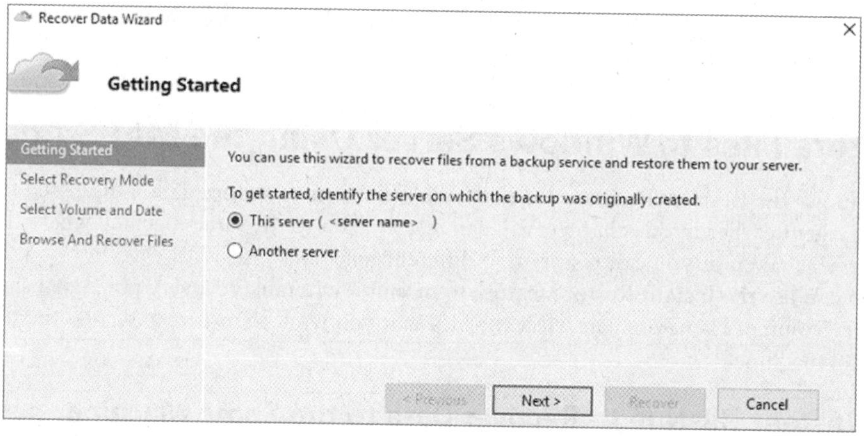

4. On the Select Recovery Mode page, choose Individual Files And Folders and then click Next, as shown in Figure 17.31.

FIGURE 17.31 Recover Data Wizard – Select Recovery Mode

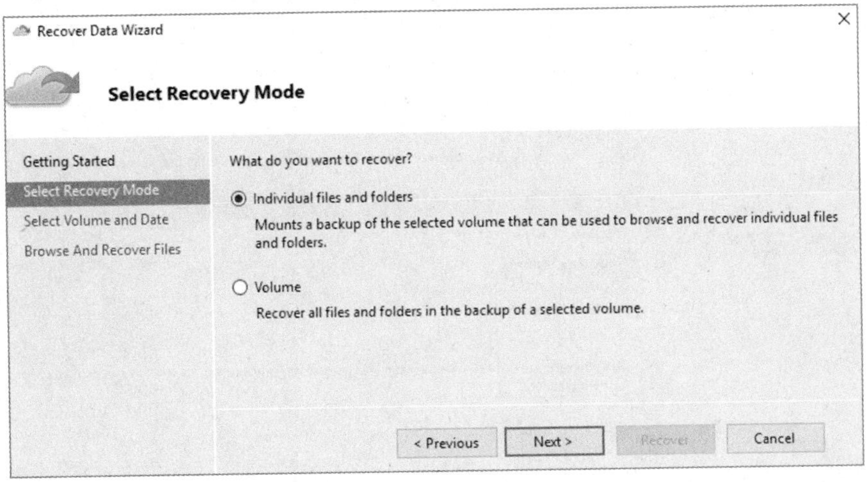

5. On the Select Volume And Date page, select the volume that contains the files and folders you want to restore. On the calendar, you can select a recovery point.

6. After choosing the recovery point to restore, click Mount.

7. On the Browse And Recover Files page, click Browse to open Windows Explorer, and locate the files and folders you want to restore.

8. In Windows Explorer, copy the files and folders you want to restore, and paste them to any location local to the server or computer.

9. When you are done restoring your desired files and folders, on the Browse And Recover Files page, click Unmount. Then select Yes to confirm that you want to unmount the volume, as shown in Figure 17.32.

FIGURE 17.32   Recover Data Wizard – Browse And Recover Files

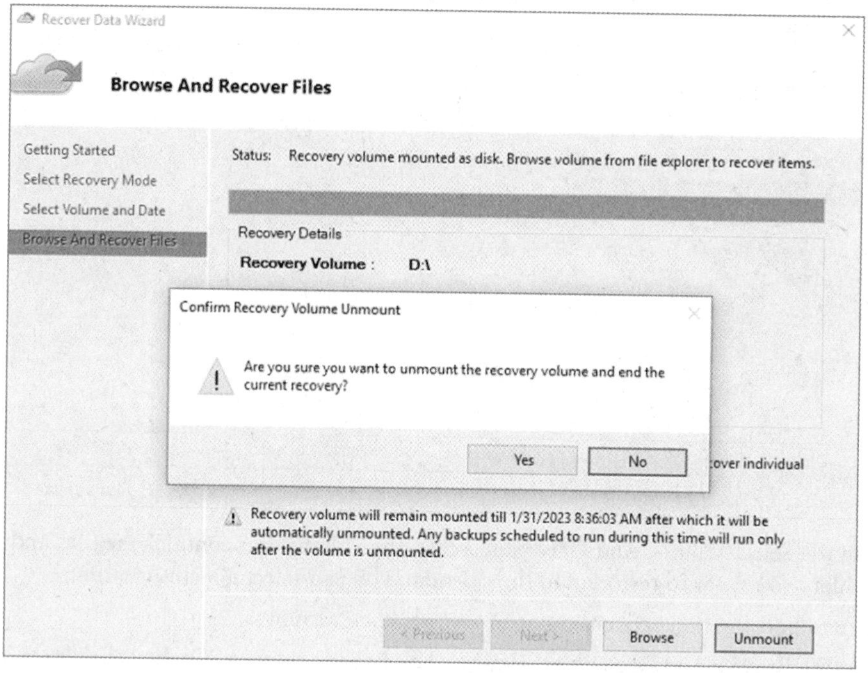

Use Instant Restore to Recover Data to an Alternate Machine

If an entire server is lost, you can still recover the data from Azure Backup to a different machine. To do so, perform the following steps:

1. Open the Microsoft Azure Backup snap-in on the target machine. If you don't know where the snap-in was installed, just search the computer or server for Microsoft Azure Backup.

2. Make sure that the target and source machines are registered to the same Recovery Services Vault.

3. Click Recover Data to start the wizard.

4. On the Getting Started page, select Another Server and then provide the Vault Credentials file by clicking Browse. Then click Next.

5. On the Select Backup Server page, select the source machine from the list of displayed machines and provide the passphrase. Then click Next, as shown in Figure 17.33.

FIGURE 17.33   Recover Data Wizard – Select Backup Server

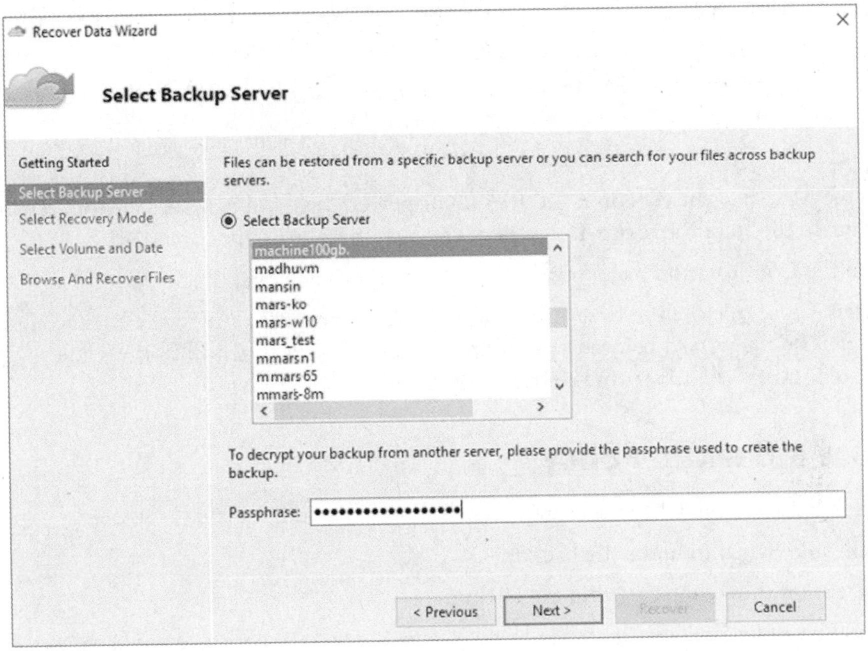

6. On the Select Recovery Mode page, choose Individual Files And Folders and then click Next

7. On the Select Volume And Date page, select the volume that contains the files and folders you want to restore. On the calendar, you can select a recovery point.

8. To locally mount the recovery point as a recovery volume on your target machine, click Mount.

9. On the Browse And Recover Files page, click Browse to open Windows Explorer, and locate the files and folders you want to restore.

10. In Windows Explorer, copy the files and folders you want to restore, and paste them to your target machine computer.

11. When you are done restoring your desired files and folders, on the Browse And Recover Files page, click Unmount. Then select Yes to confirm that you want to unmount the volume.

Run an On-Demand Backup

You can perform an on-demand backup using the MARS agent. To do so, perform the following steps:

1. Open the Microsoft Azure Backup snap-in. If you don't know where the snap-in was installed, just search the computer or server for Microsoft Azure Backup.

2. Click Back Up Now to start the wizard.

3. If the MARS agent version is 2.0.9169.0 or newer, then you can set a custom retention date. In the Retain Backup Till section, choose a date from the calendar.

4. On the Confirmation page, review the settings, and then click Back Up.

5. Click Close to close the wizard. The wizard will continue to run in the background if you close the wizard before the backup finishes. After the backup finishes, the Job Completed status will appear in the Backup console.

Create a Backup Policy

An Azure backup policy has two components:

- Schedule (when to make the backup)
- Retention (how long to retain the backup)

A backup policy will specify when to take snapshots of the data to create recovery points. It also specifies how long to keep recovery points. You will use the MARS agent to configure a backup policy.

To create a backup policy, perform the following:

1. After you download and register the MARS agent, open the agent console. You can find it by searching your machine for Microsoft Azure Backup.

2. Under Actions, select Schedule Backup, as shown in Figure 17.29 earlier.

3. In the Schedule Backup Wizard, select Getting Started and then click Next.

4. Under Select Items To Back Up, select Add Items, as shown in Figure 17.34.

FIGURE 17.34 Schedule Backup Wizard – Select Items To Backup

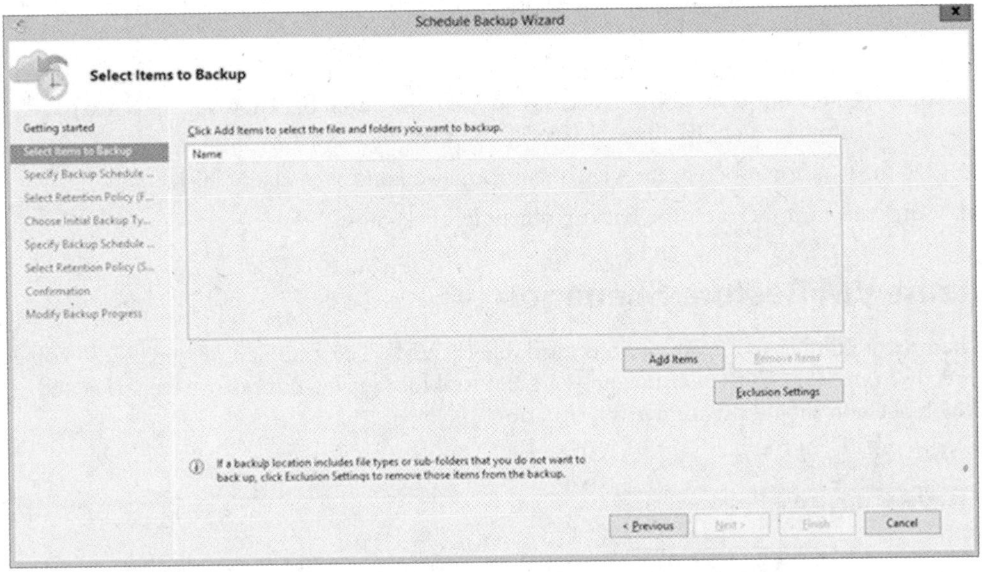

5. In the Select Items box, select items to back up, and then click OK.

6. On the Select Items To Back Up page, click Next.

7. On the Specify Backup Schedule page, specify when to take schedule backups. You can schedule up to three daily backups per day or schedule weekly backups. Then, click Next, as shown in Figure 17.35.

FIGURE 17.35 Schedule Backup Wizard – Specify Backup Schedule

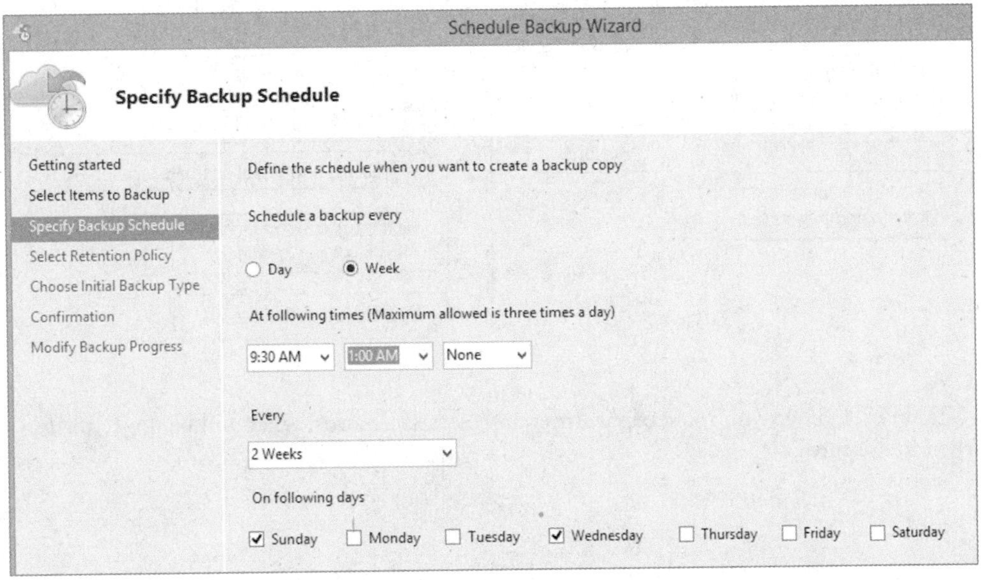

8. On the Select Retention Policy page, specify how to store historical copies of your data. Then click Next. Retention settings specify which recovery points to store and how long to store them.

9. On the Choose Initial Backup Type page, decide if you want to take the initial backup over the network or use offline backup. To take the initial backup over the network, select Automatically Over The Network, and then click Next.

10. On the Confirmation page, review the information and then click Finish.

11. After the wizard creates the backup schedule, click Close.

Azure VM Restore Scenarios

There are a number of restore options available for VMs. The graphic in Figure 17.36 comes directly from Microsoft's website and is a great tool for figuring out restore scenarios and which one you should use for a given situation.

FIGURE 17.36 Restore Scenarios

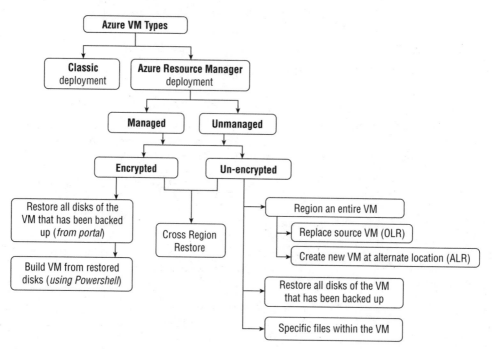

Table 17.1 shows you some of the different restore scenarios, what will be done, and when to use them.

TABLE 17.1 Restore scenarios

Scenario	What is done	When to use
Create a new VM	Creates and gets a basic VM up and running from a restore point	When you need to create a new VM.
Restore to create a new virtual machine	Restores the entire VM to Original Location Recovery (OLR) (if the source VM still exists) or Alternate-Location Recovery (ALR)	If the source VM is lost or corrupted, then you can restore the entire VM. You can create a copy of the VM. You can perform a restore drill for audit or compliance. If your license for Marketplace Azure VM has expired, the Create VM Restore option can't be used.
Restore disks of the VM	Restore disks attached to the VM	All disks: This option creates the template and restores the disk. You can edit this template with special configurations (e.g., availability sets) to meet your requirements and then use both the template and restore the disk to re-create the VM.
Restore specific files within the VM	Choose restore point, browse, select files, and restore them to the same (or compatible) OS as the backed-up VM	If you know which specific files to restore, then use this option instead of restoring the entire VM.
Cross Region Restore (CRR)	Create a new VM or restore disks to a secondary region (Azure paired region)	Full outage: With the CRR feature, there's no wait time to recover data in the secondary region. You can initiate restores in the secondary region even before Azure declares an outage. Partial outage: Downtime can occur in specific storage clusters where Azure Backup stores your backed-up data or even in-network, connecting Azure Backup and storage clusters associated with your backed-up data. With CRR, you can perform a restore in the secondary region using a replica of backed-up data in the secondary region. No outage: You can conduct business continuity and disaster recovery (BCDR) drills for audit or compliance purposes with the secondary region data. This allows you to perform a restore of backed-up data in the secondary region even if there isn't a full or partial outage in the primary region for business continuity and disaster recovery drills.

Select a Restore Point

A VM restore point stores VM configuration from a particular point in time. Basically, it's a snapshot of all the managed disks that are attached to the VM. You can use VM restore points to capture multi-disk-consistent backups. VM restore points contain a disk restore point for each of the attached disks. A disk restore point consists of a snapshot of an individual managed disk.

To select a restore point, perform the following steps:

1. Sign into the Azure portal at `https://portal.azure.com`.

2. Search for Backup Center, and then go to the Backup Center dashboard.

3. On the Overview pane, select Restore, as shown in Figure 17.37.

FIGURE 17.37   Backup Center – Restore

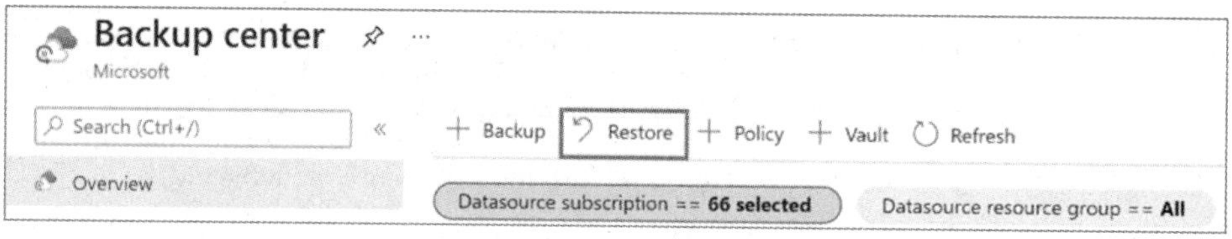

4. Select Azure Virtual Machines as the data source type, and then select a backup instance.

5. Select a VM and then click Continue.

6. On the next screen, select a restore point to use for the recovery, as shown in Figure 17.38.

FIGURE 17.38   Restore Virtual Machine – Select Restore Point

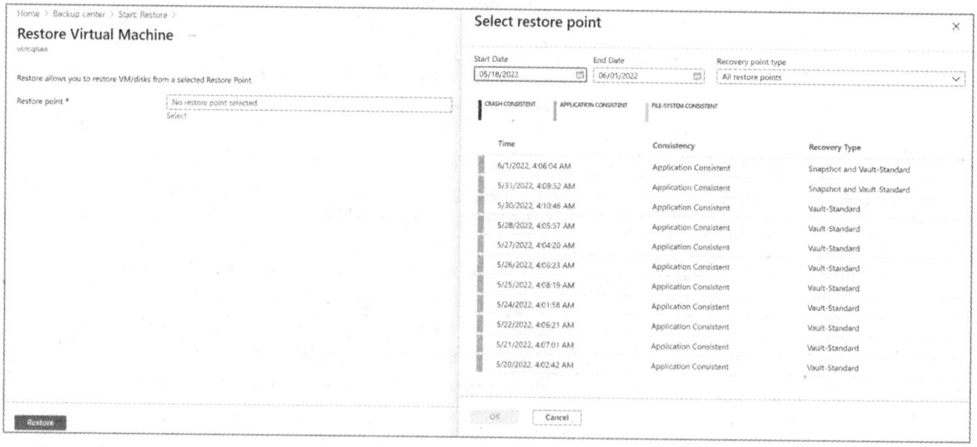

Choosing a VM Restore Configuration

When restoring a VM, you will see two restore options, as shown in Figure 17.39:

- **Create New:** You can use this option if you want to create a new VM. You can create a VM with simple settings, or restore a disk and create a customized VM.

- **Replace Existing:** You can use this option if you want to replace disks on an existing VM.

FIGURE 17.39   Restore Configuration options

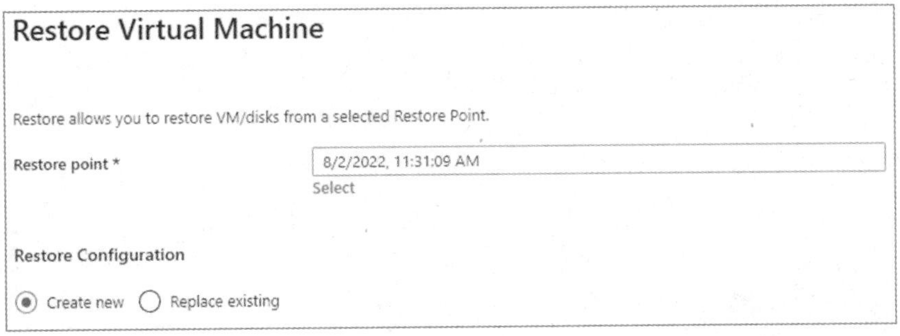

> ### Restore Virtual Machine
>
> Restore allows you to restore VM/disks from a selected Restore Point.
>
> Restore point *   8/2/2022, 11:31:09 AM
>   Select
>
> Restore Configuration
>
> ◉ Create new   ○ Replace existing

As one of the restore options, you can create a VM using settings from a restore point. To do so, perform the following:

1. In Restore Virtual Machine, click Create New.

2. In the Restore Type section, select Create New Virtual Machine, as shown in Figure 17.40.

FIGURE 17.40 Restore Virtual Machine

Restore Virtual Machine

Restore allows you to restore VM/disks from a selected Restore Point.

Restore point *

8/2/2022, 11:31:09 AM
Select

Restore Configuration

⦿ Create new ○ Replace existing

ⓘ To create an alternate configuration when restoring your VM (from the following menus), use PowerShell cmdlets.

Restore Type * ⓘ

Create new virtual machine

Virtual machine name * ⓘ

Resource group * ⓘ

Virtual network * ⓘ

Subnet * ⓘ

Staging Location * ⓘ

Can't find your storage account ?

Restore

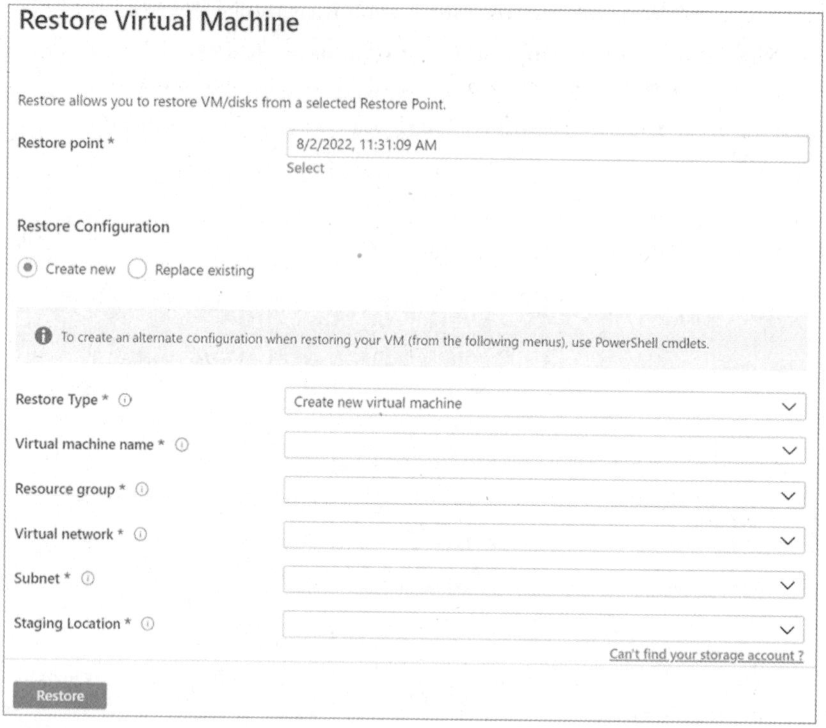

3. Continue to fill out the following sections of the Restore Virtual Machine page:

Virtual Machine Name—Specify a VM that doesn't exist in the subscription.

Resource Group—Select an existing resource group for the new VM, or create a new one with a globally unique name. If you assign a name that already exists, Azure assigns the group the same name as the VM.

Virtual Network—Select the VNet in which the VM will be placed. All VNets associated with the subscription in the same location as the vault, which is active and not attached with any affinity group, are displayed.

Subnet—The first subnet is selected by default.

Staging Location—Specify the storage account for the VM.

4. Click Restore to start the restore operation.

Implement Disaster Recovery by using Azure Site Recovery

Azure Site Recovery adds to your Business Continuity and Disaster Recovery (BCDR) strategy by providing:

- A Site Recovery service that keeps business apps and workloads running during outages. Site Recovery will replicate workloads that are running on physical and VMs from a primary site to a secondary location. If an outage occurs at the primary site, then you will fail over to a secondary location, and access apps from there. After the primary location is back up, you can fail back to it.

- A backup service, Azure Backup, that will keep your data safe and recoverable.

Site Recovery can be used to manage replication for

- Azure VMs replicating between Azure regions

- Replication from Azure Public Multi-Access Edge Compute (MEC) to the region

- Replication between two Azure Public MECs

- On-premises VMs, Azure Stack VMs, and physical servers

Table 17.2 shows Site Recovery features along with a brief description. This information came directly from Microsoft's website.

TABLE 17.2   Site Recovery features

Feature	Description
Azure automation integration	A rich Azure Automation library provides production-ready, application-specific scripts that can be downloaded and integrated with Site Recovery.
Azure VM replication	You can set up disaster recovery of Azure VMs from a primary region to a secondary region or from Azure Public MEC to the Azure region or from one Azure Public MEC to another Azure Public MEC connected to the same Azure region.
BCDR integration	Site Recovery integrates with other BCDR technologies. For example, you can use Site Recovery to protect the SQL Server backend of corporate workloads, with native support for SQL Server Always On, to manage the failover of availability groups.
Customized recovery plans	Using recovery plans, you can customize and sequence the failover and recovery of multitier applications running on multiple VMs. You group machines together in a recovery plan, and optionally add scripts and manual actions. Recovery plans can be integrated with Azure Automation runbooks.

TABLE 17.2   Site Recovery features *(Continued)*

Feature	Description
Data resilience	Site Recovery orchestrates replication without intercepting application data. When you replicate to Azure, data is stored in Azure storage, with the resilience that provides. When failover occurs, Azure VMs are created based on the replicated data.
Flexible failovers	You can run planned failovers for expected outages with zero-data loss or unplanned failovers with minimal data loss, depending on replication frequency, for unexpected disasters. You can easily fail back to your primary site when it's available again.
Keep apps consistent over failover	You can replicate using recovery points with application-consistent snapshots. These snapshots capture disk data, all data in memory, and all transactions in process.
Network integration	Site Recovery integrates with Azure for application network management. For example, to reserve IP addresses, configure load balancers and use Azure Traffic Manager for efficient network switchovers.
On-premises VM replication	You can replicate on-premises VMs and physical servers to Azure, or to a secondary on-premises datacenter. Replication to Azure eliminates the cost and complexity of maintaining a secondary datacenter.
RTO and RPO targets	Keep recovery time objectives (RTOs) and recovery point objectives (RPOs) within organizational limits. Site Recovery provides continuous replication for Azure VMs and VMware VMs, and replication frequency as low as 30 seconds for Hyper-V. You can reduce RTO further by integrating with Azure Traffic Manager.
Simple BCDR solution	Using Site Recovery, you can set up and manage replication, failover, and failback from a single location in the Azure portal.
Testing without disruption	You can easily run disaster recovery drills, without affecting ongoing replication.
VMware VM replication	You can replicate VMware VMs to Azure using the improved Azure Site Recovery replication appliance, which offers better security and resilience than the configuration server.
Workload replication	Replicate any workload running on supported Azure VMs, on-premises Hyper-V and VMware VMs, and Windows/Linux physical servers.

Configure Azure Site Recovery Networking

A VM in Azure must have at least one network interface attached to it, but it can have as many as the VM size supports. The first network interface, attached to an Azure VM, is called the primary network interface and all other network interfaces are called secondary network interfaces. All outbound traffic from the VM uses the IP address of the primary network interface.

Azure Site Recovery, by default, will create the same number of network interfaces as the amount of Azure VMs on an on-premises server. During migration or failover, you can avoid creating redundant network interfaces by editing the network interface settings under the settings for the replicated VM.

Select the Target Network

You can specify the target VNet for individual VMs for VMware and physical machines, and for Hyper-V (without System Center Virtual Machine Manager) VMs. To do so, perform the following:

1. In a Recovery Services Vault, under Replicated Items, select any replicated item to access the settings for that replicated item.

2. Select the Compute And Network tab to access the network settings for the replicated item, as shown in Figure 17.41.

FIGURE 17.41   Compute And Network tab

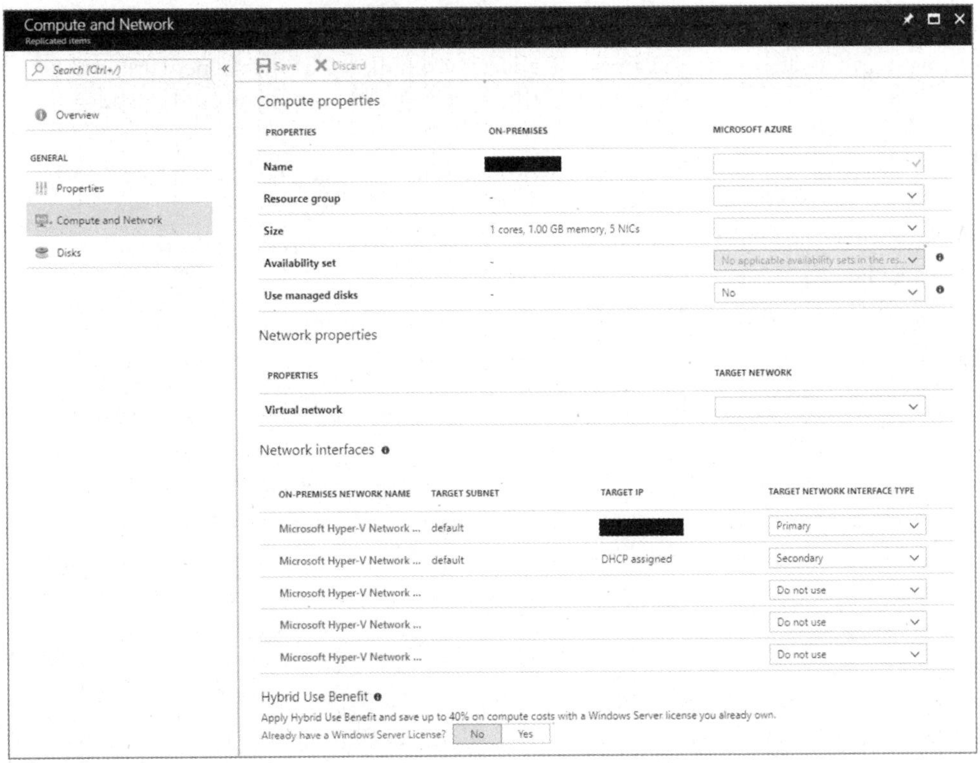

3. Under Network Properties, choose a virtual network from the list of available network interfaces. When you modify the target network, it will affect all other network interfaces on that VM.

Select the Target Interface Type

When you are enabling replication, Site Recovery selects all detected network interfaces on the on-premises server by default. It will mark one as the Primary and all others as Secondary. By default, any interfaces added to the on-premises server are marked Do Not Use.

If you want to view and edit the network interface settings and specify the target network interface type, you can do so by following these steps:

1. In a Recovery Services Vault, under Replicated Items, select any replicated item to access the settings for that replicated item.

2. Select the Compute And Network tab to access the network settings for the replicated item.

3. Look in the Network Interfaces section to view and edit the network interface settings. From here, you can also specify the target network interface type, as shown in Figure 17.41 earlier. The target network interface type options include Primary, Secondary, and Do Not Use.

Modify the Network Interface Settings

You can also change the subnet and IP address for a replicated item's network interfaces. Site Recovery will assign the next available IP address from the subnet to the network interface at failover if an IP address is not specified. In order to change the subnet and IP address, perform the following:

1. In a Recovery Services Vault, under Replicated Items, select any replicated item to access the settings for that replicated item.

2. Select the Compute And Network tab to access the network settings for the replicated item.

3. In the Network Interfaces section, view and edit the network interface settings.

4. Select any available network interface to open Network Interface Card Properties, as shown in Figure 17.42.

FIGURE 17.42   Network Interface Card Properties

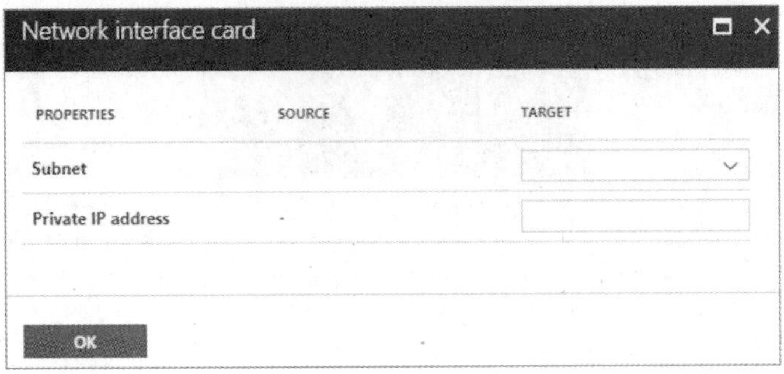

5. Select your desired subnet from the list of available subnets.

6. Enter the desired IP address (as required).

7. When done, click OK to return to the Compute And Network tab.

8. Repeat steps 4–7 for any other network interfaces that you wish to change.

9. When done, click Save to save all changes.

Configure Site Recovery for On-Premises VMs

To set up disaster recovery of on-premises physical Windows and Linux servers to Azure, there are a number of steps. I have covered most of these throughout this chapter. The steps include:

- Set up Azure and on-premises prerequisites.

- Create a Recovery Services Vault for Site Recovery.

- Set up the source and target replication environments.

- Create a replication policy.

- Enable replication for a server.

To create a Recovery Services Vault to be used for Site Recovery, perform the following:

1. Sign into the Azure portal at https://portal.azure.com.

2. Search for and select Recovery Services Vault.

3. Click Create A Resource. Then select Monitoring + Management. Select Backup And Site Recovery to open the Recovery Services Vault window, as shown in Figure 17.43.

FIGURE 17.43   Recovery Services Vault

4. Perform the following:

   - In the Name section, specify a name to identify the vault.
   - In the Subscription section, if you have more than one subscription, select the appropriate one.
   - For Create A New Resource Group, type a name for the new group or select an existing one.
   - In Location, specify your Azure region.

5. If you want to quickly access the vault from the dashboard, click Pin To Dashboard and then click Create. The new vault will appear on the dashboard under All Resources and on the main Recovery Services Vaults page.

Configure a Recovery Plan

For the purpose of failover, a recovery plan gathers machines into recovery groups and helps define the recovery process. The recovery plan will determine how the machines failover and the order in which they start after failover. Recovery plans can be used for both failover to and failback.

To create a recovery plan, perform the following:

1. Sign into the Azure portal at `https://portal.azure.com`.

2. Search for and select Recovery Services Vault.

3. In the Recovery Services Vault, select Recovery Plans (Site Recovery), and then select +Recovery Plan.

4. In Create Recovery Plan, enter a name for the plan.

5. Choose a source and target based on the machines in the plan, and then select Resource Manager for the deployment model.

   Table 17.3 shows the failover, source, and target information for a recovery plan.

TABLE 17.3   Failover source and target

Failover	Source	Target
Azure to Azure	Select the Azure region	Select the Azure region
VMware to Azure	Select the configuration server	Select Azure
Physical machines to Azure	Select the configuration server	Select Azure
Hyper-V to Azure	Select the Hyper-V site name	Select Azure
Hyper-V (managed by VMM) to Azure	Select the VMM server	Select Azure

6. In Select Items Virtual Machines, select the machines (or replication group) that you want to add to the plan. Then click OK.

7. When done, click OK again to create the plan.

   To add a group to a recovery plan, perform the following:

1. In Recovery Plans, right-click the plan and select Customize. By default, after creating a plan all the added machines are located in default Group 1.

2. Click +Group. By default, a new group is numbered in the order in which it is added. You can have up to seven groups.

3. Select the machine you want to move to the new group, click Change Group, and then select the new group. You can also right-click the group name and select Protected Item, and then add machines to the group. A machine or replication group can only belong to one group in a recovery plan.

Configure Site Recovery for Azure Virtual Machines

To set up site recovery for Azure VMs, there are a number of steps. I have covered most of these throughout this chapter. The steps include:

- Verify Azure settings and permissions.
- Prepare VMs you want to replicate.
- Create a Recovery Services Vault.
- Enable Site Recovery.
- Enable VM replication.

To enable site recovery, in the vault settings, select Enable Site Recovery, as shown in Figure 17.44.

FIGURE 17.44   Enable Site Recovery

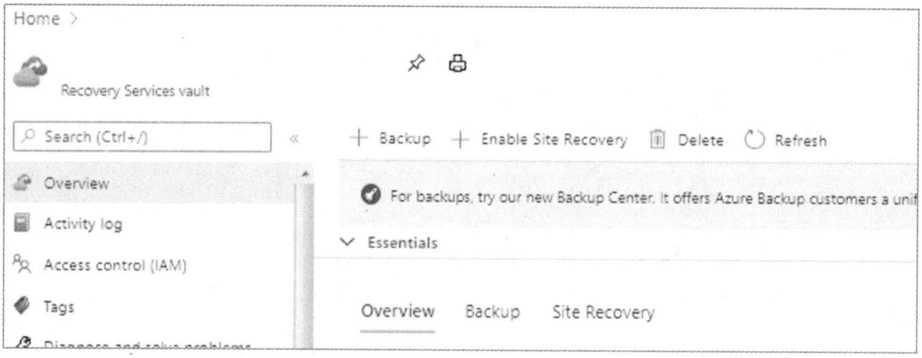

The next step in enabling Site Recovery for an Azure VM is to enable replication. Enabling replication has several steps that include:

- Selecting source settings
- Selecting the VMs
- Reviewing the replication settings
- Managing the replication policy
- Reviewing the VM settings

I will be covering each of these, starting with selecting the source.

Select the Source Settings

To select the source settings, perform the following:

1. Sign into the Azure portal at `https://portal.azure.com`.

2. Search for and select Recovery Services Vault.

3. In the vault, select Site Recovery from the menu, and then under Azure Virtual Machines, select Enable Replication, as shown in Figure 17.45.

FIGURE 17.45   Enable Replication

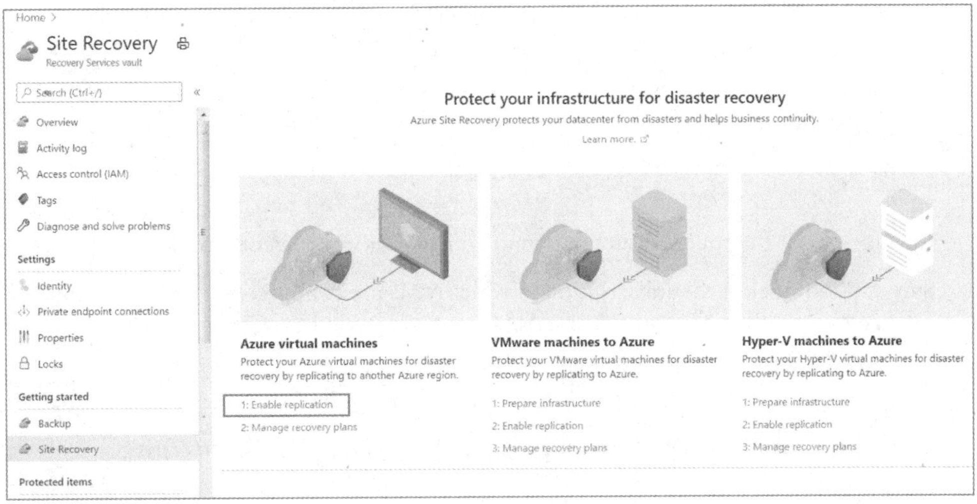

4. On the Enable Replication page, on the Source tab, enter the following, as shown in Figure 17.46.

FIGURE 17.46   Enable Replication – Source

Region—Select the source Azure region in which VMs are currently running.

Subscription—Select the subscription in which VMs are running. You can select any subscription that's in the same Azure AD tenant as the vault.

Resource Group—Select the desired resource group from the drop-down list.

Virtual Machine Deployment Model—Retain the default Resource Manager setting.

Disaster Recovery Between Availability Zones—Retain the default No setting.

5. Click Next.

Select the VMs

Site Recovery retrieves the VMs associated with the selected subscription/resource group. To select the VMs, perform the following:

1. In Virtual Machines, select the VMs you want to enable for disaster recovery, as shown in Figure 17.47. You can select up to 10 VMs.

FIGURE 17.47   Enable Replication – Virtual Machines

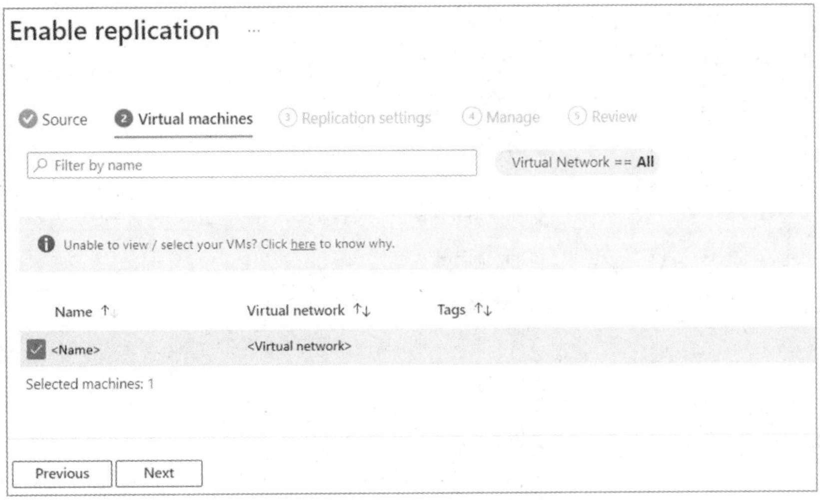

2. Click Next.

Review the Replication Settings

To review the replication settings, perform the following:

1. In Replication Settings, review the settings, as shown in Figure 17.48. Site Recovery creates default settings/policy for the target region.

FIGURE 17.48   Enable Replication – Replication Settings

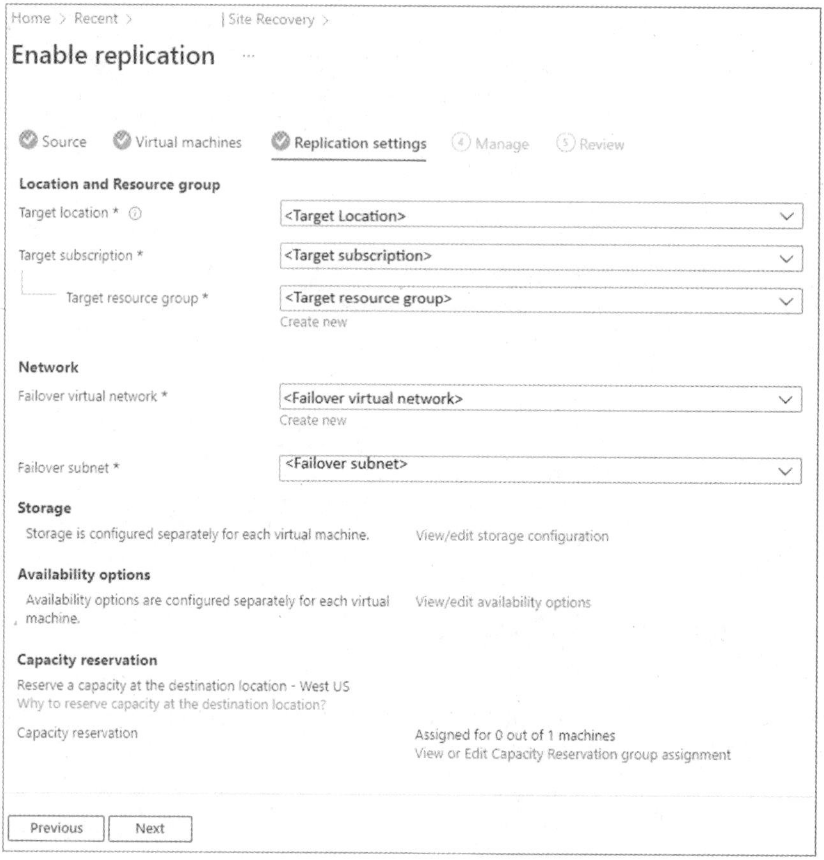

2.   When done reviewing the replication settings, click Next.

Managing the Replication Policy

To manage the replication policy, perform the following:

1.   In the Manage options, as shown in Figure 17.49, enter the following:

FIGURE 17.49   Enable Replication – Manage

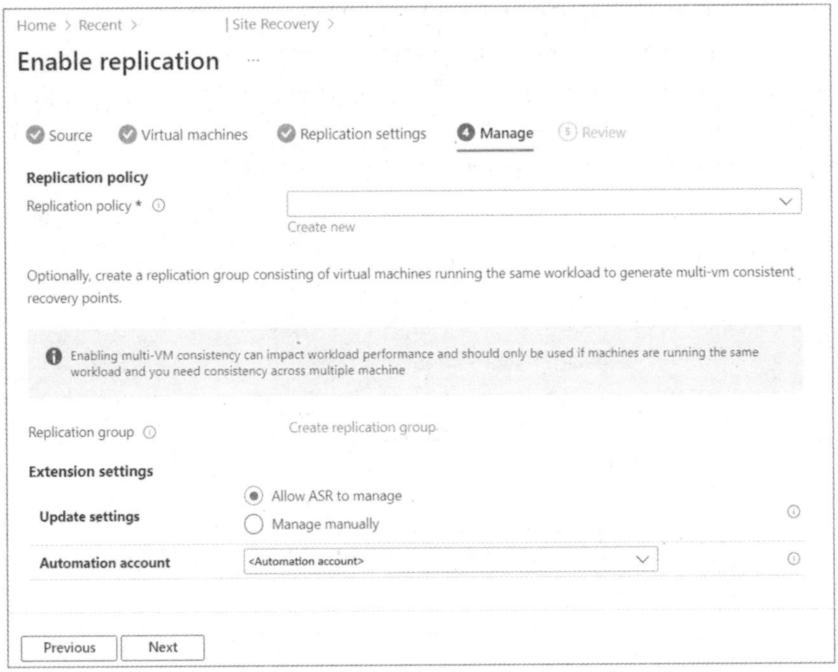

Under Replication Policy:

Replication Policy—Select the replication policy.

Replication Group—Create a replication group to replicate VMs together to generate multi-VM consistent recovery points.

Under Extension Settings:

Select Update Settings and Automation Account.

2.   When done, click Next.

Review the VM Settings

On the Review tab, review all the VM settings and select Enable Replication. The VMs that you enabled will appear in the Vault on the Replicated Items page.

Implement VM Replication to Secondary Datacenter or Azure Region

In this section, I discuss how to set up Site Recovery on an Azure VM by replicating it to a secondary Azure region.

Enable Replication for the Azure VM

To enable VM replication to a secondary location, perform the following:

1. Sign into the Azure portal at `https://portal.azure.com`.

2. On the Azure portal, from the Home page, go to the Virtual Machines menu, and select the VM you want to replicate.

3. In Operations, select Disaster Recovery, as shown in Figure 17.50.

FIGURE 17.50   Azure Disaster Recovery

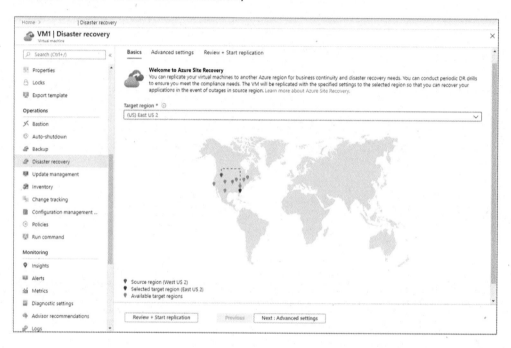

4. From Basics, go to the Target region and choose the target region.

5. To view the replication settings, select Review + Start Replication. If you need to change any defaults, click Advanced Settings.

6. Click Start Replication to start the VM replication.

Configure Azure Site Recovery Policies

Azure Policies help enforce rules on your Azure resources and checks the compliance of those resources. You can enable Site Recovery through a process called remediation for all the VMs already existing in the resource group. A scope determines the resources or the grouping of resources where the policy assignment is enforced. The scope of this policy can be at a subscription level or a resource group level. An assignment is a policy that has been assigned to run on a specific scope.

Create a Policy Assignment

To create a policy assignment for the built-in Azure Site Recovery policy that enables replication for all newly created VMs in a subscription or resource group, perform the following:

1. Sign into the Azure portal at `https://portal.azure.com`.

2. In the Azure portal, go to Azure Policy.

3. Select Assignments on the left side of the Azure Policy page.

4. Select Assign Policy from the top of the Policy – Assignments page, as shown in Figure 17.51.

FIGURE 17.51   Azure Policy – Assignments

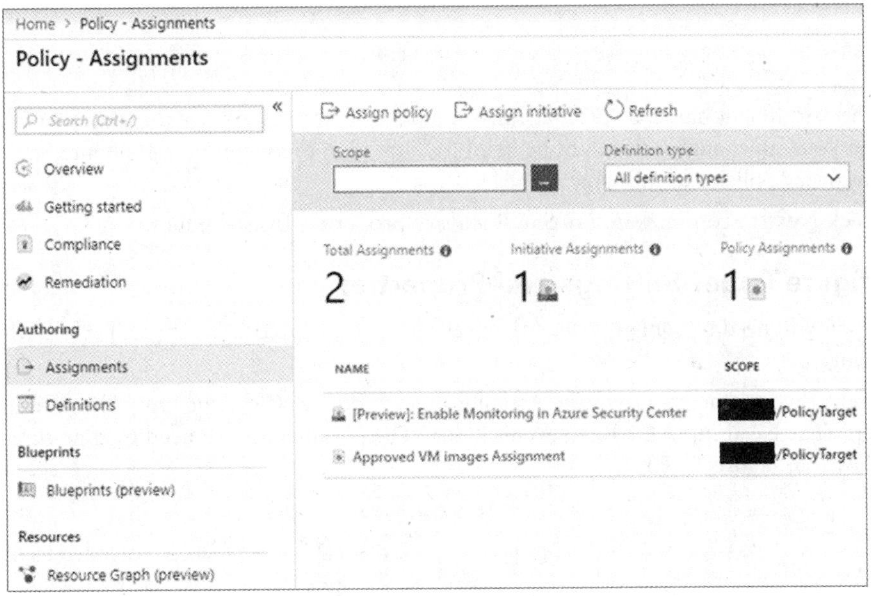

5. On the Assign Policy page, set the Scope information by clicking the ellipsis, selecting a subscription, and optionally selecting a resource group. Then, click Select at the bottom of the Scope page.

6. Open the policy definition picker by clicking the ellipsis next to Policy Definition. Search for **disaster recovery** or **site recovery**. You'll find a built-in policy titled Configure Disaster Recovery On Virtual Machines By Enabling Replication Via Azure Site Recovery. Select it and click Select, as shown in Figure 17.52.

FIGURE 17.52 Azure Policy – Available Definitions

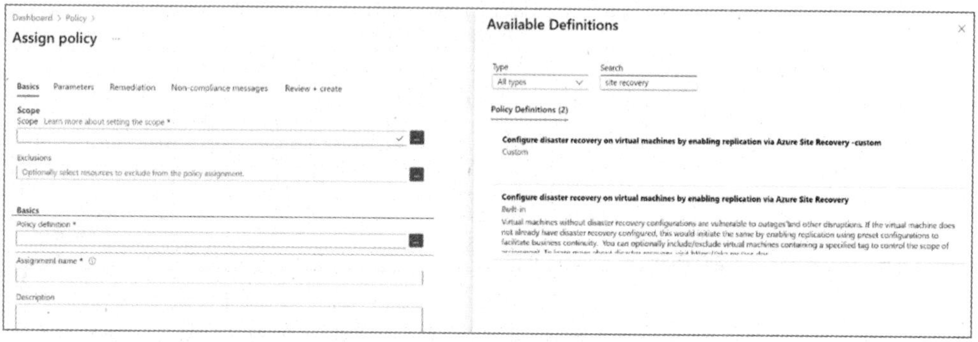

7. The assignment name is automatically populated with the policy name that you selected, but you can change it. It might be helpful if you plan to assign multiple Azure Site Recovery policies to the same scope.

8. Click Next to configure Azure Site Recovery properties for the policy.

Configure Target Settings and Properties

Next, you will need to configure the target settings and properties. To do so, perform the following:

1. Select the Parameters tab in the Assign Policy workflow. Clear the Only Show Parameters That Need Input Or Review check box. The parameters you need to configure are shown in Figure 17.53.

FIGURE 17.53   Assign Policy – Parameters

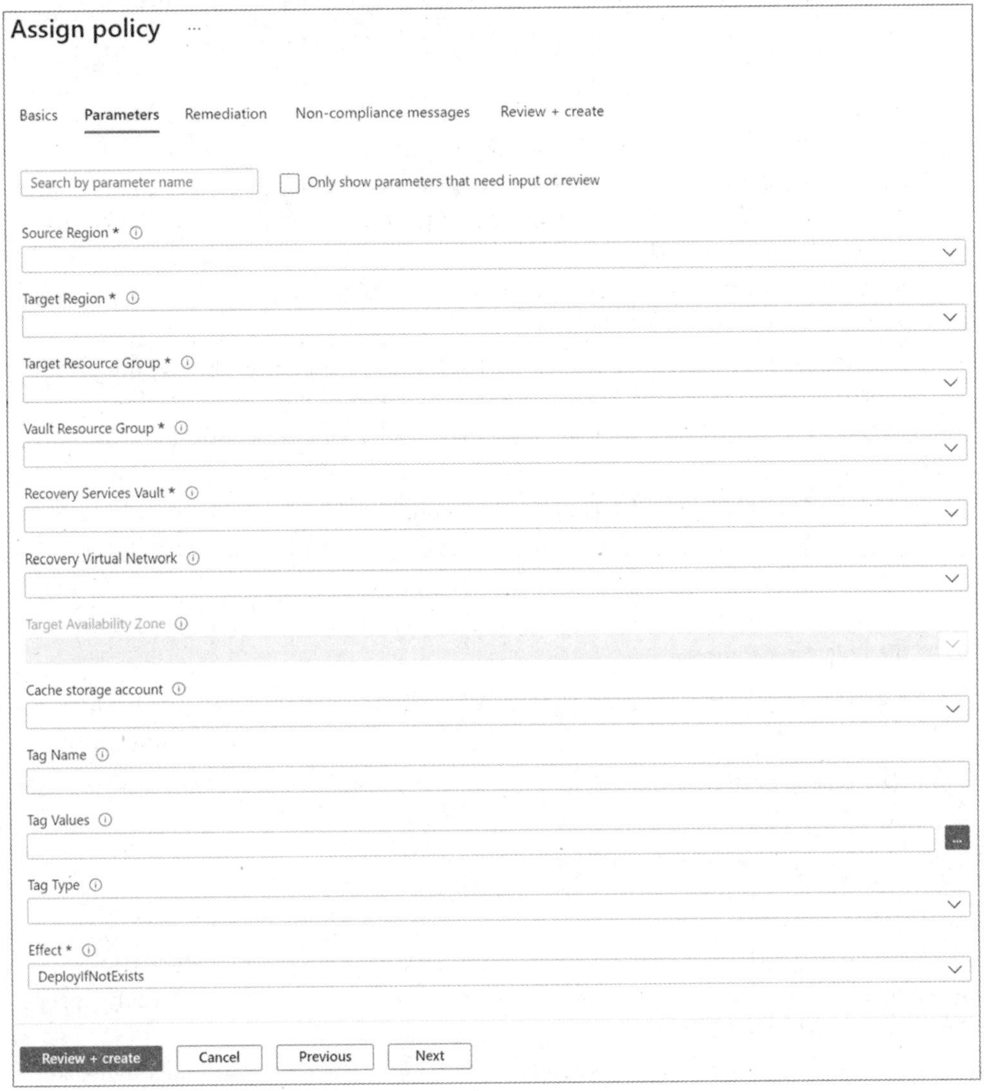

2. Select the appropriate values for the parameters:

    Source Region—Enter the source region of the VMs for which the policy will apply.

    Target Region—Enter the location where your source VM data will be replicated. Site Recovery provides the list of target regions that you can replicate to.

Target Resource Group—Enter the resource group where all your replicated VMs belong. By default, Site Recovery creates a new resource group in the target region.

Vault Resource Group—Enter the resource group in which the Recovery Services vault exists.

Recovery Services Vault—This is the vault where all the VMs of the scope will be protected. The policy can create a new vault on your behalf, if required.

Recovery Virtual Network (optional)—Choose an existing virtual network in the target region to be used for the recovery virtual machine. The policy can create a new virtual network for you, if required.

Target Availability Zone (optional)—Enter the availability zone of the target region where the virtual machine will fail over.

Cache Storage Account (optional)—Azure Site Recovery uses a storage account for caching replicated data in the source region. Select an account.

Tag Name (optional)—You can apply tags to your replicated VMs to help organize them.

Tag Values (optional)—Use this field to enter a tag value.

Tag Type (optional)—Use tags to include VMs as part of the policy assignment. You can choose:

> Tag type = Inclusion—Ensures that only the VMs that have the tag are included in the policy assignment.

> Tag type = Exclusion—Ensures that the VMs that have the tag are excluded from the policy assignment.

Effect—Enable or disable the execution of the policy. Select DeployIfNotExists to enable the policy as soon as it's created.

3. Click Next to decide on remediation tasks.

Configure Remediation

Next comes remediation. Replication on preexisting VMs is not automatically enabled, so you will need to create a remediation task. To create a remediation task and set other properties, perform the following:

1. On the Remediation tab in the Assign Policy workflow, select the Create A Remediation Task check box. Azure Policy will create a managed identity, which will have owner permissions to enable Azure Site Recovery for the resources in the scope.

2. You can configure a custom noncompliance message for the policy on the Noncompliance Messages tab.

3. Click Next on the Review + Create tab at the top of the page to move to the next segment of the assignment wizard.

4. Review the selected options, and then click Create at the bottom of the page.

After the policy is assigned, you will have to wait for up to 1 hour for replication to be enabled. After an hour you can go to the Recovery Services Vault and check for the replication job.

Summary

Azure has a wide variety of security tools and features that allow you to customize security in order to meet your company's security needs and make it possible to create secure solutions by using the Azure subscription platform.

Microsoft Sentinel provides security analytics and threat intelligence as well as providing attack detection, threat visibility, proactive hunting, and threat response. Microsoft Sentinel collects data for users, devices, applications, and infrastructure, both on-premises and in multiple clouds.

Microsoft Defender for Cloud helps you find and fix security vulnerabilities, block malicious activity by applying access and application controls, detect threats by using analytics, and if you are under attack, helps you to respond. With Microsoft Defender for Cloud's enhanced security features enabled, you can have Advanced Detection, which triggers security alerts.

Microsoft Defender for Cloud has a workflow automation feature that can trigger Logic Apps on items such as security alerts, recommendations, and changes to regulatory compliance.

Organizations can protect against data loss by using the practice of backup and recovery. A backup creates a copy of data that can be recovered in the event of a failure. Recovery involves restoring lost or damaged data to the original location from a backup.

Azure Backup can be used to back up and restore your data in the Microsoft cloud. You can manage and monitor Azure Backup by using the Backup Center.

To back up and recover files, folders, volumes, or system state data from an on-premises computer to Azure, Azure Backup uses the Microsoft Azure Recovery Services (MARS) agent.

A Recovery Services Vault is an Azure storage entity that holds data. It stores recovery points that have been created over a period of time.

Microsoft Azure Backup Server (MABS) is a server product that you can use to protect application workloads using a single console. A backup policy will specify when to take snapshots of the data to create recovery points. It also specifies how long to keep recovery points.

A recovery plan gathers machines into recovery groups and helps define the recovery process. The recovery plan determines how the machines fail over and the order in which they start after failover. Recovery plans can be used for both failover to and failback.

Azure Policies help enforce rules on your Azure resources and check the compliance of those resources.

Exam Essentials

Understand Azure Security.   Know the six functional levels of Azure security: Applications, Computer, Identity and Access, Networking, Operations, and Storage. Know some of the tools and features of each. Know how to identify and remediate security issues by using Azure services.

Know how to monitor on-premises servers and Azure IaaS VMs by using Microsoft Sentinel.   Understand how to use Microsoft Sentinel. Know how to onboard and how to enable Microsoft Sentinel and set up data connectors.

Know how to identify and remediate security issues on-premises servers and Azure IaaS VMs by using Microsoft Defender for Cloud.   Understand how to use Microsoft Defender for Cloud. Know how to enable Microsoft Defender for Cloud and how to manage and respond to security alerts. Understand Azure Logic Apps and how to create them. Know about vulnerability assessment solutions and how to deploy an integrated scanner to your Azure and hybrid machines.

Understand how to manage backup and recovery for Windows Server.   Know how to install and manage Azure Backup. Understand how to work with the Microsoft Azure Recovery Services (MARS) agent, including how to download, install, and register. Know how to back up using the Azure Recovery Services Vault and how to create a recovery services vault. Understand how to monitor and manage Recovery Services Vaults. Know how to manage backup alerts.

Know how to use the Azure Backup Center.   Know how to move around the Azure Backup Center. Understand how to configure and manage backups in a Recovery Services Vault using the Backup Center. Know how to configure a backup vault. Know how to perform different restore and backup options using the Recovery Services Vault.

Know how to back up and recover using Azure Backup Server.   Understand how to install and manage Azure Backup Server. Know how to extract and install the Azure Backup Server. Know how to configure backup for Azure virtual machines using the built-in backup agents. Understand how to use Instant Restore.

Understand how to create a backup policy.   Know how to create a backup policy and restore a VM. Understand the different Azure VM Restore scenarios and how to select a restore point.

Understand how to recover a VM using temporary snapshots and recover VMs to new Azure VMs.   Know how to restore a VM. Understand how to choose a VM restore configuration. Understand how to recover a VM using snapshots.

Understand how to implement disaster recovery by using Azure Site Recovery.   Know Site Recovery features. Know how to configure Azure Site Recovery networking. Understand how to modify the network interface settings.

Know how to configure site recovery for on-premises VMs, configure a recovery plan, and configure Site Recovery for Azure VMs. Understand how to create a Recovery Services Vault to be used for Site Recovery. Know how to configure a recovery plan. Know how to configure site recovery for Azure VMs. Understand how to implement VM Replication to a secondary datacenter or Azure Region. Know how to enable replication for an Azure VM.

Know how to configure Azure Site recovery policies. Understand what an Azure Policy is. Understand how to create a policy assignment. Know how to configure target settings and properties. Understand remediation.

Review Questions

1. You have a Microsoft Sentinel deployment and 100 Azure Arc-enabled on-premises servers. All the Azure Arc–enabled resources are in the same resource group. You need to onboard the servers to Microsoft Sentinel. What should you use to onboard the servers to Microsoft Sentinel if you want to minimize administrative effort?

   A. Azure automation

   B. Azure policy

   C. Azure VM extensions

   D. Microsoft Defender for Cloud

2. You have 100 Azure VMs that run Windows Server. The virtual machines are onboarded to Microsoft Defender for Cloud. What should you use in Microsoft Defender for Cloud if you want to automatically shut down the VM if Microsoft Defender for Cloud generates a security alert?

   A. Adaptive network hardening

   B. Logic App

   C. Security policy

   D. Workbook

3. You and a colleague are discussing Azure Site Recovery Networking. All outbound traffic from the VM uses the IP address of which of the following?

   A. The initial network interface

   B. The default gateway

   C. The primary network interface

   D. The secondary network interface

4. You have an on-premises server named Svr1 that runs Windows Server and has the Hyper-V server role installed. You have an Azure subscription. You are planning to back up Svr1 to Azure by using Azure Backup. Which two Azure Backup options require you to deploy Microsoft Azure Backup Server (MABS)?

   A. Bare-Metal Recovery

   B. Files And Folders

   C. Hyper-V Virtual Machines

   D. System State

5. You have an Azure subscription that has Microsoft Defender for Cloud enabled. You have received a security recommendation that states "Machines should have a vulnerability assessment solution." You are taking the steps needed to deploy an integrated scanner. You proceed through the steps and click Remediate. Once set up, scans will run every _____ hours?

   A. 3

   B. 6

   C. 12

   D. 24

6. You and a colleague are discussing Microsoft Defender for Cloud. Microsoft Defender for Cloud has two main pillars for cloud security. What are they called? (Choose two.)

   A. Cloud Security Posture Management (CSPM)

   B. Cloud Workload Protection Platform (CWPP)

   C. Security Information and Event Management (SIEM)

   D. Security Orchestration, Automation, and Response (SOAR)

7. You have 200 Azure virtual machines. You create a recovery plan in Azure Site Recovery to fail over all the VMs to an Azure region. The plan has three manual actions. What should you use if you need to replace one of the manual actions with an automated process?

   A. An Azure Automation runbook

   B. An Azure Desired State Configuration (DSC) virtual machine extension

   C. An Azure PowerShell function

   D. A Custom Script Extension on the virtual machines

8. You and a colleague are discussing Azure Security and the tool/feature that can help with replication, failover, and the recovery of workloads and apps from a secondary location. What is this tool called?

   A. Azure Load Balancer

   B. Azure Site Recovery

   C. Virtual Machine Backup

   D. Virtual Networking

9. You and a colleague are discussing using Microsoft Sentinel. You have successfully onboarded Microsoft Sentinel. What is the next step?

   A. Isolate the workspace.

   B. Monitor the Overview dashboard.

   C. Move the workspace.

   D. Set up data connectors.

10. You have three Azure virtual machines, named VM1, VM2, and VM3, that host a multitier application. You are planning to implement Azure Site Recovery. What should you configure if you need to ensure that the virtual machines failover as a group?

    A. An availability set

    B. An availability zone

    C. A RAID array

    D. A recovery plan

11. You have 100 Azure VMs that run Windows Server. The virtual machines are onboarded to Microsoft Defender for Cloud. You are in the middle of creating a Security Alert and you are now on the Take Action tab. You want to view the resource's activity logs. What section should you go to?

    A. Inspect Resource Context

    B. Mitigate The Threat

    C. Prevent Future Attacks

    D. Trigger Automated Response

12. You and a colleague are discussing managing backup and recovery. There are a number of tools to help with this. However, you are discussing Azure Backup and Azure Site Recovery. Both of these use a centralized management interface. What is this interface known as?

    A. Azure Backup Collector

    B. Backup Center

    C. Recovery Services Vault

    D. VM Backup Tool

13. You want to back up from an on-premises computer to Azure. What do you need in order to be able to do this?

    A. Azure Backup and Restore (ABR) Agent

    B. Azure Data Management (ADM) Agent

    C. Microsoft Azure Recovery Services (MARS) Agent

    D. Microsoft Protection Agent

14. You and a colleague are discussing the Backup Center and the different alert levels that the Backup Alerts can show. The Backup Alerts report will list all the alerts for the vault and display an alert severity. All of the following are alert severity levels, except which one?

    A. Critical

    B. Danger

    C. Informational

    D. Warning

15. You and a colleague are discussing setting up a Microsoft Azure Backup Server. This server will be onsite. How much RAM does Microsoft recommend for this backup server as a minimum?

   A. 4 GB

   B. 8 GB

   C. 10 GB

   D. 16 GB

16. You and a colleague are discussing some of the different Site Recovery features. One feature is described as being able to run disaster recovery drills without affecting ongoing replication. What feature is being discussed?

   A. Azure automation integration

   B. Data resilience

   C. On-premises VM replication

   D. Testing without disruption

17. You have an Azure subscription that has Microsoft Defender for Cloud enabled. You have 50 Azure VMs that run Windows Server. You need to ensure that any security exploits detected on the VMs are forwarded to Defender for Cloud. What extension should you enable on the virtual machines?

   A. Guest Configuration agent

   B. Log Analytics agent for Azure VMs

   C. Microsoft Dependency agent

   D. Vulnerability scanner

18. You and a colleague are discussing the Microsoft Defender for Cloud Overview page. There is a graph-based algorithm that will scan the cloud security graph and show you all the possible paths that an attacker can use to breach your workload. What is this called?

   A. Attack Path Analysis

   B. Attack Route Assessment

   C. Breach Path Evaluation

   D. Hacker Highway

19. You and a colleague are discussing how a vulnerability scanner extension works and the different parts associated with it. One of the parts monitors your machines and provides recommendations on how to deploy the extension. Which part is being discussed?

   A. Analyze

   B. Deploy

   C. Gather Information

   D. Report

20. You and a colleague are discussing Microsoft Sentinel. Microsoft Sentinel provides which of the following? (Choose two.)

   A.   Cloud Security Posture Management (CSPM)

   B.   Cloud Workload Protection Platform (CWPP)

   C.   Security information and event management (SIEM)

   D.   Security orchestration, automation, and response (SOAR)

Appendix

Answers to Review Questions

Chapter 1: Introduction to Windows Server 2022

1. **B.** Windows Server 2022 Datacenter Server Core is a more secure, slimmed-down version of Windows Server. Web versions of Windows Server 2022 are not available. You would use Windows Server 2022 Standard as a web server.

2. **A.** The only way you can change between Server Core and the Desktop Experience is to reinstall the server. Converting from Server Core to Desktop Experience by running a PowerShell command is no longer an option.

3. **B.** Microsoft recommends that you upgrade your Windows Server 2012 R2 Standard server to Windows Server 2022 Standard.

4. **A.** Windows Server 2022 Datacenter was designed for organizations that are seeking to migrate to a highly virtualized, private cloud environment. Windows Server 2022 Datacenter has full Windows Server functionality with unlimited virtual instances.

5. **D.** Windows Server 2022 Essentials is ideal for small businesses that have as many as 25 users and 50 devices. Windows Server 2022 Essentials has a simpler interface and preconfigured connectivity to cloud-based services but no virtualization rights.

6. **C.** Windows Server 2022 Essentials is ideal for small businesses that have as many as 25 users and 50 devices. It has a simple interface, preconfigured connectivity to cloud-based services, and no virtualization rights.

7. **A, B, C, D.** All four answers are advantages of using Windows Server 2022. Server Core is a smaller installation of Windows Server and therefore all four answers apply.

8. **B.** Windows Server 2022 Features on Demand allows you not only to disable a role or feature but also to remove the role or feature's files completely from the hard disk.

9. **D.** Windows Server 2022 Nano Server uses the Current Branch for Business (CBB) servicing model. This version of servicing is a more aggressive version and was specifically designed with the cloud in mind. As the cloud continues to quickly evolve, the CBB servicing model is meant for that lifecycle.

10. **C.** Windows Server 2022 has a type of server called Server Core. This gives an organization the ability to install a server in an area or location (onsite or offsite) where security is a concern. Server Core has no GUI and can be set up more securely than a server version with the GUI.

11. **B.** Windows Deployment Services (WDS) allows an IT administrator to install a Windows operating system without using an installation disc. Using WDS allows you to deploy the operating system through a network installation or an image.

12. C, D. Using Windows Server 2022 Server Core allows you to have reduced management, minimal installation files, and tighter security. Server Core is a smaller installation than Windows Server 2022 with Desktop Experience, and it has a smaller attack surface.

13. C. Windows Server 2022 allows you to set up a type of server installation called Nano Server. With Nano Server, you can remotely administer the server operating system. Nano Server has no local logon and must be administered remotely. It is very similar to Server Core, but the Nano Server operating system uses significantly smaller hard drive space and only supports 64-bit applications and tools.

14. D. Windows Server 2022 Nano Server uses the Current Branch for Business (CBB) servicing model. This version of servicing is a more aggressive version and was specifically designed with the cloud in mind. As the cloud continues to quickly evolve, the CBB servicing model is meant for that lifecycle.

15. B. Windows Server 2022 (Server Core) is a more secure, slimmed-down version of Windows Server. Windows Server 2022 versions with Desktop Experience are versions with a GUI interface. Server Core versions do not have a GUI interface, making the server more secure. Nano Server installations are also a good option for securing your server. But if that is not an available option, Server Core is another good way to help secure a server.

Chapter 2: Understanding Hyper-V

1. B, D. Hyper-V can be installed on the Standard or Datacenter editions of Windows Server 2022. The Itanium, x86, and Web editions are not supported.

2. C. The external virtual network type will allow the virtual machine to communicate with the external network as it would with the Internet, so A is wrong. The internal-only network type allows communication between the virtual machines and the host machine. Because the question says that only communication between the virtual machines should be allowed, the only valid answer is private virtual machine network. The last option, public virtual machine network, does not exist in Hyper-V.

3. A. This question focuses on the fact that you cannot change the memory if the virtual machine is running, paused, or saved. The only valid answer is to shut it down and then change the memory.

4. A. The only virtual hard disk that increases in size is the dynamically expanding disk. Thus, this is the only valid answer to this question. The fixed-size disk creates a disk of the size you specify, the differencing disk is a special disk that stores only the differences between it and a parent disk, and the physical disk uses a physical drive and makes it available to the virtual machine.

5. C. Physical hard disks cannot be configured using the Virtual Hard Disk Wizard, the Edit Virtual Hard Disk Wizard, or the New Virtual Machine Wizard. You can configure and attach a physical disk only by using the virtual machine's settings.

6. B. Hyper-V is not supported on Itanium-based systems, which means Rich cannot install it.

7. A, B, C. The minimum CPU requirement for running Hyper-V is an x64-based processor (Itanium is not supported), hardware Data Execution Protection must be enabled, and hardware-assisted virtualization must be enabled. There is no minimum requirement for a dual-core processor.

8. C. This question relates to the setup command used to install the Hyper-V server role on a Windows Server 2022 Server Core machine. It's important to remember that these commands are case sensitive, and that the correct command is `start /wocsetup Microsoft-Hyper-V`, which is option C. All of the other commands will fail to install Hyper-V on a Server Core machine.

9. A, C, D. The Hyper-V Manager is available only for Windows Server 2022/2019/2016/2012 R2/2012/2008 R2/2008, Windows 11, Windows 10, Windows 8, and Windows 7. There is no version available that runs on Windows Server 2003.

10. C. The virtual network type in which the machines communicate with each other and with the host machine is called *internal only*. In a private virtual network, the virtual machines can communicate only with each other, not with the network or the host machine. The external network type defines a network where the virtual machines can communicate with each other, with the host machine, and with an external network like the Internet.

11. B. To properly work with Hyper-V, you must make sure that your system meets minimum requirements, and this includes the network adapter.

12. A, B, C, D. Integration Services includes those services that you want to offer to the Hyper-V virtual machine. To take advantage of these services, they must be supported by the operating system that is installed on the virtual machine. The following services are offered using Integration Services: Operating System Shutdown, Time Synchronization, Data Exchange, Heartbeat, and Backup (volume snapshot).

13. A, B. Hyper-V Manager supports copying a physical disk to a virtual disk by using only dynamically expanding or fixed-size virtual hard disks. You can perform this task in the New Virtual Hard Disk Wizard. Differencing and physical disks are not available for this feature.

14. C. A legacy network adapter is a virtual network adapter that allows you to boot from the network. All other options are misleading and only point to different virtual network types.

15. A. The only supported way to move virtual machines between host machines listed here is to use Export And Import Virtual Machine. The option to move the virtual machine files cannot be used anymore because you will lose the configuration of your virtual machines. You cannot apply a snapshot to a different host machine, nor is a Save command available in Hyper-V.

16. B. Integration Services are those services that you want to offer to the Hyper-V virtual machine. One of the services that Integration Services offers is Time Synchronization.

The following services are offered using Integration Services: Operating System Shutdown, Data Exchange, Heartbeat, and Backup (volume snapshot).

17. D. Integration Services are services that you want to offer to the Hyper-V virtual machine. One of the services that Integration Services offers is Data Exchange.

The following services are offered using Integration Services: Operating System Shutdown, Time Synchronization, Heartbeat, and Backup (volume snapshot).

18. D. A differencing disk is associated in a parent-child relationship with another disk. The differencing disk is the child and the associated virtual disk is the parent. Differencing disks include only the differences to the parent disk. By using this type, you can save a lot of disk space in similar virtual machines.

19. D. Legacy network adapters can't have bandwidth specifications assigned to them. So to give a network adapter a specific amount of bandwidth to use, you must remove the old adapter and install the new adapter.

20. A. The PowerShell command `Restart-VM` restarts a virtual machine.

Chapter 3: Installing Windows Server 2022

1. B. Windows Server 2022 Datacenter Server Core is a more secure, slimmed-down version of Windows Server. Web versions of Windows Server 2022 are not available. You would use Windows Server 2022 Standard as a web server.

2. D. NTFS can work with file encryption and disk quotas. ReFS cannot work with filesystem compression, filesystem encryption, transactions, object IDs, Offloaded Data Transfer (ODX), short names, extended attributes, disk quotas, bootable drives, page file support, and support on removable media.

3. B. Microsoft allows you to upgrade any Windows Server above Windows Server 2012 R2 Standard to Windows Server 2022 Standard.

4. A. Windows Server 2012 R2 Datacenter was designed for organizations that are seeking to migrate to a highly virtualized, private cloud environment. Windows Server 2012 R2 Datacenter has full Windows Server functionality with unlimited virtual instances.

5. D. Windows Server 2022 Essentials is ideal for small businesses that have as many as 25 users and 50 devices. Windows Server 2022 Essentials has a simpler interface and preconfigured connectivity to cloud-based services but no virtualization rights.

6. C. Windows Server 2022 Essentials is ideal for small businesses that have as many as 25 users and 50 devices. It has a simple interface, preconfigured connectivity to cloud-based services, and no virtualization rights.

7. A, B, C, D. All four answers are advantages of using Windows Server 2022. Server Core is a smaller installation of Windows Server and therefore all four answers apply.

8. B. Windows Server 2022 Features on Demand allows you not only to disable a role or feature but also to remove the role or feature's files completely from the hard disk.

9. C, D. Using Windows Server 2022 Server Core allows you to have reduced management, minimal installation files, and tighter security. Server Core is a smaller installation than Windows Server 2022 with Desktop Experience and it has a smaller attack surface.

10. D. The `Get-WindowsFeature` cmdlet allows you to view a list of available and installed roles and features on the local server.

11. B. Windows Server 2022 (Server Core) is a more secure, slimmed-down version of Windows Server. Windows Server 2022 versions with Desktop Experience are versions with a GUI interface. Server Core versions do not have a GUI interface, making the server more secure.

12. A. The iSCSI default port is TCP 3260. Port 3389 is used for RDP, port 1433 is used for Microsoft SQL, and port 21 is used for FTP.

13. D. NTFS has file-level security, and it makes efficient usage of disk space. Since this machine is to be configured as a domain controller, the configuration requires at least one NTFS partition to store the SYSVOL information.

14. A, D. To convert the system partition to NTFS, you must first use the `CONVERT` command-line utility and then reboot the server. During the next boot, the filesystem will be converted.

15. A, B, C, D. Improved security, quotas, compression, and encryption are all advantages of using NTFS over FAT32. These features are not available in FAT32. The only security you have in FAT32 is shared folder permissions.

16. B. Disk quotas allow you to limit the amount of space on a volume or partition. You can set an umbrella quota for all users and then implement individual users' quotas to bypass the umbrella quota.

17. D. The `Get-WindowsFeature` cmdlet allows you to view a list of available and installed roles and features on the local server.

18. D. The `iscsicli addisnsserver server_name` command manually registers the host server to an iSNS server. `refreshisnsserver` refreshes the list of available servers. `removeisnsserver` removes the host from the iSNS server. `listisnsservers` lists the available iSNS servers.

19. D. The `iscsicli addisnsserver server_name` command manually registers the host server to an iSNS server. refreshisnsserver refreshes the list of available servers. `removeisnsserver` removes the host from the iSNS server. `listisnsservers` lists the available iSNS servers.

20. E. NTFS and ReFS can both work with BitLocker. ReFS can't work with filesystem compression, filesystem encryption, transactions, object IDs, Offloaded Data Transfer (ODX), short names, extended attributes, disk quotas, bootable drives, page file support, and support on removable media.

Chapter 4: Understanding IP

1. A. The port that's responsible for handling all unencrypted HTTP web traffic is port 80. When we use a TLS certificate, the communication channel between the browser and the server gets encrypted to protect all sensitive data exchanges. All such secure transfers are done using port 443.

2. B. The port that's responsible for handling Secure Shell (SSH) is port 22. Ports 20 and 21 are used for FTP.

3. B. The port that's responsible for handling Simple Mail Transfer Protocol (SMTP) is port 25. Port 53 is used for DNS.

4. A. The port that's responsible for handling Post Office Protocol version 3 (POP3) is port 110.

5. D. To calculate the network mask, you need to figure out which power number (2^x) is greater than or equal to the number you need. Since we are looking for 1,000, $2^{10} = 1,024$. You then add the power (10) to the current network mask (53 + 10 = 63).

6. A. When you look at an IPv6 address, the first sections tell you the IPv6 address space prefix. Fd00:: /8 is the unique local unicast prefix, and this allows the server to communicate with all local machines within your intranet.

7. C. The unique local address can be FC00 or FD00, and it is used like the private address space of IPv4. Unique local addresses are not expected to be routable on the global Internet, but they are used for private routing within an organization.

8. A. A Class B address with a default subnet mask of 255.255.0.0 will support up to 65,534 hosts. To increase the number of networks that this network will support, you need to subnet the network by borrowing bits from the host portion of the address. The subnet mask 255.255.252.0 uses 6 bits from the host's area, and it will support 64 subnets while leaving enough bits to support 1,022 hosts per subnet. The subnet mask 255.255.248.0 uses 5 bits from the hosts and will support 32 subnetworks while leaving enough bits to support 2,046 hosts per subnet. 255.255.252.0 is the better answer because it leaves quite a bit of room for further growth in the number of networks while still leaving room for more than 1,000 hosts per subnet, which is a fairly large number of devices on one subnet. The subnet mask 255.255.254.0 uses 7 bits from the host's area and will support 126 networks, but it will leave only enough bits to support 500 hosts per subnet. The subnet mask 255.255.240.0 uses 4 bits from the hosts and will support only 16 subnetworks, even though it will leave enough bits to support more than 4,000 hosts per subnet.

9. A. The network mask applied to an address determines which portion of that address reflects the number of hosts available to that network. The balance with subnetting is always between the number of hosts and individual subnetworks that can be uniquely represented within one encompassing address. The number of hosts and networks that are made available

depends on the number of bits that can be used to represent them. This scenario requires more than 35 networks and fewer than 1,000 workstations on each network. If you convert the subnet masks as described in the chapter, you will see that the mask in option A allows for 64 networks and more than 1,000 hosts. All of the other options are deficient in either the number of networks or the number of hosts that they represent.

10. A. The subnet mask 255.255.255.192 borrows 2 bits from the hosts, which allows you to build four separate networks that you can route through the Windows server. This will allow you to have 62 hosts on each segment. A mask of 255.255.255.128 would have been even better, with two subnets of 126 hosts each, but that wasn't an option and this solution gives you room for growth in the number of subnets. The subnet mask 255.255.255.224 borrows 3 bits from the hosts. This allows you to create 8 networks, which you don't need, and it leaves only enough bits for 30 hosts. The subnet mask 255.255.255.252 borrows 6 bits from the hosts. This allows you to create 64 networks, which you don't need, and it leaves only enough bits for 2 hosts. The subnet mask 255.255.255.240 borrows 4 bits from the hosts. This allows you to create 16 networks, which you don't need, and it leaves only enough bits for 14 hosts per subnet.

11. B, C, D. When you add up the locations that currently need to be given a network address, the total is 3,150, and the maximum number of hosts at any one of these locations is fewer than 1,000. The subnet masks need to support those requirements. Assuming that you choose the Class A private address space 10.0.0.0/8, the subnet masks given in options B, C, and D will provide the address space to support the outlined requirements. The subnet mask 255.255.240.0 supports 4,096 subnets and more than 4,000 hosts. The subnet mask 255.255.248.0 supports 8,192 subnets and 2,046 hosts. The subnet mask 255.255.252.0 supports more than 16,000 subnets and more than 1,000 hosts. Although each of these subnet masks will work, at the rate that this company is growing, 255.255.252.0 is probably the best mask to prepare for the future. It's unlikely that there will ever be more than 1,000 hosts on any given network. In fact, that number would probably cause performance problems on that subnet. Therefore, it's better to have more subnets available to deploy as the company grows. The subnet mask 255.255.224.0 supports 2,048 subnets—an insufficient number to cover the locations. The subnet mask 255.255.254.0 supports 32,768 subnets, but only 500 hosts per subnet, which are not enough hosts to cover all of the locations.

12. C. The CIDR /27 tells you that 27 1s are turned on in the subnet mask. Twenty-seven 1s equals 11111111.11111111.11111111.11100000. This would then equal 255.255.255.224.

The network address 192.168.11.192 with a subnet mask of 255.255.255.224 is perfect for Subnet A because it supports up to 30 hosts. The network address 192.168.11.128 with a subnet mask of 255.255.255.192 is perfect for Subnet B because it supports up to 62 hosts. The network address 192.168.11.0 with a subnet mask of 255.255.255.128 is perfect for Subnet C because it supports up to 126 hosts.

13. C. You need to configure a subnet mask that can accommodate 3,500 clients. The way to figure it out is to use the formula of $2^x - 2 =$ Mask Number. So 3,500 clients means it is $2^{12} - 2 = 4,094$. 4,094 (power of 12) is the first power number that is greater than 3,500. So since it is 2^{12}, that means that our subnet mask has 12 0s. So it looks like the following: 11111111.11111111.11110000.00000000. This translates to 255.255.240.0.

14. B, D. If the first word of an IPv6 address is FE80 (actually the first 10 bits of the first word yields 1111 1110 10, or FE80:: /10), then the address is a link-local IPv6 address. If it's in EUI-64 format, then the MAC address is also available (unless it's randomly generated). The middle FF:FE is the filler and indicator of the EUI-64 space, with the MAC address being 00:03:FF:11:02:CD. Remember also the 00 of the MAC becomes 02 in the link-local IPv6 address, flipping a bit to call it local.

15. B. The port that's responsible for handling DNS is port 53. Port 80 is used for HTTP communications.

Chapter 5: Implementing DNS

1. B. Because of the `.(root)` zone, users will not be able to access the Internet. The DNS forwarding option and DNS root hints will not be configurable. If you want your users to access the Internet, you must remove the `.(root)` zone.

2. C. Active Directory Integrated zones store their records in Active Directory. Because this company only has one Active Directory forest, it's the same Active Directory that both DNS servers are using. This allows ServerA to see all of the records of ServerB and ServerB to see all the records of ServerA.

3. D. The Secure Only option is for DNS servers that have an Active Directory Integrated zone. When a computer tries to register with DNS dynamically, the DNS server checks Active Directory to verify that the computer has an Active Directory account. If the computer that is trying to register has an account, DNS adds the host record. If the computer trying to register does not have an account, the record gets tossed away and the database is not updated.

4. A. If you need to complete a zone transfer from Microsoft DNS to a BIND (Unix) DNS server, you need to enable BIND secondaries on the Microsoft DNS server.

5. B. Conditional forwarding allows you to send a DNS query to different DNS servers based on the request. Conditional forwarding lets a DNS server on a network forward DNS queries according to the DNS domain name in the query.

6. B. On a Windows Server 2022 DNS machine, debug logging is disabled by default. When it is enabled, you have the ability to log DNS server activity, including inbound and outbound queries, packet type, packet content, and transport protocols.

7. D. Active Directory Integrated zones give you many benefits over using primary and secondary zones including less network traffic, secure dynamic updates, encryption, and reliability in the event of a DNS server going down. The Secure Only option is for dynamic updates to a DNS database.

8. A. Windows Server 2022 DNS supports two features called DNS Aging and DNS Scavenging. These features are used to clean up and remove stale resource records. DNS zone or DNS server aging and scavenging flags old resource records that have not been updated in a certain amount of time (determined by the scavenging interval). These stale records will be scavenged at the next cleanup interval.

9. C. The `dnscmd /zoneexport` command creates a file using the zone resource records. This file can then be given to the Compliance department as a copy.

10. D. Stub zones are very useful for slow WAN connections. These zones store only three types of resource records: NS records, glue host (A) records, and SOA records. These three records are used to locate authoritative DNS servers.

11. B. Manual settings override DHCP options.

12. C. A default gateway allows devices on one subnet to communicate with devices on another subnet. The default gateway is the router's IP address. This question states that you can access computers on one network but not on the remote network. This is an indicator that the issue is with the IP address of the default gateway.

13. D. A Domain Name System (DNS) server has the DNS service running on it. DNS is a name-resolution service that resolves a hostname to a TCP/IP address (called *forward lookup*). DNS can also resolve a TCP/IP address to a name (called *reverse lookup*). If you can connect to a machine by using its TCP/IP address but not the name, then DNS is the issue.

14. D. Computers can communicate only by using a series of numbers. The Domain Name System (DNS) is basically like the phonebook of the Internet. Web browsers use Internet Protocol (IP) addresses, and DNS translates those domain names into IP addresses so that the browsers can load the web pages. The `ipconfig` command displays a computer's IP address configuration. Using `ipconfig` with the `/registerdns` switch will automatically register the Windows client machine with the DNS server. The registration includes the Windows client machine name and the IP address.

15. C. A Domain Name System (DNS) server has the DNS service running on it. DNS is a name-resolution service that resolves a hostname to a TCP/IP address (called *forward lookup*). DNS can also resolve a TCP/IP address to a name (called *reverse lookup*). The `ipconfig` command displays your IP configuration. Using `ipconfig` with the `/flushdns` switch will purge the DNS resolver cache on the machine.

16. B. Using the `ipconfig` command displays all of current TCP/IP network configuration values and refreshes Dynamic Host Configuration Protocol (DHCP) and Domain Name System (DNS) settings. Used without parameters, it will display the Internet Protocol version 4 (IPv4) and IPv6 addresses, subnet mask, and default gateway for all adapters. In this case, notice that the DNS server has an IP address that is not in the same network as the rest of the IP addresses. It starts with a 131.107.10 network versus a 192.168.0 network. So, the issue is that the primary DNS server is wrong.

17. A. If you need to complete a zone transfer from Microsoft DNS to a BIND (Unix) DNS server, you need to enable BIND secondaries on the Microsoft DNS server.

18. D. Active Directory Integrated zones give you many benefits over using primary and secondary zones including less network traffic, secure dynamic updates, encryption, and reliability in the event of a DNS server going down. The Secure Only option is for dynamic updates to a DNS database.

19. A. Windows Server 2022 DNS supports two features called DNS Aging and DNS Scavenging. These features are used to clean up and remove stale resource records. DNS zone or DNS server aging and scavenging flags old resource records that have not been updated in a certain amount of time (determined by the scavenging interval). These stale records will be scavenged at the next cleanup interval.

20. C. The `dnscmd /zoneexport` command creates a file using the zone resource records. You can then give a copy of this file to the Compliance department.

Chapter 6: Configuring DHCP and IPAM

1. C. Out of the possible answers provided, the only DHCP configuration option that would be both fault-tolerant and redundant is DHCP failover.

2. C. You can use the `Set-DhcpServerv4Scope` command to configure the settings of an existing IPv4 scope.

3. D. Microsoft recommends the 80/20 rule for redundancy of DHCP services in a network. Implementing the 80/20 rule calls for one DHCP server to make approximately 80 percent of the addresses for a given subnet available through DHCP while another server makes the remaining 20 percent of the addresses available.

4. A. DHCP can become a single point of failure within a network if there is only one DHCP server. If that server becomes unavailable, clients will not be able to obtain new leases or renew existing leases. For this reason, it is recommended that you have more than one DHCP server in the network. However, more than one DHCP server can create problems if they both are configured to use the same scope or set of addresses. Microsoft recommends the 80/20 rule for redundancy of DHCP services in a network. To do this, you run the Configure Failover Wizard.

5. B. DHCP can't be loaded onto a Nano server. You can load DHCP on a Server Core server (a server with no GUI desktop) or a server with the GUI desktop.

6. A. 003 Router is used to provide a list of available routers or default gateways on the same subnet.

7. D. You can use the `Set-DhcpServerv4Scope` command to configure the settings of an existing IPv4 scope.

8. B. 006 DNS is used to provide a list of available DNS servers to your scope settings or to your server settings.

9. B. Reservations are set up by using the machine's network adapter's MAC address. Every network adapter has its own MAC address. So, when the network card is replaced, the new MAC address needs to be put into the current reservation.

10. C. Conflict Detection Attempts specifies how many ICMP echo requests (pings) the server sends for an address it is about to offer. The default is 0. Conflict detection is a way to verify that the DHCP server is not issuing IP addresses that are already being used on the network. Since you only have one DHCP server, lower the value to 0.

11. B. You can use the `Set-IpamBlock` PowerShell command to configure an IP address block in IPAM.

12. C. You can use the `Add-IpamRange` PowerShell command to add an IP address range to an IPAM server.

13. D. You can use the `Set-IpamDiscoveryDomain` PowerShell command to change the IPAM discovery configuration.

14. A. You can use the `Get-IpamDnsZone` PowerShell command to view the DNS zone information from IPAM database.

15. C. You need to create and link IPAM Group Policy Objects (GPOs) for provisioning. To do this, you can either manually create the GPOs or run the `Invoke-IpamGpoProvisioning` PowerShell command.

16. C. The IPAM ASM Administrators group is specifically designed for the delegation of IPAM Address Space Management. The IPAM Administrators group would give Noelle's domain account way too much access within the environment, and the other two possible answers would not provide her with enough permissions to perform her required responsibilities.

17. B. Out of the three real possible deployment methods—Distributed, Centralized, and Hybrid—only the Centralized deployment method allows one primary IPAM server to manage the entire enterprise. The Distributed method places an IPAM server at each site location, and the Hybrid method uses a primary server with an additional IPAM server at each site location within the enterprise.

18. B. The `Get-IpamDnsServer` command allows you to view DNS server information from IPAM databases.

19. C. After you have successfully installed and provisioned your IPAM server, the next logical step in the IPAM deployment configuration is to configure and run server discovery.

20. A. The `Move-IpamDatabase` command allows you to move an IPAM database to a SQL Server database.

Chapter 7: Understanding Active Directory

1. A, B, C, D. The forest and function levels have to be Windows 2003 or newer to install an RODC.

2. B. A domain controller can contain Active Directory information for only one domain. If you want to use a multidomain environment, you must use multiple domain controllers configured in either a tree or a forest setting.

3. D. NTFS has file-level security, and it makes efficient usage of disk space. Since this machine is to be configured as a domain controller, the configuration requires at least one NTFS partition to store the Sysvol information.

4. A, D. To convert the system partition to NTFS, you must first use the `CONVERT` command-line utility and then reboot the server. During the next boot, the filesystem will be converted.

5. B, E. The use of LDAP and TCP/IP is required to support Active Directory. TCP/IP is the network protocol favored by Microsoft, which determined that all Active Directory communication would occur on TCP/IP. DNS is required because Active Directory is inherently dependent on the domain model. DHCP is used for automatic address assignment and is not required. Similarly, NetBEUI and IPX/SPX are not available network protocols in Windows Server 2022.

6. A, C. The Sysvol directory must be created on an NTFS partition. If such a partition is not available, you will not be able to promote the server to a domain controller. An error in the network configuration might prevent the server from connecting to another domain controller in the environment.

7. B, C. You need to run the `adprep` command when installing your first Windows Server 2022 domain controller onto a Windows Server 2008 R2 domain. `adprep /rodcprep` actually gets the network ready to install a read-only domain controller and not a GUI version.

8. A. You'll need to use Active Directory Federation Services (AD FS) in order to implement federated identity management. Federated identity management is a standards-based and information technology process that will enable distributed identification, authentication, and authorization across organizational and platform boundaries. The AD FS solution in Windows Server 2022 helps you address these challenges by enabling your organization to share a user's identity information securely.

9. B. The HOSTS file is a text-file-based database of mappings between hostnames and IP addresses. It works like a file-based version of DNS. DNS resolves a hostname to an IP address.

10. A. You only need to give them rights to the `WillPanek.com` zone using the DNS snap-in. If they do not have any rights to the `WillPanekAD.com` zone, they will not be able to configure this zone in any way.

11. A. A computer account and the domain authenticate each other by using a password. The password resets every 30 days. Since the machine has not connected to the domain for 16 weeks, the computer needs to be rejoined to the domain.

12. C. Selecting Account Never Expires will prevent this user's account from expiring again.

13. D. The `dsadd` command allows you to add an object (user's account) to the Active Directory database.

14. A. Distribution groups are for emails only, and distribution groups cannot be assigned rights and permissions to objects.

15. A. Inheritance is the process by which permissions placed on parent OUs affect child OUs. In this example, the permissions change for the higher-level OU (Texas) automatically caused a change in permissions for the lower-level OU (Austin).

16. B, E. Enabling the Advanced Features item in the View menu will allow Isabel to see the `LostAndFound` and `System` folders. The `LostAndFound` folder contains information about objects that could not be replicated among domain controllers.

17. A. Through the use of filtering, you can choose which types of objects you want to see using the Active Directory Users and Computers tool. Several of the other choices may work, but they require changes to Active Directory settings or objects.

18. A. To allow the junior admin to do backups, their account needs to be part of the Backup Operators local group. To add their account to the local group, you need to use Computer Management.

19. A, B, C, D. All of the options listed are common tasks presented in the Delegation Of Control Wizard.

20. D. The Delegation Of Control Wizard is designed to allow administrators to set up permissions on specific Active Directory objects.

Chapter 8: Understanding Group Policies

1. C. The Delegation Of Control Wizard can be used to allow other system administrators permission to add GPO links.

2. C. The system administrator can specify whether the application will be uninstalled or whether future installations will be prevented.

3. B. You would use `GPUpdate.exe /force`. The `/force` switch forces the GPO to reapply all policy settings. By default, only policy settings that have changed are applied.

4. A. You would use the Windows PowerShell `Invoke-GPUpdate` cmdlet. This cmdlet allows you to force the GPO to reapply the policies immediately.

5. D. DVD Present Targeting is not one of the options that you may consider when using item-level targeting.

6. B. You have the ability to apply individual preference items only to selected users or computers using a GPO feature called item-level targeting. Item-level targeting allows you to select specific items that the GPO will look at and then apply that GPO only to the specific users or computers. You have the ability to include multiple preference items, and each item can be customized for specific users or computers to use.

7. D. If you assign an application to a user, the application does not get automatically installed. To have an application automatically installed, you must assign the application to the computer account. Since Finance is the only OU that should receive this application, you would link the GPO to Finance only.

8. C. The Resultant Set of Policy (RSoP) utility displays the exact settings that apply to individual users, computers, OUs, domains, and sites after inheritance and filtering have taken effect. Desktop wallpaper settings are under the User section of the GPO, so you would run the RSoP against the user account.

9. B. The Enforced option can be placed on a parent GPO, and this option ensures that all lower-level objects inherit these settings. Using this option ensures that Group Policy inheritance is not blocked at other levels.

10. A. If the data transfer rate from the domain controller providing the GPO to the computer is slower than what you have specified in the Slow Link Detection setting, the connection is considered to be a slow connection, and the application will not install properly.

11. A, B. If you want your clients to be able to edit domain-based GPOs by using the ADMX files that are stored in the ADMX Central Store, you must be using any version of Windows above Vista, or Windows Server 2008 or higher.

12. D. If you assign an application to a user, the application does not get automatically installed. To have an application installed automatically, you must assign the application to the computer account. Since Finance is the only OU that should receive this application, you would link the GPO to Finance only.

13. C. The Resultant Set of Policy (RSoP) utility displays the exact settings that apply to individual users, computers, OUs, domains, and sites after inheritance and filtering have taken effect. Desktop wallpaper settings are under the User section of the GPO, so you would run the RSoP against the user account.

14. B. The Enforced option can be placed on a parent GPO, and this option ensures that all lower-level objects inherit these settings. Using this option ensures that Group Policy inheritance is not blocked at other levels.

15. A. If the data transfer rate from the domain controller providing the GPO to the computer is slower than what you have specified in the slow link detection setting, the connection is considered to be a slow connection and the application will not install properly.

16. D. To disable the application of Group Policy on a security group, you should deny the Apply Group Policy option. This is particularly useful when you don't want GPO settings to apply to a specific group, even though that group may be in an OU that includes the GPO settings.

17. A. GPOs at the OU level take precedence over GPOs at the domain level. GPOs at the domain level, in turn, take precedence over GPOs at the site level.

18. B. The Block Policy Inheritance option prevents group policies of higher-level Active Directory objects from applying to lower-level objects as long as the Enforced option is not set.

19. A, B, C, D. GPOs can be set at all of the levels listed. You cannot set GPOs on security principals such as users or groups.

20. D, E. Administrative templates are used to specify the options available for setting Group Policy. By creating new administrative templates, Ann can specify which options are available for the new applications. She can then distribute these templates to other system administrators in the environment.

Chapter 9: Introduction to Microsoft Azure

1. D. IaaS, PaaS, and SaaS are all built-in Azure services. If you need to implement SaaS for your organization, all you must do is configure the needed SaaS solution.

2. C. The advantage of a public cloud is that the cloud provider is responsible for the physical servers. Private clouds give you the option of having your company manage all the equipment.

3. C. When choosing a cloud subscription, you choose a subscription based on cost and guarantee. Microsoft guarantees (except for the Azure Free Account) that your service will remain available. If Azure becomes unavailable, for any reason, due to a Microsoft issue, your organization will be given a credit on a future bill.

4. C. This is a cloud service that automatically scales resources as needed. It is the ability to automatically increase or decrease computer processing, memory, and storage resources to meet the current demand. With cloud elasticity, a business can avoid for paying for resources that aren't being used and they don't have to worry about purchasing new equipment or maintaining current systems.

5. B. According to Microsoft, "platform as a service (PaaS) is a complete development and deployment environment in the cloud, with resources that enable you to deliver everything from simple cloud-based apps to sophisticated, cloud-enabled enterprise applications."

6. C. Infrastructure-as-a-service (IaaS) encompasses the components in your network that physically make the network function properly. This includes hardware (routers, gateways, firewalls, etc.) and servers/VMs.

7. D. Hybrid clouds are the best of both worlds. Administrators can use both onsite resources and Azure resources while still maintaining the company's domain.

8. A. The cloud providers provide backup, disaster recovery, and replication services. The SLA that you chose for your Azure subscription will determine the amount of acceptable uptime from Microsoft.

9. A. Software-as-a-service (SaaS) lets you use software on a subscription basis instead of just purchasing the software. O365 is a perfect example of SaaS.

10. C. This is a cloud service that automatically scales resources as needed. It is the ability to automatically increase or decrease computer processing, memory, and storage resources to meet the current demand. With cloud elasticity, a business can avoid paying for resources that aren't being used, and they don't have to worry about purchasing new equipment or maintaining current systems.

Chapter 10: Understanding Azure Active Directory

1. B. Azure AD Identity Protection is a tool that allows a company to achieve these three key tasks:

- Automate the detection and remediation of identity-based risks.

- Investigate risks using data in the portal.

- Export risk detection data to third-party utilities for further analysis.

Azure AD Identity Protection identifies risks. The risk signals that can trigger remediation efforts may include requiring users to perform Azure Multifactor Authentication, requiring users to reset their password by using self-service password reset, or blocking until you take action. Azure AD Identity Protection allows you to use the same type of protection that Microsoft uses to protect and secure users' identities.

2. D. Azure AD is Microsoft's cloud-based identity and access management service. It helps users sign in and access resources. You can use the Windows PowerShell command `New-AzureADPolicy` to create a new Azure AD policy. The syntax is as follows:

```
New-AzureADPolicy -Definition <Array of Rules> -DisplayName <Name of
Policy> -IsTenantDefault
```

3. A. Windows PowerShell is a Windows command-line shell designed especially for system administrators. By using the `Get-AzureADPolicy` command, you can view an Azure AD policy.

4. C. The Password Reset section allows you to control if they want to enable self-service password reset (SSPR). If you enable this feature, then users will be able to reset their own passwords or unlock their accounts. You can allow all accounts to use SSPR, or they can just choose certain groups to have the ability to use SSPR.

5. B. Azure AD Connect is a Microsoft utility that allows you to set up a hybrid design between Azure AD and an onsite AD. It allows both versions of Active Directory to connect to each other. Azure AD Connect provides the following features:

- Federation integration

- Health monitoring

- Pass-through authentication

- Password hash synchronization
- Synchronization

6. B. Azure AD simplifies the way that you manage your applications by providing a single identity system for your cloud and on-premises apps. You can use the `Add-AzureADApplicationPolicy` command to add an application policy.

7. D. Azure AD simplifies the management of applications by providing a single identity system for cloud and on-premises apps. You can use the `Set-AzureADPolicy` command to update an Azure AD policy.

8. D. The Custom Domain Names section allows you to add and verify new domain names. When it is first built, the Azure subscription comes with an Azure AD tenant that originates with an initial domain name. You cannot change or delete the initial domain name once it's been created. However, you can add a domain name to the list of supported names.

9. A. You can use the Custom Domain Names section of Azure AD to add an organization's new or existing domain names to the list of supported names. The Custom Domain Names section allows you to add and verify new domain names. When the Azure subscription is first created, it comes with an Azure AD tenant that has an initial domain name. You cannot change or delete the initial domain name once it has been created, but you can add a domain name to the list of supported names. For the steps on how to add a custom domain name to Azure AD, check out the following Microsoft website:

`http://docs.microsoft.com/en-us/azure/active-directory/`
`fundamentals/add-custom-domain#add-your-custom-domain-name-`
`to-azure-ad`

10. B. Azure AD simplifies the way that you manage your applications by providing a single identity system for your cloud and on-premises apps. You can use the `Get-AzureADDirectorySetting` command to view the directory settings.

11. B. Azure AD simplifies the way that you manage your applications by providing a single identity system for your cloud and on-premises apps. You can use the `Get-AzureADApplicationPolicy` command to view an Azure AD application policy.

12. A. With Windows 10/11, Azure AD users can synchronize their user settings and application settings data to the cloud. Enterprise State Roaming provides users with a unified experience across their Windows devices. Using Enterprise State Roaming ensures that the desktop background, the Favorites folder, and the browsing history will be available on the new computers.

13. A. Azure AD includes features such as Azure Multifactor Authentication (Azure MFA) and Azure AD Self-Service Password Reset (SSPR). These allow you to protect their organizations and users with secure authentication methods. The use of security questions is available only in Azure AD SSPR. If security questions are used, Microsoft recommends that they be used in conjunction with another security method. Security questions are stored privately and securely on a user object in the directory, and they can only be answered by users during registration. There is no way for you to read or modify a user's questions or answers.

14. C. Azure AD Terms of Use provide a method that you can use to present information to end users. Azure AD Terms of Use are in PDF format. The PDF file can be any content, such as existing contract documents, that allows you to collect end-user agreements during the user sign-in process. To add a Terms of Use document, check out the following Microsoft website: `http://docs.microsoft.com/en-us/azure/active-directory/ conditional-access/terms-of-use#add-terms-of-use`

15. C. Windows 10/11 allows devices to be registered in Azure AD and enrolled into Mobile Device Management (MDM) automatically. Automatic enrollment lets users enroll their Windows client devices. To enroll, users add their work account to their personally owned devices or join corporate-owned devices to Azure AD. To configure automatic MDM enrollment, sign into the Azure portal.

16. C. Conditional access policies use conditions and controls that are used to build the rules that will be evaluated by Azure AD when determining access to resources. Assignments are the rules that are checked in accordance with conditional access requirements, such as device encryption or password requirements. Some conditions are based on the following:

- The client apps that are used to access the data
- The client browser type
- The device platform being used
- The location where the data is being accessed

17. A. Conditional access is the feature used by Azure AD to bring together signals, to make decisions, and to enforce organizational policies. Conditional access policies are basically "if-then" statements; if a user wants to access a resource, then they must complete an action. By using conditional access policies, you can apply the precise access controls needed to keep the organization secure. Conditional access takes into account signals when making a policy decision.

18. B. With Windows 10/11, Azure AD users have the ability to securely synchronize their user settings and application settings data to the cloud using Enterprise State Roaming. Enterprise State Roaming provides users with a unified experience across their Windows devices and diminishes the time required for configuring a new device. When you enable Enterprise State Roaming, your organization is automatically granted a free, limited-use license for Azure Rights Management protection from Azure Information Protection.

19. B. Azure AD Identity Protection is a tool that allows a company to achieve these three key tasks:

- Automate the detection and remediation of identity-based risks.
- Investigate risks using data in the portal.
- Export risk detection data to third-party utilities for further analysis.

Azure AD Identity Protection identifies risks. The risk signals that can trigger remediation efforts may include requiring users to perform Azure Multifactor Authentication, requiring users to reset their password by using self-service password reset, or blocking until you take action.

20. C. Conditional access is a feature used by Azure AD to bring signals together, to make decisions, and to enforce policies. To manage conditional access abilities, you should assign the Conditional Access Administrator role. Users who have the Conditional Access Administrator role have permissions to view, create, modify, and delete conditional access policies. The Conditional Access Administrator can perform the following tasks:

Create: Create conditional access policies

Read: Read conditional access policies

Update: Update conditional access policies

Delete: Delete conditional access policies

Chapter 11: Configuring Storage

1. A. The iSCSI default port is TCP 3260. Port 3389 is used for RDP, port 1433 is used for Microsoft SQL, and port 21 is used for FTP.

2. A. The `Get-ShieldedVMProvisioningStatus` command allows you to view the provisioning status of a shielded virtual machine.

3. B. The `Set-VMNetworkAdapter` cmdlet allows you to configure features of the virtual network adapter in a virtual machine or the management operating system.

4. C. This `Set-VMProcessor` command allows you to configure the processors of a virtual machine. While the virtual machine is in the OFF state, run the `Set-VMProcessor` command on the physical Hyper-V host. This enables nested virtualization for the virtual machine.

5. C. The `Set-VMSwitch` cmdlet allows you to configure a virtual switch.

6. D. The `Optimize-VHD` cmdlet allows you to optimize the allocation of space in virtual hard disk files, except for fixed virtual hard disks.

7. B. The `Get-Package` command allows you to view a list of all software packages that have been installed by using Package Management.

8. D. The `Get-WindowsFeature` cmdlet allows you to view a list of available and installed roles and features on the local server.

9. D. The `iscsicli addisnsserver server_name` command manually registers the host server to an iSNS server. `refreshisnsserver` refreshes the list of available servers. `removeisnsserver` removes the host from the iSNS server. `listisnsservers` lists the available iSNS servers.

10. D. The `Set-VMHost` cmdlet allows you to configure a Hyper-V host. These settings include network settings network adapters.

11. A, B, C, D. Improved security, quotas, compression, and encryption are all advantages of using NTFS over FAT32. These features are not available in FAT32. The only security you have in FAT32 is shared folder permissions.

12. B. Disk quotas allow you to limit the amount of space on a volume or partition. You can set an umbrella quota for all users and then implement individual users' quotas to bypass the umbrella quota.

13. D. NTFS has file-level security, and it makes efficient usage of disk space. Since this machine is to be configured as a domain controller, the configuration requires at least one NTFS partition to store the SYSVOL information.

14. D. The `iscsicli addisnsserver server_name` command manually registers the host server to an iSNS server. `refreshisnsserver` refreshes the list of available servers. `removeisnsserver` removes the host from the iSNS server. `listisnsservers` lists the available iSNS servers.

15. C, E. The Admin group needs Full Control on the NTFS security and shared permission settings in order to do their job. To be able to give other users permissions, you must have the Full Control permission.

16. E. By giving Moe Modify on the NTFS security setting, Will is giving Moe just enough to do his job. Will could also give Sales or Finance the Modify permission, but then everyone in those groups would be able to delete, change, and do more than they all need. Also, Moe does not need Full Control to change or delete files.

17. A, D. To convert the system partition to NTFS, you must first use the CONVERT command and then reboot the server. During the next boot, the filesystem will be converted.

18. B. Compression helps compact files or folders to allow for more efficient use of hard drive space. For example, a file that usually takes up 20 MB of space might use only 13 MB after compression. To enable compression, just open the Advanced Attributes dialog box for a folder and select the Compress Contents To Save Disk Space option.

19. D. The `Get-WindowsFeature` cmdlet allows you to view a list of available and installed roles and features on the local server.

20. D. The default port for RDP is 3389. The iSCSI default port is 3260 and port 1433 is used for Microsoft SQL, and port 21 is used for FTP.

Chapter 12: Building an Azure Infrastructure

1. B. The docker rm command is used to delete an image. You should run docker images first and get the ID number or name of the image that you want to delete.

2. A. The docker create command lets you create a new container.

3. D. The Get-Container PowerShell command allows you to view information about containers.

4. A. The docker images command gives you the ability to see your images. The docker info command lets you see how many images you have on a host, but it does not give you details about the images.

5. C. The Docker build command allows you to compile and create an image. The docker run command executes commands in a Dockerfile, and the docker rm command allows you to delete an image.

6. A. The Docker run command executes commands in a Dockerfile. The Docker build command allows you to compile and create an image, and you use docker rm to delete an image.

7. C. The Remove-Container command gives you the ability to delete a container.

8. B. The docker pull microsoft/windowsservercore command allows you to grab an image of Windows Server Core from the Docker website.

9. D, C, A. The first step is to create a new Dockerfile. After the Dockerfile is complete, you need to build the container using the docker build command and push the container out using docker push.

10. C. Physical hard disks cannot be configured using the Virtual Hard Disk Wizard in Azure. To set up a new hard drive, choose the VM and from the left-side menu, choose Disks.

Chapter 13: Managing Data in a Hybrid Network

1. A. To create a new NLB cluster, use the PowerShell cmdlet New-NlbCluster.

2. C. You and your colleague are discussing Azure Load Balancer. It is a network-layer load balancer that improves network performance and availability of your applications by using low-latency Layer 4 load balancing capabilities. Azure Load Balancer can balance traffic between virtual machines inside your virtual networks and across multitiered hybrid apps. It supports TCP, UDP, Layer 4, and global/regional apps.

3. A. The maximum number a single cluster can support is 32 computers.

4. B. If you decide to use the `drainstop` command, the cluster stops after answering all of the current NLB connections. So, the current NLB connections are finished but no new connections to that node are accepted.

5. D. If you want to stop the entire cluster from running, while in the NLB manager (type `NLBmgr` in the Run command), right-click the cluster, point to Control Hosts, and then choose Stop.

6. A. The PowerShell command `Stop-VMReplication` will stop virtual machine replication from happening.

7. D. The `Enable-VMReplication` cmdlet allows you to enable virtual machine migration on a virtual machine host.

8. B. To use unicast communication between NLB cluster nodes, each node must have a minimum of two network adapters.

9. D. Setting the cluster affinity to Single will send all traffic from a specific IP address to a single cluster node. Using this affinity will keep a client on a specific node where the client should not have to authenticate again. Setting the filtering mode to Single would remove the authentication problem but would not distribute the load to other servers unless the initial server was down.

10. C. When setting the affinity to Class C, NLB links clients with a specific member based on the Class C part of the client's IP address. This allows you to set up NLB so that clients from the same Class C address range can access the same NLB member. This affinity is best for NLB clusters using the Internet.

11. C. Quorum determines the number of failures that the cluster can sustain while still remaining online. In this question, there are six nodes and one witness, so there are seven votes. In order to maintain quorum, there needs to be four votes available (four votes is the majority of seven). This means that a minimum of three nodes plus the witness need to remain online for the cluster to function. This means that the maximum number of simultaneous failures is three. This question asks about nodes failing "simultaneously," not nodes failing one after the other.

12. D. You can use the following tools to manage and monitor Storage Spaces Direct:

- Windows Admin Center
- Server Manager and Failover Cluster Manager
- Windows PowerShell
- System Center Virtual Machine Manager (SCVMM) and Operations Manager

13. A. To view all of the information for an NLB cluster, use the PowerShell command `Get-NlbCluster`.

14. D. Microsoft Cloud Witness is a high-availability (HA) feature for failover clusters that uses storage in Azure so that clusters will continue to work if there is an onsite outage. It is a type of failover cluster quorum witness that uses Azure. You can't use Azure Premium Storage for a cloud witness.

15. A. Microsoft Cloud Witness is a high-availability (HA) feature for failover clusters that uses storage in Azure so that clusters will continue to work if there is an onsite outage. It is a type of failover cluster quorum witness that uses Azure. When you create an Azure Storage Account, it is associated with two access keys that are automatically generated: the Primary Access key and the Secondary Access key.

16. A. To change the settings for Hyper-V replication, use the PowerShell cmdlet `Set-VMReplication`.

17. D. Software Load Balancing allows you to have multiple servers hosting the same virtual networking workload in a multitenant environment. This allows you to set up high availability.

18. C, E, and F. Only three of these options are needed. To configure Storage Spaces Direct:

- Clean the drives.
- Validate the cluster.
- Create the failover cluster.
- Configure a cluster witness.
- Enable Storage Spaces Direct.
- Create volumes.
- Enable the CSV cache (optional).
- Deploy virtual machines for hyper-converged deployments.

19. F. Given the options, the answer would be F, all of these. To configure Storage Spaces Direct:

- Clean the drives.
- Validate the cluster.
- Create the failover cluster.
- Configure a cluster witness.
- Enable Storage Spaces Direct.
- Create volumes.
- Enable the CSV cache (optional).
- Deploy virtual machines for hyper-converged deployments.

20. B. Once a cluster is created, there are several actions that are available. However, this question is asking which one is irreversible and that would be to evict the node. Eviction is an irreversible process. Once you evict the node, it must be readded to the cluster. You would evict a node when it is damaged beyond repair or is no longer needed in the cluster. If you evict a damaged node, you can repair or rebuild it and then add it back to the cluster using the Add Node Wizard.

Chapter 14: Hybrid Data and Servers

1. A, D. When enabling cloud tiering, you can set up two policy types: volume free space policy and the date policy. The volume free space policy tells Azure File Sync to tier cool files to the cloud once a certain amount of space is used up on your local disk. With the date policy, cool files are tiered to the cloud if they haven't been accessed for a set number of days.

2. C. You can use Storage Migration Service to easily migrate data to a Windows Server or to an Azure subscription. Storage Migration Service gives you a graphical utility that will do an inventory of data on Windows, Linux, and NetApp CIFS servers. Using that inventory, Storage Migration Service will help transfer the data to newer servers or to Azure virtual machines. Storage Migration Service will also give you the option to transfer the identity of a server to the destination server. This will allow applications and users to access their data without needing to change links or paths of the data's location.

3. A. The Azure Migrate appliance is a lightweight appliance that is used by the Azure Migrate Discovery and Assessment tool. This tool is used to help discover and assess physical or virtual servers on your network. The Azure Migrate Appliance is also used in the migration and modernization tool.

4. A. You can use Storage Migration Service to easily migrate data to a Windows Server or to an Azure subscription. Storage Migration Service gives you a graphical utility that will do an inventory of data on Windows, Linux, and NetApp CIFS servers. Using that inventory, Storage Migration Service will help transfer the data to newer servers or to Azure virtual machines. Storage Migration Service will also give you the option to transfer the identity of a server to the destination server. This will allow applications and users to access their data without needing to change links or paths of the data's location.

5. A. Use the Storage Migration Service to easily migrate data to a Windows Server or to an Azure subscription. Storage Migration Service gives you a graphical utility that will do an inventory of data on Windows, Linux, and NetApp CIFS servers. Using that inventory, Storage Migration Service will help transfer the data to newer servers or to Azure virtual machines. Storage Migration Service will also give you the option to transfer the identity of a server to the destination server. This will allow applications and users to access their data without needing to change links or paths of the data's location.

6. D. Use the Storage Migration Service to easily migrate data to a Windows Server or to an Azure subscription. Storage Migration Service gives you a graphical utility that will do an inventory of data on Windows, Linux, and NetApp CIFS servers.

7. B. Windows Autopilot profiles allow you to choose how the Windows client system will be set up and configured on Azure AD and Intune. Windows Autopilot simplifies enrolling devices. With Windows Autopilot you can give new devices to end users without the need to build, maintain, and apply custom operating system images.

8. B. Windows Autopilot is a way to set up and preconfigure devices. You can use Windows Autopilot to reset, repurpose, and recover devices. Windows Autopilot user-driven mode is designed to enable Windows client devices to be converted from their initial state into a ready-to-use state without you working on the device. The process is designed to be user friendly so that anyone can complete it.

9. D. Windows Autopilot profiles allow you to choose how the Windows client system will be set up and configured. Windows Autopilot simplifies enrolling devices. With Windows Autopilot you can give new devices to end users without the need to build, maintain, and apply custom operating system images.

10. B. Deployment scenarios are assigned to one of three categories. The three categories are as follows:

Modern: Using Modern deployment methods is recommended by Microsoft unless there is a specific need to use a different procedure. Modern deployment scenarios include Windows Autopilot and In-Place Upgrades.

Dynamic: Using Dynamic deployment methods enables you to configure applications and settings for specific use cases. Dynamic deployment scenarios include Subscription Activation, Azure Active Directory Join (Azure AD) with Automatic Mobile Device Management (MDM), and Provisioning Packages.

Traditional: Traditional deployment methods use existing tools to deploy operating system images. Traditional deployment scenarios include Bare-Metal, Refresh, and Replace.

11. D. Using Microsoft Intune and Windows Autopilot, you can give devices to your end users without the need to build, maintain, and apply custom operating system images. When you use Intune to manage Autopilot devices, you can manage policies, profiles, applications, and more.

12. B. Windows Autopilot is a way to set up and preconfigure devices. You can use Windows Autopilot to reset, repurpose, and recover devices. Autopilot Reset removes all of the files, apps, and settings on a device (including the user profile), but it retains the connection to Azure AD, Intune, or a third-party mobile device management (MDM). Autopilot Reset will retain the following:

- The region/language and keyboard
- Any applied provisioning packages
- Wi-Fi connections

Autopilot Reset is the best option when reusing a device within your network. So, the app will be removed by using Autopilot Reset.

13. C. Windows Autopilot is a way to set up and preconfigure devices. You can use Windows Autopilot to reset, repurpose, and recover devices. Windows Autopilot user-driven mode is designed to enable Windows client devices to be converted from their initial state into a ready-to-use state without you working on the device.

14. C. Windows Autopilot is a collection of technologies used to set up and preconfigure new devices, getting them ready for productive use. It is a zero-touch, self-service Windows deployment platform introduced with Windows 10/11. You can also use Windows Autopilot to reset, repurpose, and recover devices.

15. D. The User State Migration Tool (USMT) uses configurable migration rule (XML) files to control what user accounts, user files, operating system settings, and application settings are migrated. They can be written to improve efficiency and customized with settings and rules. USMT migration XML files include the following:

   - `MigApp.xml`
   - `MigDocs.xml`
   - `MigUser.xml`
   - Custom XML files that are created

Chapter 15: Implementing Security

1. C. Microsoft Defender Application Guard is designed for Windows 10/11 and Microsoft Edge. Application Guard uses an approach that performs hardware isolation. This allows untrusted site navigation to launch inside a container. You can use Microsoft Defender Application Guard to ensure that only applications that you explicitly allow can run on your Windows client computers.

2. A. Microsoft Defender Application Guard is designed for Windows 10/11 and Microsoft Edge. Application Guard uses an approach that performs hardware isolation. This allows untrusted site navigation to launch inside a container. Hardware isolation allows companies to protect their network and corporate data just in case a user visits a site that is compromised or is malicious. You can define what sites are trusted, cloud resources, and internal networks. If something is not trusted, it is considered untrusted, and these sites will be isolated from the network and corporate data on the user's device. You can use Windows Defender Application Control to ensure that only applications that you explicitly allow can run on your Windows client.

3. A. Windows Defender Credential Guard is a virtualization-based security tool that helps isolate critical files so that only system software that is privileged can access those critical files. Once it's enabled, a Windows client machine that is part of Active Directory or Azure AD will have the systems credentials protected by Windows Defender Credential Guard. Windows Defender Credential Guard can be enabled by using Group Policy, the Registry, or the Hypervisor-Protected Code Integrity (HVCI) and Windows Defender Credential Guard hardware readiness tool.

4. A. Windows Defender Credential Guard is a virtualization-based security service designed to help isolate critical files so that only system software that is privileged can access those critical files.

5. C. Windows Defender Credential Guard is a Windows 10/11 Enterprise and Windows Server 2016 and newer security feature that uses virtualization-based security to protect credentials. Hyper-V is Microsoft's hardware virtualization product that allows you to create and run a software version of a computer, called a virtual machine.

6. B. Microsoft Defender Exploit Guard helps protect your system from common malware hacks that use executable files and scripts that attack applications like Microsoft Office. Microsoft Defender Exploit Guard also looks for suspicious scripts or behavior that is not normal on the Windows client system.

7. C. Microsoft Defender Application Guard was designed for Windows 10/11 and Microsoft Edge. It uses a hardware isolation approach. This lets untrusted site navigation launch inside a container, thus safeguarding corporate networks and data. You determine which sites are trusted sites, cloud resources, and internal networks. Anything that is not on the trusted sites list is considered untrusted. If a user goes to an untrusted site through using Microsoft Edge it will open the site in an isolated Hyper-V-enabled container, which is separate from the host operating system. To use Microsoft Defender Application Guard, the environment has a few hardware requirements that must be met. This question is asking what the minimum amount of RAM is to use Microsoft Defender Application Guard and the answer is that Microsoft recommends 8 GB of RAM.

8. C. To configure your Windows Firewall to allow DNS inbound and outbound traffic, you would set up port 53. Port 20 is for FTP data, port 25 is for SMTP (mail), and port 80 is for HTTP.

9. B. You can onboard the following operating systems using Microsoft Endpoint Configuration Manager:

- Windows 8.1
- Windows 10, version 1709 or later
- Windows 11
- Windows Server 2012 R2
- Windows Server 2016
- Windows Server Semi-Annual Channel (SAC), version 1803 or later
- Windows Server 2019
- Windows Server 2022

Because this question is asking what devices can be onboarded using Microsoft Endpoint Configuration Manager, then the answer would be devices 1, 2, and 3 since they are Windows machines.

10. B. Microsoft Defender for Endpoint is designed to help enterprise networks prevent, detect, investigate, and respond to advanced threats. Microsoft Defender for Endpoint has a number of built-in features and capabilities. These include the following:

- Automated Investigation and Remediation
- Attack Surface Reduction

- Configuration Score
- Endpoint Detection and Response
- Microsoft Threat Experts
- Next Generation Protection
- Threat & Vulnerability Management

Endpoint Detection and Response capabilities are put in place to detect, investigate, and respond to advanced threats.

11. C. Microsoft Defender Antivirus can help protect devices by actively detecting spyware, malware, and viruses on both operating systems and Windows 10/11 installed on Hyper-V virtual machines. It runs in the background and installs new definitions automatically as they are released. Microsoft Defender Antivirus can manually scan for malware using the Microsoft Defender scan options. The scan options include the following:

- Custom
- Full
- Quick
- Microsoft Defender Offline Scan

In this question, you are discussing a quick scan that will scan the most likely areas on a hard disk that spyware, malware, and viruses are commonly known to infect.

12. B. Windows Security provides the latest antivirus protection. Devices will be actively protected from the moment the Windows client is started. Windows Security constantly scans for malware, viruses, and security threats. The App & Browser Control section covers the Microsoft Defender SmartScreen settings and Exploit Protection mitigations.

13. C. In Intune, security baselines are preconfigured groups of settings that are best practice recommendations from the Microsoft security teams for that product. These recommendations protect your users and devices. Intune supports security baselines for Windows 10/11 device settings, Microsoft Edge, Microsoft Defender for Endpoint Protection, and more. Security baselines are supported for devices that run Windows 10 version 1809 and later, and Windows 11. In order to manage security baselines in Intune, you must have an account with the Policy and Profile Manager built-in role.

14. A. Endpoints include desktops, laptops, tablets, mobile devices, servers, IoT devices, virtual machines, and more. Endpoint security helps to protect these endpoints from cyberattacks by using a wide variety of services and solutions. This question is asking about drive-by downloads. This type of attack uses the automated download of software to a device without the user's knowledge or consent.

15. C. Microsoft Defender Application Guard functionality is turned off by default. You can quickly install it on a user's device by using Control Panel, PowerShell, or your mobile device management (MDM) solution. To install Microsoft Defender Application Guard by using Control Panel, perform the following steps:

1. Open Control Panel, click Programs And Features, and then click Turn Windows Features On Or Off.

2. Select the check box next to Microsoft Defender Application Guard and then click OK.

3. Click OK. You will be prompted to restart the computer.

16. C. Microsoft Defender Application Guard was designed for Windows 10/11 and Microsoft Edge. Application Guard helps protect the corporation while users browse the Internet by segregating untrusted sites. You can configure Microsoft Defender Application Guard in one of two modes:

- Standalone mode: In this mode, users can use hardware-isolated browsing sessions without any administrative or management policy configurations.

- Enterprise mode: In this mode, you define the company limitations by adding trusted domains and by customizing Application Guard to meet and enforce the needs on the users' devices.

17. B. Microsoft Defender for Endpoint provides you with near-real-time detection and response capabilities. It collects process information, network activity, user login activity, Registry and filesystem changes, and more. To view threats, you can use the Security Operations dashboard. Here you will see an overview of threats that have been detected and when response actions are required. This question is asking which tile shows you a list of devices that have the most active alerts—that would be the Devices At Risk tile.

18. A. Microsoft Defender Exploit Guard helps protect Windows client devices against malware, ransomware, and other types of attacks. It does this by reducing the attack surface of a device. There are a number of ways that you can turn it on. Microsoft Defender Exploit Guard consists of four components:

- Attack surface reduction rules

- Controlled folder access

- Exploit protection

- Network protection

In this question, attack surface reduction rules are being discussed. Attack surface reduction rules help prevent attack vectors that are applied by scripts, email, and Office-based malware.

19. C. Windows Defender Firewall, which is included with Windows 10/11, helps to prevent unauthorized users or malicious software from accessing your computer. Windows Defender Firewall does not allow unsolicited traffic (traffic that was not sent in response to a request) to pass through the firewall.

20. C. Windows Defender Credential Guard can be enabled by using Group Policy, the Registry, or the Hypervisor-Protected Code Integrity (HVCI) and the Windows Defender Credential Guard hardware readiness tool. You can use Group Policy to enable Windows Defender Credential Guard. This will add and enable the virtualization-based security features. This question is asking which setting you need to enable in Group Policy, and the answer is Turn On Virtualization Based Security.

Chapter 16: Understanding Monitoring

1. D. All of the applications that are running on the Windows Server 2022 machine will show up on the Details tab. Right-click the application and end the process.

2. C. Windows PowerShell is one way to remotely configure and maintain client machines. You need to make sure that your Windows systems can accept remote PowerShell commands. If this feature is not already enabled on a system, you can enable this feature by running the `Enable-PSRemoting` cmdlet. To enable remote PowerShell commands, you must be an administrator to run this cmdlet. After PowerShell is enabled, you can then enter a Power-Shell session on the Windows client system to run the `Invoke-Command` cmdlet.

3. A. Performance Monitor allows you to watch the resources on your system. You can add as many objects and counters that you want to view.

4. B. `Perfmon.exe` is the command-line command used to start Performance Monitor.

5. D. All of the users that are running applications on the Windows Server 2022 machine will show up on the Users tab of Task Manager. Right-click the user and click the Disconnect button if you need them to be disconnected.

6. B. The Resource Monitor allows you to view the resources on your server. You can use Resource Monitor to watch the system's CPU, Memory, Disk, and Network.

7. D. `Resmon.exe` is the command-line command used to start Resource Monitor.

8. D. By using the Microsoft Message Analyzer, you can view all of the network packets that are being sent to or from the local server. Based on this information, you can determine the source of certain types of traffic, such as pings. The other types of monitoring can provide useful information, but they do not allow you to drill down into the specific details of a network packet, and they don't allow you to filter the data that has been collected based on details about the packet.

9. A. Azure Monitor was created to perform analytics, diagnostics, and monitoring. The core components consist of collectors, metrics and logs store, and analytics. Azure Monitor maximizes the availability and performance of apps and services by delivering a solution for collecting, analyzing, and acting on telemetry from your cloud and on-premises environments.

10. D. All of the users who are running applications on the Windows Server 2022 machine will show up on the Users tab of Task Manager. Right-click the user and click the Disconnect button if you need them to be disconnected.

11. A, B. C, D. Resource Monitor will monitor the system's CPU, Memory, Disk, and Network.

12. B. Task Manager allows you to see all of the applications that are currently running on a Windows system. You can terminate any of those applications by using Task Manager.

13. B. The term that you and your colleague are discussing is known as second-hop remoting. Second-hop remoting is when you are in a PowerShell Remoting session and you attempt to access a resource that is outside of that remote computer.

14. D. Resmon.exe is the command-line command used to start Resource Monitor.

15. B. Perfmon.exe is the command-line command used to start Performance Monitor.

16. A. Performance Monitor allows you to watch the resources on your system. You can add as many objects and counters that you want to view.

17. D. All of the users that are running applications on the Windows Server 2022 machine will show up on the Users tab. Right-click the user and click the Disconnect button if you need them to be disconnected.

18. B. The Windows Admin Center is installed on a dedicated gateway server. The client browser is the machine where the Windows Admin Center is being accessed from. Operating systems include Windows Server Semi-Annual Channel, Windows Server 2016, Windows Server 2019, and Windows Server 2022.

19. D. All of the applications that are running on the Windows Server 2022 machine will show up on the Details tab. You would right-click on the application and choose Priority.

20. D. All of the applications that are running on the Windows Server 2022 machine will show up on the Details tab. Right-click the application and choose Affinity.

Chapter 17: Understanding Disaster Recovery

1. B. For this question, you will want to assign an Azure policy. Use Azure Arc–enabled servers to assign Azure policies to VMs outside of Azure, whether they are on-premises or on other clouds. This approach can be used to make sure all your servers are onboarded to services such as Azure Monitor, Microsoft Defender for Cloud, and Microsoft Sentinel.

2. B. Microsoft Defender for Cloud has a workflow automation feature that can trigger Logic Apps on items such as security alerts and recommendations, and if there are any changes to regulatory compliance. Trigger Automated Response provides the option to trigger a Logic App as a response to a security alert.

3. C. A VM in Azure must have at least one network interface attached to it, but it can have as many as the VM size supports. The first network interface, attached to an Azure VM, is called the primary network interface and all other network interfaces are called secondary network interfaces. All outbound traffic from the VM uses the IP address of the primary network interface.

4. A, D. Microsoft Azure Backup Server (MABS) backs up system state and provides bare-metal recovery (BMR) protection. MABS, also called Azure Backup Server, is a server product that you can use to protect application workloads such as Hyper-V VMs, Microsoft SQL Server, SharePoint Server, Microsoft Exchange, and Windows clients using a single console.

5. C. It will only take a few minutes for the scanner extension to be installed on the selected machines and scanning will start as soon as the extension is deployed. Scans will run every 12 hours (this time interval cannot be changed).

6. A, B. Microsoft Defender for Cloud helps you find and fix security vulnerabilities, block malicious activity by applying access and application controls, detect threats by using analytics, and if you are under attack, helps you to respond. Microsoft Defender for Cloud has two main pillars for cloud security: Cloud Security Posture Management (CSPM) and Cloud Workload Protection Platform (CWPP).

7. A. Using recovery plans, you can customize and sequence the failover and recovery of multi-tier applications running on multiple VMs. You group machines together in a recovery plan, and optionally add scripts and manual actions. Recovery plans can be integrated with Azure Automation runbooks.

8. B. Azure Site Recovery can help with replication, failover, and the recovery of workloads and apps from a secondary location if your primary location fails.

9. D. Once Microsoft Sentinel is onboarded, you can use data connectors to start obtaining your information. Microsoft Sentinel comes with numerous out-of-the-box connectors for Microsoft services, which you can then integrate in real time.

10. D. For the purpose of failover, a recovery plan gathers machines into recovery groups and helps define the recovery process. The recovery plan will determine how the machines failover and the order in which they start after failover. Recovery plans can be used for both failover to and failback.

11. A. The Take Action tab allows you to take further actions regarding the security alert, such as:

    - Inspect Resource Context sends you to the resource's activity logs that support the security alert.

    - Mitigate The Threat provides manual remediation steps for this security alert.

    - Prevent Future Attacks provides security recommendations to help reduce the attack surface, increase security posture, and thus prevent future attacks.

    - Trigger Automated Response provides the option to trigger a logic app as a response to this security alert.

    - Suppress Similar Alerts provides the option to suppress future alerts with similar characteristics if the alert isn't relevant for your organization.

12. B. Azure Backup and Azure Site Recovery use a centralized management interface, known as the Backup Center, to make it easier to create policies to protect, monitor, and manage enterprise workloads across hybrid and cloud networks.

13. C. To back up and recover files, folders, volumes, or system state data from an on-premises computer to Azure, Azure Backup uses the Microsoft Azure Recovery Services (MARS) agent.

14. B. The Backup Alerts report will list all the alerts for the vault and display an alert severity. There are three different alert levels:

Critical—You will see this alert when backup jobs or recovery jobs fail, and when you stop protection on a server but retain the data.

Warning—You will see this alert when backup jobs finish with warnings.

Informational—Currently, no informational alerts are generated by the Azure Backup service.

15. B. Microsoft Azure Backup Server (MABS) is a server product that you can use to protect application workloads such as Hyper-V VMs, Microsoft SQL Server, SharePoint Server, Microsoft Exchange, and Windows clients using a single console. For a server on-premises:

- The Azure Backup Server must be located on-premises and be connected to the domain.
- MABS can run on a Hyper-V VM, a VMware VM, or a physical host.
- Microsoft recommends at least a minimum of two cores and 8 GB of RAM for the server.
- The supported operating systems for the on-premises server are Windows Server 2019/2022, 64-bit, Standard, Datacenter, or Essentials or Windows Server 2016 with the latest service packs, 64-bit, Standard, Datacenter, or Essentials.

16. D. Azure Site Recovery can help with replication, failover, and the recovery of workloads and apps from a secondary location if your primary location fails. There are a number of Site Recovery features, but the one being discussed is testing without disruption. It allows you to run disaster recovery drills without affecting ongoing replication.

17. D. The vulnerability scanner included with Microsoft Defender for Cloud is powered by Qualys. Microsoft Defender for Cloud includes vulnerability scanning for your machines at no extra cost. The VMs would be listed as unhealthy resources, meaning that a vulnerability scanner extension can be deployed to the machines. Deploy the integrated scanner to your Azure and hybrid machines.

18. A. There is a graph-based algorithm that scans the cloud security graph; it is called an Attack Path Analysis. This graph will show you possible paths that an attacker may use to breach your workload. The Attack Path Analysis will expose the paths and make recommendations on how to best remediate the problems to prevent the breach.

19. B. Microsoft Defender for Cloud consistently checks your connected machines to make sure that they are running vulnerability assessment tools. How the vulnerability scanner extension works:

1. Deploy—Microsoft Defender for Cloud monitors your machines and provides recommendations to deploy the extension.

2. Gather information—The extension collects artifacts and sends them for analysis.

3. Analyze— Qualys's cloud service conducts the vulnerability assessment and sends its findings to Microsoft Defender for Cloud.

4. Report—The findings are listed in Microsoft Defender for Cloud.

20. C, D. Microsoft Sentinel was previously known as Azure Sentinel. It is a cloud-native solution that is scalable and provides security information and event management (SIEM), and security orchestration, automation, and response (SOAR).

Index

H

N

O

X

Z

Online Test Bank

To help you study for your MCA Windows Server Hybrid Administrator certification exams, register to gain one year of FREE access after activation to the online interactive test bank—included with your purchase of this book! All of the practice questions in this book are included in the online test bank so you can study in a timed and graded setting.

Register and Access the Online Test Bank

To register your book and get access to the online test bank, follow these steps:

1. Go to www.wiley.com/go/sybextestprep. You'll see the **"How to Register Your Book for Online Access"** instructions.
2. Click "here to register" and then select your book from the list.
3. Complete the required registration information, including answering the security verification to prove book ownership. You will be emailed a pin code.
4. Follow the directions in the email or go to www.wiley.com/go/sybextestprep.
5. Find your book on that page and click the "Register or Login" link with it. Then enter the pin code you received and click the "Activate PIN" button.
6. On the Create an Account or Login page, enter your username and password, and click Login or, if you don't have an account already, create a new account.
7. At this point, you should be in the test bank site with your new test bank listed at the top of the page. If you do not see it there, please refresh the page or log out and log back in.